Road map symbols

Motorways

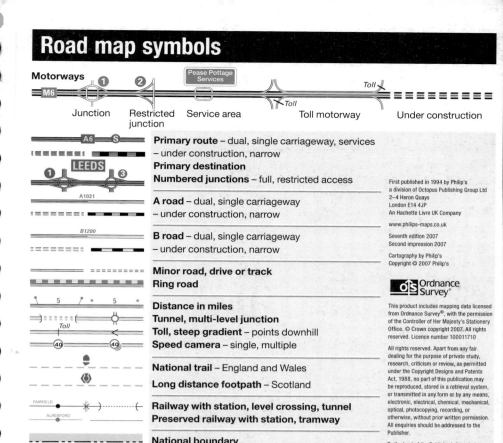

Junction   Restricted junction   Service area   Toll motorway   Under construction

Primary route – dual, single carriageway, services
– under construction, narrow
Primary destination
Numbered junctions – full, restricted access

A road – dual, single carriageway
– under construction, narrow

B road – dual, single carriageway
– under construction, narrow

Minor road, drive or track
Ring road

Distance in miles
Tunnel, multi-level junction
Toll, steep gradient – points downhill
Speed camera – single, multiple

National trail – England and Wales
Long distance footpath – Scotland

Railway with station, level crossing, tunnel
Preserved railway with station, tramway

National boundary
County or unitary authority boundary

Car ferry, catamaran
Passenger ferry, catamaran
Hovercraft, freight ferry
Internal ferry – car, passenger

Principal airport, other airport or airfield

Area of outstanding natural beauty – England and Wales, **Forest park, National park, National scenic area** – Scotland, **Regional park**

Woodland

Beach – sand, shingle

Navigable river or canal
Lock, flight of locks, canal bridge number

Viewpoint, spot height – in metres
Site and date of battle, RAC or AA telephone box
National nature reserve, major sporting venue
Shopping village, park and ride
World Heritage site, caravan site, camping site

First published in 1994 by Philip's
a division of Octopus Publishing Group Ltd
2–4 Heron Quays
London E14 4JP
An Hachette Livre UK Company
www.philips-maps.co.uk

Seventh edition 2007
Second impression 2007

Cartography by Philip's
Copyright © 2007 Philip's

Ordnance Survey®

This product includes mapping data licensed from Ordnance Survey®, with the permission of the Controller of Her Majesty's Stationery Office. © Crown copyright 2007. All rights reserved. Licence number 100011710

Printed in Spain by Cayfosa-Quebecor

All rights reserved. Apart from any fair dealing for the purpose of private study, research, criticism or review, as permitted under the Copyright Designs and Patents Act, 1988, no part of this publication may be reproduced, stored in a retrieval system, or transmitted in any form or by any means, electronic, electrical, chemical, mechanical, optical, photocopying, recording, or otherwise, without prior written permission. All enquiries should be addressed to the Publisher.

To the best of the Publisher's knowledge, the information in this atlas was correct at the time of going to press. No responsibility can be accepted for any errors or their consequences.

The representation in this atlas of any road, drive or track is no evidence of the existence of a right of way.

Data for the speed cameras provided by PocketGPSWorld.com Ltd.

Information for Tourist Attractions in England supplied by the British Tourist Authority / English Tourist Board.

Information for National Parks, Areas of Outstanding Natural Beauty, National Trails and Country Parks in Wales supplied by the Countryside Council for Wales.

Information for National Parks, Areas of Outstanding Natural Beauty, National Trails and Country Parks in England supplied by the Countryside Commission.

Data for Regional Parks, Long Distance Footpaths and Country Parks in Scotland provided by Scottish Natural Heritage.

Data for National Scenic Areas in Scotland provided by the Scottish Executive Office. Crown copyright material is reproduced with the permission of the Controller of HMSO and the Queen's Printer for Scotland. Licence number C02W0003960.

Gaelic name forms used in the Western Isles provided by Comhairle nan Eilean.

Information for canal bridge numbers supplied by GEOprojects (UK) Limited.

Tourist information 1:100 000 road maps

- ⚓ **Abbey or priory**
- 🐬 **Aquarium or dolphinarium**
- 🏛 **Art gallery**
- ⊠ **Art collection or museum**
- 🦒 **Bird sanctuary or aviary**
- 🏰 **Castle**
- ✝ **Cathedral**
- ⛪ **Church of interest**
- 🏛 **Country park** – England and Wales
- 🏛 **Country park** – Scotland
- **County show ground**
- 🐑 **Farm park**
- ❀ **Garden**

- ⛳ **Golf course**
- 🚢 **Historic ship**
- 🏠 **House**
- 🏠 **House and garden**
- 🏛 **Local museum**
- ⚓ **Marina**
- ◈ **Maritime museum / Military museum**
- ⚑ **Motor racing circuit**
- 🏛 **Museum**
- ⊘ **Picnic area**
- **Racecourse**
- ⚔ **Roman antiquity**
- ⛲ **Safari park**

- 🚂 **Preserved railway**
- ⛲ **Theme park**
- **Tourist information centre** — *i* – open all year — *i* – open seasonally
- **Transport collection**
- ★ **Viewpoint**
- △ **Youth hostel**
- 🦁 **Zoo**
- **Ancient monument**
- **Earthwork**
- **Windmill**
- **Watermill**
- **Other place of interest**

Tourist information 1:200 000 road maps

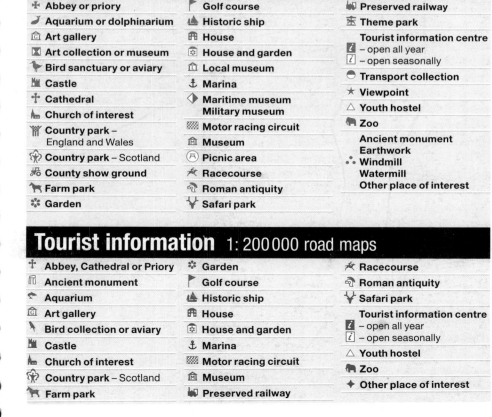

- ✝ **Abbey, Cathedral or Priory**
- 🏛 **Ancient monument**
- **Aquarium**
- 🏛 **Art gallery**
- **Bird collection or aviary**
- 🏰 **Castle**
- ⛪ **Church of interest**
- 🏛 **Country park** – Scotland
- 🐑 **Farm park**

- ❀ **Garden**
- ⛳ **Golf course**
- 🚢 **Historic ship**
- 🏠 **House**
- 🏠 **House and garden**
- ⚓ **Marina**
- ⚑ **Motor racing circuit**
- 🏛 **Museum**
- 🚂 **Preserved railway**

- **Racecourse**
- ⚔ **Roman antiquity**
- ⛲ **Safari park**
- **Tourist information centre** — *i* – open all year — *i* – open seasonally
- △ **Youth hostel**
- 🦁 **Zoo**
- ✦ **Other place of interest**

PHILIP'S
NAVIGA
Britain

C000157008

Contents

Route-finding system

Town names printed in yellow on a green background are those used on Britain's signposts to indicate primary destinations. To find your route quickly and easily, simply follow the signs to the primary destination immediately beyond the place you require.
Below Driving from Totnes to Berry Pomeroy, follow the signs to Paignton, the first primary destination beyond Berry Pomeroy. These will indicate the most direct main route to the side turning for Berry Pomeroy.

Shetland Islands

314 Mainland
315

ABERDEEN
BERGEN
KIRKWALL
TORSHAVN
SEYDISFJÖRDUR (May–Sept)
Lerwick

Orkney Islands

312
Kirkwall Mainland
313
Pentland Firth
Thurso
Wick

ABERDEEN
LERWICK

NORTH SEA

AMSTERDAM
BERGEN
STAVANGER
HAUGESUND

KIRKWALL
LERWICK

STROMNESS
Pentland Firth

310 Thurso Wick
311 Helmsdale

308
309 Tain

306
307 Ullapool Gairloch

Little Minch
North Minch

Outer Hebrides

304 Stornoway Lewis
305 Tarbert (Tairbeart)

296 North Uist
297 South Uist Loch Baghasdail (Lochboisdale)

298 Uig Portree
299

295 Kyle of Lochalsh Mallaig

294

Inner Hebrides
Sea of the Hebrides

288

289 Loch na Keal
Mull

274
Islay
Jura

254 Campbeltown

275 Tarbert
Arran

255

303 Fraserburgh Peterhead
302 Elgin
301 Nairn Grantown-on-Spey
300 Inverness
291 Fort Augustus
290 Fort William
299 Glencoe
285 Oban
284

293 Stonehaven
Aberdeen
292 Brechin Forfar
286 Pitlochry Perth
287 Dundee St. Andrews

Moray Firth

Firth of Forth

280 Kirkcaldy
281 EDINBURGH
282 Dunbar
283 Berwick-upon-Tweed

279 Dunfermline Falkirk
278 Stirling Cumbernauld
277 Clydebank GLASGOW
276 Greenock Port Glasgow Paisley
266 Dunoon
256

269 Hamilton
268 East Kilbride
267 Kilmarnock
257 Ayr Irvine
244

270 Livingston
271
272
273

260 Biggar
261 Hawick
262 Galashiels
263
264 Alnwick
265

259
258
246
245

247
248
249
250 Carlisle
251 Otterburn
252 Morpeth
253 Ashington

NEWCASTLE
UPON TYNE
Gateshead
241
252
253 Tynemouth South Shields
Sunderland

236 Newton Stewart
237 Castle Douglas
238 Dumfries
239
240
241

Solway Firth

228 Workington Whitehaven
229 Cockermouth Keswick
230 Penrith
231 Brough
232 Bishop Auckland Barnard Castle
233 Darlington
234 Stockton-On-Tees Middlesbrough
235 Hartlepool Redcar

Firth of Clyde

219
220 Windermere Kendal
221
222
223
224
225 Guisborough
226
227 Whitby

Peterlee

A1(M)
Consett

Stranraer

LIVERPOOL
DOUGLAS

Isle of Man

FLEETWOOD

BELFAST
Lisburn
Bangor
Larne
Antrim
Coleraine
Derry/Londonderry
Omagh
Armagh
Downpatrick

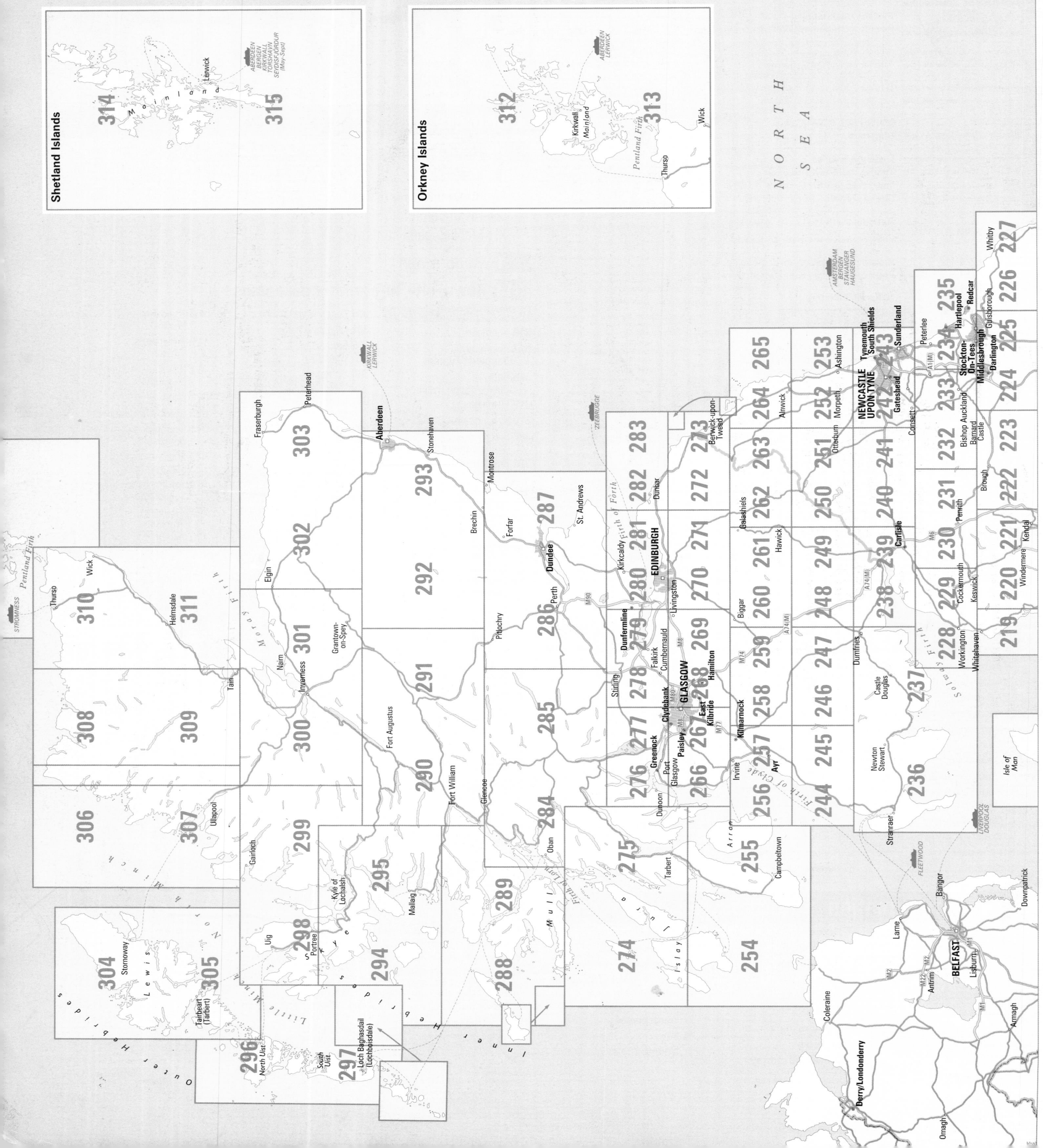

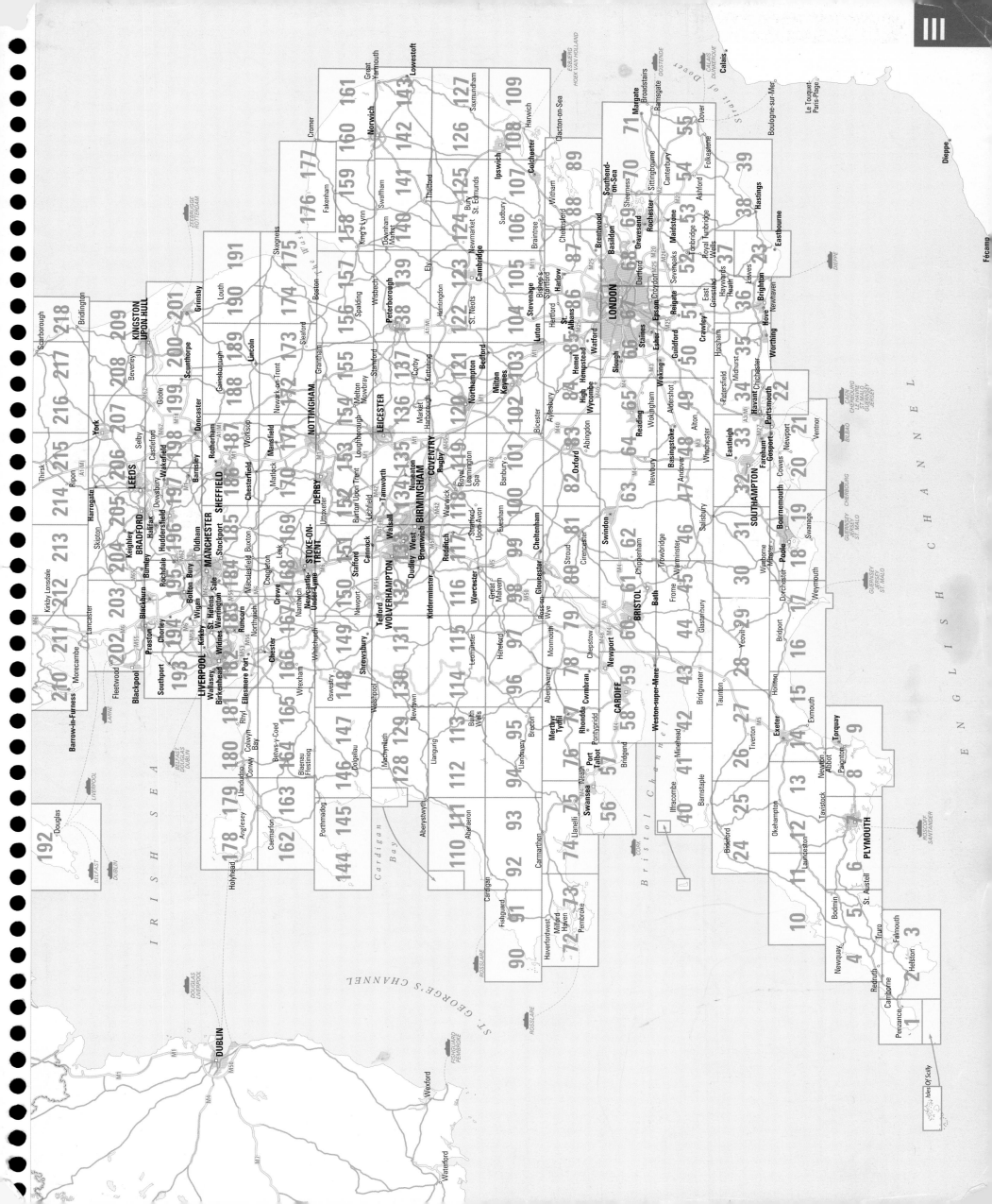

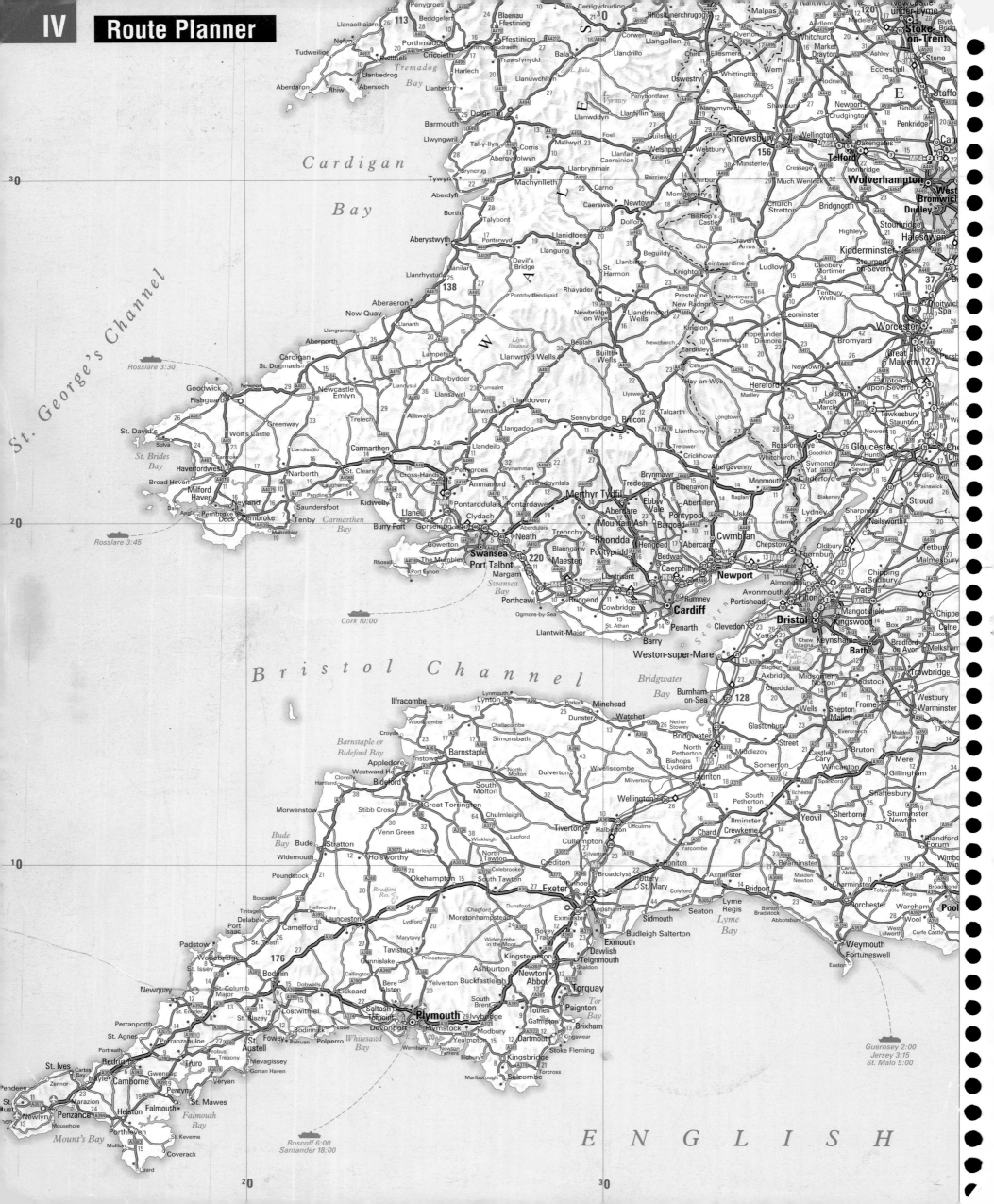

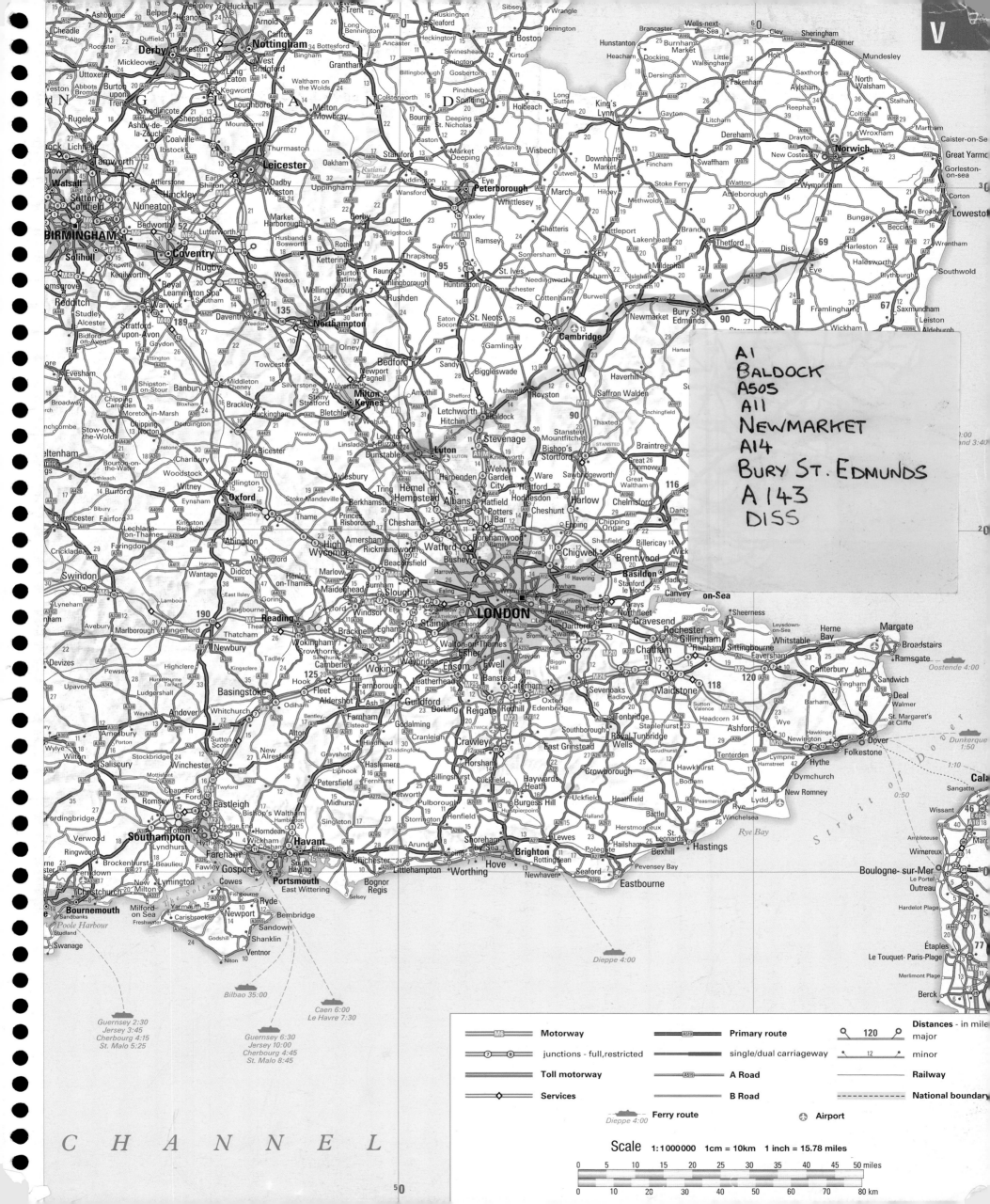

A1
BALDOCK
A505
A11
NEWMARKET
A14
BURY ST. EDMUNDS
A143
DISS

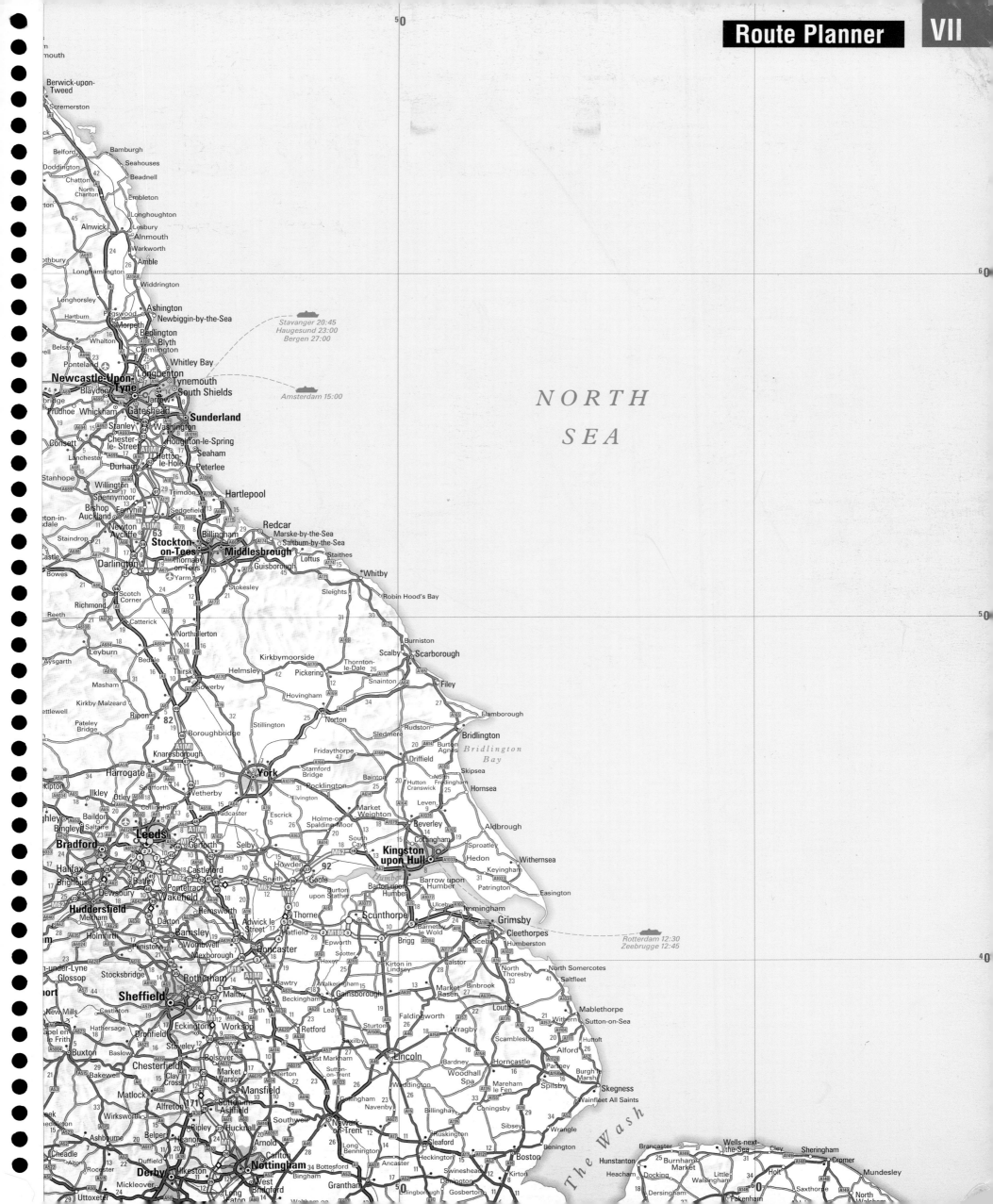

Pentland Firth

Stromness 1:30

Scrabster
Mey
John o'Groats
Thurso
Dunnet
Castletown
Nybster
Halkirk
Sordale
Hastigrow
Keiss
Olgrinmore
Watten
Reiss
Mybster
Watten
Wick
Thrumster
Achavanich
Ulbster
Latheron
Lybster
Dunbeath
Berriedale
Ousdale
Helmsdale

Firth

Burghead
Lossiemouth
Spey B.
Findochty
Portknockie
Portsoy
Rosehearty
Fraserburgh
Kingston
Buckie
Macduff
Banff
New Aberdour
Inverallochy
Elgin
Fochabers
Craibstone
A97
New Pitsligo
Crimond
Forres
Kinloss
Mulben
Aberchirder
Strichen
New Deer
Peterhead
Kellas
Rothes
Keith
Turriff
Maud
Mintlaw
Charlestown of Aberlour
161
Huntly
Fortrie
Old Deer
Boddam
Dufftown
Methlick
Cruden Bay
Marypark
Colpy
Insch
Tarves
Ellon
Newburgh
Tomnavoulin
Cabrach
Rhynie
Oldmeldrum
Lettoch
Lumsden
Inverurie
Newmachar
Strathdon
Alford
Kemnay
Kintore
Dyce
Balmedie
Tomintoul
Ordhead
Bridge of Don
of Garten
Tarland
Westhill
Cults
Aberdeen
Braemar
Crathie
Torphins
Petercutler
Aboyne
Ballater
Banchory
Portlethen
Strachan
Newtonhill
Stonehaven
Spittle of Glenshee
135
Fettercairn
Inverbervie
Clova
Laurencekirk
Johnshaven
Kirkton of Glenisla
Marykirk
michael
Dykehead
Tannadice
Brechin
Montrose
chry
Bridge of Cally
Kirriemuir
Friockheim
Inverkeilor
Lunan B.
allinluig
Alyth
Glamis
Forfar
Blairgowrie
Rattray
Meigle
Carmylie
Dunkeld
Coupar Angus
Monikie
Arbroath
nkfoot
Balbeggie
Carnoustie
Dundee
Monifieth
Scone
Invergowrie
Perth
Tayport
Newport-on-Tay
Bridge of Earn
Wormit
Leuchars
Newburgh
Auchtermuchty
Cupar
St. Andrews
Falkland
Ladybank
Ceres
Kinross
Leslie
Markinch
Crail
Anstruther
Glenrothes
Leven
St. Monance
63
Lochgelly
Buckhaven
Elie
nfermline
Cowdenbeath
Kirkcaldy
Burntisland
Firth of Forth
North Berwick
Boness
Inverkeithing
Gullane
Dunbar
South Rosyth
Queensferry
Zeebrugge 17:30
Prestonpans
Edinburgh
Musselburgh
Tranent
Haddington
Cockburnspath
Dalkeith
Gifford
Grantshouse
St. Abb's
Coldingham
Eyemouth
Bonnyrigg
Penicuik
Gorebridge
Preston
Ayton
Chirnside
Leadburn
West Linton
Westruther
Lauder
Duns
Swinton
Berwick-upon-Tweed
Carnwath
Blyth Bridge
Peebles
Fountainhall
Greenlaw
Gordon
Coldstream
Innerleithen
Stow
Earlston
Broughton
Galashiels
Scremerston

Kirkwall 6:00
Lerwick 14:00

Shetland Islands
Norwick
Haroldswick
Baltasound
Cullivoe
Unst
Gutcher
Belmont
Isbister
Mid Yell
Fetlar
Hillswick
Ulsta
Burravoe
Funzie
St. Magnus Bay
Brae
Voe
Vidlin
Whalsay
Sandness
Aith
Symbister
Neap
Dale
Walls
Foula
Easter Skeld
Scalloway
Lerwick
Hamnavoe
West Burra
Bergen 12:00
Torshavn 12:30
Seyðisfjörður 30:00
Scousburgh
Northpunds
Aberdeen 14:00
Kirkwall 6:00
Boddam
Toloh
Sumburgh
Fair Isle

Orkney Islands
Westray
Hollandstoun
Pierowall
The North Sound 2:40
N. Ronaldsay
Midbea
Burness
Rapness
Overbister
The Barony
Wasbister
Rousay
Eday
Sanday
Store
Twatt
Redland
Brinyan
Odin
Aith
Dounby
Finstown
Shapinsay
Stronsay
Voy
Balfour
Stromness
M a i n l a n d
Kirkwall
Gritley
Linkness
Orphir
St. Mary's
Aberdeen 8:00
Lerwick 6:00
Hoy
Scapa Flow
Lyness
St. Margaret's Hope
Longhope
South Ronaldsay
South Walls
Burwick
Pentland Firth

Scrabster
Mey
John o'Groats
Thurso
Dunnet
Castletown
Nybster
Halkirk
Sordale
Hastigrow
Keiss
Olgrinmore
Watten
Reiss
Mybster
Wick

Distance table

How to use this table

Distances are shown in miles and kilometres with estimated journey times in hours and minutes.

For example: the distance between Aberdeen and Birmingham is 420 miles or 676 kilometres with an estimated journey time of 8 hours, 30 minutes.

Estimated driving times are based on an average speed of 60mph on Motorways and 40mph on other roads. Drivers should allow extra time when driving at peak periods or through areas likely to be congested.

	London	Aberdeen	Aberystwyth	Ayr	Berwick-upon-Tweed	Birmingham	Blackpool	Bournemouth	Braemar	Brighton	Bristol	Cambridge	Cardiff	Carlisle	Doncaster	Dover	Dundee	Edinburgh	Exeter	Fishguard	Fort William	Glasgow	Gloucester	Great Yarmouth	Harwich	Holyhead	Inverness	John o' Groats	Kingston upon Hull	Kyle of Lochalsh	Land's End	Leeds	Leicester	Lincoln	Liverpool	Manchester	Newcastle upon Tyne	Norwich	Nottingham	Oban	Oxford	Plymouth	Portsmouth	Sheffield	Shrewsbury	Southampton	Stranraer	Swansea
Aberdeen	517 / 832 / 11:20																																															
Aberystwyth	211 / 340 / 4:40	445 / 716 / 8:40																																														
Ayr	394 / 634 / 7:20	183 / 295 / 4:20	317 / 510 / 6:10																																													
Berwick-upon-Tweed	352 / 567 / 7:30	182 / 293 / 4:40	311 / 501 / 6:20	134 / 216 / 3:00																																												
Birmingham	117 / 188 / 2:50	420 / 676 / 8:30	114 / 183 / 2:50	289 / 465 / 5:30	274 / 441 / 5:30																																											
Blackpool	226 / 364 / 4:30	308 / 496 / 6:20	153 / 246 / 3:20	180 / 290 / 3:30	181 / 291 / 3:50	123 / 198 / 2:40																																										
Bournemouth	107 / 172 / 2:40	564 / 908 / 10:20	207 / 333 / 4:30	436 / 702 / 8:00	412 / 663 / 7:50	147 / 237 / 3:10	270 / 435 / 5:00																																									
Braemar	482 / 776 / 10:30	59 / 95 / 1:30	405 / 652 / 7:50	143 / 230 / 3:00	148 / 238 / 3:20	385 / 620 / 7:10	281 / 452 / 5:20	524 / 843 / 9:30																																								
Brighton	52 / 84 / 1:50	573 / 922 / 10:30	253 / 407 / 5:10	446 / 718 / 8:00	409 / 658 / 7:40	163 / 262 / 3:20	286 / 460 / 5:20	92 / 148 / 2:10	534 / 859 / 9:40																																							
Bristol	122 / 196 / 2:50	493 / 793 / 9:10	125 / 201 / 3:00	370 / 595 / 6:40	362 / 583 / 6:50	81 / 130 / 2:00	204 / 328 / 3:50	82 / 132 / 2:30	477 / 768 / 8:40	147 / 237 / 4:10																																						
Cambridge	54 / 87 / 1:30	471 / 758 / 10:00	214 / 344 / 4:20	357 / 575 / 6:20	306 / 493 / 5:40	100 / 161 / 2:10	208 / 335 / 3:50	154 / 248 / 3:00	438 / 705 / 7:50	116 / 187 / 2:20	169 / 272 / 3:10																																					
Cardiff	157 / 253 / 3:20	505 / 813 / 9:20	105 / 169 / 2:40	382 / 615 / 7:00	368 / 592 / 7:00	103 / 166 / 2:20	209 / 336 / 4:00	117 / 188 / 3:00	483 / 778 / 8:40	182 / 293 / 3:40	45 / 72 / 1:20	190 / 306 / 3:30																																				
Carlisle	301 / 484 / 5:40	221 / 356 / 4:30	224 / 360 / 4:30	93 / 150 / 2:00	87 / 140 / 2:10	196 / 315 / 3:50	87 / 140 / 1:50	343 / 552 / 6:20	196 / 316 / 3:50	370 / 596 / 6:40	277 / 446 / 5:00	264 / 425 / 4:40	289 / 465 / 5:20																																			
Doncaster	171 / 275 / 3:30	344 / 554 / 6:50	176 / 283 / 3:40	235 / 378 / 4:20	184 / 296 / 3:50	94 / 151 / 2:00	94 / 151 / 1:50	235 / 378 / 4:20	310 / 499 / 5:40	236 / 380 / 4:30	175 / 282 / 3:20	116 / 187 / 2:10	209 / 336 / 4:00	142 / 229 / 3:00																																		
Dover	71 / 114 / 2:00	588 / 947 / 10:40	297 / 478 / 5:50	478 / 769 / 8:30	424 / 683 / 7:50	194 / 312 / 3:50	312 / 502 / 5:40	174 / 280 / 4:30	553 / 890 / 9:50	82 / 132 / 2:20	202 / 325 / 3:50	125 / 201 / 2:30	238 / 383 / 4:30	389 / 626 / 7:00	242 / 390 / 4:30																																	
Dundee	448 / 721 / 8:40	67 / 108 / 1:50	376 / 605 / 7:10	117 / 188 / 2:30	113 / 182 / 2:40	349 / 562 / 6:20	239 / 385 / 4:30	495 / 797 / 8:50	52 / 84 / 1:20	517 / 832 / 9:10	430 / 692 / 7:40	406 / 654 / 7:10	441 / 710 / 8:00	152 / 245 / 3:00	275 / 443 / 5:00	523 / 842 / 9:10																																
Edinburgh	390 / 628 / 7:20	125 / 201 / 3:10	320 / 515 / 6:20	73 / 117 / 1:50	57 / 92 / 1:40	292 / 470 / 5:30	183 / 295 / 3:30	439 / 707 / 8:00	91 / 146 / 2:10	456 / 734 / 8:20	373 / 600 / 6:50	345 / 555 / 6:10	385 / 620 / 7:00	96 / 154 / 2:00	219 / 352 / 4:00	462 / 744 / 8:10	56 / 90 / 1:30																															
Exeter	181 / 291 / 3:40	569 / 916 / 10:20	201 / 323 / 4:10	446 / 718 / 7:50	428 / 689 / 7:50	157 / 253 / 3:10	282 / 454 / 5:10	82 / 132 / 2:20	550 / 885 / 9:40	184 / 296 / 5:00	76 / 122 / 1:40	249 / 401 / 4:30	121 / 195 / 2:30	353 / 568 / 6:20	251 / 404 / 4:30	248 / 399 / 4:40	518 / 834 / 9:10	450 / 724 / 8:00																													
Fishguard	260 / 418 / 5:20	504 / 811 / 10:10	56 / 90 / 1:30	373 / 600 / 7:00	371 / 597 / 7:20	170 / 274 / 3:40	209 / 336 / 4:10	222 / 357 / 4:40	493 / 794 / 9:10	291 / 468 / 5:40	154 / 248 / 3:20	270 / 435 / 5:10	112 / 180 / 2:40	297 / 478 / 5:40	247 / 398 / 4:50	331 / 533 / 6:20	460 / 740 / 8:30	399 / 642 / 7:30	230 / 370 / 4:30																												
Fort William	510 / 821 / 9:50	149 / 240 / 3:50	430 / 692 / 8:40	133 / 214 / 3:20	190 / 306 / 4:40	392 / 631 / 7:40	296 / 476 / 6:00	539 / 867 / 10:10	125 / 201 / 3:10	575 / 926 / 10:50	486 / 782 / 9:10	479 / 771 / 9:00	485 / 781 / 9:10	206 / 332 / 4:30	357 / 575 / 7:00	596 / 959 / 11:00	127 / 204 / 3:10	144 / 232 / 3:30	560 / 901 / 10:20	486 / 782 / 9:30																											
Glasgow	397 / 639 / 7:30	145 / 233 / 3:30	320 / 515 / 6:20	33 / 53 / 1:10	101 / 163 / 2:40	292 / 470 / 5:30	183 / 295 / 3:40	439 / 707 / 8:00	110 / 177 / 2:30	468 / 753 / 8:30	373 / 600 / 6:50	372 / 599 / 6:40	385 / 620 / 7:00	96 / 154 / 2:10	249 / 401 / 4:40	488 / 786 / 8:40	83 / 134 / 2:00	44 / 71 / 1:20	449 / 723 / 8:00	376 / 605 / 7:10	101 / 163 / 2:50																										
Gloucester	109 / 175 / 2:30	468 / 753 / 8:30	102 / 164 / 2:30	330 / 531 / 5:50	318 / 512 / 6:00	56 / 90 / 1:20	174 / 280 / 3:10	99 / 159 / 2:40	443 / 713 / 8:00	159 / 256 / 3:10	35 / 56 / 1:00	123 / 198 / 2:20	56 / 90 / 1:20	247 / 398 / 4:20	150 / 241 / 2:50	191 / 307 / 3:30	410 / 660 / 7:10	349 / 562 / 6:10	111 / 179 / 2:10	153 / 246 / 3:10	454 / 731 / 8:30	346 / 557 / 6:10																									
Great Yarmouth	128 / 206 / 3:40	517 / 832 / 10:50	294 / 473 / 6:20	402 / 647 / 7:40	345 / 555 / 7:00	180 / 290 / 4:10	252 / 406 / 5:10	240 / 386 / 5:00	477 / 768 / 9:10	180 / 290 / 4:10	275 / 443 / 5:40	82 / 132 / 2:10	284 / 457 / 5:50	320 / 515 / 6:20	167 / 269 / 3:40	185 / 298 / 4:00	484 / 779 / 9:00	386 / 621 / 7:30	335 / 539 / 6:30	366 / 589 / 7:20	527 / 848 / 10:20	419 / 674 / 8:00	225 / 362 / 4:40																								
Harwich	76 / 122 / 2:20	535 / 861 / 11:20	281 / 452 / 5:50	425 / 684 / 8:00	372 / 599 / 7:20	167 / 269 / 3:40	275 / 443 / 5:20	187 / 301 / 4:00	504 / 811 / 9:20	128 / 206 / 3:00	217 / 349 / 4:30	67 / 108 / 1:50	246 / 396 / 5:00	336 / 541 / 6:20	194 / 312 / 4:00	125 / 201 / 2:50	469 / 755 / 8:40	413 / 665 / 7:40	279 / 449 / 5:20	337 / 542 / 6:40	543 / 874 / 10:30	432 / 695 / 8:10	196 / 316 / 4:00	82 / 132 / 2:10																							
Holyhead	269 / 433 / 5:40	439 / 707 / 8:40	111 / 179 / 2:50	305 / 491 / 6:10	311 / 501 / 6:30	148 / 238 / 3:30	141 / 227 / 3:20	288 / 463 / 5:50	426 / 686 / 8:20	334 / 538 / 6:40	206 / 332 / 4:30	270 / 435 / 5:20	216 / 348 / 5:40	231 / 372 / 4:50	181 / 291 / 3:50	360 / 580 / 7:00	394 / 634 / 7:30	333 / 536 / 6:40	282 / 454 / 5:40	167 / 269 / 4:00	438 / 705 / 8:50	330 / 531 / 6:40	191 / 307 / 4:00	334 / 538 / 7:00	349 / 562 / 7:10																						
Inverness	550 / 885 / 10:40	105 / 169 / 2:50	486 / 782 / 9:40	199 / 320 / 4:30	215 / 346 / 5:10	458 / 737 / 9:00	348 / 560 / 7:00	597 / 961 / 11:20	75 / 121 / 2:00	617 / 993 / 11:30	539 / 867 / 10:10	505 / 813 / 9:30	549 / 884 / 10:20	262 / 422 / 5:30	383 / 617 / 7:30	622 / 1001 / 11:30	132 / 212 / 3:20	158 / 254 / 3:50	618 / 995 / 11:30	542 / 872 / 10:30	66 / 106 / 1:40	166 / 267 / 4:00	504 / 811 / 9:30	553 / 890 / 11:00	569 / 916 / 11:00	474 / 763 / 9:40																					
John o' Groats	663 / 1067 / 13:30	232 / 373 / 5:50	601 / 967 / 12:40	328 / 528 / 7:40	342 / 550 / 8:10	574 / 924 / 11:50	478 / 769 / 10:00	724 / 1165 / 14:20	202 / 325 / 5:00	741 / 1193 / 14:40	668 / 1075 / 13:20	630 / 1014 / 12:30	680 / 1094 / 13:30	391 / 629 / 8:40	507 / 816 / 10:30	746 / 1201 / 14:40	259 / 417 / 6:30	285 / 459 / 7:00	744 / 1197 / 14:30	671 / 1080 / 13:40	195 / 314 / 5:00	295 / 475 / 7:10	628 / 1011 / 12:30	677 / 1090 / 14:00	693 / 1116 / 14:00	603 / 970 / 12:40	129 / 208 / 3:20																				
Kingston upon Hull	184 / 296 / 3:50	364 / 586 / 7:20	223 / 359 / 4:40	251 / 404 / 4:40	185 / 298 / 3:50	134 / 216 / 2:50	127 / 204 / 2:30	264 / 425 / 5:00	327 / 526 / 6:10	245 / 394 / 4:40	233 / 375 / 4:20	139 / 224 / 3:10	244 / 393 / 4:40	158 / 254 / 3:00	47 / 76 / 1:10	256 / 412 / 4:50	295 / 475 / 5:30	234 / 377 / 4:30	309 / 497 / 5:40	280 / 451 / 5:30	369 / 594 / 7:20	254 / 409 / 4:50	169 / 272 / 3:10	207 / 333 / 5:20	196 / 316 / 4:10	231 / 372 / 4:50	394 / 634 / 7:50	518 / 834 / 10:50																			
Kyle of Lochalsh	586 / 943 / 11:40	189 / 304 / 4:50	499 / 803 / 10:20	212 / 341 / 5:10	263 / 423 / 6:20	471 / 758 / 9:40	372 / 599 / 7:50	618 / 995 / 12:10	159 / 256 / 4:00	651 / 1048 / 12:40	552 / 888 / 10:50	555 / 893 / 10:50	564 / 908 / 11:10	275 / 443 / 6:10	432 / 695 / 8:40	671 / 1080 / 12:50	186 / 299 / 4:40	216 / 348 / 5:20	628 / 1011 / 12:00	567 / 913 / 11:20	79 / 127 / 2:00	179 / 288 / 4:40	528 / 850 / 10:20	602 / 969 / 12:10	611 / 983 / 12:10	514 / 827 / 10:40	84 / 135 / 2:10	189 / 304 / 4:40	445 / 716 / 9:00																		
Land's End	297 / 478 / 6:30	692 / 1114 / 13:10	313 / 504 / 6:50	570 / 917 / 10:50	552 / 888 / 10:40	281 / 452 / 6:00	405 / 652 / 8:00	205 / 330 / 5:20	665 / 1070 / 12:30	308 / 496 / 7:50	200 / 322 / 4:40	374 / 602 / 7:20	245 / 394 / 5:20	477 / 768 / 9:10	374 / 602 / 7:20	381 / 613 / 7:40	642 / 1033 / 12:00	574 / 924 / 10:50	123 / 198 / 3:20	353 / 568 / 7:20	686 / 1104 / 13:20	573 / 922 / 10:50	235 / 378 / 5:00	446 / 718 / 9:10	390 / 628 / 8:00	405 / 652 / 8:30	741 / 1193 / 14:20	868 / 1397 / 17:20	421 / 678 / 8:20	763 / 1228 / 15:10																	
Leeds	189 / 304 / 3:50	327 / 526 / 6:50	169 / 272 / 3:40	212 / 341 / 4:00	156 / 251 / 3:20	113 / 182 / 2:30	72 / 116 / 1:40	255 / 410 / 4:50	293 / 472 / 5:30	260 / 419 / 5:00	194 / 312 / 3:50	145 / 233 / 2:50	232 / 373 / 4:20	119 / 192 / 2:30	29 / 47 / 0:50	260 / 418 / 4:50	258 / 415 / 4:50	202 / 325 / 4:00	270 / 435 / 5:00	237 / 381 / 4:40	329 / 530 / 6:40	215 / 346 / 4:10	174 / 280 / 3:20	196 / 315 / 4:20	223 / 359 / 4:30	176 / 283 / 4:00	360 / 579 / 7:10	487 / 784 / 10:20	55 / 89 / 1:30	394 / 634 / 8:20	405 / 652 / 8:00																
Leicester	97 / 156 / 2:20	414 / 666 / 7:40	153 / 246 / 3:20	299 / 481 / 5:20	252 / 406 / 5:00	39 / 63 / 1:10	140 / 225 / 2:40	158 / 254 / 3:10	389 / 626 / 7:00	166 / 267 / 3:20	120 / 193 / 2:30	68 / 109 / 1:20	154 / 248 / 3:00	206 / 332 / 3:50	74 / 119 / 1:30	185 / 298 / 3:30	349 / 562 / 6:20	296 / 476 / 5:20	196 / 315 / 3:40	209 / 336 / 4:10	422 / 679 / 8:00	314 / 505 / 5:40	85 / 137 / 1:40	140 / 225 / 3:20	147 / 237 / 3:10	190 / 306 / 4:00	461 / 742 / 8:50	588 / 947 / 11:50	102 / 164 / 2:10	500 / 805 / 9:50	320 / 515 / 6:30	95 / 153 / 2:00															
Lincoln	131 / 211 / 3:10	383 / 616 / 7:20	199 / 320 / 4:20	274 / 441 / 5:10	224 / 360 / 4:40	90 / 145 / 2:10	128 / 206 / 2:40	209 / 336 / 4:10	357 / 575 / 6:40	197 / 317 / 4:00	183 / 295 / 3:40	85 / 137 / 2:20	208 / 335 / 4:10	191 / 307 / 3:40	39 / 63 / 1:10	202 / 325 / 4:00	314 / 505 / 5:50	258 / 415 / 5:00	247 / 398 / 4:40	272 / 438 / 5:30	399 / 642 / 7:50	291 / 468 / 5:30	159 / 256 / 3:10	128 / 206 / 3:20	155 / 249 / 3:30	216 / 348 / 4:40	427 / 687 / 8:30	554 / 892 / 11:30	44 / 71 / 1:20	476 / 766 / 9:40	371 / 597 / 7:30	68 / 109 / 1:50	51 / 82 / 1:20														
Liverpool	202 / 325 / 4:10	341 / 549 / 6:40	104 / 167 / 2:40	213 / 343 / 4:10	219 / 352 / 4:30	93 / 150 / 2:10	49 / 79 / 1:20	234 / 377 / 4:30	318 / 512 / 6:00	272 / 438 / 5:10	161 / 259 / 3:10	194 / 312 / 3:40	169 / 272 / 3:20	120 / 193 / 2:30	86 / 138 / 1:50	299 / 481 / 5:30	286 / 460 / 5:20	216 / 348 / 4:10	237 / 381 / 4:30	160 / 257 / 3:30	329 / 530 / 6:40	216 / 348 / 4:10	140 / 225 / 2:40	240 / 386 / 5:00	265 / 427 / 5:20	102 / 164 / 2:40	382 / 615 / 7:40	511 / 822 / 10:40	130 / 209 / 2:40	407 / 655 / 8:30	361 / 581 / 7:20	75 / 121 / 1:50	130 / 209 / 2:40	129 / 208 / 2:50													
Manchester	185 / 298 / 3:50	340 / 547 / 6:30	129 / 208 / 3:00	212 / 341 / 4:00	196 / 315 / 4:00	80 / 129 / 2:00	48 / 77 / 1:20	227 / 365 / 4:20	318 / 512 / 6:00	257 / 414 / 4:50	161 / 259 / 3:10	165 / 266 / 3:10	183 / 295 / 3:40	119 / 192 / 2:30	61 / 98 / 1:30	276 / 444 / 5:10	285 / 459 / 5:20	215 / 346 / 4:10	236 / 380 / 4:20	197 / 317 / 4:00	329 / 530 / 6:40	215 / 346 / 4:10	126 / 203 / 2:30	212 / 341 / 4:30	228 / 367 / 4:40	124 / 200 / 3:00	373 / 600 / 7:30	500 / 805 / 10:30	95 / 153 / 2:10	406 / 654 / 8:30	361 / 581 / 7:20	40 / 64 / 1:10	92 / 148 / 2:00	84 / 135 / 2:00	35 / 56 / 1:10												
Newcastle upon Tyne	286 / 460 / 5:40	235 / 378 / 4:50	257 / 414 / 5:20	149 / 240 / 3:00	64 / 103 / 1:50	207 / 333 / 4:10	129 / 208 / 2:40	347 / 558 / 6:30	201 / 323 / 4:00	352 / 567 / 6:30	299 / 481 / 5:30	241 / 388 / 4:20	325 / 523 / 6:00	57 / 92 / 1:50	114 / 183 / 2:20	358 / 576 / 6:30	166 / 267 / 3:20	110 / 177 / 2:20	364 / 586 / 6:30	329 / 529 / 6:20	253 / 407 / 5:20	148 / 238 / 3:10	266 / 428 / 4:50	281 / 452 / 5:40	308 / 496 / 6:00	272 / 438 / 5:40	268 / 431 / 5:40	395 / 636 / 8:50	132 / 212 / 2:50	318 / 512 / 7:00	498 / 802 / 9:40	92 / 148 / 2:10	187 / 301 / 3:40	159 / 256 / 3:20	168 / 270 / 3:20	132 / 212 / 2:50											
Norwich	114 / 183 / 3:30	496 / 798 / 9:40	276 / 444 / 6:00	382 / 615 / 7:20	328 / 528 / 6:40	166 / 267 / 3:50	232 / 373 / 4:50	214 / 344 / 4:40	457 / 735 / 8:40	175 / 282 / 4:00	252 / 406 / 5:10	62 / 100 / 1:50	262 / 422 / 5:20	289 / 465 / 5:40	147 / 237 / 3:20	174 / 280 / 3:50	422 / 679 / 8:00	366 / 589 / 7:00	308 / 496 / 6:00	343 / 552 / 7:00	504 / 811 / 10:00	385 / 620 / 9:00	204 / 328 / 4:10	20 / 32 / 0:40	73 / 117 / 2:00	311 / 501 / 6:40	529 / 852 / 10:30	654 / 1053 / 13:30	149 / 240 / 4:00	582 / 937 / 11:50	421 / 678 / 8:40	176 / 283 / 3:50	119 / 192 / 3:20	105 / 169 / 2:50	220 / 354 / 4:40	185 / 298 / 4:30	264 / 425 / 5:20										
Nottingham	122 / 196 / 2:40	393 / 633 / 7:30	164 / 264 / 3:40	274 / 441 / 5:10	221 / 356 / 4:30	50 / 80 / 1:20	111 / 179 / 2:20	183 / 295 / 3:40	353 / 568 / 6:30	193 / 311 / 3:50	145 / 233 / 3:00	83 / 134 / 1:40	172 / 277 / 3:20	194 / 312 / 3:40	43 / 69 / 1:10	205 / 330 / 3:50	328 / 528 / 6:00	262 / 422 / 4:50	221 / 356 / 4:10	220 / 354 / 4:30	401 / 646 / 7:50	293 / 472 / 5:30	110 / 177 / 2:10	153 / 246 / 3:30	150 / 241 / 3:20	185 / 298 / 4:00	430 / 692 / 8:20	557 / 896 / 11:30	90 / 145 / 2:00	479 / 771 / 9:40	345 / 555 / 7:00	70 / 113 / 1:40	25 / 40 / 0:50	35 / 56 / 1:10	98 / 158 / 2:10	73 / 118 / 1:40	157 / 253 / 3:10	130 / 209 / 3:40									
Oban	499 / 803 / 9:30	178 / 286 / 4:20	412 / 663 / 8:10	94 / 151 / 2:20	180 / 290 / 4:20	384 / 618 / 7:30	285 / 459 / 5:40	530 / 853 / 9:50	141 / 227 / 3:30	565 / 910 / 10:30	465 / 748 / 8:40	468 / 753 / 8:40	477 / 768 / 9:00	188 / 303 / 4:00	346 / 557 / 6:40	585 / 942 / 10:40	117 / 188 / 2:50	67 / 108 / 2:00	549 / 884 / 10:00	481 / 774 / 9:10	49 / 79 / 1:20	92 / 148 / 2:30	441 / 710 / 8:10	515 / 829 / 10:00	524 / 843 / 10:00	427 / 687 / 8:30	117 / 188 / 3:00	244 / 393 / 6:10	346 / 557 / 6:40	128 / 206 / 3:10	665 / 1070 / 12:50	307 / 494 / 6:00	419 / 674 / 7:50	387 / 623 / 7:30	308 / 496 / 6:10	307 / 494 / 6:00	233 / 375 / 4:50	492 / 792 / 9:40	390 / 628 / 7:30								
Oxford	57 / 92 / 1:40	483 / 777 / 8:50	154 / 248 / 3:20	353 / 568 / 6:20	324 / 521 / 6:10	64 / 103 / 1:30	187 / 301 / 3:30	90 / 145 / 2:00	465 / 749 / 8:20	108 / 174 / 2:20	74 / 119 / 1:40	83 / 134 / 1:40	108 / 174 / 2:20	260 / 418 / 4:40	145 / 233 / 2:40	141 / 227 / 2:50	433 / 697 / 7:40	372 / 599 / 6:40	156 / 251 / 3:00	205 / 330 / 4:10	472 / 760 / 9:00	356 / 573 / 6:30	52 / 84 / 1:30	200 / 322 / 4:20	145 / 233 / 3:10	238 / 383 / 4:50	532 / 856 / 10:00	656 / 1056 / 13:00	192 / 309 / 3:40	550 / 885 / 10:40	274 / 441 / 5:40	168 / 270 / 3:10	73 / 117 / 1:30	137 / 221 / 2:50	172 / 277 / 3:20	144 / 232 / 2:50	260 / 418 / 4:50	145 / 233 / 3:50	109 / 175 / 2:10	462 / 744 / 8:30							
Plymouth	218 / 351 / 4:40	615 / 990 / 11:20	237 / 382 / 5:10	492 / 792 / 9:00	474 / 763 / 9:00	203 / 327 / 4:20	328 / 528 / 6:10	128 / 206 / 3:30	587 / 945 / 10:40	224 / 361 / 6:00	122 / 196 / 2:50	293 / 472 / 5:30	167 / 269 / 3:40	399 / 642 / 7:20	297 / 478 / 5:40	300 / 483 / 5:50	552 / 888 / 10:00	496 / 798 / 9:00	46 / 74 / 1:30	264 / 425 / 5:30	595 / 958 / 11:20	495 / 797 / 9:10	157 / 253 / 3:20	365 / 588 / 7:20	309 / 497 / 6:10	328 / 528 / 6:40	664 / 1069 / 12:30	790 / 1271 / 15:40	355 / 571 / 6:40	674 / 1085 / 13:10	89 / 143 / 2:20	316 / 509 / 6:00	242 / 389 / 4:40	293 / 472 / 5:50	283 / 455 / 5:30	283 / 455 / 5:30	410 / 660 / 7:40	343 / 552 / 7:00	267 / 430 / 5:10	587 / 945 / 11:00	199 / 320 / 4:00						
Portsmouth	70 / 113 / 2:00	560 / 901 / 10:10	222 / 357 / 4:40	430 / 692 / 7:40	401 / 645 / 7:30	141 / 227 / 3:00	264 / 425 / 4:50	52 / 84 / 1:30	547 / 881 / 9:50	48 / 77 / 1:40	97 / 156 / 2:10	144 / 232 / 2:50	142 / 229 / 3:00	348 / 560 / 6:10	234 / 377 / 4:20	130 / 209 / 2:50	514 / 827 / 9:00	453 / 729 / 8:10	135 / 217 / 2:40	251 / 404 / 5:00	555 / 893 / 10:20	448 / 721 / 8:10	119 / 192 / 3:00	221 / 356 / 4:40	166 / 267 / 3:40	311 / 501 / 6:10	613 / 987 / 11:30	737 / 1186 / 14:30	269 / 433 / 5:00	633 / 1019 / 12:10	259 / 417 / 5:40	257 / 414 / 4:50	162 / 261 / 3:10	201 / 323 / 4:00	254 / 409 / 4:50	236 / 380 / 4:30	337 / 542 / 6:10	207 / 333 / 4:20	191 / 307 / 3:40	545 / 877 / 10:00	77 / 124 / 1:40	176 / 283 / 4:50					
Sheffield	159 / 256 / 3:20	360 / 579 / 6:50	159 / 256 / 3:30	245 / 394 / 4:30	190 / 306 / 4:00	76 / 122 / 1:50	86 / 138 / 1:50	216 / 348 / 4:10	320 / 515 / 6:00	226 / 364 / 4:20	161 / 259 / 3:10	120 / 193 / 2:20	194 / 312 / 3:40	152 / 245 / 3:00	18 / 29 / 0:40	245 / 394 / 4:30	291 / 468 / 5:20	235 / 378 / 4:20	237 / 381 / 4:20	215 / 346 / 4:20	348 / 560 / 6:50	248 / 399 / 4:40	126 / 203 / 2:20	166 / 267 / 3:40	187 / 301 / 3:50	168 / 270 / 3:40	393 / 632 / 7:40	520 / 837 / 10:50	65 / 105 / 1:30	427 / 687 / 8:40	361 / 581 / 7:10	33 / 53 / 1:00	62 / 100 / 1:20	46 / 74 / 1:20	72 / 116 / 1:40	38 / 61 / 1:00	125 / 201 / 2:40	146 / 235 / 3:20	37 / 60 / 1:00	339 / 546 / 6:30	135 / 217 / 2:40	283 / 455 / 5:30	230 / 370 / 4:20				
Shrewsbury	160 / 258 / 3:20	399 / 642 / 7:30	77 / 124 / 2:10	269 / 433 / 5:00	265 / 426 / 5:10	45 / 72 / 1:20	98 / 158 / 2:00	185 / 298 / 3:40	371 / 597 / 6:50	226 / 364 / 4:20	103 / 166 / 2:50	159 / 256 / 3:00	111 / 179 / 2:20	176 / 283 / 3:20	109 / 175 / 2:10	251 / 404 / 4:30	330 / 531 / 6:00	274 / 441 / 5:00	179 / 288 / 3:20	145 / 233 / 3:10	382 / 615 / 7:20	272 / 438 / 5:00	77 / 124 / 1:30	225 / 362 / 4:40	240 / 386 / 4:40	113 / 182 / 2:50	438 / 705 / 8:20	567 / 912 / 11:30	169 / 272 / 3:10	451 / 726 / 9:00	303 / 488 / 6:10	109 / 175 / 2:20	84 / 135 / 1:40	133 / 214 / 2:50	58 / 93 / 1:50	69 / 111 / 1:40	201 / 323 / 3:50	205 / 330 / 4:20	93 / 150 / 2:00	364 / 586 / 7:00	106 / 171 / 2:10	225 / 362 / 4:40	207 / 333 / 3:50	82 / 132 / 2:10			
Southampton	77 / 124 / 2:00	547 / 880 / 10:00	201 / 323 / 4:10	417 / 671 / 7:30	388 / 624 / 7:10	128 / 206 / 2:40	251 / 404 / 4:40	31 / 50 / 1:00	532 / 856 / 9:30	61 / 98 / 1:50	76 / 122 / 2:20	148 / 238 / 2:50	121 / 195 / 2:30	324 / 521 / 5:50	209 / 336 / 3:50	143 / 230 / 2:50	500 / 805 / 8:50	438 / 705 / 7:50	105 / 169 / 3:00	233 / 375 / 4:40	541 / 871 / 10:00	433 / 697 / 7:40	105 / 169 / 2:40	220 / 354 / 4:40	164 / 264 / 3:30	293 / 472 / 5:50	598 / 963 / 11:10	723 / 1164 / 14:10	256 / 412 / 4:40	618 / 995 / 12:00	228 / 367 / 5:00	232 / 373 / 4:20	137 / 220 / 2:40	204 / 328 / 4:00	239 / 385 / 4:30	221 / 356 / 4:10	324 / 521 / 5:50	206 / 332 / 4:20	176 / 283 / 3:20	530 / 853 / 9:40	64 / 103 / 1:30	151 / 243 / 4:10	21 / 34 / 0:50	199 / 320 / 3:40	185 / 298 / 4:10		
Stranraer	402 / 647 / 7:50	228 / 367 / 5:10	325 / 523 / 6:50	51 / 82 / 1:20	170 / 274 / 4:10	297 / 478 / 6:00	188 / 303 / 4:00	444 / 715 / 8:30	194 / 312 / 4:20	475 / 765 / 9:00	378 / 608 / 7:20	379 / 610 / 7:10	390 / 628 / 7:30	101 / 163 / 2:40	257 / 414 / 5:10	496 / 798 / 9:10	167 / 269 / 3:40	124 / 200 / 3:00	454 / 731 / 8:30	392 / 631 / 7:50	195 / 314 / 4:50	84 / 135 / 2:30	343 / 552 / 6:30	426 / 686 / 8:40	410 / 660 / 8:10	338 / 544 / 7:00	262 / 422 / 6:00	379 / 610 / 9:00	259 / 417 / 5:20	263 / 423 / 6:30	585 / 942 / 11:30	220 / 354 / 4:40	330 / 531 / 6:20	298 / 480 / 6:00	221 / 356 / 4:40	220 / 354 / 4:40	158 / 254 / 3:40	403 / 649 / 8:10	290 / 467 / 5:50	148 / 238 / 3:40	379 / 610 / 7:10	500 / 805 / 9:40	461 / 742 / 8:40	263 / 423 / 5:20	277 / 446 / 5:30	445 / 716 / 8:20	
Swansea	194 / 312 / 4:00	507 / 816 / 9:20	73 / 117 / 2:00	379 / 610 / 6:50	383 / 616 / 7:10	119 / 192 / 2:30	216 / 348 / 4:00	167 / 269 / 3:20	505 / 813 / 9:00	222 / 357 / 4:20	85 / 137 / 1:50	227 / 365 / 4:10	41 / 66 / 1:10	309 / 497 / 5:30	232 / 373 / 4:10	274 / 441 / 5:00	473 / 761 / 8:20	412 / 663 / 7:20	161 / 259 / 3:00	67 / 108 / 1:50	496 / 798 / 9:20	409 / 658 / 7:20	89 / 143 / 1:50	329 / 530 / 6:30	267 / 430 / 5:10	184 / 296 / 4:50	572 / 921 / 10:40	696 / 1120 / 13:40	264 / 425 / 4:50	594 / 956 / 11:30	285 / 459 / 6:00	248 / 399 / 4:40	177 / 285 / 3:20	233 / 375 / 4:30	195 / 314 / 3:40	187 / 301 / 3:30	347 / 559 / 6:20	301 / 485 / 6:00	192 / 309 / 3:40	506 / 815 / 9:20	141 / 227 / 2:40	206 / 332 / 4:10	182 / 293 / 3:30	217 / 349 / 4:00	118 / 190 / 2:20	161 / 259 / 3:00	417 / 671 / 7:50
York	207 / 333 / 4:10	319 / 513 / 6:10	195 / 314 / 4:10	214 / 344 / 4:00	148 / 238 / 3:10	130 / 209 / 2:40	96 / 154 / 2:00	269 / 433 / 5:00	285 / 459 / 5:20	275 / 443 / 5:10	222 / 357 / 4:10	165 / 266 / 3:10	244 / 393 / 4:40	121 / 195 / 2:30	34 / 55 / 1:00	282 / 454 / 5:10	250 / 402 / 4:40	194 / 312 / 3:40	287 / 462 / 5:10	261 / 420 / 5:10	330 / 531 / 6:30	217 / 349 / 4:10	189 / 304 / 3:30	201 / 323 / 4:20	228 / 367 / 4:40	204 / 328 / 4:20	352 / 566 / 7:00	479 / 771 / 10:10	37 / 60 / 1:10	407 / 655 / 8:20	411 / 661 / 8:00	24 / 39 / 0:50	108 / 174 / 2:10	75 / 121 / 1:50	99 / 159 / 2:10	64 / 103 / 1:30	84 / 135 / 2:20	181 / 291 / 4:20	77 / 124 / 1:40	309 / 497 / 6:00	181 / 291 / 3:20	333 / 536 / 6:20	278 / 448 / 5:10	52 / 84 / 1:20	133 / 214 / 2:40	258 / 415 / 5:10	222 / 357 / 4:40	272 / 438 / 5:10

Going far?
Make time for a break every two hours.
THINK!
Tiredness Kills

Mobile speed camera sites

The vast majority of speed cameras used on Britain's roads are operated by safety camera partnerships. These comprise local authorities, the police, Her Majesty's Court Service (HMCS) and the Highways Agency.

This table lists the sites where each safety camera partnership may enforce speed limits through the use of mobile cameras or detectors. These are usually set up on the roadside or a bridge spanning the road and operated by a police or civilian enforcement officer. The speed limit at each site (if available) is shown in red type, followed by the approximate location in black type.

Abbreviations

adj	adjacent
btwn	between
Dr	Drive
Ind Est	Industrial Estate
jct	junction
j/w	junction with
nr	near
o/s	outside
opp	opposite
rdbt	roundabout
twds	towards

England

Avon and Somerset

Bath and North East Somerset, Bristol, North Somerset, Somerset, South Gloucestershire

M32
60 Bristol Stadium

A4
30 Bath, Newbridge Rd
30 Bristol, Anchor Rd
30 Bristol, Totterdown Bridge
50 Nr Keynsham, Keynsham Bypass jct A4175 Durley Hill
50 Portway
30 Portway, nr A4176 Bridge Valley Rd

A4/B4054
30 Bristol, Avonmouth Rd

A30
50 Cricket St Thomas
30 East Chinnock
40 Roundham
40 Yeovil, Hospital Rdbt
30 Yeovil, Sherborne Rd

A37
30 Bristol, Wells Rd (nr jct Airport Rd)
30 Bristol, Wells Rd (nr St Johns La)
60 Chilthorne Domer (east)
50 Emborough
30 Gurney Slade (north)
60 Lydford to Bristol
40 Lydford to Yeovil
60 Nr Podimore, Fosse Way, north of Podimore Rdbt
30 Shepton Mallet

A38
40 Aztec West, nr Bradley Stoke Way
30 Bathpool
40 Bedminster Down, Bridgwater Rd
40 Bristol, Bedminster Down Rd nr Bishopsworth Rd
30 Bristol, Bedminster Down Rd/West St
30 Bristol, Cheltenham Rd/Gloucester Rd, nr Cranbrook Rd
30 Bristol, Gloucester Rd nr B4052 Ashley Down Rd
30 Bristol, Stokes Croft nr Bond St
40 Churchill – Langford
40 Cross
30 East Reach/Toneway
40 Filton, Gloucester Rd (north) nr B4057 Gypsy Patch Lane
50 Heatherton Grange
40,30 North Petherton
40 Patchway, Gloucester Rd nr Highwood Rd
50 Pawlett (south)
50 Redhill
30 Rooks Bridge (east)
30 Taunton – Bridgwater
30 Taunton, Wellington Rd (inbound)
30 Taunton, Wellington Rd (outbound)
30 West Huntspill (north)

A39
30 Ashcott
30 Bilbrook
30 Bridgwater, Bath Rd
30 Bridgwater, North Broadway nr A38 Taunton Rd
30 Bridgwater, North Broadway/Broadway/Monmouth St
30 Chewton Mendip
40 Coxley nr Wells
50 Green Ore (south)
40 Horsey, Bath Rd
30 Quantock Rd
30 Walton

A46
60 Bath to Wickwar Rd
40 Dunkirk

A303
50 Buckland St Mary
50 Downhead nr Ilchester

A303/A3088
70 Cartgate Rdbt

A357
30 Templecombe

A303/A358
60 Southfields Rdbt

A358
60 Ashill
30 Donyatt
30 Henlade, nr M5 jct 25
40 Hornsbury Mill
40 Pen Elm (south)
30 Staplegrove Rd
30 Taunton Deane, Priorswood Rd
30 Taunton, Greenway Rd

A359
30 Mudford (north)

A361
30 Doulting
40 Durston
60 Frome Bypass
30 Othery
30 Pilton
30 West Pennard

A362
40 Terry Hill

A367
30 Bath, Green Park Rd
30 Bath, Bear Flat
30 Radstock, Wells Rd

A369
40 Abbots Leigh
60 Easton-in-Gordano, Martcombe Rd nr M5 jct 19

A370
30 Cleeve Village
30 Congresbury, Station Rd, Bristol Rd
30 Flax Bourton nr B3130
40 Long Ashton Bypass, Bristol End
50 West Wick, Somerset Avenue, west of M5 jct 21
30 Weston-super-Mare, Beach Rd
50 Weston-super-Mare, Herluin Way nr Winterstoke Rd
50 Weston-super-Mare, Somerset Avenue (central reservation)
50 Weston-super-Mare, Somerset Avenue, jct Moor Lane
30 Weston-super-Mare, Winterstoke Rd

A371
30 Draycott
40 Priestleigh (south)
30 Winscombe, Sidcot Lane nr jct A38,

A372
30 Aller

A378
30 Curry Rivel
40 Wrantage

A403
40 Avonmouth Docks

A420
30 Bristol, Lawrence Hill
30 Kingswood, Two Mile Hill Rd, Regent St
30 Old Market, nr Temple Way/Bond St
30 Redfield, Church Rd
30 St George, Clouds Hill Rd/Bell Hill Rd
30 Warmley, High St London Rd nr A4175 Bath Rd
60 Wick, Tog Hill

A432
30 Bristol, Fishponds Rd nr B4048 Lodge Causeway
30 Bristol, Fishponds Rd nr B4469 Royate Hill
30 Bristol, Fishponds Rd with B4469 Muller Rd
30 Bristol, Stapleton Rd nr jct A4320 Easton Way
40 Hambrook, Badminton Rd nr A4174 Avon Ring Rd
40 Kendleshire
30 Yate, Station Rd/B4059 Stover Rd

A3027
30 North St/East St

A3029
40 Bristol, Avon Bridge

A3039
30 Devonshire Rd

A3088
30 Yeovil, Lysander Rd

A3259
30 Monkton Heathfield

A4018
30 Bristol, Black Boy Hill/Whiteladies Rd
30 Bristol, Cribbs Causeway jct 17 M5
30 Bristol, Westbury Rd nr B4054 North View
30 Bristol, Whiteladies Rd into Queens Rd
30 Westbury on Trym, Falcondale Rd

A4044
30 Bristol, Temple Way/Redcliffe Way

A4081
40 Catbrain

A4162
30 Bristol, Sylvan Way/Dingle Rd/Canford Lane

A4174
50 Avon Ring Rd nr jct 1 M32
30 Bristol, Hartcliffe Way
40 Bristol, Hengrove Way/Airport Rd nr Creswicke Rd
50 Bromley Heath
50 Filton, Filton Rd/Avon Ring Rd nr Coldharbour Lane
40 Filton, Station Rd, nr Great Stoke Way

A4320
30 Bristol, at A4 Bath Rd nr Sandy Park Rd

B3124
30 Clevedon, Walton Rd

B3130
30 Nailsea, Stockway (north)/Chapel Avenue
30,40 Wraxall

B3133
30 Clevedon, Central Way

B3139
30,40 Mark Causeway
30 Chilcompton

B3140
30 Berrow, Coast Rd

B3141
30 East Huntspill

B3151
30 Compton Dundon
30 Ilchester
30 St, Somerton Rd

B3153
30 Keinton Mandeville (east Somerton)

B3170
30 Shoreditch Rd

B3440
30 Weston-super-Mare, Locking Rd/Regent St/Alexandra Parade

B4051
30 Bristol, Park Row/Perry Rd

B4054
30 Sea Mills, Shirehampton Rd

B4056
30 Bristol, Northumbria Drive/Linden Rd/Westbury Park
30 Bristol, Southmead Rd nr Pen Park Rd
30 Bristol, Southmead Rd nr Wellington Hill

B4057
30 Bristol, Crow Lane nr A4018 Passage Rd
30 Gypsy Patch Lane nr Hatchet Rd
50 Winterbourne Rd nr B4427 Gloucester Rd

B4058
30 Bristol, Frenchay Park Rd
30 Winterbourne, Winterbourne Hill/High St

B4059
30 Yate, Goose Green Way

B4060
30 Yate, Station Rd/Bowling Hill/Rounceval St

B4061
30 Thornbury, Bristol Rd

B4465
30 Mangotsfield, Broad St

B4465
30 Staple Hill, Staple Hill Rd/High St nr Forest Rd

Unclassified
30 Bristol, Bishopsworth, Whitchurch/Hareclive Rd
30 Bristol, Bishport Avenue
30 Knowle Bristol, Broadwalk
30 Bristol, Hengrove, Hawkfield Rd nr A4174 Hartcliffe Way
30 Bristol, Kingsway
30 Bristol, Long Cross, Lawrence Weston
30 Bristol, Stoke Hill/Stoke Rd nr Saville Rd, Clifton
30 Bristol, Sturminster Rd
30 Bristol, Whitchurch Lane nr Dundry Rd
30 Little Stoke, Little Stoke Lane
30 Taunton, Cheddon Rd
30 Taunton, Chestnut Drive
30 Taunton, Lisieux Way
30 Taunton, Trull Rd
50 Watergore, Harp Rd
30 Yeovil, Combe St

Bedfordshire and Luton

A5
60 Battlesden
40 Hockcliffe
60 Kensworth

A6
60 Gravenhurst, Barton Rd
30 Kempston, Ampthill Rd
30 Luton, New Bedford Rd
60 Pulloxhill, Barton Rd
60 Silsoe, Barton Rd

A421
50 Brogborough
60 Link Rd

A428
30 Bedford, Bromham Rd
30 Bedford, Goldington Rd

A505
30 Dunstable, Luton Rd
60 Leighton to Linslade Bypass

A507
30 Ridgmont, High St East
30 Ridgmont, High St West
60 Shefford, nr New Rd

A603
30 Bedford, Cardington Rd
30 Bedford, Lovell Rd
40 Willington

A1081
60 Luton, Airport Way

A4146
40 Leighton Buzzard, Billington Rd

A5120
40 Houghton Regis, Bedford Rd
30 Toddington, Station Rd

A5134
30 Kempston, High St

B530
60 Houghton Conquest

B1040
30 Biggleswade, Potton Rd

Unclassified
30 Bedford, Roff Avenue
30 Bromham, Stagsden Rd
30 Clapham, Highbury Grange
30 Cranfield, High St
30 Eaton Bray, Bower Lane
30 Flitwick, Ampthill Rd
30 Flitwick, Dunstable Rd
30 Heath and Reach, Woburn Rd
30 Leighton Buzzard, Heath Rd
30 Luton, Crawley Green Rd
30 Luton, Grange Avenue
30 Luton, Leagrave High St
30 Luton, Marsh Rd
30 Luton, Park Viaduct
30 Luton, Waller Avenue
30 Luton, Whitehorse Vale
30 Slip End, Markyate Rd

Berkshire

see Thames Valley

Buckinghamshire

see Thames Valley

Cambridgeshire

A14(E)
70 2km west of A1 Brampton Hut
70 East/Westbound

A15
30 New Fletton, London Rd

A47
60 Thorney Toll

A141
60 Clews Corner
60 Warboys
60 Wimblington/Doddington Bypass

A142
60 Soham Bypass
60 Witchford Bypass

A605
60 Elton, Bullock Rd
40 Kings Dyke

A1073
60 Eye Green, Peterborough Rd

A1123
60 Bluntisham, Needingworth Bypass

A1123
40 St Ives, Houghton Hill
40 Wiburton Village

A1307
70 Bartlow crossroads
30 Hills Rd
60 Linton Bypass

B645
40 Tilbrook Bends

Cheshire

A50
30 Grappenhall, Knutsford Rd
30 Knutsford, Manchester/Toft Rd
30 Warrington, Long Lane

A54
60 Ashton, Kelsall Rd

A56
40 Lymm, Camsley Lane

A57
40 Paddington, New Manchester Rd

A523
30 Poynton, London Rd

A532
30 Crewe, West St

A533
40 Middlewich, Booth Lane

A537
50 Macclesfield, Buxton Rd nr Wildboarclough

A5019
30 Crewe, Mill St

A5032
30 Whitby, Chester Rd

A5034
60 Mere, Mereside Rd

A5104
30 Chester, Hough Green

B5071
30 Crewe, Gresty Rd

B5078
30 Alsager, Sandbach Rd North

B5082
30 Northwich, Middlewich Rd

B5132
30 Ellesmere Port, Overpool Rd

B5463
30 Little Sutton, Station Rd

B5470
30 Macclesfield, Rainow Rd

Unclassified
30 Burtonwood, Lumber Lane
30 Ellesmere Port, Overpool Rd
30 Fearnhead, Harpers Rd
30 Hough Green, Prescot Rd
30 Howley, Battersby Lane
40 Runcorn, Astmoor Rd
30 Runcorn, Boston Avenue
30 Runcorn, Clifton Rd
30 Runcorn, Halton Rd
30 Runcorn, Heath Rd
30 Runcorn, Northwich Rd
30 Runcorn, Warrington Rd
30 Vale Royal, Woodford Lane (St John's Drive)
30 Whitecross, Lovely Lane
30 Widnes, Birchfield Rd
30 Widnes, Hough Green Rd
30 Wilmslow, Hough Lane
40 Winsford, Bradford Rd

Cleveland

Darlington, Hartlepool, Middlesbrough, Redcar and Cleveland

A171
50 Redcar, Charltons

A172
40 Middlesbrough, Morton Rd from crossroads to St Lukes
30 Middlesbrough, Morton Rd from Longlands to St Lukes
40 Middlesbrough, Stokesley – from Guisborough Rd jct to Captain Cooks Crescent

A177
50,60 Stockton, Durham Rd

A178
30 Seaton Carew, The Front

A179
30 Hartlepool, Easington Rd/Powlett Rd

A689
50 to 40 Hartlepool, from Sappers Corner

B1380
40 Middlesbrough, from Marton Crossroads to Ormesby Rd
30 Redcar, Eston

Unclassified
30 Dormanstow, Broadway
30 Eaglescliffe, Yarm Rd
30 Hartlepool, Catcote Rd
40,30 Hartlepool, Coronation Drive
30 Hartlepool, Owton Manor Lane and Wynyard Rd
30 Hartlepool, Oxford Rd
30 Hartlepool, Raby Rd
30 Hartlepool, Throston Grange Lane
30 Hartlepool, Winterbottom Avenue
30 Middlesbrough, Acklam Rd
40 Middlesbrough, Acklam Rd from Blue Bell to the Crematorium
30 Middlesbrough, Mandale Rd
30 Middlesbrough, Ormesby Rd
30 Middlesbrough, Trimdon Avenue
30 Ormesby, Normanby Rd
30 Redcar, Bankfields Rd
30 Redcar, Carlin How
30 Redcar, Church Lane
30 Redcar, Flatts Lane
30 Redcar, Greenstones Rd
30,40 Redcar, Kirkleatham Lane
30 Redcar, Marske High St
30 Redcar, Normanby Rd
30 Redcar, Ormesby Bank
30 Redcar, Redcar Lane
30 Redcar, Redcar Rd
30 Redcar, Stanghow Rd
30 Redcar, West Dyke Rd
30 Seaton Carew, Seaton Lane
30 Seaton Carew, Station Lane
40 Stockton, Bishopton Avenue
30 Stockton, Bishopton Rd West
30 Stockton, Darlington Lane
30 Stockton, Harrogate Lane
30 Stockton, Junction Rd
30 Stockton, Thames Rd
30 Stockton, Thornaby Rd
30 Stockton, Whitehouse Rd
30 Thornaby, Acklam Rd
30 Thornaby, Cunningham Drive

Cumbria

M6
70 Brunthwaite
70 Capplerigg
70 Cowperthwaite
70 Tebay

A6
60 Garnett Bridge/Hollowgate
30 Kendal, Milnthorpe Rd
30 Kendal, Shap Rd
30 London Rd
30 Penrith, Scotland Rd
60 Thiefside

A7
60 Westlinton Crossroads

A65
30 Kendal, Burton Rd
40 Kirby Lonsdale, Devils Bridge
60 Kirkby Lonsdale, Hollin Hall to Hornsbarrow

A66
60 Brigham/Broughton to Chapel Brow
60 Crackenthorpe
60 Dubwath/Bass Lake
60 Sandford Rd Ends
60 Troutbeck/Mungrisdale
60 Warcop, Brough Hill

A69
60 Aglionby
60 Scarrow Hill

A74
70 Kendal, Floriston

A590
60 Bouth Rd Ends
60 Haverthwaite/Backbarrow
70 Heaves/Levens/Gilpin
60 Newlands

A592
30,40 Rayrigg Rd

A595
60 Broughton, Wreaks End
30 Carlisle, Wigton Rd
60 Red Dial, Greenhill Hotel
60 West Woodside/Curthwaite Jct
40 Whitehaven, Loop Rd

A596
60 Micklethwaite

A683
60 Middleton to Cautley

A685
30 Kendal, Appleby Rd

A686
60 Edenhall to Meathaw Hill

A5087
30 Ulverston

B5277
30 Grange, Lindale Rd

B5299
40 Carlisle, Dalston Rd

Unclassified
30 Carlisle, Durdar Rd/Blackwell Rd
30 Barrow in Furness, Abbey Rd
30 Barrow in Furness, Michelson Rd

Derbyshire

A6
30 Allestree
30 Alvaston to Raynesway
40 Ambergate, Matlock Rd nr Chase Rd
30 Bakewell
40 Bakewell, Buxton Rd nr Holme Lane
30 Belper
40 Darley Dale, Dale Rd North nr The Parkway
40 Darley Dale, Dale Rd North opp The Parkway
30 Derby, London Rd
30 Fairfield, Fairfield Rd nr North Rd
40 Matlock Bath to Matlock, Dale Rd nr St John's Rd
40 Matlock Bath to Matlock, Dale Rd opp No. 138
40 Rock Corner, Buxton Rd
50 Taddington to Buxton

A52
30 Derby, Ashbourne Rd
40 Mackworth

A53
30 Buxton, Station Rd o/s Railway Station
30 Buxton, Station Rd opp Railway Station

A57
30 Glossop, Dinting Vale nr Primary School
30 Glossop, Dinting Vale opp Dinting Lane
30 Glossop, High St West nr Glossop Brook Rd

A61
30 Chesterfield, Derby Rd nr Herriot Drive
30 Chesterfield, Derby Rd nr Langer Lane
50 Stretton, Main Rd nr B6014
50 Stretton, Main Rd nr Straw Lane

A444
30 Overseal, Acresford Rd nr Valley Rd
30 Overseal, Burton Rd nr Lullington Rd
30 Stanton, Woodland Rd nr Piddocks Rd
30 Stanton, Woodland Rd opp Park Rd

A511
40 Bretby, Ashby Rd East nr Greary Lane
30 Hatton, Station Rd
30 Swadlincote, Ashby Rd nr Field Lane
30 Swadlincote, Burton Rd nr Eureka Rd
30 Swadlincote, Burton Rd nr Lincoln Way
30 Swadlincote, Burton Rd nr Sandcliffe Rd
30 Swadlincote, Burton Rd nr Springfield Rd
30 Woodville, Burton Rd nr Sorrel Drive
30 Woodville, High St nr Butt Lane

A514
30 Derby, Osmaston Rd nr Keble Close
30 Derby, Osmaston Rd nr Shaftesbury St
30 Derby, Osmaston Rd opp Cotton Lane
30 Hartshorne
30 Shelton Lock, Chellaston Rd nr Shelton Drive
30 Swadlincote
40 Swadlincote to Hartshorne
30 Ticknall

A516
30 Uttoxeter, New Rd

A601
30 Derby, Abbey St

A608
30 Heanor, Church St nr Hands Rd
30 Heanor, Heanor Rd nr Peatburn Ave
30 Heanor, Mansfield Rd adj Watson Ave
30 Heanor, Mansfield Rd opp Watson Ave
30 Langley Mill, Station Rd adj Aldred's Lane
30 Smalley

A609
30 Ilkeston, Nottingham Rd opp Ashdale Rd
30 Ilkeston, Nottingham Rd opp Little Hallam Lane
30 Kilburn to Horsley Woodhouse

A610
40 Codnor Gate
40 Ripley, Nottingham Rd nr Brittain Dr

A615
60 Tansley to Wessington

A616
30 Clowne
30 Creswell

A617
40 Bramley Vale
40 Glapwell to Pleasley

A6175
30 Holmewood
30 North Wingfield

A618
30 Killamarsh, Rotherham Rd

A619
50 Barlborough, Worksop Rd nr Van Dyks Hotel
40 Brimington, Chesterfield Rd opp Lansdowne Rd
30 Brimington, Ringwood Rd nr Foljambe Rd
30 Chesterfield, Chatsworth Rd nr Chatsworth Ave
30 Chesterfield, Chatsworth Rd opp Church View
30 Chesterfield, Chatsworth Rd opp Haddon Close
30 Hollingwood, Chesterfield Rd opp Ringwood Hall
40 Mastin Moor, Worksop Rd nr Norbriggs Rd
40 Mastin Moor, Worksop Rd nr Renishaw Rd
30 Middlecroft, Chesterfield Rd nr Ringwood Ave
30 Staveley, Chesterfield Rd nr Middlecroft Rd
50 Whitwell Common, Worksop Rd opp Highwood Lane
50 Whitwell, Barlborough nr Southgate Bungalows
50 Whitwell, Clinthill Lane o/s Southgate Bungalows

A623
30 Stoney Middleton

A624
40 Hayfield, Chapel Rd nr Church
40 Hayfield, Chapel Rd nr New Mills Rd

A632
30 Bolsover
30 Bolsover, Langwith Rd
30 Calow, Top Rd o/s No.33
30 Calow, Top Rd o/s No.62
40 Duckmanton, Chesterfield Rd nr Staveley Rd
40 Duckmanton, Chesterfield Rd opp Arkwright Arms Pub
30 Langwith, Main Rd nr Langwith Drive
30 Langwith, Main Rd nr Whaley Rd
30 Matlock

A5111
40 Derby, Harvey Rd nr Cockayne St North
40 Derby, Harvey Rd nr Neilson St
40 Derby, Harvey Rd nr Wyndham St
40 Derby, Harvey Rd o/s Newsagents
40 Derby, Osmaston Park Rd nr Arkwright St

A5250
30 Derby, Burton Rd
30 Littleover, Burton Rd

A6005
30 Draycott to Breaston
30 Long Eaton, Derby Rd opp Russell St
30 Long Eaton, Nottingham Rd nr Charlton Ave
30 Long Eaton, Nottingham Rd opp Cleveland Ave
30 Spondon, Derby Rd nr Derwent Rd
30 Spondon, Derby Rd o/s Asda
30 Spondon, Nottingham Rd nr Angler's Lane

A6007
30 Codnor, Heanor Rd
30 Heanor, Ilkeston Rd nr Westfield Ave
40 Ilkeston, Heanor Rd nr Broadway
40 Ilkeston, Heanor Rd nr Hospital
40 Ilkeston, Heanor Rd nr Woodside Crescent
40 Shipley, Hardy Barn o/s No.64
40 Shipley, Hassock Lane North nr Algrave Hall Farm
40 Shipley, Hassock Lane South nr Pitt Lane

A6096
30 Kirk Hallam, Ladywood Rd nr Godfrey Dr
30 Kirk Hallam, Ladywood Rd nr Goole Ave
30 Spondon, Dale Rd nr Dreyfus Close
30 Spondon, Dale Rd nr Wood Rd
30 Spondon, Dale Rd opp Sandringham Dr

B5010
30 Sandiacre, Derby Rd adj Brook St
30 Sandiacre, Derby Rd adj Friesland Drive
30 Sandiacre, Derby Rd adj Woodside Rd

B5036
30 Cromford, Cromford Rd

B5353
30 Newhall, Park Rd

B6002
30 Sandiacre, Longmoor Rd nr Springfield Ave
30 Sandiacre, Longmoor Rd o/s No.108
30 Sandiacre, Longmoor Rd nr Queen's Drive

B6019
30 Alfreton, Mansfield Rd nr Prospect St
30 South Normanton, Mansfield Rd nr Carter Lane West
30 South Normanton, Mansfield Rd nr Storth Lane
30 South Normanton, The Common nr Market St
30 South Normanton, The Common nr The Hamlet

B6051
30 Chesterfield, Newbold Rd
30 Newbold, Newbold Rd

B6052
30 Eckington, High St nr j/w School St
30 Eckington, West St nr j/w Fanshaw Rd
30 Whittington

B6056
30 Eckington, Dronfield Rd opp Ravenscar Rd
30 Marsh Lane, Main Rd nr School Lane
30 Marsh Lane, Main Rd o/s No.45

B6062
30 Chinley

B6179
30 Little Eaton
40 Lower Kilburn
50 Lower Kilburn to Little Eaton
30 Ripley to Marehay

B6407
30 Shirebrook, Portland Rd adj Ashbourne St
30 Shirebrook, Portland Rd opp Ashbourne St

B6540
30 Long Eaton, Tamworth Rd nr Charles St
30 Long Eaton, Tamworth Rd nr Wyvern Ave
30 Long Eaton, Tamworth Rd opp Draycott Rd
30 Long Eaton, Tamworth Rd opp No.559
30 Long Eaton, Tamworth Rd opp Shaftesbury Ave

Unclassified
30 Chaddesden, Nottingham Rd nr No.427 (Cemetery)
30 Chaddesden, Nottingham Rd nr Pentagon Island
30 Chaddesden, Nottingham Rd o/s No.590 (Cherry Tree)
30 Charlesworth, Long Lane
30 Chesterfield, Boythorpe Rd
30 Chesterfield, Linacre Rd
30 Chesterfield, Old Rd
30 Denby, St Lane
30 Derby, Blagreaves Lane
30 Derby, Kedleston Rd
30 Derby, Stenson Rd
30 Langley Mill, Upper Dunstead Rd
30 Shardlow, London Rd
40 Stenson Fields, Stenson Rd
30 Swadlincote, Hearthcote Rd

Devon and Cornwall

A30
60 Chiverton Cross
70 Highgate (Eastbound)
70 Highgate Hill
40 Sowton
60 Temple

A38
70 Bittaford Straight, Wrangaton
70 Deep Lane
70 Lee Mill, Lee Mill On-slip
70 Lower Clicker Tor
70 Smithaleigh
70 Smithaleigh, Smithaleigh Overbridge
70 Wrangaton, Bittaford Straight

A39
60 Barras Moor
30 Camelford, Valley Truckle
40 Perranarworthal, nr Truro

A361
50 Ashford
30 Barnstaple, Eastern Avenue
40 Knowle
30 Knowle (Westerland)
30 Wrafton

A374
30 Ebford
40 Plymouth, Plymouth Rd (Inbound)
40 Plymouth, Plymouth Rd (Outbound)
30 Torpoint, Anthony Rd

A376
30 Exmouth, Exeter Rd

A377
30 Copplestone
30 Crediton, Western Rd
30 Exeter, Alphington Rd

A379
30 Brixton Village
30 Paignton, Dartmouth Rd
30 Starcross
30 Starcross, The Strand
30 Teignmouth, Teignmouth Rd
30 Torquay, Babbacombe Rd
30 Yealmpton

A380
40 Kingskerswell, Newton Rd

A381
30 Newton Abbott, East St

A385
30 Collaton St Mary, Totnes Rd
30 Totnes, Ashburton Rd

A386
60 Chubb Tor
30 Plymouth, Outland Rd
60 Plymouth, Roborough Down
40 Plymouth, Tavistock Rd

A388
30 Kelly Bray

A390
60 Penstraze
60 Sticker Bypass

A394
40 Kenneggy Downs

A396
30 Rewe
30 Stoke Canon, Exeter Rd

A3015
30 Exeter, Topsham Rd

A3047
30 Carbis Bay
30 Pool, Trevenson Rd
30 Tuckingmill

A3058
30 Trewoon

A3064
30 Plymouth, St Budeaux Bypass

A3075
60 Rosecliston

B3165
30 Raymonds Hill, Crewkerne Rd

B3174
30 Ottery St Mary, Barrack Rd

B3183
30 Exeter, Heavitree Rd
30 Exeter, New North Rd

B3212
30 Exeter, Dunsford Rd
30 Exeter, Pinhoe Rd

B3213
30 Wrangaton Village, nr South Brent

B3233
30 Barnstaple, Bickington Rd

B3250
30 Plymouth, North Hill

B3284
60 Liskey
30 Liskey, Perranporth
30 Chudleigh, Station Hill

B3396
30 Plymouth, Milehouse Rd

Unclassified
30 Avonwick Village
30 Buddle Lane, Exwick Rd
30 Elburton, Haye Rd
30 Exeter, Exwick Lane
30 Fraddon Village, nr Indian Queens
60 Goss Moor, Castle an Dinas
30 Honicknowle, Shakespeare Rd
30 Ivybridge, Exeter Rd
40 Monkton Village
30 Paignton, Colley End Rd
30 Paignton, Preston Down Rd
30 Plymouth, Beacon Park Rd
30 Plymouth, Church Hill
30 Plymouth, Devonport Rd
30 Plymouth, Eggbuckland Rd
30 Plymouth, Glen Rd
30 Plymouth, Honicknowle Lane
30 Plymouth, Honicknowle Lane (North)
30 Plymouth, Lipson Rd
30 Plymouth, Mannamead Rd
30 Plymouth, Molesworth Rd
30 Plymouth, North Prospect Rd
40 Plymouth, Novorrossiysk Rd
30 Plymouth, Pomphlett Rd
30 Plymouth, Southway Drive
30 Plymouth, St Levan Rd
30 Plymouth, Tamerton Foliot Rd
30 Plymouth, Union St
30 Plymouth, Weston Park Rd
30 Plymouth, Wolseley Rd (Both Directions)
30 Plympton, Glen Rd
30 Saltash, Callington Rd
30 St Judes, Grenville Rd

Dorset

A30
70 Babylon Hill
40 Shaftesbury, Long Cross

A31
40 Winterbourne Zelston

A35
60 Bridport, Cross Dykes nr Whiteway Cross
60 btwn Morden Mill & Slepe
70 Christchurch Bypass
60 Dorchester, Friary Press
60 Kingston Russell
60 Lyndhurst Rd
50 Lytchett Minster, Bakers Arms
30 Poole, Upton Rd
40 Sea Rd South
60 Vinney Cross

A37
60 Holywell Cross
60 Long Ash Lane
60 Staggs Folly

A338
50 Cooper Dean, Wessex Way
70 Spur Rd

A348
40 Bear Cross, Ringwood Rd

A349
40 Poole, Gravell Hill

A350
50 Holes Bay Rd to Sterte Rd
60 Poole Rd
70 Poole, Upton Country Park
30 Stourpaine, Shashton Rd

A352
30 Wool, Dorchester Rd

A354
30 Dorchester Rd Manor Rdbt
40 Redlands, Dorchester Rd
60 Ridgeway Hill, Dorchester Rd
30 Upwey, Dorchester Rd
30 Weymouth, Buxton Rd
30 Whitechurch, Winterbourne

B3065
30 Poole, Pinecliff Rd
30 Poole, The Avenue

B3073
40 West Parley, Christchurch Rd
30 Wimborne, Oakley Hill

B3074
30 Poole, Higher Blandford Rd

B3081
30 Ebblake, Ringwood Rd

B3082
60 Bradbury Rings, Blandford Rd

B3092
n/a Gillingham, Colesbrook

B3157
30 Lanehouse Rocks Rd
50 Limekiln Hill
30 Portesham

B3369
30 Poole, Sandbanks Rd
30 Poole, Shore Rd

Unclassified
30 Blandford, Salisbury Rd
30 Bournemouth, Branksome Wood Rd
30 Bournemouth, Crabery Avenue
30 Bournemouth, Littledown Avenue
30 Bournemouth, Southbourne Overcliff Drive
30 Poole, Old Wareham Rd
30 Portland, Weston Rd
40 Staplehill, Wimborne Rd
30 Upton, Poole Rd
30 Weymouth, Chickerell Rd

Durham

A66
Bowes Moor/Galley Bank/Greta Bridge

A67
Conniscliffe

A167
Chester-le-St, North Lodge
Darlington, North Rd
Durham, Whitesmocks and Tollhouse Rd

A690
Crook, Low Willington to West Rd
Durham, West Rainton

A1086
Crimdon to Horden

B6188
Dipton, New Kyo to Flint Hill

B6280
Darlington, Yarm Rd

B6282
Bishop Auckland, Etherley and B6284 Ediscum Garth

B6288
Spennymoor/A167 Croxdale

Unclassified
Darlington, McMullen Rd
Durham, Finchale Rd
Peterlee, Essington Way

Essex

A12
Braintree, Overbridge nr Kelvedon Interchange

A13
30 Castle Point, High St (Hadleigh twds London)
30 Leigh on Sea, London Rd
Southend, Bournes Green Chase
Southend, North Shoebury Rd
Southend, Southchurch Boulevard

A113
30 Epping, High Rd

A120
Little Bentley, Pellens Corner

A121
30 Epping, High Rd
30 Loughton, Goldings Hill (j/w Monkchester Close)
Loughton, High Rd
Waltham Abbey, Farm Hill Rd
Waltham Abbey, Sewardstine Rd

A126
30 Grays, London Rd
30 Tilbury, Montreal Rd

A128
Chipping Ongar, High St
30 Ingrave/Herongate, Brentwood Rd

A129
30 Basildon, Crays Hill
Billericay, Southend Rd
Rayleigh, London Rd
30 Wickford, London Rd
Wickford, Southend Rd

A130
30 Canvey Island, Long Rd
South Benfleet, Canvey Way

A133
30 Elmstead Market, Clacton Rd

A133
Little Bentley, Colchester Rd

A134
40 Great Horkesley, Nayland Rd

A137
30 Lawford, Wignall St

A1016
30 Chelmsford, Waterhouse Lane

A1017
30 Sible Hedingham, Swan St

A1023
30 Brentwood, Chelmsford Rd
30 Brentwood, London Rd
30 Brentwood, Shenfield Rd

A1025
40 Harlow, Third Avenue

A1060
Little Hallingbury, Lower Rd

A1090
30 Purfleet, London Rd
30 Purfleet, Tank Hill Rd

A1124
30 Colchester, Lexden Rd

A1158
30 Westcliff on Sea, Southbourne Grove

A1168
30 Loughton, Rectors Lane

A1169
40 Harlow, Southern Way

A1205
40 Harlow, Second Avenue

B170
Loughton, Roding Lane
Chigwell, Chigwell Rise

B172
Theydon Bois, Coppice Row

B173
Chigwell, Lambourne Rd

B184
40 Great Easton, Snow Hill

B186
30 South Ockendon, South Rd

B1002
30 Ingatestone, High St

B1007
30 Billericay, Laindon Rd
40 Chelmsford, Stock Rd

B1007
30 Billericay, Stock Rd

B1008
30 Chelmsford, Broomfield Rd

B1013
30 Hawkwell, High Rd
30 Hawkwell, Main Rd
30 Hockley/Hawkwell, Southend Rd
Rayleigh, High Rd
30 Rayleigh, Hockley Rd

B1014
30 South Benfleet, Benfleet Rd

B1018
30 Latchingdon, The St
30 Maldon, The Causeway

B1019
30 Hatfield Peveral, Maldon Rd

B1021
Burnham on Crouch, Church Rd

B1022
30 Colchester, Maldon Rd
30 Heckfordbridge, Maldon Rd
30 Maldon, Colchester Rd
30 Tiptree Heath, Maldon Rd

B1027
30 Clacton-on-Sea, Valley Rd/Old Rd
30 St Osyth, Pump Hill
40 Wivenhoe, Brightlingsea Rd

B1028
30 Wivenhoe, Colchester Rd
30 Wivenhoe, The Avenue

B1033
30 Kirby Cross, Frinton Rd

B1335
40 South Ockendon, Stifford Rd

B1352
Harwich, Main Rd

B1383
30 Newport, London Rd
Stansted Mountfitchet, Cambridge Rd

B1389
30 Witham, Colchester Rd
30 Witham, Hatfield Rd

B1393
30 Epping, Palmers Hill

B1441
30 Clacton-on-Sea, London Rd

B1442
30 Clacton-on-Sea, Thorpe Rd

B1464
30 Bowers Gifford, London Rd

Unclassified
40 Alresford, St Osyth Rd
30 Aveley, Purfleet Rd
Aveley, Romford Rd
30 Barstable, Sandon Rd
30 Basildon, Ashlyns
40 Basildon, Cranes Farm Rd (j/w Honywood Rd)
Basildon, Crayhill Rd
30 Basildon, Felmores
Basildon, London Rd, Wickford
30 Basildon, Vange Hill Drive
30 Basildon, Whitmore Way
30 Basildon, Wickford Avenue
30 Billericay, Mountnessing Rd
30 Bowers Gifford, London Rd
30 Braintree, Coldnailhurst Avenue
30 Brentwood, Eagle Way (nr j/w Clive Rd twds Warley Rd)
30 Buckhurst Hill, Buckhurst Way/Albert Rd
30 Canvey Island, Dovervelt Rd
30 Canvey Island, Link Rd
30 Canvey Island, Thorney Bay Rd
Chadwell St Mary, Brentwood Rd
30 Chadwell St Mary, Linford Rd
30 Chadwell St Mary, Riverview
30 Chelmsford, Baddow Rd
30 Chelmsford, Chignall Rd
30 Chelmsford, Copperfield Rd
Chelmsford, Galleywood Rd
30 Chelmsford, Longstomps Avenue
30 Clacton-on-Sea, St Johns Rd
30 Clacton, Kings Parade
30 Clacton, Marine Parade East
30 Colchester, Abbots Rd
30 Colchester, Avon Way
30 Colchester, Bromley Rd
Colchester, Ipswich Rd
30 Colchester, Old Heath Rd
30 Colchester, Shrub End Rd
30 Corringham, Southend Rd
30 Corringham, Springhouse Rd
Danbury, Maldon Rd
30 Daws Heath, Daws Heath Rd
30 Eastwood, Green Lane j/w Kendal Way
30 Eastwood, Western Approaches j/w Rockall
30 Grays, Blackshots Lane
30 Grays, Lodge Lane
Grays, London Rd (nr Angel Rd)
Grays, London Rd (nr Bransons Way)
40 Harlow, Abercrombie Way, twds Southern Way
40 Harlow, Howard Way
30 Hullbridge, Coventry Hill
30 Laindon, Durham Rd
30 Laindon, Nightingales
30 Laindon, Wash Rd
Langdon Hills, High Rd
30 Leigh on Sea, Belton Way East
30 Leigh on Sea, Belton Way West
30 Leigh on Sea, Blenheim Chase
30 Leigh on Sea, Grand Parade/Cliff Parade
30 Leigh on Sea, Hadleigh Rd
30 Leigh on Sea, Highlands Boulevard
30 Leigh on Sea, Manchester Drive
30 Leigh on Sea, Mountdale Gardens
30 Leigh on Sea, Western Rd
30 Loughton, Alderton Hill
30 Loughton, Loughton Way
Loughton, Valley Hill
30 Maldon, Fambridge Rd
30 Maldon, Holloway Rd
30 Maldon, Mundon Rd
30 Pitsea, Rectory Rd
30 Prittlewell, Kenilworth Gardens
30 Prittlewell, Prittlewell Chase
30 Rayleigh, Bull Lane
Rayleigh, Downhall Rd
30 Rayleigh, Trinity Rd, nr Church Rd
30 Rochford, Ashingdon Rd
30 Rochford, Rectory Rd
Rush Green, St Osyth Rd
30 Shoeburyness, Ness Rd
30 South Woodham Ferrers, Hullbridge Rd
30 South Woodham Ferrers, Inchbonnie Rd
30 Southend on Sea, Lifstan Way
Southend, Bournemouth Park Rd
30 Southend, Hamstel Rd
Southend, Western Esplanade/Westcliff on Sea
30 Southend, Woodgrange Drive j/w Sandringham Rd
30 Springfield, New Bowers Way
30 Stanford le Hope, London Rd
30 Tendring, Burrs Rd, Clacton
Tendring, Harwich Rd, Wix Arch Cottages to Cansey Lane
Theydon Bois, Piercing Hill
30 Thorpe Bay, Barnstaple Rd
30 Thorpe Bay, Thorpe Hall Avenue
Waltham Abbey, Paternoster Hill
Weeley Heath, Clacton Rd
30 West Thurrock, London Rd
30 Westcliff on Sea, Chalkwell Avenue
30 Westcliff on Sea, Kings Rd
30 Wickford, Radwinter Avenue
30 Witham, Powers Hall End
30 Witham, Rickstones Rd

Gloucestershire

A38
40 Twigworth

A40
60 Andoversford
50 Churcham
60 Farmington
40 Gloucester Rd
60 Hampnett
60 Hazleton
60 Northleach
60 The Barringtons
60 Whittington Area

A46
30 Ashchurch
40 North of Nailsworth

A48
60 Stroat

A417
70 Burford Jct
40 Corse, Gloucester Rd
70 Dartley Bottom
40 Lechlade
30 Maisemore
40 North of Hartpury

A419
40 Oldends Lane to Stonehouse Court

A429
60 Nr Bourton-on-the-Water
40 Fossebridge

A430
40 Hempsted Bypass

A435
40 Colesbourne

A436
60 Jct with B4068

A4013
30 Gloucester, Princess Elizabeth Way
30 Gloucester, Princess Elizabeth Way (Arle)

A4019
50 Uckington

A4136
40 Brierley
40 Coleford, Lower Lane
40 Harrow Hill
40 Little London

A4151
40 Steam Mills

A4173
30 nr St Peters School

B4008
40 Hardwicke, Bristol Rd south of Tesco rdbt
30 Olympus Park Area, Bristol Rd
30 Stonehouse, Gloucester Rd

B4060
30 Katharine Lady Berkeley's School

B4215
50 South east of Rudford
50 South of Newent Bypass

B4221
30 Picklenash School
40 Kilcot Village

B4226
60 Speech House

B4228
30 Coleford, Old Station Way
40 Perrygrove

B4231
30 Bream, Coleford Rd

B4633
30 Cheltenham, Gloucester Rd

Unclassified
30 Gloucester, Abbeymead Avenue
30 Gloucester, Barrow Hill
30 Gloucester, Chesterton Lane
30 Gloucester, Parkend Fancy Rd
30 Gloucester, St Georges Rd
30 Gloucester, Swindon Lane
30 Gloucester, Wymans Lane
30 Lydney, Highfield Rd
40 Minchinhampton Common
30 Siddington
40 Tewkesbury, Gloucester Rd

Greater Manchester

A6
Manchester, Stockport Rd
Salford, Manchester Rd

A34
Manchester, Birchfield Road

A49
Marus Bridge, Warrington Rd

A56
Bury, Bury New Rd
Bury, Walmersley Rd
Bury, Whalley Rd

A57
Manchester, Hyde Rd
Salford, Liverpool Rd
Tameside, Manchester Rd

A58
Bury, Bury & Bolton Rd
Bury, Rochdale Rd

A62
Manchester, Oldham Rd
Oldham, Oldham Rd
Oldham, Oldham Way

A575
Salford, Walkden Rd

A580
Salford, East Lancashire Rd

A627
Oldham, Chadderton Way
Oldham, Ashton Rd

A662
Manchester, Ashton New Rd

A663
Oldham, Broadway

A664
Manchester, Rochdale Rd

A665
Bury, New Rd
Bury, Radcliffe New Rd

A666
Bolton, Blackburn Rd
Bolton, St Peter's Way
Salford, Manchester Rd

A667
Bury, Ringley Rd West

A5103
Manchester, Princess Parkway/Road

A6010
Manchester, Alan Turing Way

A6044
Prestwich, Sheepfoot Lane
Prestwich, Hilton Lane

A6053
Radcliffe, Dumers Lane

A6104
Blackley, Victoria Avenue

B6196
Ainsworth, Church Street
Ainsworth, Cockey Moor Rd

B6213
Tottington, Turton Rd

B6214
Greenmount, Brandlesholme Rd
Holcombe, Helmshore Rd
Holcombe Brook, Longsight Rd

B6226
Horwich, Chorley Old Rd

Unclassified
Ashton on Mersey, Ashton Lane
Bolton, Chorley Old Rd
Bolton, Hardy Mill Rd
Bolton, Hulton Lane
Bolton, Lever Park Avenue
Bolton, Plodder Lane
Bolton, Stitch Mi Lane
Bredbury, Ashton Rd
Bury, Croft Lane
Bury, Higher Lane
Bury, Stand Lane
Bury, Walshaw Rd
Manchester, Blackley New Rd
Manchester, Kingsway
Manchester, Mancunian Way
Oldham, Abbey Hills Rd
Oldham, Manchester Rd
Rochdale, Bagslate Moor Rd
Rochdale, Broad Lane
Rochdale, Bury Old Rd
Rochdale, Caldershaw Rd
Rochdale, Edenfield Rd
Rochdale, Halifax Rd
Rochdale, Heywood Old Rd
Rochdale, Hollin Lane
Rochdale, Manchester Rd
Rochdale, Queens Park Rd
Rochdale, Shawclough Rd
Rochdale, Smithybridge Rd
Rochdale, Todmorden Rd
Rochdale, Wildhouse Lane
Salford, Belvedere Rd
Salford, Langley Rd
Stockport, Birdhall Lane
Stockport, Bridge Lane
Stockport, Buxton Rd
Stockport, Chester Rd
Stockport, Councillor Lane
Stockport, Dialstone Lane
Stockport, Harrytown
Stockport, Jacksons Lane
Stockport, Kingsway
Stockport, Longhurst Lane
Stockport, Marple Rd
Stockport, Sandy Lane
Stockport, Schools Hill
Stockport, Strines Rd
Stockport, Styal Rd
Stockport, Wellington Rd North
Tameside, Mossley Rd
Tameside, Mottram Old Rd
Tameside, Mottram Rd
Tameside, Stamford Rd
Tameside, Stamford Street
Trafford, Church Rd
Trafford, Edge Lane
Trafford, Glebelands Rd
Trafford, Hope Rd
Trafford, Mosley Rd
Trafford, Norris Rd
Trafford, Park Rd
Trafford, Seymour Grove
Trafford, Warburton Lane
Trafford, Westinghouse Rd
Wigan, Almond Brook Rd
Wigan, Bickershaw Lane
Wigan, Bolton Rd
Wigan, Chaddock Lane
Wigan, Chorley Rd
Wigan, Crow Orchard Rd
Wigan, Lily Lane
Wigan, Newton Rd
Wigan, Pemberton Rd
Wigan, Scot Lane
Wigan, Victoria Street
Wigan, Wigan Rd

Hampshire and Isle of Wight

A3
70 Liphook
30 Petersfield

A27
40 Fareham (east and west bound)
30 Fareham, Portchester Rd (eastbound)
30 Fareham, Portchester Rd (westbound)
30 Fareham, The Avenue

A30
30 Blackwater
30 Hook, London Rd

A32
30 West Meon

A33
50 Basingstoke
50 Chandlers Green
50 Sherfield on Loddon
50 Southampton, Millbrook Rd (western end of Flyover to Regents Park Rd)
30 West Quay Rd

A35
50 Totton

A325
40 East Hampshire (south)
70 Farnborough, Farnborough Rd
40 Rushmoor (north)

A334/B2177
40 Wickham

A335
30 Eastleigh

A337
30 New Forest (east)
40 New Forest (west)

A338
40 New Forest (south and north bound)

A339
60 Lasham

A340
30 Basingstoke
30 Tadley

A343
30 Hurstbourne Tarrant

A3020
40 Blackwater Rd

A3024
40 Bursledon Rd
30 Northam Rd to southern river bank

A3054
30 Newport, Fairlee Rd
30 Wootton / Lushington Hill, High St

B3037/A335
30,40 Eastleigh

B3055
40 New Forest

B3395
30 Sandown, Culver Parade

Unclassified
30 Apse Heath
30 Binstead Hill
30 Brading, High St New Rd
30 East Cowes, Victoria Grove/Adelaide Grove
30 East Cowes, York Avenue
40 Fareham, Western Way
30 Fleet, Reading Rd South
30 Newport, Staplers Rd/Long Lane
30 Portsmouth, Northern Rd (north and south bound)
40 Southampton, The Avenue (north and south bound)
30 Swanick, Swanick Lane
50 Totton / Redbridge, Redbridge Flyover

Herefordshire

see West Mercia

Hertfordshire

A119
30 Hertford, North Rd

A409
30 Bushey, Heathbourne Rd

A411
30 Bushey, London Rd
30 Elstree, Barnet Lane
30 Watford, Hempstead Rd

A414
40 Hemel Hempstead, St Albans Rd
40 Hertford, Hertingfordbury Rd

A505
30 Hitchin, Cambridge Rd

A600
30 Hitchin, Bedford Rd

A602
40 Hitchin, Stevenage Rd
40 Stevenage, Broadhall Way
40 Stevenage, Monkswood Way

A1000
40 Bishops Stortford, Barnet Rd

A1057
40 Hatfield, St Albans Rd West
30 St Albans, Hatfield Rd

A1170
30 Turnford, High Rd

A4125
40 South Oxhey, Sandy Lane
30 Watford, Eastbury Rd

A4145
30 Watford, Tolpits Lane

A4147
30 Hemel Hempstead, Leverstock Green Rd

A4251
30 Bourne End, London Rd

A5183
30 St Albans, Frogmore Rd

A6141
60 Letchworth, Letchworth Gate

B156
30 Cheshunt, Goffs Lane

B176
30 Cheshunt, High Street

B197
30 Baldock, London Rd
30 Stevenage, North Rd

B462
30 Bushey, Aldenham Rd

B487
30 Harpenden, Redbourn Lane
40 Hemel Hempstead, Queensway

B488
40 Tring, Icknield Way

B556
30 Potters Bar, Mutton Lane

B1004
30 Bishops Stortford, Windhill

B1197
30 Hertford, London Rd

B1502
30 Hertford, Stansted Rd

B4505
30 Bovingdon, Chesham Rd

B4630
30 St Albans, Watford Rd

B5378
30 Elstree, Allum Lane
40 London Colney, Shenleybury

B6426
30 Hatfield, Cavendish Way

Unclassified
30 Cheshunt, Hammond St Rd
30 Hemel Hempstead, Bennetts End Rd
30 Hemel Hempstead, High Street Green
30 Hemel Hempstead, Long Chaulden
30 Hoddesdon, Essex Rd
30 Letchworth, Pixmore Way
30 Royston, Old North Rd
30 South Oxhey, Hayling Rd
30 St Albans, Sandpit Lane
30 Stevenage, Clovelly Way
30 Stevenage, Grace Way
40 Stevenage, Gresley Way
30 Watford, Radlett Rd
30 Watford, Whippendell Rd
30 Welwyn Garden City, Heronswood Rd
30 Welwyn Garden City, Howlands

Humberside

East Riding of Yorkshire, Hull, North East Lincolnshire, North Lincolnshire

M180
70 North Lincolnshire, West of River Trent
A18
60 North East Lincolnshire, Barton St Central
60 North East Lincolnshire, Barton St North
60 North East Lincolnshire, Barton St South
30 North Lincolnshire, Wrawby
A63
50 East Riding, Melton
40 Hull, Castle St
40 Hull, Daltry St Flyover
A161
30 Belton
A163
30 Holme on Spalding Moor
A164
30 Leconfield
A165
30 Beeford
40 East Riding, Coniston
30 Freetown Way
40 Holderness Rd
30 Skirlaugh
A180
70 Great Coates Jct
A614
40 Holme on Spalding Moor
30 Middleton on the Wolds
60 Shiptonthorpe, north of rdbt
60 Shiptonthorpe, south of the village
A1033
40 Thomas Clarkson Way
30 Thorngumbald, Main St
30 Withernsea
A1077
30 Barton
A1079
50 Barmby Moor
30 Bishop Burton
30 Hull, Beverley Rd (Desmond Ave to Riverdale Rd)
40 Hull, Beverley Rd (Sutton Rd to Mizzen Rd)
A1084
30 Brigg, Bigby High Rd
A1174
30 Dunswell
30 Woodmansey
B1206
30 Barrow, Wold Rd
B1230
40 Gilberdyke
40 Newport
B1398
40 Greetwell
Unclassified
30 Ashby, Grange Lane South
30 Ashby, Messingham Rd
30 Belton, Westgate Rd
30 Beverley, Hull Bridge Rd
30 Bilton, Main Rd
30 Bridlington, Kingsgate
30 Bridlington, Quay Rd/St John's St
30 Broughton, High St
30 Cleethorpes, Clee Rd
30 East Halton, College Rd
30 Goole, Airmyn Rd
30 Grimsby, Cromwell Rd
30 Grimsby, Great Coates Rd
30 Grimsby, Laceby Rd
30 Grimsby, Louth Rd
30 Grimsby, Waltham Rd
30 Grimsby, Weelsby Rd
30 Hessle, Beverley Rd
30 Hornsea, Rolston Rd
30 Howden, Thorpe Rd
30 Hull, Anlaby Rd
40 Hull, Boothferry Rd
30 Hull, Bricknell Avenue
30 Hull, Greenwood Avenue
30 Hull, Hall Rd
30 Hull, John Newton Way/Bude Rd
30 Hull, Leads Rd
30 Hull, Marfleet Lane
30 Hull, Marfleet Lane/Marfleet Avenue
30 Hull, Priory Rd
30 Hull, Saltshouse Rd
40 Hull, Spring Bank West
30 Hull, Wawne Rd
30 Humberston, Tetney Rd
30 Immingham, Pelham Rd
70 Laceby Bypass
30 Preston, Station Rd
30 Scunthorpe, Ashby Rd
30 Scunthorpe, Cambridge Avenue
30 Scunthorpe, Cottage Beck Rd
40 Scunthorpe, Doncaster Rd
30 Scunthorpe, Luneburg Way
40 Scunthorpe, Queensway
30 Scunthorpe, Rowland Rd
30 South Killingholme, Top Rd
30 Yaddlethorpe, Moorwell Rd

Kent and Medway

A2
70 Canterbury
60 Dover, Guston
70 Dover, Lydden
40 Medway, London Rd
A20
70,40 Dover, Dover Rd/Archcliffe
40,50 Tonbridge and Malling, London Rd
A21
70 Sevenoaks Bypass
60 Tonbridge and Malling, Castle Hill
60 Tunbridge Wells, Key's Green
A25
30 Sevenoaks, Seal Rd
A26
40 Tonbridge and Malling, Maidstone Rd
A28
40 Ashford, Ashford Rd
A224
30 Sevenoaks, Tubs Hill
A225
30 Sevenoaks, Sevenoaks Rd
A226
50 Gravesham, Rochester Rd/Gravesend Rd through Chalk
50 Gravesham, Rochester Rd/Gravesend Rd through Shorne
40 Gravesham, Rochester Rd/Gravesend Rd through Higham
A227
30 Gravesham, through Culverstone Green
40 Gravesham, through Istead Rise
30 Gravesham, through Meopham Green
A228
40 Medway, Ratcliffe Highway
A229
50 Maidstone, Bluebell Hill
40,30 Maidstone, Linton Rd/Loose Rd
30 Medway, City Way
40 Tunbridge Wells, Angley Rd (Hartley Rd)
A249
70 Maidstone, Chalky Rd/Rumstead Lane, South St
70 Swale, Chestnut St
A253
30 Thanet, Canterbury Rd West
A256
70 Dover
30 Dover, London Rd
40 Thanet, Haine Rd
A258
50 Dover, Dover Rd
A259
40 Shepway
60 Shepway, Guldeford Lane
30 Shepway, High St
A262
30 Ashford, High St
A268
30 Tunbridge Wells, Queen St
A289
50 Medway, Medway Tunnel
70 Medway, Wainscott Bypass
A290
30 Canterbury, Blean
A291
30 Canterbury, Canterbury Rd
A292
30 Ashford, Mace Lane
A2033
30 Shepway, Dover Rd
A2990
60 Canterbury, Old Thanet Way
B258
30 Dartford, Barn End Lane
B2015
40 Nettlestead Green, Maidstone Rd
B2017
30 Tunbridge Wells, Badsell Rd
B2067
60 Ashford, Ashford Rd
30 Ashford, Woodchurch Rd
B2071
30 Shepway, Littlestone Rd
B2097
30 Rochester, Maidstone Rd
B2205
30 Swale, Mill Way
Unclassified
30 Canterbury, Mickleburgh Hill
30 Canterbury, Rough Common Rd
30 Dartford, Ash Rd/Hartley Rd
30 Gravesham, Sole St
30 Medway, Beechings Way
30 Medway, Esplanade
30 Medway, Maidstone Rd
30 Medway, St End Rd
30 Medway, Walderslade Rd
30 Sevenoaks, Ash Rd/Hartley Rd
30 Swale, Lower Rd
30 Thanet, Shottendane Rd

Lancashire

A6
40 Broughton, Garstang Rd (north of M55)
30 Chorley, Bolton Rd
30 Fulwood, Garstang Rd (south of M55)
30 Fulwood, Garstang Rd, north of Blackpool Rd
30 Lancaster, Greaves Rd
50 Lancaster, Scotforth Rd nr Burrow Lane Bailrigg
30 Preston, North Rd
30 Preston, Ringway
A56
30 Colne, Albert Rd
30 Colne, Burnley Rd
30 Nelson, Leeds Rd
A59
60 Gisburn, Gisburn Rd
50 Hutton, Liverpool Rd
30 Preston, New Hall Lane
A65
40 Lancaster, Cowan Bridge
A570
40 Scarisbrick, Southport Rd, Brook House Farm
A581
40 Ulnes Walton, Southport Rd
A583+A5073
30 Blackpool, Whitegate Drive/Waterloo Rd
A583+B5266
30 Blackpool, Church St/Newton Drive
A584
30 Blackpool, Promenade
30 Lytham, West/Central Beach
30 Warton, Lytham Rd
A584+A587
30 Blackpool, Promenade/Fleetwood Rd
A587
30 Blackpool, East/North Park Drive
30 Cleveleys, Rossall Rd/Crescent East
A588
60 Pilling, Head Dyke Lane
60 Wyre, Lancaster Rd, Cockerham at Gulf Lane
A666
30 Darwen, Blackburn Rd
30 Darwen, Bolton Rd nr Cross St
30 Darwen, Duckworth St
A671
30 Read, Whalley Rd
A674
30 Cherry Tree, Preston Old Rd
A675
50 Belmont, Belmont Rd (south of village)
50 Darwen, Belmont Rd, north of Belmont Village
60 Withnell, Bolton Rd (Dole Lane to Calf Hey Bridge)
A680
40 Edenfield, Rochdale Rd
A682
60 Barrowford, Gisburn Rd nr Moorcock Inn
30 Brierfield, Colne Rd
40 Crawshawbooth, Burnley Rd
60 Gisburn, Gisburn Rd
60 Gisburn, Long Preston Rd
A683
30 Lancaster, Morecambe Rd
A5073
30 Blackpool, Waterloo Rd
A5085
30 Lane Ends, Blackpool Rd
A5209
30 Newburgh, Course Lane/Ash Brow
A6068
50 Barrowford, Barrowford Rd
A6114
30 Burnley, Casterton Avenue
A6177
50 Haslingden, Grane Rd West of Holcombe Rd
50 Hyndburn, Haslingden Rd/Elton Rd
B5192
30 Kirkham, Preston St
B5251
30 Chorley, Pall Mall
B5254
30 Lostock Hall, Leyland Rd/Watkin Lane
30 South Ribble, Leyland Rd (north of Talbot Rd to A59 Golden Way Rdbt, Penwortham)
B5256
30 Leyland, Turpin Green Lane
B5269
40 Goosnargh, Whittingham Lane
B6231
30 Oswaldtwistle, Union Rd
Unclassified
60 Belmont, Egerton Rd
30 Blackburn, East Park Rd
30 Blackburn, Whalley Old Rd, west of Railway Bridge
30 Blackpool, Dickson Rd, Queens St to Pleasant St
30 Briercliffe, Burnley Rd
30 Darwen, Lower Eccleshill Rd
60 Galgate, Bay Horse Rd
30 Nelson, Netherfield Rd
30 Preston, Lytham Rd
30 Preston, St Georges Rd
30 St Anne's, Church Rd to Albany Rd, nr High School

Leicestershire and Rutland

A1
70 Empingham, Great North Rd
70 Stretton, Great North Rd
A5
60 Hinckley, Watling St (B578 to M69)
50 Hinckley, Watling St (M69 to A47)
70 Sharnford, Watling St (Highcross to B4114)
A6
40 Birstall, Loughborough Rd
40 Leicester, Abbey Lane
30 Leicester, London Rd (Knighton Drive)
30 Loughborough, Derby Rd
40 Oadby, Glen Rd/Harborough Rd
A47
60 Barrowden, Peterborough Rd
60 Bisbrooke, Uppingham Rd
30 Earl Shilton, Hinckley Rd
40 Houghton on the Hill, Uppingham Rd
30 Leicester, Hinckley Rd
30 Leicester, Humberstone Rd
50 Morcott, Glaston Rd
50 Skeffington, Uppingham Rd
50 Tugby, Uppingham Rd
A50
70 Hemmington to Lockington
40 Leicester/Glenfield, Groby Rd/Leicester Rd
30 Woodgate
A426
50 Dunton Bassett, Lutterworth Rd
40 Glen Parva, Leicester Rd
60 Lutterworth, Leicester Rd
60 Whetstone, Lutterworth Rd
A444
60 Fenny Drayton, Atherstone Rd
30 Twycross Village, Main St
60 Twycross, Norton Juxta
A447
60 Cadeby, Hinckley Rd
40 Ravenstone, Wash Lane
A512
30 Loughborough, Ashby Rd
40 Shepshed, Ashby Rd Central
A563
30 Leicester, Attlee Way
30 Leicester, Colchester Rd/Hungarton Boulevard
30 Leicester, Glenhills Way
40 Leicester, Krefield Way
30 Leicester, New Parks Way
A594
30 Leicester, St Georges Way
A606
60 Barnsdale, Stamford Rd
60 Leicester, Broughton/Old Dalby
60 Tinwell, Stamford Rd
A607
30 Leicester, Melton Rd
30 Melton, Norman Way
70 Thurmaston, Newark Rd
60 Waltham on the Wolds, Melton Rd
60 Waltham/Croxton Kerrial, Melton Rd
A4304
40 Market Harborough, Lubbenham Hill
A5199
30 Leicester, Welford Rd
30 Wigston, Bull Head St
30 Wigston, Leicester Rd
A5460
40 Leicester, Narborough Rd
A6004
30 Loughborough, Alan Moss Rd
A6030
30 Leicester, Wakerley Rd/Broad Avenue
A6121
30 Ketton, Stamford Rd
B568
30 Leicester, Victoria Park Rd
B581
30 Broughton Astley, Broughton Way
B582
30 Blaby, Little Glen Rd
B590
30 Hinckley, Rugby Rd
B591
60 Charley, Loughborough Rd
B676
60 Freeby, Saxby Rd
B4114
40 Enderby/Narborough, Leicester Rd/King Edward Avenue
30 Leicester, Sharnford
B4616
30 Leicester, East Park Rd
B4666
30 Hinckley, Coventry Rd
B5003
40 Norris Hill, Ashby Rd
B5366
30 Leicester, Saffron Lane
B5350
30 Loughborough, Foreset Rd
30 Loughborough, Nanpantan Rd
Unclassified
30 Barrow upon Soar, Sileby Rd
30 Blaby, Lutterworth Rd
30 Ibstock, Leicester Rd
30 Leicester, Fosse Rd South
30 Shepshed, Leicester Rd

Lincolnshire

A15
60 Ashby Lodge
60 Aswarby
A15-B1191
60 Dunsby Hollow
A16
60 Boston, Boston Tytton Lane
40 Burwell
60 Deeping Bypass
60 Grainsby to Holton-le-Clay
60 North Thoresby
A17
60 Fleet Hargate
60 Hoffleet Stow
60 Moulton Common
A52
60 Bridge End
60 Horbling and Swaton
60 Ropsley
A153
40 Billinghay
50 Tattershall
A158
50 Scremby to Candlesby
A631
60 Hemswell
60 West Rasen, Dale Bridge
B1188
30 Branston
60 Canwick, Highfield House
60 Potterhanworth

London

M11
Chadwell
M25
Egham
Elmbridge, Byfleet
Hillingdon
Hillingdon, Colnbrook
Runneymeade
Spelthorne
Wraysbury
A3
Kingston Bypass
Wandsworth, Kingston Rd
A4
Hounslow, Brentford, Great West Rd
Hounslow, Great West Rd
A5
Barnet, Hendon Broadway
Brent, Edgware Rd
A10
Enfield, Great Cambridge Rd
Hackney, Stamford Hill
A13
Barking and Dagenham, Alfreds Way
Barking and Dagenham, Ripple Rd
Dagenham, Ripple Rd
Newham, Alfreds Way
A20
Bexley, Sidcup Rd
Bromley, Sidcup Bypass
Greenwick, Sidcup Rd
A21
Lewisham, Bromley Rd
A22
Croydon, Godstone Rd
A40
City of Westminster, Westway
Ealing, Perivale
Ealing, Western Avenue
Hammersmith and Fulham, Westway
Hillingdon, Ruislip, Western Avenue
A110
Enfield, Enfield Rd
A124
Newham, Barking Rd
A205
Richmond upon Thames
Richmond upon Thames, Upper Richmond Rd West
A213
Bromley, Croydon Rd
A214
Wandsworth, Trinity Rd
A215
Croydon, Beulah Hill
A217
Croydon, Garratt Lane
A219
Hammersmith and Fulham, Scrubs Lane
A222
Bromley, Bromley Rd
A232
Sutton, Cheam Rd
A298
West Barnes, Bushey Rd
A312
Hillingdon
A315
Hounslow, High St
A406
Barking and Dagenham, Barking Relief Rd
Barnet, North Circular Rd
Redbridge, Southend Rd
A501
Camden, Euston Rd
A503
Haringey, Seven Sisters Rd
A3220
Wandsworth, Latchmere Rd
A4006
Brent, Kenton Rd
B178
Barking and Dagenham, Ballards Rd
B272
Sutton, Foresters Rd
B278
Sutton, Green Lane
B279
Sutton, Tudor Drive
Unclassified
Barnet, Oakleigh Rd South
Bexley, Abbey Rd
Bexley, Bellegrove Rd
Bexley, Erith Rd
Bexley, Farady Avenue
Bexley, King Harolds Way
Bexley, Lower Rd
Bexley, Penhill Rd
Bexley, Pickford Lane
Bexley, Well Hall Rd
Bexley, Woolwich Rd
Brent, Crest Rd
Brent, Hillside
Brent, Kingsbury Rd
Brent, Kingsbury, Fryent Way
Brent, Sudbury, Watford Rd
Brent, Wembley, Watford Rd
Brent, Woodcock Hill
Bromley, Beckenham Rd
Bromley, Burnt Ash Lane
Bromley, Crystal Palace Park Rd
Bromley, Elmers End Rd
Bromley, Main Rd
Bromley, Sevenoaks Way
Bromley, Wickham Way
City of Westminster, Great Western Rd
City of Westminster, Millbank
City of Westminster, Vauxhall Bridge Rd
Croydon, Addiscombe, Long Lane
Croydon, Brigstock Rd
Croydon, Coulsdon, Coulsdon Rd
Croydon, Coulsdon, Portnalls Rd
Croydon, Thornton Rd
Ealing, Greenford, Greenford Rd
Ealing, Horn Lane
Ealing, Lady Margaret Rd
Ealing, Ruislip Rd
Ealing, Southall, Greenford Rd
Ealing, Uxbridge Rd
Eastcote, Field End Rd
Enfield, Fore St
Forest Hill, Stanstead Rd
Forest Hill, Stanstead Rd
Greenwick, Beresford St
Greenwick, Court Rd
Greenwick, Creek Rd
Greenwick, Glenesk Rd
Greenwick, Rochester Way
Greenwick, Rochester Way
Greenwick, Woolwich Church St
Hackney, Clapton Common
Hackney, Seven Sisters Rd
Hackney, Upper Clapton Rd
Hammersmith and Fulham, Fulham Palace Rd
Hammersmith and Fulham, Uxbridge Rd
Hammersmith and Fulham, Westway
Haringey, Belmont Rd
Haringey, Bounds Green Rd
Haringey, Seven Sisters Rd
Haringey, White Hart Lane
Harrow, Alexandra Avenue
Harrow, Harrow View
Harrow, Harrow Weald, Uxbridge Rd
Harrow, Honeypot Lane
Harrow, Porlock Avenue
Harrow, Watford Rd
Havering, Chase Cross Rd
Havering, Eastern Avenue
Havering, Eastern Avenue East
Havering, Hall Lane
Havering, Hornchurch, Parkstone Avenue
Havering, Ockenden Rd
Havering, Romford, Brentwood Rd
Havering, Wingletye Lane
Hillingdon, Cowley, Cowley Rd
Hillingdon, Cowley, High Rd
Hillingdon, Harefield, Church Hill
Hillingdon, Hayes, Kingshill Avenue
Hillingdon, Hayes, Uxbridge Rd
Hillingdon, Northwood Hills, Joel St
Hillingdon, Park Rd
Hillingdon, Stockley Rd
Hillingdon, Uxbridge, Cowley Rd
Hounslow, Bedfont, Hatton Rd
Hounslow, Great West Rd
Hounslow, Hanworth, Castle Way
Hounslow, Harlington Rd West
Islington, Holloway Rd
Islington, Seven Sisters Rd
Islington, Upper St
Kensington and Chelsea, Barlby Rd
Kensington and Chelsea, Chelsea Embankment
Kensington and Chelsea, Chesterton Rd
Kensington and Chelsea, Holand Park Avenue
Kensington and Chelsea, Holland Villas Rd
Kensington and Chelsea, Kensington Park Rd
Kensington and Chelsea, Kensington Rd
Kensington and Chelsea, Ladbroke Grove
Kensington and Chelsea, Latimer Rd
Kensington and Chelsea, Royal Hospital Rd
Kensington and Chelsea, Sloane St
Kensington and Chelsea, St Helens Gardens
Kingston upon Thames, Kingston Rd
Kingston upon Thames, Manor Drive North
Kingston upon Thames, Richmond Rd
Lambeth, Atkins Rd
Lambeth, Brixton Hill
Lambeth, Brixton Rd
Lambeth, Clapham Rd
Lambeth, Herne Hill Rd
Lambeth, Kennington Park Rd
Lambeth, Kings Avenue
Lambeth, Streatham High Rd
Lewisham, Brockley Rd
Lewisham, Brownhill Rd
Lewisham, Burnt Ash Hill
Lewisham, Lee High Rd
Lewisham, Lewisham Way
Lewisham, Westwood Hill
Merton, Central Rd
Merton, Colliers Wood, High St
Merton, Hillcross Avenue
Merton, London Rd
Merton, Martin Way
Merton, Ridgway Place
Merton, West Barnes Lane
Newham, Barking Rd
Newham, Romford Rd
Newham, Royal Albert Dock, Spine Rd
Newham, Royal Docks Rd
North Dagenham, Rainham Rd
Redbridge, Hainault, Manford Way
Redbridge, Woodford Avenue
Redbridge, Woodford Rd
Richmond upon Thames, Kew Rd
Richmond upon Thames, Sixth Cross Rd
Richmond upon Thames, Uxbridge Rd
Southwark, Albany Rd
Southwark, Alleyn Park
Southwark, Brenchley Gardens
Southwark, Camberwell New Rd
Southwark, Denmark Hill
Southwark, Kennington Park Rd
Southwark, Linden Grove
Southwark, Old Kent Rd
Southwark, Peckham Rye
Southwark, Salter Rd
Southwark, Sunray Avenue
Streatham, Streatham High Rd
Sutton, Beddington Lane
Sutton, Cheam Common Rd
Sutton, Maiden Rd
Sutton, Middleton Rd
Tower Hamlets, Bow Rd
Tower Hamlets, Cambridge Heath Rd
Tower Hamlets, Homerton High Rd
Tower Hamlets, Manchester Rd
Tower Hamlets, Mile End Rd
Tower Hamlets, Upper Clapton Rd
Tower Hamlets, Westferry Rd
Waltham Forest, Chingford Rd
Waltham Forest, Hoe St
Waltham Forest, Larksall Rd
Wandsworth, Battersea Park Rd
Wandsworth, Garratt Lane
Wandsworth, Upper Richmond Rd
Woolwich, Woolwich Church St

Norfolk

A10
60 Stow Bardolph
60 Tottenhill/Watlington
A11
60 Attleborough Bypass
70 Ketteringham
70 Roundham
70 Snetterton
70 Wymondham/Bestthorpe
A12
70 Hopton
A17
60 Terrington St Clement
A47
60 East Winch
60 Emneth
60 Honington/Easton
50 Lingwood/Acle
60 Mautby/Halvergate
60 Narborough
70 Postwick
70 Pullover Rdbt
70 Scarning
60 Swaffham/Sporle
70 Terrington St John
70 Tuddenham
60 Wendling/Framsham
A140
60 Aylsham
60 Dickleburgh Moor
60 Erpingham
60 Long Stratton/Tivetshall St Mary
60 Newton Flotman
40 Newton Flotman/Saxlingham Thorpe
30 Norwich, Harford Bridge
40 Roughton village
70 Scole Bypass
60 St. Faiths
A143
60 Billingford/Brockdish
A146
60 Hales
A148
60 Bodham
60 Fakenham Bypass
40 King's Lynn, Grimston Rd
60 Pretty Corner
50 Thursford
A149
70 Caister Bypass
60 Catfield
40 Catfield/Potter Heigham
30 Hunstanton
60 Kings Lynn/Nth Runcton
60 Knights Hill
60 Little Snoring
60 Roughton (N and S Repps)
60 Sandringham
50 Wayford Bridge East
50 Wayford Bridge West/Smallburgh
A1065
60 Hilbrough
60 South Acre
60 Weeting with Broomhill
A1066
60 Rushford
60 South Lopham
40 Thetford, Mundford Rd
A1067
50 Bawdeswell
60 Morton/Attlebridge
A1075
60 Wretham (heath)
A1082
30 Sheringham
A1122
60 Swaffham/Beachamwell
A1151
60 Rackheath/Wroxham
B1111
30 East Harling
B1108
30 Norwich, Earlham Rd
B1135
50 Wymondham/Wreningham
B1149
60 Horsford Woods
B1150
50 Scottow
50 Westwick
B1152
60 Orby
B1332
50 Ditchingham
Unclassified
70 Caister, High St/Norwich Rd
30 Caister, Ormesby Rd
60 Drayton, Reepham Rd
30 Shipdham, High St
30 Walton

North Yorkshire

A1
70 Catterick
A59
60 Beamsley
A64
70 Malton
A65
60 Clapham
60 Settle
Unclassified
30 Tunstall, Main St

Northamptonshire

A5
60 DIRFT to County Boundary
60 Norton/Whilton Crossroads
30/40 Towcester Racecourse to A43
A6
60 Burton Latimer Bypass
A14
70 Kelmarsh
70 Kettering Junctions 7-10

A43
60 Laxton Turn to A47 Duddington
60 Mawsley to A14 Junction 8 (inc Mawsley spur)
70 Towcester to M1 Junction 15a

A45
60 M1 Junction 16 to Weedon
60 Stanwick to Raunds

A361
60 Byfield to Chipping Warden

A422
60 Brackley West to A43

A428
60 East Haddon
30/60 Great Houghton to Yardley Hastings

A508
30 Northampton, Plough Gyratory
30 Northampton, St Georges Avenue to Holly Lodge Rd
30 Northampton, St Peters Way to Georges Avenue
30/60 Northampton, Stoke Bruerne to A5
70 Northampton, Wootton Flyover to M1 Junction 15

A509
60 Wellingborough to Isham

A605
40/60 Thrapston to Warmington

A4256
30 Daventry, Eastern Way

A4500
40/60 Great Billing to Earls Barton
30 Northampton, Abington Park to York Rd
30 Northampton, Park Avenue to Booth Lane South
30 Northampton, Weedon Rd to Duston Rd

A5076
40 Northampton, Mere Way
40 Northampton, Great Billing Way South

A5193
30/40 Wellingborough, London Rd

A6003
50/60 Kettering to Corby

A6014
40/60 Corby, Oakley Rd

B569
50 Irchester to Rushden

B576
60 Desborough to Rothwell

B4038
30/60 Rugby Rd

B4525
40/60 Welsh Lane

B5385
60 Watford to West Haddon

Unclassified
30 Brackmills Industrial Estate
30 Northampton, Grange Rd

Northumbria

Gateshead, Newcastle-upon-Tyne, North Tyneside, Northumberland, South Tyneside, Sunderland

A1
60 Berwick Bypass, Dunns Jct (N)

A68
60 Colt Crag

A69
60 Haltwhistle Bypass
70 Hexham, Two Mile Cottage

A167
30 Newcastle, Stamfordham Rd

A182
30 Sunderland, Houghton Rd

A183
30 Broadway, Chester Rd

A186
40 Denton Burn, West Rd
30 Newcastle, City Rd at Beamish House
40 Newcastle, West Rd at Turret Rd
30 Newcastle, Westgate Rd at Elwick Row

A189
70 Cramlington, High Pitt
70 Cramlington, Spine Rd
30 South Gosforth, Haddricks Mill Rd

A191
30 Benton, Whitley Rd

A193
30 Wallsend, Church Bank

A194
40 Simonside, Newcastle Rd

A196
30 Blackclose Bank

A690
30 Sunderland, Durham Rd
50 Sunderland, Stoneygate, Houghton, Durham Rd

A694
30 Gateshead, Rowlands Gill, Station Rd
40 Gateshead, Winlaton Mill (Spa Well Rd)

A695
60 Gateshead, Crawcrook Bypass
40 Prudhoe Jct B6395

30 Belsay Village
60 Blaxter Cottages
60 Kirkwhelpiington
60 Otterburn Monkridge

A697
60 Morpeth, Heighley Gate
60 Northumberland

A1018
30 Sunderland, Ryhope Rd, Irene Avenue

A1058
30 Newcastle, Jesmond Rd at Akenside Terrace

A1068
30 Amble Ind Est

A1147
30 Stakeford, Gordon Terrace

A1171
30 Cramlington, Dudley Lane

A1290
30 Sunderland, Southwick, Keir Hardie Way

A1300
30 South Tyneside, Nook, Prince Edward Rd

A6085
40 Newcastle, Lemington Rd

A6127
30 Gateshead, Barley Mow, Durham Rd

B1288
40 Gateshead, Leam Lane/ A195

B1296
30 Gateshead, Sheriffs Highway, QE Hospital
30 Gateshead, Sheriffs Highway, Split Crow Rd

B1298
30 South Tyneside, Boldon Colliery, New Rd

B1301
30 South Tyneside, Dean Rd (John Clay St)
30 South Tyneside, Laygate, Eglesfield Rd

B1316
30 North Tyneside, Lynn Rd

B1318
30 North Tyneside, Seaton Burn, Bridge St

B1426
30 Gateshead, Felling, Sunderland Rd

B1505
30 North Tyneside, West Moor, Great Lime Rd

B6315
30 Gateshead, High Spen, Hookergate Lane

B6317
30 Gateshead, Ryton, Main Rd
30 Gateshead, Whickham Highway

B6318
60 Whitchester, Military Rd
60 Whittington Fell, Military Rd

B6324
40 Newcastle, Stamfordham Rd southeast of Walbottle Rd

B6918
30 Newcastle, Woolsington Village

Unclassified
30 Ashington, Station Rd
30 Benton, Coach Lane
30 Gateshead, Blaydon, Shibdon Bank
30 Gateshead, Crawcrook, Greenside Rd
30 Gateshead, Felling, Watermill Lane
30 Gateshead, Whickham, Fellside Rd
30 Gateshead, Askew Rd West
30 Hebburn, Campbell Park Rd
70 Nafferton Eastbound
60 Newcastle, Dinnington Rd North Brunton Lane
40 Newcastle, West Denton Way east of Hawksley
30 North Shields, Norham Rd
30 South Tyneside, Harton Lane
40 South Tyneside, Hedworth Lane, Abingdon Way
40 Sunderland, Farringdon, North Moor Lane
40 Sunderland, North Hylton Rd, Castletown Way
30 Sunderland, Silksworth Rd, Rutland Avenue
30 Sunderland, Springwell Rd
30 Sunderland, Warwick Terrace

30 Wallsend, Battle Hill Drive
30 Whiteleas, Nevinson Avenue

Nottinghamshire

A1(T)
70 East Markham (Northbound)

A52(T)
40 Clifton Boulevard

A60
30 Carlton in Lindrick
30 Mansfield, Nottingham Rd
60 Market Warsop/Cuckney Nottingham, Bellar Gate to Woodthorpe Drive
30 Nottingham, London Rd
50 Ravenshead
30 South, Nottingham

A609
30 Nottingham, Ilkeston Rd/Wollaton Rd/Russell Drive

A610
30 Nottingham, Bobbers Mill

A611
30 Annelsey, Derby Rd
30 Nottingham, Hucknall Rd

A612
30 Southwell, Nottingham Rd

A614
60 Arnold, Burnt Stump

A617
40 Mansfield, Chesterfield Rd South

A620
40 Retford, Welham Rd

A631
50 Beckingham Bypass
50 Beckingham, Flood Plain Rd
50 Beckingham, nr Wood Lane
60 Gringley to Beckingham, nr Mutton Lane
50 West of Beckingham

A6005
30 Nottingham, Castle Boulevard/Abbey Bridge/ Beeston Rd

A6008
30 Nottingham, Canal St

A6130
30 Nottingham, Gregory Boulevard
30 Nottingham, Radford and Lenton Boulevards

A6200/A52
30 Nottingham, Derby Rd

B679
30 West Bridgford, Wilford Lane

B682
30 Nottingham, Sherwood Rise/Nottingham Rd/ Vernon Rd

B6004
30 Arnold, Oxclose Lane

B6010
30 Giltbrook, Nottingham Rd

B6011
30 Hucknall, Annesley Rd/ Nottingham Rd/Portland Rd

B6020
30 Rainworth, Kirklington Rd

B6040
30 Worksop, Retford Rd

B6166
30 Newark on Trent, Lincoln Rd/Northgate

B6326
40 Newark on Trent, London Rd

Unclassified
30 Newark, Balderton, Hawton Lane
30 Nottingham, Beechdale Rd/Wigman Rd
30 Nottingham, Bestwood Park Drive Nottingham, Radford Boulevard/Lenton Boulevard
30 Nottingham, Ridge Way/Top Valley Drive

Oxfordshire

see Thames Valley

Shropshire

see West Mercia

Somerset

see Avon and Somerset

South Yorkshire

A18
60 Doncaster, Slay Pits to Tudworth, Epworth Rd
40 Doncaster, Carr House Rd/Leger Way

A57
40,60 Anston, Sheffield Rd/Worksop Rd
60 Rotherham, Worksop Rd
60 Sheffield, Mosborough Parkway

A60
60 Tickhill, Doncaster Rd
30,60 Tickhill, Worksop Rd

A61
30 Cutting Edge, Park Rd
30,40 Sheffield, Chesterfield Rd/Chesterfield Rd South
30,40 Sheffield, Halifax Rd
30 Sheffield, Penistone Rd

A614
60 Thorne, Selby Rd

A618
40 Wales Bar, Mansfield Rd

A628
30,40 Barnsley, Cundy Cross to Shafton Two Gates
40,60 Barnsley, Dodworth
40 Penistone, Barnsley Rd

A629
60 Barnsley, Wortley
30 Burncross, Hallwood Rd/Burncross Rd
40 Rotherham, New Wortley Rd
30,40 Rotherham, Wortley Rd/Upper Wortley Rd

A630
30,40,60 Dalton/Thrybergh, Doncaster Rd
30,40,60 Doncaster, Balby Flyover to Hill Top
40 Doncaster, Wheatley Hall Rd
40,50 Rotherham, Centenary Way

A631
40 Brinsworth, Bawtry Rd
30,40 Hellaby/Maltby, Bawtry Rd/Rotherham Rd
50 Rotherham, West Bawtry Rd
40 Wickersley/Brecks, Bawtry Rd

A633
30 Athersley South, Rotherham Rd
40 Monk Bretton, Rotherham Rd
30 Wath upon Dearne, Sandygate
30,40 Wombwell, Barnsley Rd

A635
30,40,60 Barnsley, Doncaster Rd/Saltersbrook Rd

A638
40 Doncaster, Bawtry Rd
30,40,50 Doncaster, Great North Rd/York Rd

A6022
30 Rotherham, Swinton

A6101
40 Sheffield, Rivelin Valley Rd

A6102
30,40 Hillsborough/Deepcar, Manchester Rd/Langsett Rd

A6109
40 Rotherham, Meadow Bank Rd

A6123
40 Rotherham, Herringthorpe Valley Rd

A6135
40 Sheffield, Ecclesfield Rd/Chapeltown Rd

B6059
30,40 Rotherham, Kiveton/ Wales

B6089
40 Thorn Hill/Greasbrough, Greasbrough Rd/ Greasbrough St

B6096
30 Barnsley, Wombwell to Snape Hill

B6097
30,60 Wath upon Dearne, Doncaster Rd

B6100
30 Barnsley, Ardsley Rd/ Hunningley Lane

B6411
30 Thurnscoe, Houghton Rd

B6463
60 Tickhill, Stripe Rd

Unclassified
30 Armthorpe, Hatfield Lane/Mill St
30 Armthorpe, Nutwell Lane
30 Barnsley, Pogmoor Rd
30 Bolton upon Dearne, Dearne Rd
30 Doncaster, Melton Rd/Sprotbrough Rd
30 Doncaster, Urban Rd
30,60 Edlington/ Warmsworth, Broomhouse Lane/Springwell Lane
40,60 Finningley, Hurst Lane
30 Grimethorpe, Brierley Rd
30,60 Rotherham, Fenton Rd
30,40 Rotherham, Haugh Rd
30 Rotherham, Kilnhurst Rd

30 Stainforth, Station Rd
40 Wath upon Dearne, Barnsley Rd
30 Wheatley, Thorne Rd

Staffordshire

A5
60 A5127 to A38 – Wall Island to Weeford Island
60 Brownhills, Watling St
60,70,60,30 btwn A34 Churchbridge and The Turf Pub Island (B4154)
50 Cannock, Watling St
50,40 from A38 to Hints Lane
70 from A461 to A5127 (Muckley Corner Island to Wall Island Lichfield/ Tamworth)
60,70,60 Hanney Hay/ Barracks Lane Island to Muckley Corner Island
50 M6 jct 12 to A460/A4601 Island
50,30 South Cannock, A460/ A4601 to A34 Longford Island to A34 Bridgetown
60 Wall, Watling St
60 Weeford, Watling St

A34
30 Cannock North, North of Holly Lane jct to A34/ B5012 rdbt
30,50,30 Cannock South to County Boundary
30 Cannock South, A34 from south of jct of A5 Walsall Rd to north of jct with Jones Lane
40 Newcastle North, from Wolstanton Rd/Dimsdale Parade west Island to Milehouse Lane/B5367
30,40 Newcastle Rd btwn Hanford Island to London Rd Bowling Club
40 Newcastle South, Barracks Rd to Stoke City Boundary
70,40 Newcastle under Lyme to Talke, btwn Wolstanton Rd/Dimsdale Parade West Island to Jct of A500
30,40 Stafford South, from A449 jct to Acton Hill Lane Jct
30 Stafford, btwn A5013 and A518
40 Stafford, Queensway
40,30 Stone Rd from jct of Longton Rd/A5035 to Handford Island/A500
40,30 Stone Rd Redhill (A513/A34) island to Lloyds Island, Eccleshall Rd
30,60 Talke, Jct A500 to Jct A5011

A38
40 Alrewas, btwn Rradley Lane and Wychnor Lane
70 btwn London Rd Lichfield and A5121 Burton
70 btwn Weeford Island and Bassetts Pole Island (Community Concern Site)

A50
30 Kidsgrove, btwn City Boundary and Oldcott Drive
30 Kidsgrove, Liverpool Rd
30 Stoke on Trent, Victoria Rd btwn Leek Rd and City Rd

A51
60 btwn Armitage Lane Rugeley and A515 nr Lichfield
30,40,60 Lichfield, from A5127 Birmingham Rd to Heath Rd
30 Lichfield, Tamworth Rd
50 Pasturefields, A51 from south of jct with Amerton Lane to south of Hoomill Lane
40,30 Rugeley North, from A51 jct with Bower Lane to island of A460 Sandy Lane and B5013 Elmore Lane
30,40 Rugeley South, from south of island of A460/ Sandy Lane and B5013 Elmore Lane to Brereton Island
30 Tamworth, A51 Tamworth Rd/Dosthill Rd from south of jct with Peelers Way to jct with A51 Ascot Drive
60,40,50 Weston, btwn New Rd and 500m past Sandy Lane (going north)

A52
30 Stoke on Trent, Werrington Rd – btwn jct of B5040 to half mile east of Brookhouse Lane (Ashbank)
30,40 Stoke, Werrington Rd, btwn Brookhouse Lane and Kingsley Rd

A53
40,30,40,60 Endon, from A53 Leek New Rd from jct with Nursery Avenue to jct with Dunwood Lane
60,40,30 Longsden, from A53 jct with Dunwood Lane to A53 jct with Wallbridge Drive

A444
30 Stanton Rd – St Peters Bridge to Derbyshire boundary

A449
70,40 Coven, btwn Station Drive by Four Ashes to just before M54 island
40 Coven, Wolverhampton Rd
60,70 Gailey, btwn Rodbaston Drive and Station Drive
60 Galley, Wolverhampton Rd
40 Penkridge, Lynehill Lane to 0.5mile north of Goodstation Lane
30 Stafford, Lichfield Rd to Gravel Lane

A454
50 Trescott, Bridgenorth Rd btwn Brantley Lane and Shop Lane

A458
40,50 Gilberts Cross, btwn Six Ashes Rd, Six Ashes and Morfe Lane

A460
30 Rugeley, A460 from A51/A460 jct of Sandy Lane/Hednesford Rd to south of jct A460 Stile Cop Rd

A500
40 btwn M6 jct 16 and A34

A511
40,30 Burton North, btwn Anslow Lane to island of A5121
30 Burton South, island of A5121 to Brizlincote Lane (by Derbyshire boundary)

A518
30 Stafford, btwn M6 and Bridge St
30,40 Stafford, Riverway to Blackheath Lane

A519
40 Newcastle, Clayton Rd – from south of A519 Clayton Rd/Friars Wood and Brook Lane to rdbt on A519

A519
30 Woodseaves, btwn Moss Lane and Lodge Lane (Community Concern Site)

A520
30 Sandon Rd btwn Grange Rd and A50
30 Weston Rd – from north of the A50 to City boundary (Park Hall) through Meir and Weston Coyney

A522
50,40 Beamhurst, btwn Fole Lane and Grange Rd, nr Uttoxeter

A4601
30 Cannock, btwn A34 Walsall Rd jct to Longford Island A5
30 Old Hednesford Rd btwn jct with A5190 Lichfield Rd and jct with A460 Eastern Way
30,40 Wedges Mill, Longford Island twd jct 11 to just before Saredon Rd

A5005
Stoke on Trent, Lightwood Rd btwn A520 and A50

A5013
30 Stafford, Eccleshall Rd btwn A34 and M6

A5035
30 Trentham, Longton Rd btwn Trentham Rdbt A34 and A50 jct at Longton

A5121
30 Burton, Derby Rd
50,40,30 Burton, from Island Junction with B5108 Branston to Borough Rd
30,40 Burton, from jct with Byrkley St, Horninglow to jct with Hillfield Lane
30 Burton, Wellington Rd

A5127
30 Lichfield, Trent Valley Rd
30 Lichfield, from jct with Upper St John St towards Streethay (incs change in speed limit over railway bridge)

A5189
30 Burton, St Peters Bridge
30,40 Burton, btwn Wellington Rd jct along St Peters Bridge to Stapenhill Rd rdbt

A5190
30 Burntwood, Cannock Rd from Attwood Rd to Stockhay Lane Jct
30 Cannock, Cannock Rd
30,40,60 Cannock, from Five Ways Island to Hednesford Rd

B5027
30 Stone Rd btwn Byrds Lane and Springfield Rd

B5044
30 Silverdale, btwn Sneyd Terrace and the jct of the B5368 (Church Lane/ Cemetery Rd)

B5051
30 btwn Sneyd Hill Rd and Brown Edge
30 Stoke on Trent, Ford Green Rd

B5066
30 Hilderstone, btwn B5027 and Hall Lane
60 Sandon, Sandon Rd btwn A51 and Salt Lane
30 Stafford, Sandon Rd btwn A513 and Marston Rd

B5080
30,40 Tamworth, Pennine Way btwn B5000 and Pennymoor Rd

B5404
40,30 Tamworth, from Sutton Rd to jct of A4091 (Coleshill Rd/Fazeley Rd)
30 Tamworth, Watling St btwn jct with A51 and A5

B5500
30 Audley btwn Barthomley Rd and Park Lane (Community Concern Site)
30,40 Bignall End/Bignall Hill, btwn Boons Hill Rd and Alsager Lane

Unclassified
30 Burntwood, Church Rd btwn Rugeley Rd and Farewell Lane
30 Burton on Trent, Violet Way/Beaufort Rd btwn A444 and A511
30 Burton, Rosliston Rd btwn A5189 St Peters Bridge and County Boundary by Railway Bridge
30 Cannock, Pye Green Rd
30 Cedar Rd btwn Crackley Bank and B5500 Audley Rd
30 Cheadle Rd btwn Uttoxeter Rd and Quabbs Lane
40 Cresswell, Sandon Rd btwn Severley Green Rd and Uttoxeter Rd
30 Hednesford, Rawnsley Rd btwn A460 and Littleworth Rd
30,40 Leek New Rd – btwn B5049 Hanley Rd and B5051 jct with A53 at Endon
30 Oxford Rd/Chell Heath Rd btwn A527 and B5051
30 Stoke on Trent, Chell Heath Rd
30 Stoke on Trent, Dividy Rd – btwn B5039 and A52

Suffolk

A11
50 Barton Mills Elveden
40 Elveden Cross Rds Elveden, Chalk Hall Worlington

A12
40 Blythburgh Kelsale
30 Little Glemham
50 Little Glemham, North Lound
40 Marlesford
40 Melton Saxmundham

A14
Exning Newmarket Rougham

A134
40 Barnham
30 Little Welnetham Long Melford
40 Nowton

A137
30 Brantham

A140
50 Thwaite
40 Wetheringsett

A143
30 Bury St Edmunds
30 Chedburgh
40 Stanton
40 Stanton Bypass
40 Stradishall, Highpoint Prison

A144
30 Ilketshall St Lawrence

A145
40 Felixstowe, Trinity Avenue

A146
50 Barnby Bends

A1065
40 Eriswell Mildenhall North of RAF Lakenheath

A1071
40 Boxford Hadleigh, Lady Lane

A1088
30 Honington

A1092
30 Cavendish
30 Clare
40 Glemsford, Skates Hill

A1101
30 Flempton
30 Mildenhall
50 Shippea Hill

A1117
30 Lowestoft, Saltwater Way

A1120
30 Stonham Aspal

A1156
30 Ipswich, Norwich Rd

A1156
40 Nacton

A1214
40 Ipswich, London Rd

A1302
30 Bury St Edmunds

A1304
Newmarket, Golf Club

A1307
40 Haverhill

B1078
30 Barking
30 Needham Market

B1106
30 Fornham

B1113
40 Bramford

B1115
40 Chilton

B1384
30 Carlton Colville

B1385
30 Corton

B1438
30 Melton Hill

B1506
40 Kentford Moulton

Unclassified
30 Felixstowe, Grange Farm Avenue
30 Felixstowe, High Rd
30 Ipswich, Ellenbrook Rd
30 Ipswich, Foxhall Rd
30 Ipswich, Landseer Rd
30 Ipswich, Nacton Rd
30 Kesgrave, Ropes Drive

Surrey

A23
30 Horley, Brighton Rd
40 Salfords, Brighton Rd

A31
60 Hogs Back, (Central and Eastern Sections)

A308
50 Staines Bypass

Unclassified
30 Staines, Kingston Rd

Sussex

A24
30 Worthing, Broadwater Rd nr Cecilian Avenue

A27
70 Angmering, Hammerpot n/side
60 Firle, Firle Straight
70 Shoreham, Holmbush

A29
30 Aldingbourne, Westergate St/Elmcroft Place
30 Aldingbourne, Westergate St/Nook Lane
40 Bognor, Shripney Rd

A259
30 Bognor, Hotham Way
30 Brighton, Marine Parade/ Eaton Place
30 Fishbourne, Main Rd
30 Saltdean, Marine Drive

A280
40 Patching

A281
30 Horsham, Guildford Rd

A283
30 Northchapel
30 Pulborough, Lower St

A285
30 Petworth, Station Rd

A2031
30 Worthing, Offington Lane/Rogate Rd
30 Worthing, Offington Lane/The Plantation

A2032
30 Worthing, Littlehampton Rd nr Little Gables

A2280
40 Eastbourne, Lottbridge Drove

B2093
30 Hastings, The Ridge

B2104
30 Hallsham, Ersham Rd

B2138
30 Fittleworth, Lower St

B2166
30 Bognor, Aldwick Rd

Unclassified
30 Bognor, Hawthorn Rd/Amberley Drive
30 Brighton, Ditching Rd/Balfour Rd
30 Brighton, Falmer Rd Woodingdean
30 Crawley, Breezhurst Drive
30 Crawley, Gatwick Rd nr Hazlewick Flyover
30 Crawley, Gossops Drive
30 Crawley, Manor Royal/ Faraday Rd
30 Heathfield, Hallsham Rd
30 Horsham, Pondtail Rd/Haybarn Drive
30 Horsham, Pondtail Rd/Pondtail Close
30 Hove, New Church Rd/Wish Rd
30 Hove, Shirley Drive/Onslow Rd
30 Shirley, Shirley Drive/ Shirley Rd
30 Worthing, The Boulevard

Thames Valley

Bracknell Forest, Buckinghamshire, Milton Keynes, Oxfordshire, Reading, Slough, West Berkshire, Windsor and Maidenhead, Wokingham

A5
70 Wolverton
70 Bletchley

A30(T)
30 Sunningdale, London Rd

A34
70 Radley
70 Kennington

A40
60 Cassington
70 Forest Hills

A41
70 Buckland

A44
50 Kiddington with Asterleigh

A338
50 Hungerford

A361
30 Chipping Norton, Burford Rd
60 Little Faringdon

A404
70 Little Marlow, Marlow Bypass

A413
60 Swanbourne
60 Weedon
60 Hardwick
60 Wendover Bypass

A421
70 Tingewick Bypass
60 Wavendon

A422
50 Radclive cum Chackmore

A509
70 Newport Pagnell
60 Emberton Bypass

A4074
60 Dorchester
50 Nuneham Courteney

A4095
40 Freeland, Witney Rd

A4130
60 Nuffield
40 Remenham Hill

A4155
30 Shipiake

A4260
50 Shipton on Cherwell, Banbury Rd
60 Rousham, Banbury Rd
60 Steeple Aston

B4009
50 Ewelme

B4011
60 Piddington

B4494
60 Leckhampstead

Unclassified
30 Abingdon, Drayton Rd
30 Abingdon, Oxford Rd
30 Aylesbury, Buckingham Rd
30 Aylesbury, Gatehouse Rd
30 Aylesbury, Oakfield Rd
30 Aylesbury, Tring Rd
30 Aylesbury, Walton St
30 Aylesbury, Wendover Rd
30 Barkham, Barkham Rd
60 Beenham, Bath Rd
30 Blackbird Leys, Watlington Rd
30 Bletchley, Buckingham Rd
40 Bracknell, Bagshot Rd

50 Bracknell, Nine Mile Ride
30 Bracknell, Opladen Way
30 Buckingham, Stratford Rd
50 Burnham, Bath Rd
30 Chalfont St Peter, Gravel Hill
40 Chipping Norton, London Rd
40 Curbridge, Bampton Rd
40 Denham, North Orbital Rd
30 Denham, Oxford Rd
40 Earley, 30 London Rd
30 Great Missenden, Rignall Rd
60 Hardmead, Newport Rd
30 Hazelmere, Sawpit Hill
30 High Wycombe, Holmers Farm Way
30 High Wycombe, Marlow Hill
30 High Wycombe, New Rd
30 High Wycombe, West Wycombe Rd
60 Hungerford, Bath Rd
30 Kidlington, Oxford Rd
60 Kintbury, Bath Rd
30 Long Crendon, Bicester Rd
40 Maidenhead, Braywick Rd
70 Milton Keynes, Woughton on the Green, Standing Way
30 Milton Keynes, Avebury Boulevard
30 Milton Keynes, Midsummer Boulevard
30 Milton Keynes, Silbury Boulevard
30 Monks Risborough, Aylesbury Rd
30 Oxford, Church Cowley Rd
30 Oxford, Headington Rd
30 Oxford, London Rd
30 Oxford, Windmill Rd
30 Reading, Berkeley Avenue
30 Reading, Castle Hill
30 Reading, Kings Rd
30 Reading, Park Lane
30 Reading, Vastern Rd
30 Reading, Wokingham Rd
30 Slough, Buckingham Rd
30 Slough, Cippenham Lane
40 Slough, London Rd
30 Slough, Parlaunt Rd
30 Slough, Sussex Place
60 Speen, Bath Rd
30 Stanford in the Vale, Faringdon Rd
40 Sunninghill, Brockenhurst Rd
30 Tiddington, Oxford Rd
40 Tilehurst, Bath Rd
30 Wantage, Charlton Rd
70 Winkfield, Bagshot Rd
30 Witney, Corn St
30 Wokingham, London Rd
60 Wroxton, Stratford Rd

Warwickshire

A5
50 North Warwickshire, Grendon to Hinckley
60 Rugby, Churchover

A45
50 Rugby, nr Ryton

A46
60 Stratford upon Avon, nr Snitterfield
60 Warwick, nr Stoneleigh

A47
30 Nuneaton and Bedworth, Hinckley Rd
40 Nuneaton and Bedworth, Longshoot, Nuneaton Radial Route

A422
30 Stratford upon Avon, Stratford, Alcester Rd

A423
60 Rugby, nr Marton
30 Rugby, Marton
60 Stratford upon Avon, nr Fenny Compton
60 Stratford upon Avon, South of Southam

A425
30 Stratford upon Avon, Ufton
30 Warwick, Radford Semele

A426
30 Rugby, Dunchurch Rd
60 Stratford upon Avon, nr Stockton

A428
30 Rugby, Binley Woods
60 Rugby, Church Lawford
40 Rugby, Long Lawford

A429
60 Stratford upon Avon, Stretton on Fosse
60 Stratford upon Avon, Wellesbourne

A435
40 Stratford upon Avon, Mappleborough Green

A439
50 Stratford upon Avon, Stratford to A46

A446
60 North Warwickshire, Allen End

A452
60 Warwick, Greys Mallory
60 Warwick, Heathcote

A3400
50 Stratford upon Avon, Alderminster
60 Stratford upon Avon, Little Wolford
40 Stratford upon Avon, North of Henley in Arden
50 Stratford upon Avon, Pathlow

A4091
60 North Warwickshire, Middleton

A4189
60 Stratford upon Avon, Outhill to Lower Norton

B4089
Stratford upon Avon, Alcester, Arden Rd

B4098
40 North Warwickshire, Corley, Tamworth Rd

B4100
60 Stratford upon Avon, Gaydon

B4110
60 Warwick, Bishops Tachbrook

B4112
40 Nuneaton and Bedworth, Nuneaton Radial Route, Ansley Rd

B4113
30 Nuneaton and Bedworth, Hilltop, Nuneaton Radial Route

B4114
60 North Warwickshire, Church End
30 Nuneaton and Bedworth, Ansley Common, Coleshill Rd
30 Nuneaton and Bedworth, Tuttle Hill
60 Rugby, Burton Hastings, Lutterworth Rd

B4429
40 Rugby, Ashlawn Rd

B4455
60 Rugby, Fosse Way south of Princethorpe

B5414
30 Rugby, Clifton Rd

Unclassified
30 Nuneaton and Bedworth, Donnithorne Avenue
30 Warwick, Primrose Hill

West Mercia

Herefordshire, Shropshire, Telford and Wrekin, Worcestershire

A5
60 Aston towards Oswestry
60 Aston towards Shrewsbury
60 Moreton Bridge towards Chirk
60 West Felton

A40
50 Pencraig

A41
40,60 Albrighton Bypass
60 Chetwynd
60 Prees Heath
40 Tern Hill
60 Whitchurch Bypass

A44
40 Wickhamford towards Broadway
30 Worcester, Bromyard Rd towards Bromyard

A46
50 Beckford, Cheltenham Rd
60 Evesham Bypass

A49
60 Ashton towards Leominster
60 Ashton towards Ludlow
60 Dorrington
30 Dorrington towards Shrewsbury
40 Herefordshire, Harewood End

A417
40 Ledbury, Parkway

A442
40 Crudgington

A456
30 Blakedown
30 Newnham Bridge towards Tenbury Wells

A458
40 Morville
30 Much Wenlock
30 Shrewsbury, The Mount towards Town Centre

A465
60 Allensmore

A483
30 Pant

A491
60 Bromsgrove, Sandy Lane nr Hagley
50 Bromsgrove, Stourbridge Rd

A528
30 Shrewsbury, Ellesmere Rd towards Town Centre

A4103
60 Hereford, Lumber Lane towards Lugg Bridge
60 Hereford, west of Lumber Lane towards Great Malvern
40 Newtown Cross towards Hereford
60 Ridgeway Cross towards Hereford
50 Stiffords Bridge to Storridge
50 Stiffords Bridge towards Worcester

A4104
30 Welland, Drake St
30 Welland, Marlbank Rd

A4110
30 Hereford, Three Elms Rd towards City Centre
40 Hereford, Three Elms Rd towards Leominster

A5064
30 Shrewsbury, London Rd

B4096
30 Lower Marlbrook, Old Birmingham Rd

B4211
30 Great Malvern, Church St

B4349
60 Clehonger

B4373
40 Telford, Castlefield Way
40 Telford, Wrockwardine Wood Way

B4386
30 Shropshire, Mytton Oak Rd

B4638
30 Worcester, Woodgreen Drive

B5060
40 Telford, Castle Farm Way

B5061
40 Telford, Holyhead Rd

B5062
30 Shrewsbury, Sundorne Rd

B5069
30 Shropshire, Gobowen Rd

Unclassified
30 Hadley, Britannia Way
30 Hereford, Yazor Rd
30 Newport, Wellington Rd
50 Pencraig, towards Monmouth
50 Pencraig, towards Ross on Wye
30 Redditch, Birchfield Drive
40 Redditch, Coldfield Drive
30 Redditch, Studley Rd
30 Redditch, Studley Rd towards Park Farm
30 Shrewsbury, Monkmoor Rd
30 Shropshire, Longden Rd (Rural)
30 Snedshill, Holyhead Rd
30 Telford, Britannia Way
30 Telford, Hollinsgate
40 Telford, Stafford Park 1
30 Telford, Trench Rd

West Midlands

Birmingham, Coventry, Dudley, Sandwell, Solihull, Walsall, Wolverhampton

A5
60 Brownhills, Watling St
50 Cannock, Watling St
60 Wall, Watling St

A41
40 Albrighton Bypass towards Wolverhampton
40,60 Albrighton, Albrighton Bypass towards Newport

A46
70 Stoneleigh, Kenilworth Bypass

A51
30 Lichfield, Tamworth Rd
60 Weeford, Watling St

A446
60 Allens End, London Rd
60 Bassetts Pole, London Rd

A449
40 Coven, Wolverhampton Rd
60 Gailey, Wolverhampton Rd

A4177
60 Hasley Knob, Honiley Rd

A5127
30 Lichfield, Trent Valley Rd

B4065
30 Ansty, Main Rd

B4098
40 Fillongley, Coventry Rd
60 Fillongley, Tamworth Rd

B4101
40 Tanworth, Broad Lane

B4103
30 Kenilworth, Castle Rd
30 Kenilworth, Clinton Lane

B4109
40 Bulkington, Coventry Rd

Unclassified
30 Ash Green, Royal Oak Lane
30 Ash Green, St Giles Rd
30 Ash Green, Vicarage Lane
30 Coleshill, Station Rd

West Yorkshire

A58
40 Leeds, Easterley Rd

A61
40 Leeds, Scott Hall Rd
60 Rothwell, Wakefield Rd northbound carriageway lamp post 140
40 Rothwell, Wakefield Rd southbound carriageway jct Castlefields
60 Rothwell, Wakefield Rd southbound carriageway nr Wood Lane lamp post 124

A62
30 Huddersfield, Manchester Rd

A64
40 Leeds, York Rd

A616
30 Huddersfield, Woodhead Rd

A629
50 Elland, Calderdale Way southbound carriageway north of Huddersfield Way
50 Halifax, Keighley Rd
40 Shelley, Pennistone Rd

A636
30 Wakefield, Denby Dale Rd southbound carriageway jct Cotton St

A638
50 Ossett Bypass westbound carriageway layby location lamp post 39

A638
30 Wakefield, Dewsbury Rd eastbound carriageway jct Broadway

A644
30 Mirfield, Huddersfield Rd

A646
30 Portsmouth, Burnley Rd jct Durn St
30 Todmorden, Halifax Rd jct Hallroyd Rd

A651
40 Birkenshaw, Bradford Rd

A652
30 Batley, Bradford Rd
30 Batley, Bradford Rd opp Hampson St
30 Batley, Bradford Rd opp no.253 Lucas Yard
40 Birstall, Bradford Rd

A653
40 Shaw Cross, Leeds Rd

A657
30 Shipley, Leeds Rd eastbound carriageway nr jct Cragg Rd
30 Shipley, Leeds Rd westbound carriageway jct Little Cote Farm

A6025
50 Elland, Park Wood, Elland Rd

A6038
40 Baildon, Otley Rd opp lamp post 117

B6145
30 Bradford, Greenside, Thornton Rd
30 Bradford, Thornton, Thornton Rd

B6269
40 Shipley, Cottingley Cliffe Rd westbound carriageway jct New Brighton

Unclassified
30 Huddersfield, Dalton, Long Lane o/s No.144
30 South Elmsall, Minsthorpe Lane jct Ash Grove
30 South Kirby, Minsthorpe twds A180 jct Minsthorpe Vale
60 Walton, Wetherby Rd

Wiltshire and Swindon

M4
70 approx 1.8km west of jct 15
70 approx 6.9km east of jct 15
70 at jct 15
70 approx 3km east of jct 16
70 approx 8.4km west of jct 16
70 approx 3.1km east of jct 17
70 approx 8.3km east of jct 17

A4
40 Froxfield
60 West Overton

A30
40 Fovant
60 The Pheasant

A36
60 Brickworth
60 Hanging Langford
50 Knook
30 Salisbury, Wilton Rd
60 south of Whaddon
60 Stapleford to East Clyffe

A303
50 Chicklade
60 Parsonage Down
60 Willoughby Hedge

A338
40 Bosscombe
30 nr Little Woodbury
60 nr Southgrove Copse

A342
60 Chirton to Charlton
30 Ludgershall, andover Rd
50 Lydeway

A346
60 Cadley Firs
60 Whitefield

A350
60 Heywood
70 Pretty Chimneys

A354
40 Coombe Bissett

A360/A344
60 Airmans Corner

A361
60 Inglesham
60 nr Blackland Turning
70 nr jct with B3101
60 nr Shepherds Shore
30 Southwick
30 Trowbridge, Frome Rd
60 west of Beckhampton

A363
30 Bradford on Avon, Trowbridge Rd
30 North Bradley, Woodmarsh
40 Trowle Common

A419
70 Cricklade
70 nr Covingham
70 Widhill

A420
60 Giddeahall to Ford

A3026
40 Ludgershall, Tidworth Rd

A3028
40 Durrington, Larkhill Rd

A3102
30 Calne, Oxford Rd
30 Lyneham
30 Melksham, Sandridge Rd
30 Wootten Bassett

A4259
50 nr Coate
40 Swindon 2, Queens Drive (nr to jct with Rushton Rd)

A4361
60 Broad Hinton
60 Uffcott Xrd
30 Wroughton, Swindon Rd

B390
60 Maddington Farm

B3105
30 Hilperton, Hill St/Marsh St

B4006
40 Swindon, Marlborough Rd

B3098
30 Bratton

B3106
30 Hilperton, Hammond Way

B3107
30 Bradford on Avon, Holt Rd

B4006
30 Stratton St Margaret, Swindon Rd
30 Swindon, Whitworth Rd

B4040
50 Leigh

B4041
30 Wootten Bassett, Station Rd

B4143
30 Swindon, Bridge End Rd

B4192
50 Liddington

B4289
40 Great Western Way nr Bruce St Bridges

B4553
40 Swindon, Tewkesbury Way

B4587
30 Swindon, Akers Way

Unclassified
30 Corsham, Park Lane
30 Swindon, Ermin St
30 Swindon, Merlin Way
30 Swindon, Moredon Rd
30 Trowbridge, Wiltshire Drive

Worcestershire

see West Mercia

Wales

Mid and South Wales

Blaenau Gwent, Bridgend, Caerphilly, Cardiff, Carmarthenshire, Merthyr Tydfil, Monmouthshire, Neath Port Talbot, Newport, Pembrokeshire, Rhondda Cynon Taff, Swansea, Torfaen, Vale of Glamorgan

M4
70 1.1km east of Jct33 where Llantrisant Rd crosses M4
70 1.5km east of Jct37
70 2km east of Jct35
70 at Jct36 overpass
70 Cherry Orchard Overbridge Jct30-32
70 Llanmartin
70 Rhiwbina Hill overpass (Jct30-32)
50 Toll Plaza

A40
60 Buckland Hall, Brecon to Abergavenny
70 from 1.2km east to 100m west of Bancyfelin Jct
70 Johnstown, Carmarthen to St Clears
60 Llanhamlac, Brecon to Abergavenny
60 Llansantffried Jct
70 Mitchel Troy
70 Monmouth, opp. Llangattock Lodge
60 Rhosmaen, Llandeilo
60 Scethrog, Brecon to Abergavenny
40 Trecastle
60 Whitemill

A40 to B4302
30 Rhosmaen, jct to N

A44
60 Forest Bends
30 Llanbadarn Fawr
60 Llanfihangel Nant Melan
60 Sweet Lamb, West of Llangurig
60 The Gwystre opp Gwystre Farm

A48
70 300m South of Bristol House Layby to Pont Abraham Rdbt
30 Baglan, Dinas Baglan
30 Belle Vue, Cardiff Rd
50 Berryhill
40 Bonvilston
40 Brocastle
30 Castleton
70 Cowbridge Bypass
40 Crosshands to Cwmgwili
70 Cwmgwili, Pontarddulais Rd Jct.to Bristol House Layby
70 from 1.7km west to 300m east of Llanddarog Jct
70 from 1.8km west to 300m east of Foelgastell Jct
70 from 700m east to 2.2km west of Nantycaws Jct
40 Langstone
30 Pontarddulais, Bolgoed Rd
30 Pontardualais, Carmarthen Rd
30 Pontardualais, Fforest Rd
30 Port Talbot, Margam Rd (Rhanallt S)
30 St Nicholas

A438
40 Three Cocks

A449
70 Llandenny
70 Llantrissent nr Usk
70 nr Coldra

A458
60 Cefn Bridge
60 Llanfair Caereinion (Neuadd Bridge)
40 Trewern

A465
60 btwn Aberbaden and Llanfoist
60 llanfoist nr Abergavenny
50 Llanelly
40 Pandy
50 Pandy (50mph area)
60 Triley Mill nr Abergavenny

A466
40 High Beech Rdbt to Old Hospital
30 Llandogo
30 Monmouth, Redbrook Rd
30 St. Arvans
30 Tintern

A467
60 Abertillery
40 Blaina
70 Danycraig, Risca
40 Warm Tum (changing from 40 to 30 soon)

A468
30 Machen Village

A469
70 Caerphilly, Lower Rhymney Valley Relief Rd
30 Tir-Y-Birth

A470
70 Abercynon (southbound)
70 at Aberfan overbridge
30 at Cilfynydd
70 at overbridge of Cilfynydd
60 Brecon to Merthyr (Storey Arms)
40 Cardiff, Manor Way
30 Erwood
60 Erwood South
40 Llandinam to Caersws Jct
40 Llandinam Village
40 Llanidloes to Llandinam
30 Llyswen
30 Newbridge on Wye
60 Newbridge to Rhayader
70 nr Taffs Well North
70 nr Taffs Well South
60 Powys, Beacons Reservoir
70 Rhydyfelin overbridge, Dynea Rd
60 South of Builth (Aberduhonw)
60 South of Builth (Abernant)
60 South of Builth (Ysgiog)

A472
30 Hafodrynys
30 Maescwmmer
60 Monkswood
30 Usk Bridge to Old Saw Mill

A473
30 Bridgend, Bryntirion Hill
30 Pencoed, Penybont Rd

A474
30 All the village of Glanaman
40 Alltwen, Graig Rd
30 Ammanford to Portamman, Heol Wallasey Jct
30 Glanffrwd Est Jct. to Garnant
30 Heol-Y-Gors
30 Neath, Penywern Rd
30 Rhyd y Fro, Commercial St

A475
40 Llanwnen
40 Lampeter, Pentrebach, County Rd

A476
30 Carmel to N at Temple Bar
40 Carmel, Stag and Pheasant
30 Ffairfach, 30 mph to the Square
30 Gorslas, Cross Hands Rdbt to the Phoenix Inn
40 Gorslas, The Gate
30 Heol Bryngwili, Cross Hands
30 Llannon, Erw Non Jct to Clos Rebecca Jct
30 Swiss Valley, Thomas Arms, Llanelli to North
30 Upper Tumble, Llannon Rd and Bethania Rd

A477
40 Bangeston to Nash Fingerpost Roadworks
30 Llanddowror

A478
30 Clunderwen
30 Llandissilio
30 Pentlepoir

A479
30 Bronllys

A482
30 Aberaeron, Lampeter Rd
30 Cwmann, North
30 Cwmann, South
30 Village of Llanwrda

A482 and A475
30 Lampeter

A483
60 Abbey Cwm Hir Jct
30 Ammanford, Tycroes to Villiers Jct
30 Ffairfach, N to Llandeilo Bridge
30 Llandeilo, Rhosmaen St

A483
50 Garthmyl, Refail Garage
60 Garthmyl, Welshpool
60 Llandrindod, Midway Bends
60 North of Crossgates

A484
40 Bronwydd Village
30 Burry Port
30 Cenarth
40 Cwmffrwd
30 Cynwyl Elfed
30 from 80m west of New Rd Jct, east to N N.C.E
40 Idole, from 200m s.w. of B4309 Jct south to N
30 Llanelli, Sandy Rd
60 Llanelli, Trostre Rdbt to Berwick Rdbt
60 Pembrey
30 Pembrey, Danybanc Jct to St Illtyds Rise Jct
40 Pentrecagel
40 Rhos
40 Saron

A485
40 Alltwalis
30 Cwmann, from the A482 Jct N
40 Llanllwwni
30 Llanybydder (North)
30 Llanybydder (South)
40 Peniel

A487
40 Approach to Llanrhystud from the south
30 Central Aberaeron
30 Central Aberystwyth
30 Ceredigion, Bow St
30 Eglwyswrw
40 Furnace
30 Llanarth
30 Llanfarian
30 Newgale
30 Newport
40 Penglais Hill/Waunfawr
40 Penparc, Trunk Rd
40 Rhydyfelin
30 Rhydypennau
30 Talybont

A489
60 Caersws Jct to Penstrowed
60 Kerry, County Rd, Glanmule Garage
40 Newtown, west of Hafren coll
60 Penstrowed to Newtown

A4042
60 Llanover

A4046
40 Ebbw Vale (nr Tesco's)
30 Ebbw Vale, College Rd
30 Waynllwyd

A4048
30 Argoed
30 Blackwood (Sunnybank)
30 Cwmfelinfach Village
30 Hollybush
30 Pontllanfraith, Blackwood Rd

A4054
30 Edwardsville, Nantddu, Tec
30 Merthyr Vale, Cardiff Rd

A4061
30 Ogmore Vale, Cemetery Rd

A4066
40 Broadway
40 Llanmiloe, Pendine
40 Pendine, Llanmiloe
30 Pendine, Marsh Rd

A4067
60 Abercraf
60 Crai

A4068
30 Cwmtwrch, Bethel Rd
30 Cwmtwrch, Heol Gleien

A4069
30 Llandovery, Broad St
30 Llangadog, East
30 Llangadog, North, Station Rd
30 Llangadog, South
30 Station Rd to the Remploy Factory

A4074
30 Milford Haven, St Lawrence Hill

A4075
30 Pembroke

A4076
30 Carew
30 Johnston

A4093
30 Glynogwr

A4102
30 Gellideg, Swansea Rd

A4106
30 Porthcawl, Newton Nottage Rd
Porthcawl, The Porthway

A4107
30 Abergwynfi, High St

A4109
Aberdulias, Main Rd
30 Crynant, Main Rd
30 Glynneath
30 Seven Sisters, Dulais Rd

A4118
60 Fairwood Common

A4119
50 Llantrisant, Mwyndy Cross

A4120
30 Aberystwyth

A4138
30 Hendy, Loughor Bridge to 40mph speed limit
40 Talyclun, from the 30mph at Hendy to the B4297 Jct

A4139
30 Pembroke
30 Pembroke Dock
30 Tenby

A4216
30 Cockett, Cockett Rd

A4221
60 Caehopkin

A4222
30 Cowbridge, Abertin Rd
30 Maendy

A4226
40 Barry, Five Mile Lane

A4233
30 Ferndale, The Parade

B4181
30 Bridgend, Coity Rd

B4223
30 Ton Pentre, Pentwyn Rd

B4235
60 Gwernesney nr Usk

B4242
30 Pontneddfechan, Gwyn Neath

B4245
30 Caldicot Bypass
30 Langstone, Magor Rd
60 Leechpool
30 Rogiet, Caldicot Rd
30 Undy

B4254
30 Penpedairheol, Pengam Rd

B4265
30 St Brides Major

B4281
30 Kenfig Hill, High St

B4282
30 Bridgend, Bridgend Rd and Castle St
30 Bryn, Measteg Rd

B4290
30 Skewen, Pen-yr-Heol and Crymlyn Rd

B4295
40 btwn Gowerton and Penclawdd
60 btwn Penclawdd and Llanrhidian

B4297
40 Bynea, Lougher Bridge Rdbt to Station Rd Jct
30 Capel Hendre
30 Fforest
30 Llanedi
30 Llangennech, Cleviston Park Jct to Park Lane Jctct
30 Llwynhendy, from Capel Soar to the Police Station

B4301
30 Bronwydd Village

B4302
30 Talley

B4303
30 Llanelli, Dafen Rdbt to Felinfoel Rdbt

B4304
40 Llanelli, Copperworks Rdbt to Morfa Rdbt
30 Llanelli, Lower Trostre Rd Rdbt to Trostre Rd Rdbt

B4306
30 Bancffosfelen, Heol Y Banc
30 Llangendeirn
30 Pontyberem, Llanon Rd

B4308
40 Penmynnydd

B4309
30 Five Roads

B4310
30 Drefach, Heol Caegwyn
40 Nangaredig, Station Rd

B4312
30 Johnstown, from the Square to N
30 Llangain

B4314
30 Narberth
30 Pendine

B4317
30 Carway, East
30 Carway, West
30 Ponthenri, Myrtle Hill
30 Pontyberem, Heol Capel Ifan
30 Pontyberem, Station Rd

B4320
30 Hundleton

B4322
40 Pembroke Dock, Pembroke Rd

B4325
30 Neyland

B4328
30 Whitland, Trevaughan

B4333
30 Cynwyl Elfed (North)
30 Hermon
30 Newcastle Emlyn, Aber-arad

B4336
30 All the village of Llanfihangel Ar Arth
30 Llandysul, Pont-tyweli

B4337
30 Llanybydder (East)
30 Llanybydder (West)
40 Talsarn

B4347
30 Newcastle Village

B4350
60 Glasbury to Hay on Wye, County Rd

B4436
40 Kittle, Pennard Rd

B4459
30,40 Pencader
B4524
30 Corntown
B4556
30 All the village of Caerbryn
30 Blaenau, Penygroes Rd
30 Pengroes, Norton Rd
B4560
30 Beaufort, Ebbw Vale, Llangynidr Rd
B4591
30 High Cross, Risca Rd
B4598
60 Horse and Jockey nr Abergavenny
60 Llancayo
B4599
30 Ystradgynlais
B4622
30 Broadlands Link Rd
Unclassified
Aberbargoed, Bedwwellty and Coedymoeth Rd Jct
30 Abercwmboi, Park View Terrace
30 Abercynon, Abercynon Rd
30 Abergavenny, Hereford Rd
30 Abergwili, Ambulance Station to the Bypass Rdbt
30 Abertillery, Gwern Berthi
30 Ammanford, Layby outside Saron Church, Saron Rd
30 Ammanford, New Rd and Pantyffynnon Rd
30 Argoed, Penylan Rd
30 Barry, Barry Rd
30 Barry, Buttrills Rd
30 Barry, Gladstone Rd
30 Barry, Holton Rd
30 Barry, Jenner Rd
30 Beddau, Bryniteg Hill
30 Beddau, Gwaunmiskin Rd
30 Betws, Betws Rd
30 Betws, Maesquarre Rd
30 Birchgrove, Birchgrove Rd
40 Bishopston, Northway
30 Brackla, Brackla Way
30 Bridgend Ind Est, Kingsway
30 Bridgend Ind Est, North Rd
30 Bridgend Ind Est, South Rd
30 Bridgend Ind Est, Western Avenue
30 Bridgend Inner Bypass
30 Bridgend, Coychurch Rd
30 Bridgend, Pen-Y-Cae Lane
30 Britton Ferry, Old Rd
30 Brynamman, Brynamman Rd
30 Brynmawr, Beaufort Hill and High St
30 Brynna, Brynna Rd
30 Caerleon, Ponthir Rd
30 Caerleon, Usk Rd
30 Caerphilly, 2 Llanbradach
30 Caerphilly, Kendon Hill
30 Caerphilly, Mountain Rd
30 Caldicot, Chepstow Rd
30 Cardiff, Circle Way E/W Llanedeym
30 Cardiff, Cyncoed Rd
30 Cardiff, Excalibur Drive
30 Cardiff, Heol Isaf
30 Cardiff, Leckwith Rd
30 Cardiff, Newport Rd
30 Cardiff, North Rd
30 Cardiff, Pencisely Rd
30 Cardiff, Penylan, Colchester Avenue
30 Cardiff, Rhiwbina, Heol y Deri
30 Cardiff, Rhyd-y-pennau Rd
30 Cardiff, Roath, Lake Rd East/West
30 Cardiff, Rumney, Wentloog Avenue
30 Cardiff, St Fagans Rd
30 Cardiff, Willowbrook Drive
30 Carmarthen, Lime Grove Avenue and Fountain Head Tce
30 Cefn Criwber, Cefn Rd
30 Cefn Glas, Llangewydd Rd
30 Cefn Glas, Merlin Crescent
30 Cefncoed, High St
30 Cefncoed, Vaynor Rd
30 Cefneithin
30 Ceredigion, Cardigan, North
30 Ceredigion, Llandysul Central
30 Ceredigion, New Quay Central
30 Church Village, Main Rd
30 Cilfynydd, Cilfynydd Rd
30 Clydach, Pontarddawe Rd
30 Clydach, Vadre Rd
30 Cockett, Cwmbach Rd
30 Coity, Heol Spencer
60 Coldharbour, Usk to Raglan Rd
30 Cowbridge, Primrose Hill
30 Crofty, New Rd
30 Crumlin, Hafodyrynys Hill
40 Cwmbwria, Carmarthen Rd
30 Cwmgovilon
30 Cwmgwili
30 Cwmgwili, Thornhill Rd
30 Deri, New Rd
30 Derwen Fawr, Rhy-Y-Defaid Drive
30 Dinas, Dinas Rd
30 Dowlais, High St
30 Drefach, Heol Blawnhirwaun
30 Ebbw Vale, Letchwworth Rd
30 Ebbw Vale, Newchurch Rd
30 Ebbw Vale, Steelworks Rd
30 Farm Shop, Pentregethin Rd
30 Felinfoel, Llethri Rd
30 Ferndale, Highfield Jct
30 Ferndale, Oakland Terrace
30 Fforest Fach, Carmarthen Rd
40 Five Mile Lane
30 Fochrie, Olgivie Terrace
30 Foelgastell
30 Forden
60 from 120m s.e. of Heol Login for 1.2km s.e. along Nantycaws Hill
40 Gelligaer, Church Rd
30 Gelli, Gelli Ind Est
30 Gelli, Gelli Rd
30 Gilwern, Cae Meldon (aka Ty Mawr Lane)
30 Gorseinon, Frampton Rd
30 Gorslas, Pengroes Rd
30 Haverfordwest, New Rd/Uzmaston Rd
30 Heath, Maescoed Rd
30 Hendreforgan, Gilfach Rd
30 Hopkinstown, Hopkinstown Rd
30 Jersey Marine, New Rd
30 Johnstown, St Clears Rd
30 Killay, Goetre Fawr Rd
30 Llanelli, Denham Avenue
30 Llanelli, Heol Goffa (from the A476 Jct to the A484 Jct)
30 Llanfihangel Ar Arth (South)
30 Llangonoed, Bridgend Rd
30 Llangyfelach, Swansea Rd
30 Llangynwyd, Bridgend Rd
30 Llanharan, Brynna Rd
30 Llanharen, Bridgend Rd
60 Llanhenock, Caerleon to Usk Rd – Apple tree farm
30 Llantrisant, Cross Inn Rd
50 Llantwit Major Bypass
30 Llantwit Major, Llanmaes Rd
30 Maesteg, Heol Ty-With
30 Maesteg, Heol-Ty-Gwyn
30 Malpas, Rowan Way
30 Merthyr Tdyfil, Brecon Rd
30 Merthyr Tdyfil, Goatmill Rd
30 Merthyr Tdyfil, Goitre Lane
30 Merthyr Tdyfil, Gurnos Rd
30 Merthyr Tdyfil, Heol-Tai-Mawr
30 Merthyr Tdyfil, Heolgerrig Rd
30 Merthyr Tdyfil, Pant Rd
30 Merthyr Tdyfil, Plymouth St
30 Merthyr Tdyfil, Rocky Rd
30 Merthyr Tdyfil, The Walk
30 Milford Haven, Priory Rd
40 Milford Haven, Thornton Rd
40 Monmouth, Bend at Green Farm
30 Monmouth, Devauden Village
30 Monmouth, Dixton Rd
30 Monmouth, Hereford Rd
30 Monmouth, Magor (West)
60 Monmouth, Parkwall
30 Monmouth, Usk Bridge to Llanbadoc
30 Morriston, Caemawr Rd
30 Morriston, Clasemont Rd
30 Mount Pleasant, Cardiff Rd
30 Mountain Ash, Llanwonno Rd
30 Mountain Ash, Miskin Rd
30 Mountain Ash, New Rd
30 Nantgarw, Oxford St
30 Nash Village, West Nash Rd
30 New Tredegar, White Roase Way
30 Newbridge, Park Rd
30 Newport, Allt-Yr-Yn Avenue
30 Newport, Caerleon Rd (east of Beaufort Rd)
30 Newport, Chepstow Rd nr Aberthaw Rd
40 Newport, Chepstow Rd nr Royal Oak Hill
30 Newport, Corporation Rd
30 Newport, Lighthouse Rd
30 Newport, opp Power Station, Risca Rd
30 Newport, Rhiwderin
30 Newport, Wharf Rd
30 North Cornelly, Heol Fach
30 Pembroke, Merlins Bridge
30 Pencoed, Felindre Rd
30 Pendarren, High St
30 Pendine
30 Penrhiwceiber, 2 Penrhiwceiber Rd
40 Pentrecagel
30 Ponthir, Caerleon Rd
30 Pontllanfraith, Bryn Rd
30 Pontyclun, Cowbridge Rd
30 Pontymister, Welsh Oak PH
30 Pontymister, Welsh Oak PH
30 Pontypool, Little Mill
30 Pontypridd, The Broadway
40 Porthcawl, Bridgend Rd
30 Porthcawl, Fulmar Rd
30 Rassau, Reservoir Rd
30 Rhondda Cynon Taff, Tonteg Rd
30 Rhymney, Llys Joseph Parry (nr Farmers Arms)
30 Rhymney, Wellington Way
30 Risca, Cromwell Rd
30 Risca, Holly Rd
30 Risca, Waun Fawr Park Rd
30 Rogerstone, Pontymason Lane
30 Sandfields, Village Rd
30 Saron Village, Dyffryn Rd
30 Skewen, Burrows Rd
30 St Athan, Cowbridge Rd
30 Steynton
30 Sully, Haynes Rd
30 Sully, South Rd
30 Swansea, Fabian Way
30 Swansea, Grovesend
40 Swansea, Mumbles Rd (A4067) Sketty Lane to St Helens Sports Gr.
30 Swansea, Mynydd Newydd Rd, Caemawr Rd, Parry Rd, Vicarage Rd (Heol Ddu to Clasemont Rd)
30 Swansea, Peniel Green Rd (nr Station Rd o/s TOTAL Garage)
60 Tiers Cross
30 Ton Pentre, Maindy Rd
30 Tonteg, Church Rd
30 Tonyrefail, Gilfach Rd
30 Tonyrefail, Penrhiwfer Rd
30 Torfaen
30 Treboeth, Llangyfelach Rd
30 Tredegar, Vale Terrace
30 Trelewis, Gelligaer Rd
30 Upper Boat, Cardiff Rd Upper Church Village, Pen yr Eglwys
30 Usk, Porthycame St
30 Vale of Glamorgan, Pen-y-turnpike Rd
30 Waungren, Pentre Rd
30 Whitland (East), Spring Gardens
30 Whitland (west)
30 Whitland, Market St
30 Whitland, North Rd
30 Wick, St Brides Rd
30 Willowtow, Gwaun Helyg Rd
30 Ynystawe, Clydach Rd
30 Ynyswdre, Heol-Yr-Ysgol
30 Ynysybwl, New Rd

North Wales

Ceredigion, Conwy, Denbighshire, Flintshire, Gwynedd, Isle of Anglesey, Powys, Wrexham

A5
30 Holyhead
A5/A5025
50 Holyhead to Llanfachraeth
A470
30,60 Conwy Valley
40,60 Dolgellau
40,60 (30 at rdbts) Llandudno to the A55
30,40,60 Tal-y-waenydd to Congl-y-wal (Blaenau)
A483/A5
60 Ruabon to Chirk
A487
30,40,50,60 Caernarfon to Dolbenmaen
30,40,60 Penmorfa to Gellilydan
A494
40,60 Bala to Glanrafon
30,40 Llyn Tegid, Bala
40,60 Ruthin to Llanferres
A496
30,40,60 Harlech to Llanbedr
A499
30,40,60 Pwllheli
A525
40,60 Denbigh to Ruthin
30,40,60 Llanfair Dyffryn Clwyd to Llandegla
30,60 Wrexham to Minera
30,40,60 Wrexham to Redbrook Maelor
A534
30 Holt Rd
A539
30,60 Llangollen, Mill St
30,40,60 Trevor to Erbistock
A541
30 Mold Rd
30,40,60,70 Mold to Caergwrle
30,40,60,70 Wrexham to Cefn-y-bedd
A541/525
30,40,60 St Asaph to Bodfari
A545
30,40 Menai Bridge to Beaumaris
A547
30,40,50 Colwyn Bay
30,40,60 Prestatyn to Rhuddlan
30 Rhyl, Vale Rd/Rhuddlan Rd
A548
30,40 Abergele to Kinmel Bay
30 Abergele, Dundonald Avenue
30,40,50,60,70 Gronant to Flint (Oakenholt)
30,40 Rhyl to Prestatyn
A549
30,60 Mynydd Isa to Buckley
A550/B5125
30 Hawarden
A4086
30,40,60 Cwm-y-glo to Llanrug
A4212
60 Graig Las/Tryweryn to Trawsfynydd
A4244
60 Ty Mawr to Cym-y-glo
A5025
30,40,50,60 Amlwch, Menai Bridge
A5104
30 Coed-Talon to Leeswood
A5112
30,40 Llandygai to Bangor
A5119
30,50,60 Mold to Flint
A5152
30,60 Bala
30 Chester Rd
30,40 Rhostyllen
B4545
30,40 Kingsland to Valley
B5108
30,60 Benllech
B5109
30 Llangefni
B5113
30 Colwyn Bay, Kings Rd/Kings Drive
B5115
30 Llandrillo, Llandudno Rd
30,40 Llandudno Promenade to Rhos Point
B5118
30 Rhyl Promenade
B5120
30 Prestatyn, Pendyffryn Rd
B5129
30,60 Kelsterton to Saltney Ferry
B5420
30 Menai Bridge
B5425
30,60 Llay, New Rd
B5443
30 Rossett
Unclassified
30,40,60 Johnstown
30,60 Kinmel Bay, St Asaph Avenue
30,40,60 Menai Bridge to Gwalchmai

Scotland

Dumfries and Galloway

A74(M)
70 Cogries
A7
60 Langholm
A76
Auldgirth
60 Closeburn
30 Dumfries, Glasgow Rd Gateside
A77
60 Balyett
60 Cairnryan
60 Whiteleys
A701
30 Moffat
60 Mollinburn/St Anns
A709
60 Burnside
A711
50 Beeswing
30 Kirkcudbright
A716
60 Stoneykirk
A718
60 Craichmore
B721
30 Eastriggs

Fife

A91
Deer Centre to Stratheden Jct
Guardbridge to St Andrews
Melville Lodges to St Andrews
A92
Cadham to New Inn
Cardenden Overbridge to Chapel
Cowdenbeath to Lochgelly
Crossgates to New Inn
Melville Lodges to Lindifferon
New Inn to Tay Bridge
Rathillet (south) to Easter Kinnear
A823
Dunfermline, Queensferryroad
Dunfermline, St Margaret Drive
A907
Dunfermline, Halbeath Rd
A911
Glenrothes to Leslie
Glenrothes to Milton
A914
Edenwood to Cupar
Forgan to St Michaels
Kettlebridge
New Inn to Cupar
Pitlessie to Clushford Toll
A915
Checkbar Jct to Percival Jcts
A921
Kirkcaldy, Esplanade
Kirkcaldy, High St/Path
Kirkcaldy, Rosslyn St
Kirkcaldy, St Clair St
A977
Kincardine, Fere Gait
A985
Culross (west) to C38 Valleyfield
Kincardine to Rosyth
Rosyth, Admiralty Rd
Waukmill to Brankholm
B914
Redcraigs to Greenknowes
B942
East of Collinsburgh
B980
Rosyth, Castlandhill Rd
B981
Cowdenbeath, Broad St
Gosshill to Ballingry
Kirkcaldy, Dunnikier Way
B9157
Bankhead of Pitheadle to Kirkcaldy
Orrock to East Balbairdie
Sheriff Rdbt to Kirkcaldy
White Lodge Jct to Croftgary
Unclassified
Buckhaven, Methilhaven Rd
Dunfermline, Townhill Rd
Glenrothes, Formonthills Rd
Glenrothes, Woodside Rd
Glenrothes, Woodside Way
Kirkcaldy, Hendry Rd
Leven, Glenlyon Rd
Methil, Methilhaven Rd

Lothian and Borders

East Lothian, Edinburgh, Midlothian, Scottish Borders, West Lothian

A8
40 Edinburgh, at Ratho station
A7
60 Crookston
NSL Galashiels, Buckholmside to Bowland
30 Hawick Sandbed to Galalaw
30 Stow to Bowland
A68
30 Jedburgh
NSL Soutra Hill
A70
30 Edinburgh, Balerno between Bridge Rd and Stewart Rd
A71
30 Breich
30 Polbeth
A72
NSL Borders, Holylee nr Walkerburn
NSL Castlecraig nr Blyth bridge
30 Peebles, Innerleithen Rd
A90
40 Edinburgh, Southbound from Burnshot flyover to Cammo Rd
A697
30 Greenlaw and south approach
NSL Orange Lane
NSL Ploughlands to Hatchednize
A697/8
30 Coldstream
A698
NSL Ashybank
NSL Crailinghall
A699
40 Maxton Village
A701
NSL Blyth Bridge to Cowdenburn
30 Rachan Mill, Broughton to A72
A702
NSL Dolphinton to Medwyn Mains
A703
30 Eddleston and approaches
NSL Leadburn to Shiplaw
30 Peebles to Milkieston
30 Peebles, Edinburgh Rd
A705
30 between Whitburn and East Whitburn
A706
30 Whitburn, Carnie Place
A720
50 Edinburgh, City Bypass, east of Gogar Rdbt
A899
50 btwn Lizzie Bryce Rdbt and Almond Interchange
50 South of Deer Park Rdbt
A6091
NSL Melrose bypass
A6105
30 Gordon and approaches
B6374
30 Galashiels, Station Bridge to Lowood Bridge
Unclassified
30 Edinburgh, Bruntsfield place btwn Thorneybauk and Merchiston place
40 Edinburgh, Comiston Rd btwn Oxgangs Rd and Buckstone Dr
40,60 Edinburgh, Frogston Rd west btwn Mounthooly loan and Mortonhall gate
30 Edinburgh, Lower Granton Rd btwn Granton Square and Trinity Rd
30 Edinburgh, Muirhouse Parkway
40 Edinburgh, West Approach Rd btwn Morrison St Link and Dundee St
30 Edinburgh, West Granton Rd
30 Whitburn, West Main St

North East Scotland

Aberdeen, Aberdeenshire, Moray

A90
40 Aberdeen, Midstocket Rd to Whitestripes Avenue Rdbt
60 btwn bend at South of Leys and Bogbrae
60 btwn Bogbrae and north of Bridgend
70 btwn Candy and Upper Criggie
60 btwn Jct with B9032 and A98 at Fraserburgh
70 btwn Laurencekirk and north of Fourdon
70 btwn Mill of Barnes and Laurencekirk
60 btwn St Fergus and access Rd to Bilbo
70 Dundee to Aberdeen Rd at Jct with B9120 Laurencekirk
70 north of Newtonhill Jct to South of Schoolhill Rd
60 Peterhead and St Fergus, btwn A982 North Rd
60 Peterhead, btwn north of Bridgend and Blackhills
70 Portlethen to South Damhead (southbound), south of Schoolhill Rd
70 south of Schoolhill Rd, Portlethen to South Damhead (northbound)
A92
60 btwn Johnshaven and Inverbervie
60 btwn rdside of Kinneff and Mill of Uras
A93
30 Aboyne
40 at Banchory eastbound from Caravan Site
30 at Banchory westbound from Church
60 btwn Cambus O'May and Dinnet
60 btwn Dinnet to Aboyne
60 btwn Kincardine O'Neil and Haugh of Sluie
A95
30 Cornhill
60 btwn 30mph at Keith and Davoch of Grange
A96
60 btwn East Mill of Carden at B9002 Jct and north of Pitmachie
60 btwn Forgie and A98 Jct at Fochabers
60 btwn north of Pitmachie and Jct with A920 at Kirton of Culsalmond
30 Haudigain rdbt to Chapel of Stoneywood
60 Mosstodloch to Lhanbryde (East)
40 South Damhead to Midstocket Rd
A98
30 Banff
60 btwn Carnoch Farm Rd, Buckie and 30mph at Cullen
60 btwn Fochabers 30mph and Mill of Tynet
60 Buckie, btwn Mill of Tynet and Barhill Rd Jct
A941
60 btwn 30mph at Lossiemouth and 40mph at Elgin
60 btwn Clackmarras Rd and South Netherglen
60 btwn Glassgreen and Clackmarras Rd
60 from South Netherglen and Rothes
A947
60 btwn Mains of Tulloch Jct and Fyvie
A948
60 btwn Newmachar and Whiterashes
A948
60 btwn Ellon to Auchnagatt
A952
60 btwn New Leeds and Jct with A90 at Cortes
B9040
60 btwn Silver Sands Caravan Park to Jct with B9012
B9089
60 from Kinloss and crossroads at Roseisle Maltings
Unclassified
30 Aberdeen, Beach Boulevard to Links Rd
30 Aberdeen, Beach Boulevard to Wales St
30 Aberdeen, Great Northern Rd
30 Aberdeen, Great Southern Rd
30 Aberdeen, King St
30 Aberdeen, Springhill Rd
30 Aberdeen, St Machar Drive
40 Aberdeen, Wellington Rd
40 Aberdeen, West Tullos Rd

Northern Scotland

Highland, Orkney, Shetland, Western Isles

A9
Altnasleanach by Inverness
Caulmaillie, Golspie, Sutherland
Cuaich by Dalwhinnie
Daviot, by Inverness
Fearn, by Tain
North Kessock jct (both directions)
North of Dalwhinnie junction
nr Dalwhinnie
South of the Mound, by Golspie
A82
Altsigh Youth Hostel, by Inverness
Drumnadrochit, Temple Pier
Invergarry Power Station
Kingshouse Hotel, Glencoe
White Corries, Rannoch Moor, Lochaber
A87
West of Bunloyne jct
A95
by Grantown on Spey, Congash
Drumuillie by Boat of Garten
North of Cromdale
A96
East Auldearn jct, by Nairn
Gollanfield, by Nairn
Nairn, West Auldern Jct
West of Allanfearn jct, by Inverness
A99
Hempriggs, south of Wick
A834
Dingwall, nr Foddarty Bridge
Dingwall, Strathpeffer Rd
A835
Inverlael straight nr Ullapool
A939
Ferness to Grantown, Spey Rd
B9006
Sunnyside, Culloden, Inverness

Strathclyde

Argyll & Bute, East Ayrshire, East Dunbartonshire, East Renfrewshire, Glasgow, Inverclyde, North Ayrshire, North Lanarkshire, Renfrewshire, South Ayrshire, South Lanarkshire, West Dunbartonshire

M74
Abington, Jct 13 (northbound)
A70
East Tarelgin
A73
Airdrie, Carlisle Rd
A76
New Cumnock, nr Lime Rd
A78
Fairlie, Main Rd
A82
Bridge of Orchy
Milton, Dunbarton Rd
A85
west of Tyndrum
A89
Airdrie, Forrest St
A706
South of Forth
A730
Rutherglen, Blairbeth Rd
A737
Dairy, New St/Kilwinning Rd
A749
East Kilbride Rd btwn Cathkin Rd and Cairnmuir Rd
A807
Bardowie, Balmore Rd
A814
Dunbarton, Cardross Rd
A815
nr Ardkinglass
B768
Rutherglen, Burnhill St
B803
Airdrie to Glenmavis, Coatbridge Rd
B814
Duntocher Rd
B8048
Kirkintilloch, Waterside Rd
Unclassified
Bargeddie, Glasgow Rd
Barrhead, Aurs Rd
Bishopbriggs, Woodhill Rd
Clydebank, Glasgow Rd
Coatbridge, Townhead Rd
Drymen Rd/Duntocher Rd
East Kilbride, Maxwelton Rd at Kirkoswald (South)
Johnstone, Beith Rd
Neilston, Kingston Rd
Newton Mearns, Mearns Rd
Paisley, Glasgow Rd nr Newtyle Rd
Rutherglen, Glasgow Rd
Rutherglen, Mill St
Troon, Craigend Rd

Tayside

Angus, Dundee, Perth & Kinross

A9
60 Inverness to Perth road, nr Balnansteuartach
70 Perth to Inverness road, nr Inveralmond Industrial Estate
70 Stirling to Perth road, btwn Broom of Dalreoch and Upper Cairnie
70 Stirling to Perth road, Tibbermore jct
A90
40 Dundee nr Fountainbleau Drive, Forfar Rd
70 Dundee to Perth road, Walnut Grove to Inchyra
70 Dundee to Perth road, west of Longforgan village
50 Dundee, Kingsway
50 Dundee, Swallow rdbt to Strathmartine Rd rdbt
A91
60 Milnathort to Devon Bridge
A92
60 Arbroath to Montrose
30 Dundee btwn Arbroath Rd and Craigie Avenue, Greendykes Rd
40 Dundee, East Dock St
A93
60 Guildtown to Blairgowrie
60 Old Scone to Guildtown
A94
60 Scone to Coupar Angus
A822
60 Crieff to Braco
A923
60 Blairgowrie to Tullybaccart
A933
60 Colliston to Redford
A935
60 Brechin to Montrose
A972
40 Dundee, Kingsway East to Pitairlie Rd
A977
60 Kinross to Crook of Devon
B961
30 Dundee, Drumgeith Rd
B996
60 Kinross to Kelty
Unclassified
30 Dundee, Broughty Ferry Rd
30 Dundee, Charleston Drive
30 Dundee, Laird St
30 Dundee, Old Glamis Rd
30 Dundee, Perth Rd
30 Dundee, Strathmartine Rd

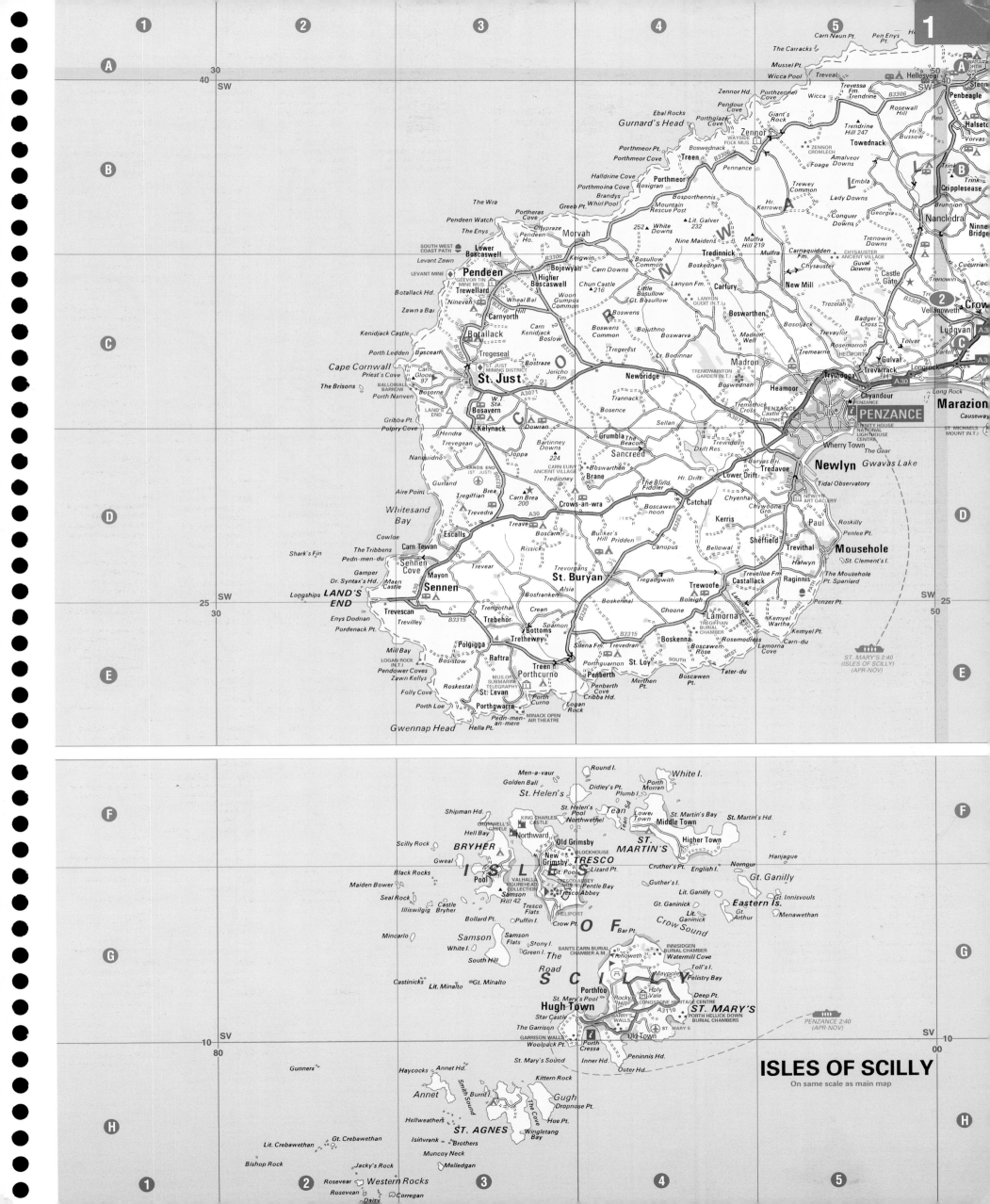

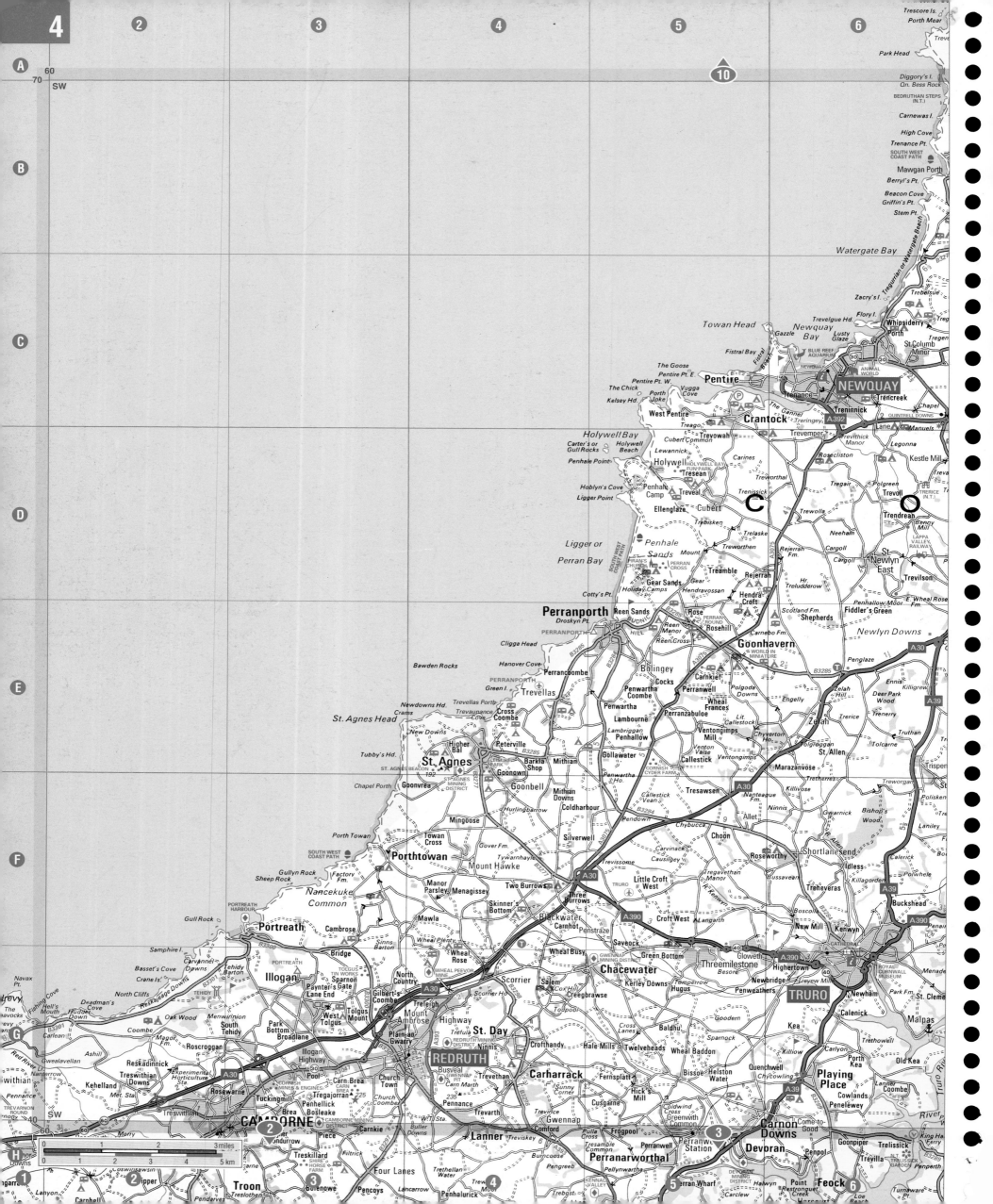

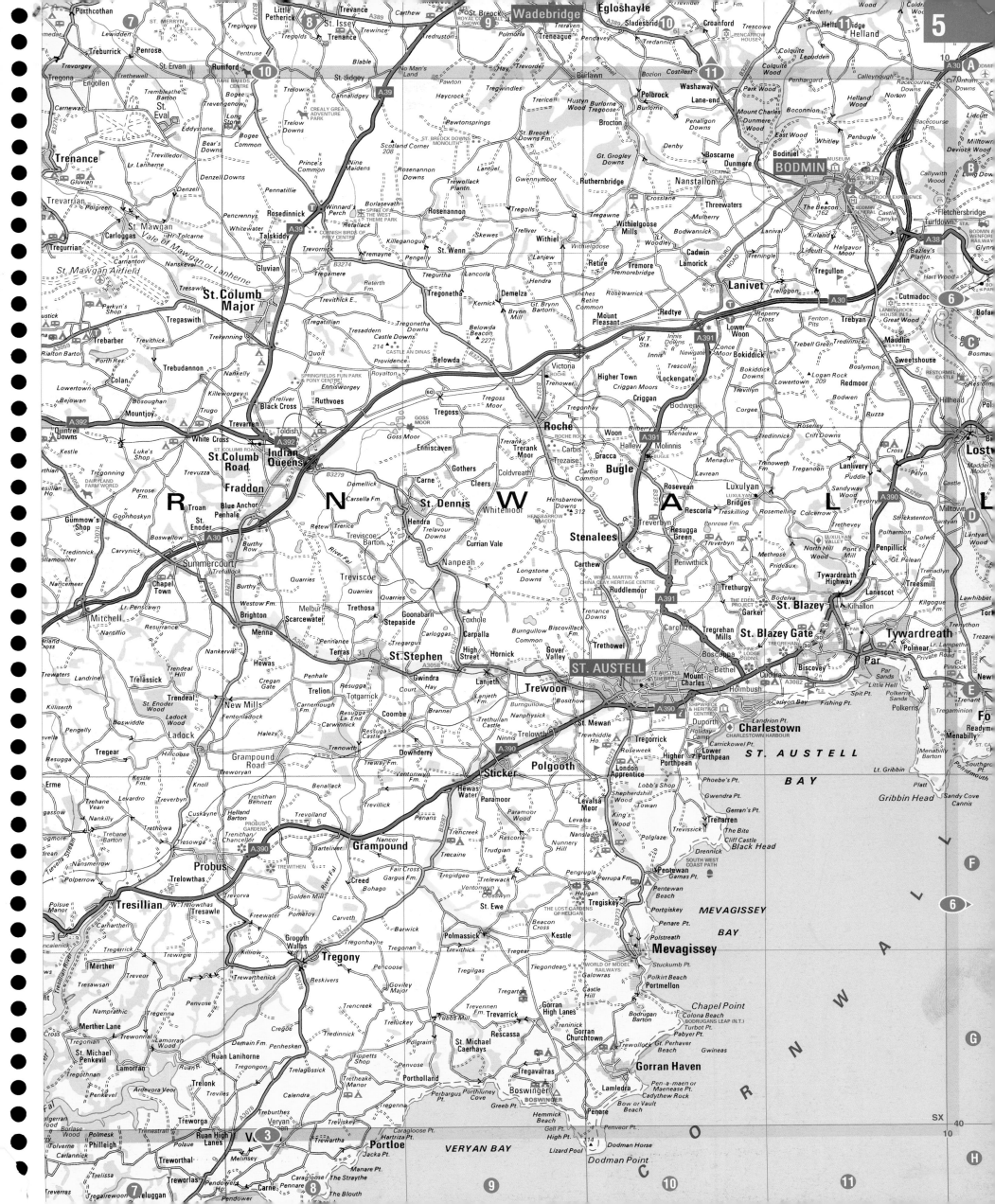

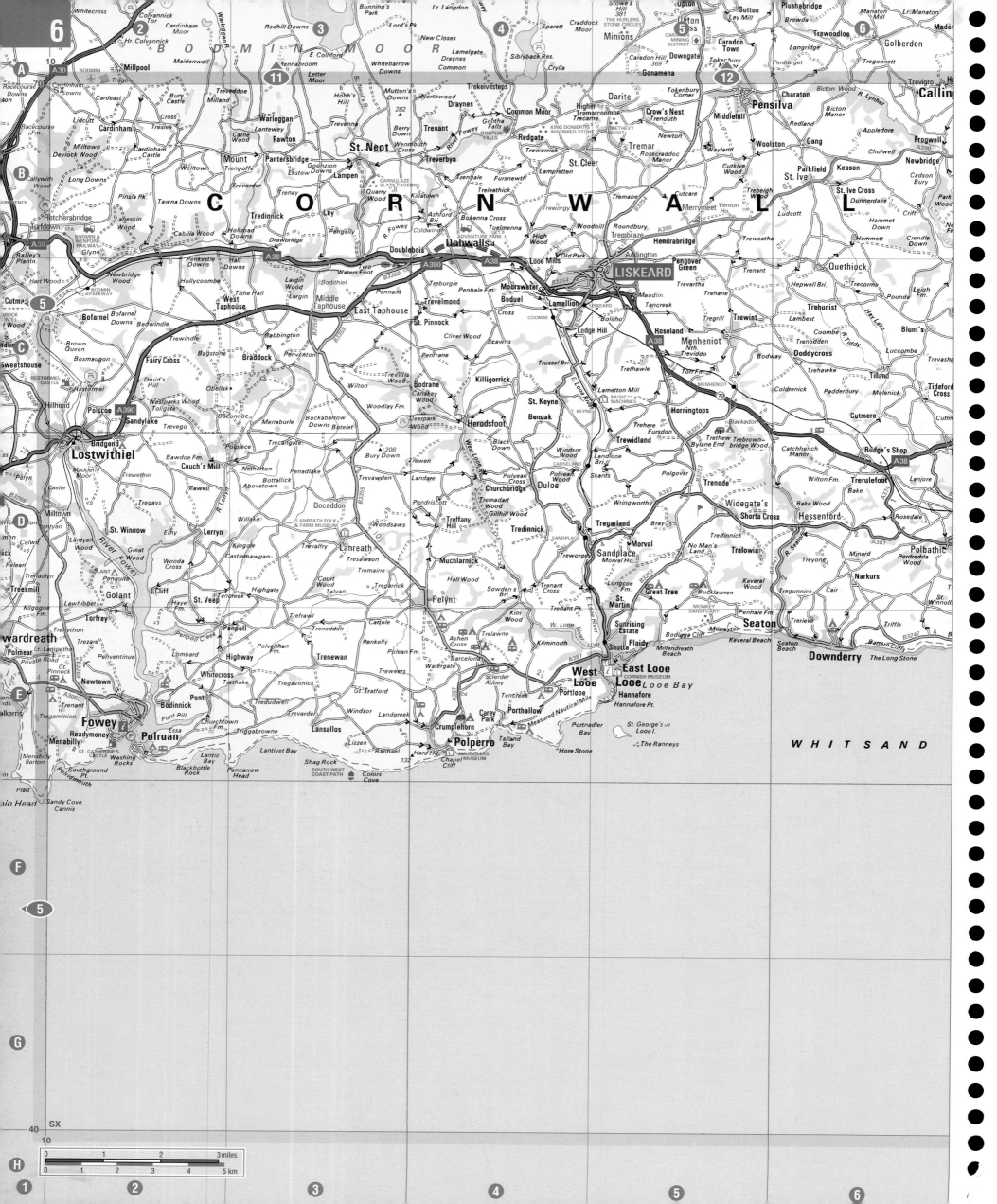

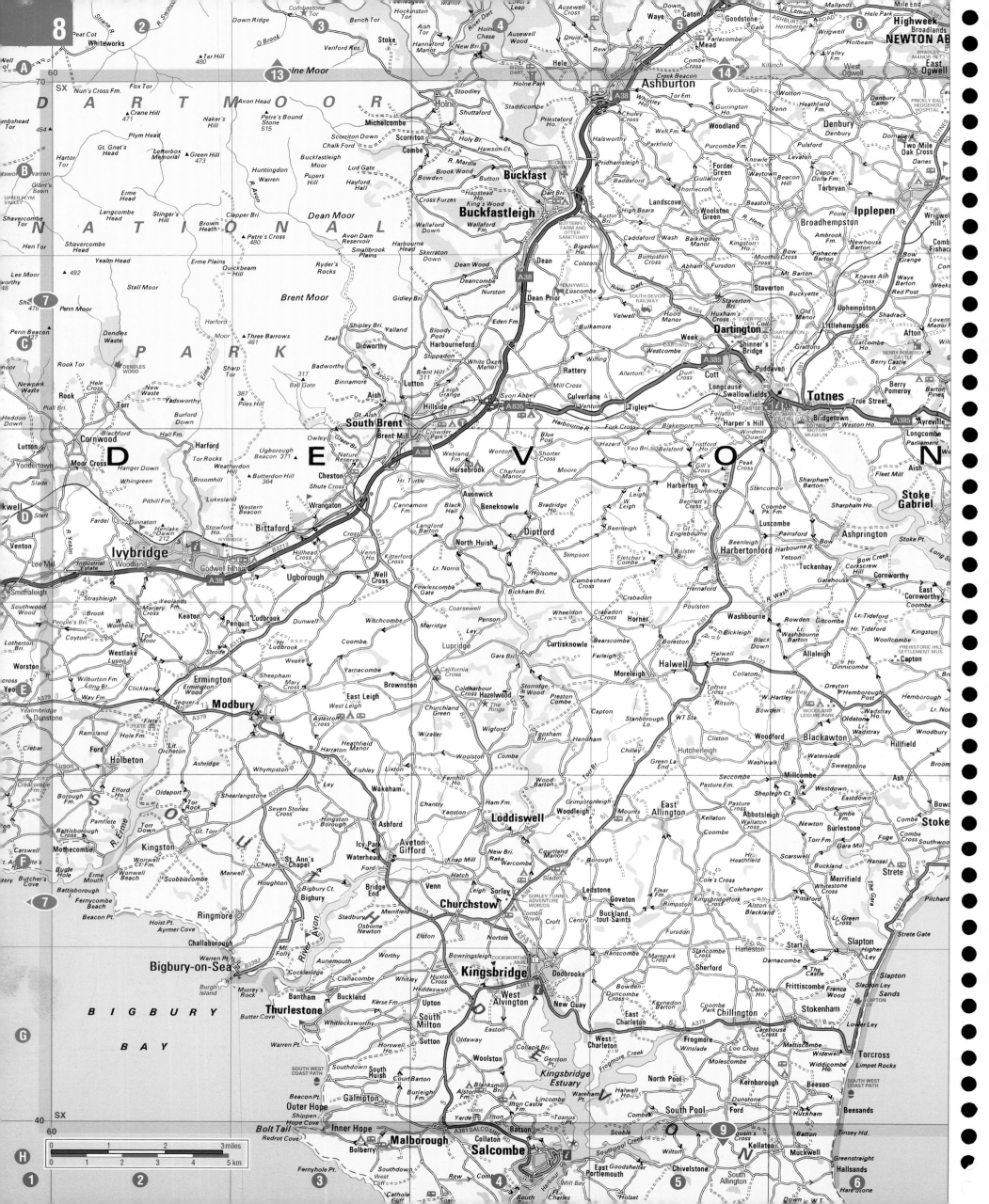

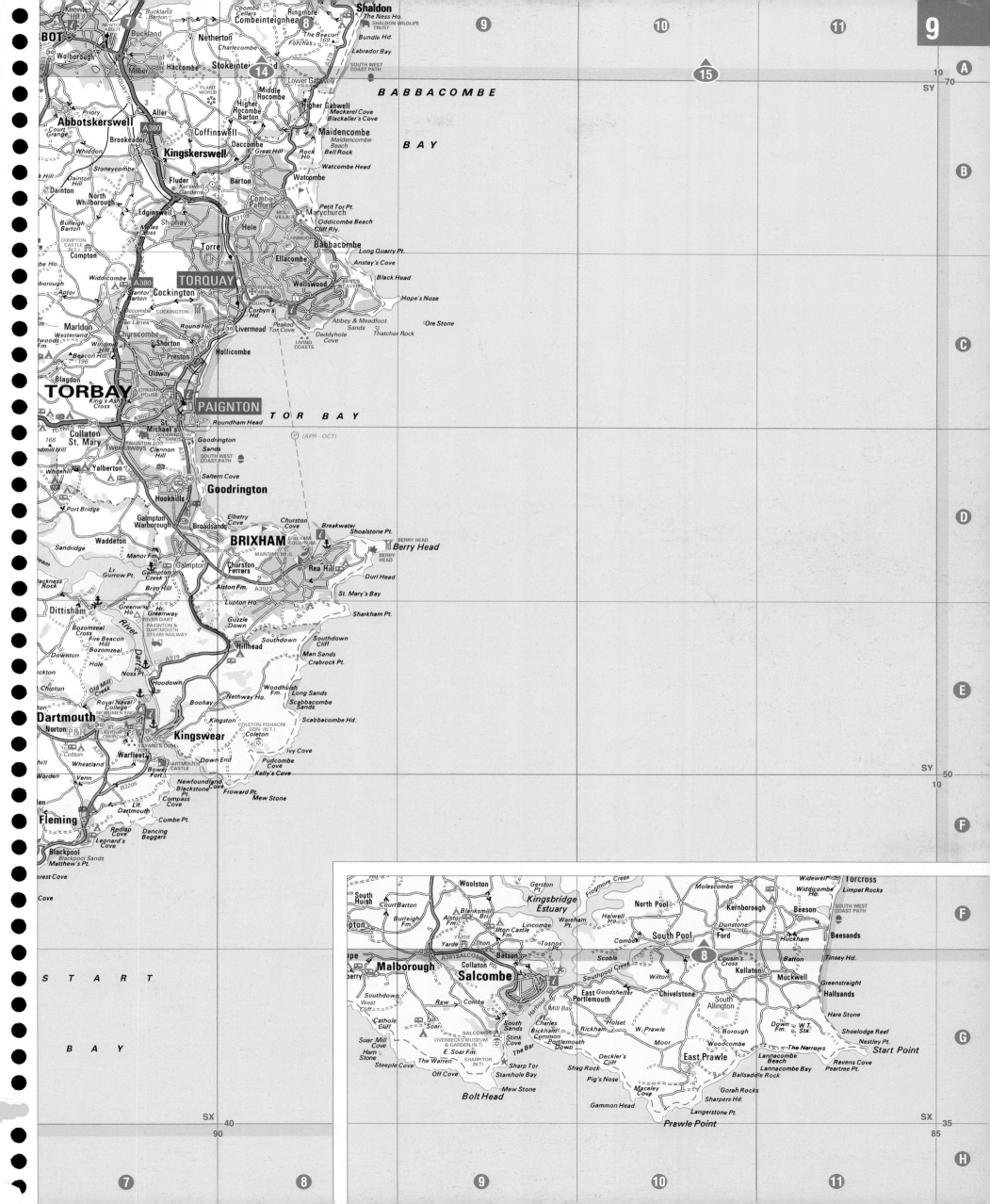

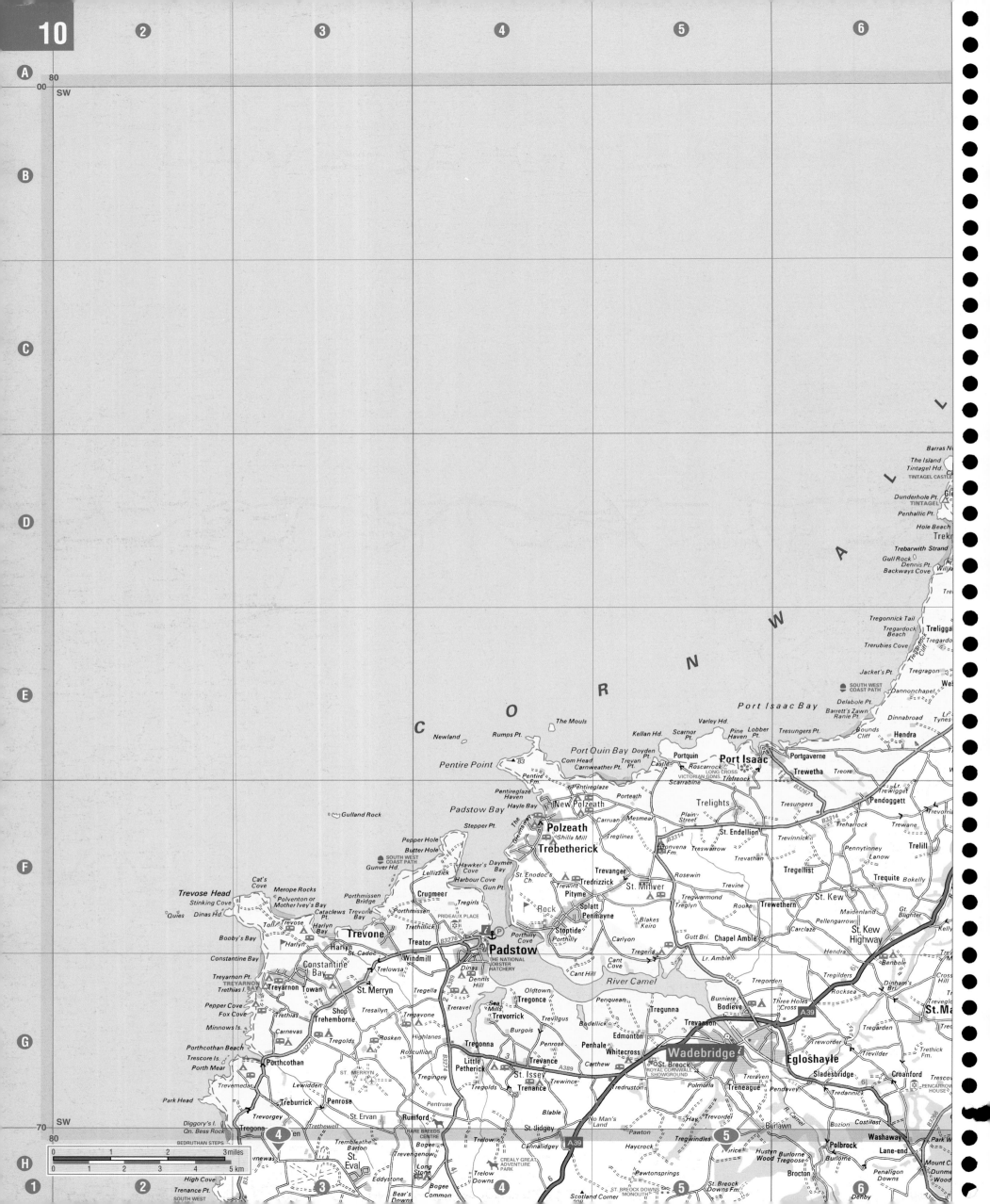

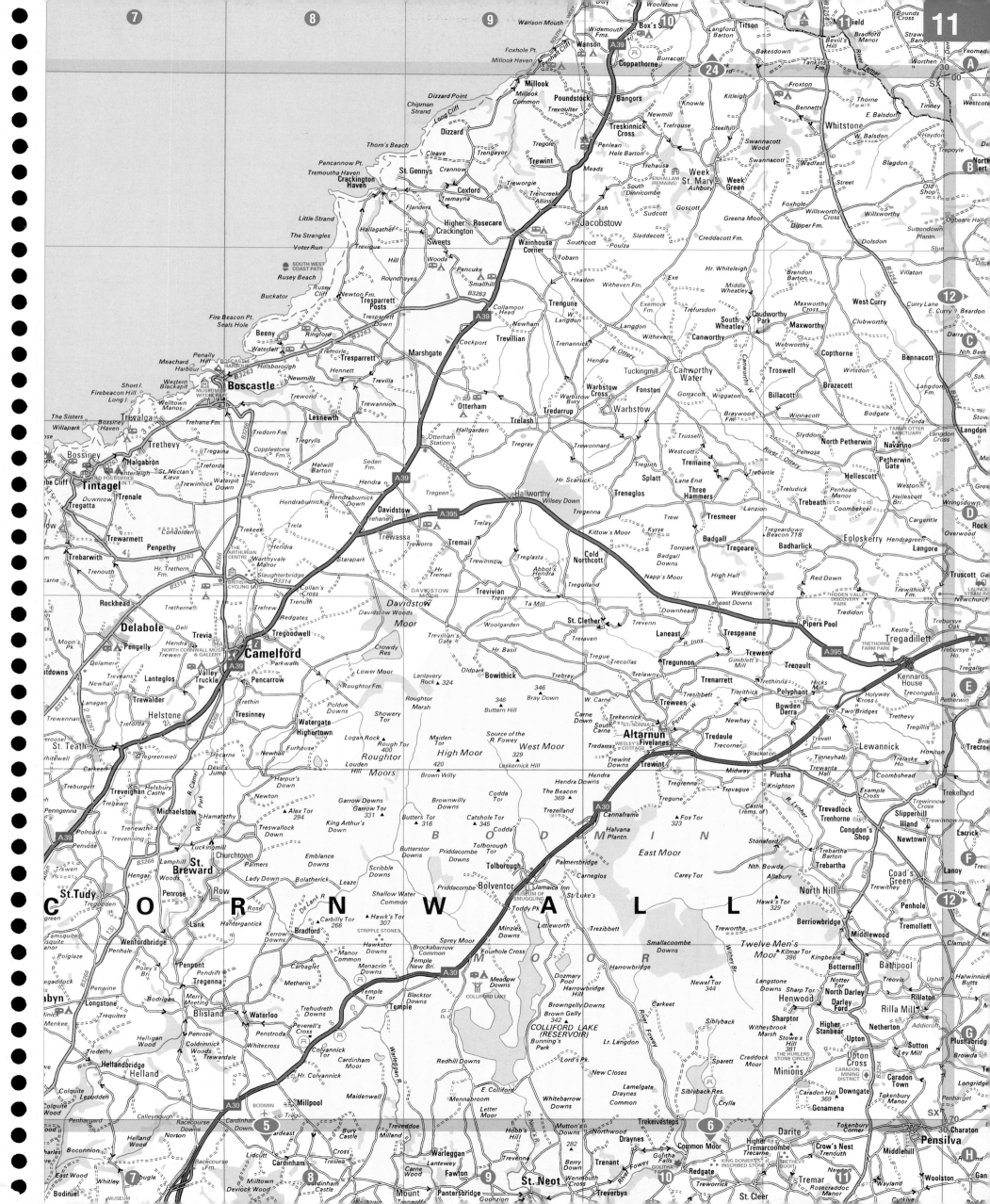

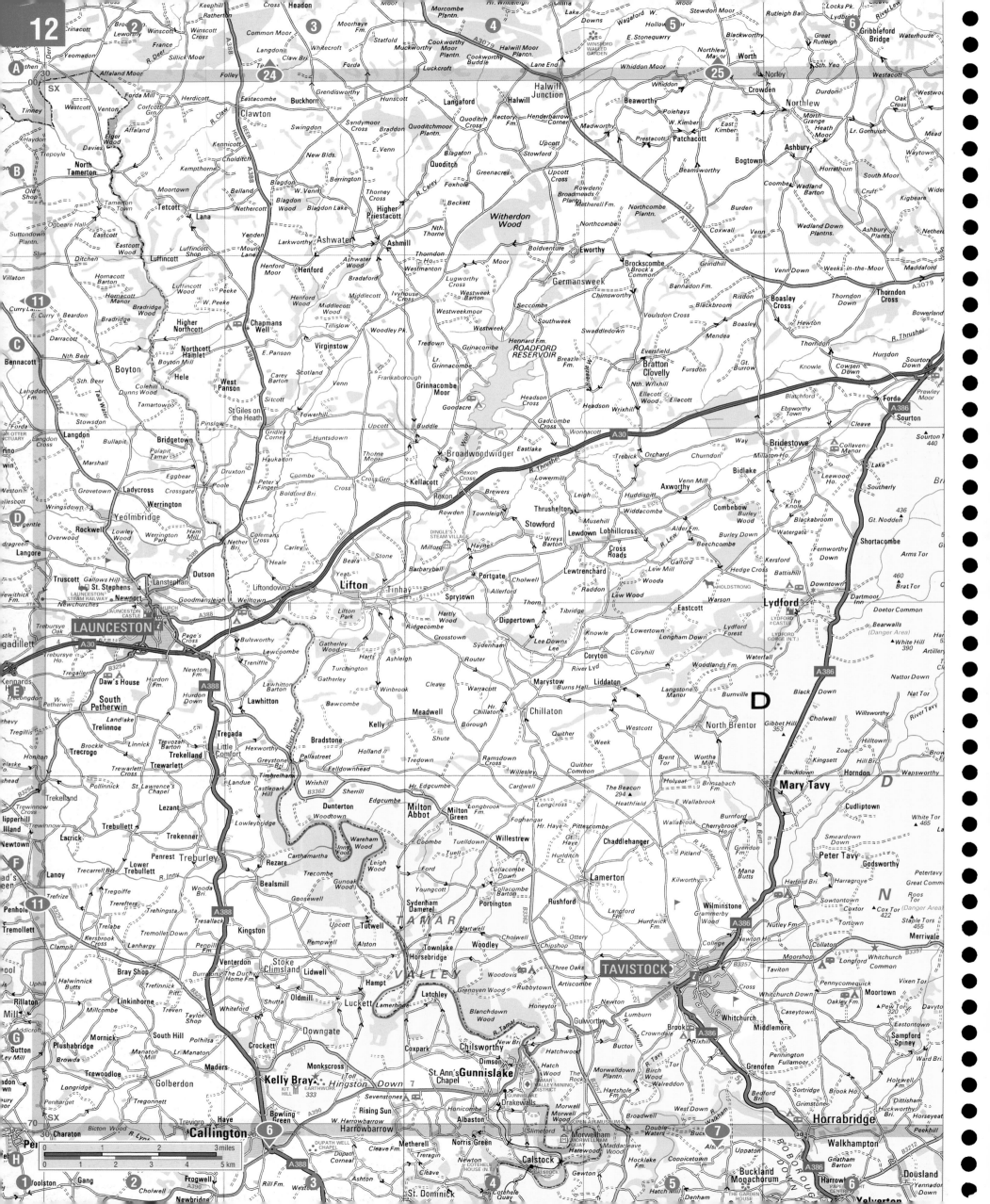

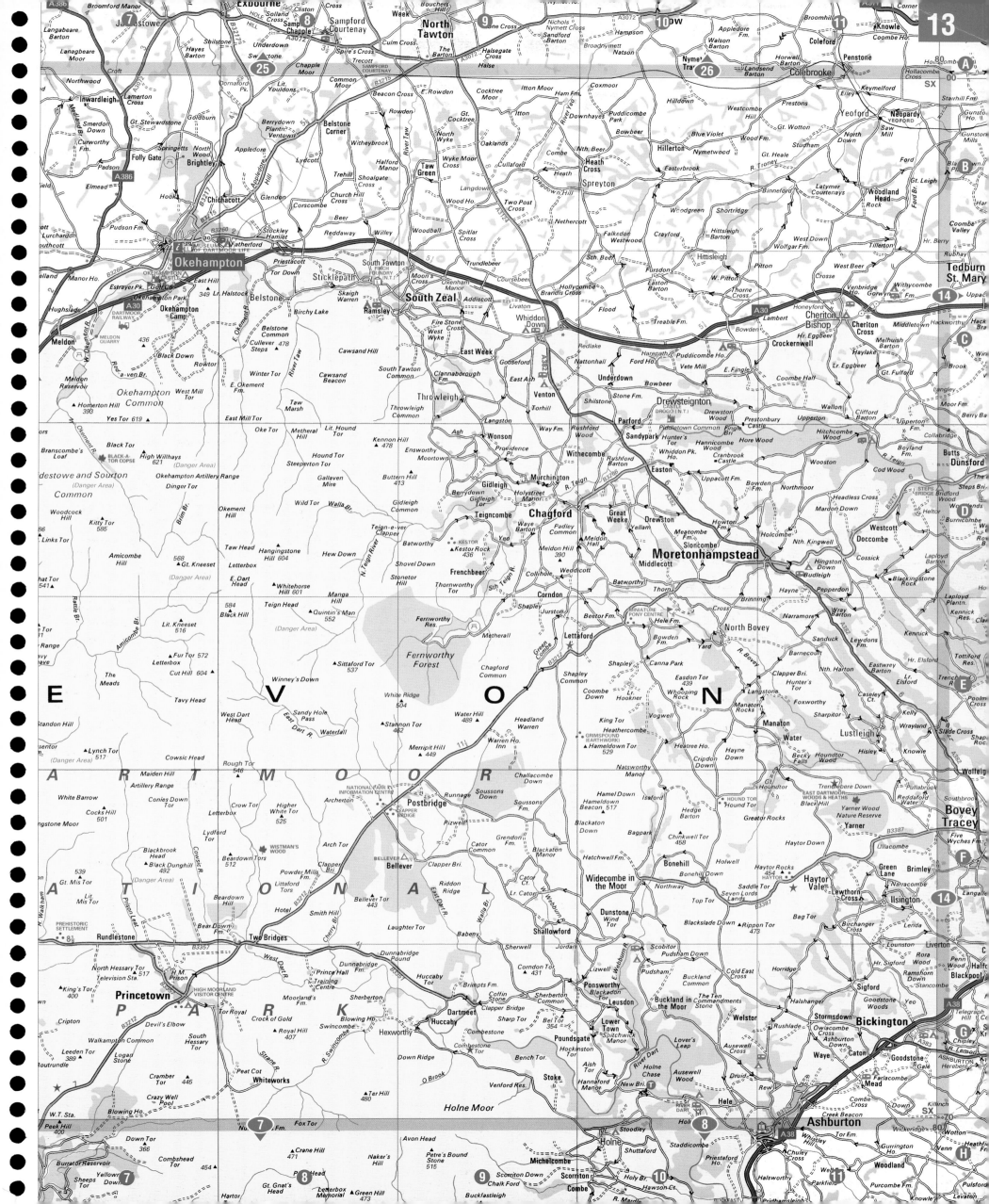

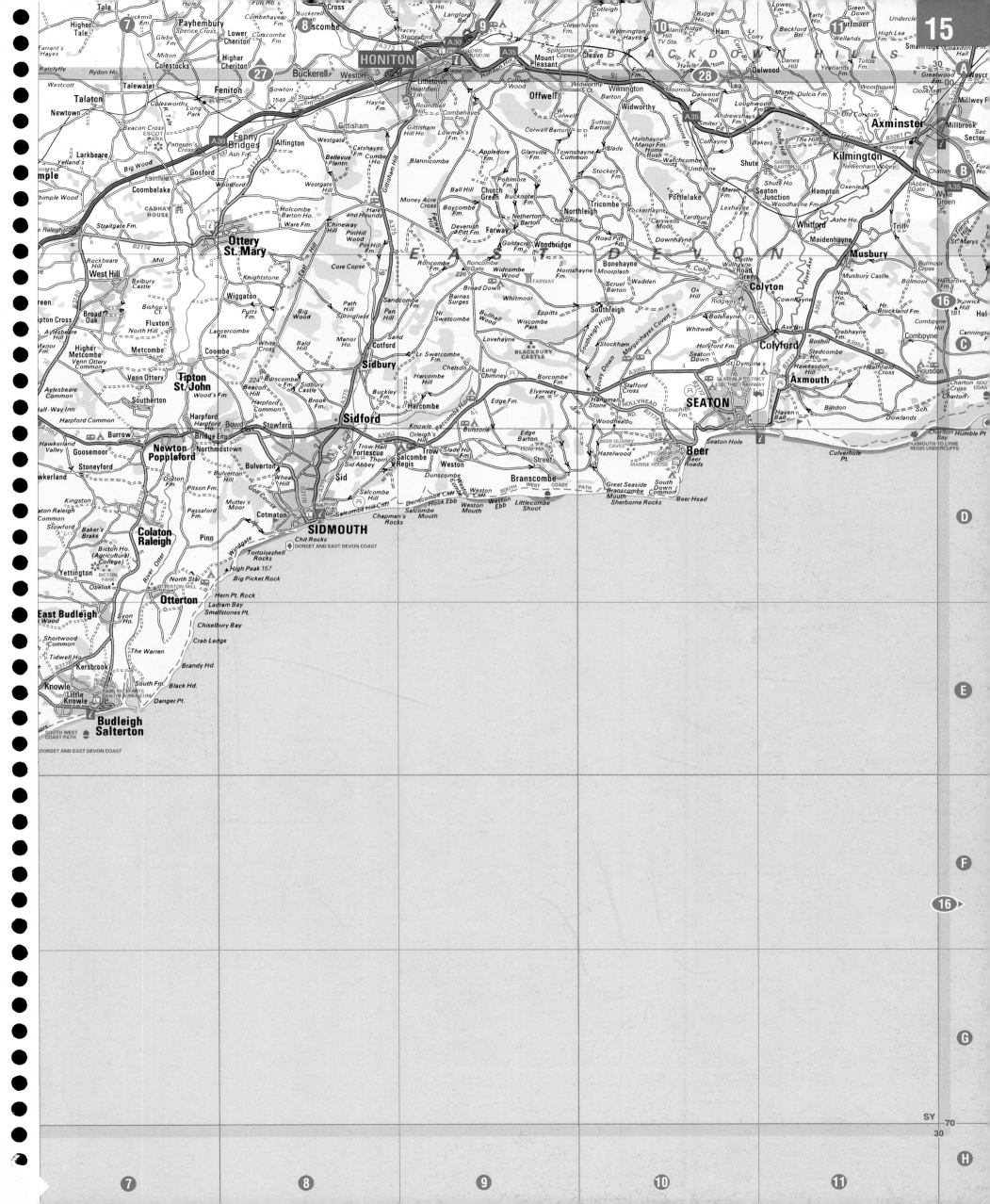

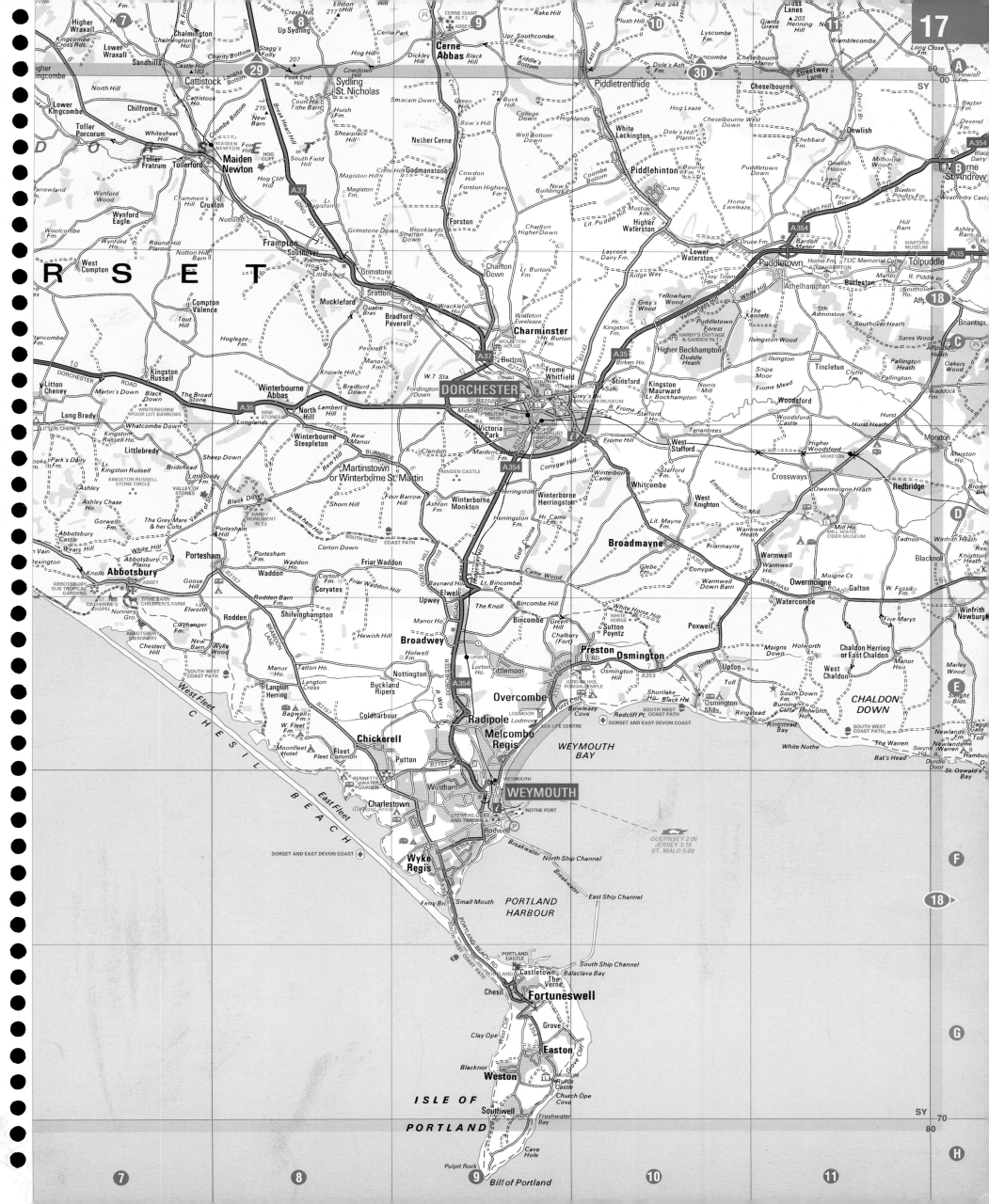

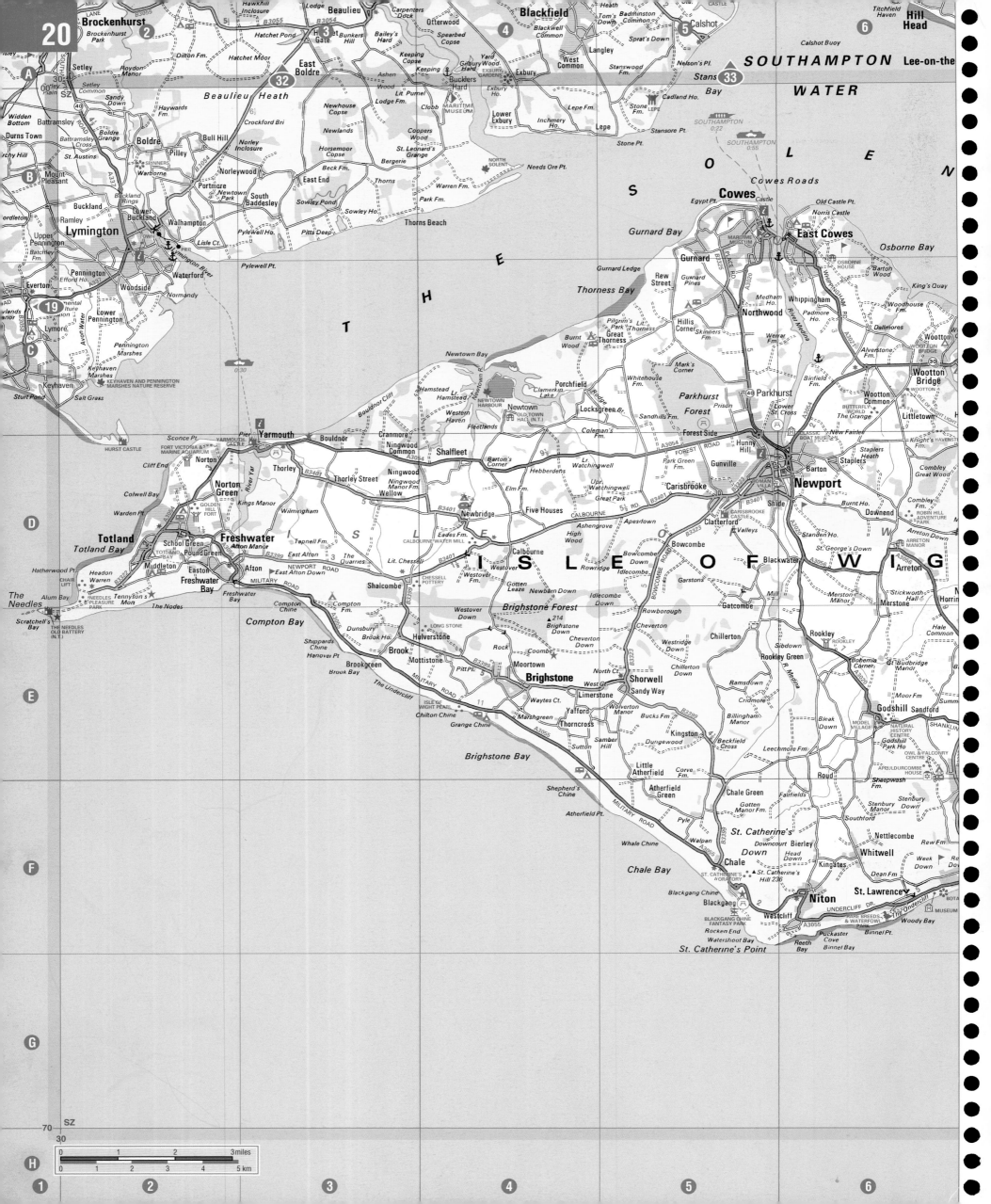

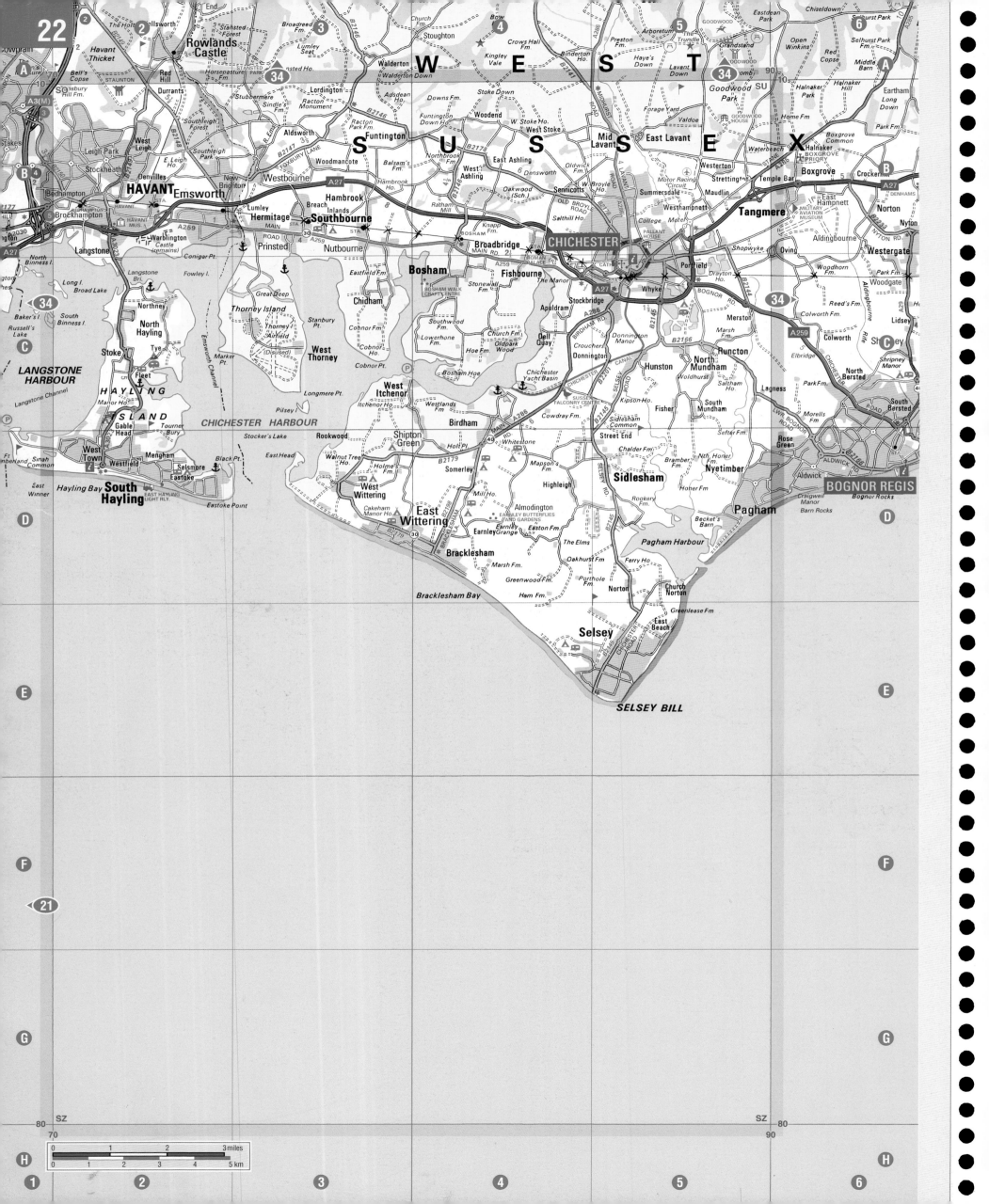

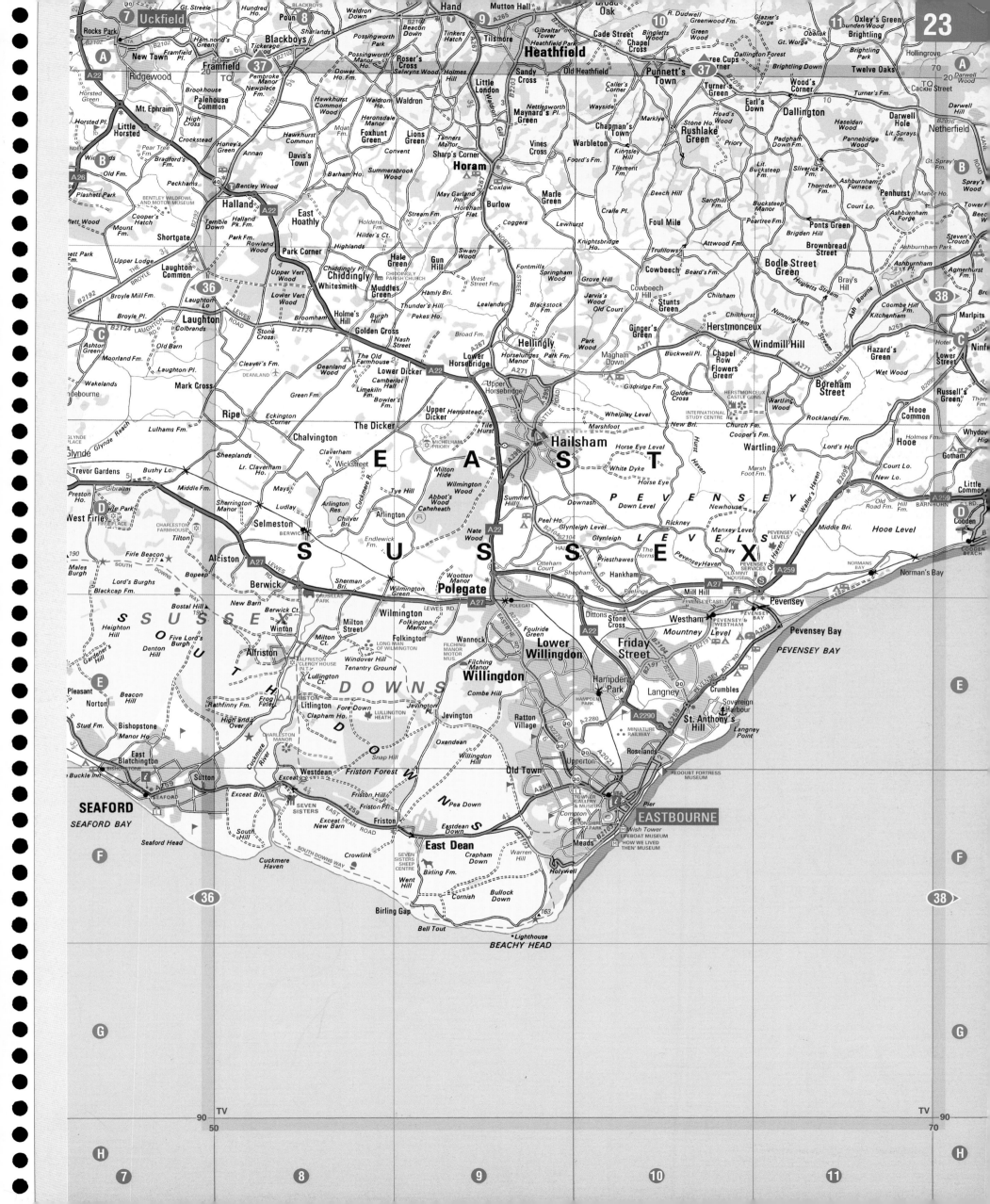

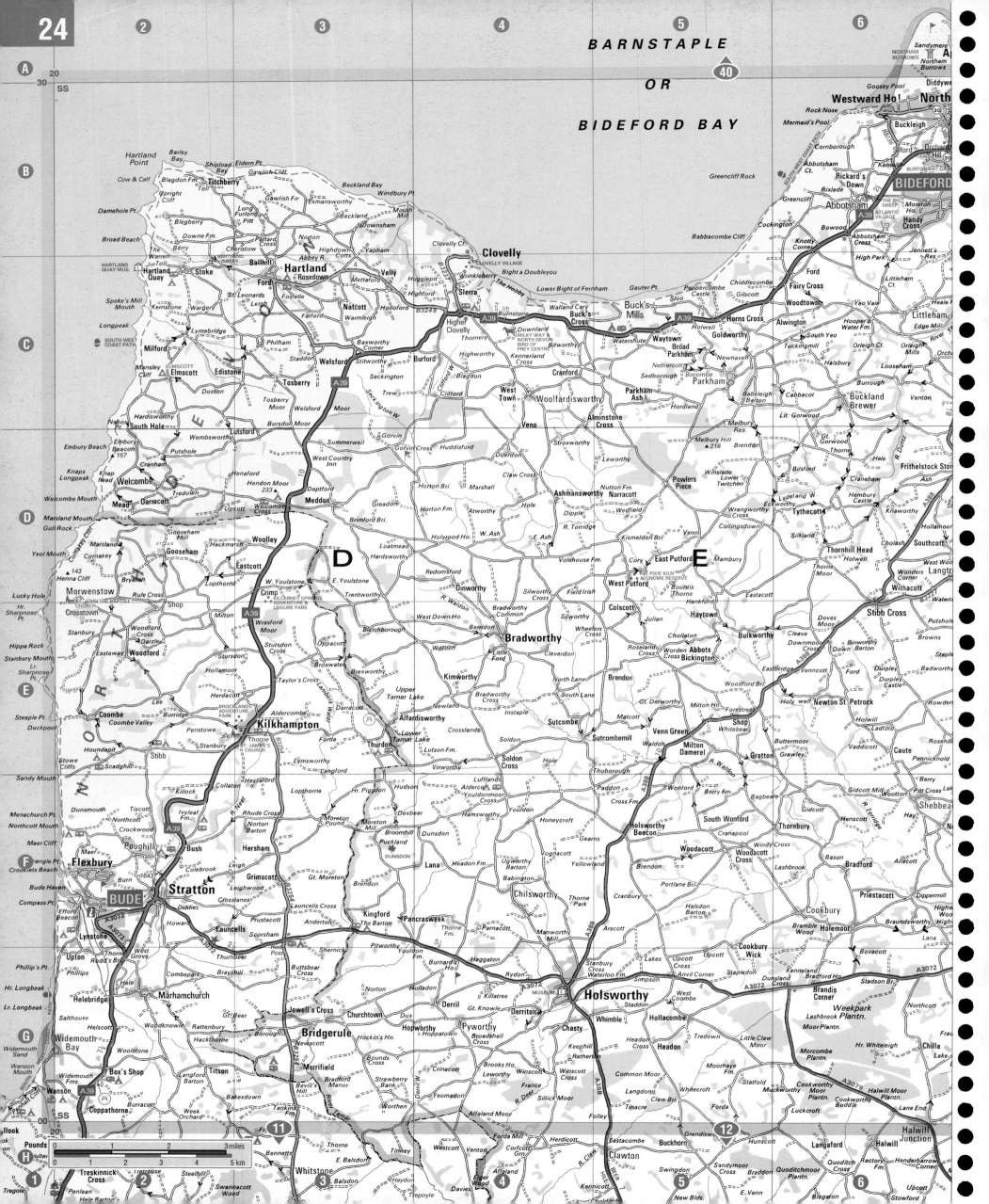

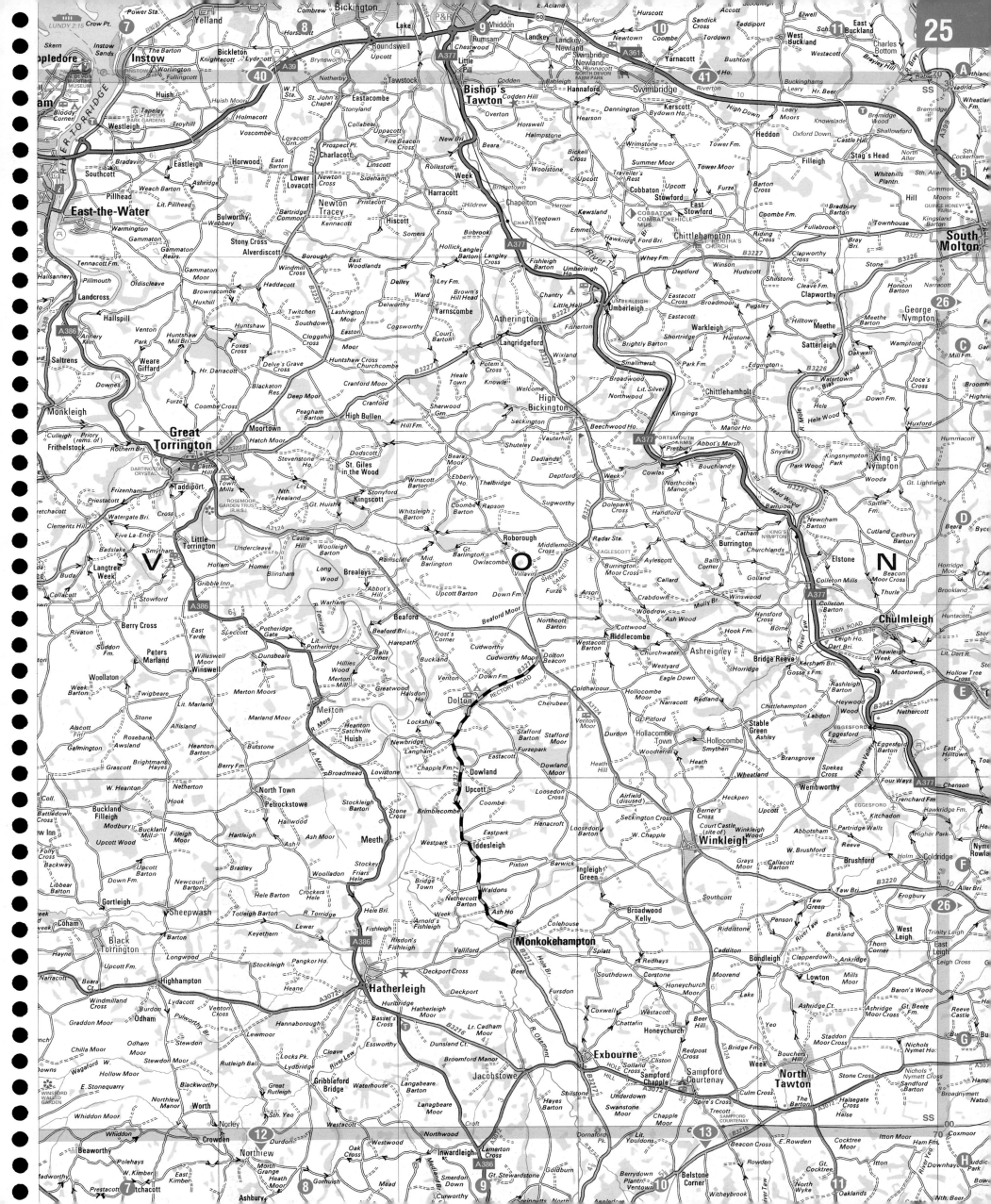

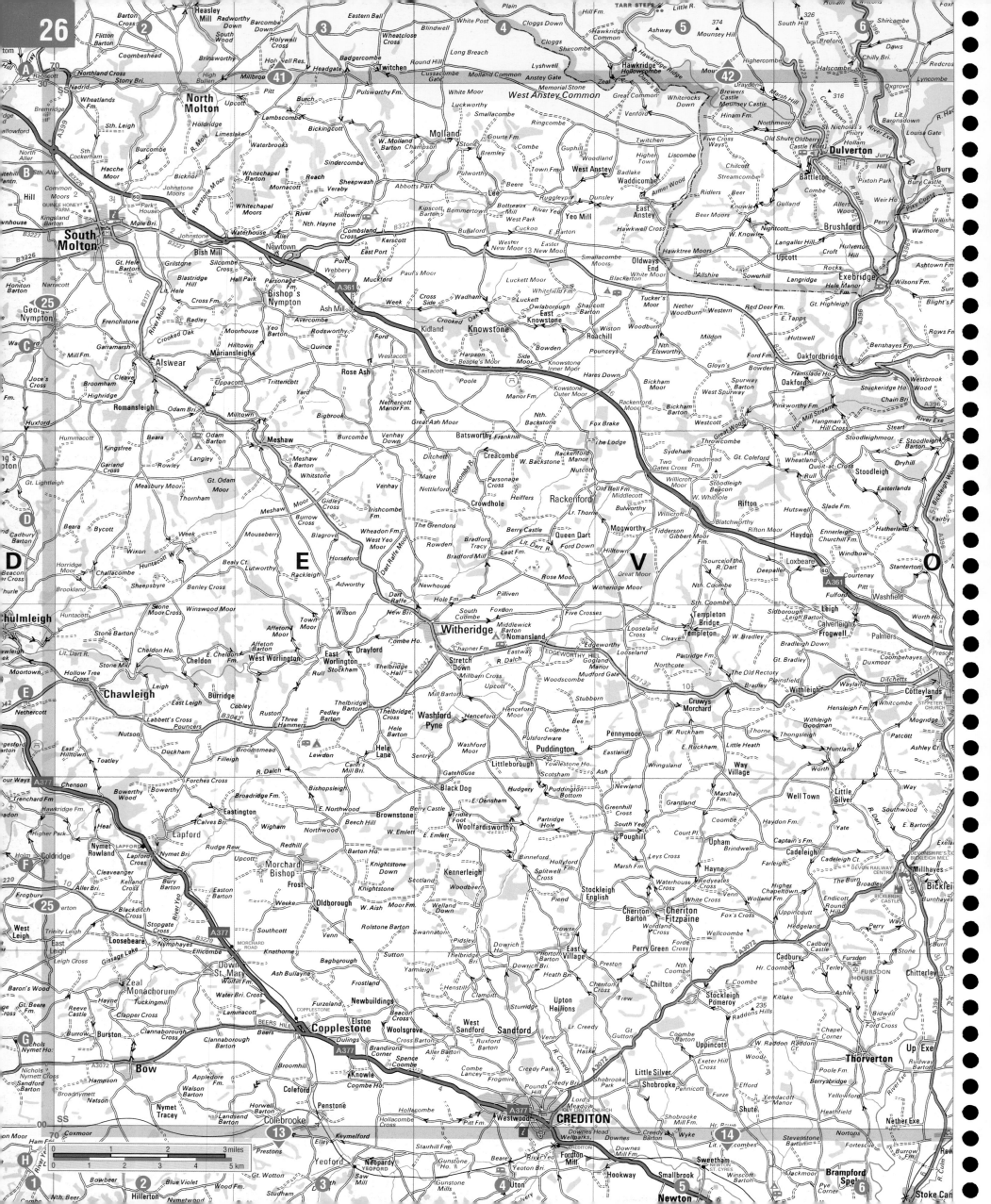

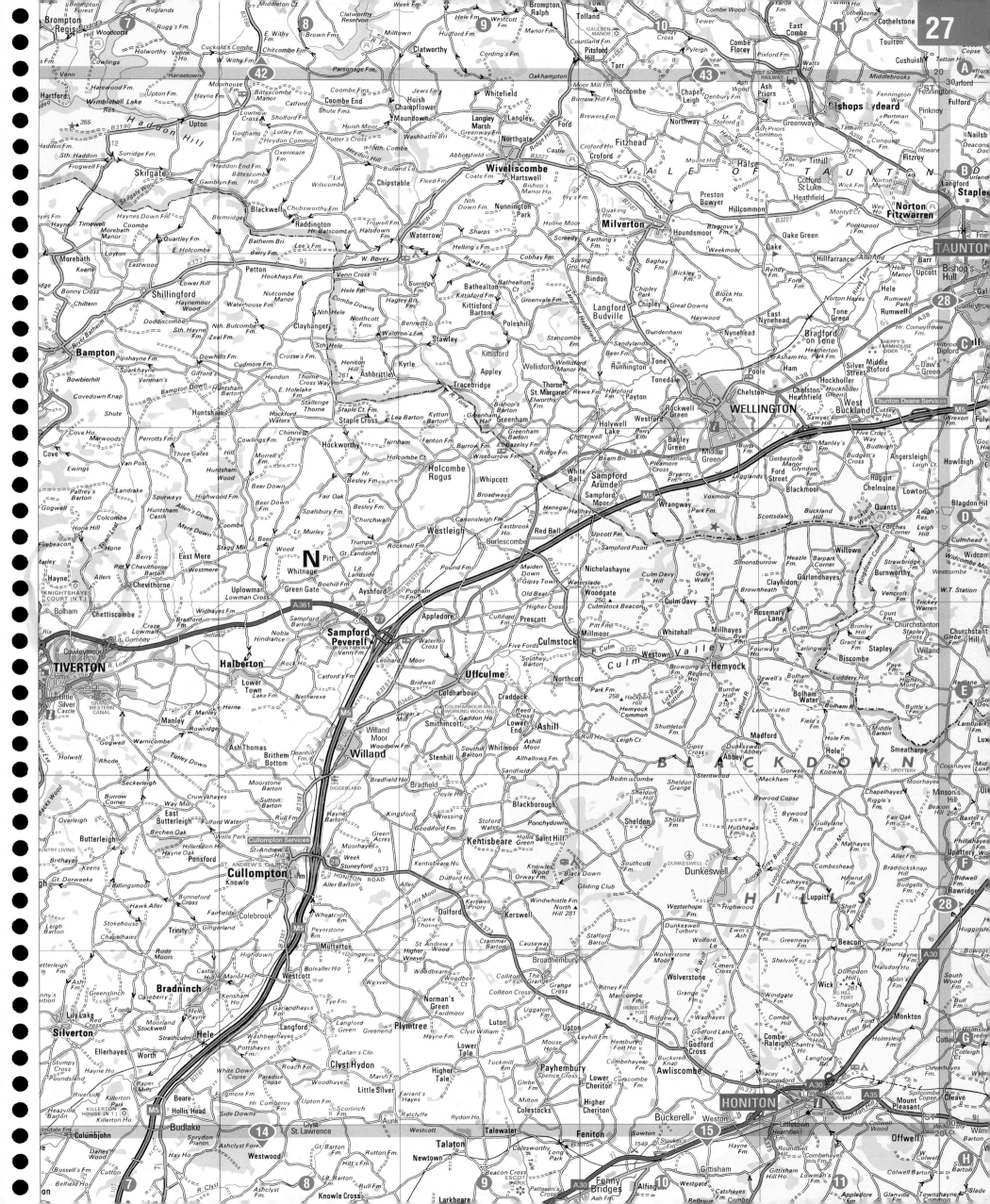

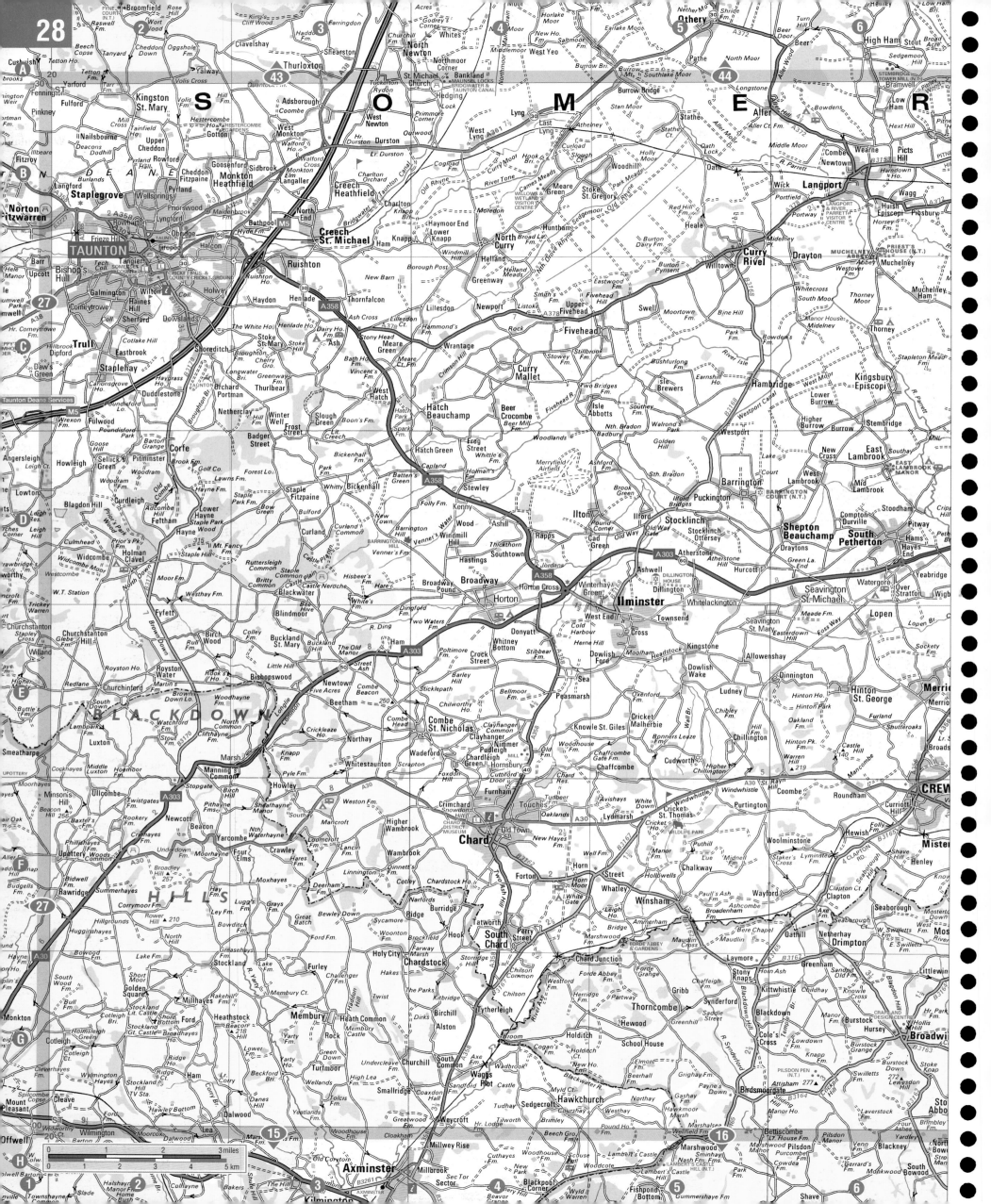

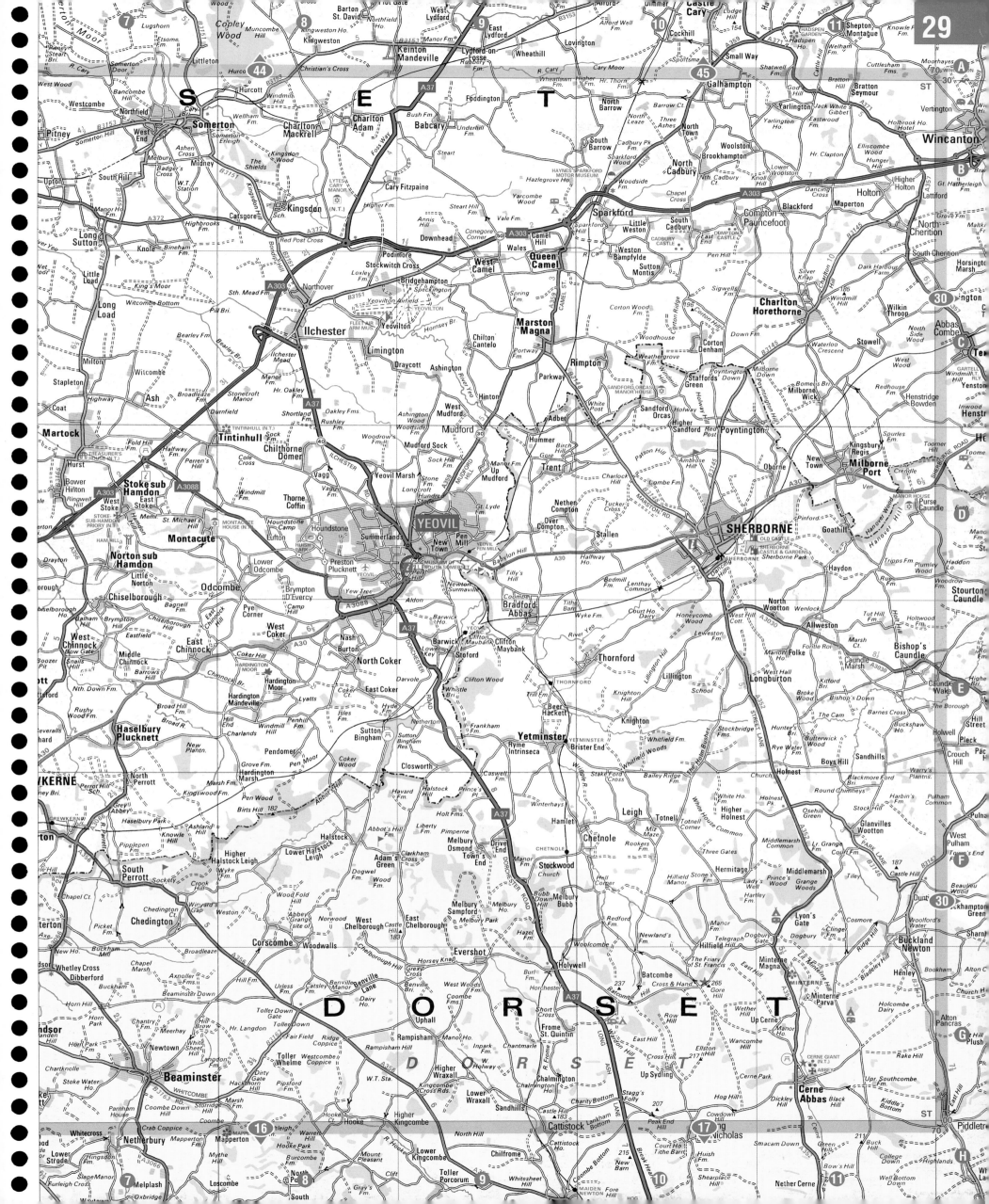

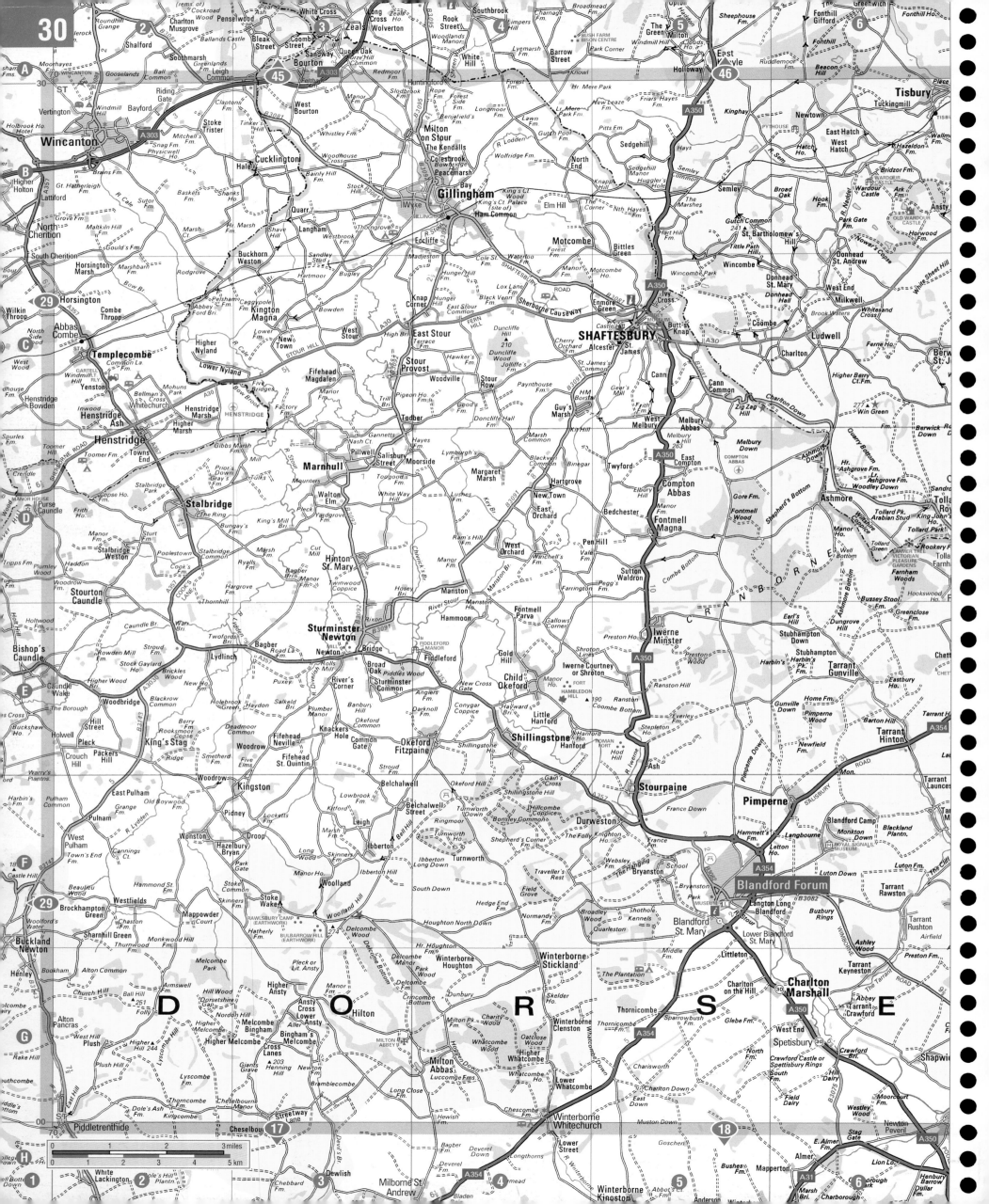

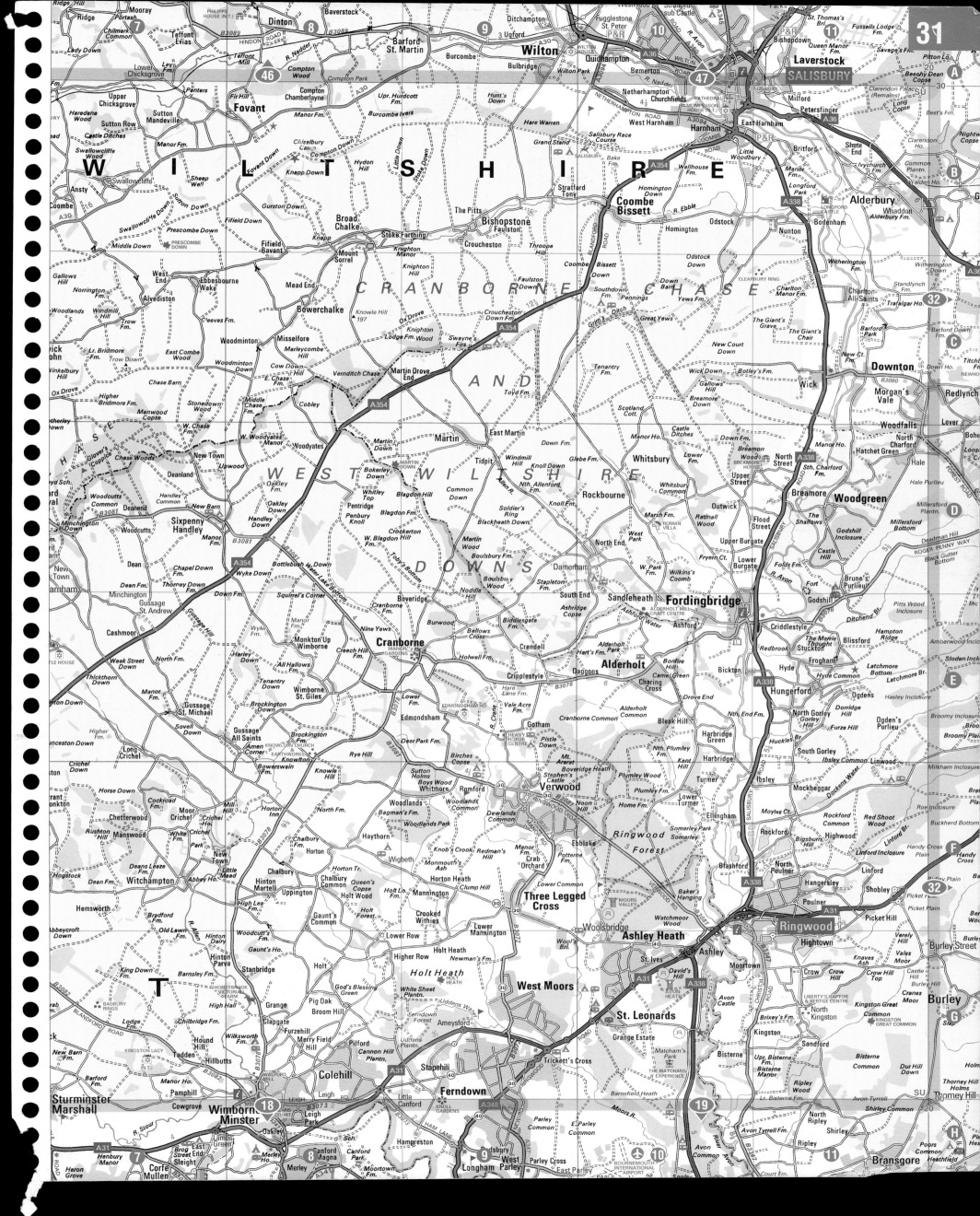

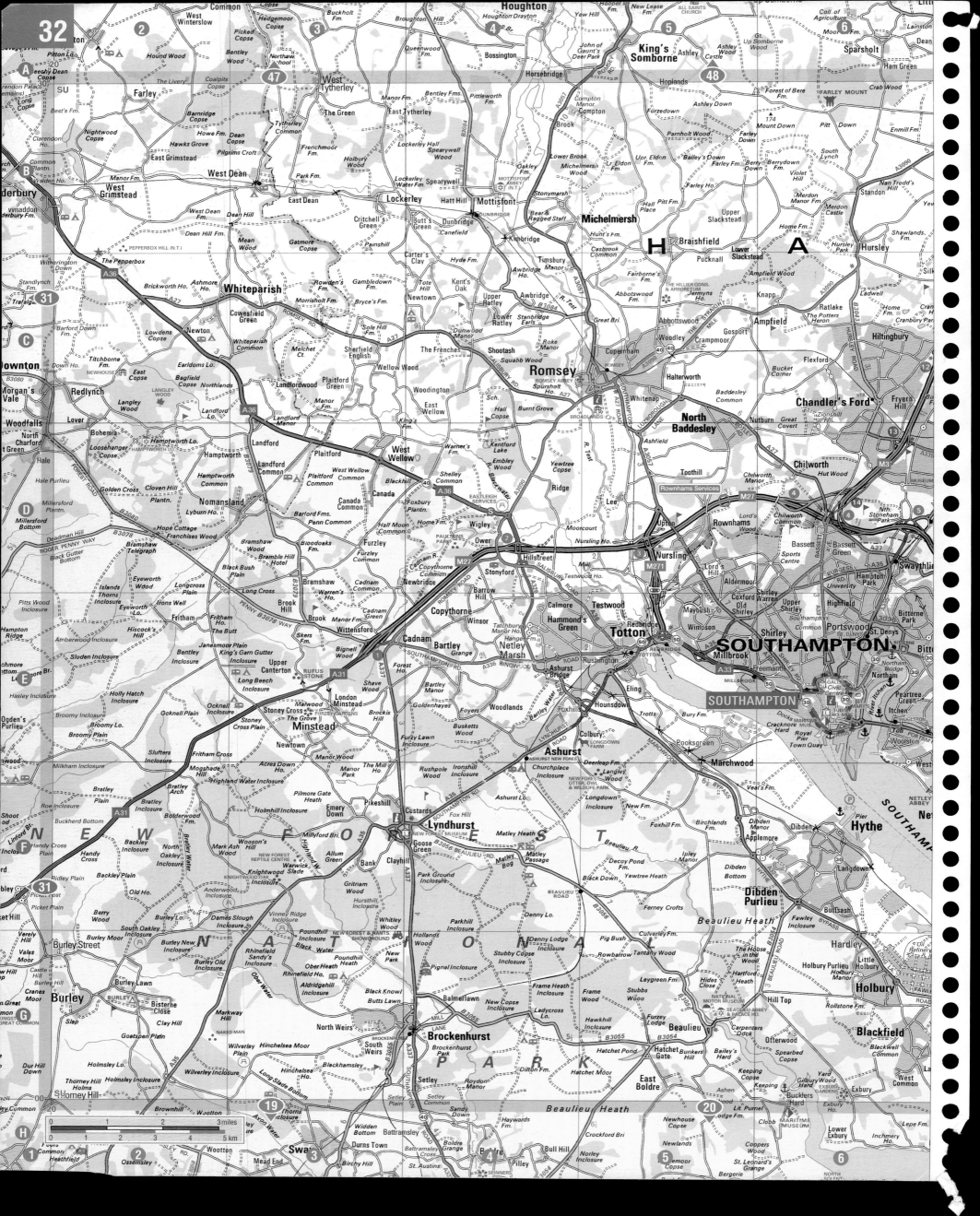

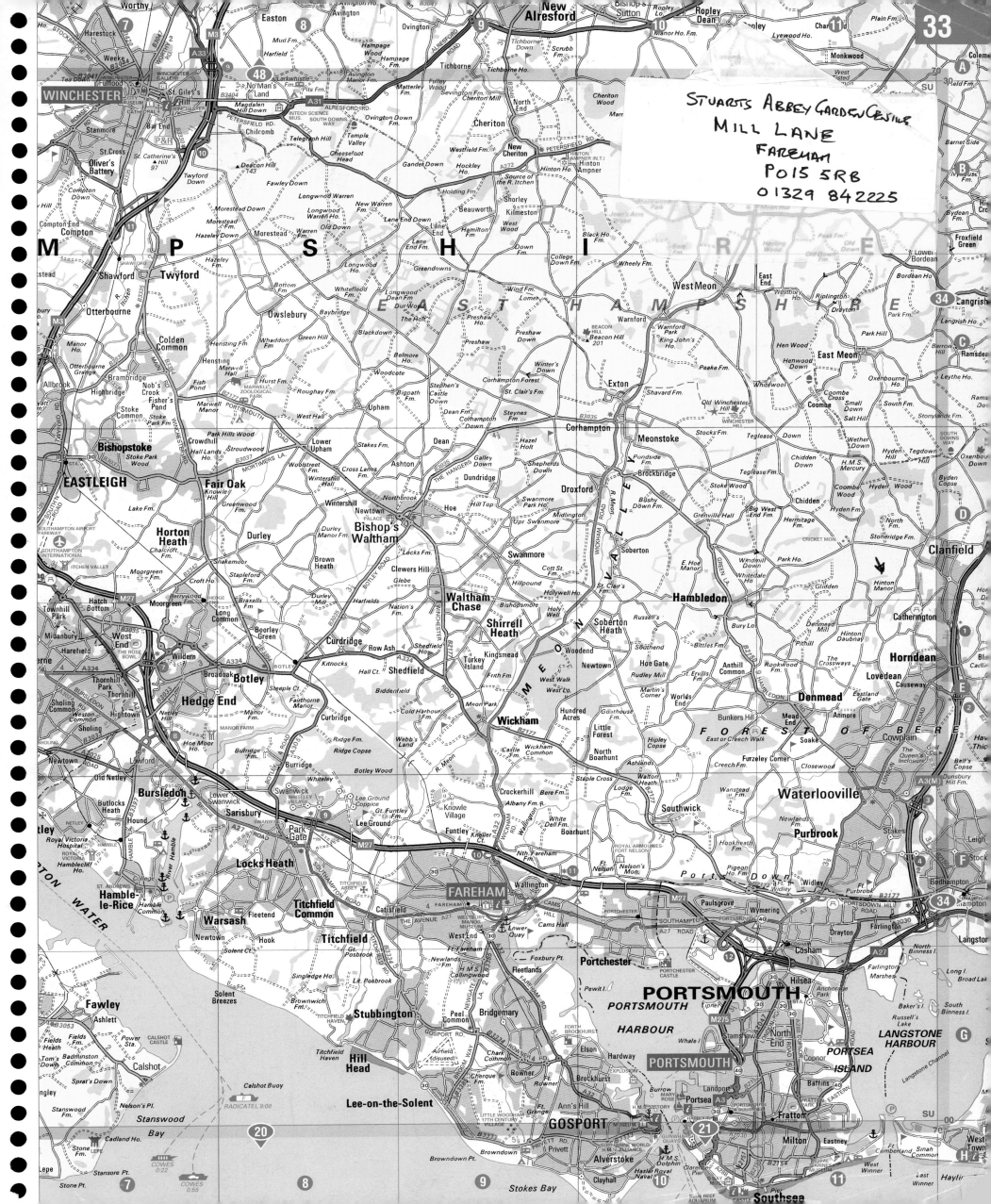

STUARTS ABBEY GARDEN CENTRE
MILL LANE
FAREHAM
PO15 5RB
01329 842225

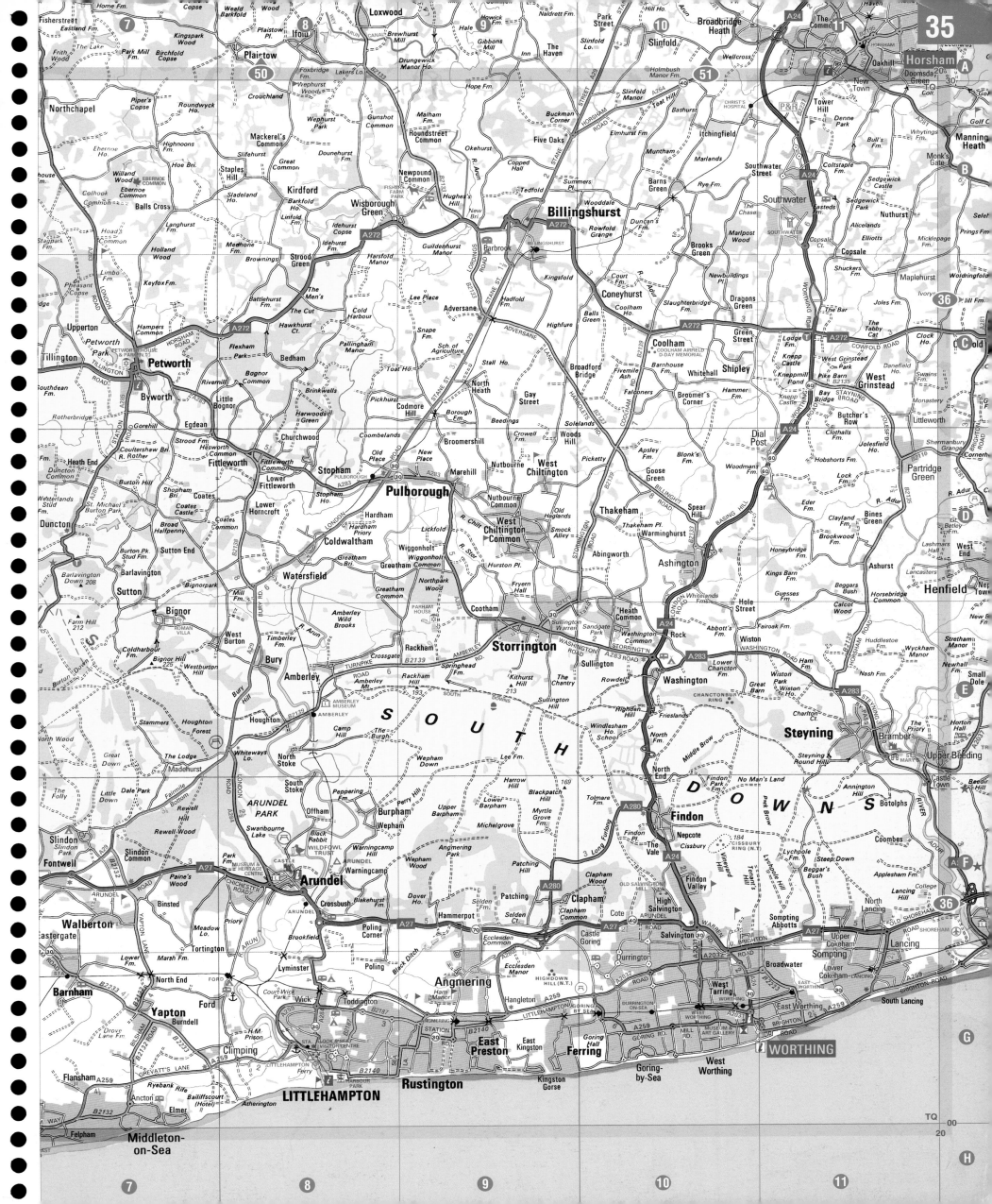

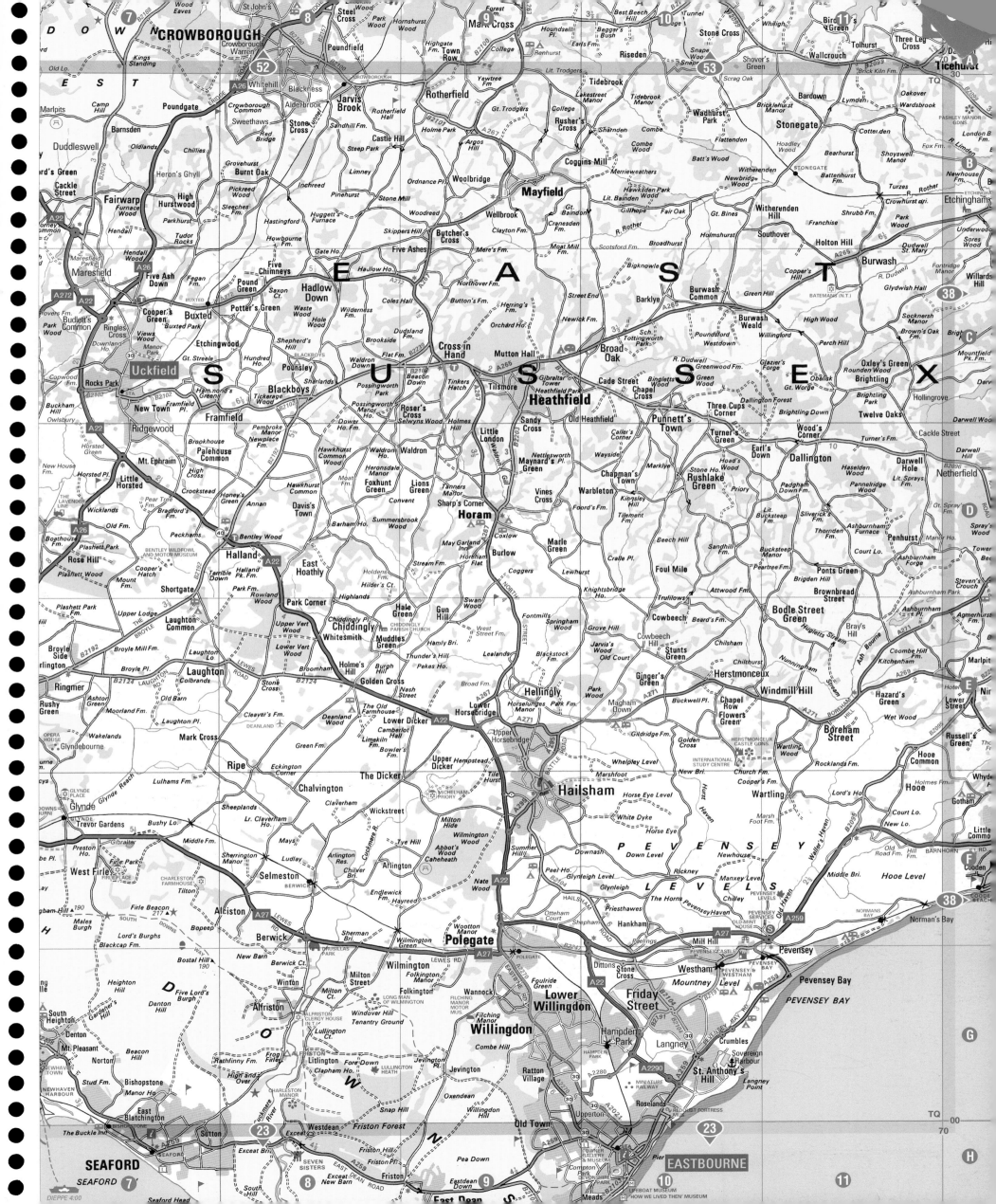

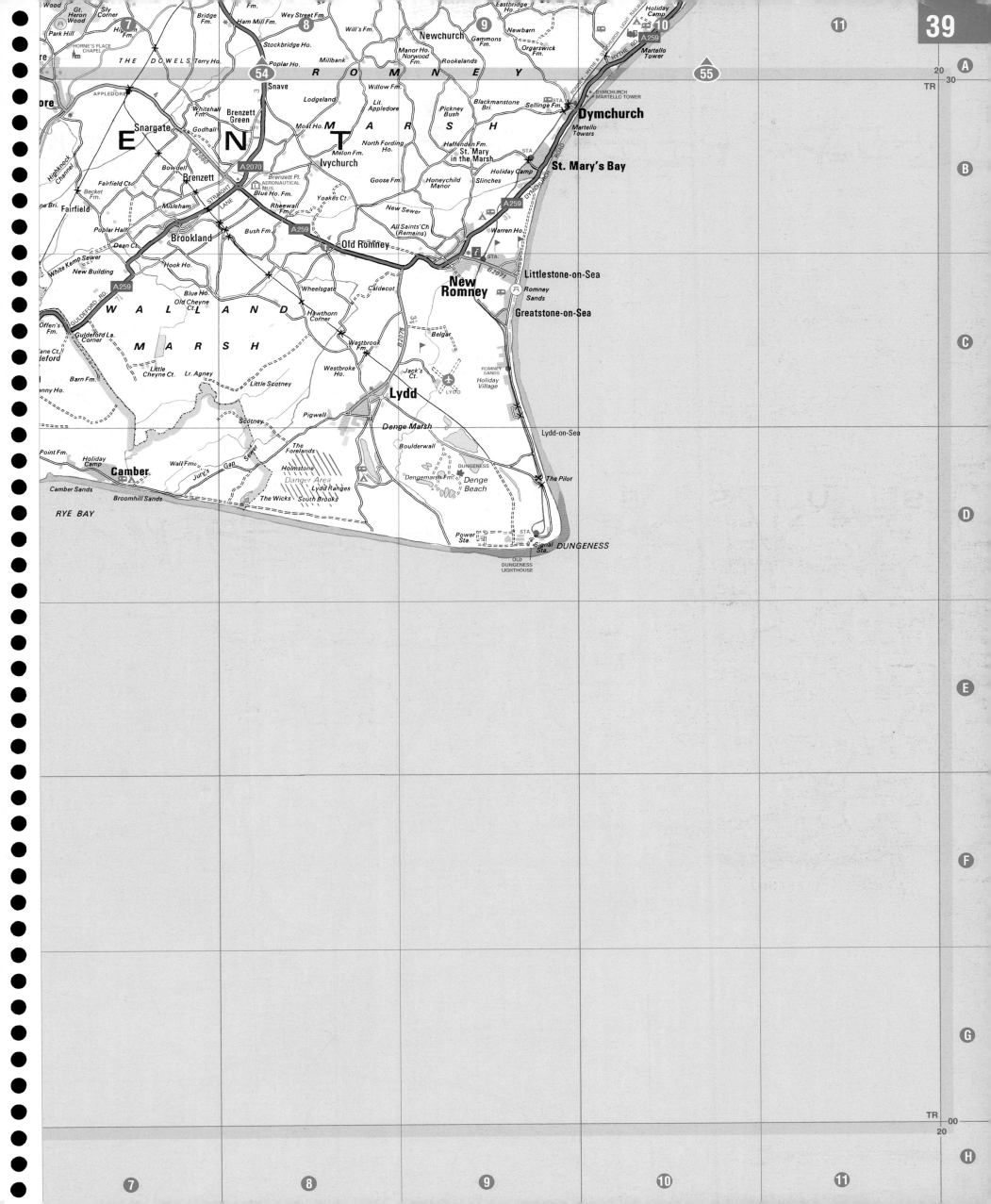

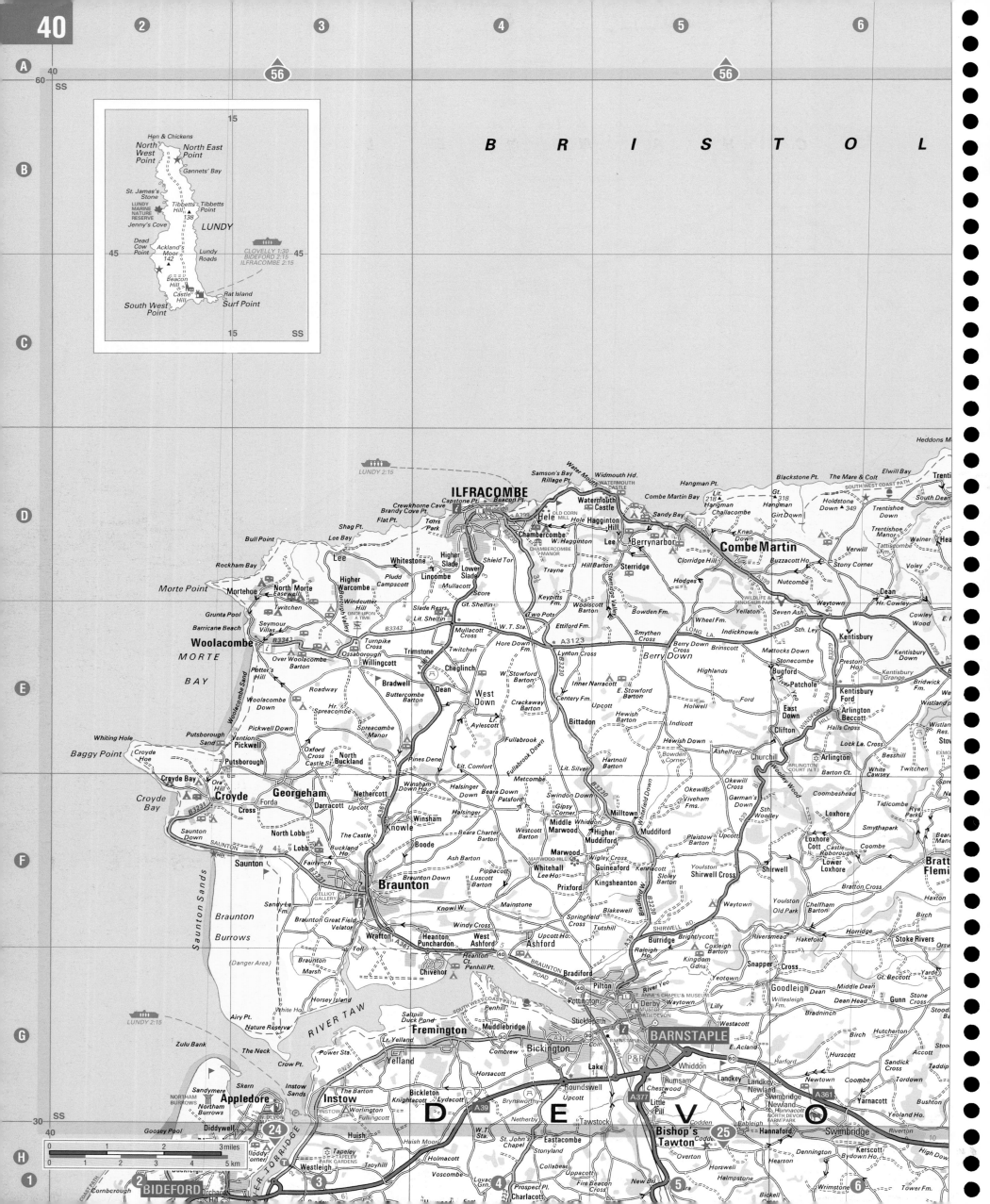

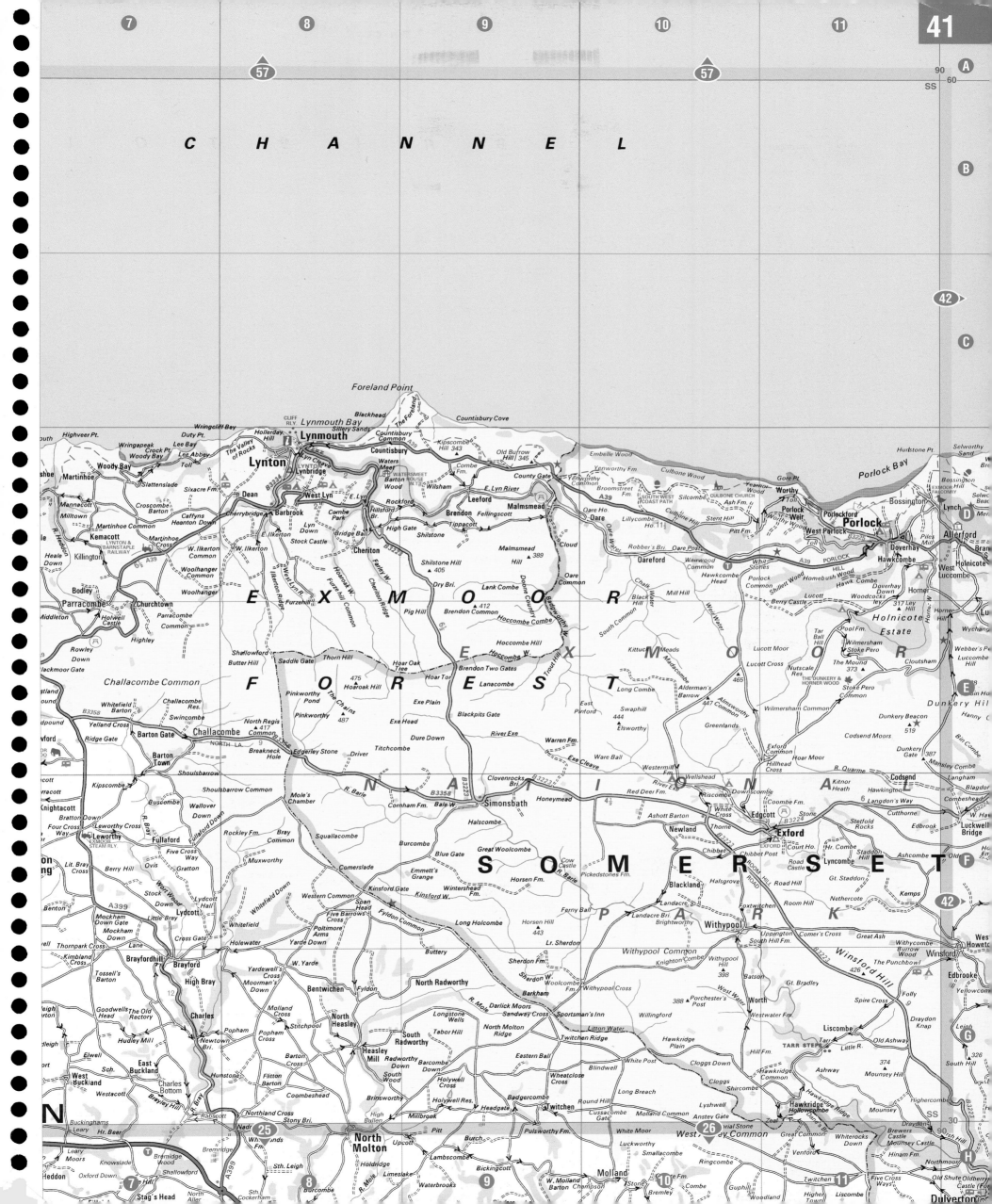

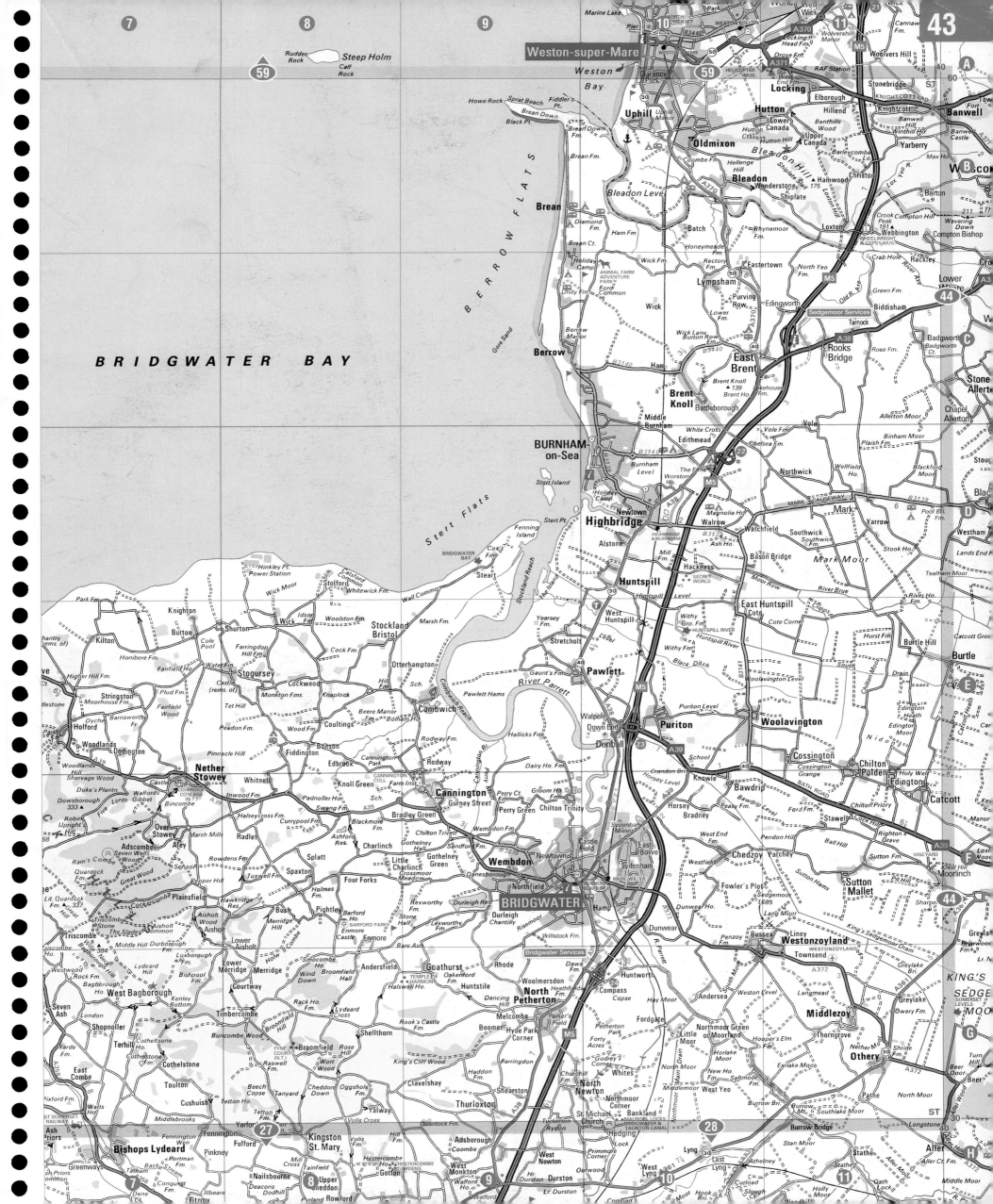

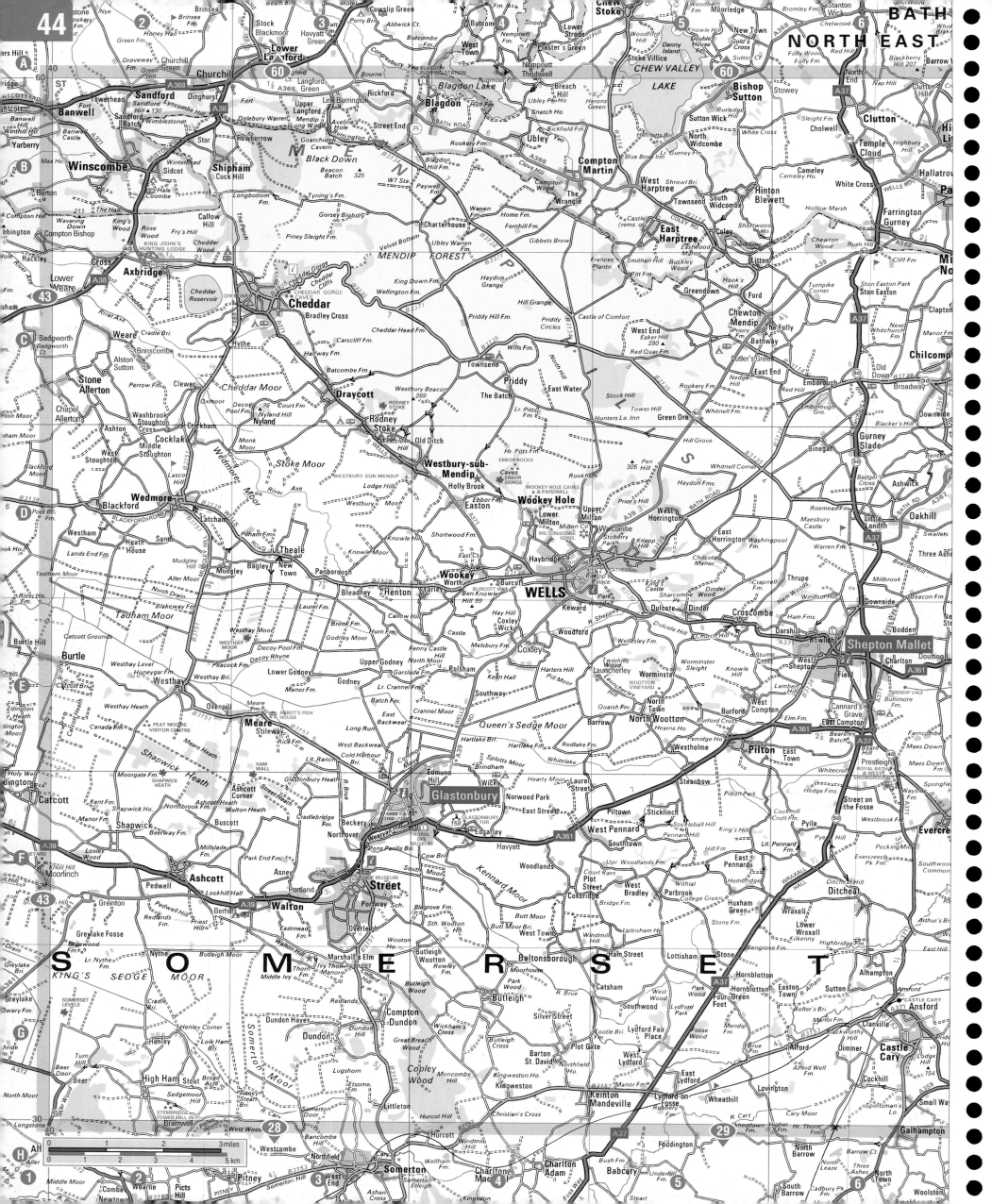

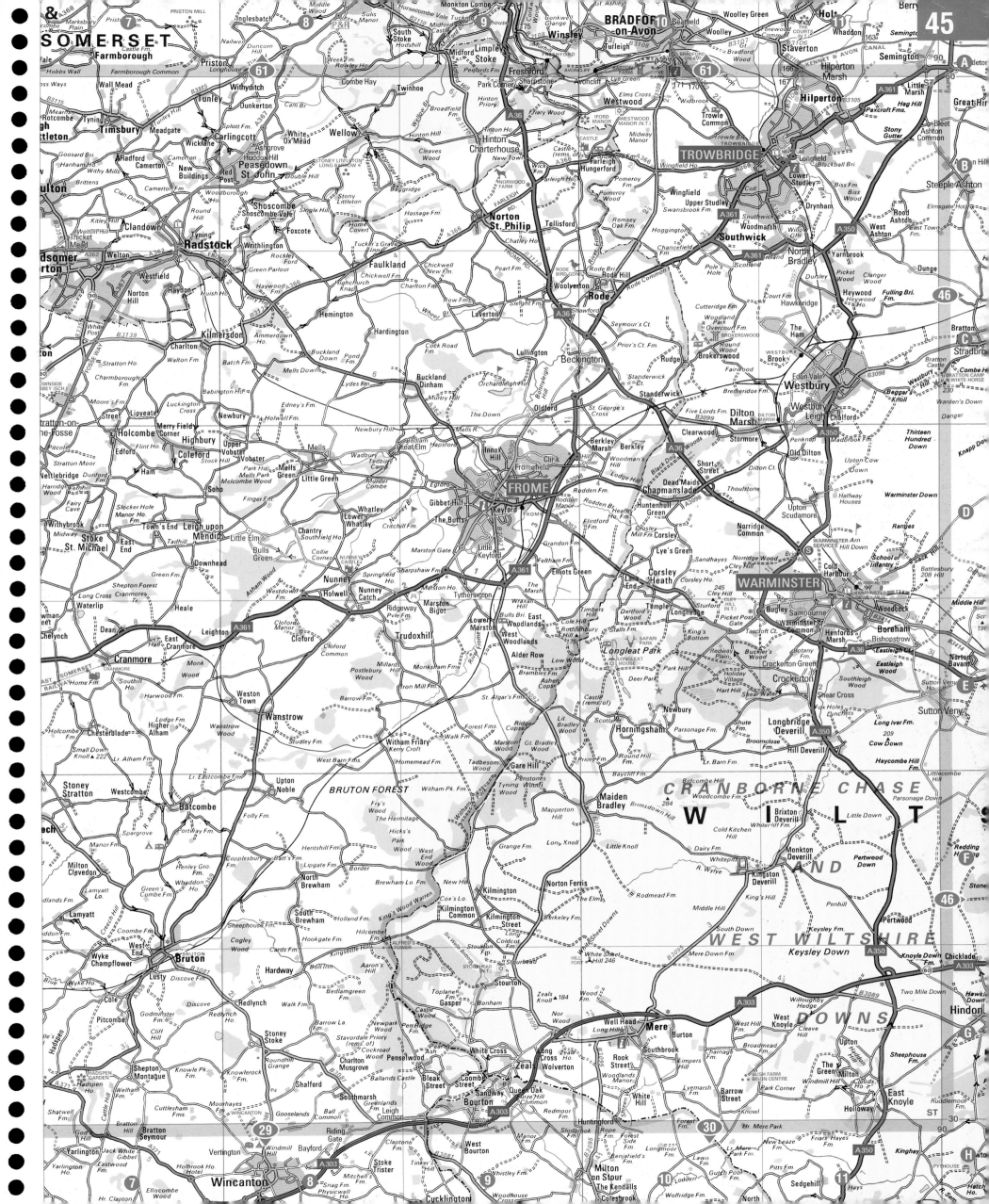

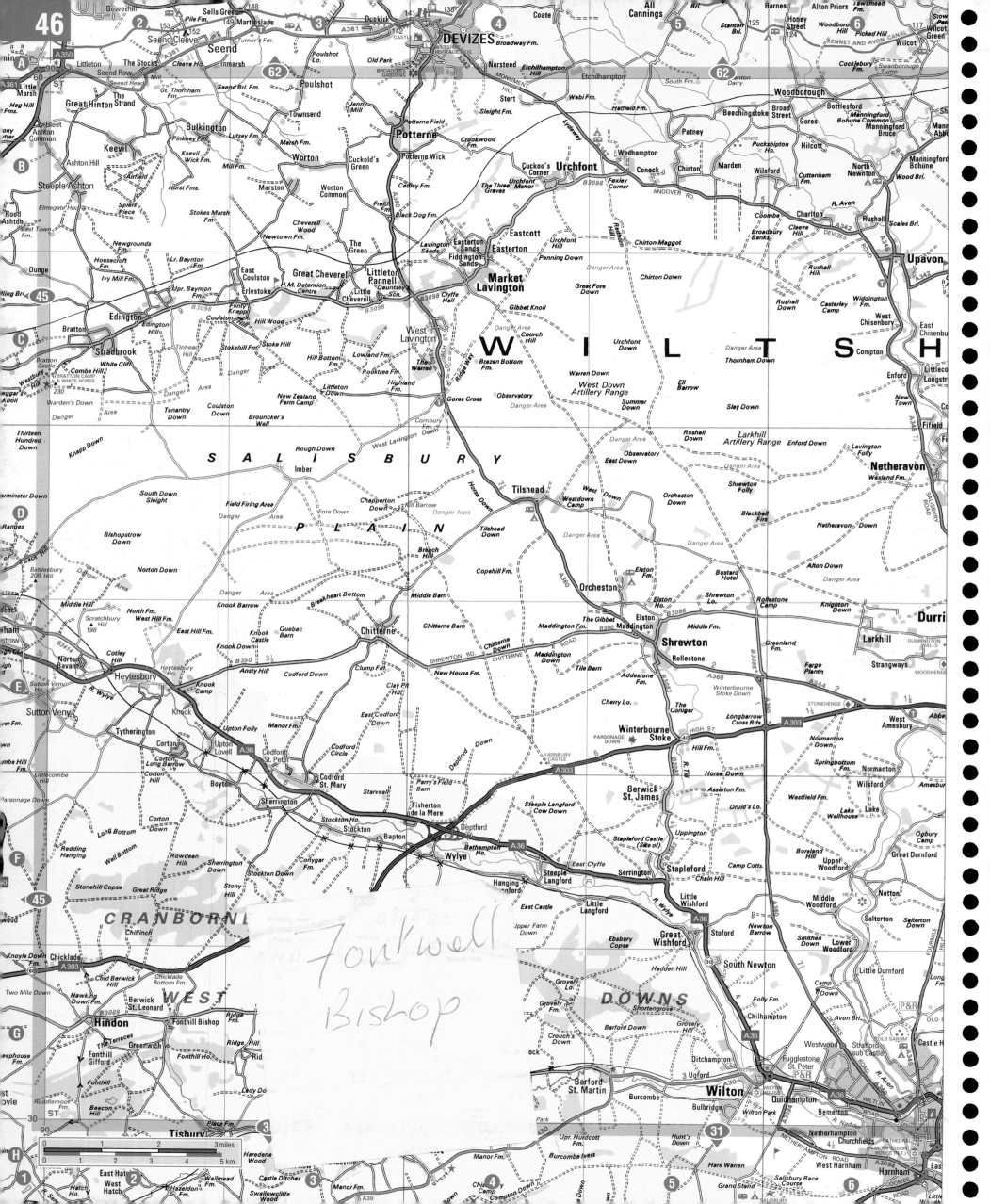

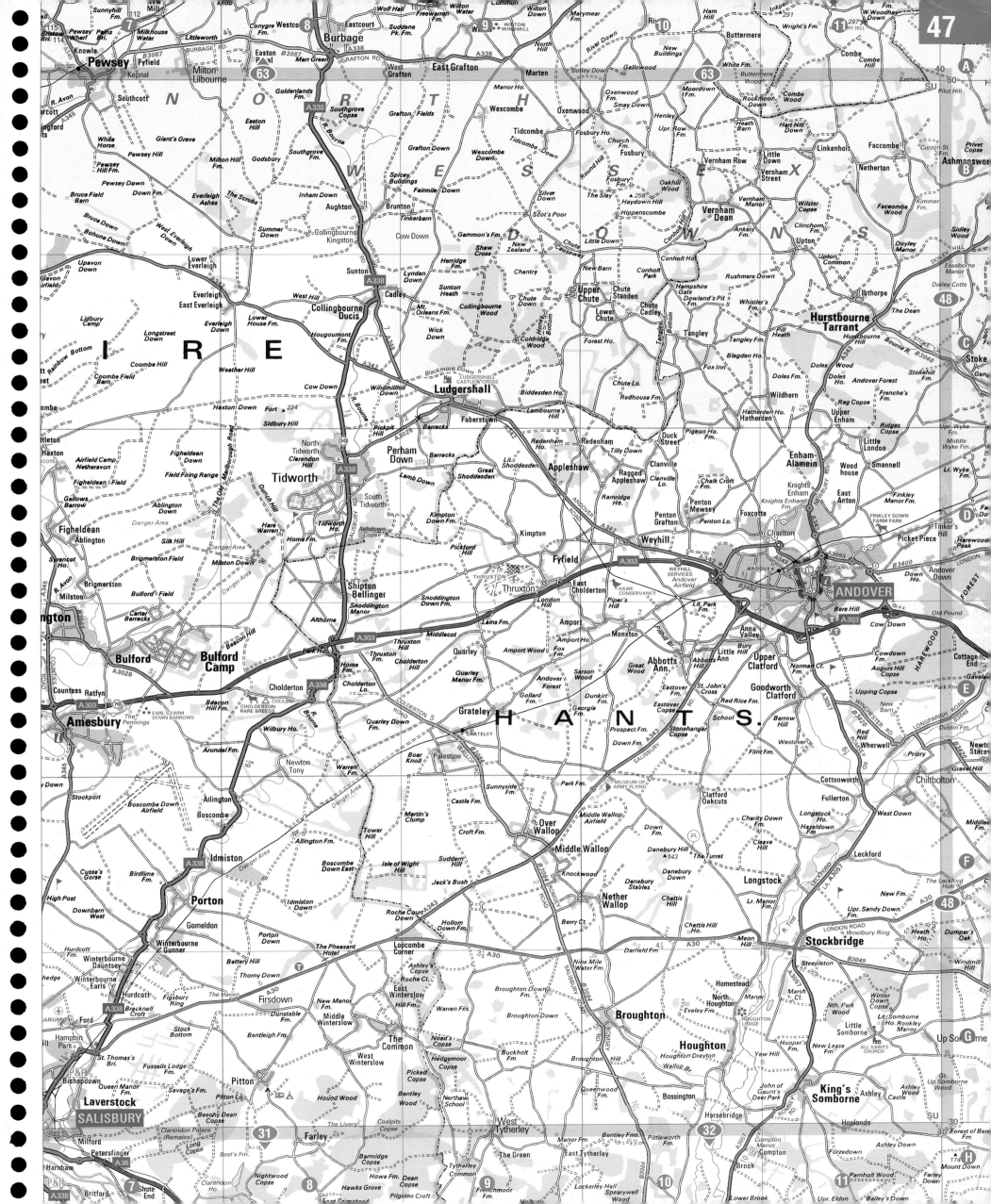

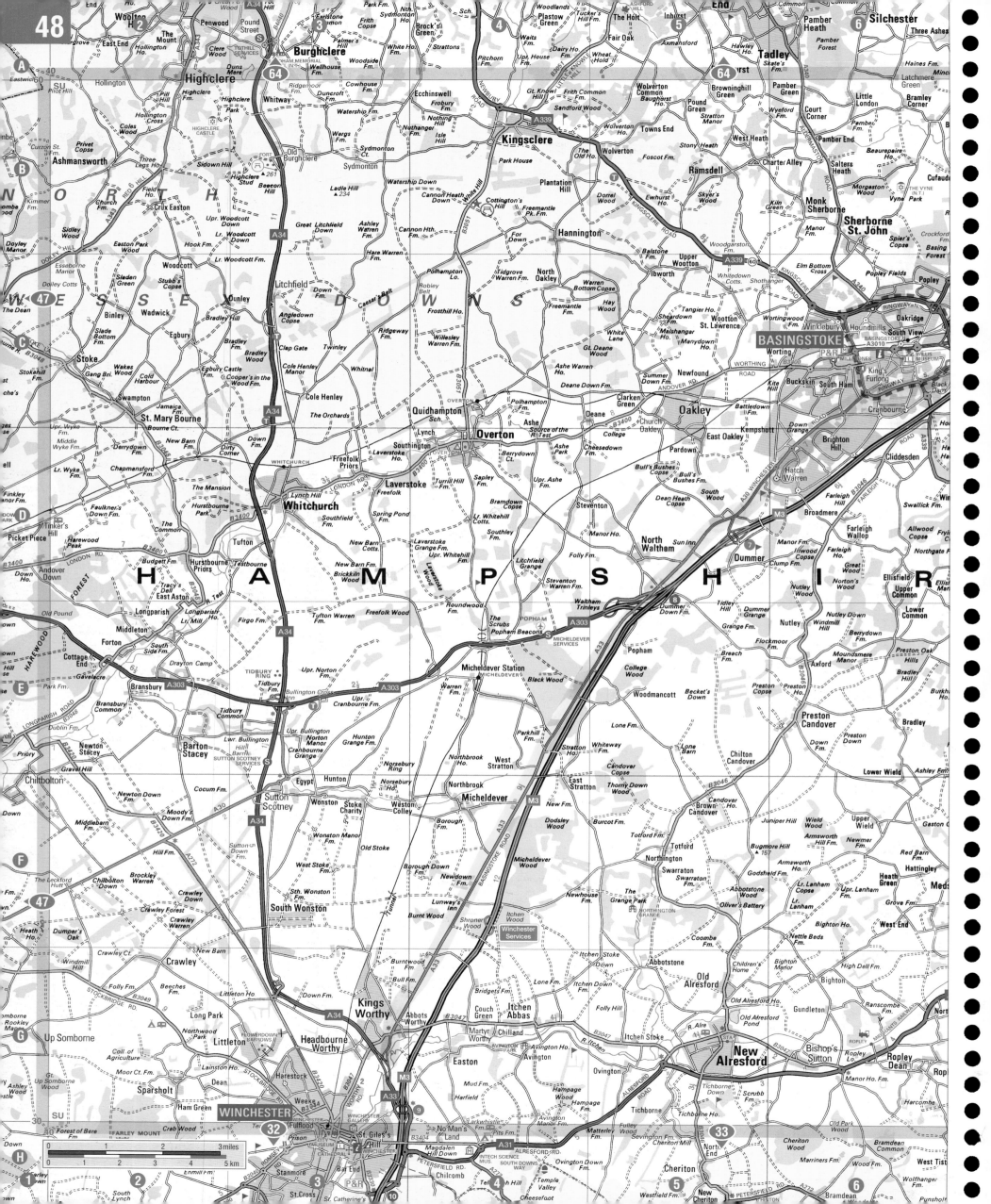

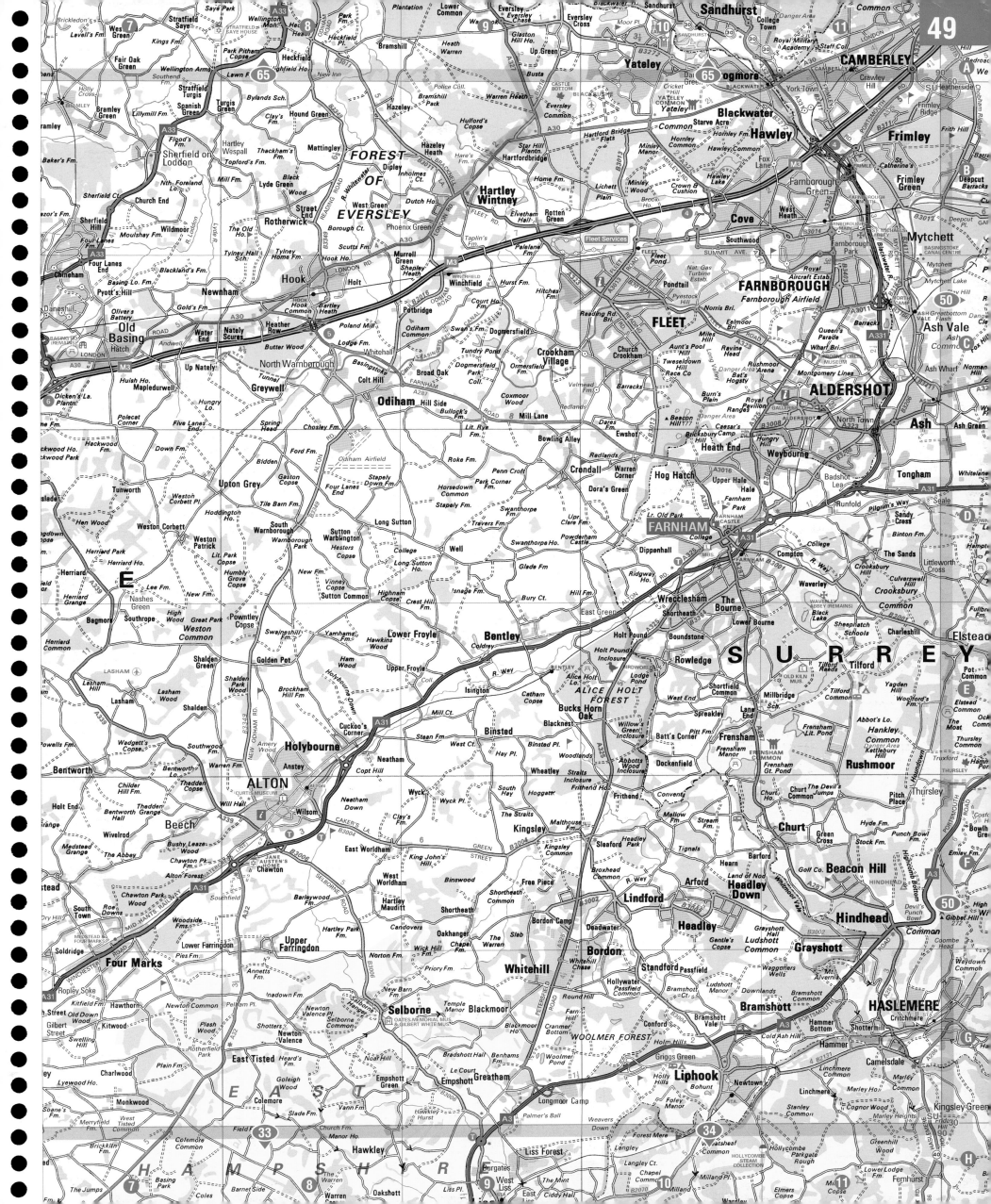

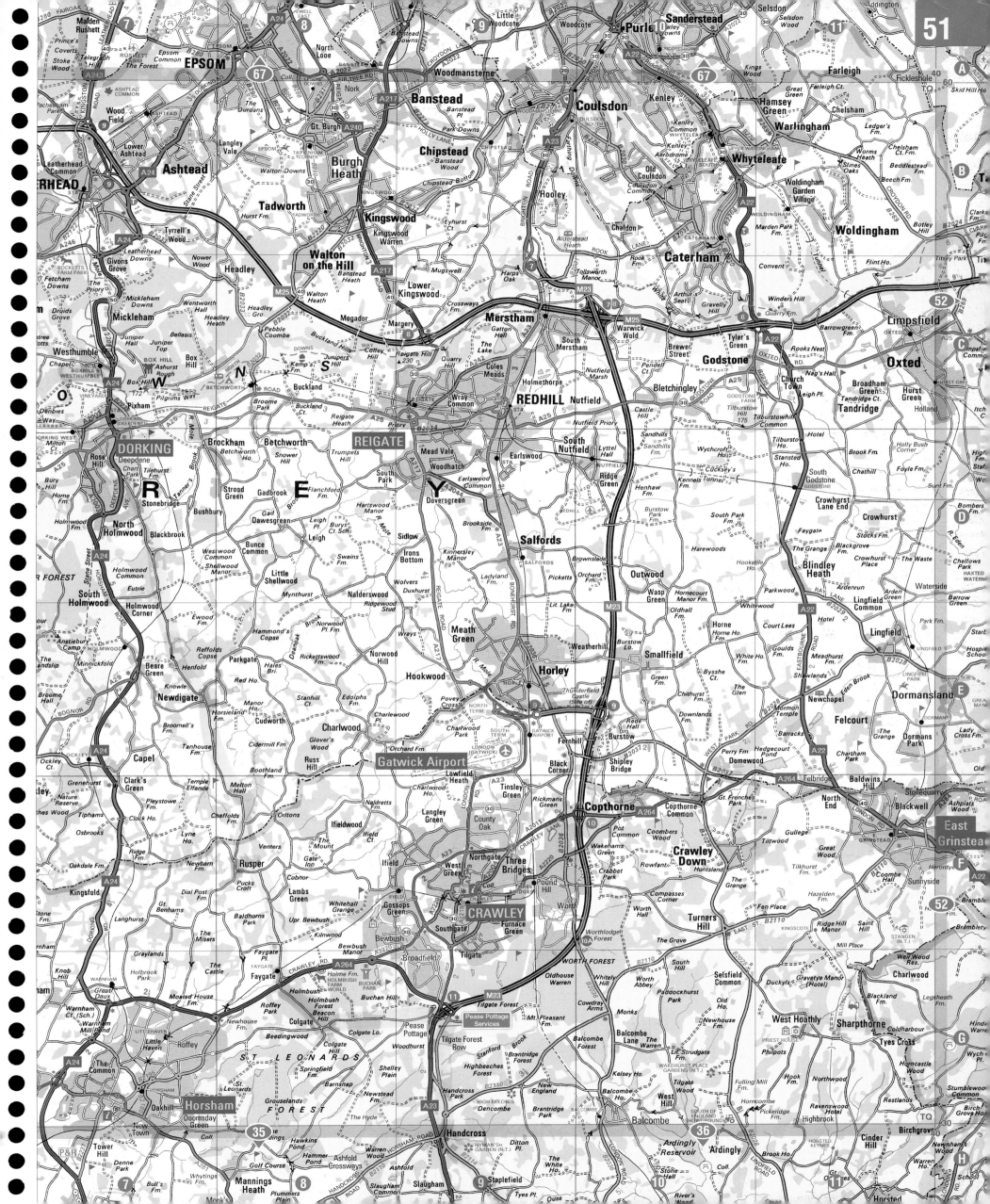

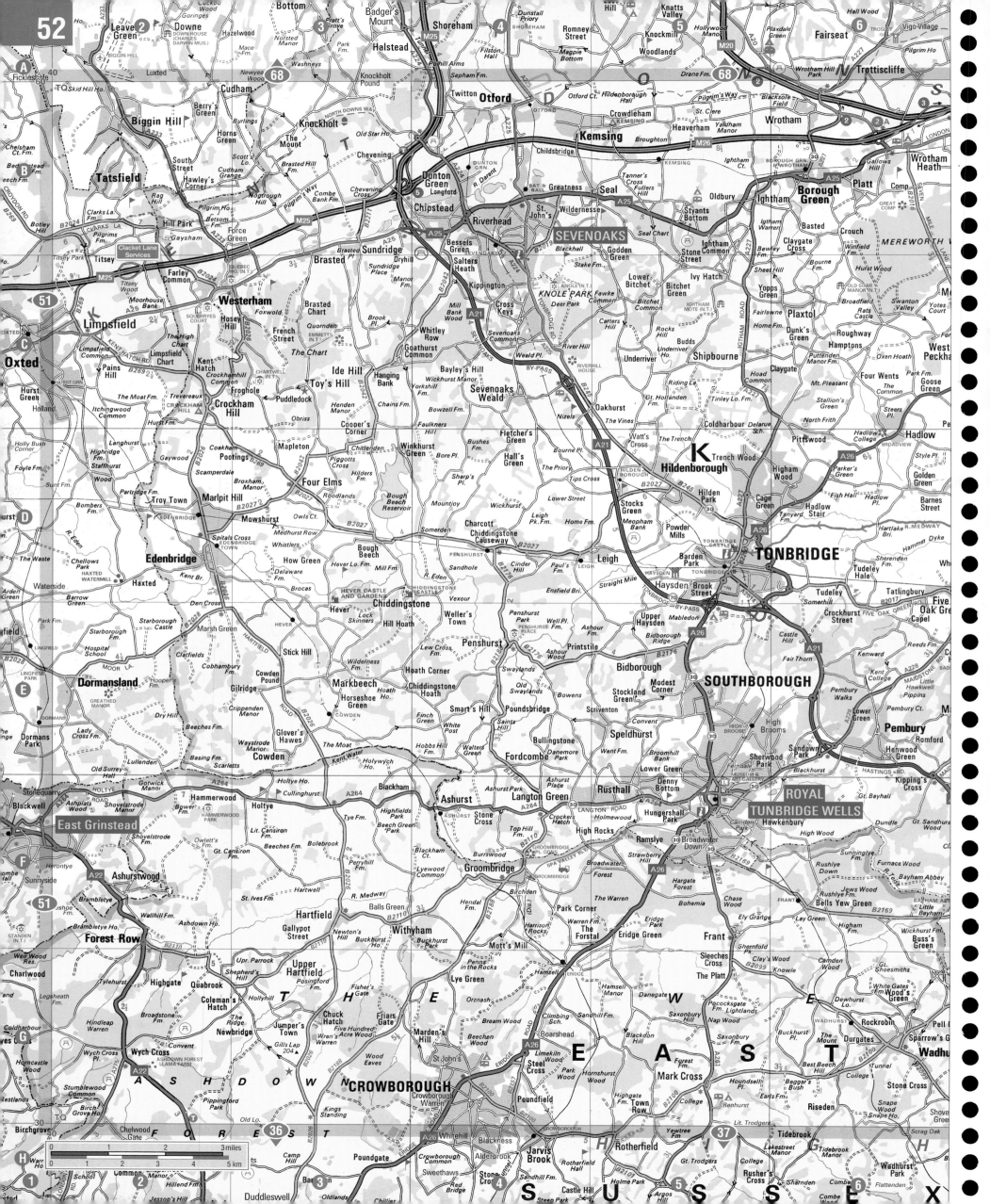

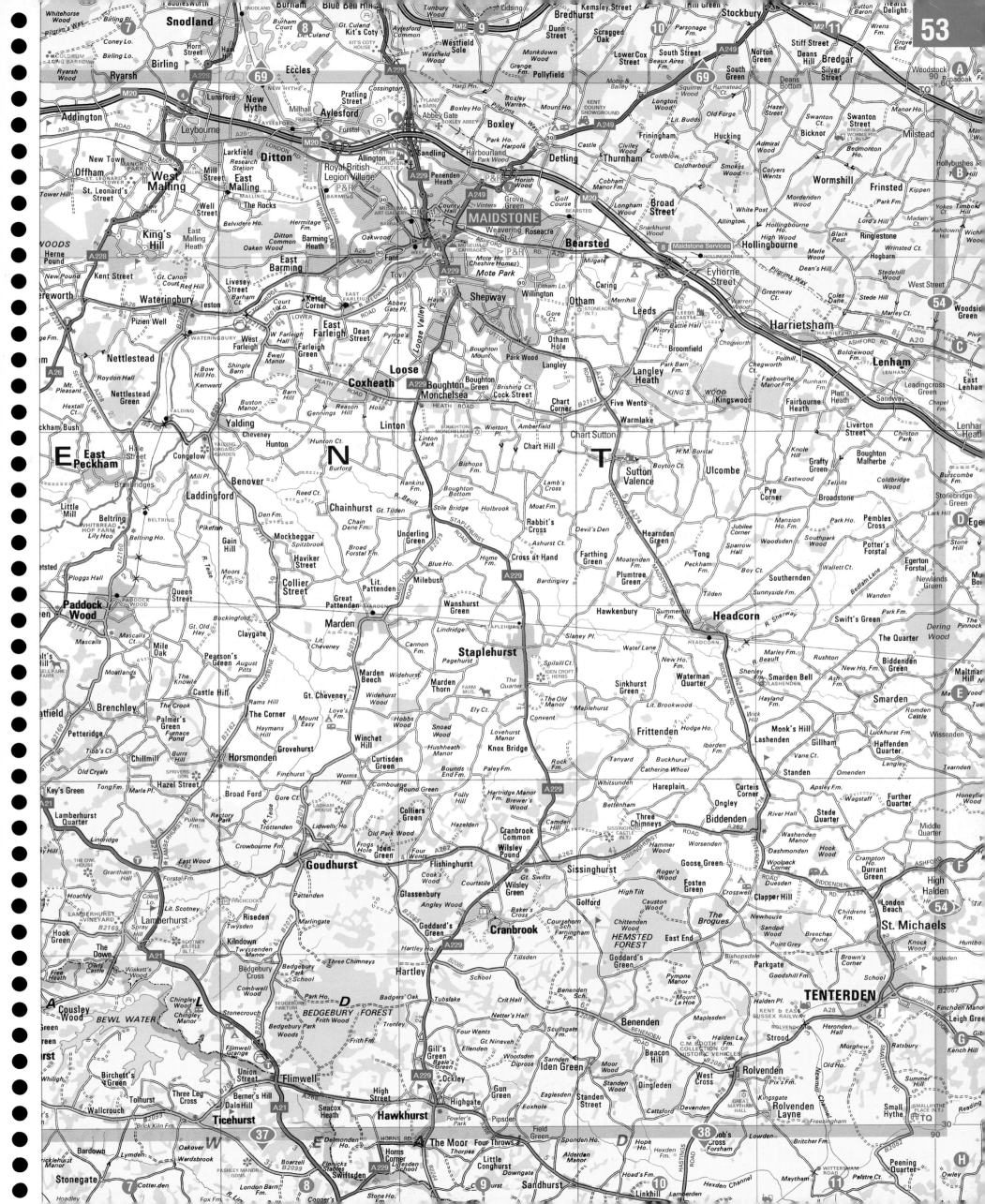

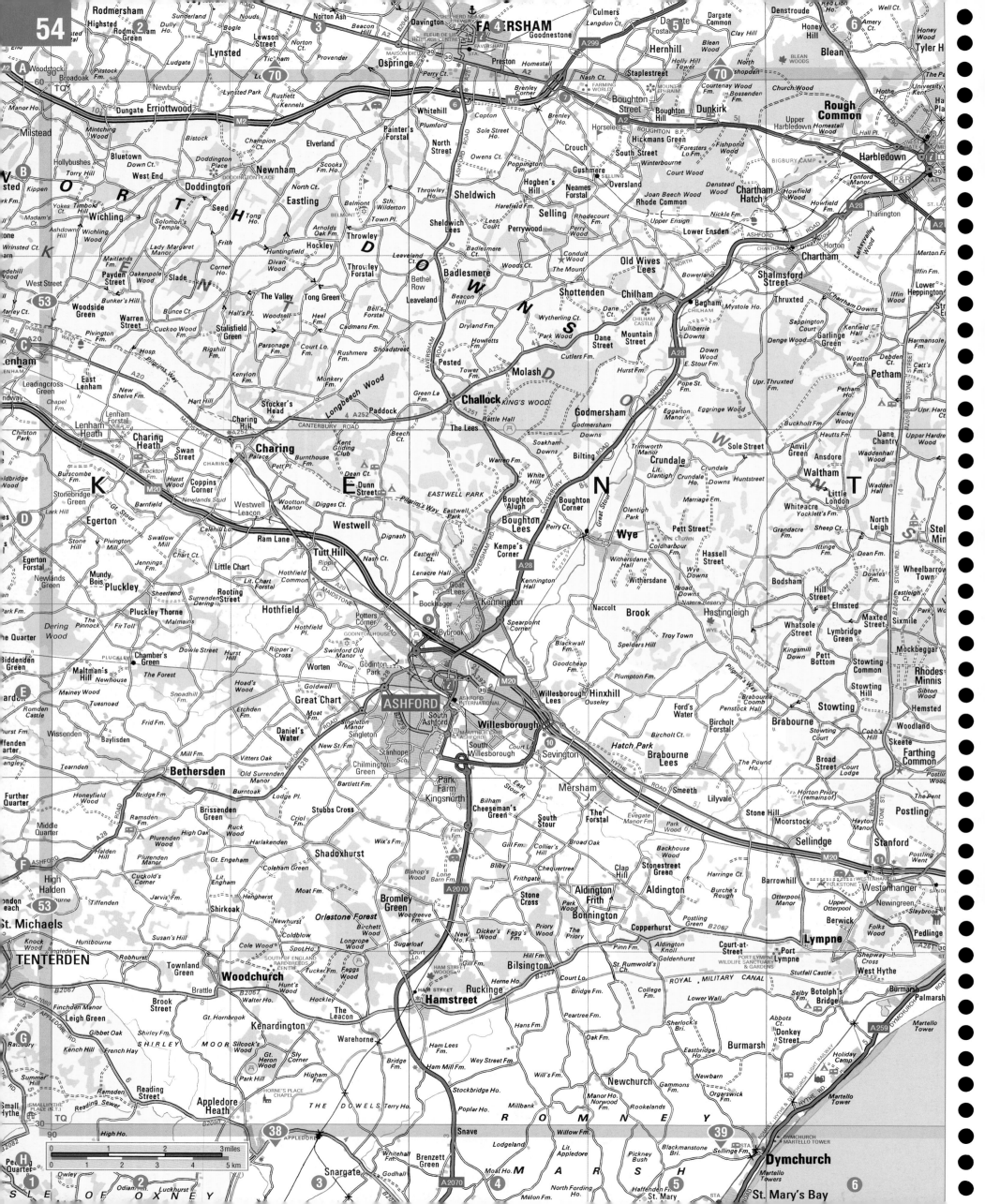

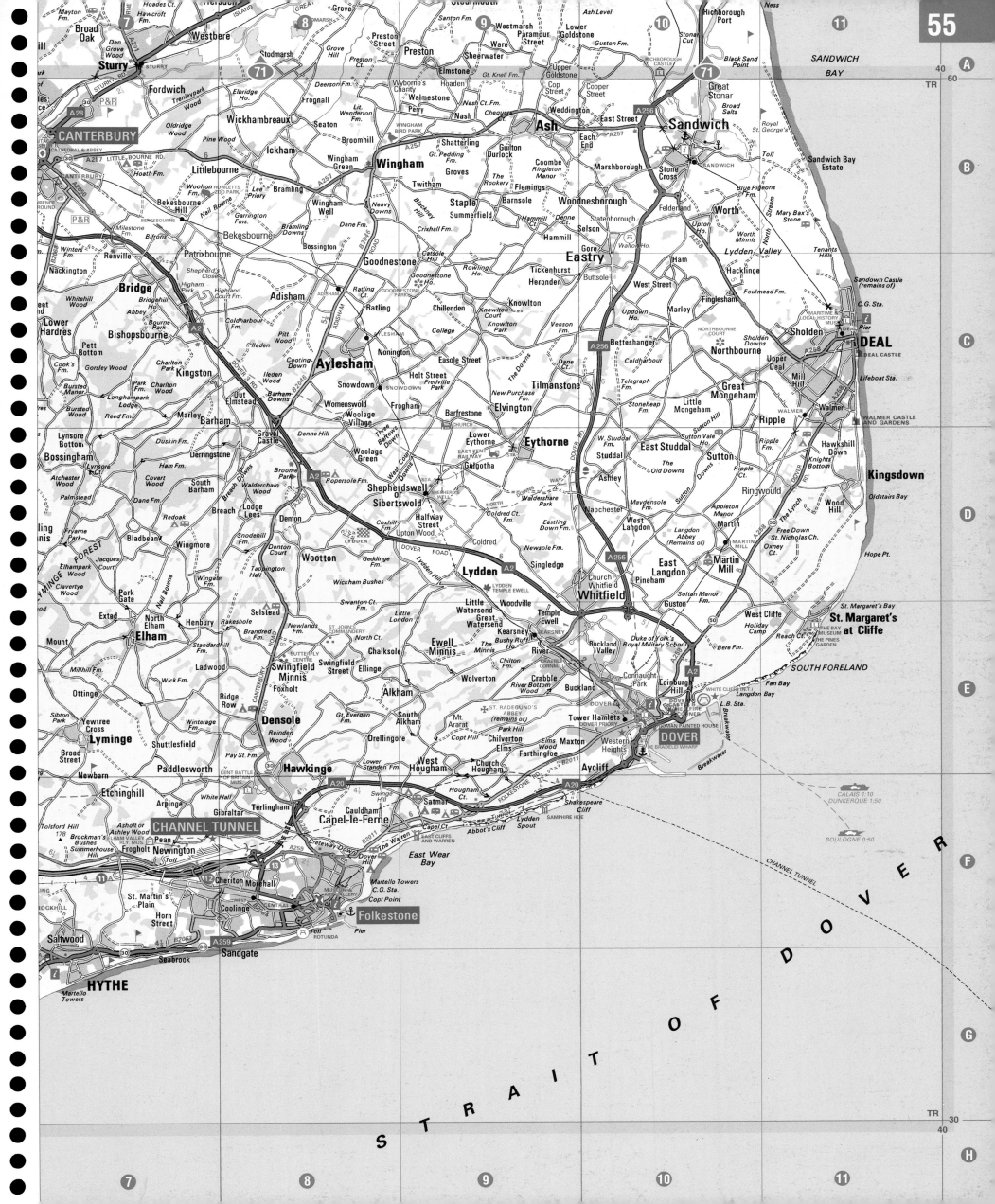

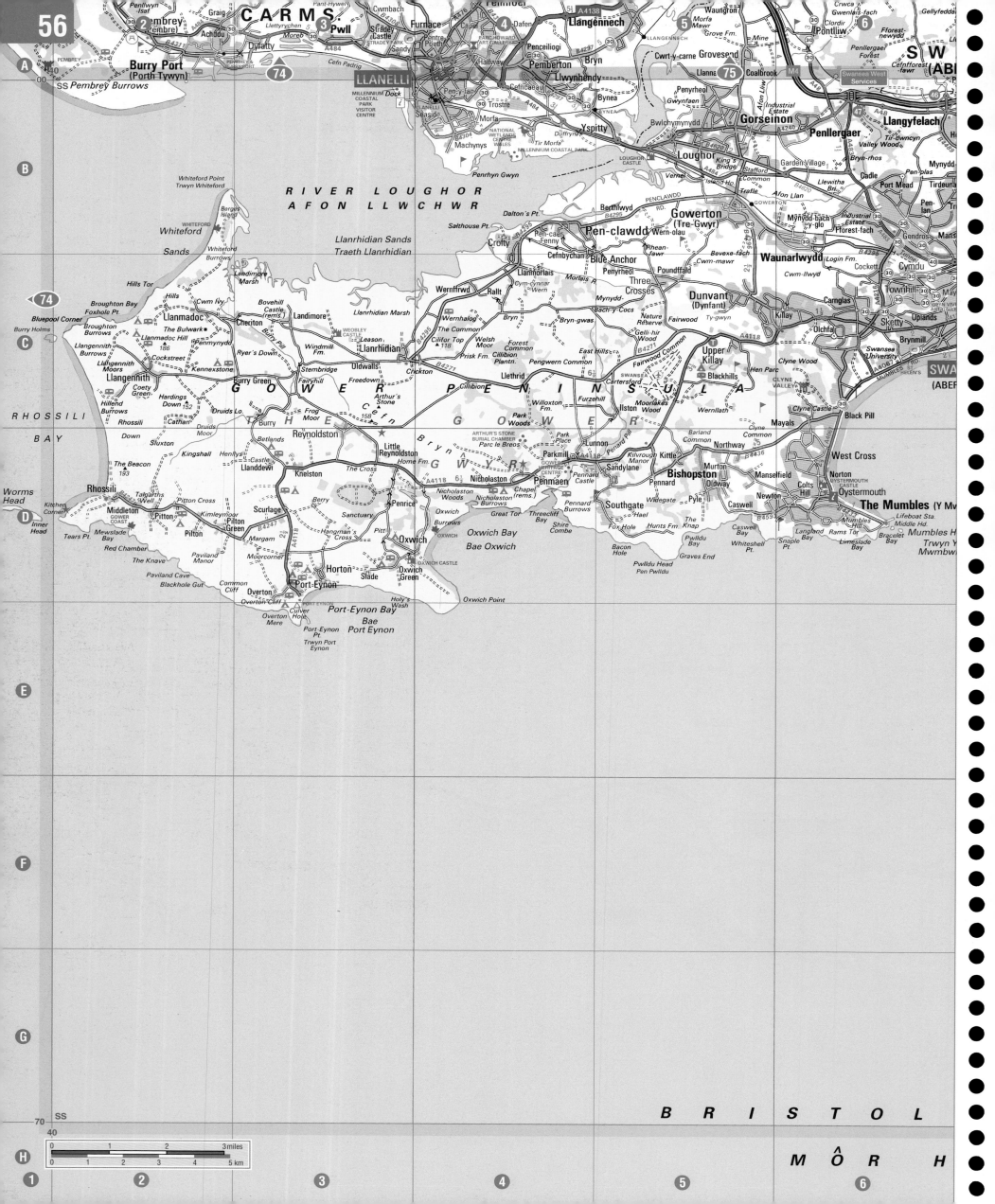

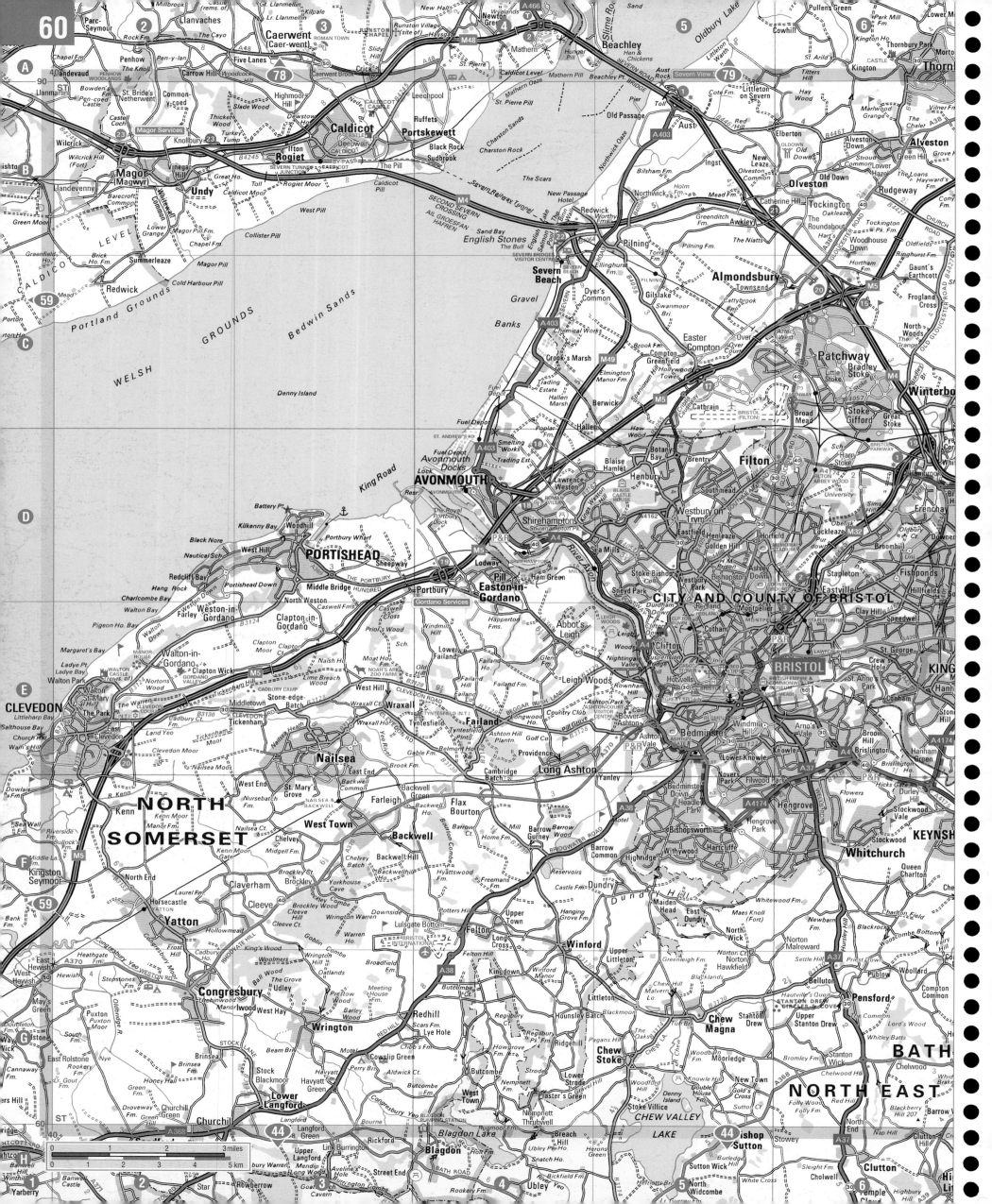

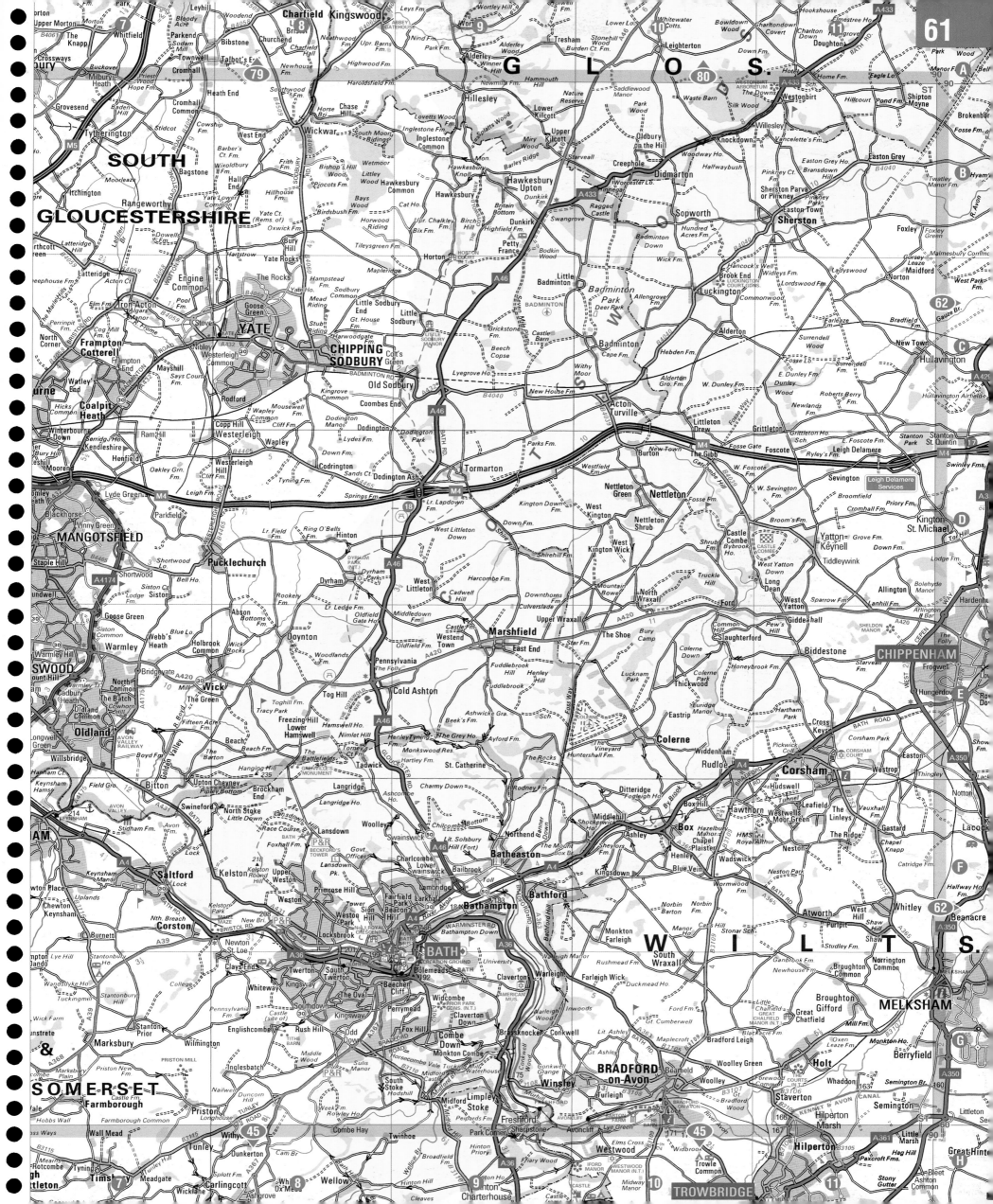

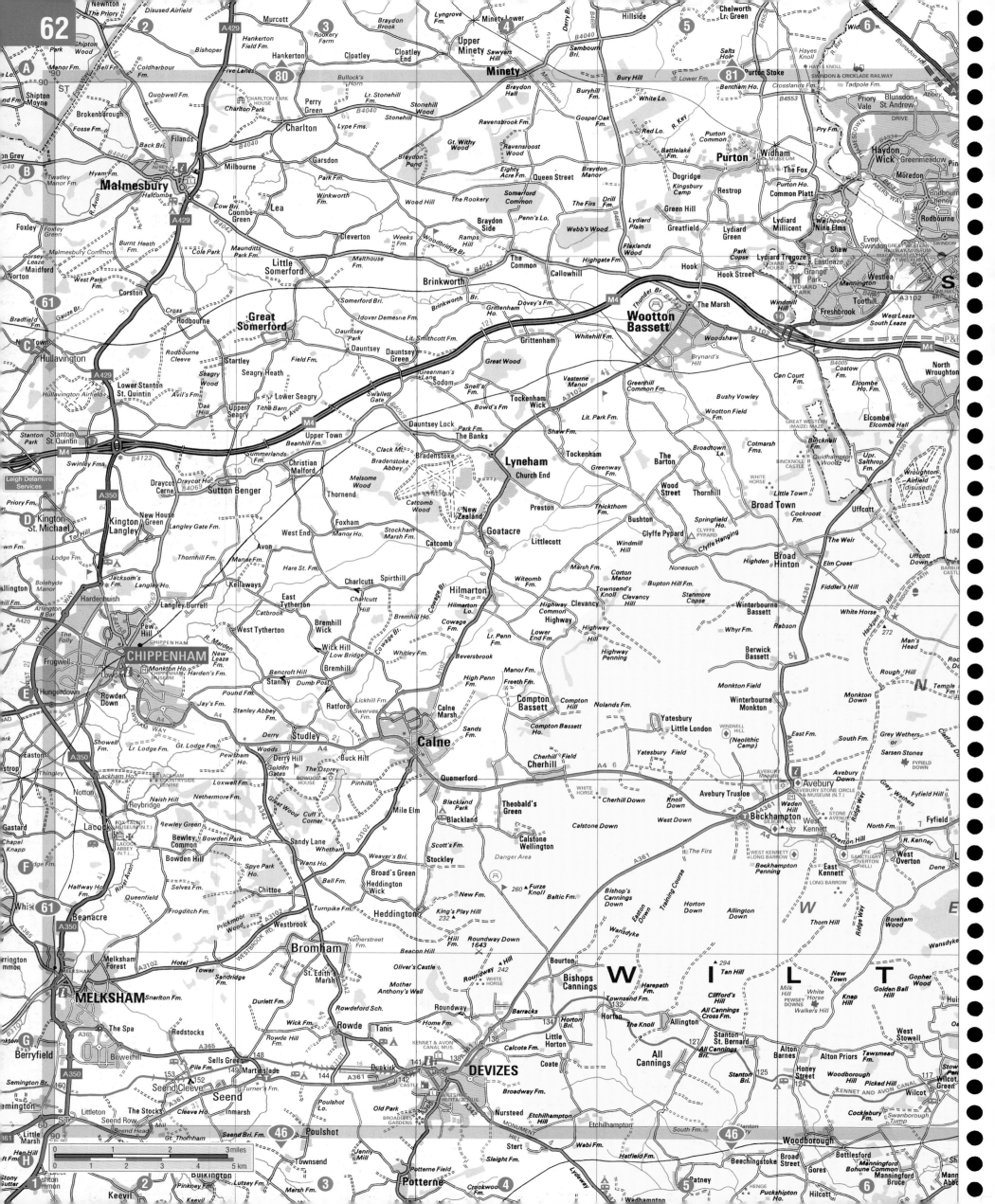

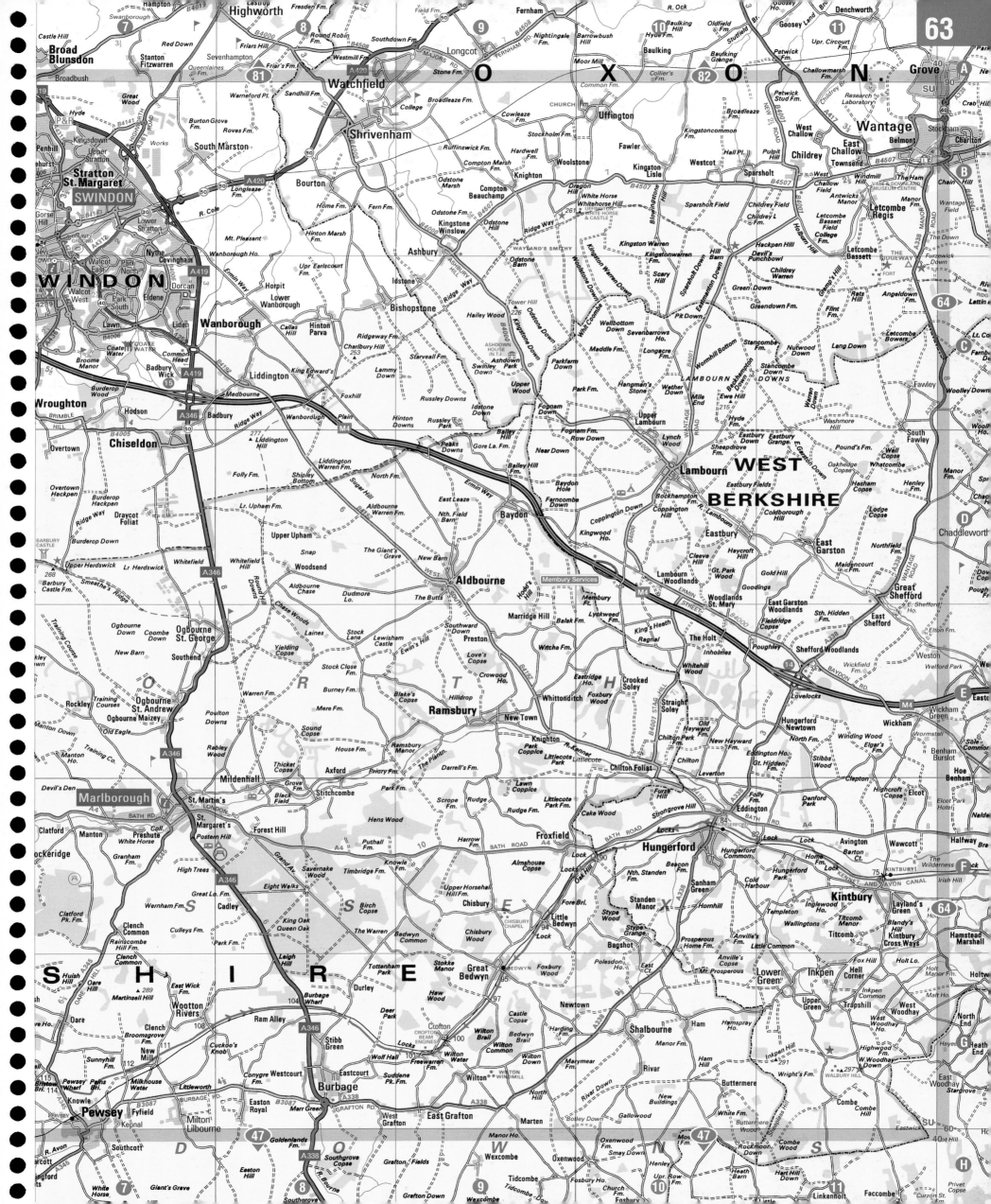

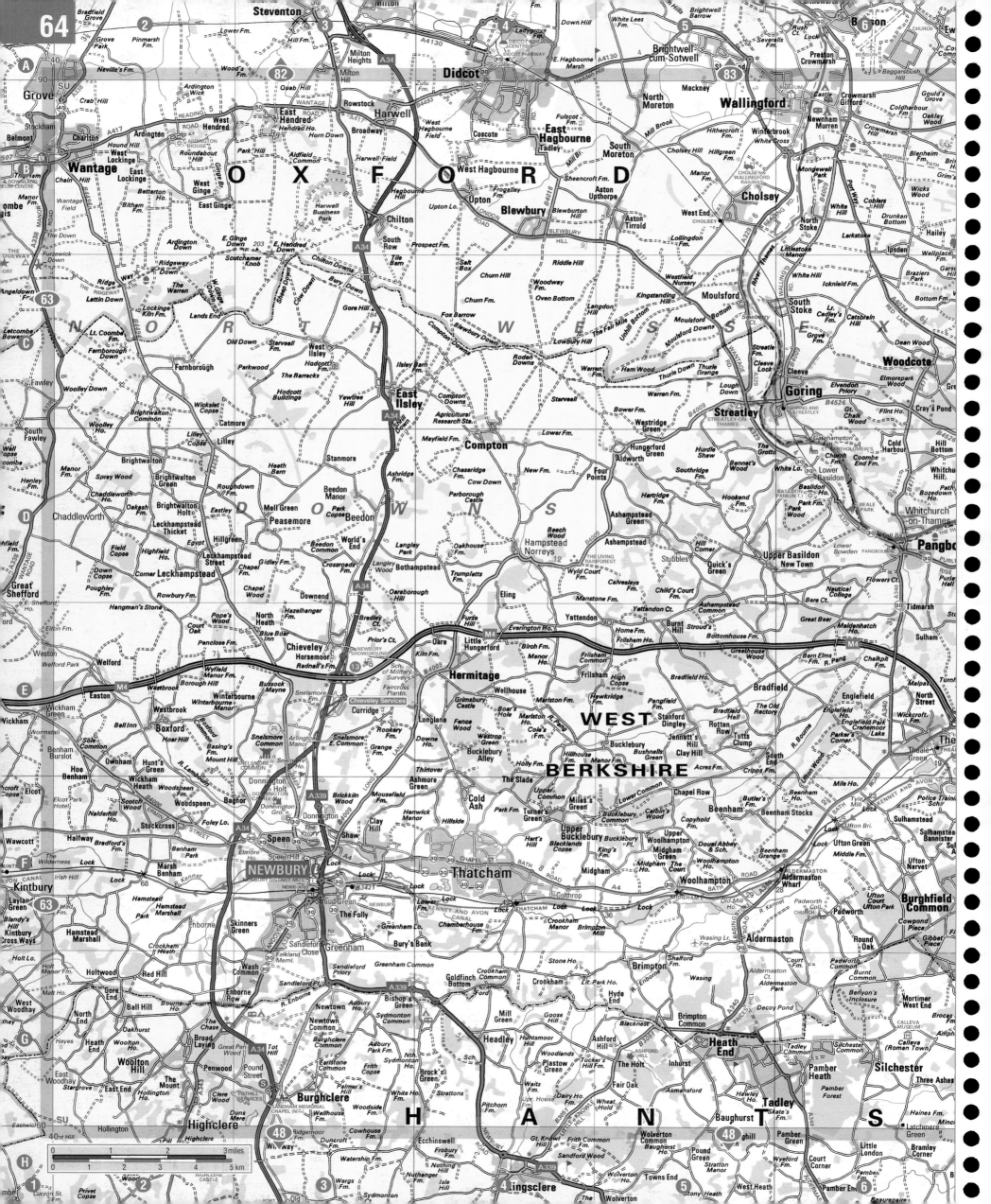

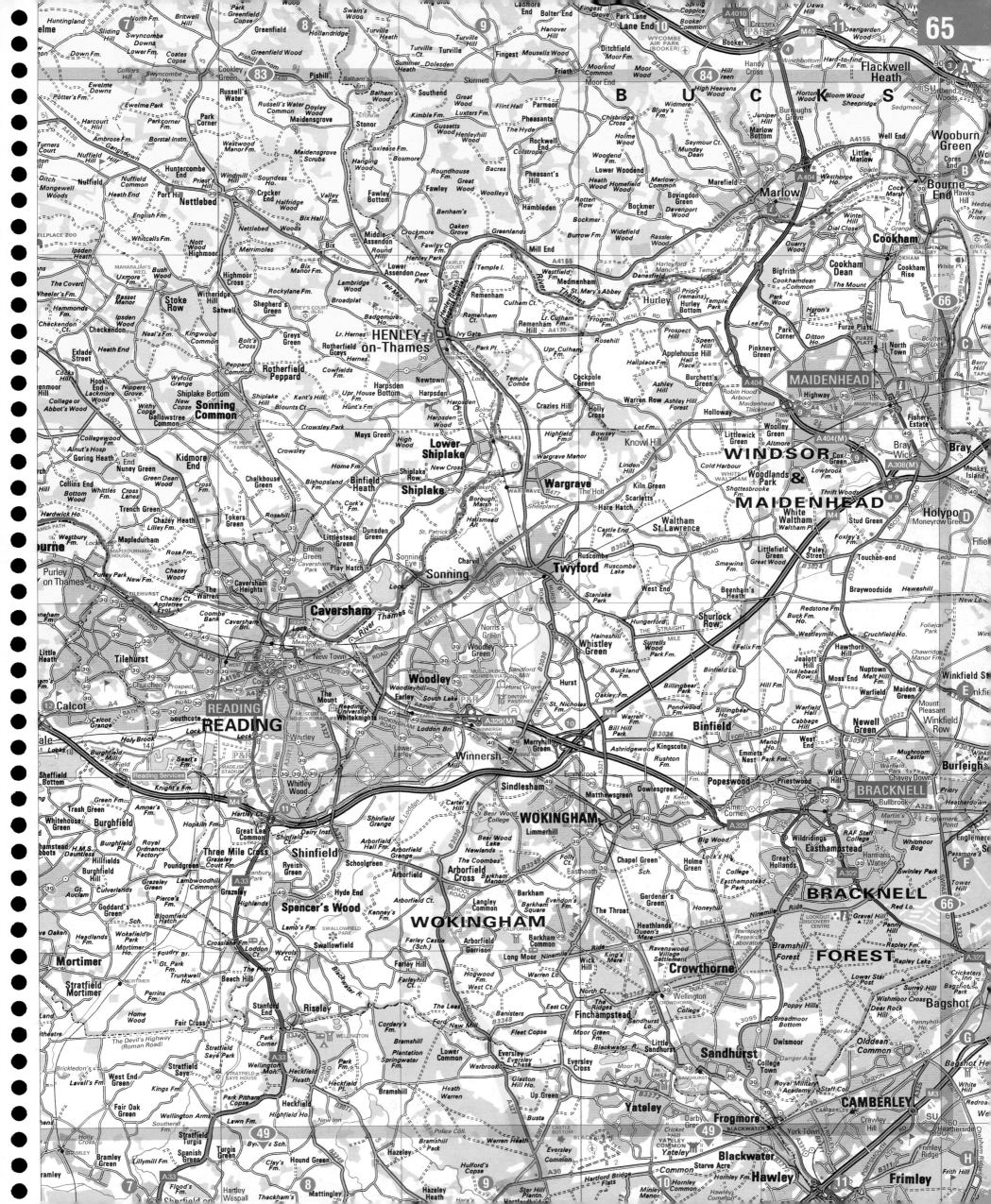

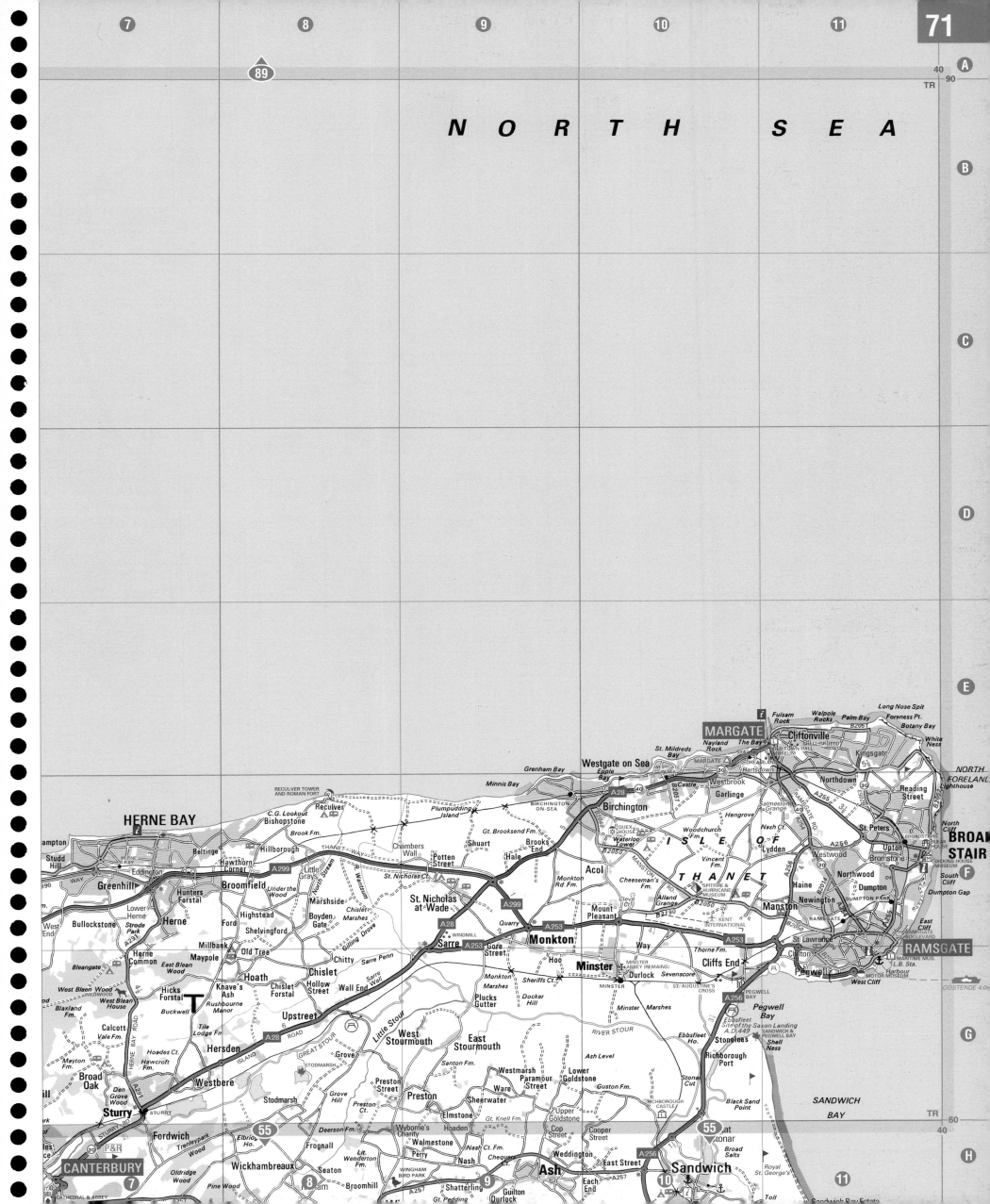

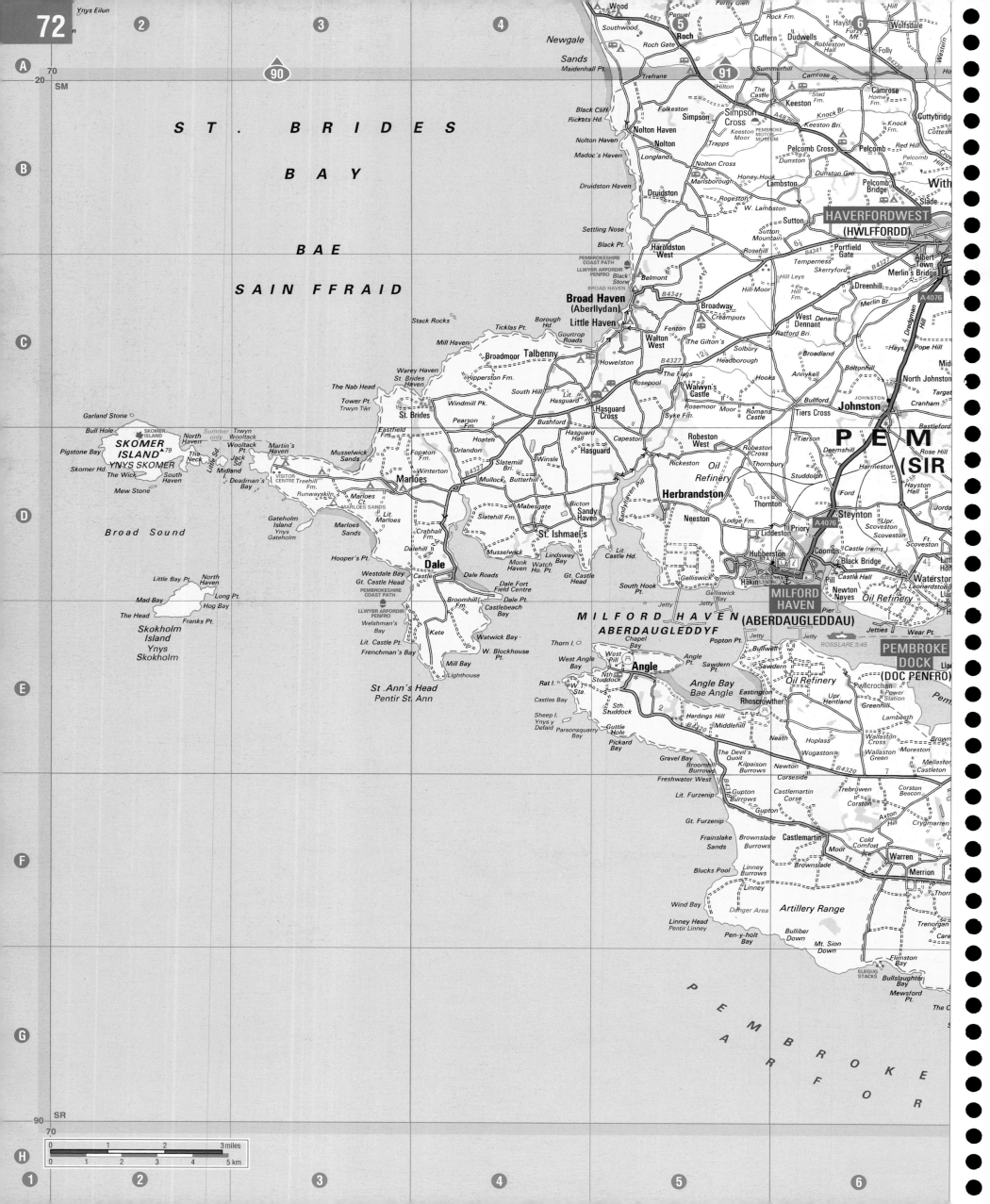

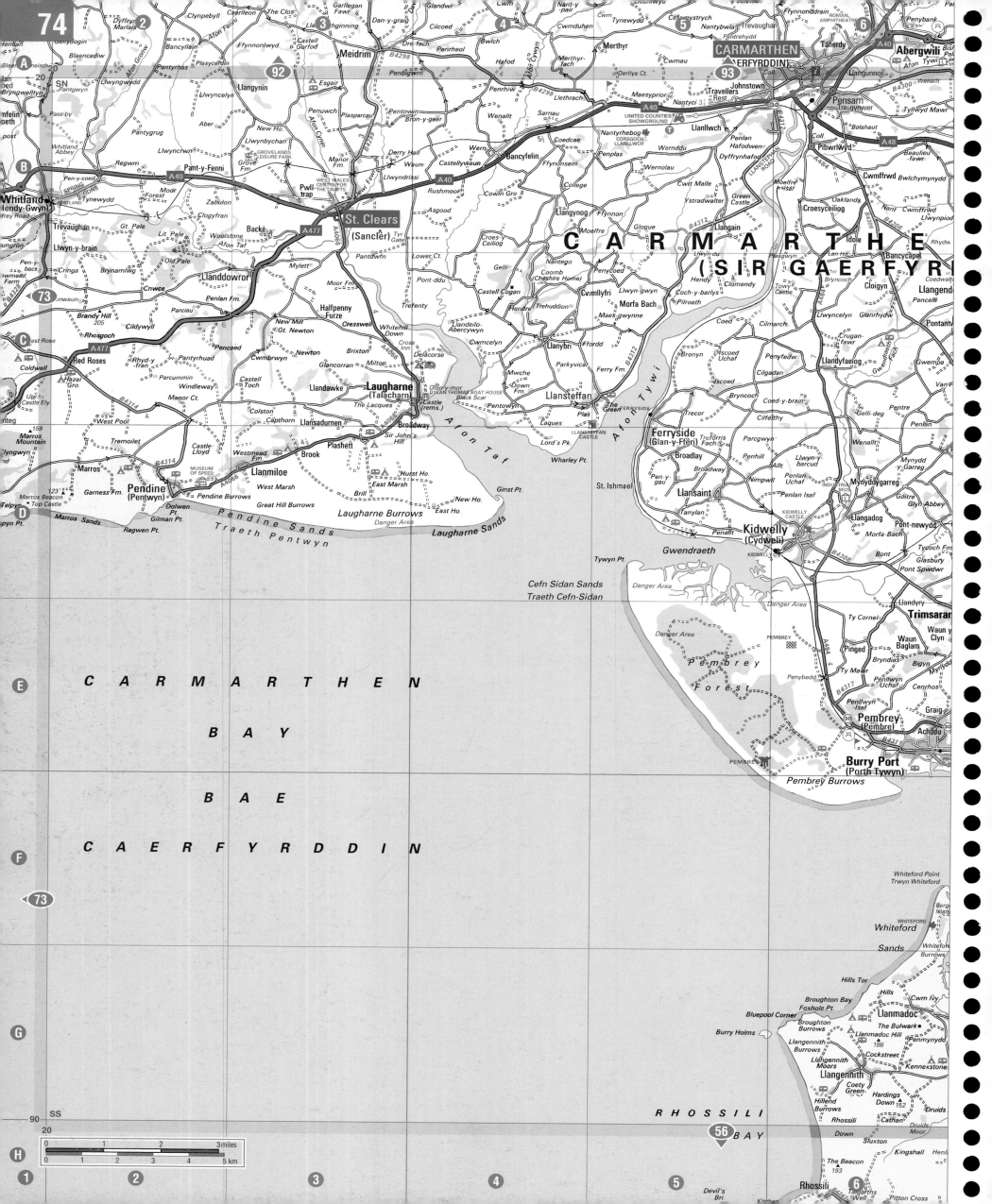

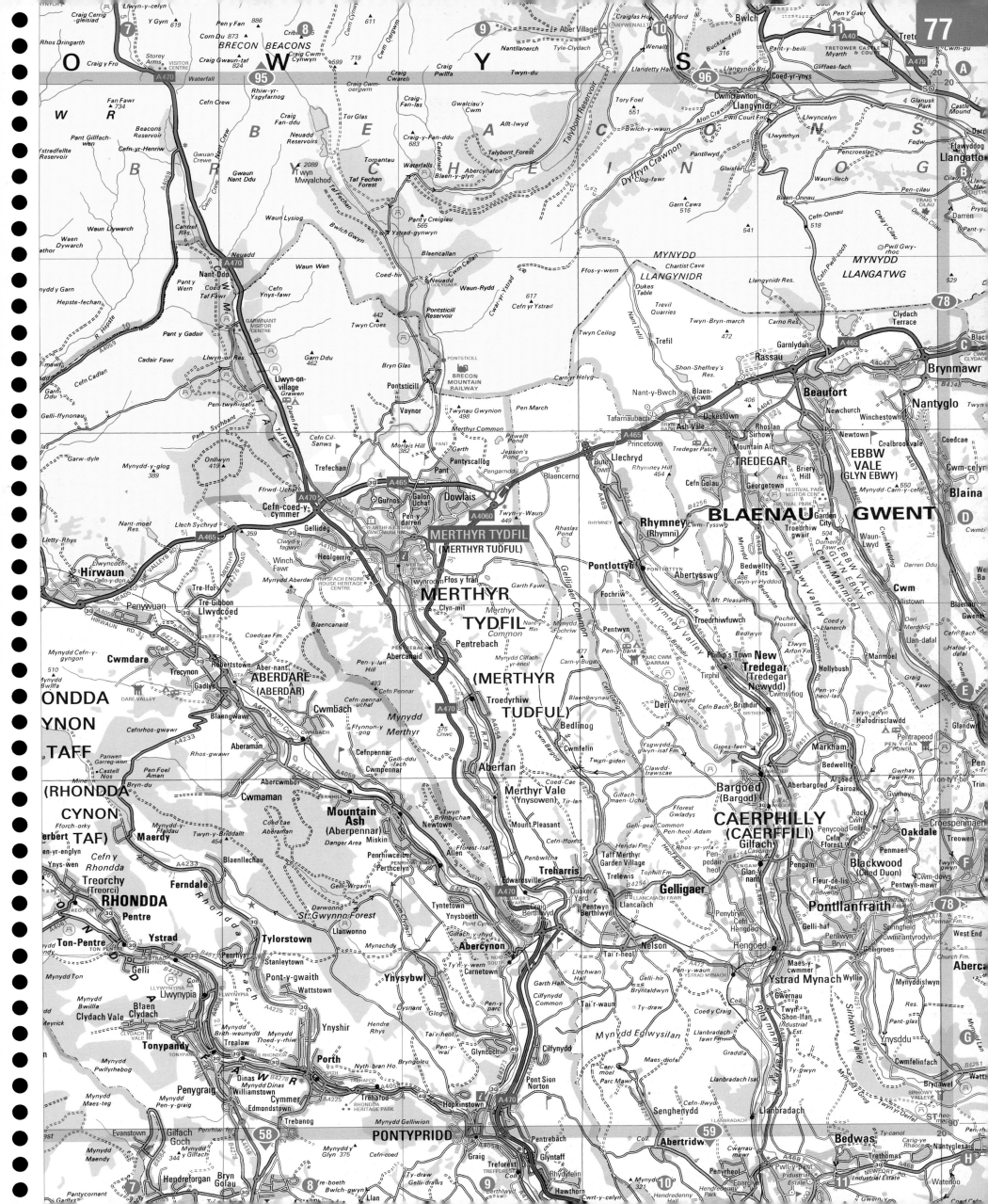

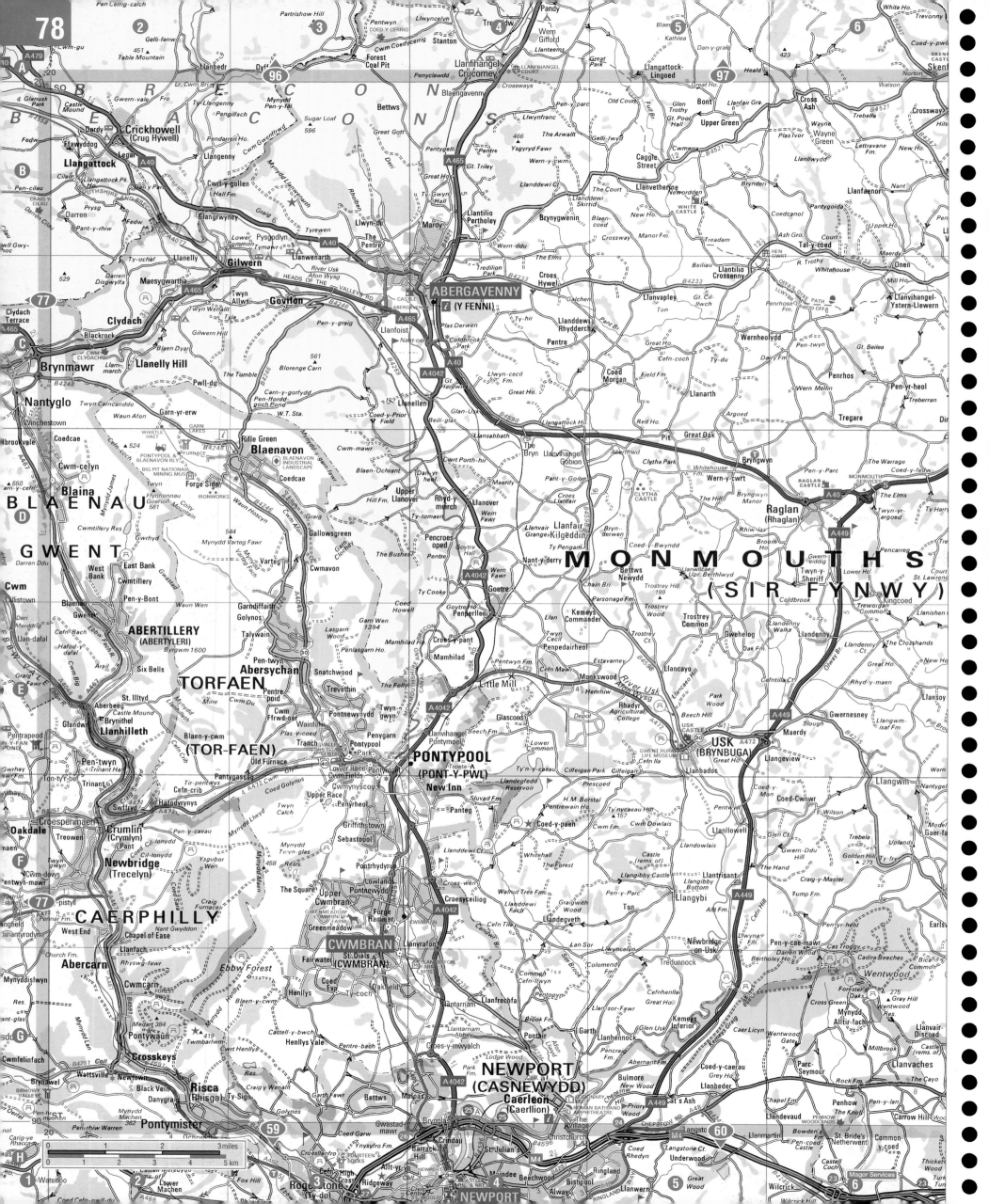

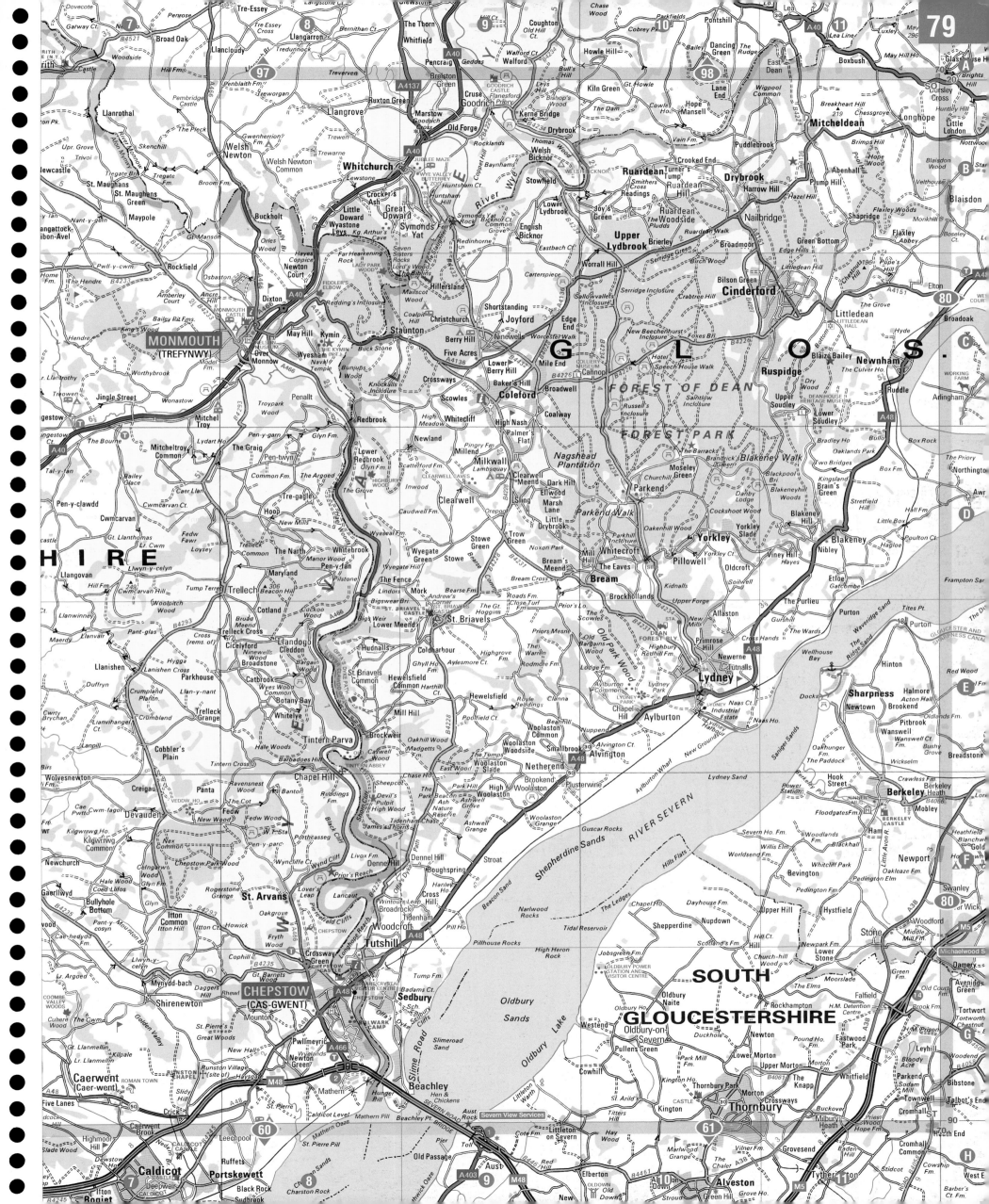

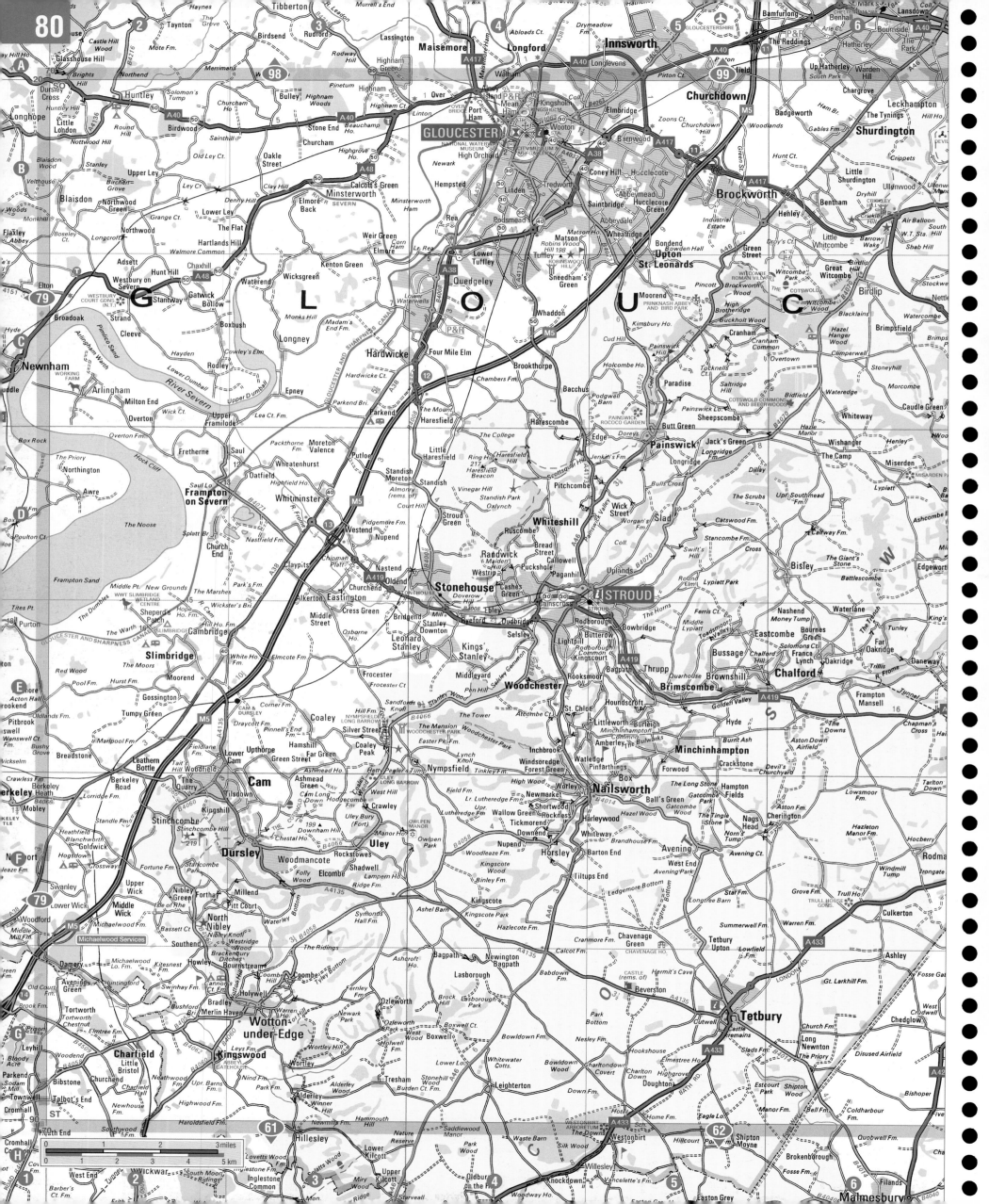

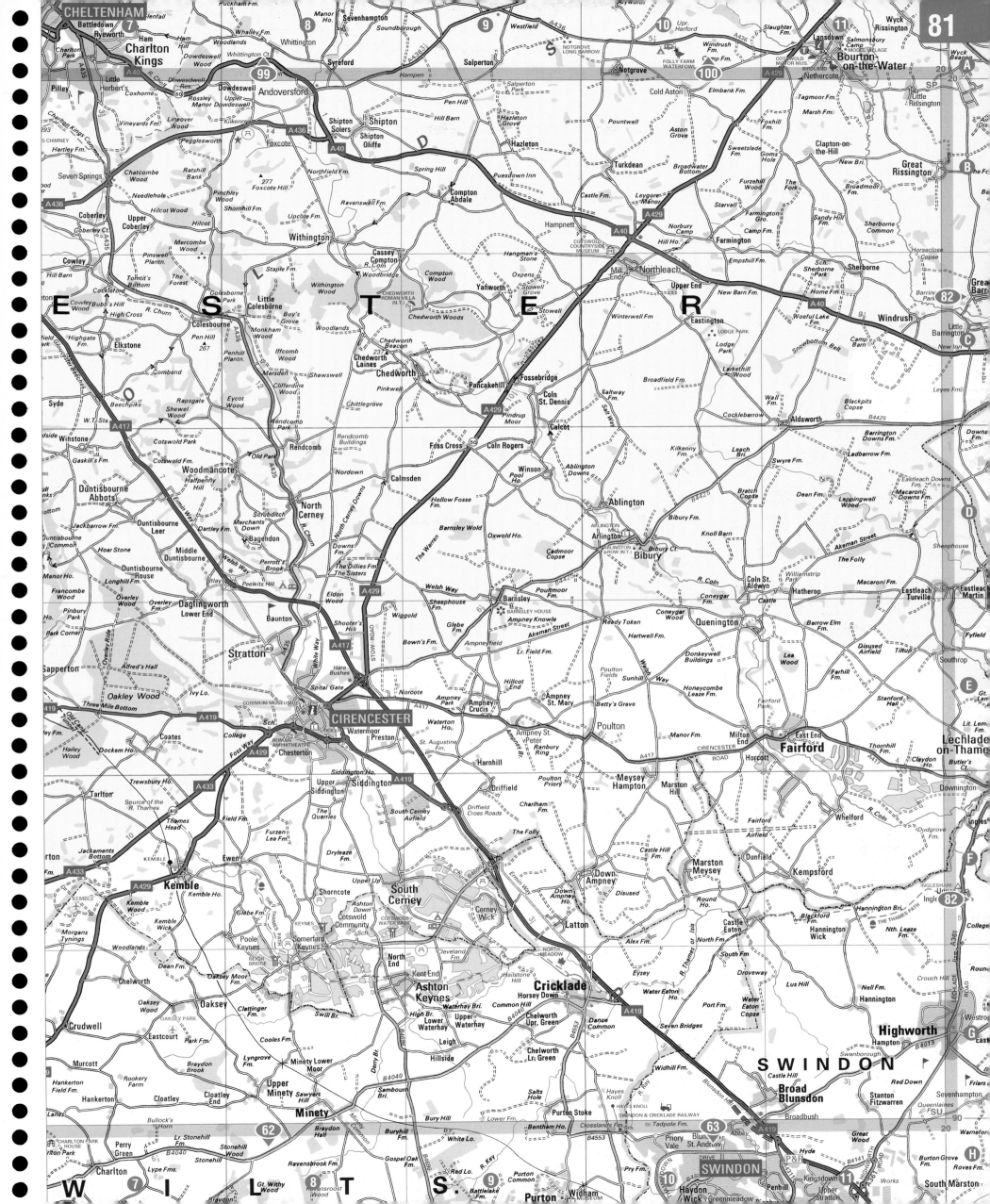

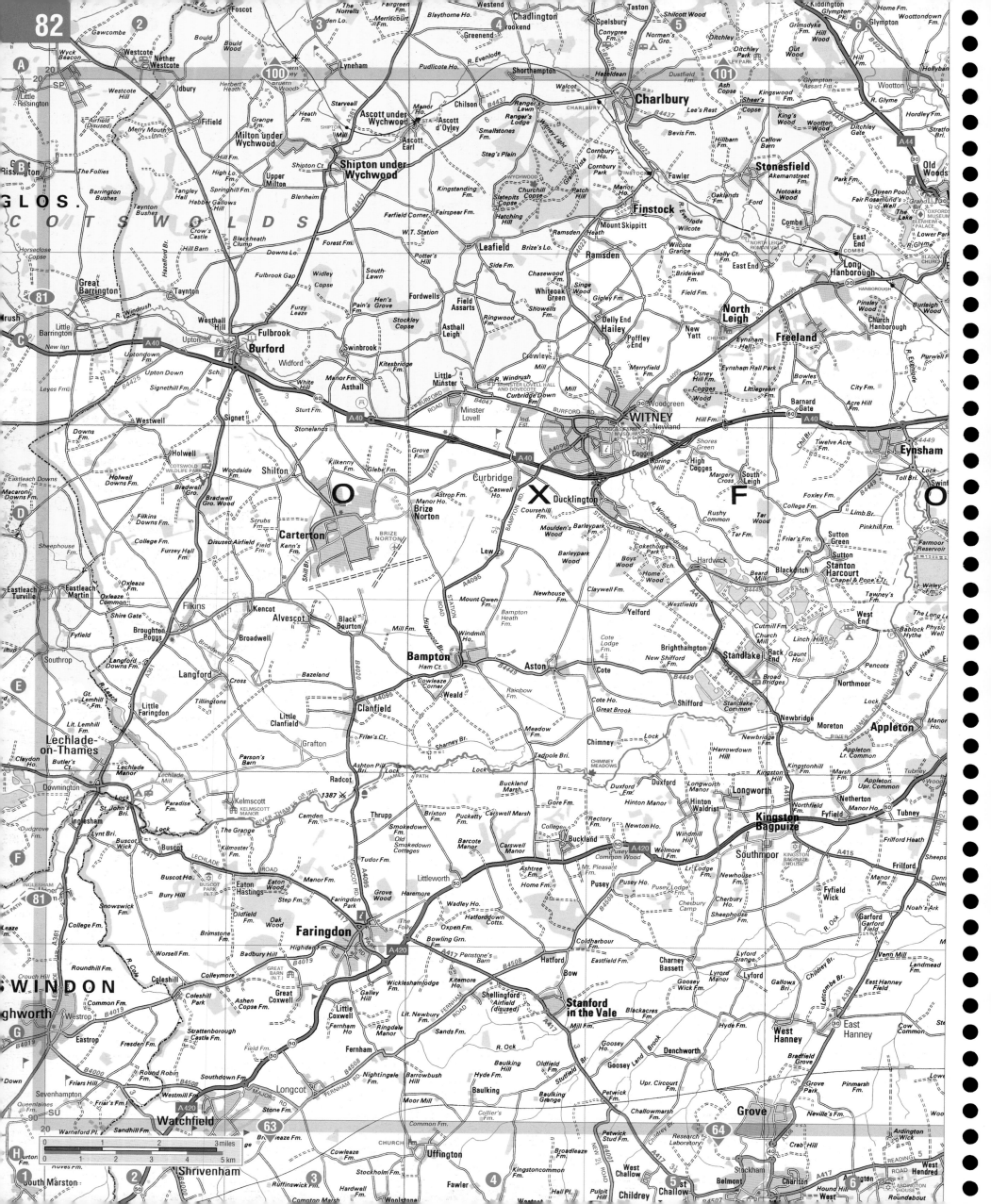

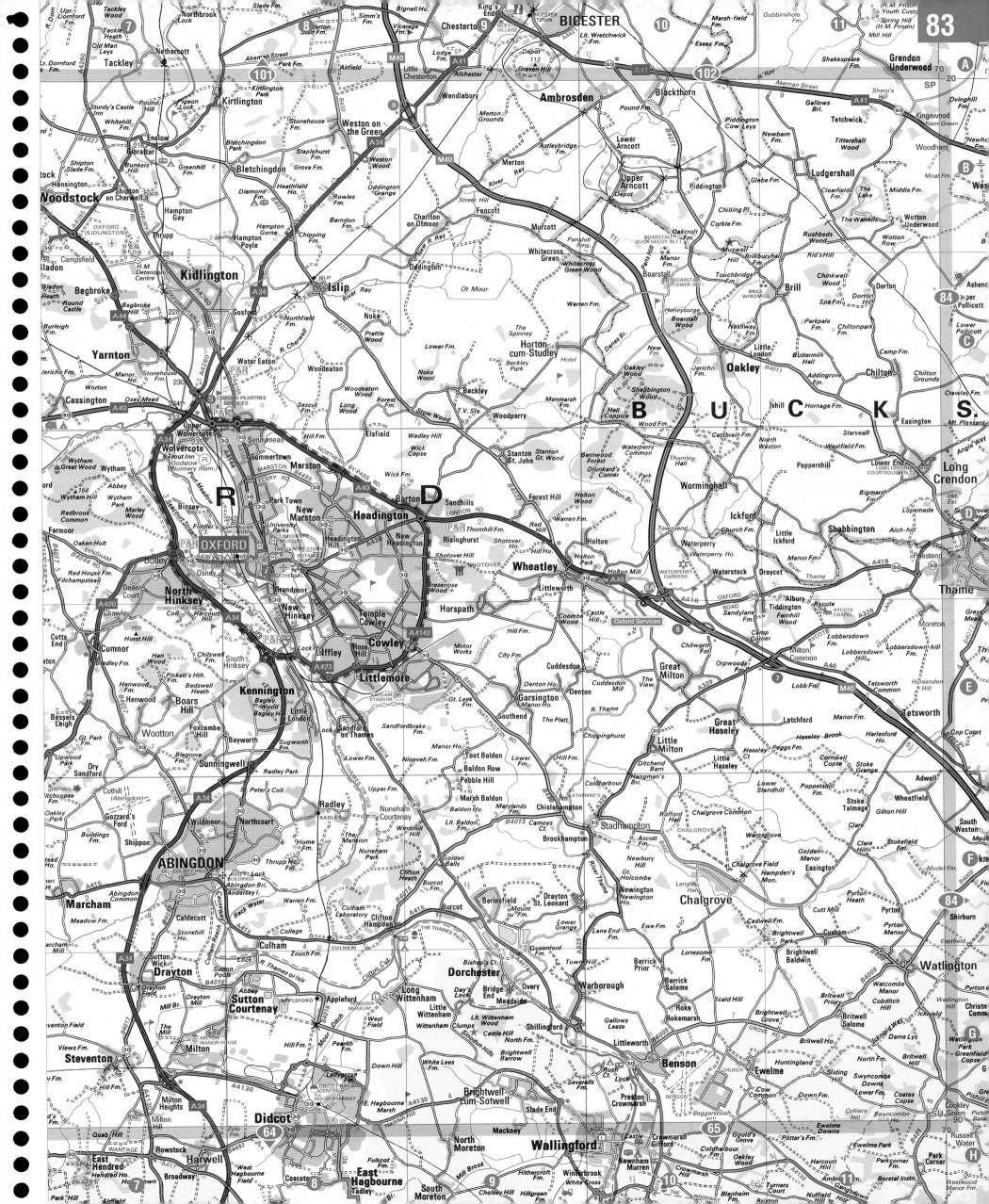

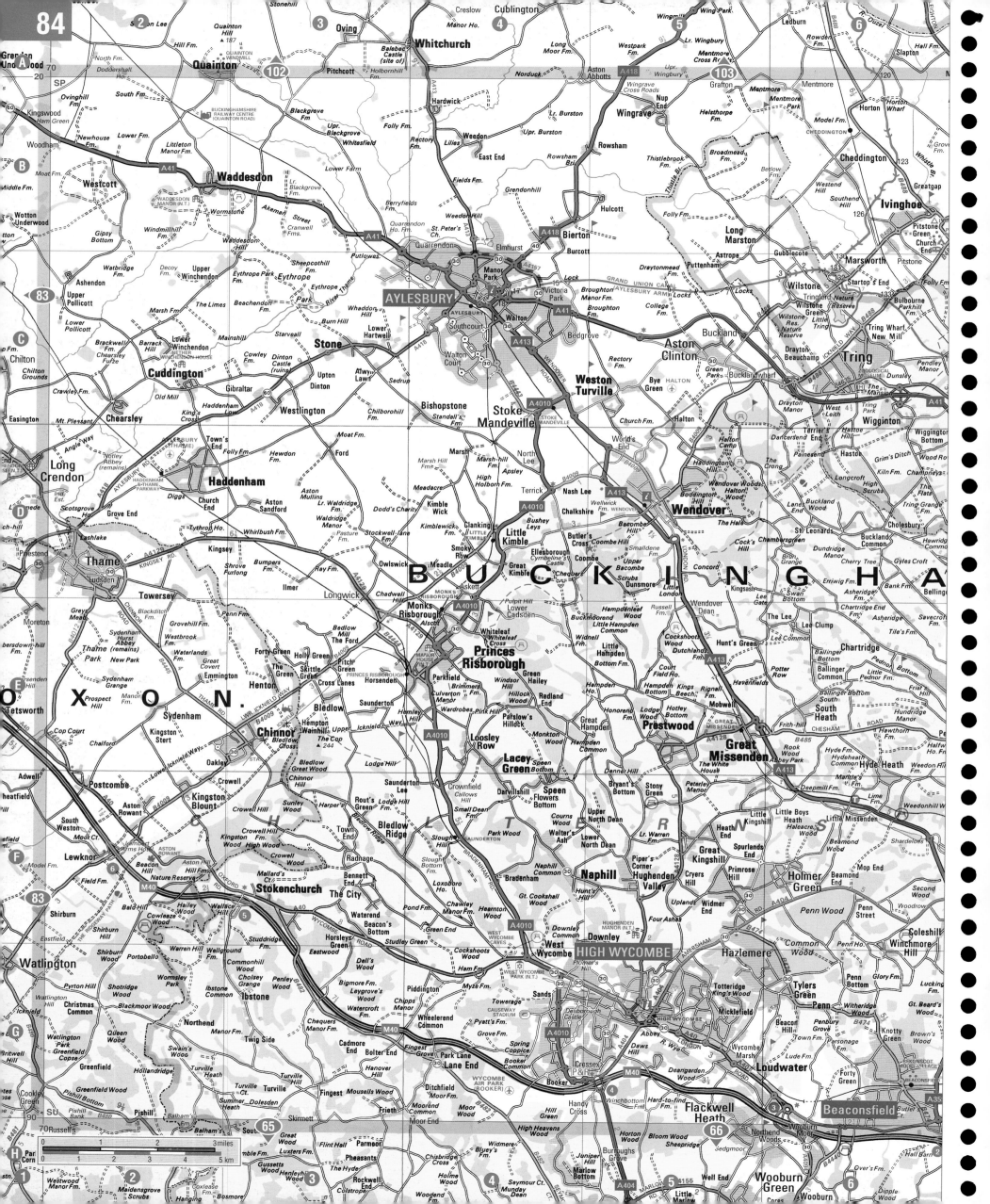

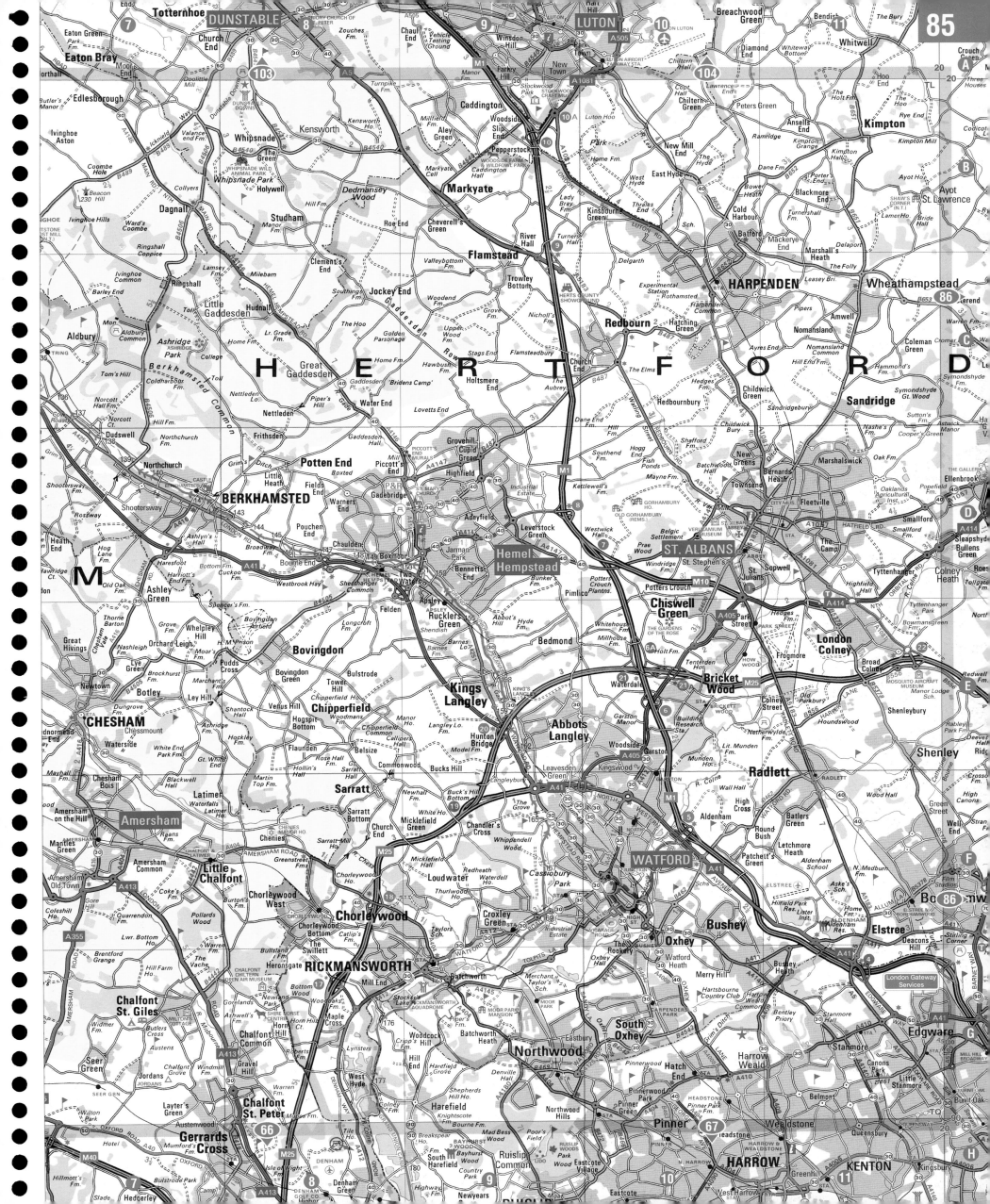

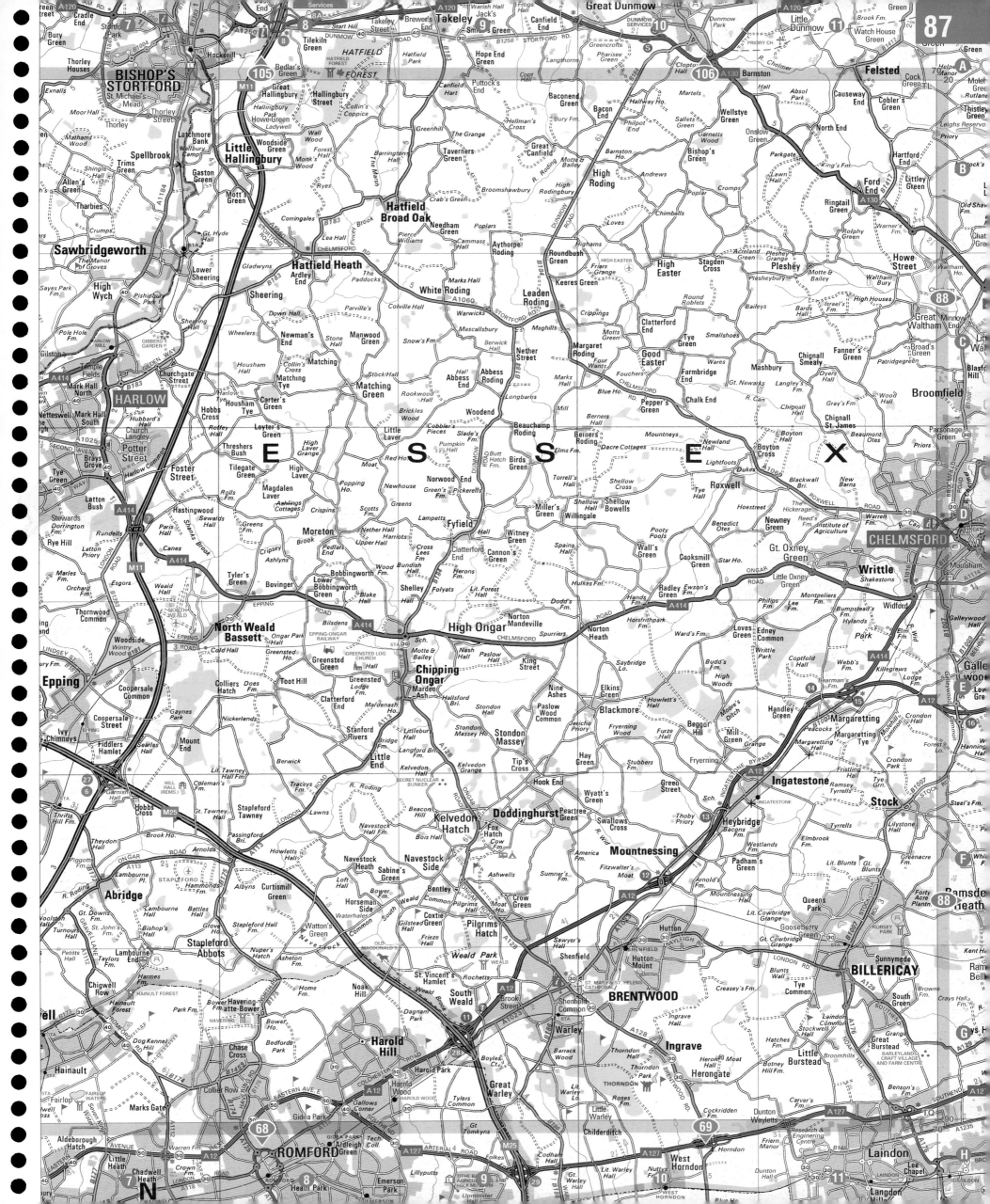

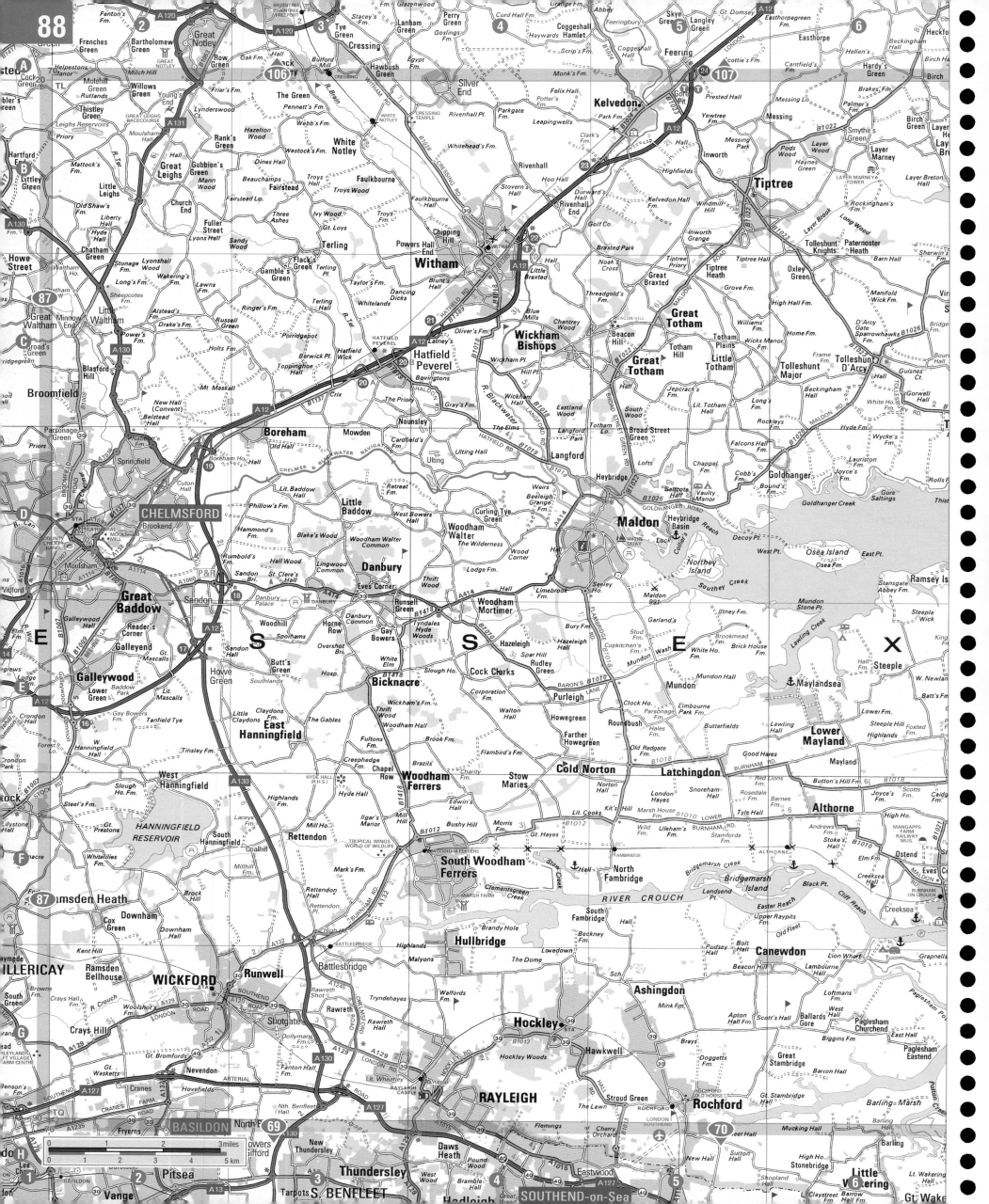

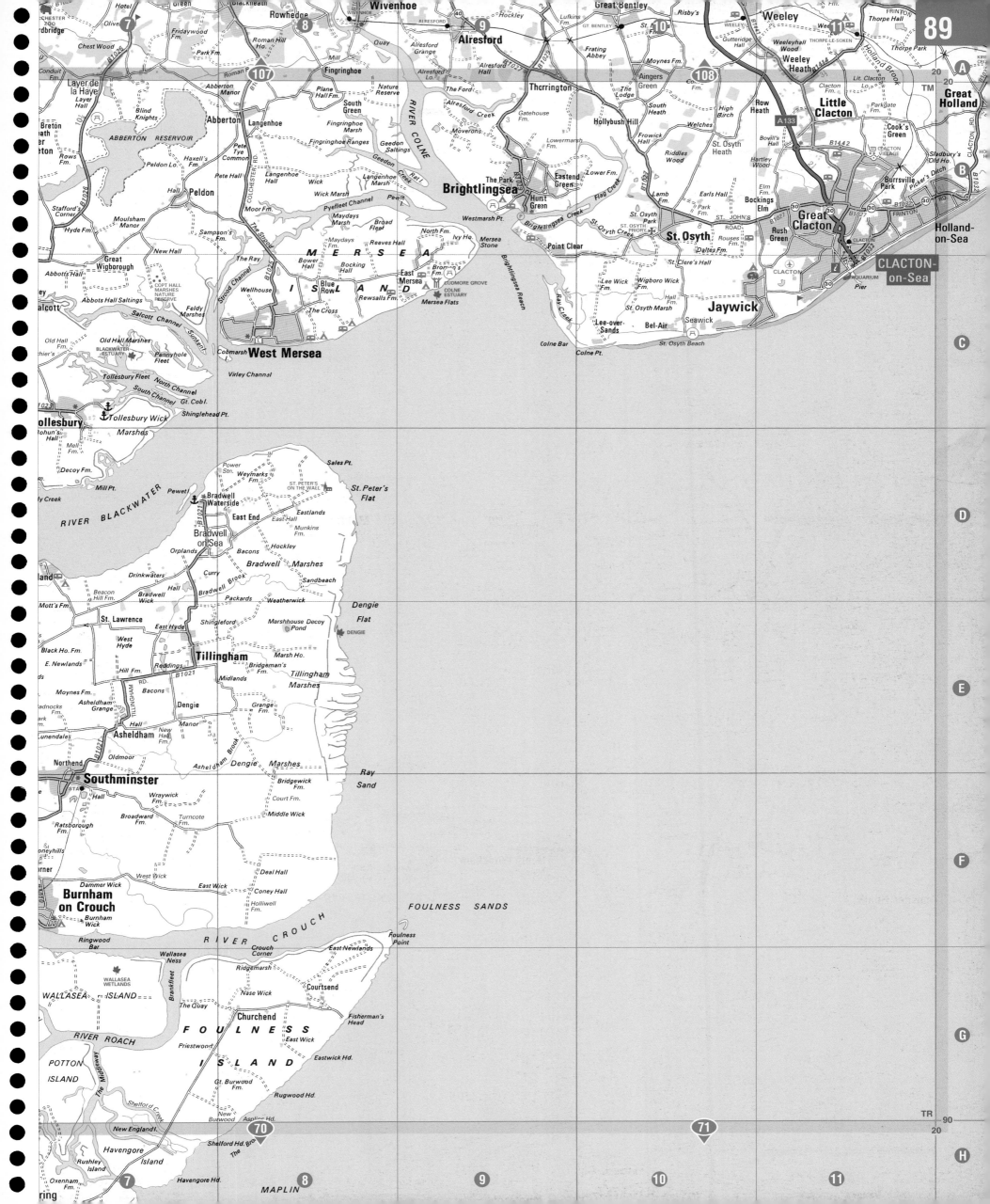

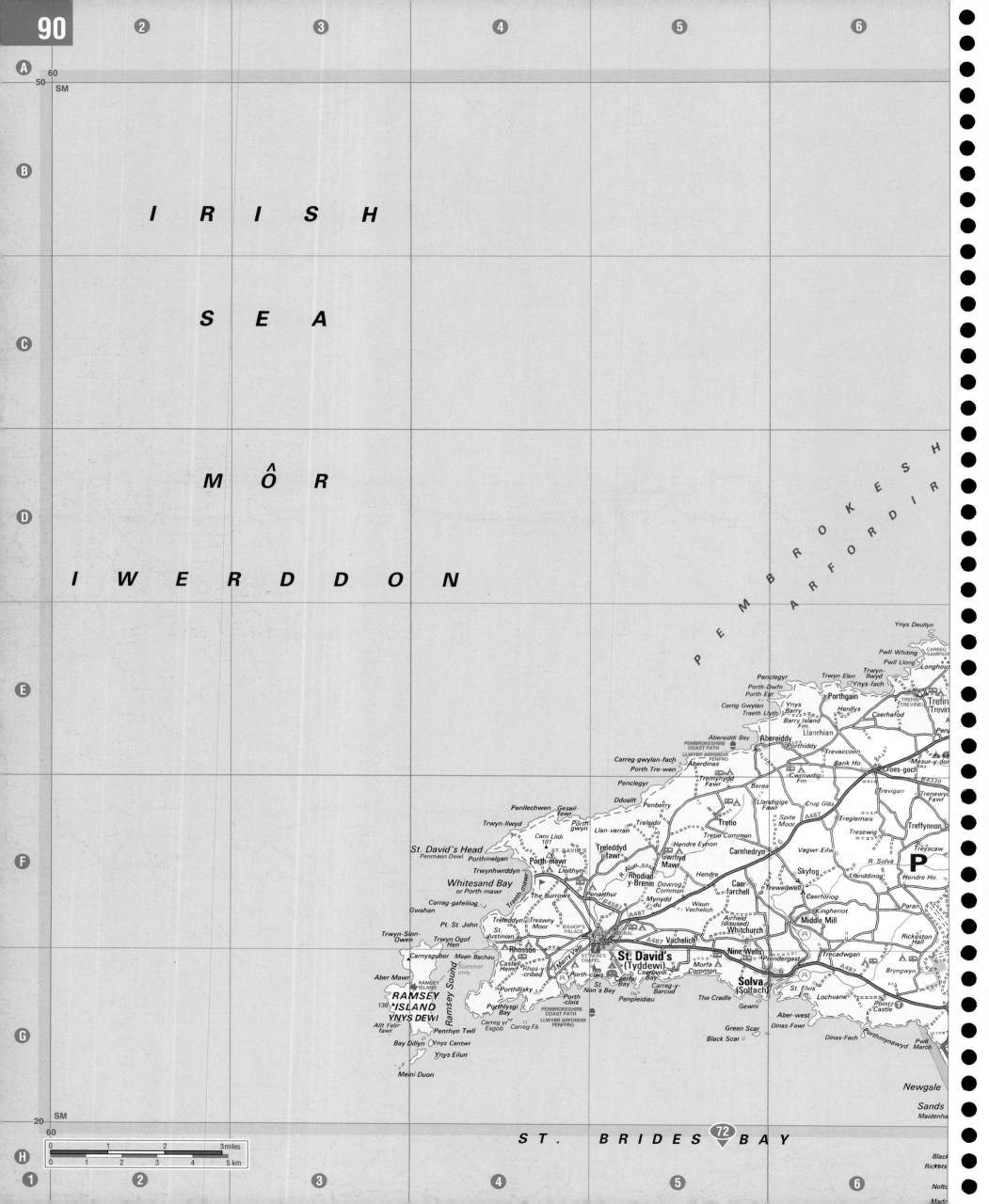

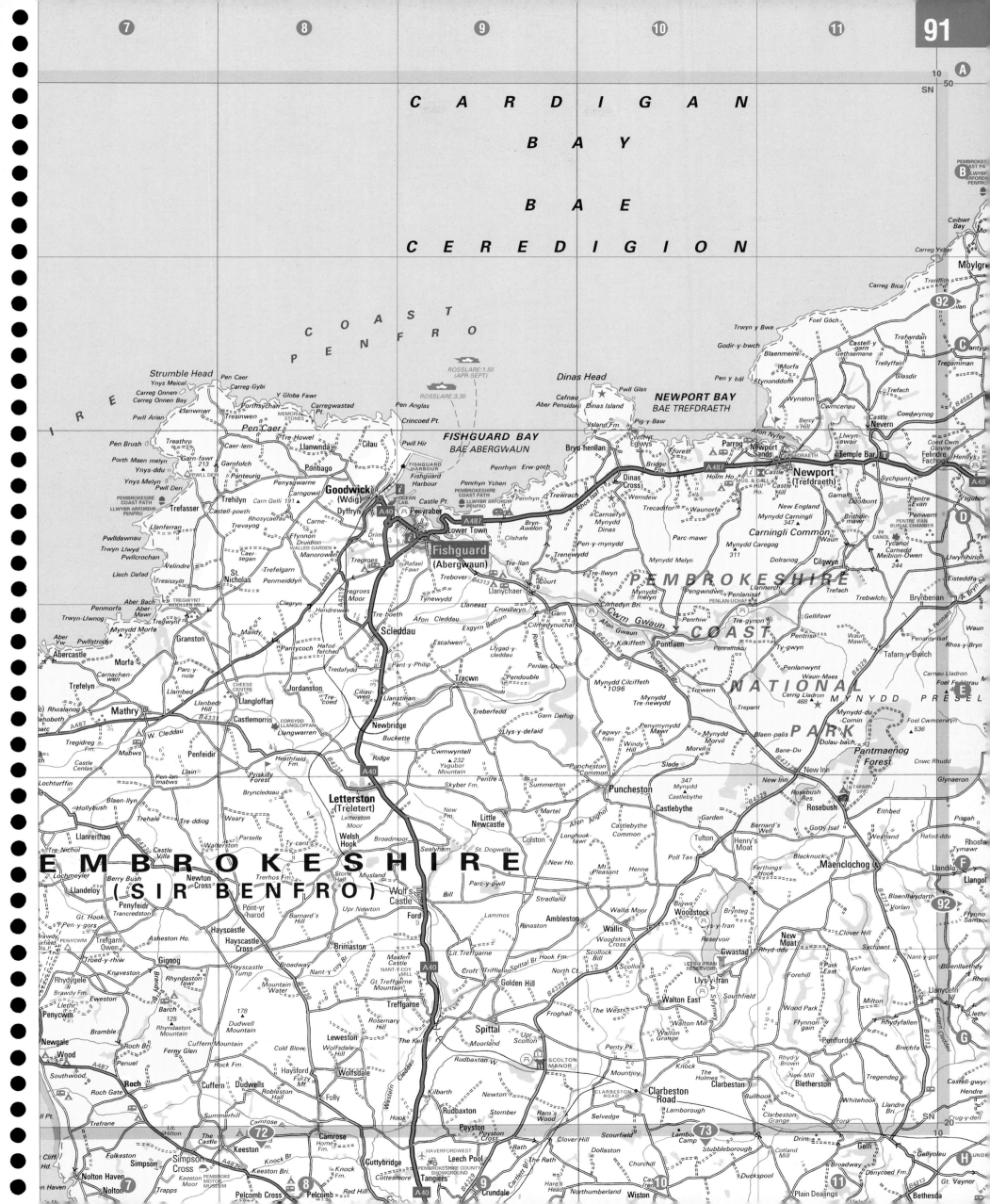

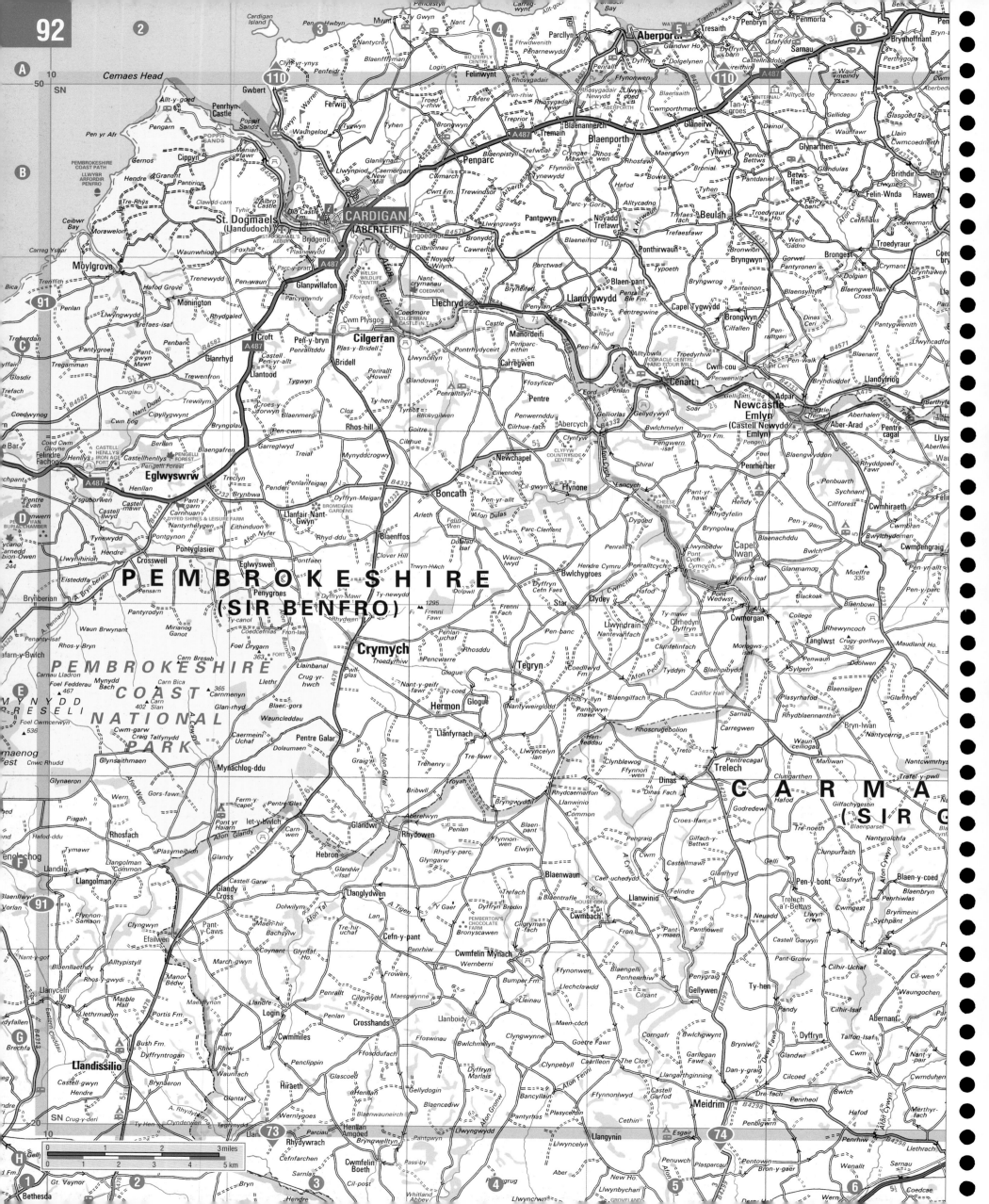

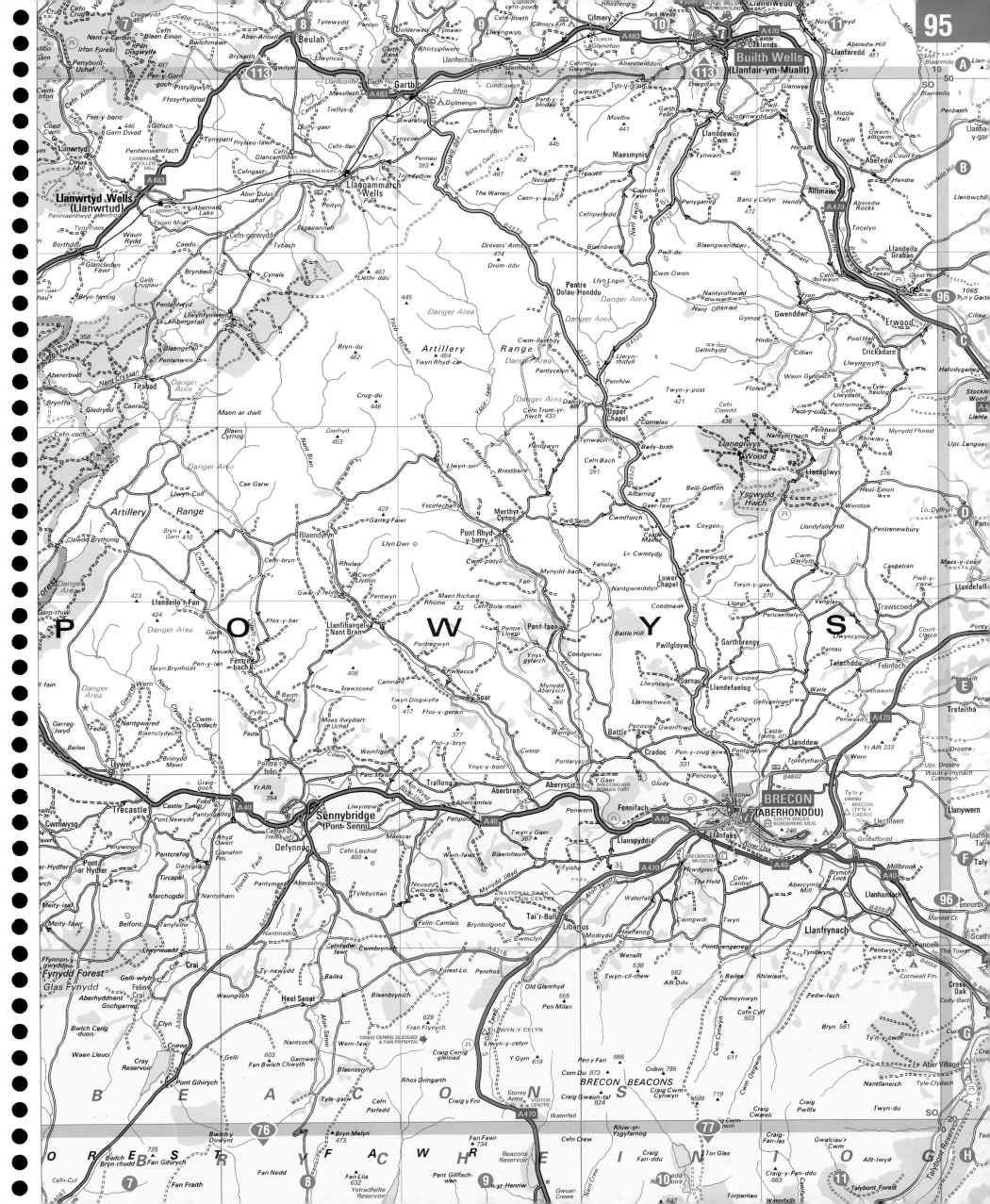

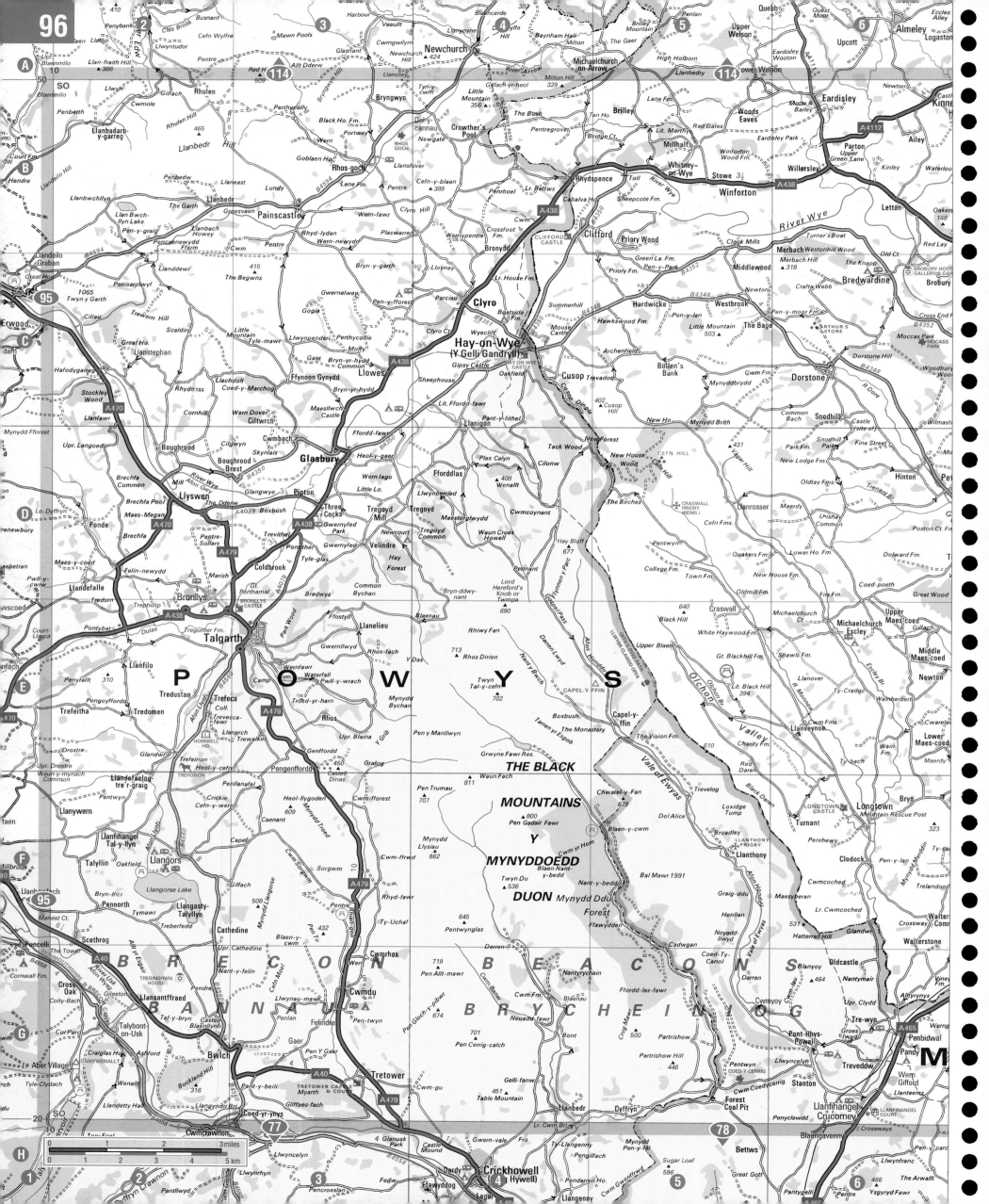

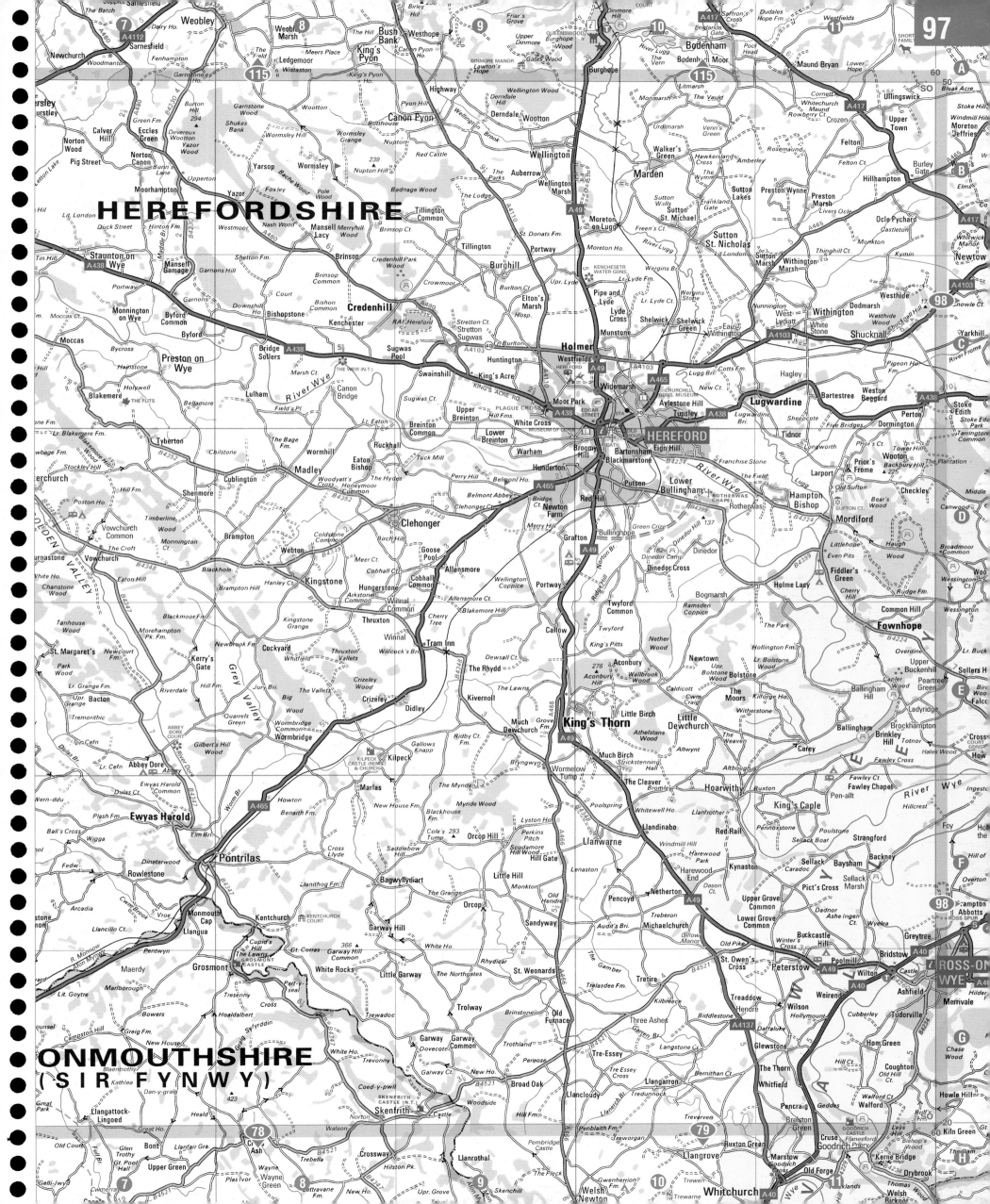

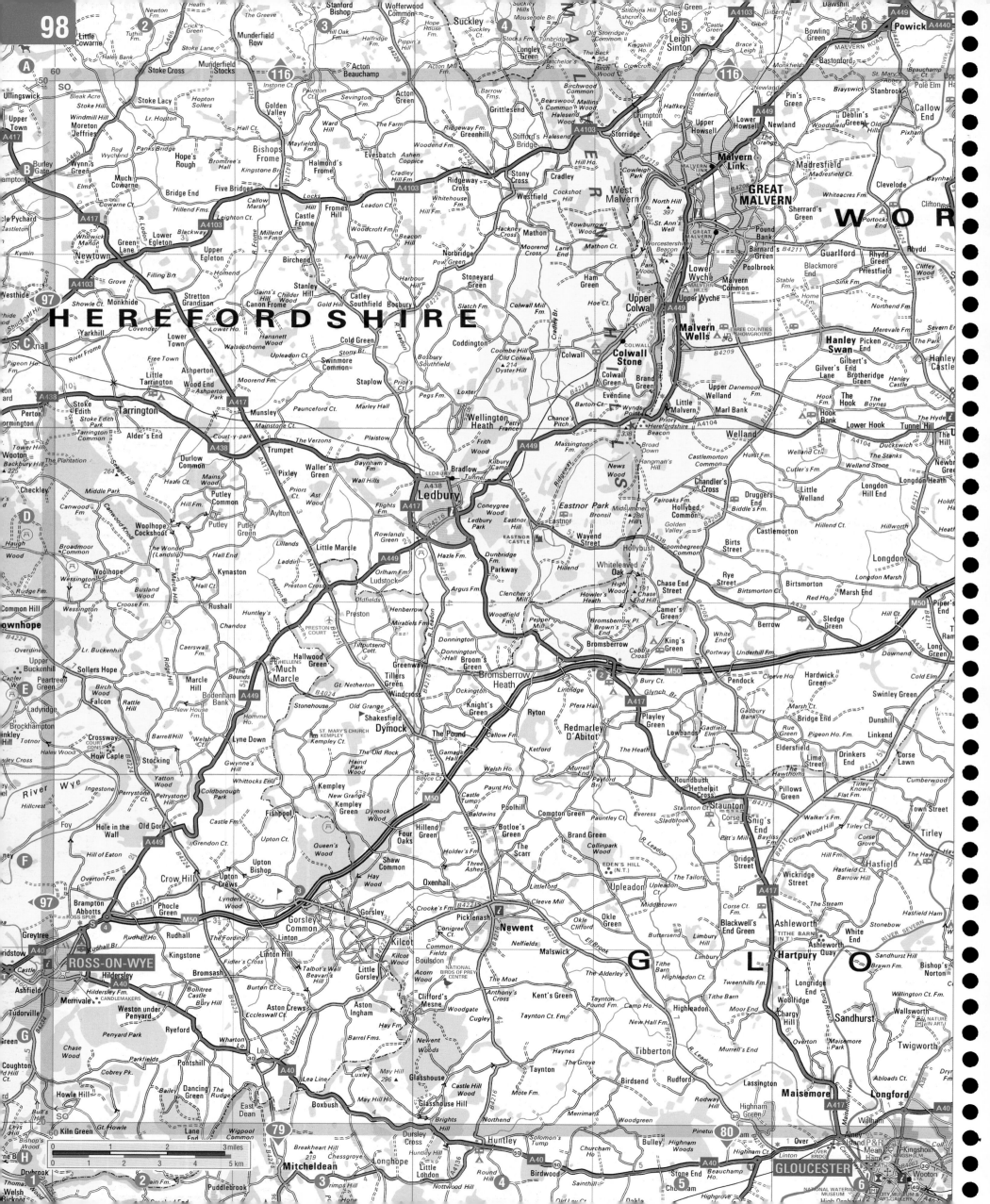

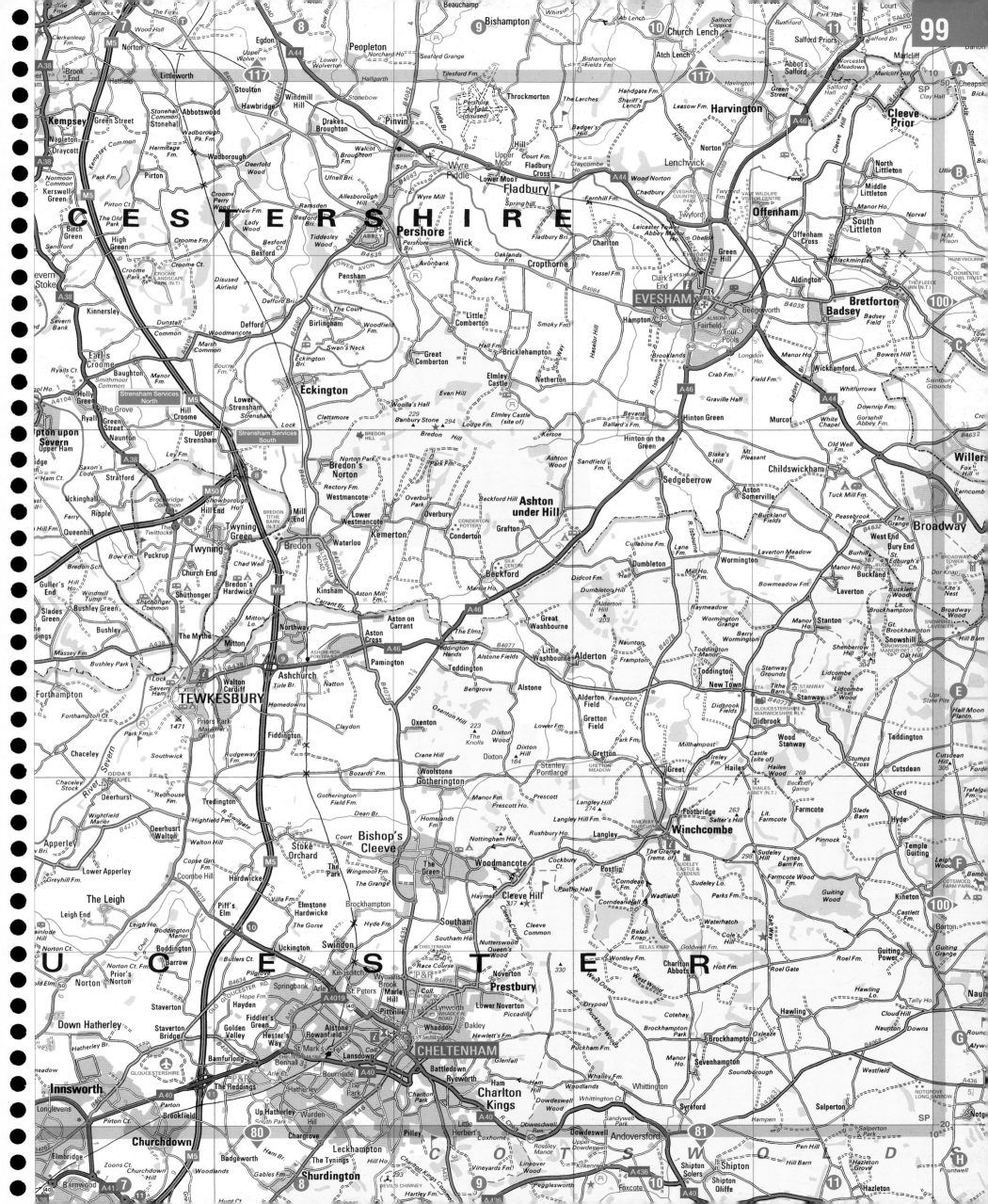

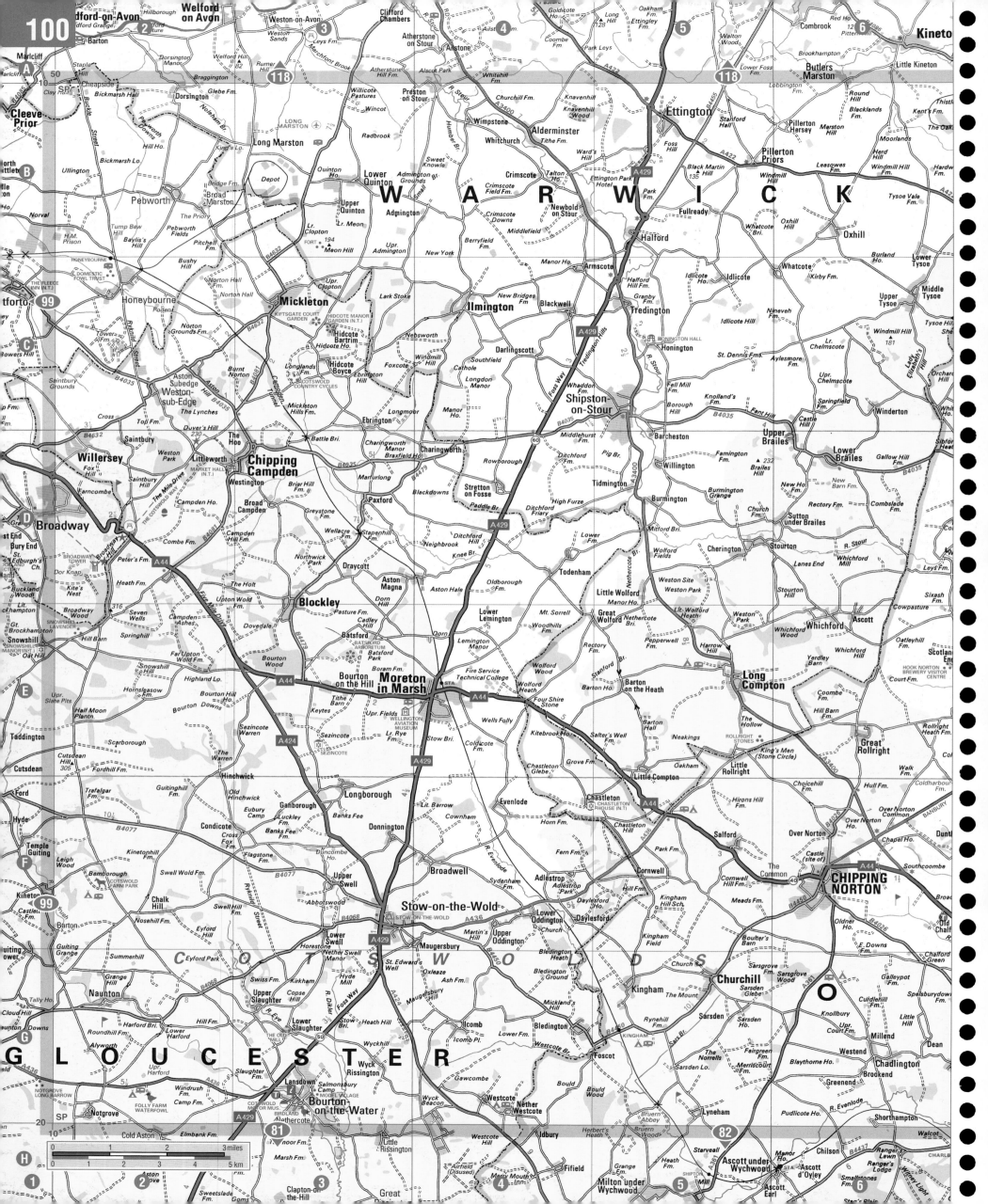

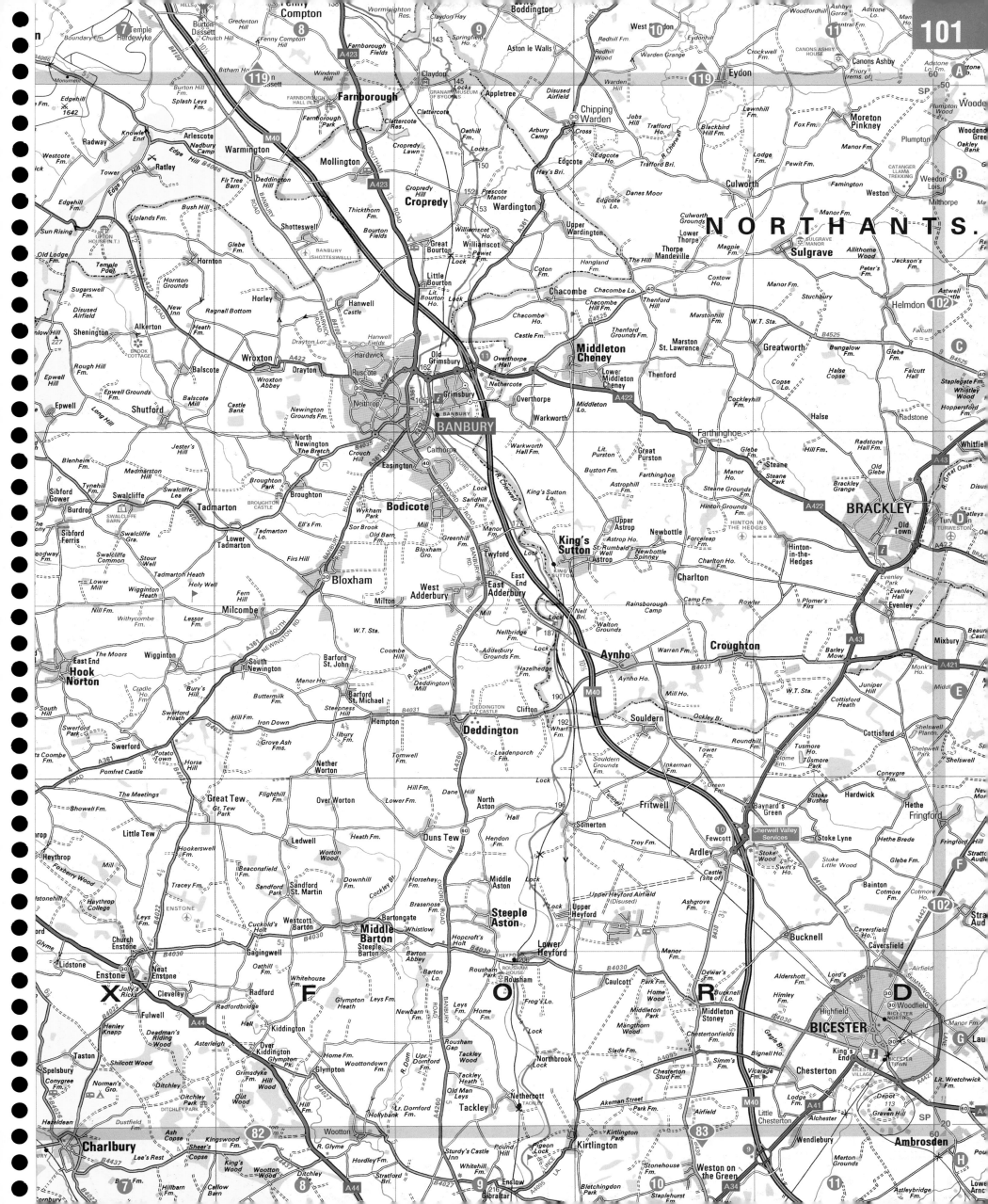

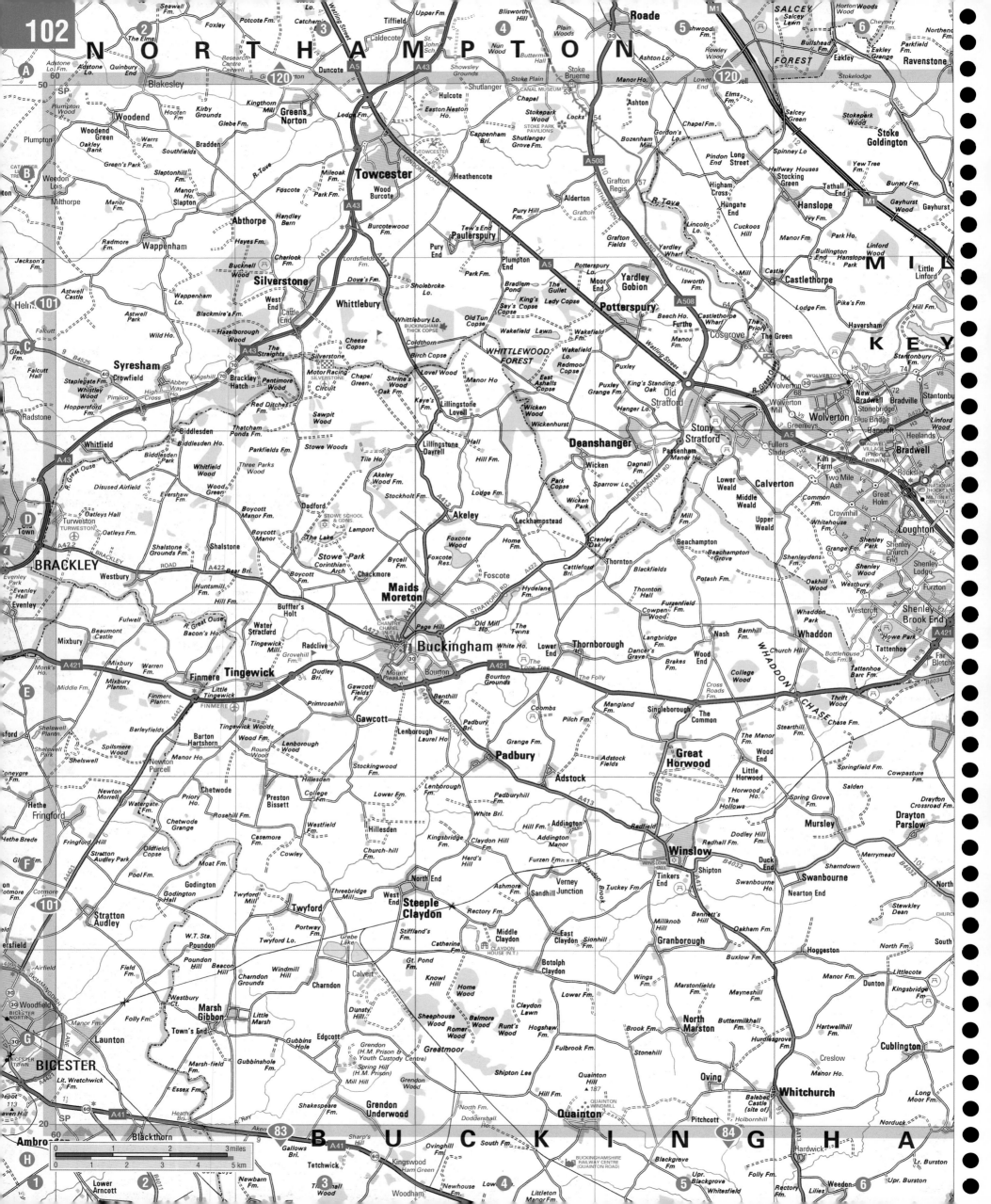

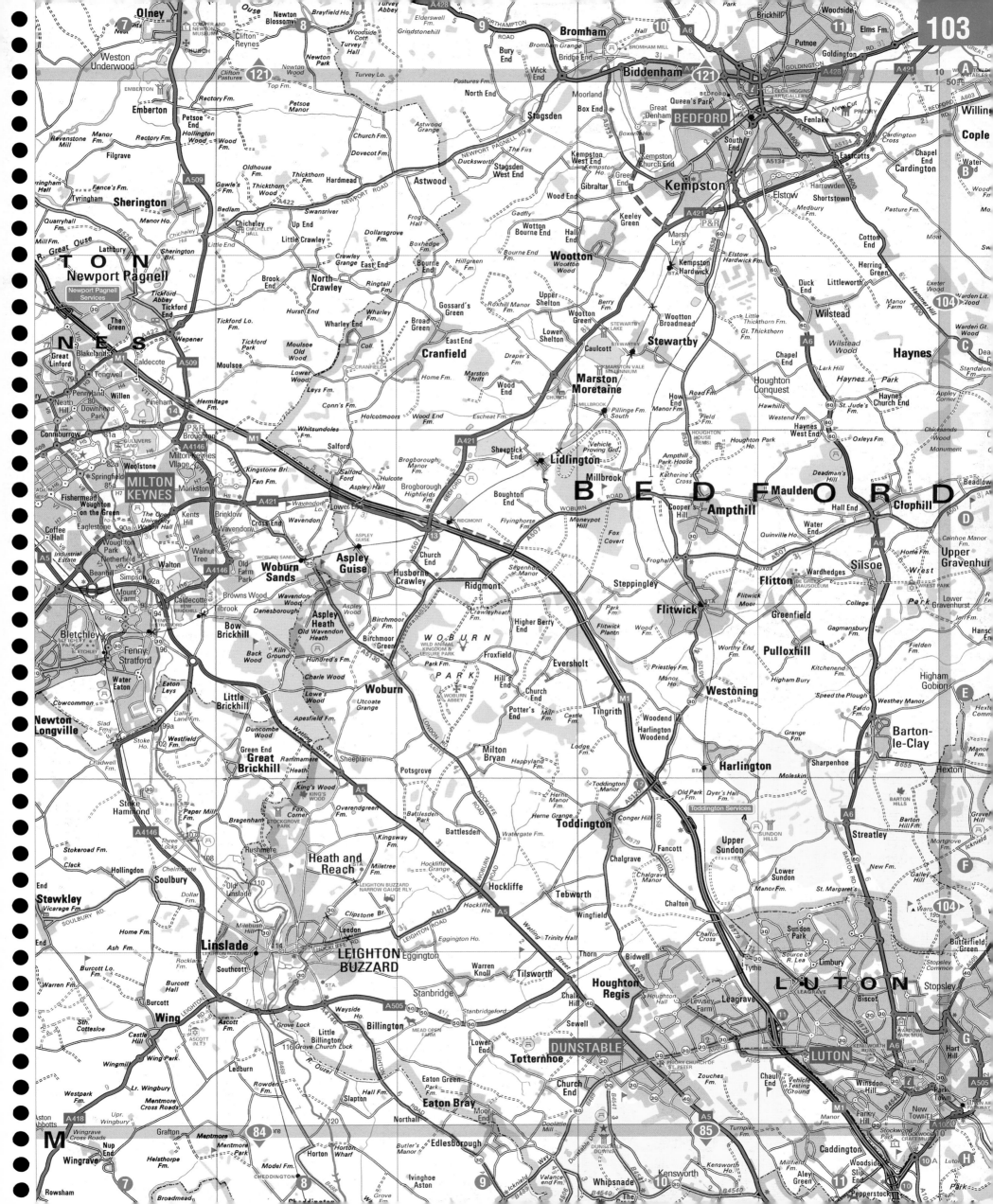

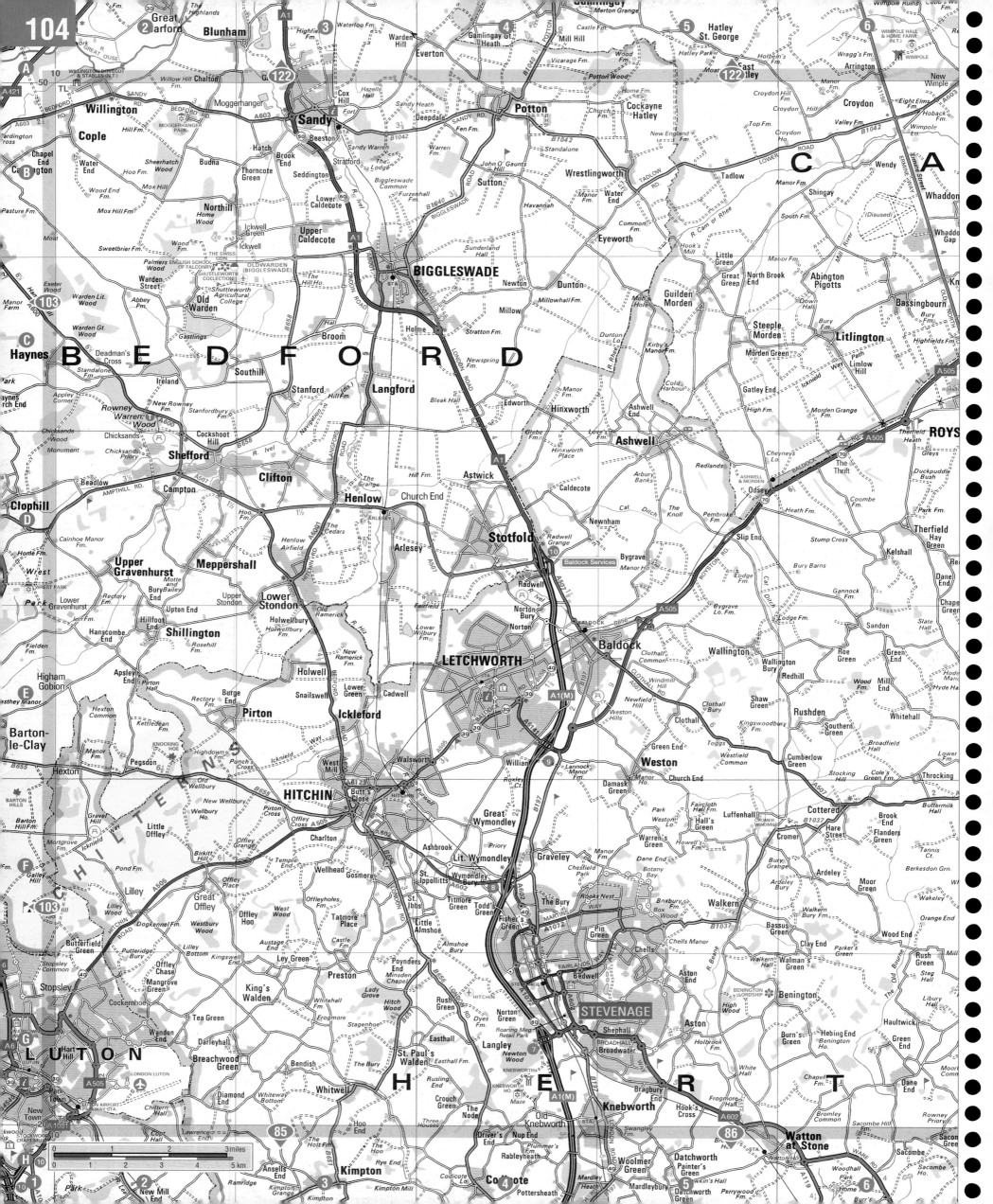

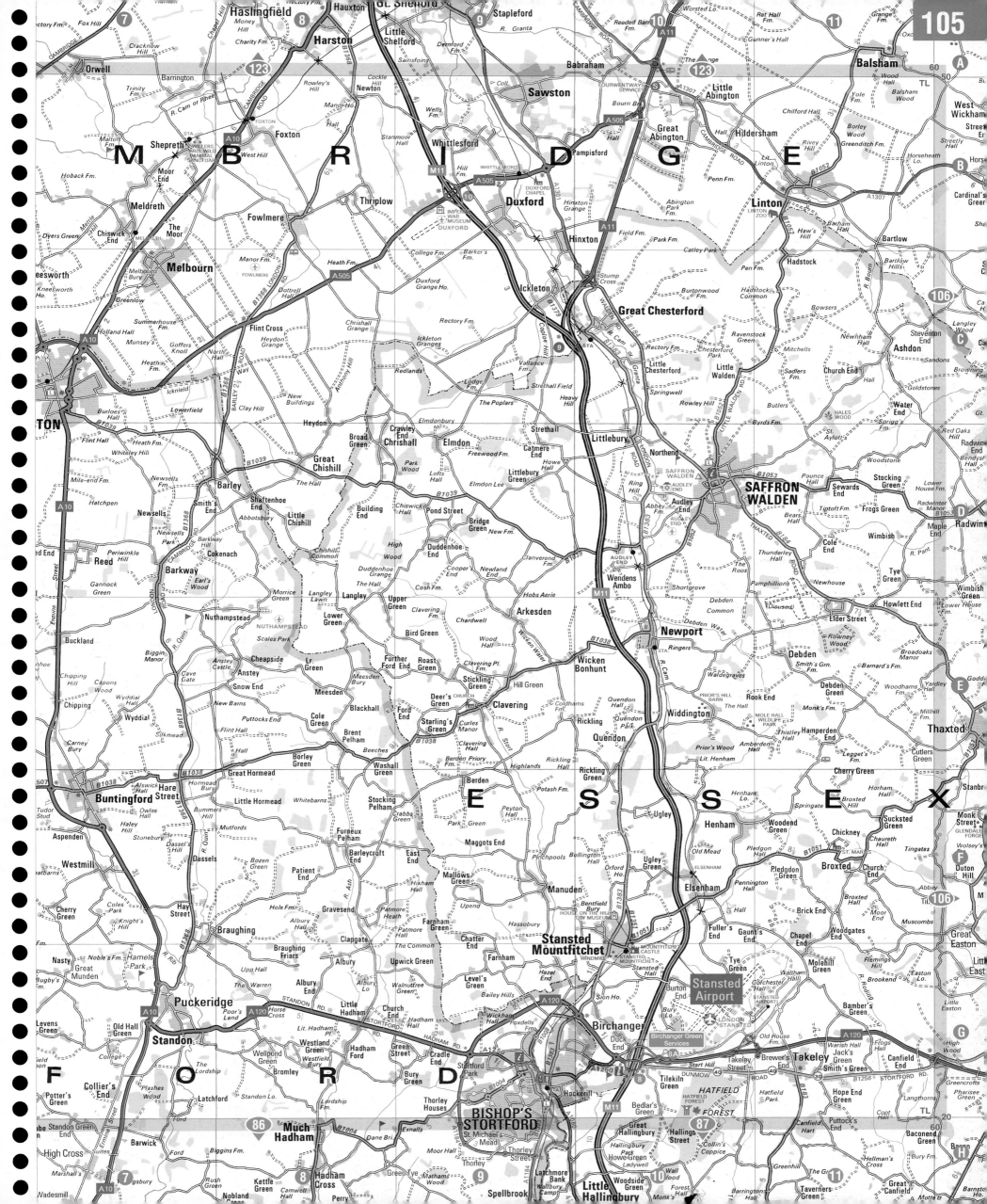

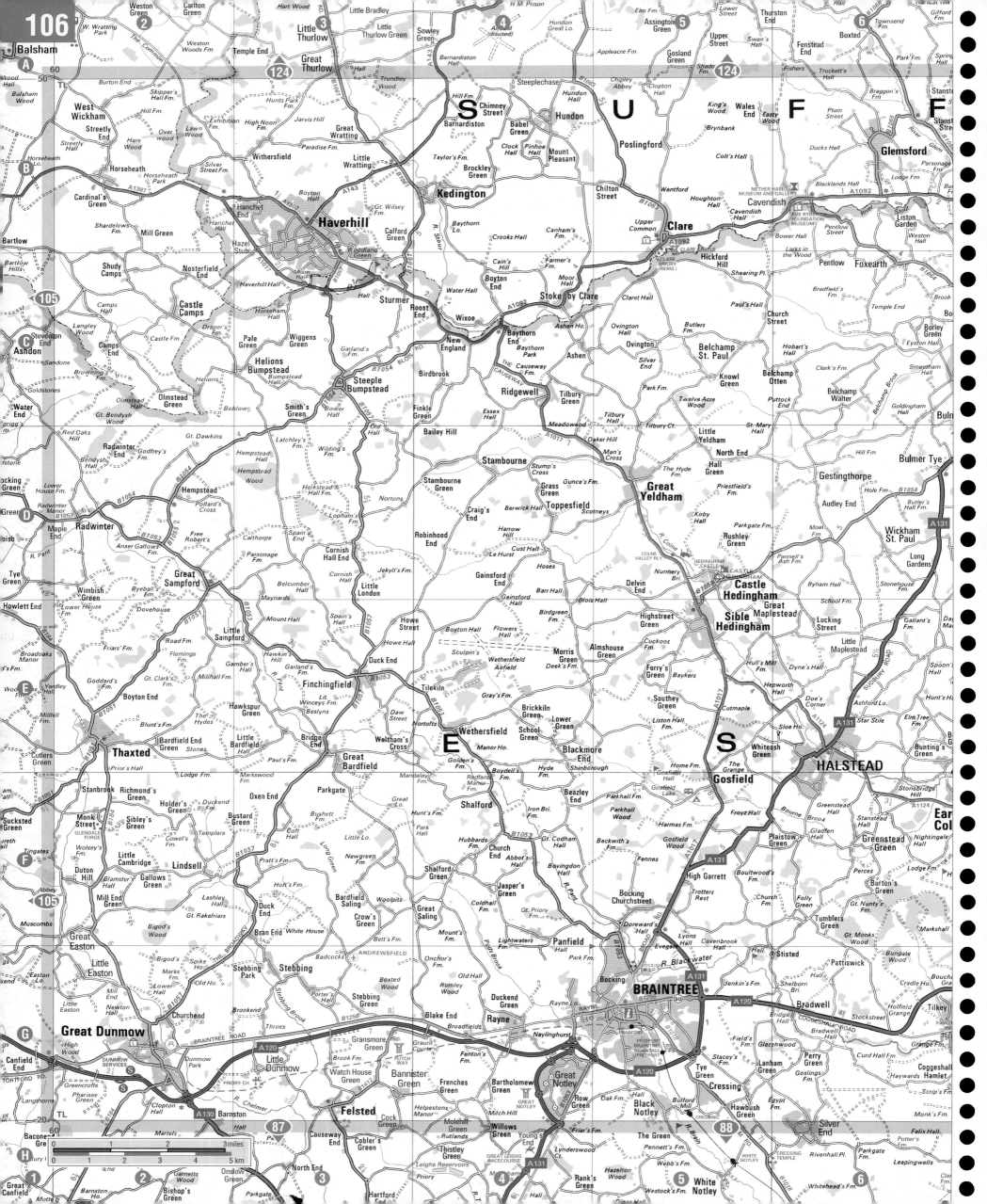

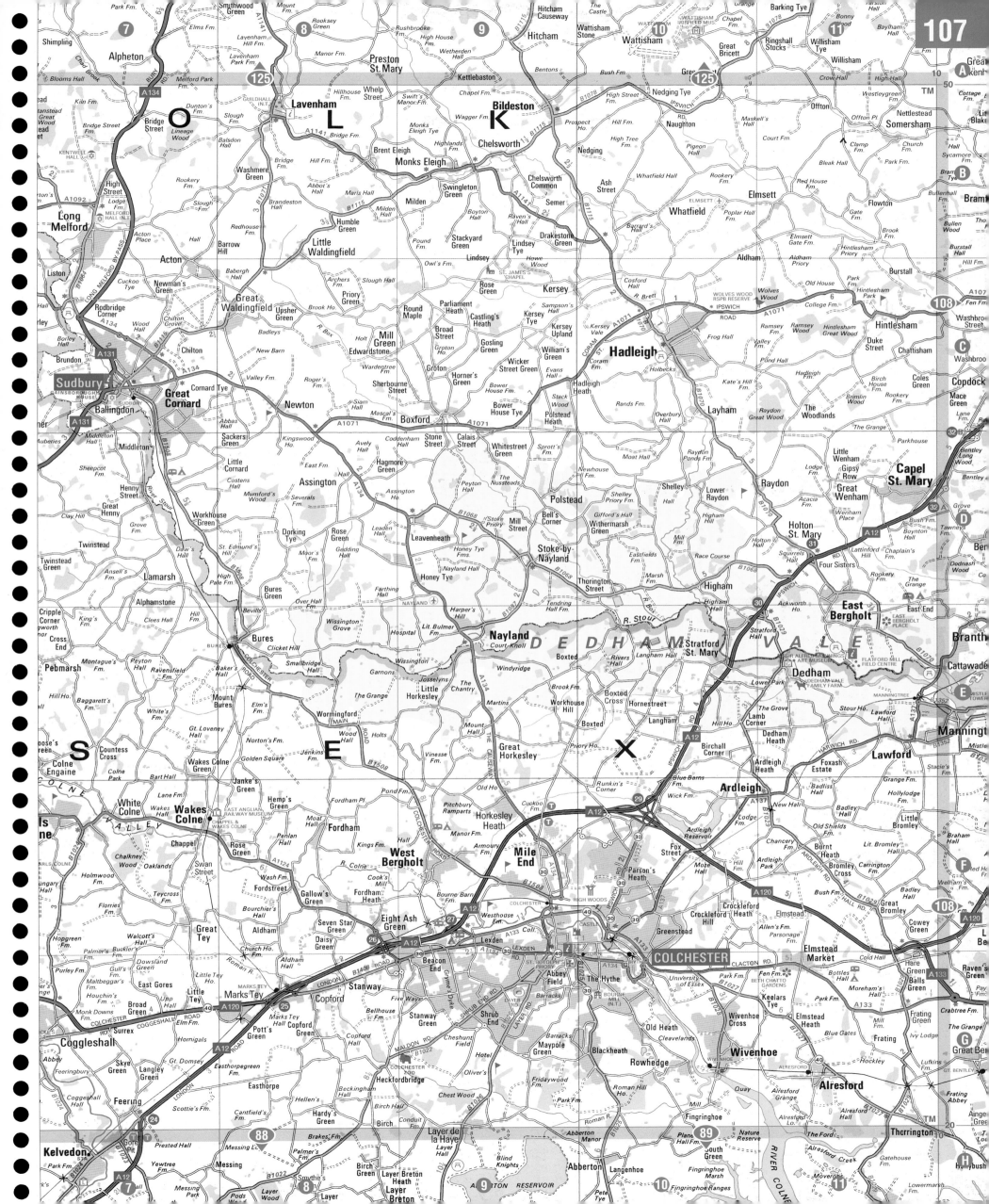

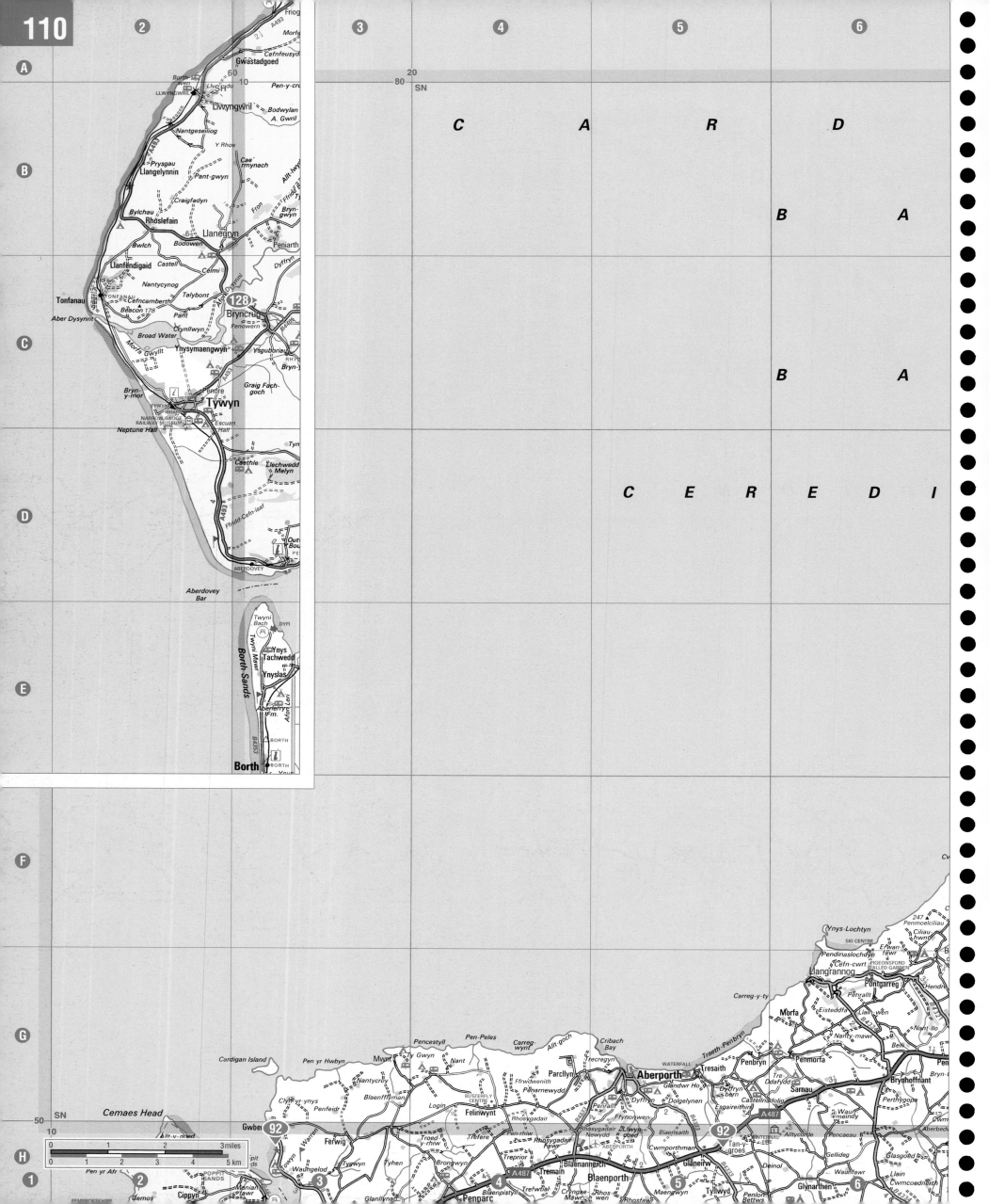

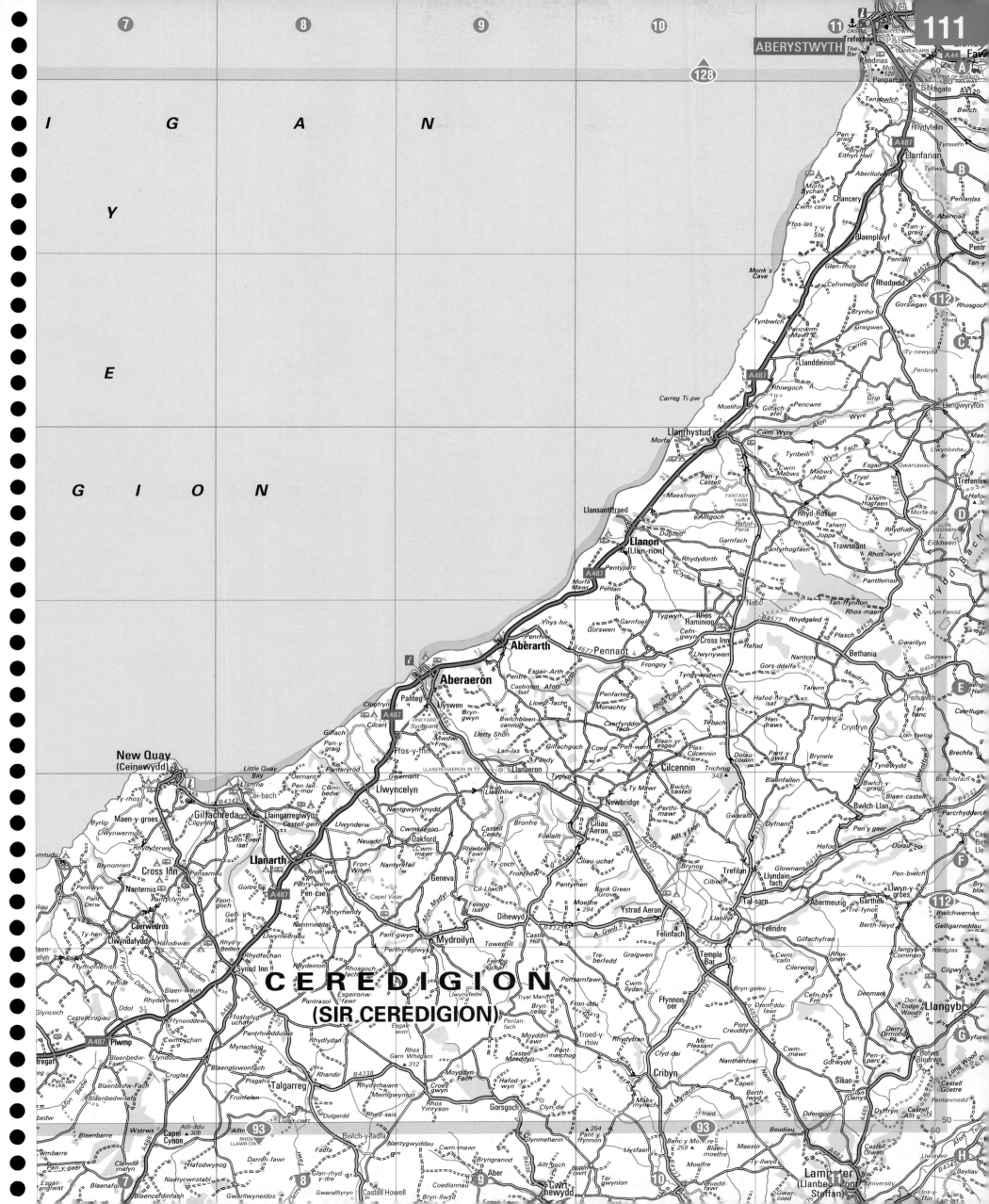

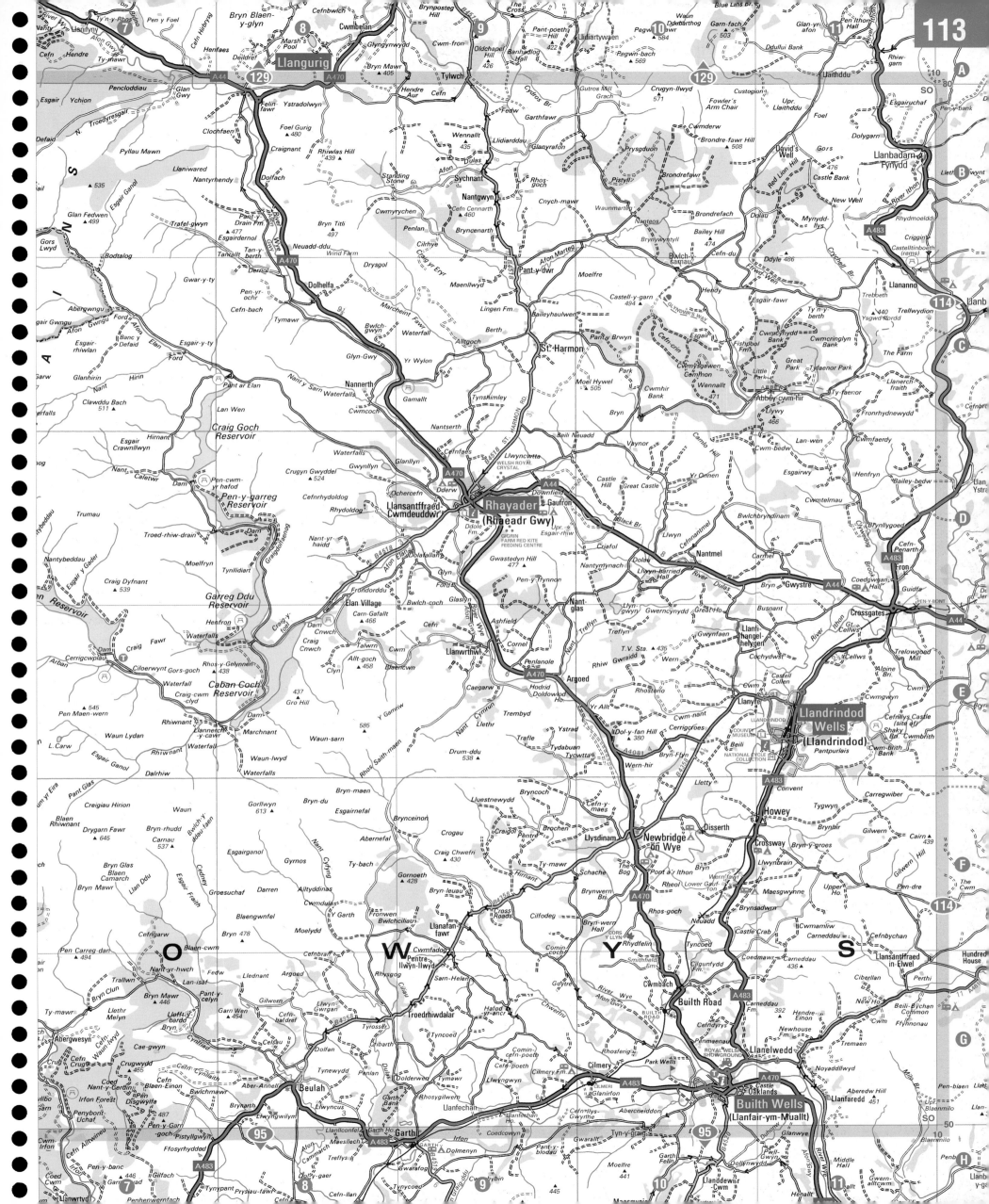

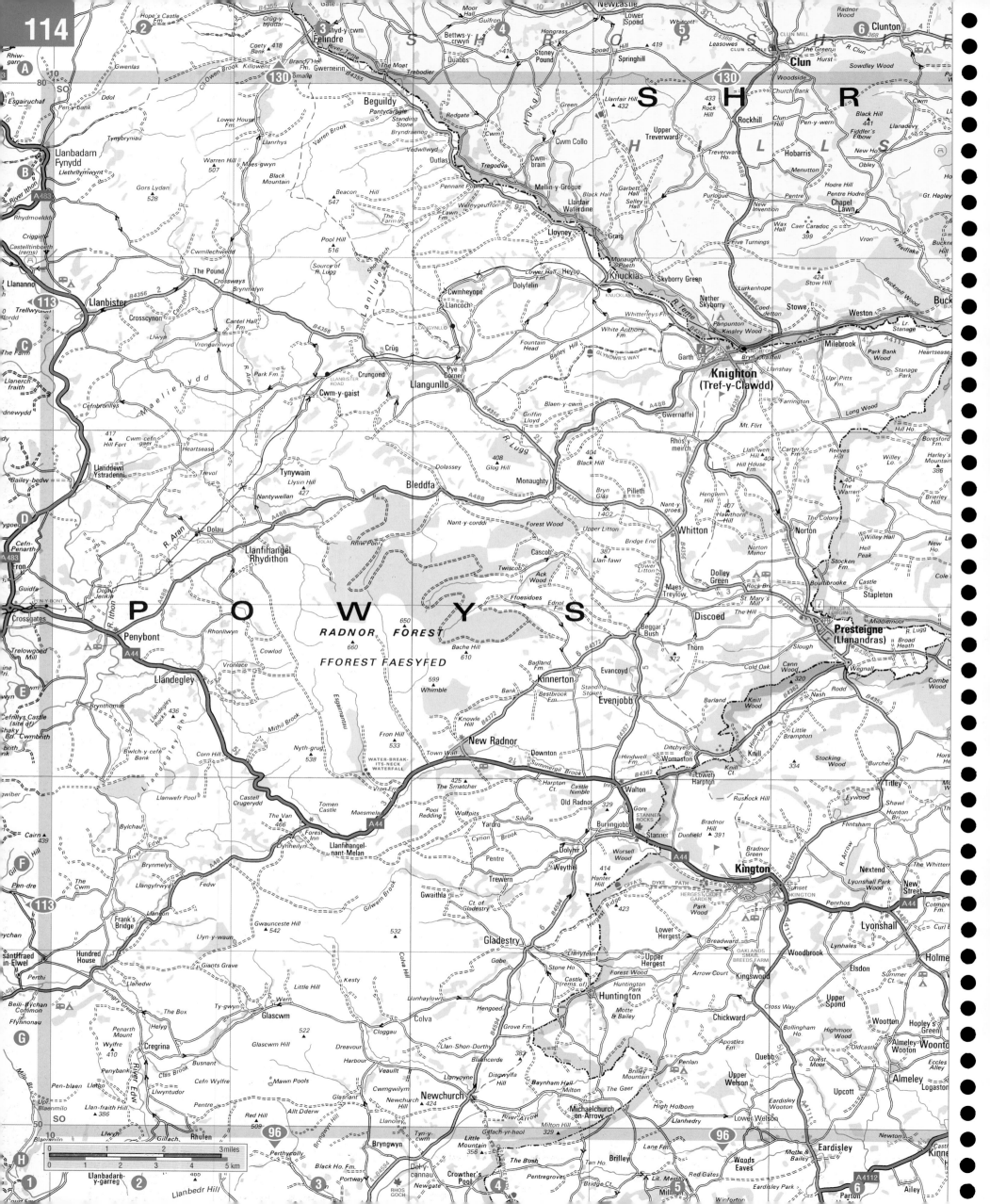

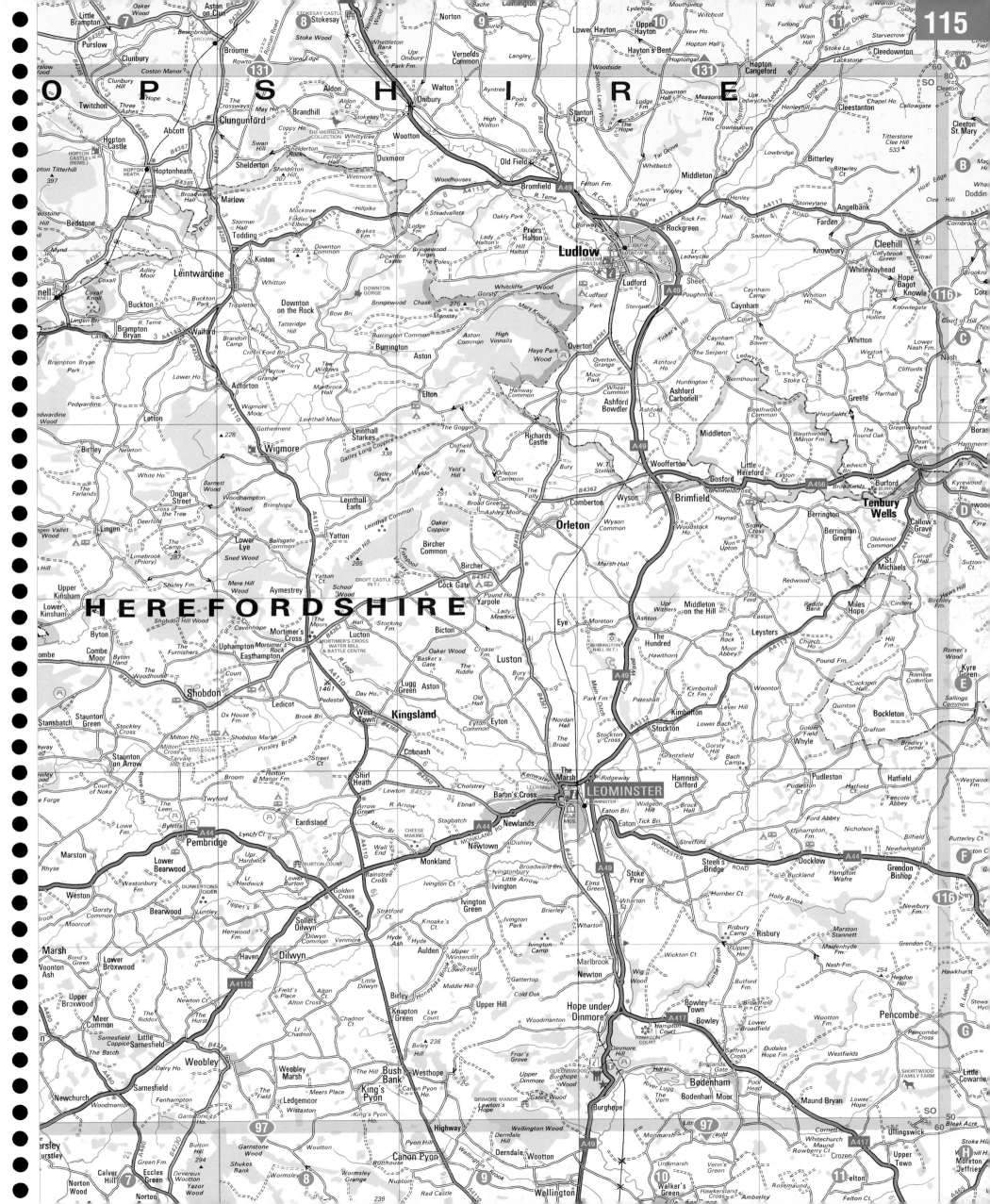

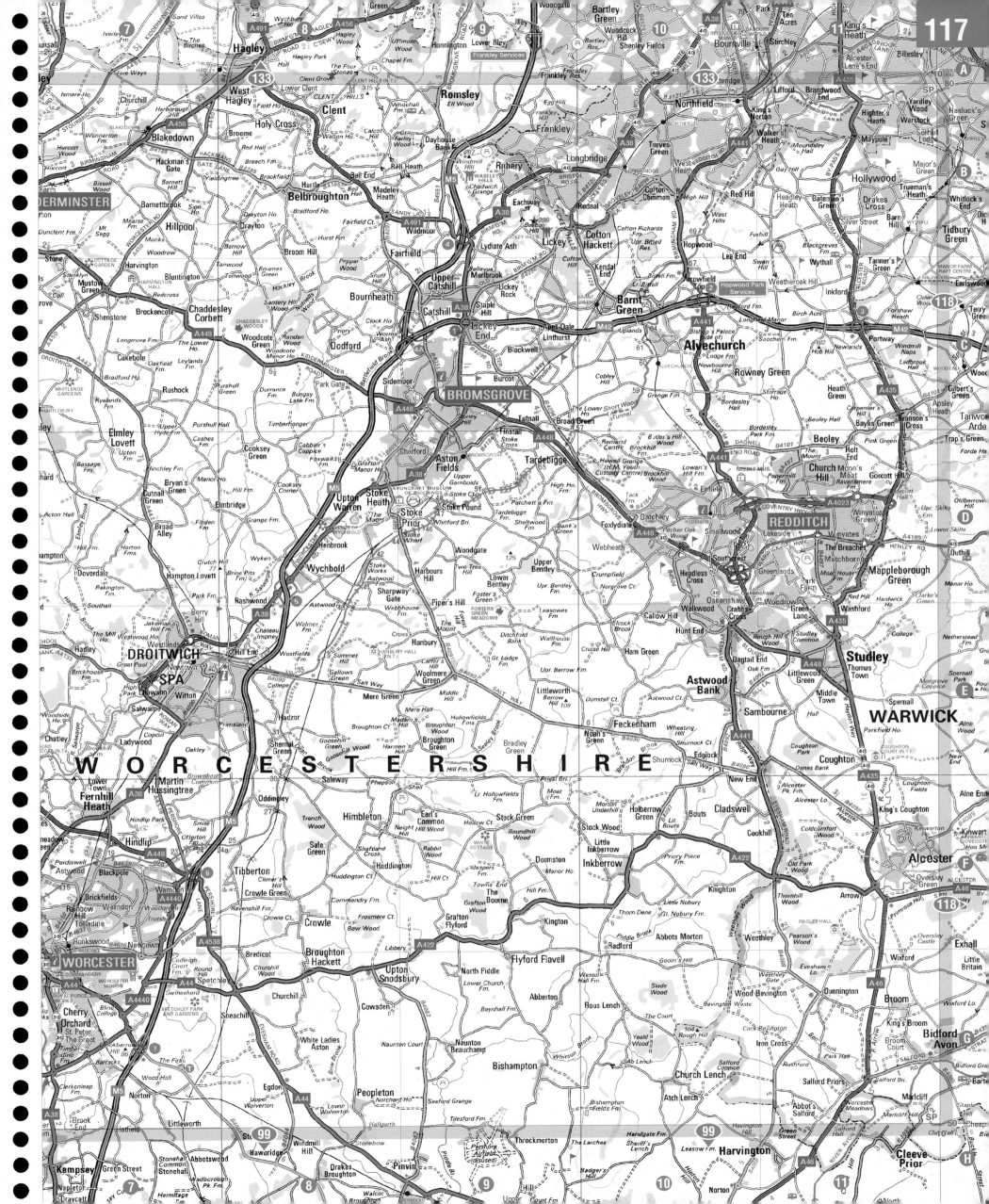

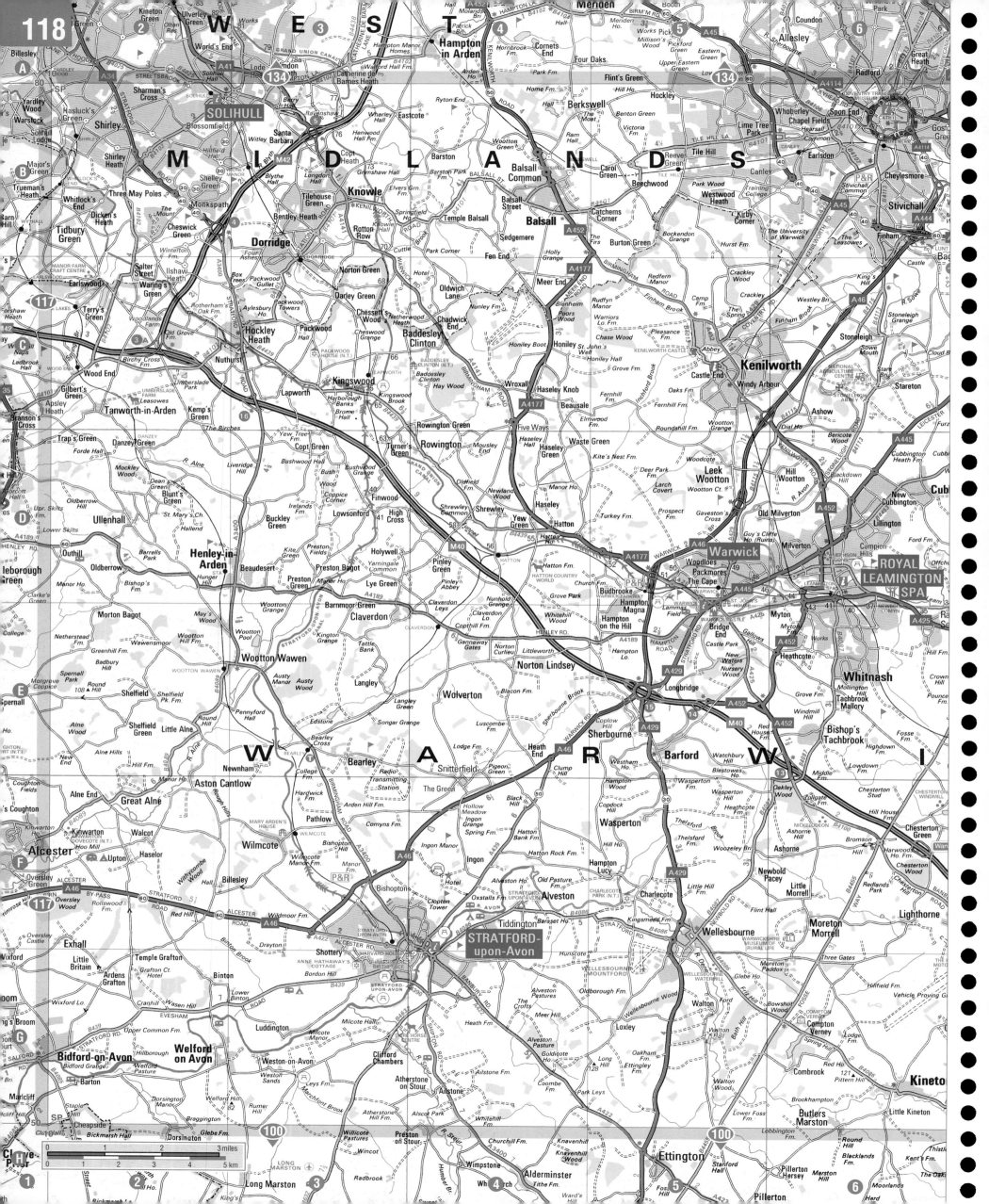

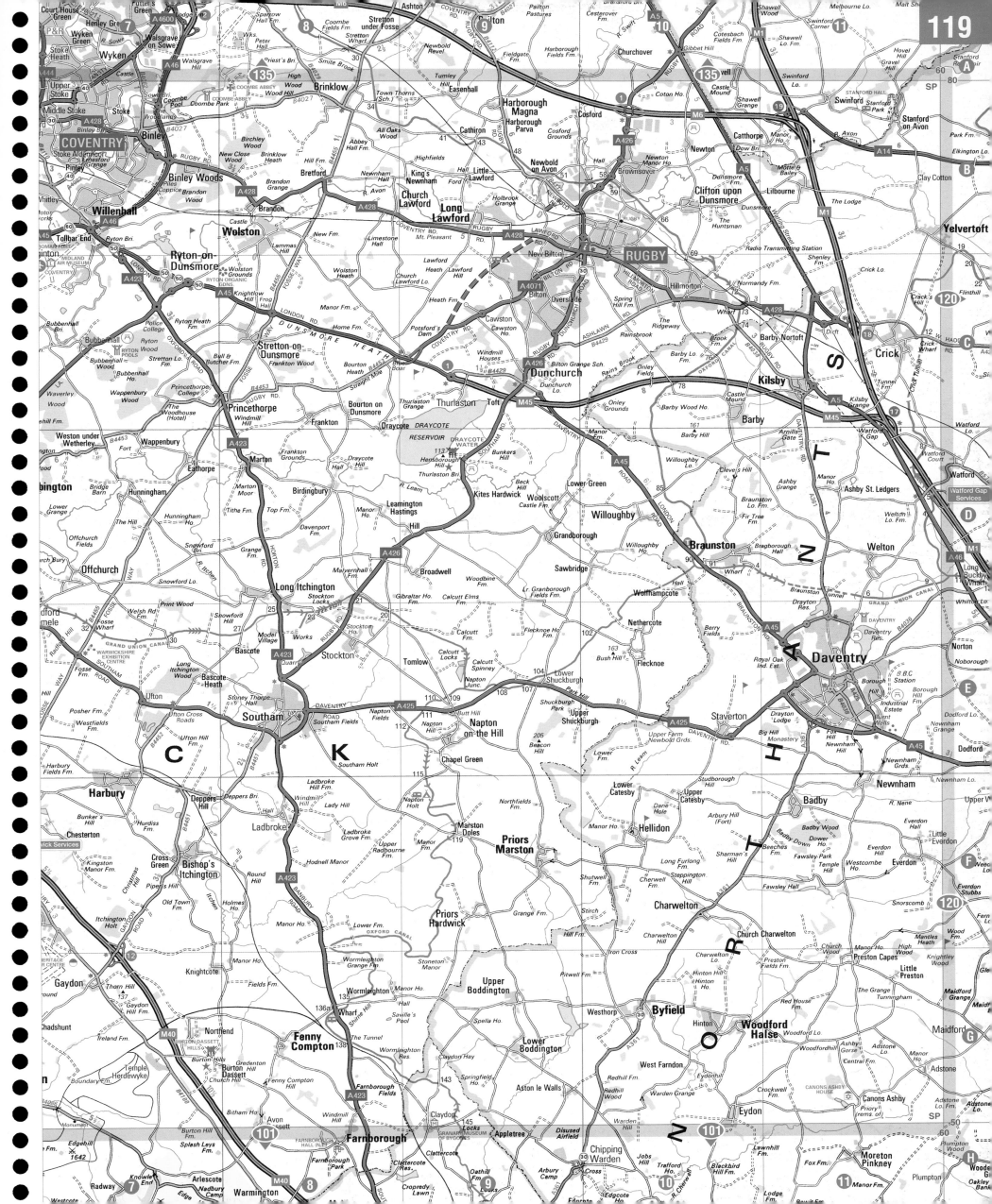

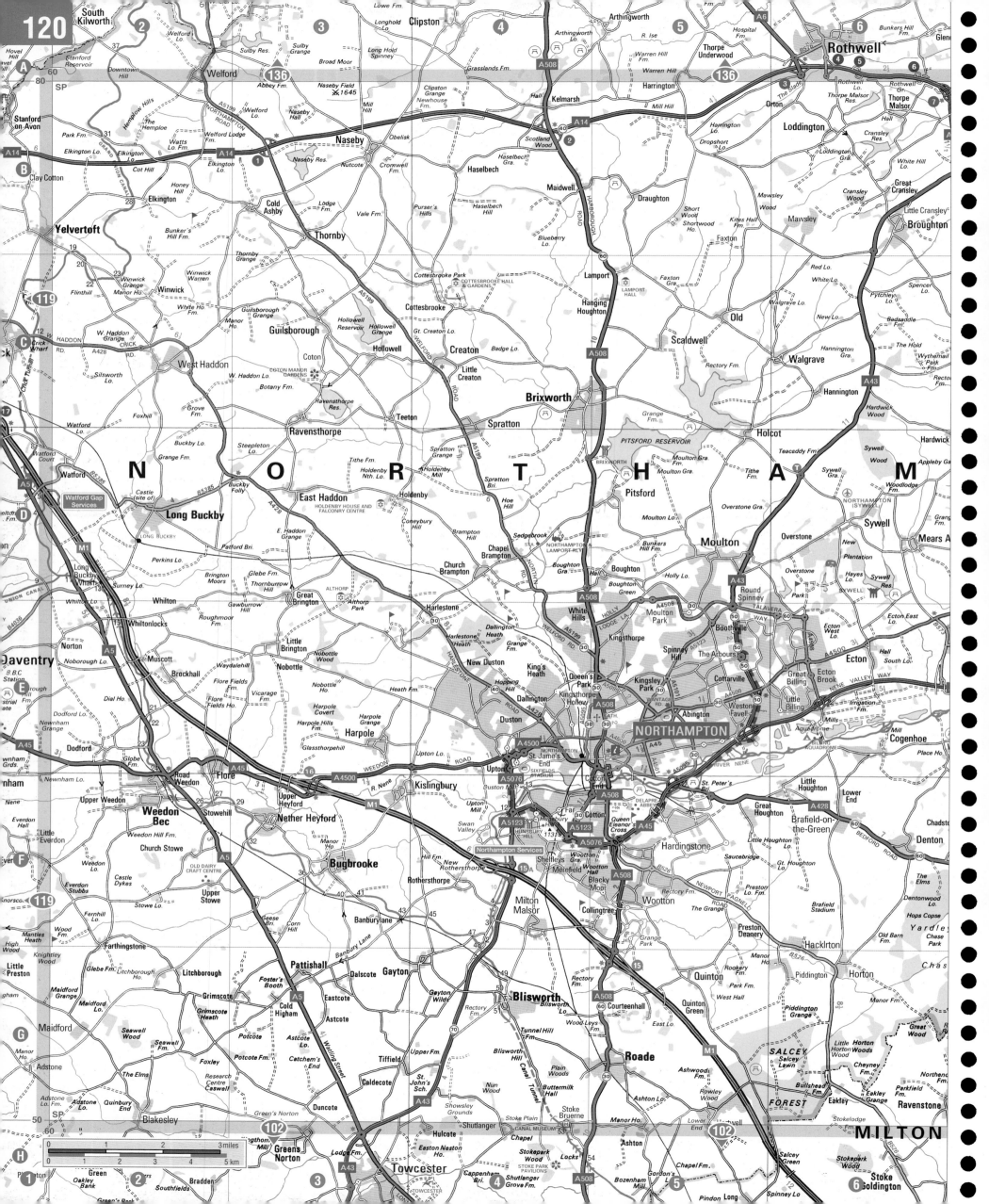

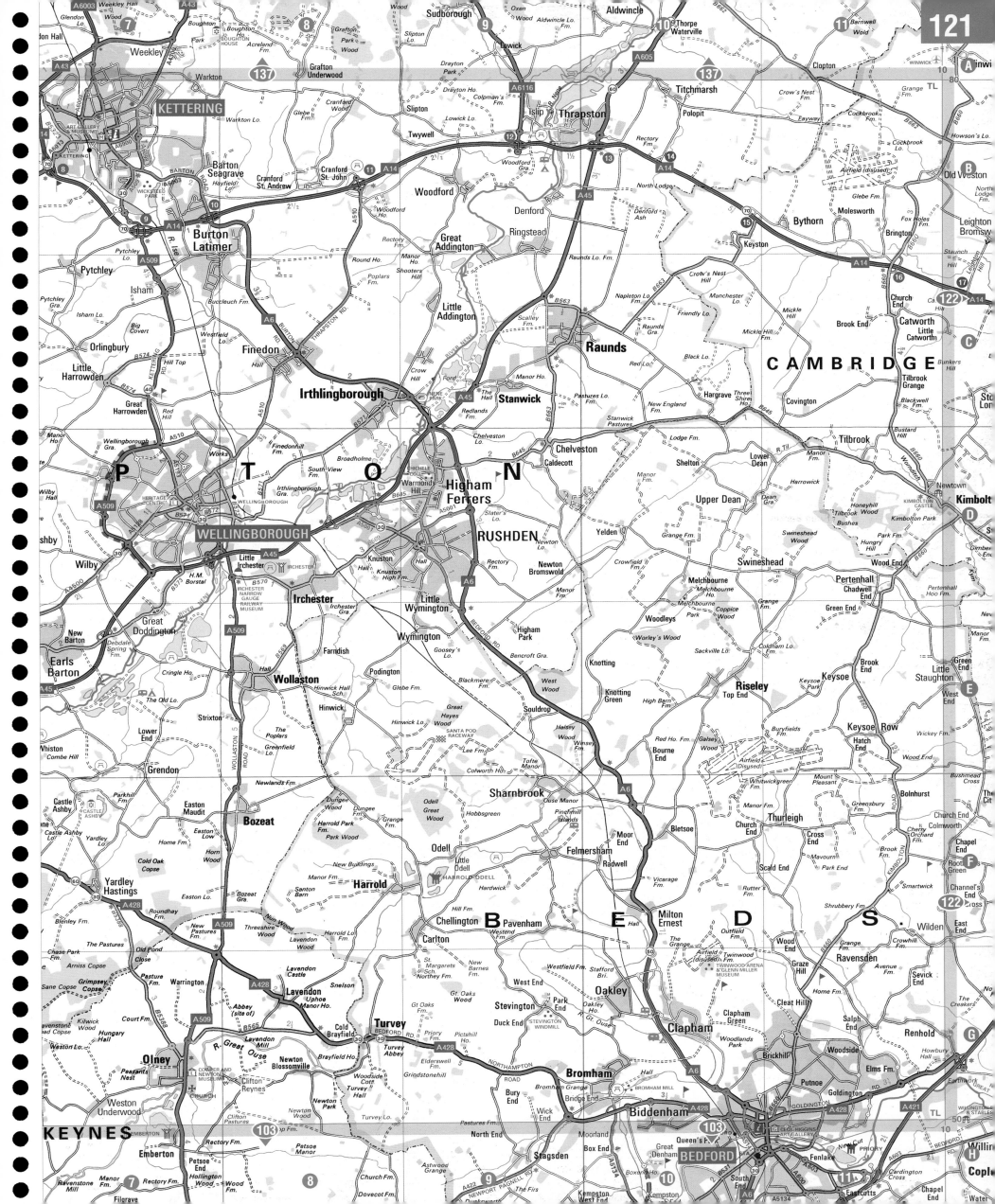

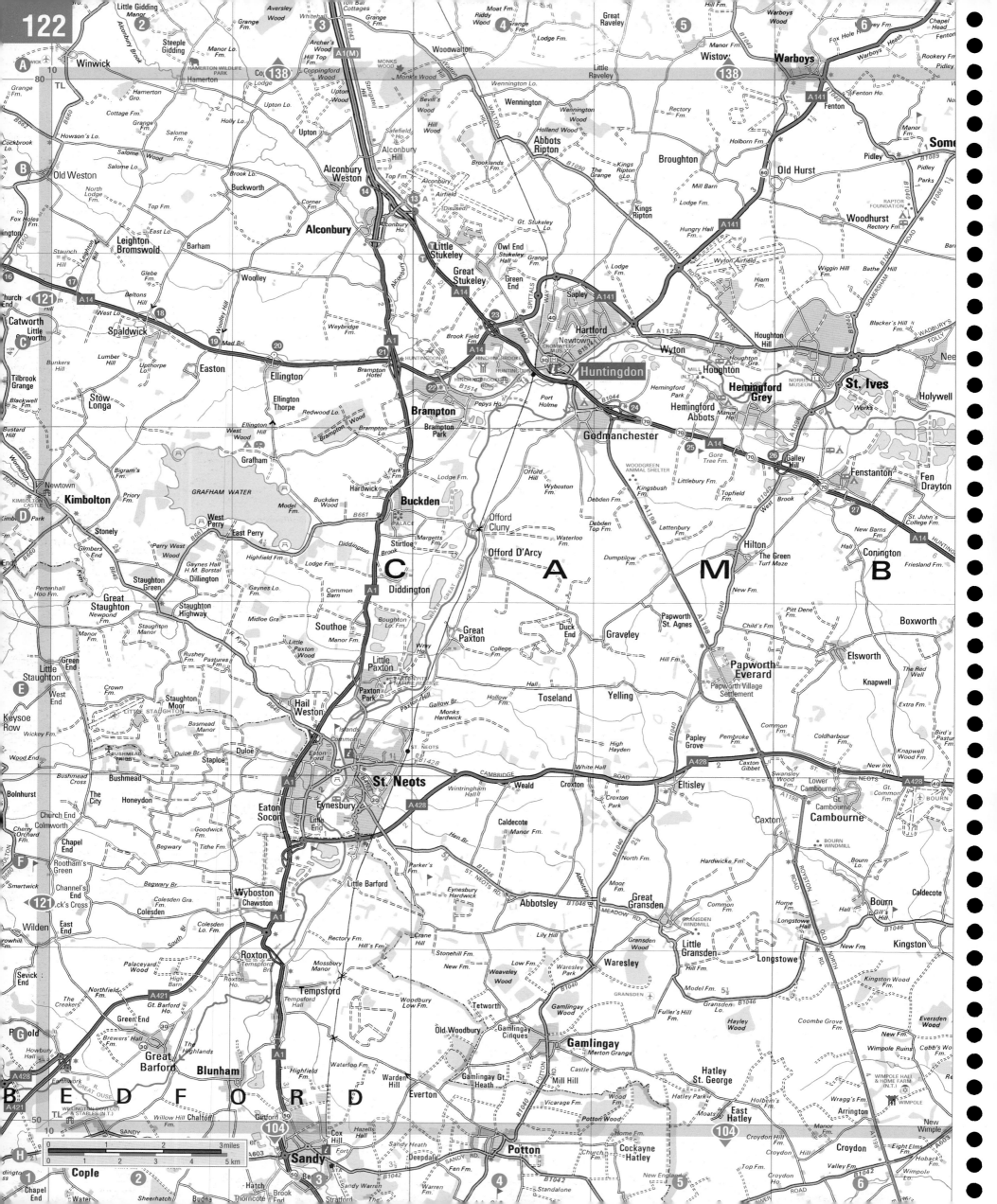

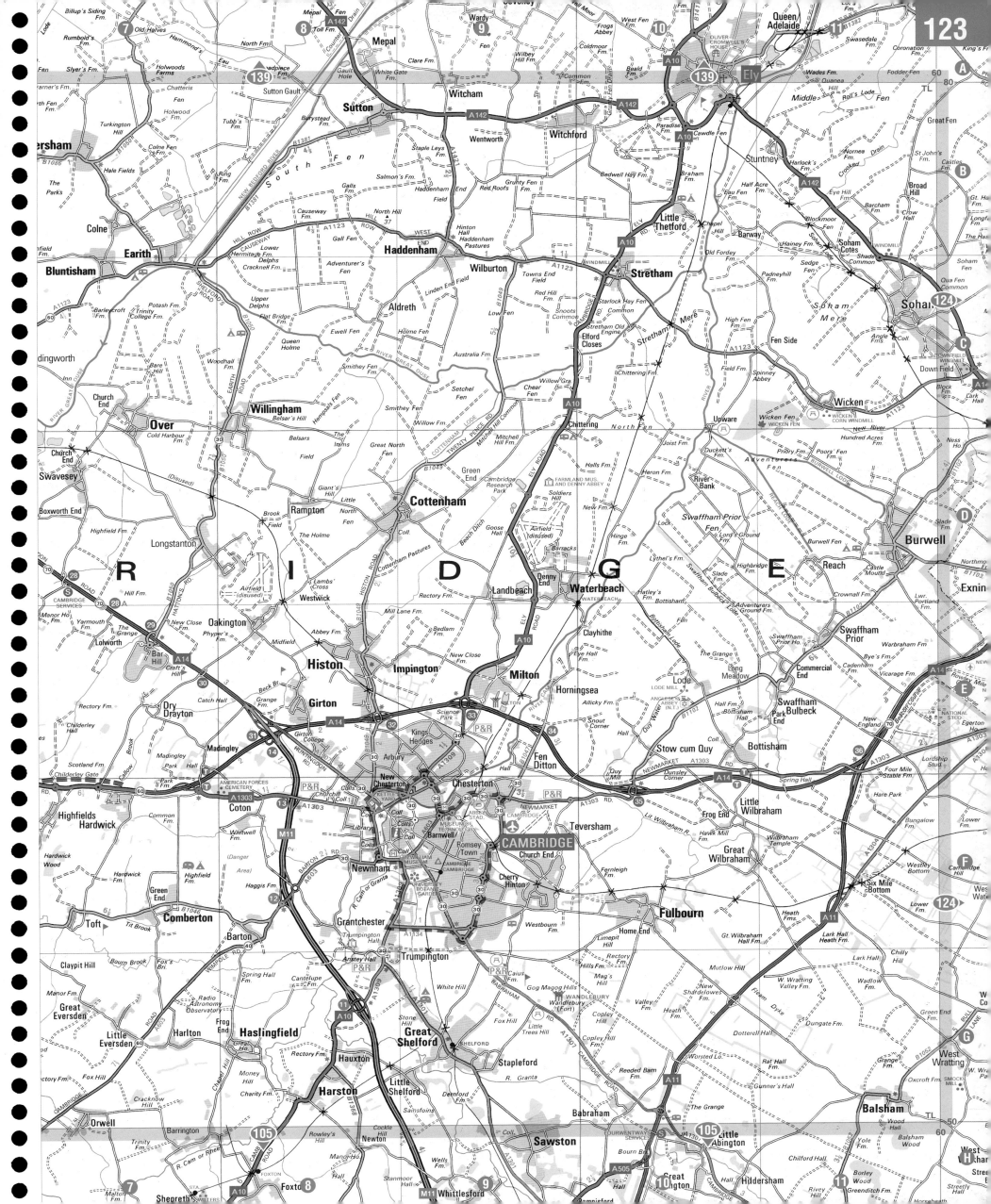

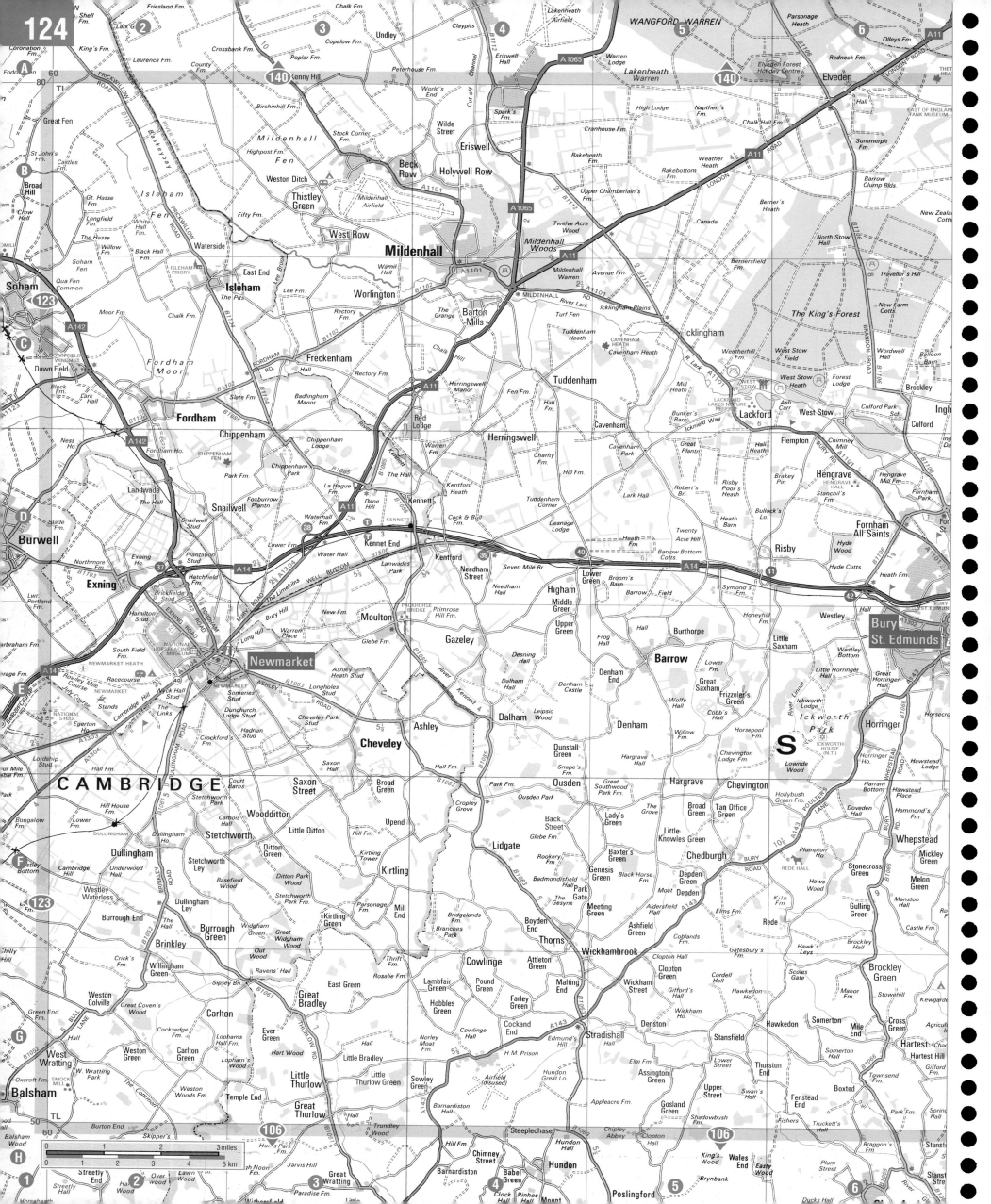

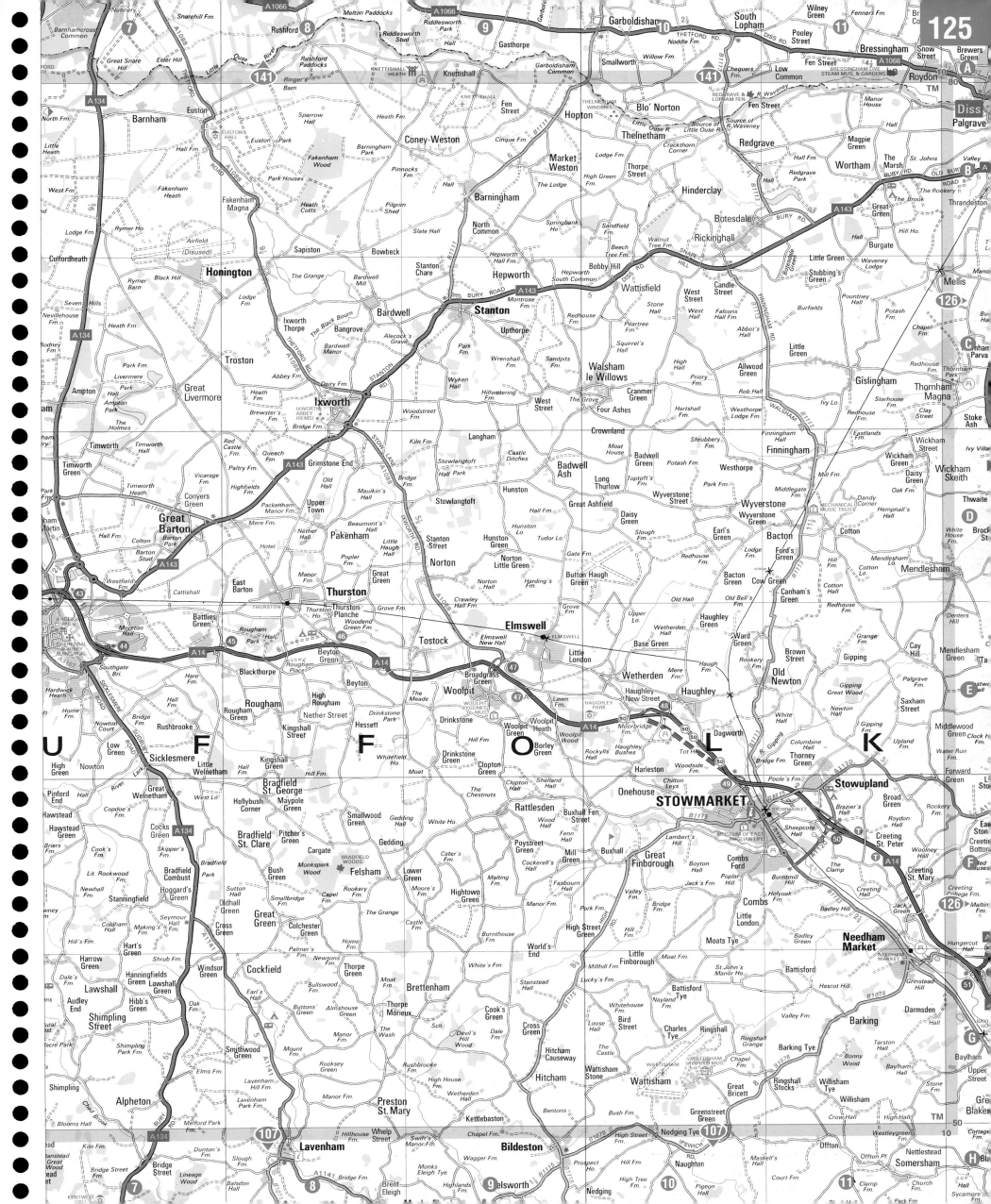

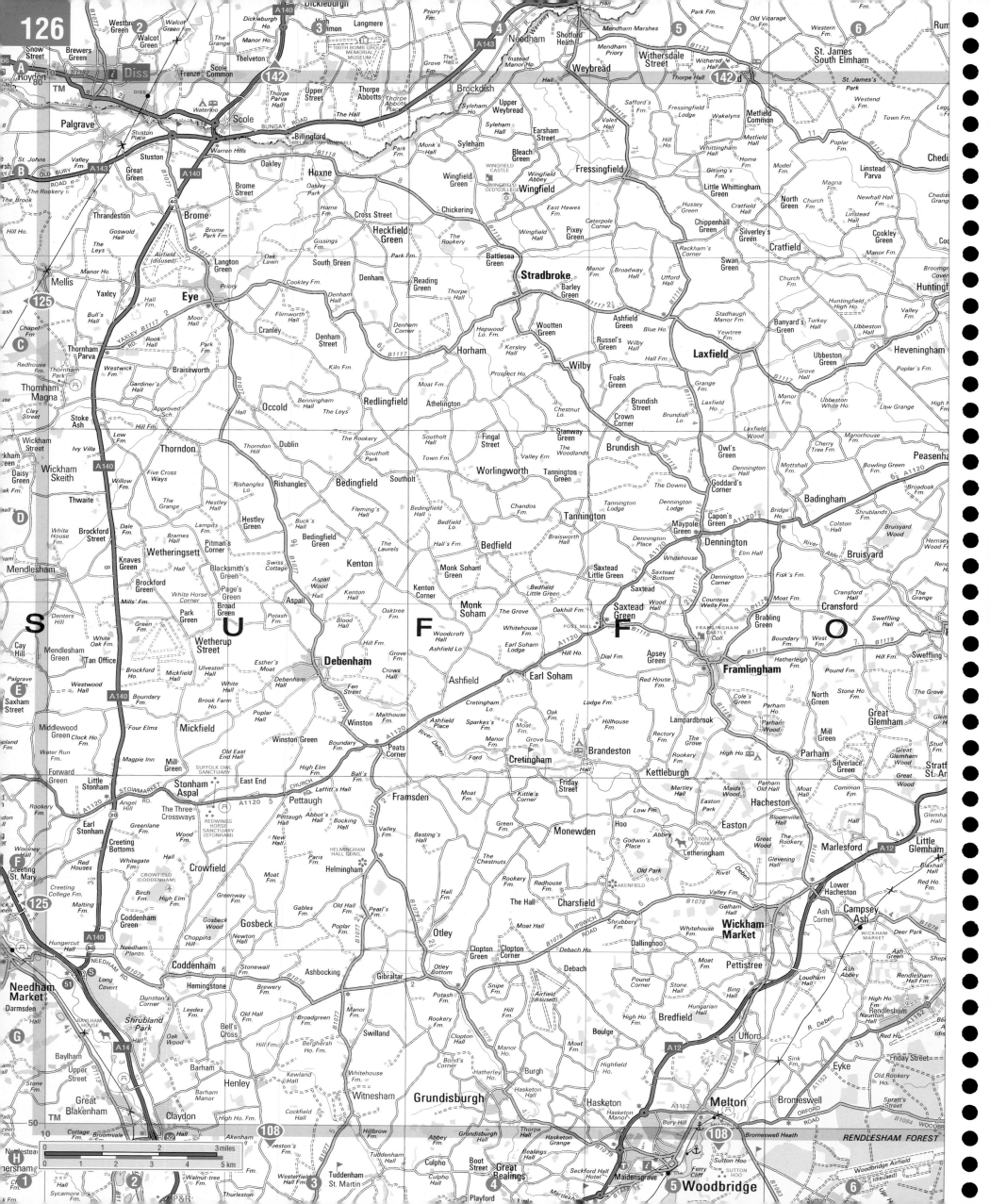

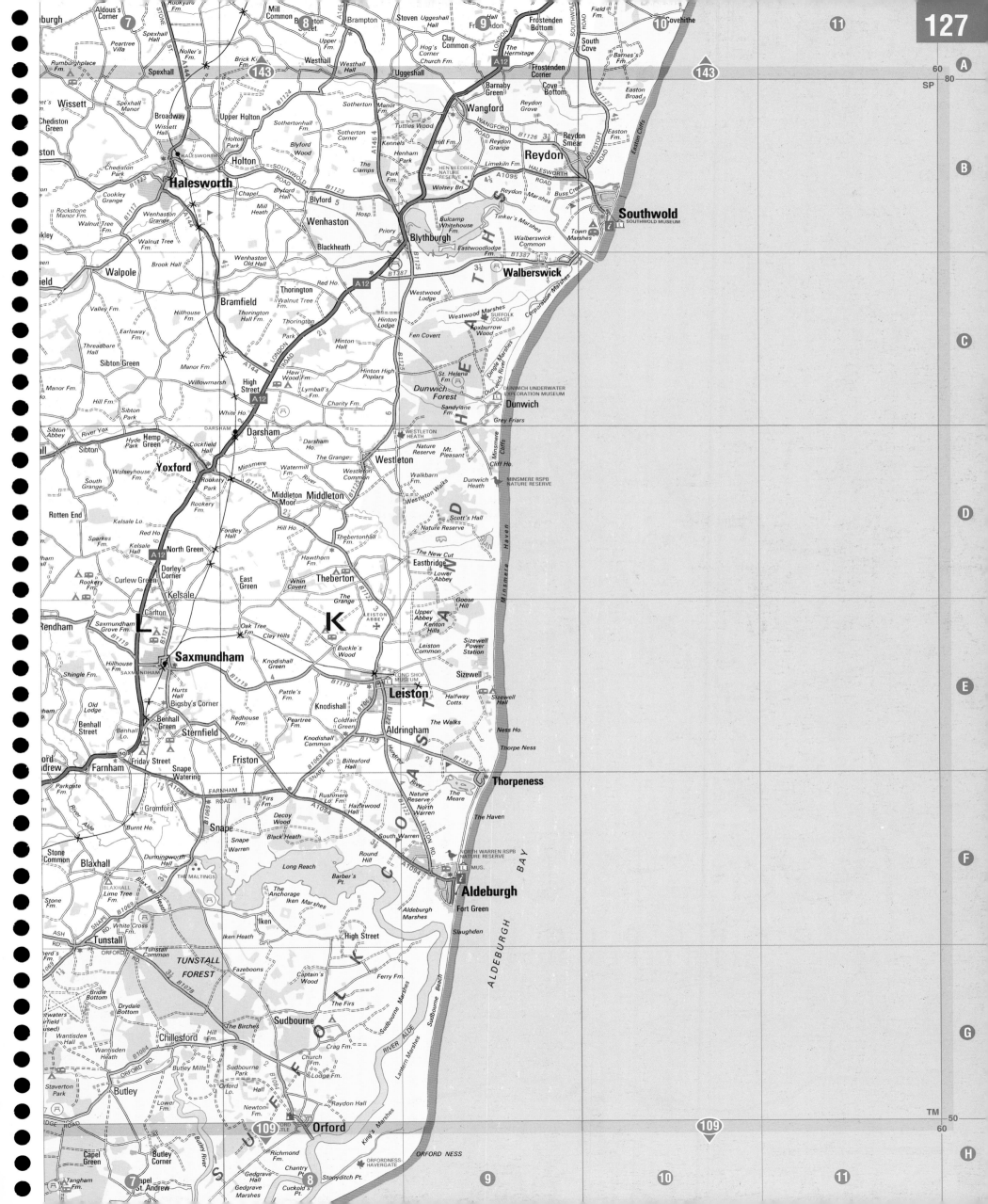

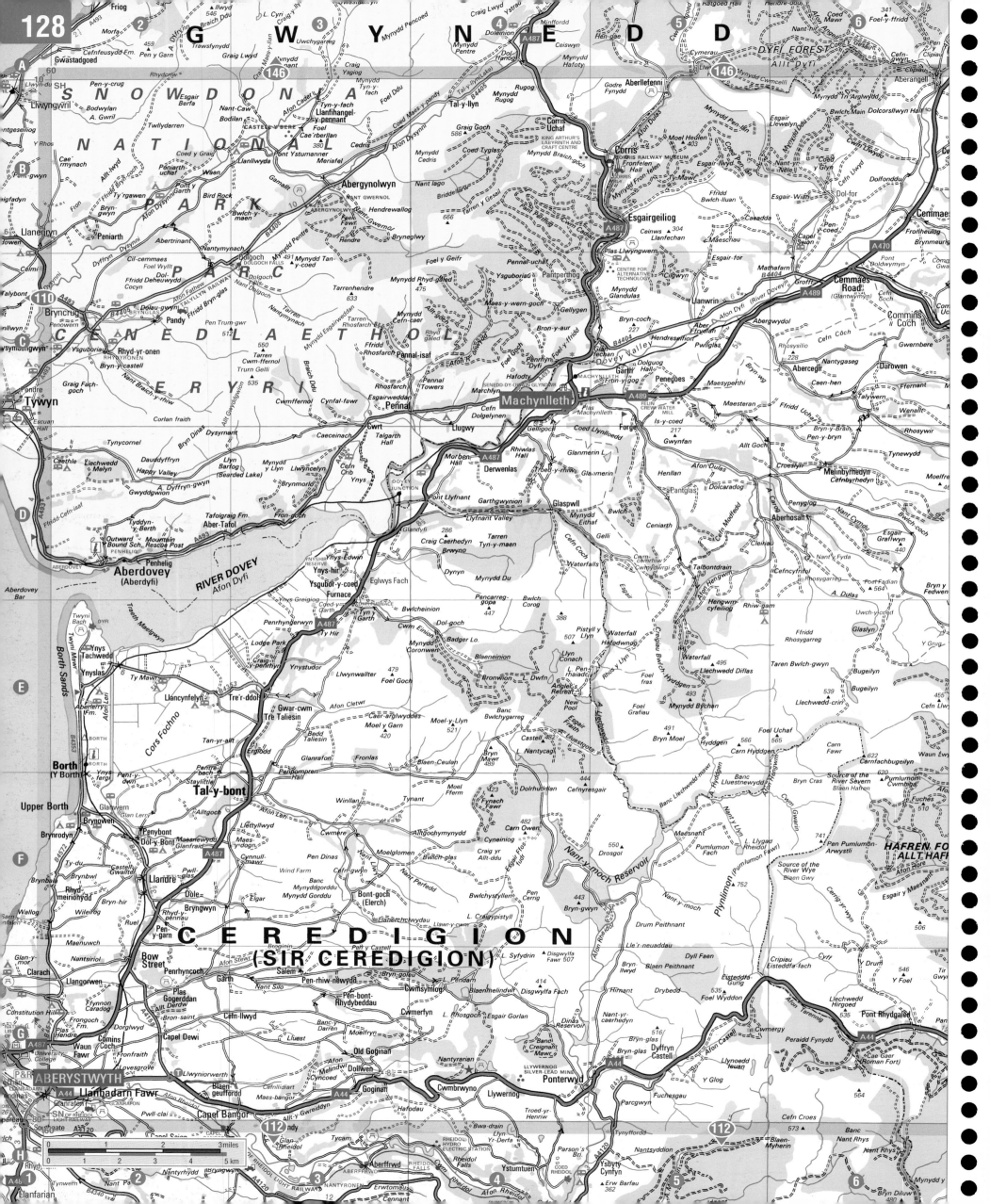

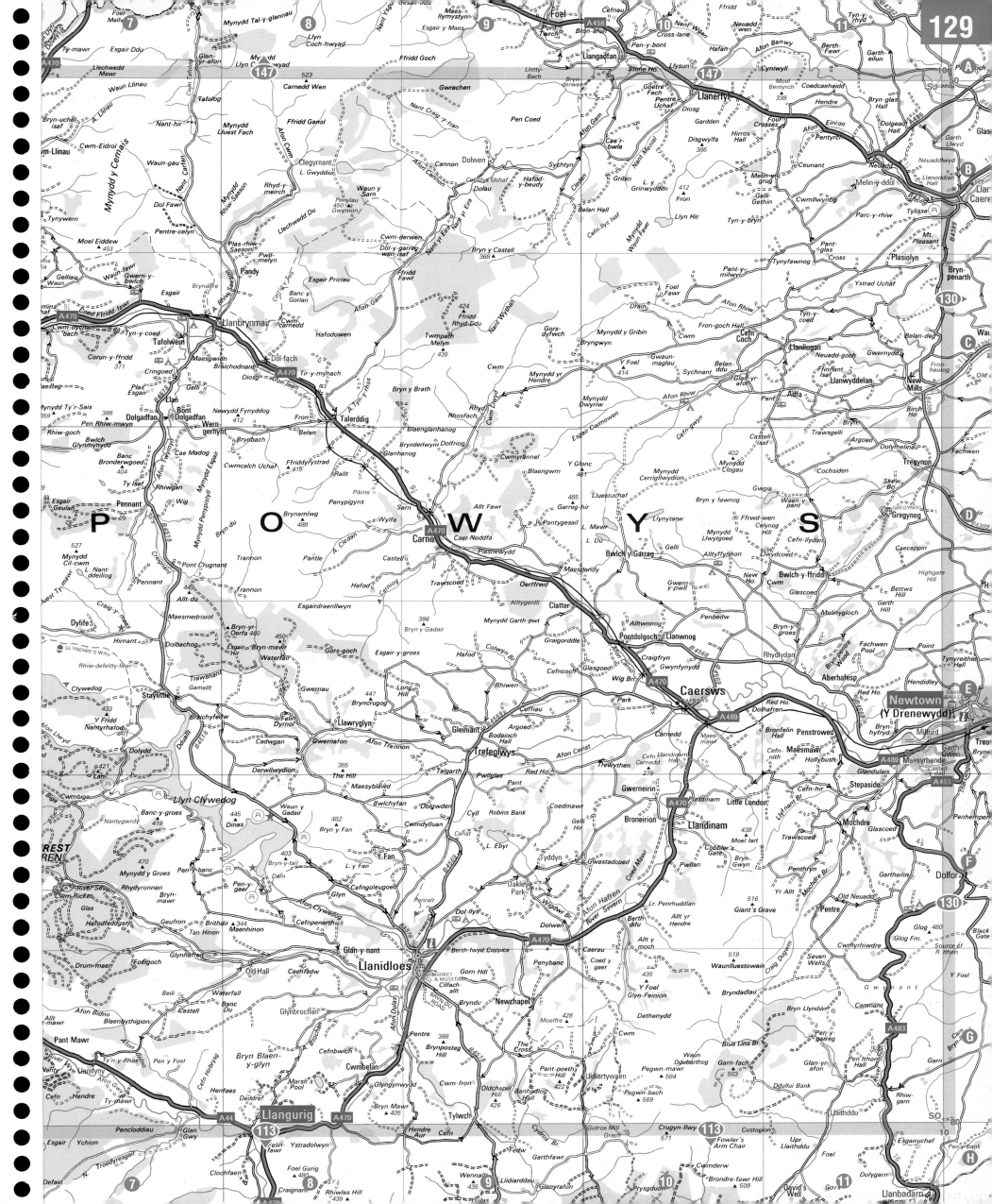

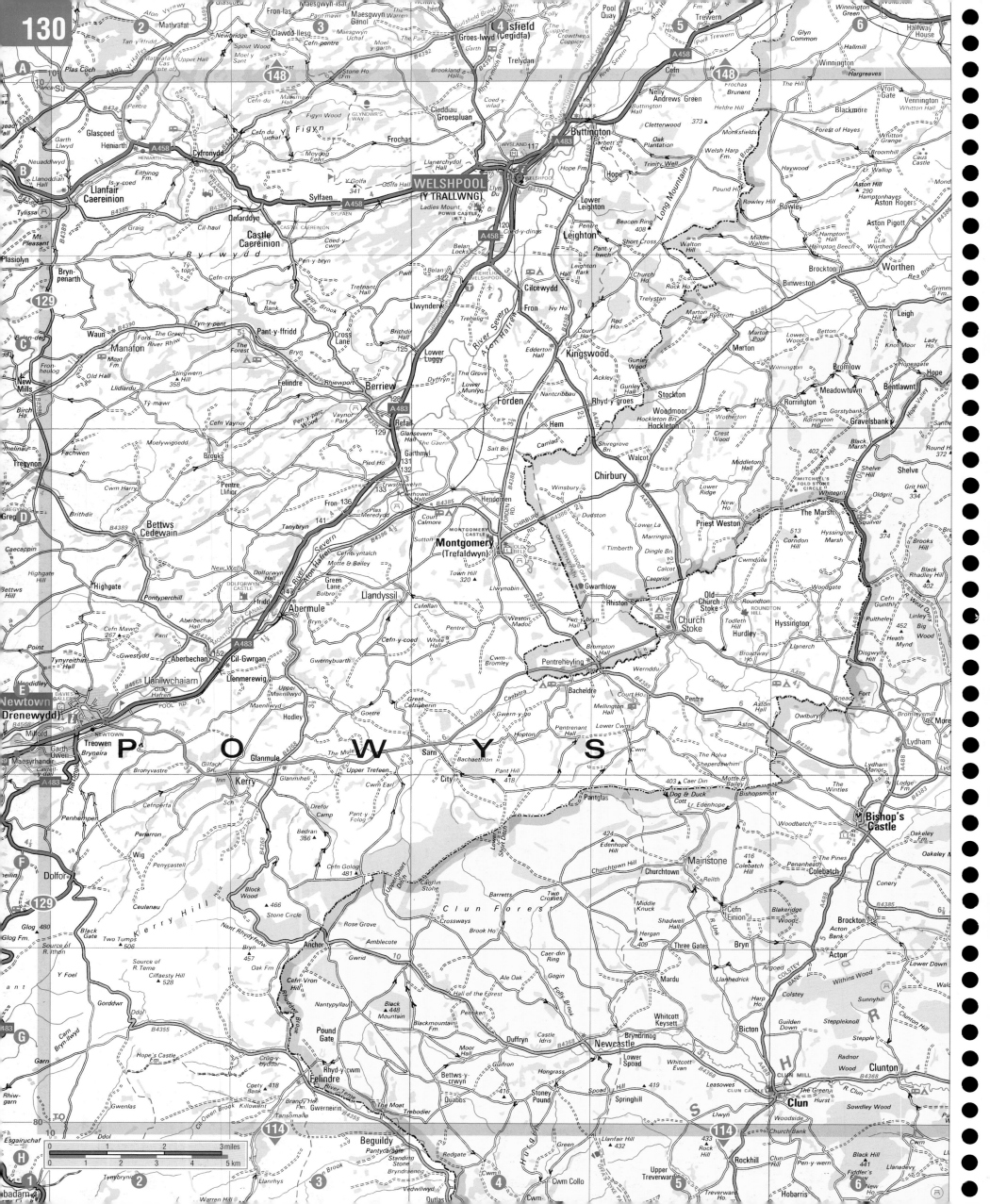

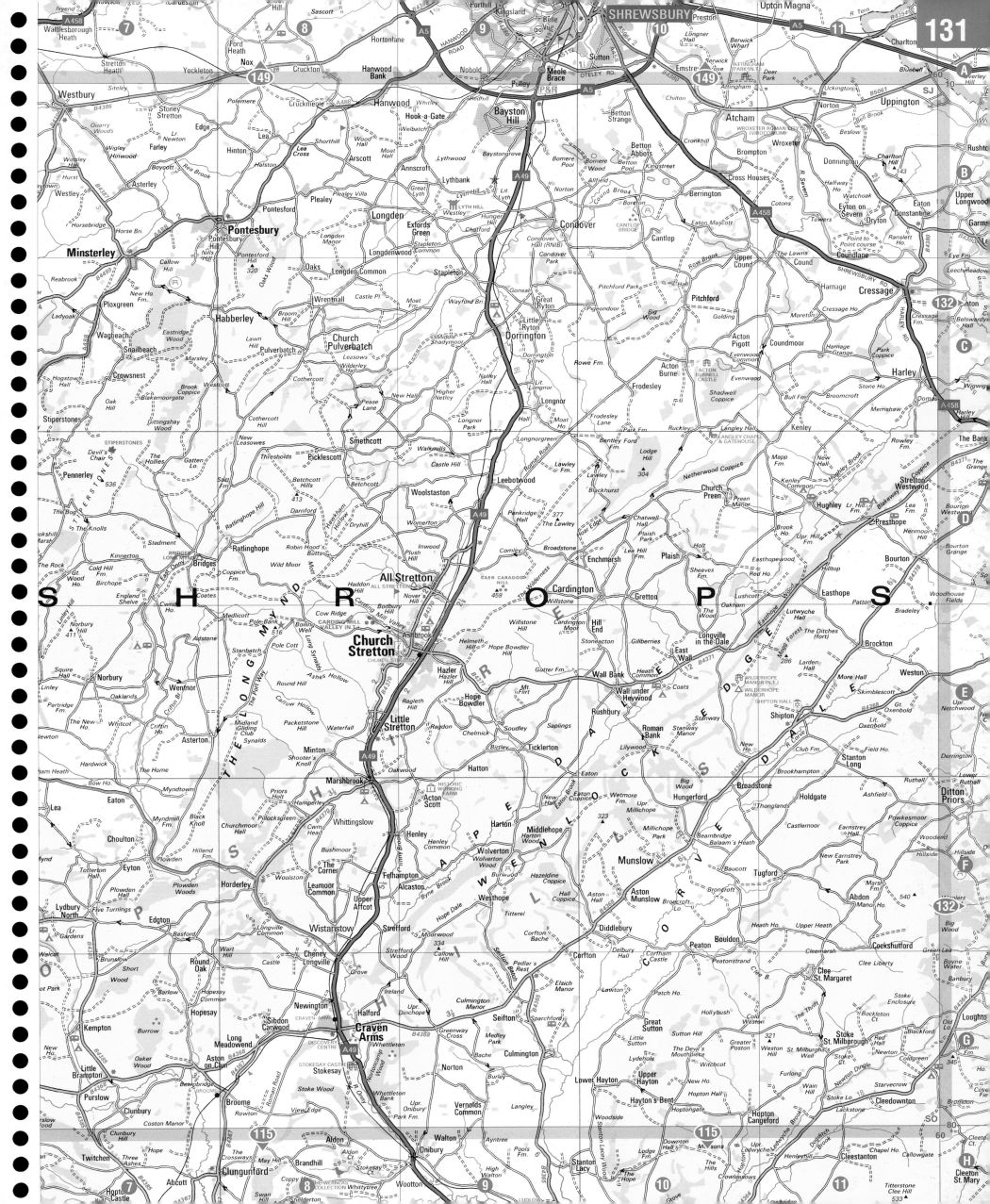

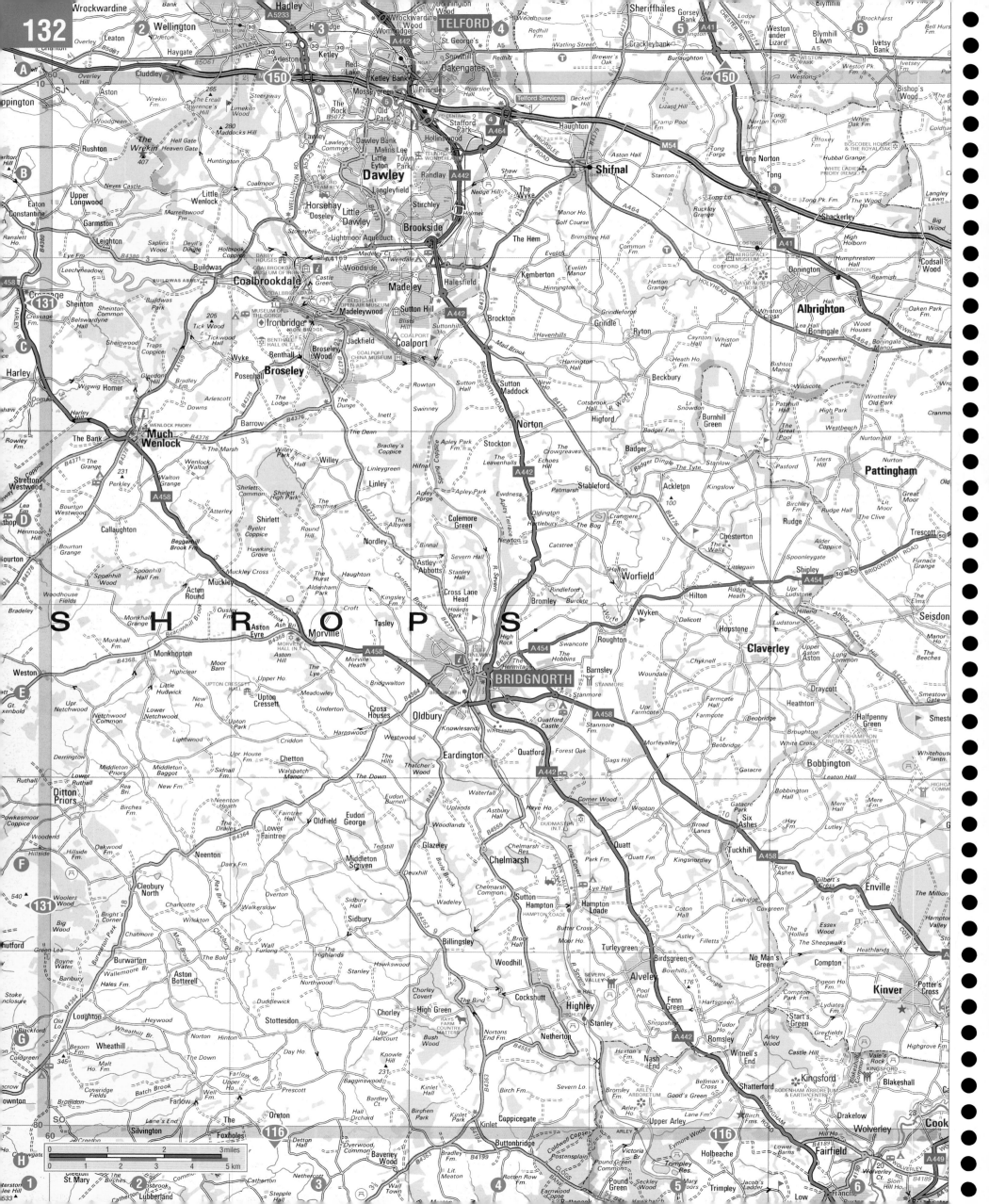

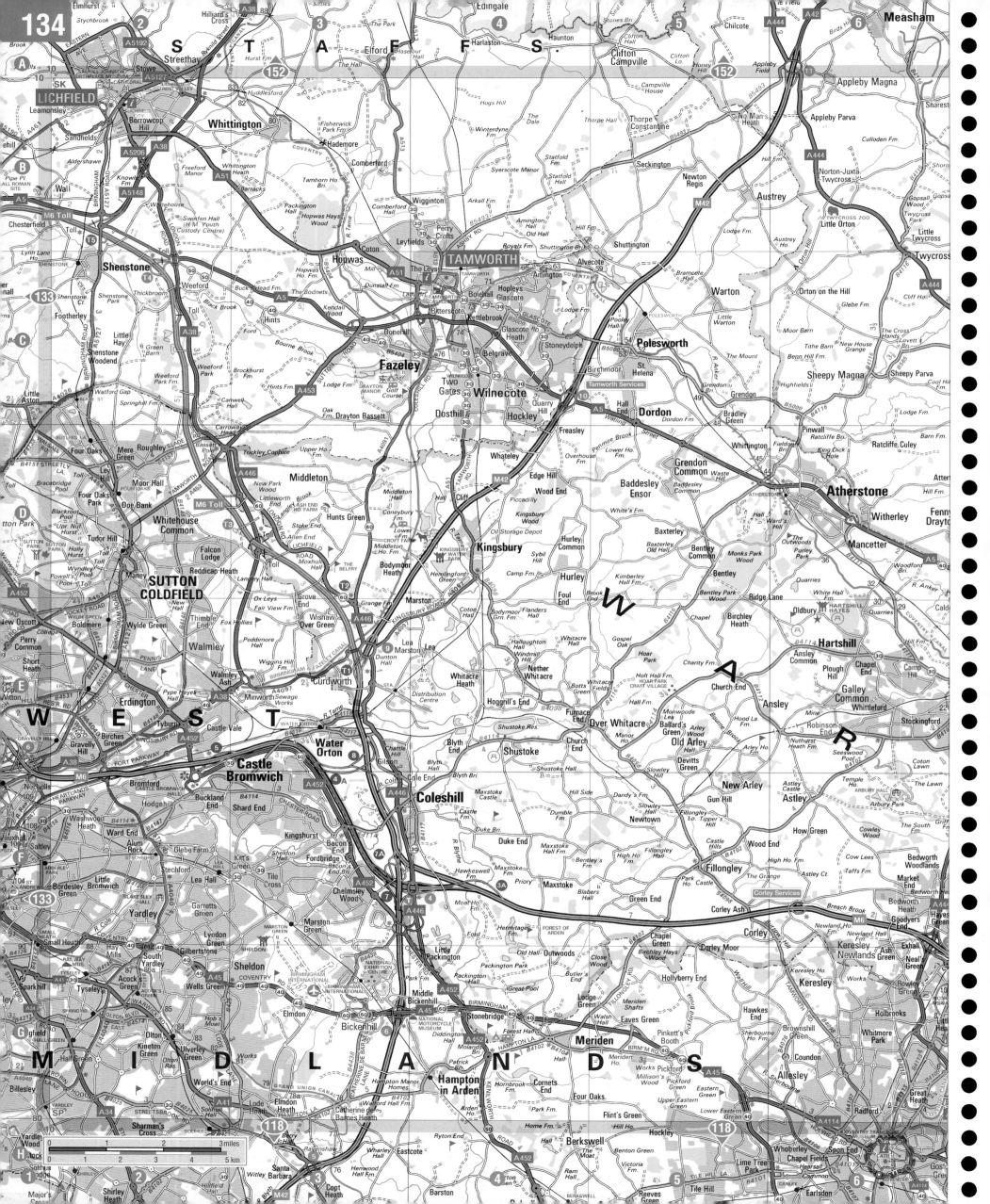

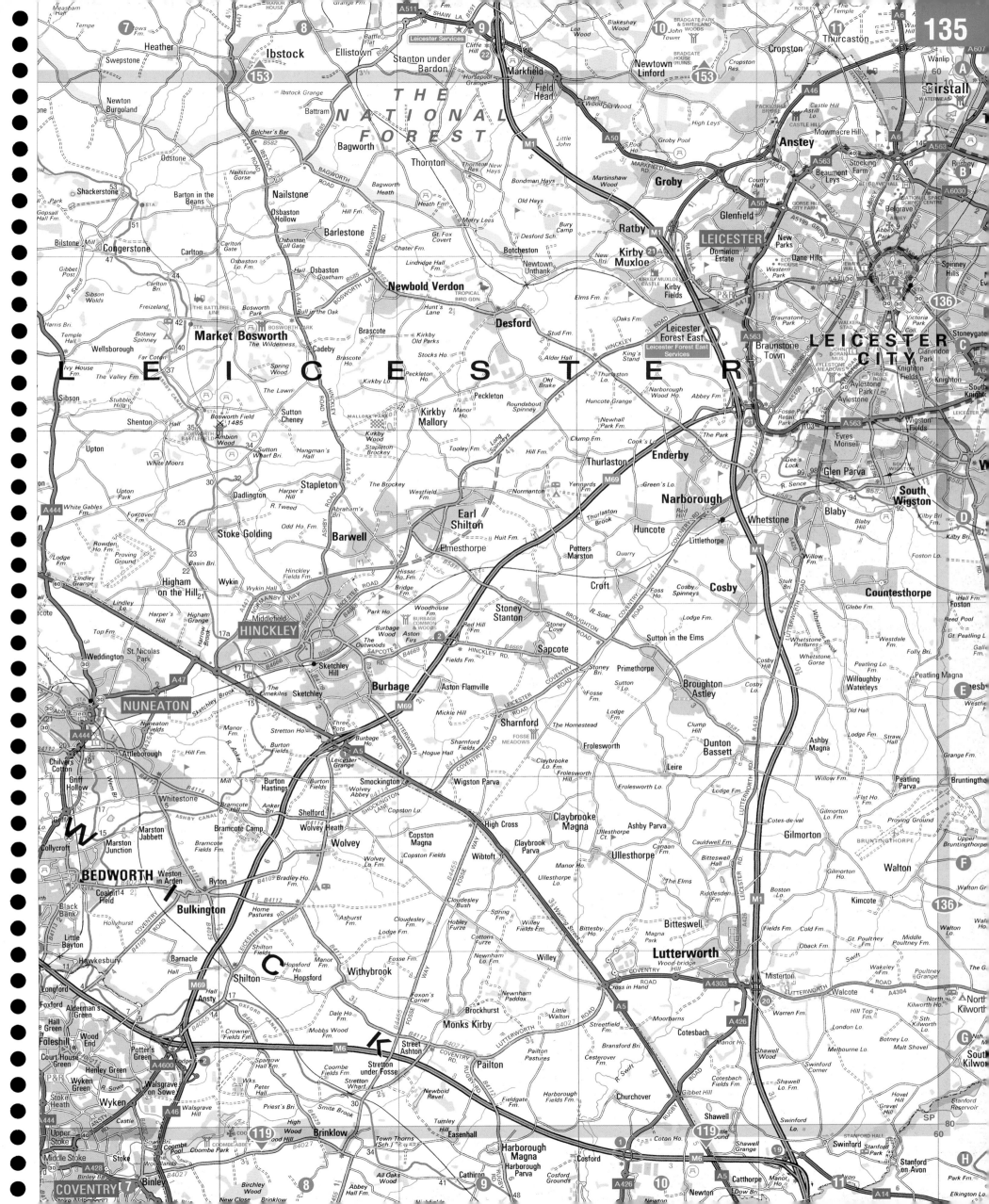

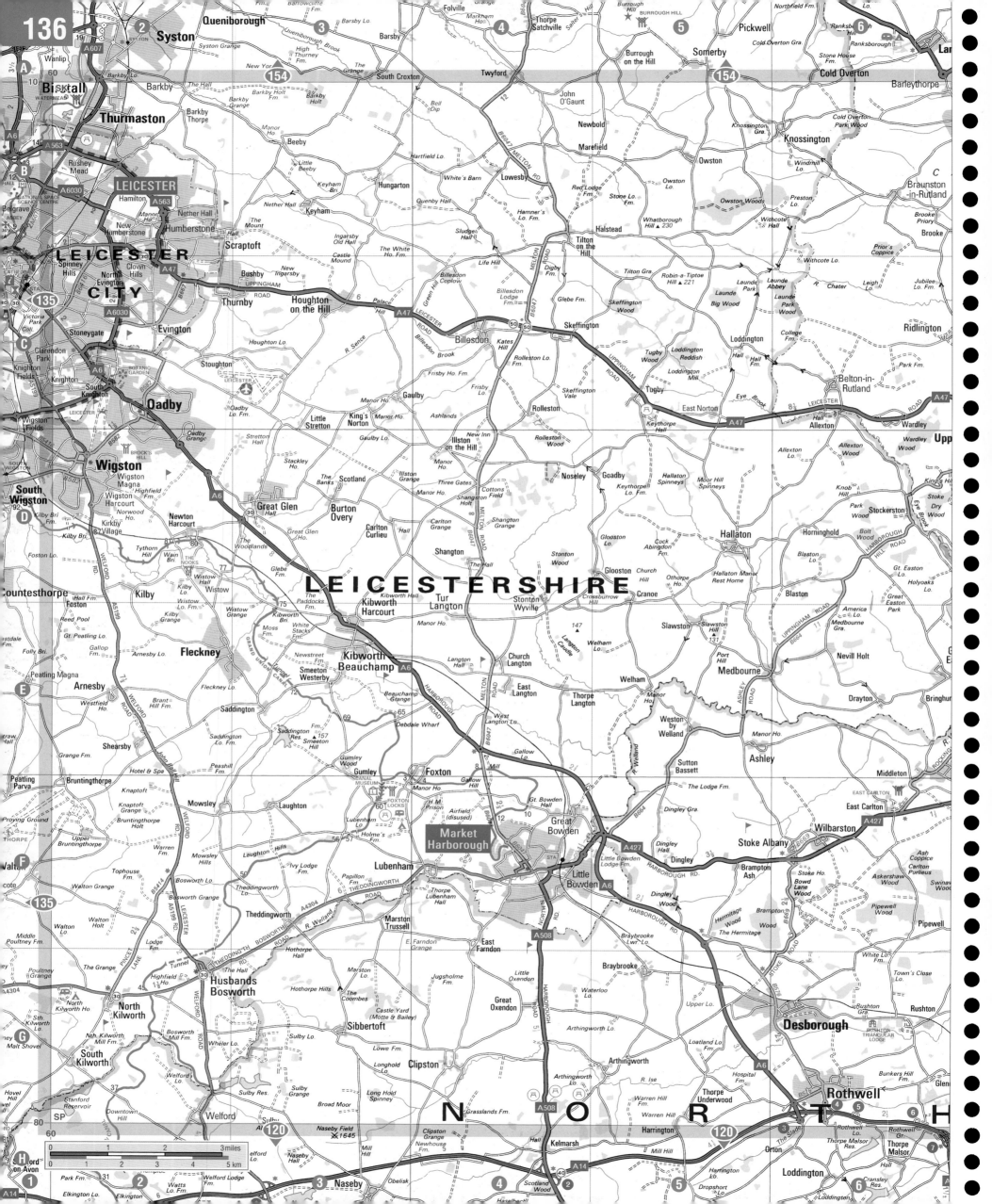

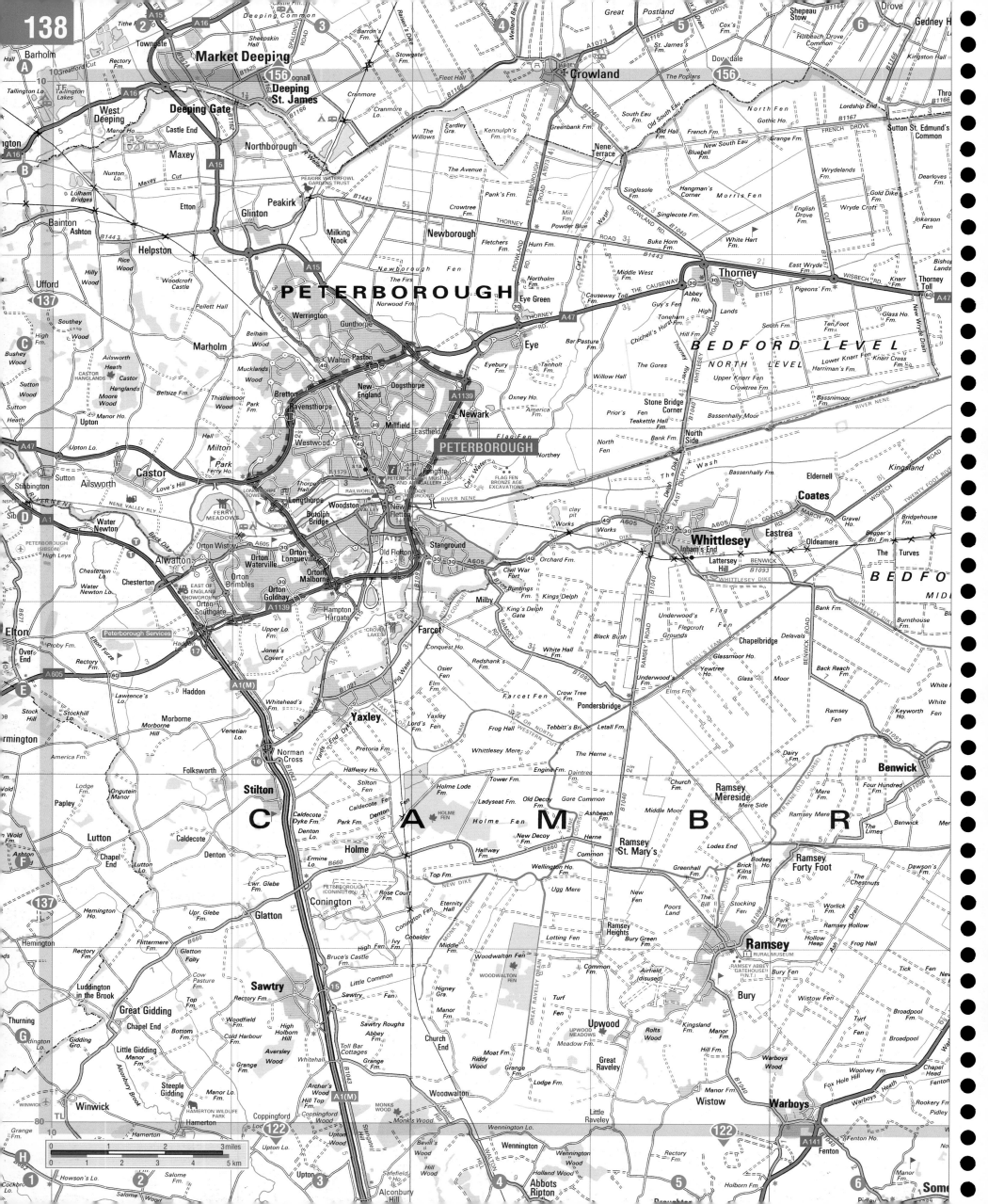

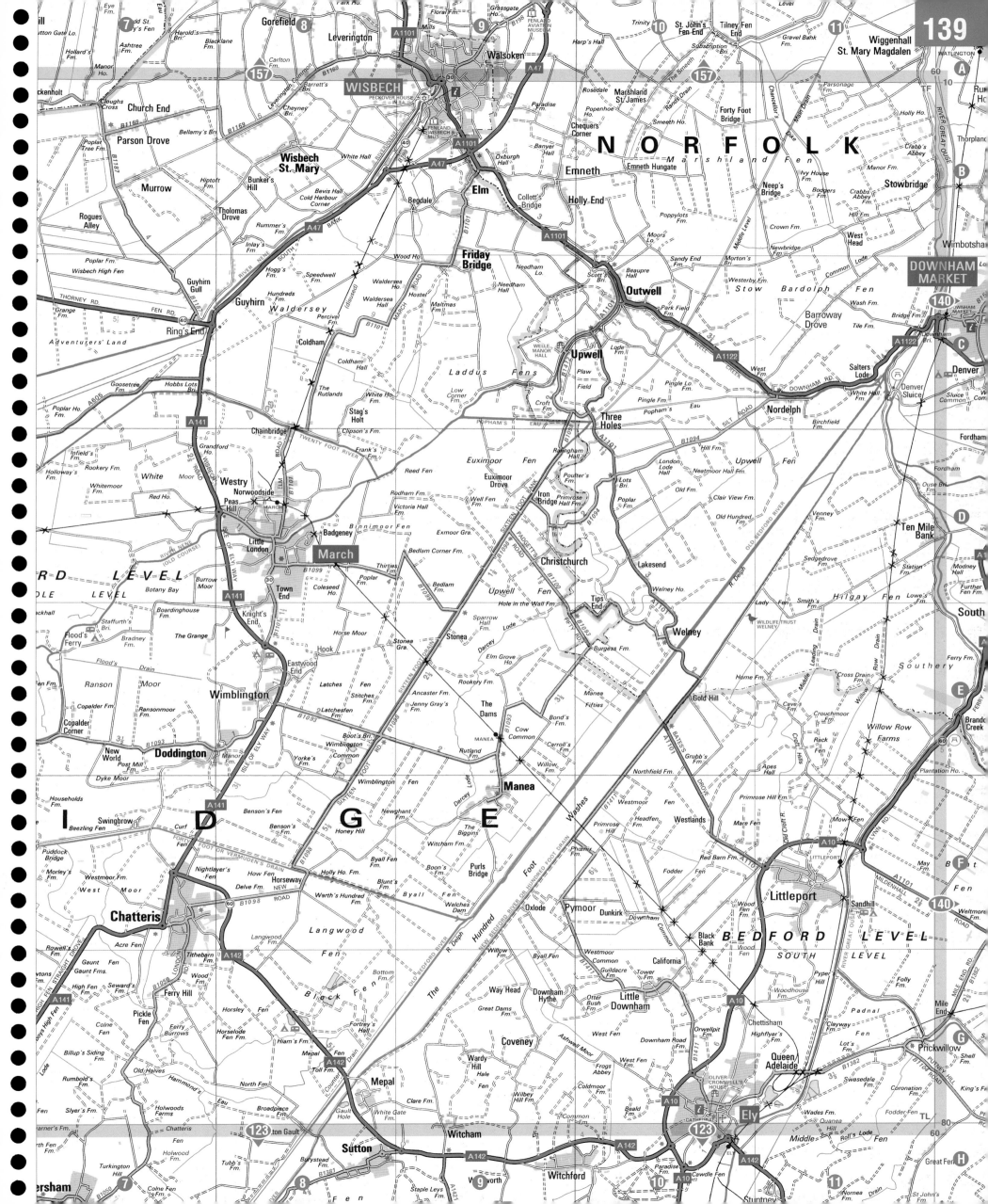

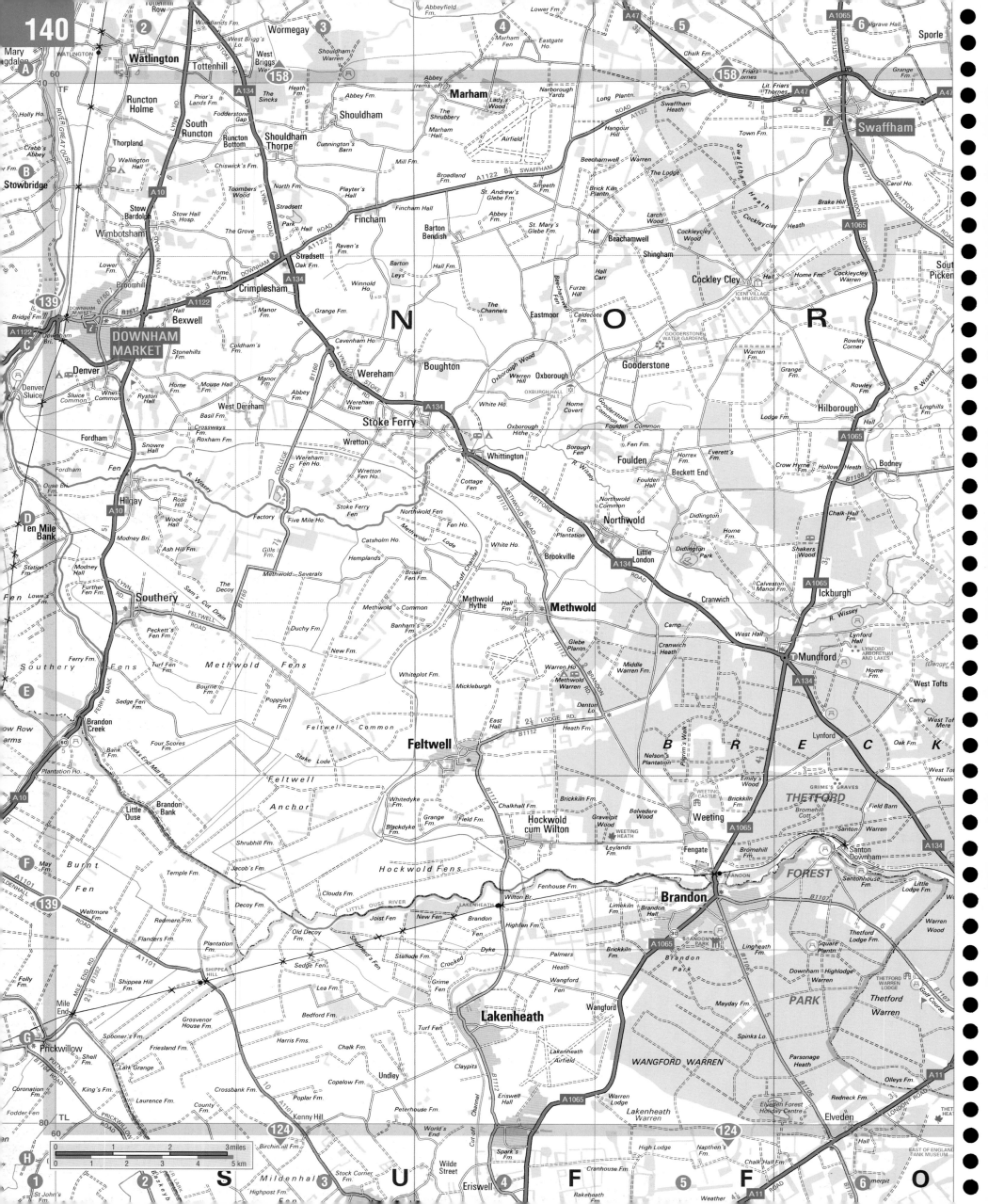

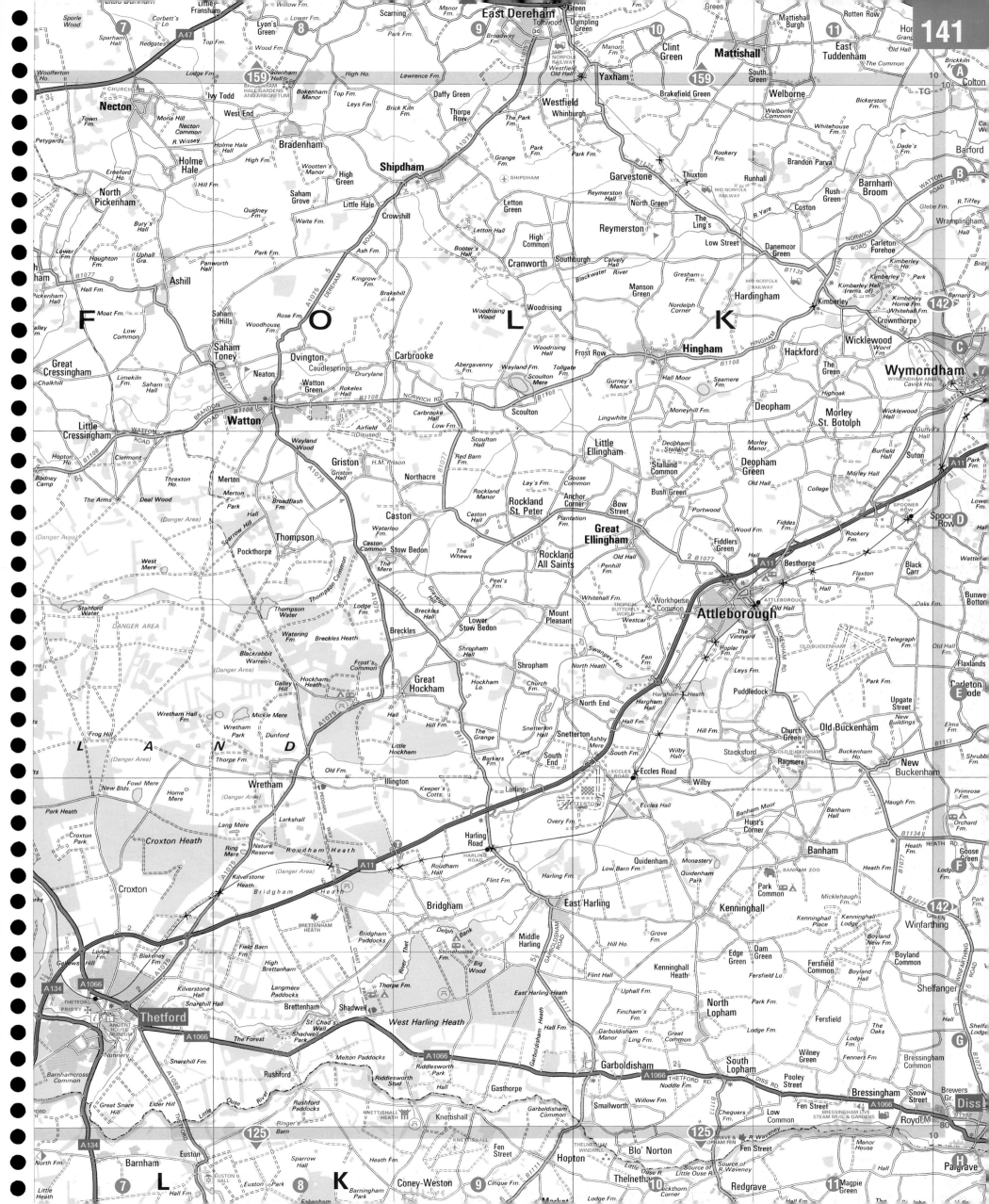

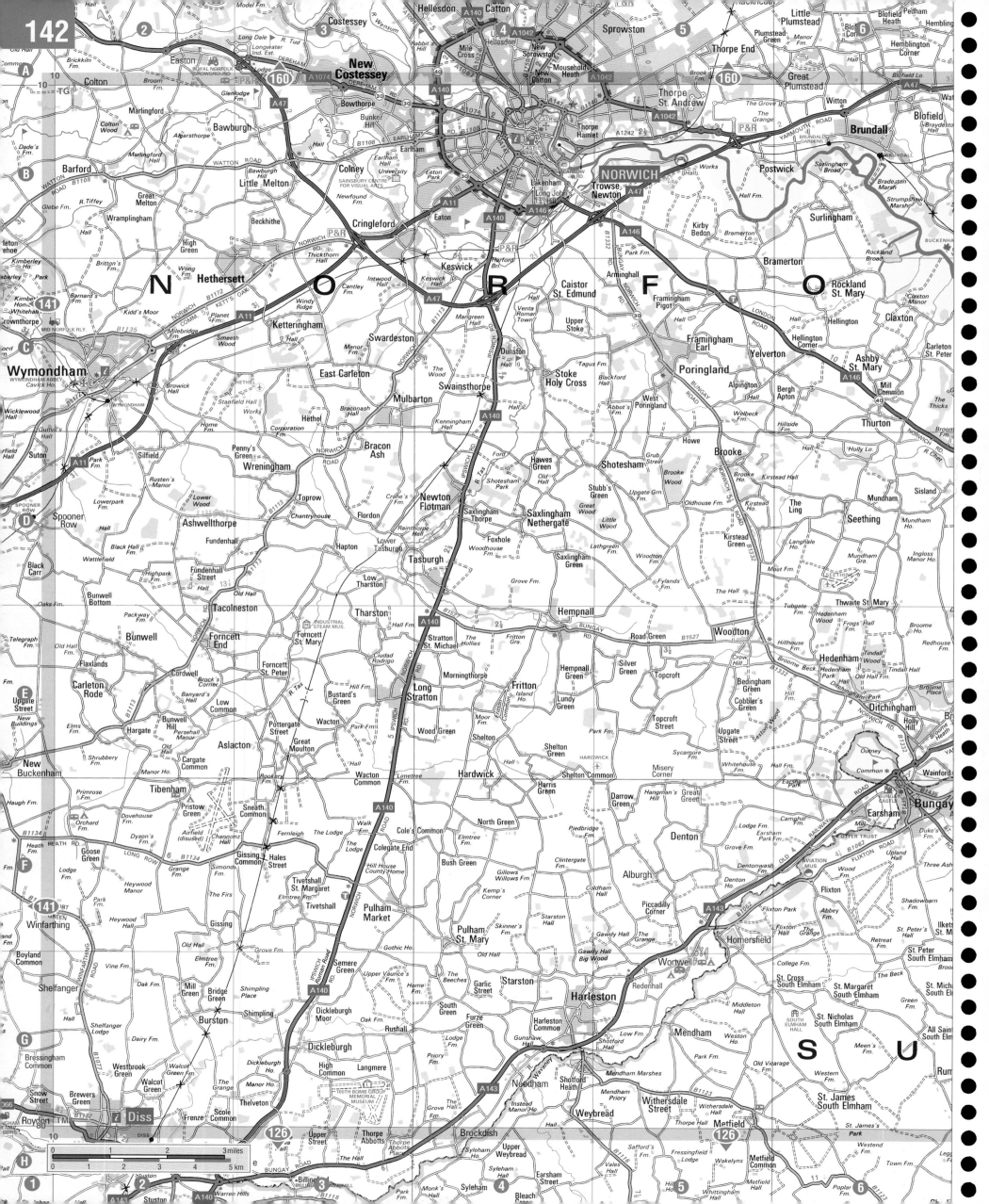

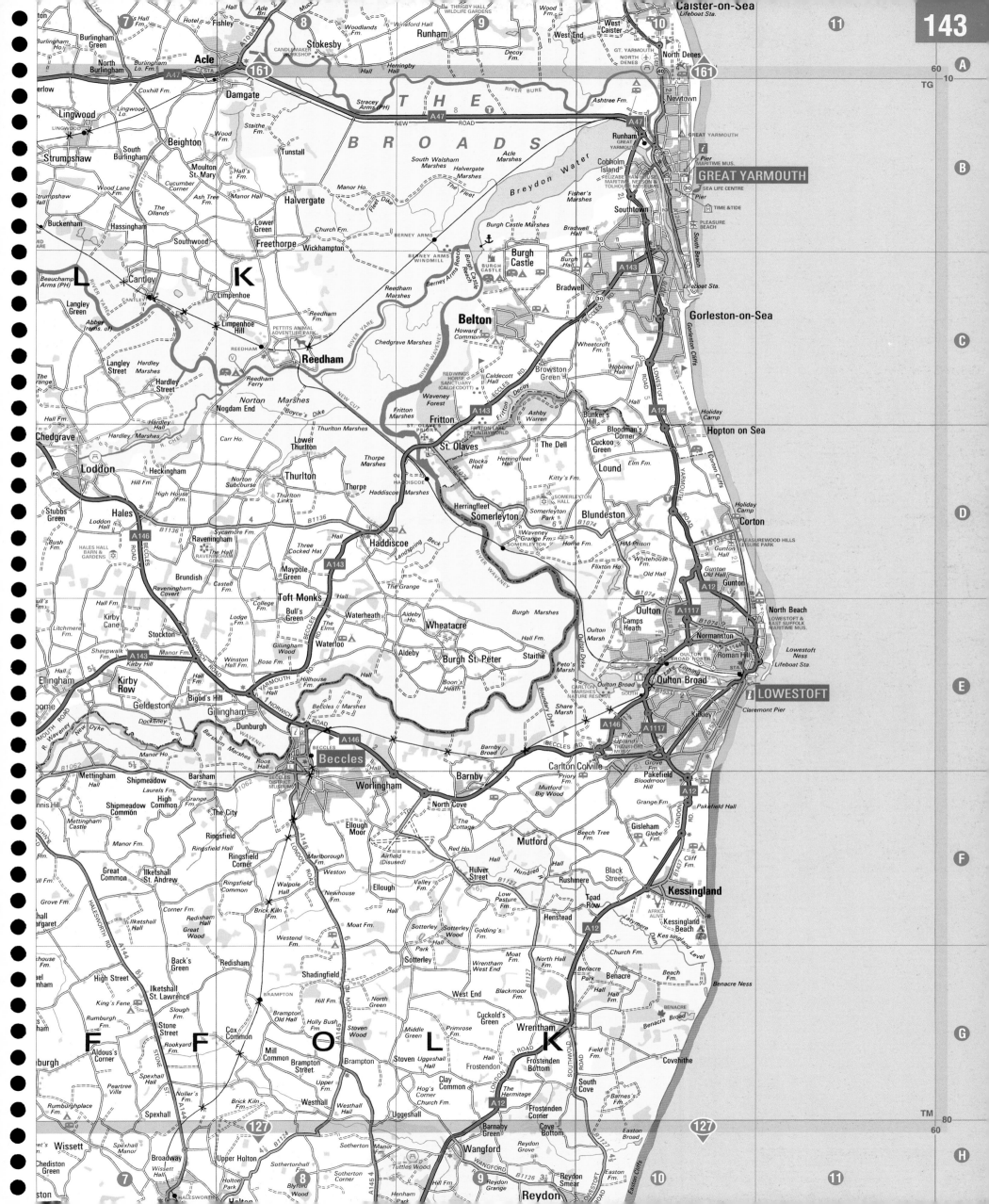

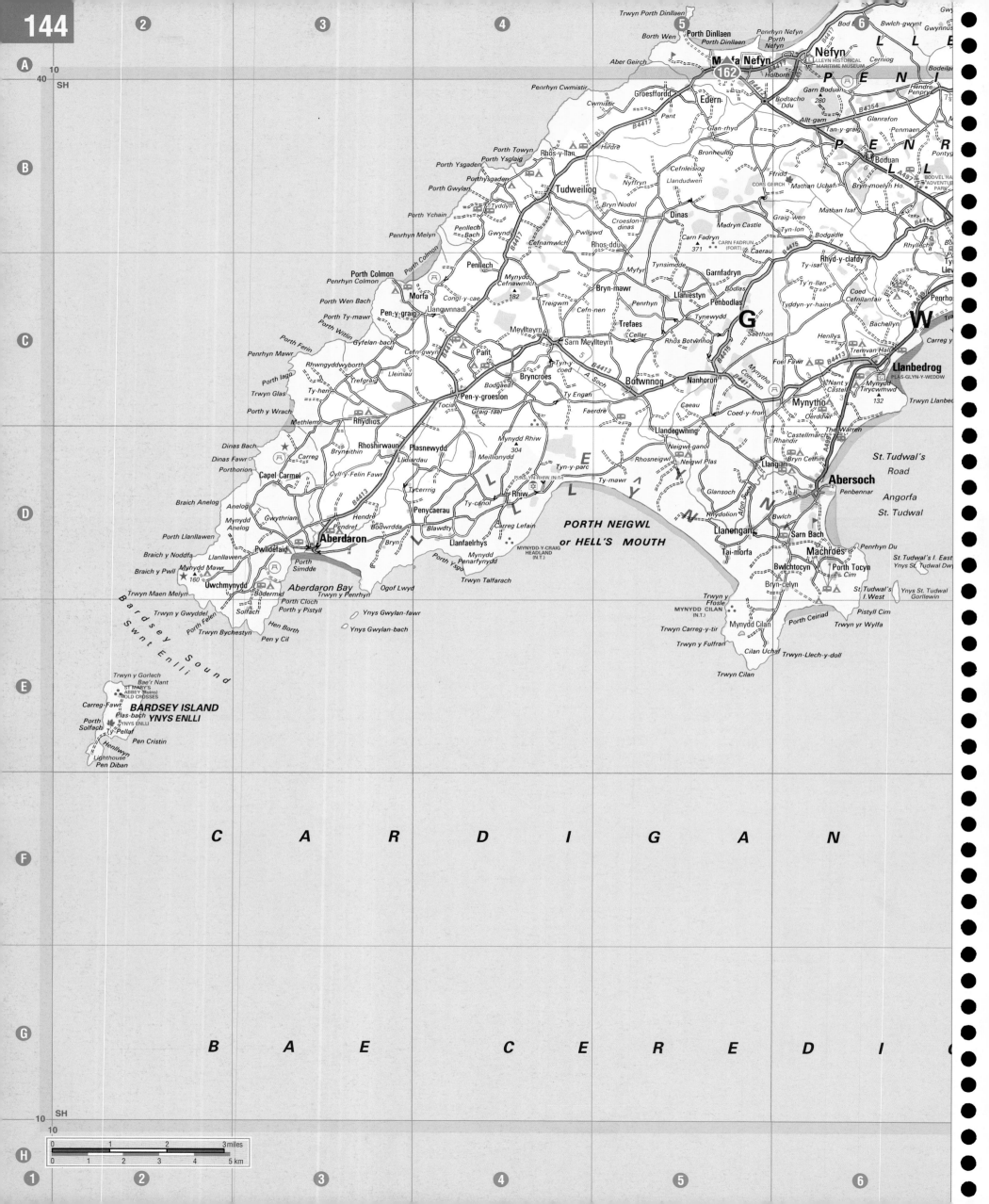

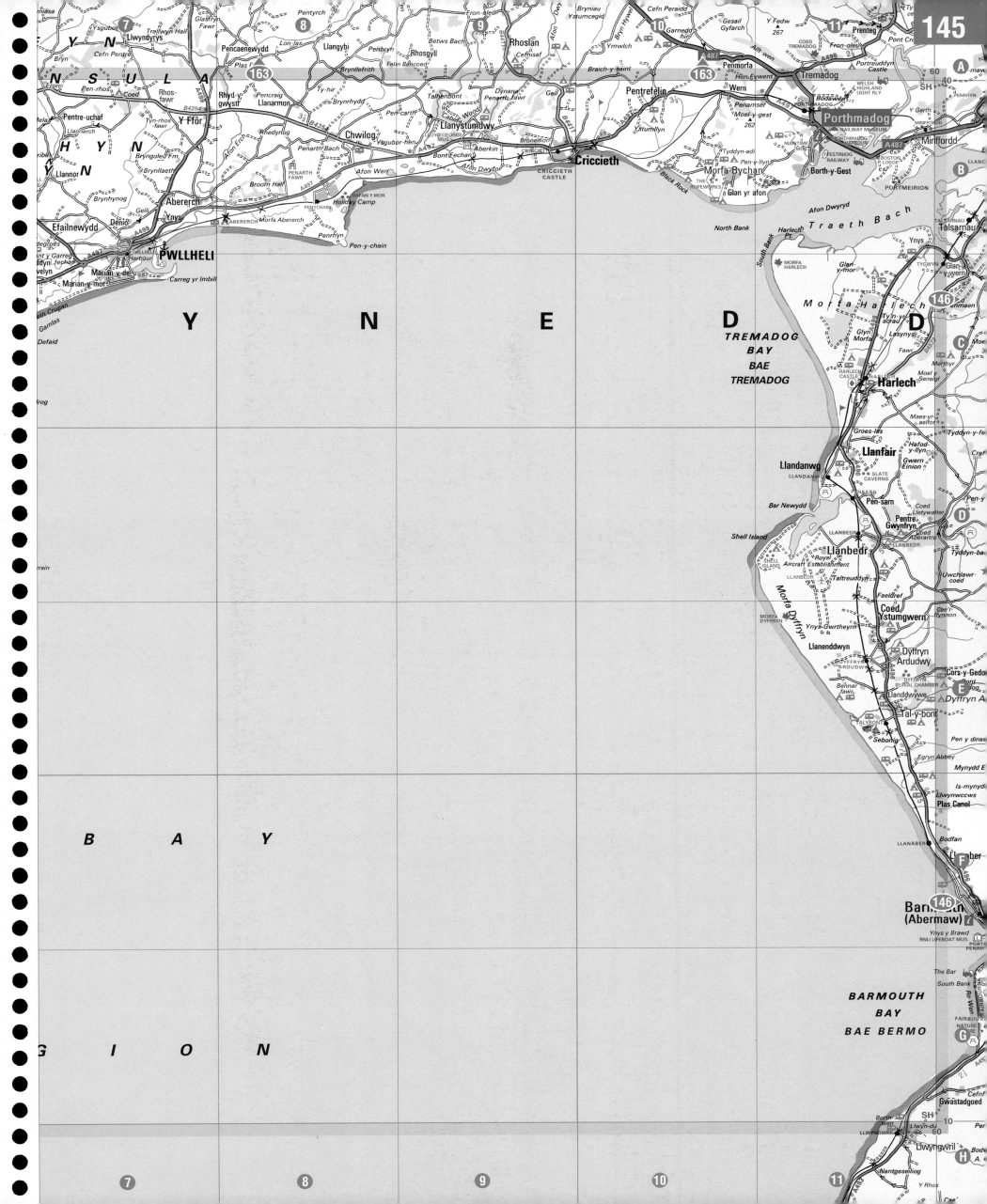

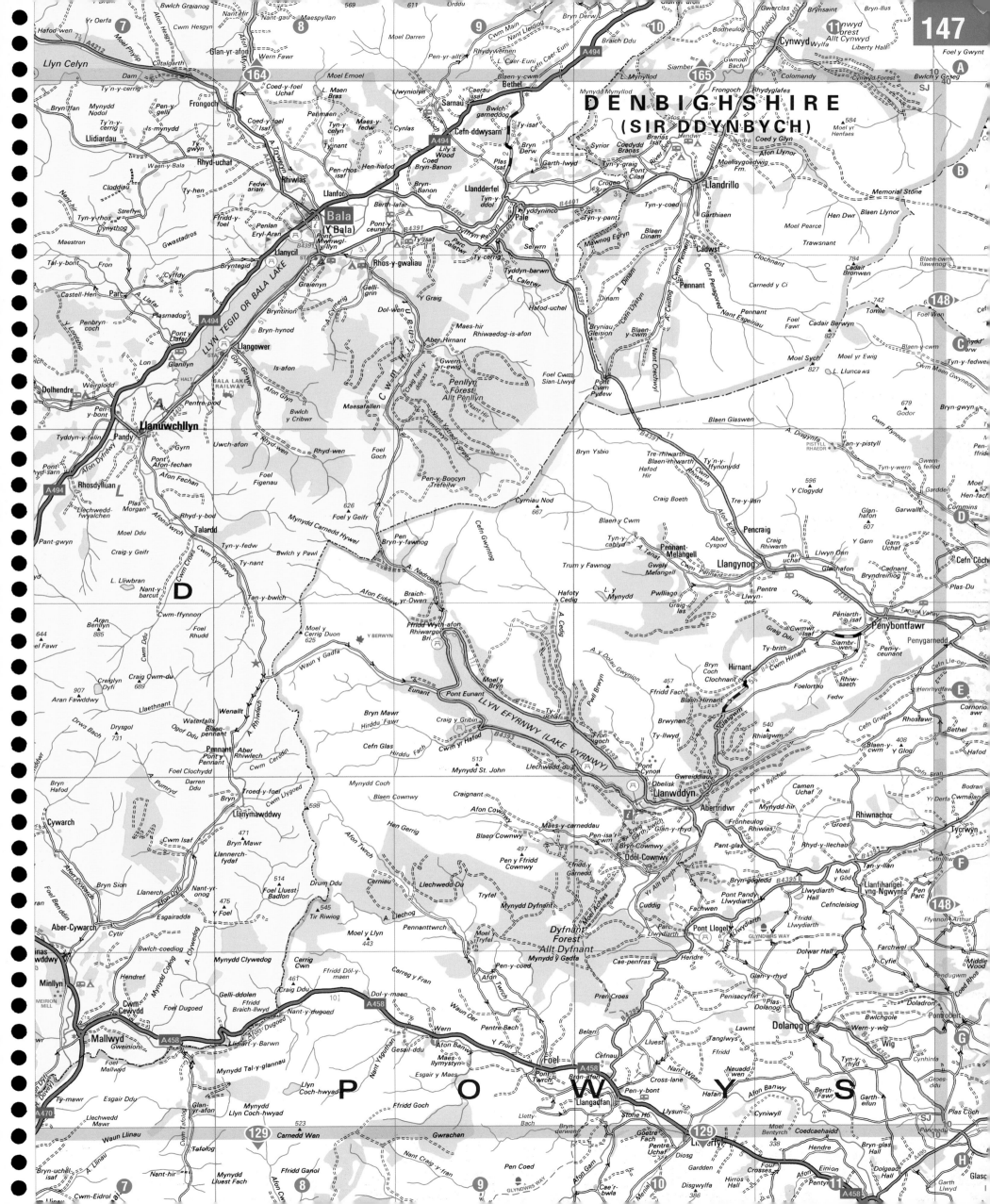

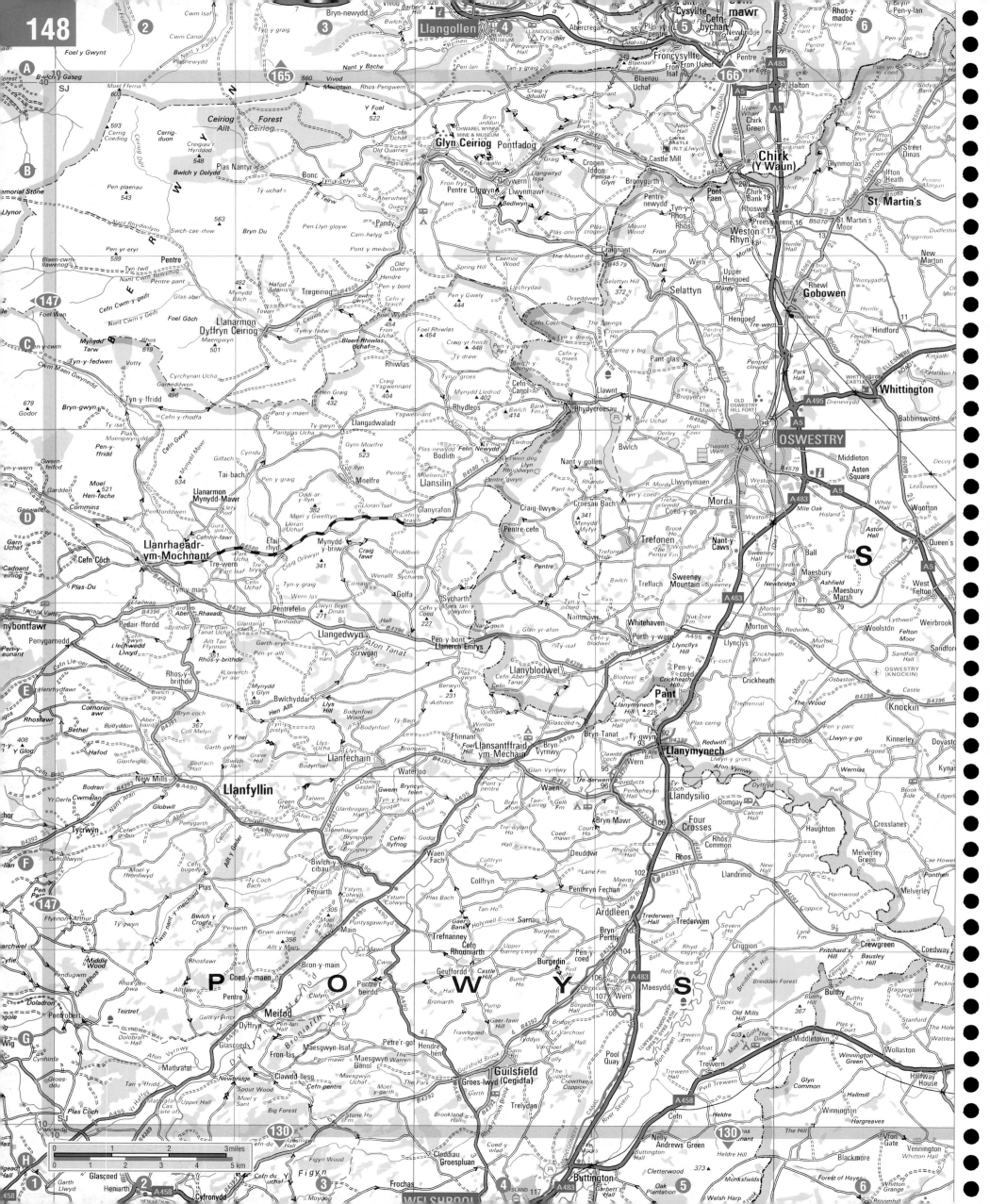

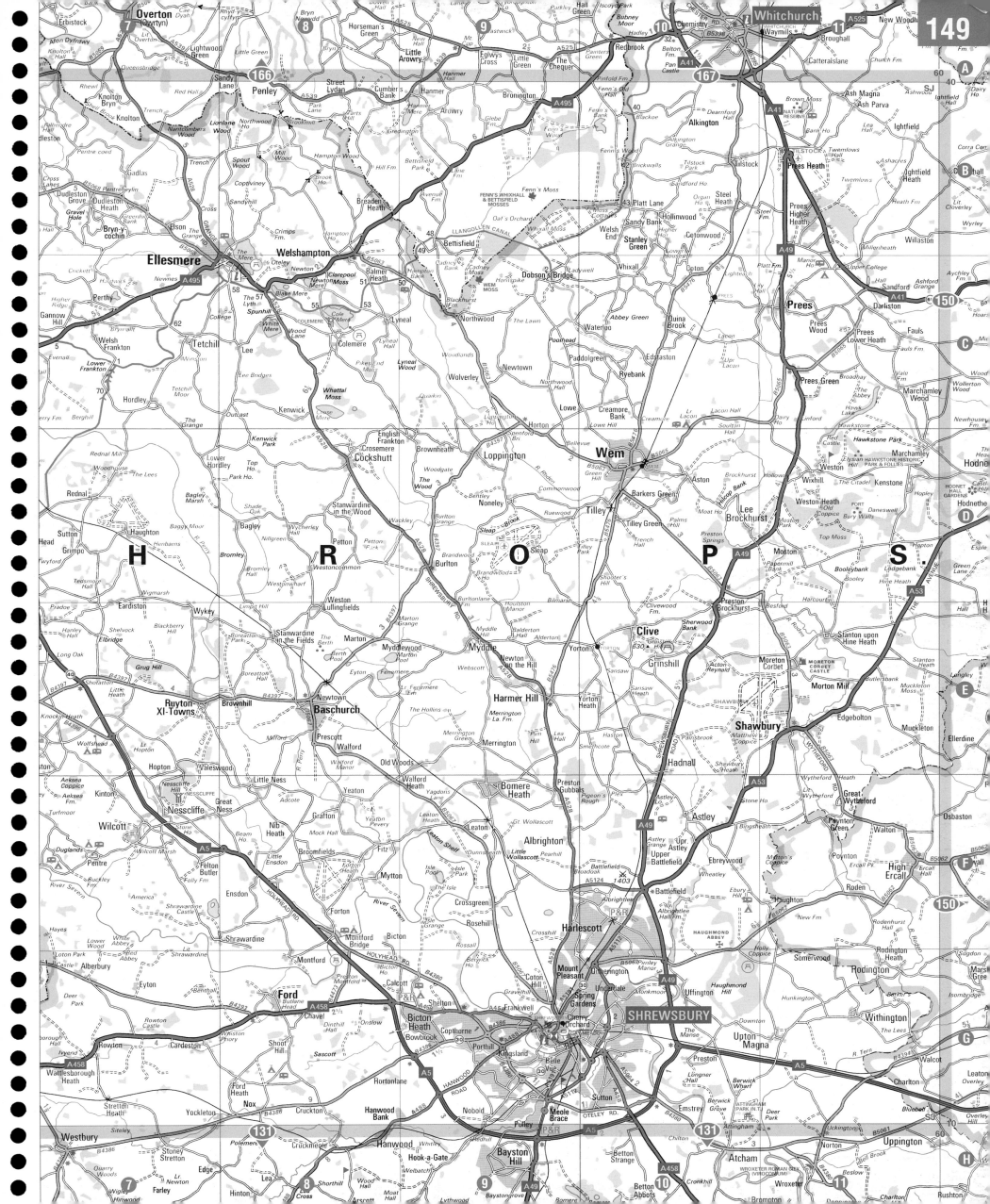

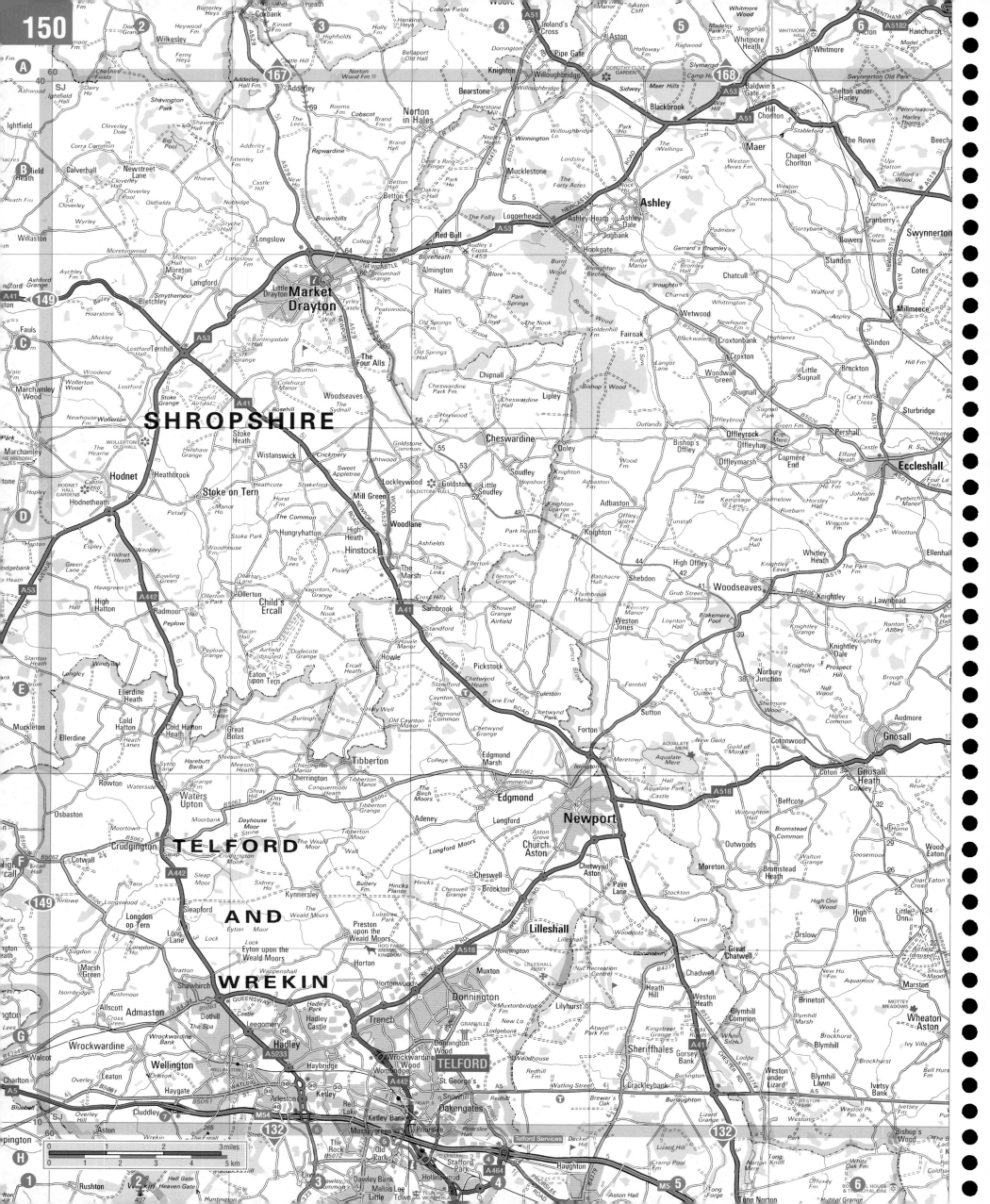

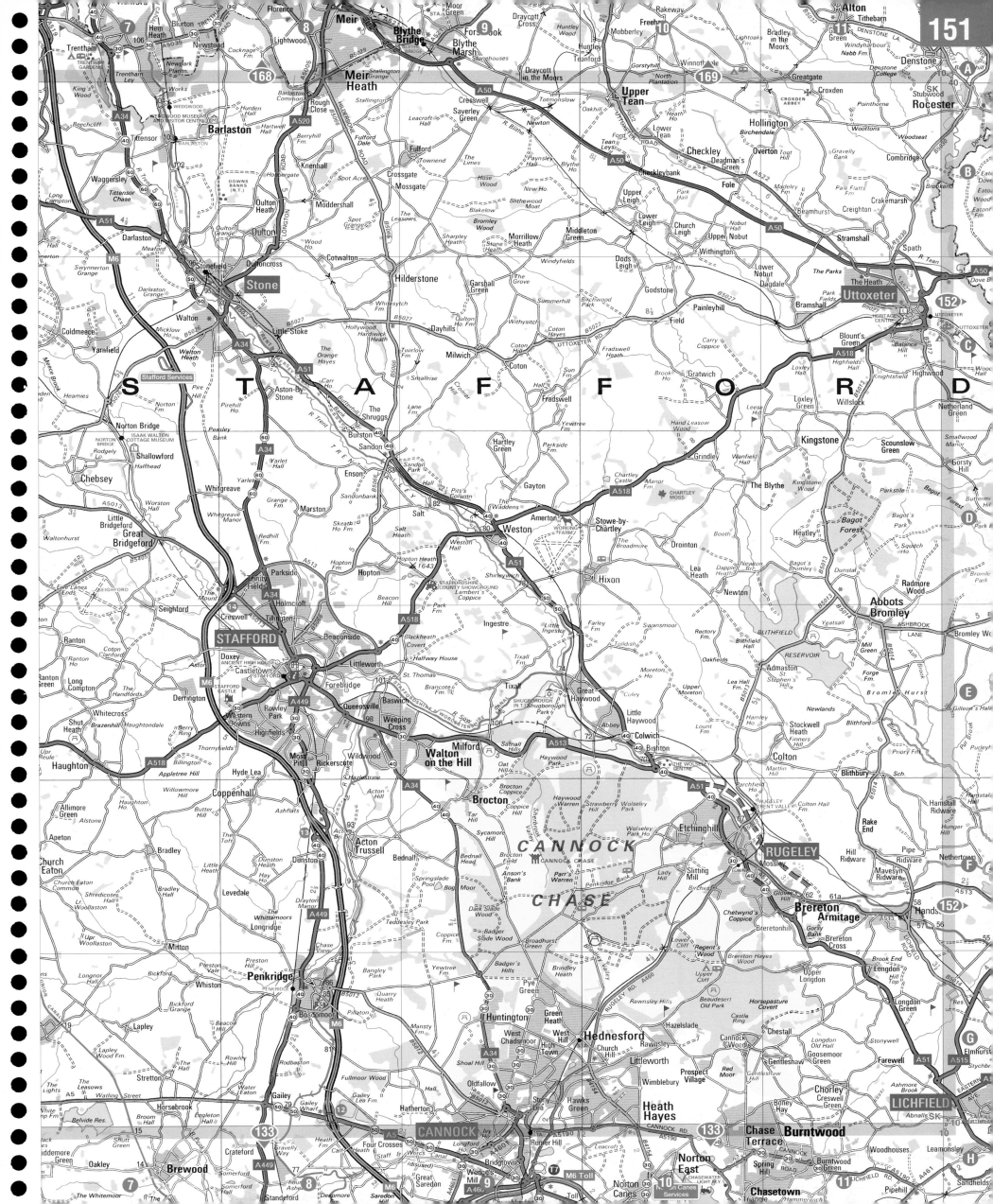

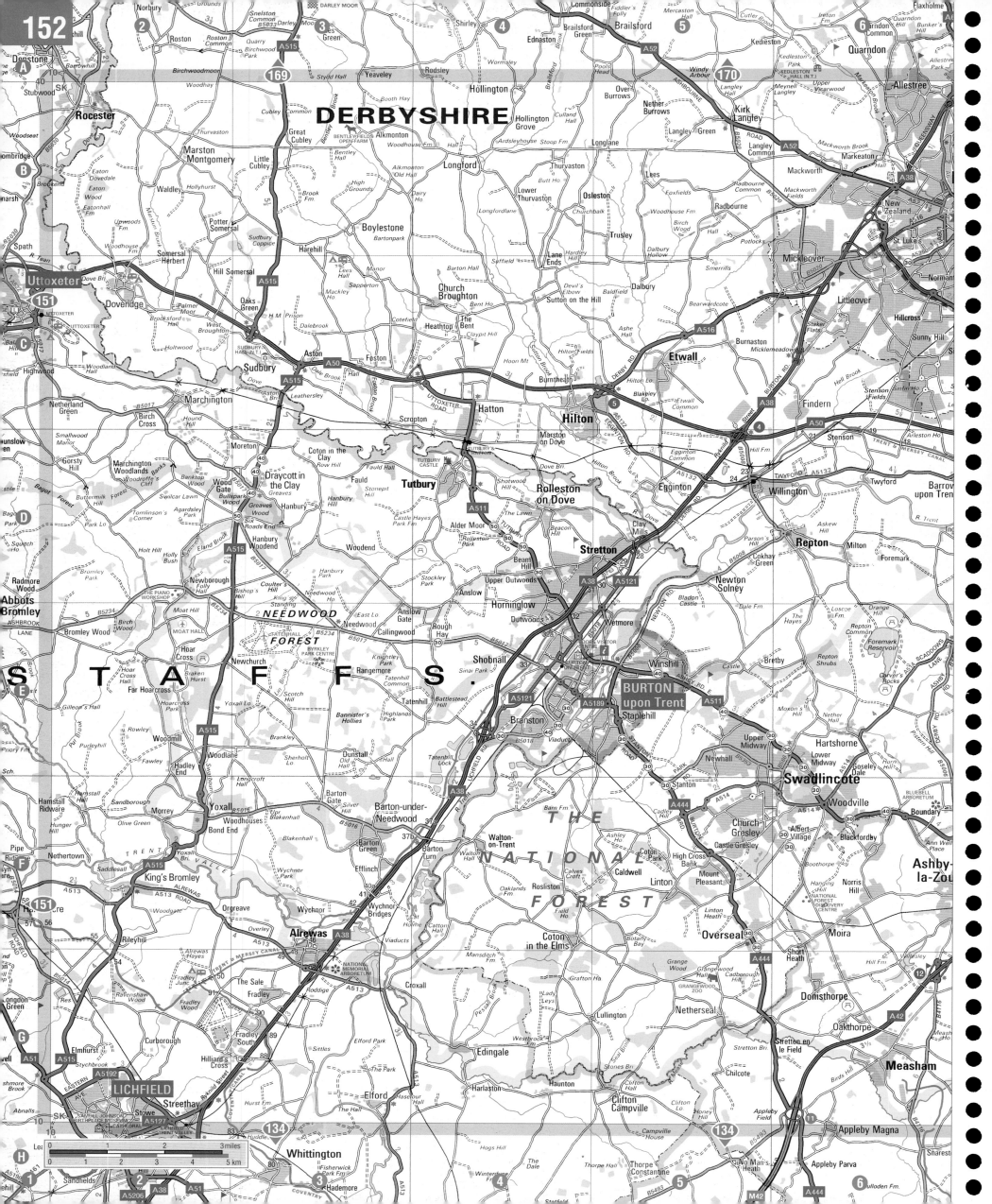

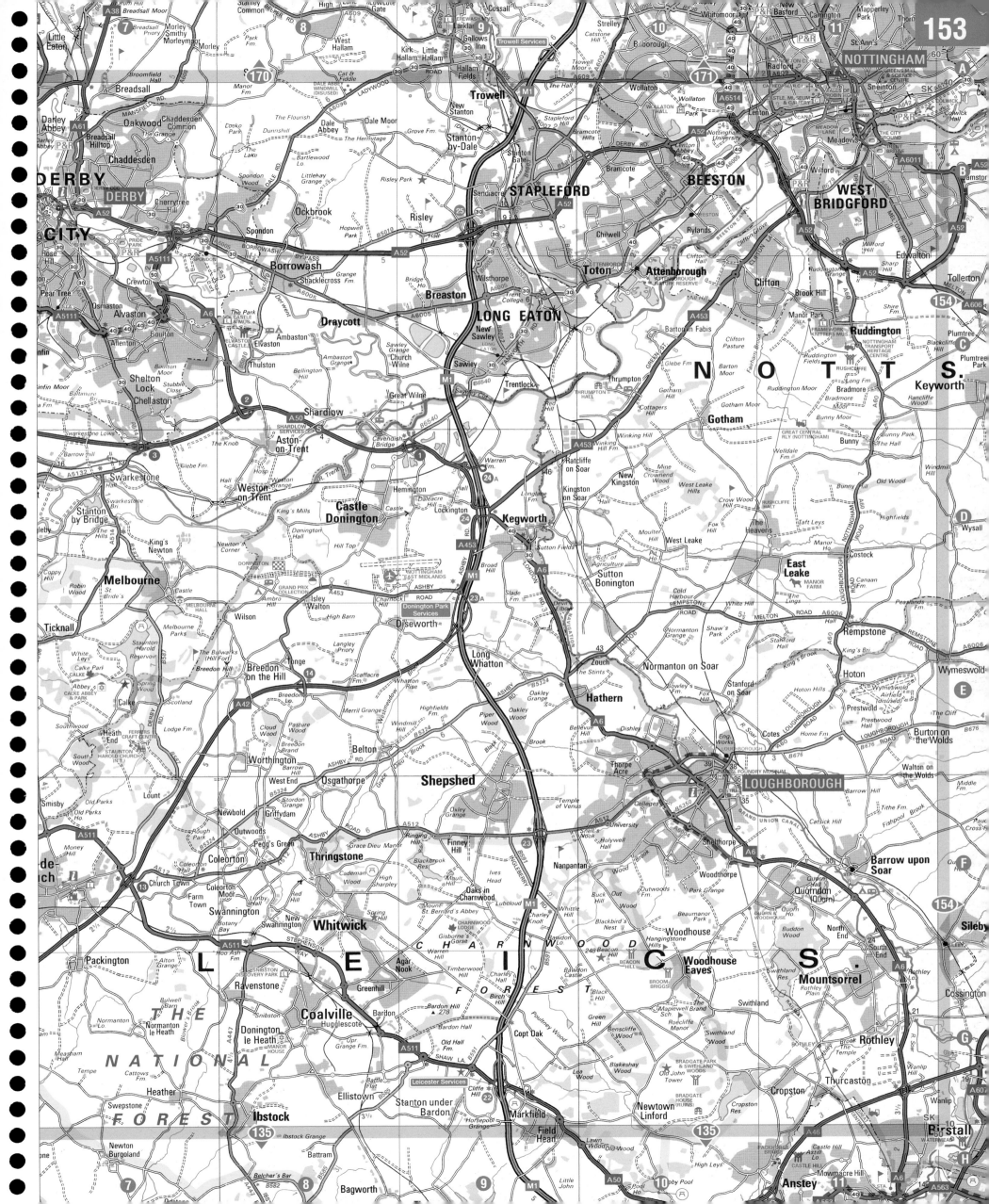

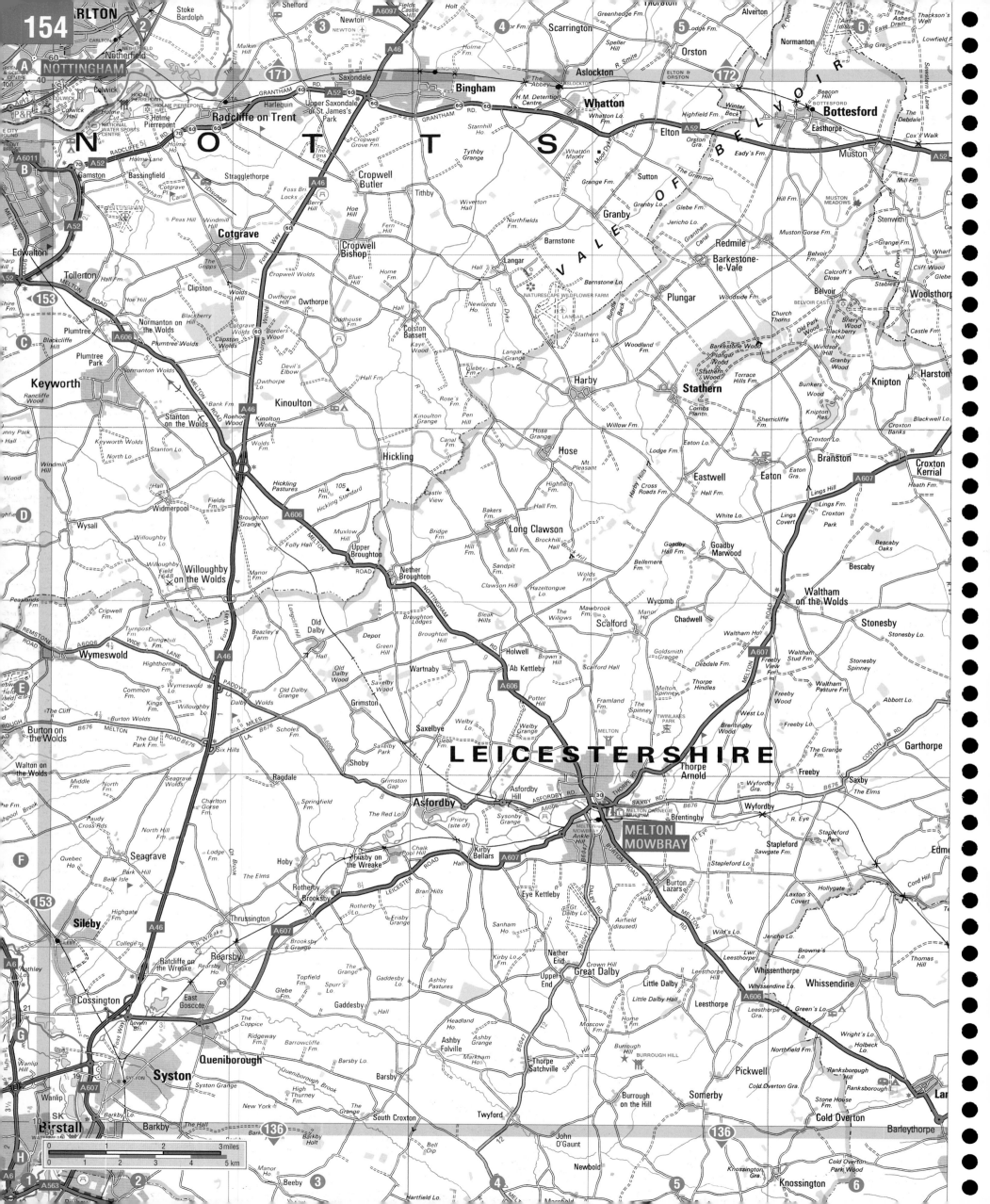

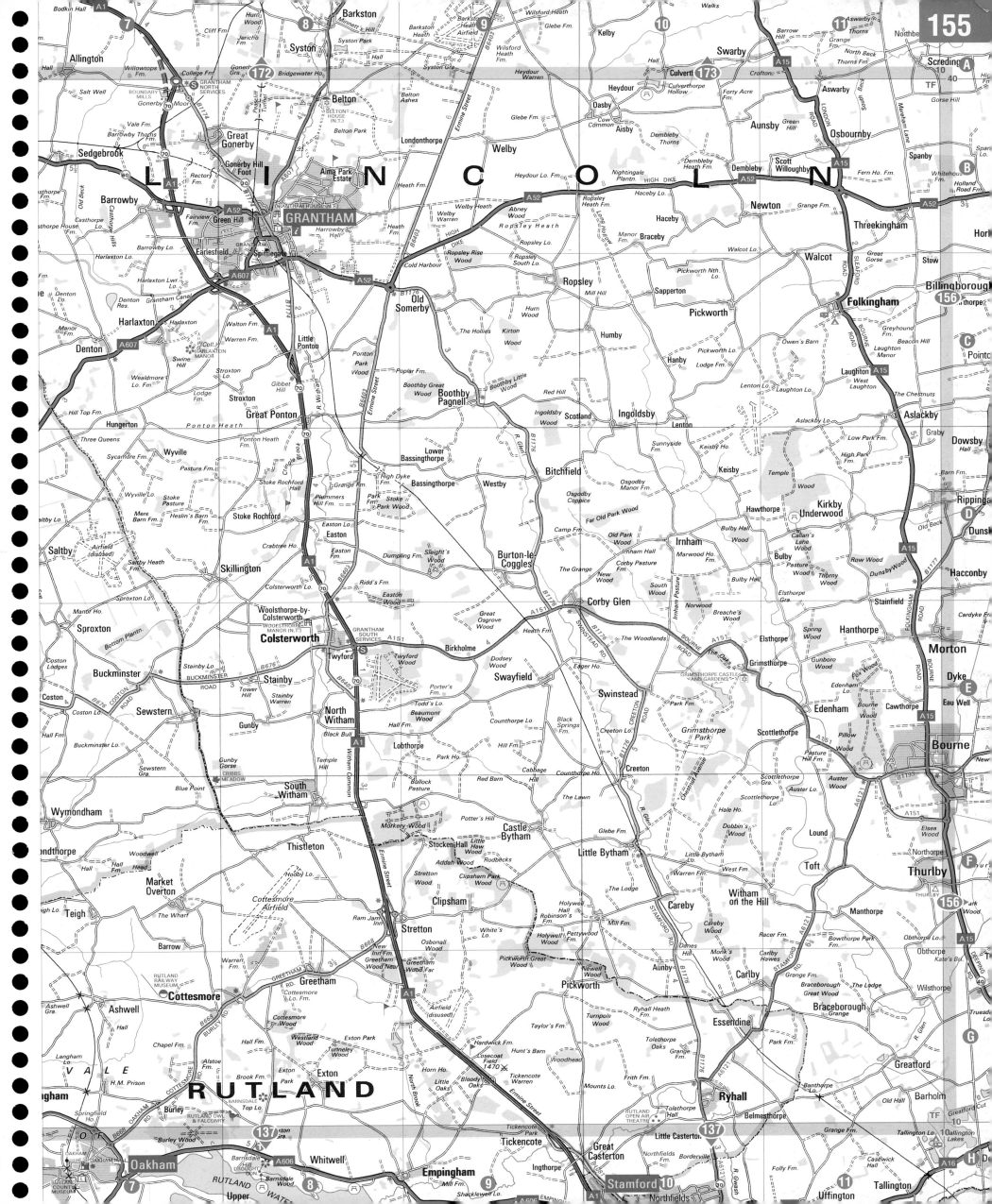

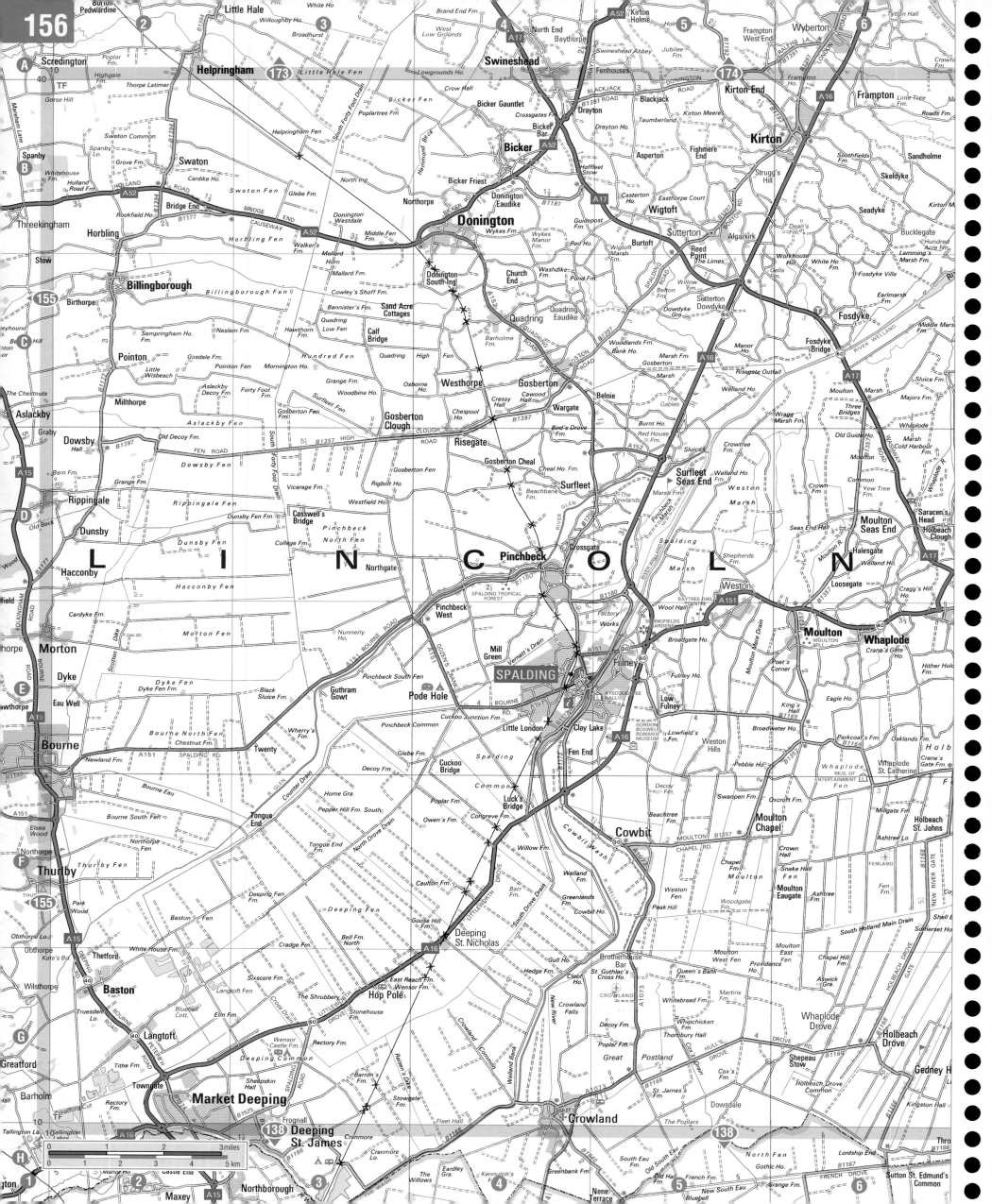

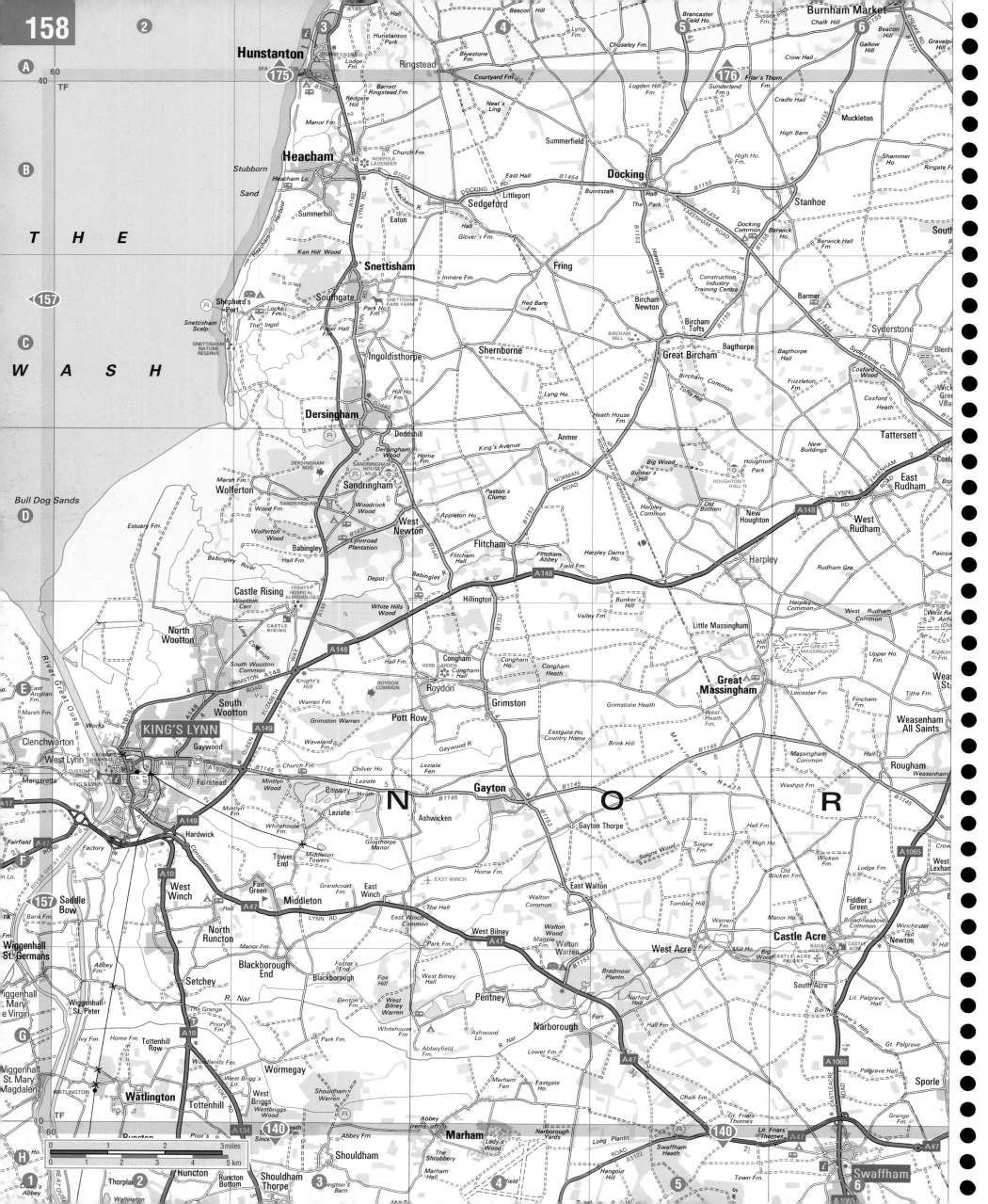

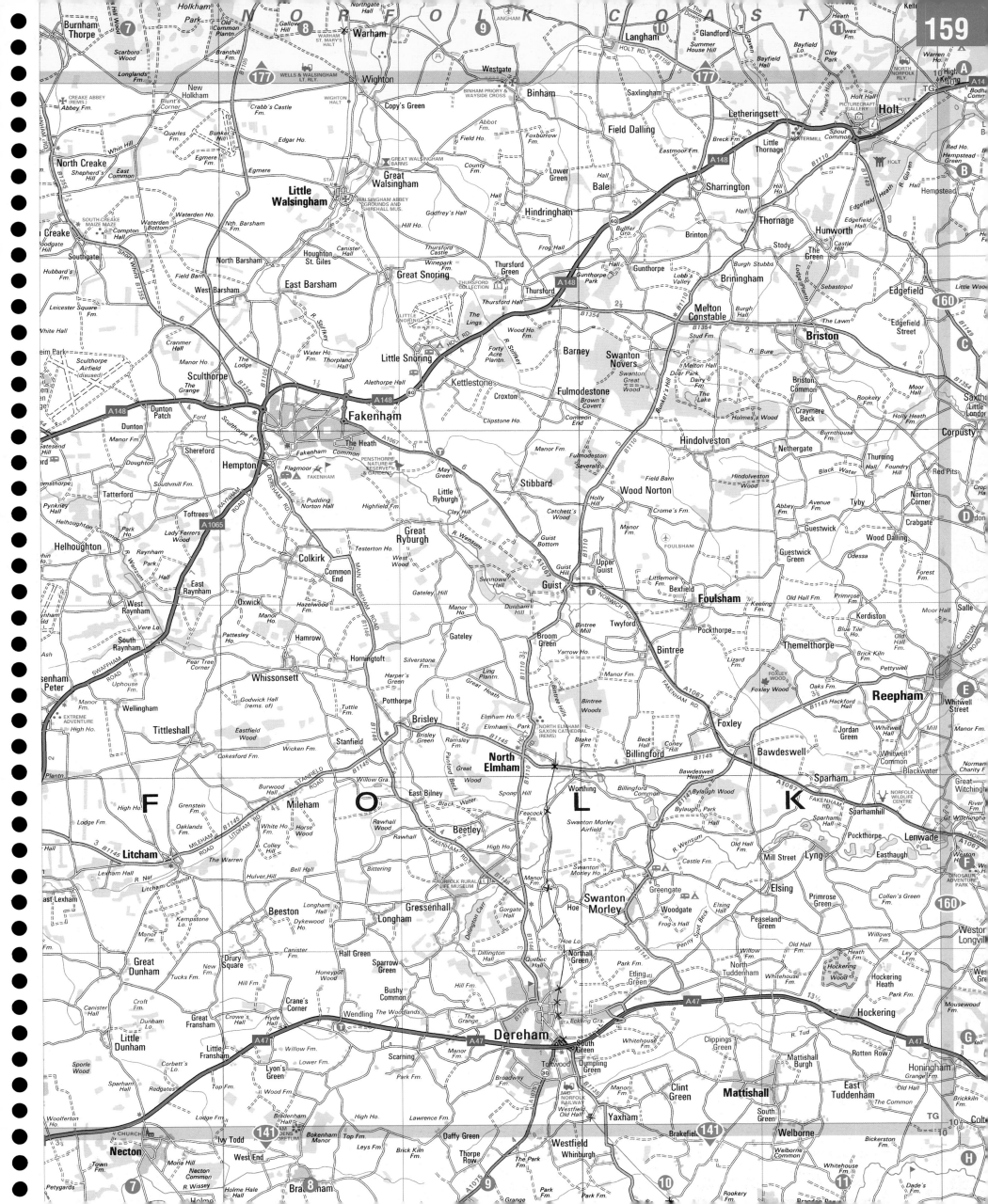

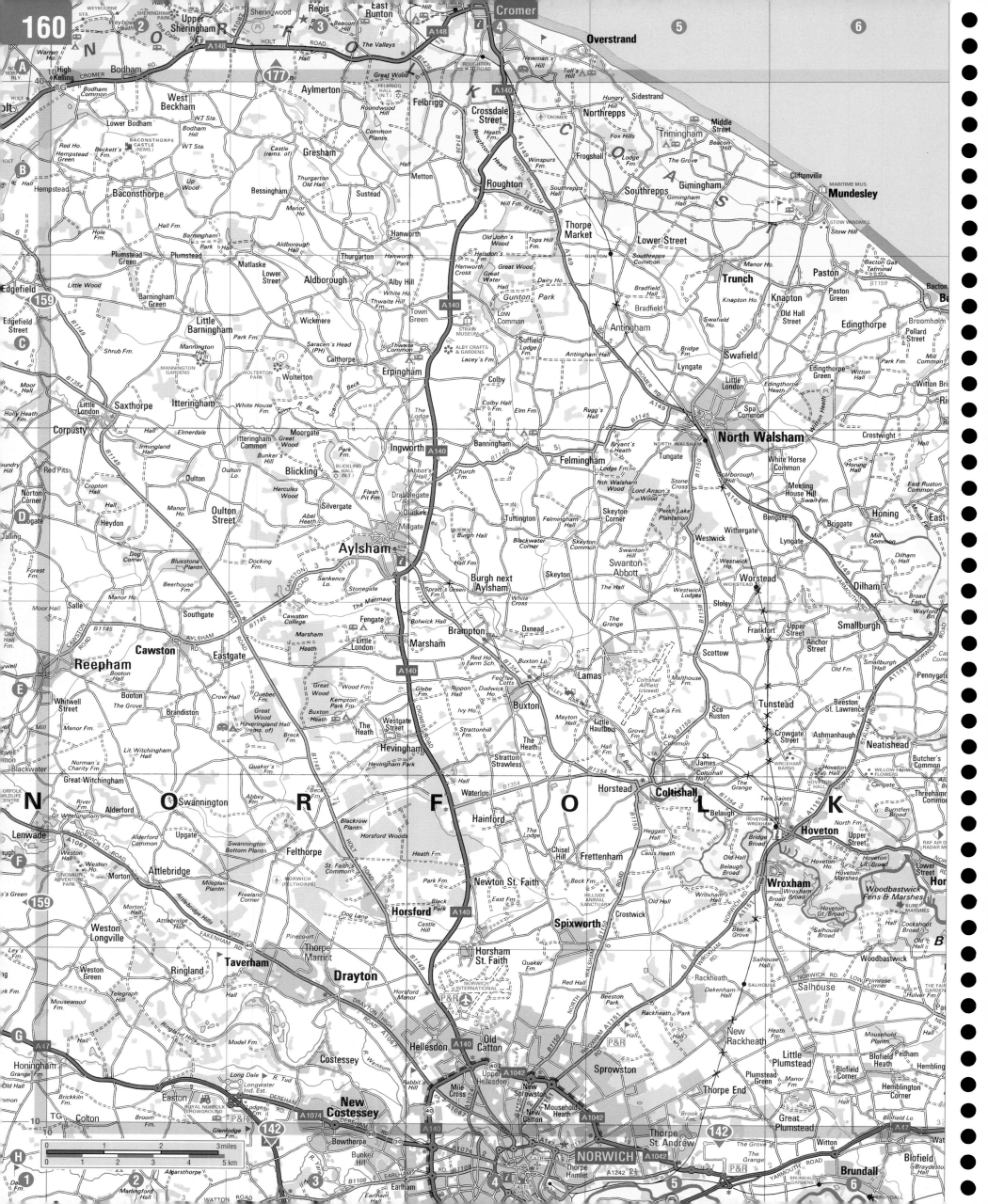

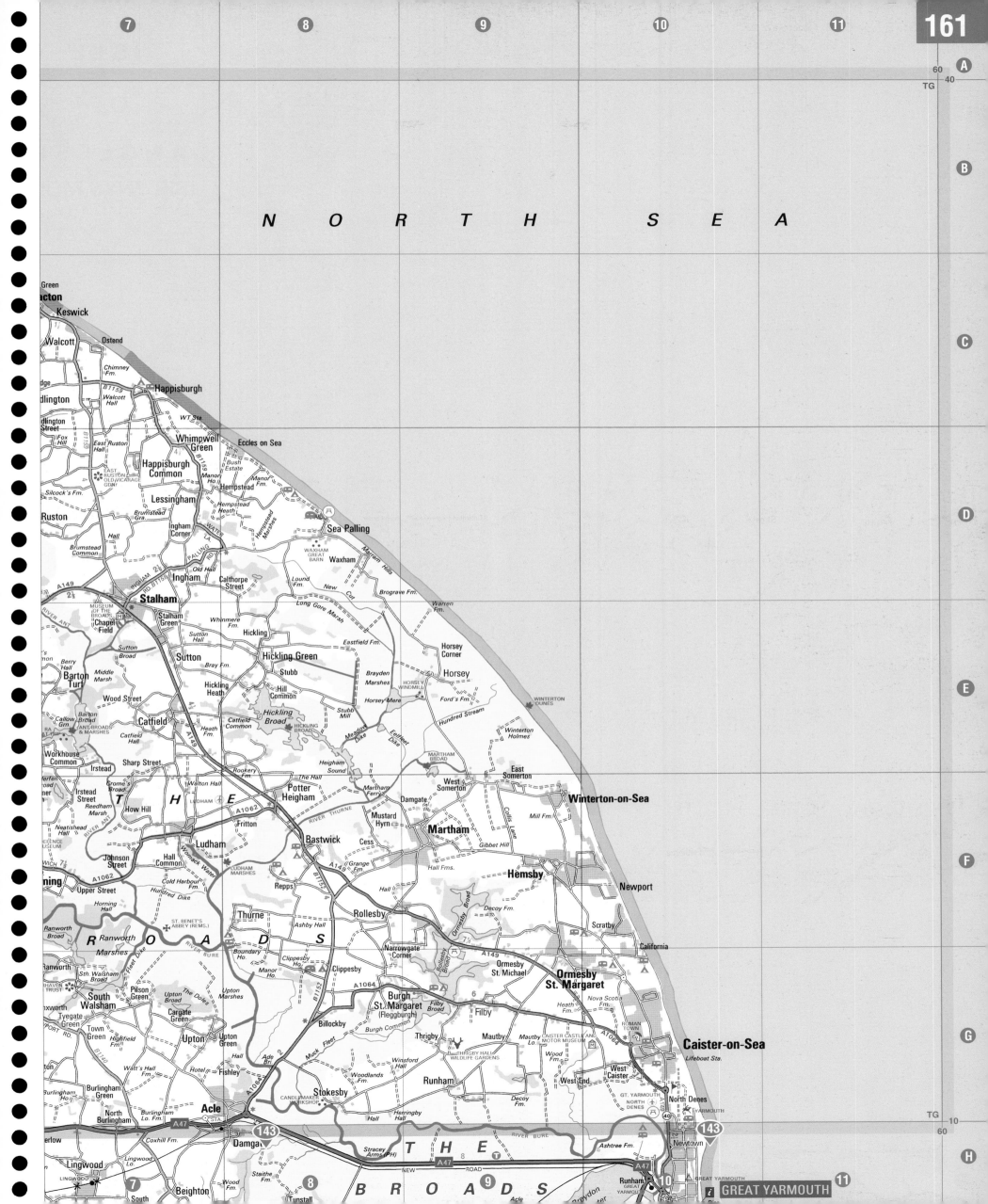

NORTH SEA

THE BROADS

GREAT YARMOUTH

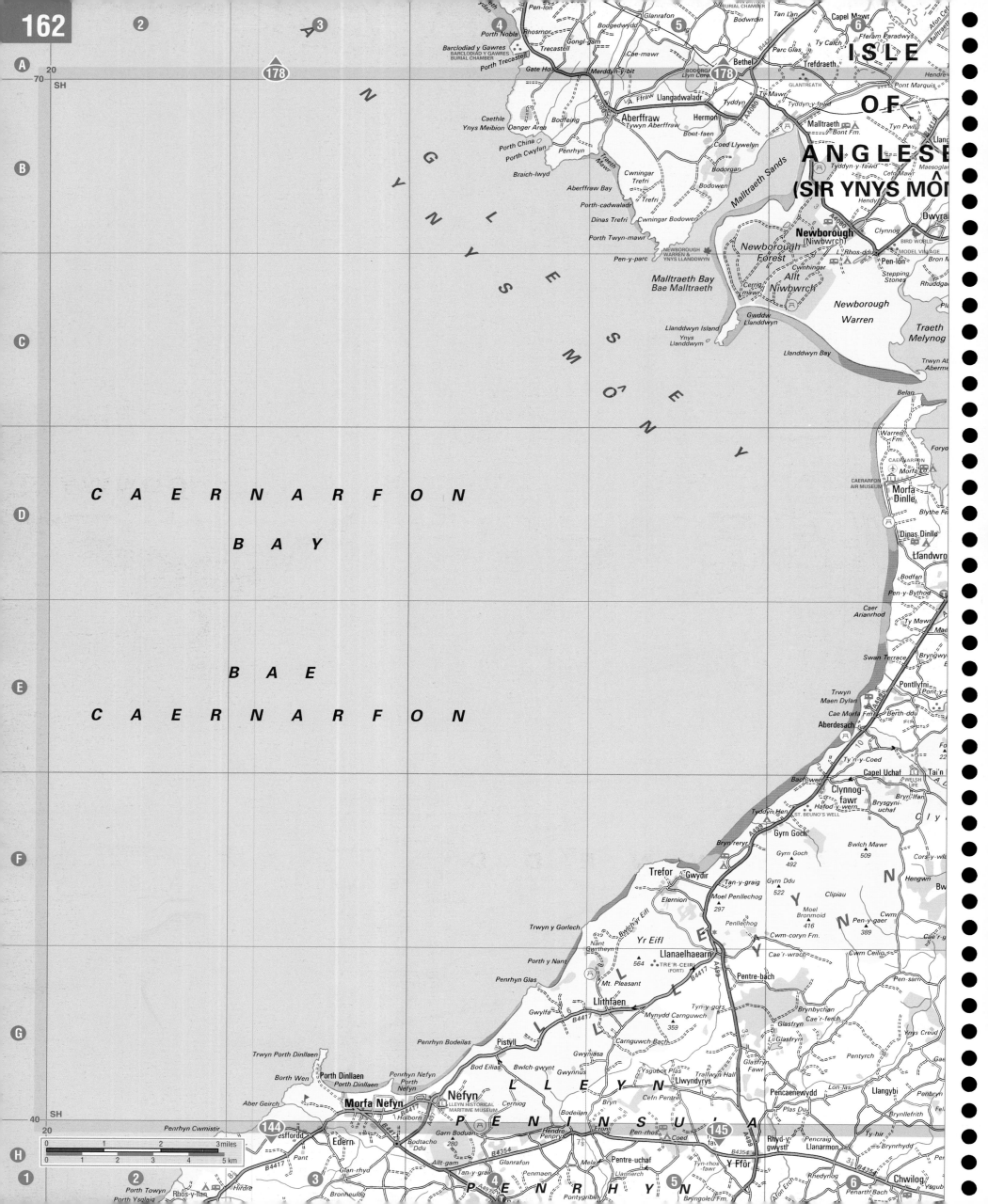

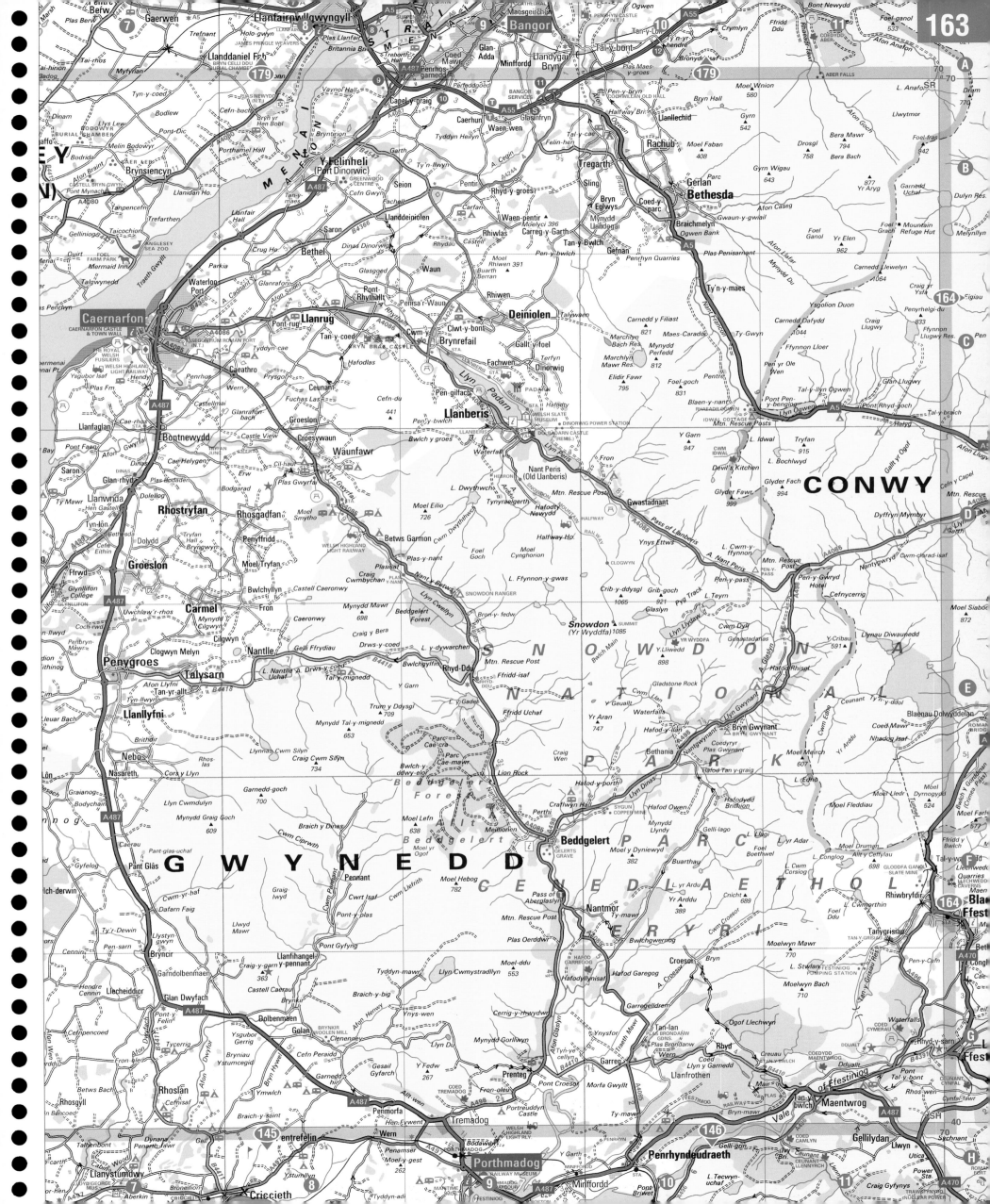

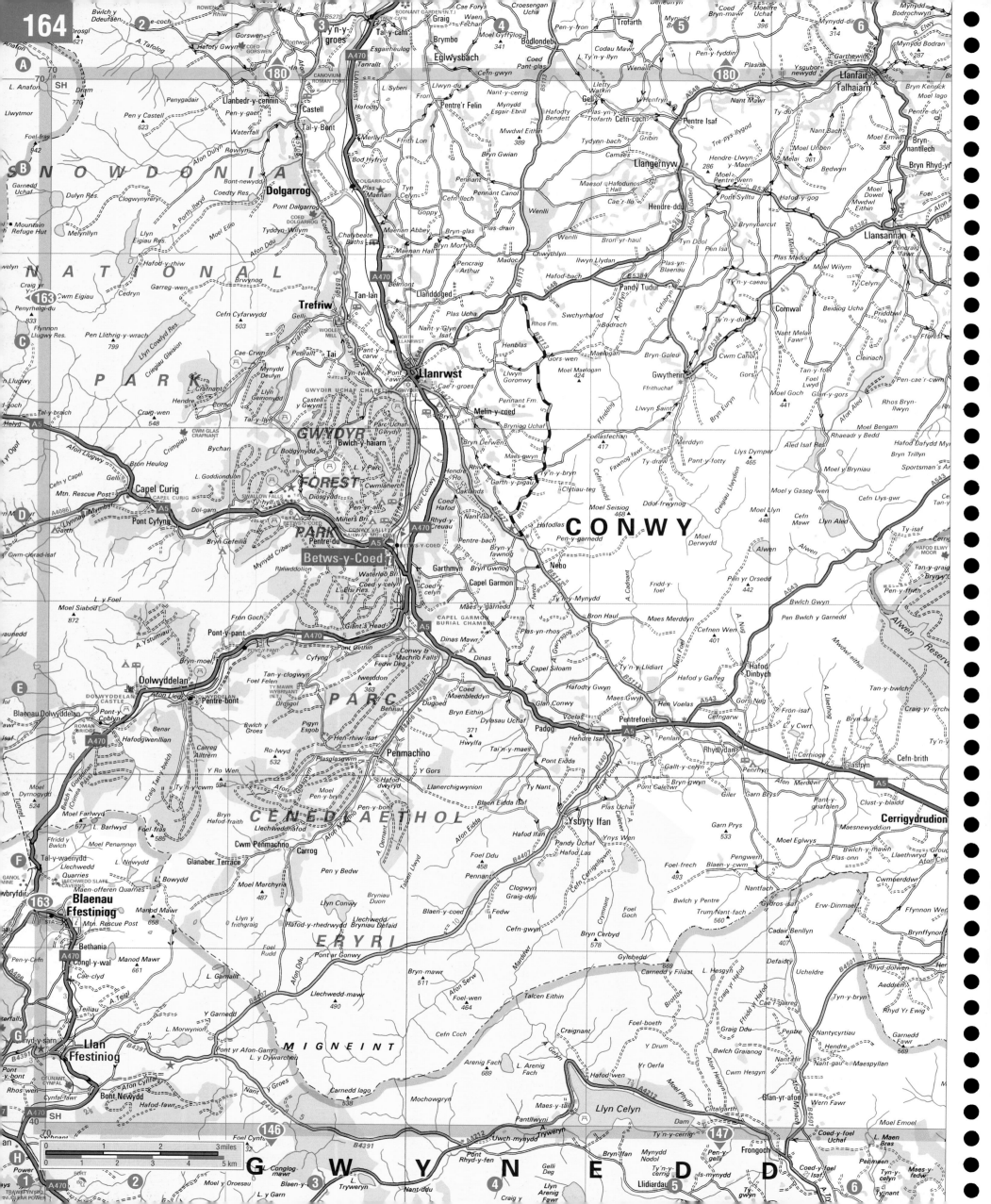

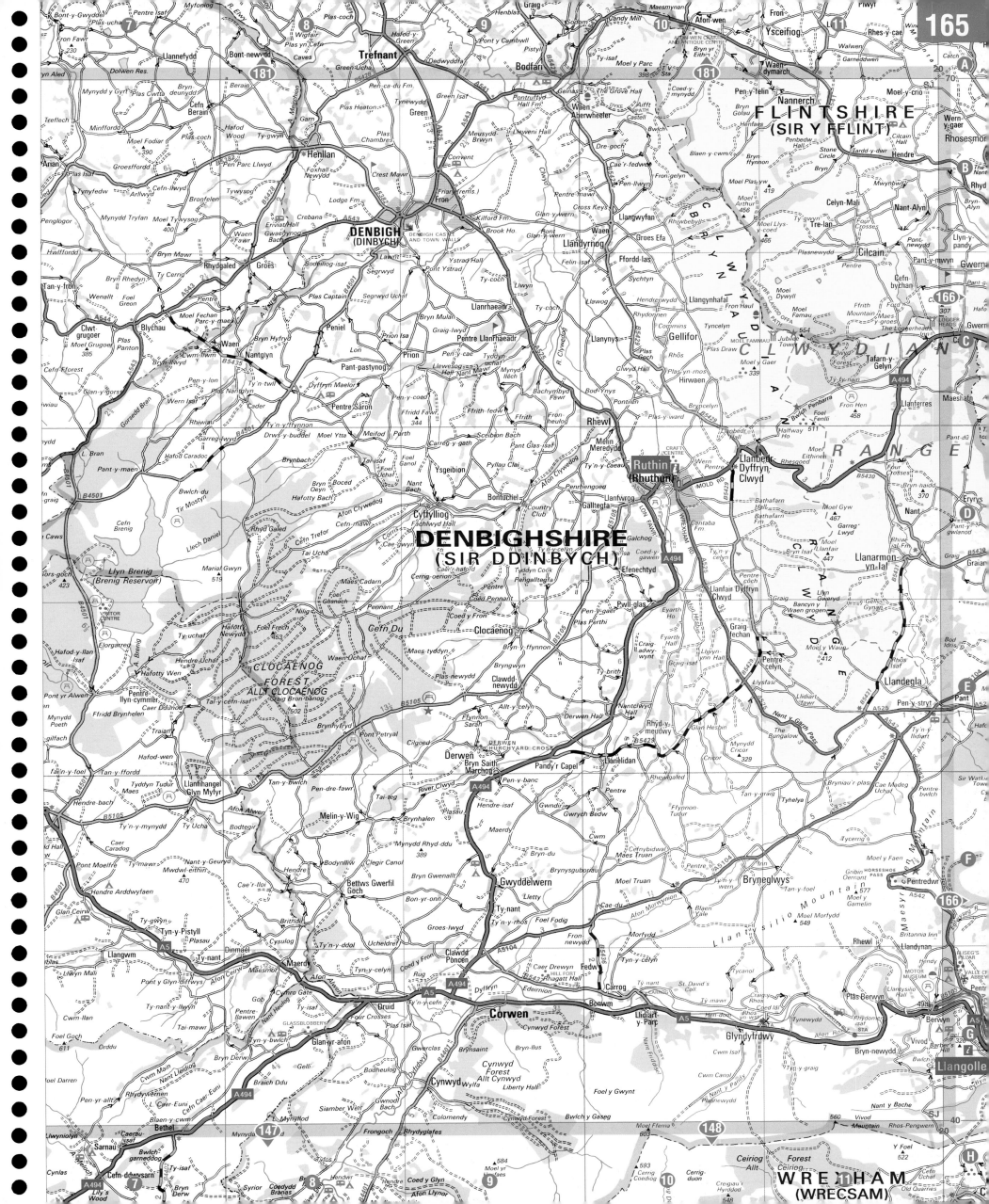

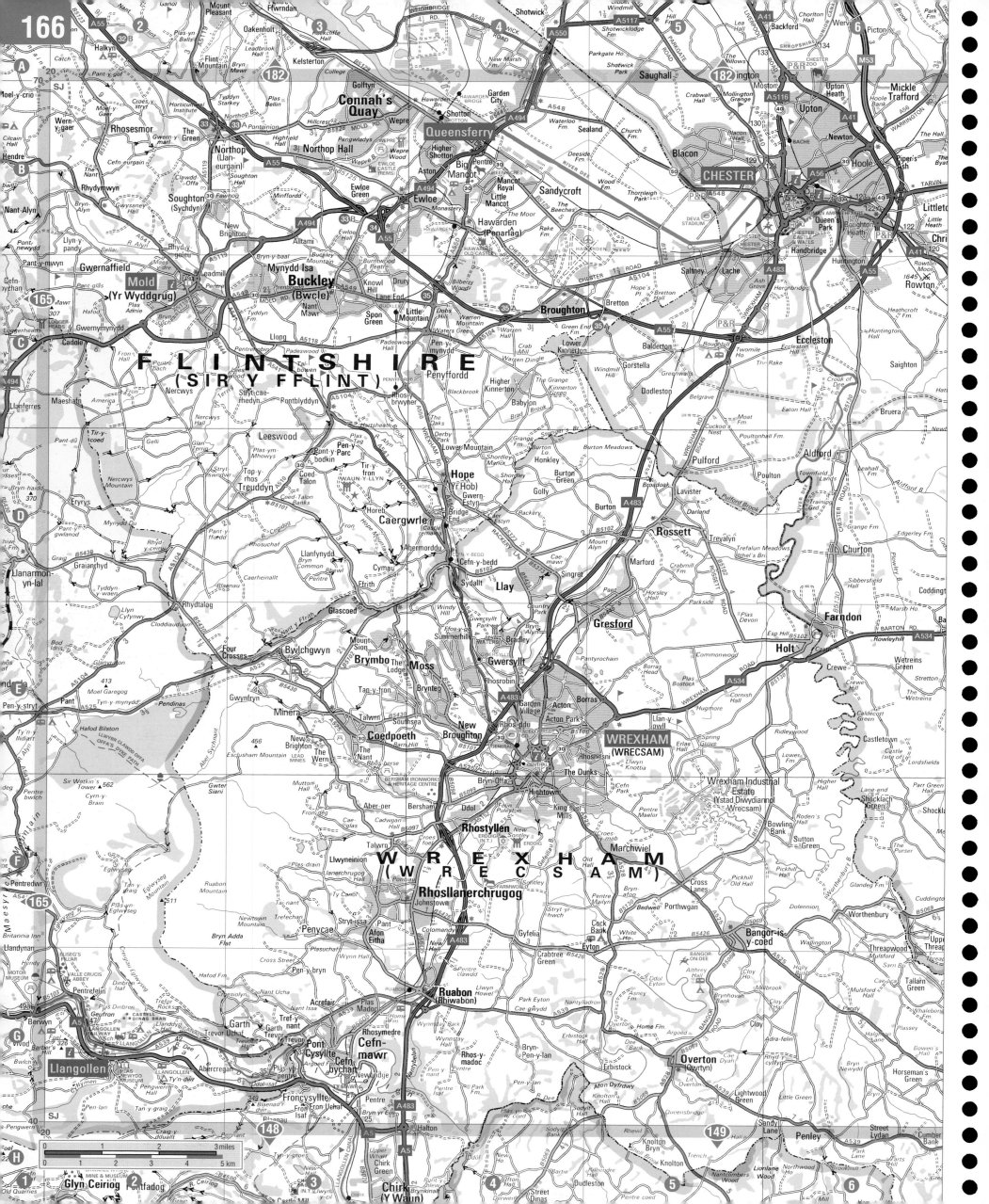

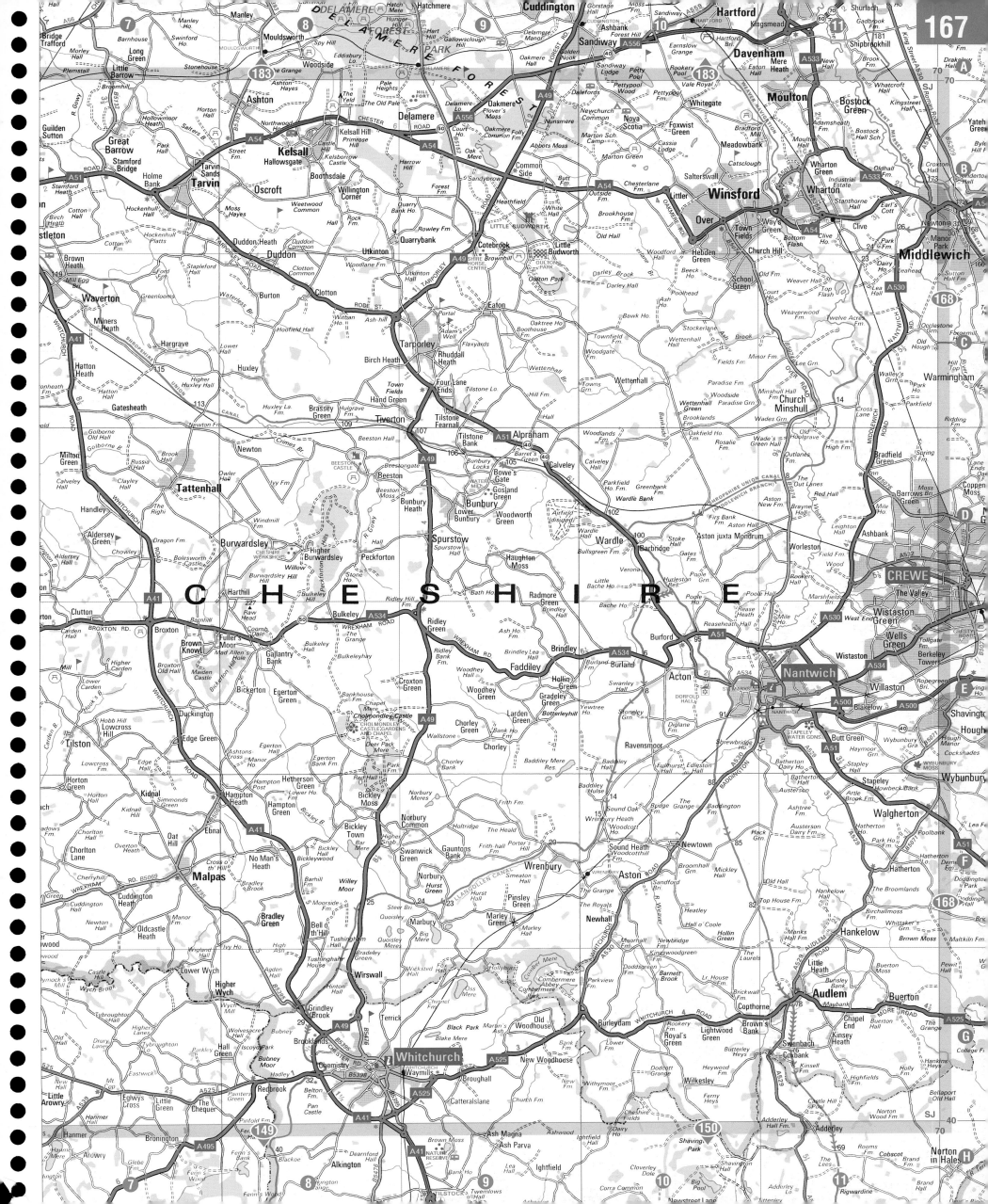

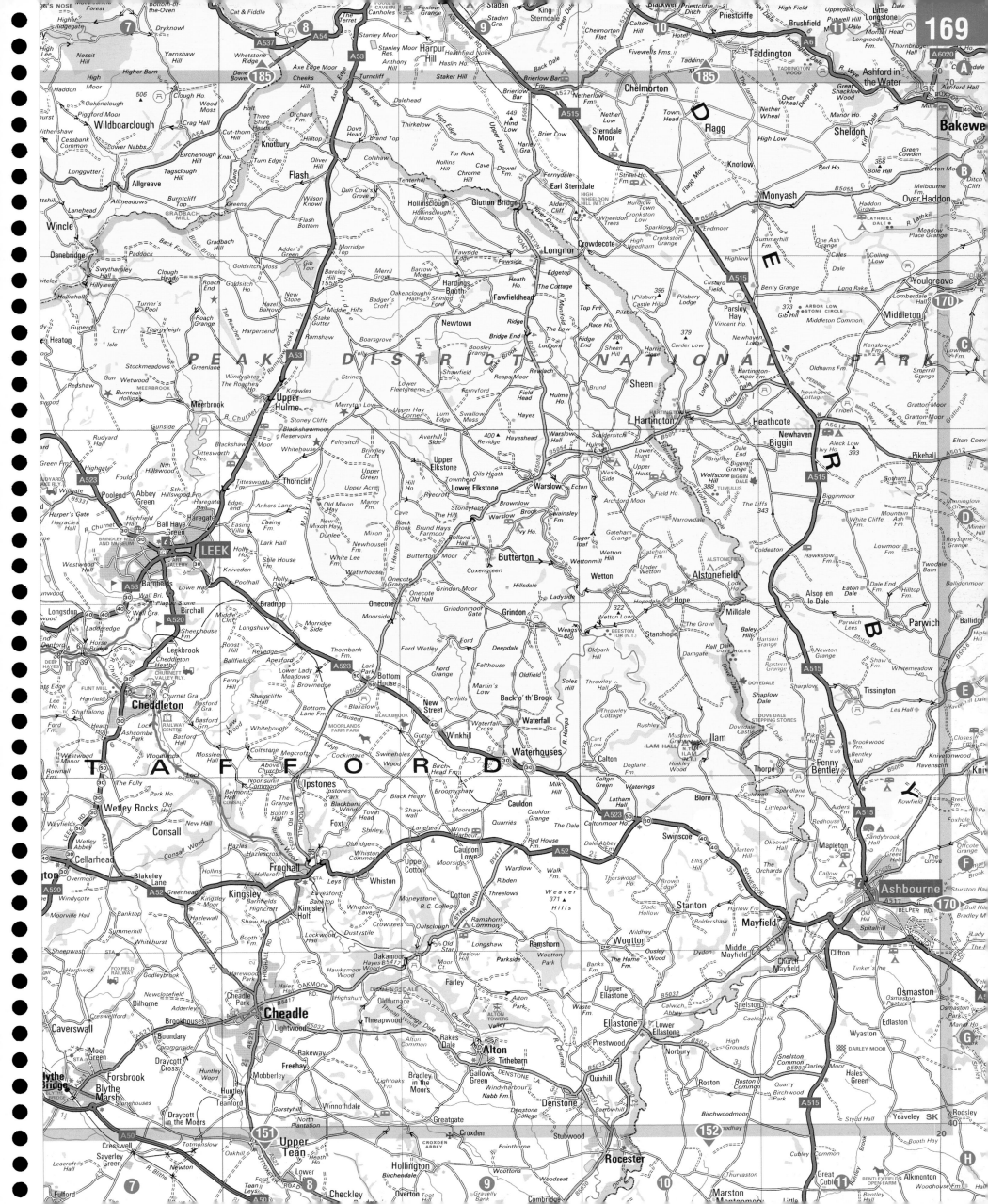

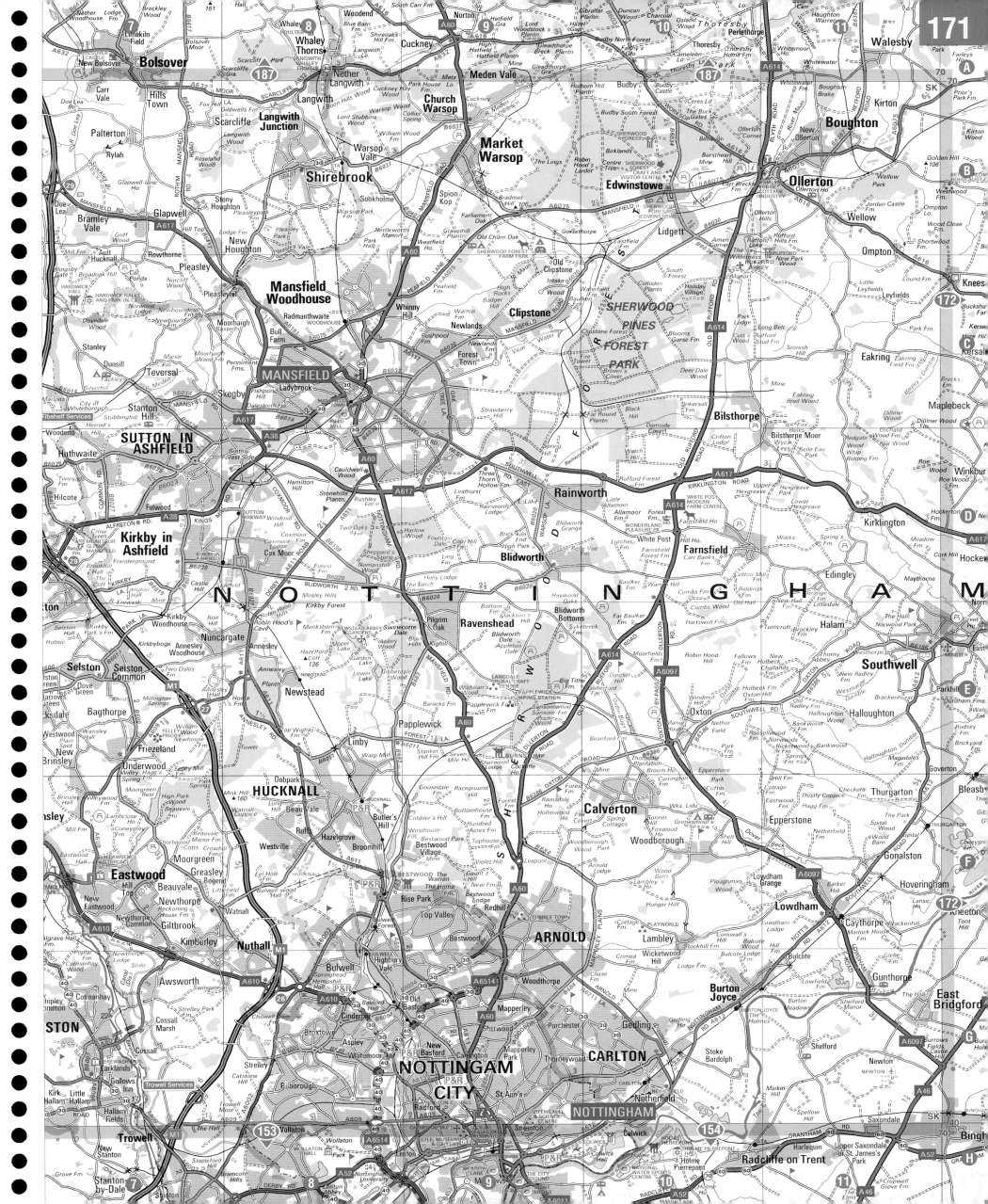

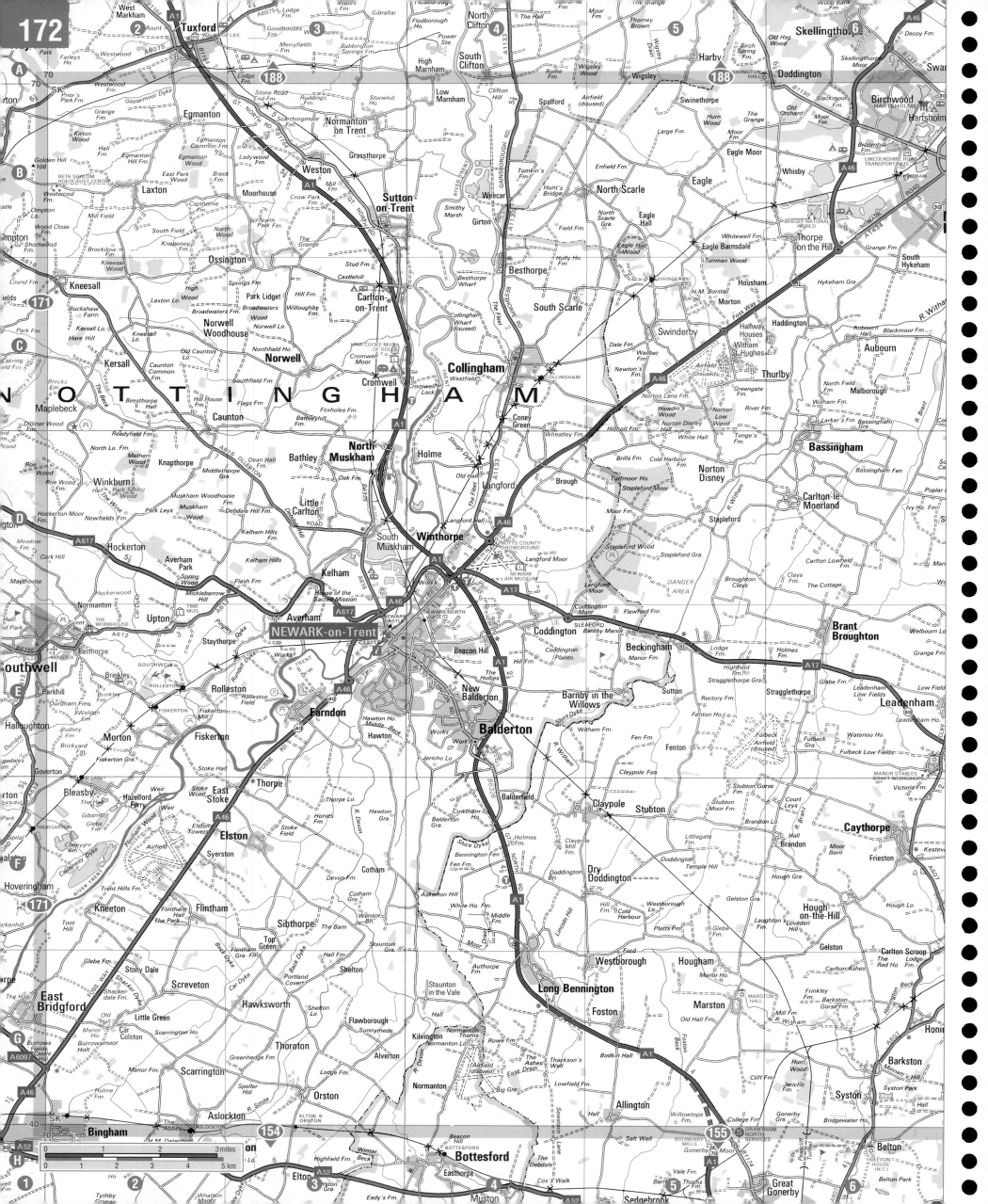

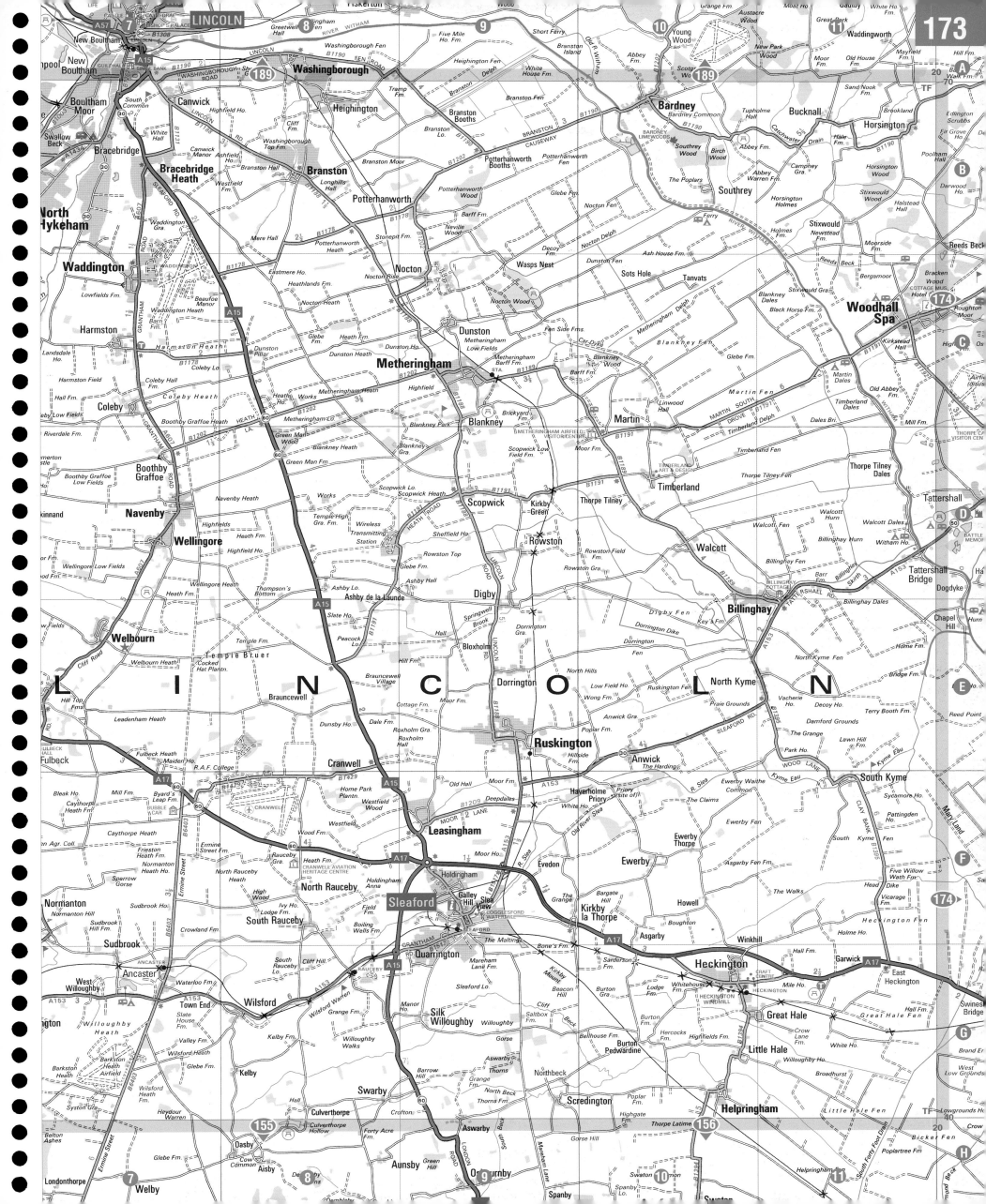

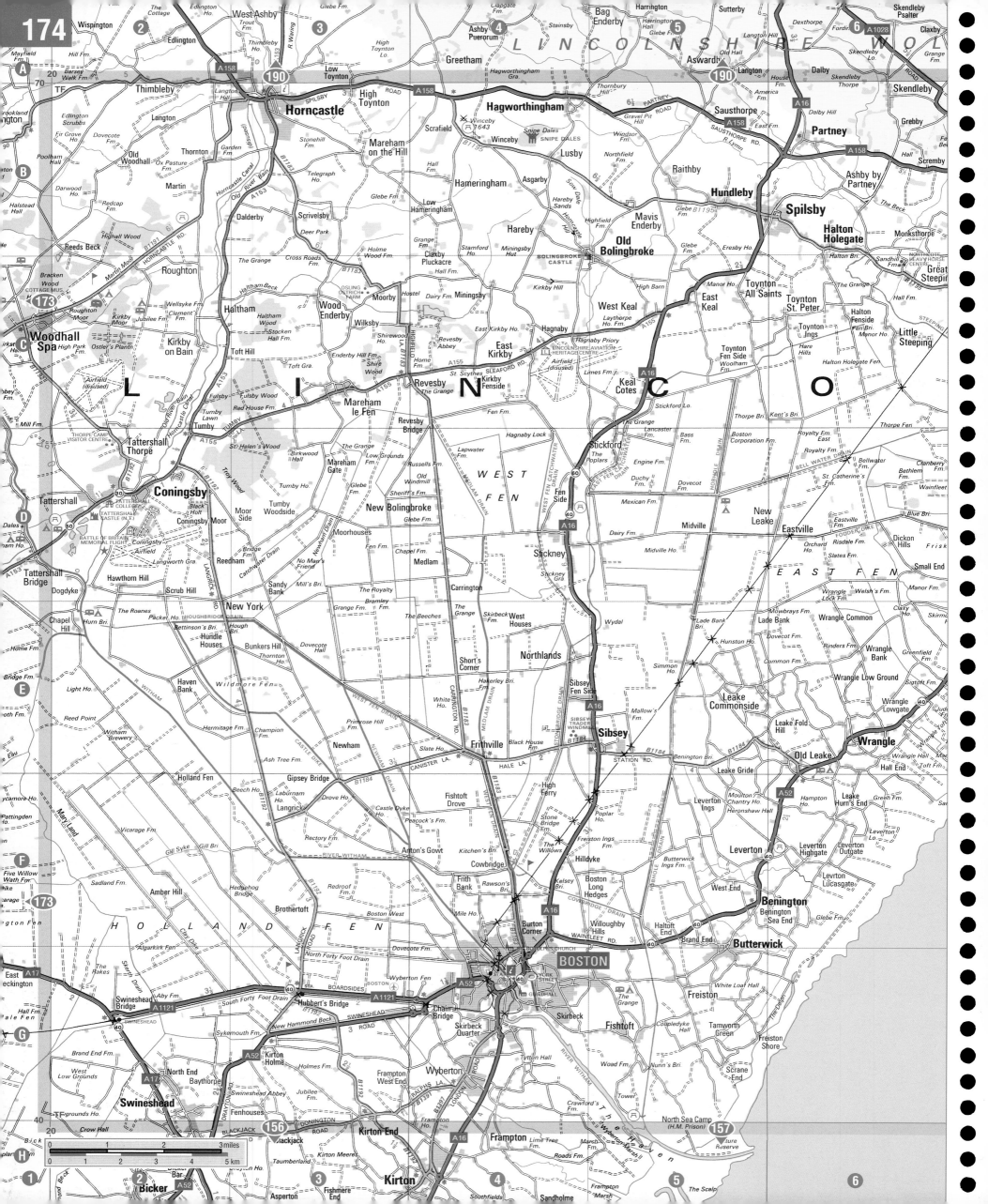

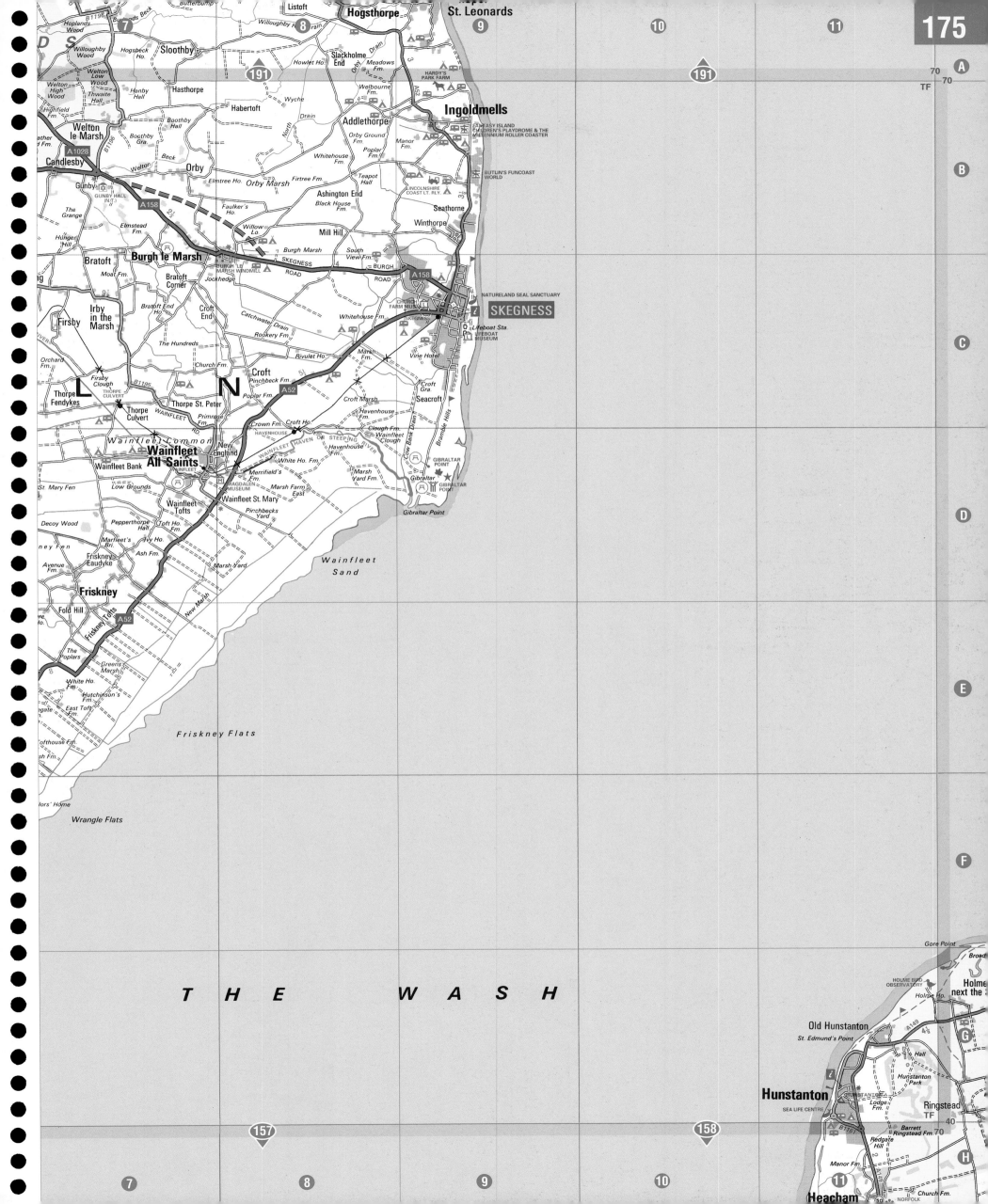

THE WASH

SKEGNESS

Hogsthorpe
St. Leonards
Ingoldmells
Seathorne
Winthorpe
Addlethorpe
Orby Marsh
Ashington End
Burgh le Marsh
Bratoft
Croft
Seacroft
Wainfleet All Saints
Wainfleet St. Mary
Wainfleet Tofts
Friskney
Hunstanton
Old Hunstanton
Heacham

BRANCASTER BAY

HOLKHAM BAY

N O R

N O R F

N O R

BRANCASTER BAY

Gore Point

HOLME
DUNES

Broad Water

HOLME BIRD
OBSERVATORY

Holme
next the Sea

Holme Ho.

The Drove
Ho.

A149 Titchwell

Marsh Side

Brancaster Marsh

Scolt Head
SCOLT HEAD
ISLAND

Brancaster Harbour

Norton Creek

Trowland Creek

Burnham Harbour
Gun Hill

Deepdale Marsh

Norton Marsh

Burnham
Overy Staithe

Overy Marshes

Marsh Ho.
Fm.

West Sands

The Run

Bob Hall's
Sand

Lodge
Marsh

Holkham Meals

Warham Salt Marshes

Stonemeal
Creek

Warham Green

HOLKHAM
WELLS
HARBOUR
MINIATURE
RAILWAY

Thornham

NORFOLK
LAVENDER

A149

Brancaster

Brancaster
Staithe

Burnham
Deepdale

Burnham
Norton

Burnham Market

A149

Burnham
Overy

Holkham

HOLKHAM HALL

Holkham
Park

WELLS-
NEXT-
THE-SEA

A149

STA.

Wells
next-the-Sea

THE MIDDEN

Northgate
Hall

N O R

Hunstanton
Park

Beacon Hill

Bluestone
Fm.

Lyng
Fm.

Ringstead

Courtyard Fm.

Barrett
Ringstead Fm.

Neat's
Ling

B1153

Brancaster
Hall

Barrow
Common

Brancaster
Field Ho.

Choseley Fm.

Sussex Fm.

Chalk Hill

Crow Hall

Cradle Hall

Friar's Thorn

Lugden Hill
Fm.

Sunderland
Fm.

Beacon
Hill

Gallow
Hill

CREAKE RD.

B1355

Leath Ho.

Burnham
Thorpe

Gravelpit
Hill

Lucas Hill Wood

Scarboro'
Wood

Longlands
Fm.

Branthill
Fm.

B1105

Gallow
Hill

Old
Common
Plantn.

WARHAM
ST. MARY'S
HALT

Warham

N O R

Wighton

WELLS & WALSINGHAM
LT. RLY.

WIGHTON
HALT

Crabb's Castle

Copy

Church Fm.

East Hall

DOCKING

Muckleton

High Barn

High Ho.
Fm.

Shammer
Ho.

Ringate Fm.

North Creake

Shepherd's
Hill

East
Common

New
Holkham

Blunt's
Corner

Quarles
Fm.

Whin Hill

Bunker's
Hill

Egdar Ho.

Egmere

GR
BA

Gre
Walsin

Docking

Burntstalk

B1454

FAKENHAM
ROAD

B1155

Hall

The
Park

Stanhoe

Docking
Common

Barwick
Ho.

Barwick Hall
Fm.

South Creake

Bloodgate
Hill

Southgate

SOUTHCREAKE
MAIZE MAZE

Compton
Hall

Waterden Ho.

Waterden
Bottom

Nth. Barsham
Fm.

Houghton
St. Giles

Little
Walsingham

WALSINGHAM ABBEY
GROUNDS AND
SHIREHALL MUS.

STA.

F

B1454

Sedgeford

Littleport

Eaton

158

Snettisham

SNETTISHAM
PARK FARM

Park Ho.

Inmere Fm.

Fring

Honey Hills

B1153

B1454

Bircham
Newton

Syderstone

Blenheim Park

Hubbard's
Fm.

White Hall

Leicester Square
Fm.

Field Barn

B1355

West Barsham

North Barsham

East Barsham

Houghton
Hall

Canister
Hall

Little

Ingoldisthorpe

N

Shernborne

Glover's Fm.

Red Barn
Fm.

Lyng Ho.

BIRCHAM
MILL

Bircham
Tofts

Great Bircham

Bagthorpe

Frizleton
Fm.

Bircham Common

Tofts Hill

O

Bagthorpe
Fm.

Coxford
Wood

Coxford

Coxford
Heath

Syderstone

R

Southgate

Short Whins

Scarboro'

Cranmer
Hall

Manor Ho.

Sculthorpe

The
Grange

The
Lodge

Thorpland
Hall

Water Ho.
Fm.

F

Alethorpe
Hall

A148

Fakenham

Dersingham

Hill Ho.

Doddshill

TF

Anmer

158

Big Wood

Bunker's
Hill

HOUGHTON
HALL

New
Houghton

Houghton
Park

Wicken
Green
Village

SCULTHORPE
AIRFIELD
(disused)

Coxford
Common

A148

Tattersett

Dunton
Patch

Dunton

Gatesend
Hill

Ford

Sculthorpe Fen

159

Shereford

The Heath

A1067

Hempton

A1065

Fakenham

B1146

FAKENHAM

PENSTHORPE
NATURE
RESERVE
& GARDEN

East
Rudham

LYNN

Broomsthorpe

Pynkney

Southmill Fm.

Tatter

Flagmoor

Pudding
Norton

0 miles scale 3 miles

0 1 2 3 4 5 km

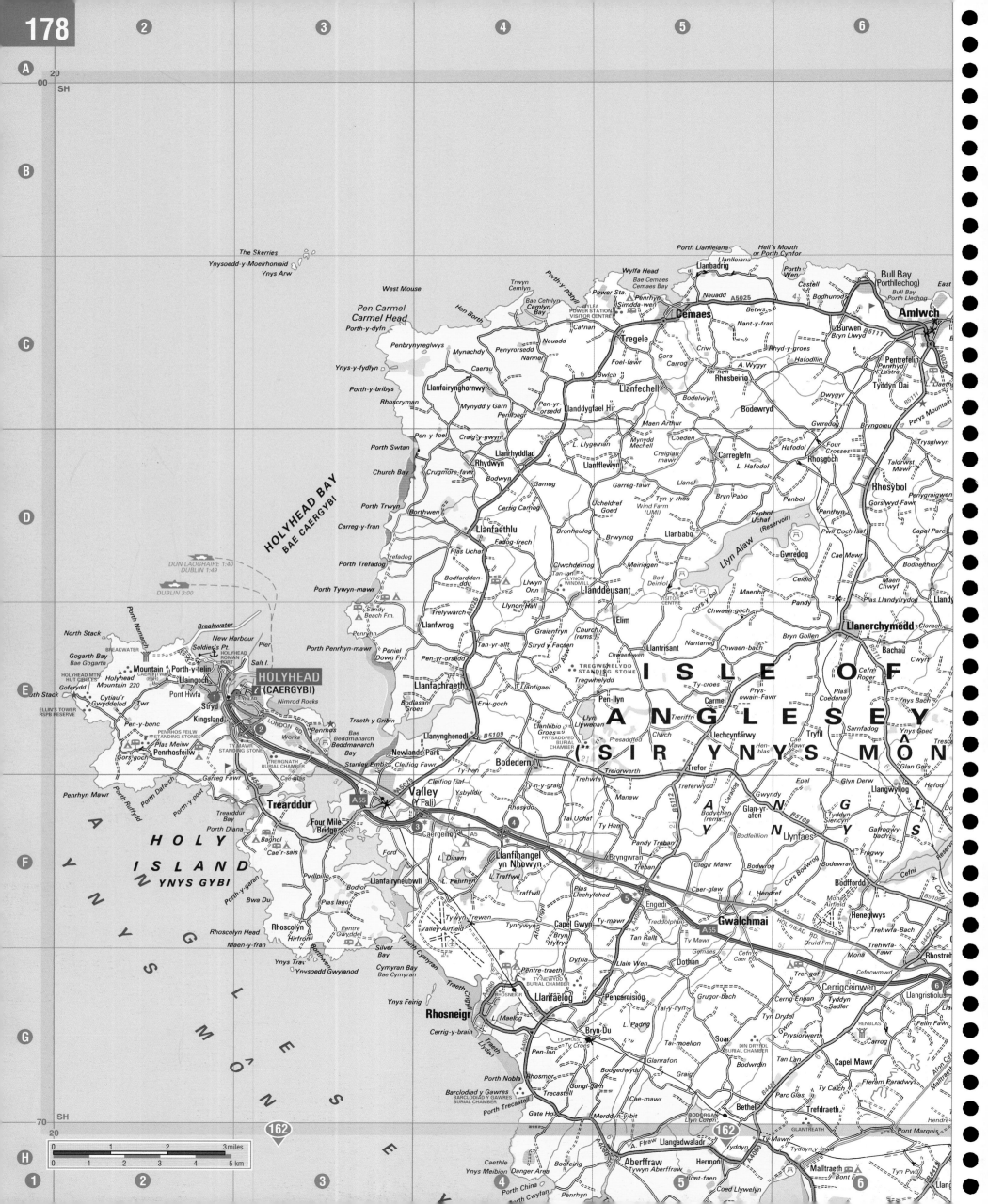

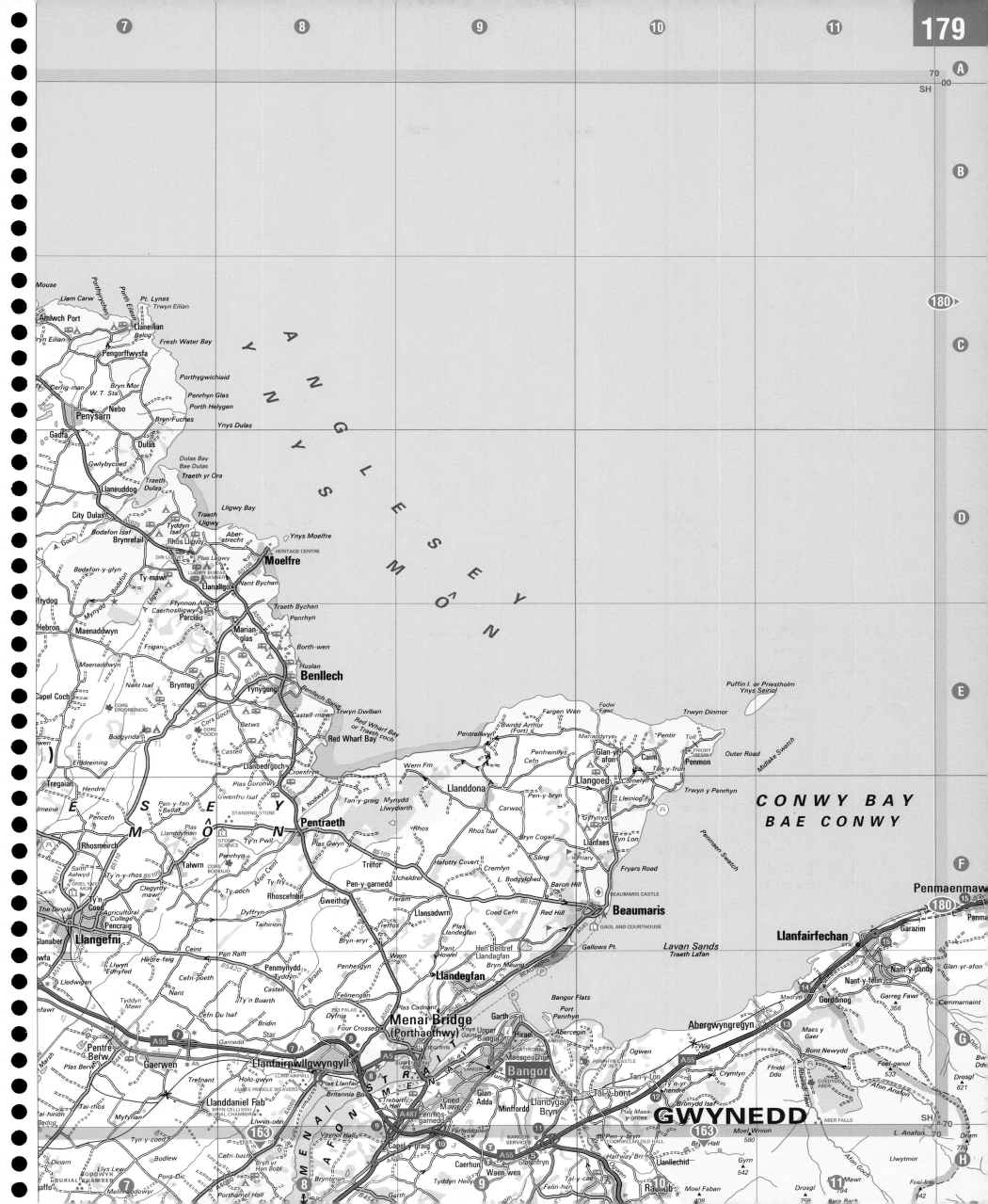

IRISH SEA

MÔR IWERDDO

Great Ormes Head
Pen-y-Gogarth

Hornby Cave

Marine Drive

GREAT
ORME

GREAT ORME
TRAMWAY

CABIN LIFT

Toll

Gogarth
Happy
Valley

Bishop's Palace (rems.)

Maes-y-
facrell

Little Ormes Head
Pen-yr-Gogarth

Ormes Bay or Llandudno Bay

Cregiau Rhiwledyn

Penrhyn Bay
(Bae Penrhyn)

GREAT ORME COPPER MINE

ALICE IN WONDERLAND

ORIEL
MOSTYN

COLWYN   141

LLANDUDNO

LLANDUDNO

RD.

Craig-y-don

Penrhynside

Rhôs-on-Sea

Penrhyn Uchaf

Gloddaeth-isaf

Llanrhos

Gloddaeth Hall

Glanwydden

Dinarth Hall

Llandrillo-yn-Rhôs

Conwy
Sands
Traeth Conwy

Deganwy

Deganwy Castle

Pen-y-bont

Bryn Euryn

131

Colwyn Bay
Bae Colwyn

Abergele Roads
Angorfa Abergele

ABERGELE & PENSARN

DEGANWY

A470

Llangwstenin
Hall

Pydew
Pabo

20

COLWYN BAY

COLWYN BAY (BAE COLWYN)

Penmaen-bach Pt.

17

Tywyn

Esgyryn
Hendre-wen

A541

22

Civic
Cen.

A547

A55   23

16

PENMAENMAWR

245

247

Conwy Mt.

Llandudno
Junction
(Cyffordd
Llandudno)

Mochdre

WELSH
MOUNTAIN
ZOO

21

DINOSAUR
WORLD

Nant-y-glyn Hall

Penmaen-Rhôs

Old Colwyn

Ty-mawr

Mynydd Marian

23

Llanddulas

Terfyn

Cefn yr Ogof

204

Allt-wen

255

Conwy

Grianllyn

Pant-y-
gloch

Bryn
Dulas

Abe

F

Penmaenmawr

A55

16

Dwygyfylchi

362

Foel Lus

Sychnant
Pass

Crow's
Nest

Conwy

STA.

Gyffin

Benarth
Hall

18

A55

19

Bryn

Dolwyd

Cilglasin

Pen-y-Bryn
Uchaf

Nantuchaf

Tal Llan

Llanelian-
yn-Rhos

Pendared

Rhyd-y-foel

Plas-newydd

Bryngwenallt

179

15

Penmaen

Garazim

Llechwedd

Iolyn
Park

Groesffordd

GLAN
CONWY

A470

Bryn-rhys

Llansanffraid
Glan Conwy

Eisteddfod

Caethiwed

Ffridd y
Mynydd

Bryn-y-maen

B5381

Ty-newydd

Gloddaeth

Bryn-y-maen Fm.

Plas
Uchaf

Llety'r Adar

Tal Rallt

Pant Idda

Ffynhonnau

Nant-y-pandy

Glan-yr-afon

Moelfre

435

Cefn Côch

Cerrig
Gwynion

Garned-wen

Ty 'n-y-ffrith

Hafodty

Henryd

Fachleidiog

Pentrefelin

Graig

Penrhyn Uchaf

Croesau

Nant-y-
cywarch

Geufron

Mynydd
Glyn-Lws

347

Grugfryn

Dawn

Gloddaeth

Coed
Bryndansi

Sarn

Coed Côch

Bron Pistyll

Mynydd
Glyn-Lws

Moelfre
Uchaf

396

Pant-y-
gwydr

Plas Newydd

Betws-yn-Rhos

Sirior Goch

Gwreiddyn

Sirior
Bach

S N O W D O N I A

Foel
Lwyd

Tal y Fan

Glyn Isaf

Tan-y-bryn

Llwydfaen

Bodnant

Cae Forys

Croesengan
Ucha

Hafodunos

Bryn-mawr

Trofarth

Mynydd-dir

314

Plas
Bodrochwyn

Mynydd
Bodran

287

Cammarnaint

356

Drosgl

621

Cae-coch

ROWEN

Rowen

Pontwgan

Tal-y-cafn

BODNANT GARDEN (N.T.)

TY'N-Y-CAFN

Graig

Moel Gyffylog

341

Codau Mawr

Deneufryn

Mynydd
Bodran

533

Bwlchy
Ddeufaen

Cae-coch

Gorswen

Ty-ny-
groes

A470

Esgairheulog

Tanralt

Eglwysbach

Coed
Pant-glas

Ty'n-y-llyn

Wenallt

Garthewin

Llanfair
Talhaiarn

NATIONAL

PARK

164

CANOVIUM
ROMAN FORT

LLANRWST
RD.

L. Anafon

Castell

Tal-y-Bont

y-cenn.

Fron

Pentre'r Felin

Henfryn

Gell

164

Nant Mawr

Ysgubor
newydd

Bryn Kenrick

Moel Iago

Pentre-du

Waterfall

Merllyn

L. Syberi

Llwyn-du

Nant-y-cerrig

Nant Esgair-Ebrill

Hafodty
Bennett

Llety
Watkin

Plas-yn-
Cefn-coch

Pentre Isaf

Nant Bach

Ty-du

Moel Unben

358

Bryn-
nantllech

L. Anafon

533

0   1   2   3 miles
0 1 2 3 4 5 km

442

Dulyn Rowlyn

Mwdwl Eithin

389

Frith Lon

Tydynn-bach

Nant Gwian

Gribin

Tre-pys-llygod

Moel Emwnt

Camarn

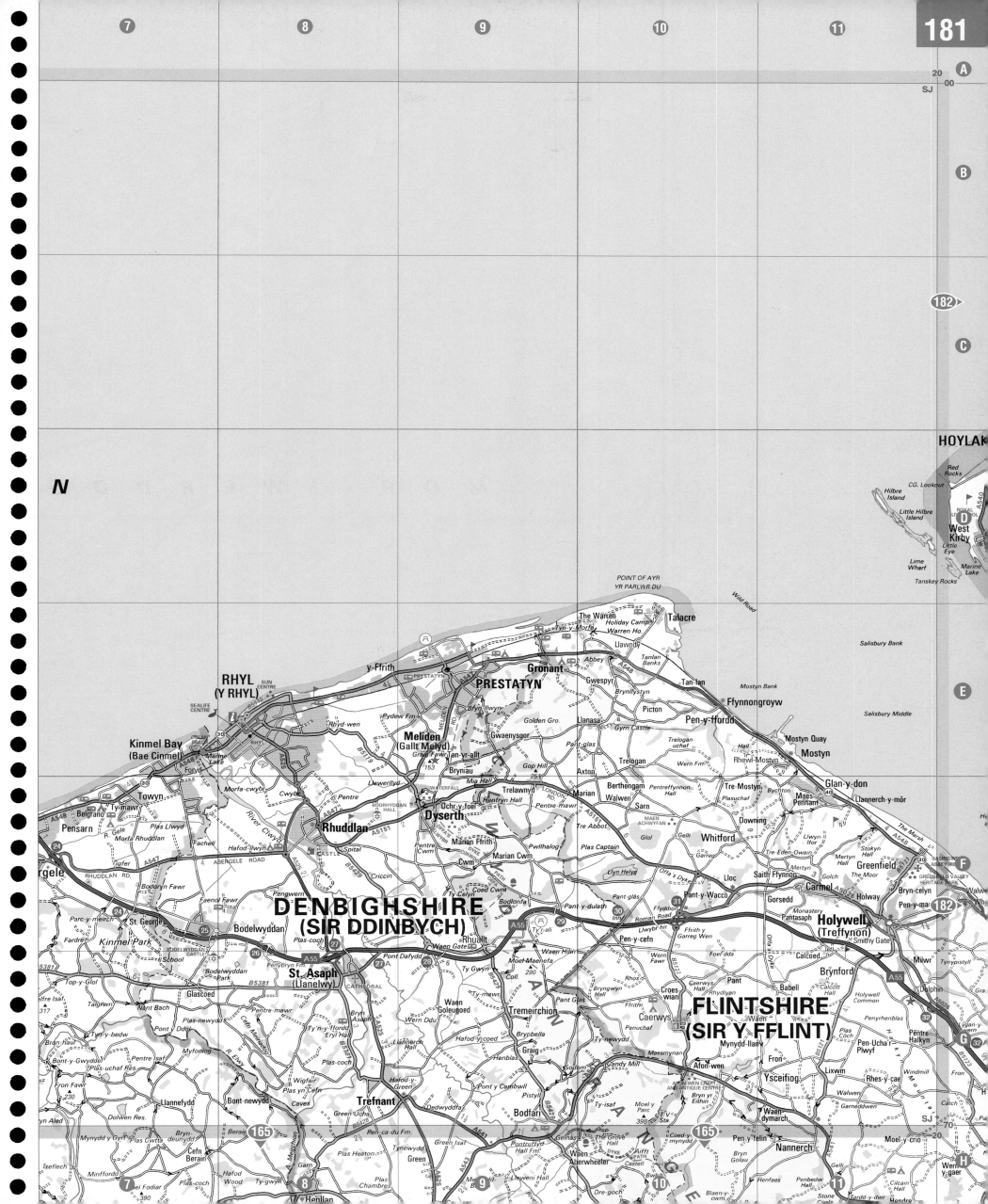

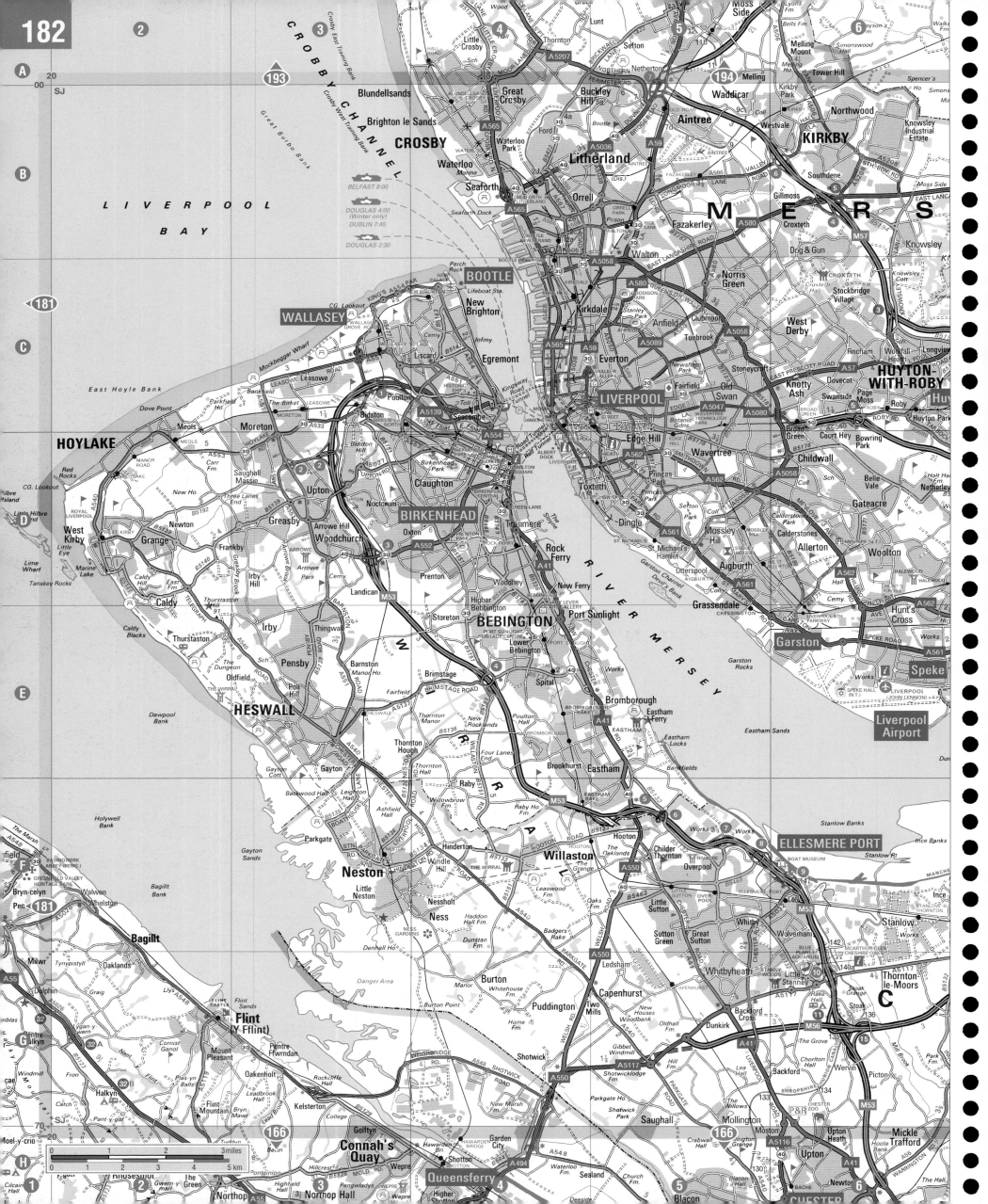

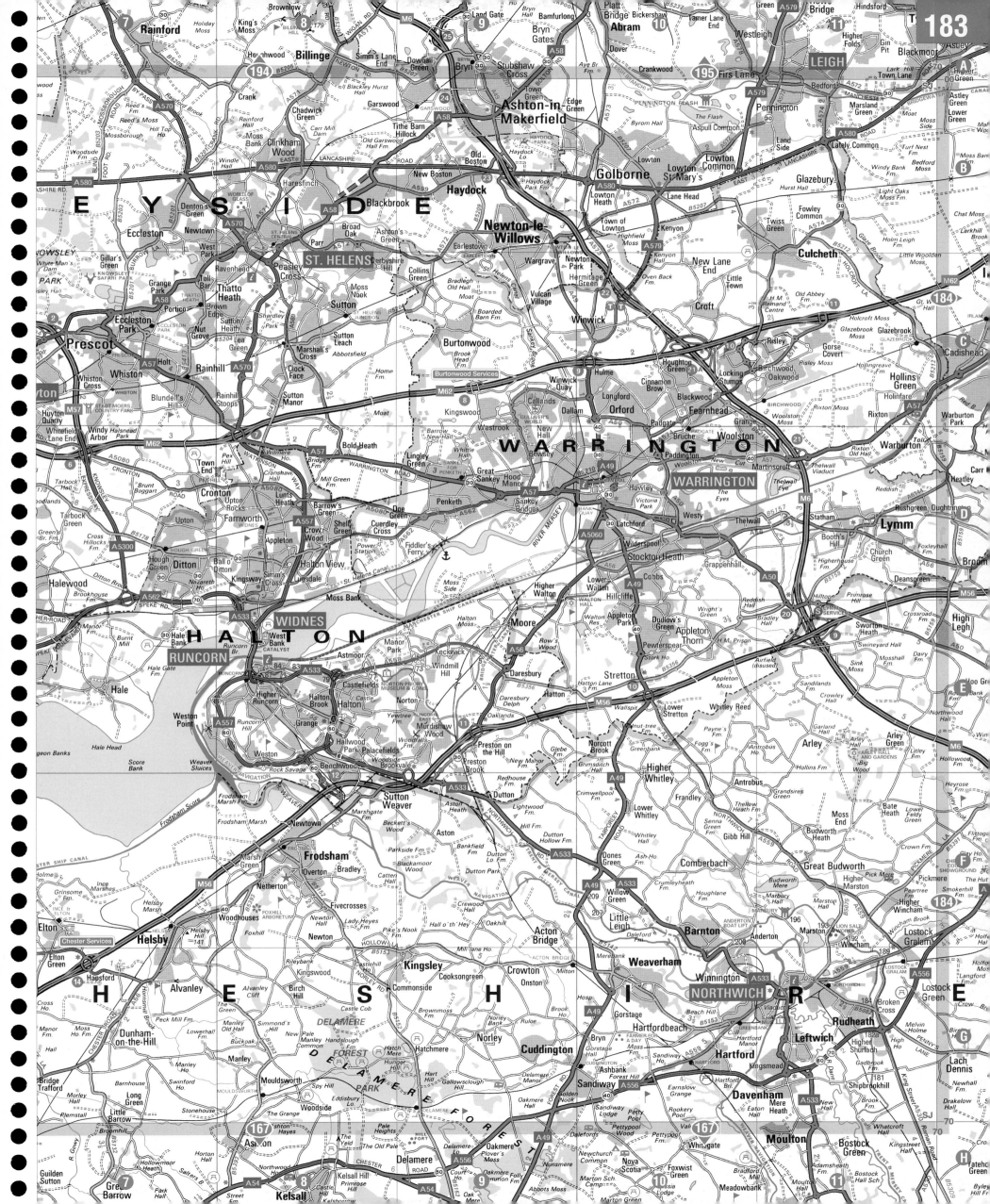

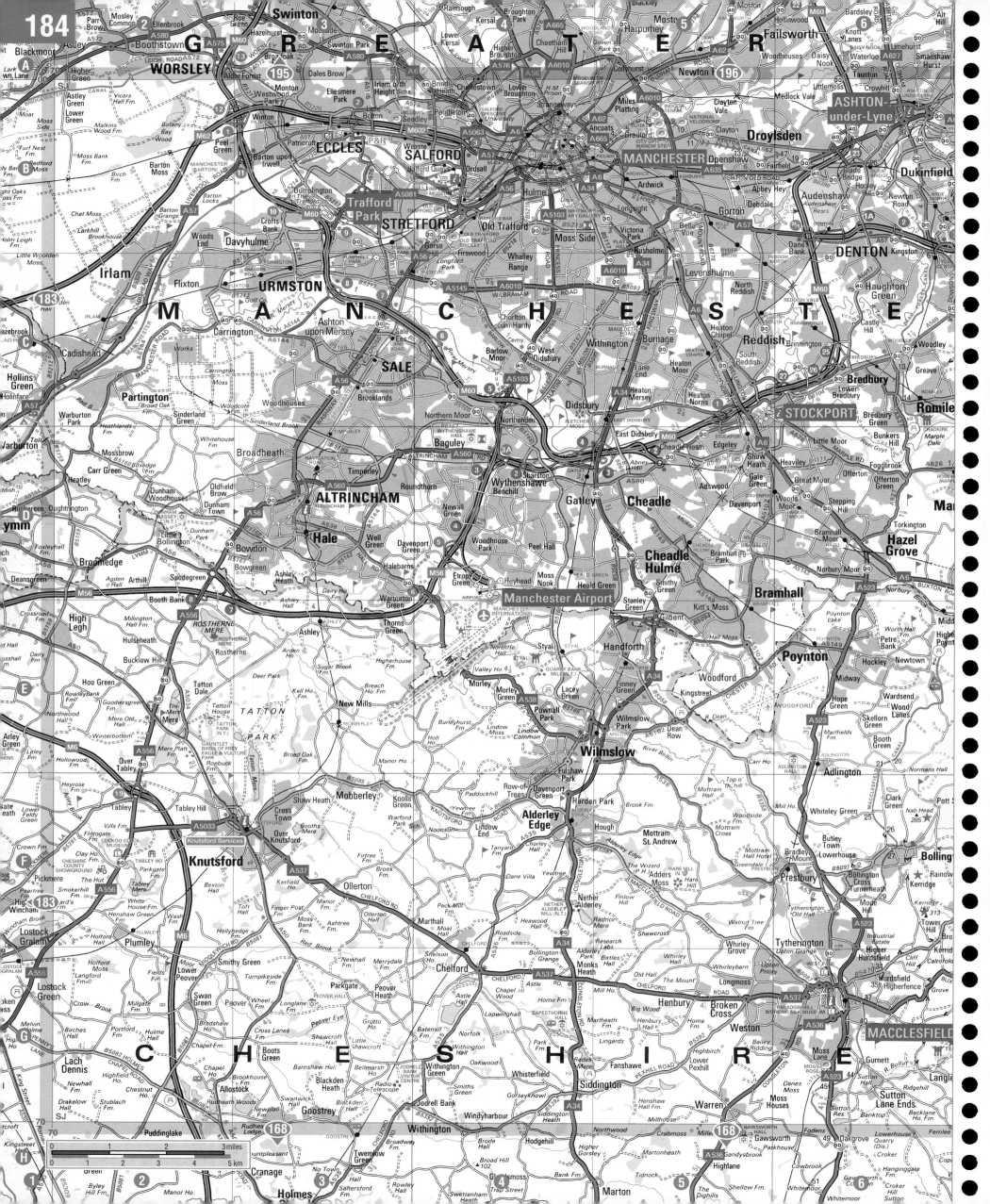

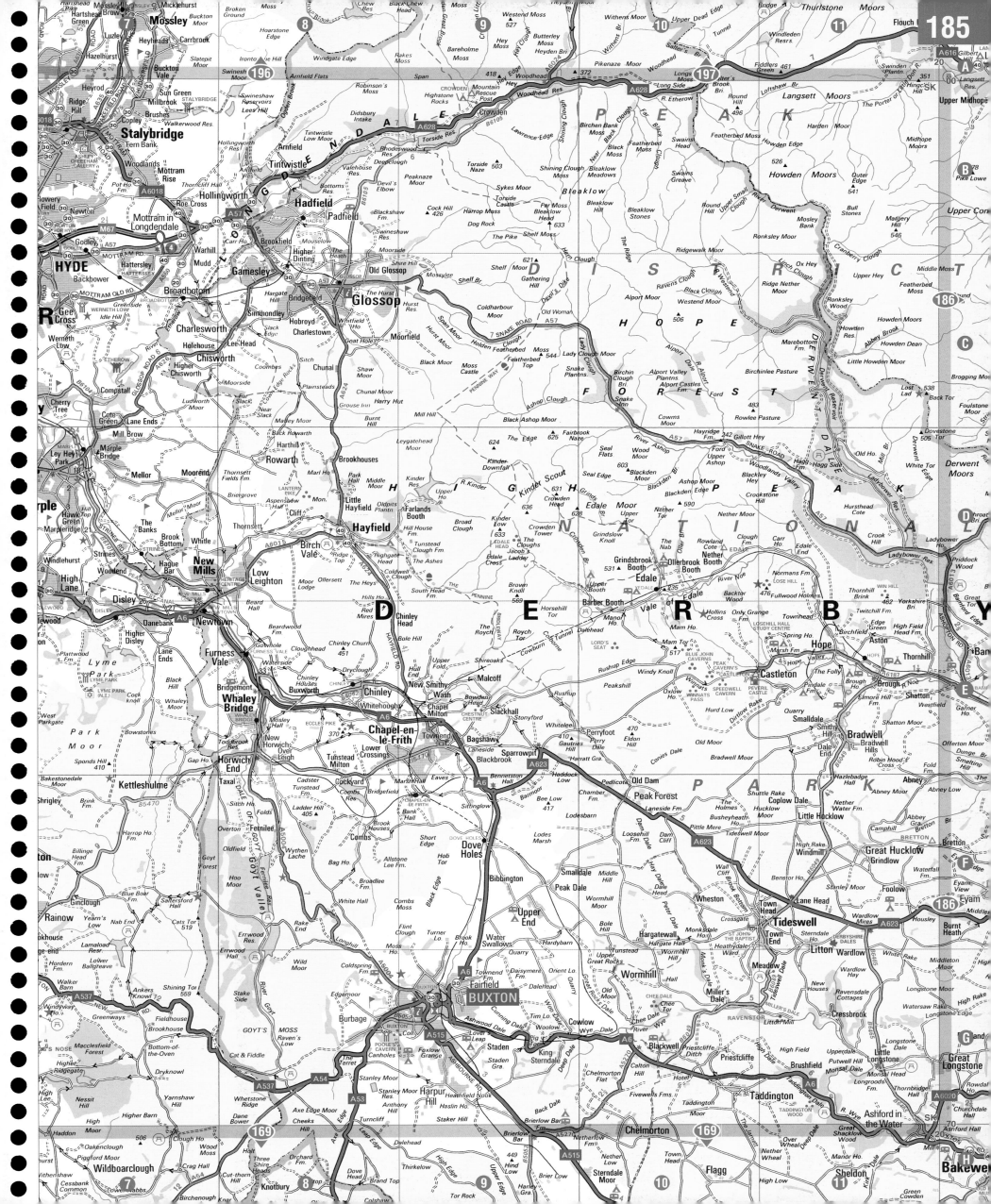

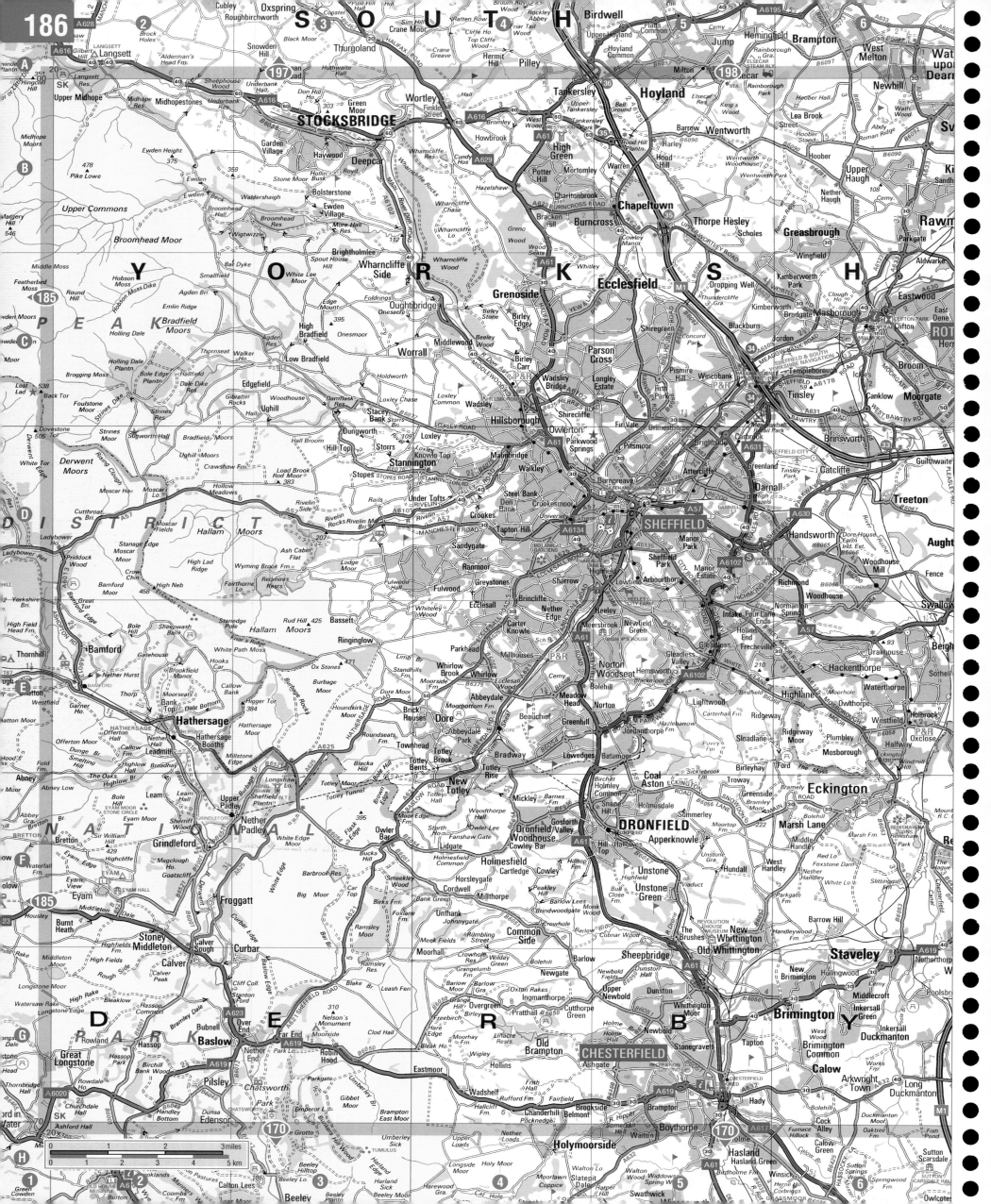

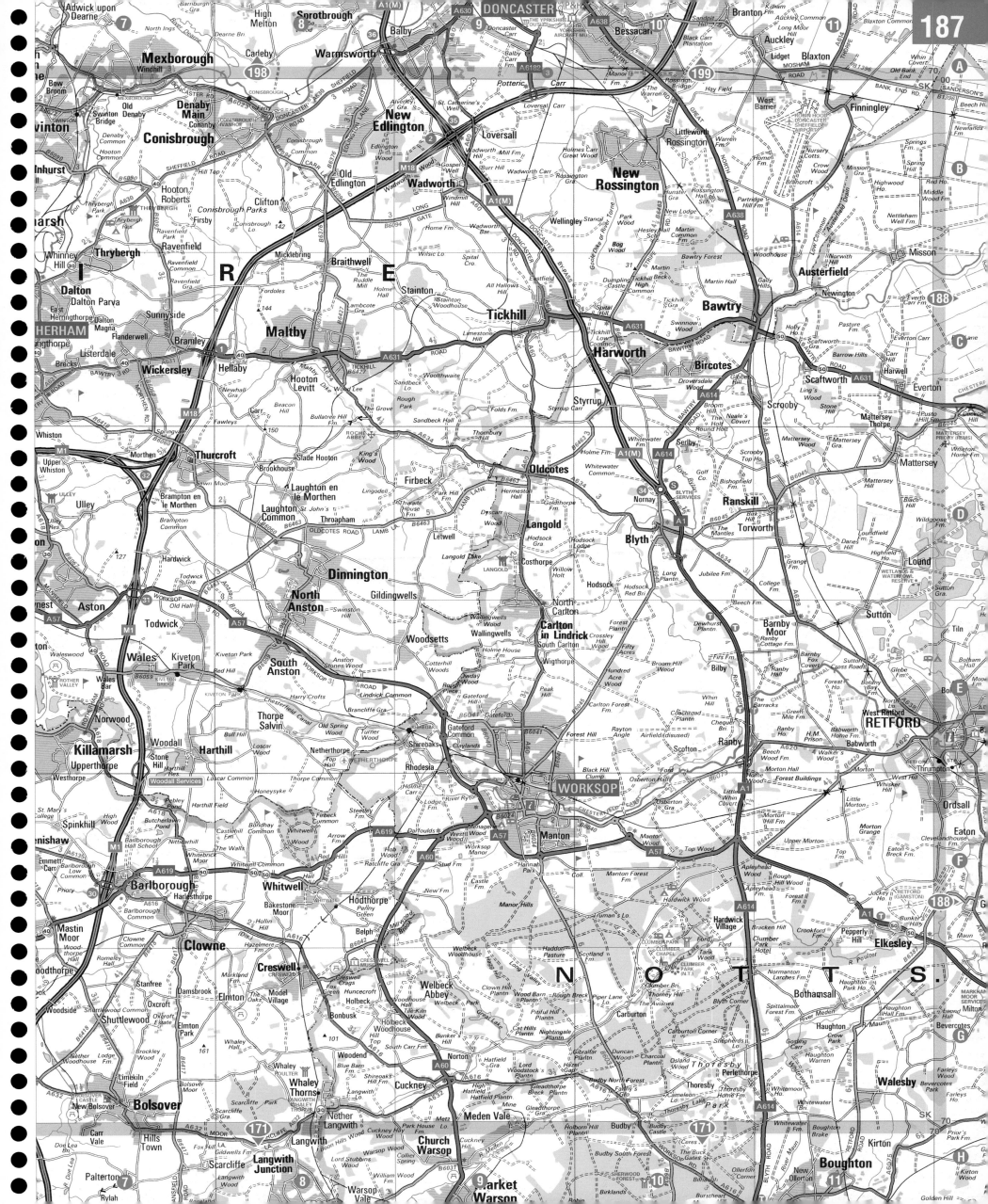

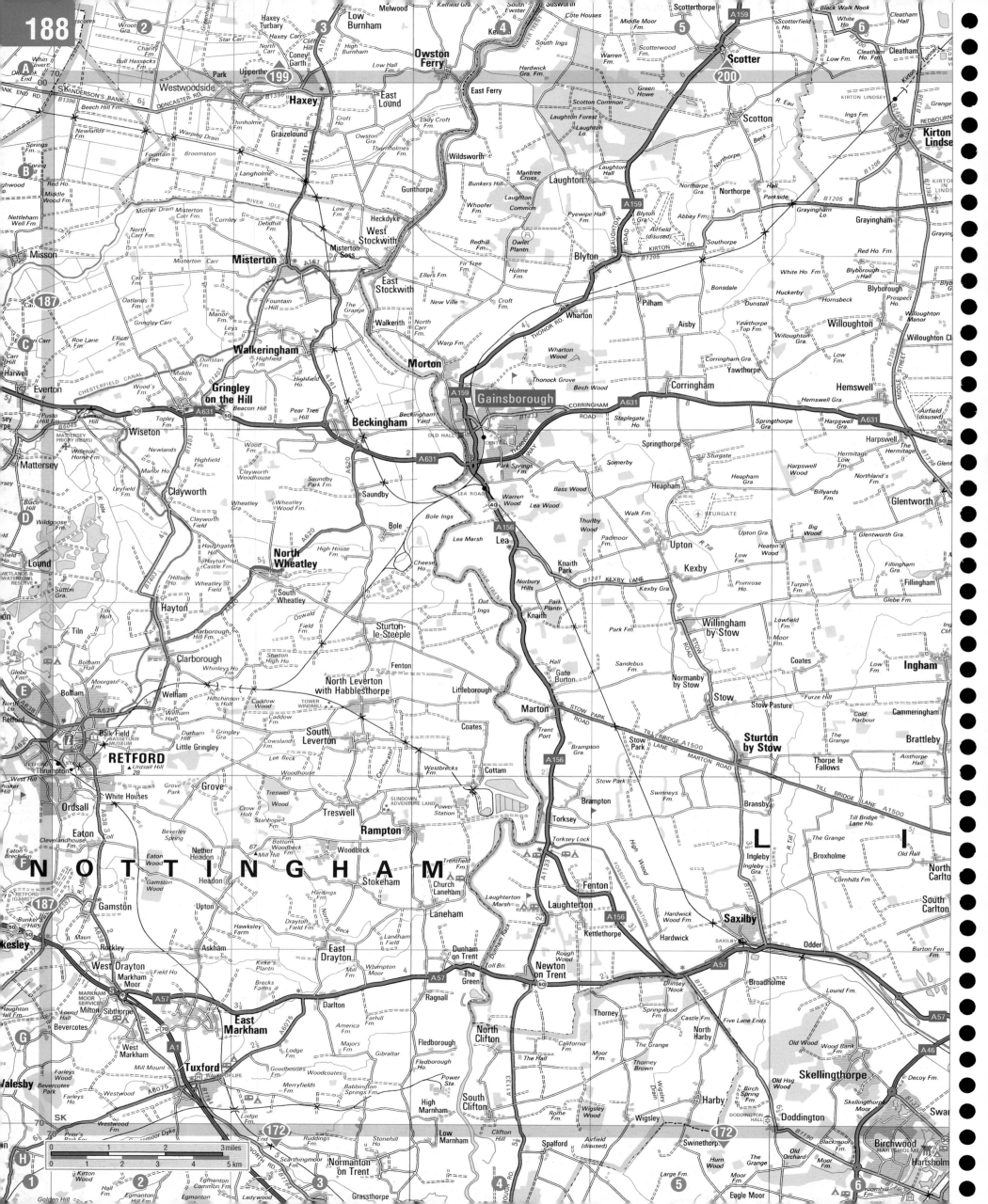

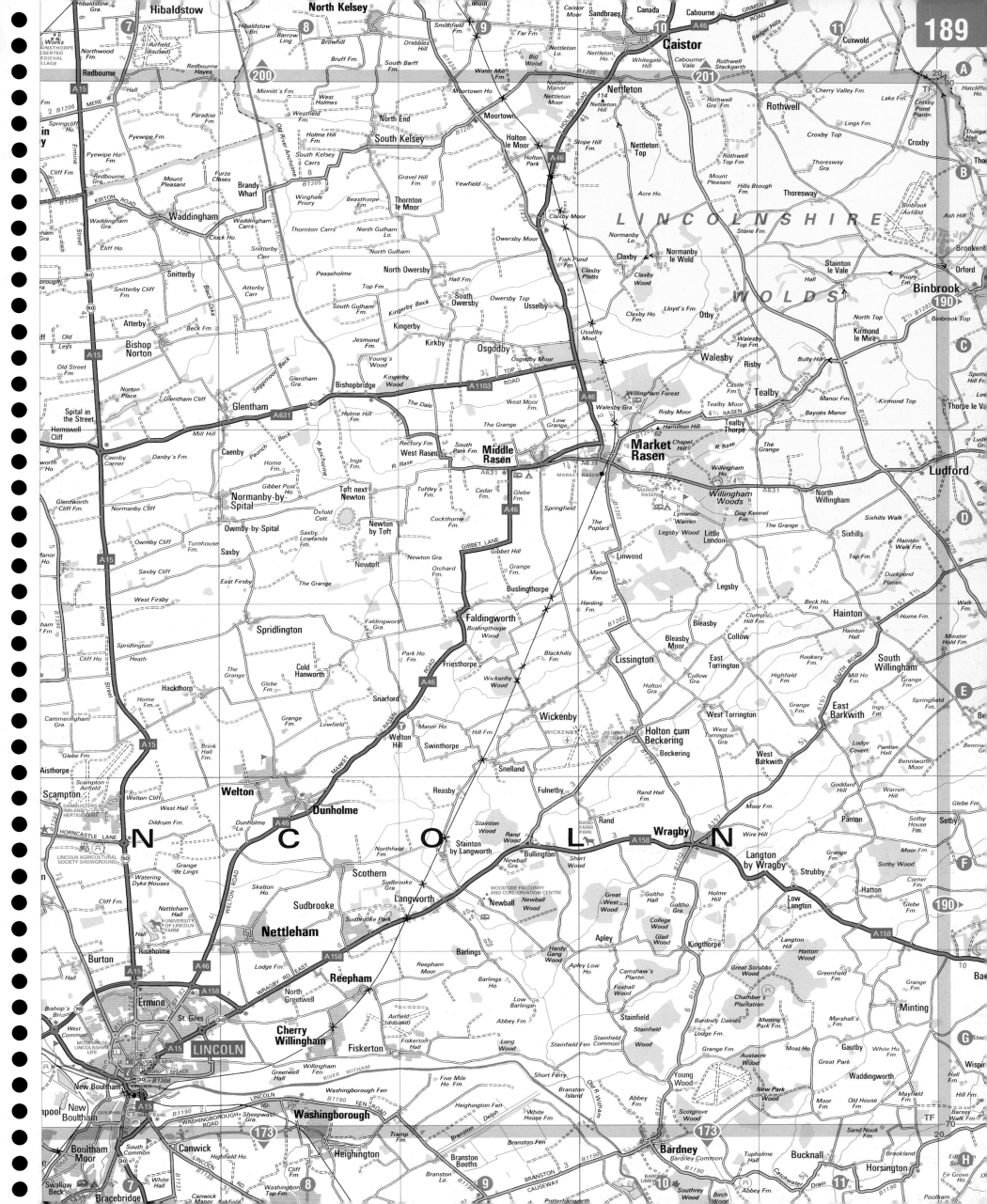

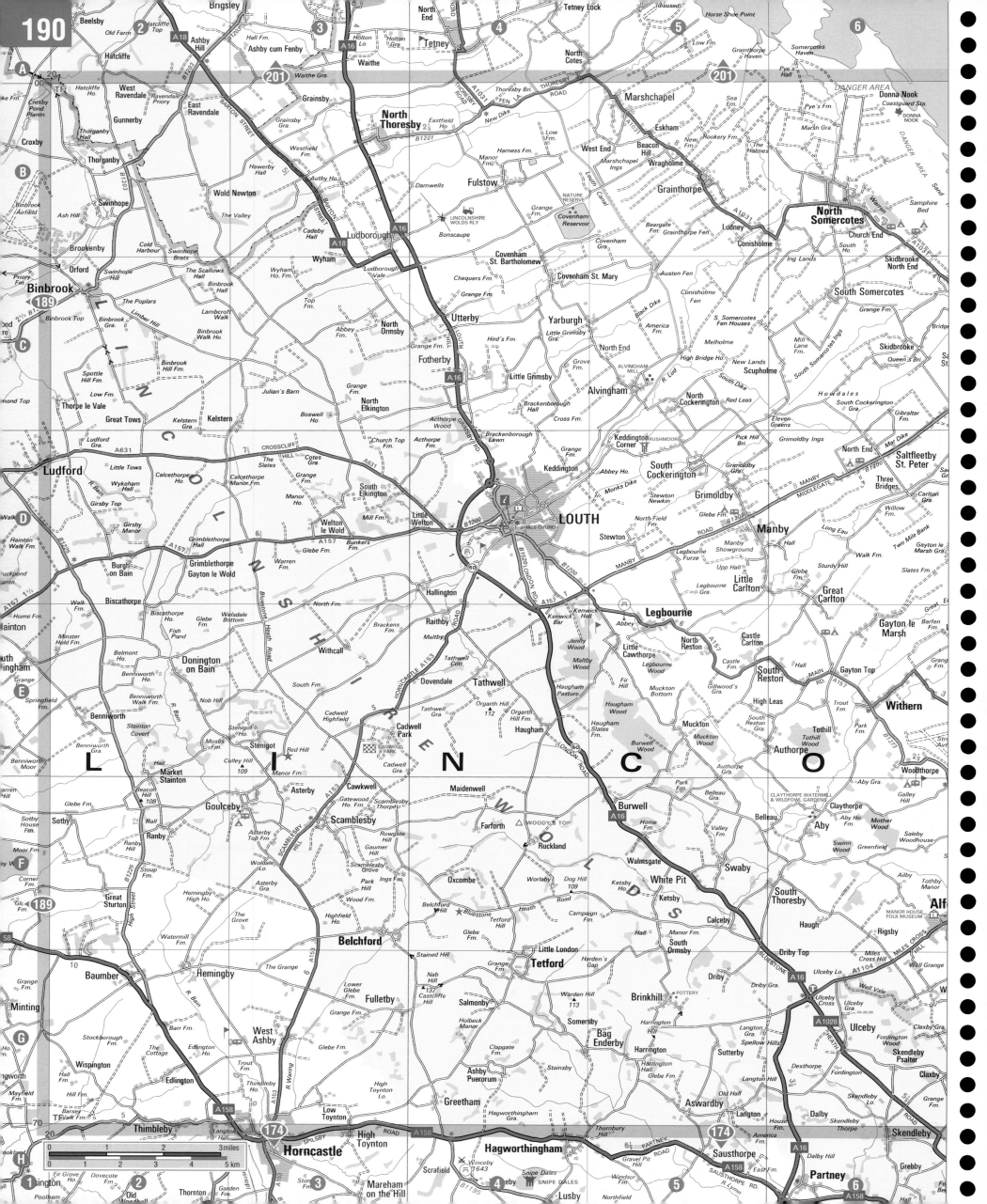

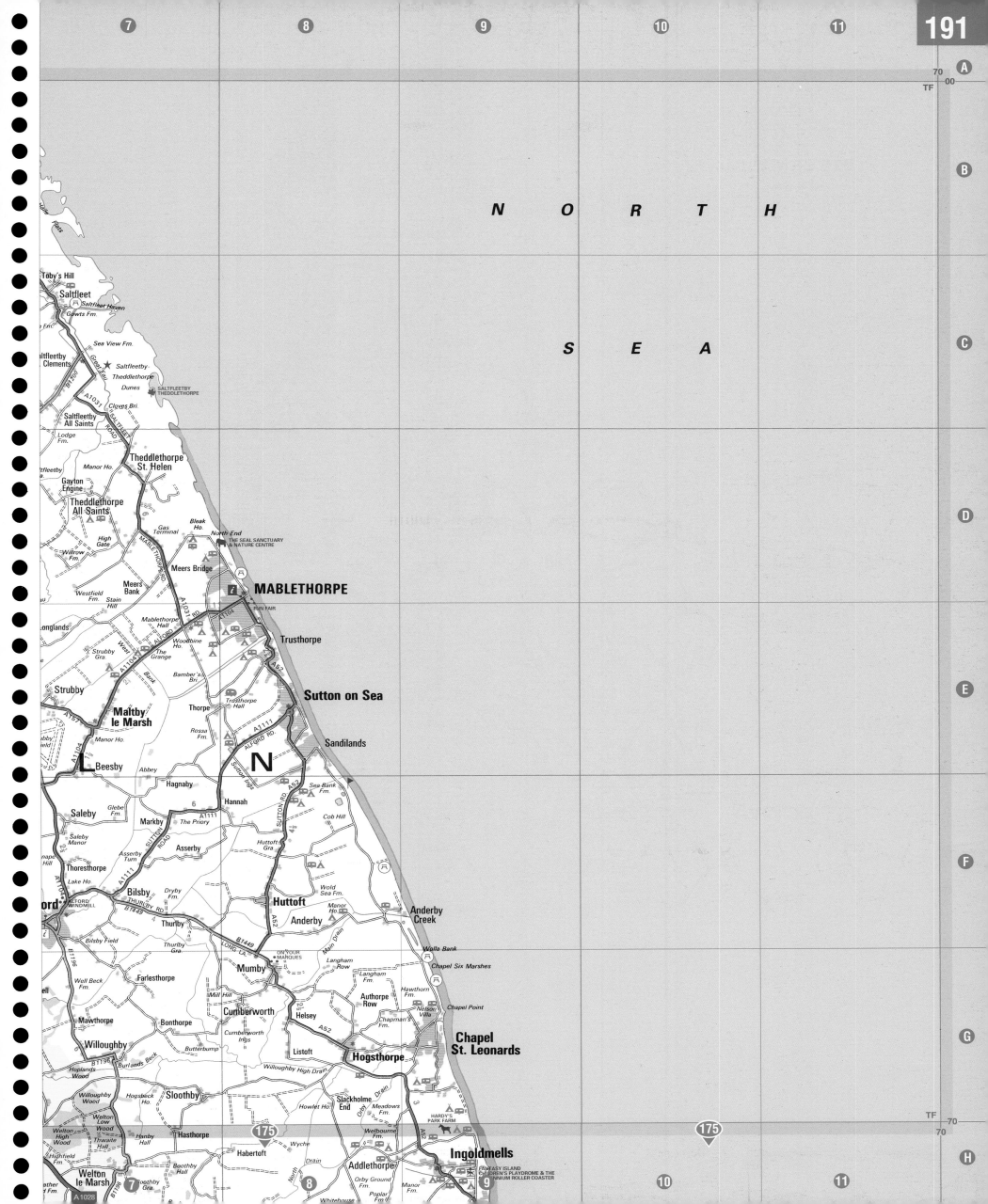

NORTH SEA

Toby's Hill
Saltfleet
Saltfleet Haven
Gowts Fm.
Fm.
Sea View Fm.
Saltfleetby
St. Clements
Saltfleetby
Theddlethorpe
Dunes
SALTFLEETBY
THEDDLETHORPE
Cloves Bri.
Saltfleetby
All Saints
Lodge Fm.
Saltfleetby
Theddlethorpe
St. Helen
Gayton
Engine
Manor Ho.
Theddlethorpe
All Saints
High
Gate
Willrow
Fm.
Bleak
Ho.
Gas
Terminal
North End
THE SEAL SANCTUARY
& NATURE CENTRE
Meers Bridge
Meers
Bank
Westfield
Fm.
MABLETHORPE
Stain
Hill
FUN FAIR
Longlands
Mablethorpe
Hall
Woodbine
Ho.
Strubby
Gra.
The
Grange
Trusthorpe
Bamber's
Bri.
Strubby
Thorpe
Trusthorpe
Hall
Sutton on Sea
**Maltby
le Marsh**
Rossa
Fm.
Sandilands
Manor Ho.
Leesby
Abbey
Hagnaby
Sea Bank
Fm.
Hannah
Saleby
Glebe
Fm.
Cob Hill
Markby
The Priory
Saleby
Manor
Huttoft
Gra.
Asserby
Turn
Asserby
Thoresthorpe
Lake Ho.
Bilsby
Dryby
Fm.
Wold
Sea Fm.
Huttoft
Manor
Ho.
Anderby
Creek
ALFORD
WINDMILL
Anderby
Thurlby
Bilsby Field
Thurlby
Gra.
Wolla Bank
ON YOUR
MARQUES
Langham
Row
Chapel Six Marshes
Mumby
Langham
Fm.
Well Beck
Fm.
Farlesthorpe
Mill Hill
Authorpe
Row
Hawthorn
Fm.
Chapel Point
Nelson
Villa
Cumberworth
Helsey
Chapman's
Fm.
**Chapel
St. Leonards**
Mawthorpe
Bonthorpe
Cumberworth
Ings
Willoughby
Butterbump
Listoft
Hogsthorpe
Hoplands
Wood
Willoughby High Drain
Hogsbeck
Wood
Sloothby
Willoughby High Drain
Slackholme
End
Howlet Ho.
Orby
Meadows
Fm.
HARDY'S
PARK FARM
Welton
Low
Wood
Welton
High
Wood
175
Welbourne
Fm.
175
Hanby
Hall
Wyche
Thwaite
Hall
Hasthorpe
175
Highfield
Hall
Habertoft
Ingoldmells
FANTASY ISLAND
CHILDREN'S PLAYDROME &
THE MILLENNIUM ROLLER COASTER
**Welton
le Marsh**
Boothby
Gra.
Addlethorpe
Orby Ground
Fm.
Manor
Fm.
Whitehouse
Poplar
Fm.

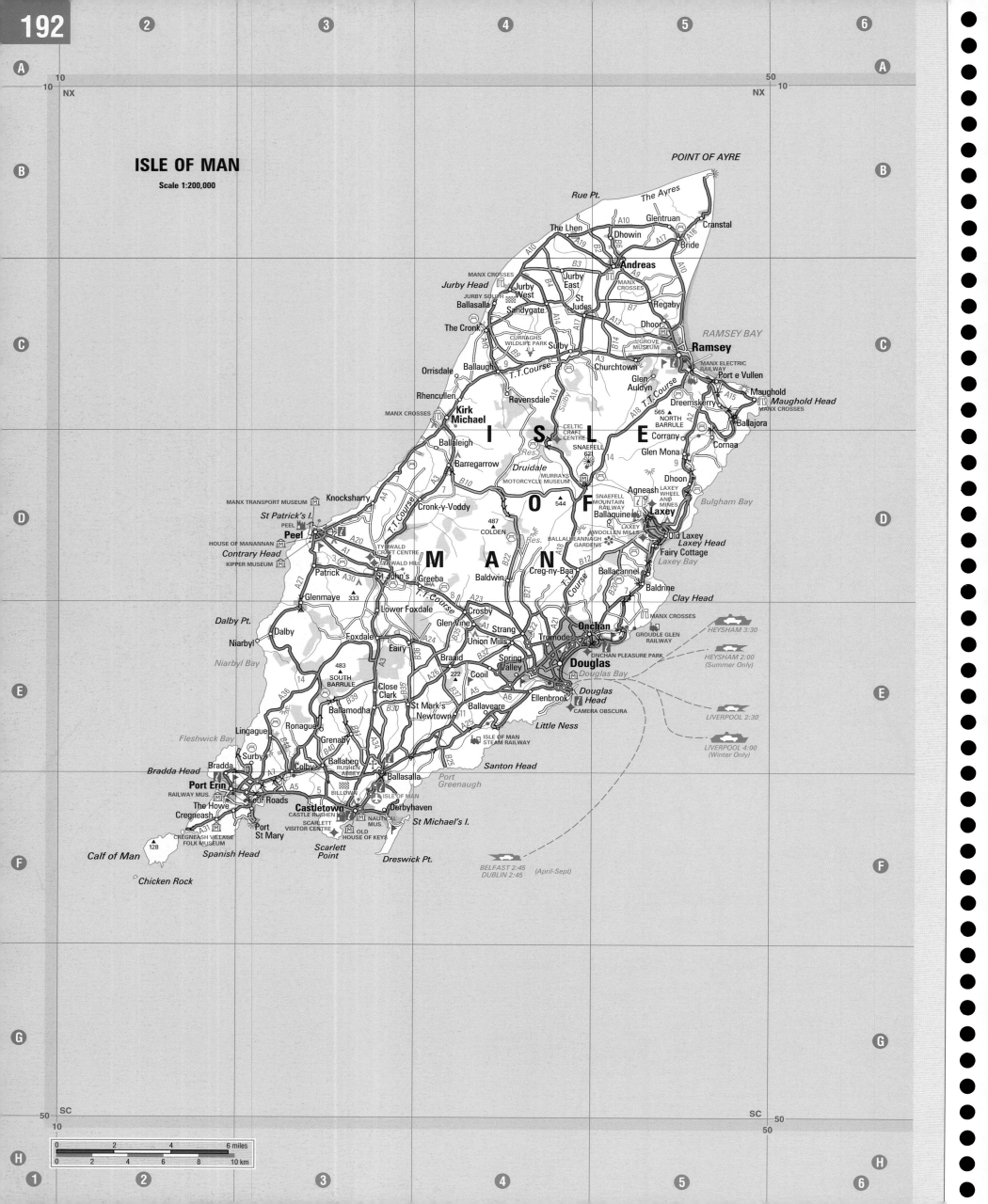

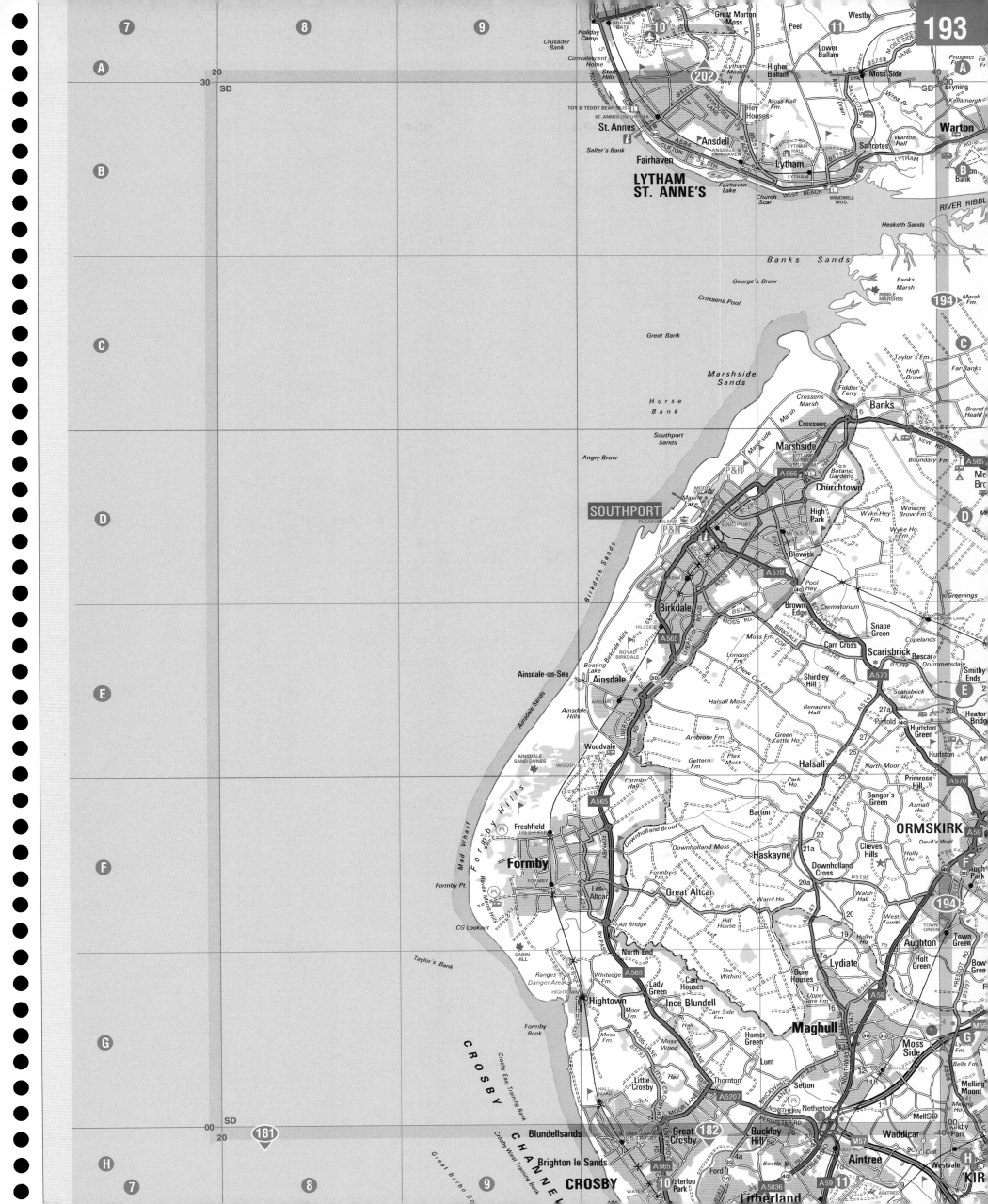

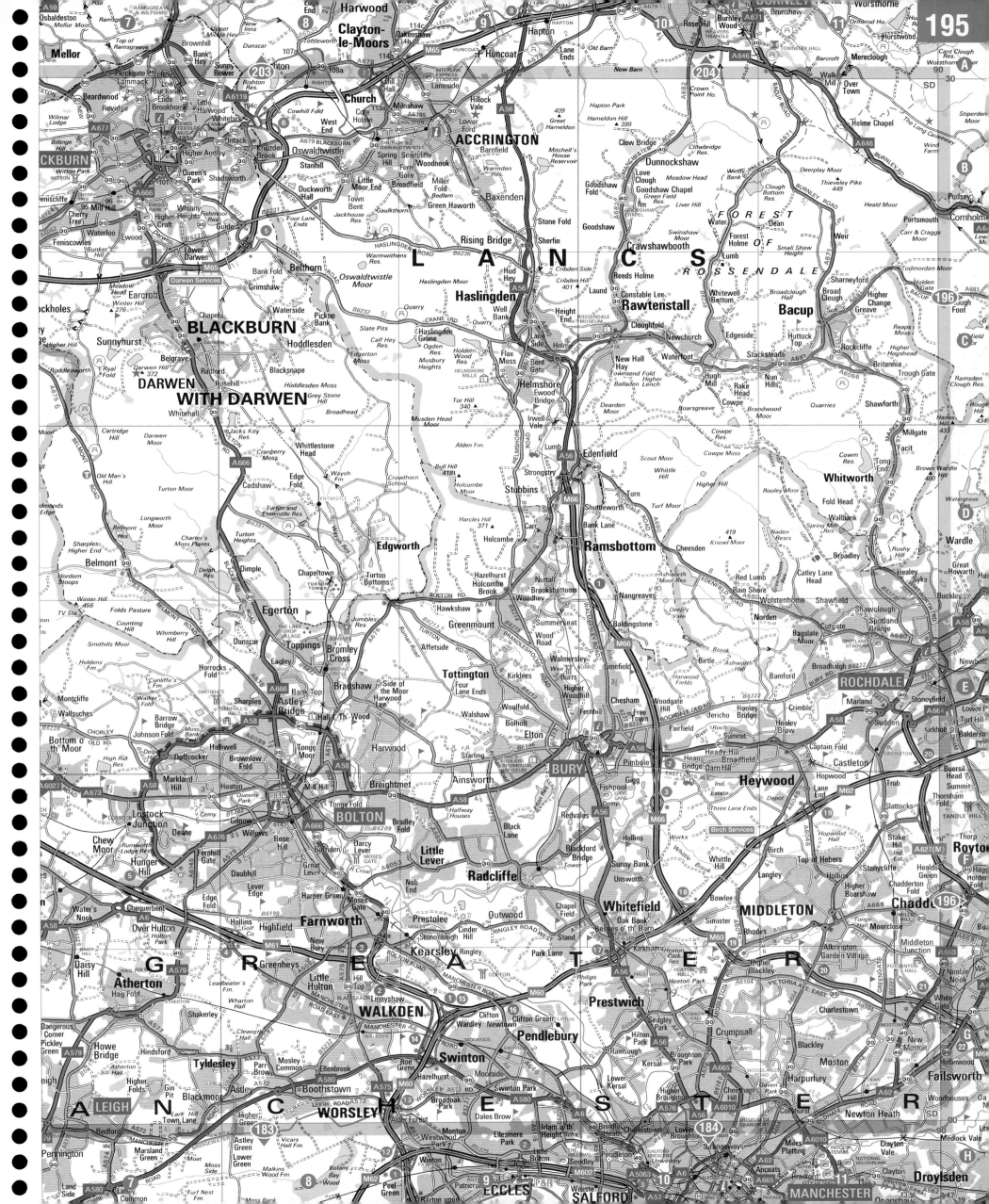

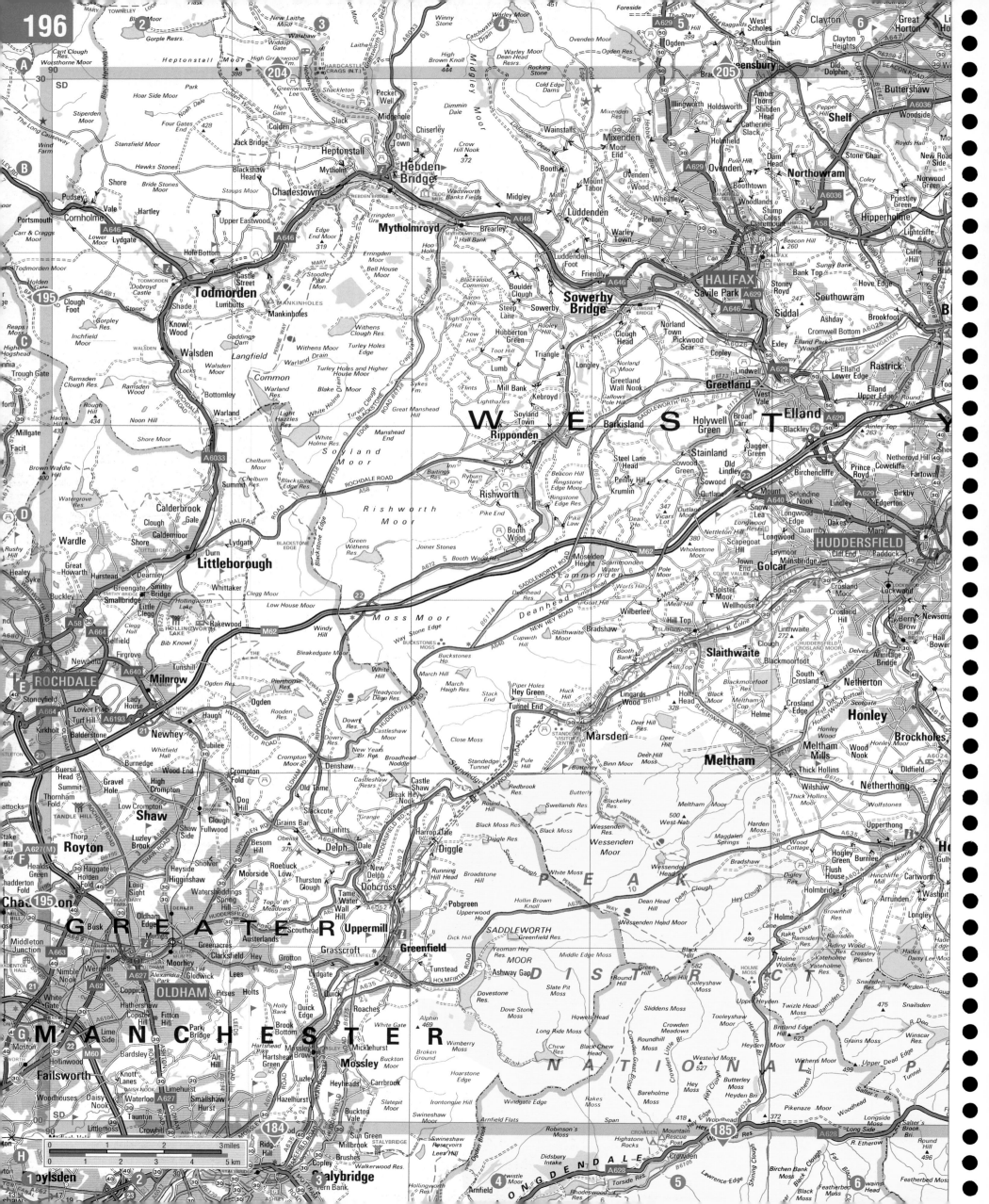

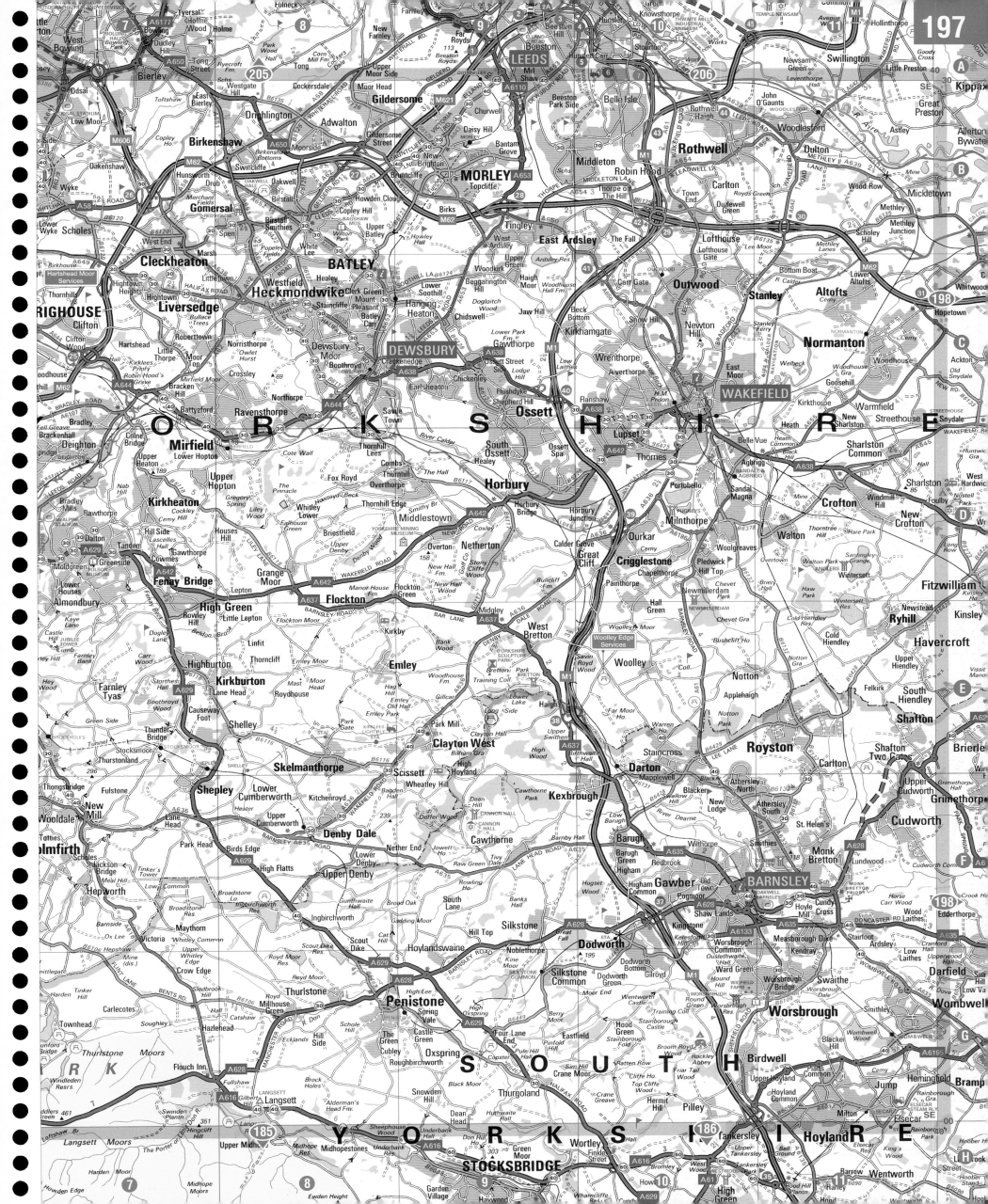

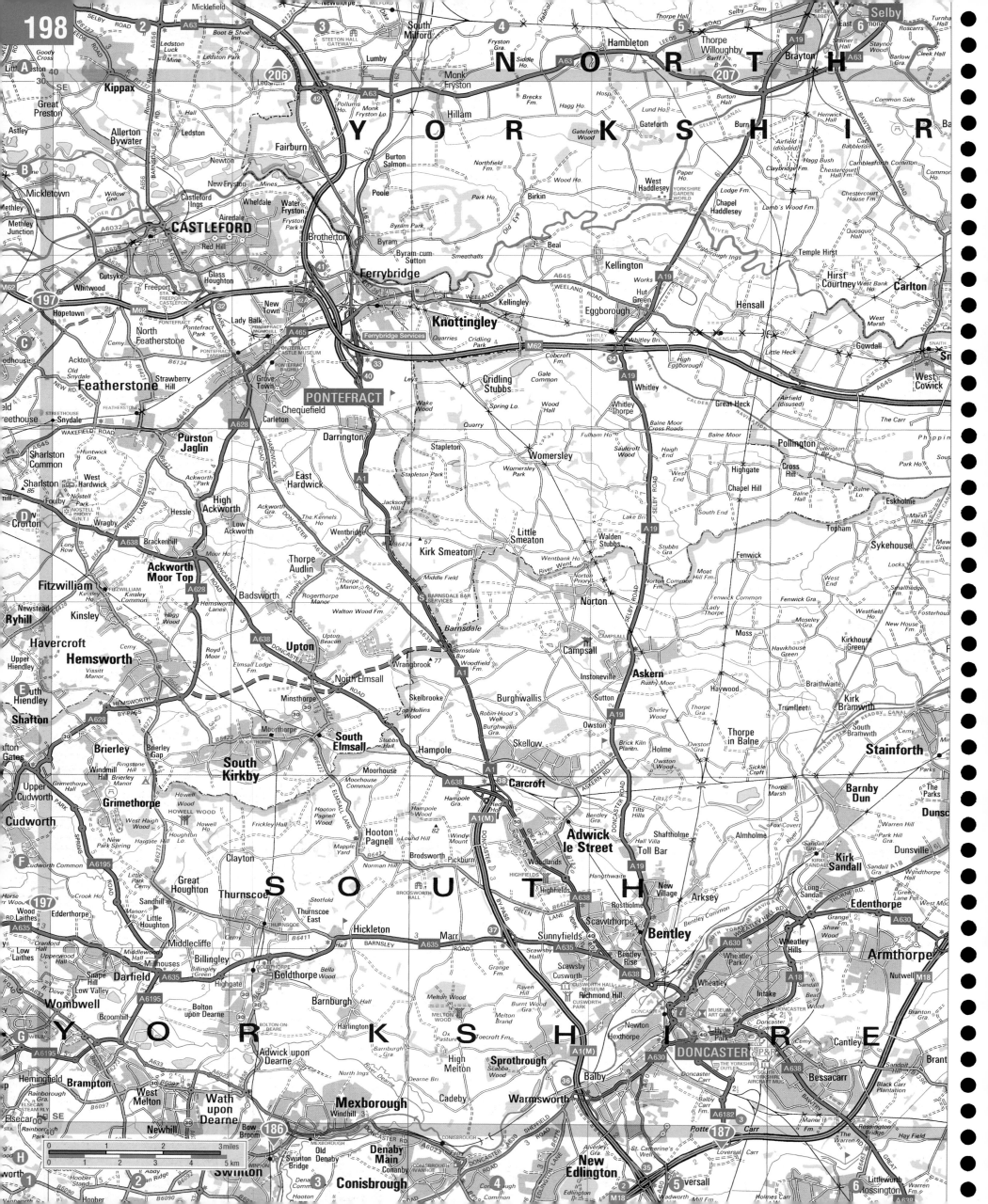

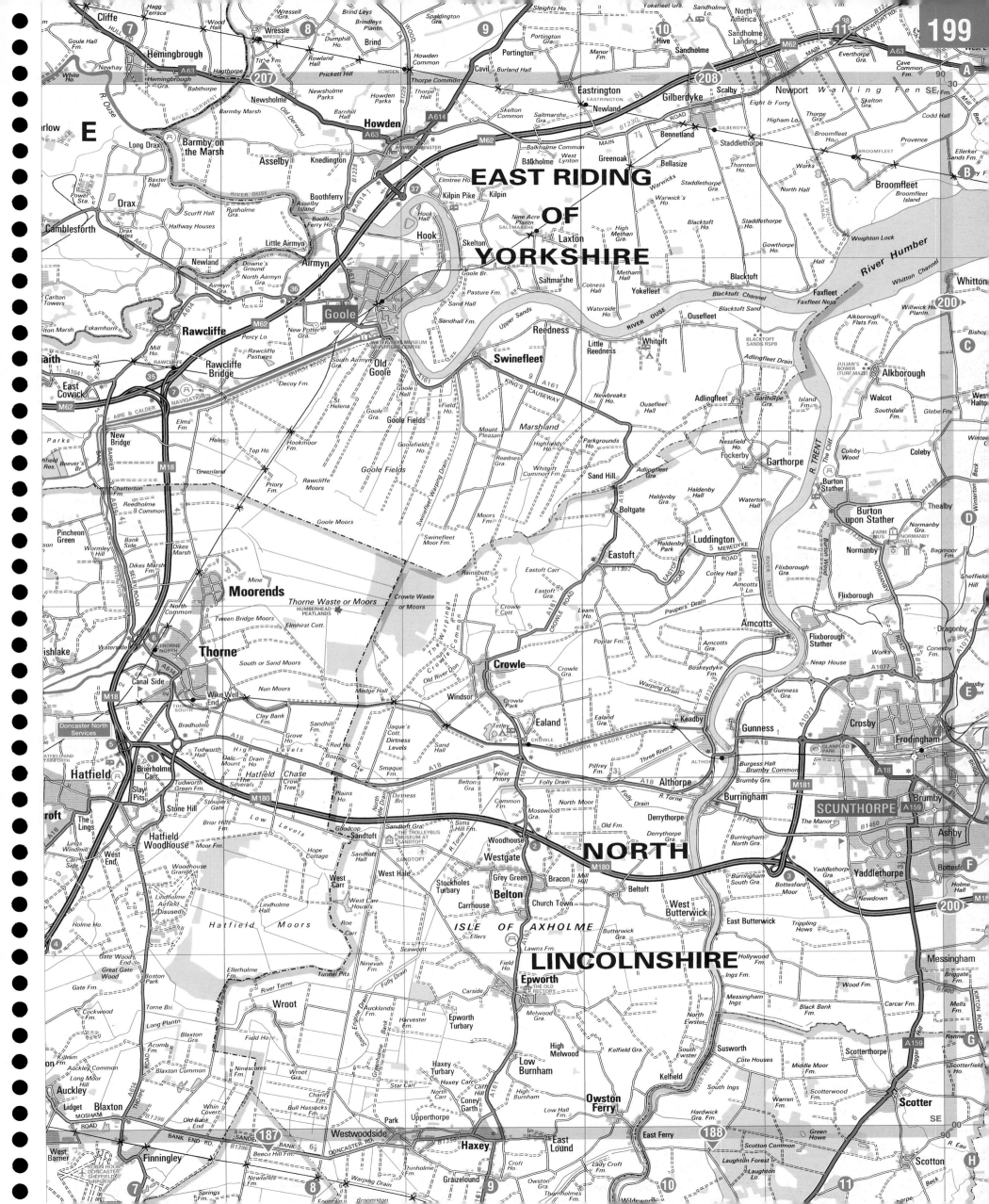

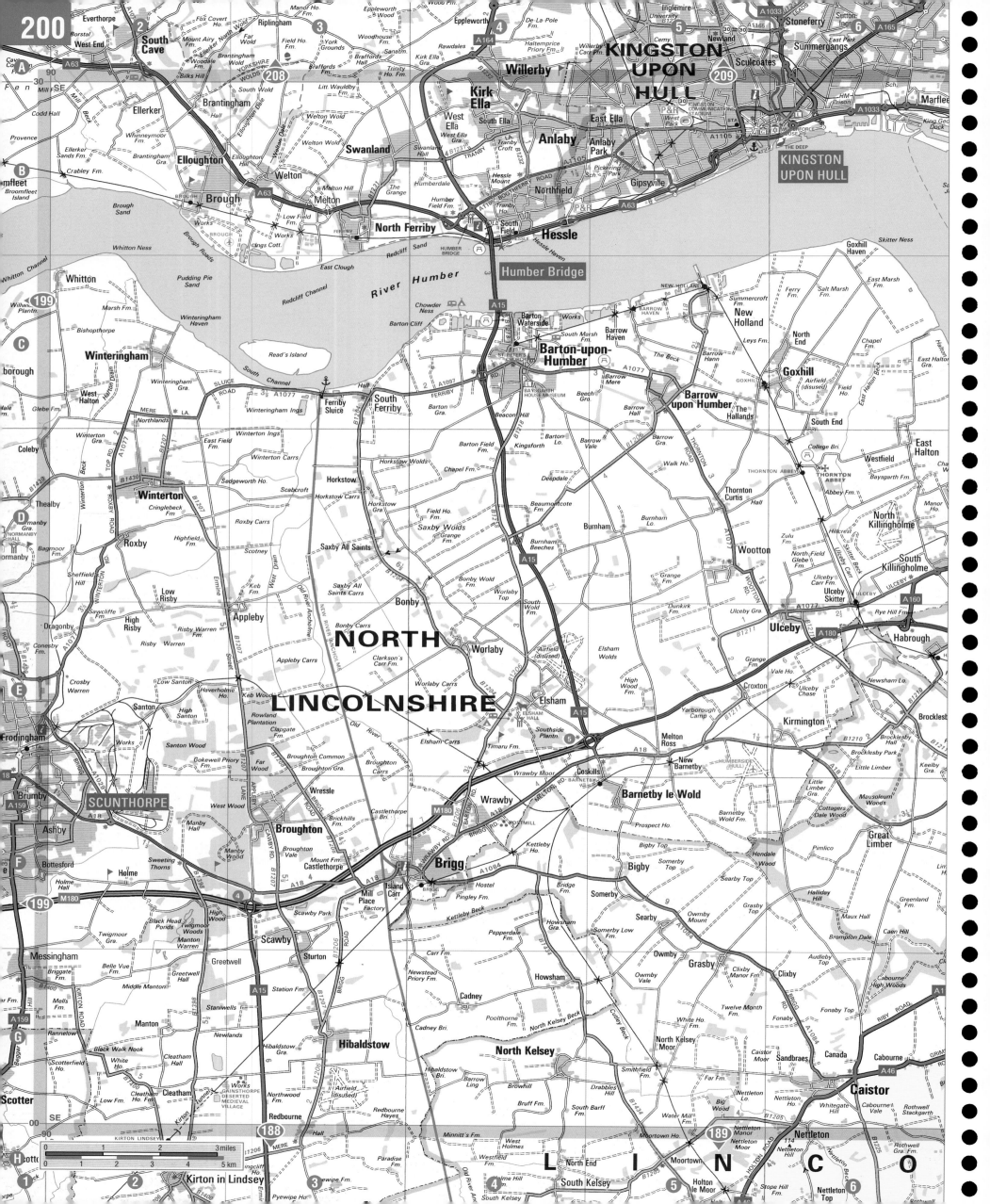

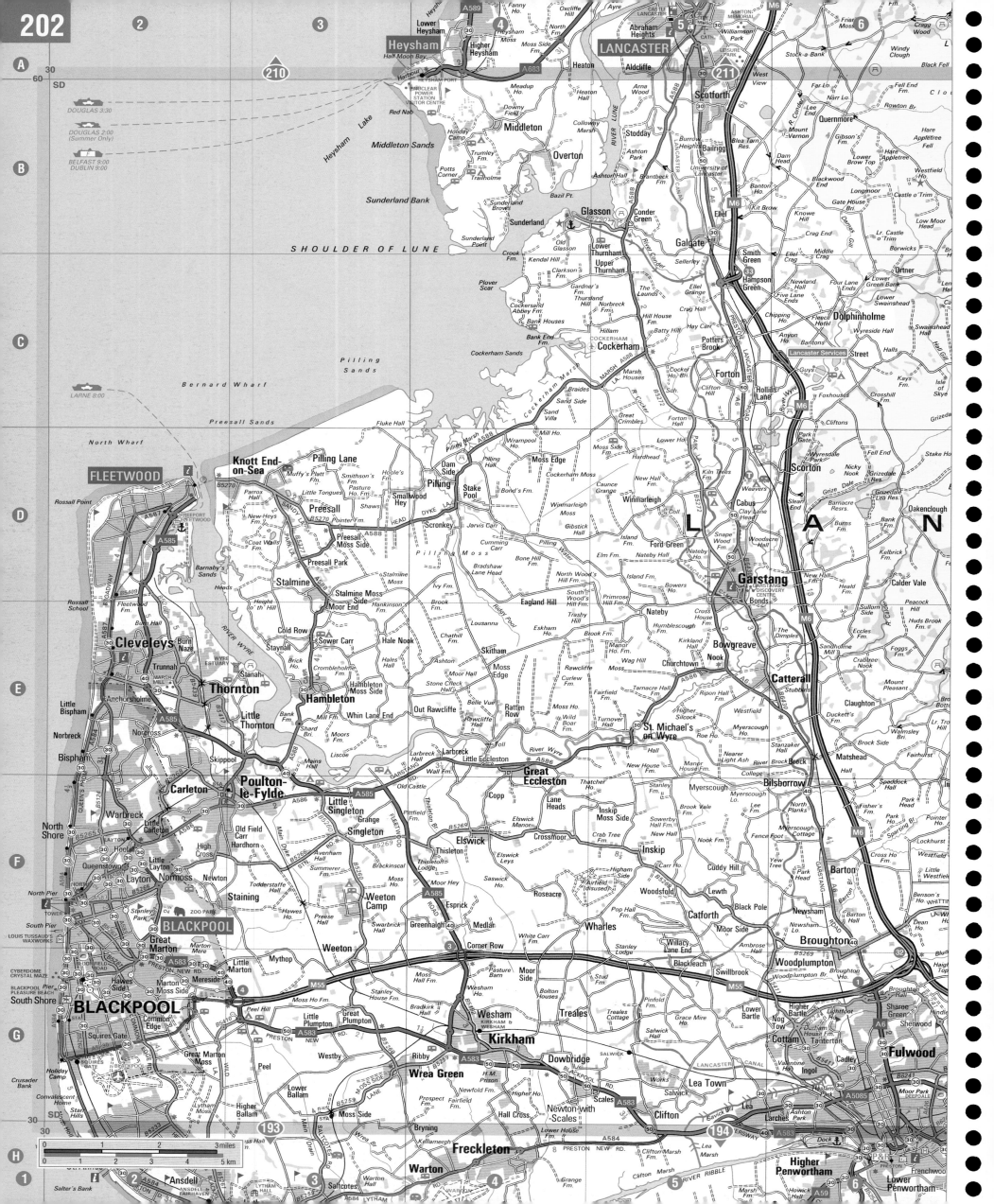

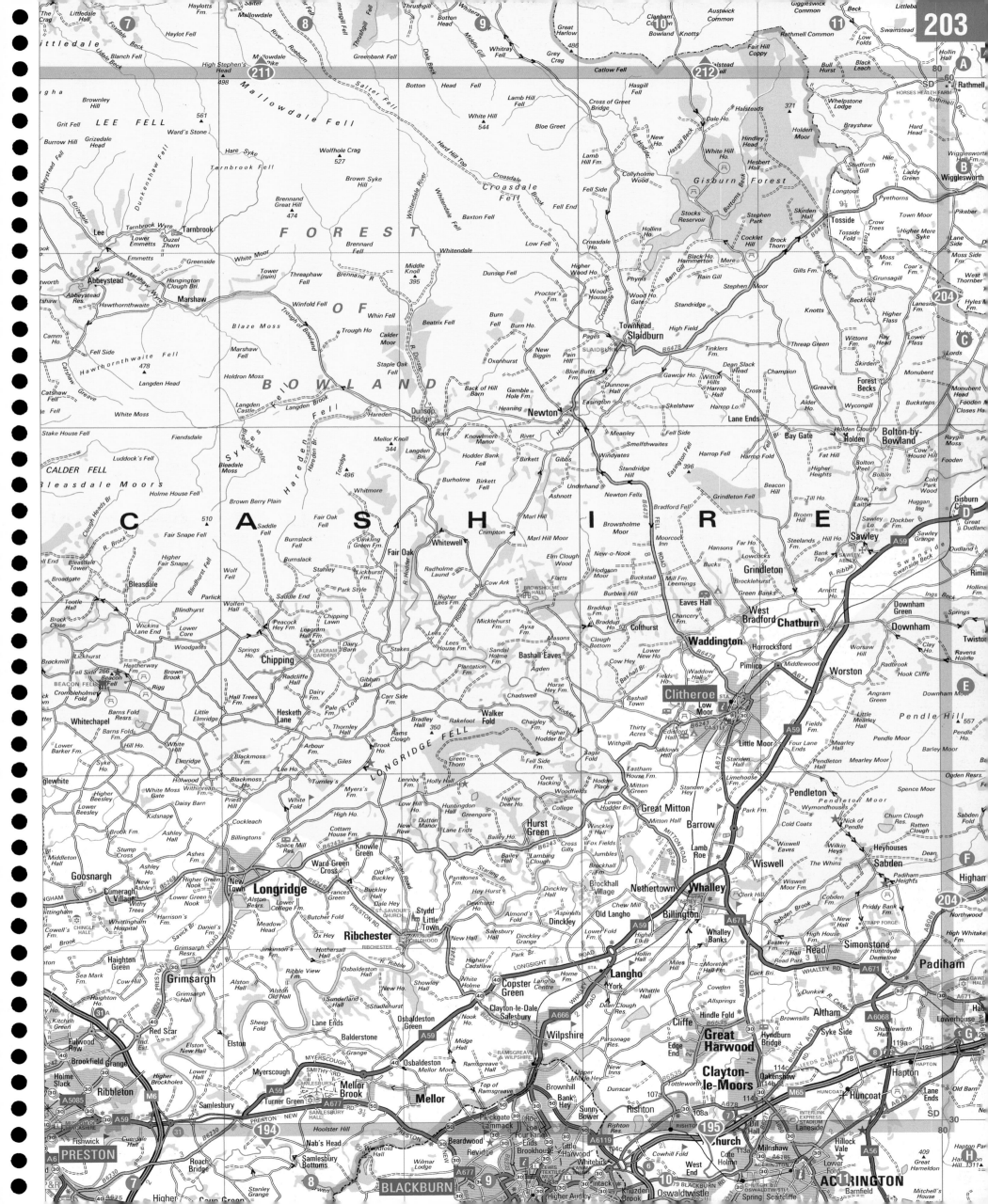

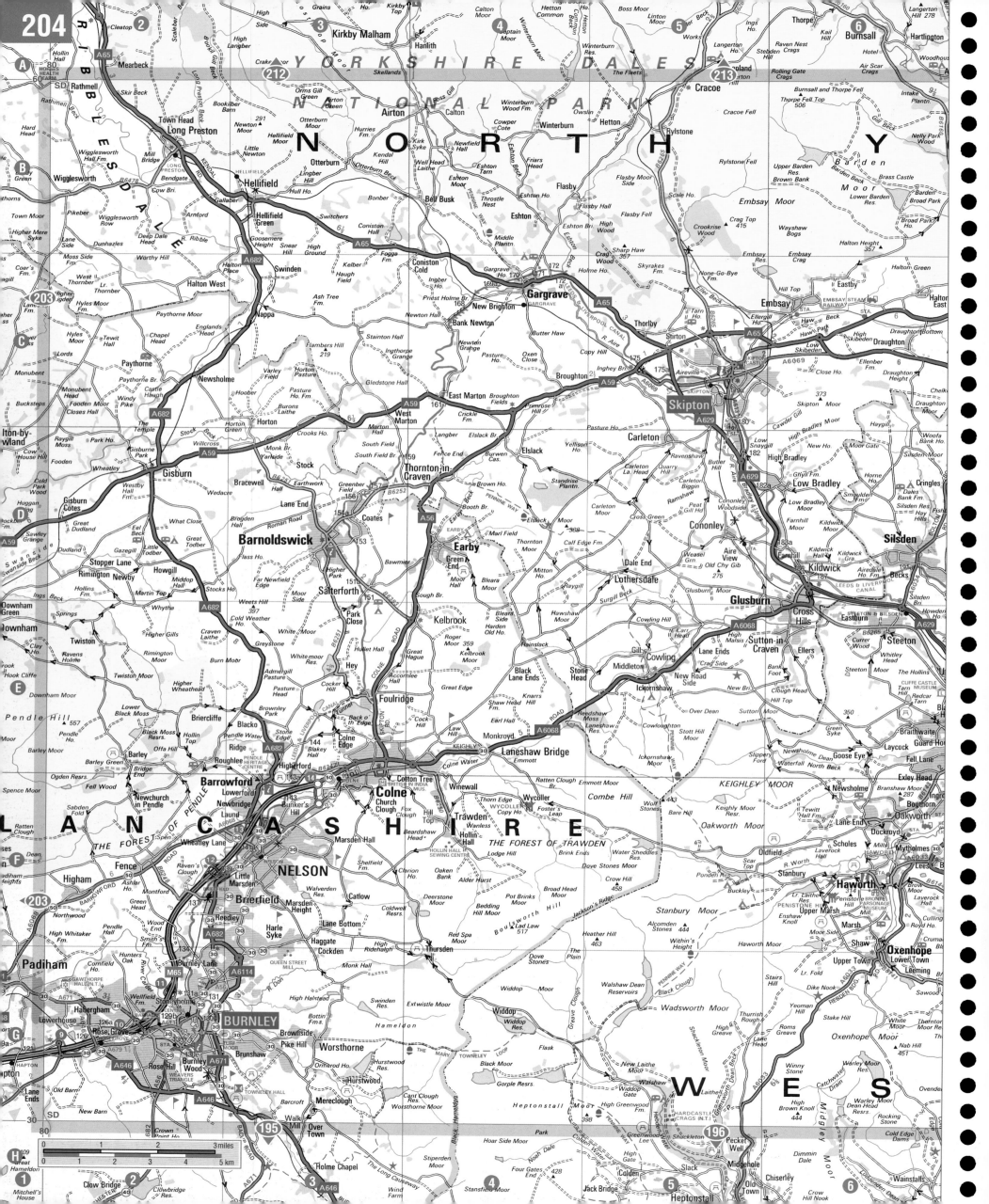

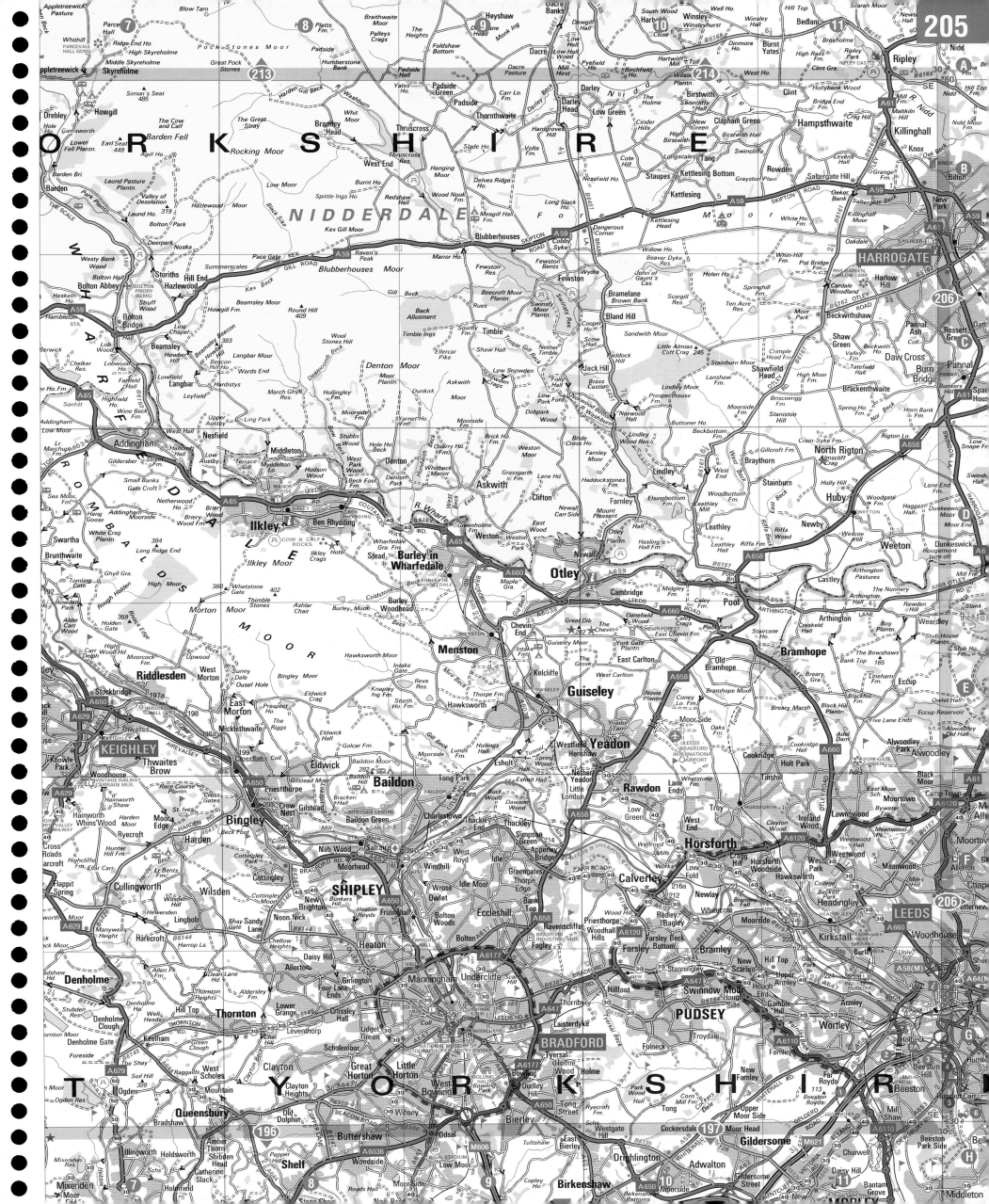

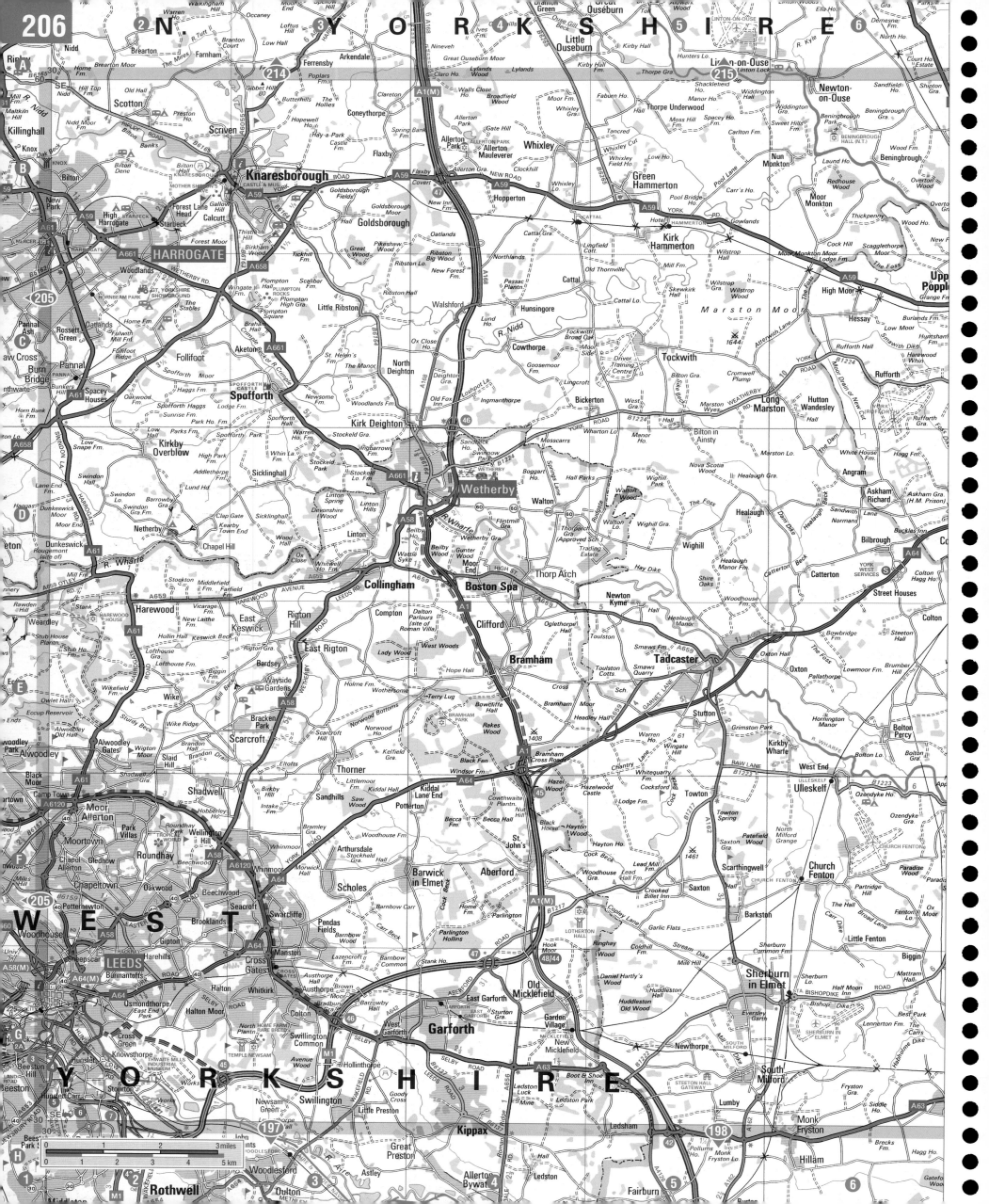

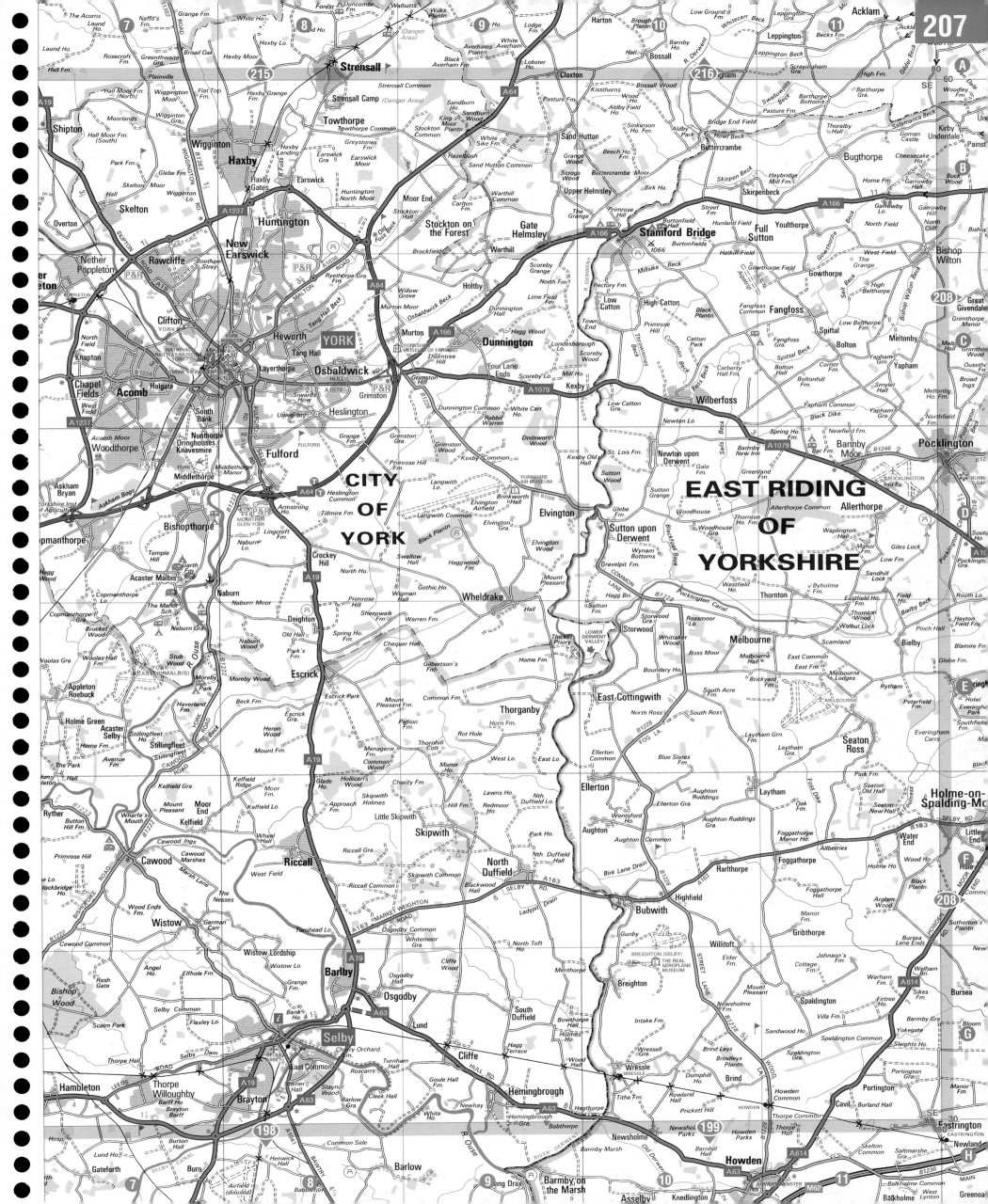

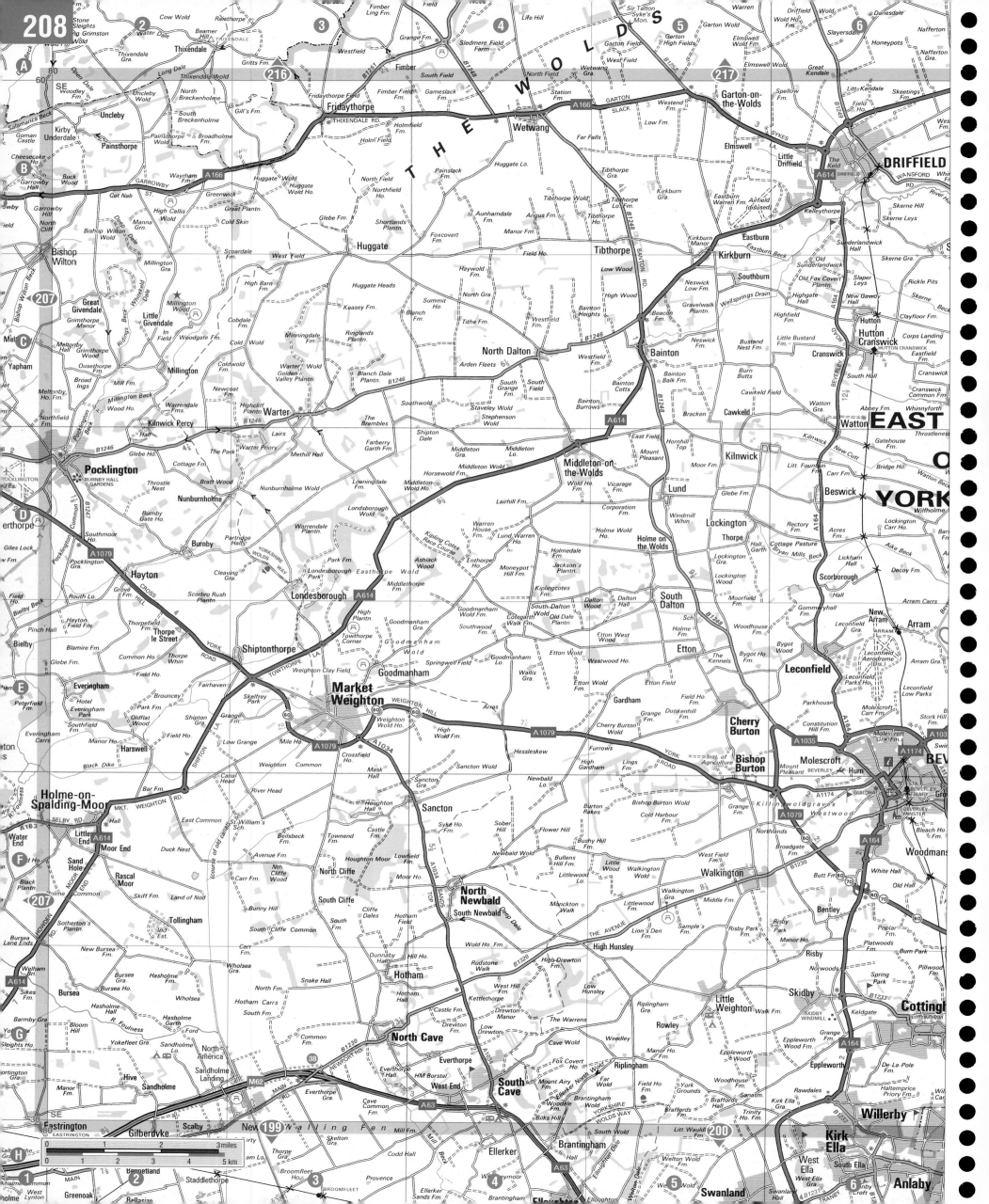

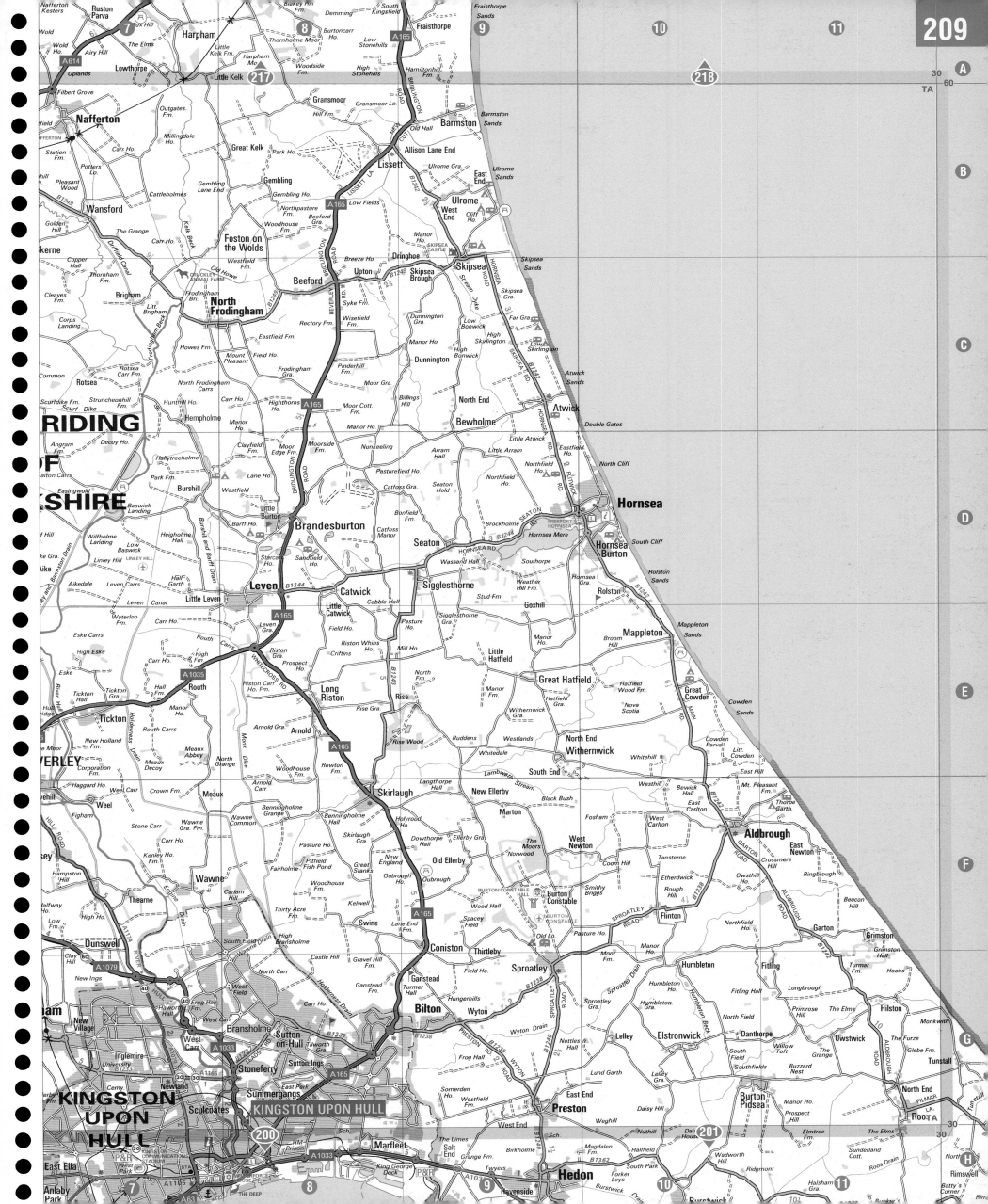

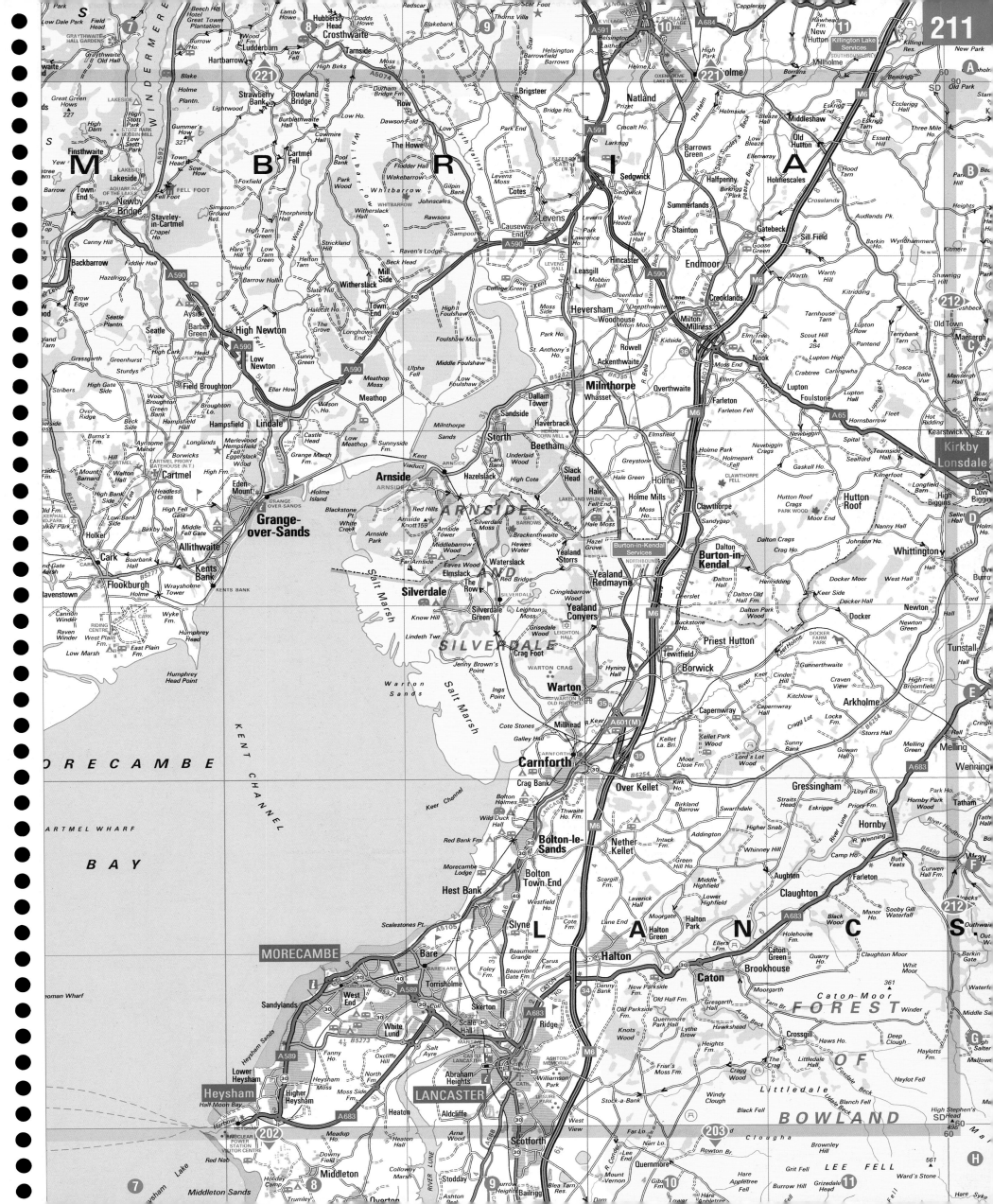

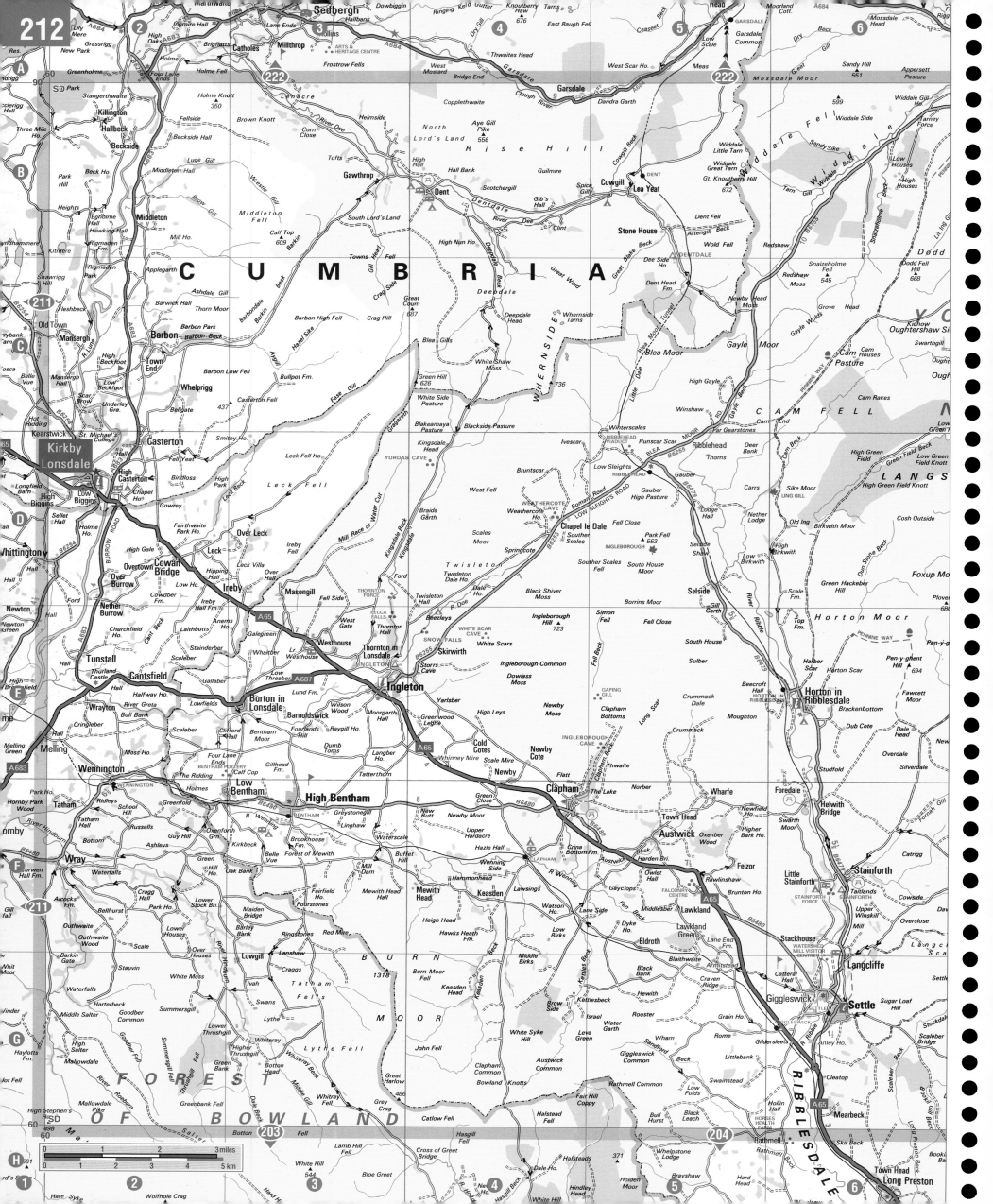

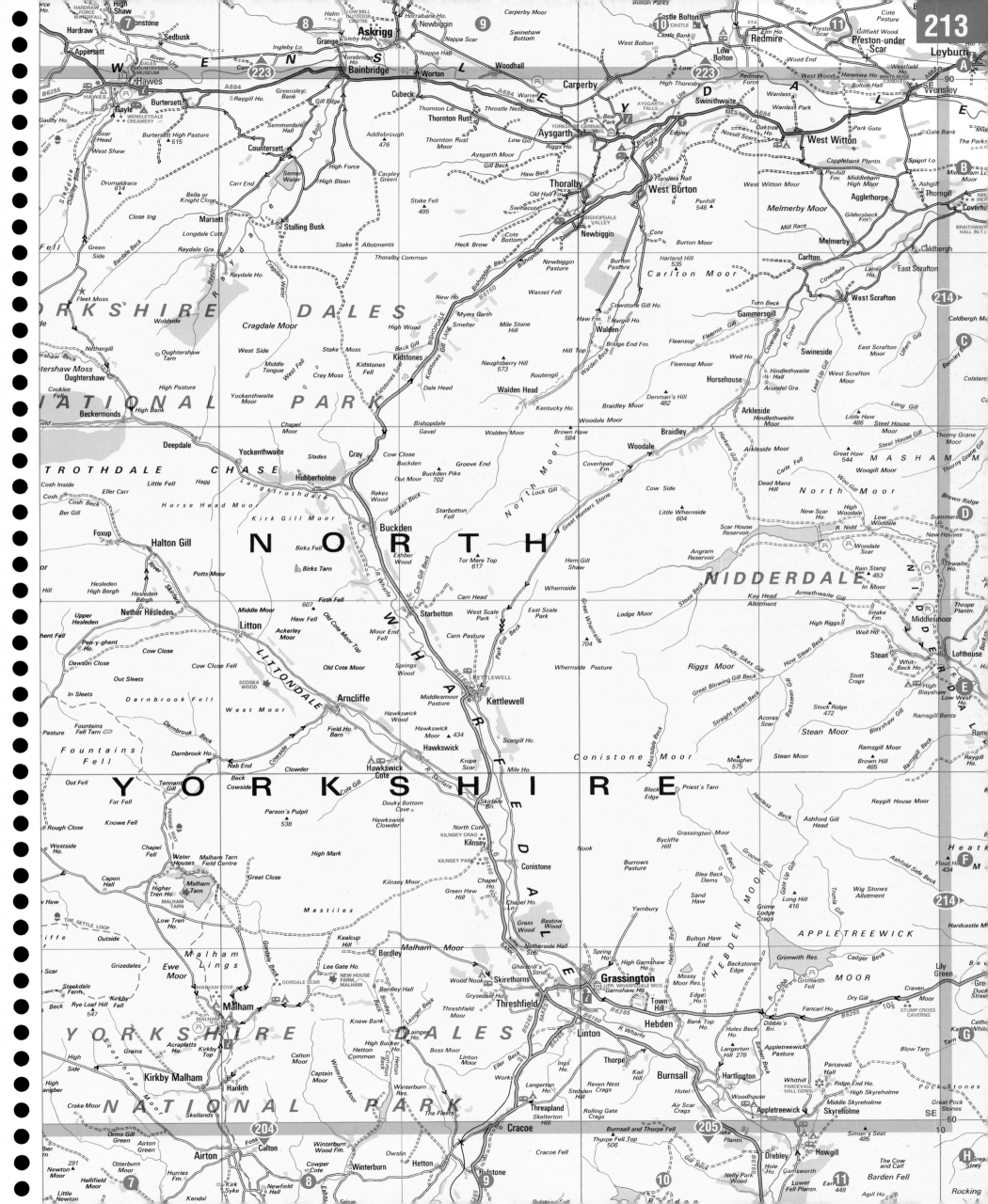

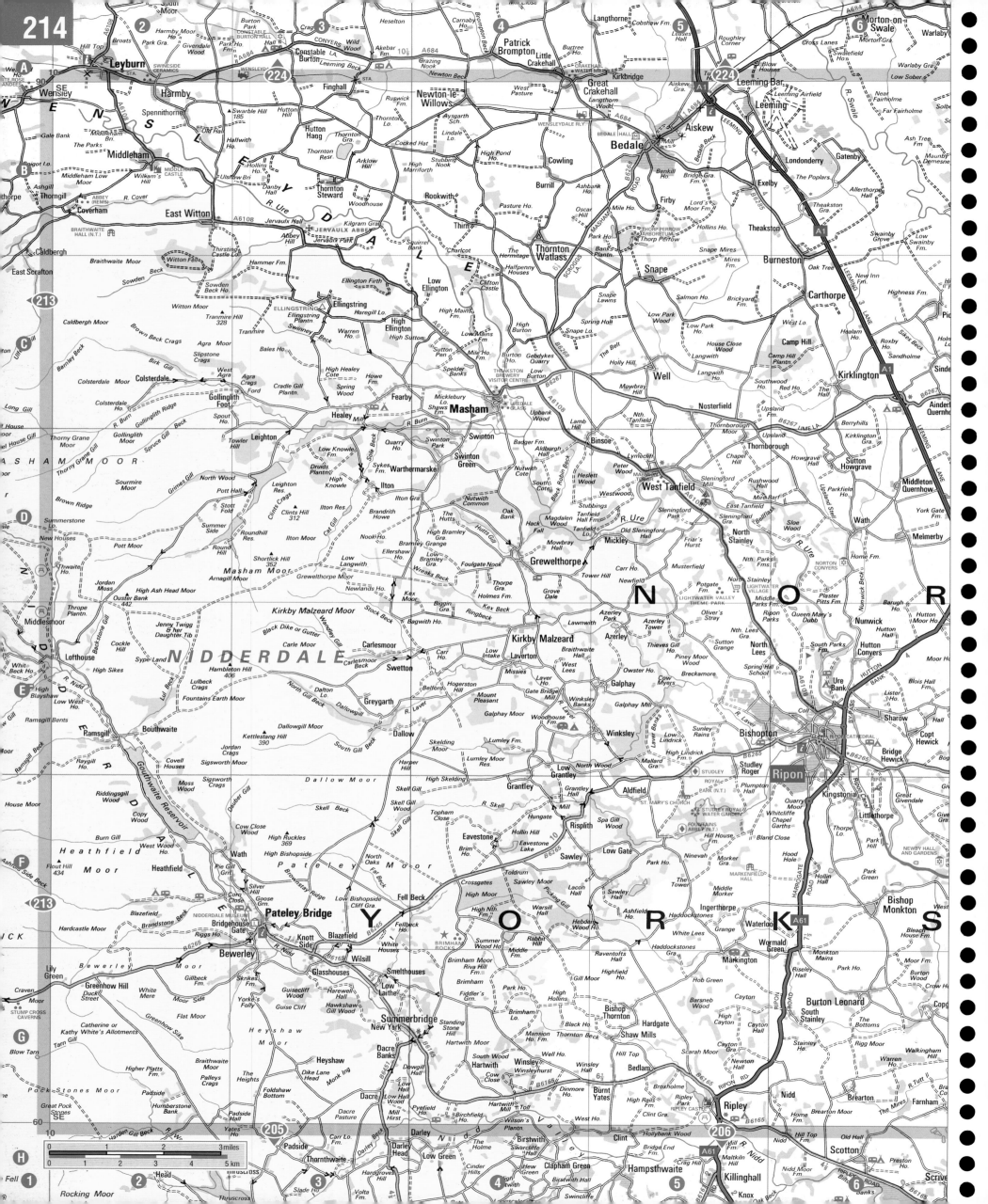

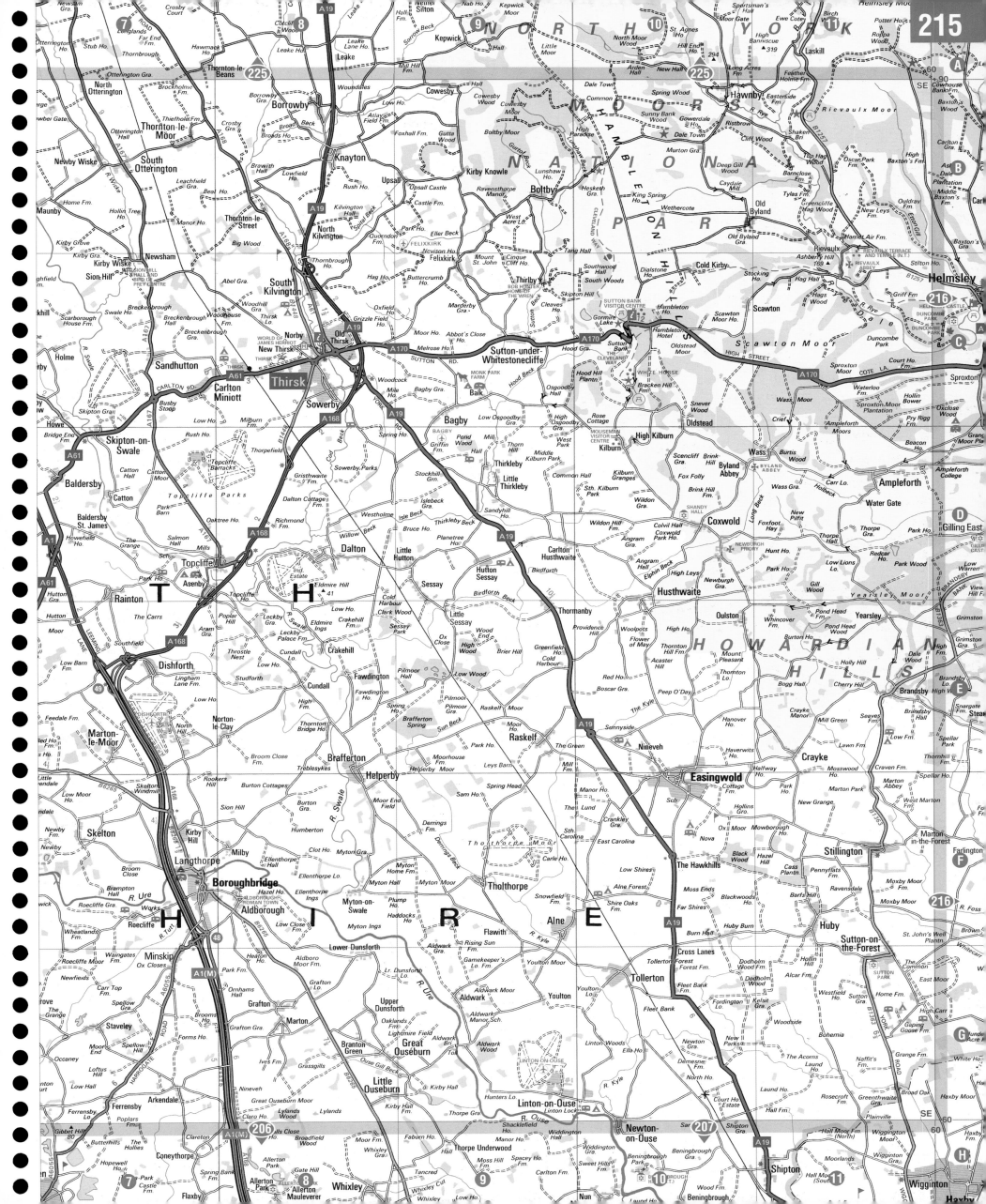

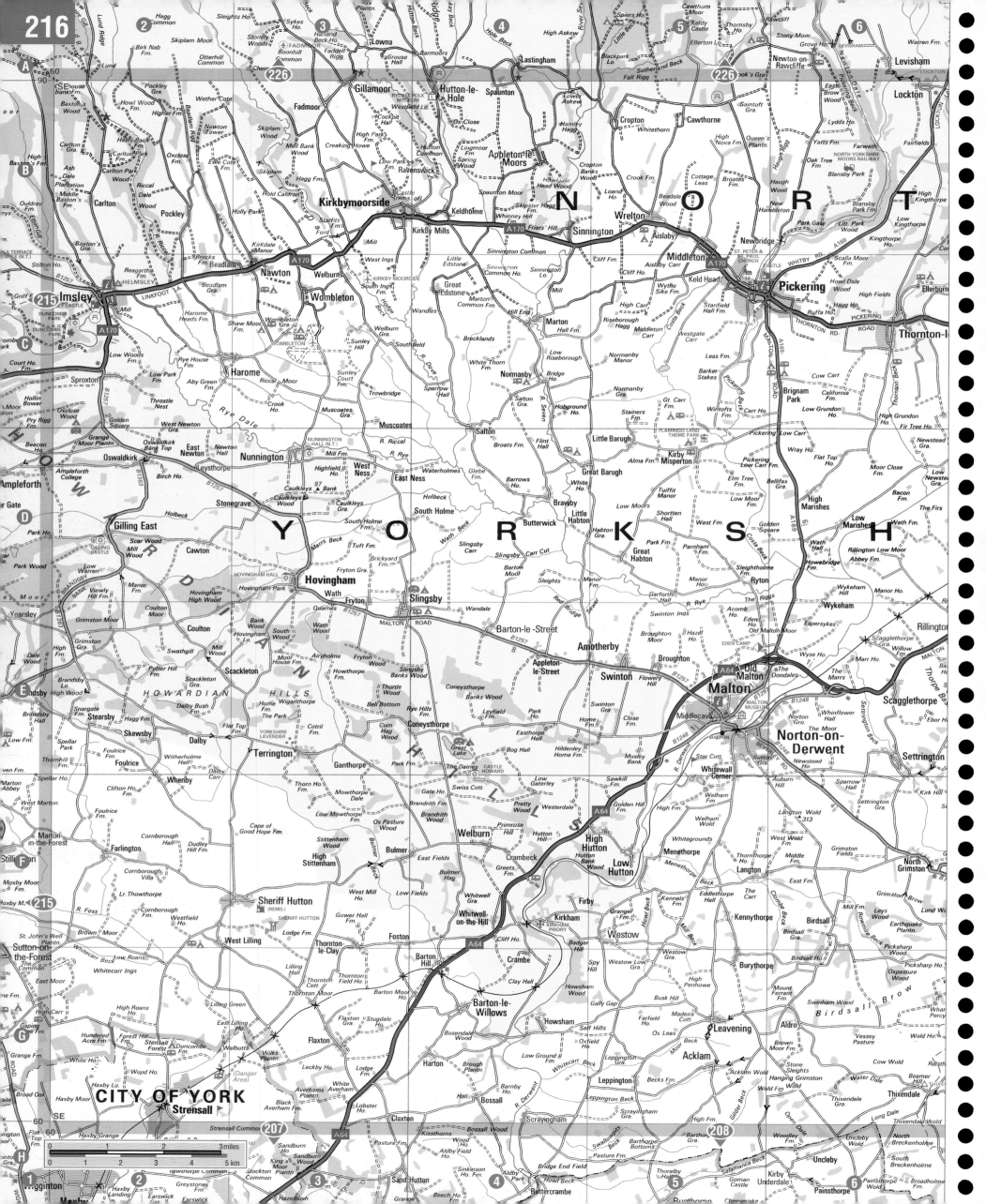

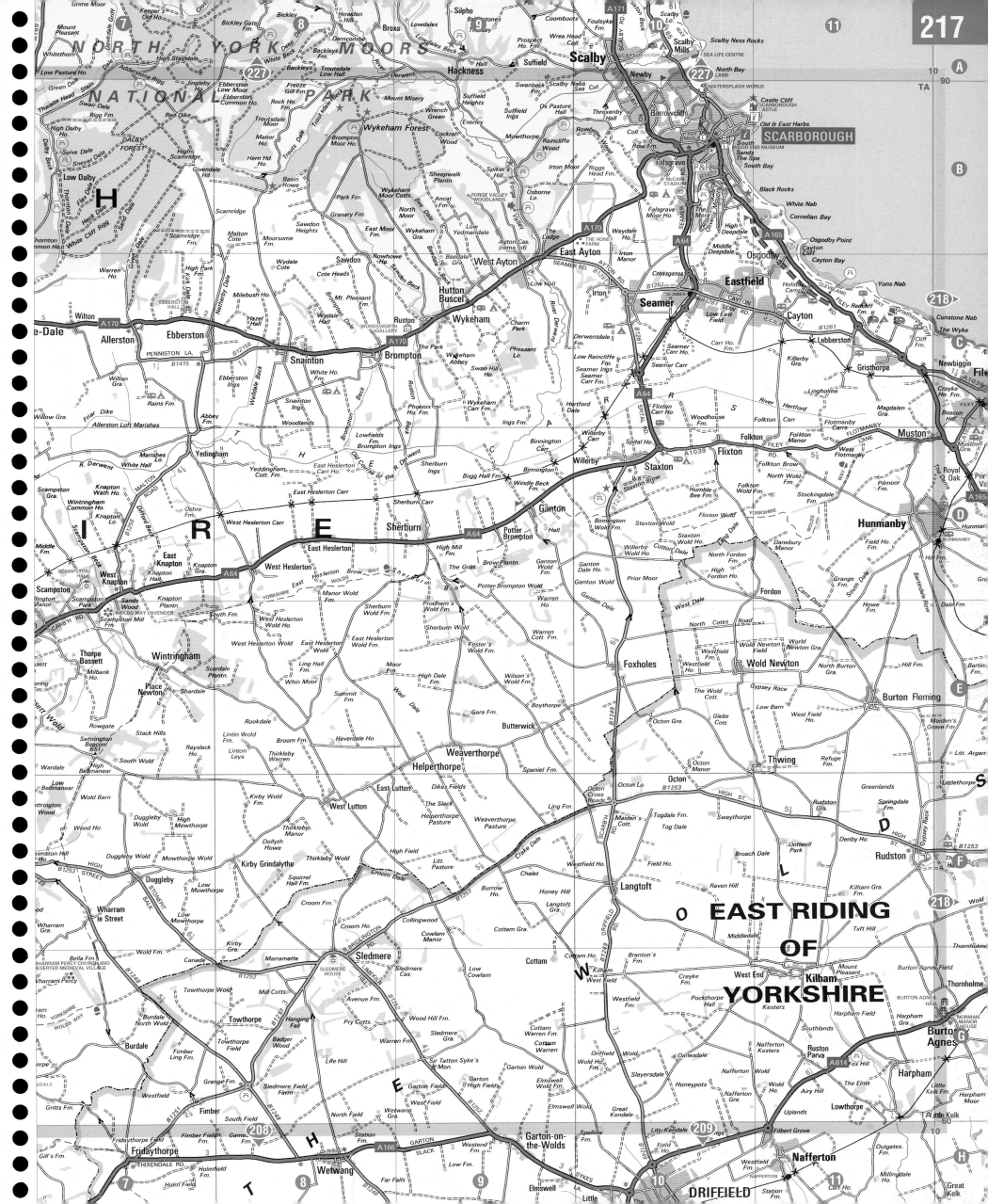

NORTH

SEA

FILEY
BAY

EAST RIDING

OF

YORKSHIRE

BRIDLINGTON

BRIDLINGTON
BAY

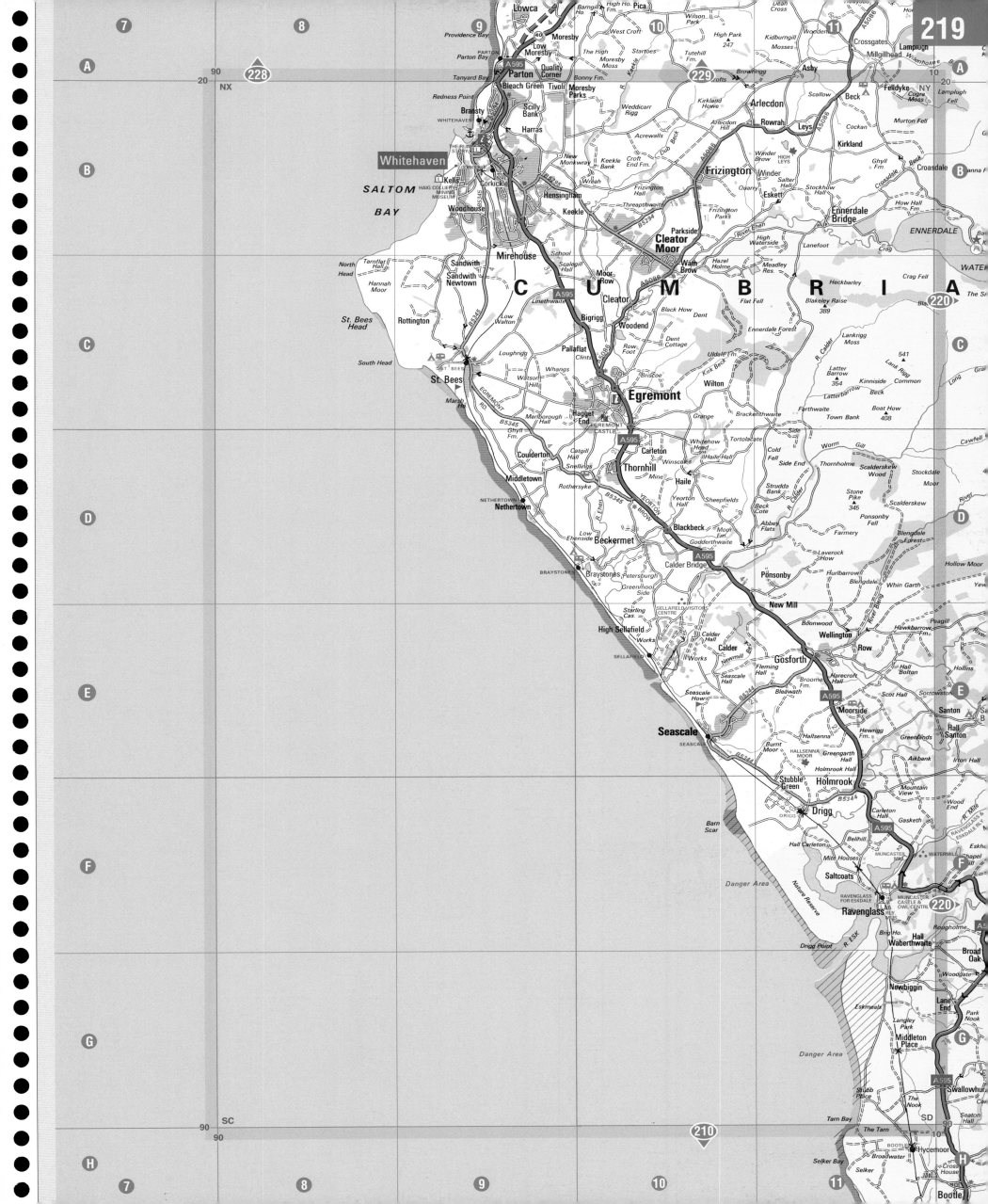

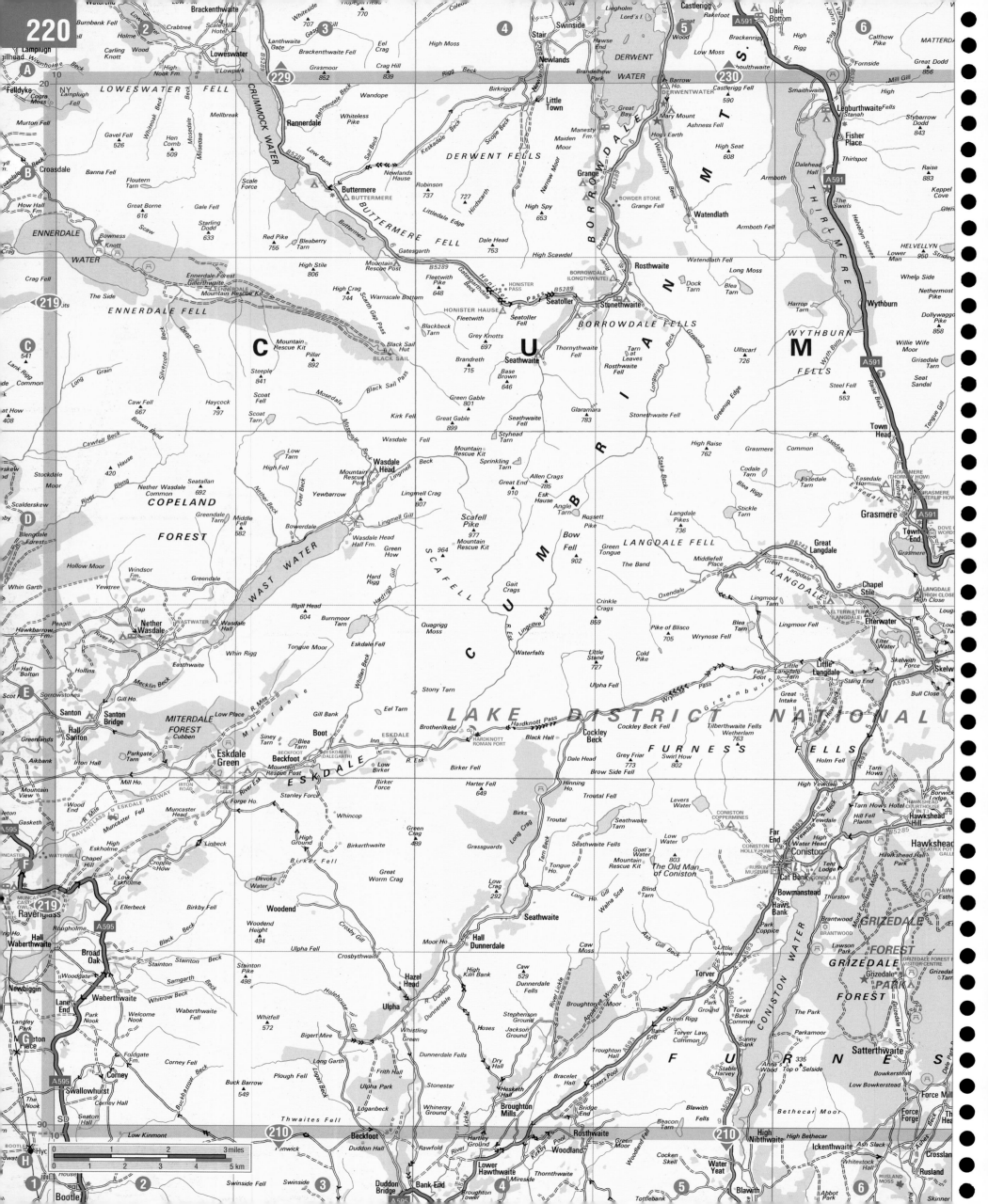

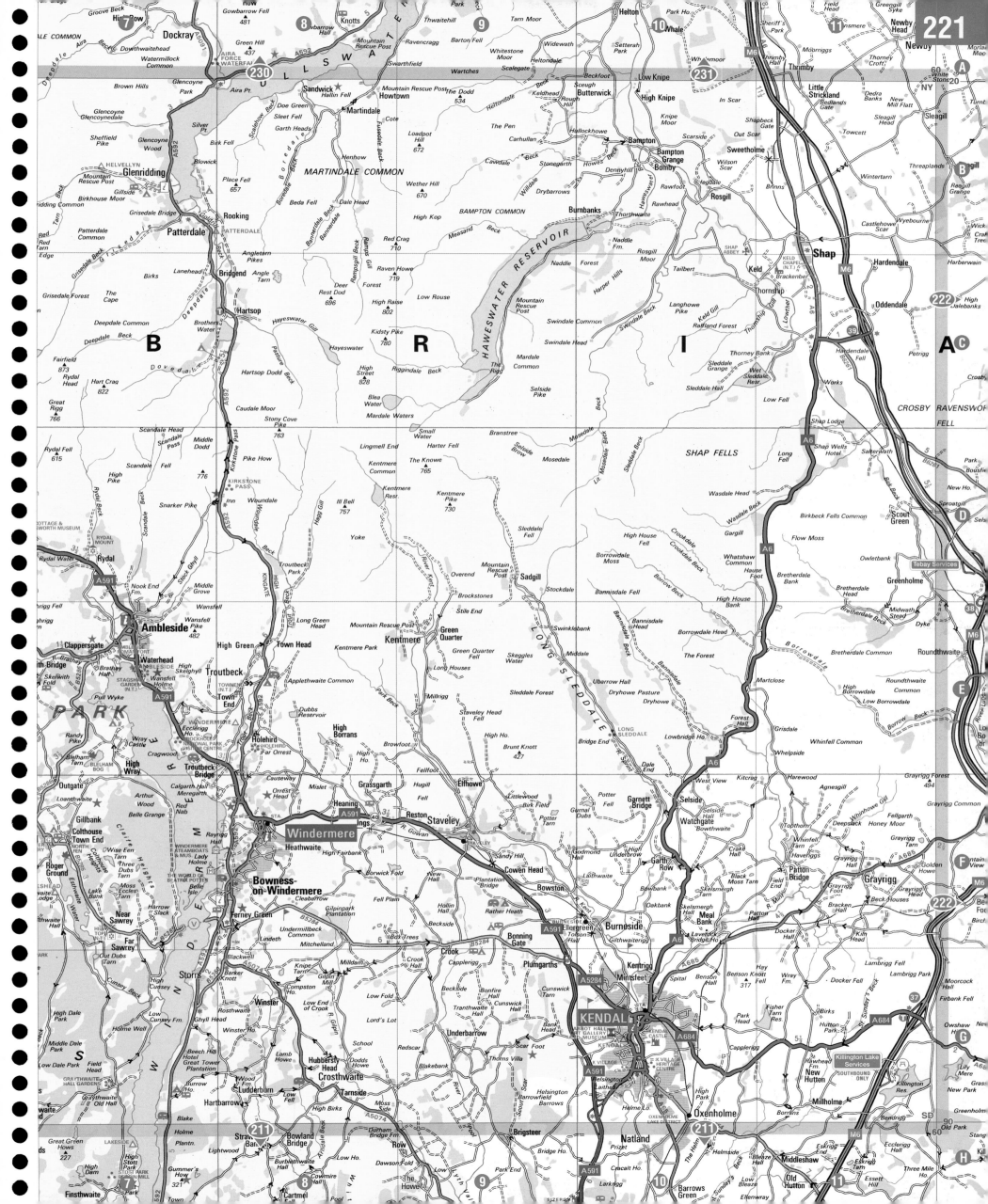

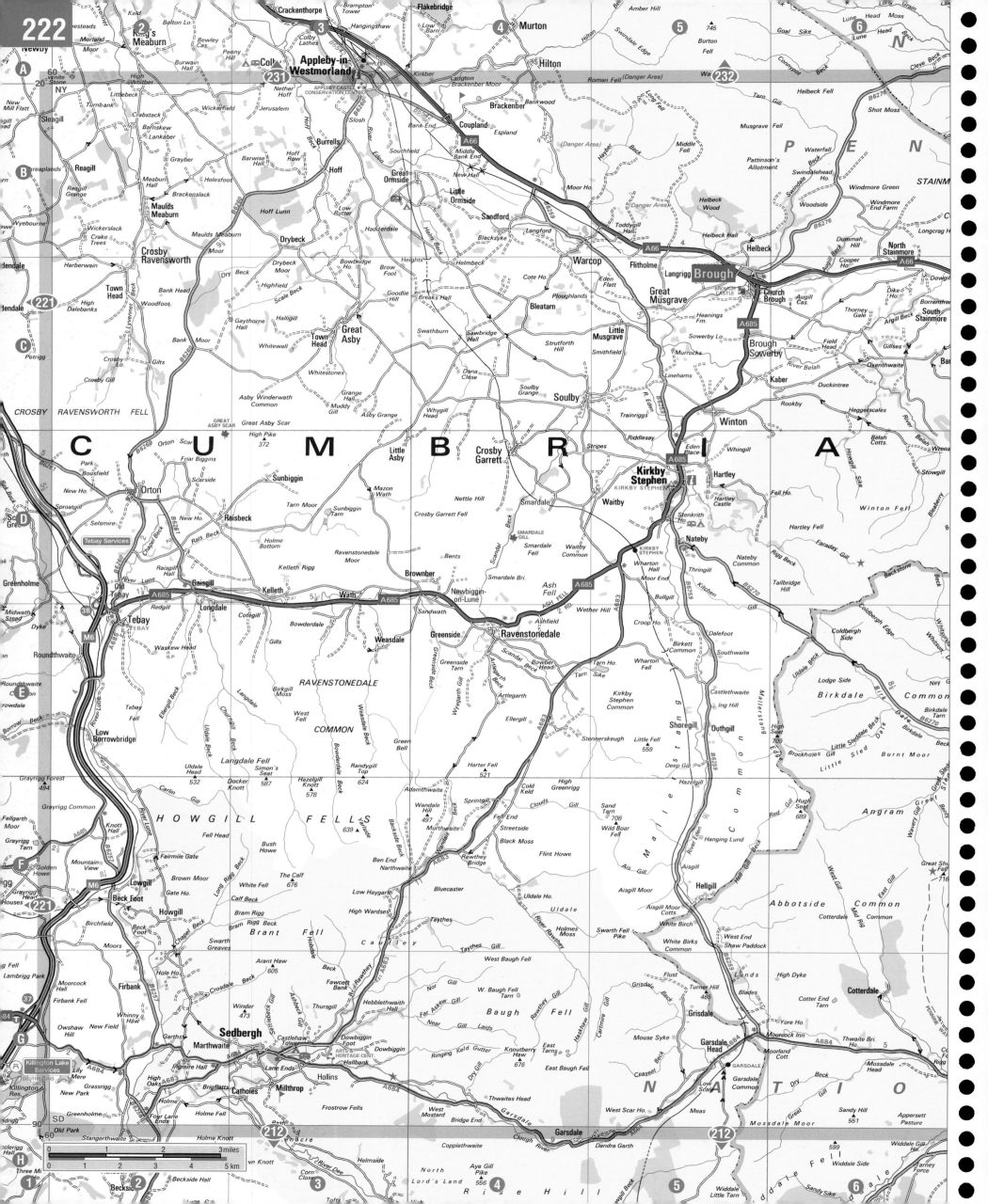

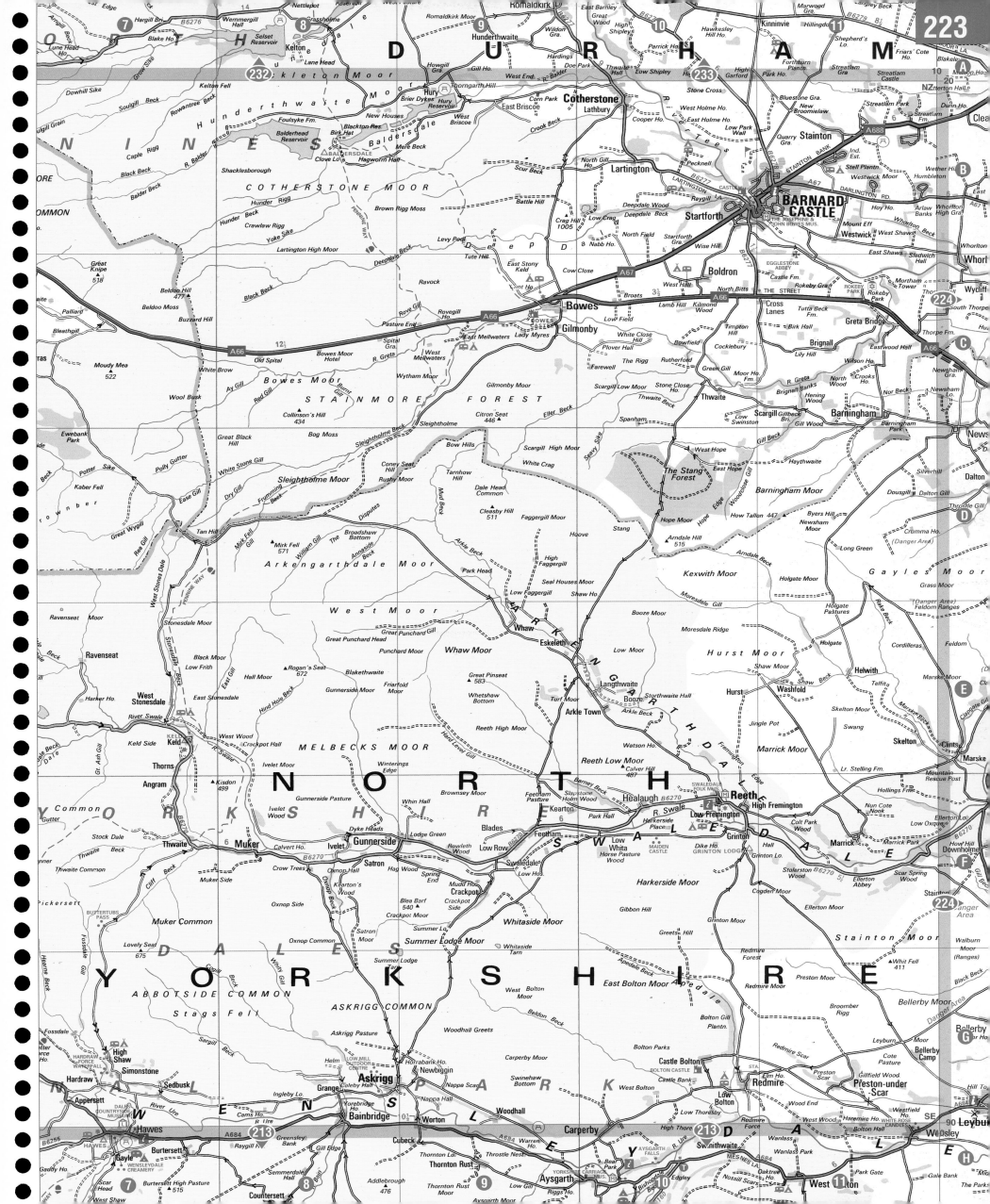

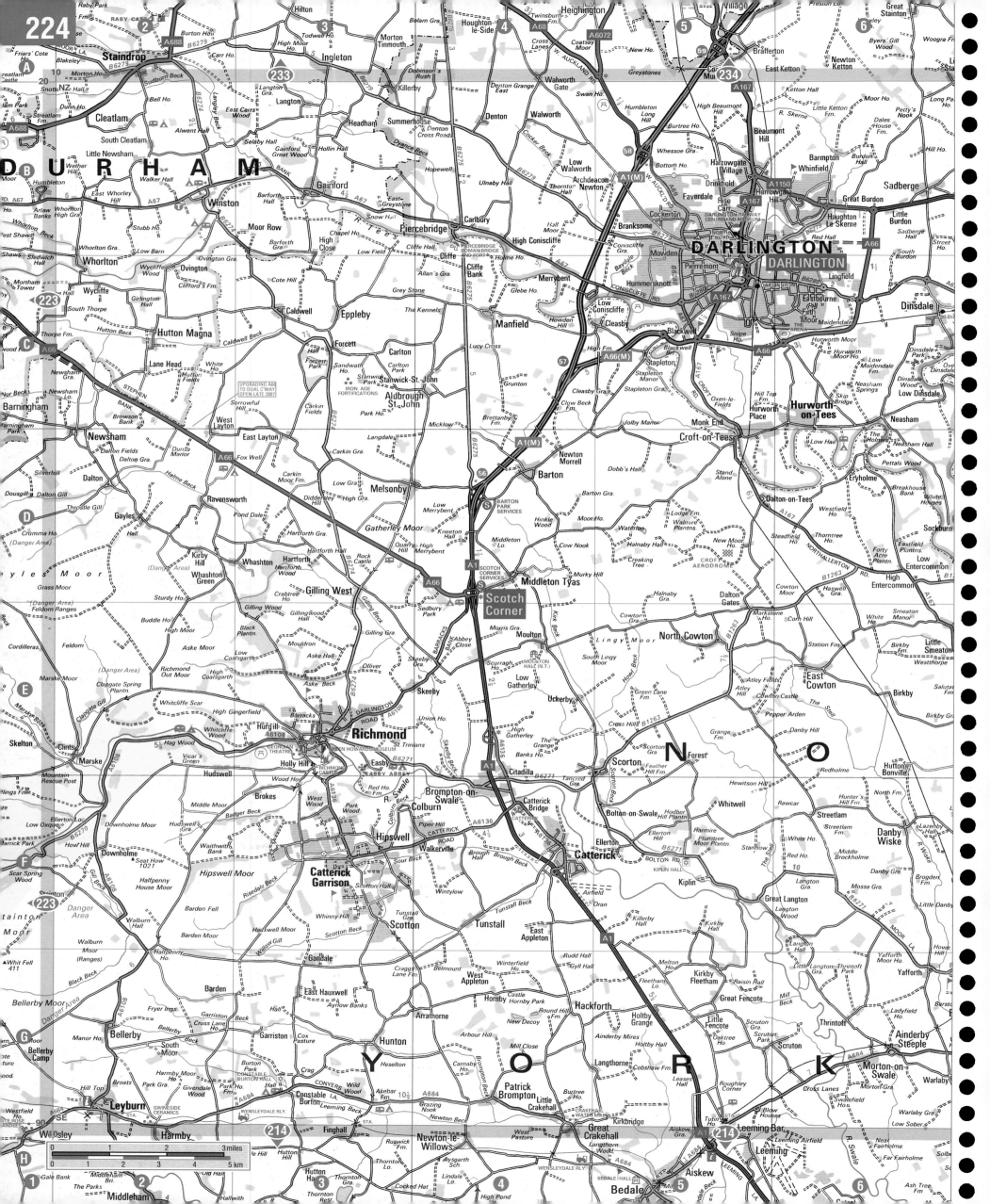

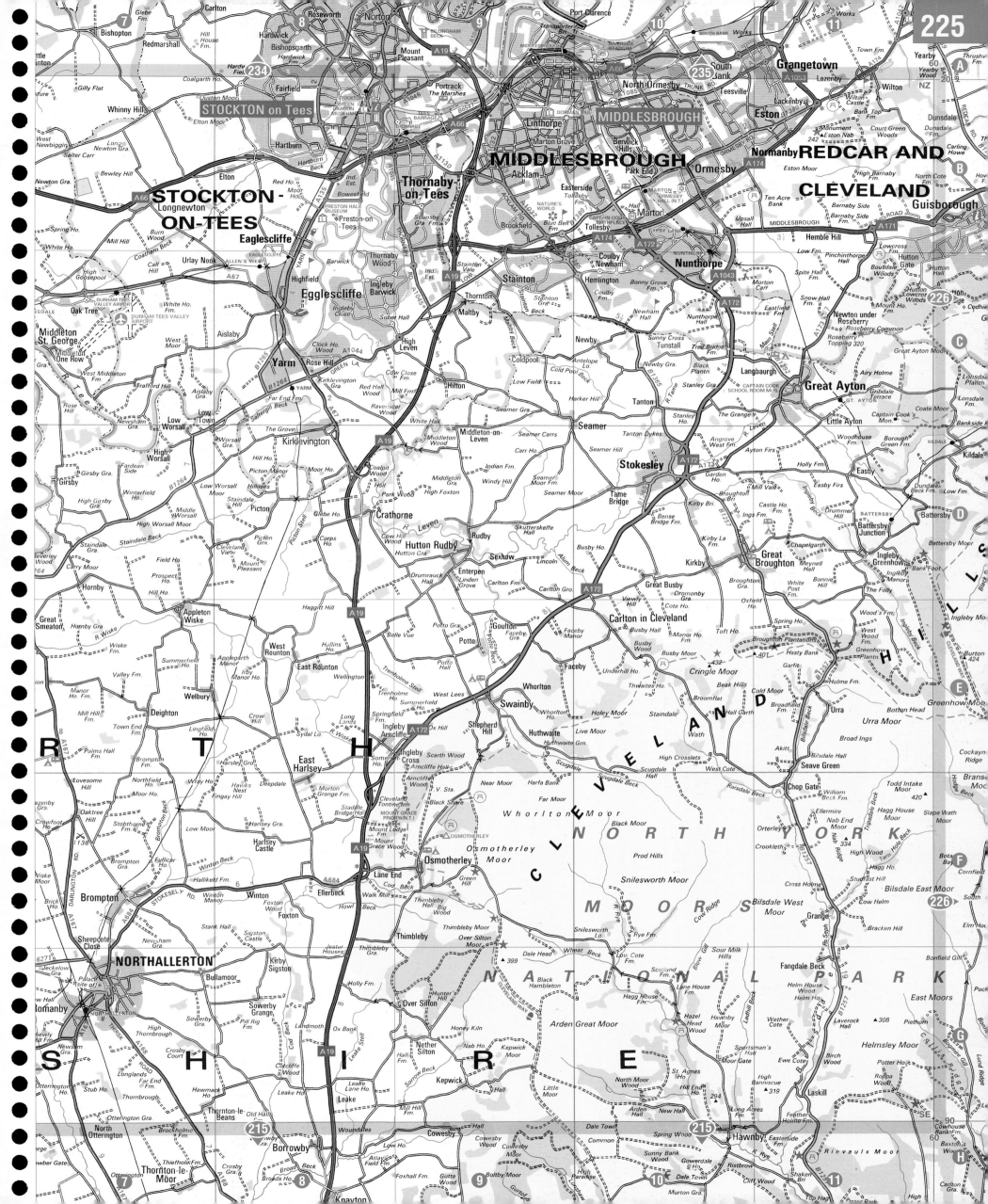

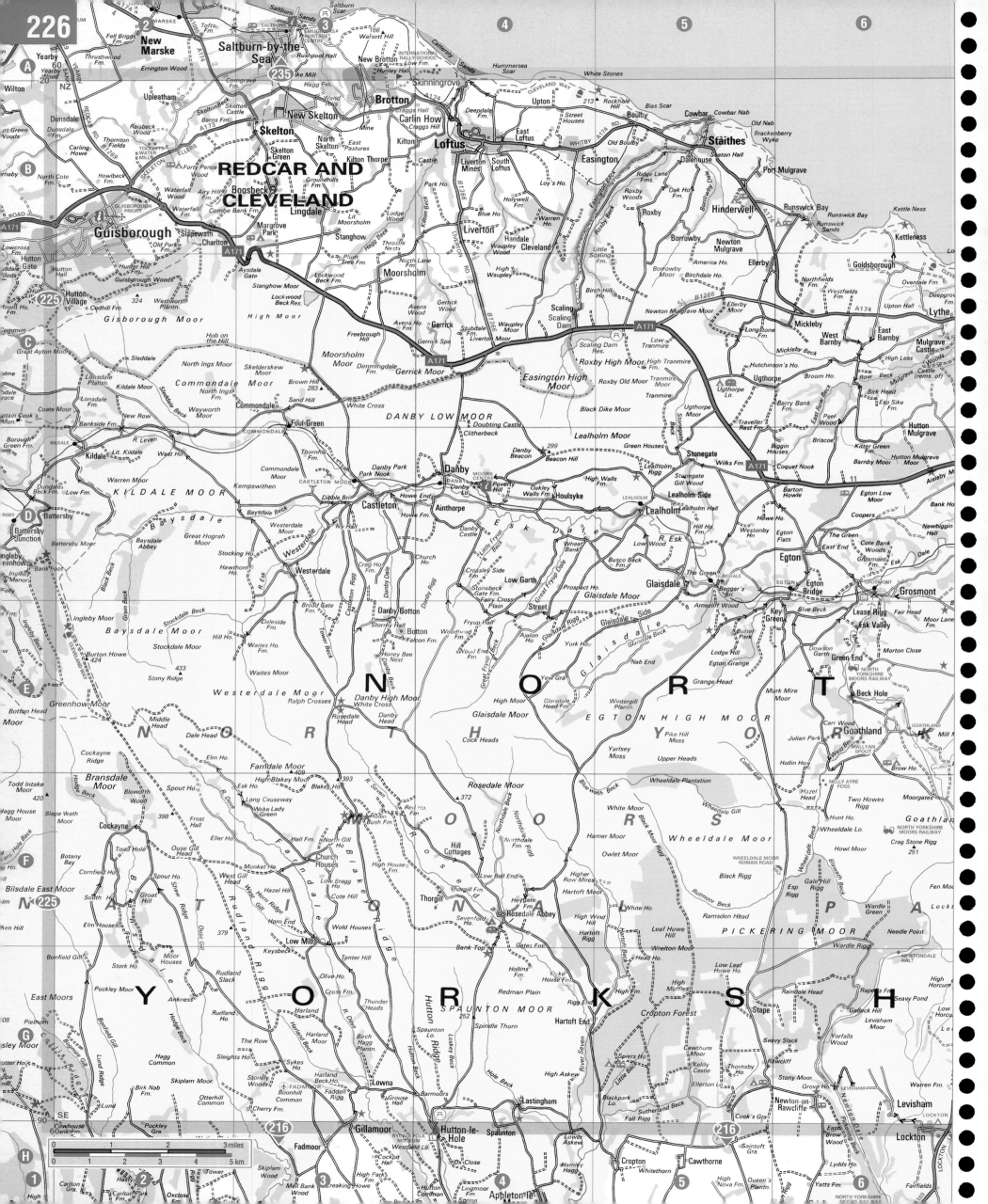

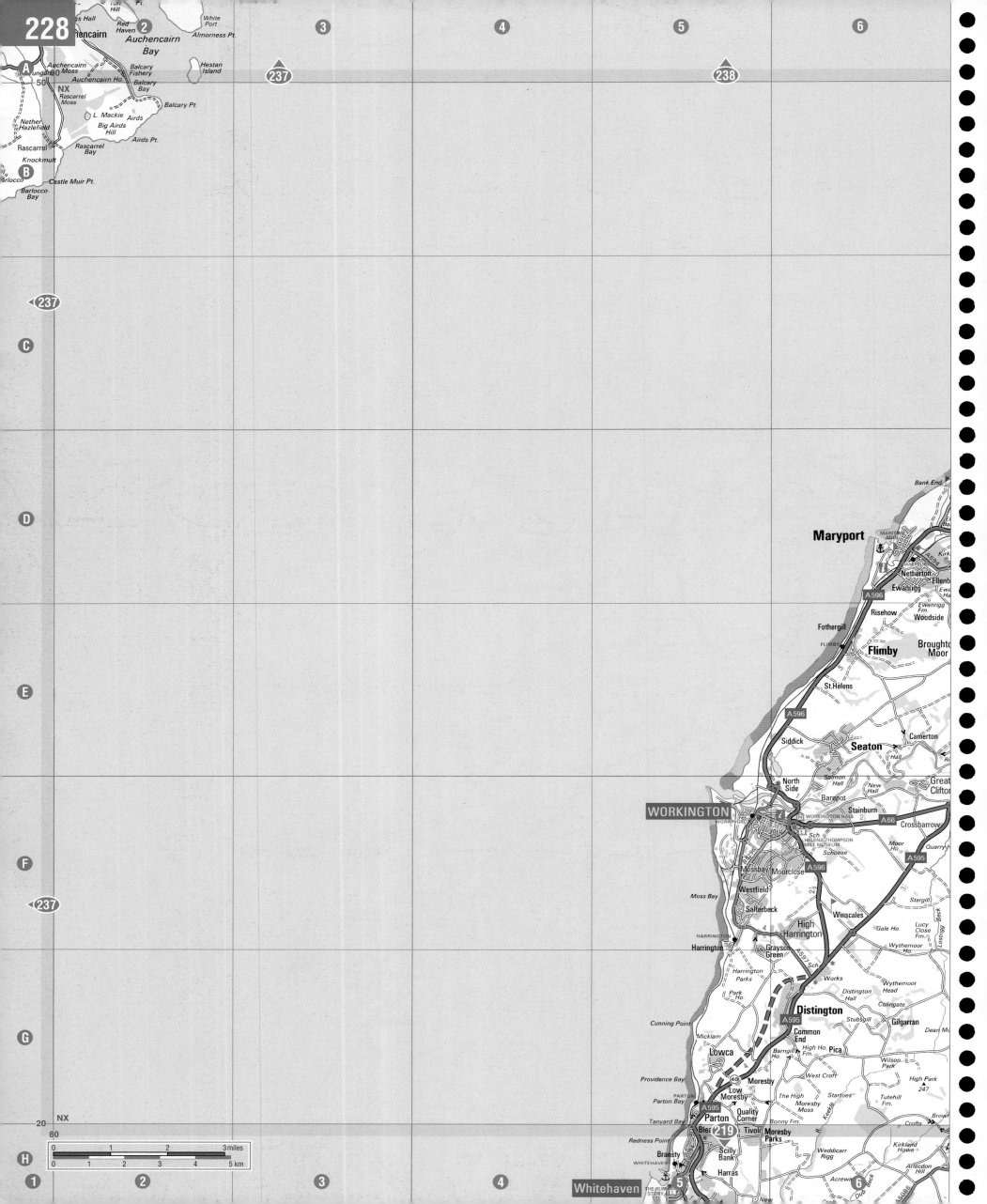

Maryport

Flimby

Broughton Moor

St.Helens

Siddick

Seaton

Camerton

North Side

WORKINGTON

Mossbay

Moorclose

Westfield

Salterbeck

Moss Bay

Winscales

High Harrington

Harrington

Grayson Green

Cunning Point

Micklam

Distington

Common End

Lowca

Gilgarran

Pica

Moresby

Low Moresby

Quality Corner

Parton

Tivoli

Moresby Parks

Tanyard Bay

Redness Point

Bransty

Scilly Bank

Harras

Whitehaven

Auchencairn Bay

Auchencairn

Balcary Bay

Balcary Pt.

Hestan Island

Rascarrel

Knockmult

Castle Muir Pt.

Barlocco Bay

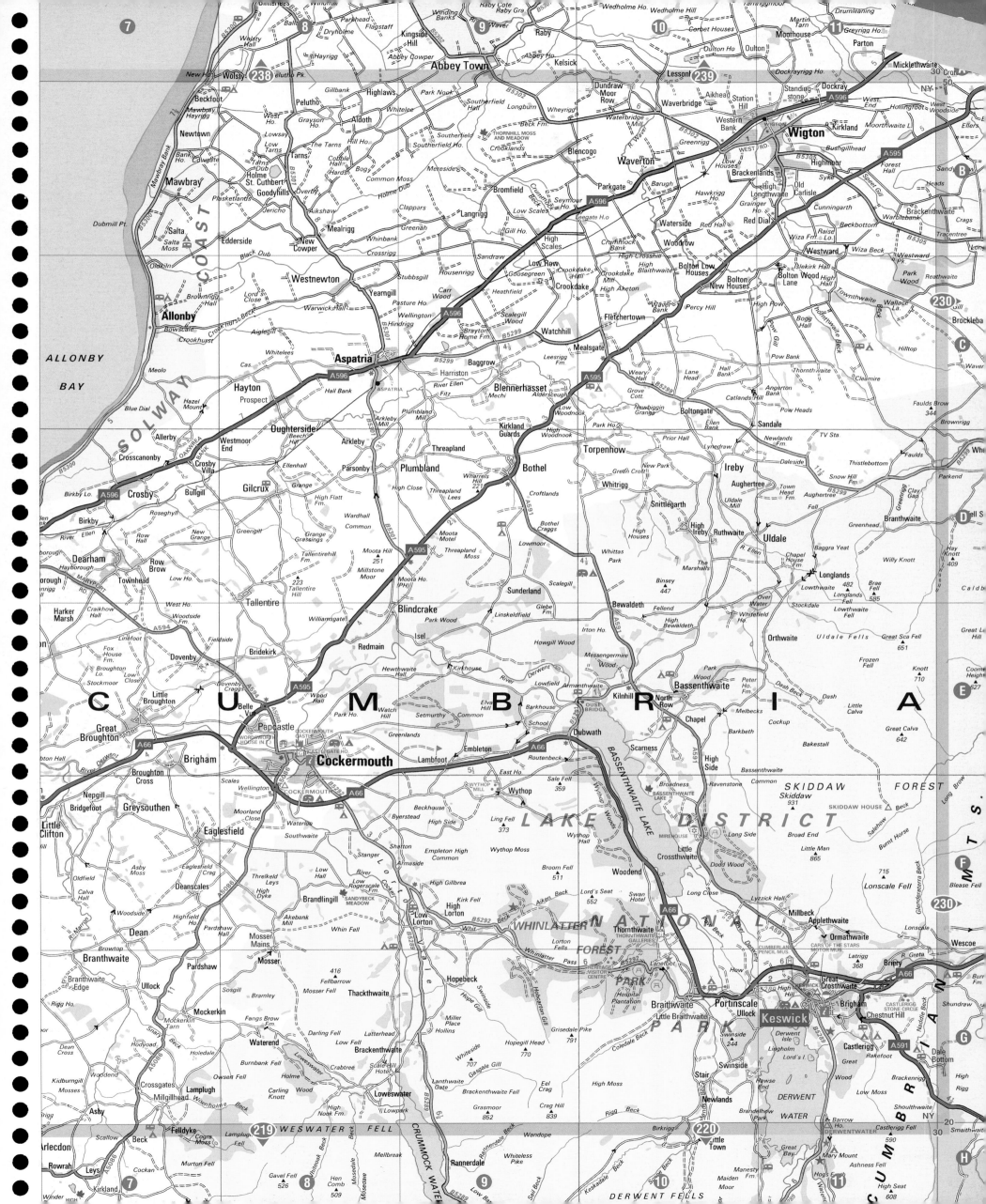

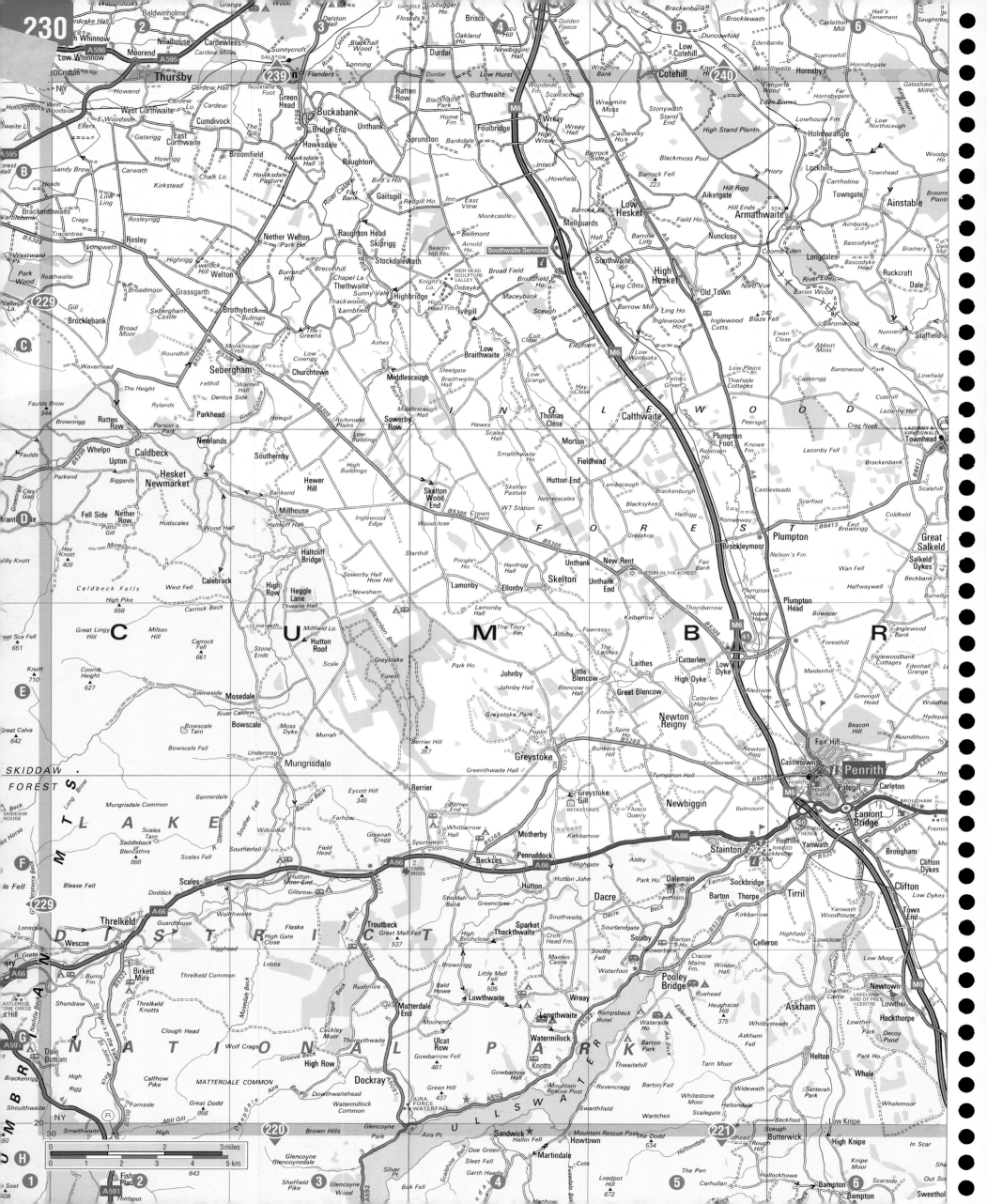

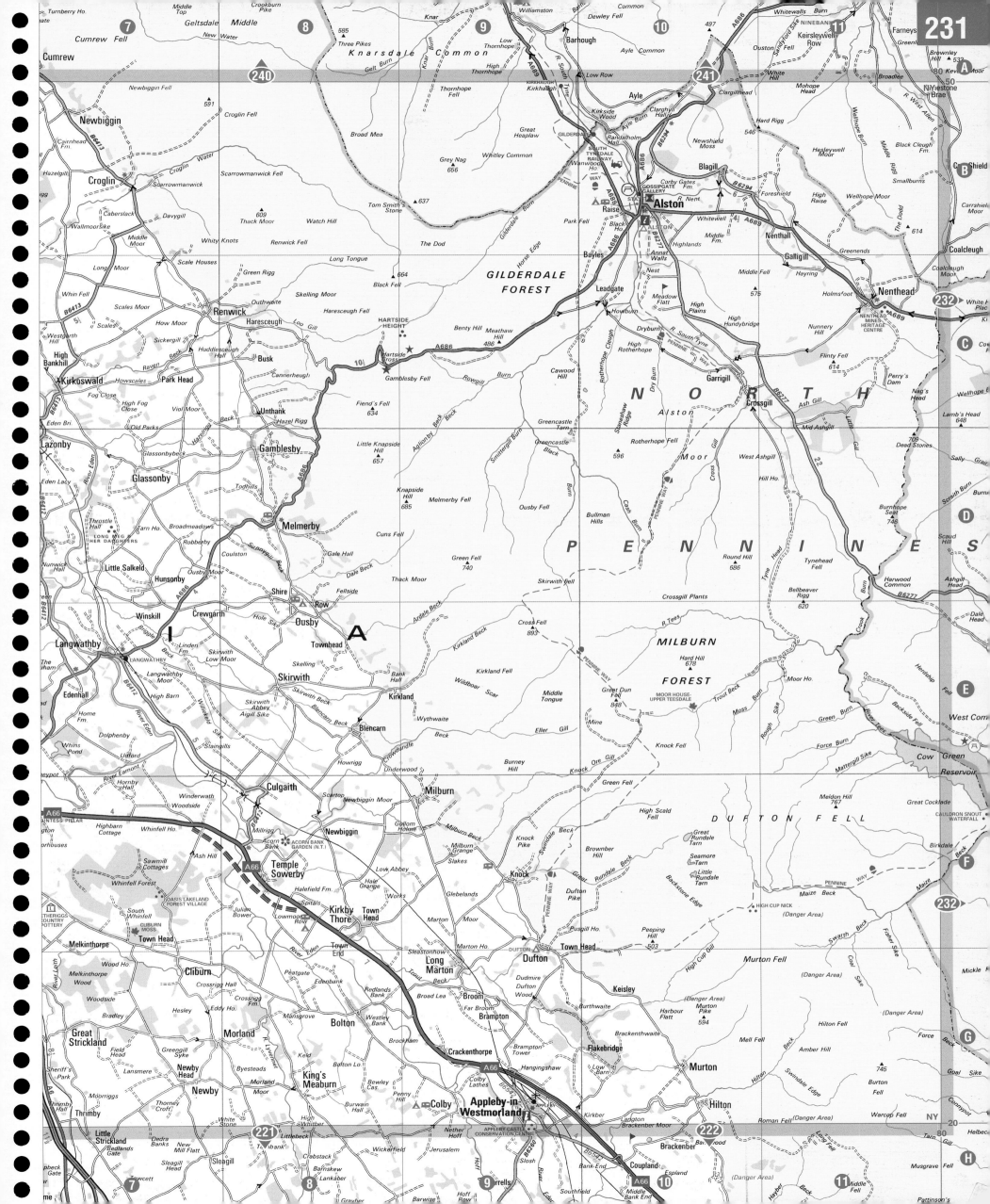

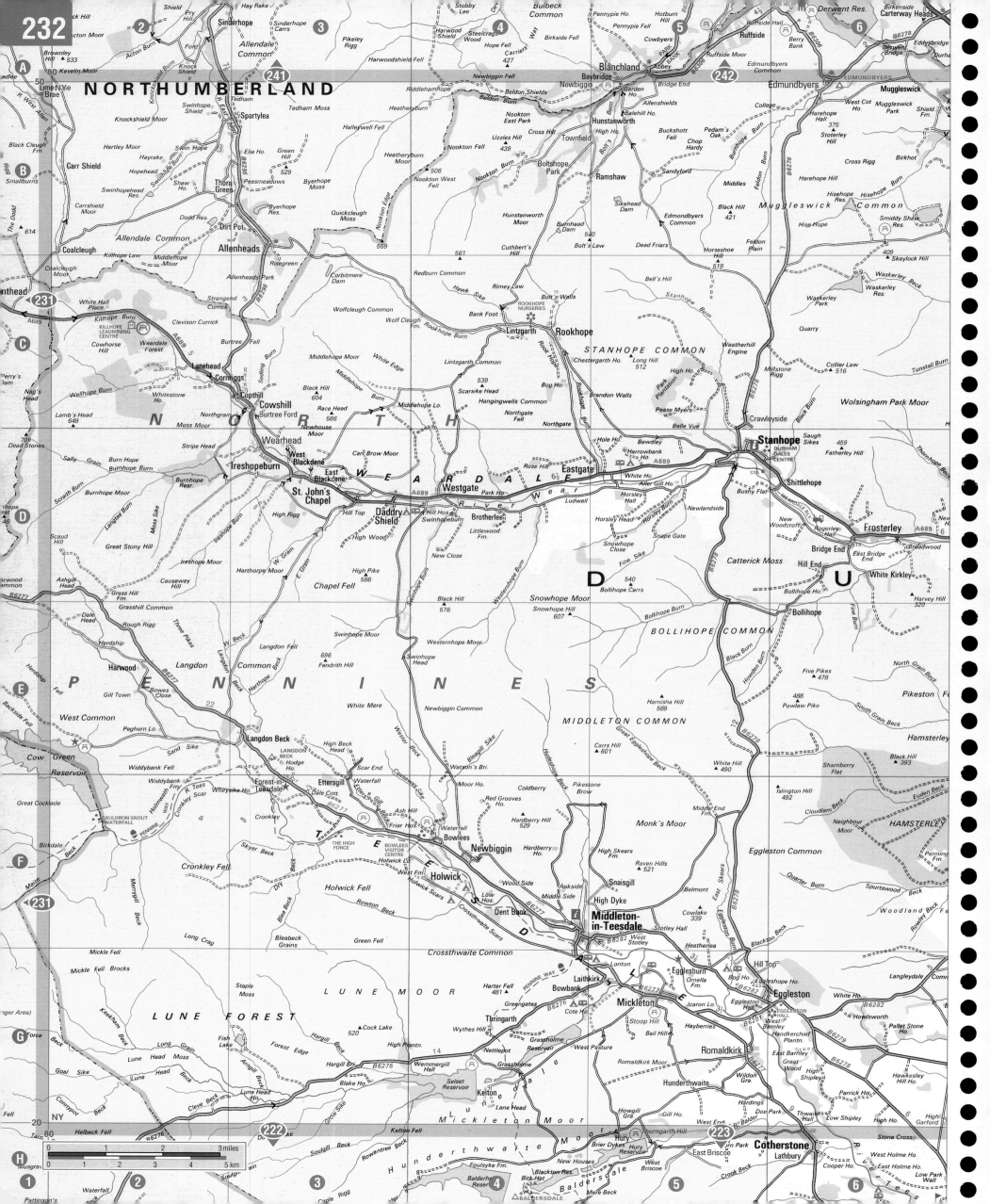

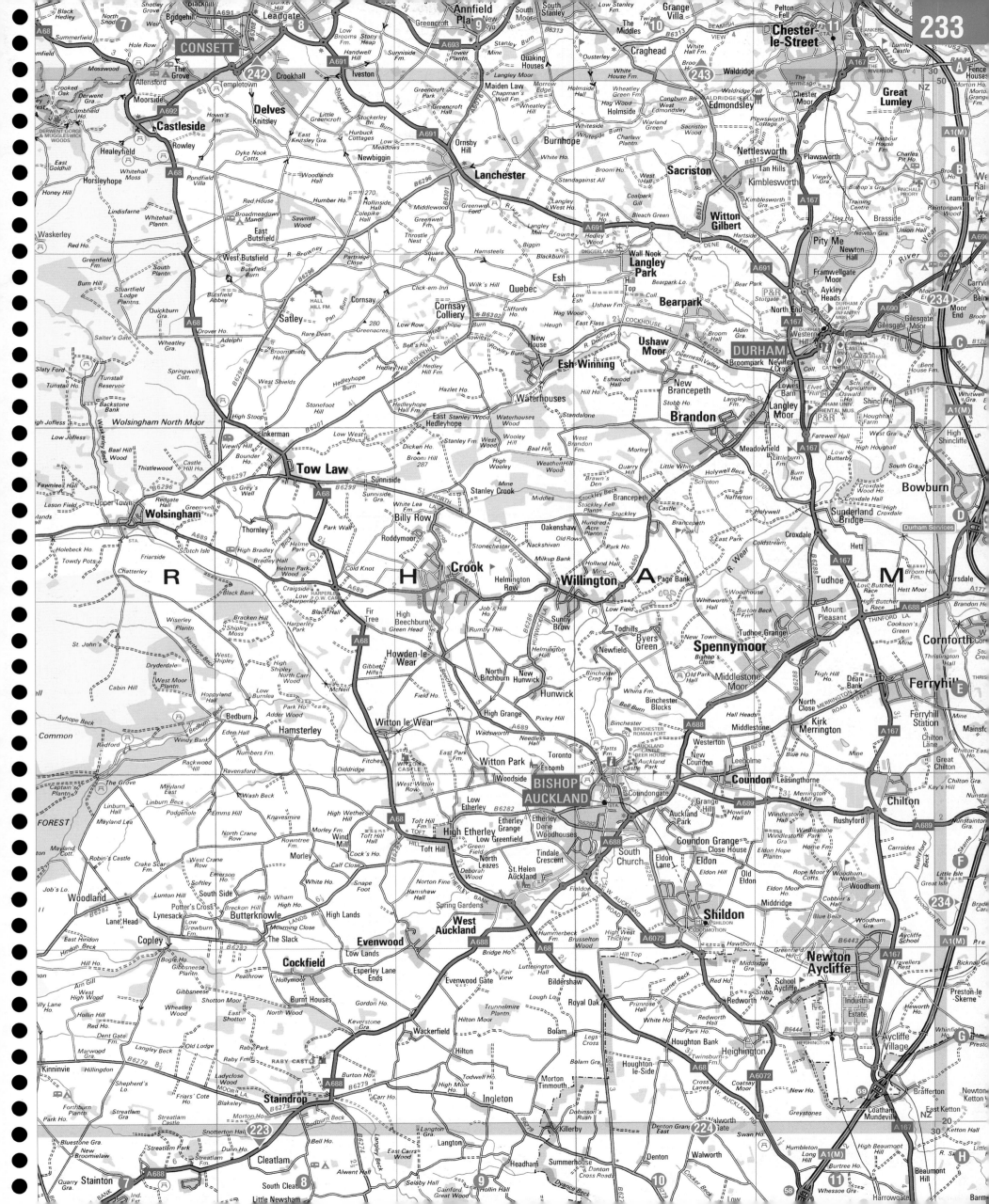

N O R T H

S E A

ROTTERDAM 16:00
ZEEBRUGGE 16:30

South Gare
Breakwater

EES BAY

Bran
Sands

Coatham Sands

Salt Scar

Coatham
Rocks

Redcar Rocks

Works

Coatham

REDCAR

Warrenby

Redcar
Sands

BRITISH STEEL
REDCAR

Coatham
Marsh

Westfield

Redcar East

REDCAR RACECOURSE

Dormanstown

REDCAR

Steel
Works

Manor
Fm.

Marske-by-the
-Sea

Marske Sands

Saltburn-by-the
-Sea

Pier

Saltburn
Sands

Saltburn
Scar

AND

Chemical
Works

Kirkleatham
HALL MUSEUM

Marske

Tofts
Fm.

SMUGGLERS
HERITAGE
CENTRE

Warsett Hill

CLEVELAND

Fell Briggs
Fm.

New
Marske

SALTBURN

Rushpool Hall

New Brotton

INTERNATIONAL
RALLY SCHOOL
Low Fm.

Hummersea
Scar

Cattersty Sands

White Stones

Town Fm.

Yearby

Thrushwood
Fm.

Errington Wood

Marske Mill

Hagg Fm.

Hunley Hall

NZ

Grangetown

A 1053

Lazenby

Wilton

Yearby
Wood

YEARBY BANK

Corngrave Fm.

Wand
Hills

Skinningrove

226

Lackenby

Wilton
Castle

Bank Top

Upleatham

225

SkeltonBeck

Skelton
Castle

Barns Fm.

Brotton

A174

Upton

213

Rockhole
Hill

Bias Scar

Cowbar

Cowbar Nab

Eston

A 1085

Dunsdale

Raisbeck
Fm.

New Skelton

Carlin How

Deepdale
Fm.

Street
Houses

Boulby

Old Nab

Monument

242

Court Green
Woods

Dunsdale
Fm.

Thornton
Fields

Carling
Howe

7

Skelton

8

TOCKETTS
WATER MILL

9

th
Skelton

Skelton
Green

East
Pastures

Mine

Craggs Hill

Kilton

10

East
Loftus

Loftus

WHITBY

Old Boulby

11

Stäithes

Brackenberry
Wyke

Normanby

Seaton Hall

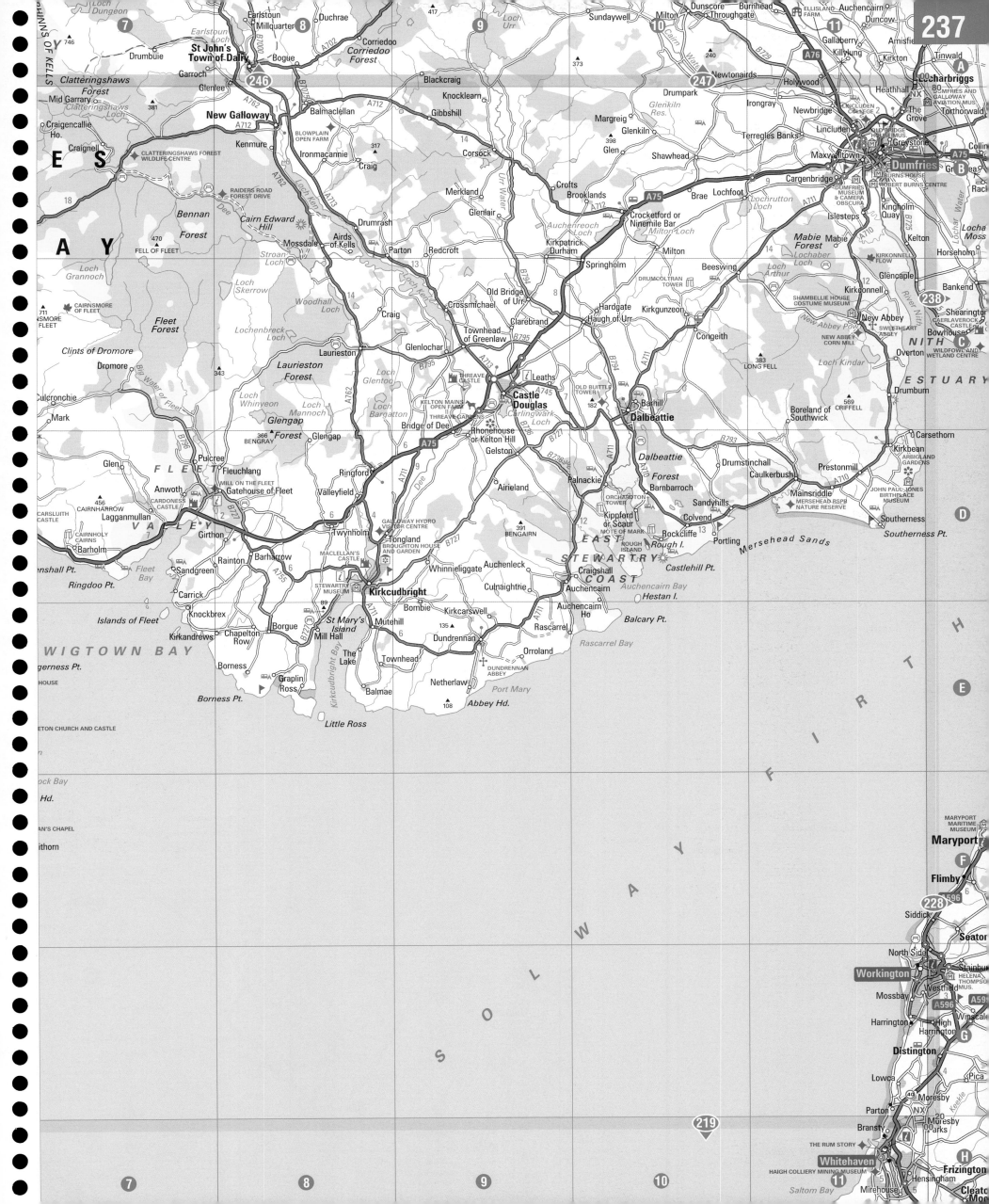

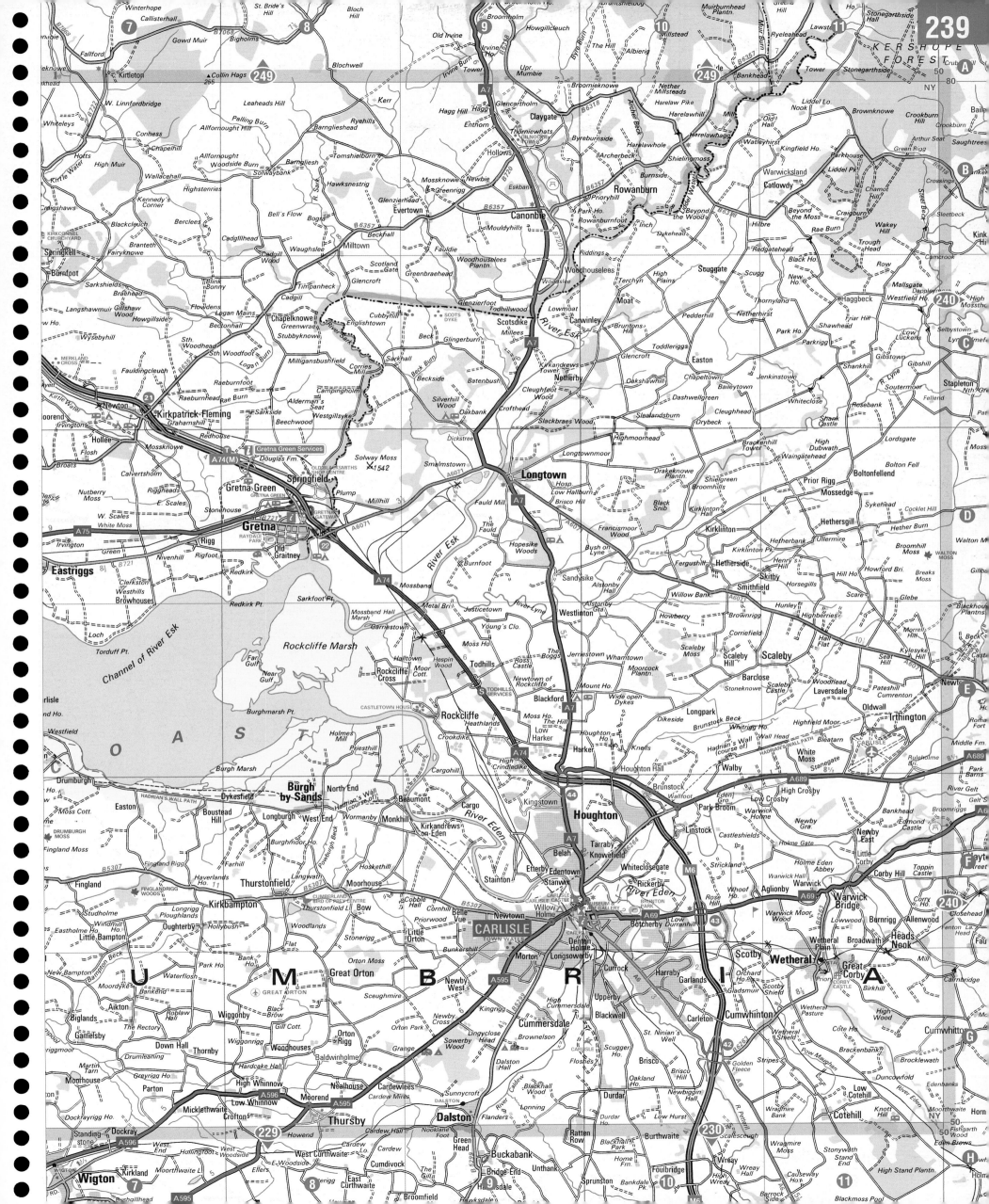

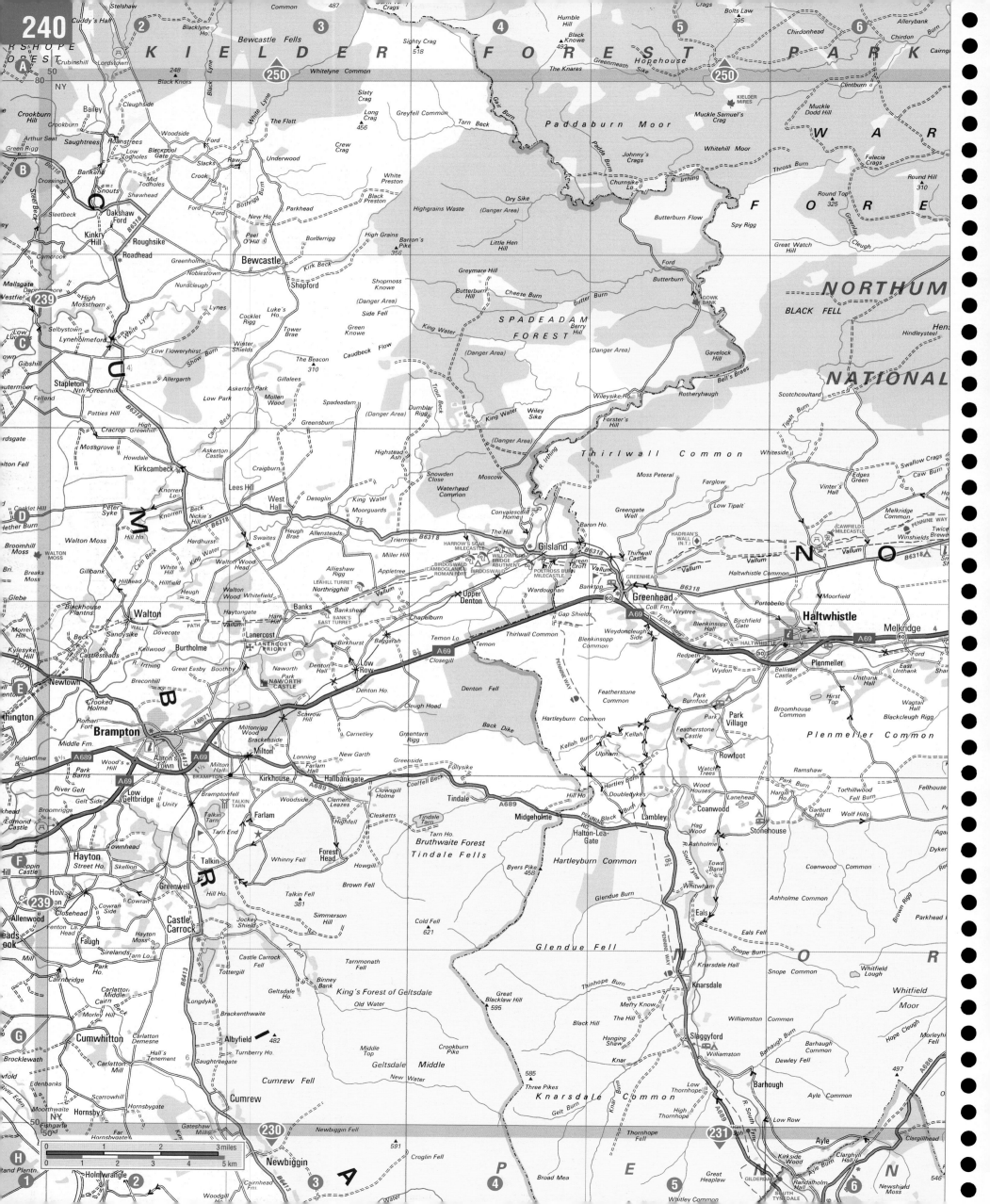

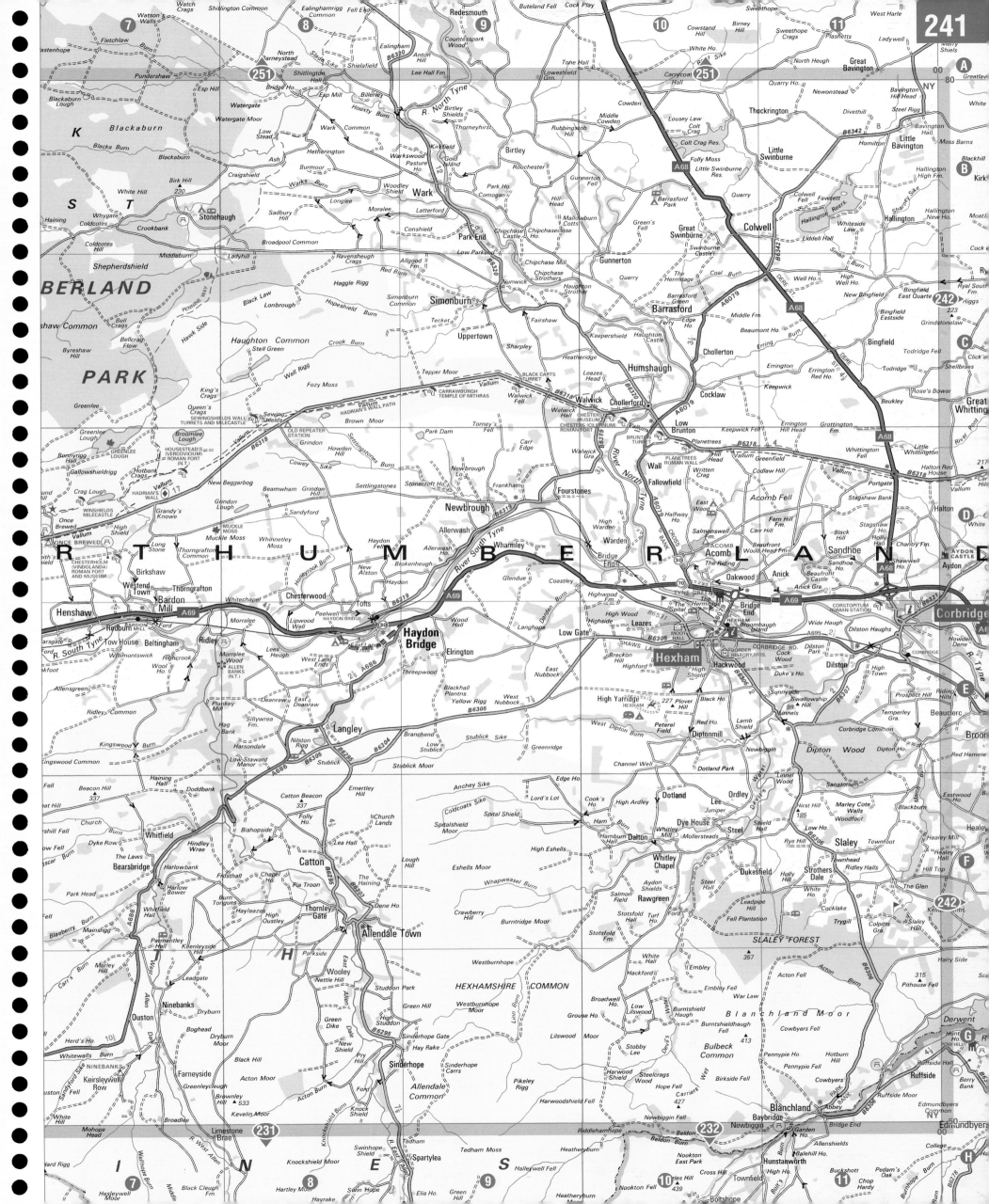

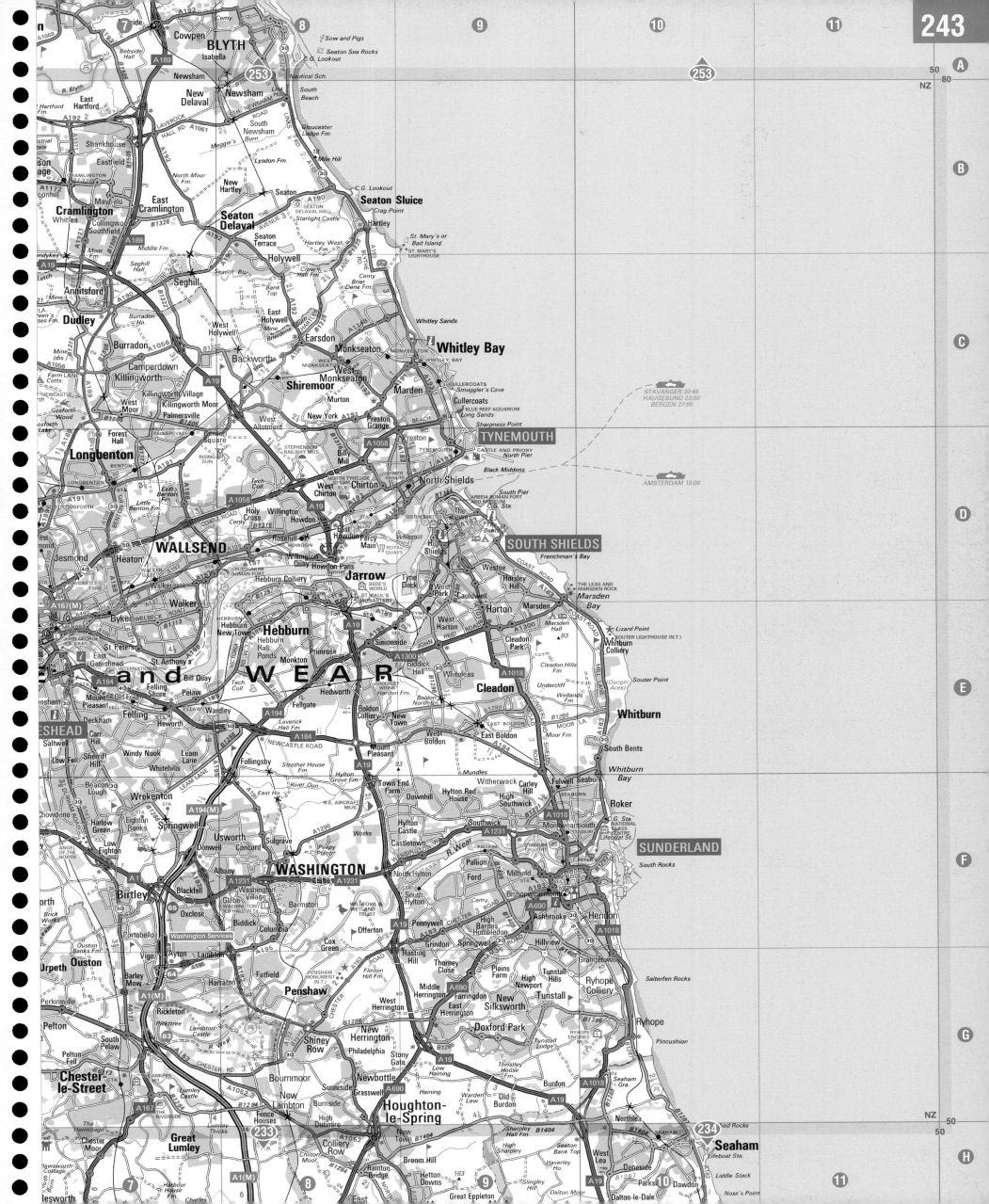

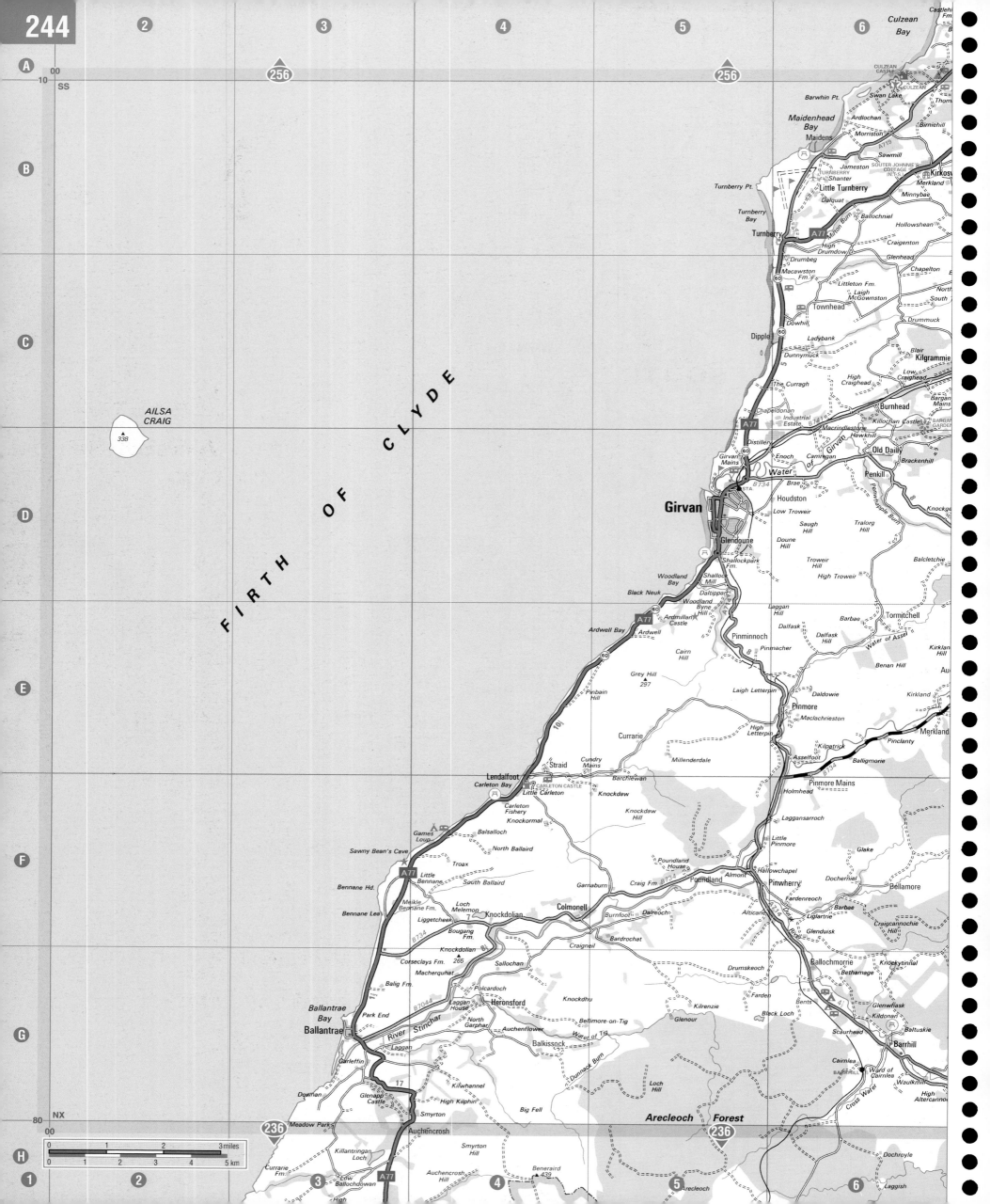

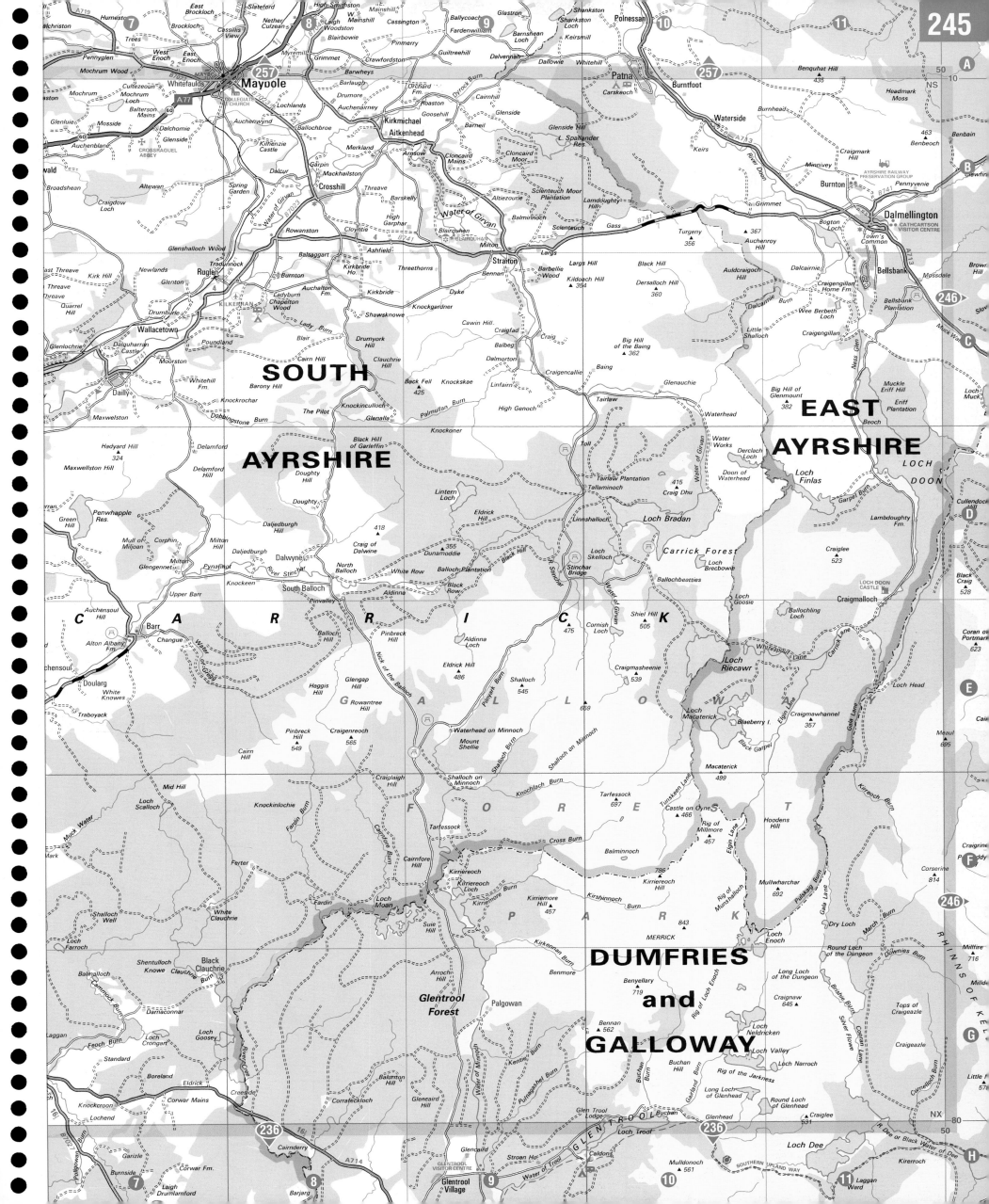

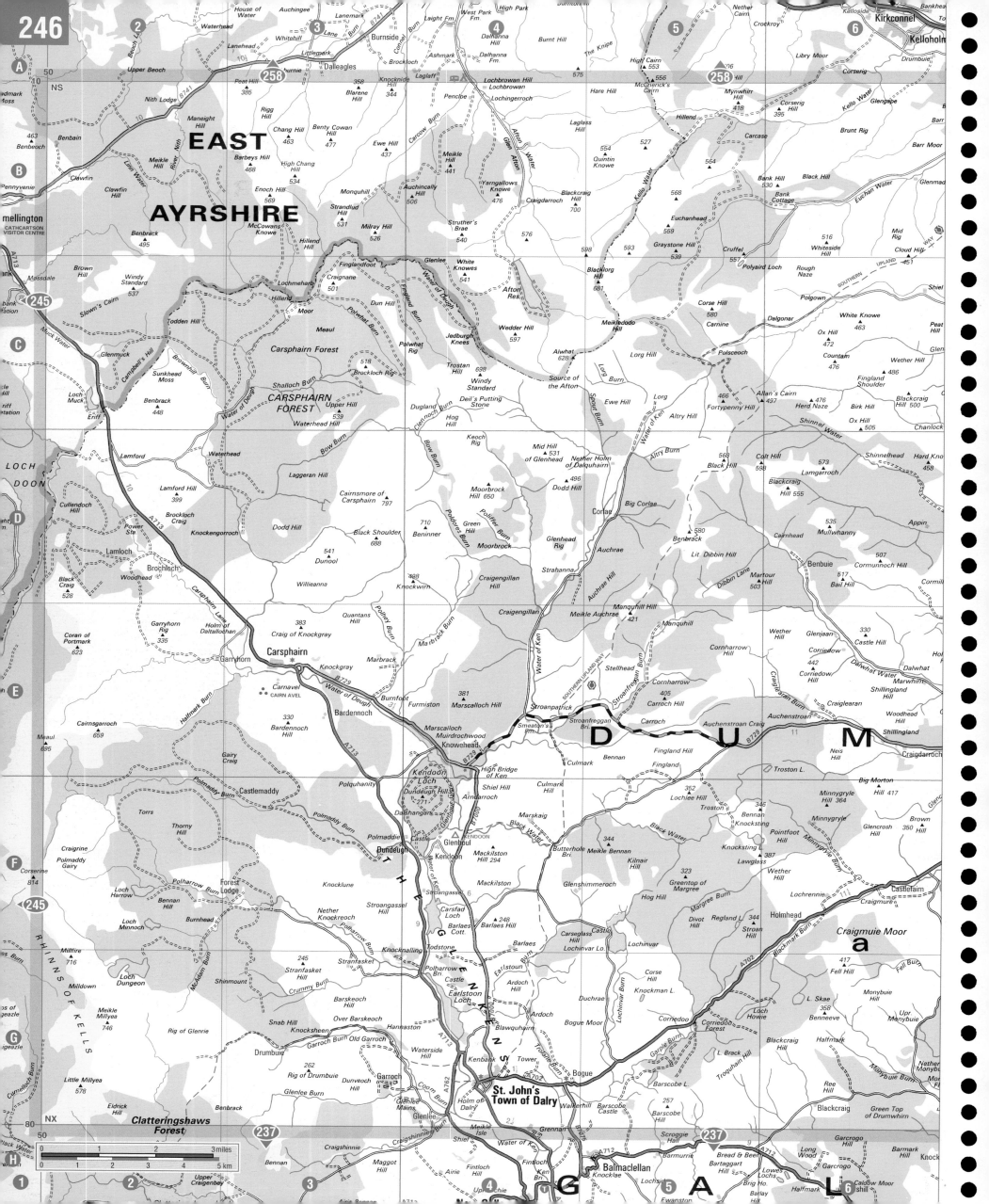

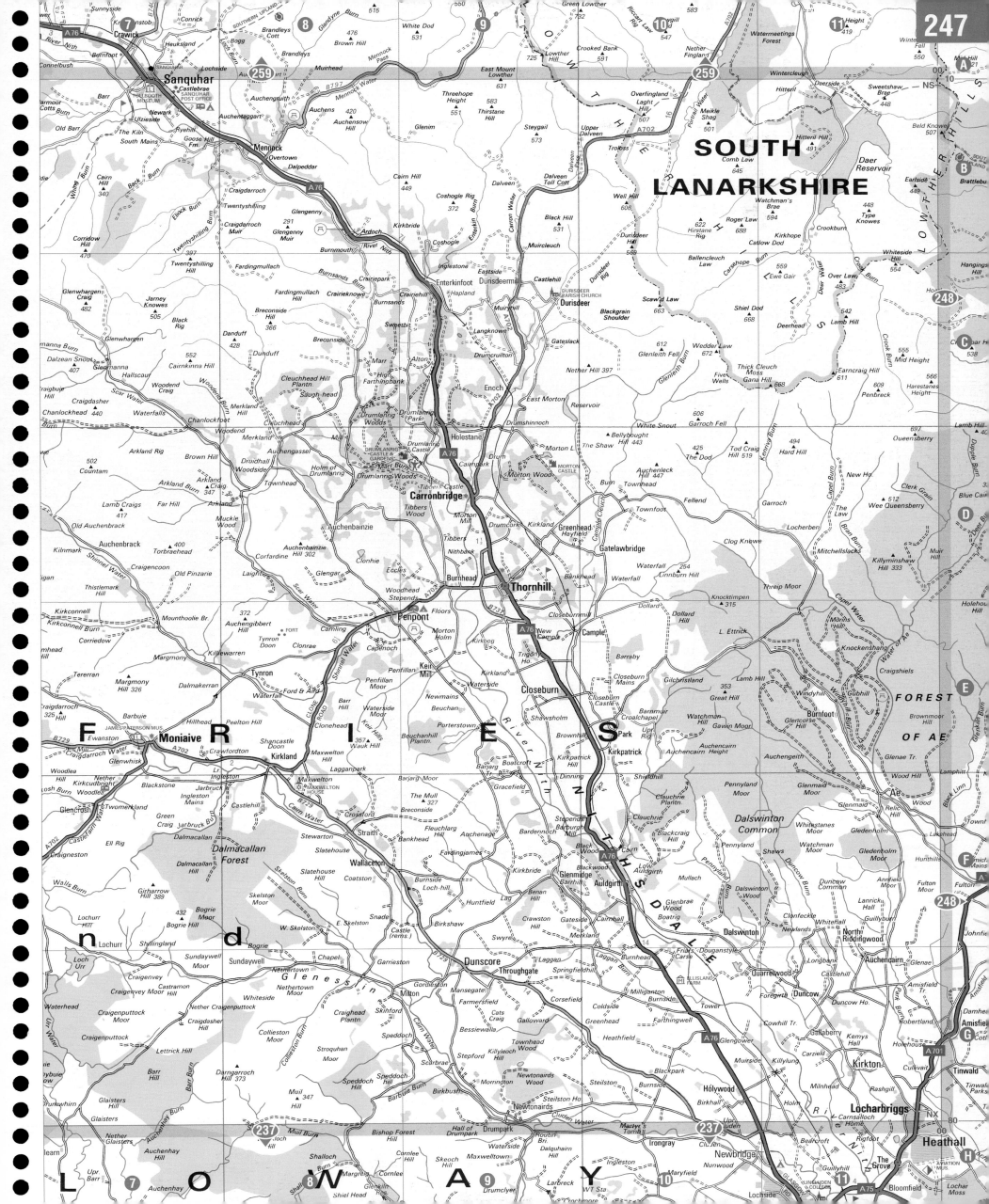

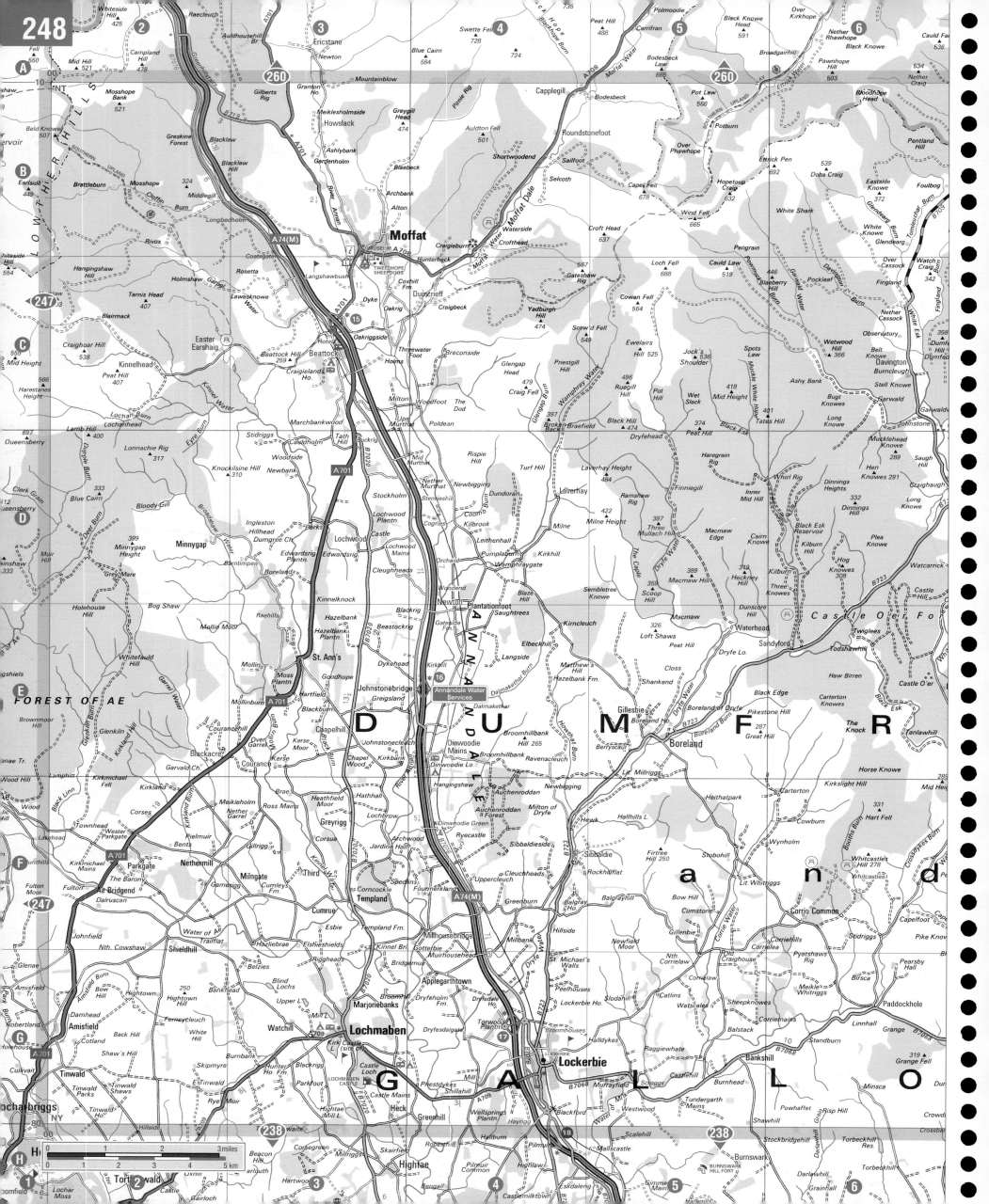

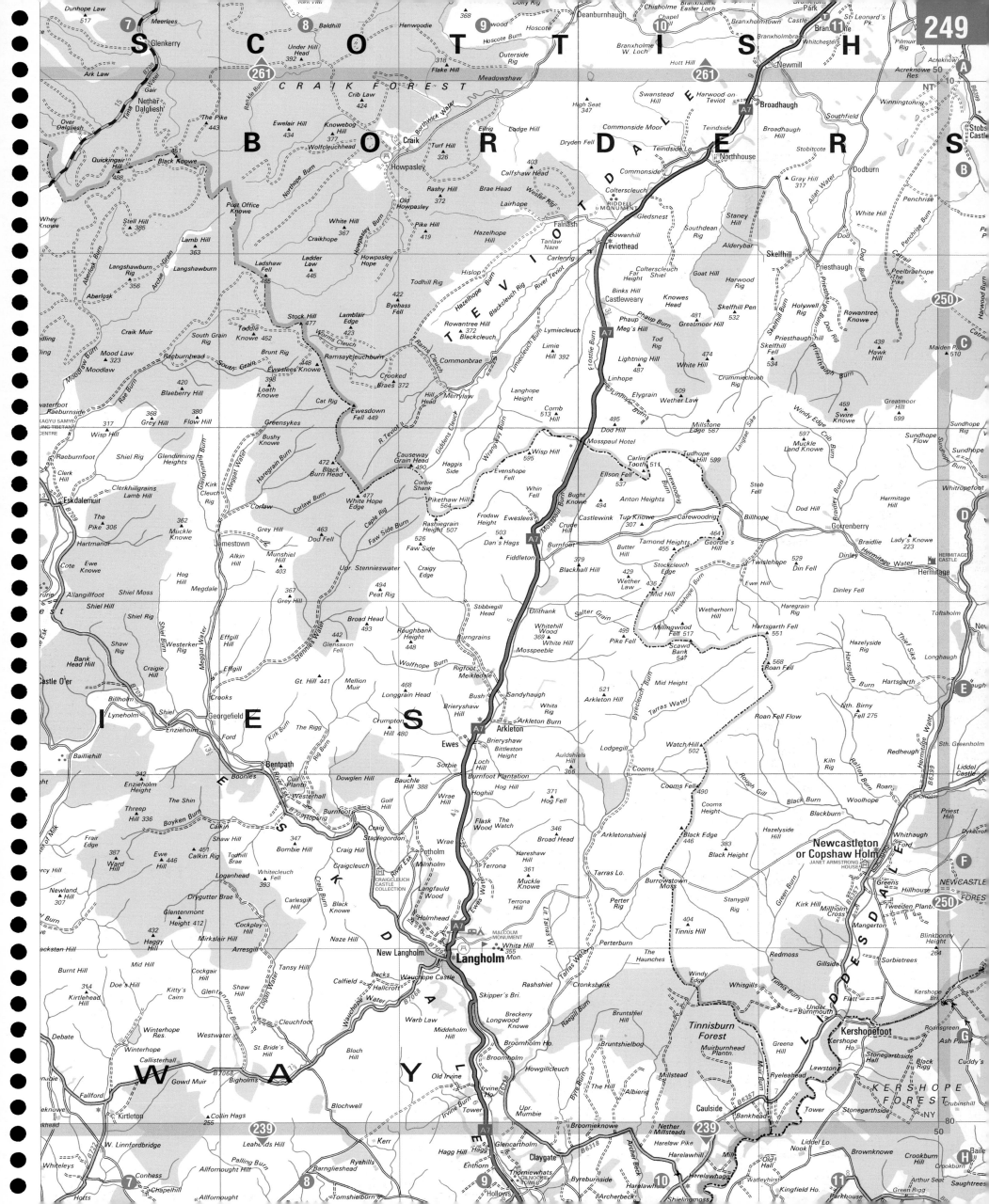

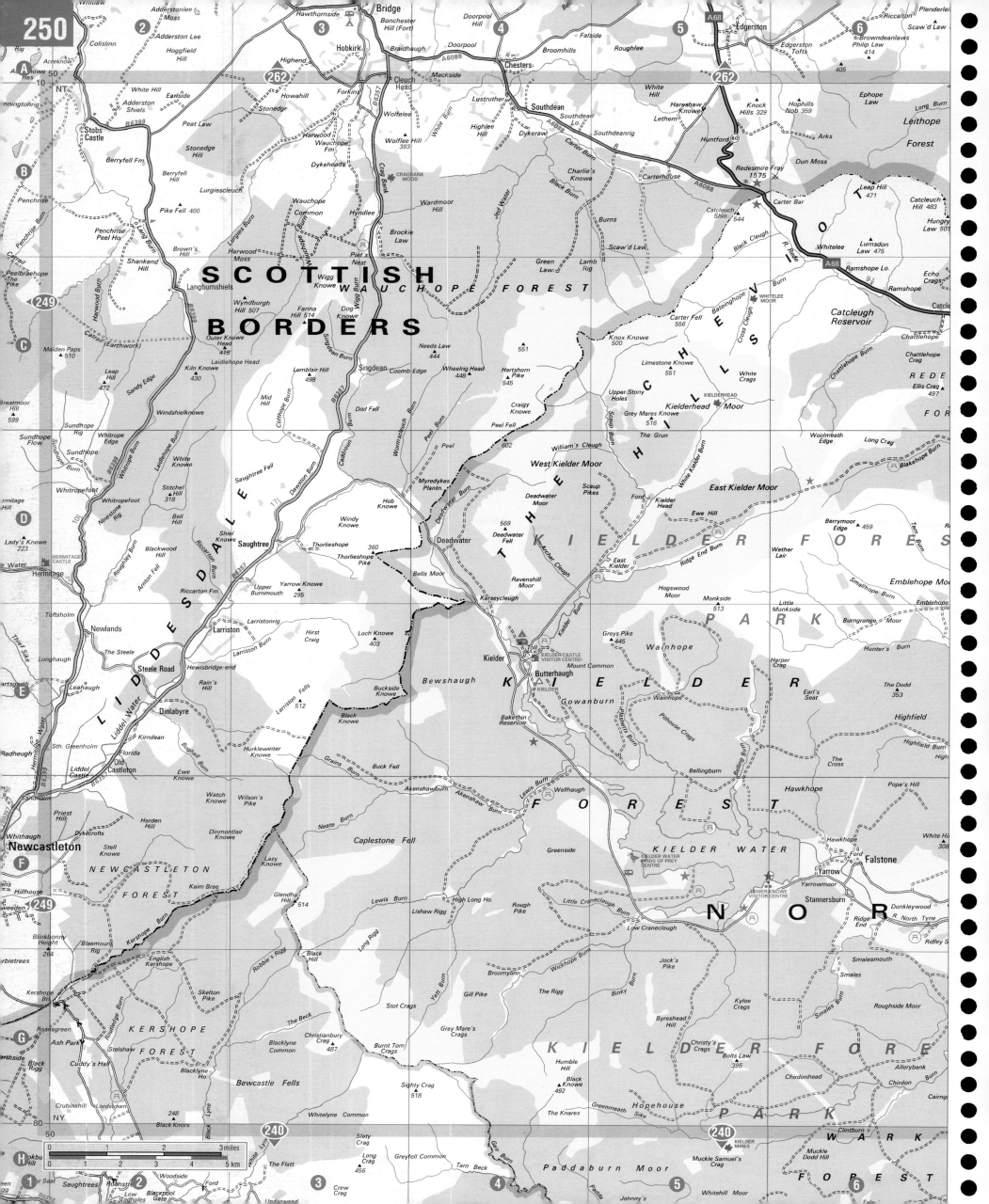

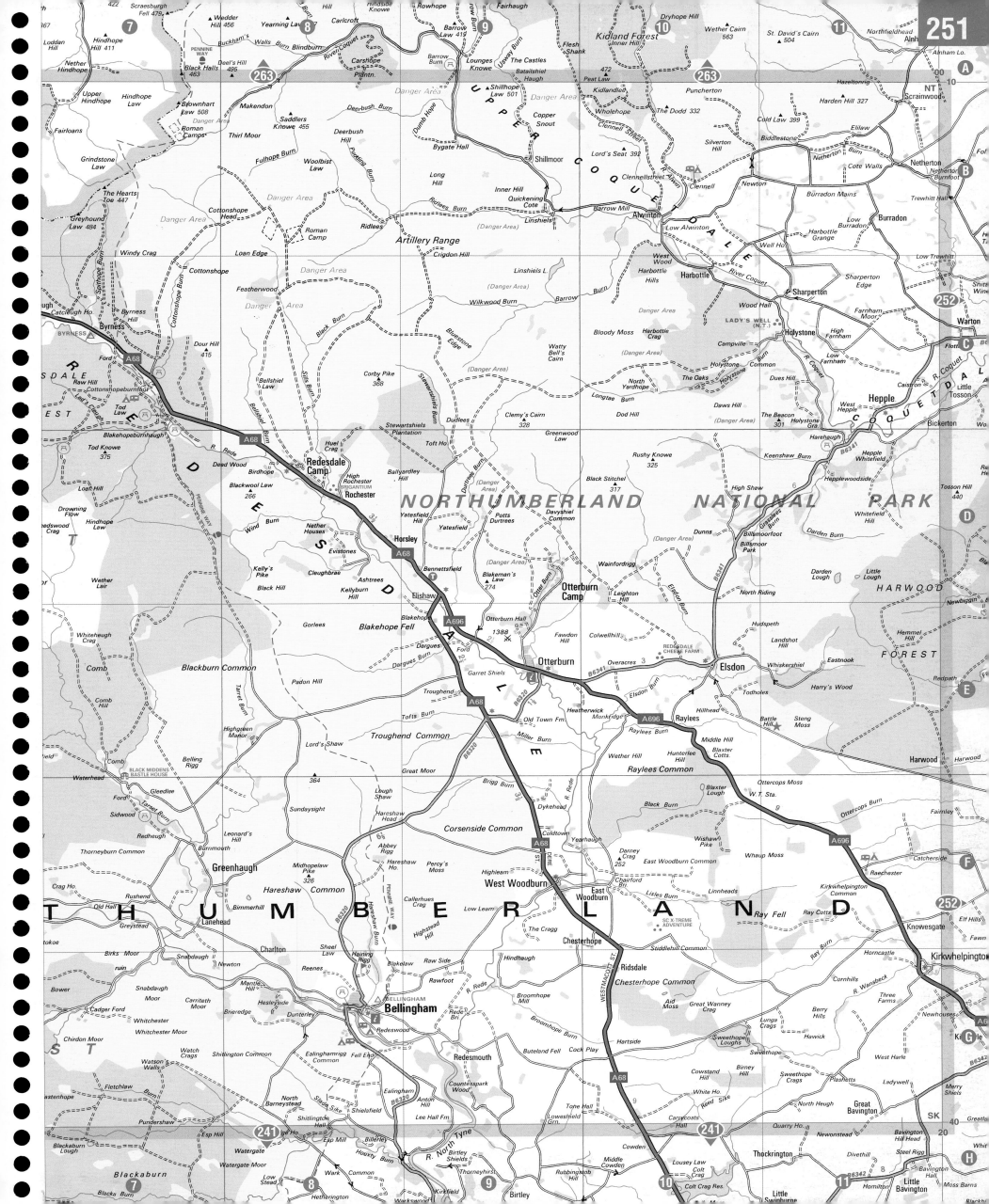

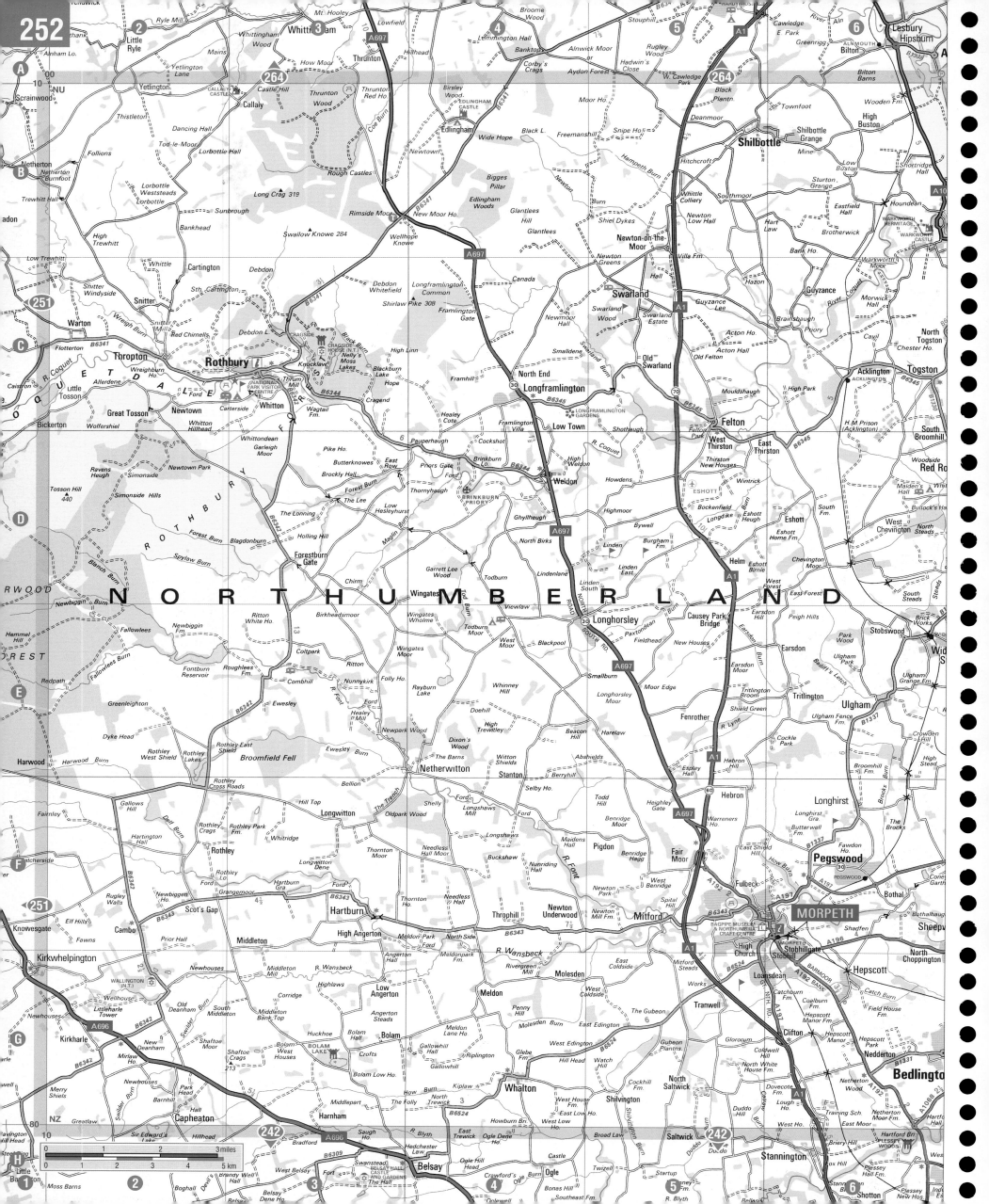

Inmouth

Alnmouth Bay

NORTH

Birling Carrs

Birling

Warkworth

Warkworth Hill
Warkworth Harbour
Gloster Hill

Amble

Coquet Island

New Hall

High Hauxley
Moor Ho.
Mine
Radcliffe
Low Hauxley
Hauxley Haven
Togston Barns
A1068
Togston East Fm.
(Danger Area)
Hadston Carrs

Broomhill
Coldrife
Hadston
DRURIDGE BAY

W
efield Ho.
Chevington Burn

SEA

Chibburn
A1068

Druridge Bay

High Chibburn
(Danger Area)
Durridge

Widdrington

Hemscott Hill
Houndalee
drington
RDINGTON
Blakemoor Fm.
The Scars
drington ation
Cresswell
Warkworthlane Cott.
Hagg Fm.
Snab Point
Lyne
Ellington
Cresswell Fm.
Linton
A1068

Old Moor Stead
Lynemouth
Mine
Lyne Sands
Works
Blue Holes
Beacon Point
Potland Burn
A189
QUEEN ELIZABETH II
COLLIERY MUS.
Woodhorn
Mine
CHURCH MUS.
A197
Newbiggin Point
A197
Woodbridge
Newbiggin-by-the-Sea
ASHINGTON
Hirst
North Seaton
Ashington Fm.
WANSBECK
R Wansbeck
B1334
1½
North Seaton Colliery
wash
A196
Stakeford
West Sleekburn
A189
2
Guide Post
Scotland Gate
Bomarsund
Choppington
East Sleekburn
Cambois
Bedlington Station
The Rockers
Green Skeer
River Blyth
North Blyth
A193
Cemy.
BLYTH
Sow and Pigs
n
Bebside
Cowpen
Seaton Sea Rocks
C.G. Lookout
Bebside Hall
A189
Isabella
Newsham
Nautical Sch.
New Delaval
243
South Beach
Hartford
East Hartford
A192
LAVEROCK
HALL RD.
A1061
STH. NEWSHAM
ROAD
South Newsham Burn
Gloucester dge Fm.
ndustrial ate
Shankhou
7
8
9
Meggie's
Mile Hill
Lysdon Fm.

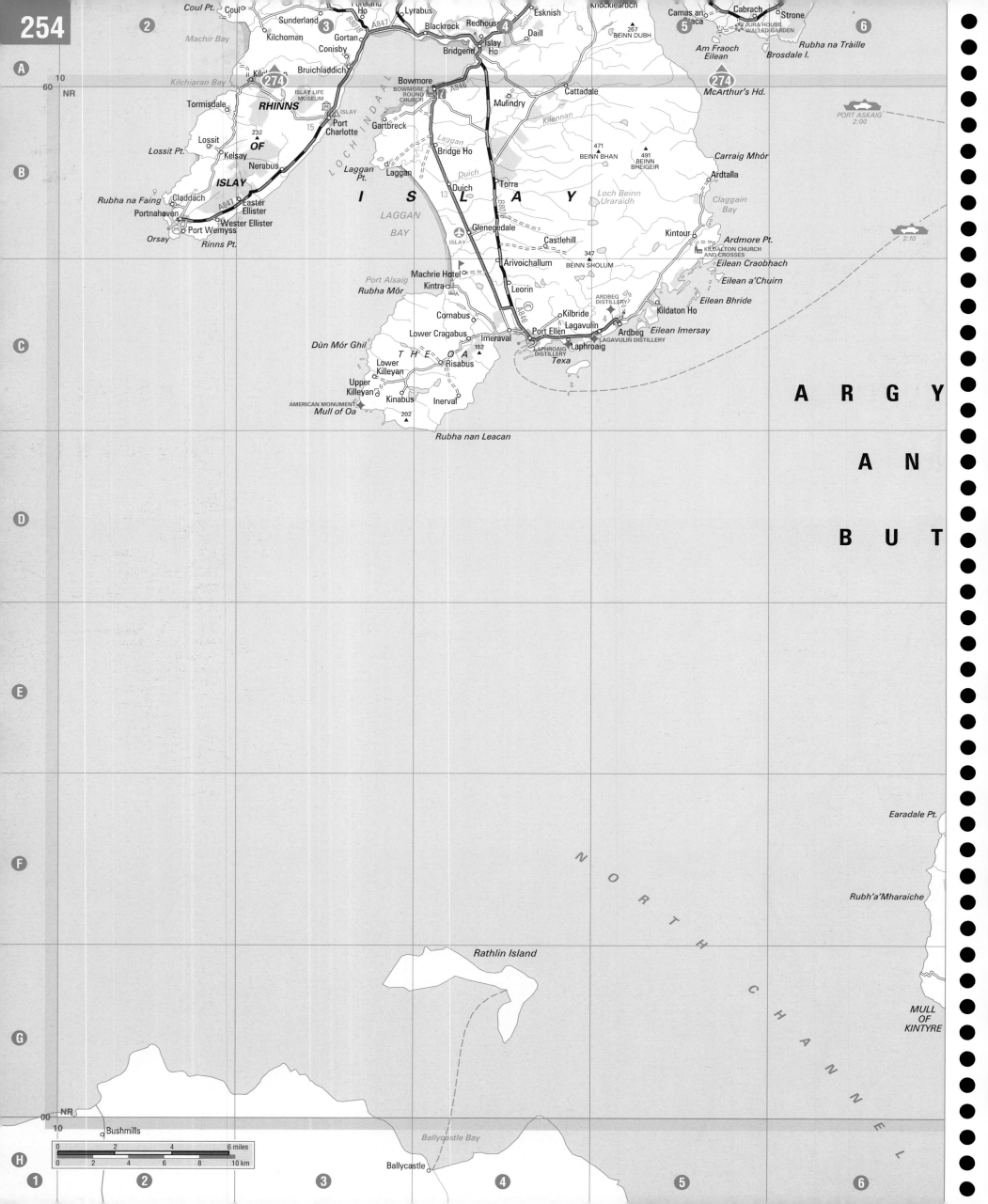

ISLAY

RHINNS OF ISLAY

THE OA

ARGY
AN
BUT

NORTH CHANNEL

Rathlin Island

MULL OF KINTYRE

Bushmills

Ballycastle

Ballycastle Bay

0   2   4   6 miles
0 2 4 6 8 10 km

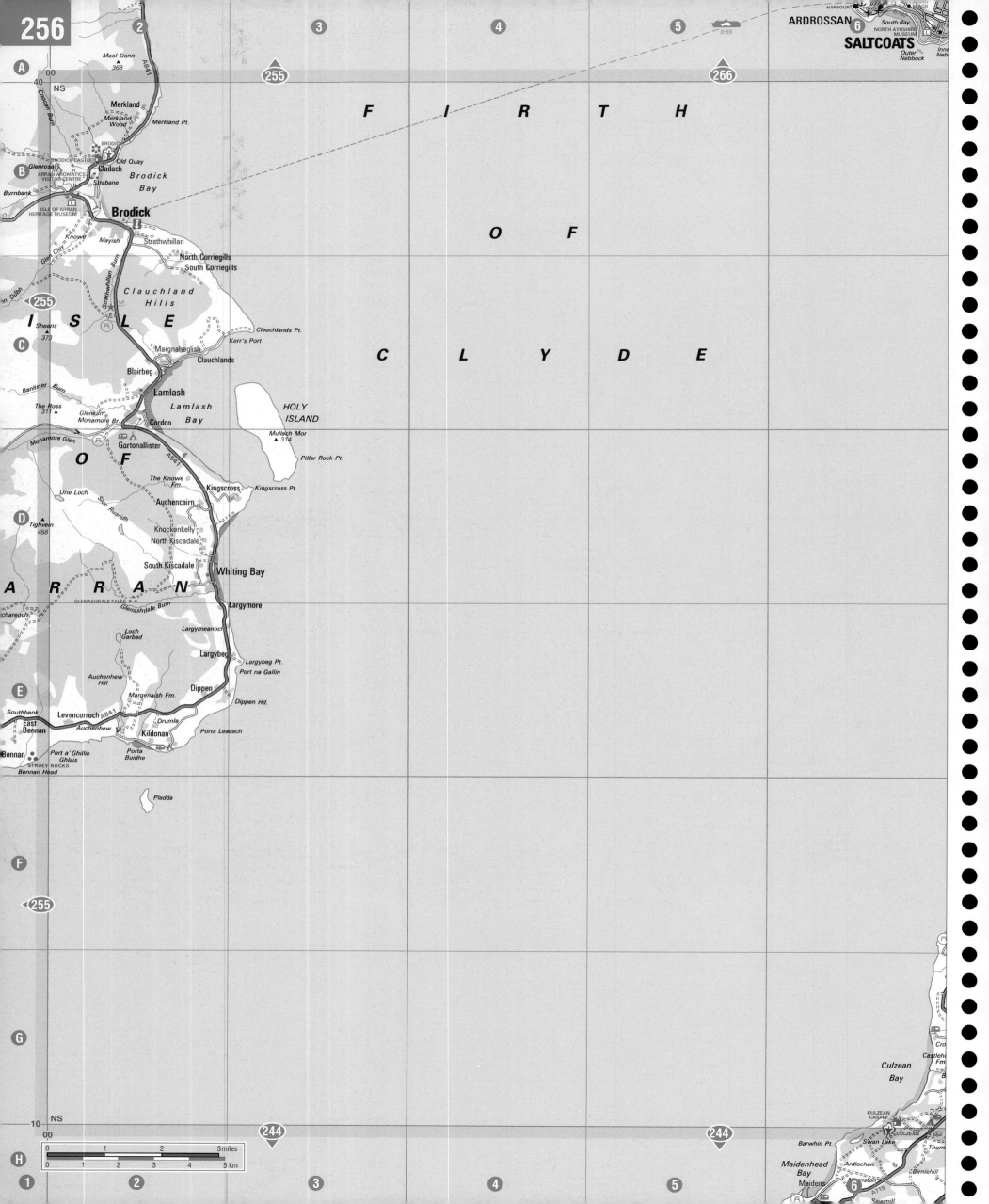

ARDROSSAN

SALTCOATS

NORTH AYRSHIRE MUSEUM

South Bay

Outer Nebbock

A 255

B 266

F I R T H

O F

C L Y D E

Maol Donn
368

Merkland

Merkland Wood

Merkland Pt.

BRODICK

BRODICK CASTLE

Glenrosa

Cladach

Old Quay

Strabane

Brodick Bay

Burnbank

ISLE OF ARRAN HERITAGE MUSEUM

ARRAN AROMATICS VISITOR CENTRE

Brodick

Knowe

Mayish

Strathwhillan

North Corriegills

South Corriegills

255

Clauchland Hills

Sheans
373

Clauchlands Pt.

Margnaheglish

Kerr's Port

Clauchlands

Blairbeg

Lamlash

Banlister Burn

The Ross
311

Glenkiln

Monamore Br.

Cordon

Lamlash Bay

HOLY ISLAND

Mullach Mor
314

Monamore Glen

Gortonallister

O F

Pillar Rock Pt.

The Knowe Fm.

Kingscross

Kingscross Pt.

Urie Loch

Spc. Ruaridh

Auchencairn

Tighvein
458

Knockenkelly

North Kiscadale

South Kiscadale

Whiting Bay

A R R A N

GLENASHDALE FALLS

Glenashdale Burn

Largymore

Loch Garbad

Largymeanoch

Largybeg

Largybeg Pt.

Port na Gallin

Auchenhew Hill

Dippen

Margenaish Fm.

Dippen Hd.

Southbank

Levencorroch

A841

East Bennan

Auchenhew

Drumla

Kildonan

Porta Leacach

Bennan

Port a' Ghillie Ghlais

Porta Buidhe

STRUEY ROCKS

Bennan Head

Pladda

255

F

244

Culzean Bay

G

CULZEAN CASTLE

NS 10 00

244

Barwhin Pt.

Swan Lake

Maidenhead Bay

Ardlochan

Maidens

H

0 1 2 3 miles
0 1 2 3 4 5 km

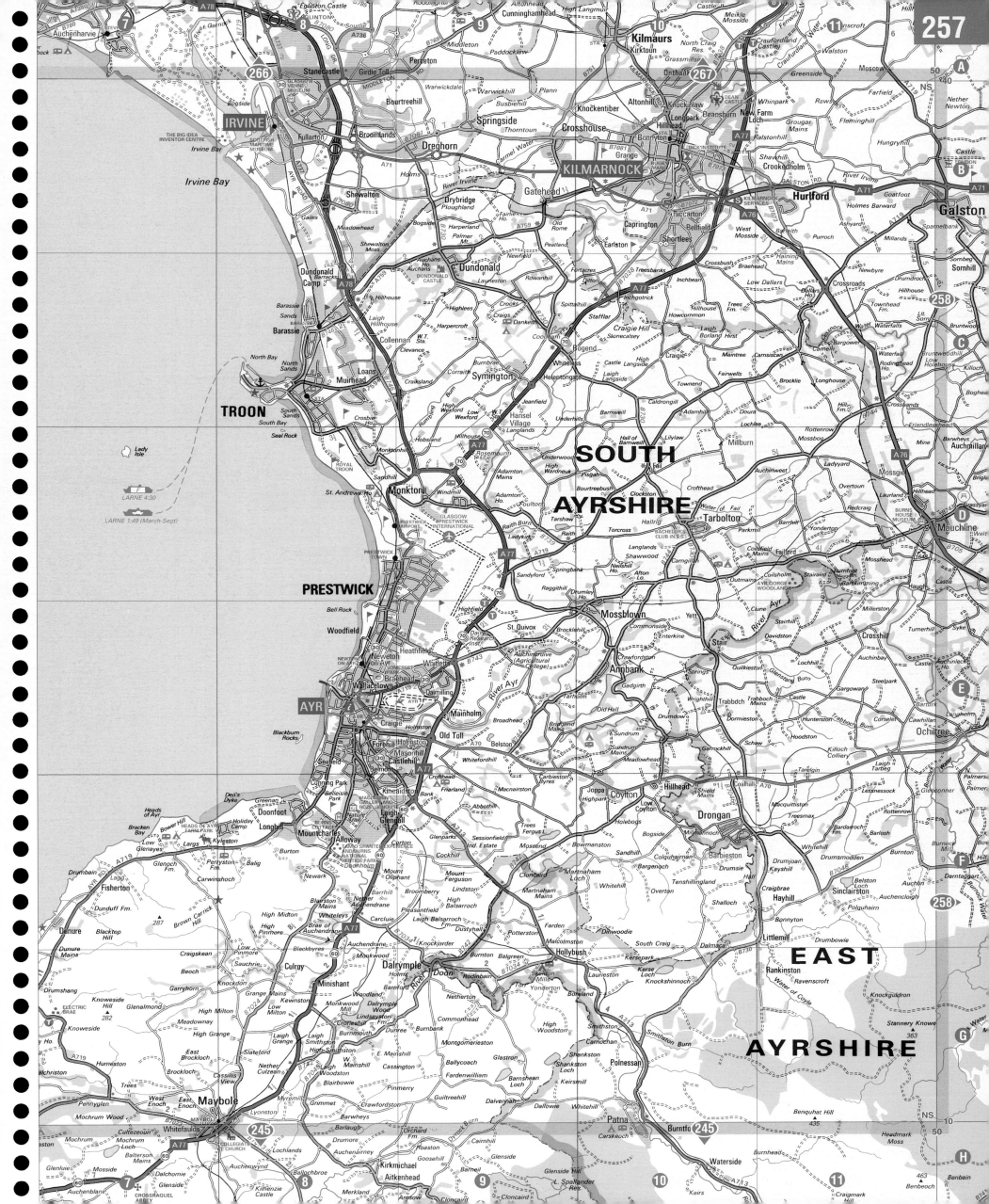

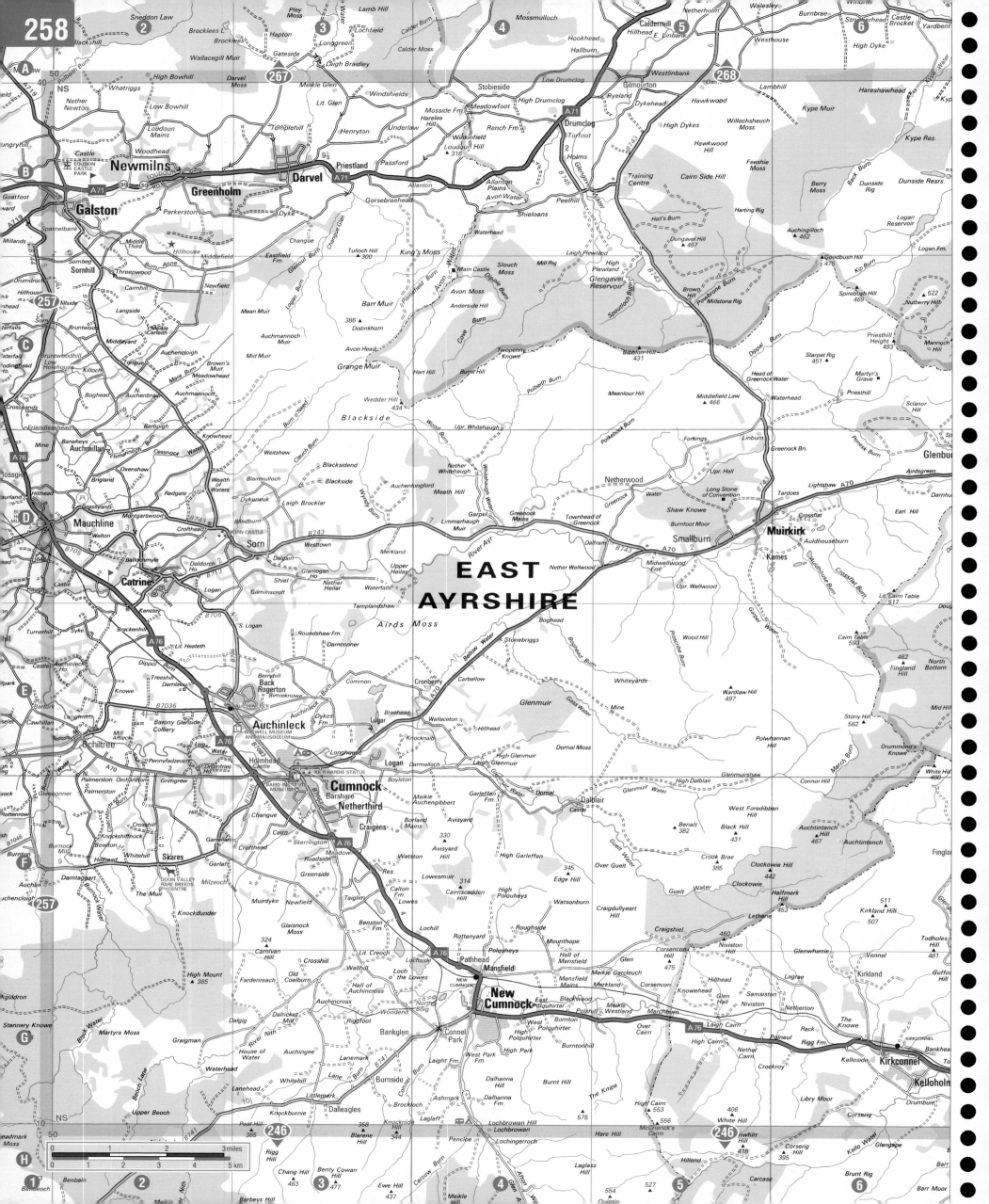

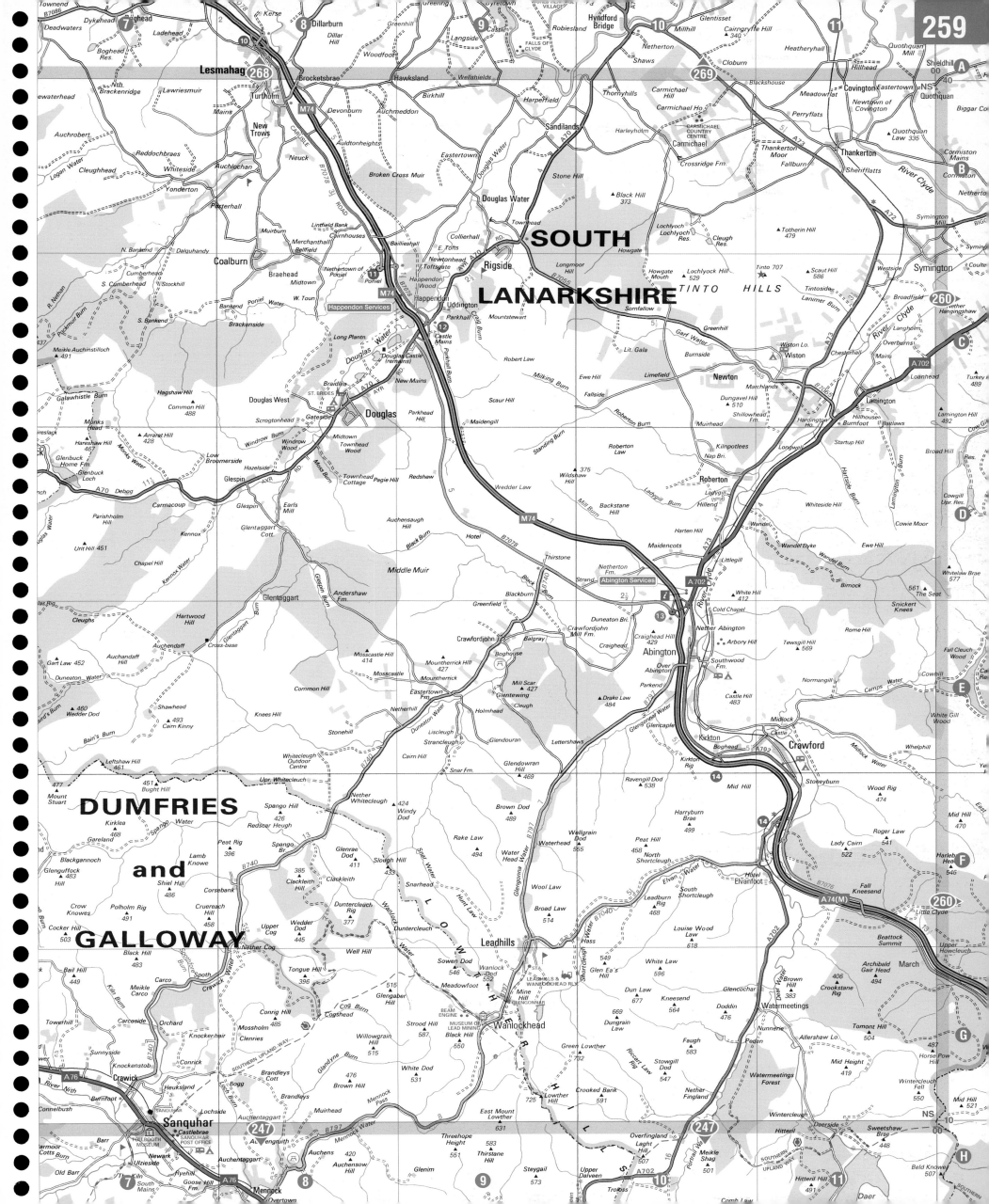

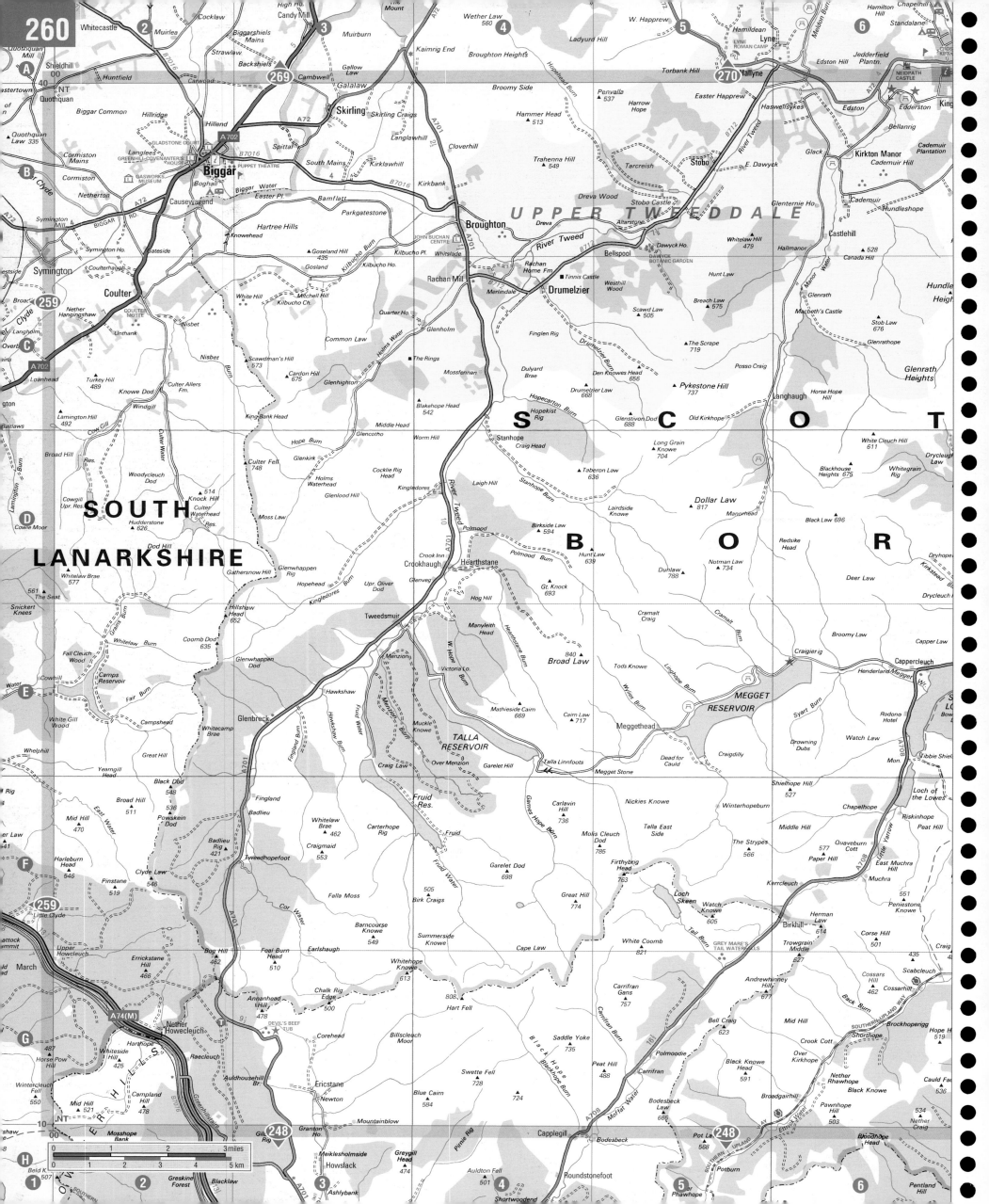

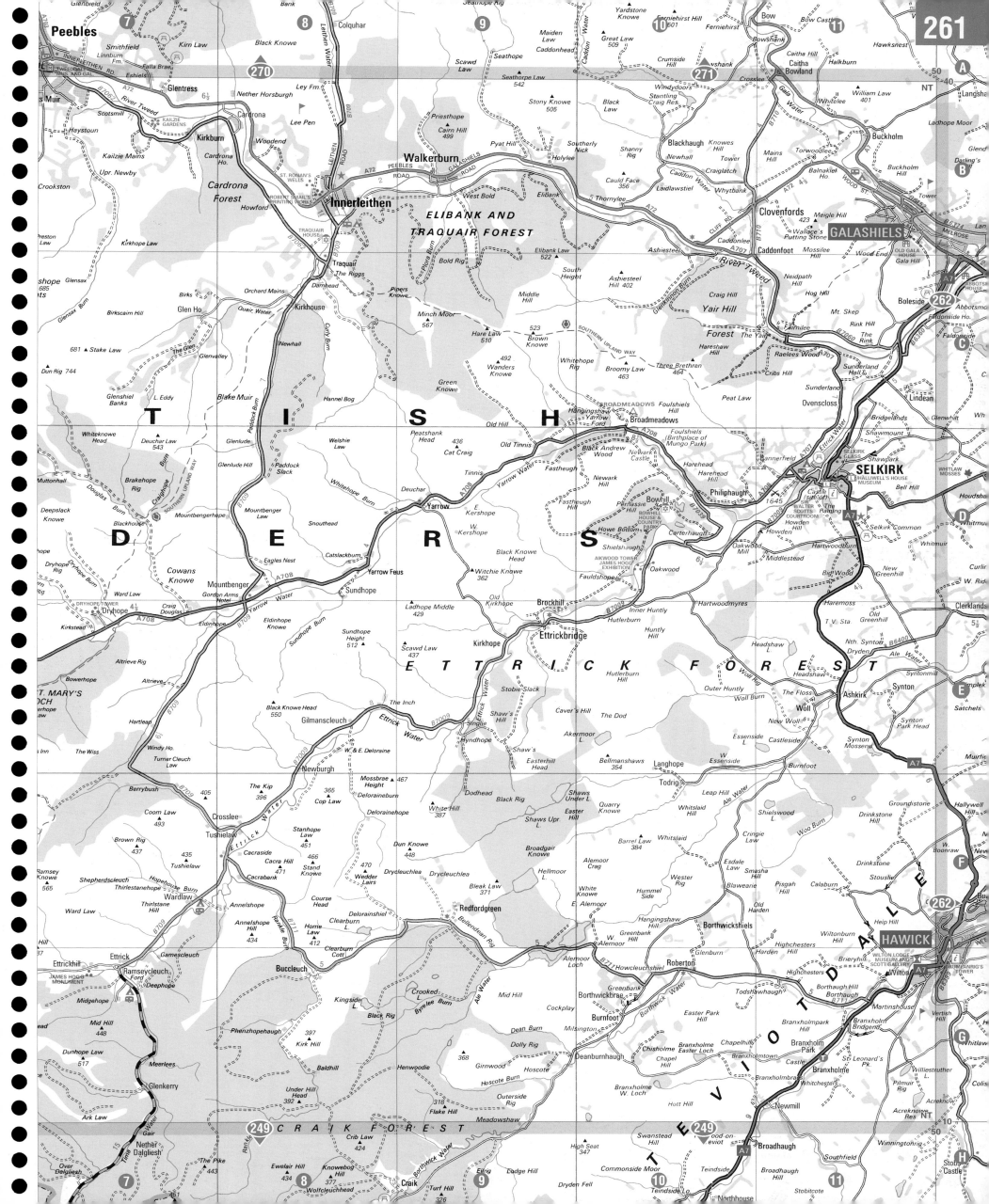

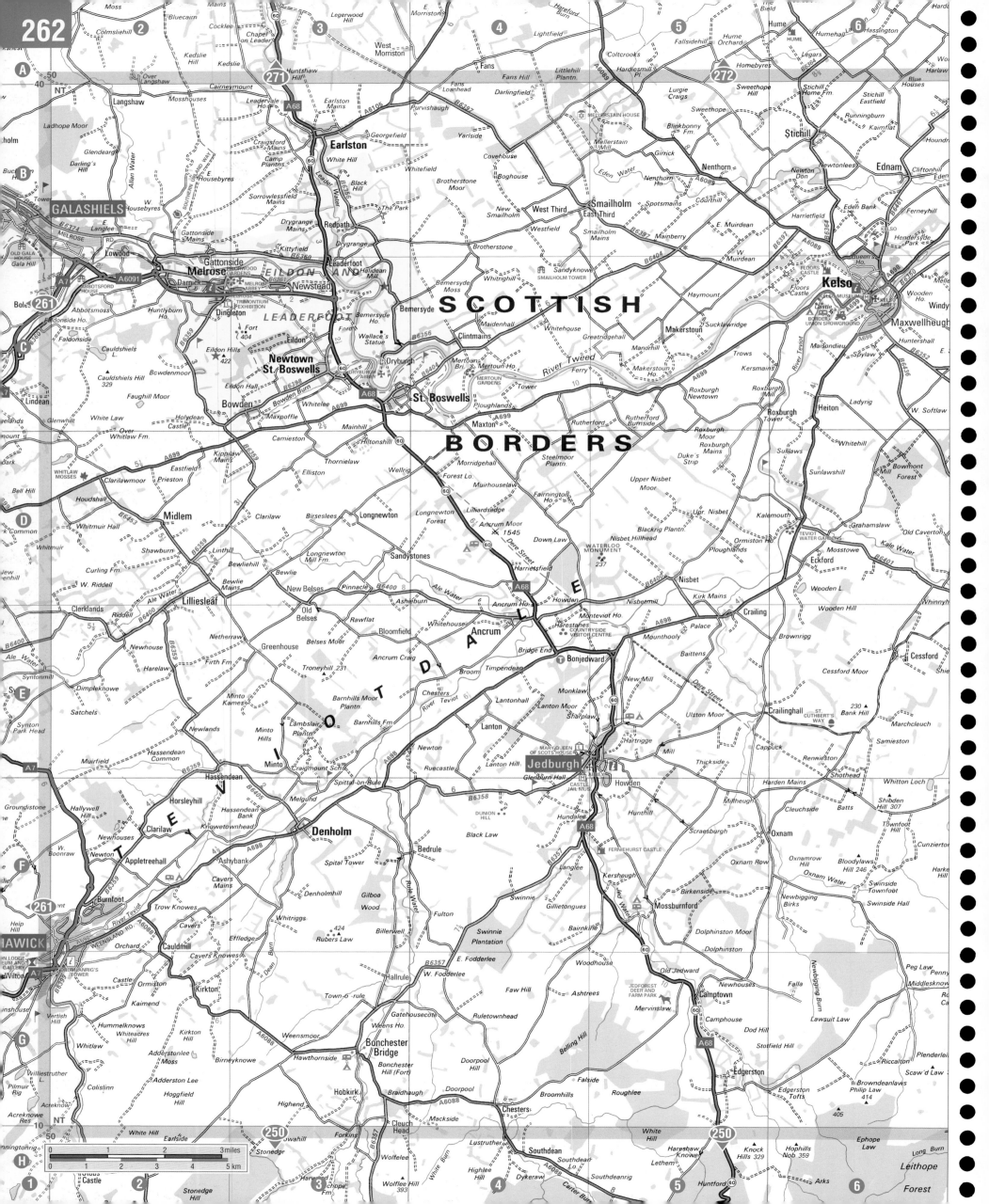

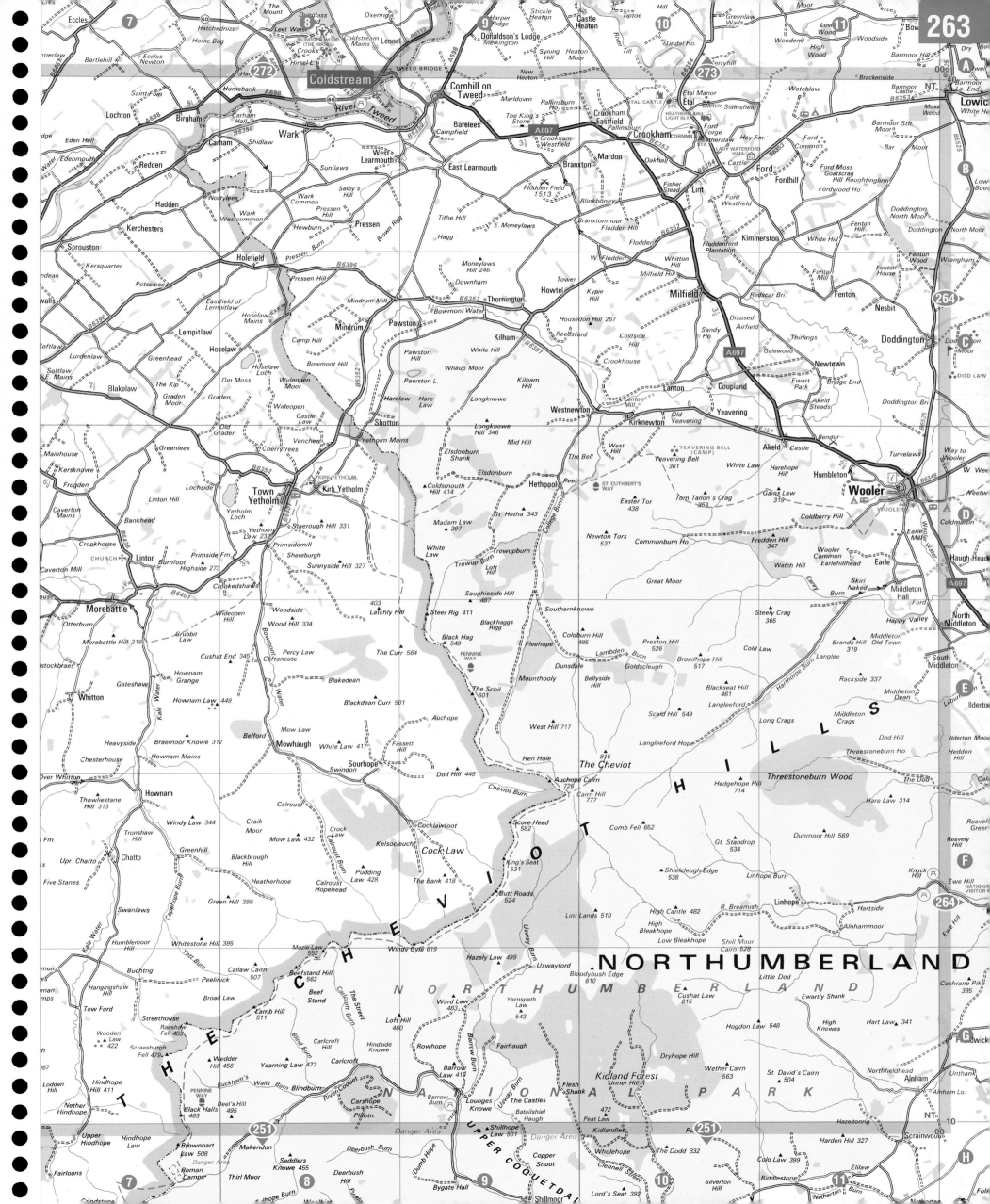

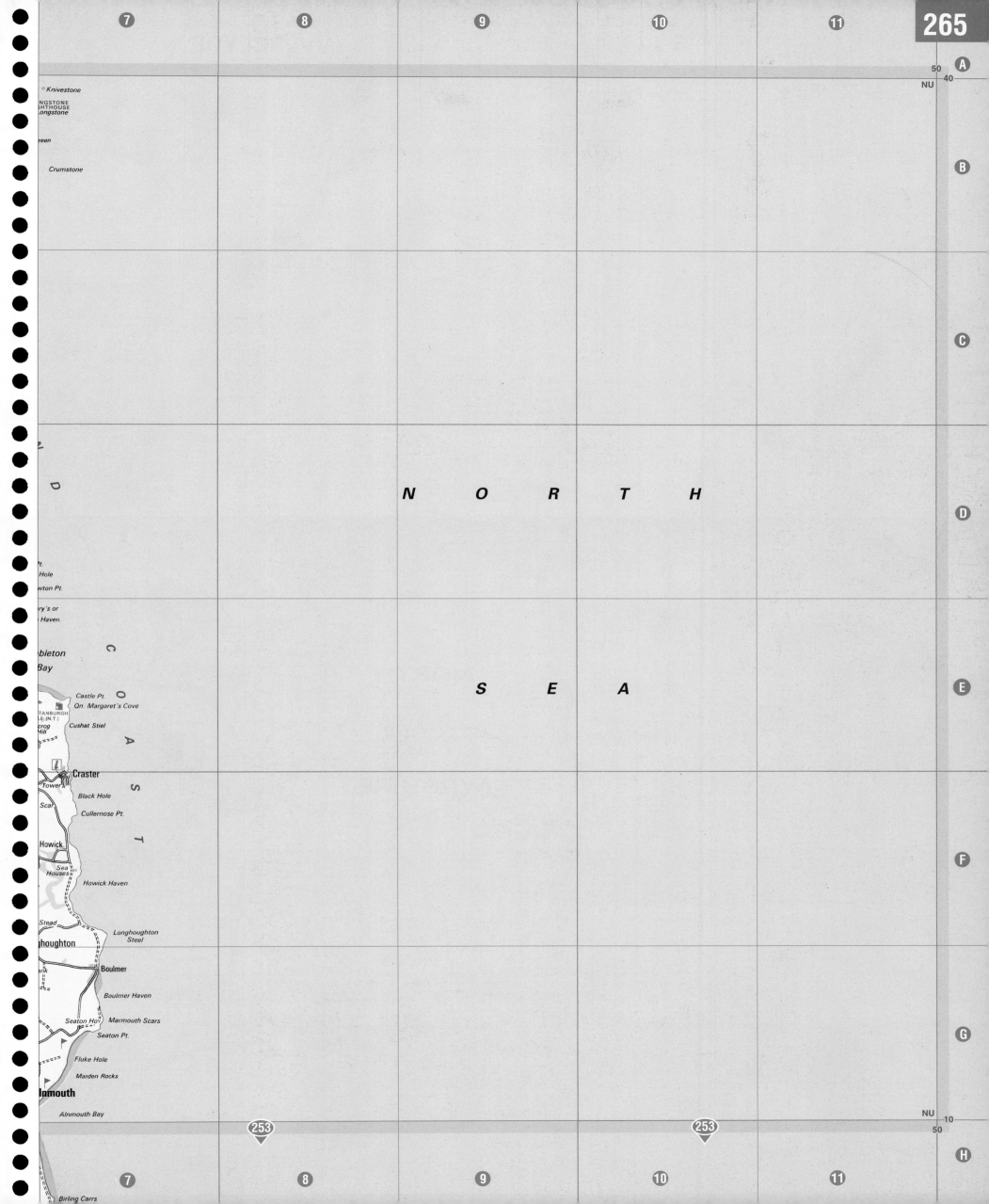

NORTH

SEA

Knivestone

NGSTONE
HTHOUSE
Longstone

reen

Crumstone

N D

D

Pt.
Hole
wton Pt.

ry's or
Haven

bleton
Bay

C

Castle Pt.
Qn. Margaret's Cove
TANBURGH
LE (N.T.)
crog
Hill
Cushat Stiel

Craster

Tower
Black Hole
Scar
Cullernose Pt.

Howick

O

A

S

T

Sea
Houses
Howick Haven

Stead
Longhoughton
Steel
houghton

rik
Boulmer
Boulmer Haven

Seaton Ho
Marmouth Scars
Seaton Pt.

Fluke Hole
Marden Rocks

lnmouth

Alnmouth Bay

253

253

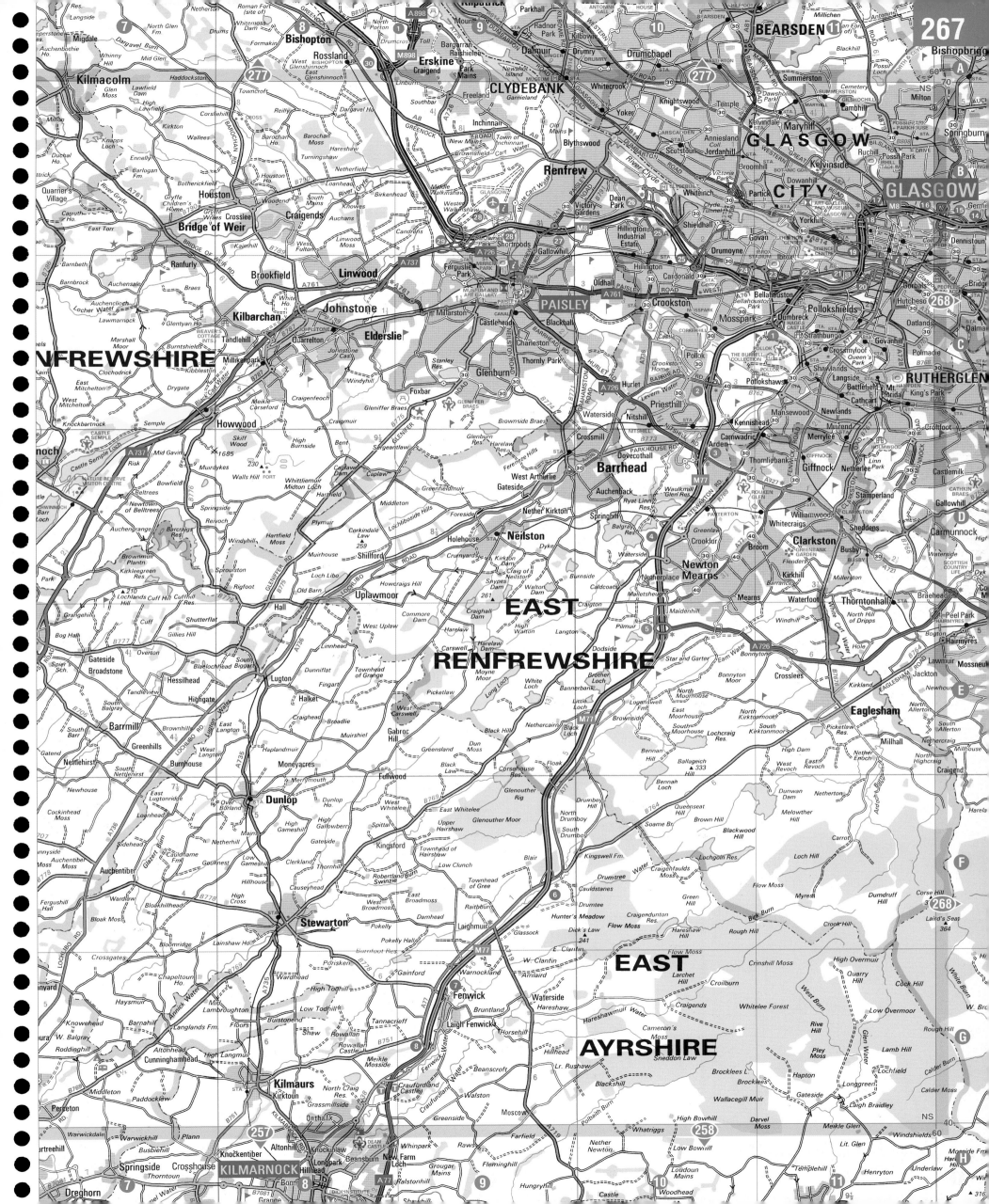

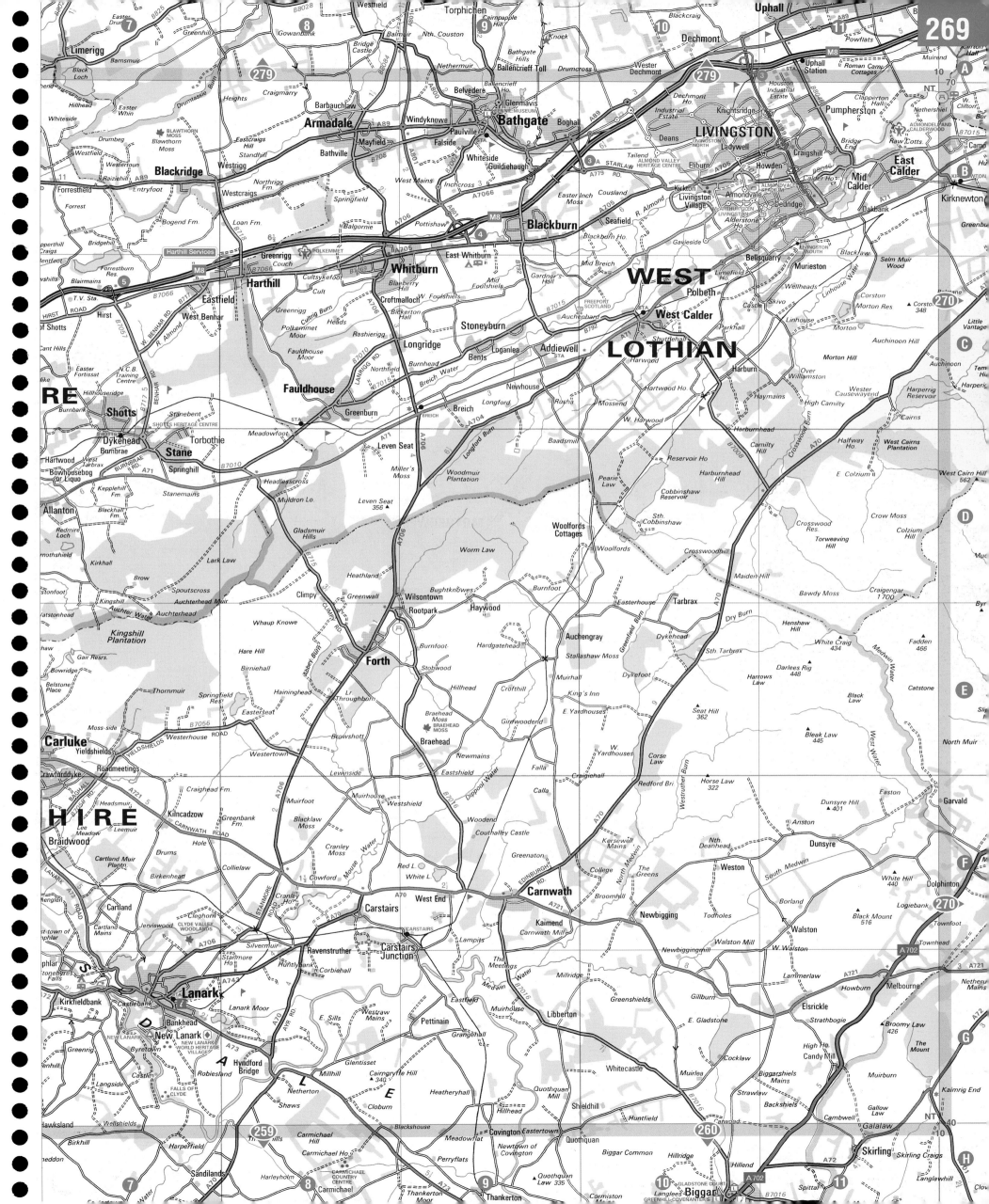

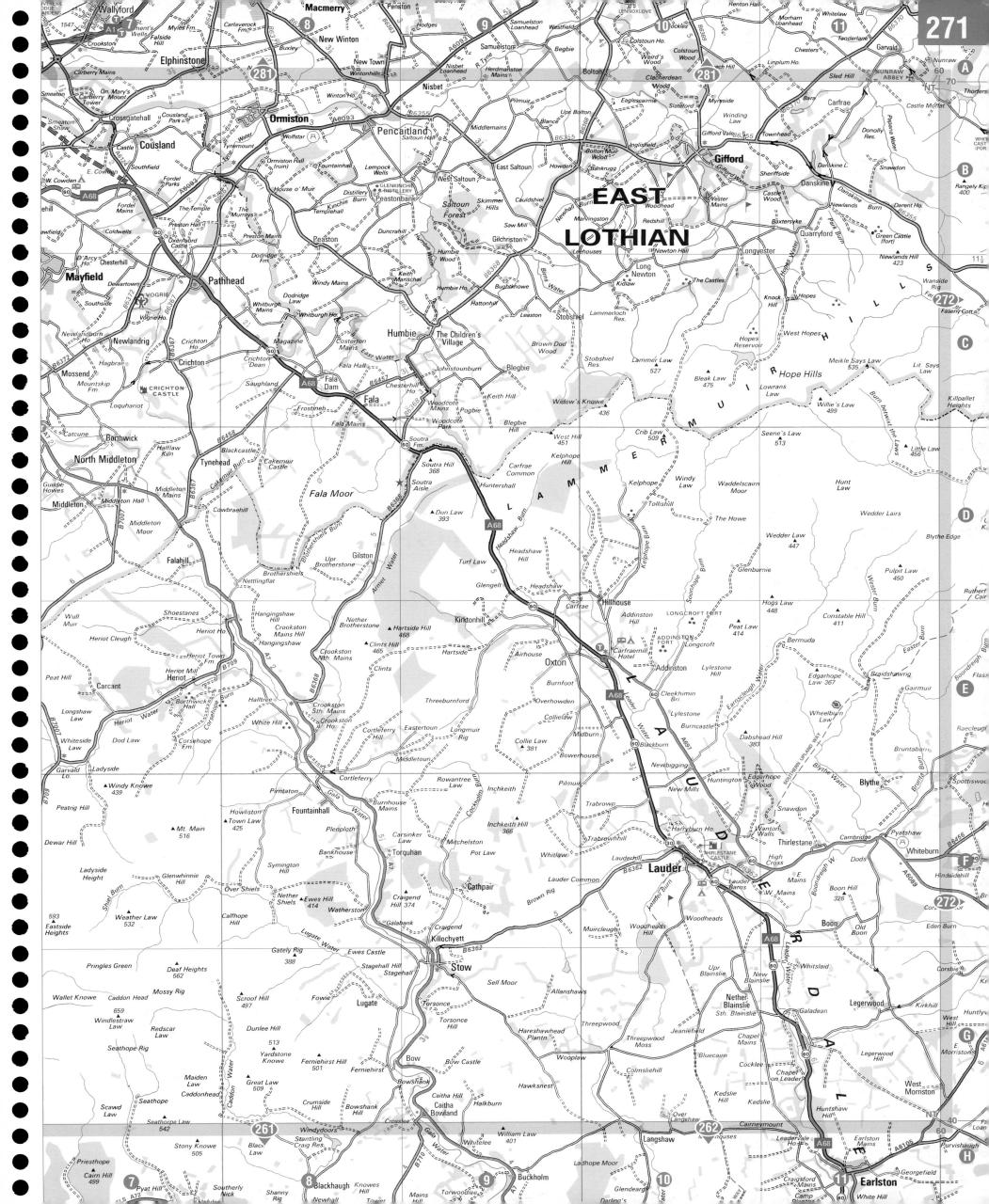

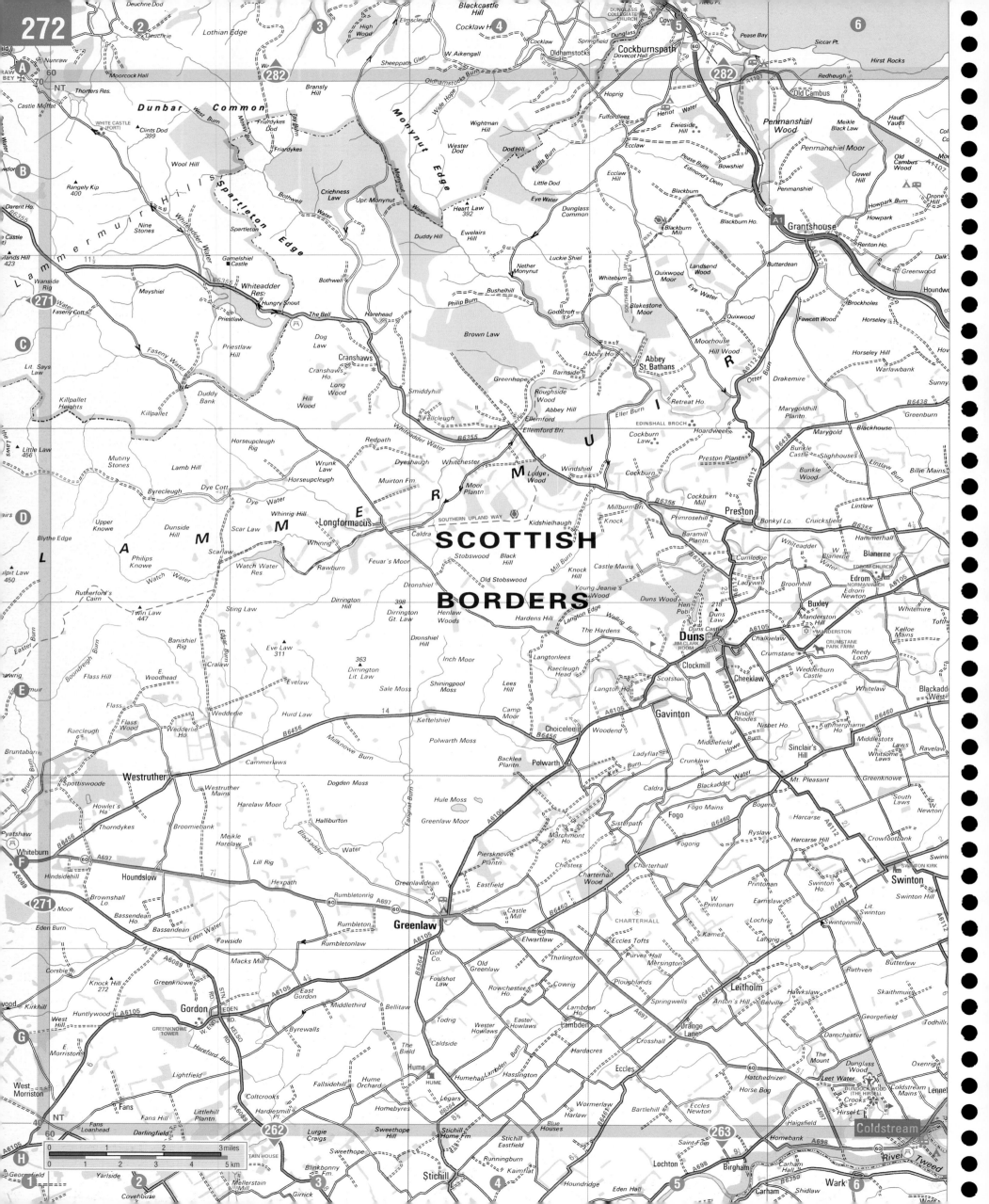

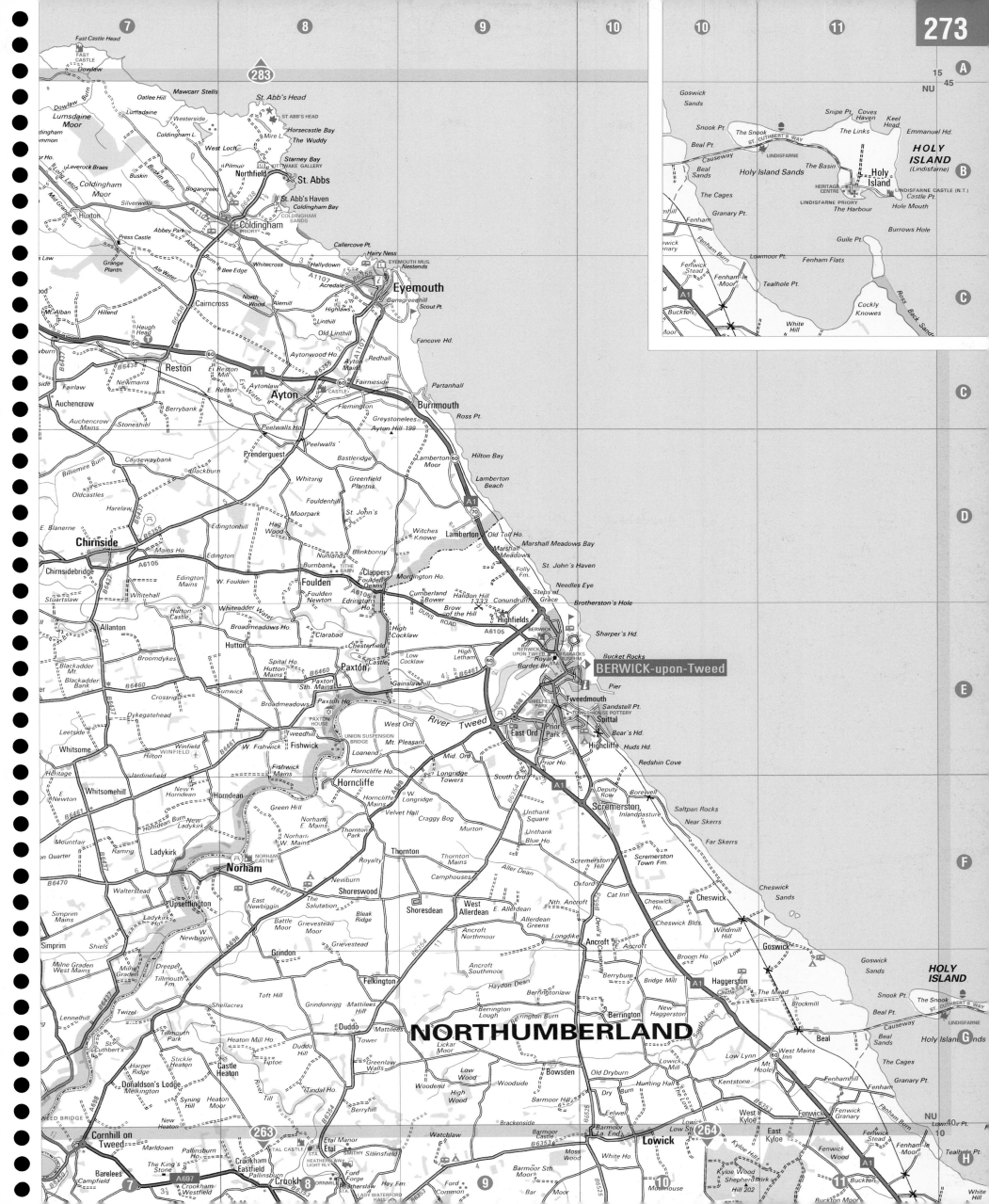

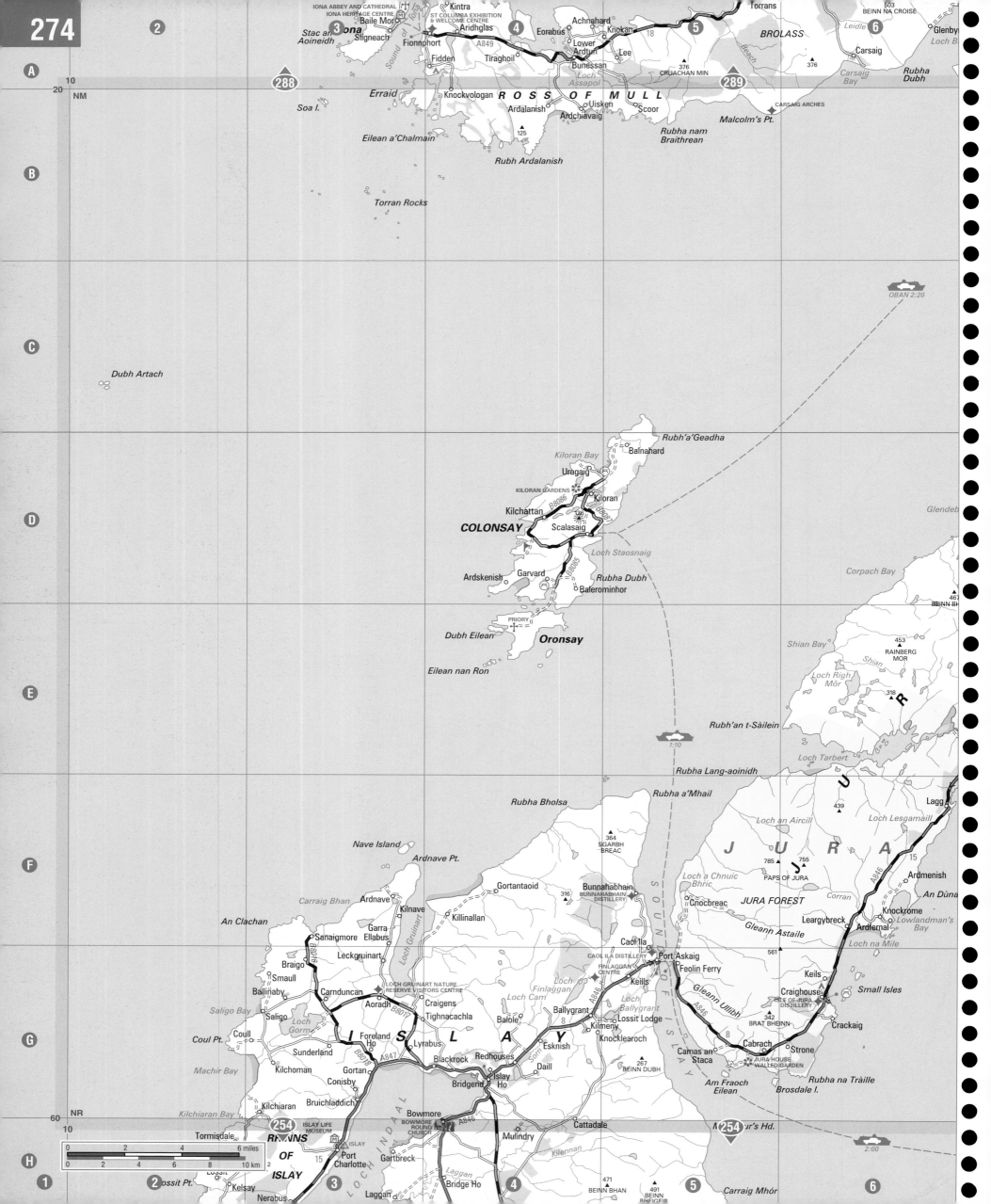

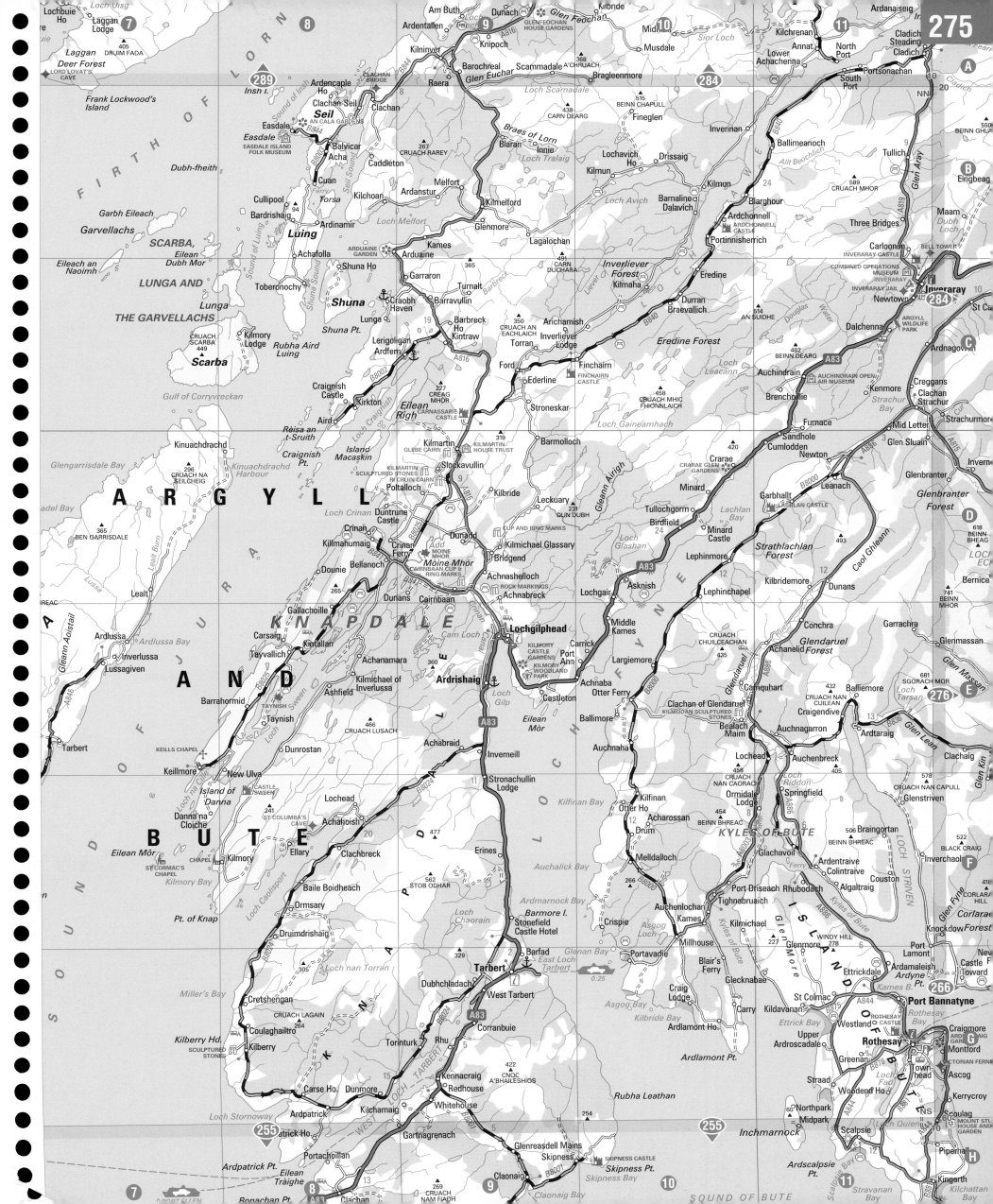

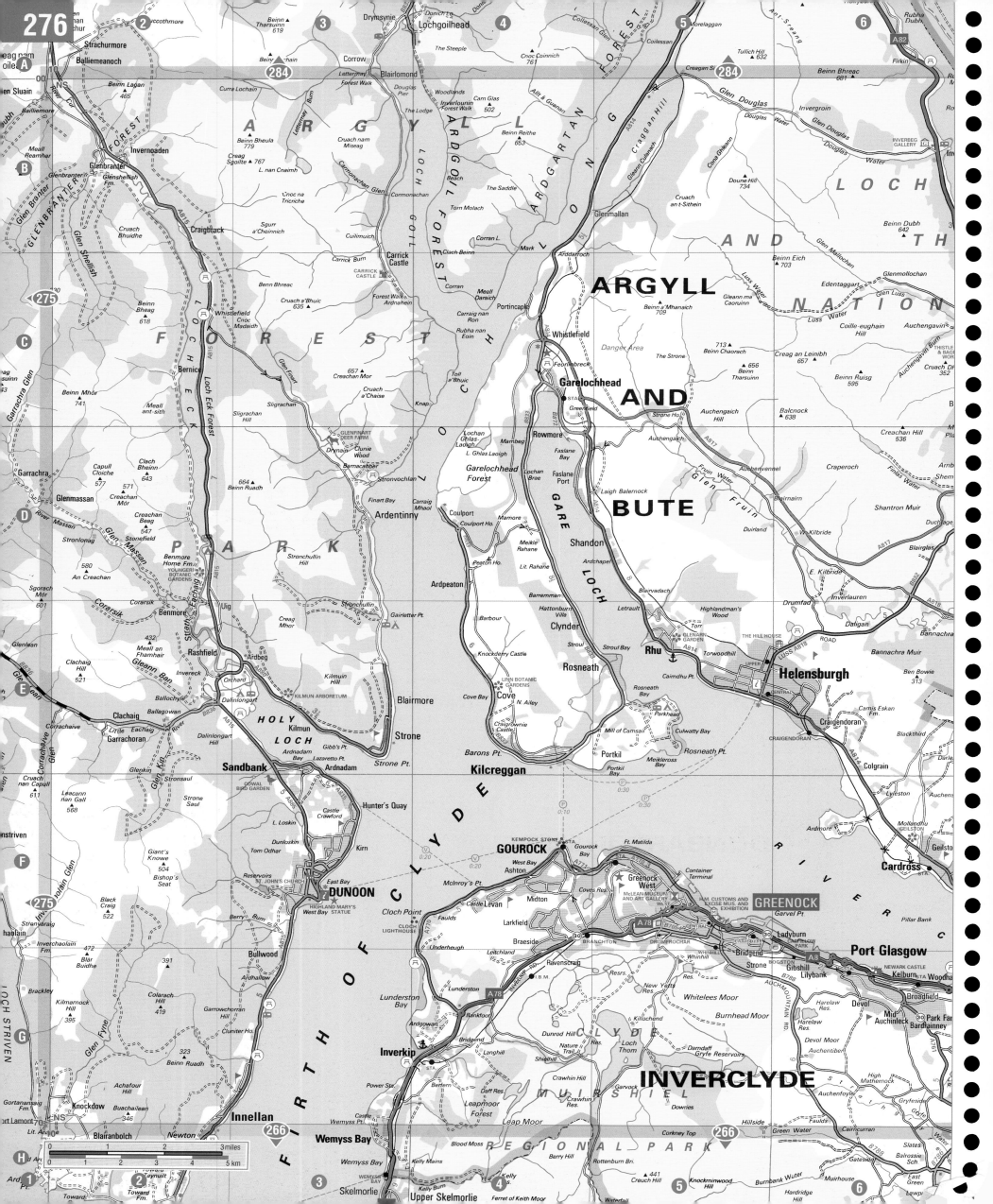

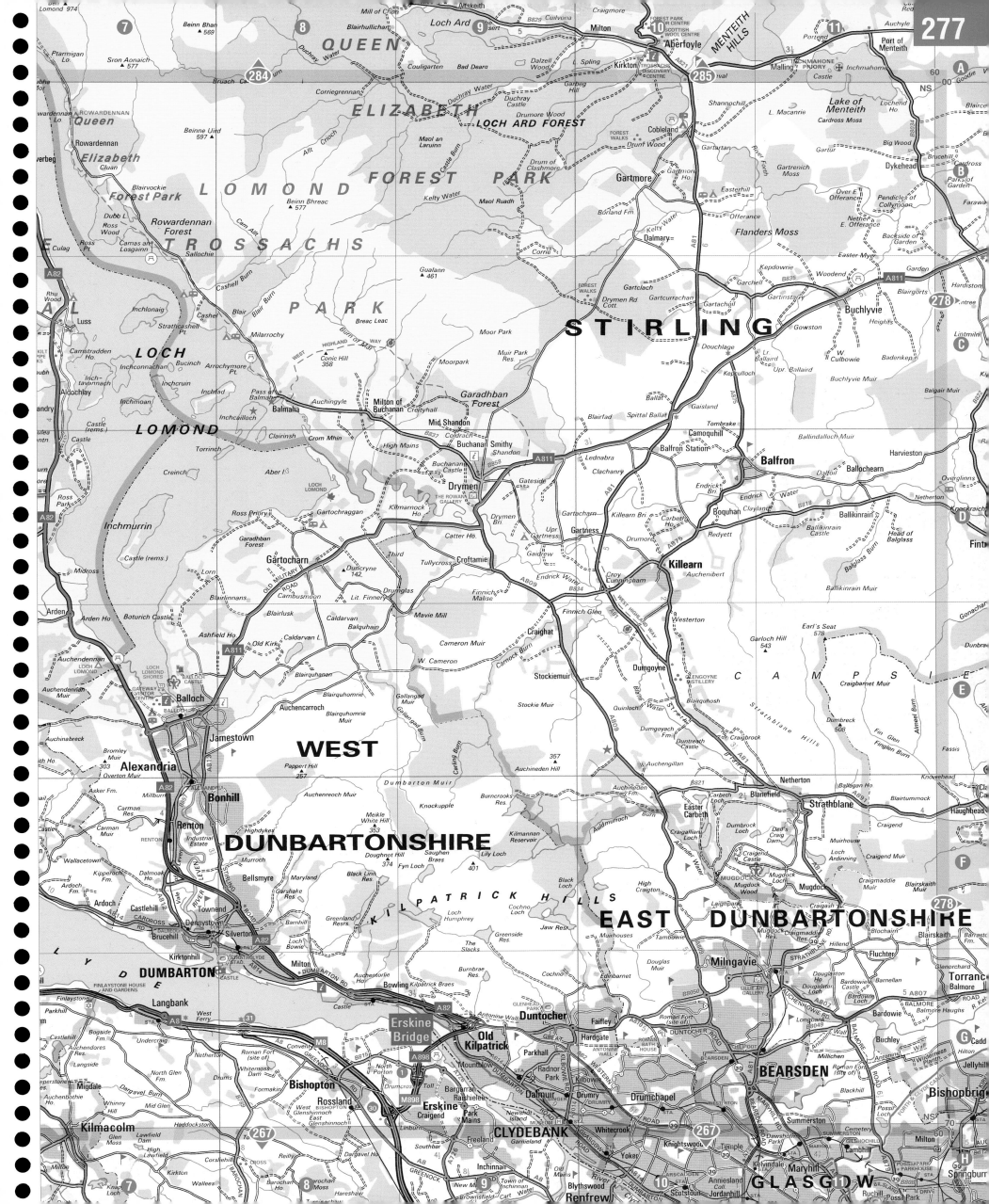

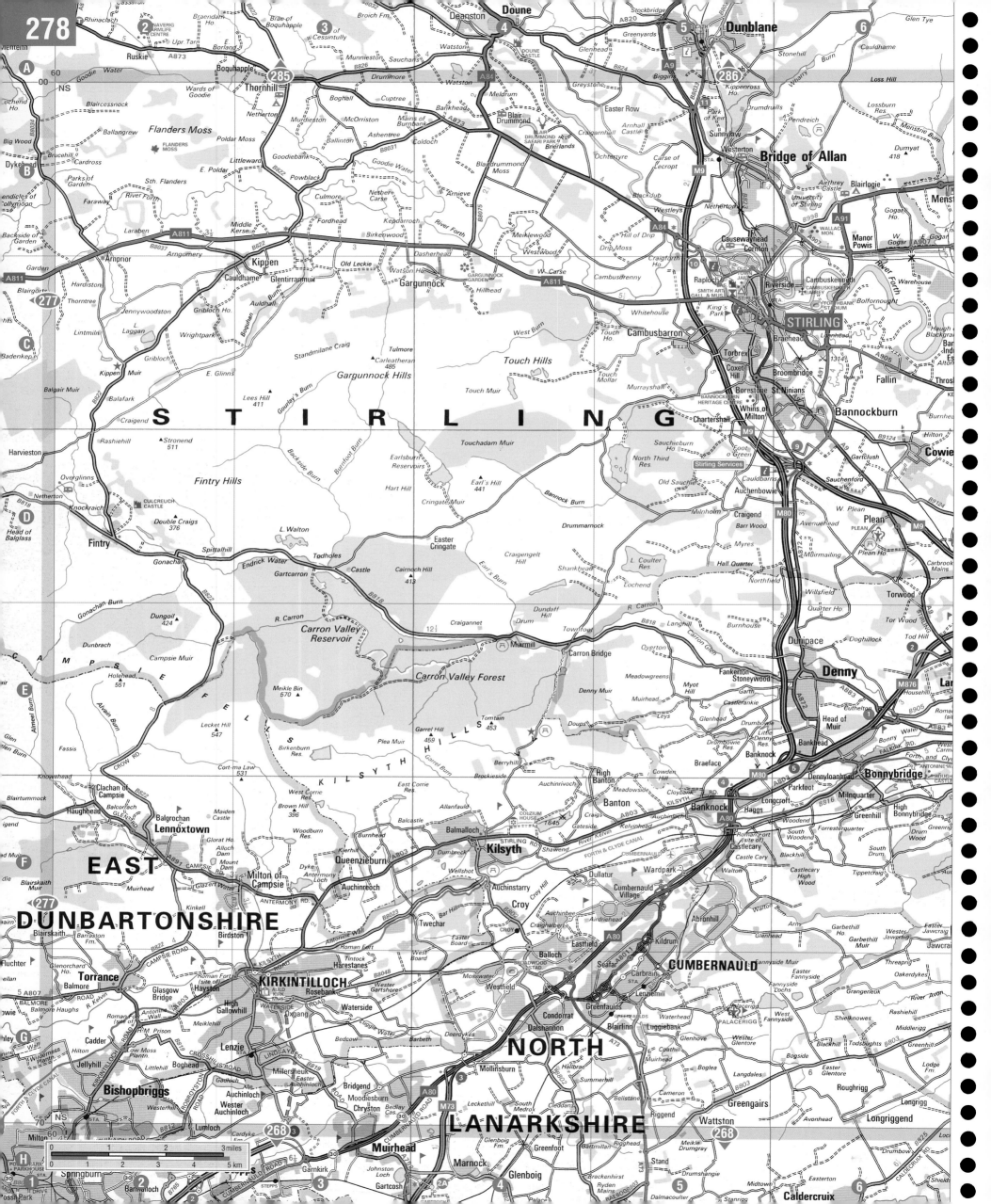

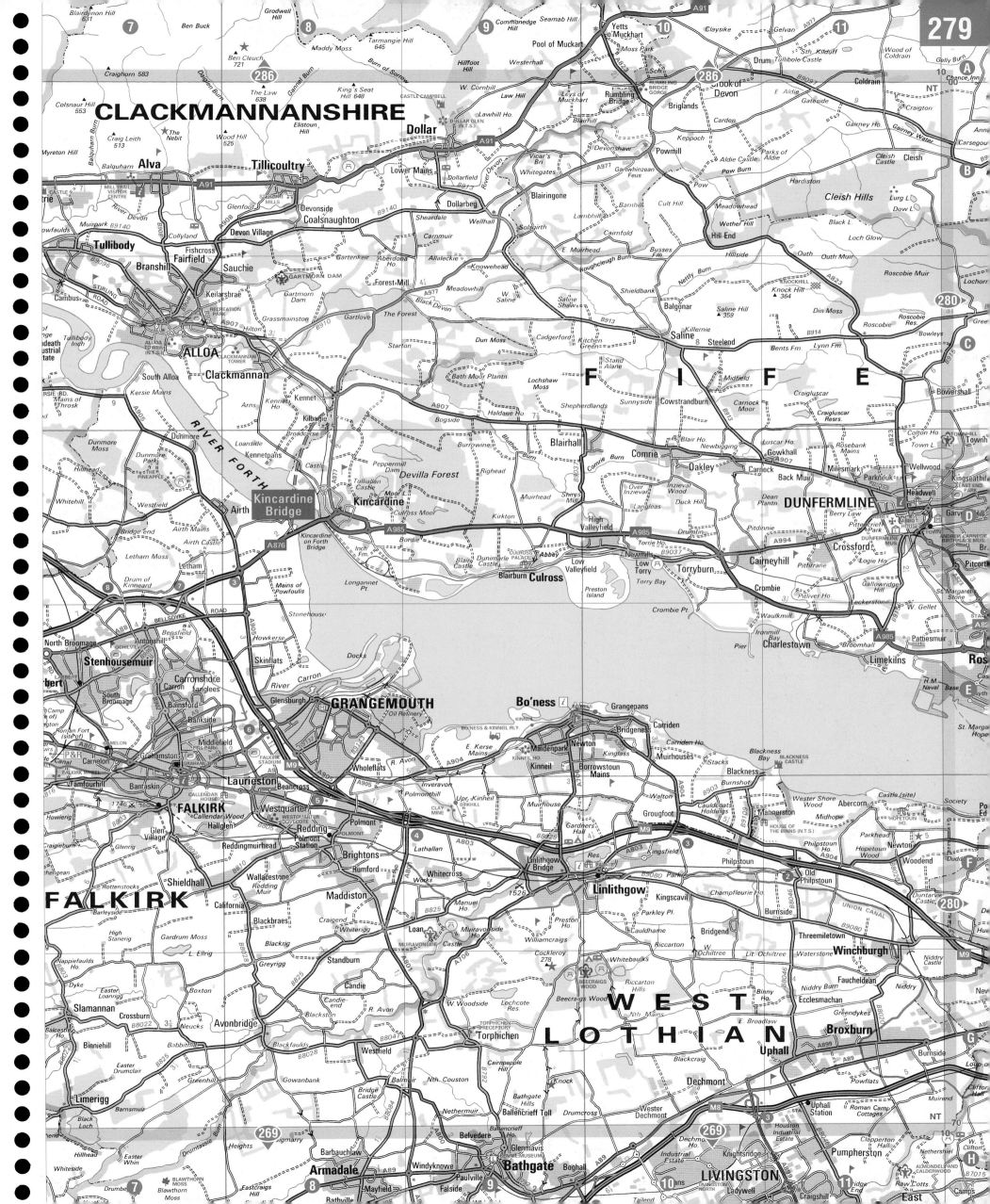

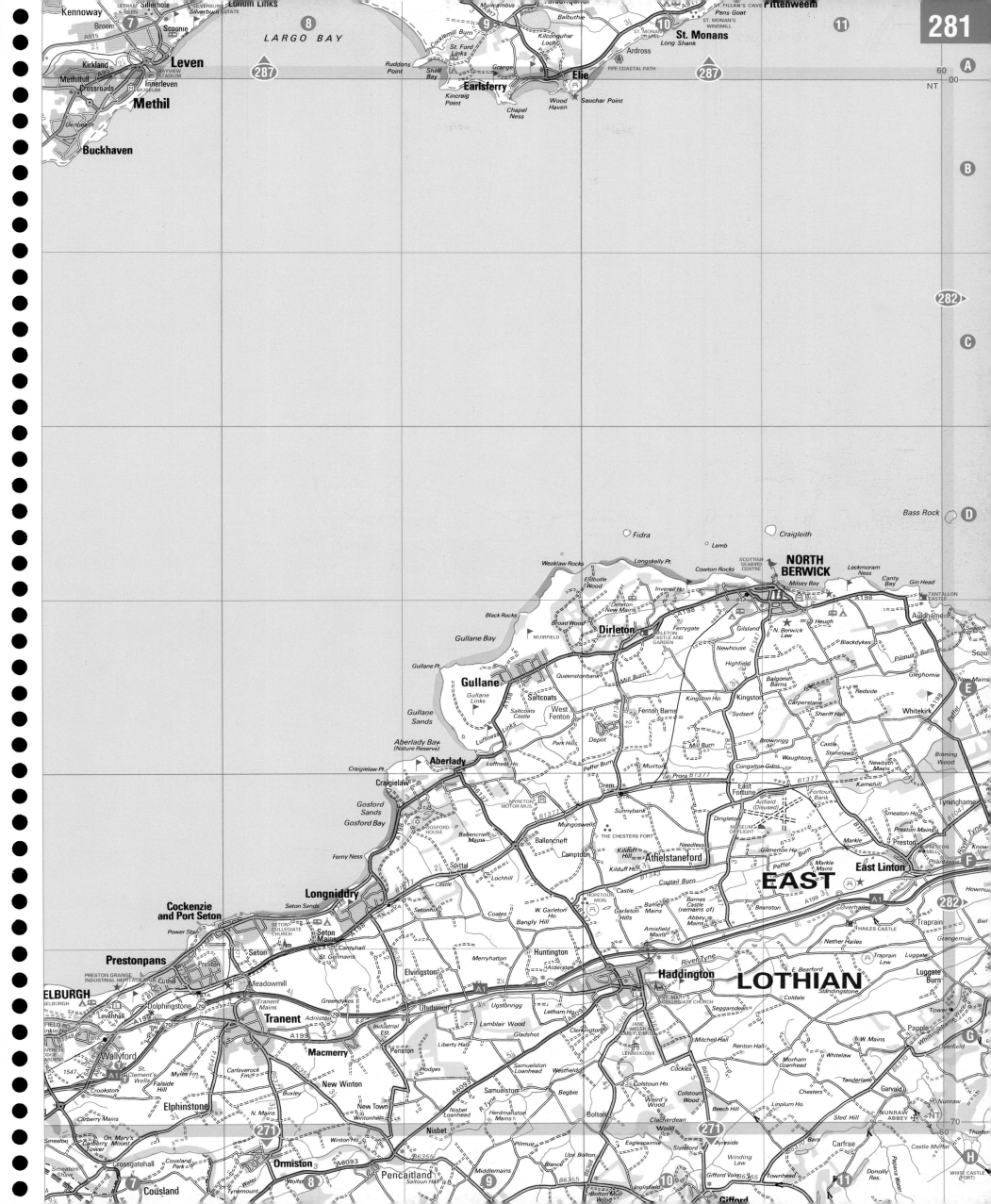

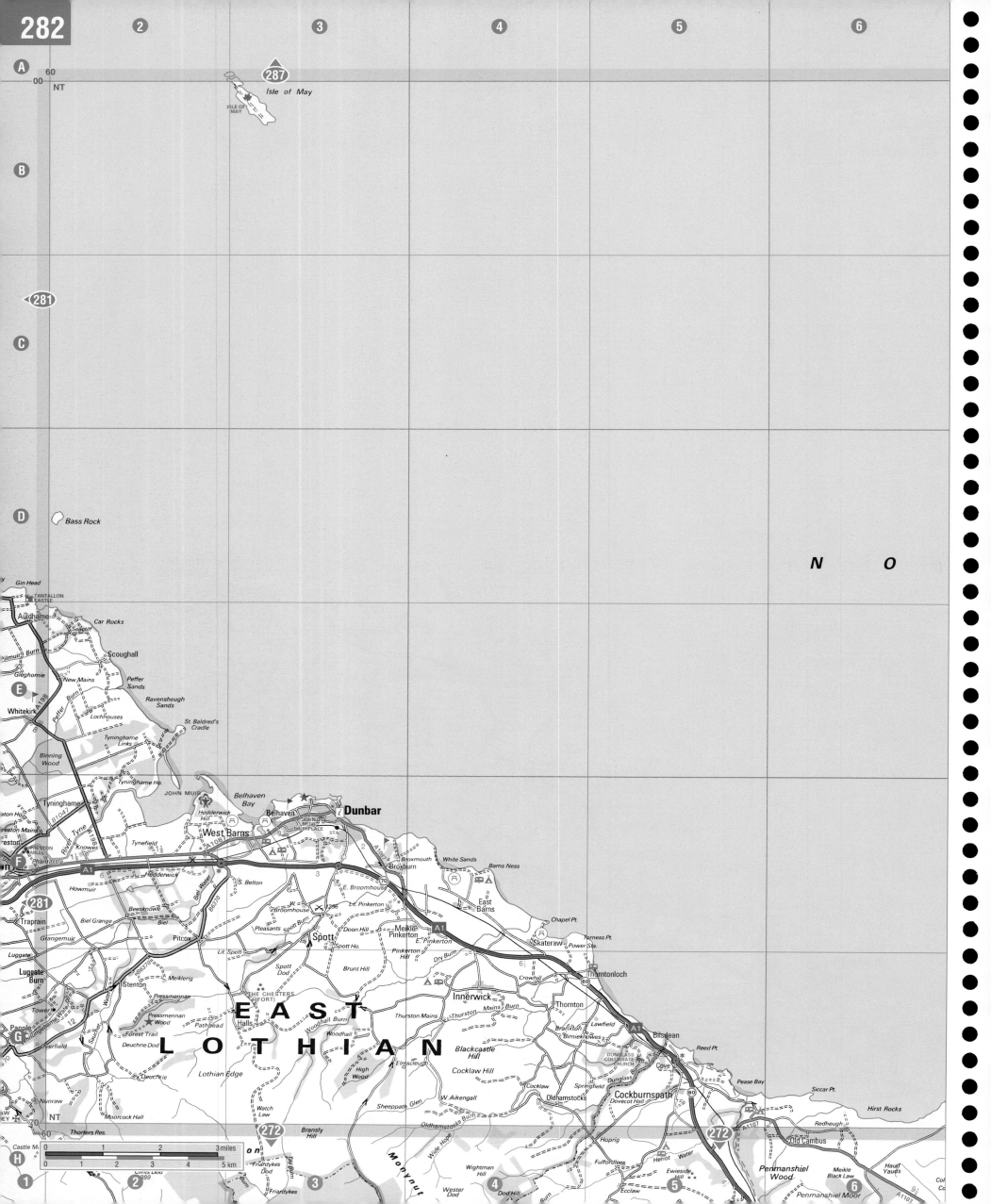

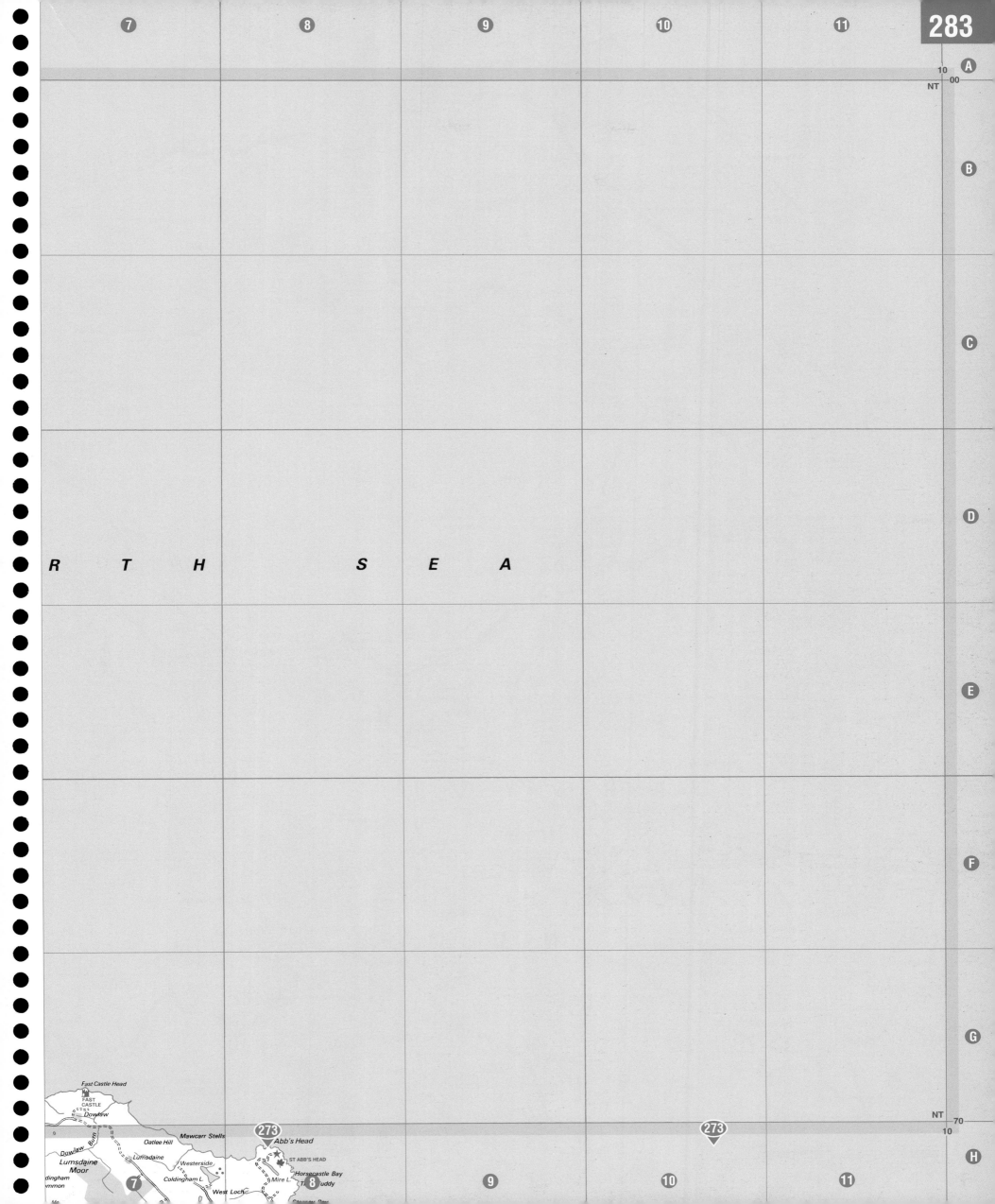

A
10
NT 00

B

C

D

R   T   H   S   E   A

E

F

G

Fast Castle Head
FAST
CASTLE
Dowlaw

NT 70
10

Mawcarr Stells
273 Abb's Head
ST ABB'S HEAD
273

Dowlaw Burn
Oatlee Hill
Lumsdaine
Horsecastle Bay
Lumsdaine
Moor
Westerside
Coldingham L
Mire L
uddy

dingham
mmon
West Loch

H

7 8 9 10 11

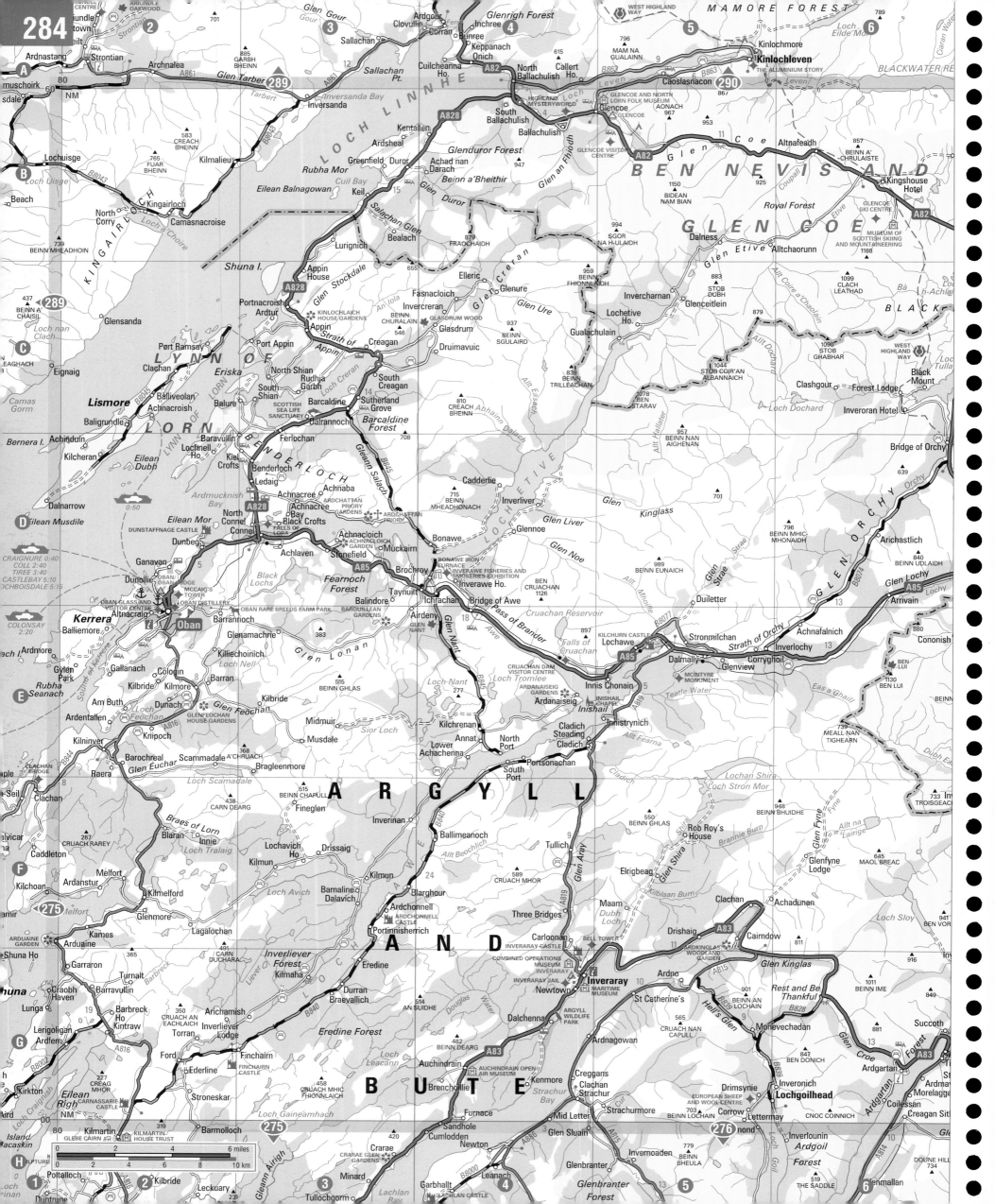

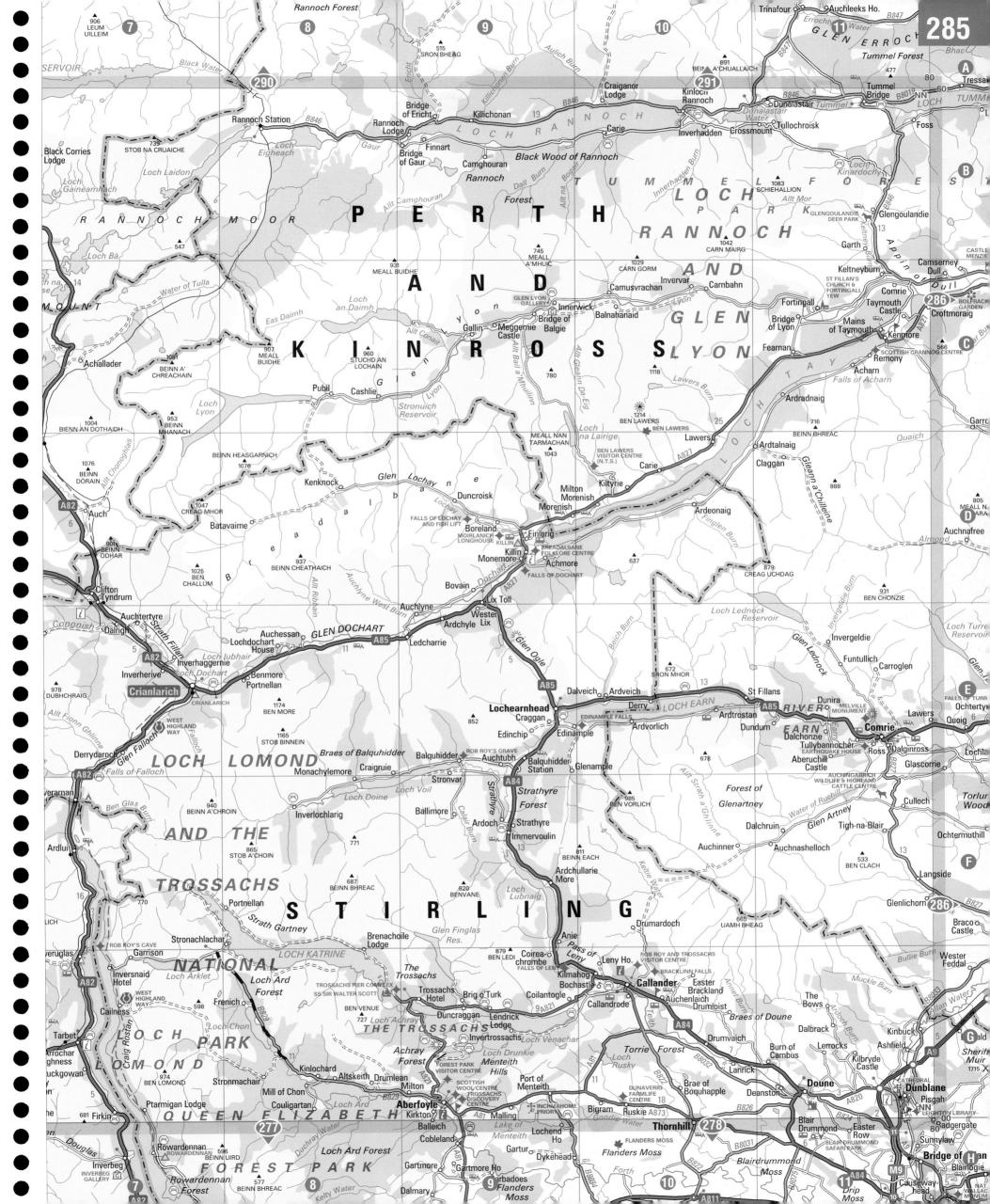

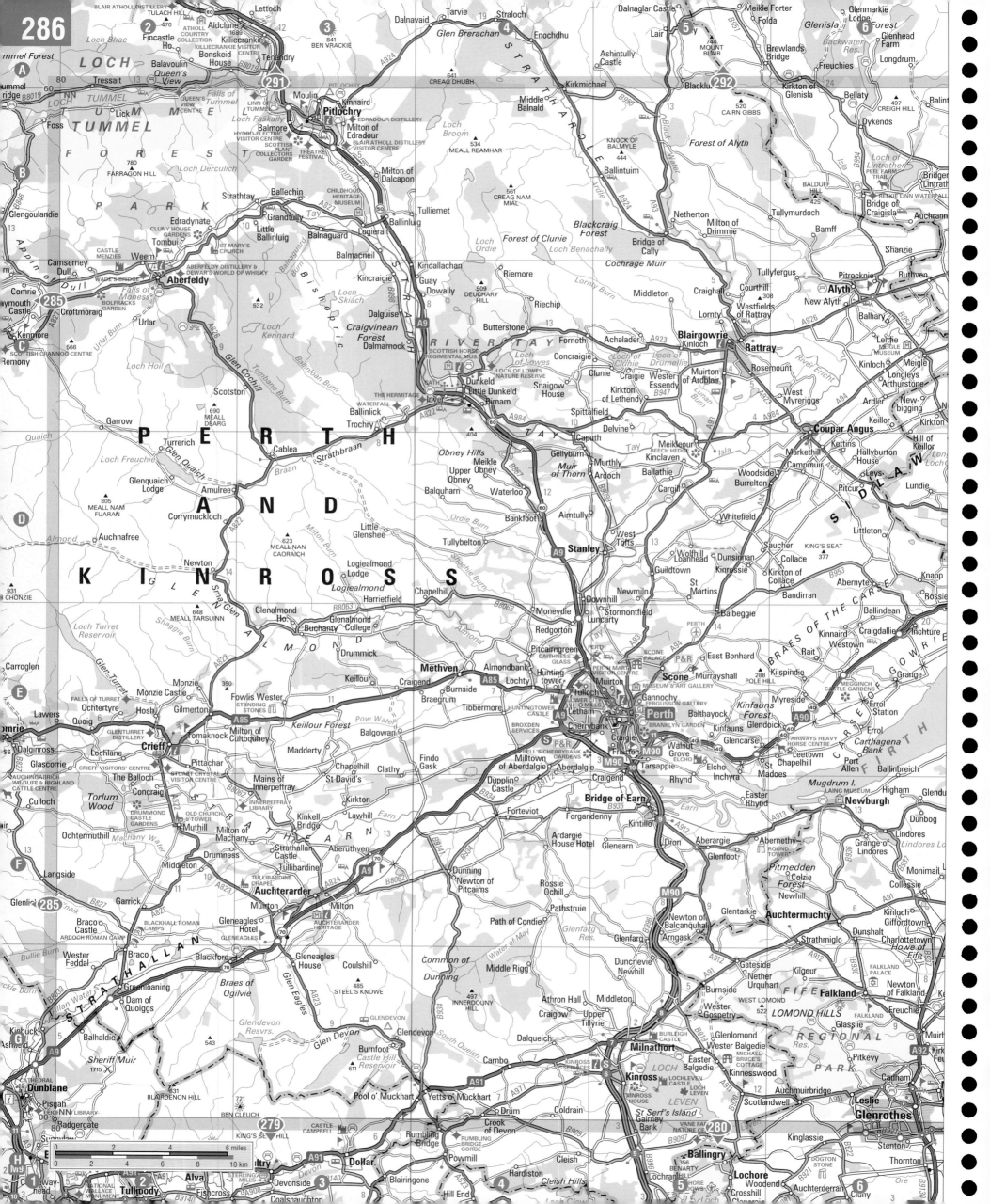

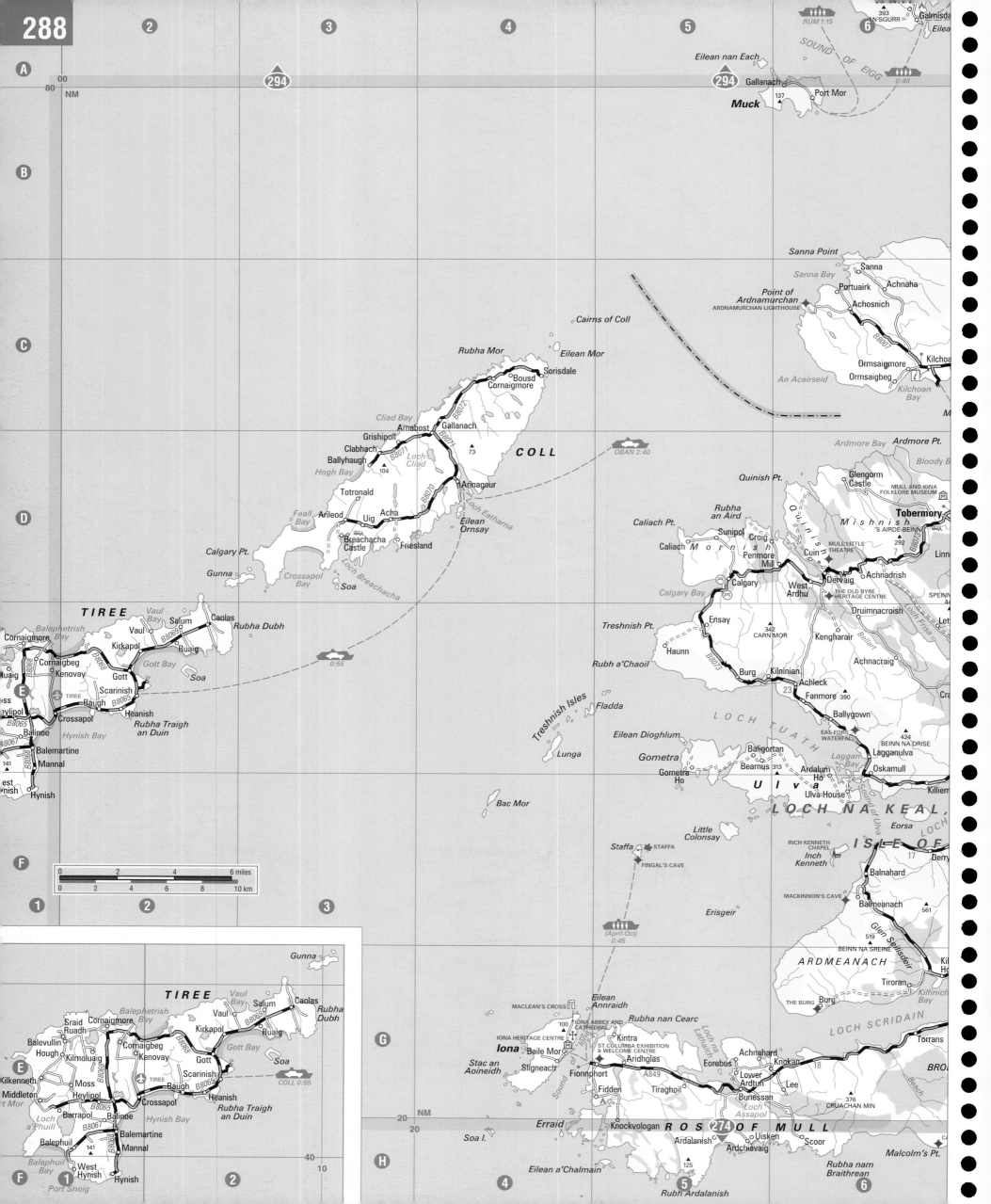

A

294
00
80 NM

Muck
Eilean nan Each
Gallanach
Port Mor
137

B

Sanna Point
Sanna
Sanna Bay
Portuairk
Achnaha
Point of
Ardnamurchan
ARDNAMURCHAN LIGHTHOUSE
Achosnich
Ormsaigmore
Ormsaigbeg
An Acairseid
Kilchoan
Kilchoan
Bay

C
Cairns of Coll
Rubha Mor
Eilean Mor
Sorisdale
Bousd
Cornaigmore

Clad Bay
Arnabost
Gallanach
Grishipoll
Clabhach
73
Ballyhaugh
Loch
Clad
COLL
OBAN 2:40
Ardmore Bay
Ardmore Pt.
Bloody B
Hogh Bay
104
Quinish Pt.
Glengorm
Castle
MULL AND IONA
FOLKLORE MUSEUM

D
Totronald
Arinagour
Tobermory
Mishnish
'S AIRDE-BEINN
292
7
Feall
Bay
Arileod
Uig
Acha
Rubha
an Aird
Sunipol
Croig
Penmore
Mill
Cuin
MULL LITTLE
THEATRE
Achnadrish
Calgary Pt.
Breachacha
Castle
Friesland
Eilean
Ornsay
Caliach Pt.
Caliach
Mornish
Dervaig
West
Ardhu
THE OLD BYRE
HERITAGE CENTRE
SPEINN
Gunna
Crossapol
Bay
Soa
Loch Breachacha
Loch Eatharna
Calgary Bay
Calgary
Druimnacroish
Loch Frisa
Let

TIREE
Vaul
Bay
Salum
Caolas
Rubha Dubh
Ensay
342
CARN MOR
Kengharair
Achnacraig
Cornaigmore
Balephetrish
Bay
Vaul
Kirkapol
Ruaig
Treshnish Pt.
Haunn
Burg
Kilninian
B8073
Achleck
23
Fanmore
390
E
Cornaigbeg
Kenovay
Gott
Scarinish
Soa
Gott Bay
Soa
Rubh a'Choil
Ballygown
Baugh
Heanish
Treshnish Isles
Fladda
0:55
Ballygown
EAS FORS
WATERFALL
424
BEINN NA DRISE
Laggan
Bay
Lagganulva
Crossapol
Rubha Traigh
an Duin
Lunga
Eilean Dioghlum
LOCH TUATH
Oskamull
Balinoe
Hynish Bay
Gometra
Baligortan
Bearnus
313
Ardalum
Ho
Uiva
Killiem
Balemartine
141
Mannal
Gometra
Ho
Ulva
House
LOCH NA KEAL
Hynish
Bac Mor
Little
Colonsay
INCH KENNETH
CHAPEL
Inch
Kenneth
Eorsa
ISLE OF
Derr
17

F
0   2   4   6 miles
0   2   4   6   8 10 km
Staffa
STAFFA
Fingal's Cave
FINGAL'S CAVE
Erisgeir
MACKINNON'S CAVE
Balnahard
Balmeanach
561

1   2   3
(April-Oct)
0:45
519
BEINN NA SREINE
ARDMEANACH
Glen Seilisdeir
Tiroran
Kil
Ho

G
Gunna
TIREE
Vaul
Bay
Salum
Caolas
Rubha
Dubh
MACLEAN'S CROSS
Eilean
Annraidh
Rubha nan Cearc
THE BURG
Burg
Sraid
Ruadh
Cornaigmore
Kirkapol
Ruaig
IONA HERITAGE CENTRE
IONA ABBEY AND
CATHEDRAL
100
Kintra
ST COLUMBA EXHIBITION
& WELCOME CENTRE
Loch
Scridain
Balevullin
Hough
Kilmoluaig
Cornaigbeg
Kenovay
Gott
Scarinish
Soa
Iona
Baile Mor
Stac an
Aoineidh
Stigneach
Aridhglas
Achnahard
Knokan
18
Kilkenneth
Middleton
Moss
Heylipol
TIREE
Baugh
Heanish
COLL 0:55
Fionnphort
Eorabus
Lower
Ardtun
Lee
Barrapol
Balinoe
Rubha Traigh
an Duin
Fidden
Tiraghoil
A849
Bunessan
376
CRUACHAN MIN
Balephuil
Balemartine
Mannal
141
Hynish Bay
20 NM
20
Erraid
Knockvologan
ROS
OF MULL
274
F
West
Hynish
Hynish
Soa I.
Eilean a'Chalmain
Ardalanish
Uisken
Scoor
Ardchiavaig
Rubha nam
Braithrean
Balephuil
Bay
Port Snoig
40
10
Rubh Ardalanish
Malcolm's Pt.

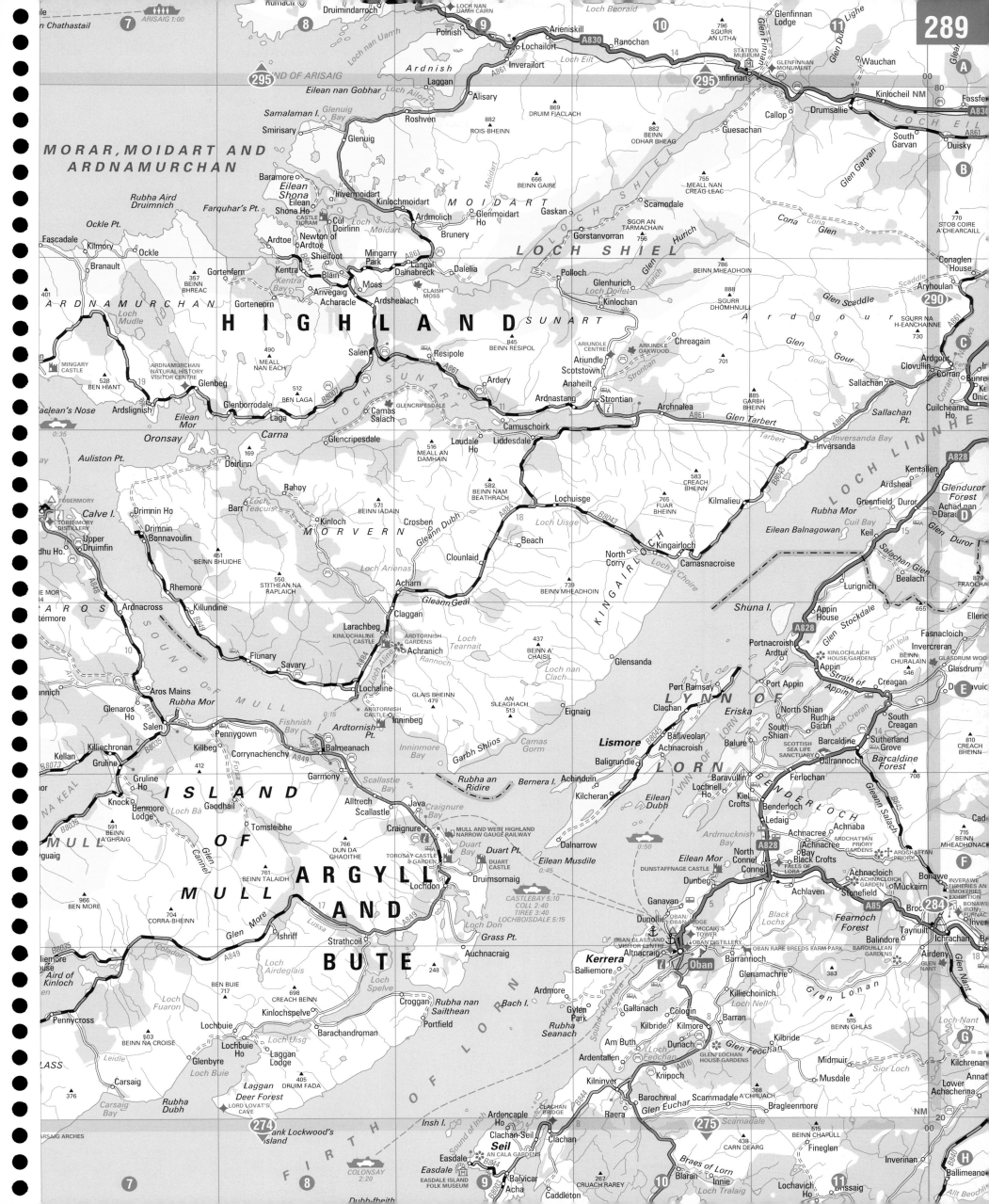

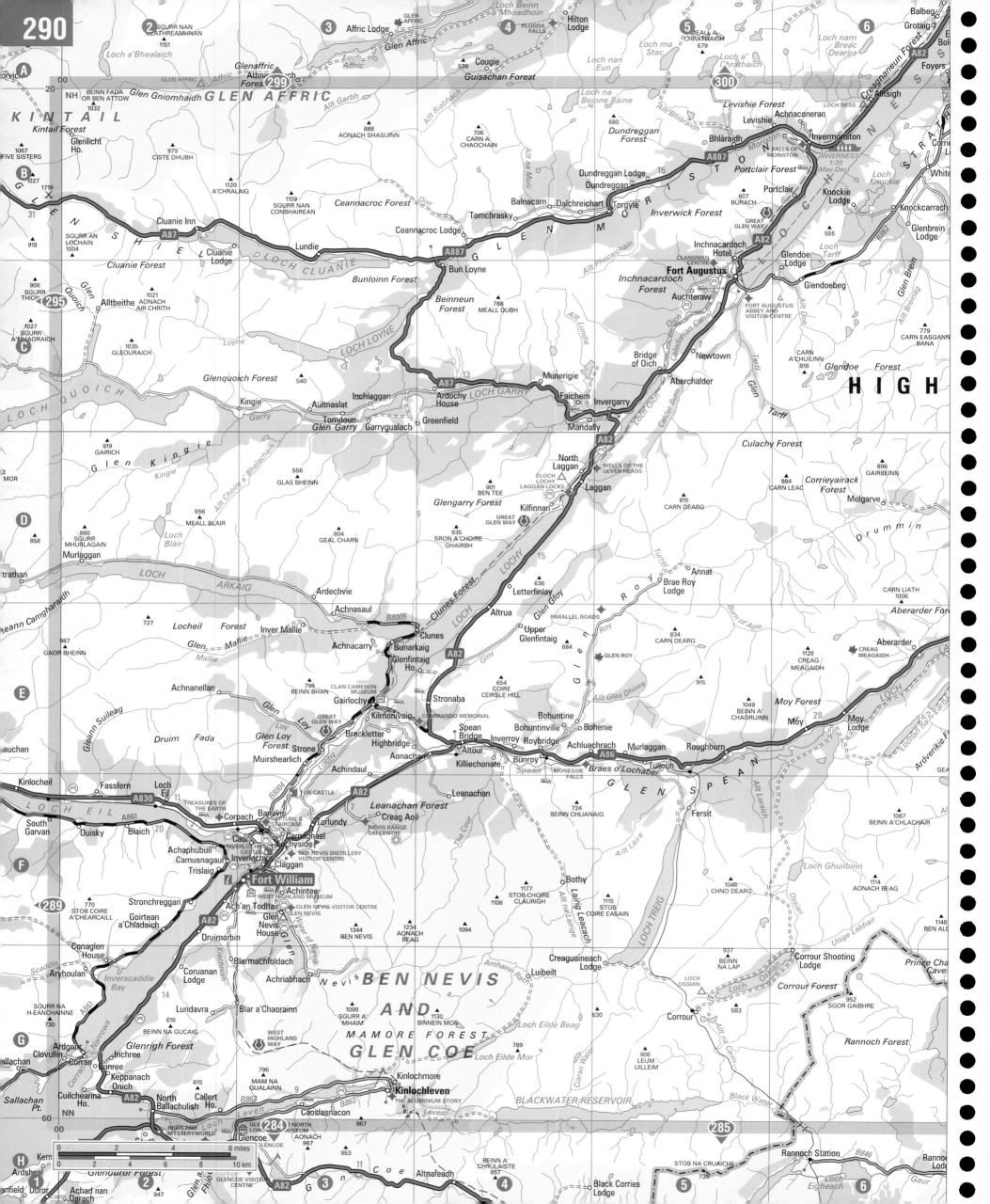

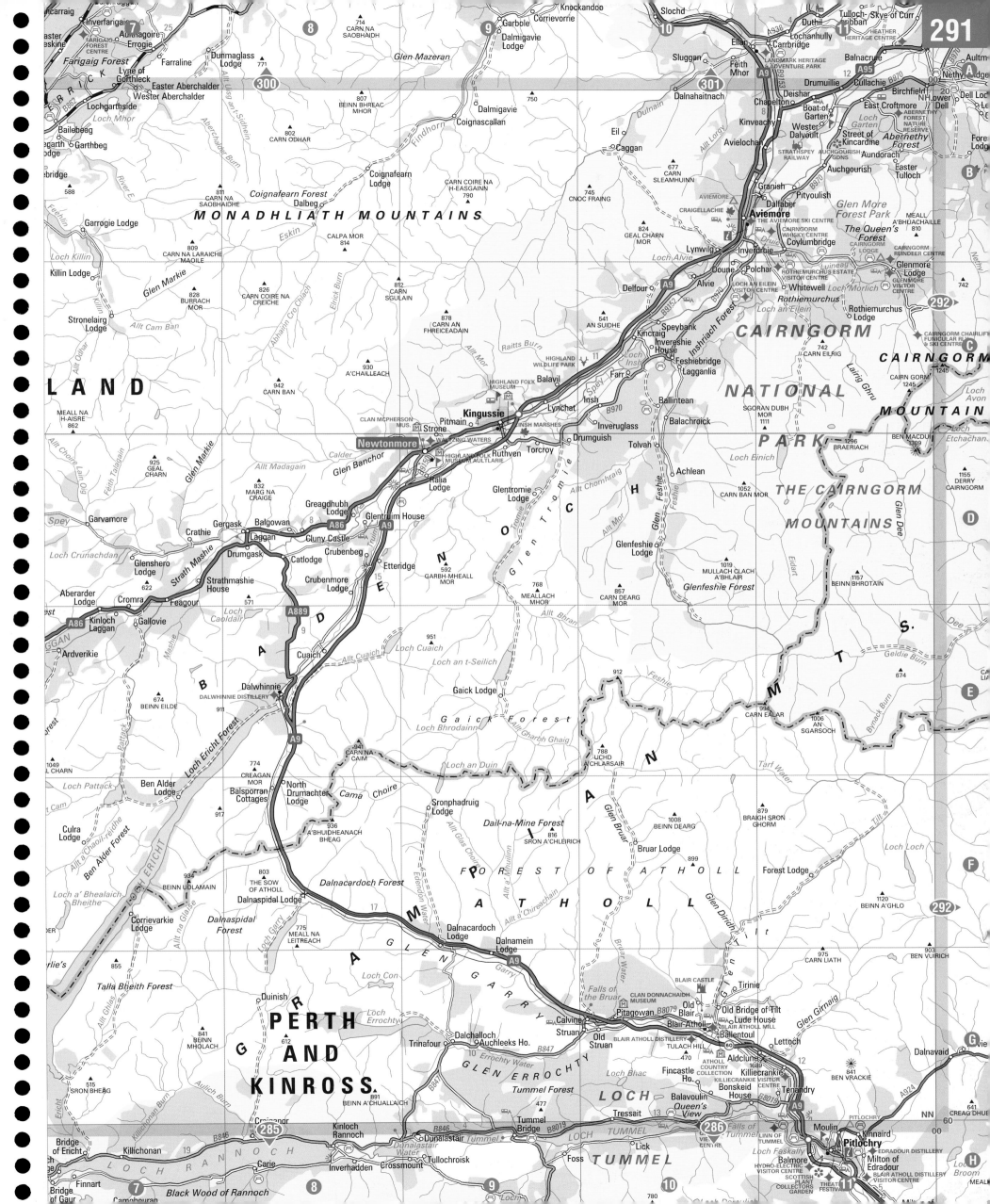

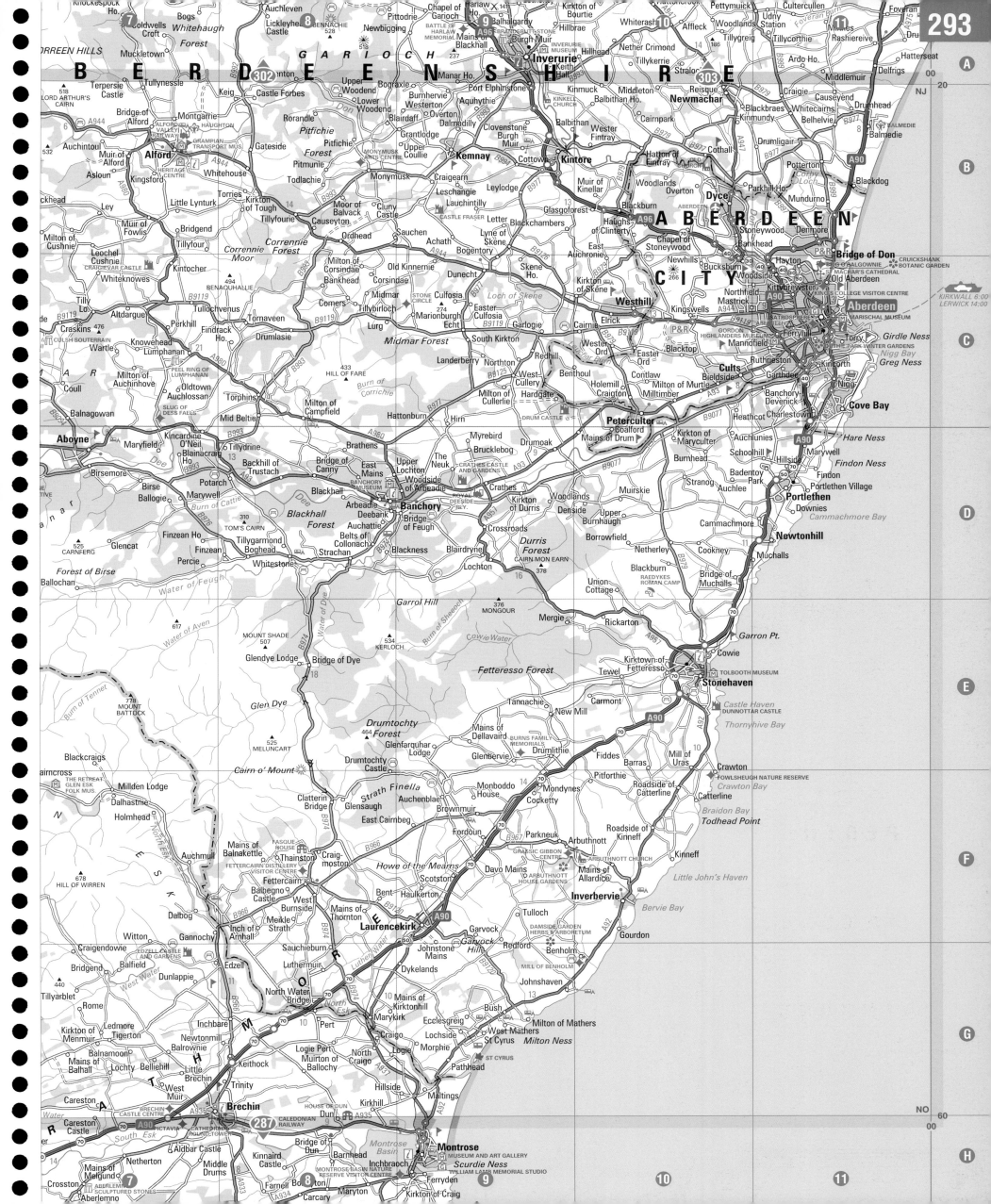

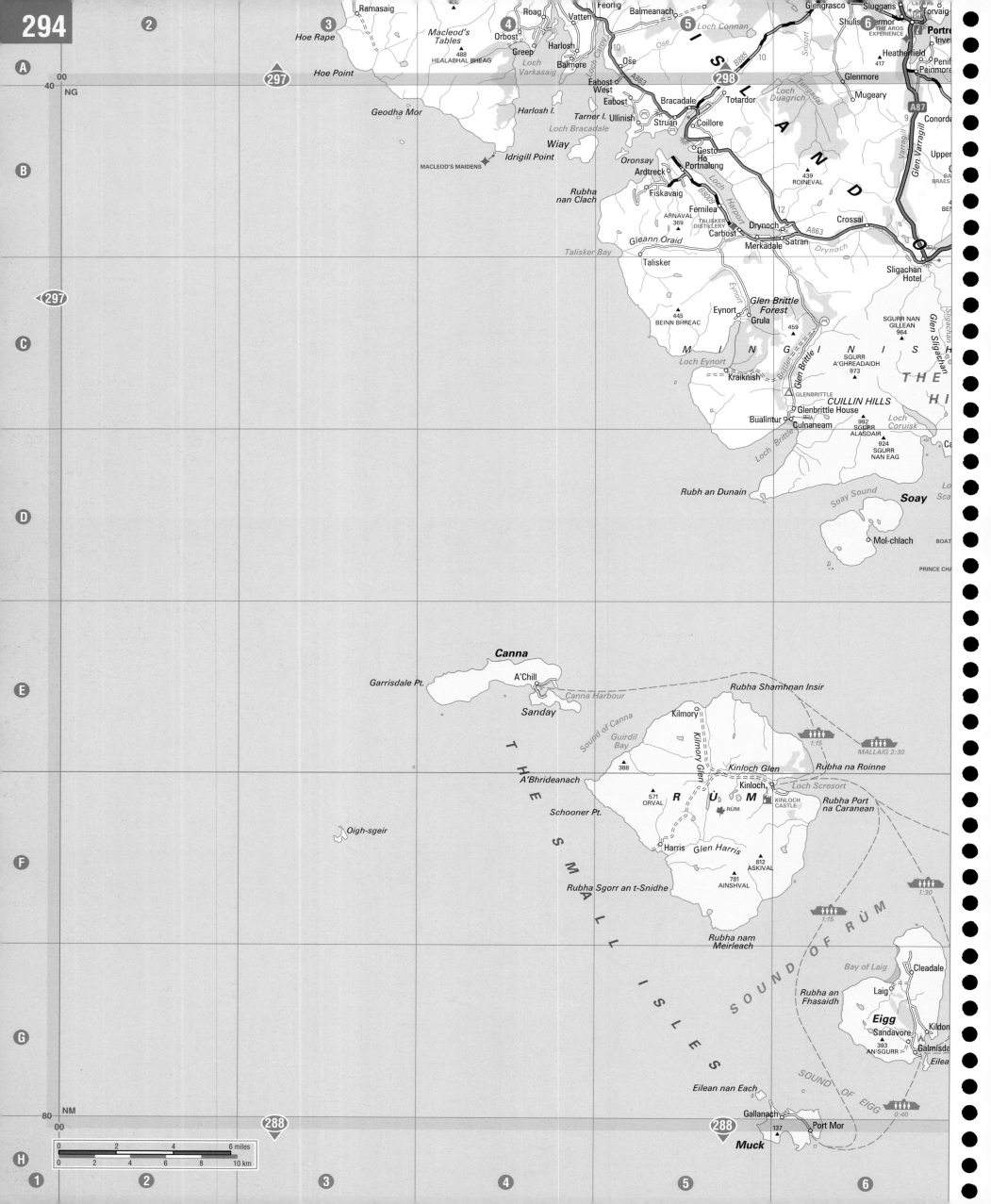

Ramasaig
Roag
Vatten
Feorlig
Balmeanach
Glengrasco
Sluggans
Torvaig
Portre

Hoe Rape
Macleod's Tables
Orbost
Greep
Harlosh
Orbost
Loch Connan
Shulis
THE AROS EXPERIENCE
Inver

488 HEALABHAL BHEAG
Loch Caroy
Ose
Ose
Heatherfield
417
Penif
Peinmore

A
00
40
Hoe Point
Eabost West
Bracadale
Totardor
Glenmore
Mugeary
A87

NG
297
Hoe Point
298
ISLAND
Loch Duagrich
A87

Geodha Mor
Harlosh I.
Eabost
Tarner I.
Ullinish
Struan
Coillore

Wiay
Loch Bracadale
Gesto
Ho
Portnalong

B
MACLEOD'S MAIDENS
Idrigill Point
Oronsay
Ardtreck
439
ROINEVAL
Upper
BRAES

Rubha nan Clach
Fiskavaig
Fernilea
Loch Harport
Crossal

ARNAVAL 369
Drynoch
A863

Talisker Distillery
Carbost
Satran
Drynoch

Talisker Bay
Gleann Oraid
Merkadale
Sligachan Hotel

Talisker
Glen Brittle Forest
Sligachan

C
297
Eynort
Grula
459
SGURR NAN GILLEAN 964
Glen Sligachan

445 BEINN BHREAC
SGURR A'GHREADAIDH 973
THE HI

Loch Eynort
Kraiknish
Glen Brittle
GLENBRITTLE
CUILLIN HILLS

Glenbrittle House
992 SGURR ALASDAIR
Loch Coruisk

Bualintur
Culnaeam
924 SGURR NAN EAG

D
Rubh an Dunain
Soay Sound
Soay
Sca

Mol-chlach
BOAT

PRINCE CHA

Canna

E
Garrisdale Pt.
A'Chill
Rubha Shamhnan Insir

Canna Harbour
Kilmory
1:15
MALLAIG 2:30

Sanday
Sound of Canna
Guirdil Bay
Kilmory Glen
Kinloch Glen
Rubha na Roinne

A'Bhrideanach
388
Kinloch
Loch Scresort

571 ORVAL
R Ü M
KINLOCH CASTLE
Rubha Port na Caranean

Schooner Pt.
RÜM

F
Oigh-sgeir
Harris
Glen Harris
812 ASKIVAL

Rubha Sgorr an t-Snidhe
781 AINSHVAL
1:30

1:15

Rubha nam Meirleach
SOUND OF RÜM

Bay of Laig
Cleadale

Rubha an Fhasaidh
Laig

G
Eigg
Sandavore
393 AN SGURR
Galmisda
Eilea

Eilean nan Each
SOUND OF EIGG

H
80
NM
00
288
288
Gallanach
Port Mor
0:40

137

Muck

0   2   4   6 miles
0   2   4   6   8   10 km

1   2   3   4   5   6

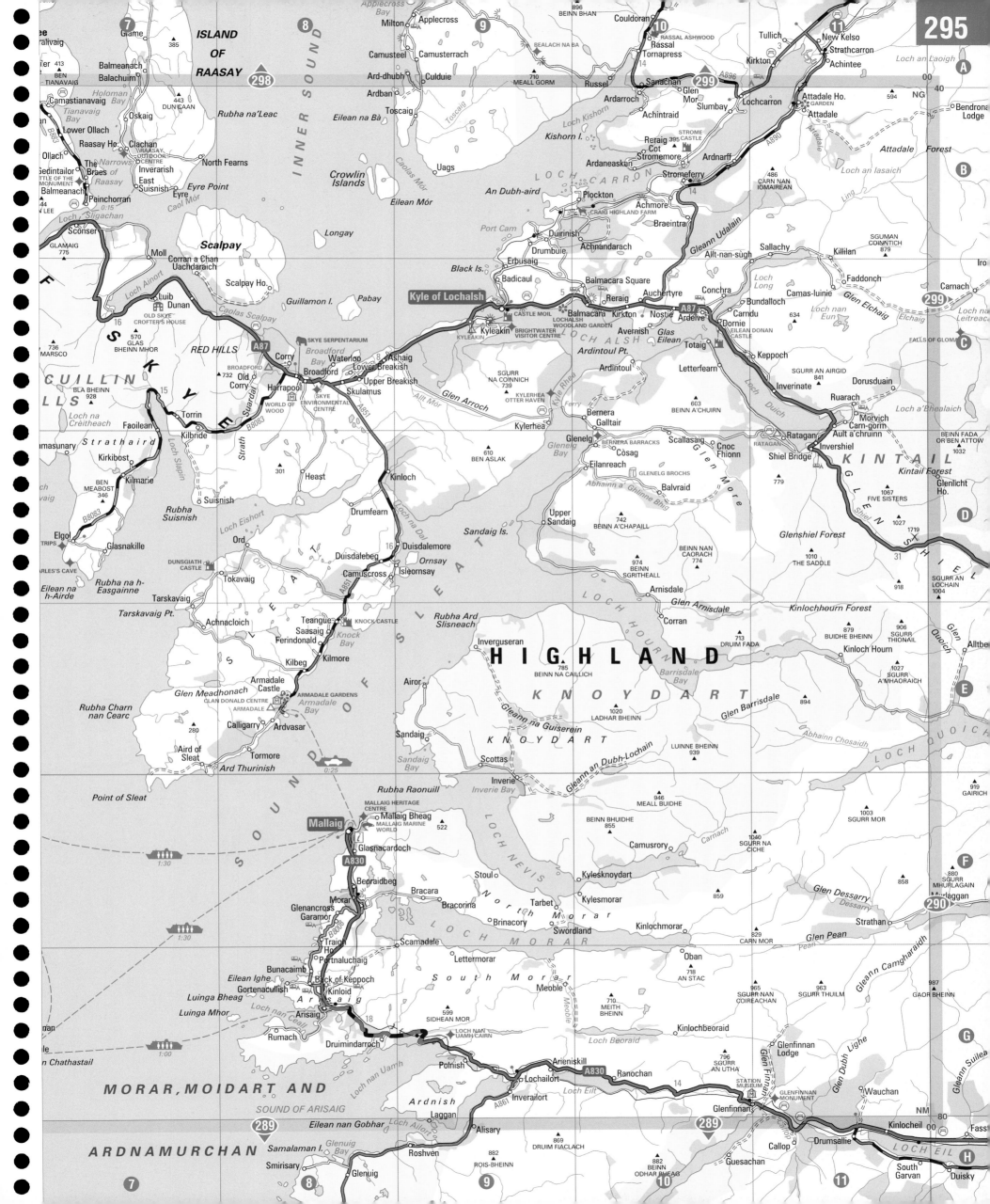

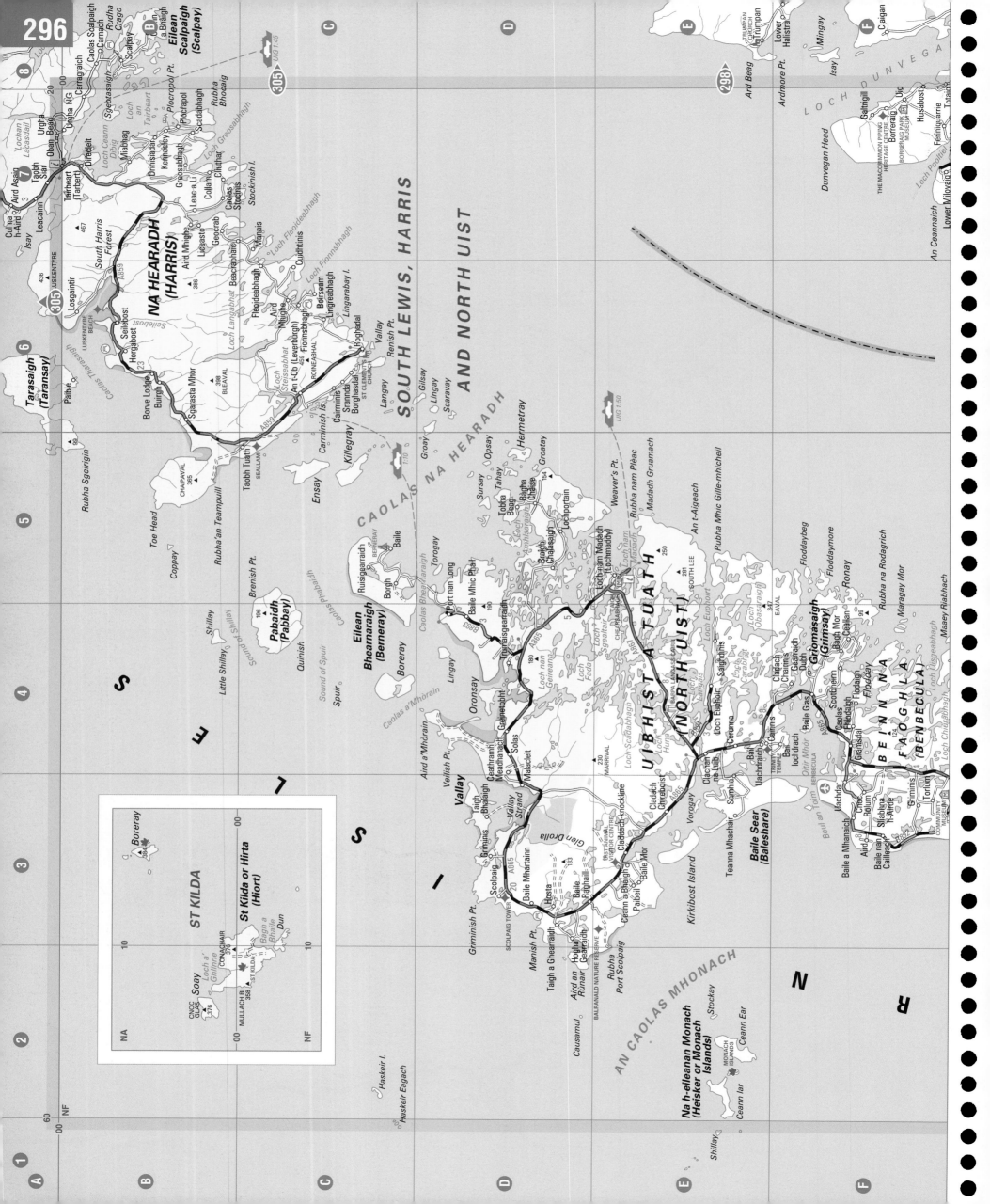

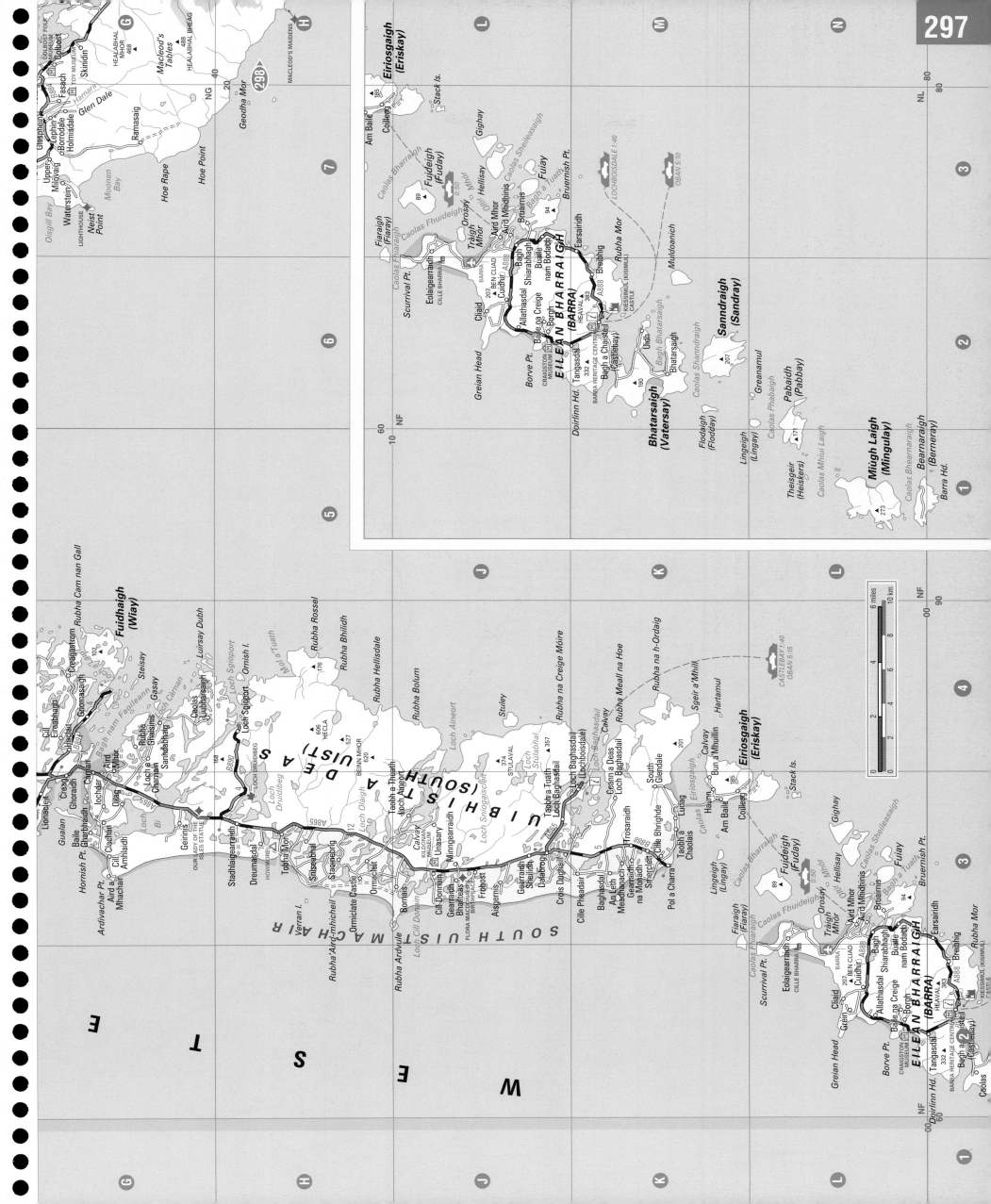

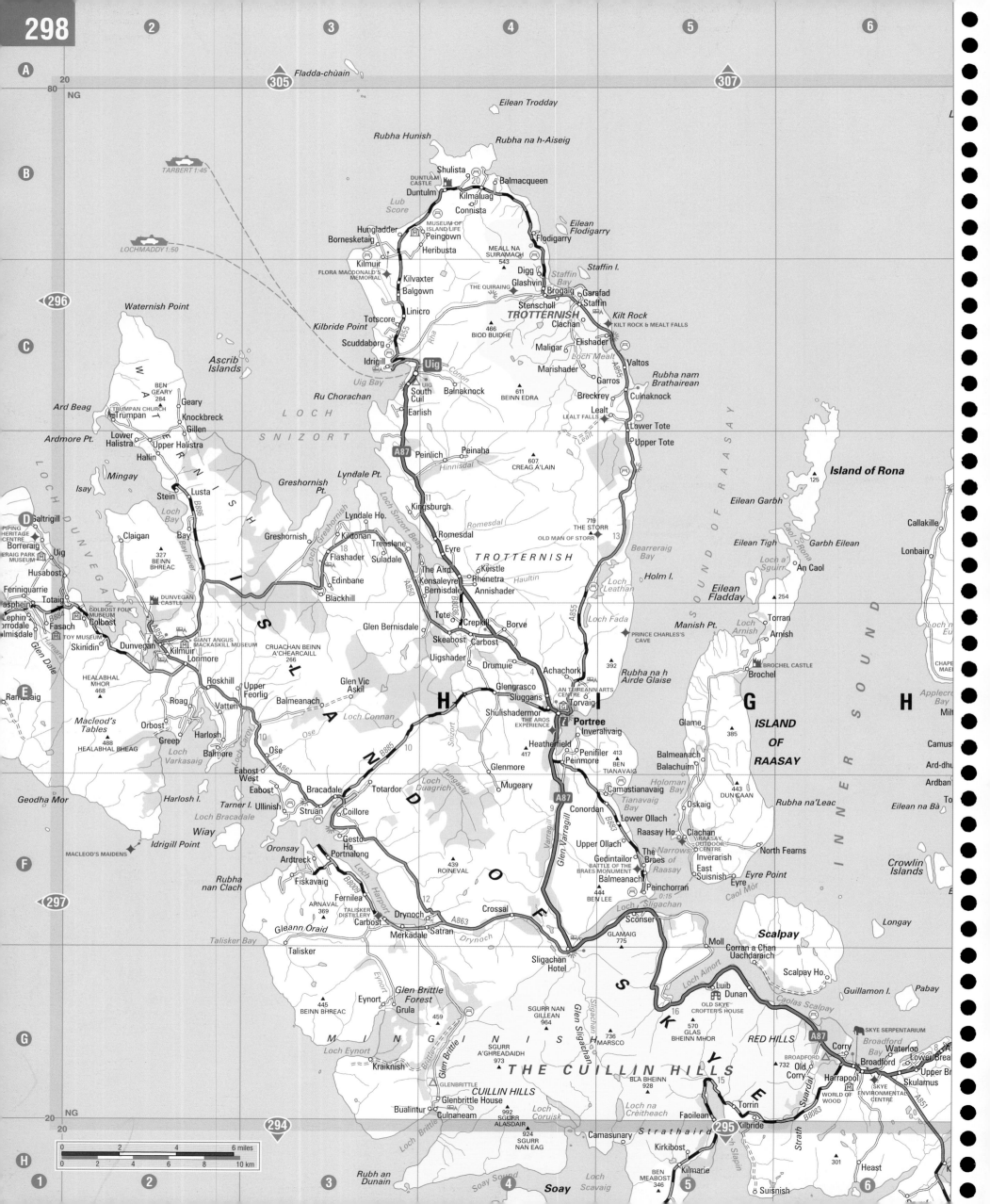

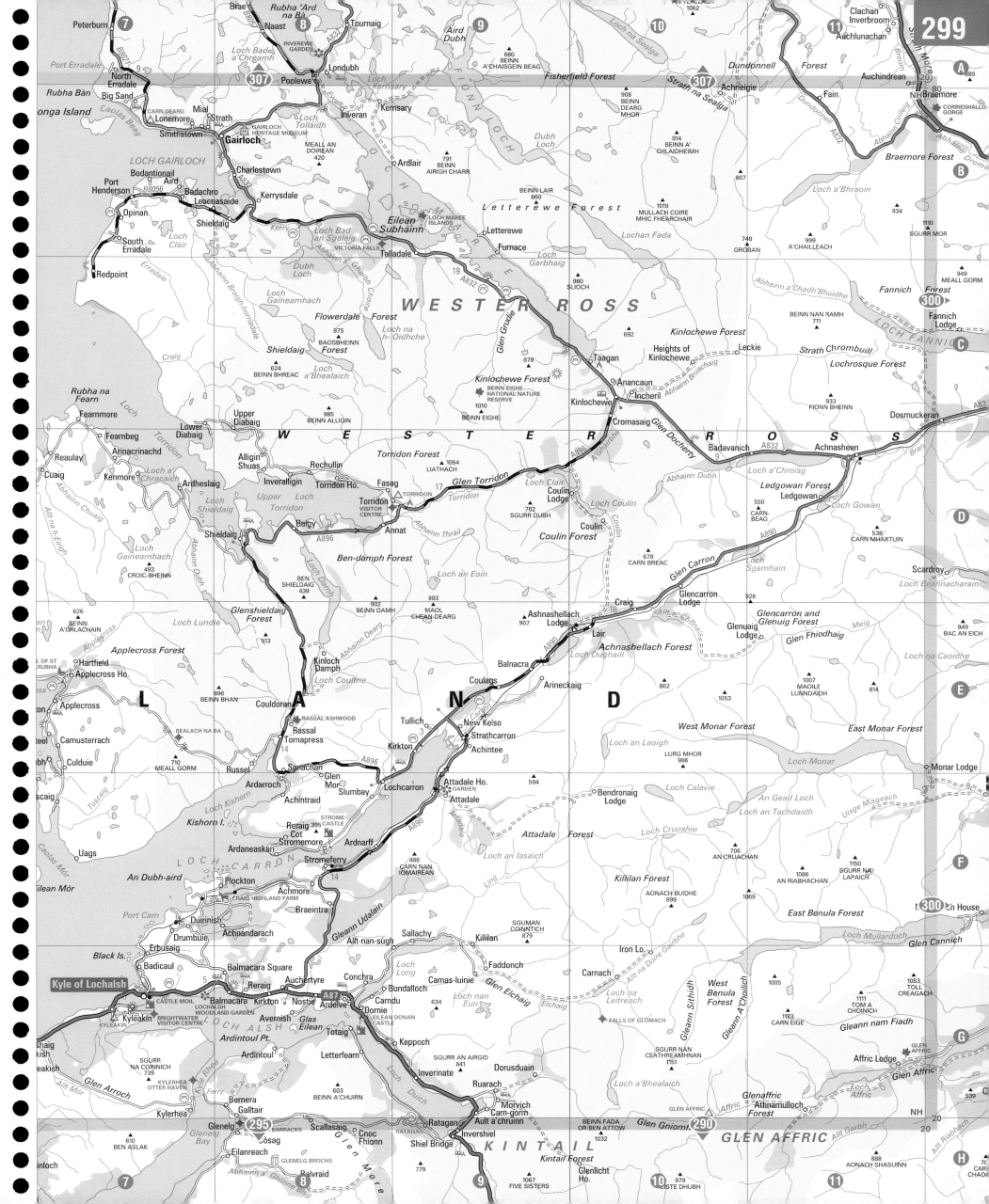

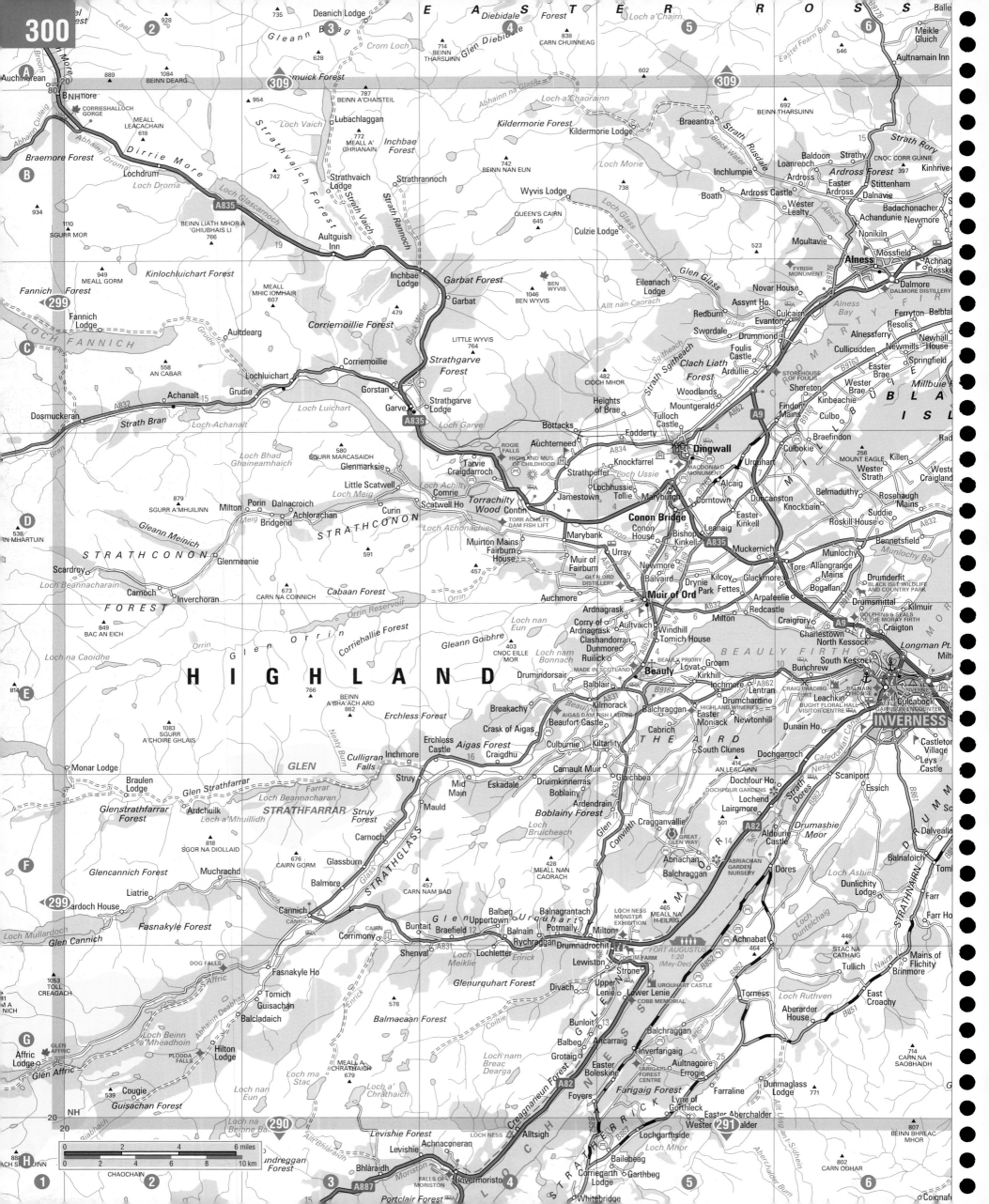

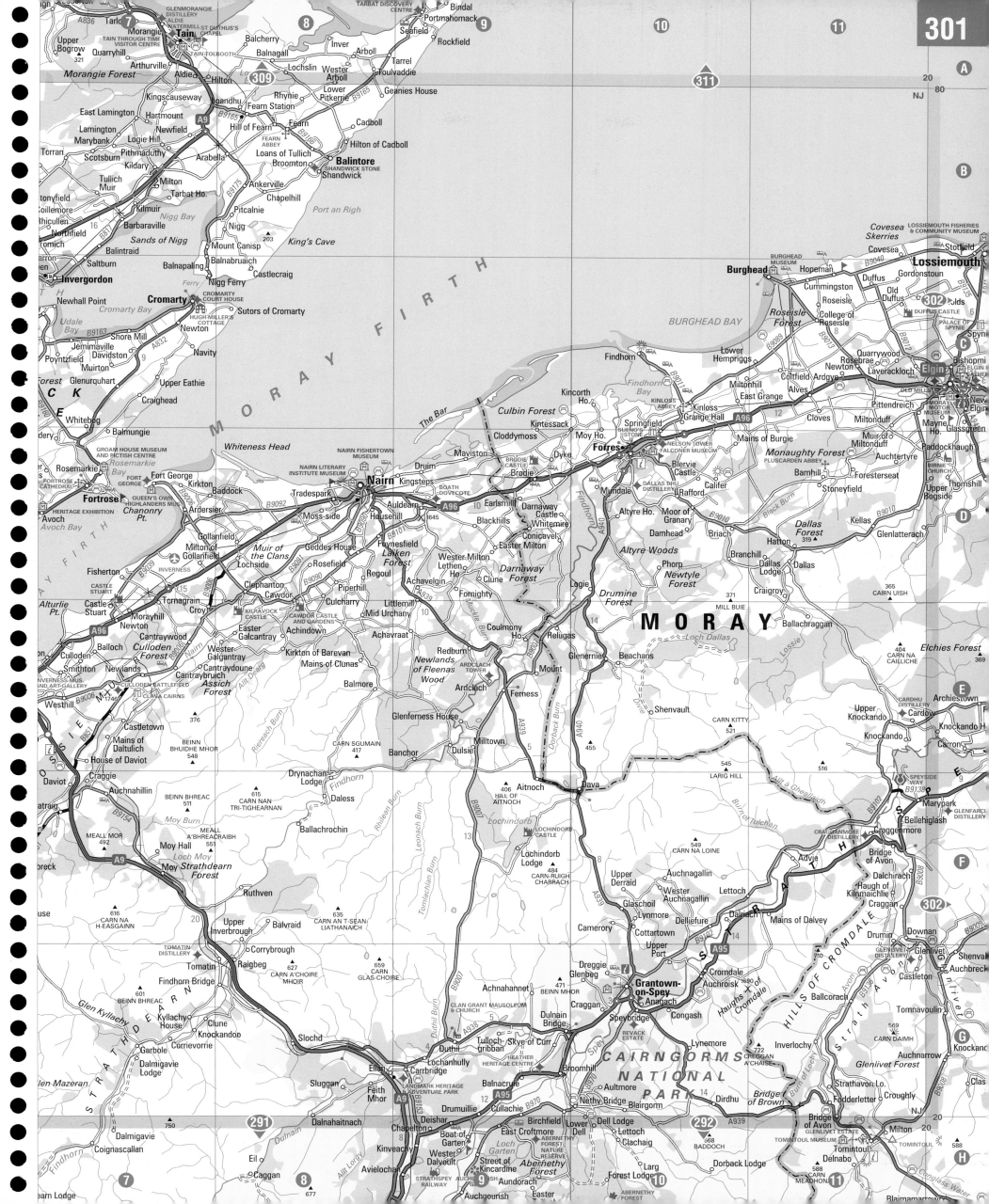

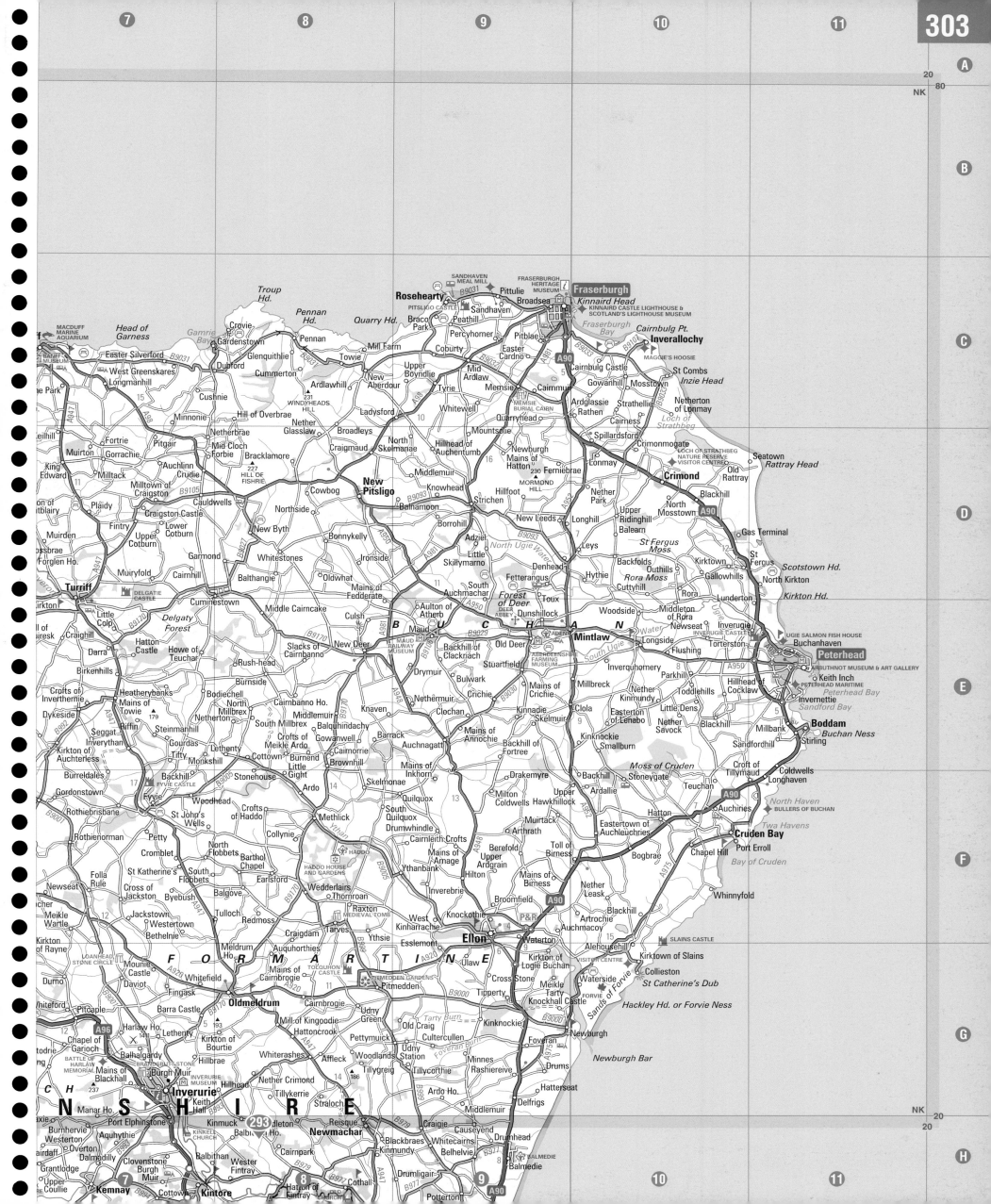

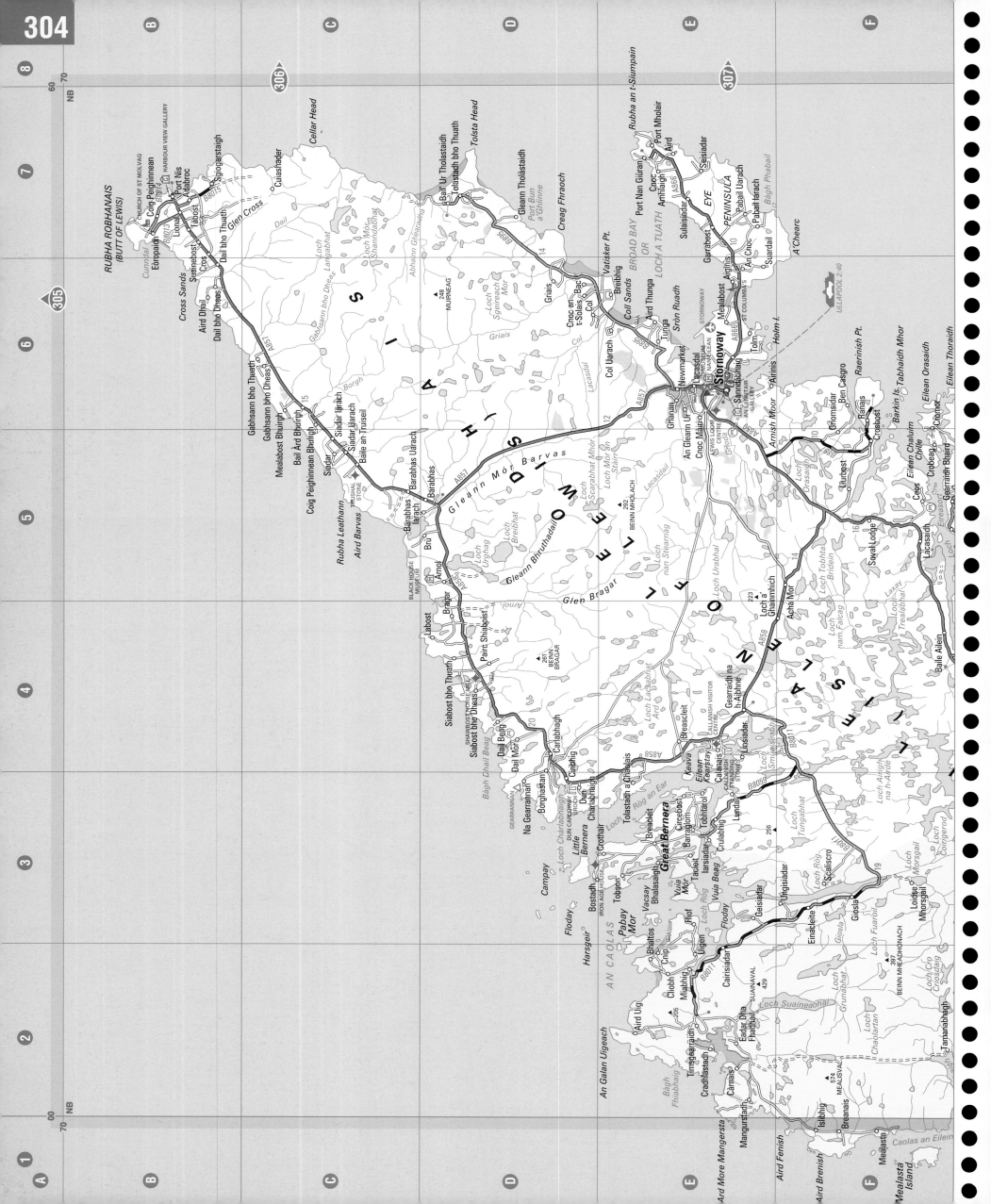

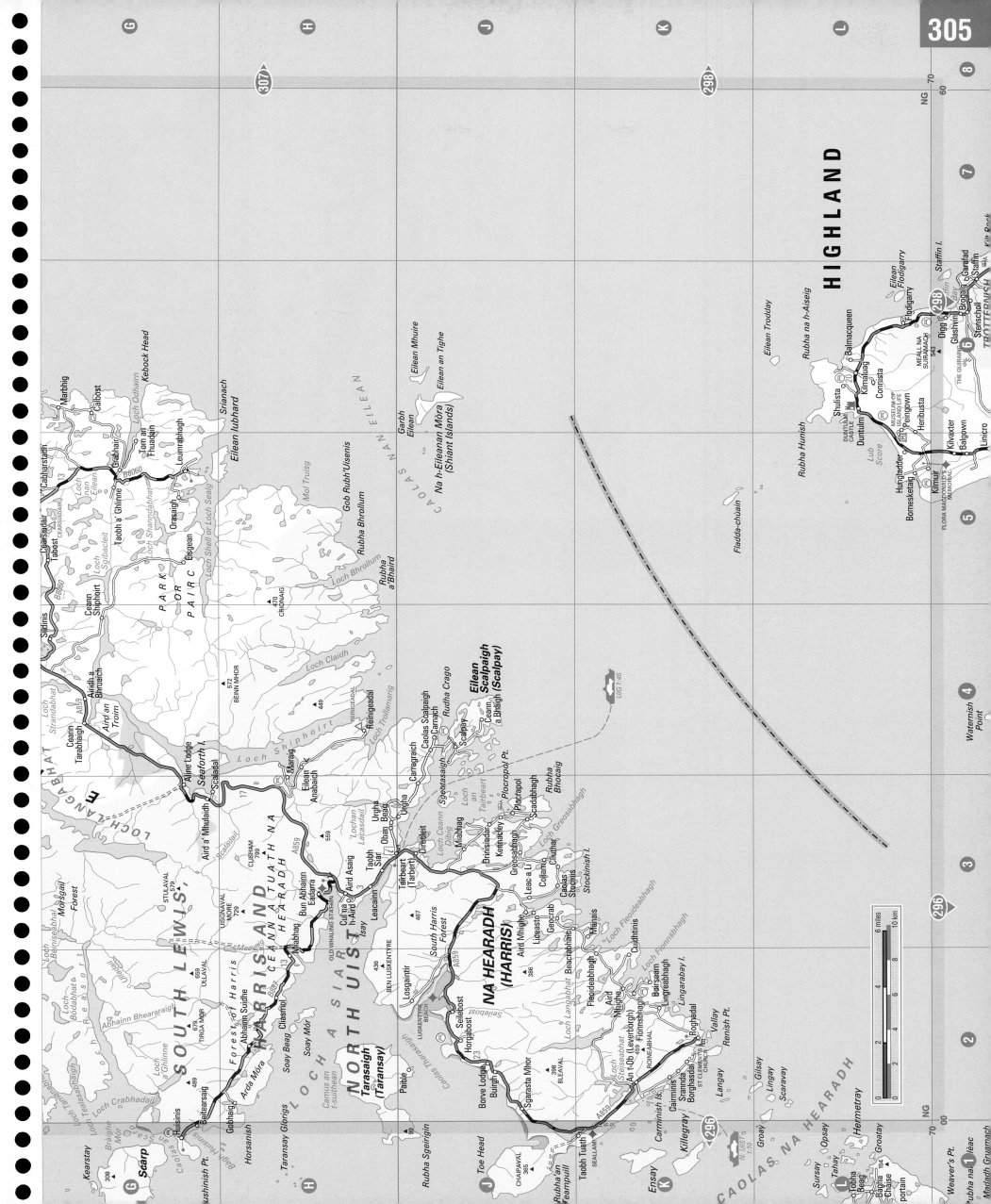

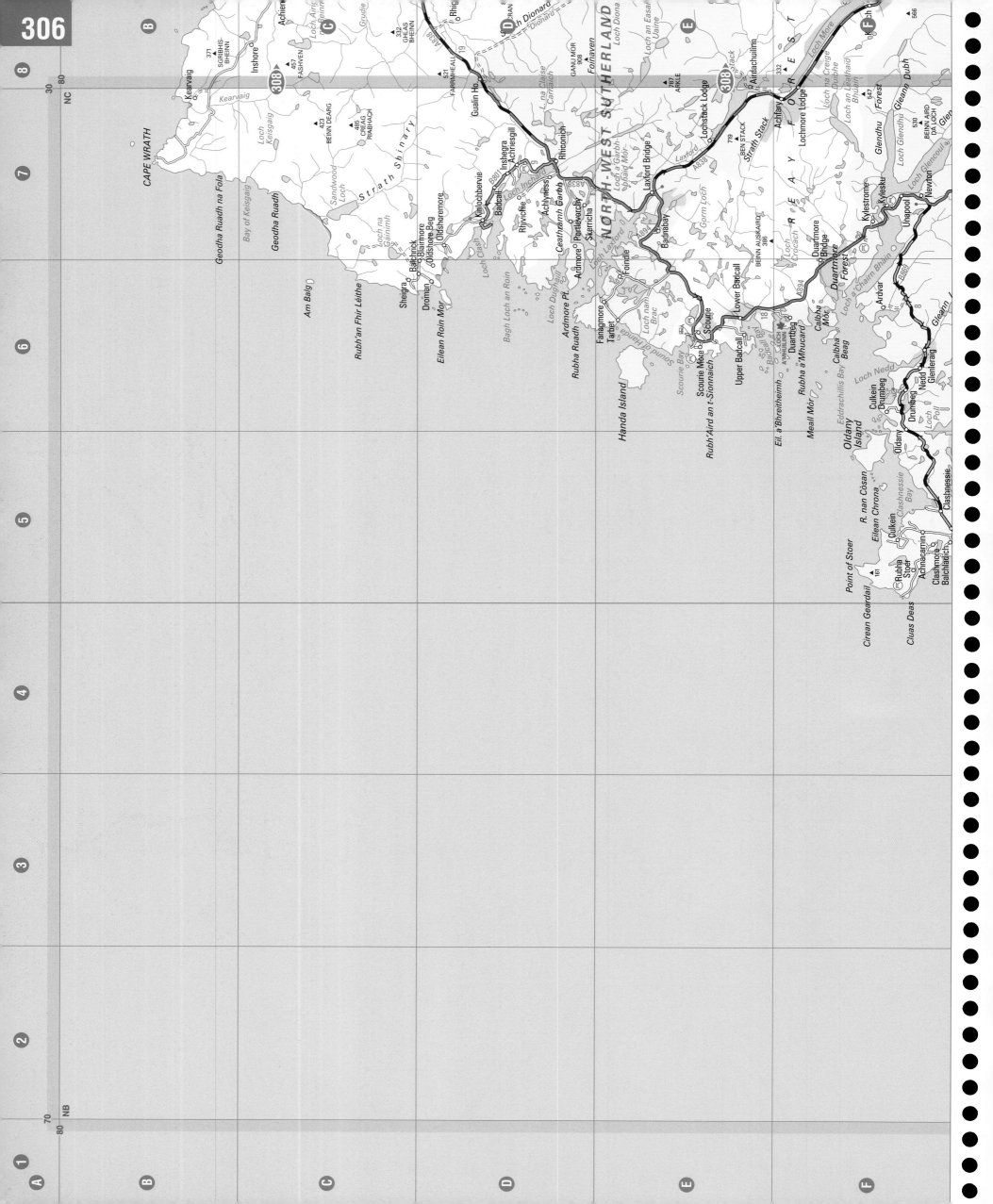

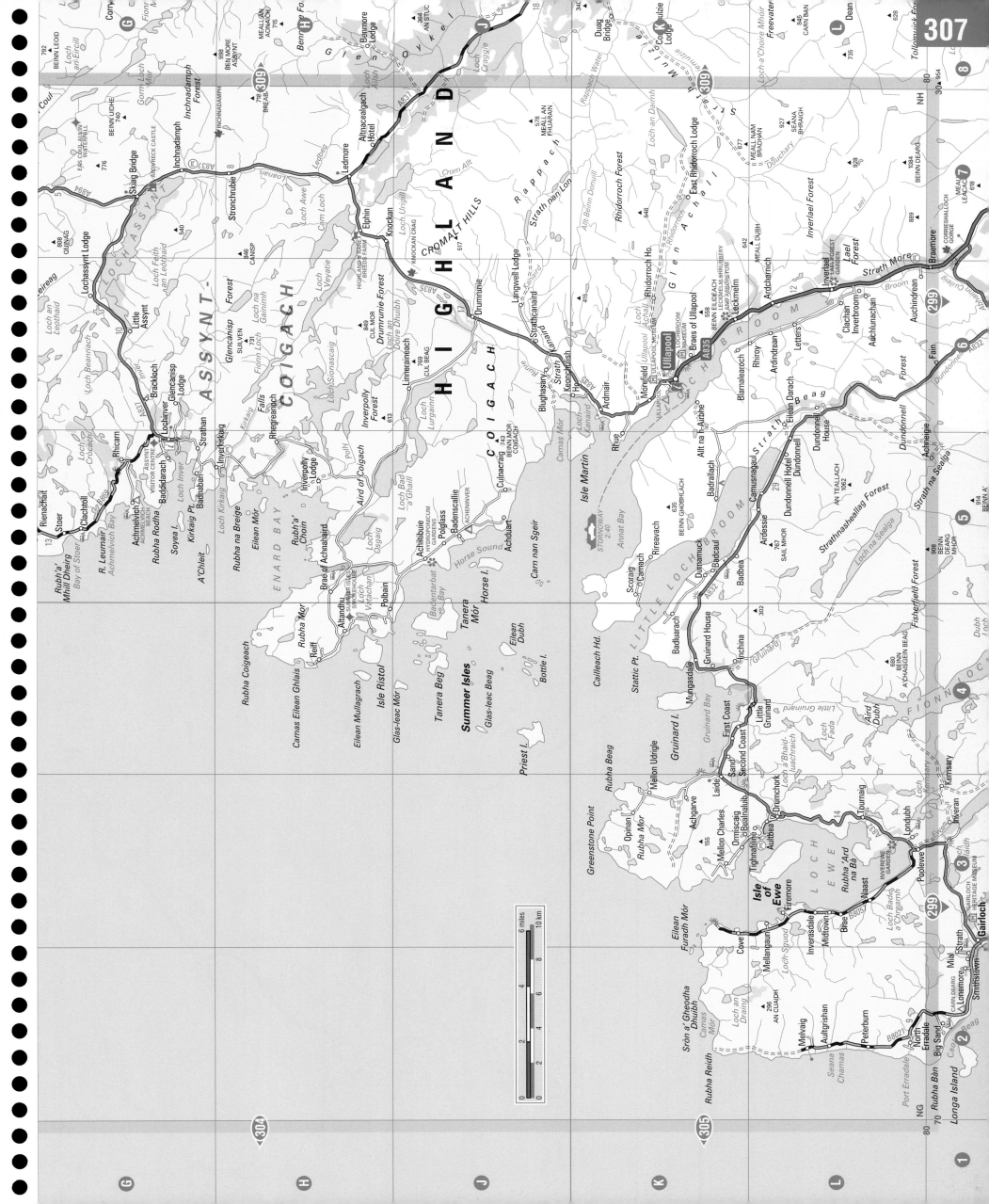

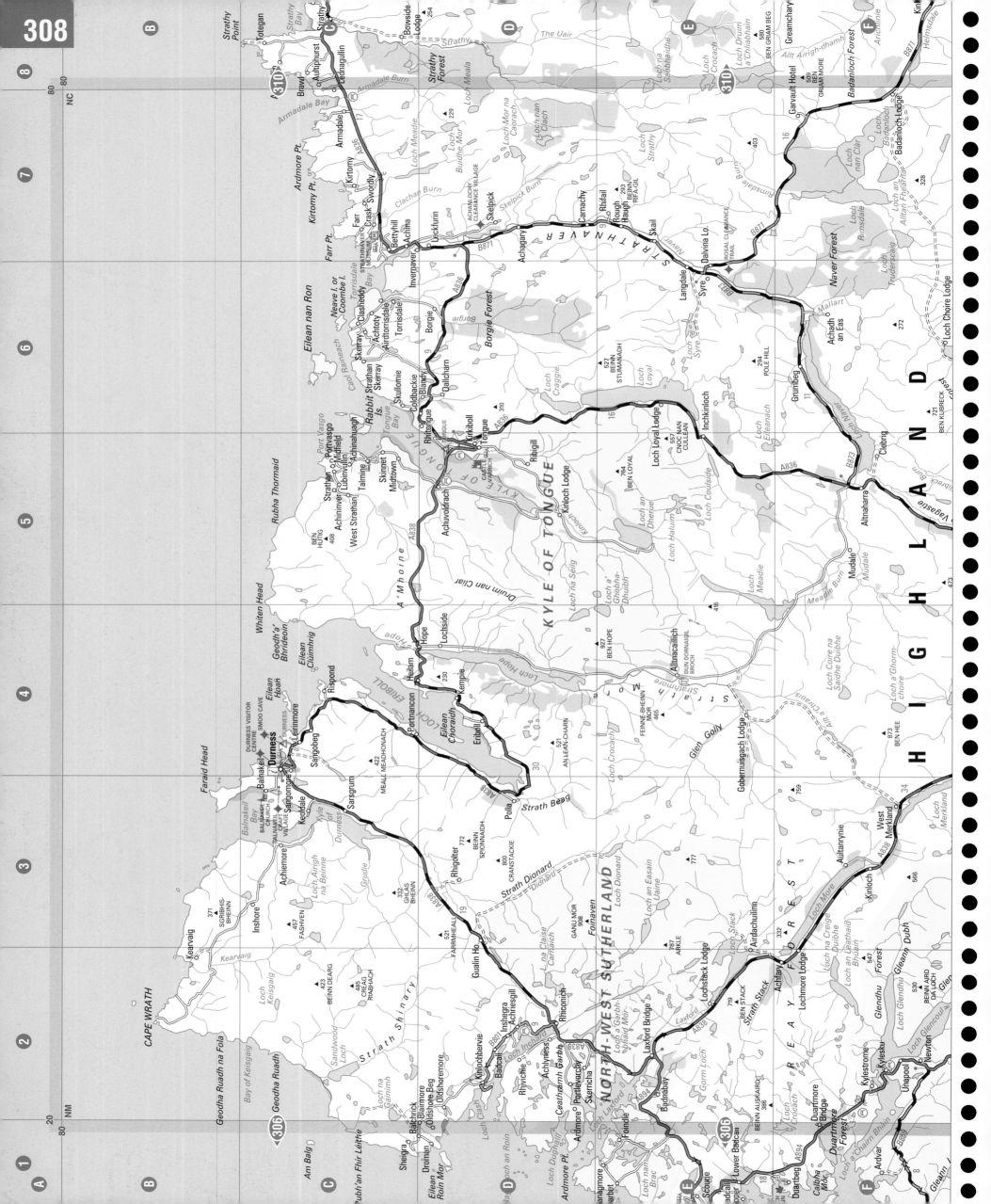

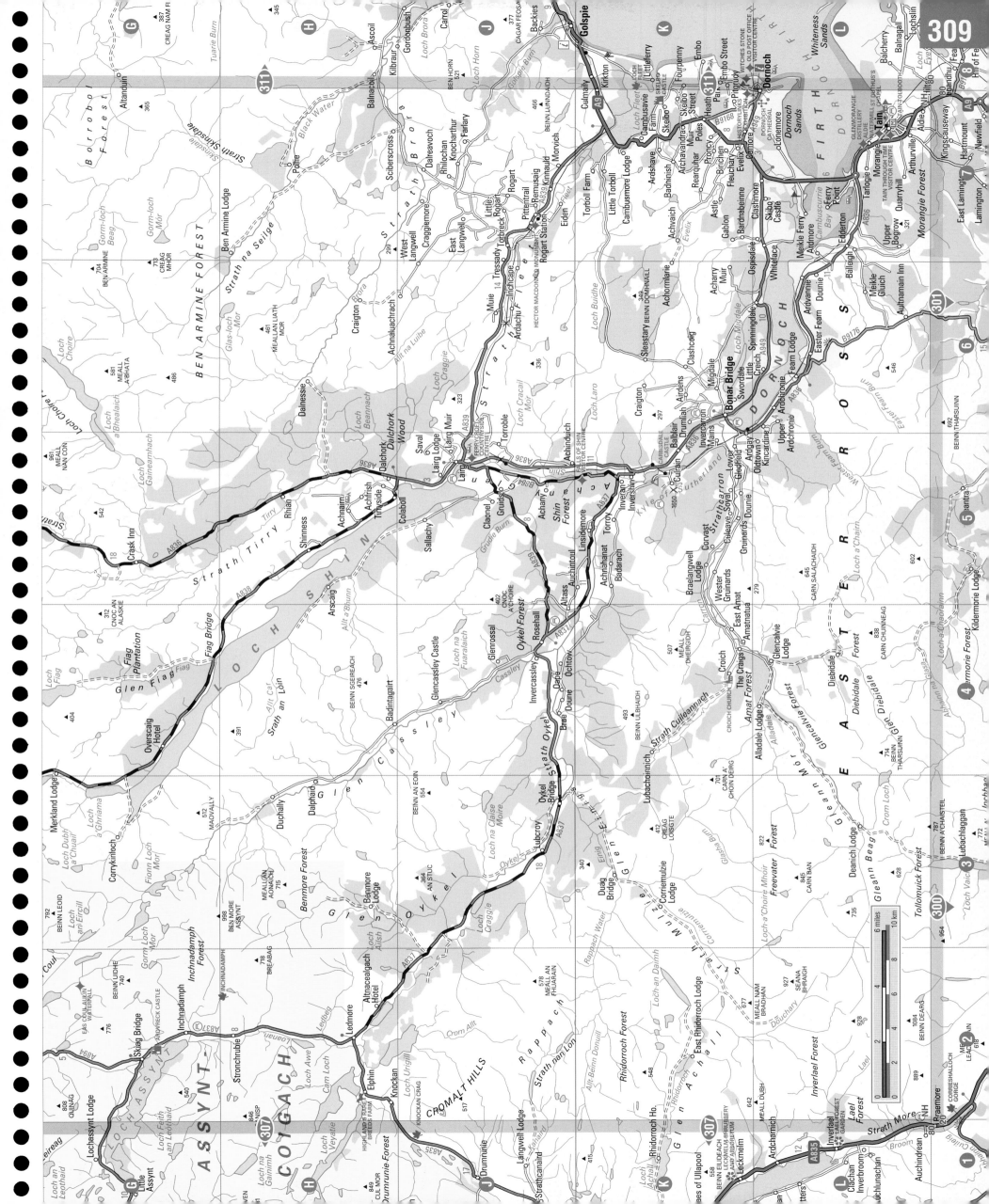

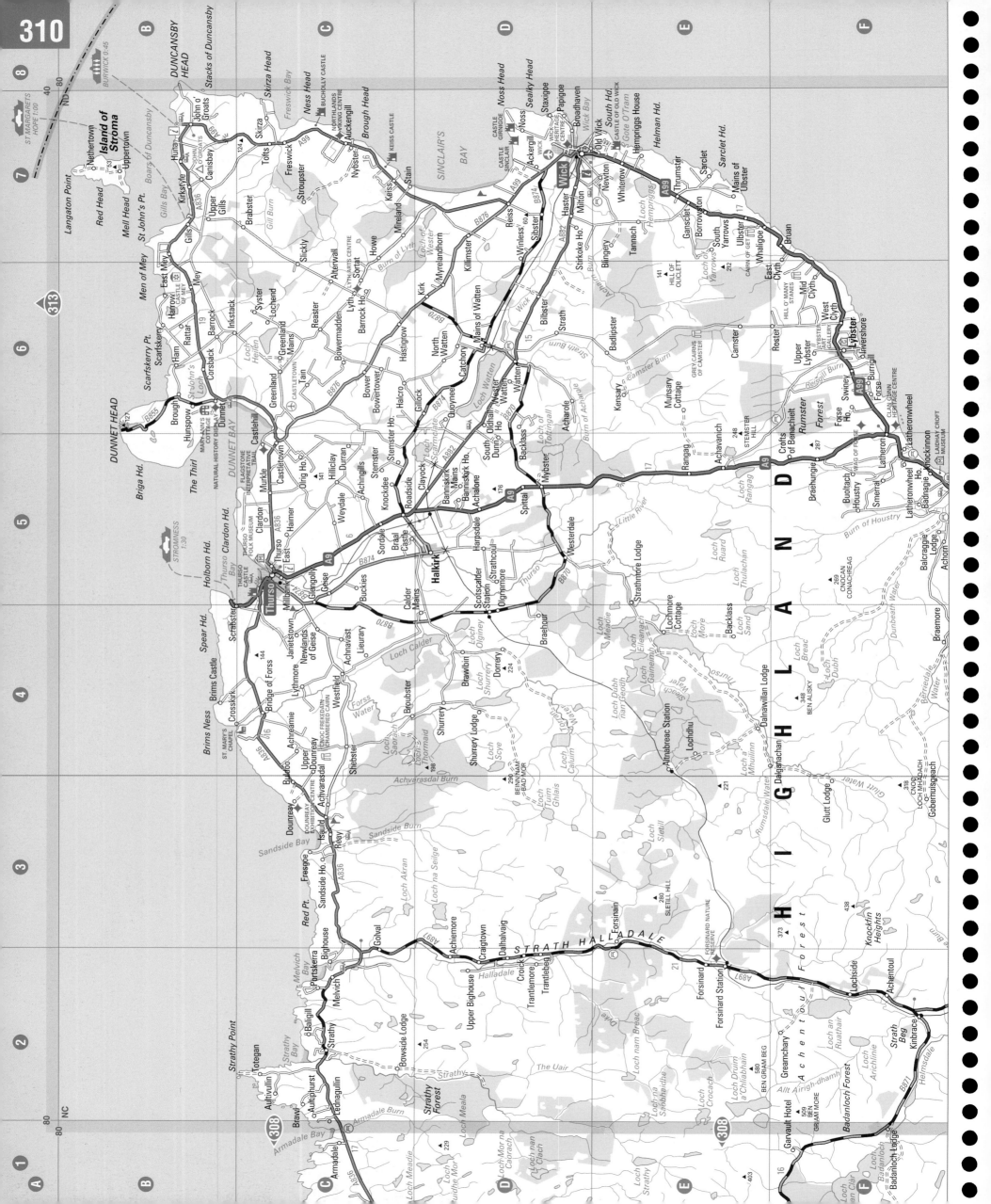

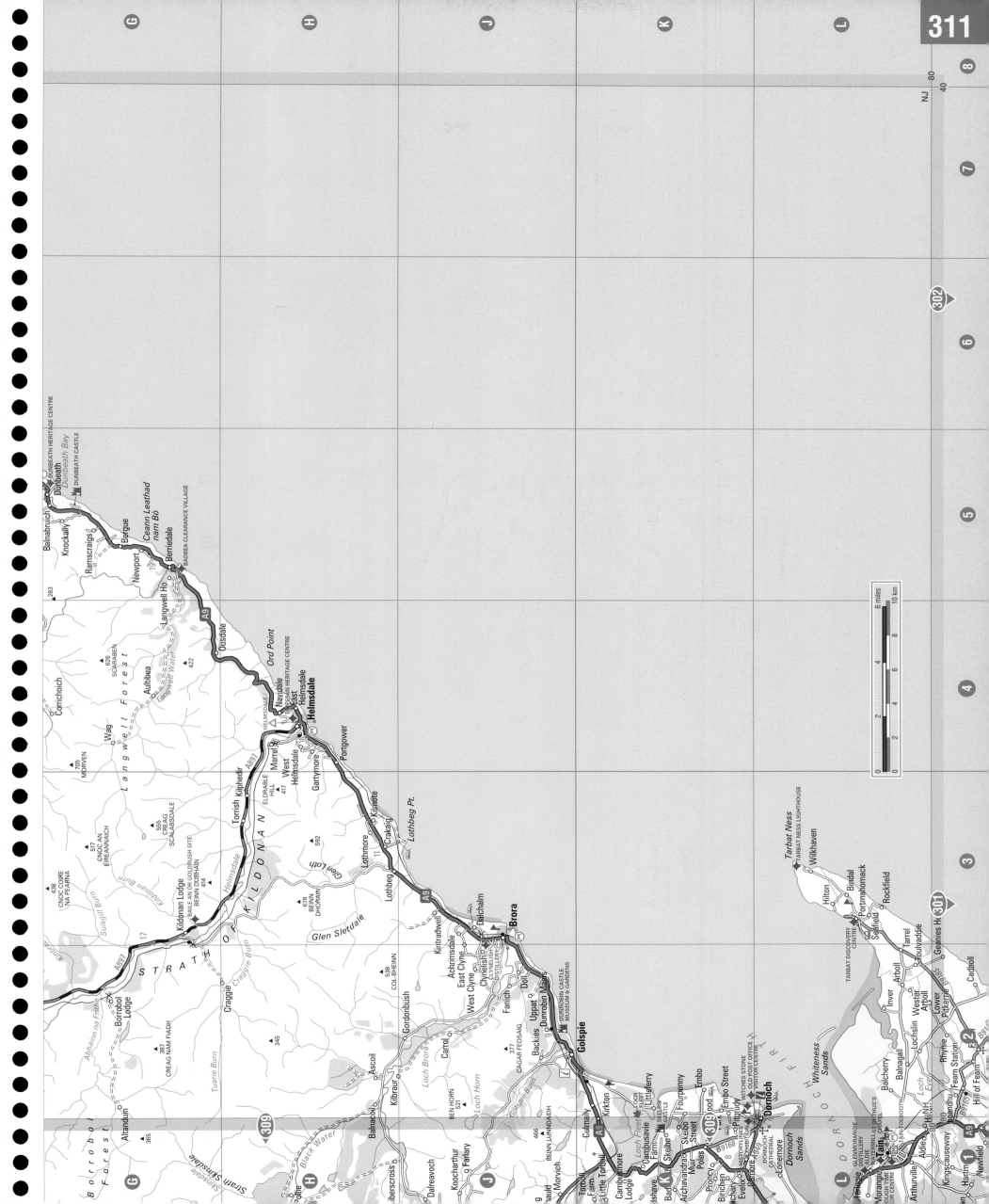

G   H   J   K   L

NJ 40   80

302

301

309

6 miles
10 km

DUNBEATH HERITAGE CENTRE
Dunbeath
DUNBEATH CASTLE
Dunbeath Bay

Balnabruich
Knockally
Ramscraigs
Borgue
Newport
Berriedale
Ceann Leathad nam Bò
BADBEA CLEARANCE VILLAGE

283
Langwell Ho.
A9
Ousdale

626 SCARABEN
422
Aultibea
Corrichoich

L a n g w e l l   F o r e s t

Navidale
East Helmsdale
Helmsdale
HELMSDALE
TIMESPAN HERITAGE CENTRE

Ord Point

Wag
705 MORVEN

555 CREAG SCALABSDALE
517 CNOC AN EIREANNAICH

438 CNOC COIRE NA PEARNA

Torrish Kilphedir
Marrel
West Helmsdale
Portgower
Gartymore

ELDRABLE HILL 417

A897

Kildonan Lodge
BAILE AN OR GOLDRUSH SITE
BEINN DUBHAIN 414

592
Lothmore
Kilmote
Crakaig
Kinbrace

Suisgill Burn

Kildonan Burn

S T R A T H   O F   K I L D O N A N

628 BEINN DHORAIN

Glen Loth

Lothbeg
Lothbeg Pt.
11

A9

Craggie Burn
438

Borrobol Lodge
A897

Abhainn na Frithe

Altanduin

365

387 CREAG NAM FIADH

538 COL-BHEINN

Craggie
Kintradwell
Achrimsdale
East Clyne
West Clyne
Clynelish
CLYNELISH DISTILLERY
Balchalm
Brora

Gordonbush
Carrol
Fanich
Doll
Upat
Backies
Dunrobin Mains
DUNROBIN CASTLE MUSEUM & GARDENS

Tarbat Ness
TARBAT NESS LIGHTHOUSE
Wilkhaven
Portmahomack
TARBAT DISCOVERY CENTRE
Rockfield
Seafield
Hilton
Balintore
Geanies Ho

Borrobol Forest

Tuarie Burn

Strath Sletdale

Strath Brora

CAGAR FEOSAG
377

Ascoil
Kilbraur
Balnacoil
BEN HORN 521

Loch Brora

Loch Horn

345

466

Dalreavoch
Knocharthur
Farlary

Morvich
BEINN LUNNDAIDH

Golspie
Backies

Kirkton
Culmaily
LOCH FLEET
Littleferry
Fourpenny
Embo
Embo Street
WITCHES STONE
OLD POST OFFICE
Dornoch
DORNOCH CATHEDRAL
Dornoch Sands

Whiteness Sands

D O R N O C H   F I R T H

Skelbo
SKELBO CASTLE
Skibo Castle
Cambusavie
Cambusmore
Poles
Pitgrudy
Evelix
Birichen
Proncy
Clashmore

Loch Evelix

Inver
Arboll
Wester Arboll
Lower Pitkerrie
Rhynie
Balchery
Bahagall
Lochslin
Cadboll
Fearn Station
Hill of Fearn

Tain
GLENMORANGIE DISTILLERY
Morangie
Arthurville
Aldie
Newfield
Kingscauseway

NH 80
NH
A9
B9175
B9165
B9168

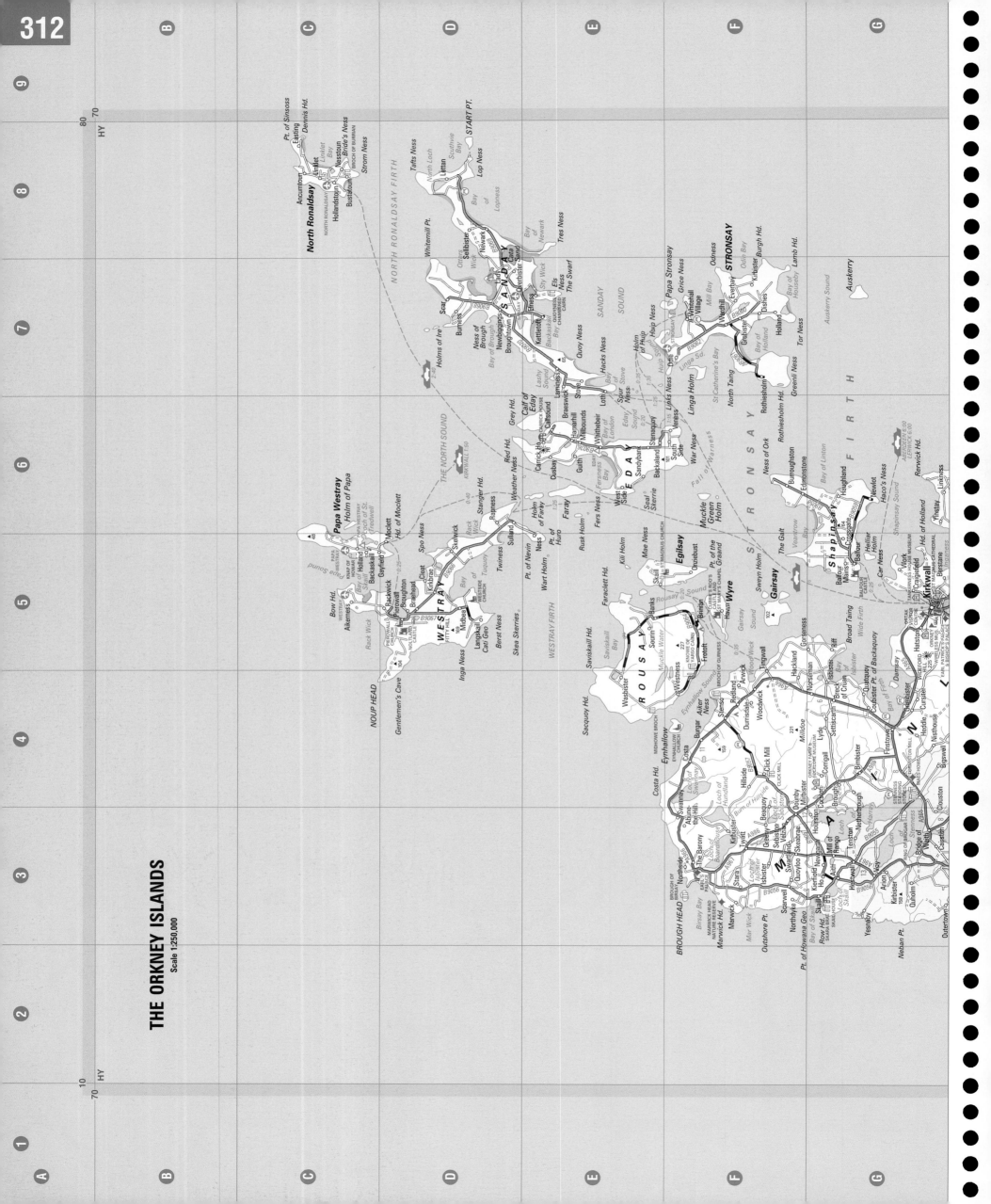

THE ORKNEY ISLANDS

Scale 1:250,000

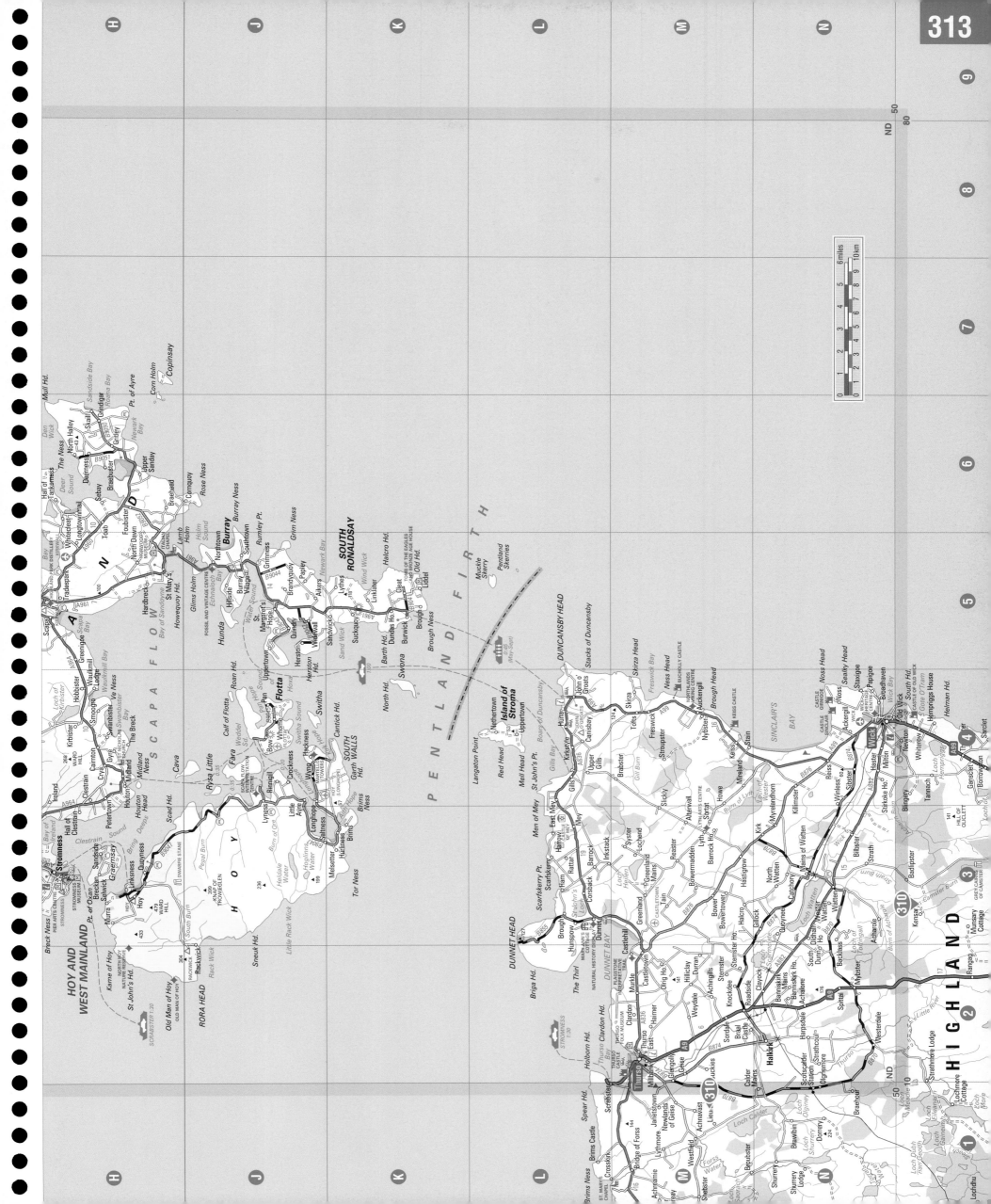

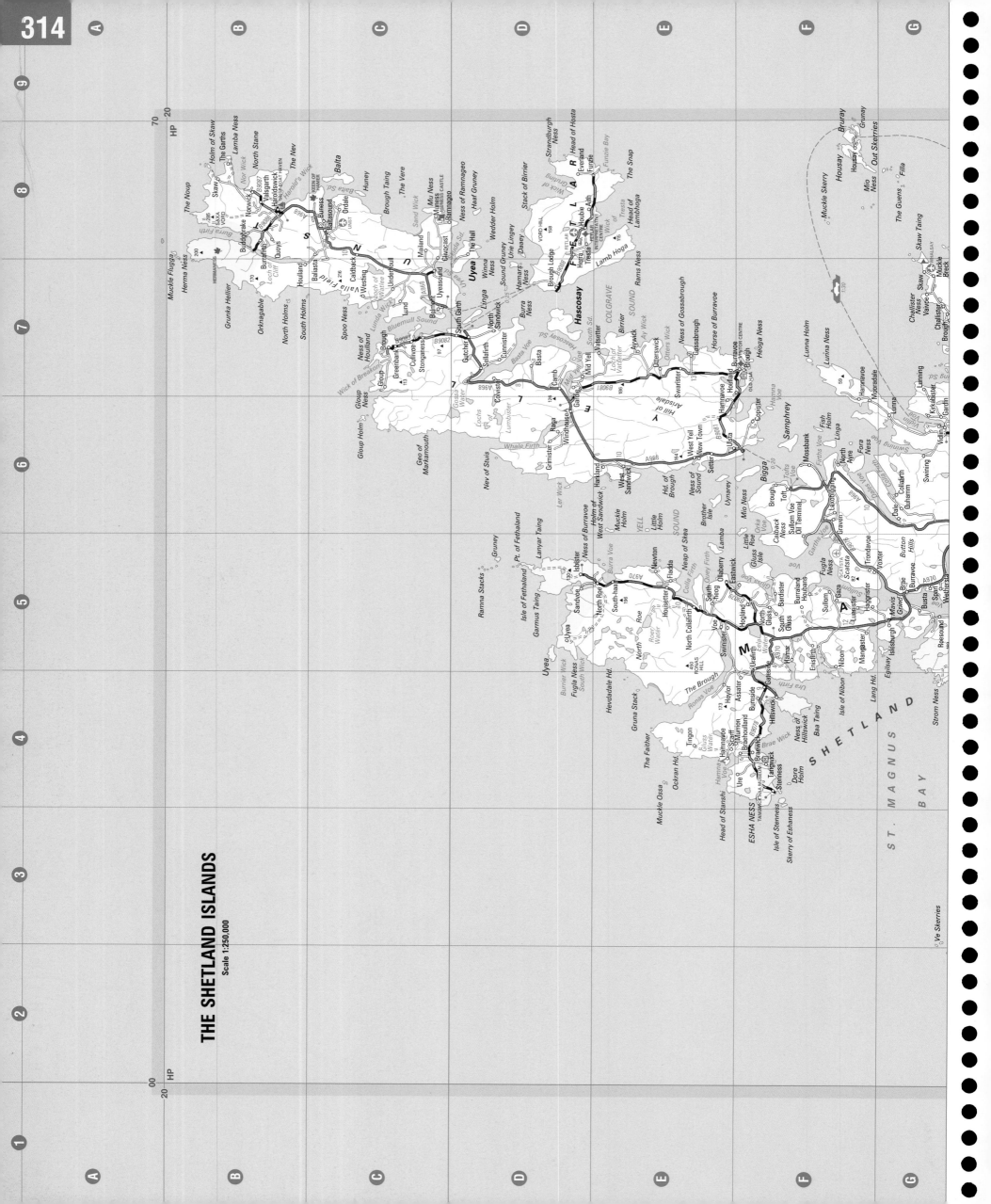

THE SHETLAND ISLANDS

Scale 1:250,000

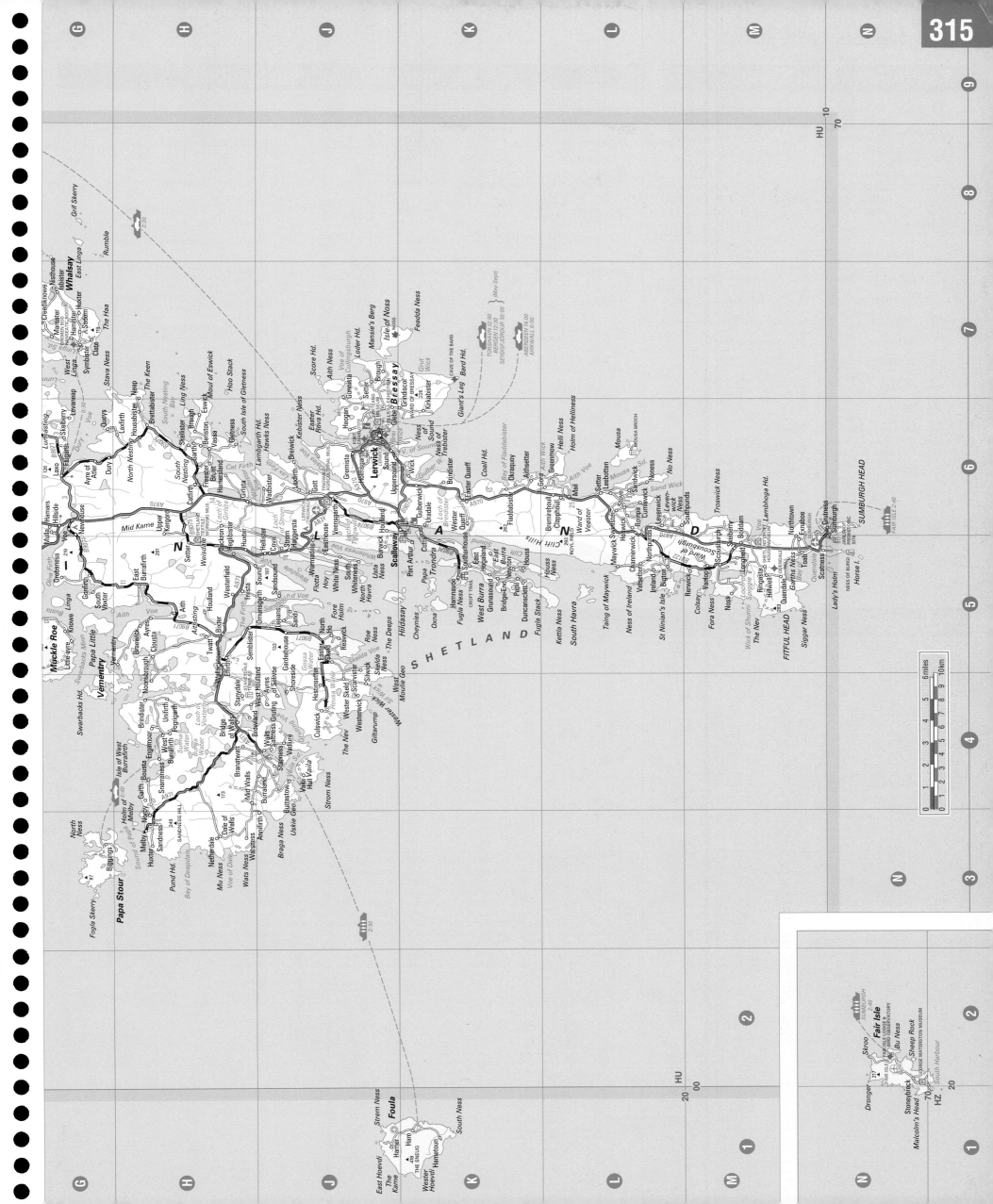

Key to Town Plan Symbols

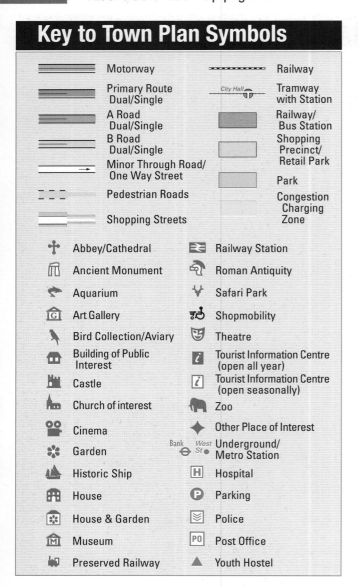

Motorway
Primary Route Dual/Single
A Road Dual/Single
B Road Dual/Single
Minor Through Road/ One Way Street
Pedestrian Roads
Shopping Streets

Railway
Tramway with Station
Railway/ Bus Station
Shopping Precinct/ Retail Park
Park
Congestion Charging Zone

✝ Abbey/Cathedral
⌂ Ancient Monument
🐟 Aquarium
Ⓖ Art Gallery
🦅 Bird Collection/Aviary
⌂ Building of Public Interest
🏰 Castle
⛪ Church of interest
📷 Cinema
❀ Garden
⛴ Historic Ship
🏠 House
🏠 House & Garden
🏛 Museum
🚂 Preserved Railway

🚉 Railway Station
Roman Antiquity
Safari Park
Shopmobility
Theatre
ℹ Tourist Information Centre (open all year)
ℹ Tourist Information Centre (open seasonally)
🐘 Zoo
✦ Other Place of Interest
Ⓤ Underground/ Metro Station
Ⓗ Hospital
Ⓟ Parking
Police
PO Post Office
▲ Youth Hostel

Key to Approach Mapping Symbols

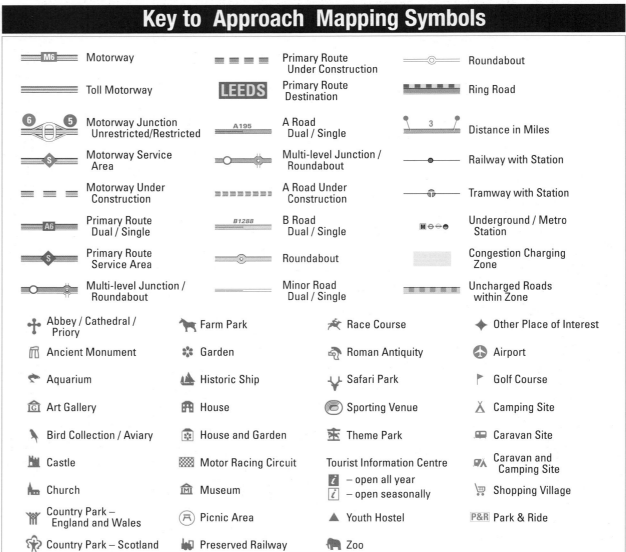

M6 Motorway
Toll Motorway
6 5 Motorway Junction Unrestricted/Restricted
Ⓢ Motorway Service Area
Motorway Under Construction
A6 Primary Route Dual / Single
Ⓢ Primary Route Service Area
Multi-level Junction / Roundabout

Primary Route Under Construction
LEEDS Primary Route Destination
A195 A Road Dual / Single
Multi-level Junction / Roundabout
A Road Under Construction
B1288 B Road Dual / Single
Roundabout
Minor Road Dual / Single

Roundabout
Ring Road
3 Distance in Miles
Railway with Station
Tramway with Station
Underground / Metro Station
Congestion Charging Zone
Uncharged Roads within Zone

✝ Abbey / Cathedral / Priory
⌂ Ancient Monument
🐟 Aquarium
Ⓖ Art Gallery
🦅 Bird Collection / Aviary
🏰 Castle
⛪ Church
Country Park – England and Wales
Country Park – Scotland

🐕 Farm Park
❀ Garden
⛵ Historic Ship
🏛 House
🏠 House and Garden
Motor Racing Circuit
🏛 Museum
Ⓟ Picnic Area
🐘 Preserved Railway

🏃 Race Course
Roman Antiquity
Safari Park
Ⓢ Sporting Venue
Theme Park
Tourist Information Centre
ℹ – open all year
ℹ – open seasonally
▲ Youth Hostel
🐘 Zoo

✦ Other Place of Interest
✈ Airport
⛳ Golf Course
⛺ Camping Site
Caravan Site
Caravan and Camping Site
Shopping Village
P&R Park & Ride

Aberdeen

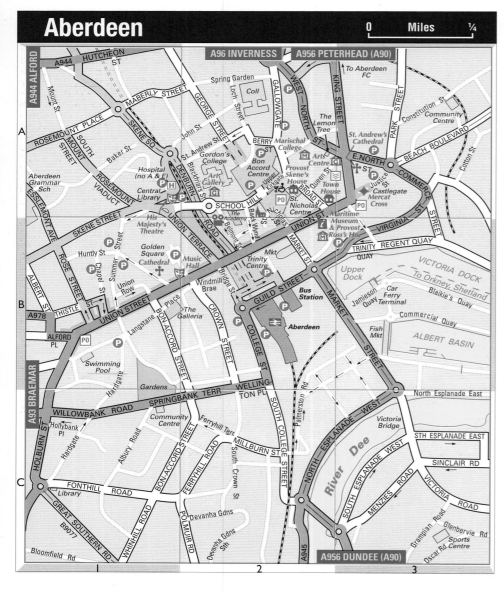

0   Miles   ¼

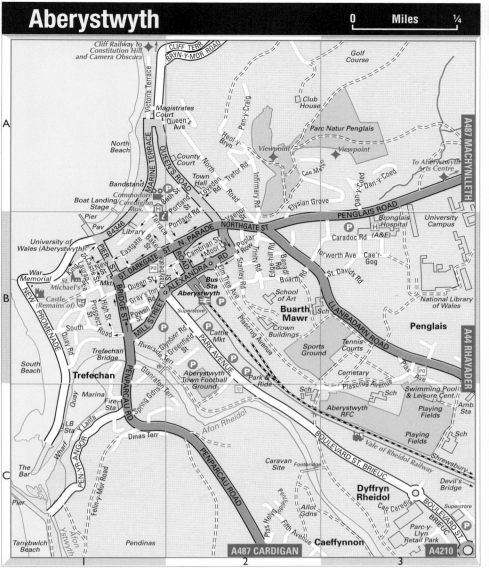

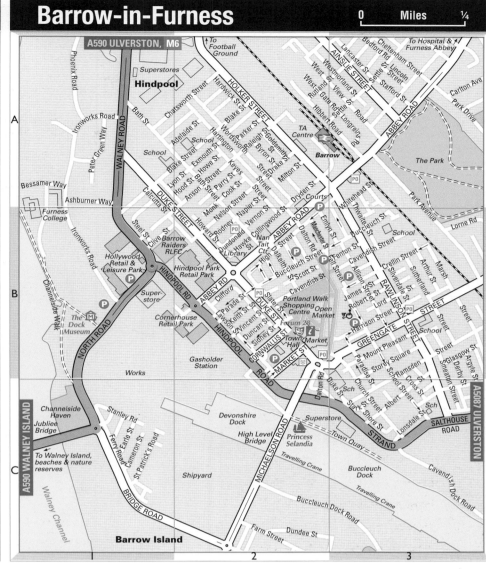

Aberystwyth

Aberystwyth RFC C3
Aberystwyth
  Station ⇌ B2
Aberystwyth Town
  Football Ground B2
Alexandra Rd B2
Ambulance Station . . . C3
Baker St B1
Banadl Rd B2
Bandstand A1
Bath St A2
Boat Landing Stage . . A1
Boulevard St. Brieuc . . C3
Bridge St B1
Bronglais Hospital H . B3
Bryn-y-Mor Rd A2
Buarth Rd B2
Bus Station B2
Cae Ceredig C3
Cae Melyn A2
Cae'r-Gog B3
Cambrian St B2
Caradoc Rd B3
Caravan Site C2
Castle
  (Remains of) ⊠ B1
Castle St B1
Cattle Market B2
Cemetary B3
Ceredigion
  Museum ⚏ A1
Chalybeate St B1

Cliff Terr A2
Club House A2
Commodore ⚏ A1
County Court A2
Crown Buildings B2
Dan-y-Coed A3
Dinas Terr C1
Eastgate B1
Edge-hill Rd B2
Elm Tree Ave. B2
Elysian Gr A2
Felin-y-Mor Rd C1
Fifth Ave C2
Fire Station C1
Glanrafon Terr. B1
Glyndwr Rd B2
Golf Course A3
Gray's Inn Rd B1
Great Darkgate St B1
Greenfield St B2
Heol-y-Bryn A2
High St B1
Infirmary Rd A2
Information Ctr ⓘ B1
Iorwerth Ave B3
King St B1
Lauraplace B1
Library B1
Lifeboat Station C1
Llanbadarn Rd B3
Loveden Rd A2
Magistrates Court A1
Marina C1
Marine Terr A1

Market B1
Mill St B1
Moor La B2
National Library
  of Wales B3
New Promenade. B1
New St B1
North Beach A1
North Parade B2
North Rd B1
Northgate St B2
Parc Natur Penglais . . A3
Parc-y-Llyn
  Retail Park C3
Park & Ride B2
Park Ave B2
Pavillion B1
Pendinas C1
Penglais Rd B3
Penparcau Rd C1/C2
Penrheidol C2
Pen-y-Craig A2
Pen-yr-angor C1
Pier St B1
Plas Ave B3
Plas Helyg C2
Plascrug Ave B2/C3
Police Station ⚲ C2
Poplar Row B1
Portland Rd B2
Portland St A2
Powell St B1
Prospect St B1

Quay Rd B1
Queen St B1
Queen's Ave A2
Queen's Rd A2
Riverside Terr B1
St. Davids Rd B3
St. Michael's ⛪ B1
School of Art B2
South Beach B1
South Rd B1
Sports Ground B2
Spring Gdns C1
Stanley Rd B2
Swimming Pool &
  Leisure Centre C3
Tanybwlch Beach C1
Tennis Courts B3
Terrace Rd B1
The Bar C1
Town Hall A2
Trefechan Bridge B1
Trefor Rd A2
Trinity Rd B2
University Campus . . . B3
University of Wales
  (Aberystwyth) B1
Vaenor St B2
Vale of Rheidol
  Railway ⚙ C3
Victoria Terr A1
Viewpoint ◆ A2
Viewpoint ◆ A3
War Memorial B1
Y Lanfa C1

Barrow-in-Furness

Abbey Rd A3/B2
Adelaide St A2
Ainslie St A3
Albert St C3
Allison St B3
Anson St A2
Argyle St B3
Arthur St B3
Ashburner Way A1
Barrow Raiders
  RLFC B1
Barrow Station ⇌ . . . A2
Bath St A1/B2
Bedford Rd A3
Bessamer Way A1
Blake St A1/A2
Bridge Rd C1
Buccleuch Dock C3
Buccleuch
  Dock Rd C2/C3
Buccleuch St B2
Byron St B2
Calcutta St A1
Cameron St C1
Carlton Ave. A2
Cavendish Dock Rd . . C3
Cavendish St B2/B3
Channelside Walk. . . . B1
Channelside Haven . . C1
Chatsworth St A2
Cheltenham St A3
Church St C3
Clifford St B2
Clive St. B1
Collingwood St B2
Cook St A2
Cornerhouse
  Retail Park B2

Cornwallis St B2
Courts. A2
Crellin St B3
Cross St C2
Dalkeith St B2
Dalton Rd B2/C2
Derby St B3
Devonshire Dock C2
Dock Museum,
  The ⚏ B1
Drake St A2
Dryden St A3
Duke St A1/B2/C3
Duncan St B2
Dundee St C1
Dundonald St B2
Earle St C1
Emlyn St A2
Exmouth St A2
Farm St C2
Fell St B3
Fenton St B3
Ferry Rd C1
Forum 28 ⚏ B2
Furness College B1
Glasgow St B3
Goldsmith St A2
Greengate St B3
Hardwick St A2
Harrison St B3
Hartington St A2
Hawke St A2
Hibbert Rd A2
High Level Bridge C2
High St B2
Hindpool Park
  Retail Park B2
Hindpool Rd B2
Holker St A2
Hollywood Retail &
  Leisure Park B1
Hood St A2

Howard St B2
Howe St A2
Information Ctr ⓘ B2
Ironworks Rd A1/B1
James St B3
Jubilee Bridge C1
Keith St. B2
Keyes St A2
Lancaster St A3
Lawson St B2
Library B2
Lincoln St A3
Longreins Rd A3
Lonsdale St C3
Lord St B2
Lorne Rd B3
Lyon St A2
Manchester St B2
Market B2
Market St B2
Marsh St B3
Michaelson Rd C2
Milton St A2
Monk St B2
Mount Pleasant B3
Nan Tait Centre B2
Napier St B2
Nelson St B2
North Rd B1
Open Market B2
Parade St B2
Paradise St A3
Park Ave A3
Park Dr A3
Parker St A2
Parry St A2
Peter Green Way A1
Phoenix Rd A1
Police Station ⚲ B2
Portland Walk
  Shopping Centre . . . B2
Post Office ⓟ . A3/B2/B3

Princess Selandia ⚓ . C2
Raleigh St A2
Ramsden St B3
Rawlinson St B3
Robert St B3
Rodney St. B2
Rutland St A2
St Patrick's Rd C1
Salthouse Rd C3
School St B3
Scott St B2
Settle St A3
Shore St C3
Sidney St B2
Silverdale St B3
Slater St B2
Smeaton St B3
Stafford St A3
Stanley Rd C1
Stark St C3
Steel St B1
Storey Sq B3
Strand. C3
Sutherland St B3
TA Centre A2
The Park A3
Thwaite St B3
Town Hall B2
Town Quay C3
Vernon St B2
Vincent St B2
Walney Rd A1
West Gate Rd A3
West View Rd A3
Westmorland St A3
Whitehead St A3
Wordsworth St A2

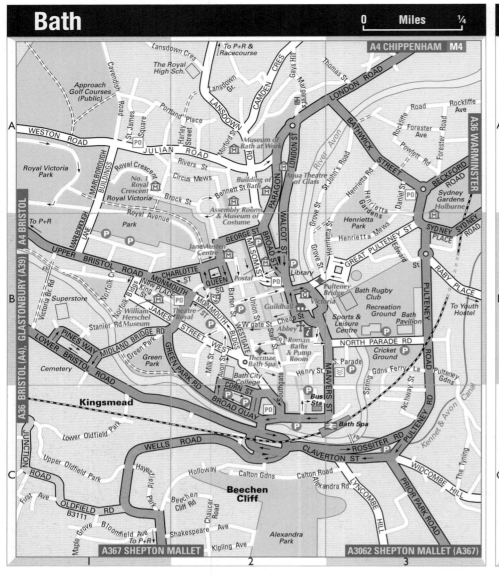

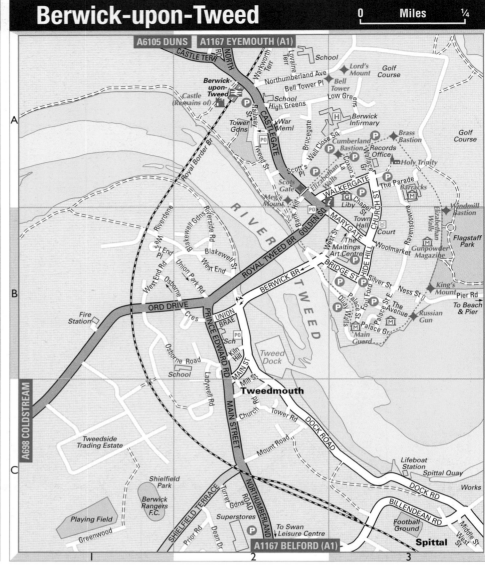

Bath

Alexandra Park C2	Corn St C2	Lower Oldfield Park . . C1	Rockliffe Rd A3
Alexandra Rd C2	Cricket Ground B3	Lyncombe Hill C3	Roman Baths &
Approach Golf	Daniel St A3	Manvers St B3	Pump Room 🏛 B2
Courses (Public) A1	Edward St A3	Maple Gr A1	Rossiter Rd C3
Aqua Theatre	Ferry La B3	Margaret's Hill A2	Royal Ave A1
of Glass 🏛 A2	First Ave C1	Marlborough	Royal Cr A1
Archway St C3	Forester Ave A3	Buildings A1	Royal High
Assembly Rooms	Forester Rd A3	Marlborough La B1	School, The A2
& Museum of	Gays Hill A2	Midland Bridge Rd . . . B1	Royal Victoria Park . . A1
Costume 🏛 A2	George St B3	Milk St B2	St James Sq A1
Avon St B2	Great Pulteney St B3	Milsom St B2	St John's Rd A3
Barton St B2	Green Park B1	Monmouth St B2	Shakespeare Ave . . . C2
Bath Abbey †. B2	Green Park Rd B2	Morford St A2	Southgate C2
Bath City College B2	Grove St B2	Museum of Bath	South Pde B3
Bath Pavilion B3	Guildhall 🏛 B2	at Work 🏛 B1	Sports & Leisure
Bath Rugby Club B3	Harley St A2	New King St B1	Centre B3
Bath Spa Station ≈ . . C3	Hayesfield Park C1	No. 1 Royal	Spring Gdns C3
Bathwick St A3	Henrietta Gdns A3	Crescent 🏛 A1	Stall St B2
Beechen Cliff Rd C2	Henrietta Mews A3	Norfolk Bldgs A1	Stanier Rd A1
Bennett St A2	Henrietta Park A3	Norfolk Cr B1	Sydney Gdns A3
Bloomfield Ave C1	Henrietta Rd A3	North Parade Rd B3	Sydney Pl B3
Broad Quay C2	Henrietta St B3	Oldfield Rd C1	Theatre Royal 🎭 B2
Broad St B2	Henry St B2	Paragon A2	Thermae
Brock St A1	Holburne Museum 🏛 . B3	Pines Way A1	Bath Spa ♦ B2
Building of Bath	Holloway C2	Police Station 🏢 B3	The Tyning C3
Museum 🏛 A2	Information Ctr 🅸 B2	Portland Pl A2	Thomas St A3
Bus Station C2	James St West B1/B2	Post Office 🄿🄾	Union St B2
Calton Gdns C2	Jane Austen	A1/A3/B2/C2	Upper Bristol Rd B1
Calton Rd C2	Centre 🏛 B2	Postal Museum 🏛 . . . B2	Upper Oldfield Park . . C1
Camden Cr A2	Julian Rd A1	Powlett Rd A3	Victoria Art
Cavendish Rd A1	Junction Rd C1	Prior Park Rd C3	Gallery 🏛 B2
Cemetery B1	Kipling Ave C2	Pulteney Bridge ♦ . . . B2	Victoria Bridge Rd . . . B1
Charlotte St B2	Lansdown Cr A1	Pulteney Gdns B3	Walcot St B2
Chaucer Rd C2	Lansdown Gr A2	Pulteney Rd B3	Wells Rd C1
Cheap St B2	Lansdown Rd A2	Queen Sq B2	Westgate St B2
Circus Mews A2	Library B2	Raby Pl B3	Weston Rd A1
Claverton St C2	London Rd A3	Recreation Ground . . . B3	Widcombe Hill C3
	London St A2	Rivers St A2	William Herschel
	Lower Bristol Rd B1	Rockliffe Ave A3	Museum 🏛 B1

Berwick-upon-Tweed

Bank Hill B2	Dean Dr C2	Middle St C3	Shielfield Park C1
Barracks 🏛 A3	Dock Rd C2/C3	Mill St C2	Shielfield Terr C2
Bell Tower ♦ A3	Elizabethan Walls . A2/B3	Mount Rd C2	Silver St B3
Bell Tower Pl A2	Fire Station B1	Museum 🏛 B3	Spittal Quay C3
Berwick Br ≈ B2	Flagstaff Park B3	Ness St B3	Superstores C2
Berwick Infirmary Ⓗ . A3	Football Ground C3	North Rd A2	The Avenue B3
Berwick	Foul Ford B3	Northumberland Ave . A2	The Parade A3
Rangers F.C. C1	Gallery 🏛 A3	Northumberland Rd . . C2	Tower Gdns A2
Berwick-upon-	Golden Sq B2	Ord Dr B1	Tower Rd C2
Tweed ≈ A2	Golf Course A3	Osborne Cr B1	Town Hall B3
Billendean Rd C3	Greenwood C1	Osborne Rd B1	Turret Gdns C2
Blakewell Gdns B2	Gunpowder	Palace Gr B3	Tweed Dock B2
Blakewell St B2	Magazine 🏛 B3	Palace St B3	Tweed St A2
Brass Bastion ♦ A3	Hide Hill B3	Palace St East B3	Tweedside Trading
Bridge St B3	High Greens A2	Pier Rd B3	Estate C1
Brucegate St A2	Holy Trinity ⛪ A3	Playing Field C1	Union Brae B2
Castle	Information Ctr 🅸 A2	Police Station 🏢 B3	Union Park Rd B2
(Remains of) 🏛 . . . A2	Kiln Hill B2	Post Office 🄿🄾 . A2/B2/B2	Walkergate A3
Castle Terr A2	King's Mount ♦ B3	Prince Edward Rd . . . B2	Wallace Gr A3
Castlegate A2	Ladywell Rd C2	Prior Rd C2	War Meml A2
Chapel St A3	Library A3	Quay Walls B3	Warkworth Terr A2
Church Rd C2	Lifeboat Station C3	Railway St A2	Well Close Sq A2
Church St B3	Lord's Mount ♦ A3	Ravensdowne B3	West End B2
Court B3	Lovaine Terr A2	Records Office A3	West End Pl B1
Coxon's La A3	Low Greens A3	Riverdene B1	West End Rd B1
Cumberland	Main Guard 🏛 B3	Riverside Rd B2	West St B3
Bastion ♦ A3	Main St B2/C2	Royal Border Br A2	West St C3
	Maltings Art	Royal Tweed Br B2	Windmill Bastion ♦ . . B3
	Centre, The B3	Russian Gun ♦ B3	Woolmarket B3
	Marygate B3	Scots Gate ♦ A2	Works C3
	Meg's Mount ♦ A2	Scott's Pl A2	

Birmingham

Abbey St A2	Allcock St C5	Bagot St B4	Berkley St C3
Aberdeen St A1	Allesley St A4	Banbury St B5	Bexhill Gr C3
Acorn Gr A2	Allison St C4	Barford Rd B1	Birchall St C5
Adams St A5	Alston Rd C1	Barford St C4	Birmingham City F.C.
Adderley St C5	Arcadian Centre C4	Barn St C5	(St Andrew's) C6
Albert St B4/B5	Arthur St C6	Barnwell Rd C6	Birmingham City
Albion St A3	Assay Office 🏛 B3	Barr St A3	Hospital (A&E) Ⓗ . . . A1
Alcester St C5	Aston Expressway . . . A5	Barrack St B4	Bishopsgate St C3
Aldgate Gr A3	Aston Science Park . . . B5	Bartholomew St C4	Blews St A4
Alexandra Theatre 🎭 . C3	Aston St B4	Barwick St B4	Bloomsbury St A6
All Saint's St A2	Avenue Rd A5	Bath Row C3	Blucher St C3
All Saints Rd A2	BT Tower ♦ B3	Beaufort Rd C1	Bordesley St C4
	Bacchus Rd A1	Belmont Row B5	Bowyer St C5
		Benson Rd A1	Bradburne Way A5

Bradford St C5	Browning St C2	Cato St A6	Church St B4
Branston St A3	Bryant St A1	Cato St North A6	Claremont Rd A2
Brearley St A4	Buckingham St A3	Cattell Rd C6	Clarendon Rd C1
Brewery St A4	Bullring C4	Cattells Gr A6	Clark St C1
Bridge St A3	Bull St B4	Cawdor Cr C1	Clement St B3
Bridge St C3	Cambridge St C3	Cecil St B4	Clissold St B2
Bridge St West B4	Camden Dr B3	Cemetery A2/B2	Cleveland St B4
Brindley Dr B3	Camden St B3	Cemetery La A2	Coach Station C5
Broad St C3	Cannon St C4	Centre Link	College St B3
Broad St UGC 🎬 C2	Cardigan St B5	Industrial Estate A6	Colmore Circus B4
Broadway Plaza ♦ . . . C2	Carlisle St A1	Charlotte St B3	Colmore Row B4
Bromley St C5	Carlyle Rd C1	Cheapside C4	Commercial St C3
Bromsgrove St C4	Caroline St B3	Chester St A5	Constitution Hill B3
Brookfield Rd A2	Carver St B2	Children's Hospital Ⓗ . B4	Convention Centre . . . C3

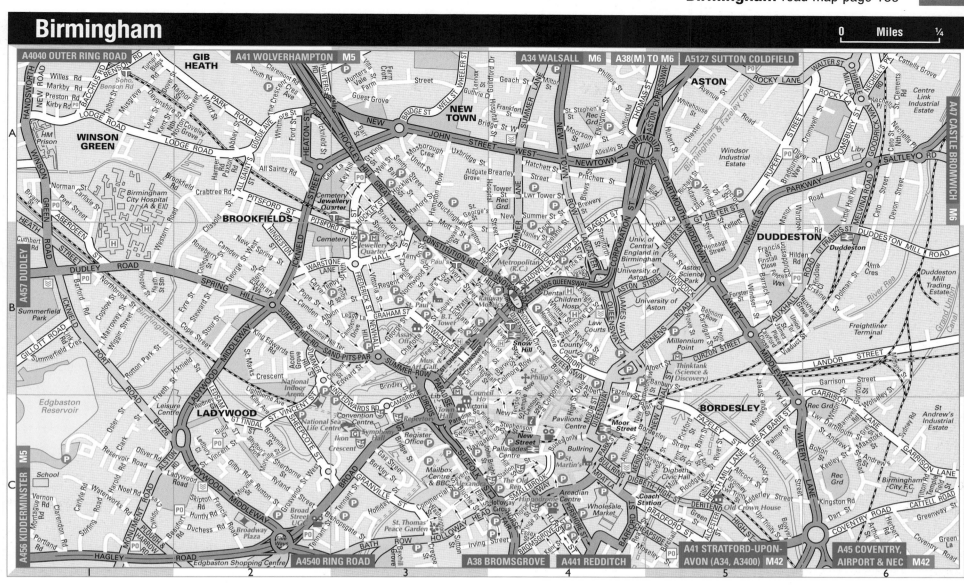

Birmingham

Birmingham continued

Cope St B2
Coplow St. B1
Corporation St B4
Council House 🏛 . . . B3
County Court B4
Coveley Gr A2
Coventry Rd C6
Coventry St C5
Cox St B3
Crabtree Rd A2
Cregoe St C3
Crescent Ave A2
Crescent Theatre 🎭 . C3
Cromwell St A6
Cromwell St B3
Curzon St B5
Cuthbert Rd B1
Dale End B4
Dart St C6
Dartmouth Circus . . . A4
Dartmouth
   Middleway A5
Dental Hospital 🏥 . . B4
Deritend C5
Devon St. A6
Devonshire St. A1
Digbeth Civic Hall. . . C5
Digbeth High St C4
Dolman St. B6
Dover St A1
Duchess Rd C2
Duddeston ≈ B6
Duddeston
   Manor St B5
Duddeston Mill Rd . . B6
Duddeston Mill
   Trading Estate . . . B6
Dudley Rd. B1
Edgbaston Shopping
   Centre C2
Edmund St. B3
Edward St. B3
Elkington St A4
Ellen St. B2
Ellis St. C3
Erskine St B6
Essex St C4
Eyre St B2
Farm Croft A3
Farm St A3
Fazeley St B4

Felstead Way B5
Finstall Cl B5
Five Ways. C2
Fleet St B3
Floodgate St. C5
Ford St A2
Fore St B4
Forster St B5
Francis Rd C2
Francis St. B5
Frankfort St A4
Frederick St B3
Freeth St. C1
Freightliner Terminal . B6
Garrison La. C6
Garrison St B6
Gas St C3
Geach St A4
George St. B3
George St West B2
Gibb St C5
Gillott Rd B1
Gilby Rd C2
Glover St C6
Goode Ave A2
Goodrick Way. A6
Gordon St. B6
Graham St B3
Granville St. C3
Gray St C5
Great Barr St C5
Great Charles St. B3
Great Francis St B6
Great Hampton Row . A3
Great Hampton St . . . A3
Great King St A3
Great Lister St A5
Great Tindal St C2
Green La. C6
Green St C5
Greenway St. C6
Grosvenor St West . . . C2
Guest Gr A3
Guild Cl. A3
Guildford Dr A4
Guthrie Cl. A3
Hagley Rd. C1
Hall St. B3
Hampton St B3
Handsworth New Rd . A1
Hanley St B4
Harford St A3
Harmer Rd A3
Harold Rd C1
Hatchett St A4

Heath Mill La C5
Heath St B1
Heath St South. B1
Heaton St A2
Heneage St. B4
Henrietta St B4
Herbert Rd C6
High St B4
High St C5
Hilden Rd B5
Hill St C3
Hindlow Cl B6
Hingeston St B2
Hippodrome
   Theatre 🎭. C4
HM Prison A1
Hockley Circus A2
Hockley Hill A3
Hockley St A3
Holliday St C3
Holloway Circus C4
Holloway Head C4
Holt St B5
Hooper St. B1
Horse Fair C4
Hospital St A4
Howard St B3
Howe St B5
Hubert St A5
Hunters Rd A2
Hunters Vale A3
Huntly Rd C2
Hurst St C4
Icknield Port Rd B1
Icknield Sq. B2
Icknield St. A2
Inge St C4
Irving St C3
Ivy La C5
James Watt
   Queensway B4
Jennens Rd B5
Jewellery
   Quarter ≈ A3
Jewellery Quarter
   Museum 🏛 B3
John Bright St C4
Keeley St C6
Kellett Rd B5
Kent St C4
Kent St North A1
Kenyon St B3
Key Hill A3

Kilby Ave C2
King Edwards Rd B2
King Edwards Rd C3
Kingston Rd C6
Kirby Rd A1
Ladywood
   Middleway C2
Ladywood Rd. C1
Lancaster St B4
Landor St B6
Law Courts B4
Lawford Cl B5
Lawley Middleway . . . B5
Ledbury Cl C2
Ledsam St B2
Lees St A1
Legge La B3
Lennox St. A3
Library A6/C3
Library Walk B2
Lighthorne Ave B2
Link Rd B1
Lionel St B3
Lister St B5
Little Ann St C5
Little Hall Rd A6
Liverpool St C5
Livery St B3
Lodge Rd A1
Lord St A5
Love La. A5
Loveday St B4
Lower Dartmouth St. . C6
Lower Loveday St . . . B4
Lower Tower St A4
Lower Trinty St C5
Ludgate Hill B3
Mailbox Centre
   & BBC C3
Margaret St. B3
Markby Rd A1
Marroway St. B1
Maxstoke St C6
Melvina Rd A6
Meriden St C4
Metropolitan
   (R.C.) ✝ B4
Midland St B6
Milk St C5
Mill St A5
Millennium Point. . . . B5
Miller St A4
Milton St A4
Moat La C4
Montague Rd C1

Montague St. C5
Monument Rd C1
Moor Street ≈ C4
Moor St Queensway. . C4
Moorsom St A4
Morville St C2
Mosborough Cr A3
Moseley St C4
Mott St B3
Museum &
   Art Gallery 🏛 B3
Musgrave Rd A1
National Indoor
   Arena ✦ B2
National Sea Life
   Centre C3
Navigation St C3
Nechell's Park Rd. . . . A6
Nechells Parkway. . . . A5
Nechells Pl A6
New
   Bartholomew St . . . C4
New Canal St B5
New John St West . . . A3
New Spring St B2
New St C4
New Street ≈ C4
New Summer St A4
New Town Row A4
Newhall Hill B3
Newhall St B3
Newton St B4
Newtown A4
Noel Rd C1
Norman St A1
Northbrook St. B1
Northwood St B3
Norton St A2
Old Crown House 🏛 .C5
Old Rep Theatre,
   The 🎭 C4
Old Snow Hill B4
Oliver Rd C1
Oliver St A5
Osler St C1
Oxford St C5
Pallasades Centre . . . C4
Palmer St C5
Paradise Circus C3
Paradise St C3
Park Rd A2
Park St C4
Pavilions Centre C4
Paxton Rd A2
Peel St A1

Penn St B5
Pershore St C4
Phillips St A4
Pickford St C4
Pinfold St C4
Pitsford St A2
Plough & Harrow Rd . C1
Police Station
   . . . . . A4/B1/B4/C2/C4
Pope St B2
Portland Rd C1
Post Office 🏤 . A1/A3/A5/
   B1/B5/C1/C2/C3/C6
Preston Rd A1
Price St. B4
Princip St B4
Printing House St B4
Priory Queensway . . . B4
Pritchett St A4
Proctor St A5
Queensway. C4
Radnor St A2
Railway Mosaics ✦ . . B4
Rea St C5
Regent Pl B3
Register Office C3
Repertory Theatre 🎭 . C3
Reservoir Rd C1
Richard St A5
River St. C5
Rocky La A5
Rodney Cl C2
Roseberry St B2
Rotton Park St B1
Rupert St A5
Ruston St C2
Ryland St C2
St Andrew's Industrial
   Estate. C6
St Andrew's Rd C6
St Andrew's St C6
St Bolton St C6
St Chads Circus B4
St Chads
   Queensway B4
St Clements Rd A6
St George's St A3
St James Pl B5
St Marks Cr C2
St Martin's 🏛 C4
St Paul's 🏛 B3
St Paul's (Metro) B3
St Paul's Sq B3
St Philip's ✝ B4
St Stephen's St A4

St Thomas' Peace
   Garden ✿ C3
St Vincent St C2
Saltley Rd A6
Sand Pits Pde B3
Severn St C3
Shadwell St B4
Sheepcote St C2
Shefford Rd A4
Sherborne St C2
Shylton's Croft C2
Skipton Rd C2
Smallbrook
   Queensway C4
Smith St A3
Snow Hill ≈ B4
Snow Hill
   Queensway B4
Soho, Benson Rd
   (Metro) A1
South Rd A2
Spencer St B3
Spring Hill B2
Staniforth St B4
Station St C4
Steelhouse La. B4
Stephenson St C4
Steward St B2
Stirling Rd. C1
Stour St B2
Suffolk St C3
Summer Hill Rd B2
Summer Hill St B2
Summer Hill Terr. . . . B2
Summer La. A4
Summer Row B3
Summerfield Cr B1
Summerfield Park. . . . B1
Sutton St C3
Swallow St C3
Sydney Rd C6
Symphony Hall 🎭 . . . C3
Talbot St A1
Temple Row C4
Temple St C4
Templefield St. C6
Tenby St B3
Tenby St North B2
Tennant St C2
The Crescent A2
Thimble Mill La A6
Thinktank (Science
   & Discovery) 🏛 . . . B5
Thomas St A4
Thorpe St C4

Tilton Rd C6
Tower St A4
Town Hall 🏛 C3
Trent St C5
Turner's Buildings. . . . A1
Unett St A3
Union Terr. A3
University of Central
   England in
   Birmingham B4
University of
   Aston B4/B5
Upper Trinity St C5
Uxbridge St A3
Vauxhall Gr B5
Vauxhall Rd B5
Vernon Rd C1
Vesey St B4
Viaduct St. B5
Victoria Sq C3
Villa St A3
Vittoria St B3
Vyse St B3
Walter St. A6
Wardlow Rd A5
Warstone La B2
Washington St C3
Water St B3
Waterworks Rd. C1
Watery La C5
Well St A3
Western Rd. B1
Wharf St A2
Wheeler St A3
Whitehouse St A4
Whitmore St A2
Whittall St B4
Wholesale Market. . . . C4
Wiggin St B1
Willes Rd A1
Windsor Industrial
   Estate. A5
Windsor St A5
Windsor St B5
Winson Green Rd . . . A1
Witton St C6
Wolseley St. C6
Woodcock St B5

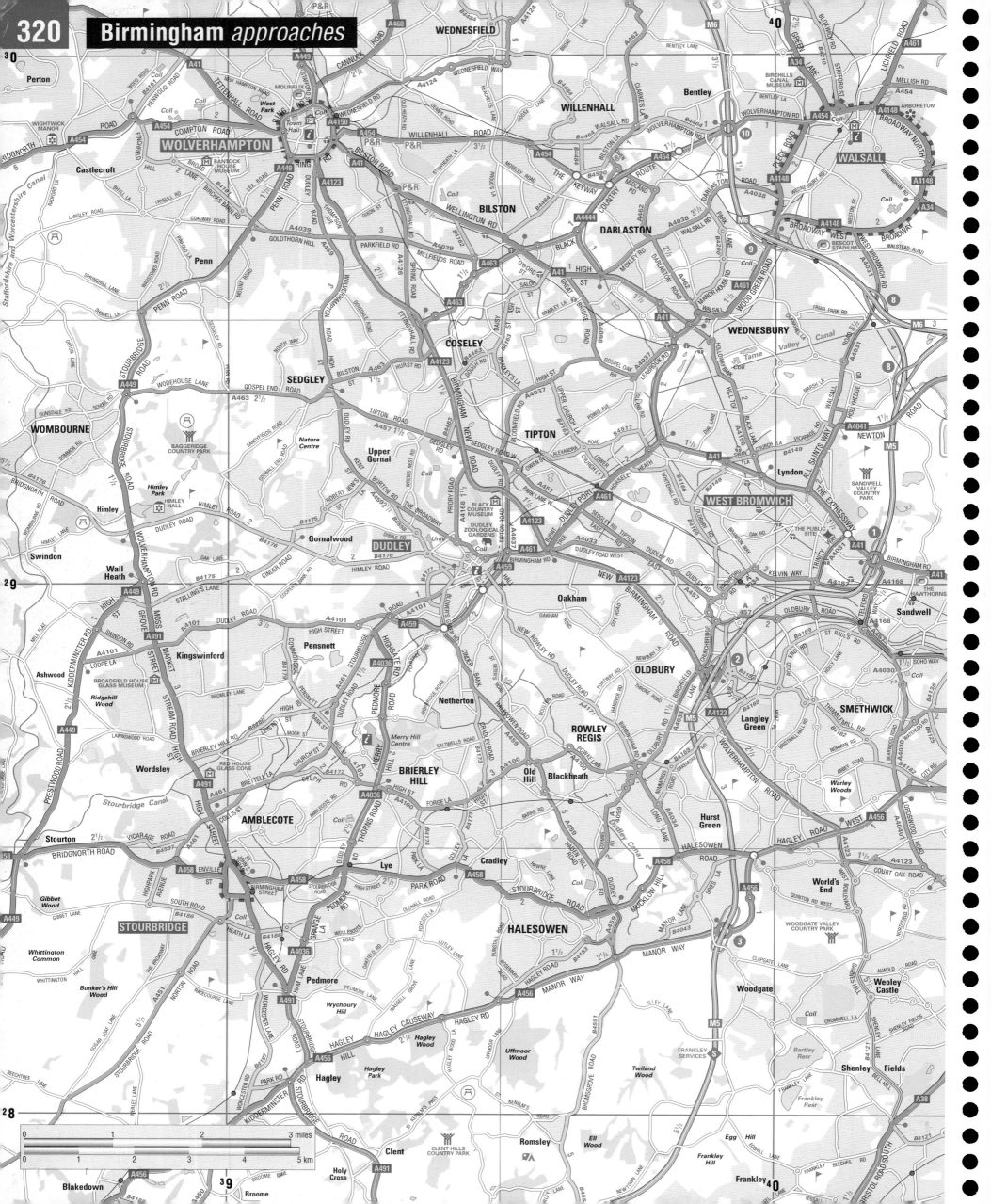

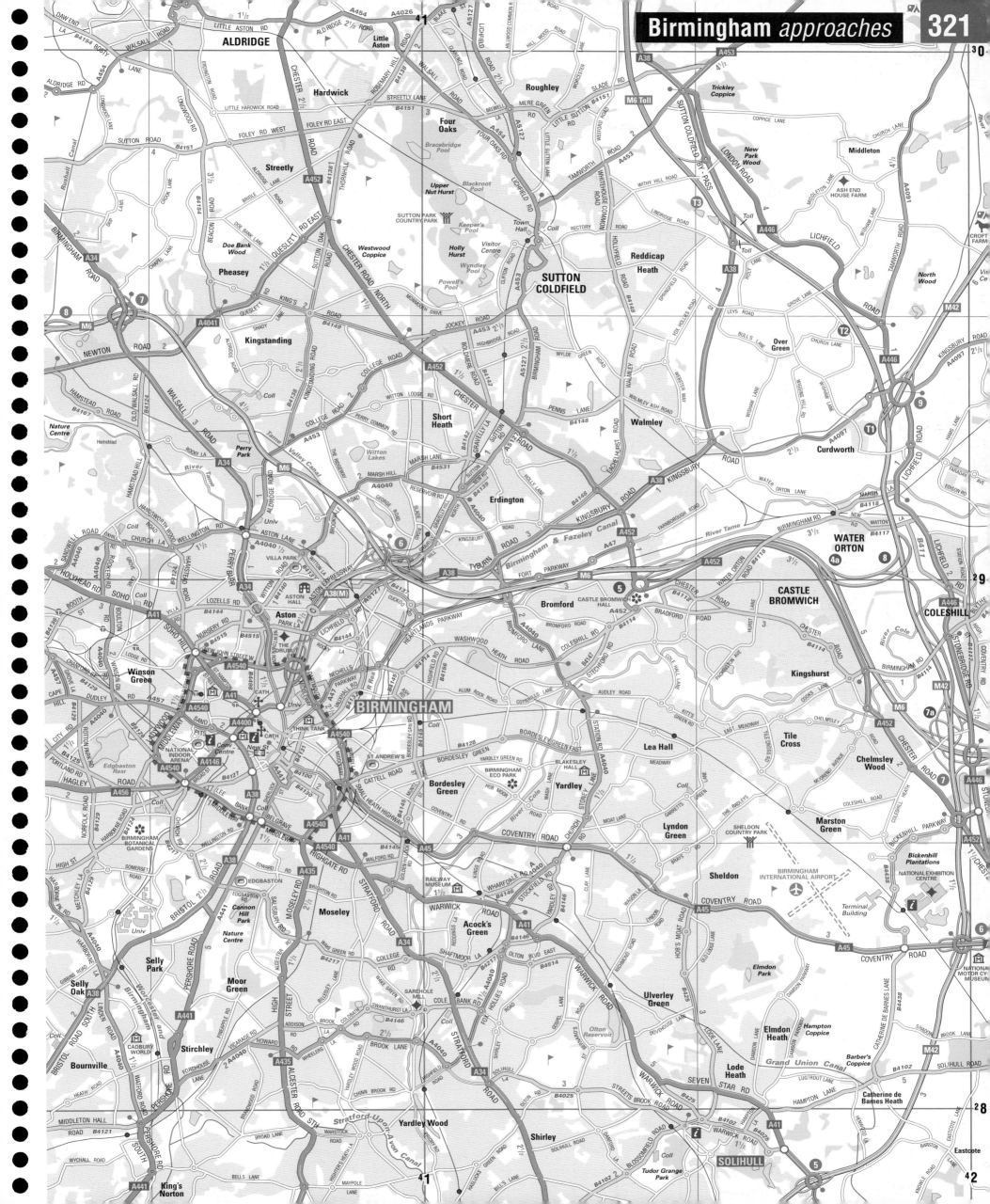

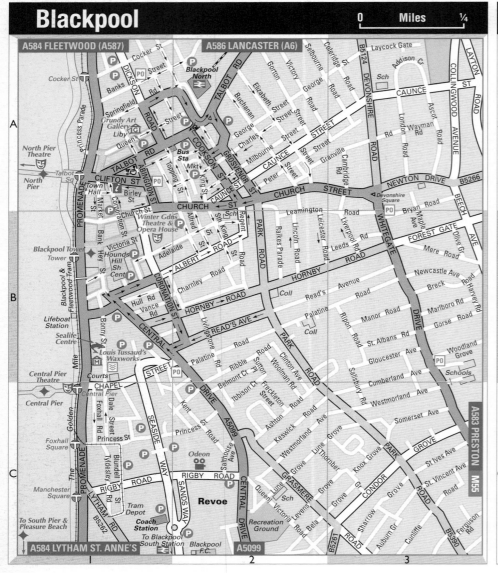

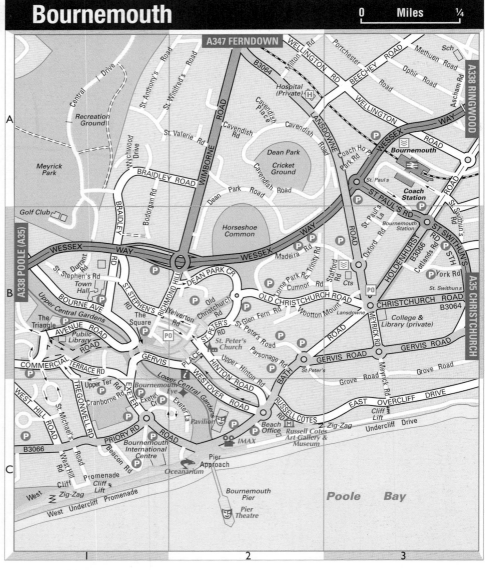

Blackpool

Abingdon St A1	
Addison Cr A3	
Adelaide St B1	
Albert Rd B2	
Alfred St B2	
Ascot Rd A3	
Ashton Rd C2	
Auburn Gr C3	
Bank Hey St B1	
Banks St A1	
Beech Ave B3	
Bela Gr C2	
Belmont Ct B2	
Birley St A1	
Blackpool &	
Fleetwood Tram B1	
Blackpool F.C. C2	
Blackpool North ⇌ . . A2	
Blackpool Tower ✦ . . B1	
Blundell St C1	
Bonny St B1	
Breck Rd B3	
Bryan Rd A3	
Buchanan St. A2	
Bus Station. A2	
Cambridge Rd A3	
Caunce St A2	
Central Dr B1	
Central Pier ✦ C1	
Central Pier	
(Tram stop) C1	
Central Pier	
Theatre 🎭 C1	
Chapel St C1	
Charles St A2	
Charnley Rd B2	
Church St A1	
Clifton St A1	
Clinton Ave. B2	
Coach Station C1	

Cocker St A1	
Cocker St	
(Tram stop) A1	
Coleridge Rd A3	
Collingwood Ave A3	
Condor Rd C3	
Cookson St A2	
Coronation St. B1	
Corporation St A1	
Courts. B1	
Cumberland Ave. B3	
Cunliffe Rd C3	
Dale St C1	
Devonshire Rd A3	
Devonshire Sq A3	
Dickson Rd. A1	
Elizabeth St A2	
Ferguson Rd. C3	
Forest Gate. B3	
Foxhall Rd C1	
Foxhall Sq	
(Tram stop). C1	
Freckleton St C2	
George St A2	
Gloucester Ave. B3	
Golden Mile, The C1	
Gorse Rd B3	
Gorton St A2	
Granville Rd A2	
Grasmere Rd C2	
Grosvenor St A2	
Grundy Art	
Gallery 🏛 A1	
Harvey Rd. B3	
Hornby Rd B2	
Hounds Hill Shopping	
Centre B1	
Hull Rd B1	
Ibbison Ct. C2	
Information Ctr ℹ . . . A1	
Kent Rd C2	
Keswick Rd C2	

King St A2	
Knox Gr C3	
Laycock Gate. A3	
Layton Rd. A3	
Leamington Rd. B2	
Leeds Rd B3	
Leicester Rd B2	
Levens Gr C2	
Library A1	
Lifeboat Station B1	
Lincoln Rd B2	
Liverpool Rd B2	
Livingstone Rd. B2	
London Rd A3	
Lune Gr C2	
Lytham Rd C1	
Manchester Sq	
(Tram stop) C1	
Manor Rd B3	
Maple Ave B3	
Market A2	
Market St A1	
Marlboro Rd B3	
Mere Rd B3	
Milbourne St A2	
Newcastle Ave B3	
Newton Dr A3	
North Pier ✦ A1	
North Pier Theatre 🎭 . A1	
Odeon 🎬 C2	
Olive Gr B3	
Palatine Rd. B2	
Park Rd B2	
Peter St A2	
Police Station 🚓 . . . B1	
Post Office 📮 . A1/B2/B3	
Princess Pde A1	
Princess St C1/C2	
Promenade. A1/C1	
Queen St A1	

Queen Victoria Rd . . . C2	
Raikes Pde B2	
Read's Ave B2	
Regent Rd B2	
Ribble Rd B2	
Rigby Rd. C1	
Ripon Rd B3	
St Albans Rd B3	
St Ives Ave B3	
St Vincent Ave C3	
Salisbury Rd. B3	
Salthouse Ave C2	
Sands Way C2	
Sealife Centre ⚓ . . . B1	
Seaside Way. C1	
Selbourne Rd A2/A3	
Sharrow Gr. C2	
Somerset Ave. C3	
Springfield Rd. A1	
South King St B2	
Sutton Pl. B1	
Talbot Rd A1	
Talbot Sq	
(Tram stop) A1	
Thornber Gr C2	
Topping St A1	
Tower (Tram stop). . . . B1	
Town Hall A1	
Tram Depot. C1	
Tyldesley Rd C1	
Vance Rd B1	
Victoria St B1	
Victory Rd. A2	
Wayman Rd A3	
Westmorland Ave C2	
Whitegate Dr B3	
Winter Gardens Theatre	
& Opera House 🎭 . . B1	
Woodland Gr B3	
Woolman Rd. B2	

Bournemouth

Ascham Rd. A3	
Avenue Rd B1	
Bath Rd C2	
Beacon Rd C1	
Beach Office. C2	
Beechey Rd A3	
Bodorgan Rd B1	
Bourne Ave. B1	
Bournemouth Eye ✦ . C2	
Bournemouth	
International Ctr C1	
Bournemouth Pier . . . C2	
Bournemouth	
Station ⇌ A3	
Bournemouth Station	
(r'about) B3	
Braidley Rd. A1	
Cavendish Place A2	
Cavendish Rd. A2	
Central Drive. A1	
Christchurch Rd B3	
Cliff Lift C1/C3	
Coach House La A3	
Coach Station A3	
College & Library A3	
Commercial Rd B1	
Cotlands Rd. B3	
Courts. B3	

Cranborne Rd. C1	
Cricket Ground. A2	
Cumnor Rd. B2	
Dean Park. A2	
Dean Park Cr B2	
Dean Park Rd. A2	
Durrant Rd B1	
East Overcliff Dr C3	
Exeter Cr C1	
Exeter La C2	
Exeter Rd C1	
Gervis Place B1	
Gervis Rd B3	
Glen Fern Rd B2	
Golf Club A1	
Grove Rd B3	
Hinton Rd. C2	
Holdenhurst Rd B3	
Horseshoe Common . B2	
Hospital (Private) 🏥 . . A2	
IMAX 🎬 C2	
Information Ctr ℹ. . . . B2	
Lansdowne (r'about) . B3	
Lansdowne Rd. A2	
Lorne Park Rd B2	
Lower Central Gdns . . B2	
Madeira Rd. B2	
Methuen Rd A3	
Meyrick Park A1	
Meyrick Rd B3	

Milton Rd A2	
Oceanarium ⚓ C2	
Old Christchurch Rd. . B2	
Ophir Rd A3	
Oxford Rd. B3	
Park Rd B2	
Parsonage Rd. B2	
Pavilion 🎭 C2	
Pier Approach C2	
Pier Theatre 🎭 C2	
Police Station 🚓 . . A3/B3	
Portchester Rd A3	
Post Office 📮 B1/B3	
Priory Rd C1	
Recreation Ground. . . A1	
Richmond Hill Rd B1	
Russell Cotes Art Gallery	
& Museum 🏛 C2	
Russell Cotes Rd C2	
St Anthony's Rd A1	
St Michael's Rd. C1	
St Paul's (r'about). . . . B3	
St Paul's La B3	
St Paul's Rd A3	
St Peter's ⛪ B2	
St Peter's (r'about) . . . B2	
St Peter's Rd B2	
St Stephen's Rd B1	
St Swithun's	
(r'about) B3	

St Swithun's Rd A3	
St Swithun's	
Rd South B3	
St Valerie Rd. A2	
St Winifred's Rd A2	
Stafford Rd. B3	
Terrace Rd B1	
The Square. B1	
The Triangle B1	
Town Hall B1	
Tregonwell Rd. C1	
Trinity Rd B2	
Undercliff Drive. C3	
Upper Central Gdns . . B1	
Upper Hinton Rd B2	
Upper Terr Rd C1	
Wellington Rd A3	
Wessex Way B2	
West Cliff	
Promenade. C1	
West Hill Rd C1	
West Undercliff	
Promenade. C1	
Westover Rd. B2	
Wimborne Rd A2	
Wootton Mount B1	
Wychwood Dr. A1	
Yelverton Rd. B2	
York Rd. B3	
Zig-Zag Walks . . . C1/C3	

Bradford

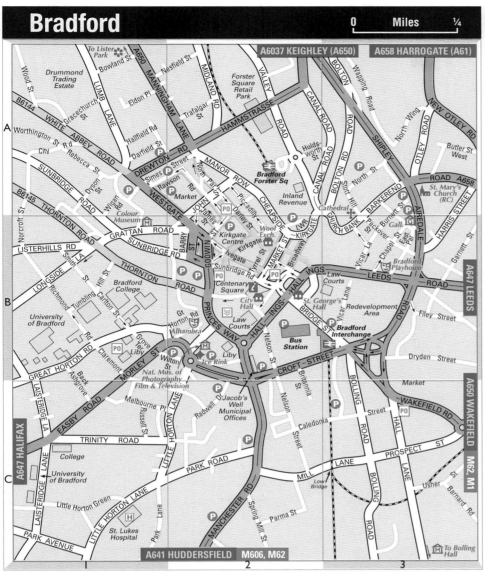

Brighton

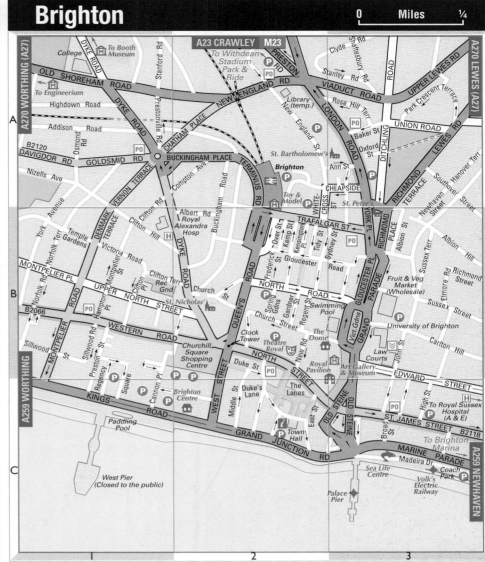

Bradford

Brighton

Bristol

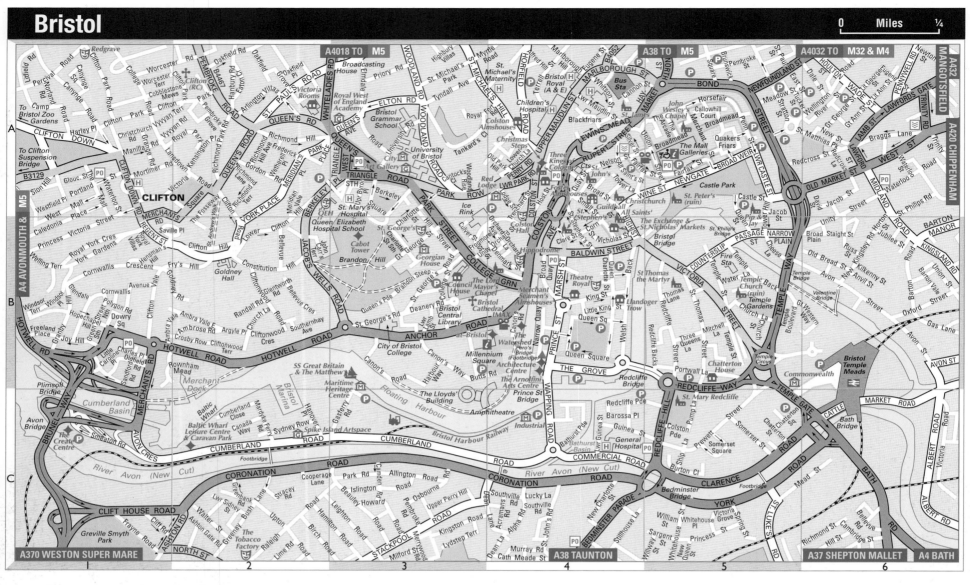

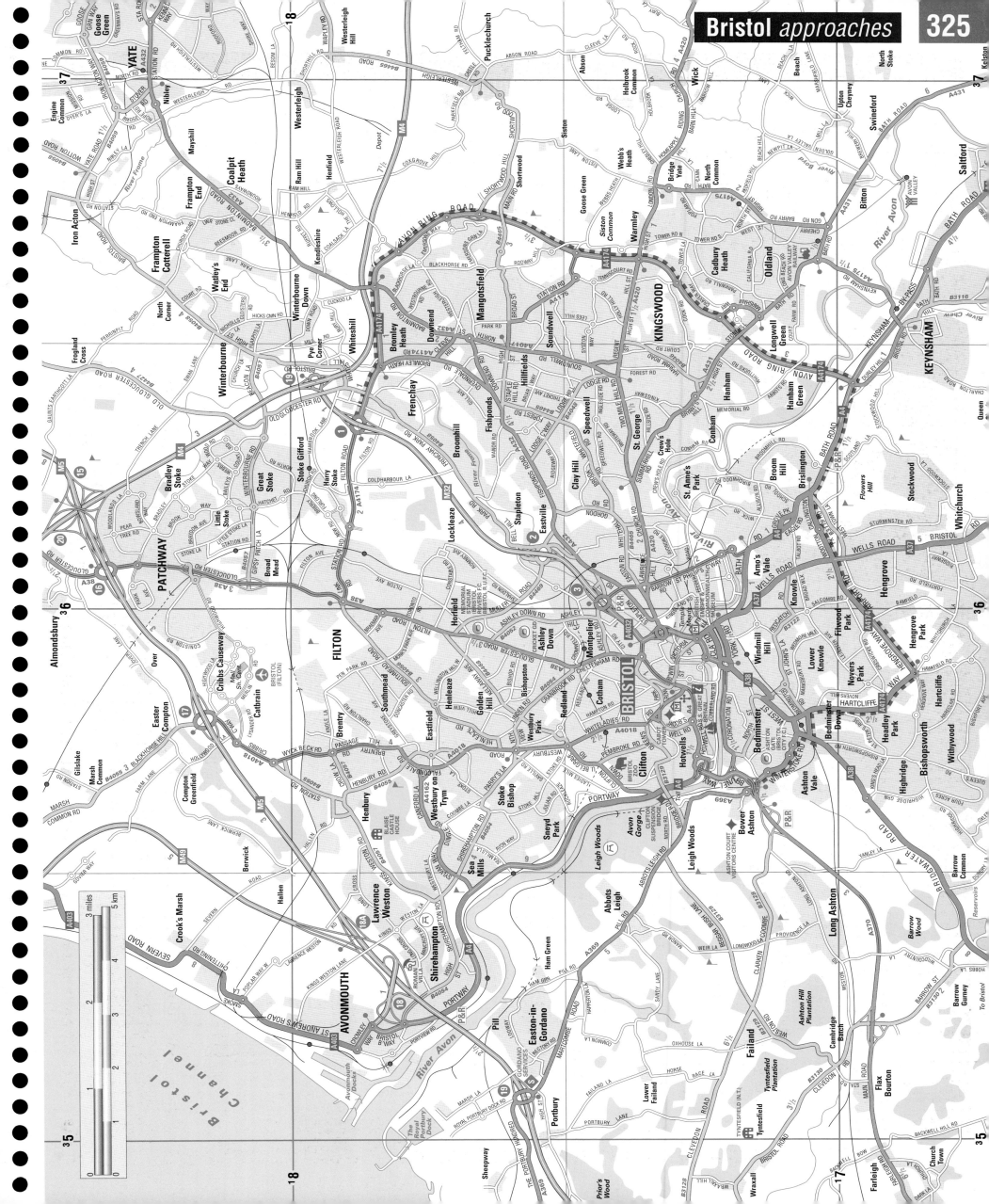

Cardiff / Caerdydd

0 Miles ¼

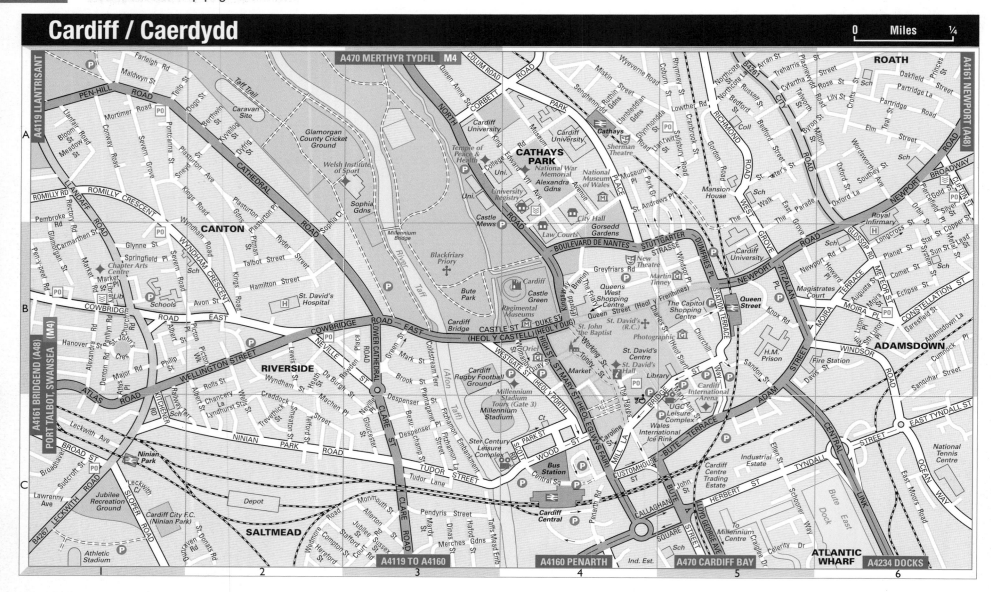

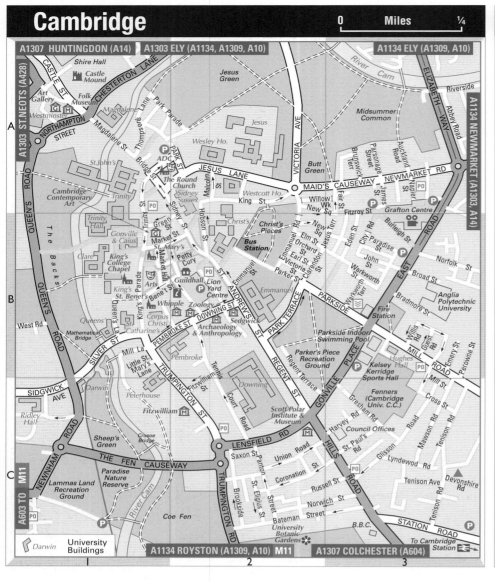

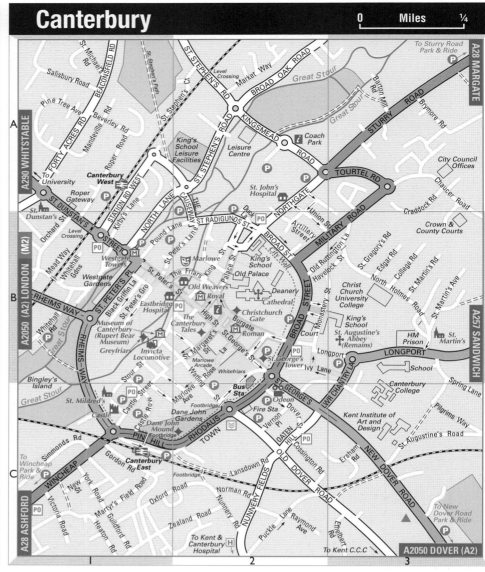

Cambridge

Abbey Rd A3
ADC ♦ A2
Anglia Polytechnic
 University B3
Archaeology &
 Anthropology ⌂ B2
Art Gallery ⌂ A1
Arts Theatre ♦ B1
Auckland Rd A3
Bateman St C2
B.B.C. C3
Bene't St B1
Bradmore St B3
Bridge St A1
Broad St B3
Brookside C2
Brunswick Terr A3
Burleigh St B3
Bus Station B2
Butt Green A2
Cambridge
 Contemporary
 Art Gallery ⌂ B1
Castle Mound ⌂ A1
Castle St A1
Chesterton La. A1
Christ's (Coll) B2
Christ's Pieces B2
City Rd B3
Clare (Coll) B1
Clarendon St B2
Coe Fen C2
Coronation St C2
Corpus Christi (Coll) . . B1
Council Offices C3
Cross St C3
Crusoe Bridge C1
Darwin (Coll) C1
Devonshire Rd C3
Downing (Coll) B2
Downing St B2
Earl St B2
East Rd B3
Eden St B3
Elizabeth Way A3
Elm St B2

Emery St B3
Emmanuel (Coll) B2
Emmanuel Rd. B2
Emmanuel St B2
Fair St A3
Fenners (Cambridge
 Univ. C. C.) C3
Fire Station B3
Fitzroy St A3
Fitzwilliam
 Museum ⌂ C1
Fitzwilliam St C1
Folk Museum ⌂ A1
Glisson Rd C3
Gonville &
 Caius (Coll) B1
Gonville Place B3
Grafton Centre A3
Gresham Rd C3
Green St B1
Guest Rd B3
Guildhall ⌂ B2
Harvey Rd. C3
Hills Rd C3
Hobson St B2
Hughes Hall (Coll) . . . B3
Information Ctr ⓘ B2
James St A3
Jesus (Coll) A2
Jesus Green A2
Jesus La A2
Jesus Terr B3
John St B3
Kelsey Kerridge
 Sports Hall B3
King St A2
King's (Coll) B1
King's College
 Chapel ⌂ B1
King's Parade B1
Lensfield Rd C2
Lion Yard Centre B2
Little St Mary's La . . . B1
Lyndewod Rd C3
Magdalene (Coll) A1
Magdalene St A1
Maid's Causeway A3
Malcolm St A2

Market Hill B1
Market St B1
Mathematical Bridge . B1
Mawson Rd C3
Midsummer
 Common A3
Mill La. B1
Mill Rd B3
Napier St A3
New Square A2
Newmarket Rd A3
Newnham Rd C1
Norfolk St B3
Northampton St A1
Norwich St C2
Orchard St B2
Panton St C2
Paradise Nature
 Reserve C1
Paradise St B3
Park Parade A1
Park St A2
Park Terr B2
Parker St B2
Parker's Piece B2
Parkside B2
Parkside Swimming
 Pool B3
Parsonage St A3
Pembroke (Coll) B2
Pembroke St B1
Perowne St B3
Peterhouse (Coll) C1
Petty Cury B2
Police Station ⌂ B3
Post Office ⓟ A1/A3/
 B2/B3/C1/C2/C3
Queens' (Coll) B1
Queen's La B1
Queen's Rd B1
Regent St B2
Regent Terr B2
Ridley Hall (Coll) C1
Riverside A3
Round Church,
 The ⌂ A1
Russell St C2
St Andrew's St B2

St Benet's ⌂ B1
St Catharine's (Coll) . . B1
St Eligius St C2
St John's (Coll) A1
St Mary's B1
St Paul's Rd C3
Saxon St C2
Scott Polar Institute
 & Museum ⌂ C2
Sedgwick
 Museum ⌂ B2
Sheep's Green C1
Shelly Row A1
Shire Hall A1
Sidgwick Ave C1
Sidney St B1
Sidney Sussex (Coll) . A2
Silver St B1
Station Rd C3
Tenison Ave C3
Tenison Rd C3
Tennis Court Rd B2
The Backs B1
The Fen Causeway . . . C1
Thompson's La A1
Trinity (Coll) A1
Trinity Hall (Coll) B1
Trinity St B1
Trumpington Rd C2
Trumpington St C2
Union Rd C2
University Botanic
 Gardens ❀ C3
Victoria Ave A2
Victoria St B2
Warkworth St B2
Warkworth Terr B3
Wesley House (Coll) . . A2
West Rd B1
Westcott House
 (Coll) A2
Westminster (Coll) . . . A1
Whipple ⌂ B2
Willis Rd B3
Willow Walk A2
Zoology ⌂ B2

Canterbury

Artillery St B2
Barton Mill Rd A3
Beaconsfield Rd. A1
Beverley Rd A1
Bingley's Island B1
Black Griffin La. B1
Broad Oak Rd A2
Broad St B2
Brymore Rd A3
Burgate B2
Bus Station C2
Canterbury College . . C3
Canterbury East ⌁ . . . C1
Canterbury Tales,
 The ♦ B2
Canterbury West ⌁ . . . A1
Castle ⌂ C1
Castle Row C1
Castle St C1
Cathedral † B2
Chaucer Rd A3
Christ Church
 University College . . B3
Christchurch Gate ♦ . . B2
City Council Offices . . A3
City Wall B2
Coach Park A2
College Rd B3
Cossington Rd C2
Court. B2
Craddock Rd A3
Crown & County
 Courts B3
Dane John Gdns C2
Dane John
 Mound ♦ C1
Deanery B2
Dover St C2
Duck La B2

Eastbridge
 Hospital ⌂ B1
Edgar Rd B3
Ersham Rd C3
Ethelbert Rd C3
Fire Station C2
Forty Acres Rd A1
Gordon Rd C1
Greyfriars ♦ B1
Guildford Rd C1
Havelock St B2
Heaton Rd C1
High St B2
HM Prison B3
Information Ctr ⓘ . . . A2/B2
Invicta
 Locomotive ⌂ B1
Ivy La B2
Kent Institute of
 Art and Design C3
King St B2
King's School B3
Kingsmead Rd A2
Kirby's La B1
Lansdown Rd C2
Leisure Centre A2
Longport B3
Lower Chantry La. . . . C3
Mandeville Rd. A1
Market Way A2
Marlowe Arcade B2
Marlowe Ave. C2
Marlowe Theatre ♦ . . B2
Martyr's Field Rd C1
Mead Way B1
Military Rd B2
Monastery St B2
Museum of Canterbury
 (Rupert Bear
 Museum) ⌂ B1
New Dover Rd C3

New St C1
Norman Rd C2
North Holmes Rd B3
North La B1
Northgate. A2
Nunnery Fields C2
Nunnery Rd C2
Oaten Hill C2
Odeon Cinema ⌂ C2
Old Dover Rd C3
Old Palace B2
Old Ruttington La. . . . B2
Old Weavers ⌂ B2
Orchard St B1
Oxford Rd C1
Palace St B2
Pilgrims Way. C3
Pin Hill C1
Pine Tree Ave A1
Police Station ⌂ C2
Post Office ⓟ
 . . . . . . B1/B2/C1/C2
Pound La B1
Puckle La C2
Raymond Ave. C2
Rheims Way B1
Rhodaus Town C1
Roman Museum ⌂ . . . B2
Roper Gateway A1
Roper Rd A1
Rose La B2
Royal Museum ⌂ B2
St Augustine's Abbey
 (remains) † B3
St Augustine's Rd. . . . C3
St Dunstan's ⌂ A1
St Dunstan's St A1
St George's Pl C2
St.George's St B2
St.George's
 Tower ♦ B2

St Gregory's Rd B3
St John's
 Hospital ⌂ A2
St Margaret's St B2
St Martin's ⌂ B3
St Martin's Ave B3
St Martin's Rd B3
St Michael's Rd A1
St Mildred's ⌂ C1
St Peter's Gr. B1
St Peter's La. B2
St Peter's Pl B1
St Peter's St B1
St Radigunds St B2
St Stephen's Ct A1
St Stephen's Path . . . A1
St Stephen's Rd A2
Salisbury Rd A1
Simmonds Rd C1
Spring La C3
Station Rd West B1
Stour St B1
Sturry Rd A3
The Causeway A1
The Friars B2
Tourtel Rd A3
Union St B2
Vernon Pl C2
Victoria Rd C1
Watling St B2
Westgate Towers ⌂ . . B1
Westgate Gdns B1
Whitefriars B2
Whitehall Gdns B1
Whitehall Rd B1
Wincheap C1
York Rd C1
Zealand Rd C2

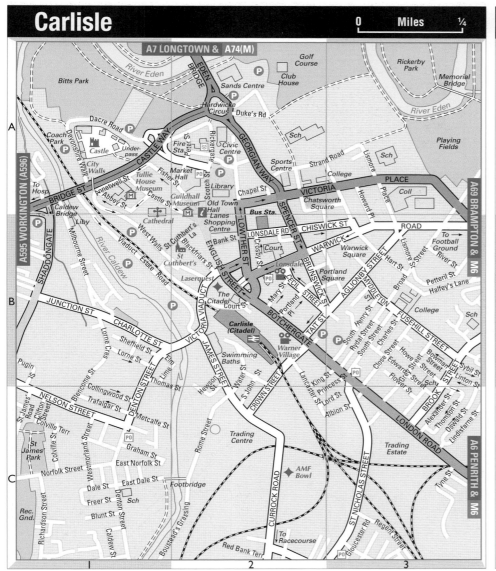

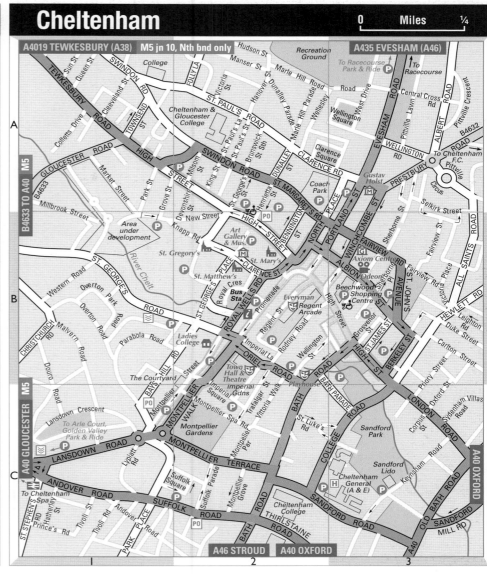

Carlisle

Abbey St. A1
Aglionby St. B3
Albion St. C3
Alexander St. A3
AMF Bowl ✦ C2
Annetwell St A1
Bank St. B2
Bitts Park A1
Blackfriars St B2
Blencome St. C1
Blunt St. C1
Botchergate B2
Boustead's Grassing . C2
Bowman St. B3
Broad St. B3
Bridge St A1
Brook St C3
Brunswick St B2
Bus Station B2
Caldew Bridge A1
Caldew St. C1
Carlisle (Citadel)
   Station B2
Castle 🏰 A1
Castle St. A1
Castle Way A1
Cathedral ✝ A1
Cecil St. B2
Chapel St. A2
Charles St. B3
Charlotte St B1
Chatsworth Square . . A2
Chiswick St B2
Citadel, The B2
City Walls A1
Civic Centre A2
Clifton St C1
Close St B3

Collingwood St C1
Colville St C1
Colville Terr. C1
Court. B2
Court St B2
Crosby St B2
Crown St C2
Currock Rd C2
Dacre Rd A1
Dale St C1
Denton St C1
Devonshire Walk. A1
Duke's Rd. A1
East Dale St C1
East Norfolk St C1
Eden Bridge A2
Edward St B3
Elm St B1
English St. B2
Fire Station A2
Fisher St. A2
Flower St C3
Freer St. C1
Fusehill St B3
Georgian Way A2
Gloucester Rd C3
Golf Course A2
Graham St C1
Grey St B3
Guildhall Museum 🏛 . A2
Halfey's La B3
Hardwicke Circus A2
Hart St B3
Hewson St C2
Howard Pl. A3
Howe St B3
Information Ctr ℹ A2
James St B2
Junction St B1
King St B2

Lancaster St C2
Lanes Shopping
   Centre A2/B2
Laserquest ✦ B2
Library A2/B1
Lime St B1
Lindisfarne St C3
Linton St B3
Lismore Pl A3
Lismore St B3
London Rd C3
Lonsdale 🎦 B2
Lonsdale Rd B1
Lord St C3
Lorne Cres B1
Lorne St B1
Lowther St B2
Market Hall A2
Mary St B3
Memorial Bridge. A3
Metcalfe St C1
Milbourne St. B1
Myddleton St B3
Nelson St C1
Norfolk St C1
Old Town Hall A2
Oswald St. C3
Peter St B2
Petteril St B3
Police Station 🚔 A2
Portland Pl B2
Portland Sq B2
Post Office 🅿️
   . . . . . . A2/B2/B3/C1/C3
Princess St C3
Pugin St B1
Red Bank Terr. C2
Regent St C3
Richardson St C1
Rickergate A2

Rickergate A2
River St. B3
Rome St C2
Rydal St B3
St Cuthbert's 🕍 B2
St Cuthbert's La B2
St James' Park C1
St James' Rd C1
St Nicholas St C3
Sands Centre A2
Scotch St A2
Shaddongate B1
Sheffield St. B1
South Henry St. B3
South John St C2
South St. C2
Spencer St B2
Sports Centre A2
Strand Rd A2
Swimming Baths B2
Sybil St. B3
Tait St B2
Thomas St B1
Thomson St C3
Trafalgar St C1
Tyne St C3
Viaduct Estate Rd. . . . B1
Victoria Pl A2/A3
Victoria Viaduct B2
Warner Village 🎦 B2
Warwick Rd B3
Warwick Sq B3
Water St B2
West Walls B1
Westmorland St C1

Cheltenham

Albert Rd A3
Albion St. B3
All Saints Rd B3
Andover Rd C1
Art Gallery &
   Museum 🏛 B2
Axiom Centre 🏛 B3
Bath Pde B2
Bath Rd C2
Bays Hill Rd B1
Beechwood Shopping
   Centre B3
Bennington St B2
Berkeley St B3
Brunswick St South . . A2
Bus Station B2
Carlton St B3
Cheltenham &
   Gloucester College . A2
Cheltenham College. . C2
Cheltenham F.C. A3
Cheltenham General
   (A & E) 🏥 C3
Christchurch Rd B1
Clarence Rd A3
Clarence Sq A2
Clarence St B2
Cleeveland St A1
Coach Park A2
College Rd C2
Colletts Dr A1
Corpus St C3
Devonshire St A2
Douro Rd B1
Duke St B3
Dunalley Pde A2
Dunalley St A2
Everyman 🎭 B2

Evesham Rd A3
Fairview Rd B3
Fairview St B3
Folly La A1
Gloucester Rd A1
Grosvenor St B3
Grove St A2
Gustav Holst 🏛 A3
Hanover St A2
Hatherley St C1
Henrietta St A2
Hewlett Rd B3
High St B2/B3
Hudson St A2
Imperial Gdns C2
Imperial La C2
Imperial Sq C2
Information Ctr ℹ B2
Keynsham Rd C3
King St A2
Knapp Rd A2
Ladies College 🏛 B2
Lansdown Cr C1
Lansdown Rd C1
Leighton Rd B3
London Rd C3
Lypiatt Rd C1
Malvern Rd B1
Manser St A3
Market St A1
Marle Hill Pde A2
Marle Hill Rd. A2
Millbrook St A1
Milsom St A2
Montpellier Gdns C2
Montpellier Gr. C2
Montpellier Pde C2
Montpellier Spa Rd . . C2
Montpellier Pde C2
Montpellier Terr C2

Montpellier Walk. C2
New St B2
North Pl B2
Odeon 🎦 B3
Old Bath Rd C3
Oriel Rd B2
Overton Park Rd. B1
Overton Rd. B1
Oxford St C3
Parabola Rd B1
Park Pl B1
Park St A1
Pittville Circus. A3
Pittville Cr. A3
Pittville Lawn A3
Pittville Pump Room &
   Racecourse ✦ A3
Playhouse 🎭 B2
Police Station 🚔 . B1/C1
Portland St B3
Post Office 🅿️ . B2/C1/C2
Prestbury Rd A3
Prince's Rd C1
Priory St B3
Promenade. B2
Queen St A1
Recreation Ground . . . A2
Regent Arcade B2
Regent St B2
Rodney Rd B2
Royal Cr B2
Royal Wells Rd B2
Sandford Lido. C3
Sandford Park C3
Sandford Rd C2
Selkirk St A3
Sherborne Pl B3
Sherborne St B3
St George's Pl B2
St George's Rd B1

St George's St A1
St Gregory's 🕍 B2
St James St B3
St John's Ave B3
St Luke's Rd C2
St Margaret's Rd A2
St Mary's 🕍 B2
St Matthew's 🕍 B2
St Paul's La A2
St Paul's Rd A2
St Paul's St. A2
St Stephen's Rd C1
Suffolk Pde C2
Suffolk Rd C1
Suffolk Sq. C1
Sun St A1
Swindon Rd B2
Sydenham Villas Rd . . C3
Tewkesbury Rd A1
The Courtyard B1
Thirlstaine Rd C2
Tivoli Rd C1
Tivoli St. C1
Town Hall &
   Theatre B2
Townsend St. A1
Trafalgar St. C2
Victoria Pl B3
Victoria St. A2
Vittoria Walk C2
Wellesley Rd A2
Wellington Rd A3
Wellington Sq A3
Wellington St B2
West Drive A3
Western Rd. B1
Winchcombe St B3

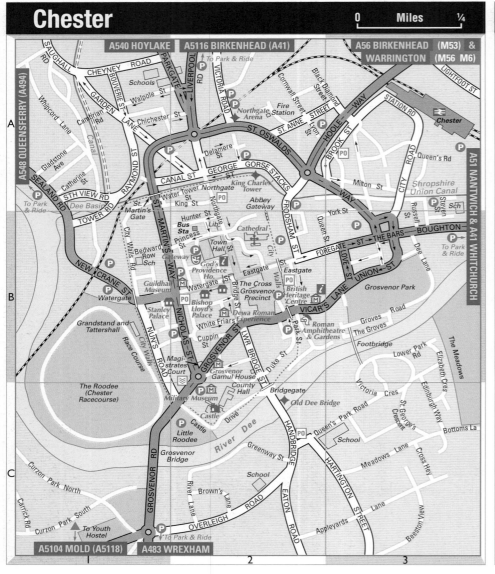

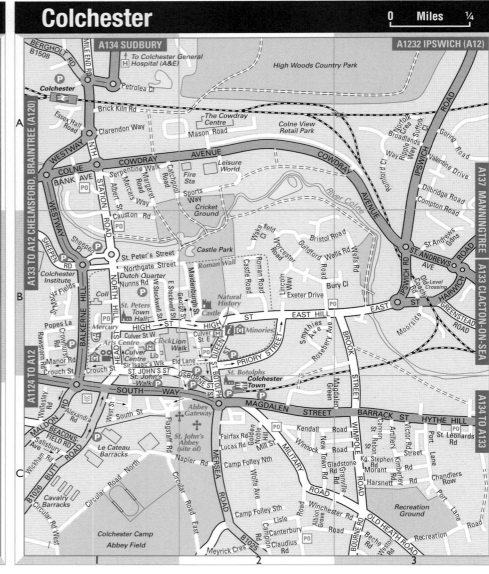

Chester

Abbey Gateway A2
Appleyards La C3
Bedward Row B1
Beeston View C3
Bishop Lloyd's
 Palace 🏛 B2
Black Diamond St . . . A2
Bottoms La. C3
Boughton B3
Bouverie St A1
Bridge St B2
Bridgegate C2
British Heritage
 Centre 🏛 B2
Brook St A3
Brown's La C2
Bus Station B2
Cambrian Rd A1
Canal St A2
Carrick Rd C1
Castle 🏰 C2
Castle Dr C2
Cathedral † B2
Catherine St A1
Chester 🚉 A3
Cheyney Rd A1
Chichester St A1
City Rd A3
City Walls B1/B2
City Walls Rd B1
Cornwall St. A2
County Hall. C2
Cross Hey C3
Cuppin St B2

Curzon Park North . . . C1
Curzon Park South. . . C1
Dee Basin A1
Dee La B3
Delamere St A2
Dewa Roman
 Experience 🏛 B2
Duke St. B2
Eastgate B2
Eastgate 🏛 B2
Eaton Rd C2
Egerton St A3
Elizabeth Cr A3
Fire Station A2
Foregate St. B2
Frodsham St. B2
Gamul House B2
Garden La. A1
Gateway Theatre 🎭 . . A2
George St A2
Gladstone Ave A1
God's Providence
 House 🏛 B2
Gorse Stacks A2
Greenway St. C2
Grosvenor Bridge. . . . C1
Grosvenor
 Museum 🏛 B2
Grosvenor Park B3
Grosvenor Precinct . . B2
Grosvenor Rd C1
Grosvenor St B2
Groves Rd B3
Guildhall Museum 🏛 . B1
Handbridge. C2
Hartington St. C3

Hoole Way A2
Hunter St B2
Information Ctr 🅈 . . . B2
King Charles'
 Tower ♦ A2
King St A2
Library A2
Lightfoot St A3
Little Roodee C2
Liverpool Rd A2
Love St B3
Lower Bridge St B2
Lower Park Rd B3
Lyon St A2
Magistrates Court. . . . B2
Meadows La. C3
Military Museum 🏛 . . C2
Milton St. A3
New Crane St. B1
Nicholas St B2
Northgate A2
Northgate Arena ♦ . . A2
Northgate St. A2
Nun's Rd B1
Old Dee Bridge ♦ . . . C2
Overleigh Rd. C2
Park St B2
Police Station 🅟 B2
Post Office 🅟 . . . .
 . . . . A2/A3/B2/C2
Princess St. B2
Queen St B2
Queen's Park Rd C3
Queen's Rd A3
Raymond St A1
River La C2

Roman Amphitheatre
 & Gardens 🏛 B2
Roodee, The (Chester
 Racecourse) B1
Russell St A3
St Anne St A2
St George's Cr C3
St Martin's Gate A1
St Martin's Way A1
St Oswalds Way A2
Saughall Rd A1
Sealand Rd. A1
South View Rd A1
Stanley Palace 🏛 . . . B1
Station Rd A3
Steven St A2
The Bars B3
The Cross B2
The Groves B3
The Meadows. B3
Tower Rd B1
Town Hall B2
Union St B3
Vicar's La B2
Victoria Cr. C3
Victoria Rd A2
Walpole St A1
Water Tower St B1
Watergate B1
Watergate St. B2
Whipcord La. A1
White Friars B2
York St B3

Colchester

Abbey Gateway † . . . C2
Albert St A1
Albion Grove. C2
Alexandra Rd C1
Artillery St. C3
Arts Centre 🏛 B1
Balkerne Hill B1
Barrack St C3
Barrington Rd. C2
Beaconsfield Rd. C1
Beche Rd C3
Bergholt Rd A1
Bourne Rd C3
Brick Kiln Rd A1
Bristol Rd B2
Broadlands Way A3
Brook St B3
Bury Cl B2
Butt Rd C1
Camp Folley North . . C2
Camp Folley South. . . C2
Campion Rd C2
Cannon St C3
Canterbury Rd C2
Castle 🏰 B2
Castle Rd B2
Catchpool Rd A1
Causton Rd B1
Cavalry Barracks C1
Chandlers Row C3
Circular Rd East C2
Circular Rd North . . . C1
Circular Rd West C1
Clarendon Way A1
Claudius Rd C2
Clock 🏛 B2
Colchester Institute . . B1
Colchester 🚉 A1
Colchester Town 🚉 . . C2
Colne Bank Ave A1
Colne View
 Retail Park A2

Compton Rd A3
Cowdray Ave A1/A3
Cowdray Centre,
 The A2
Crouch St. B1
Crowhurst Rd. B1
Culver Centre B1
Culver St East B2
Culver St West B1
Dilbridge Rd A3
East Hill B2
East St B3
East Stockwell St . . . B1
Eld La B1
Essex Hall Rd A1
Exeter Dr B2
Fairfax Rd C2
Fire Station A2
Flagstaff Rd C1
George St B2
Gladstone Rd. C2
Golden Noble Hill . . . C2
Goring Rd. A3
Granville Rd C3
Greenstead Rd. B3
Guildford Rd B2
Harsnett Rd C3
Harwich Rd. B3
Head St B1
High St B1
Hythe Hill C3
Information Ctr 🅈 . . . B2
Ipswich Rd A3
Kendall Rd C2
Kimberley Rd C3
King Stephen Rd C3
Le Cateau Barracks . . C1
Leisure World A2
Library B1
Lincoln Way B2
Lion Walk Shopping
 Centre B1
Lisle Rd C2
Lucas Rd C2

Magdalen Green. C3
Magdalen St. C2
Maidenburgh St B2
Maldon Rd C1
Manor Rd A1
Margaret Rd A1
Mason Rd A2
Mercers Way A1
Mersea Rd C2
Meyrick Cr C2
Mile End Rd A1
Military Rd C2
Mill St C3
Minories 🏛 B2
Moorside B3
Morant Rd C2
Napier Rd C2
Natural History 🏛 . . . B2
New Town Rd C2
Norfolk Cr. A3
North Hill B1
North Station Rd A1
Northgate St. B1
Nunns Rd B1
Odeon 🎬 B1
Old Coach Rd. B3
Old Heath Rd C3
Osborne St B2
Petrolea Cl A1
Police Station 🅟 B2
Popes La B1
Port La C3
Post Office 🅟 . . . . . .
 . . . . . . A1/B1/B2/C2/C3
Priory St B2
Queen St B2
Rawstorn Rd B1
Rebon St C3
Recreation Rd C3
Ripple Way A3
Roman Rd B2
Roman Wall B2
Romford Cl. A3

Rosebery Ave B2
St Andrews Ave B3
St Andrews Gdns . . . B3
St Botolph St B2
St Botolphs 🏛 B2
St John's Abbey
 (site of) † C2
St John's St B1
St John's Walk Shopping
 Centre B1
St Leonards Rd C3
St Marys Fields B1
St Peters 🏛 B1
St Peter's St B1
Salisbury Ave C1
Serpentine Walk A1
Sheepen Pl. B1
Sheepen Rd B1
Sir Isaac's Walk B1
Smythies Ave B2
South St C1
South Way C1
Sports Way A2
Suffolk Cl A3
Town Hall B1
Turner Rd A1
Valentine Dr A3
Victor Rd. C3
Wakefield Cl B2
Wellesley Rd. C1
Wells Rd B2
West St C1
West Stockwell St . . . B1
Weston Rd C3
Westway. A1
Wickham Rd C1
Wimpole Rd C3
Winchester Rd C2
Winnock Rd C2
Wolfe Ave C2
Worcester Rd B2

Coventry

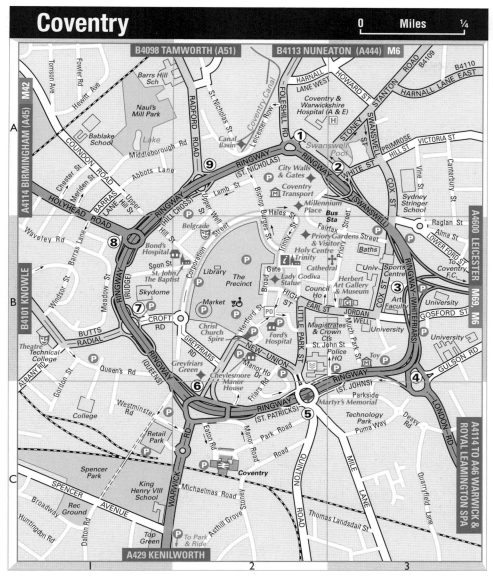

Derby

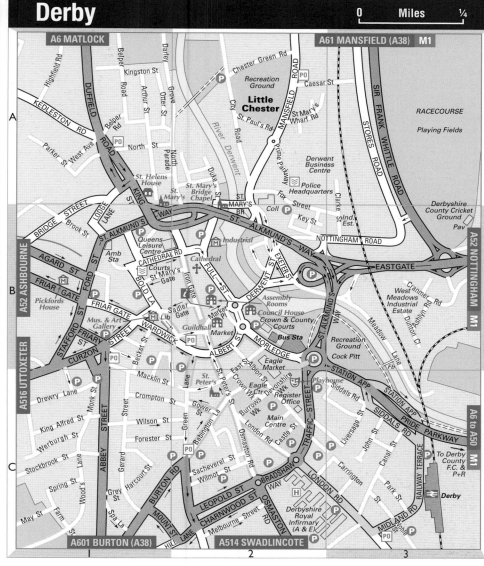

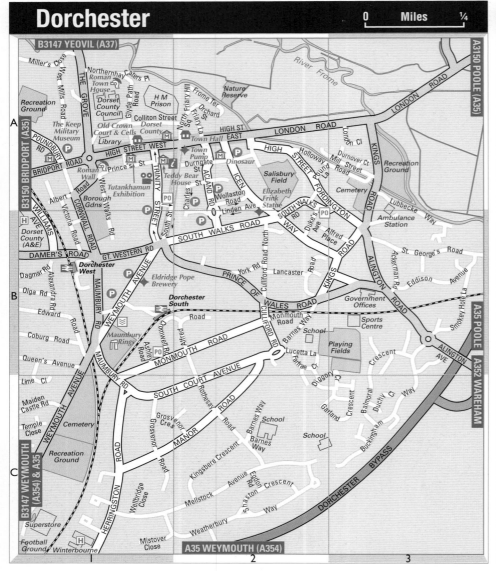

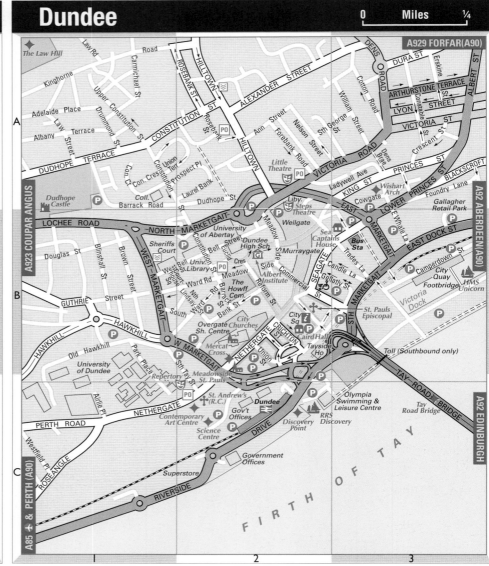

Dorchester

Ackerman Rd B3
Acland Rd. A2
Albert Rd A1
Alexandra Rd B1
Alfred Place B3
Alfred Rd B2
Alington Ave B3
Alington Rd B3
Ambulance Station . . . B3
Ashley Rd B1
Balmoral Cres C3
Barnes Way B2/C2
Borough Gdns A1
Bridport Rd A1
Buckingham Way C3
Caters Place A1
Charles St. A2
Coburg Rd B1
Colliton St. A1
Cornwall Rd A1
Cromwell Rd B1
Culliford Rd B2
Culliford Rd North . . . B2
Dagmar Rd B1
Damer's Rd B1
Diggory Cres B2
Dinosaur Museum 🏛 . . A2
Dorchester Bypass. . . C3
Dorchester South
 Station 🚆 B1
Dorchester West
 Station 🚆 B1

Dorset County
 Council Offices. A1
Dorset County
 (A+E) 🏥 B1
Dorset County
 Museum 🏛 A1
Duchy Close. C3
Duke's Ave B2
Durngate St A2
Durnover Court. A2
Eddison Ave B3
Edward Rd B1
Egdon Rd C2
Eldridge Pope
 Brewery ✦ B1
Elizabeth Frink
 Statue ✦ B2
Farfrae Cres A2
Friary Hill A2
Friary Lane A2
Frome Terr A2
Garland Cres C3
Glyde Path Rd A1
Gt. Western Rd. B1
Grosvenor Cres C1
Grosvenor Rd. C1
H M Prison A1
Herrington Rd. C1
High St East A2
High Street
 Fordington A2
High Street West A1
Holloway Rd A1
Icen Way. A2

Keep Military
 Museum, The 🏛 . . . A1
Kings Rd A3/B3
Kingsbere Cres C2
Lancaster Rd B2
Library A1
Lime Cl B1
Linden Ave B2
London Cl A3
London Rd A3
Lubbecke Way A3
Lucetta La B2
Maiden Castle Rd. . . . C1
Manor Rd C2
Maumbury Rd B1
Maumbury Rings 🏛 . . B1
Mellstock Ave. C2
Mill St A3
Miller's Cl A1
Mistover Cl C1
Monmouth Rd B1
North Sq A2
Northernhay A1
Old Crown Court
 & Cells A1
Olga Rd B1
Orchard St A2
Police Station 🚓 . . . B1
Post Office 📮 . . A1/B1/B2
Pound Lane A1
Poundbury Rd A1
Prince of Wales Rd. . . B2
Prince's St B1
Queen's Ave B1

Roman Town
 House 🏺 A1
Roman Wall 🏺 A1
Rothesay Rd. C2
St George's Rd. B3
Salisbury Field A2
Shaston Cres C2
Smokey Hole La. A2
South Court Ave. C1
South St. B1
South Walks Rd B2
Teddy Bear
 House 🏛 A1
Temple Cl C1
The Grove. A1
Town Hall 🏛. A2
Town Pump ✦ A2
Trinity St A1
Tutankhamun
 Exhibition 🏛 A1
Victoria Rd B1
Weatherbury Way . . . C2
Wellbridge Cl C1
West Mills Rd A1
West Walks Rd A1
Weymouth Ave C1
Williams Ave B1
Winterbourne
 Hospital 🏥 C1
Wollaston Rd A2
York Rd. B2

Dundee

Adelaide Pl A1
Airlie Pl C1
Albany Terr A1
Albert Institute 🏛 . . . B2
Albert St A3
Alexander St. A2
Ann St. A2
Arthurstone Terr A3
Bank St. B2
Barrack Rd A1
Barrack St B2
Bell St. B2
Blackscroft A3
Blinshall St B1
Brown St. B1
Bus Station. B3
Caird Hall B2
Camperdown St B3
Candle La. B3
Carmichael St. A1
Carnegie St A2
City Churches 🏛 B2
City Quay B3
City Sq B2
Commercial St B2
Constable St. A3
Constitution Ct A1
Constitution Cres A1
Constitution St . . . A1/B2
Contemporary
 Art Centre ✦ C2
Cotton Rd A3

Courthouse Sq B1
Cowgate. A3
Crescent St A3
Crichton St B2
Dens Brae A3
Dens Rd A3
Discovery Point ✦ . . . C2
Douglas St B1
Drummond St. A1
Dudhope Castle 🏰. . . A1
Dudhope St A2
Dudhope Terr A2
Dundee 🚆. C2
Dundee High School . B2
Dura St A3
East Dock St B3
East Whale La B3
East Marketgait B3
Erskine St A3
Euclid Cr. B2
Forebank Rd. A3
Foundry La A3
Gallagher Retail Park . B3
Gellatly St. B3
Government Offices . . C2
Guthrie St B1
Hawkhill B1
Hilltown. A2
Howff Cemetery, The . B2
HMS Unicorn ✦ B3
Information Ctr ℹ B2
King St A3
Kinghorne Rd A1
Ladywell Ave A3

Laurel Bank A2
Law Hill, The ✦ A1
Law Rd A1
Law St A2
Library A2
Little Theatre 🎭 A2
Lochee Rd A1
Lower Princes St A3
Lyon St. A3
Meadow Side B2
Meadowside St.
 Pauls 🏛 B2
Mercat Cross ✦ B2
Murraygate. B2
Nelson St A2
Nethergate B2/C1
North Marketgait B2
North Lindsay St B2
Old Hawkhill B1
Olympia Swimming
 & Leisure Centre . . . C3
Overgate Shopping
 Centre B2
Park Pl B1
Perth Rd C1
Police Station 🚓 . . A2/B1
Post Office 📮 . . A2/B2/C2
Princes St. A3
Prospect Pl A2
Reform St B2
Repertory 🎭 C1
Riverside Dr C2
Roseangle. C1
Rosebank St. A2

RRS Discovery ⚓ C2
St Andrew's ✝ C2
St Pauls
 Episcopal ✝ B3
Science Centre ✦ C2
Sea Captains
 House 🏛 B3
Sheriffs Court B1
South Ward Rd B2
South George St A2
South Marketgait B3
South Tay St B2
Steps 🚆 A2
Tay Road Bridge ✦ . . C3
Tayside House B2
Trades La B3
Union St B2
Union Terr A1
University Library B2
University of Abertay . B2
University of Dundee . B1
Upper
 Constitution St. A1
Victoria Rd A2
Victoria St A3
West Marketgait . . . B1/B2
Ward Rd B1
Wellgate B2
West Bell St B1
Westfield Pl. C1
William St A3
Wishart Arch ✦ A3

Durham

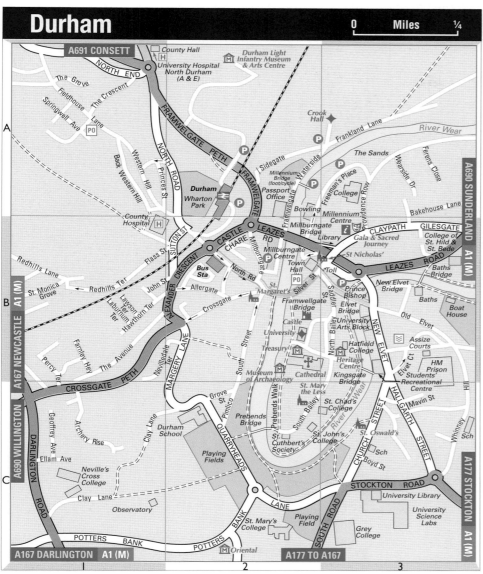

Miles 0 — ¼

Exeter

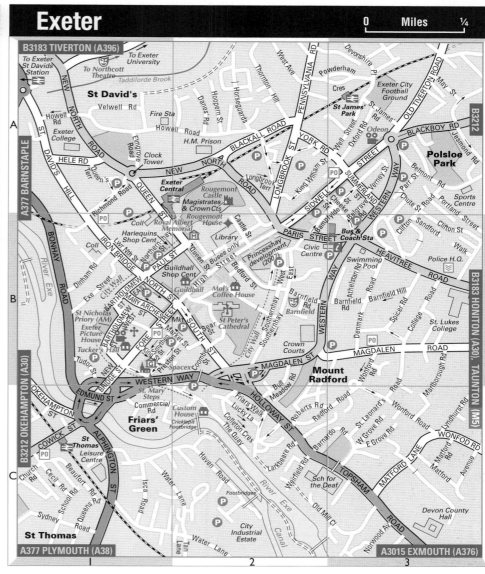

Miles 0 — ¼

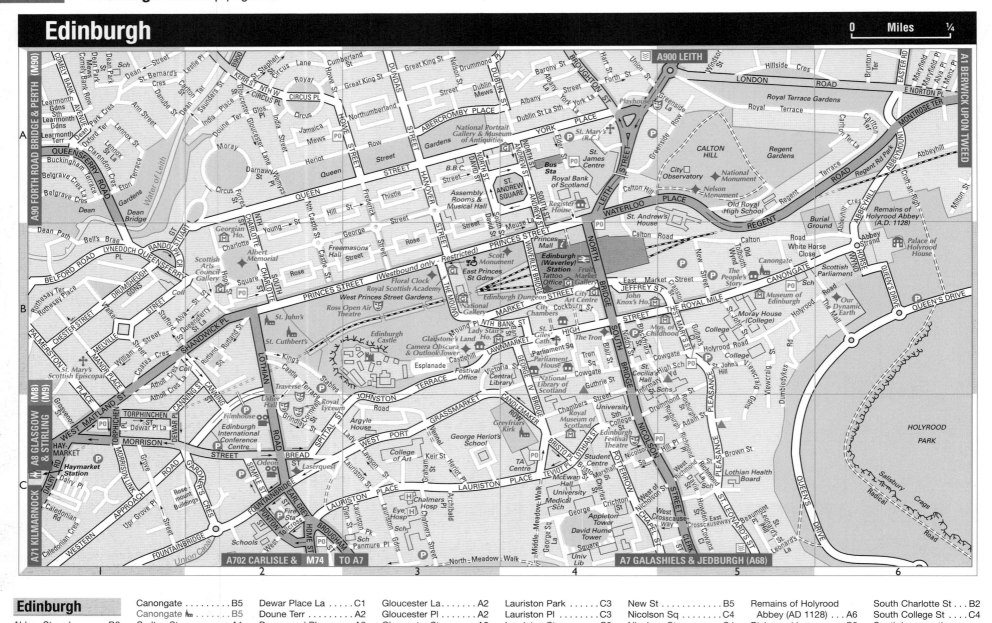

Edinburgh

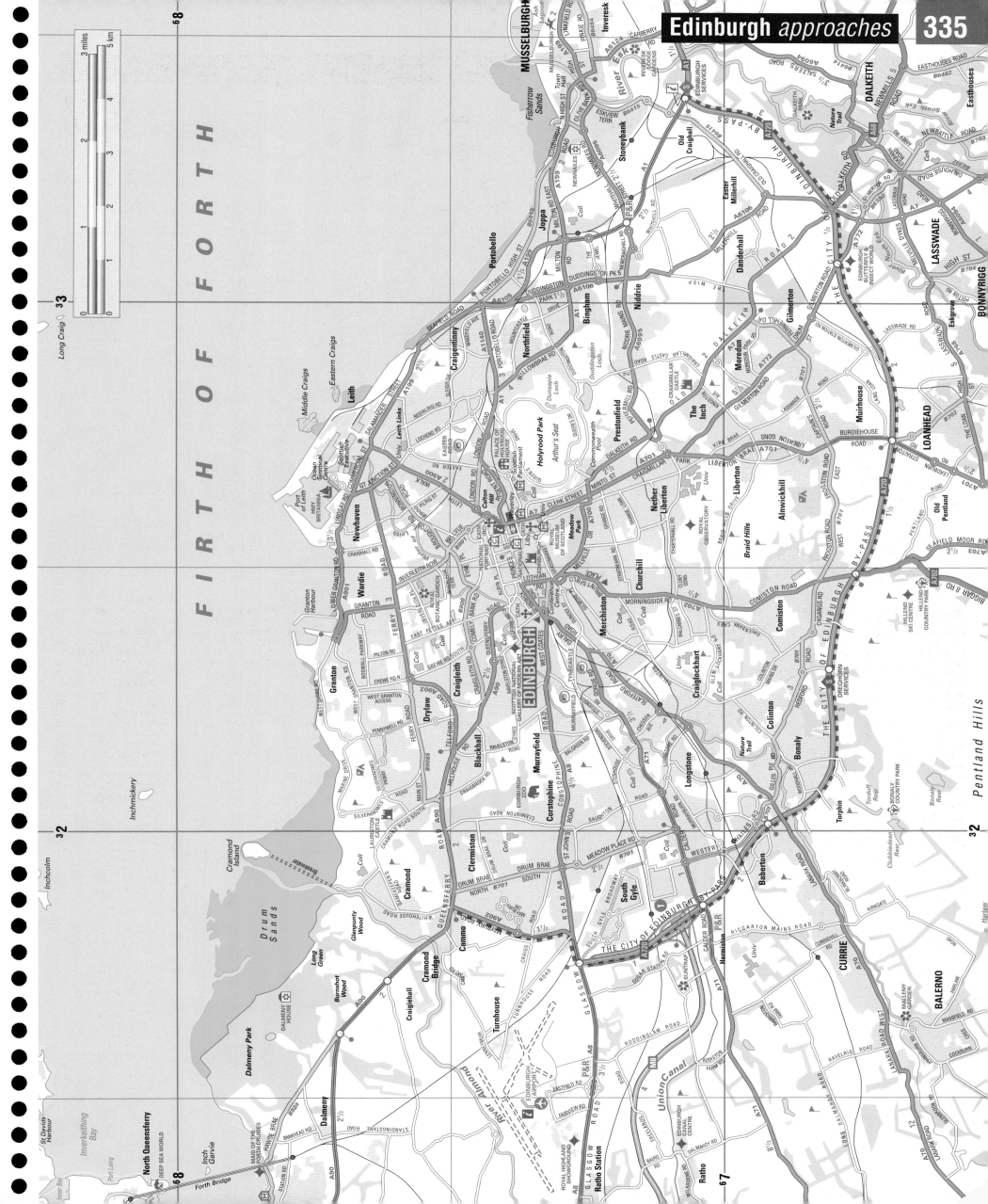

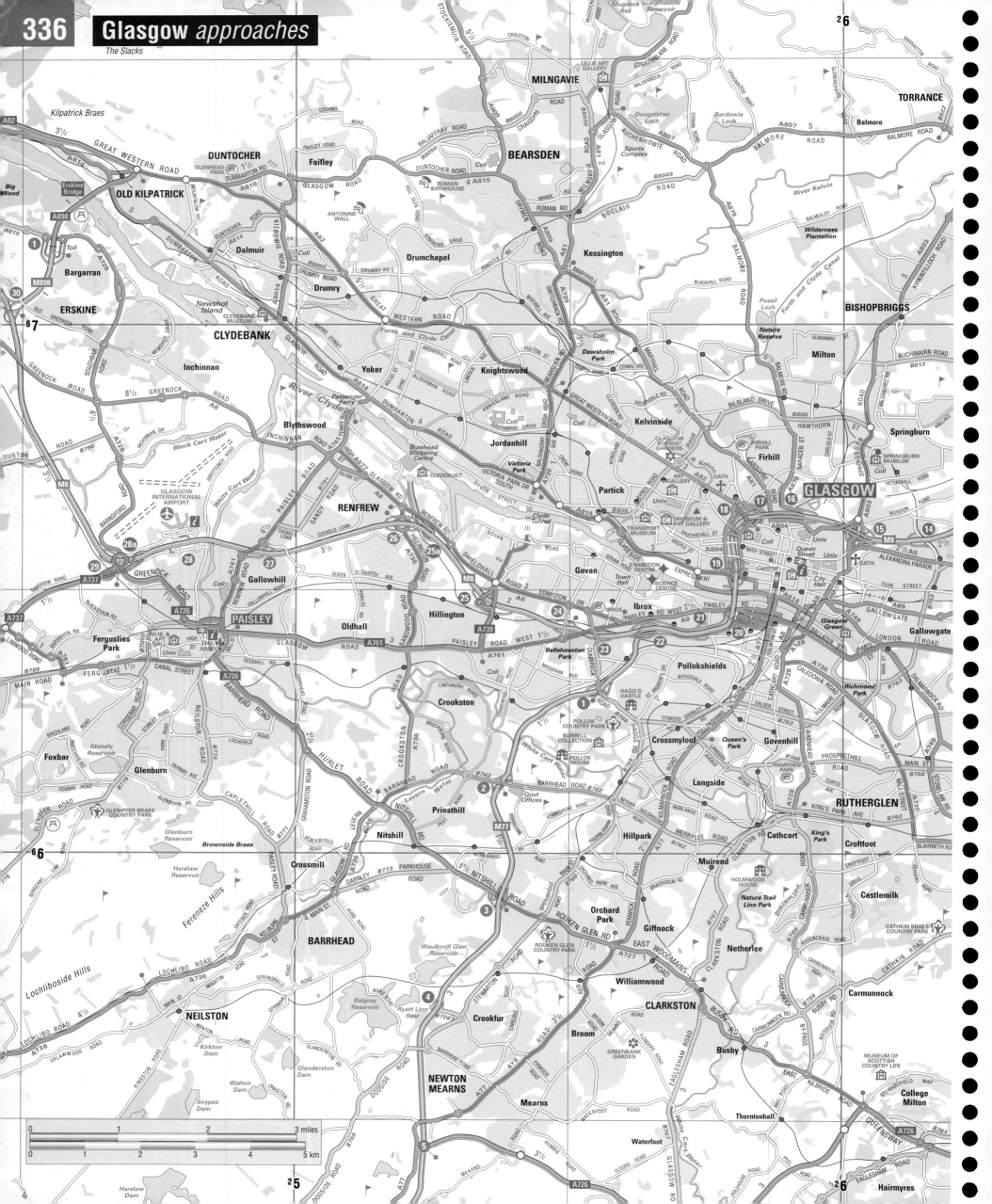

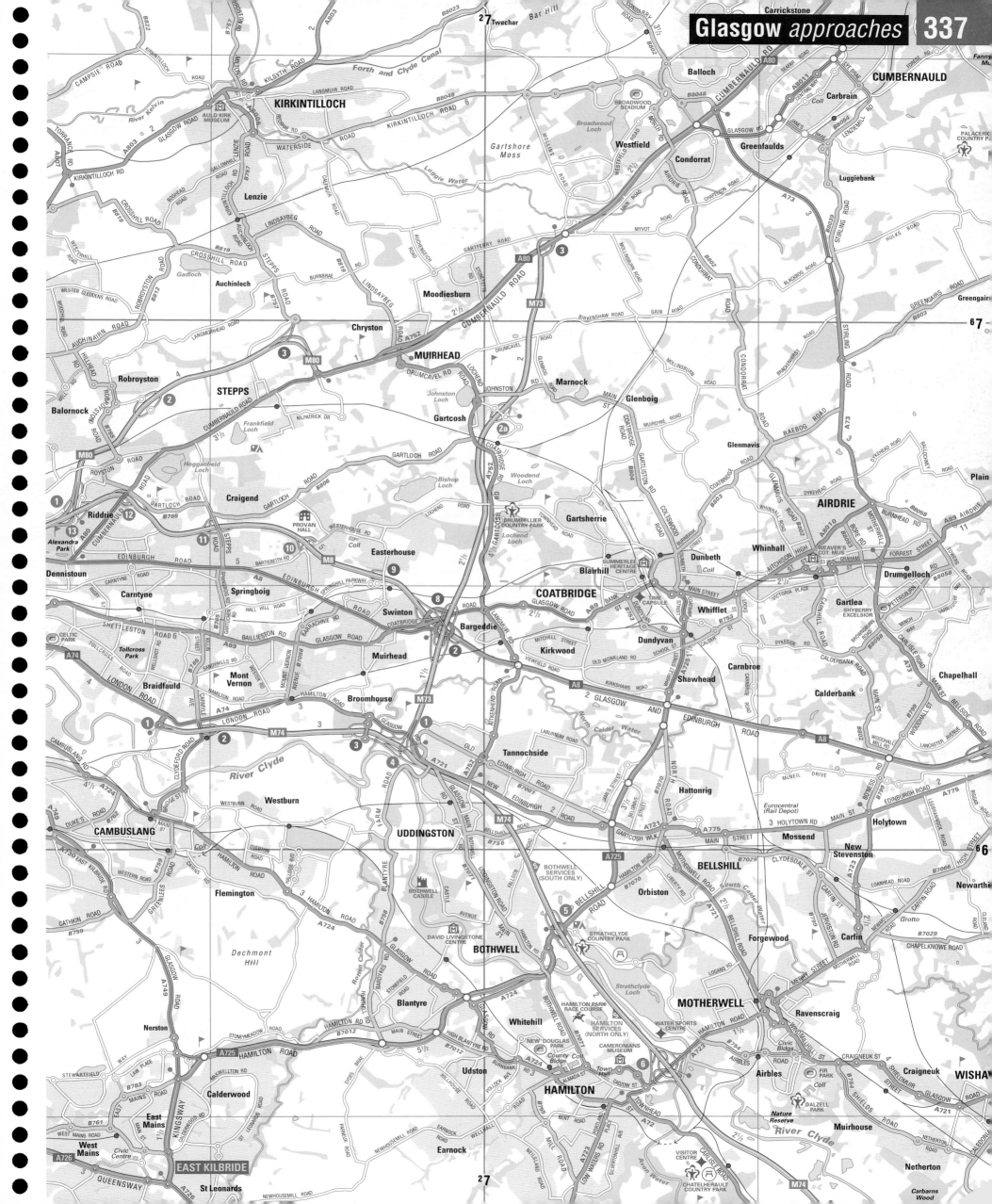

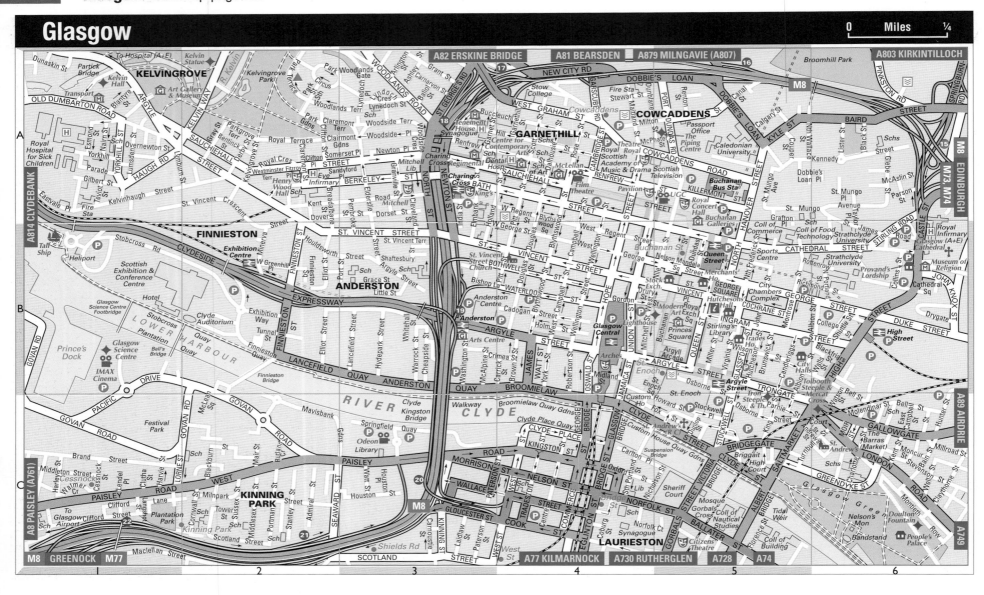

Glasgow

Admiral St. C2
Albert Bridge C5
Albion St. B5
Anderston Centre B3
Anderston Quay B3
Anderston B3
Arches B4
Argyle St . . . .
. . . . . A1/A2/B3/B4/B5
Argyle Street ⇌ B4
Argyll Arcade B5
Arlington St. A3
Art Gallery & Mus 🏛 . A1
Arts Centre 🏛 B3
Ashley St A3
Bain St C6
Baird St A6
Baliol St A3
Ballater St C5
Barras, The (Market). . C6
Bath St B5
Bell St C6
Bell's Bridge B1
Bentinck St A2
Berkeley St A3
Bishop La B3
Black St A6
Blackburn St. C2
Blackfriars St B6
Blantyre St A1
Blythswood Sq. B4
Blythswood St B4
Bothwell St B4
Brand St C1
Breadalbane St A2
Bridge St C4
Bridge St (Metro) C4
Bridgegate C5
Briggait C5
Broomhill Park A6
Broomielaw B4
Broomielaw Quay
. . Gdns. B3
Brown St C4
Brunswick St. B5
Buccleuch St A3
Buchanan Bus
. . Station A5
Buchanan Galleries 🏛 A5
Buchanan St A5
Buchanan St (Metro) . B5
Cadogan St B4
Caledonian University A5

Calgary St A5
Cambridge St A4
Campbell St B4
Canal St B3
Candleriggs B5
Carlton Pl C4
Carnarvon St A3
Carnoustie St C3
Carrick St B4
Castle St B6
Cathedral Sq B6
Cathedral St. B5
Centre for Contemporary
. . Arts 🏛 A4
Centre St C4
Cessnock (Metro) C1
Cessnock St. C1
Charing Cross ⇌ A3
Charlotte St C6
Cheapside St B3
Citizens' Theatre 🎭 . . C5
City Chambers
. . Complex B5
City Halls 🏛 B5
Clairmont Gdns A2
Claremont St A2
Claremont Terr A2
Claythorne St C6
Cleveland St A3
Clifford La. C1
Clifford St C1
Clifton Pl. A2
Clifton St A2
Clutha St C1
Clyde Auditorium B2
Clyde Pl C4
Clyde Place Quay C4
Clyde St C5
Clyde Walkway. C5
Clydeside
. . Expressway B2
Coburg St C4
Cochrane St B5
College of Building . . . C5
College of Commerce B5
College of Food
. . Technology. B5
College of Nautical
. . Studies B5
College St B6
Collins St B6
Commerce St C4
Cook St C4
Cornwall St. C2
Couper St A5

Cowcaddens (Metro) . A4
Cowcaddens Rd. A4
Crimea St B3
Custom House 🏛 C4
Custom House Quay
. . Gdns. C4
Dalhousie St A4
Dental Hospital 🏥 . . . A4
Derby St A2
Dobbie's Loan . . . A4/A5
Dobbie's Loan Pl A5
Dorset St A3
Douglas St B4
Dover St A2
Drury St B4
Drygate B6
Duke St B6
Dunaskin St A1
Dunblane St A4
Dundas St B5
Dunlop St C5
East Campbell St C6
Eastvale Pl A1
Eglinton St C4
Elderslie St A3
Elliot St B2
Elmbank St A3
Esmond St A1
Exhibition Centre ⇌ . . B2
Exhibition Way B2
Eye Infirmary 🏥 A2
Festival Park C1
Film Theatre 🎭 A4
Finnieston Bridge B2
Finnieston Quay B2
Finnieston Sq B2
Finnieston St B2
Fitzroy Pl. A2
Florence St C5
Fox St C5
Gallowgate C6
Garnet St A3
Garnethill St A4
Garscube Rd A4
George Sq B5
George St B5
George V Bridge C4
Gilbert St A1
Glasgow Bridge C4
Glasgow Cathedral ✝ B6
Glasgow Central ⇌ . . . B4
Glasgow Green C6
Glasgow Science
. . Centre ✦ B1

Glasgow Science Centre
. . Footbridge B1
Glassford St B5
Glebe St A6
Gloucester St C3
Gorbals Cross C5
Gorbals St C5
Gordon St B4
Govan Rd . . . B1/C1/C2
Grace St B3
Grafton Pl A5
Grant St A3
Granville St A3
Gray St A2
Greendyke St C6
Harley St C1
Harvie St C1
Haugh Rd A1
Heliport B1
Henry Wood Hall 🎭 . . A2
High St A3
Holland St A3
Holm St B4
Hope St A5
Houldsworth St B2
Houston Pl C3
Houston St C3
Howard St C5
Hutcheson St B5
Hutcheson St B5
High Street ⇌ B6
Hill St A3
Hunter St B6
Hydepark St B3
Imax Cinema 🎦 B1
India St A4
Information Ctr ℹ B5
Ingram St B5
Jamaica St B4
James Watt St B4
John Knox St B6
John St B5
Kelvin Hall ✦ A1
Kelvin Statue ✦ A2
Kelvin Way A2
Kelvingrove Park A2
Kelvingrove St A2
Kelvinhaugh St A1
Kennedy St A6
Kent Rd A2
Killermont St. A5
King St B5
King's 🎭 A4
Kingston Bridge C3
Kingston St. C4
Kinning Park (Metro). . C2

Kinning St C3
Kyle St A5
Laidlaw St C3
Lancefield Quay B2
Lancefield St B3
Langshot St C1
Lendel Pl C1
Lighthouse ✦ B4
Lister St A6
Little St B3
London Rd C6
Lorne St C1
Lower Harbour B1
Lumsden St A1
Lymburn St A1
Lyndoch Cr. A3
Lyndoch Pl A3
Lyndoch St A3
Maclellan St C1
Mair St C2
Maitland St A4
Mavisbank Gdns C2
Mcalpine St B3
Mcaslin St A6
McLean Sq C2
McLellan Gallery 🏛 . . A4
McPhater St A4
Merchants' House 🏛 . B5
Middlesex St C2
Middleton St C1
Midland St B4
Miller St B5
Millroad St C6
Milnpark St C2
Milton St A4
Minerva St A2
Mitchell Library. A3
Mitchell St B5
Mitchell St West B5
Mitchell Theatre 🎭 . . . A3
Modern Art Gallery 🏛 B5
Moir St C6
Molendinar St C6
Moncur St C6
Montieth Row C6
Montrose St B5
Morrison St C3
Mosque C5
Museum of
. . Religion 🏛 B6
Nairn St A1
Nelson Mandela Sq . . B5
Nelson St C4
Nelson's Monument . . C6
New City Rd A4
Newton St A3

Newton Pl A3
Nicholson St C4
Nile St A5
Norfolk Court C4
Norfolk St C4
North Frederick St B5
North Hanover St B5
North Portland St B6
North St A3
North Wallace St A5
Odeon 🎦 C3
Old Dumbarton Rd . . . A1
Osborne St B5/C5
Oswald St. B4
Overnewton St A1
Oxford St C4
Pacific Dr B1
Paisley Rd C3
Paisley Rd West C2
Park Circus A2
Park Gdns A2
Park St South A2
Park Terr A2
Parkgrove Terr A1
Parnie St. C5
Parson St A6
Partick Bridge. A1
Passport Office. A5
Paterson St C3
Pavilion Theatre 🎭 . . . A4
Pembroke St A3
People's Palace 🏛 . . . C6
Pinkston Rd A5
Pitt St A4/B4
Plantation Park C1
Plantation Quay B1
Police Station ✦ . . . .
. . . . A4/A6/B5
Port Dundas Rd A5
Port St A3
Portman St C2
Prince's Dock B1
Princes Sq B5
Provand's
. . Lordship 🏛 B6
Queen St B5
Queen Street ⇌ B5
Renfrew St A3/A4
Renton St A5
Richmond St B5
Robertson St B4
Rose St A4
Rottenrow B5

Royal Concert Hall 🎭 . A5
Royal Cr A2
Royal Exchange Sq . . B5
Royal Hospital For Sick
. . Children 🏥 A1
Royal Infirmary 🏥 B6
Royal Scottish Academy
. . of Music & Drama . . A4
Royal Terr A2
Rutland Cr C2
St Kent St C6
St Andrew's (R.C.) ✝ . C5
St Andrew's 🏛 C5
St Andrew's St C5
St Enoch (Metro) B5
St Enoch Shopping
. . Centre B5
St Enoch Sq B4
St George's Rd A3
St James Rd B6
St Mungo Ave . . . A5/A6
St Mungo Pl A6
St Vincent Cr A2
St Vincent Pl. B5
St Vincent St B3/B4
St Vincent Street
. . Church B4
St Vincent Terr B3
Saltmarket C5
Sandyford Pl. A3
Sauchiehall St A2/A4
School of Art A4
Scotland St C2/C3
Scott St A4
Scottish Exhibition &
. . Conference Centre. . B1
Scottish Television . . . A5
Seaward St C2
Shaftesbury St B3
Sheriff Court. C5
Shields Rd C3
Shields Rd (Metro) . . . C3
Shuttle St B6
Somerset Pl A2
Springburn Rd A6
Springfield Quay. C3
Stanley St C2
Stevenson St C6
Stewart St A4
Stirling Rd B6
Stirling's Library C5
Stobcross Quay B1
Stobcross Rd B1
Stock Exchange 🏛 . . . B5

Stockwell Pl C5
Stockwell St B5
Stow College A4
Strathclyde University A5
Sussex St C2
Synagogues A3/C4
Tall Ship ⚓ B1
Taylor Pl A6
Tenement House 🏛 . . A3
Teviot St A1
Theatre Royal 🎭 A3
Tolbooth Steeple &
. . Mercat Cross ✦ C6
Tower St C2
Trades House 🏛 B5
Tradeston St C4
Transport Mus 🏛 A1
Tron Steeple &
. . Theatre C5
Trongate B5
Tunnel St B2
Turnbull St C5
UGC 🎦 A5
Union St B4
Victoria Bridge C5
Virginia St B5
Walls St B6
Walmer Cr C1
Warrock St B3
Washington St B3
Waterloo St. B4
Watson St B6
Watt St C3
Well St C6
Wellington St B4
West George St B4
West Graham St A4
West Regent St B4
West St C4
West St (Metro). C4
Westminster Terr A2
Whitehall St B3
Wilson St B5
Woodlands Gate A3
Woodlands Rd A3
Woodlands Terr A3
Woodside Cr. A3
Woodside Pl. A3
Woodside Terr A3
York St West. B4
Yorkhill Pde. A1
Yorkhill St A1

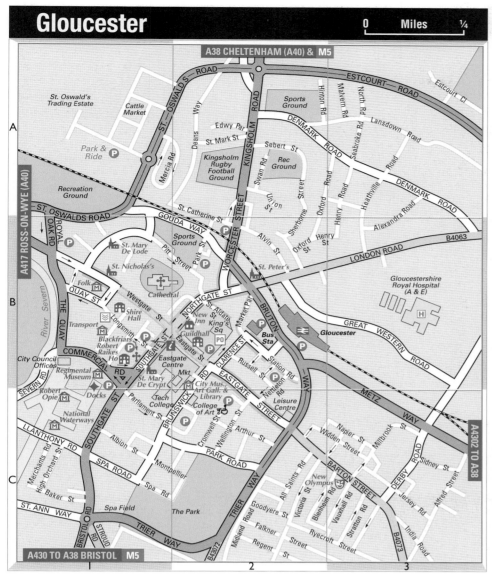

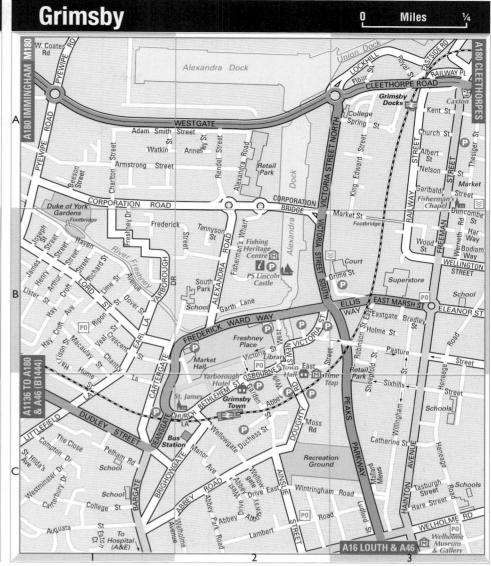

Gloucester

Albion St. C1
Alexandra Rd B3
Alfred St C3
Alvin St B2
Arthur St C3
Baker St C1
Barton St C2
Blackfriars † B1
Blenheim Rd C2
Bristol Rd C1
Brunswick Rd C2
Bruton Way. B2
Bus Station B2
Cattle Market A1
City Council Offices . .B1
City Mus., Art Gall. &
  Library 🏛 B2
Clarence St. B2
College of Art C2
Commercial Rd B1
Cromwell St C2
Deans Way A2
Denmark Rd. A3
Derby Rd C3
Docks ✦ C1
Eastgate Centre B1
Eastgate St. B2
Edwy Pde. A2
Estcourt Cl A3
Estcourt Rd A3
Falkner St. C2

Folk Museum 🏛 B1
Gloucester
  Cathedral † B1
Gloucester
  Station ≈ B2
Gloucestershire Royal
  Hospital (A & E) H . .B3
Goodyere St. C2
Gouda Way. A1
Great Western Rd. . . .B3
Guildhall 🏛 B2
Heathville Rd A3
Henry Rd B3
Henry St B2
High Orchard St C1
Hinton Rd A2
India Rd C3
Information Ctr 🛈 B1
Jersey Rd C3
King's Sq B2
Kingsholm Rd. A2
Kingsholm Rugby
  Football Ground. . . .A2
Lansdown Rd A3
Leisure Centre C2
Llanthony Rd C1
London Rd B3
Longsmith St B1
Malvern Rd A3
Market Pde. B2
Merchants Rd. C1
Mercia Rd. A1
Metz Way C3
Midland Rd. C2

Millbrook St C3
Market B2
Montpellier C1
Napier St C3
National
  Waterways 🏛 C1
Nettleton Rd. C2
New Inn 🏛 B2
New Olympus 🎭 C3
North Rd A3
Northgate St. B2
Oxford Rd A2
Oxford St B2
Park & Ride
  Gloucester A1
Park Rd C2
Park St B2
Parliament St C1
Pitt St B1
Police Station 🚓 B1
Post Office 🏤 B2
Quay St B1
Recreation Gd . . .A1/A2
Regent St C2
Regimental 🏛 B1
Robert Opie 🏛 C1
Robert Raikes
  House 🏛 B1
Royal Oak Rd. A1
Russell St B2
Ryecroft St C2
St Aldate St B2
St Ann Way C1
St Catherine St. A2

St Mark St A2
St Mary De Crypt 🏛 . .B1
St Mary De Lode 🏛 . .B1
St Nicholas's 🏛 B1
St Oswald's Rd. A1
St Oswald's Trading
  Estate. A1
St Peter's 🏛 B2
Seabroke Rd A3
Sebert St A2
Severn Rd. C1
Sherborne St B2
Shire Hall 🏛 B1
Sidney St C3
Southgate St B1/C1
Spa Field C1
Spa Rd C1
Sports Ground . . .A2/B2
Station Rd B2
Stratton Rd. C3
Stroud Rd C1
Swan Rd A2
Technical College. . . .C1
The Park C1
The Quay B1
Transport 🏛 B1
Trier Way. C1/C2
Union St A1
Vauxhall Rd C2
Victoria St. C2
Wellington St C2
Westgate St B1
Widden St. C2
Worcester St. B2

Grimsby

Abbey Drive East C2
Abbey Drive West. . . .C2
Abbey Park Rd C2
Abbey Rd C2
Abbey Walk C2
Abbotsway C2
Adam Smith St. . . .A1/A2
Ainslie St B2
Albert St A3
Alexandra Rd A2/B2
Annesley St B2
Armstrong St A1
Arthur St C1
Augusta St C1
Bargate. C1
Beeson St. A1
Bethlehem St B2
Bodiam Way B3
Bradley St. A3
Brighowgate C1/C2
Bus Station. C2
Canterbury Dr. C1
Cartergate. B1/C1
Catherine St C3
Caxton 🎭 A3
Chantry La B1
Charlton St. A1
Church La. C2
Church St A3
Cleethorpe Rd A3
College C2
College St. C1
Compton Dr C1
Corporation Bridge. . .A2
Corporation Rd. A1
Court. B3
Crescent St B1
Deansgate C1

Doughty Rd C2
Dover St B1
Duchess St. C2
Dudley St C1
Duke of York
  Gardens B1
Duncombe St B3
Earl La B1
East Marsh St. B3
East St B2
Eastgate B3
Eastside Rd A3
Eaton Ct C1
Eleanor St. B3
Ellis Way. B3
Fisherman's
  Chapel 🏛 A3
Fisherman's Wharf . . .A3
Fishing Heritage
  Centre B2
Flour Sq A3
Frederick St B1
Frederick Ward Way. .B2
Freeman St A3/B3
Freshney Dr B1
Freshney Pl. B2
Garden St. C2
Garibaldi St A3
Garth La B2
Grime St B3
Grimsby Docks
  Station ≈ A3
Grimsby Town
  Station ≈ C2
PS Lincoln Castle ⚓ . .B2
Post Office 🏤
  . . . . B1/B2/B3/C2/C3
Hainton Ave C3
Har Way. B3
Hare St. C3
Harrison St B1
Haven Ave B1
Hay Croft Ave. B1

Hay Croft St B1
Heneage Rd B3/C3
Henry St B1
Holme St B3
Hume St C1
Information Ctr 🛈 B2
James St B1
Joseph St B1
Kent St A3
King Edward St A3
Lambert Rd C2
Library B2
Lime St B1
Lister St B1
Littlefield La C1
Lockhill. A3
Lord St B1
Ludford St C3
Macaulay St B1
Mallard Mews C3
Manor Ave C2
Market A3
Market Hall B2
Market St. B3
Moss Rd C2
Nelson St A3
New St B2
Osbourne St. B2
Pasture St. B3
Peaks Parkway. C3
Pelham Rd C1
Police Station 🚓 . .A3/B2
Post Office 🏤
  . . . . .B2
Pyewipe Rd A1
Railway Pl. A3
Railway St A3
Rendel St A2
Retail Park A2

Retail Park B3
Richard St. B1
Ripon St B1
Robinson St East B3
Royal St A3
St Hilda's Ave C1
St. James 🏛 C2
Sheepfold St. B3/C3
Sixhills St C3
South Park B2
Spring St A3
Superstore B3
Tasburgh St C3
Tennyson St B2
Thesiger St A3
The Close C1
Time Trap 🏛 C2
Town Hall 🏛 B2
Veal St B1
Victoria St North. A2
Victoria St South B2
Victoria St West B2
W. Coates Rd. A1
Watkin St. A1
Welholme Ave. C2
Welholme Museum &
  Gallery 🏛 C2
Welholme Rd. C3
Wellington St B3
Wellowgate C2
Werneth Rd B3
Westgate A2
Westminster Dr. C1
Willingham St C3
Wintringham Rd C2
Wood St B3
Yarborough Dr B1
Yarborough Hotel 🏨 . .C2

Harrogate

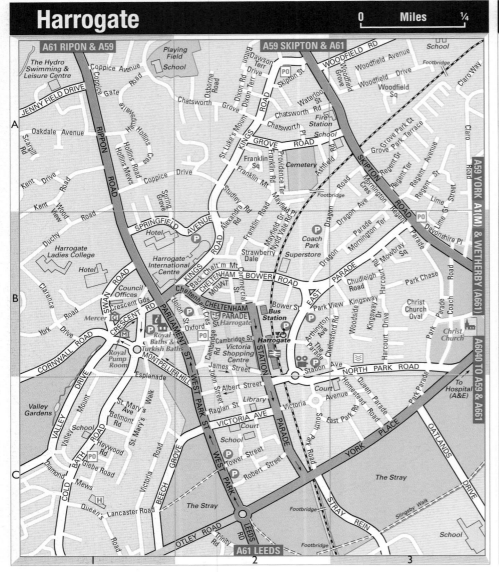

0 Miles ¼

Hull

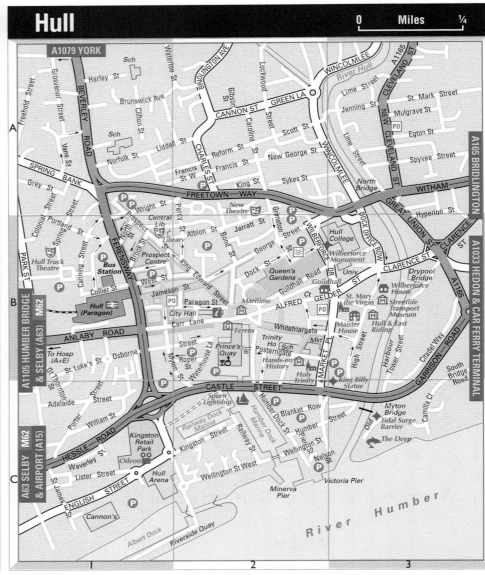

0 Miles ¼

Inverness

0 Miles ¼

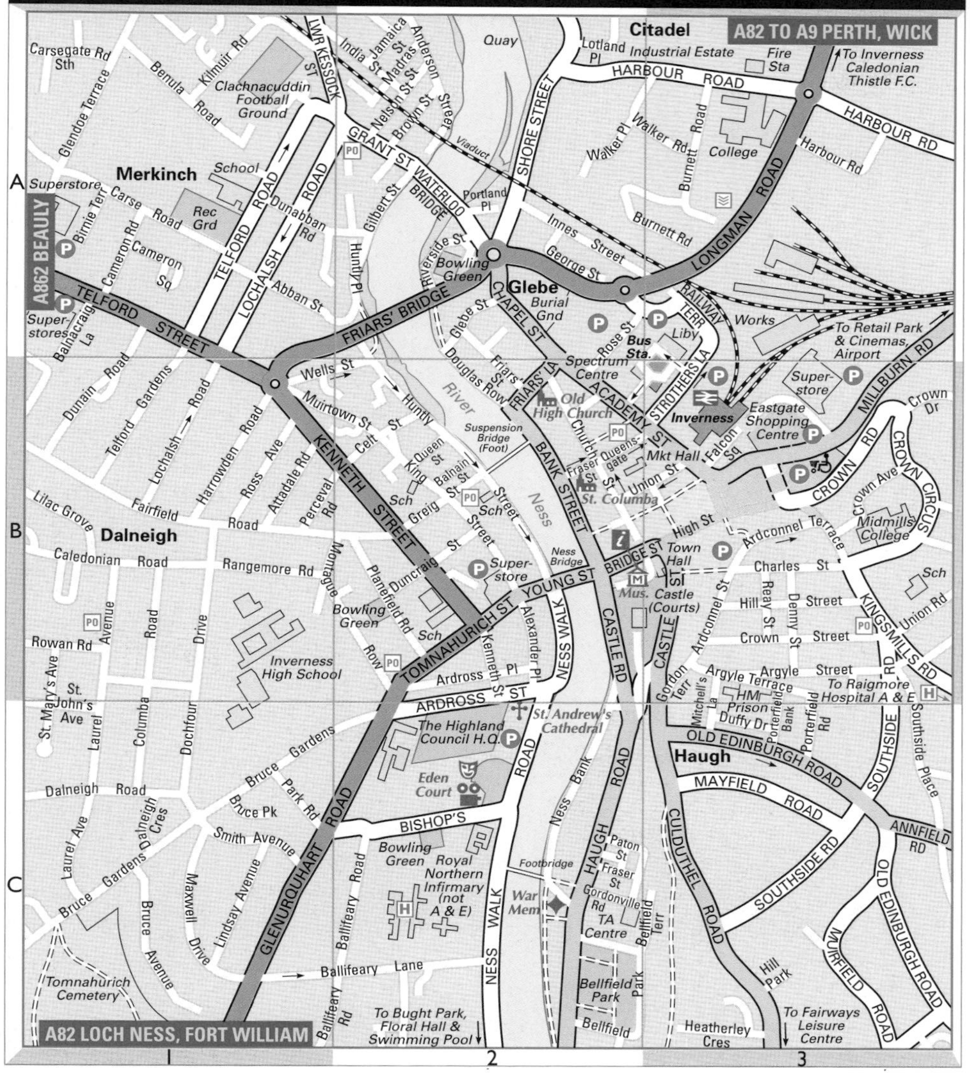

Ipswich

0 Miles ¼

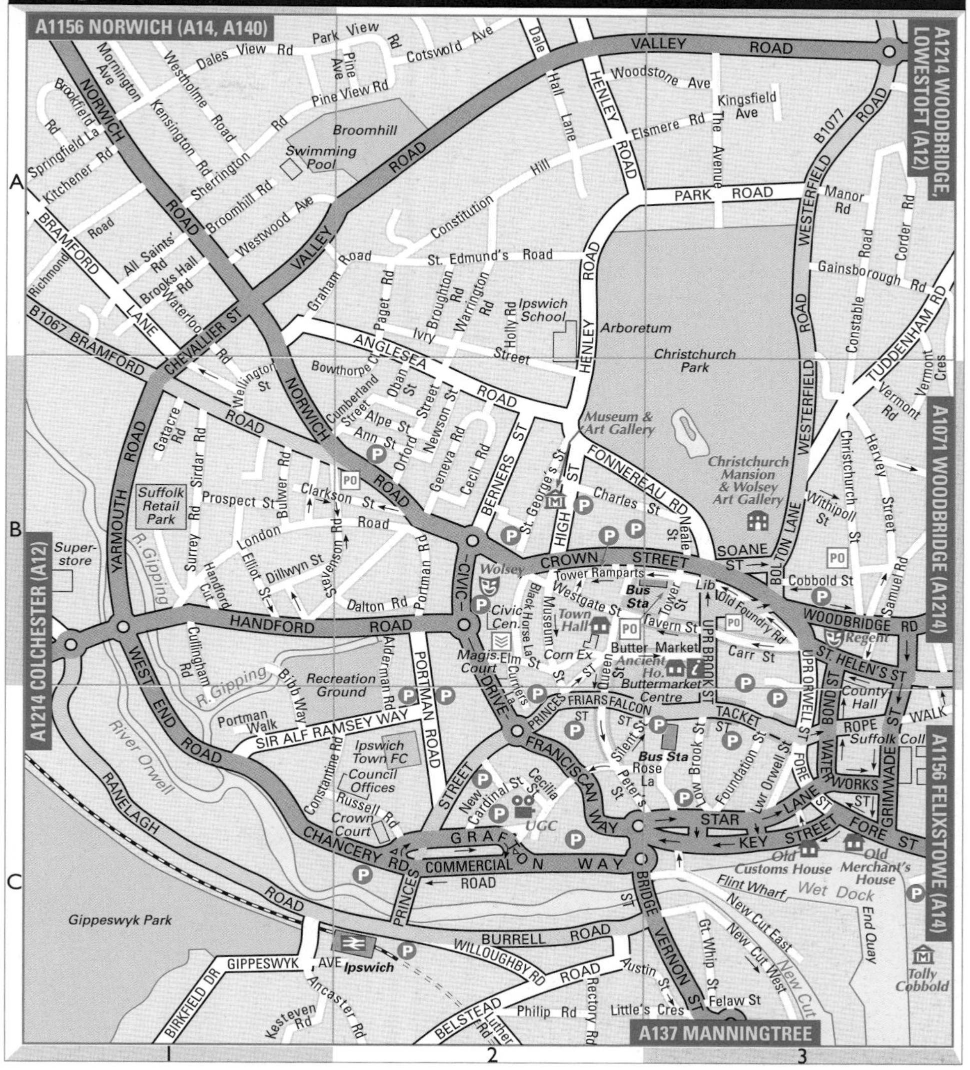

Inverness

Abban St A1
Academy St B2
Alexander Pl B2
Anderson St A2
Annfield Rd C3
Ardconnel St B3
Ardconnel Terr B3
Ardross Pl B2
Ardross St B2
Argyle St B3
Argyle Terr B3
Attadale Rd B1
Ballifeary La C2
Ballifeary Rd C1/C2
Balnacraig La A1
Balnain St B2
Bank St B2
Bellfield Park C2
Bellfield Terr C3
Benula Rd A1
Birnie Terr A1
Bishop's Rd C2
Bowling Green A2
Bowling Green B2
Bowling Green C2
Bridge St B2
Brown St A2
Bruce Ave C1
Bruce Gdns C1
Bruce Pk C1
Burial Ground A2
Burnett Rd A3
Bus Station B3
Caledonian Rd B1
Cameron Rd A1
Cameron Sq A1
Carse Rd A1
Carsegate Rd South . . A1
Castle (Courts) B3
Castle Rd B2
Castle St B3
Celt St B2
Chapel St A2
Charles St B3
Church St B2
Clachnacuddin Football Ground A1
College A3
Columba Rd B1/C1
Crown Ave B3
Crown Circus B3
Crown Dr B3
Crown Rd B3
Crown St B3
Culduthel Rd C3
Dalneigh Cres C1
Dalneigh Rd C1
Denny St B3
Dochfour Dr B1/C1
Douglas Row B2
Duffy Dr C3
Dunabban Rd A1
Dunain Rd B1
Duncraig St B2
Eastgate Shopping Centre B3
Eden Court C2
Fairfield Rd B1
Falcon Sq B3
Fire Station A3
Fraser St B2
Fraser St C2
Friars' Bridge A2
Friars' La B2
Friars' St A2
George St A2
Gilbert St A2
Glebe St A2
Glendoe Terr A1
Glenurquhart Rd C1
Gordon Terr B3
Gordonville Rd C2
Grant St A2
Greig St B2
H.M. Prison B3
Harbour Rd A3
Harrowden Rd B1
Haugh Rd C2
Heatherley Cres C3
High St B3
Highland Council H.Q., The C2
Hill Park C3
Hill St B3
Huntly Pl A2
Huntly St B2
India St A2
Industrial Estate A3
Information Ctr . . . B2
Innes St A2
Inverness High School B1
Inverness B3
Jamaica St A2
Kenneth St B2
Kilmuir Rd A1
King St B2
Kingsmills Rd B3
Laurel Ave B1/C1
Library A3
Lilac Gr B1
Lindsay Ave C1
Lochalsh Rd A1/B1
Longman Rd A3
Lotland Pl A2
Lower Kessock St . . . A1
Madras St A2
Market Hall B3
Maxwell Dr C1
Mayfield Rd C3
Midmills College B3
Millburn Rd B3
Mitchell's La C3
Montague Row B2
Muirfield Rd C3
Muirtown St B1
Museum B2
Nelson St A2
Ness Bank C2
Ness Bridge B2
Ness Walk B2/C2
Old Edinburgh Rd . . . C3
Old High Church . . . B2
Park Rd C1
Paton St C2
Perceval Rd B1
Planefield Rd B2
Police Station A3
Porterfield Bank C3
Porterfield Rd C3
Portland Pl A2
Post Office A2/B1/B2/B3
Queen St B2
Queensgate B2
Railway Terr A3
Rangemore Rd B1
Reay St B3
Riverside St A2
Rose St A2
Ross Ave B1
Rowan Rd B1
Royal Northern Infirmary C2
St. Andrew's Cathedral C2
St. Columba B2
St. John's Ave C1
St. Mary's Ave C1
Shore St A2
Smith Ave C1
Southside Pl C3
Southside Rd C3
Spectrum Centre B2
Strothers La B3
TA Centre C2
Telford Gdns B1
Telford Rd A1
Telford St A1
Tomnahurich Cemetery C1
Tomnahurich St B2
Town Hall B3
Union Rd B3
Union St B3
Walker Pl A2
Walker Rd A3
War Memorial ✦ C2
Waterloo Bridge A2
Wells St B1
Young St B2

Ipswich

Alderman Rd B2
All Saints' Rd A1
Alpe St B2
Ancaster Rd C1
Ancient House B3
Anglesea Rd B2
Ann St B2
Austin St C2
Belstead Rd C2
Berners St B2
Bibb Way B1
Birkfield Dr C1
Black Horse La B2
Bolton La B3
Bond St C3
Bowthorpe Cl B2
Bramford La A1
Bramford Rd A1
Bridge St C2
Brookfield Rd A1
Brooks Hall Rd A1
Broomhill Rd A1
Broughton Rd A2
Bulwer Rd B1
Burrell Rd C2
Bus Station B2/C3
Butter Market B2
Butter Market Centre . B3
Carr St B3
Cecil Rd B2
Cecilia St C2
Chancery Rd C2
Charles St B2
Chevallier St A1
Christchurch Mansion & Wolsey Art Gallery B3
Christchurch Park A3
Christchurch St B3
Civic Centre B2
Civic Dr B2
Clarkson St B1
Cobbold St B3
Commercial Rd C2
Constable Rd A3
Constantine Rd C1
Constitution Hill A2
Corder Rd A3
Corn Exchange B2
Cotswold Ave A2
Council Offices C2
County Hall B3
Crown Court C2
Crown St B2
Cullingham Rd B1
Cumberland St B2
Curriers La B2
Dale Hall La A2
Dales View Rd A1
Dalton Rd B2
Dillwyn St B1
Elliot St B1
Elm St B2
Elsmere Rd A3
End Quay C3
Falcon St C2
Felaw St C3
Flint Wharf C3
Fonnereau Rd B2
Fore St C3
Foundation St C3
Franciscan Way C2
Friars St C2
Gainsborough Rd A3
Gatacre Rd B1
Geneva Rd B2
Gippeswyk Ave C1
Gippeswyk Park C1
Grafton Way C2
Graham Rd A1
Grimwade St C3
Great Whip St C3
Handford Cut B1
Handford Rd B1
Henley Rd A2
Hervey St B3
High St B2
Holly Rd A2
Information Ctr B3
Ipswich School A2
Ipswich Station C2
Ipswich Town FC (Portman Road) C2
Ivry St A2
Kensington Rd A1
Kesteven Rd C1
Key St C3
Kingsfield Ave A3
Kitchener Rd A1
Magistrates Court B2
Little's Cr C2
London Rd B1
Low Brook St C3
Lower Orwell St C3
Luther Rd C2
Manor Rd A3
Mornington Ave A1
Museum & Art Gallery B2
Museum St B2
Neale St B3
New Cardinal St C2
New Cut East C3
New Cut West C3
Newson St B2
Norwich Rd A1/B1
Oban St B2
Old Customs House C3
Old Foundry Rd B3
Old Merchant's House C3
Orford St B2
Paget Rd A2
Park Rd A3
Park View Rd A2
Peter's St C2
Philip Rd C2
Pine Ave A2
Pine View Rd A2
Police Station B2
Portman Rd B2
Portman Walk C1
Post Office B2/B3
Princes St C2
Prospect St B1
Queen St B2
Ranelagh Rd C1
Rectory Rd C2
Regent Theatre B3
Richmond Rd A1
Rope Walk C3
Rose La C2
Russell Rd C1
St Edmund's Rd A2
St George's St B2
St Helen's St B3
Samuel Rd B3
Sherrington Rd A1
Silent St C2
Sir Alf Ramsey Way . . C1
Sirdar Rd B1
Soane St B3
Springfield La A1
Star La C3
Stevenson Rd B1
Suffolk College C3
Suffolk Retail Park . . . B1
Superstore B1
Surrey Rd B1
Swimming Pool A1
Tacket St C3
Tavern St B3
The Avenue A3
Tolly Cobbold Museum C3
Tower Ramparts B2
Tower St B3
Town Hall B2
Tuddenham Rd A3
UGC C2
Upper Brook St B3
Upper Orwell St B3
Valley Rd A2
Vermont Cr B3
Vermont Rd B3
Vernon St C3
Warrington Rd A2
Waterloo Rd A1
Waterworks St C3
Wellington St B1
West End Rd B1
Westerfield Rd A3
Westgate St B2
Westholme Rd A1
Westwood Ave A1
Willoughby Rd C2
Withipoll St B3
Wolsey Theatre B2
Woodbridge Rd B3
Woodstone Ave A3
Yarmouth Rd B1

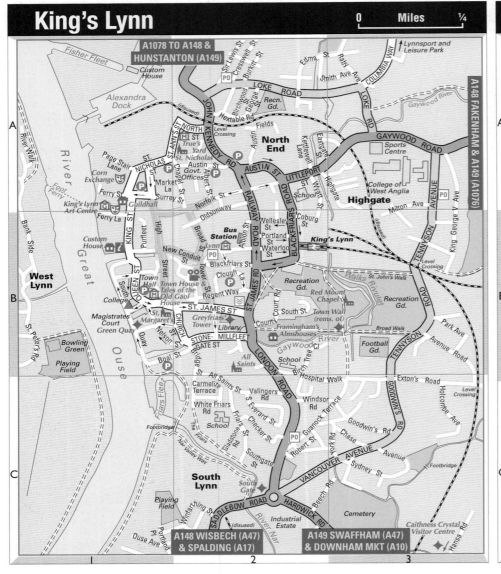

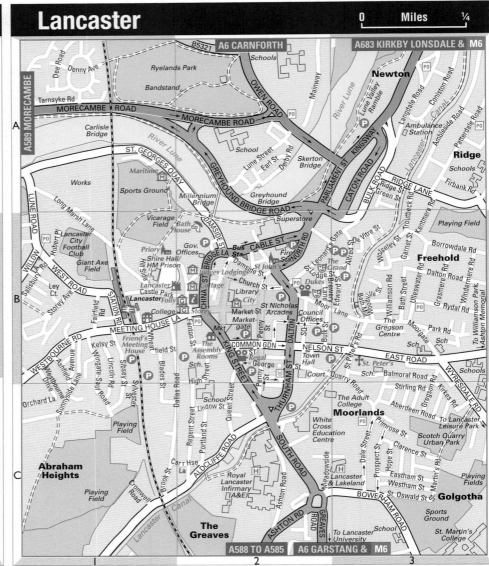

King's Lynn

Albert St A2
Albion St B2
All Saints ⛪ B2
All Saints St B2
Austin Fields A2
Austin St A2
Avenue Rd B3
Bank Side B1
Beech Rd C2
Birch Tree Cl B2
Birchwood St A2
Blackfriars Rd B2
Blackfriars St B2
Boal St B1
Bridge St B2
Broad St B2
Broad Walk B3
Burkitt St A2
Bus Station B2
Carmelite Terr C2
Chapel St A2
Chase Ave C3
Checker St C2
Church St B2
Clough La B2
Coburg St B2
College of
    West Anglia A3
Columbia Way A3
Corn Exchange ⛪ . . A1
County Court Rd C3
Cresswell St A2
Custom House ⛪ A1

Eastgate St A2
Edma St A2
Exton's Rd C3
Ferry La B1
Ferry St A1
Framingham's
    Almshouses ⛪ . . B2
Friars St B2
Gaywood Rd A3
George St A2
Gladstone Rd C2
Goodwin's Rd C3
Green Quay ✦ B1
Greyfriars' Tower ✦ . . B2
Guanock Terr C2
Guildhall ⛪ A1
Hansa Rd B2
Hardwick Rd C2
Hextable Rd A2
High St B1
Holcombe Ave C2
Hospital Walk C2
Information Ctr ℹ . . . B1
John Kennedy Rd . . . A2
Kettlewell Lane A2
King George V Ave . . B3
King's Lynn Art
    Centre ⛪ A1
King's Lynn
    Station ⚉ B2
King St B1
Library B2
Littleport St A2
Loke Rd A2
London Rd B2

Lynn Museum B2
Majestic 🎬 B2
Magistrates Court . . . B1
Market La A1
Millfleet B2
Milton Ave A3
Nar Valley Walk C2
Nelson St B1
New Conduit St B2
Norfolk St A2
North St A2
Oldsunway B2
Ouse Ave C1
Page Stair Lane A1
Park Ave B3
Police Station 🚓 . . . B1
Portland Pl C1
Portland St B2
Post Office 📮 . A3/B2/C2
Purfleet B1
Queen St B1
Raby Ave A3
Railway Rd A2
Red Mount
    Chapel ⛪ B3
Regent Way B2
River Walk A1
Robert St B2
Saddlebow Rd C2
St Ann's St A1
St James' Rd B2
St James St B2
St John's Walk B3
St Margaret's ⛪ B1
St Nicholas ⛪ A2

St Nicholas St A1
St Peter's Rd B1
S Everard St C2
Sir Lewis St A2
Smith Ave A3
South Gate ✦ C2
Southgate St C2
South Quay B1
South St B2
Stonegate St B2
Surrey St A1
Sydney St C3
Tennyson Ave B3
Tennyson Rd B3
The Friars C2
Tower St B2
Town Hall B1
Town House & Tales
    of The Old Gaol
    House 🏛 B1
Town Wall
    (Remains) ✦ B3
True's Yard
    Museum 🏛 A2
Valingers Rd C2
Vancouver Ave C2
Waterloo St B2
Wellesley St B2
White Friars Rd C2
Windsor Rd C2
Winfarthing St C2
Wyatt St A2
York Rd C3

Lancaster

Aberdeen Rd C3
Adult College, The . . . C3
Aldcliffe Rd C2
Alfred St B3
Ambleside Rd A3
Ambulance Sta A3
Ashfield Ave B1
Ashton Rd C2
Assembly Rooms,
    The 🏛 B2
Balmoral Rd C3
Bath House ⛪ B2
Bath Mill La B3
Bath St B3
Blades St B1
Borrowdale Rd B3
Bowerham Rd C3
Brewery La B2
Bridge La B2
Brook St C1
Bulk Rd A3
Bulk St B2
Bus Station B2
Cable St B2
Carlisle Bridge A1
Carr House La C2
Castle 🏰 B1
Castle Park B1
Caton Rd A3
China St B2
Church St B2
City Museum 🏛 B2
Clarence St C3
Common Gdn St B2
Coniston Rd A3
Cottage Museum 🏛 . . B2
Council Offices B2
Court B2
Cromwell Rd C1
Dale St C3
Dallas Rd B1/C1
Dalton Rd B3
Dalton Sq B2
Damside St B2

De Vitre St B3
Dee Rd A1
Denny Ave A1
Derby Rd A2
Dukes 🎬⚉ B2
Earl St A2
East Rd B3
Eastham St C3
Edward St B3
Fairfield Rd B1
Fenton St B2
Firbank Rd A3
Fire Station B1
Folly Gallery 🏛 B2
Friend's Meeting
    House ⛪ B1
Garnet St B3
George St B2
Giant Axe Field B1
Gov. Offices B2
Grand, The 🎬 B2
Grasmere Rd B3
Greaves Rd C2
Green St A3
Gregson Centre, The . B3
Gregson Rd C3
Greyhound Bridge . . . A2
Greyhound
    Bridge Rd A2
High St B2
Hill Side B1
Hope St C3
Hubert Pl B1
Information Ctr ℹ . . . B2
Judges
    Lodgings 🏛 B2
Kelsy St B1
Kentmere Rd B3
King St B2
Kingsway A3
Kirkes Rd C3
Lancaster ⚉ B1
Lancaster &
    Lakeland 🏥 C3
Lancaster City
    Football Club B1

Langdale Rd A3
Ley Ct B1
Library B2
Lincoln Rd B1
Lindow St B2
Lodge St B2
Long Marsh La B1
Lune Rd A1
Lune St A2
Lune Valley Ramble . . A3
Mainway A2
Maritime Museum 🏛 . A1
Market St B2
Marketgate Shopping
    Centre B2
Meadowside C2
Meeting House La . . . B1
Millennium Bridge . . . A2
Moor La B2
Moorgate B3
Morecambe Rd . . . A1/A2
Nelson St B2
North Rd B2
Orchard La C1
Owen Rd A3
Park Rd B3
Parliament St A3
Patterdale Rd A3
Penny St B2
Police Station 🚓 . . . B2
Portland St C2
Post Office 📮
    . . . A2/A3/B1/B2/B3/C3
Primrose St C3
Priory ⛪ B1
Prospect St B3
Quarry Rd B3
Queen St C2
Regal 🎬 B2
Regent St C2
Ridge La A3
Ridge St A3
Royal Lancaster
    Infirmary (A&E) 🏥 . C2
Rydal Rd B3
Ryelands Park A1

St. John's ⛪ B2
St. Nicholas Arcades
    Shopping Centre . . B2
St Peter's Rd B3
St Georges Quay A1
St. Leonard's Gate . . . B2
St. Martin's College . . C3
St. Martin's Rd C3
St. Oswald St C3
St. Peter's ✝ B3
Salisbury Rd B1
Scotch Quarry
    Urban Park C3
Shire Hall/HM Prison . B1
Sibsey St B1
Skerton Bridge A2
South Rd C2
Station Rd B1
Stirling Rd C3
Storey Ave B1
Storey Gallery 🏛 . . . B2
Sunnyside La C1
Sylvester St C1
Tarnsyke Rd A1
Thurnham St C2
Town Hall B2
Troutbeck Rd B3
Ulleswater Rd B3
Vicarage Field B1
West Rd B1
Westbourne Dr C1
Westbourne Rd B1
Westham St C3
Wheatfield St B1
White Cross Education
    Centre C2
Williamson Rd B3
Willow La B1
Windermere Rd B3
Wingate-Saul Rd B1
Wolseley St B3
Woodville St B3
Wyresdale Rd C3

Leeds

0   Miles   ¼

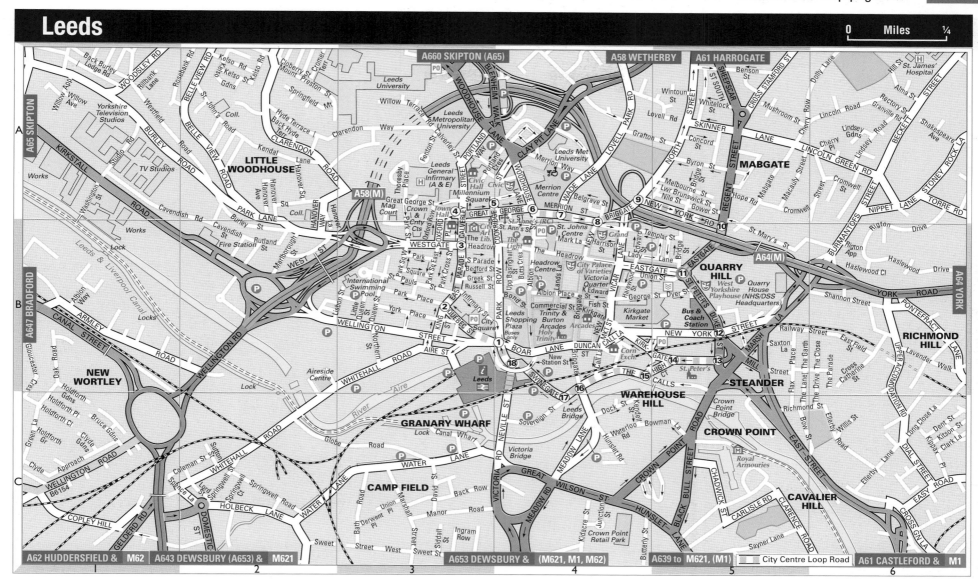

1	**2**	**3**	**4**	**5**	**6**

A62 HUDDERSFIELD & M62   A643 DEWSBURY (A653) & M621   A653 DEWSBURY & (M621, M1, M62)   A639 to M621, (M1)   City Centre Loop Road   A61 CASTLEFORD & M1

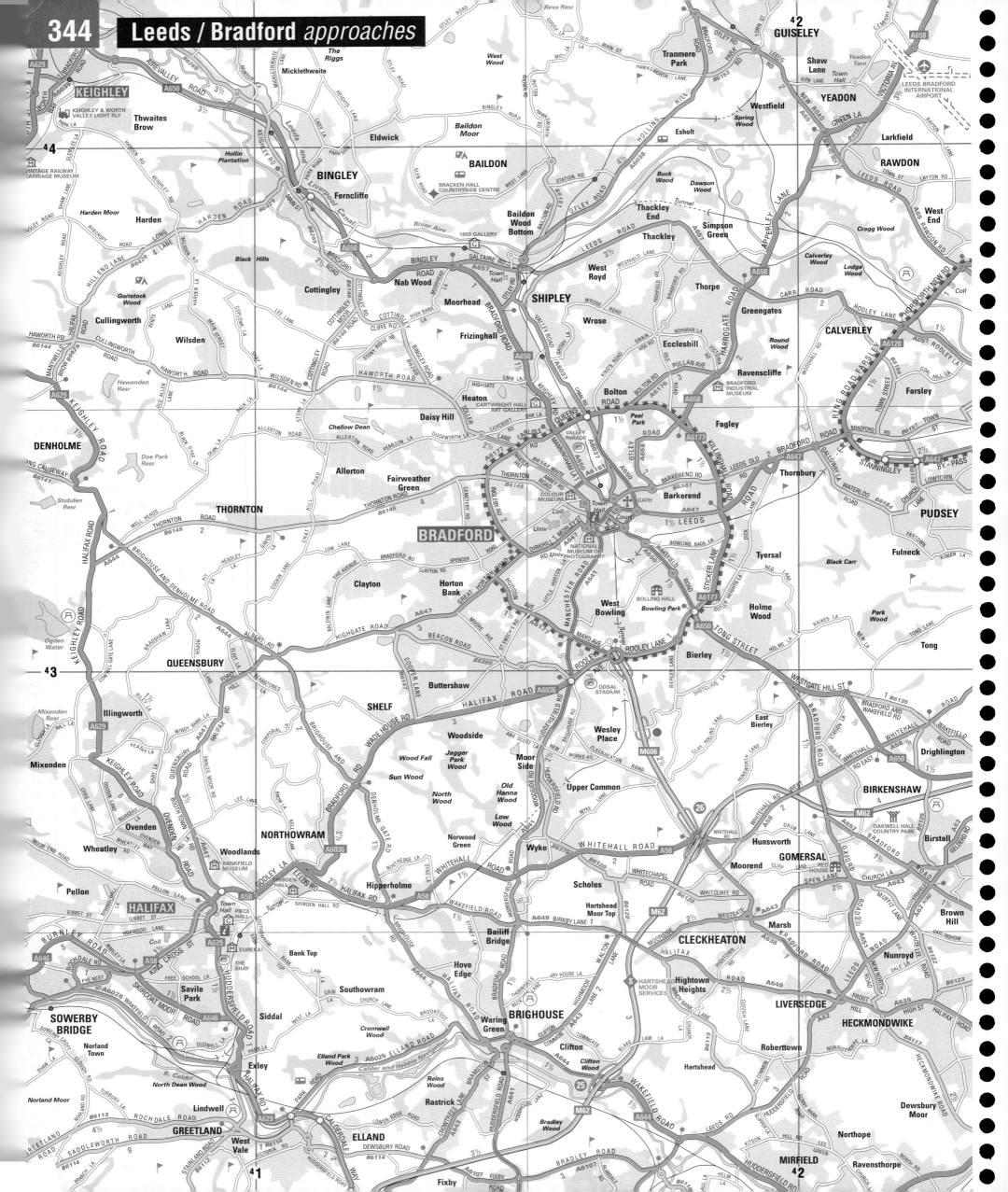

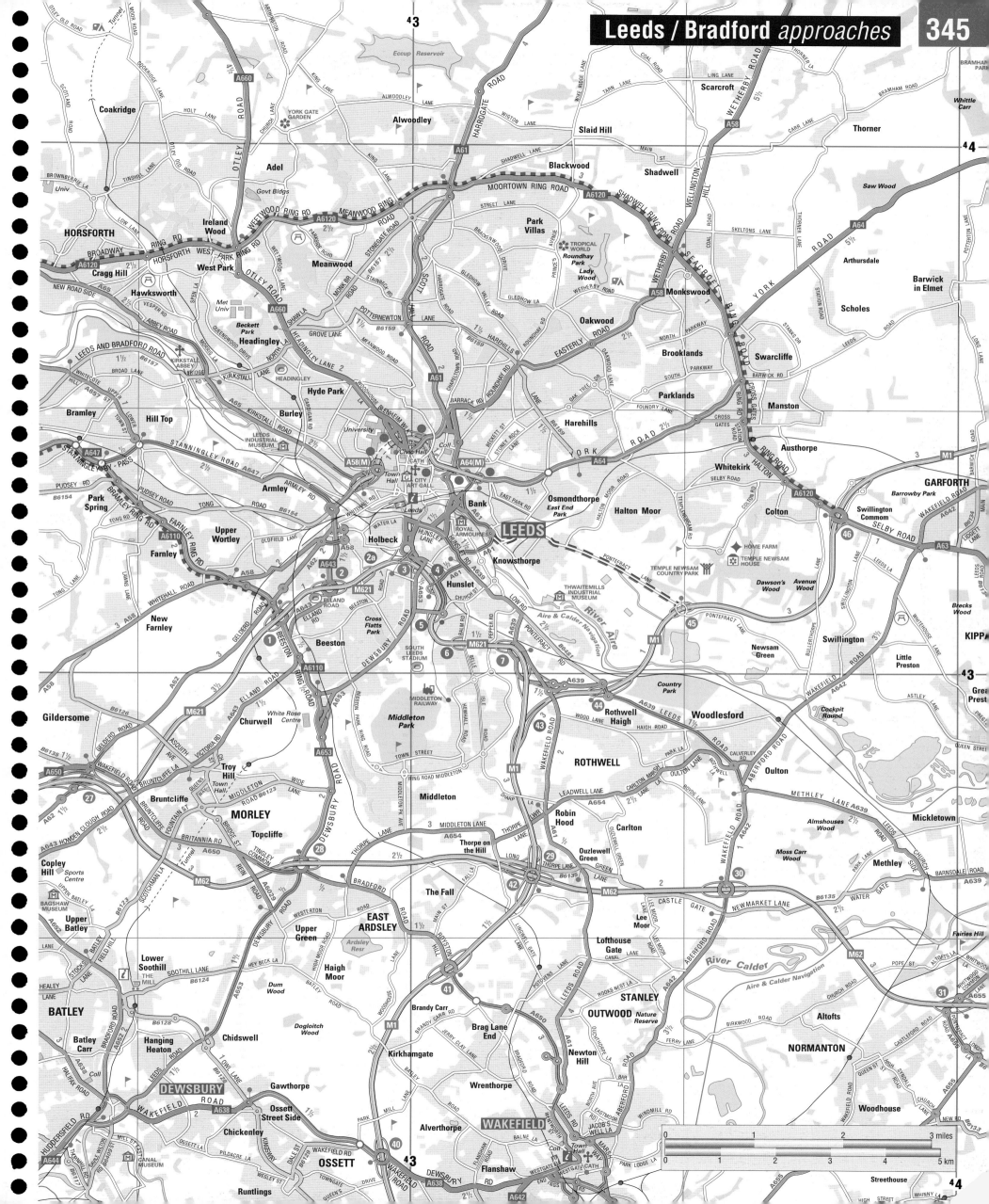

Liverpool

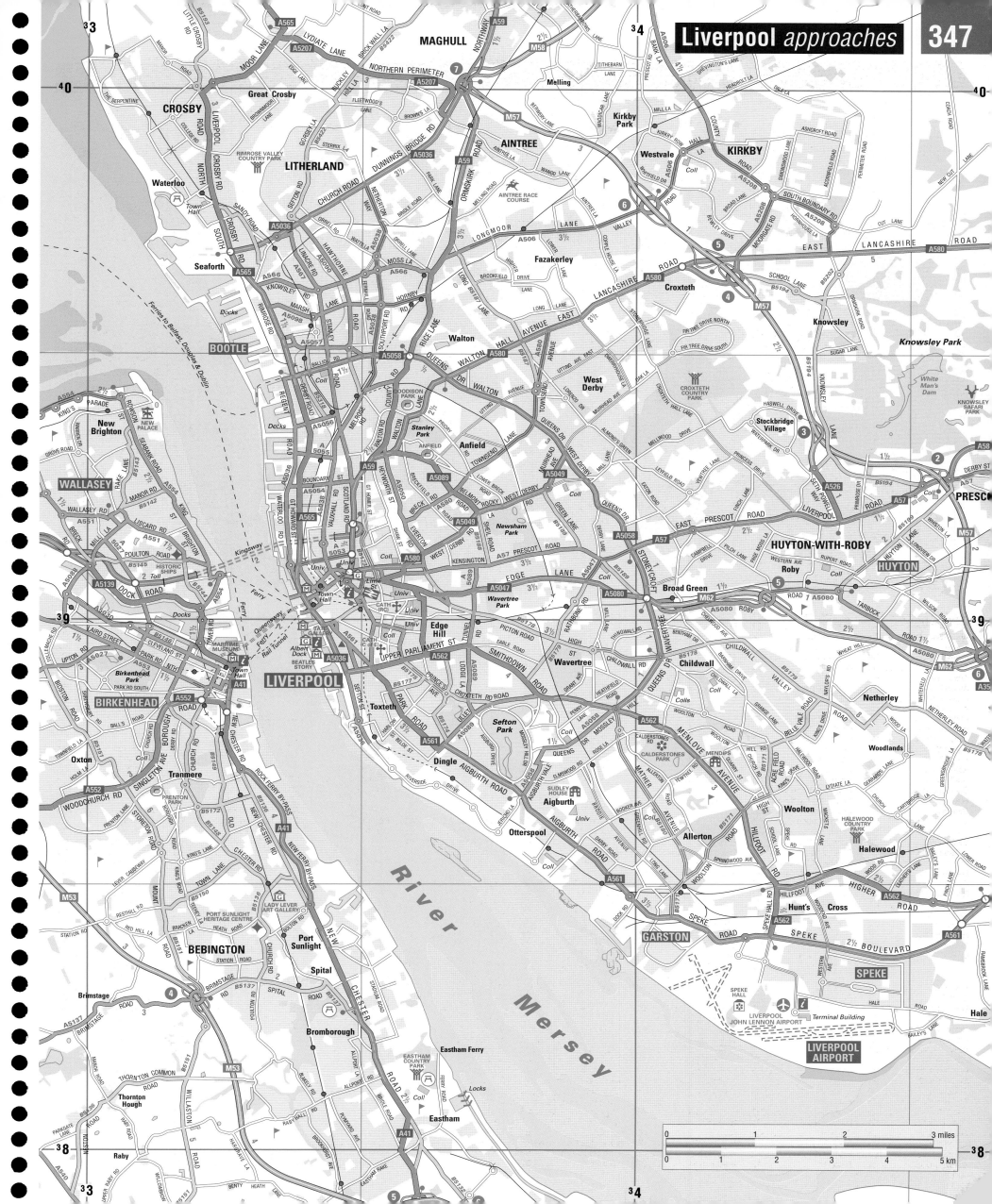

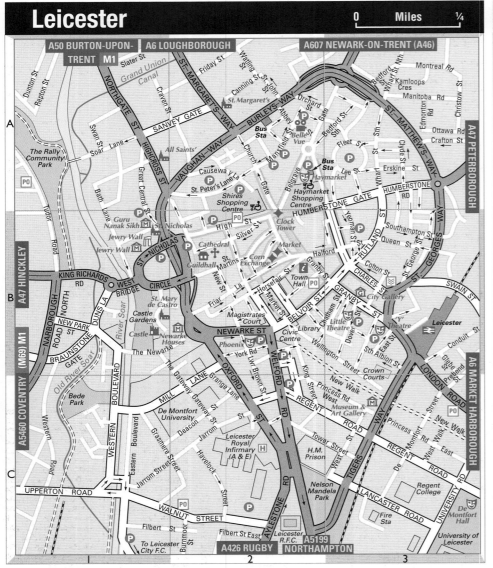

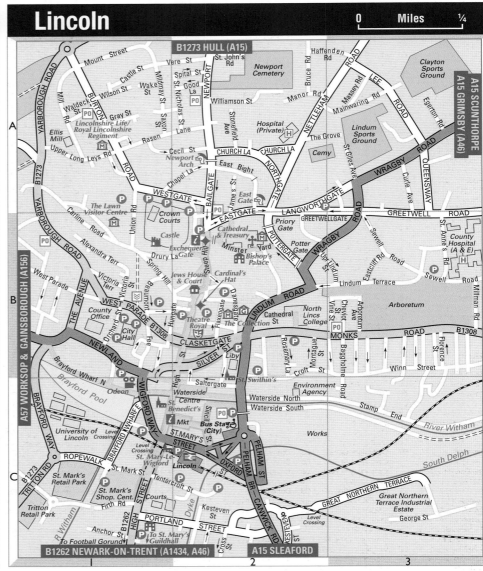

Leicester

Abbey St.	A2
All Saints'	A1
Aylestone Rd	C2
Bath La.	A1
Bede Park	C1
Bedford St	A3
Bedford St South	A3
Belgrave Gate	A2
Belle Vue	A2
Belvoir St	B2
Braunstone Gate	B1
Burleys Way	A2
Burnmoor St	C2
Bus Station	A2
Canning St	A2
Castle	B1
Castle Gardens	B1
Cathedral	B2
Causeway La	A2
Charles St	B3
Chatham St	B2
Christow St	A3
Church Gate	A2
City Gallery	B3
Civic Centre	B2
Clock Tower	B2
Clyde St	A3
Colton St	B3
Conduit St	B3
Corn Exchange	B2
Crafton St	A3
Craven St	A1
Crown Courts	B3
Deacon St	C2
De Montfort Hall	C3
De Montfort St	C3
De Montfort University	C1
Dover St	B3
Duns La	B1
Dunton St	A1
East St	B3
Eastern Boulevard	C1
Edmonton Rd	A3
Erskine St	A3
Filbert St	C1
Filbert St East	C2
Fire Station	C3
Fleet St	A3
Friar La	B2
Friday St	A2
Gateway St	C2
Glebe St	B3
Granby St	B2
Grange La	C2
Grasmere St	C1
Great Central St	A1
Guildhall	B2
Guru Nanak Sikh Museum	B1
Halford St	B2
Havelock St	C2
Haymarket	B2
Haymarket Shopping Centre	A2
High St	A2
Highcross St	A1
H.M. Prison	C2
Horsefair St	B2
Humberstone Gate	B2
Humberstone Rd	A3
Information Ctr	B2
Jarrom St	C2
Jewry Wall	B1
Kamloops Cr	A3
King Richards Rd	B1
King St	B2
Lancaster Rd	C3
Lee St	A3
Leicester Station	C2
Leicester R.F.C.	C3
Leicester Royal Infirmary (A & E)	C2
Library	B2
Little Theatre	B3
London Rd	C3
Lower Brown St	B2
Magistrates Court	B2
Manitoba Rd	A3
Mansfield St	A2
Market	B2
Market St	B2
Mill La	C2
Montreal Rd	A3
Museum & Art Gallery	C3
Narborough Rd North	B1
Nelson Mandela Park	C2
New St	B2
New Walk	C3
New Park St	B1
Newarke Houses	B1
Newarke St	B2
Northgate St	A1
Orchard St	A2
Ottawa Rd	A3
Oxford St	C2
Phoenix	B2
Police Station	B3
Post Office	A1/B2/C2/C3
Prebend St	C3
Princess Rd East	C3
Princess Rd West	C3
Queen St	B3
Regent College	C3
Regent Rd	C2/C3
Repton St	A1
Rutland St	B2
St George St	B3
St Georges Way	B3
St John St	A2
St Margaret's	A2
St Margaret's Way	A2
St Martins	B2
St Mary de Castro	B1
St Matthew's Way	A3
St Nicholas	B1
St Nicholas Circle	B1
St Peter's La	A2
Sanvey Gate	A2
Shires Shopping Centre	A2
Silver St	B2
Slater St	A1
Soar La	A1
South Albion St	B3
Southampton St	B3
Swain St	B3
Swan St	A1
The Gateway	C2
The Newarke	B1
The Rally Community Park	A2
Tigers Way	C3
Tower St	C3
Town Hall	B2
Tudor Rd	B1
University of Leicester	C3
University Rd	C3
Upperton Rd	C1
Vaughan Way	A2
Walnut St	C2
Watling St	A2
Welford Rd	B2
Wellington St	B2
West Bridge	B1
West St	C3
West Walk	C3
Western Boulevard	C1
Western Rd	C1
Wharf St North	A3
Wharf St South	A3
'Y' Theatre	B3
Yeoman St	A3
York Rd	B2

Lincoln

Alexandra Terr	B1
Anchor St	C1
Arboretum	B3
Arboretum Ave	B3
Baggholme Rd	B3
Bailgate	A2
Beaumont Fee	B1
Bishop's Palace	B2
Brayford Wharf	B1
Brayford Wharf East	C1
Brayford Wharf North	B1
Bruce Rd	A2
Burton Rd	A1
Bus Station (City)	C2
Canwick Rd	C2
Cardinal's Hat	B2
Carline Rd	B1
Castle	B1
Castle St	A1
Cathedral & Treasury	B2
Cathedral St	B2
Cecil St	A2
Chapel La	A2
Cheviot St	B3
Church La	A2
City Hall	B1
Clasketgate	B2
Clayton Sports Ground	A3
Collection, The	B2
County Hospital (A & E)	B3
County Office	B1
Courts	C1
Croft St	B2
Cross St	C2
Crown Courts	B1
Curle Ave	A3
Danesgate	B2
Drury La	B1
East Bight	A2
East Gate	A2
Eastcliff Rd	B3
Eastgate	A2
Egerton Rd	A3
Ellis Mill	A1
Environment Agency	C2
Exchequer Gate	B2
Firth Rd	C1
Flaxengate	B2
Florence St	B3
George St	C3
Good La	A2
Gray St	A2
Great Northern Terr	C3
Great Northern Terrace Industrial Estate	C3
Greetwell Rd	B3
Greetwellgate	B3
Haffenden Rd	A3
High St	B2/C1
Hospital (Private)	A2
Hungate	B2
Information Ctr	B2
James St	A2
Jews House & Court	B2
Kesteven St	C2
Langworthgate	A2
Lee Rd	A3
Lawn Visitor Centre, The	B1
Library	B2
Lincoln Station	C2
Lincolnshire Life/Royal Lincolnshire Regiment Museum	A1
Lindum Rd	B2
Lindum Sports Ground	A3
Lindum Terr	B3
Mainwaring Rd	A3
Manor Rd	A2
Massey Rd	A3
Mildmay St	A1
Mill Rd	A1
Millman Rd	B3
Minster Yard	B2
Market	B2
Monks Rd	B3
Montague St	B2
Mount St	A1
Nettleham Rd	A2
Newland	B1
Newport	A2
Newport Arch	A2
Newport Cemetery	A2
North Lincs College	B2
Northgate	A2
Odeon	C1
Orchard St	B1
Oxford St	C2
Pelham Bridge	C2
Pelham St	C2
Police Station	B1
Portland St	C2
Post Office	A1/A2/B1/B3/C2
Potter Gate	B2
Priory Gate	B2
Queensway	A3
Rasen La	A1
Ropewalk	C1
Rosemary La	B2
St Anne's Rd	B3
St Benedict's	C1
St Giles Ave	A3
St John's Rd	A2
St Mark St	C1
St Mark's Retail Park	C1
St Mark's Shopping Centre	C1
St Mary-Le-Wigford	C1
St Mary's St	C2
St Nicholas St	A2
St Swithin's	B2
Saltergate	C1
Saxon St	A1
Sewell Rd	B3
Silver St	B2
Sincil St	C2
Spital St	A2
Spring Hill	B1
Stamp End	C3
Steep Hill	B2
Stonefield Ave	A2
Tentercroft St	C1
The Avenue	B1
The Grove	A3
Theatre Royal	B2
Tritton Retail Park	C1
Tritton Rd	C1
Union Rd	B1
University of Lincoln	C1
Upper Lindum St	B3
Upper Long Leys Rd	A1
Vere St	A2
Victoria St	B1
Victoria Terr	B1
Vine St	B3
Wake St	A1
Waldeck St	A1
Waterside Centre	C2
Waterside North	C2
Waterside South	C2
West Pde	B1
Westgate	A2
Wigford Way	C1
Williamson St	A2
Wilson St	A1
Winn St	B3
Wragby Rd	A3
Yarborough Rd	A1

London

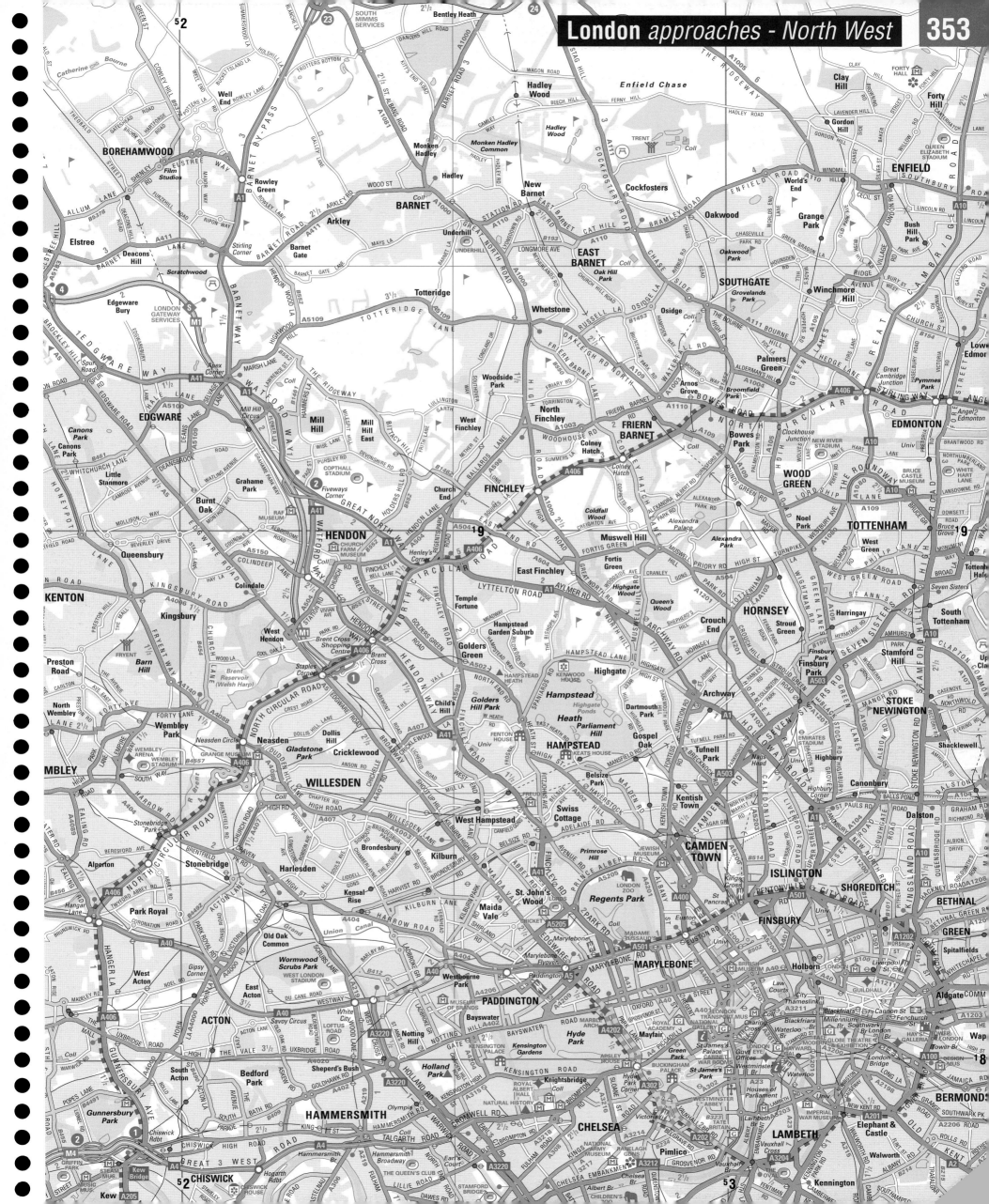

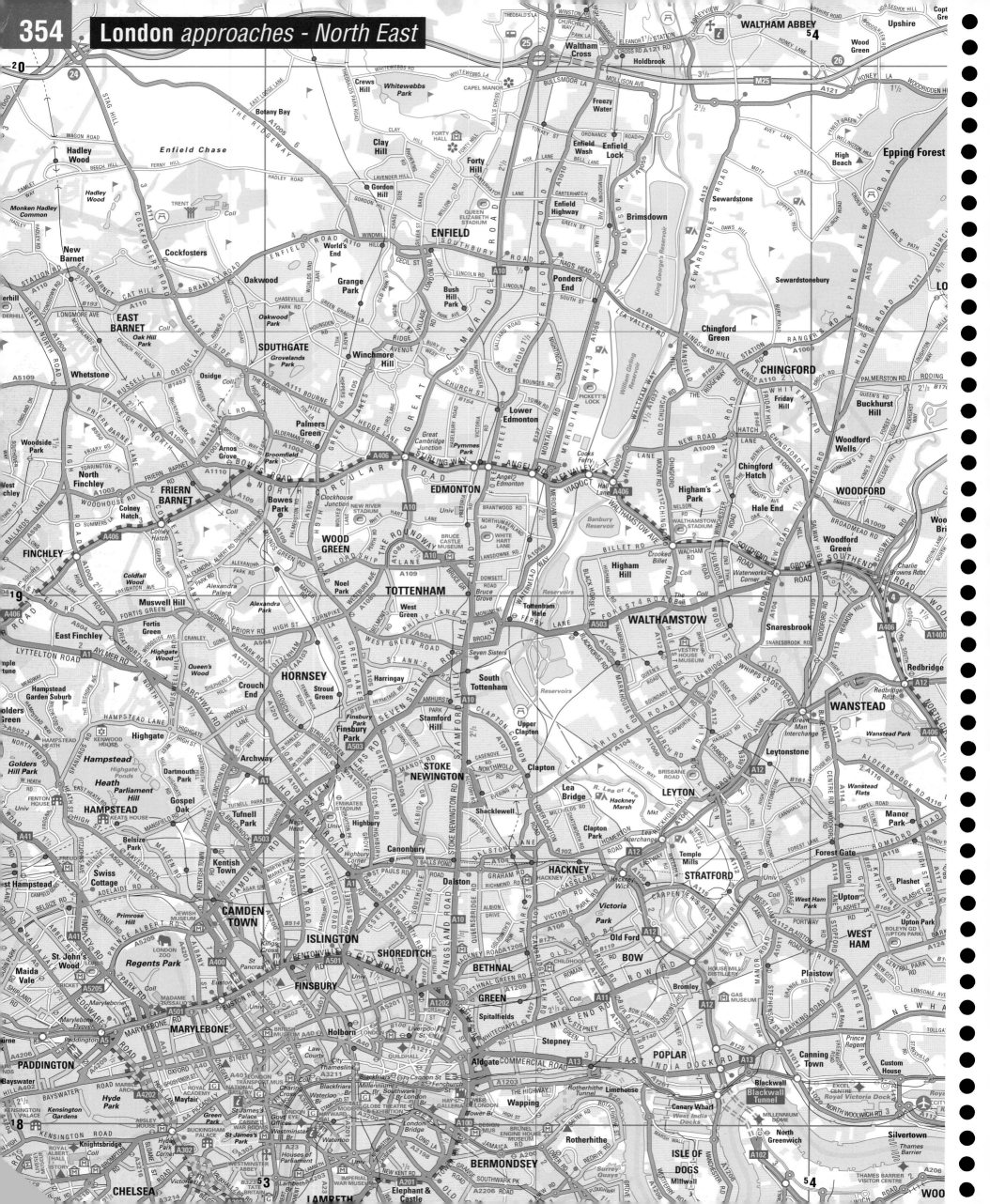

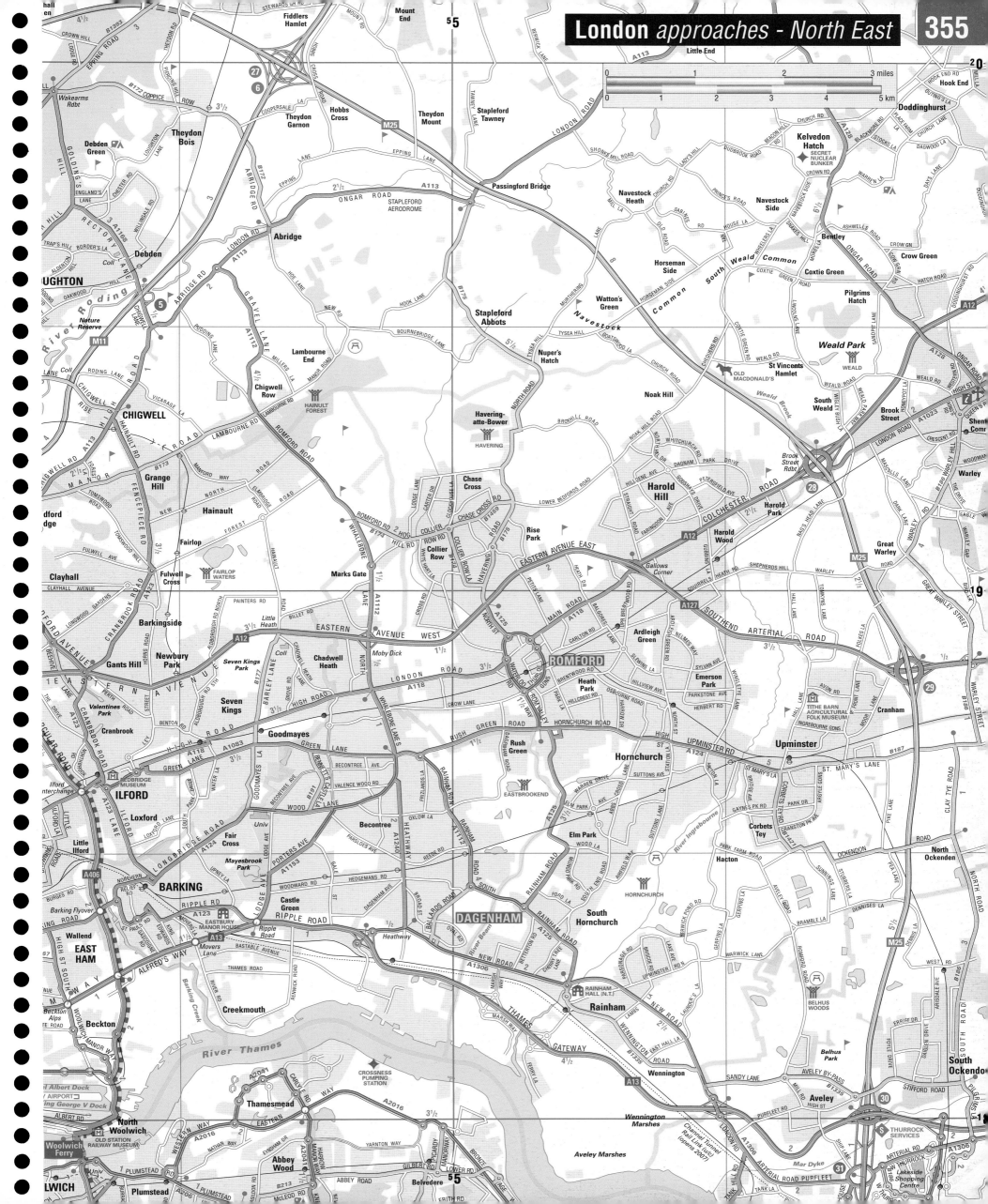

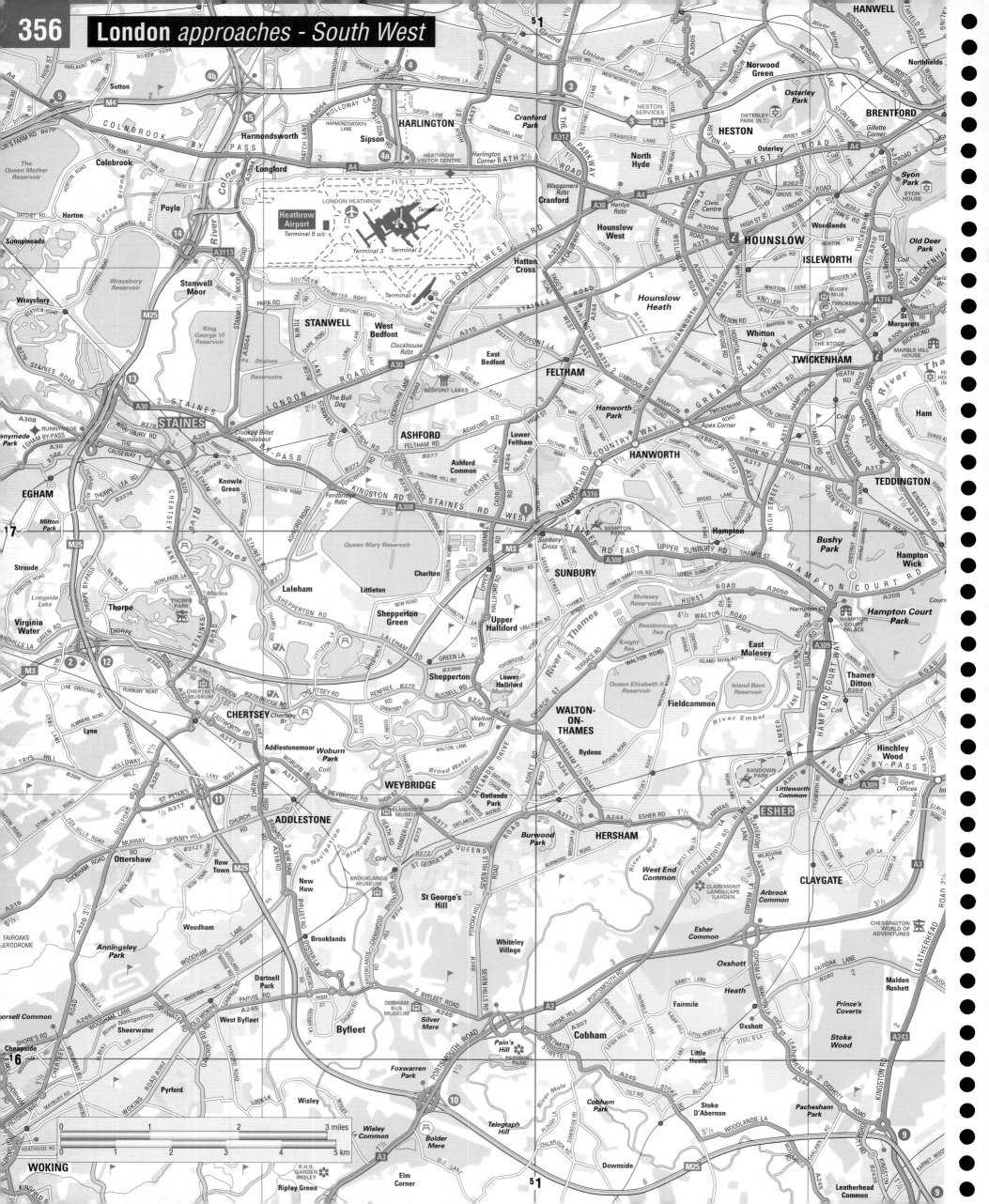

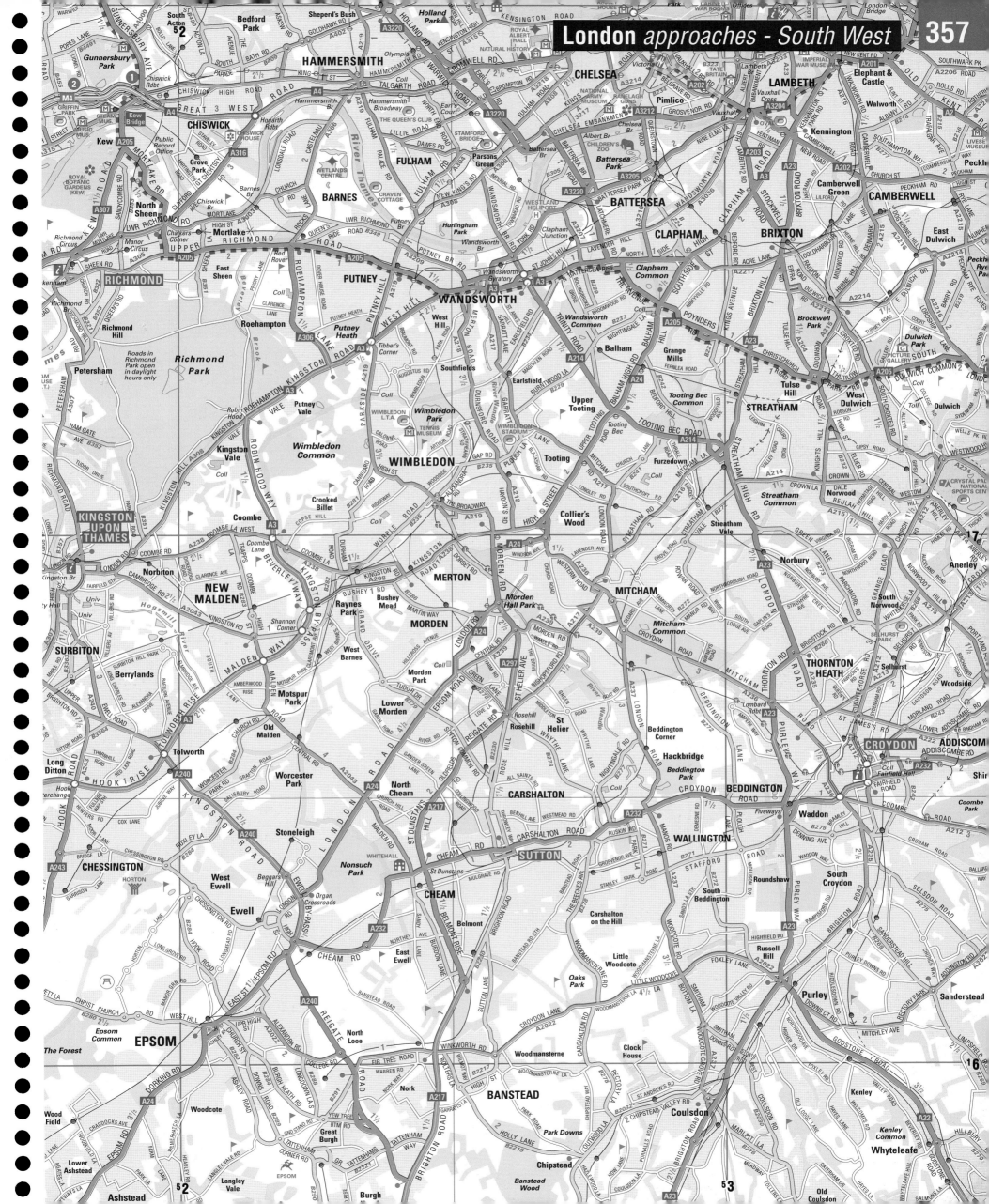

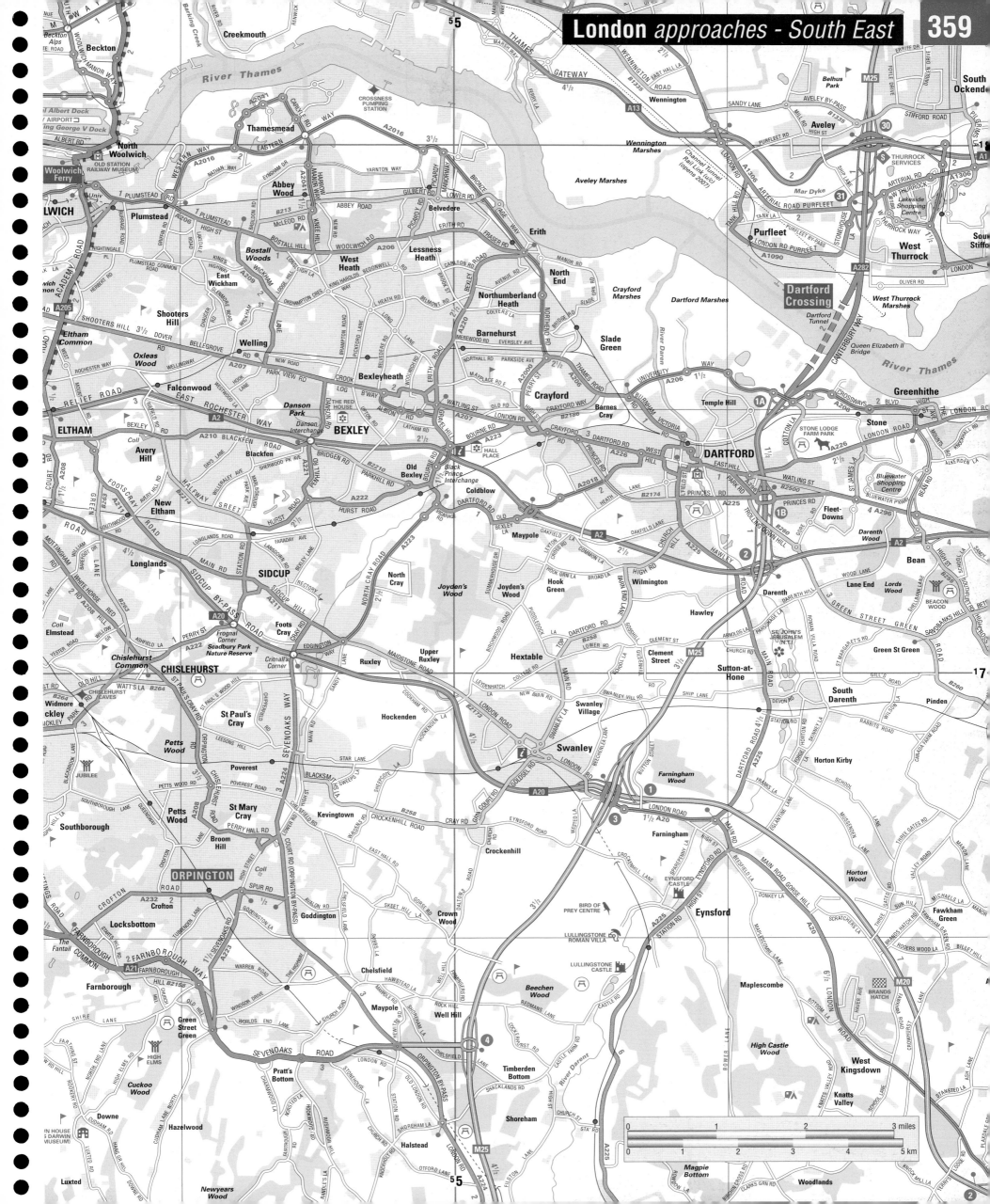

Manchester

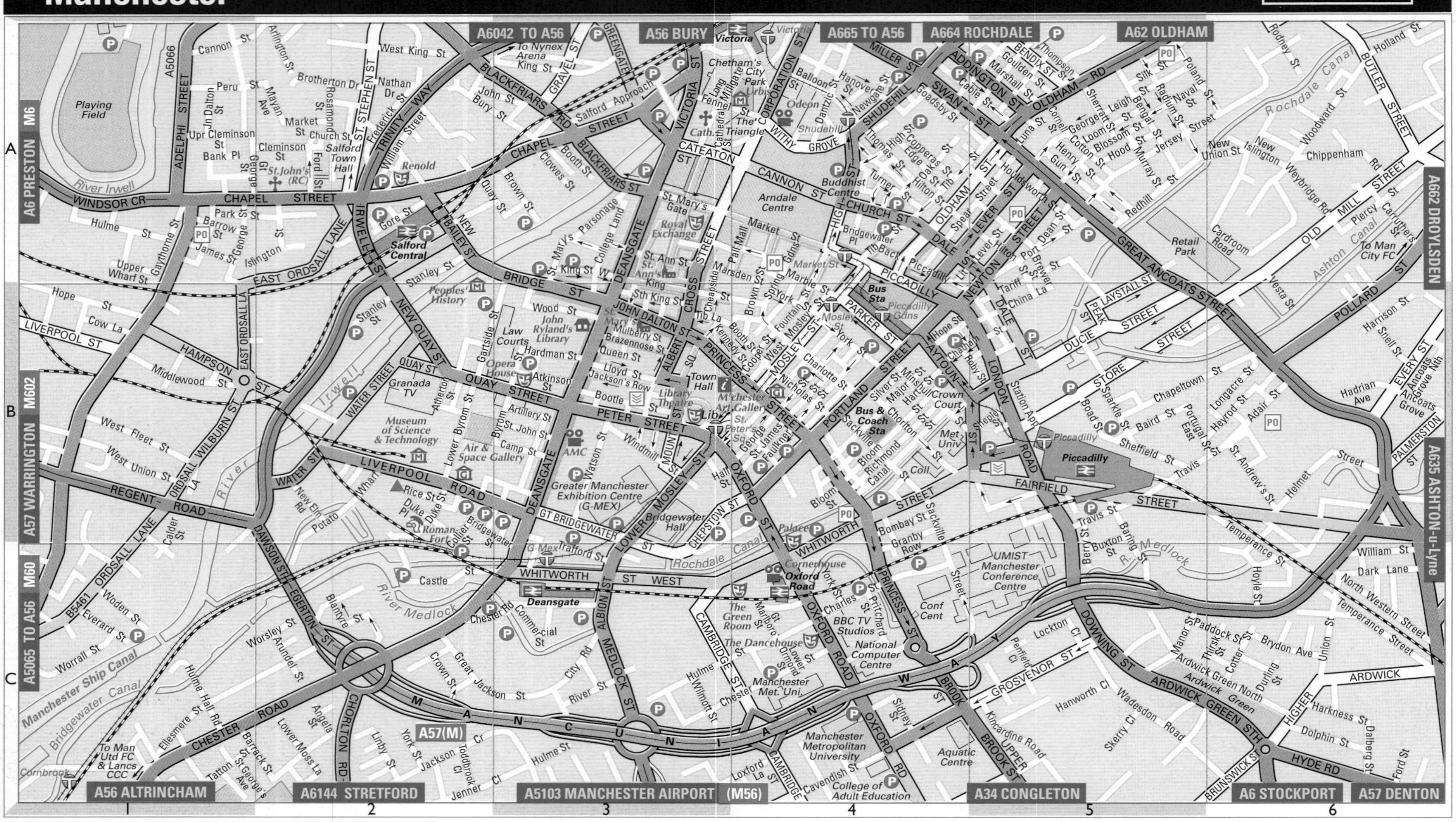

Manchester

Adair St. B6
Addington St A5
Adelphi St. A1
Air & Space Gallery B2
Albert Sq B3
Albion St. C3
AMC Great Northern B3
Ancoats Gr. B6
Ancoats Gr North . . . B6
Angela St C2
Aquatic Centre C4
Ardwick Green C5
Ardwick Green North . C5
Ardwick Green South. C5
Arlington St. A2
Arndale Centre A4
Artillery St. B3
Arundel St. C2
Atherton St B2
Atkinson St. B3
Aytoun St B4
Back Piccadilly. A4
Baird St B5
Balloon St. A4
Bank Pl. A1
Baring St B5
Barrack St C1
Barrow St A1
BBC TV Studios C4
Bendix St A5
Bengal St A5
Berry St C5
Blackfriars Rd. A3
Blackfriars St A3
Blantyre St C2
Bloom St B4
Blossom St. A5
Boad St B5
Bombay St B4
Booth St A3
Booth St B4
Bootle St B3
Brazennose St B3
Brewer St A5
Bridge St A3
Bridgewater Hall. B3
Bridgewater Pl A4
Bridgewater St B2
Brook St C4
Brotherton Dr A2
Brown St. A3
Brown St. B4
Brunswick St C6
Brydon Ave. C6
Buddhist Centre. A4
Bury St A2
Bus & Coach Station . B4
Bus Station. B4
Butler St A6
Buxton St. C5
Byrom St B3
Cable St A5
Calder St B1
Cambridge St C3/C4
Camp St B3
Canal St B4
Cannon St A1
Cannon St A4
Cardroom Rd A6
Carruthers St A6
Castle St. C2
Cateaton St A3
Cathedral A3
Cathedral St. A3
Cavendish St C4
Chapel St A1/A3
Chapeltown St B5
Charles St. C4
Charlotte St B4
Chatham St B4
Cheapside A3
Chepstow St. B3
Chester Rd C1/C2
Chester St C4
Chetham's (Dept Store) A3
China La. B5
Chippenham Rd A6
Chorlton Rd C2
Chorlton St. B4
Church St A2
Church St A4
City Park. A4
City Rd C3
Cleminson St A2
Clowes St. A3
College Land A3
College of Adult Education. C4
Collier St. B2
Commercial St C3
Conference Centre . . . C4
Cooper St. B4
Copperas St. A4
Cornbrook (Metro) . . . C1
Cornell St A5
Cornerhouse C4
Corporation St A4
Cotter St. C6
Cotton St A5
Cow La. B1
Cross St B3
Crown Court. B4
Crown St C2
Dalberg St C6
Dale St A4/B5
Dancehouse, The . . . C4
Dantzic St. A4
Dark La. C6
Dawson St C2
Dean St. A5
Deansgate A3/B3
Deansgate C3
Dolphin St. C6
Downing St. C5
Ducie St B5
Duke Pl. B2
Duke St. B2
Durling St C6
East Ordsall La. . . . A2/B1
Edge St. A4
Egerton St C2
Ellesmere St C1
Everard St. C1
Every St B6
Fairfield St B5
Faulkner St. B4
Fennel St A3
Ford St A2
Ford St C6
Fountain St. B4
Frederick St A2
Gartside St. B2
Gaythorne St A1
George Leigh St. A5
George St A1
George St B4
G-Mex (Metro) C3
Goadsby St A4
Gore St. A2
Goulden St. A4
Granada TV Studios . . B2
Granby Row B4
Gravel St. A3
Great Ancoats St A5
Great Bridgewater St B3
Great George St A1
Great Jackson St C2
Great Marlborough St C4
Greater Manchester Exhibition Centre (G-Mex) B3
Greengate. A3
Green Room, The . . . C4
Grosvenor St C5
Gun St A5
Hadrian Ave B6
Hall St. B3
Hampson St B1
Hanover St A4
Hanworth Cl C5
Hardman St B3
Harkness St C6
Harrison St B6
Hart St B4
Helmet St B6
Henry St A5
Heyrod St B6
High St A4
Higher Ardwick C6
Hilton St A4/A5
Holland St. A6
Hood St A5
Hope St B1
Hope St B4
Houldsworth St A5
Hoyle St C6
Hulme Hall Rd C1
Hulme St. A1
Hulme St. C3
Hyde Rd C6
Information Ctr B3
Irwell St. A2
Islington St A2
Jackson Cr. C2
Jackson's Row B3
James St A1
Jenner Cl C2
Jersey St A5
John Dalton St A1
John Dalton St B3
John Ryland's Library B3
John St. A2
Kennedy St. B3
Kincardine Rd. C4
King St A3
King St West. A3
Law Courts. B3
Laystall St. B5
Lever St A5
Library B3
Library Theatre B3
Linby St C2
Little Lever St A4
Liverpool Rd B2
Liverpool St B1
Lloyd St B3
Lockton Cl C5
London Rd B5
Long Millgate A3
Longacre St B6
Loom St A5
Lower Byrom St B2
Lower Mosley St B3
Lower Moss La. C2
Lower Ormond St. . . . C4
Loxford La C4
Luna St. A5
Major St B4
Manchester Art Gallery B4
Manchester Metropolitan University B4/C4
Mancunian Way C3
Manor St. C5
Marble St A4
Market St A2
Market St A4
Market St (Metro). . . . A4
Marsden St. A3
Marshall St A5
Mayan Ave A2
Medlock St. C3
Middlewood St. B1
Miller St A4
Minshull St B4
Mosley St A4
Mosley St (Metro). . . . B4
Mount St. B3
Mulberry St. B3
Murray St A5
Museum of Science & Technology B2
Nathan Dr A2
National Computer Centre C4
Naval St A5
New Bailey St. A2
New Elm Rd B2
New Islington A6
New Quay St B2
New Union St A6
Newgate St. A4
Newton St A5
Nicholas St. B4
North George St. A1
North Western St C6
Oak St A4
Odeon A4
Old Mill St. A6
Oldfield Rd A1/C1
Oldham Rd. A5
Oldham St A4
Opera House B3
Ordsall La C1
Oxford Rd. C4
Oxford Road C4
Oxford St B4
Paddock St. C6
Palace Theatre B4
Pall Mall A3
Palmerston St. B6
Park St A1
Parker St B4
Peak St. B5
Penfield Cl C5
Peoples' History Museum B2
Peru St A1
Peter St B3
Piccadilly A4
Piccadilly B5
Piccadilly (Metro) B5
Piccadilly Gdns (Metro) B4
Piercy St. A6
Poland St A5
Police Station . . . B3/B5
Pollard St B6
Port St A5
Portland St B4
Portugal St East B5
Post Office A1/A4/A5/B4/B6
Potato Wharf B2
Princess St. B3/C4
Pritchard St C4
Quay St A2
Quay St B2
Queen St B3
Radium St. A5
Redhill St A5
Regent Rd B1
Renold Theatre A2
Retail Park A5
Rice St B2
Richmond St B4
River St. C3
Roby St B5
Rodney St. A6
Roman Fort B2
Rosamond St A2
Royal Exchange A3
Sackville St. B4
St Andrew's St B6
St Ann St A3
St Ann's A3
St George's Ave C1
St James St B4
St John St B3
St John's Cathedral (RC) A2
St Mary's B3
St Mary's Gate A3
St Mary's Parsonage . A3
St Peter's Sq (Metro) . B3
St Stephen St A2
Salford Approach A3
Salford Central A2
Sheffield St B5
Shepley St B5
Sherratt St A5
Shudehill. A4
Shudehill (Metro) A4
Sidney St C4
Silk St A5
Silver St B4
Skerry Cl. C5
Snell St B6
South King St B3
Sparkle St. B5
Spear St A4
Spring Gdns A4
Stanley St A2/B2
Station Approach B5
Store St B5
Swan St A4
Tariff St. B5
Tatton St. C1
Temperance St B6/C6
The Triangle A4
Thirsk St C6
Thomas St A4
Thompson St A5
Tib La B3
Tib St A4
Toddbrook Cl C2
Town Hall (Manchester) B3
Town Hall (Salford). . . . A2
Trafford St. C3
Travis St B5
Trinity Way A2
Turner St. A4
UMIST Manchester Conference Centre. . C5
Union St C6
Upper Brook St C5
Upper Cleminson St. . A1
Upper Wharf St A1
Urbis Museum A4
Vesta St B6
Victoria (Metro) A4
Victoria A4
Victoria St. A3
Wadesdon Rd. C5
Water St B2
Watson St. B3
Wellington St A2
West Fleet St B1
West King St. A2
West Mosley St B4
West Union St B1
Weybridge Rd. A6
Whitworth St B4
Whitworth St West . . . C3
Wilburn St. B1
William St A2
William St C6
Wilmott St. C3
Windmill St. B3
Windsor Cr A1
Withy Gr A4
Woden St C1
Wood St B3
Woodward St A6
Worrall St C1
Worsley St C2
York St B4
York St C2
York St C4

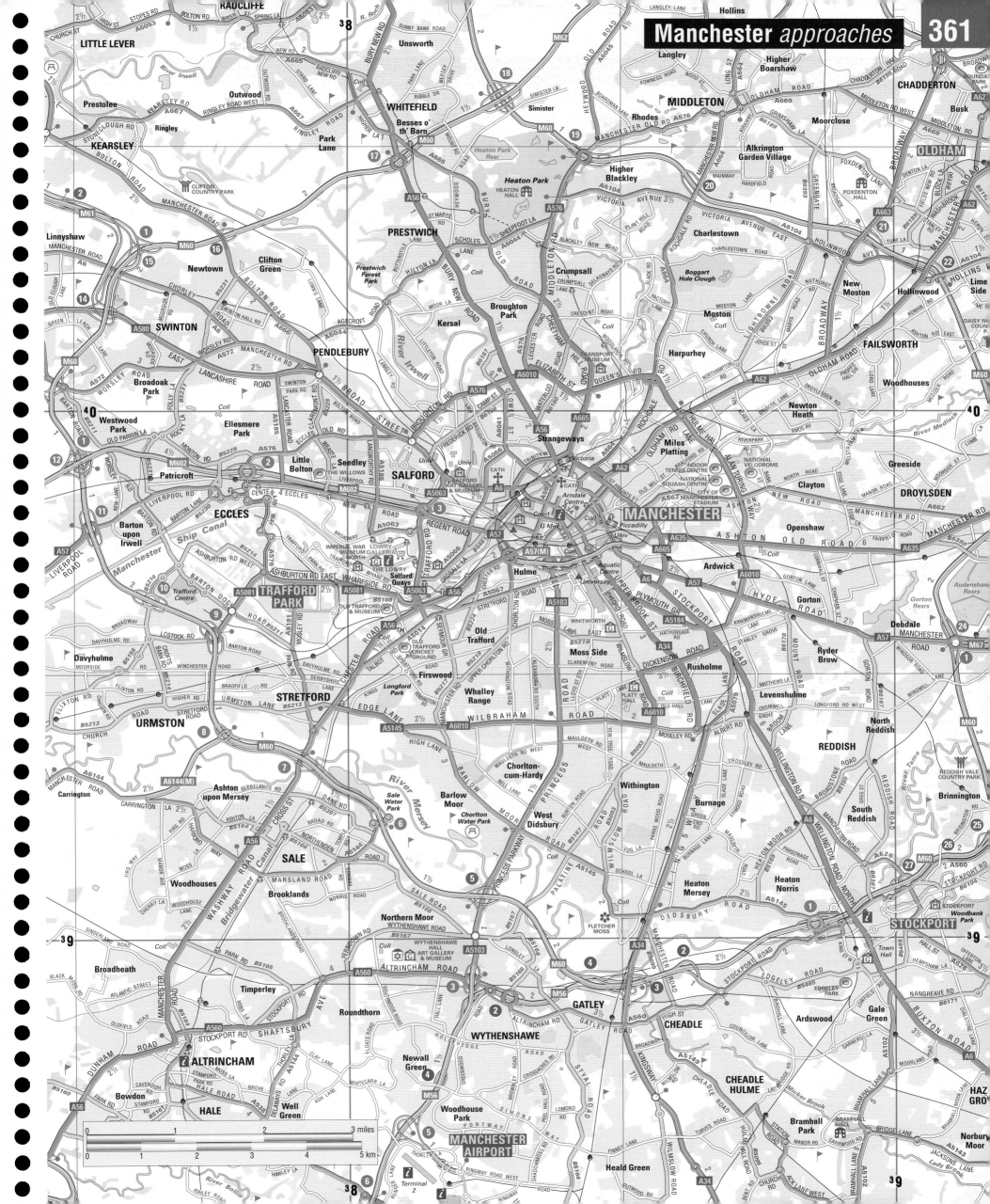

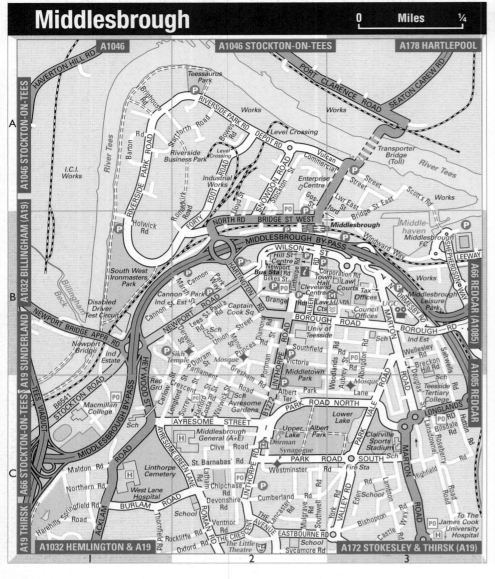

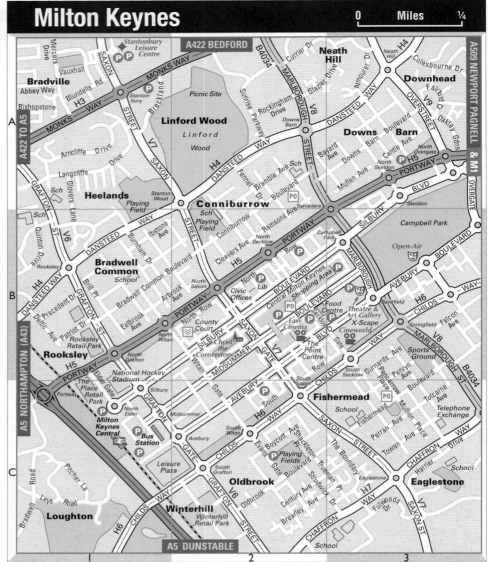

Middlesbrough

Abingdon Rd C3	Disabled Driver	Middlesbrough	Scott's Rd. A3
Acklam Rd C1	Test Circuit B1	By-Pass B2/C1	Seaton Carew Rd. . . . A3
Albert Park C2	Dorman Museum ⌂ . . C2	Middlesbrough F.C. . . B3	Shepherdson Way . . . B3
Albert Rd B2	Douglas St B3	Middlesbrough	Sikh Temple ✦ B2
Albert Terr. C2	Eastbourne Rd C2	General (A+E) 🅗 . . . C2	Snowdon Rd C1
Aubrey St C3	Eden Rd C3	Middlesbrough	South West
Ayresome Gdns C2	Enterprise Centre . . . A2	Leisure Park B3	Ironmasters Park . . B1
Ayresome Green La . . C1	Forty Foot Rd A2	Middlesbrough ⇌ . . . B2	Southfield Rd B3
Ayresome St. C2	Gilkes St B3	Middletown Park C2	Southwell Rd C2
Barton Rd A1	Gosford St A2	MIMA B3	Springfield Rd. C1
Bilsdale Rd C3	Grange Rd B2	Mosque ✦ B2	Startforth Rd. C2
Bishopton Rd C2	Gresham Rd B2	Mosque ✦ C3	Stockton Rd C1
Borough Rd B2/B3	Harehills Rd C1	Mulgrave Rd C2	Stockton St C2
Bowes Rd. A2	Harford St. C2	North Ormesby Rd. . . B3	Surrey St. C2
Breckon Hill Rd B3	Hartington Rd B2	Newport Bridge B1	Sycamore Rd C2
Bridge St East B3	Haverton Hill Rd A1	Newport Bridge	Synagogue ✦ B2
Bridge St West B2	Hey Wood St B1	Approach Rd B1	Tax Offices B3
Brighouse Rd A1	Highfield Rd C3	Newport Rd B2	Tees Viaduct B1
Burlam Rd C1	Hill St Centre B2	North Rd. B2	Teessaurus Park. . . . A2
Bus Station. B2	Holwick Rd B1	Northern Rd C1	Teesside Tertiary
Cannon Park B1	Hutton Rd C3	Outram St. B2	College C3
Cannon Park Way . . . B2	I.C.I. Works A1	Oxford Rd C2	The Avenue C2
Cannon St B1	Information Ctr 🅘 B2	Park La C2	The Crescent C2
Captain Cook Sq B2	Lambton Rd C3	Park Rd North C2	Thornfield Rd C1
Carlow St B1	Lancaster Rd C2	Park Rd South C2	Town Hall B2
Castle Way C3	Lansdowne Rd C3	Park Vale Rd C2	Transporter
Chipchase Rd C2	Latham Rd C2	Parliament Rd. B1	Bridge (Toll) A3
Clairville Sports	Law Courts B2/B3	Police Station 🄟 B3	UGC 🎬 B3
Stadium C3	Lees Rd B2	Port Clarence Rd A3	Union St B2
Cleveland Centre . . . B2	Leeway B3	Portman St. B2	University of Teesside B2
Clive Rd C2	Linthorpe Cemetery . . C1	Post Office 🄿	Upper Lake. C2
Commercial St A2	Linthorpe Rd B2	. . . . . B2/B3/C1/C2/C3	Valley Rd. C3
Corporation Rd. B2	Little Theatre, The 🎭 . C2	Princes Rd B2	Ventnor Rd C2
Costa St C2	Longford St C2	Riverside Business	Victoria Rd B2
Council Offices B3	Longlands Rd. C3	Park A2	Vulcan St A2
Crescent Rd C1	Lower East St A3	Riverside Park Rd. . . A1	Warwick St C2
Cumberland Rd C2	Lower Lake. C3	Rockliffe Rd C2	Wellesley Rd. B3
Depot Rd A2	Macmillan College . . . C1	Romaldkirk Rd B1	West Lane Hospital 🅗 C1
Derwent St B1	Maldon Rd C1	Roman Rd C2	Westminster Rd C2
Devonshire Rd C2	Manor St. B2	Roseberry Rd C3	Wilson St B2
Diamond Rd B2	Marsh St. B1	St Paul's Rd. B2	Windward Way B3
	Marton Rd B3	St Barnabas' Rd. . . . C2	Woodlands Rd B2
	Middlehaven. B3	Saltwells Rd B3	York Rd C3

Milton Keynes

Abbey Way A1	Currier Dr A2	Mullion Pl C3	Saxon Gate B2
Arbrook Ave B1	Dansteed	National Hockey	Saxon St. A1/C3
Armourer Dr A3	Way A2/A3/B1	Stadium B1	Secklow Gate. B2
Arncliffe Dr A1	Deltic Ave B1	Neath Hill (r'about) . . . A3	Shackleton Pl C2
Avebury (r'about) C2	Downs Barn	North Elder (r'about). . C1	Silbury (r'about) C1
Avebury Blvd C2	(r'about) A2	North Grafton	Silbury Blvd B2
Bankfield (r'about) . . . B3	Downs Barn Blvd . . . A2	(r'about) B1	Skeldon (r'about) A3
Bayard Ave A2	Eaglestone (r'about) . . C3	North Overgate	South Grafton
Belvedere (r'about) . . B2	Easy Cinema 🎬 B2	(r'about) A3	(r'about) C2
Bishopstone A1	Eelbrook Ave B1	North Row B2	South Row C2
Blundells Rd A1	Elder Gate B1	North Saxon	South Saxon
Boycott Ave C2	Evans Gate B2	(r'about) B2	(r'about) C2
Bradwell Common	Fairford Cr A3	North Secklow	South Secklow
Blvd B1	Falcon Ave B3	(r'about) B2	(r'about) B3
Bradwell Rd C1	Fennel Dr C2	North Skeldon	South Witan
Bramble Ave A2	Fishermead Blvd C3	(r'about) A3	(r'about) C2
Brearley Ave B2	Food Centre B3	North Witan (r'about) . B1	Springfield (r'about) . . B3
Breckland A1	Fulwoods Dr. C2	Oakley Gdns. A3	Stanton Wood
Brill Place B1	Glazier Dr A2	Oldbrook Blvd C2	(r'about) A1
Burnham Dr B1	Glovers La A1	Open-Air Theatre 🎭 . B3	Stantonbury
Bus Station. C1	Grafton Gate. B1	Overgate. A3	(r'about) A1
Campbell Park	Grafton St. A1/C2	Overstreet. A3	Stantonbury Leisure
(r'about) B3	Gurnards Ave A3	Patriot Dr B1	Centre ✦ A1
Cantle Ave A3	Harrier Dr C3	Pencarrow Pl B3	Strudwick Dr. C2
Central Milton Keynes	Ibstone Ave B1	Penryn Ave B3	Sunrise Parkway. . . . A2
Shopping Area B2	Langcliffe Dr A1	Perran Ave C2	Telephone Exchange . C3
Century Ave C2	Leisure Plaza C1	Pitcher La. C1	The Boundary C3
Chaffron Way C3	Leys Rd C1	Place Retail	Theatre & Art
Childs Way C1	Library C1	Park, The C1	Gallery 🎭 B3
Christ the	Linford Wood A2	Point Centre, The . . . B2	Tolcarne Ave. C3
Cornerstone 🏛 B2	Marlborough Gate . . . B3	Police Station 🄟 B2	Towan Ave C3
Cineworld 🎬 B2	Marlborough St . . A2/B3	Portway (r'about) B2	Trueman Pl C3
Civic Offices B2	Mercers Dr A1	Post Office 🄿 . A2/B2/C3	Vauxhall A1
Cleavers Ave B2	Midsummer (r'about) . C2	Precedent Dr B1	Winterhill Retail Park . C2
Colesbourne Dr A3	Midsummer Blvd B2	Quinton Dr B1	Witan Gate B2
Conniburrow Blvd . . . B2	Milton Keynes	Ramsons Ave B2	X-Scape B3
County Court B2	Central ⇌ C1	Rockingham Dr A2	
	Monks Way. A1	Rooksley (r'about) . . . B1	
	Mullen Ave A3	Rooksley Retail Park . C1	

Newport / Casnewydd

0 Miles ¼

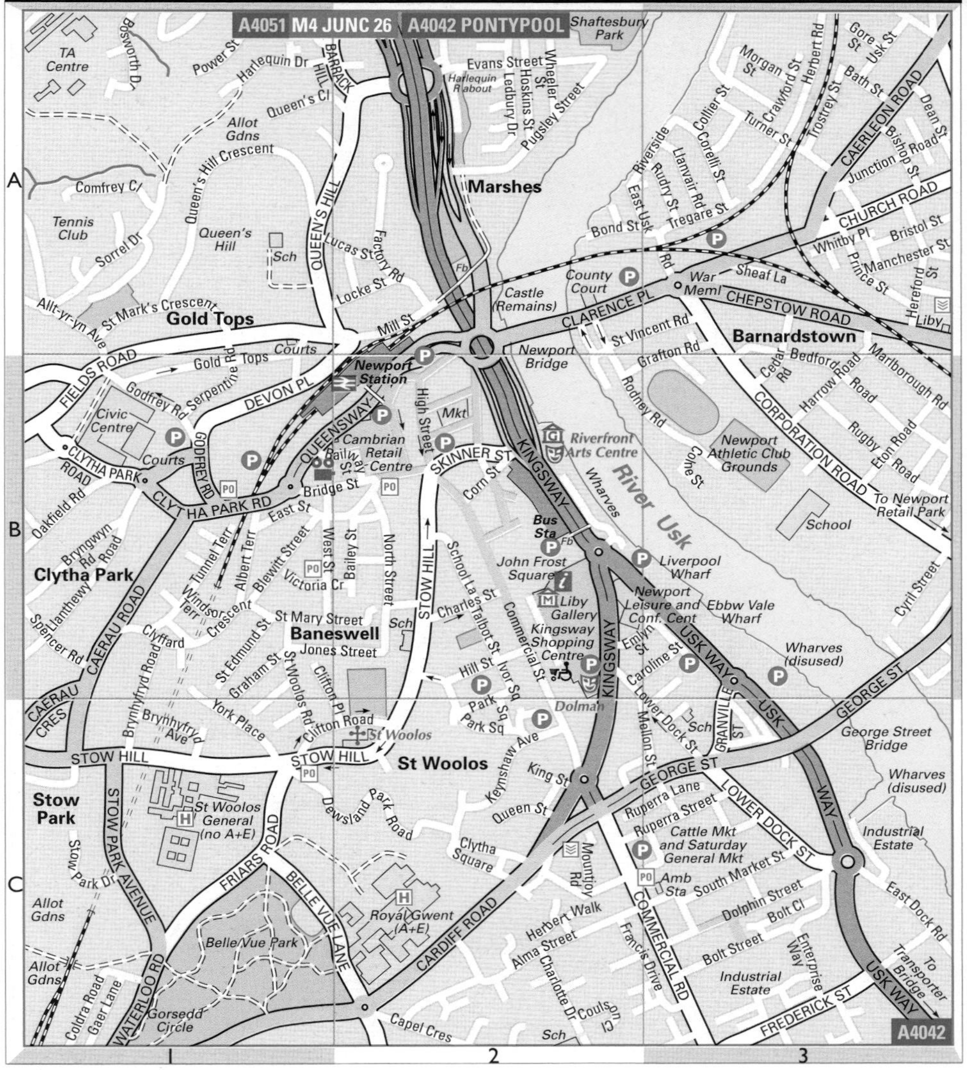
A4051 M4 JUNC 26
A4042 PONTYPOOL
Marshes
Gold Tops
Barnardstown
Newport Station
Clytha Park
Baneswell
St Woolos
Stow Park
River Usk
Kingsway
Riverfront Arts Centre
Newport Athletic Club Grounds
Royal Gwent (A+E)
Belle Vue Park
Industrial Estate
A4042

Northampton

0 Miles ¼

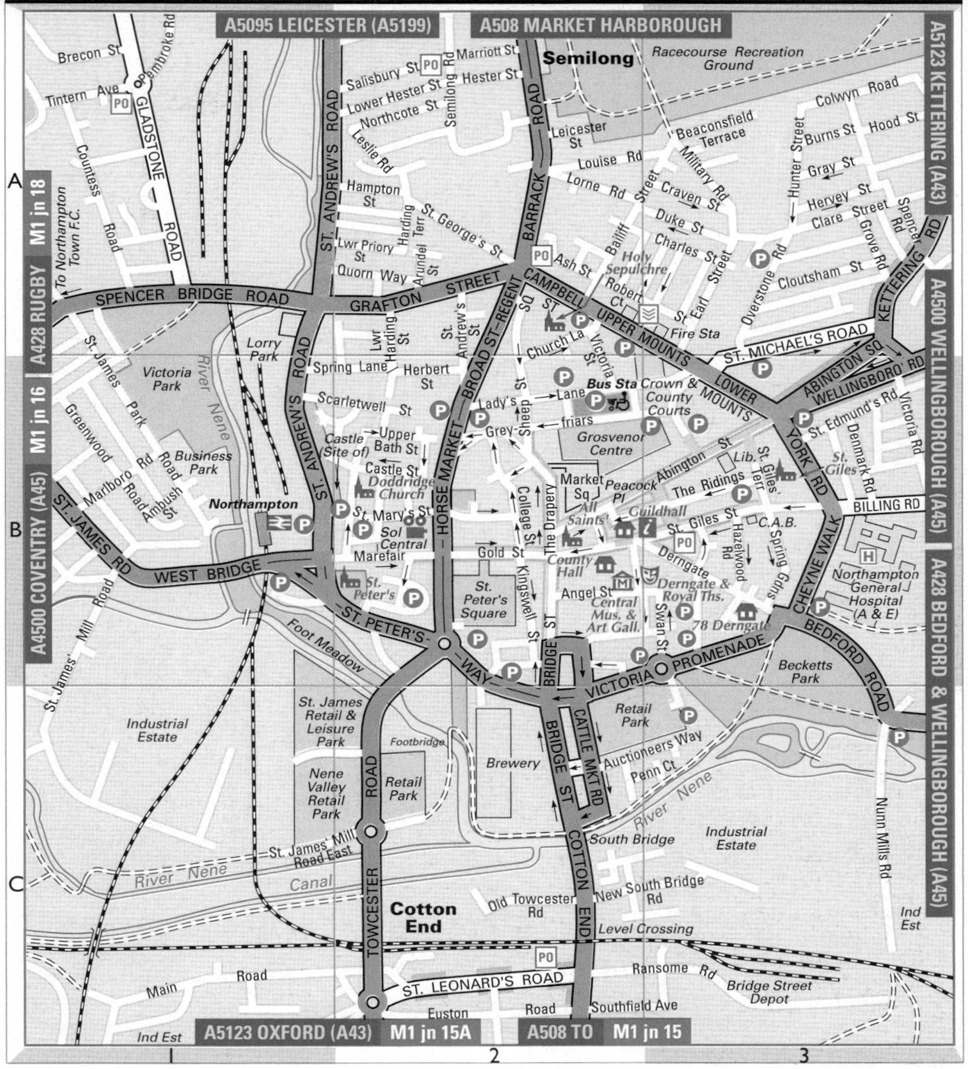
A5095 LEICESTER (A5199)
A508 MARKET HARBOROUGH
A5123 KETTERING (A43)
A4500 WELLINGBOROUGH (A45)
A428 BEDFORD & WELLINGBOROUGH (A45)
A428 RUGBY M1 jn 18
A4500 COVENTRY (A45) M1 jn 16
Semilong
Racecourse Recreation Ground
Victoria Park
Northampton
Grosvenor Centre
Becketts Park
Industrial Estate
Brewery
Cotton End
A5123 OXFORD (A43) M1 jn 15A
A508 TO M1 jn 15

Newport / Casnewydd

Albert Terr B1
Allt-yr-Yn Ave A1
Alma St C2
Ambulance Station C3
Bailey St B2
Barrack Hill A2
Bath St A3
Bedford Rd B3
Belle Vue La C1
Belle Vue Park C1
Bishop St A3
Blewitt St B1
Bolt Cl C3
Bolt St C3
Bond St A2
Bosworth Dr A1
Bridge St B1
Bristol St A3
Bryngwyn Rd B1
Brynhyfryd Ave C1
Brynhyfryd Rd C1
Bus Station B2
Caerau Cres C1
Caerau Rd B1
Caerleon Rd A3
Cambrian Retail Centre B2
Capel Cres C2
Cardiff Rd C2
Caroline St B3
Castle (Remains) A2
Cattle Market and Saturday General Market C3
Cedar Rd B3
Charles St B2
Charlotte Dr C2
Chepstow Rd A3
Church Rd A3
City Cinema B1
Civic Centre B1
Clarence Pl A2
Clifton Pl B1
Clifton Rd C1
Clyffard Cres B1
Clytha Park Rd B1
Clytha Sq C2
Coldra Rd C1
Collier St A3
Colne St B3
Comfrey Cl A1
Commercial Rd C3
Commercial St B2
Corelli St A3
Corn St B2
Corporation Rd B3
Coulson Cl C2
County Court A2
Courts A1
Courts B1
Crawford St A3
Cyril St B3
Dean St A3
Devon Pl B1
Dewsland Park Rd C2
Dolman B2
Dolphin St C3
East Dock Rd C3
East St B1
East Usk Rd A3
Ebbw Vale Wharf B3
Emlyn St B2
Enterprise Way C3
Eton Rd B3
Evans St A2
Factory Rd A2
Fields Rd B1
Francis Dr C2
Frederick St C3
Friars Rd C1
Gaer La C1
George St C3
George Street Bridge C3
Godfrey Rd B1
Gold Tops B1
Gore St A3
Gorsedd Circle C1
Grafton Rd A3
Graham St B1
Granville St C3
Harlequin Dr A1
Harrow Rd B3
Herbert Rd A3
Herbert Walk C2
Hereford St A3
High St B2
Hill St B2
Hoskins St A2
Information Ctr B2
Ivor Sq B2
John Frost Sq B2
Jones St B1
Junction Rd A3
Keynshaw Ave C2
King St C2
Kingsway B2
Kingsway Shopping Centre B2
Ledbury Dr A2
Library A3
Library, Museum & Art Gallery B2
Liverpool Wharf B3
Llanthewy Rd B1
Llanvair Rd A3
Locke St A2
Lower Dock St C3
Lucas St A2
Manchester St A3
Market B2
Marlborough Rd B3
Mellon St C3
Mill St A2
Morgan St A3
Mountjoy Rd C2
Newport Athletic Club Grounds B3
Newport Bridge A2
Newport Leisure and Conference Ctr B2
Newport Station B2
North St B2
Oakfield Rd B1
Park Sq C2
Police Station A3/C2
Post Office B1/B2/C1/C3
Power St A1
Prince St A3
Pugsley St A2
Queen St C2
Queen's Cl A1
Queen's Hill A1
Queen's Hill Cres A1
Queensway B2
Railway St B2
Riverfront Arts Centre B2
Riverside A3
Rodney Rd B2
Royal Gwent (A+E) C2
Rudry St A3
Rugby Rd B3
Ruperra La C3
Ruperra St C3
St. Edmund St B1
St. Mark's Cres A1
St. Mary St B1
St. Vincent Rd A3
St. Woolos C2
St. Woolos General (no A+E) C1
St. Woolos Rd B1
School La B2
Serpentine Rd B1
Shaftesbury Park A2
Sheaf La A3
Skinner St B2
Sorrel Dr A1
South Market St C3
Spencer Rd B1
Stow Hill B2/C1/C2
Stow Park Ave C1
Stow Park Dr C1
TA Centre A1
Talbot St B2
Tennis Club A1
Tregare St A3
Trostrey St A3
Tunnel Terr B1
Turner St A3
Usk St A3
Usk Way B3/C3
Victoria Cr B1
War Memorial A3
Waterloo Rd C1
West St B1
Wharves B2
Wheeler St A2
Whitby Pl A3
Windsor Terr B1
York Pl C1

Northampton

78 Derngate B3
Abington Sq B3
Abington St B3
All Saints' B2
Ambush St B1
Angel St B2
Arundel St A2
Ash St A2
Auctioneers Way C2
Bailiff St A2
Barrack Rd A2
Beaconsfield Terr A3
Becketts Park C3
Bedford Rd B3
Billing Rd B3
Brecon St A1
Brewery C2
Bridge St C2
Bridge St Depot C3
Broad St B2
Burns St A3
Bus Station B2
Campbell St A2
Castle (Site of) B2
Castle St B2
Cattle Market Rd C2
Central Museum & Art Gallery B2
Charles St A3
Cheyne Walk B3
Church La A2
Clare St A3
Cloutsham St A3
College St B2
Colwyn Rd A3
Cotton End C2
Countess Rd A1
County Hall B2
Court A2
Craven St A3
Crown & County Courts B3
Denmark Rd B3
Derngate B3
Derngate & Royal Theatres B3
Doddridge Church B2
Duke St A3
Earl St A3
Euston Rd C2
Fire Station A3
Foot Meadow B2
Gladstone Rd A1
Gold St B2
Grafton St A2
Gray St A3
Greenwood Rd B1
Greyfriars B2
Grosvenor Centre B2
Grove Rd A3
Guildhall B2
Hampton St A2
Harding Terr A2
Hazelwood Rd B3
Herbert St B2
Hervey St A3
Hester St A2
Holy Sepulchre A2
Hood St A3
Horse Market B2
Hunter St A3
Information Ctr B1
Kettering Rd A3
Kingswell St B2
Lady's La B2
Leicester St A2
Leslie Rd A2
Library B3
Lorne Rd A2
Lorry Park A1
Louise Rd A2
Lower Harding St A2
Lower Hester St A2
Lower Mounts B3
Lower Priory St A2
Main Rd C1
Marefair B2
Market Sq B2
Marlboro Rd B1
Marriott St A2
Military Rd A3
Nene Valley Retail Park C1
New South Bridge Rd C2
Northampton General Hospital (A & E) B3
Northampton Station B1
Northcote St A2
Nunn Mills Rd C3
Old Towcester Rd C2
Overstone Rd A3
Peacock Pl B2
Pembroke Rd A1
Penn Court C2
Police Station B3
Post Office A1/A2/B3/C2
Quorn Way A2
Ransome Rd C3
Regent Sq A2
Retail Park C2
Robert St A2
St Andrew's Rd B1
St Andrew's St A2
St Edmund's Rd B3
St George's St A2
St Giles B3
St Giles St B3
St Giles' Terr B3
St James' Mill Rd B1
St James' Mill Rd East C1
St James Park Rd B1
St James Retail & Leisure Park C1
St James Rd B1
St Leonard's Rd C2
St Mary's St B2
St Michael's Rd A3
St Peter's B2
St Peter's Square Shopping Precinct B2
St Peter's Way B2
Salisbury St A2
Scarletwell St B2
Semilong Rd A2
Sheep St B2
Sol Central (Leisure Centre) B2
South Bridge C2
Southfield Ave C2
Spencer Bridge Rd A1
Spencer Rd A3
Spring Gdns B3
Spring La B2
Swan St B3
The Drapery B2
The Ridings B3
Tintern Ave A1
Towcester Rd C2
Upper Bath St B2
Upper Mounts A2
Victoria Park A1
Victoria Promenade B2
Victoria Rd B3
Victoria St A2
Wellingborough Rd B3
West Bridge B1
York Rd B3

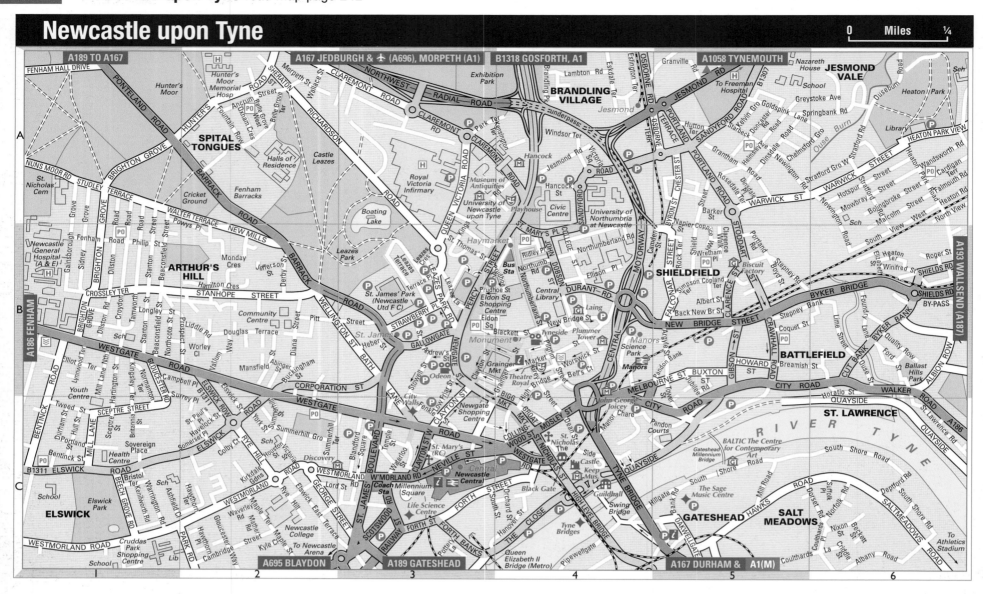

Newcastle upon Tyne

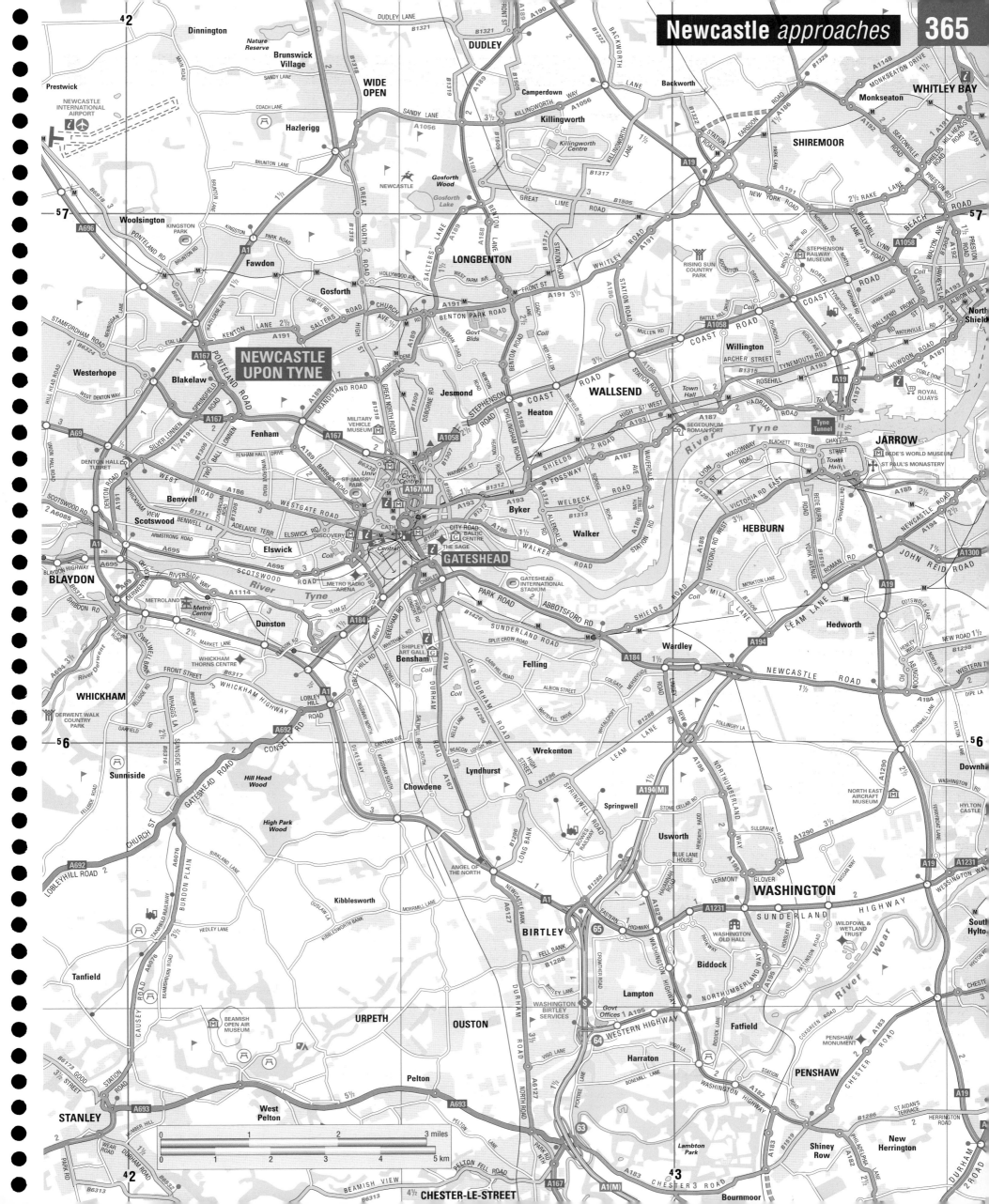

Norwich

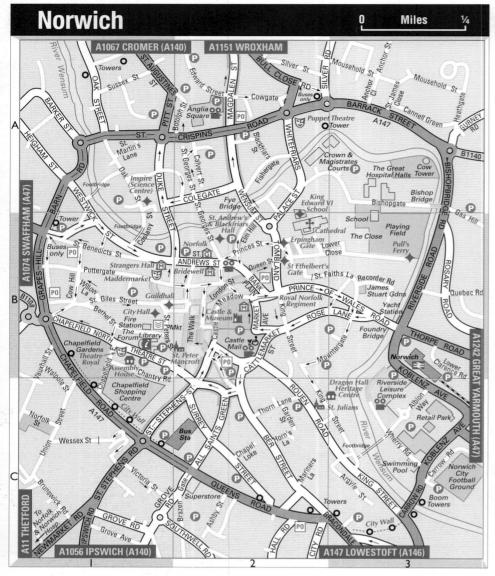

Nottingham

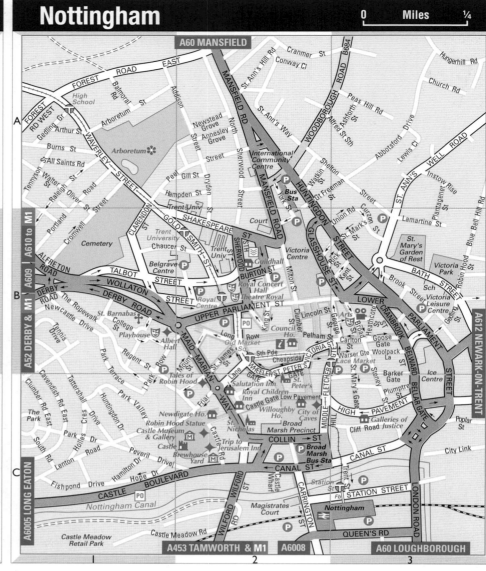

Norwich

Albion Way C3
All Saints Green C2
Anchor Cl A3
Anchor St A3
Anglia Sq B2
Argyle St C3
Ashby St C3
Assembly House 🏛 . . B1
Bank Plain B2
Barker St A1
Barn Rd A1
Barrack St A3
Ber St C2
Bethel St B1
Bishop Bridge A3
Bishopbridge Rd A3
Bishopgate A3
Blackfriars St A2
Botolph St A2
Bracondale C3
Brazen Gate C2
Bridewell 🏛 B2
Brunswick Rd C1
Bull Close Rd A2
Bus Station C2
Calvert St A2
Cannell Green A3
Carrow Rd C3
Castle Mall B2
Castle Meadow B2
Castle & Museum 🏛 . B1
Cathedral ✝ B2
Cattlemarket St B2
Chantry Rd B1
Chapel Loke C2
Chapelfield East B1
Chapelfield Gdns B1
Chapelfield North B1
Chapelfield Rd B1
Chapelfield Shopping
  Centre C1

City Hall ✦ B1
City Rd C2
City Wall C1/C3
Colegate A2
Coslany St B1
Cow Hill B1
Cow Tower A3
Cowgate A2
Crown & Magistrates
  Courts B2
Dragon Hall Heritage
  Centre 🏛 C3
Duke St A1
Edward St A2
Elm Hill B2
Erpingham Gate ✦ . . . B2
Fire Station B1
Fishergate A2
Foundry Bridge B3
Fye Bridge A2
Garden St C2
Gas Hill B3
Grapes Hill B1
Great Hospital
  Halls, The A3
Grove Ave C1
Grove Rd C1
Guildhall ✦ B1
Gurney Rd A3
Hall Rd C2
Heathgate A3
Heigham St A1
Horn's La C2
Information Ctr 🅸 . . . B1
Inspire (Science
  Centre) ✦ A1
Ipswich Rd C1
James Stewart Gdns . B3
King Edward VI
  School ✦ B2
King St B2
King St C3
Koblenz Ave C3

Library B1
London St B2
Lower Clarence Rd . . B3
Lower Cl B3
Maddermarket 🎭 . . . B1
Magdalen St A2
Mariners La C2
Market B2
Market Ave B2
Mountergate B3
Mousehold St A3
Newmarket Rd C1
Norfolk Gallery 🏛 . . . C1
Norfolk St C1
Norwich City FC C3
Norwich Station 🚉 . . B3
Oak St A1
Palace St A2
Pitt St A1
Police Station 🅿 B1
Post Office ▣
  . . . . A2/B1/B2/C2
Pottergate B1
Prince of Wales Rd . . . B2
Princes St B2
Pull's Ferry ✦ B3
Puppet Theatre 🎭 . . . A2
Quebec Rd B3
Queen St B2
Queens Rd C2
Recorder Rd B3
Retail Park C3
Riverside Leisure
  Complex C3
Riverside Rd B3
Rosary Rd B3
Rose La B2
Rouen Rd B2
Royal Norfolk Regiment
  Museum 🏛 B2
St Andrew's &
  Blackfriars Hall ✦ . . B2
St Andrews St B2

St Augustines St A1
St Benedicts St B1
St Crispins Rd A1
St Ethelbert's
  Gate ✦ B2
St Faiths La B3
St Georges St A2
St Giles St B1
St James Cl A3
St Julians C2
St Martin's La A1
St Peter Mancroft 🏛 . B2
St Peters St B1
St Stephens Rd C1
St Stephens St C1
Silver Rd A2
Silver St A2
Southwell Rd C2
Strangers Hall 🏛 B1
Superstore C2
Surrey St C2
Sussex St A1
Swimming Pool B3
The Close B3
The Forum B1
The Walk B2
Theatre Royal 🎭 B1
Theatre St B1
Thorn La C2
Thorpe Rd B3
Tombland B2
Union St C1
Vauxhall St B1
Victoria St C1
Walpole St B1
Wensum St A2
Wessex St C1
Westwick St A1
Wherry Rd C3
Whitefriars A2
Willow La B1
Yacht Station B3

Nottingham

Abbotsford Dr A3
Addison St A1
Albert Hall ✦ B1
Alfred St South A3
Alfreton Rd B1
All Saints Rd A1
Annesley Gr A2
Arboretum ❀ A1
Arboretum St A1
Arthur St A1
Arts Theatre 🎭 B3
Ashforth St A3
Balmoral Rd A1
Barker Gate B3
Bath St B3
Belgrave Centre B1
Bellar Gate B3
Belward St B3
Blue Bell Hill Rd B3
Brewhouse Yard 🏛 . . C2
Broad Marsh
  Bus Station C2
Broad Marsh
  Precinct C2
Broad St B3
Brook St B3
Burns St A1
Burton St B2
Bus Station A2
Canal St C2
Carlton St B3
Carrington St C2
Castle Blvd C1
Castle 🏰 C2
Castle Gate C2
Castle Meadow
  Retail Park C1
Castle Meadow Rd . . C1
Castle Museum
  & Gallery 🏛 C2
Castle Rd C2
Castle Wharf C2
Cavendish Rd East . . C1
Cemetery B1
Chaucer St B1
Cheapside B2
Church Rd A3
City Link C3
City of Caves ✦ C2
Clarendon St B1

Cliff Rd C3
Clumber Rd East C1
Clumber St B2
College St B1
Collin St C2
Conway Cl A2
Council House 🏛 . . . B2
Court B2
Cranbrook St B3
Cranmer St A2
Cromwell St B1
Curzon St B3
Derby Rd B1
Dryden St A2
Fishpond Dr C1
Fletcher Gate B3
Forest Rd East A1
Forest Rd West A1
Friar La C2
Galleries of
  Justice 🏛 C3
Gedling Gr A1
Gedling St B3
George St B3
Gill St A2
Glasshouse St B2
Goldsmith St B2
Goose Gate B3
Great Freeman St . . . A2
Guildhall 🏛 B2
Hamilton Dr C1
Hampden St A1
Heathcote St B3
High Pavement C3
High School
  (tram stop) A1
Holles Cr C1
Hope Dr C1
Hungerhill Rd A3
Huntingdon Dr C1
Huntingdon St A2
Ice Centre C3
Information Ctr 🅸 . . . B2
Instow Rise A3
International Community
  Centre A2
Kent St B3
King St B2
Lace Market
  (tram stop) B3
Lamartine St B3
Lenton Rd C1

Lewis Cl A3
Lincoln St B2
London Rd C3
Long Row B2
Low Pavement C2
Lower Parliament St . . B3
Magistrates Court . . . C2
Maid Marian Way . . . B2
Mansfield Rd A2/B2
Middle Hill C2
Milton St B2
Mount St B2
Newcastle Dr B1
Newdigate House 🏛 . C2
Newstead Gr A2
North Sherwood St . . A2
Nottingham
  Station 🚉 C3
Old Market Square
  (tram stop) B2
Oliver St A1
Park Dr C1
Park Row C1
Park Terr B1
Park Valley C1
Peas Hill Rd A3
Peel St A1
Pelham St B2
Peveril Dr C1
Plantagenet St A3
Playhouse
  Theatre 🎭 C1
Plumptre St C3
Police Station 🅿 B2
Poplar St C3
Portland Rd B1
Post Office ▣ B2/C1
Queen's Rd C3
Raleigh St A1
Regent St B1
Rick St B3
Robin Hood
  Statue ✦ C2
Robin Hood St B3
Royal Centre
  (tram stop) B2
Royal Children Inn 🏛 . C2
Royal Concert Hall 🎭 . B2
St Ann's Hill Rd A1
St Ann's Way A2
St Ann's Well Rd A3
St Barnabas ✝ B1

St James' St B2
St Mark's St B3
St Mary's
  Garden of Rest B3
St Mary's Gate B3
St Nicholas 🏛 C2
St Peter's 🏛 C2
St Peter's Gate B2
Salutation Inn 🏛 C2
Shakespeare St B2
Shelton St A2
South Pde B2
South Rd C1
South Sherwood St . . B2
Station St C3
Station Street
  (tram stop) C3
Stoney St B3
Talbot St B1
Tales of
  Robin Hood ✦ C2
Tattershall Dr C1
Tennis Dr B1
Tennyson St A1
The Park C1
The Ropewalk B1
Theatre Royal 🎭 B2
Trent St C3
Trent University . . A2/B2
Trent University
  (tram stop) B2
Trip To Jerusalem
  Inn ✦ C2
Union Rd B3
Upper Parliament St . . B2
Victoria Centre B2
Victoria Leisure
  Centre B3
Victoria Park B3
Victoria St B2
Walter St A1
Warser Gate B3
Watkin St A2
Waverley St A1
Wheeler Gate B2
Wilford Rd C2
Wilford St C2
Willoughby House . . . C2
Wollaton St B1
Woodborough Rd . . . A2
Woolpack La B3
York St A2

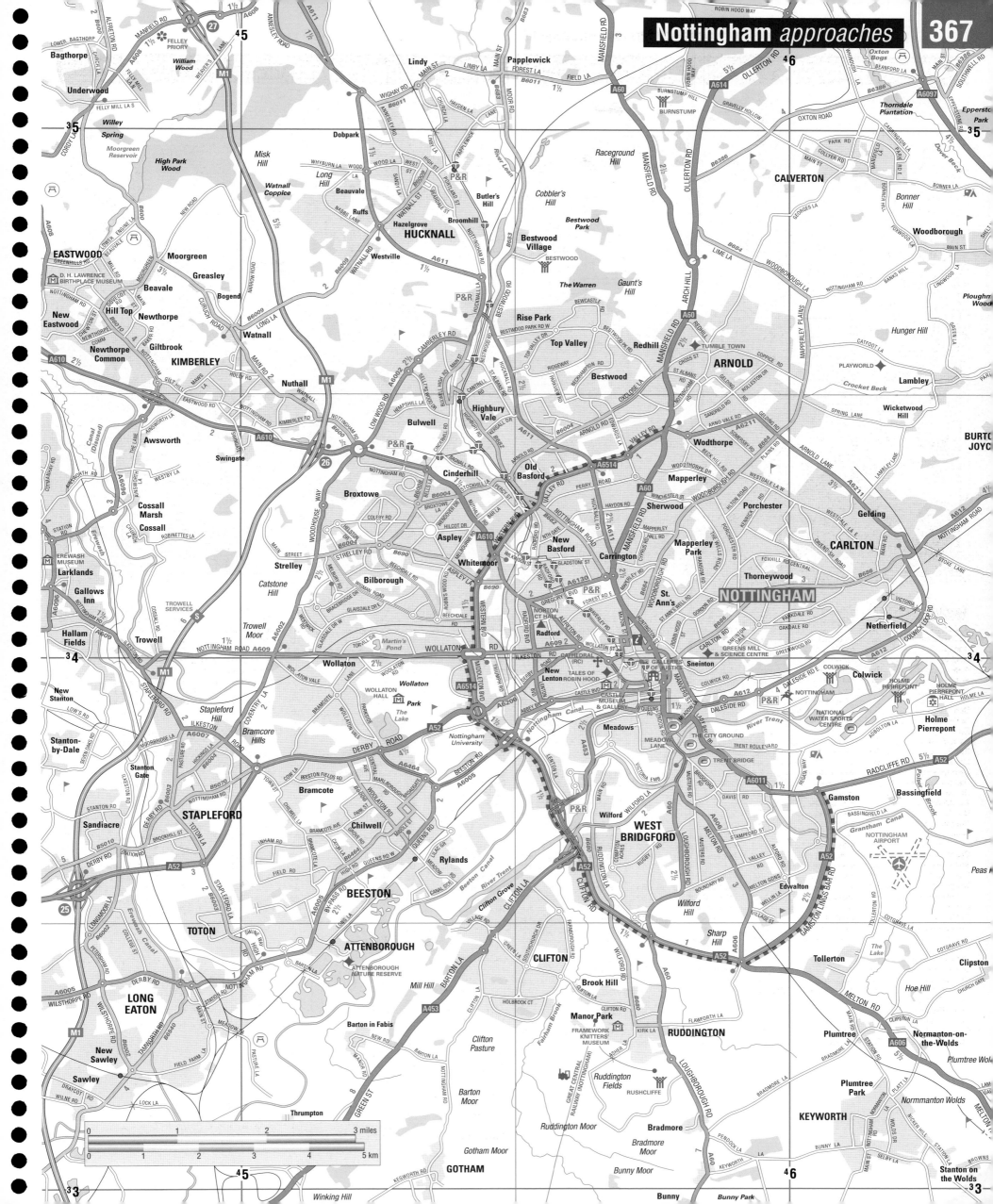

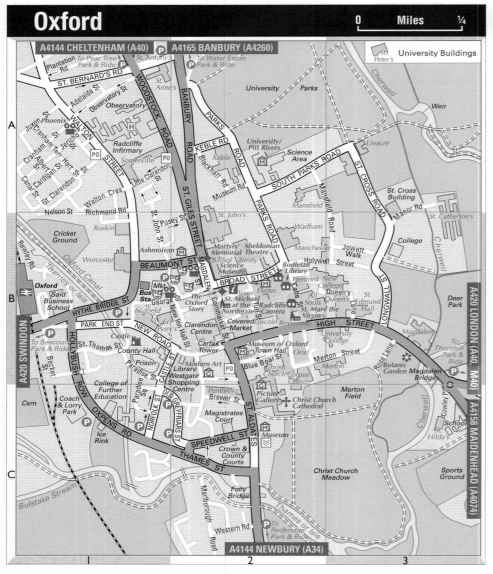

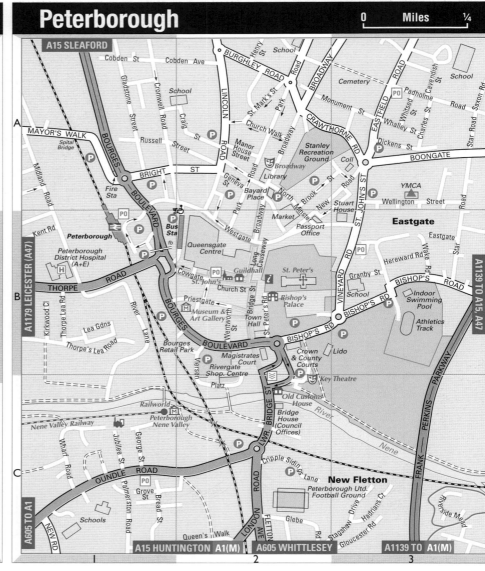

Oxford

Adelaide St A1
Albert St A1
All Souls (Coll) B2
Ashmolean
 Museum 🏛 B2
Balliol (Coll) B2
Banbury Rd A2
Beaumont St B1
Becket St B1
Blackhall Rd A2
Blue Boar St B2
Bodleian Library 📖 . . B2
Botanic Garden ❀ . . B3
Brasenose (Coll) . . . B2
Brewer St C2
Broad St B2
Burton-Taylor
 Theatre 🎭 B2
Bus Station B1
Canal St A1
Cardigan St A1
Carfax Tower B2
Castle 🏰 B1
Castle St B1
Catte St B2
Cemetery C1
Christ Church (Coll) . B2
Christ Church
 Cathedral † C2
Christ Church
 Meadow C2
Clarendon Centre . . . B2
Coach & Lorry Park . . C1
College B3
College of Further
 Education C1
Cornmarket St B2
Corpus Christi (Coll) . B2
County Hall B1
Covered Market B2
Cowley Pl C3
Cranham St A1

Cranham Terr A1
Cricket Ground B1
Crown & County
 Courts C2
Deer Park B3
Exeter (Coll) B2
Folly Bridge C2
George St B1
Great Clarendon St . . A1
Hart St A1
Hertford (Coll) B2
High St B2
HM Prison B1
Hollywell Row B1
Holywell St B2
Hythe Bridge St . . . B1
Ice Rink C1
Information Ctr 🅸 . . . B2
Jericho A1
Jesus (Coll) B2
Jowett Walk B3
Juxon St A1
Keble (Coll) A2
Keble Rd A2
Library B2
Linacre (Coll) A3
Lincoln (Coll) B2
Little Clarendon St . . A1
Longwall St B3
Magdalen (Coll) . . . B3
Magdalen Bridge . . . B2
Magdalen St B2
Magistrates Court . . . C2
Manchester (Coll) . . B2
Manor Rd B3
Mansfield (Coll) . . . A2
Mansfield Rd A3
Market B1
Marlborough Rd . . . C2
Martyrs' Memorial ✦ . B2
Merton (Coll) B3
Merton Field B3
Merton St B2
Museum 🏛 C2

Museum of
 Modern Art 🏛 . . . B2
Museum of
 Oxford 🏛 B2
Museum Rd A2
New College (Coll) . . B3
New Inn Hall St B2
New Rd B1
New Theatre 🎭 B2
Norfolk St C1
Nuffield (Coll) B1
Observatory A1
Observatory St A1
Odeon 🎬 B1/B2
Old Fire Station 🎭 . . B1
Old Greyfriars St . . . C2
Oriel (Coll) B2
Oxford 🚉 B1
Oxford Story, The ✦ . B2
Oxpens Rd C1
Paradise Sq B1
Paradise St B1
Park End St B1
Parks Rd A2/B2
Pembroke (Coll) . . . C2
Phoenix 🎬 A1
Picture Gallery 🏛 . . B2
Plantation Rd A1
Playhouse 🎭 B2
Police Station 🚓 . . . C2
Post Office 🅿 . . . A1/B2
Pusey St B1
Queen's La B2
Queen's (Coll) B3
Radcliffe Camera 🏛 . B2
Radcliffe Infirmary 🏥 . A1
Rewley Rd B1
Richmond Rd B1
Rose La B3
Ruskin (Coll) B1
Saïd Business
 School B1
St Aldates C2
St Anne's (Coll) A1

St Antony's (Coll) . . . A1
St Bernard's Rd A1
St Catherine's (Coll) . B3
St Cross Building . . . A3
St Cross Rd A3
St Edmund Hall
 (Coll) B3
St Giles St A2
St Hilda's (Coll) C3
St John St B2
St John's (Coll) B2
St Mary the Virgin 🏛 . B2
St Michael at the
 Northgate 🏛 B2
St Peter's (Coll) B1
St Thomas St B1
Science Area A2
Science Museum 🏛 . . B2
Sheldonian
 Theatre 🎭 B2
Somerville (Coll) . . . A1
South Parks Rd A2
Speedwell St C2
Sports Ground C3
Thames St C2
Town Hall B2
Trinity (Coll) B2
Turl St B2
University College
 (Coll) B3
University Museum & Pitt
 Rivers Museum 🏛 . A2
University Parks A2
Wadham (Coll) B2
Walton Cr A1
Walton St A1
Western Rd C2
Westgate Shopping
 Centre B2
Woodstock Rd A1
Worcester (Coll) . . . B1

Peterborough

Bishop's Palace 🏛 . . B2
Bishop's Rd B2/B3
Boongate A3
Bourges Boulevard . . . A1
Bourges Retail
 Park B1/B2
Bridge House
 (Council Offices) . . . C2
Bridge St B2
Bright St A1
Broadway A2
Broadway A2
Brook St A2
Burghley Rd A2
Bus Station B2
Cavendish St A3
Charles St A3
Church St B2
Church Walk A2
Cobden Ave A1
Cobden St A1
Cowgate B2
Craig St A1
Crawthorne Rd A2
Cripple Sidings La . . . C2
Cromwell Rd A1
Dickens St A3

Eastfield Rd A3
Eastgate B3
Fire Station A1
Fletton Ave C2
Frank Perkins
 Parkway C3
Geneva St A2
George St C1
Gladstone St A1
Glebe Rd C3
Gloucester Rd C3
Granby St B3
Grove St C1
Guildhall 🏛 B2
Hadrians Ct C3
Henry St A2
Hereward Rd B3
Information Ctr 🅸 . . . B2
Jubilee St C1
Kent Rd B1
Key Theatre 🎭 C2
Kirkwood Cl B1
Lea Gdns B2
Library A2
Lincoln Rd A2
London Rd C2
Long Causeway . . . B2
Lower Bridge St C2
Magistrates Court . . . B2
Manor House St A2

Mayor's Walk A1
Midland Rd A1
Monument St A2
Museum & Art
 Gallery 🏛 B2
Nene Valley
 Railway 🚂 C1
New Rd A2
New Rd C1
North Minster A2
Old Customs
 House 🏛 C2
Oundle Rd C1
Padholme Rd A3
Palmerston Rd C1
Park Rd A2
Passport Office B2
Peterborough District
 Hospital (A+E) 🏥 . . B1
Peterborough
 Station 🚉 B2
Peterborough Nene
 Valley Station 🚂 . . C1
Peterborough
 United FC C2
Police Station 🚓 . . . B2
Post Office 🅿
 . . . A3/B1/B2/B3/C1
Priestgate B2
Queen's Walk C2

Queensgate Centre . . B2
Railworld 🏛 C1
River La B1
Rivergate Shopping
 Centre B2
Riverside Mead C3
Russell St A1
St John's 🚂 B2
St John's St A3
St Mark's St A2
St Peter's † B2
St Peter's Rd B2
Saxon Rd A3
Spital Bridge A1
Stagshaw Dr C3
Star Rd B3
Thorpe Lea Rd B1
Thorpe Rd B1
Thorpe's Lea Rd B1
Town Hall B2
Viersen Platz B2
Vineyard Rd B3
Wake Rd B3
Wellington St A3
Wentworth St B2
Westgate B2
Whalley St A3
Wharf Rd C1
Whitsed St A3
YMCA A3

Plymouth

Poole

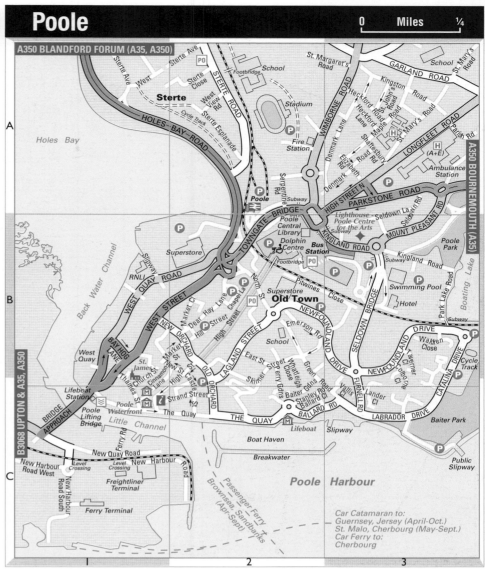

Plymouth

Poole

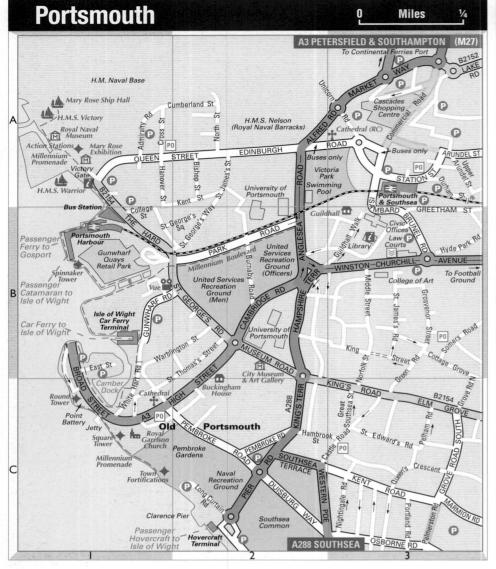

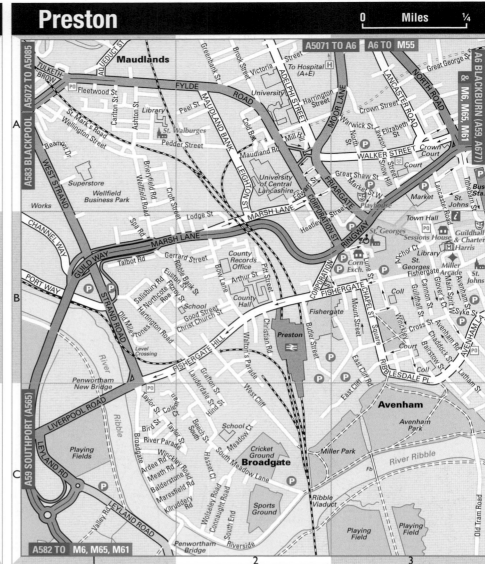

Portsmouth

Action Stations ✦ . . .C1
Admiralty Rd A1
Alfred Rd A2
Anglesea Rd B2
Arundel St B3
Bishop St A2
Broad St C1
Buckingham
  House 🏛 C2
Burnaby Rd B2
Bus Station B1
Camber Dock C1
Cambridge Rd B2
Car Ferry to
  Isle of Wight B1
Cascades Shopping
  Centre A3
Castle Rd C3
Cathedral † C1
Cathedral (RC) † A3
City Museum & Art
  Gallery 🏛 B2
Civic Offices B3
Clarence Pier C2
College of Art B3
College St. B1
Commercial Rd A3
Cottage Gr B3
Cross St A1
Cumberland St A2
Duisburg Way C2
Durham St A3
East St B1
Edinburgh Rd A2
Elm Gr C3
Great Southsea St . . .C3
Green Rd B3
Greetham St B3
Grosvenor St B3
Grove Rd North C3
Grove Rd South C3
Guildhall 🏛 B3
Guildhall Walk B3
Gunwharf Quays
  Retail Park B1
Gunwharf Rd B1
Hambrook St C2
Hampshire Terr. B2
Hanover St A1
High St C2
HM Naval Base A1
HMS Nelson (Royal
  Naval Barracks) A2
HMS Victory ⚓ A1
HMS Warrior ⚓ A1
Hovercraft Terminal . .C2
Hyde Park Rd B3
Information Ctr ℹ A1/B3
Isambard Brunel Rd . .B3
Isle of Wight Car
  Ferry Terminal B1
Kent Rd C3
Kent St A2
King St B3
King's Rd C3
King's Terr. C2
Lake Rd A3
Law Courts B3
Library B3
Long Curtain Rd C2
Market Way A3
Marmion Rd C3
Mary Rose
  Exhibition 🏛 A1
Mary Rose
  Ship Hall ⚓ A1
Middle St B3
Millennium Blvd B2
Millennium
  Promenade. A1/C1
Museum Rd B2
Naval Recreation
  Ground C2
Nightingale Rd C3
Norfolk St B3
North St A2
Osborne Rd C3
Park Rd B2
Passenger Catamaran
  to Isle of Wight. B1
Passenger Ferry
  to Gosport B1
Pelham Rd C3
Pembroke Gdns C2
Pembroke Rd C2
Pier Rd C2
Point Battery C1
Police Station 🛡 . . .B3
Portsmouth &
  Southsea ⚦ A3
Portsmouth
  Harbour ⚦ B1
Post Office 🅿 . . . . . .
  . . . . . .A1/A3/B3/C1/C3
Queen St A1
Queen's Cr C3
Round Tower ✦ C1
Royal Garrison
  Church ⛪ C1
Royal Naval
  Museum 🏛 A1
St Edward's Rd C3
St George's Rd B2
St George's Sq B1
St George's Way B2
St James's Rd B3
St James's St A2
St Thomas's St B2
Somers Rd B3
Southsea Common . .C2
Southsea Terr. C2
Station St A3
Spinnaker Tower ✦ . .B1
Square Tower ✦ C1
Swimming Pool A2
The Hard B1
Town Fortifications ✦ .C1
Unicorn Rd A2
United Services
  Recreation Ground. . .B2
University of
  Portsmouth A2/B2
Upper Arundel St A3
Victoria Park A2
Victory Gate A1
Vue 🎬 B1
Warblington St B1
Western Pde. C2
White Hart Rd C1
Winston Churchill
  Ave. B3

Preston

Adelphi St. A2
Anchor Ct B3
Aqueduct St A1
Ardee Rd C1
Arthur St B2
Ashton St A1
Avenham La B3
Avenham Park C3
Avenham Rd B3
Avenham St B3
Bairstow St. B3
Balderstone Rd C1
Beamont Dr A1
Beech St South C2
Bird St B3
Bow La B2
Brieryfield Rd A1
Broadgate. C2
Brook St A2
Bus Station. A3
Butler St B2
Cannon St B3
Carlton St A1
Chaddock St B3
Channel Way B1
Chapel St B3
Christ Church St. B2
Christian Rd B2
Cold Bath St. A2
Coleman Ct C1
Connaught Rd C2
Corn Exchange 🏛 . . .B3
Corporation St A2/B2
County Hall. B2
County Records
  Office B2
Court. A3
Court. B3
Cricket Ground. C2
Croft St A1
Cross St B3
Crown Court A3
Crown St A3
East Cliff. C3
East Cliff Rd B3
Edward St. A2
Elizabeth St A3
Euston St B1
Fishergate B2/B3
Fishergate Hill. B2
Fishergate Shopping
  Centre B2
Fitzroy St B1
Fleetwood St A1
Friargate A3
Fylde Rd A1/A2
Gerrard St B2
Glover's Ct B3
Good St B2
Grafton St B2
Great George St A3
Great Shaw St A3
Greenbank St A2
Guild Way B1
Guildhall &
  Charter 🏛 B3
Guildhall St. B3
Harrington St A2
Hartington Rd B1
Hasset Cl C2
Heatley St B2
Hind St C2
Information Ctr ℹ B3
Kilruddery Rd C1
Lancaster Rd A3/B3
Latham St B2
Lauderdale St C2
Lawson St A3
Leighton St A2
Leyland Rd C1
Library A1
Library A3
Liverpool Rd C1
Lodge St. B2
Lune St B3
Main Sprit West B3
Maresfield Rd C1
Market St West. A3
Marsh La B1/B2
Maudland Bank A2
Maudland Rd A2
Meadow Ct. C2
Meath Rd C1
Mill Hill B3
Miller Arcade ✦ B3
Miller Park C3
Moor La A3
Mount St. B3
North Rd A3
North St A3
Northcote Rd B1
Old Milestones B3
Old Tram Rd. C3
Pedder St A1/A2
Peel St A2
Penwortham Bridge . .C2
Penwortham New
  Bridge. C1
Pitt St B2
Playhouse 🎭 A3
Police Station 🛡 A3
Port Way B1
Post Office 🅿 . A1/B3/C1
Preston Station ⚦ B2
Ribble Bank St B2
Ribble Viaduct C2
Ribblesdale Pl B3
Ringway B3
River Parade C1
Riverside. C2
St Georges ⛪ B3
St Georges Shopping
  Centre B3
St Johns ⛪ B3
St Johns Shopping
  Centre A3
St Mark's Rd A1
St Walburges ⛪ A1
Salisbury Rd B1
Sessions House 🏛 . . .B3
Snow Hill A3
South End. C2
South Meadow La C2
Spa Rd B1
Sports Ground C2
Strand Rd B1
Syke St B3
Talbot St B1
Taylor St C1
Tithebarn St A3
Town Hall B3
Tulketh Brow. A1
University of Central
  Lancashire A2
Valley Rd. C1
Victoria St A2
Walker St A3
Walton's Parade B2
Warwick St A3
Wellfield Business
  Park A1
Wellfield Rd A1
Wellington St A1
West Cliff C2
West Strand A1
Winckley Rd C1
Winckley Square B3
Wolseley Rd C2

Reading

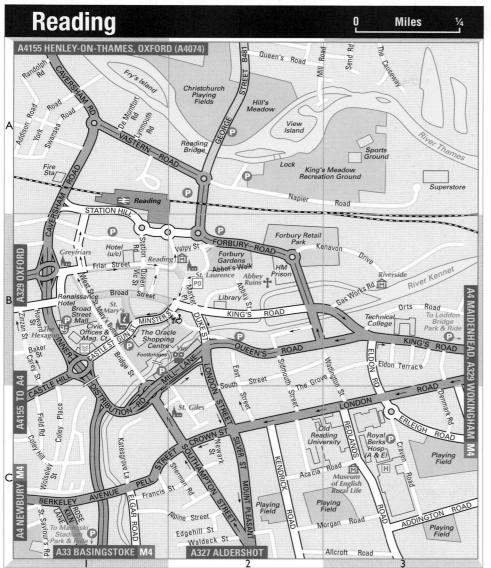

A4155 HENLEY-ON-THAMES, OXFORD (A4074)

A33 BASINGSTOKE M4　　A327 ALDERSHOT

Salisbury

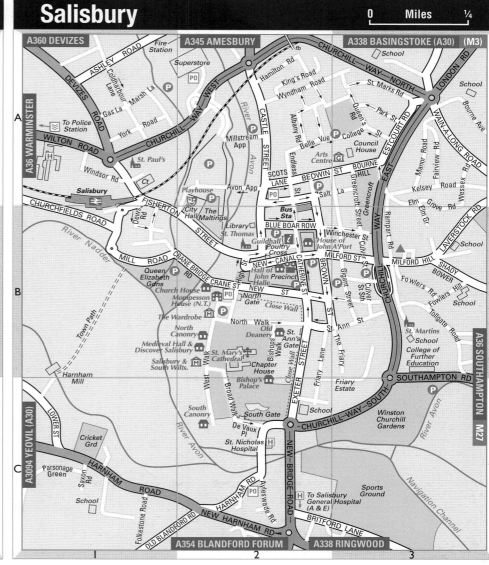

A360 DEVIZES　A345 AMESBURY　A338 BASINGSTOKE (A30) (M3)

A354 BLANDFORD FORUM　A338 RINGWOOD

Sheffield

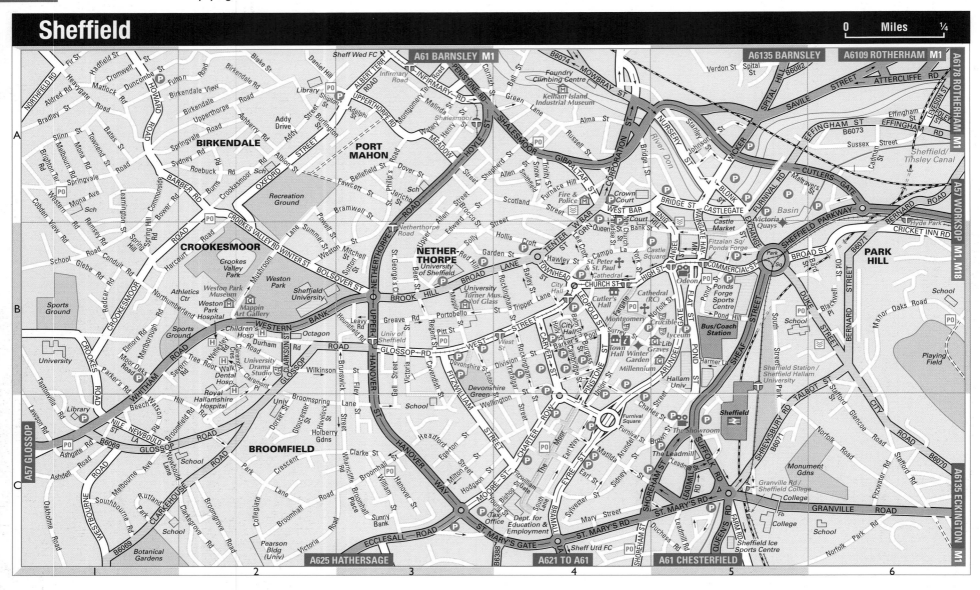

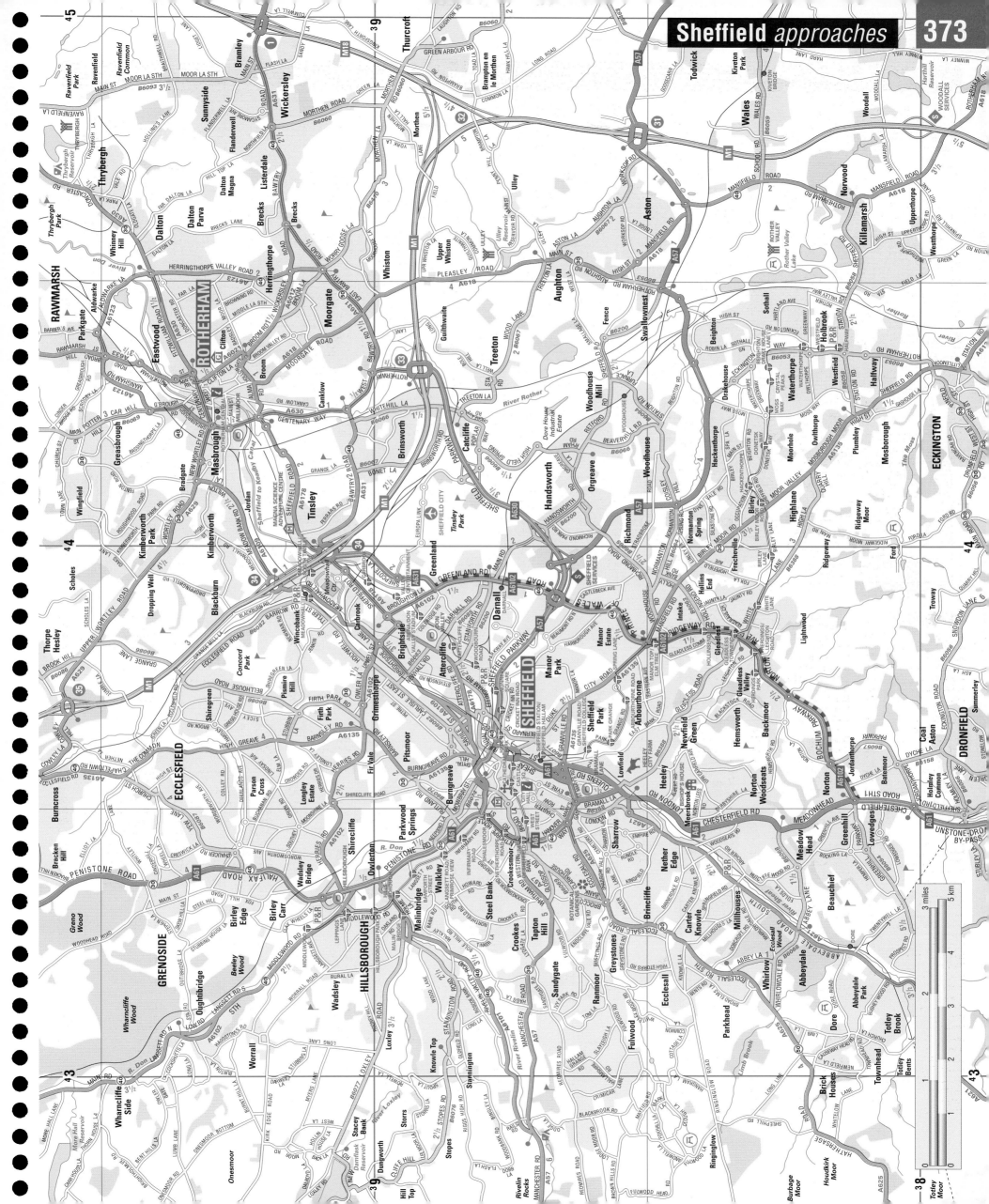

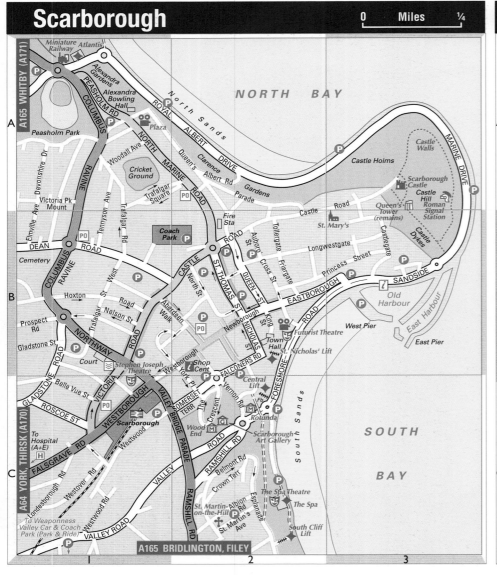

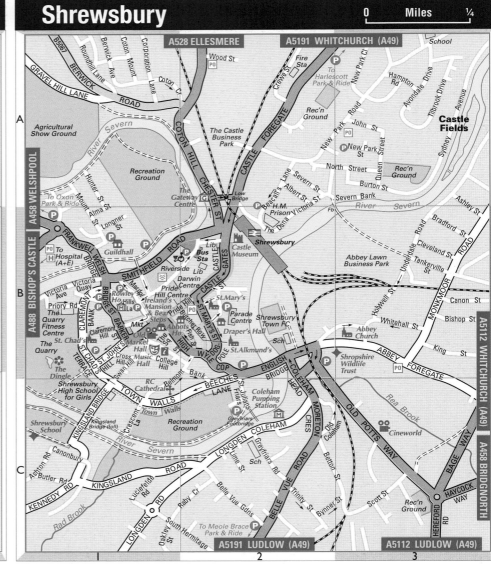

Scarborough

Aberdeen Walk B2
Albert Rd A2
Albion Rd C2
Alexandra Bowling
  Hall A1
Alexandra Gardens . . . A1
Atlantis ✦ A1
Auborough St B2
Belle Vue St C1
Belmont Rd C2
Brunswick Shopping
  Centre B2
Castle Dykes B3
Castlegate B3
Castle Holms A3
Castle Hill A3
Castle Rd B2
Castle Walls A3
Cemetery B1
Central Lift ✦ C2
Clarence Gardens A2
Coach Park B1
Columbus Ravine A1
Court B1
Cricket Ground A1
Cross St B2
Crown Terr C2
Dean Rd B1
Devonshire Dr A1
East Harbour B3
East Pier B3
Eastborough B2
Elmville Ave B1
Esplanade C2
Falconers Rd B2
Falsgrave Rd C1
Fire Station B2
Foreshore Rd B2
Friargate B2
Futurist Theatre 🎭 🎦 . . B2
Gladstone Rd B1
Gladstone St B1
Hoxton Rd B1
Information Ctr ℹ . B2/B3
King St B2
Londesborough Rd C1
Longwestgate B3
Marine Dr A3
Miniature Railway 🚂 . . A1
Nelson St B1
Newborough B2
Nicolas St B2
North Marine Rd A1
North St B1
Northway B1
Old Harbour B3
Peasholm Park A1
Peasholm Rd A1
Plaza 🎦 A1
Police Station 🚔 B1
Post Office 🅟
  . . . . A2/B1/B2/C1
Princess St B3
Prospect Rd B1
Queen St B2
Queen's Parade A2
Queen's Tower
  (Remains) 🏰 A3
Ramshill Rd C2
Roman Signal
  Station ♣ A3
Roscoe St C1
Rotunda Museum 🏛 . . C2
Royal Albert Dr A2
St Martin-on-
  the-Hill ♣ C2
St Martin's Ave C2
St Mary's ♣ B3
St Nicholas' Lift ✦ . . . B2
St Thomas St B2
Sandside B3
Scarborough Art
  Gallery 🏛 C2
Scarborough
  Castle 🏰 A3
Scarborough
  Station 🚉 C1
Somerset Terr C2
South Cliff Lift ✦ C2
Spa, The ✦ C2
Spa Theatre, The 🎭 . . C2
Stephen Joseph
  Theatre 🎭 B1
Tennyson Ave B1
The Crescent C2
Tollergate B2
Town Hall B2
Trafalgar Rd B1
Trafalgar Square A1
Trafalgar St West B1
Valley Bridge Parade . . C2
Valley Rd C1
Vernon Rd C2
Victoria Park Mount . . A1
Victoria Rd B1
West Pier B3
Westborough B2
Westover Rd C1
Westwood C1
Woodall Ave A1
Wood End
  Museum 🏛 C2
York Pl B2

Shrewsbury

Abbey Church ♣ B3
Abbey Foregate B3
Abbey Lawn
  Business Park B3
Abbots House 🏠 B2
Agricultural Show
  Ground A1
Albert St A2
Alma St B1
Ashley St A3
Ashton Rd C1
Avondale Dr A3
Bage Way C3
Barker St B1
Beacall's La A2
Beeches La C2
Belle Vue Gdns C2
Belle Vue Rd C2
Belmont Bank C1
Berwick Ave A1
Berwick Rd A1
Betton St C2
Bishop St B3
Bradford St B3
Bridge St B1
Bus Station B2
Butcher Row B2
Burton St A3
Butler Rd C1
Bynner St C2
Canon St B3
Canonbury C1
Castle Foregate A2
Castle Gates B2
Castle Museum 🏛 . . . B2
Castle St B2
Cathedral (RC) ✝ C1
Chester St A2
Cineworld 🎦 C3
Claremont Bank B1
Claremont Hill B1
Cleveland St B3
Coleham Head C2
Coleham Pumping
  Station 🏠 C2
College Hill B1
Corporation La A1
Coton Cres A2
Coton Hill A2
Coton Mount A1
Crescent La C1
Crewe St A2
Cross Hill B1
Darwin Centre B2
Dingle, The ✿ B1
Dogpole B2
Draper's Hall 🏠 B2
English Bridge B2
Fish St B2
Frankwell B1
Gateway Centre,
  The 🏠 A2
Gravel Hill La A1
Greyfriars Rd C2
Guildhall 🏠 B1
Hampton Rd A3
Haycock Way C3
HM Prison B2
Hereford Rd C3
High St B1
Hills La B1
Holywell St B3
Hunter St B1
Information Ctr ℹ B1
Ireland's Mansion
  & Bear Steps 🏠 . . . B1
John St A3
Kennedy Rd C1
King St B3
Kingsland Bridge C1
Kingsland Bridge
  (toll) C1
Kingsland Rd C1
Library B2
Lime St C2
Longden Coleham C2
Longden Rd C1
Longner St B1
Luciefelde Rd C1
Mardol B1
Market B1
Monkmoor Rd B3
Moreton Cr C2
Mount St A1
Music Hall 🎭 B1
New Park Cl A3
New Park Rd A2
New Park St A3
North St A2
Oakley St C1
Old Coleham C2
Old Market Hall 🎦 . . . B1
Old Potts Way C3
Parade Centre B2
Police Station 🚔 B1
Post Office 🅟
  . . . . A2/B1/B2/B3
Pride Hill B1
Pride Hill Centre B1
Priory Rd B1
Queen St A3
Raby Cr C2
Rad Brook C1
Rea Brook C3
Riverside B1
Roundhill La A1
Rowley's House 🏠 . . . B1
St.Alkmund's ♣ B2
St Chad's ♣ B1
St Chad's Terr B1
St John's Hill B1
St Julians Friars C2
St.Mary's ♣ B2
St Mary's St B2
Scott St C3
Severn Bank A3
Severn St A2
Shrewsbury 🚉 B2
Shrewsbury High
  School for Girls C1
Shrewsbury
  School ✦ C1
Shrewsbury
  Town FC B2
Shropshire Wildlife
  Trust ✦ B3
Smithfield Rd B1
South Hermitage C1
Swan Hill B1
Sydney Ave A3
Tankerville St B3
The Castle Business
  Park A2
The Dana B2
The Quarry B1
The Square B1
Tilbrook Dr A3
Town Walls C1
Trinity St C2
Underdale Rd B3
Victoria Ave B1
Victoria Quay B1
Victoria St B2
Welsh Bridge B1
Whitehall St B3
Wood St A2
Wyle Cop B2

Southampton

0 Miles ¼

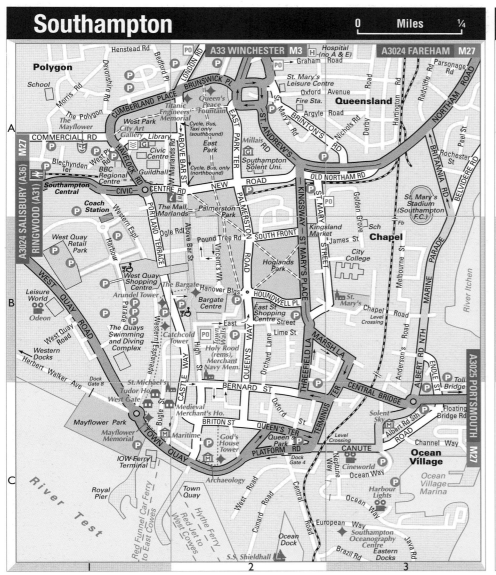

Stoke-on-Trent (Hanley)

0 Miles ¼

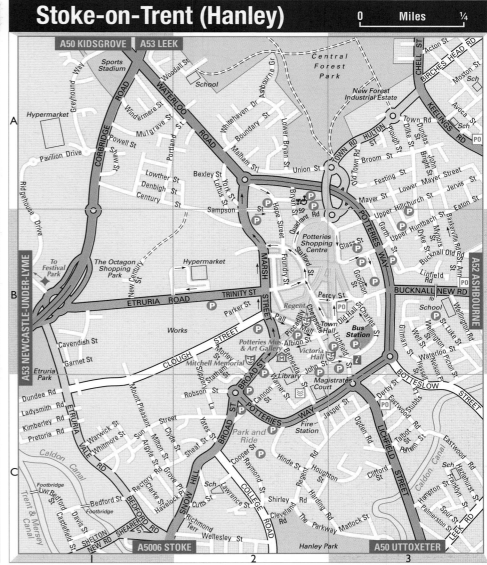

Southampton

Above Bar St A2	Dock Gate 8 . . . . B1	Marsh La B2	Rochester St A3
Albert Rd North B3	East Park A2	Mayflower	Royal Pier C1
Albert Rd South C3	East Park Terr A2	Memorial ✦ C1	St Andrew's Rd A2
Anderson's Rd B3	East St B2	Mayflower Park C1	St Mary St A2
Archaeology	East St Shopping	Mayflower Theatre,	St Mary's B3
Museum 🏛 . . . C2	Centre B2	The A1	St Mary's Leisure
Argyle Rd A2	Endle St C2	Medieval Merchant's	Centre A2
Arundel Tower ✦ . . B1	European Way C2	House 🏛 C1	St Mary's Pl A2
Bargate, The ✦ . . . B2	Fire Station A2	Melbourne St B3	St Mary's Rd A2
Bargate Centre B2	Floating Bridge Rd . . . C3	Millais 🏛 A2	St Mary's Stadium
BBC Regional	God's House	Morris Rd A1	(Southampton F.C.) . A3
Centre A1	Tower ✦ C2	Neptune Way C3	St Michael's 🏛 C1
Bedford Pl A1	Golden Gr A3	New Rd A2	Solent Sky 🏛 C3
Belvidere Rd A3	Graham Rd A3	Nichols Rd A3	South Front B2
Bernard St C2	Guildhall A1	Northam Rd A3	Southampton Central
Blechynden Terr A1	Hanover Bldgs B2	Ocean Dock C2	Station 🚂 A1
Brazil St C3	Harbour Lights 🎬 . . C3	Ocean Village	Southampton Solent
Brinton's Rd A2	Harbour Pde B1	Marina C3	University A2
Britannia Rd A3	Hartington Rd A3	Ocean Way C3	Southhampton
Briton St C2	Havelock Rd A1	Odeon 🎬 B1	Oceanography
Brunswick Pl A2	Henstead Rd A1	Ogle Rd B1	Centre ✦ C2
Bugle St C1	Herbert Walker Ave . . B1	Old Northam Rd A3	SS Shieldhall ⚓ . . . C2
Canute Rd C3	High St B2	Orchard La B2	Terminus Terr C2
Castle Way C2	Hoglands Park B2	Oxford Ave A2	The Mall, Marlands . . A1
Catchcold Twr ✦ . . B1	Holy Rood (Rems),	Oxford St C2	The Polygon A1
Central Bridge C3	Merchant Navy	Palmerston Park A2	Threefield La B2
Central Rd C2	Memorial ✦ A2	Palmerston Rd A2	Titanic Engineers'
Channel Way C3	Hospital 🏥 A2	Parsonage Rd A3	Memorial ✦ A2
Chapel Rd B3	Houndwell Pl B2	Peel St A3	Town Quay C1
Cineworld 🎬 C3	Hythe Ferry C1	Platform Rd C2	Town Walls B2
City Art Gallery 🏛 . . A1	Information Ctr ℹ . . . A1	Police Station 🏢 . . . A1	Tudor House 🏛 C1
City College B3	Isle of Wight	Portland Terr B1	Vincent's Walk B2
Civic Centre A1	Ferry Terminal C1	Post Office 🏤 . . A2/A3/B2	West Gate 🏛 C1
Civic Centre Rd A1	James St B3	Pound Tree Rd B2	West Marlands Rd . . . A1
Coach Station B1	Java Rd C3	Quays Swimming	West Park A1
Commercial Rd A1	Kingsland Market B2	& Diving Complex,	West Park Rd A1
Cumberland Pl A1	Kingsway A2	The B1	West Quay Rd B1
Cunard Rd C2	Leisure World B1	Queen's Park C2	West Quay
Derby Rd A3	Library A1	Queen's Peace	Retail Park B1
Devonshire Rd A1	Lime St B2	Fountain ✦ A2	West Quay Shopping
Dock Gate 4 . . . . . . C2	London Rd A2	Queen's Terr C2	Centre B1
	Marine Pde B3	Queen's Way B2	West Rd C2
	Maritime 🏛 C1	Radcliffe Rd A3	Western Esplanade . . B1

Stoke-on-Trent (Hanley)

Acton St A3	Dyke St B3	Lowther St A1	Rectory Rd C1
Albion St B2	Eastwood Rd C3	Magistrates Court . . . C2	Regent Rd C3
Argyle St C1	Eaton St A3	Malham St A2	Regent Theatre 🎭 . . B2
Ashbourne Gr A2	Etruria Park B1	Marsh St B2	Richmond Terr C2
Avoca St A3	Etruria Rd B1	Matlock St C3	Ridgehouse Dr A1
Baskerville Rd B3	Etruria Vale Rd C1	Mayer St A3	Robson St C2
Bedford Rd C1	Festing St A3	Milton St C1	St Ann St B3
Bedford St C1	Fire Station C2	Mitchell Memorial	St Luke St B3
Bethesda St B2	Foundry St B2	Theatre 🎭 B2	Sampson St B2
Bexley St A2	Franklyn St B3	Morley St B2	Shaw St A1
Birches Head Rd A3	Garnet St B1	Moston St A3	Sheaf St C2
Botteslow St B3	Garth St B3	Mount Pleasant C1	Shearer St C1
Boundary St A2	George St B2	Mulgrave St A1	Shelton New Rd C1
Broad St C2	Gilman St B3	Mynors St B3	Shirley Rd C3
Broom St A3	Glass St B2	Nelson Pl B3	Slippery La B2
Bryan St A2	Goodson St B3	New Century St B1	Snow Hill C2
Bucknall New Rd B3	Greyhound Way A1	New Forest Industrial	Sports Stadium A1
Bucknall Old Rd B3	Grove Pl C1	Estate A3	Spur St C3
Bus Station B3	Hampton St C3	Octagon Shopping	Stafford St B2
Cannon St C2	Hanley Park C2	Park, The B1	Statham St B2
Castlefield St C1	Harding Rd C2	Ogden Rd C3	Stubbs La C3
Hanley Park C2	Hassall St B3	Old Hall St B2	Sun St C1
Cavendish St B1	Havelock Pl C1	Old Town Rd A3	Talbot St C3
Central Forest Park . . A2	Hazlehurst St C3	Pall Mall B2	The Parkway C2
Charles St B3	Hinde St C2	Palmerston St C3	Town Hall B2
Cheapside B2	Hope St B2	Park and Ride C2	Town Rd A3
Chell St A3	Houghton St C2	Parker St C2	Trinity St B2
Clarke St C1	Hulton St A3	Pavilion Dr A1	Union St A2
Cleveland Rd C3	Hypermarket A1/B2	Pelham St C3	Upper Hillchurch St . . A3
Clifford St C3	Information Ctr ℹ . . . B2	Percy St C2	Upper Huntbach St . . B3
Clough St B2	Jasper St C2	Piccadilly B2	Victoria Hall
Clyde St C1	Jervis St A3	Picton St B3	Theatre 🎭 B3
College Rd C2	John Bright St B3	Plough St A3	Warner St C2
Cooper St B2	John St B2	Police Station 🏢 . . . C2	Warwick St C1
Corbridge Rd A1	Keelings Rd A3	Portland St A3	Waterloo Rd A1
Cutts St C2	Kimberley Rd C1	Post Office 🏤 . . A3/B3/C3	Waterloo St B3
Davis St C1	Ladysmith Rd C1	Potteries Museum &	Well St B3
Denbigh St A1	Lawrence St C2	Art Gallery 🏛 B2	Wellesley St C2
Derby St C3	Leek Rd C3	Potteries Shopping	Wellington Rd A3
Dilke St A3	Library C2	Centre B2	Wellington St B3
Dundas St A3	Lichfield St C3	Potteries Way C2	Whitehaven Dr A2
Dundee Rd C1	Linfield Rd B3	Powell St A1	Whitmore St C2
	Loftus St A2	Pretoria Rd C1	Windermere St A1
	Lower Bedford St C1	Quadrant Rd B2	Woodall St C1
	Lower Bryan St A2	Ranelagh St A3	Yates St C2
	Lower Mayer St A3	Raymond St C2	York St A2

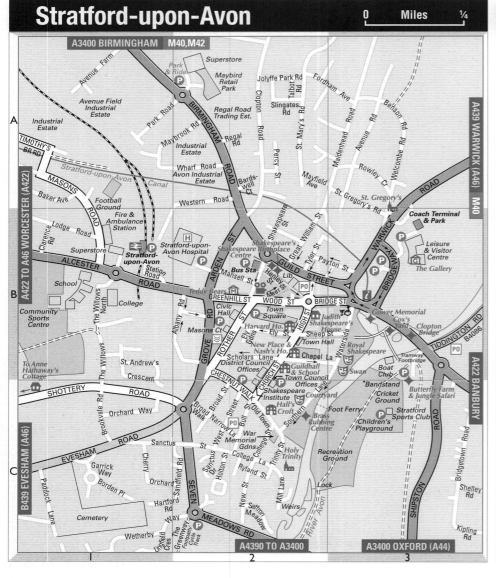

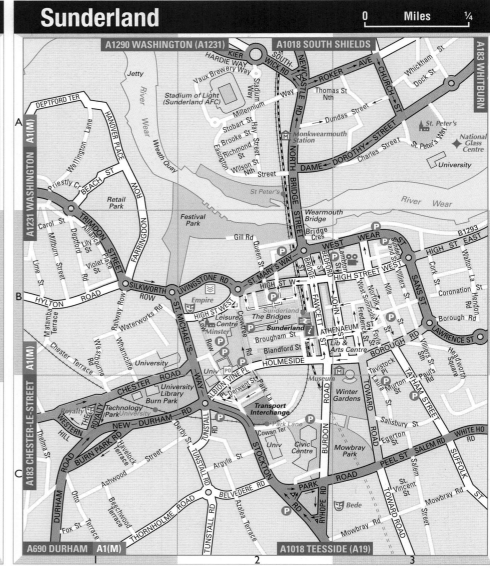

Stratford-upon-Avon

Sunderland

Swansea / Abertawe

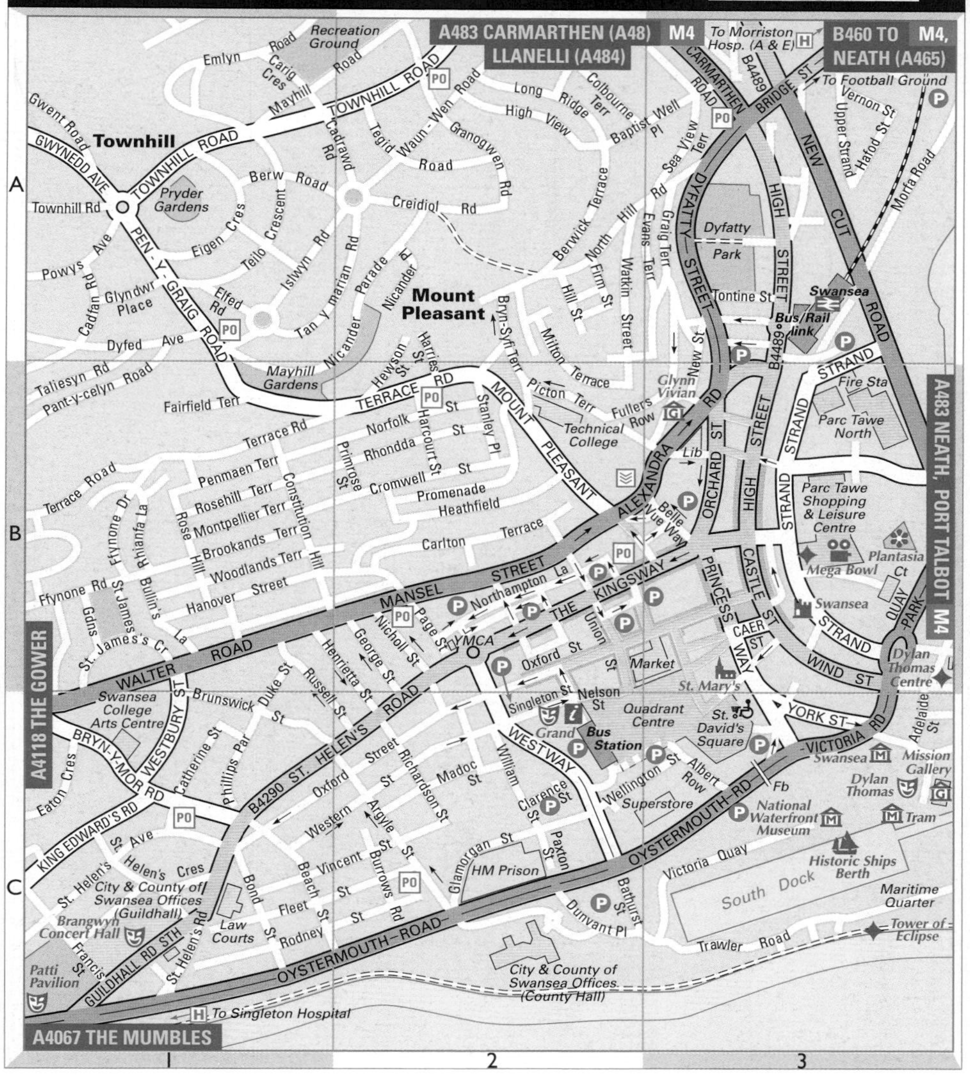

Swindon

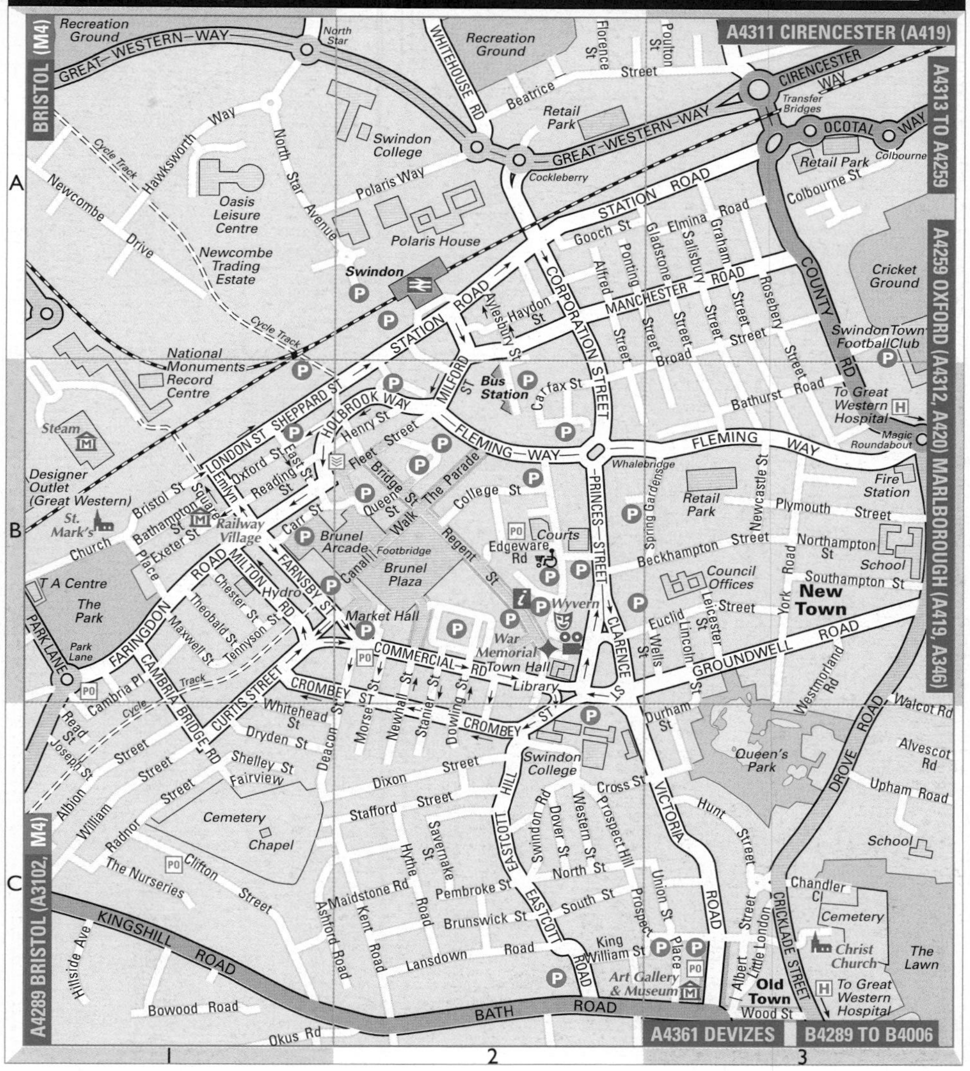

Swansea/ Abertawe

Adelaide St C3
Albert Row C3
Alexandra Rd B3
Argyle St C1
Baptist Well Pl A2
Beach St C1
Belle Vue Way B3
Berw Rd A1
Berwick Terr A2
Bond St C1
Brangwyn Concert Hall C1
Bridge St A3
Brookands Terr B1
Brunswick St C1
Bryn-Syfi Terr A2
Bryn-y-Mor Rd C1
Bullins La B1
Burrows Rd C1
Bus/Rail link A3
Bus Station C2
Cadfan Rd A1
Cadrawd Rd A1
Caer St B3
Carig Cr A1
Carlton Terr B2
Carmarthen Rd A3
Castle St B3
Catherine St C1
City & County of Swansea Offices (County Hall) C2
City & County of Swansea Offices (Guildhall) C1
Clarence St C2
Colbourne Terr A2
Constitution Hill B1
Court B3
Creidiol Rd A2
Cromwell St B2
Duke St B1
Dunvant Pl C2
Dyfatty Park A3
Dyfatty St A3
Dyfed Ave A1
Dylan Thomas Ctr ✦ B3
Dylan Thomas Theatre C3
Eaton Cr C1
Eigen Cr A1
Elfed Rd A1
Emlyn Rd A1
Evans Terr A3
Fairfield Terr B1
Ffynone Dr B1
Ffynone Rd B1
Fire Station B3
Firm St A2
Fleet St C1
Francis St C1
Fullers Row B2
George St B2
Glamorgan St C2
Glyndwr Pl A1
Glynn Vivian B3
Graig Terr A3
Grand Theatre C2
Granogwen Rd A2
Guildhall Rd South C1
Gwent Rd A1
Gwynedd Ave A1
Hafod St A3
Hanover St B1
Harcourt St B2
Harries St A2
Heathfield B2
Henrietta St B1
Hewson St B2
High St A3/B3
High View A2
Hill St A2
Historic Ships Berth C3
HM Prison C2
Information Ctr C2
Islwyn Rd A1
King Edward's Rd C1
Law Courts C1
Library B3
Long Ridge A2
Madoc St C2
Mansel St B2
Maritime Quarter C3
Market B3
Mayhill Gdns B1
Mayhill Rd A1
Mega Bowl ✦ B3
Milton Terr A2
Mission Gallery C3
Montpellier Terr B1
Morfa Rd A3
Mount Pleasant B2
National Waterfront Museum C3
Nelson St C2
New Cut Rd A3
New St A3
Nicander Pde A2
Nicander Pl A2
Nicholl St B2
Norfolk St B2
North Hill Rd A2
Northampton La B2
Orchard St B3
Oxford St B2
Oystermouth Rd C1
Page St B2
Pant-y-Celyn Rd B1
Parc Tawe North B3
Parc Tawe Shopping & Leisure Centre B3
Patti Pavilion C1
Paxton St C2
Penmaen Terr B1
Pen-y-Graig Rd A1
Phillips Pde C1
Picton Terr B2
Plantasia B3
Police Station B2
Post Office A1/A2/A3/B2/C1/C2/C3
Powys Ave A1
Primrose St B2
Princess Way B3
Promenade B2
Pryder Gdns A1
Quadrant Centre C2
Quay Park B3
Rhianfa La B1
Rhondda St B2
Richardson St C2
Rodney St C1
Rose Hill B1
Rosehill Terr B1
Russell St B1
St David's Sq C3
St Helen's Ave C1
St Helen's Cr C1
St Helen's Rd C1
St James Gdns B1
St James's Cr B1
St Mary's B3
Sea View Terr A3
Singleton St C2
South Dock C3
Stanley Pl B2
Strand B3
Swansea Castle B3
Swansea College Arts Centre C1
Swansea Museum C3
Swansea Station A3
Taliesyn Rd B1
Tan y Marian Rd A1
Technical College B2
Tegid Rd A2
Teilo Cr A1
Terrace Rd B1/B2
The Kingsway B2
Tontine St A3
Tower of Eclipse ✦ C3
Townhill Rd A1
Tram Museum C3
Trawler Rd C3
Union St B2
Upper Strand A3
Vernon St A3
Victoria Quay C3
Victoria Rd B3
Vincent St C1
Walter Rd B1
Watkin St A2
Waun-Wen Rd A2
Wellington St C2
Westbury St C1
Western St C1
Westway C2
William St C2
Wind St B3
Woodlands Terr B1
YMCA B2
York St C3

Swindon

Albert St C3
Albion St C1
Alfred St A2
Alvescot Rd C3
Art Gallery & Museum C3
Ashford Rd C1
Aylesbury St A2
Bath Rd C2
Bathampton St B1
Bathurst Rd B3
Beatrice St A2
Beckhampton St B3
Bowood Rd C1
Bristol St B1
Broad St A3
Brunel Arcade B2
Brunel Plaza B2
Brunswick St C2
Bus Station B2
Cambria Bridge Rd B1
Cambria Place B1
Canal Walk B2
Carfax St B2
Carr St B1
Cemetery C1/C3
Chandler Cl C3
Chapel C1
Chester St B1
Christ Church C3
Church Place B1
Cirencester Way A3
Clarence St B2
Clifton St C1
Cockleberry Rdbt A2
Colbourne Rdbt A3
Colbourne St A3
College St B2
Commercial Rd B2
Corporation St A2
Council Offices B3
County Rd A3
Courts B2
Cricket Ground A3
Cricklade Street C3
Crombey St B1/C2
Cross St C2
Curtis St B1
Deacon St C1
Designer Outlet (Great Western) B1
Dixon St C2
Dover St C2
Dowling St C2
Drove Rd C3
Dryden St C1
Durham St C3
East St B1
Eastcott Hill C2
Eastcott Rd C2
Edgeware Rd B2
Elmina Rd A3
Emlyn Square B1
Euclid St B3
Exeter St B1
Fairview C1
Faringdon Rd B1
Farnsby St B1
Fire Station B3
Fleet St B2
Fleming Way B2/B3
Florence St A2
Gladstone St A3
Gooch St A2
Graham St A3
Great Western Way A1/A2
Groundwell Rd B3
Hawksworth Way A1
Haydon St A2
Henry St B2
Hillside Ave C1
Holbrook Way B2
Hunt St C3
Hydro B1
Hythe Rd C2
Information Ctr B2
Joseph St C1
Kent Rd C2
King William St C2
Kingshill Rd C1
Lansdown Rd C2
Leicester St B3
Library B2
Lincoln St B3
Little London C3
London St B1
Magic Rdbt B3
Maidstone Rd C2
Manchester Rd A3
Market Hall B2
Maxwell St B1
Milford St B2
Milton Rd B1
Morse St C2
National Monuments Record Centre B1
Newcastle St B3
Newcombe Drive A1
Newcombe Trading Estate A1
Newhall St C2
North St C2
North Star Ave A1
North Star Rdbt A1
Northampton St B3
Oasis Leisure Centre A1
Ocotal Way A3
Okus Rd C1
Old Town C3
Oxford St B1
Park Lane B1
Park Lane Rdbt B1
Pembroke St C2
Plymouth St B3
Polaris House A2
Polaris Way A2
Police Station B2
Ponting St A2
Post Office B1/B2/C1/C3
Poulton St A3
Princes St B2
Prospect Hill C2
Prospect Place C2
Queen St B2
Queen's Park C3
Radnor St C1
Railway Village B1
Read St C1
Reading St B1
Regent St B2
Retail Park A2/A3/B3
Rosebery St A3
St Mark's B1
Salisbury St A3
Savernake St C2
Shelley St C1
Sheppard St B1
South St C2
Southampton St B3
Spring Gardens B3
Stafford Street C2
Stanier St C2
Station Road A2
Steam B1
Swindon Station A2
Swindon College A2/C2
Swindon Rd C2
Swindon Town Football Club A3
T A Centre B1
Tennyson St B1
The Lawn C3
The Nurseries C1
The Parade B2
The Park B1
Theobald St B1
Town Hall B2
Transfer Bridges Rdbt A3
Union St C2
Upham Rd C3
Victoria Rd C3
Walcot Rd B3
War Memorial ✦ B2
Wells St B3
Western St C2
Westmorland Rd B3
Whalebridge Rdbt B2
Whitehead St C1
Whitehouse Rd A2
William St C1
Wood St C3
Wyvern Theatre & Arts Centre B2
York Rd B3

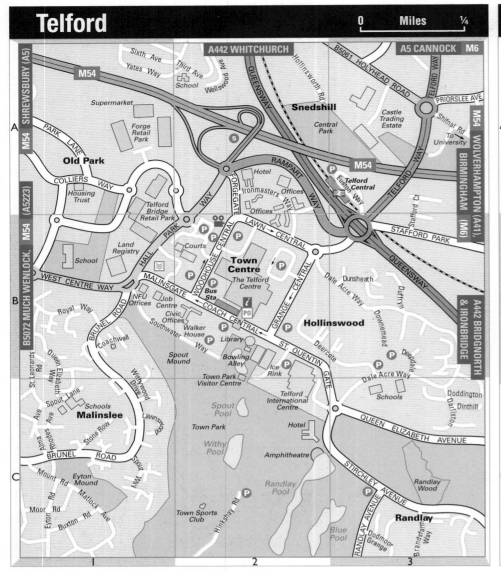

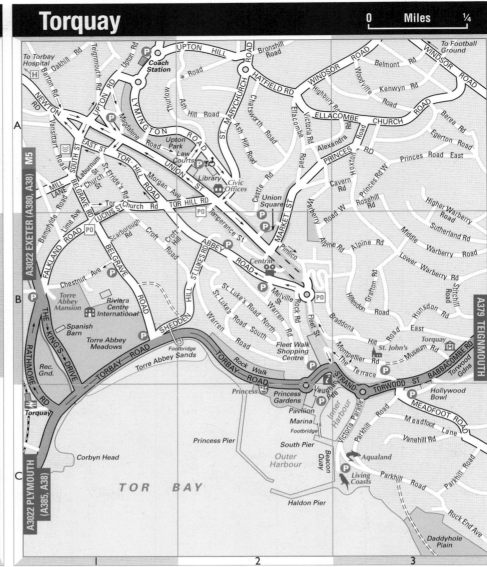

Telford

Alma Ave	. . . .	C1
Amphitheatre	. . . . . .	C2
Bowling Alley	. . . . . .	B2
Brandsfarm Way	. . . .	C3
Brunel Rd	. . . .	B1
Bus Station	. . . .	B2
Buxton Rd	. . . .	C1
Castle Trading		
Estate	. . . .	A3
Central Park	. . . . . .	B2
Civic Offices	. . . . . .	B2
Coach Central	. . . . .	B2
Coachwell Cl	. . . . . .	B1
Colliers Way	. . . . . .	A1
Courts	. . . .	B2
Dale Acre Way	. . . . .	B2
Darliston	. . . .	C3
Deepdale	. . . .	B3
Deercote	. . . .	B3
Dinthill	. . . .	C3
Doddington	. . . . . .	C3
Dodmoor Grange	. . .	C3
Downemead	. . . . . .	B3
Duffryn	. . . .	B3
Dunsheath	. . . .	B3
Euston Way	. . . . . .	A3
Eyton Mound	. . . . .	C1
Eyton Rd	. . . .	C1
Forge Retail Park	. . .	A1
Forgegate	. . . .	A2
Grange Central	. . . .	B2
Hall Park Way	. . . . .	B1
Hinkshay Rd	. . . . . .	C2
Hollinsworth Rd	. . . .	A2
Holyhead Rd	. . . . . .	A2
Housing Trust	. . . . .	A1
Ice Rink	. . . .	B2
Information Ctr ⓘ	. . .	B2
Ironmasters Way	. . . .	A2
Job Centre	. . . .	B1
Land Registry	. . . . .	B2
Lawn Central	. . . . .	B2
Lawnswood	. . . . . .	C1
Library	. . . .	B2
Malinsgate	. . . .	B1
Matlock Ave	. . . . . .	C1
Moor Rd	. . . .	C1
Mount Rd	. . . .	C1
NFU Offices	. . . . . .	B1
Park Lane	. . . .	A1
Priorslee Ave	. . . . . .	A3
Queen Elizabeth Ave	.	C3
Queen Elizabeth		
Way	. . . .	B1
Queensway	. . . . . .	A2/B3
Rampart Way	. . . . .	A2
Randlay Ave	. . . . . .	C3
Randlay Wood	. . . . .	C3
Rhodes Ave	. . . . . .	C1
Royal Way	. . . .	B1
St Leonards Rd	. . . .	B1
St Quentin Gate	. . . .	B2
Shifnal Rd	. . . .	A3
Sixth Ave	. . . .	A1
Southwater Way	. . . .	B1
Spout Lane	. . . .	C1
Spout Mound	. . . . .	B1
Spout Way	. . . .	C1
Stafford Court	. . . . .	B3
Stafford Park	. . . . . .	B3
Stirchley Ave	. . . . . .	C3
Stone Row	. . . .	C1
Telford Bridge		
Retail Park	. . . . . .	A1
Telford Central		
Station 🚆	. . . . . .	A3
Telford Centre, The	. .	B2
Telford International		
Centre	. . . .	C2
Telford Way	. . . . . .	A3
Third Ave	. . . .	A2
Town Park	. . . .	C2
Town Park Visitor		
Centre	. . . .	C2
Town Sports Club	. . .	C2
Walker House	. . . . .	B2
Wellswood Ave	. . . .	A2
West Centre Way	. . .	B1
Withywood Drive	. . .	C1
Woodhouse Central	. .	B2
Yates Way	. . . .	A1

Torquay

Abbey Rd	. . . .	B2
Alexandra Rd	. . . . . .	A2
Alpine Rd	. . . .	B3
Aqualand ⚓	. . . . . .	C3
Ash Hill Rd	. . . .	A2
Babbacombe Rd	. . . .	B3
Bampfylde Rd	. . . . .	B1
Barton Rd	. . . .	A1
Beacon Quay	. . . . . .	C2
Belgrave Rd	. . . . .	A1/B1
Belmont Rd	. . . .	A3
Berea Rd	. . . .	A3
Braddons Hill		
Rd East	. . . .	B3
Bronshill Rd	. . . . . .	A2
Castle Rd	. . . .	A2
Cavern Rd	. . . .	A3
Central 🚌	. . . .	B2
Chatsworth Rd	. . . . .	A2
Chestnut Ave	. . . . . .	B1
Church St	. . . .	A1
Civic Offices 🏛	. . . .	A2
Coach Station	. . . . .	A1
Corbyn Head	. . . . . .	C1
Croft Hill	. . . .	B1
Croft Rd	. . . .	B1
Daddyhole Plain	. . . .	C3
East St	. . . .	A1
Egerton Rd	. . . .	A3
Ellacombe		
Church Rd	. . . . . .	A3
Ellacombe Rd	. . . . . .	A2
Falkland Rd	. . . .	B1
Fleet St	. . . .	B2
Fleet Walk Shopping		
Centre	. . . .	B2
Grafton Rd	. . . .	B3
Haldon Pier	. . . . . .	C2
Hatfield Rd	. . . .	A2
Highbury Rd	. . . . . .	A3
Higher Warberry Rd	. .	A3
Hillesdon Rd	. . . . . .	B3
Hollywood Bowl	. . . .	B3
Hoxton Rd	. . . .	A3
Hunsdon Rd	. . . . . .	B3
Information Ctr ⓘ	. . .	B2
Inner Harbour	. . . . .	C3
Kenwyn Rd	. . . .	A3
Laburnum St	. . . . . .	A1
Law Courts	. . . .	A2
Library	. . . .	B2
Lime Ave	. . . .	B1
Living Coasts 🐧	. . . .	C3
Lower Warberry Rd	. .	B3
Lucius St	. . . .	B1
Lymington Rd	. . . . . .	A1
Magdalene Rd	. . . . .	A1
Marina	. . . .	C2
Market St	. . . .	B2
Meadfoot Lane	. . . . .	C3
Meadfoot Rd	. . . . . .	C3
Melville St	. . . .	B2
Middle Warberry Rd	. .	B3
Mill Lane	. . . .	A1
Montpellier Rd	. . . . .	B3
Morgan Ave	. . . . . .	A1
Museum Rd	. . . .	B3
Newton Rd	. . . .	A1
Oakhill Rd	. . . .	A1
Outer Harbour	. . . . .	C2
Parkhill Rd	. . . .	C3
Pavilion	. . . .	C2
Pimlico	. . . .	B2
Police Station 🏛	. . . .	A1
Post Office 🏤	. . . A2/B1/B2
Princes Rd	. . . .	A3
Princes Rd East	. . . .	A3
Princes Rd West	. . . .	A3
Princess Theatre 🎭	. .	C2
Princess Gdns	. . . . .	C2
Princess Pier	. . . . . .	C2
Rathmore Rd	. . . . . .	B1
Recreation Grd	. . . . .	B1
Riviera Centre		
International	. . . . . .	B1
Rock End Ave	. . . . . .	C3
Rock Rd	. . . .	B2
Rock Walk	. . . .	B2
Rosehill Rd	. . . .	A3
St Efride's Rd	. . . . .	A1
St John's ⛪	. . . . . .	B3
St Luke's Rd	. . . . . .	B2
St Luke's Rd North	. .	B2
St Luke's Rd South	. .	B2
St Marychurch Rd	. .	A2
Scarborough Rd	. . . .	B1
Shedden Hill	. . . . . .	B2
South Pier	. . . .	C2
South St	. . . .	A1
Spanish Barn	. . . . . .	B1
Stitchill Rd	. . . .	B3
Strand	. . . .	B3
Sutherland Rd	. . . . .	B3
Teignmouth Rd	. . . . .	A1
Temperance St	. . . . .	B2
The King's Drive	. . . .	B1
The Terrace	. . . . . .	B3
Thurlow Rd	. . . .	A1
Tor Bay	. . . .	B1
Tor Church Rd	. . . . .	A1
Tor Hill Rd	. . . .	A1
Torbay Rd	. . . .	B2
Torquay Museum 🏛	. .	B3
Torquay Station 🚆	. .	C1
Torre Abbey		
Mansion 🏰	. . . . .	B1
Torre Abbey		
Meadows	. . . . . .	B1
Torre Abbey Sands	. .	B1
Torwood Gdns	. . . . .	B3
Torwood St	. . . . . .	C3
Union Square	. . . . . .	A2
Union St	. . . .	A1
Upton Hill	. . . .	A2
Upton Park	. . . .	A1
Upton Rd	. . . .	A1
Vanehill Rd	. . . .	C3
Vansittart Rd	. . . . . .	A1
Vaughan Parade	. . . .	C2
Victoria Parade	. . . .	C3
Victoria Rd	. . . .	A2
Warberry Rd West	. .	B2
Warren Rd	. . . .	B2
Windsor Rd	. . . . A2/A3
Woodville Rd	. . . . . .	A3

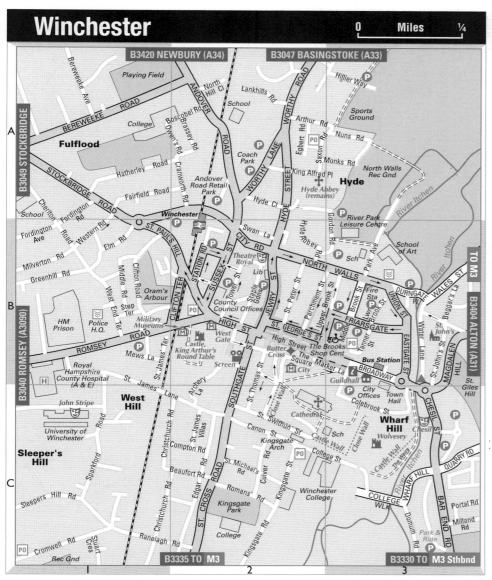

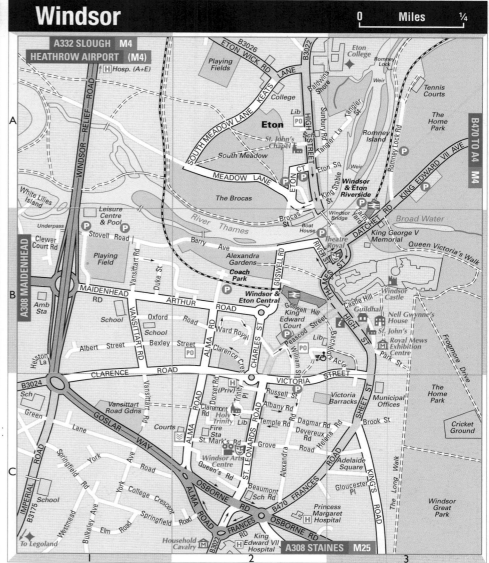

Winchester

Andover Rd A2	Cranworth Rd A2	Mews La B1
Andover Road	Cromwell Rd C1	Middle Brook St B3
Retail Park A2	Culver Rd C2	Middle Rd B1
Archery La C2	Domum Rd C3	Military Museums 🏛 . B2
Arthur Rd A2	Durngate Pl B3	Milland Rd C3
Bar End Rd C3	Eastgate St B3	Milverton Rd B1
Beaufort Rd C2	Edgar Rd C2	Monks Rd A3
Beggar's La B3	Egbert Rd A2	North Hill Cl A2
Bereweeke Ave A1	Elm Rd B1	North Walls B2
Bereweeke Rd A1	Fairfield Rd A1	North Walls
Boscobel Rd A2	Fire Station B3	Rec Gnd A3
Brassey Rd A2	Fordington Ave B1	Nuns Rd A3
Broadway B3	Fordington Rd A1	Oram's Arbour B1
Brooks Shopping	Friarsgate B3	Owen's Rd A2
Centre, The B3	Gordon Rd B3	Parchment St B2
Bus Station B3	Greenhill Rd B1	Park & Ride C3
Butter Cross ✦ B2	Guildhall 🏛 B3	Park Ave B3
Canon St C2	HM Prison B1	Parchment St B2
Castle Wall C2/C3	Hatherley Rd A1	Playing Field A1
Castle, King Arthur's	High St B2	Police H.Q. 🚓 B1
Round Table 🏛 B2	Hillier Way A3	Police Station 🚓 . . . B3
Cathedral † B2	Hyde Abbey	Portal Rd C3
Cheriton Rd A1	(Remains) † A2	Post Office 🅿 . . . .
Chesil St C3	Hyde Abbey Rd A2	. . . . A2/B2/B3/C1/C2
Chesil Theatre 🎭 C3	Hyde Cl. A2	Quarry Rd B3
Christchurch Rd C1	Hyde St A2	Ranelagh Rd C1
City Museum 🏛 B2	Information Ctr 🛈 . . . B3	River Park Leisure
City Offices C3	Jewry St B2	Centre B3
City Rd B2	John Stripe	Romans' Rd C2
Clifton Rd B1	Theatre 🎭 C1	Romsey Rd B2
Clifton Terr B2	King Alfred Pl A2	Royal Hampshire County
Close Wall C2/C3	Kingsgate Arch C2	Hospital (A & E) 🏥 . . B1
Coach Park A2	Kingsgate Park C2	St Cross Rd C2
Colebrook St C3	Kingsgate Rd C2	St George's St B2
College St C2	Kingsgate St C2	St Giles Hill C3
College Walk C3	Lankhills Rd A2	St James' La B1
Compton Rd C2	Library B2	St James' Terr B1
County Council B2	Lower Brook St B3	St James Villas C2
	Magdalen Hill B3	St John's B3
	Market La B2	St John's St B3
		St Michael's Rd C2

St Paul's Hill B1	
St Peter St B2	
St Swithun St C2	
St Thomas St C2	
Saxon Rd A2	
School of Art B3	
Screen 🎬 B2	
Sleepers Hill Rd C1	
Southgate St B2	
Sparkford Rd C1	
Staple Gdns B2	
Station Rd B2	
Step Terr B1	
Stockbridge Rd A1	
Stuart Cres C1	
Sussex St B2	
Swan Lane B2	
Tanner St B3	
The Square B2	
The Weirs C3	
Theatre Royal 🎭 B2	
Tower St B2	
Town Hall C3	
Union St B3	
University of	
Winchester C1	
Upper Brook St B3	
Wales St B3	
Water Lane B3	
West End Terr B1	
West Gate 🏛 B2	
Western Rd B1	
Wharf Hill C3	
Winchester College . . C2	
Winchester 🚉 A2	
Wolvesey Castle 🏛 . . . C3	
Worthy Lane A2	
Worthy Rd A2	

Windsor

Adelaide Sq C3	Elm Rd C1	King Stable St A2
Albany Rd C2	Eton College ✦ A3	Leisure Centre
Albert St B1	Eton Ct A2	& Pool B1
Alexandra Gdns B2	Eton Sq. A2	Library B2
Alexandra Rd C2	Eton Wick Rd A2	Maidenhead Rd B1
Alma Rd B2	Farm Yard B3	Meadow La. A2
Ambulance Station . . B1	Fire Station C2	Municipal Offices . . . C3
Arthur Rd B2	Frances Rd C2	Nell Gwynne's
Bachelors Acre B3	Frogmore Dr B3	House 🏛 B3
Barry Ave B2	Gloucester Pl C3	Osborne Rd C2
Beaumont Rd C2	Goslar Way C1	Oxford Rd B1
Bexley St B1	Goswell Hill B2	Park St B2
Boat House A2	Goswell Rd B2	Peascod St B2
Brocas St A2	Green La. C1	Police Station 🚓 . . . C2
Brook St C3	Grove Rd C2	Post Office 🅿 A2/B2
Bulkeley Ave C1	Guildhall 🏛 B3	Princess Margaret
Castle Hill B3	Helena Rd C2	Hospital 🏥 C2
Charles St B2	Helston La B1	Queen Victoria's
Claremont Rd C2	High St A2/B3	Walk B3
Clarence Cr B2	Holy Trinity 🏛 C2	Queen's Rd C2
Clarence Rd B1	Hospital (Private) 🏥 . . C2	River St A2
Clewer Court Rd B1	Household	Romney Island A3
Coach Park B2	Cavalry 🏛 C2	Romney Lock A3
College Cr C1	Imperial Rd C1	Romney Lock Rd A3
Courts C2	Information Ctr 🛈 . . . B3	Royal Mews Exhibition
Cricket Ground C3	Keats La A2	Centre 🏛 B3
Dagmar Rd C2	King Edward Ct B2	Russell St C2
Datchet Rd B3	King Edward VII Ave . . A3	St John's 🏛 B3
Devereux Rd C2	King Edward VII	St John's Chapel 🏛 . . A2
Dorset Rd C2	Hospital 🏥 C2	St Leonards Rd C2
Duke St. B1	King George V	St Mark's Rd C2
	Memorial B3	Sheet St C3
	King's Rd C3	South Meadow A2

South Meadow La . . . A3	
Springfield Rd C1	
Stovell Rd B1	
Sunbury Rd A2	
Tangier La. A2	
Tangier St A3	
Temple Rd C2	
Thames St B3	
The Brocas A2	
The Home Park . . . A3/C3	
The Long Walk C3	
Theatre Royal 🎭 B3	
Trinity Pl C2	
Vansittart Rd B1/C1	
Vansittart Rd Gdns . . . C1	
Victoria Barracks C2	
Victoria St C2	
Ward Royal B2	
Westmead C1	
White Lilies Island . . . A1	
William St B2	
Windsor Arts	
Centre 🎭 🎬 C2	
Windsor Castle 🏛 . . . B3	
Windsor & Eton	
Central 🚉 B2	
Windsor & Eton	
Riverside 🚉 A3	
Windsor Bridge B3	
Windsor Great Park . . C3	
Windsor Relief Rd . . . A1	
York Ave C1	
York Rd C1	

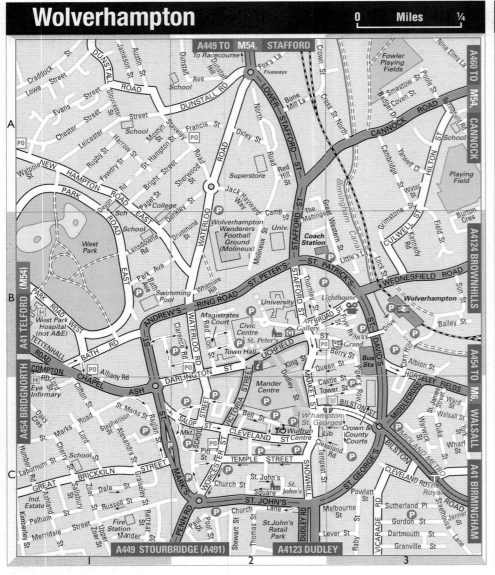

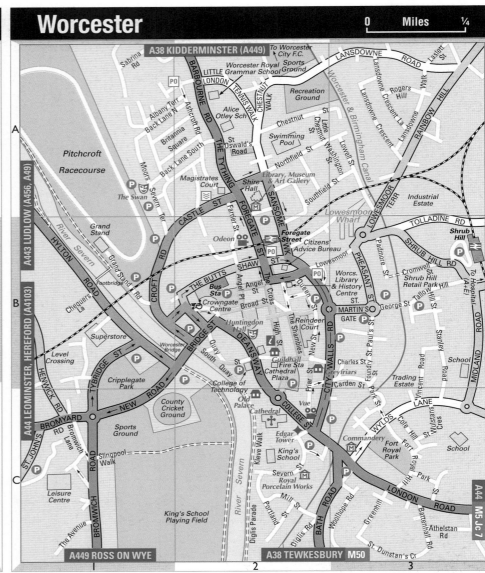

Wolverhampton

Albany Rd B1
Albion St B3
Alexandra St C1
Gallery 🏛 B2
Ashland St C1
Austin St A1
Badger Dr A3
Bailey St B3
Bath Ave B1
Bath Rd B1
Bell St C2
Berry St B3
Bilston Rd C3
Bilston St C3
Birmingham Canal . . . A3
Bone Mill La A2
Bright St A1
Burton Cres B3
Bus Station B3
Cambridge St A3
Camp St B2
Cannock Rd A3
Castle St C2
Chapel Ash C1
Cherry St C1
Chester St A1
Church La C2
Church St C2
Civic Centre B2
Clarence Rd B2
Cleveland Rd C2
Cleveland St C2
Clifton St C1
Coach Station B2
Compton Rd B1
Corn Hill B3
Coven St A3
Craddock St A1
Cross St North A2
Crown & County
  Courts C3
Crown St A2
Culwell St B3
Dale St C1
Darlington St C1
Dartmouth St C3
Devon Rd A1
Drummond St B2
Dudley Rd C2
Dudley St B2

Duke St C3
Dunkley St B1
Dunstall Ave A2
Dunstall Hill A2
Dunstall Rd A1/A2
Evans St A1
Fawdry St A1
Field St B3
Fire Station C1
Fiveways (r'about) . . . A2
Fowler Playing
  Fields A3
Fox's La A2
Francis St C1
Fryer St B3
Gloucester St A1
Gordon St C3
Graiseley St C1
Grand 🎭 B3
Granville St C3
Great Western St A2
Great Brickkiln St C1
Grimstone St B3
Gt. Hampton St A1
Harrow St A1
Hilton St A3
Horseley Fields C3
Humber Rd C1
Jack Hayward Way A2
Jameson St A1
Jenner St C3
Kennedy Rd B3
Kimberley St C1
King St B2
Laburnum St C1
Lansdowne Rd B1
Leicester St A1
Lever St C3
Library B2
Lichfield St B2
Little's La B3
Lock St B3
Lord St C1
Lowe St A1
Lower Stafford St A2
Magistrates Court B2
Mander Centre C2
Mander St C1
Market St B2
Market C2

Melbourne St C3
Merridale St C1
Middlecross C3
Molineux St B2
Mostyn St A1
New Hampton
  Rd East A1
Nine Elms La A3
North Rd A2
Oaks Cres C1
Oxley St A2
Paget St A1
Park Ave B1
Park Rd East A1
Park Road West B1
Paul St C2
Pelham St C1
Penn Rd C2
Piper's Row B3
Pitt St C2
Police Station 🚓 C3
Pool St C2
Poole St A3
Post Office 📮
  . . . . A1/A2/B2/B2/C2
Powlett St C3
Queen St B2
Raby St C3
Raglan St C1
Railway Dr B3
Red Hill St A2
Red Lion St B2
Retreat St C1
Ring Rd B2
Rugby St A1
Russell St C1
St. Andrew's B1
St. David's B3
St. George's C2
St. James St C3
St. John's C2
St. John's
  Park C2
St. John's Square C2
St. Mark's C1
St. Marks Rd C1
St. Marks St C1
St. Patrick's B2
St. Peter's B2
St. Peter's 🏛 B2
Salisbury St C1

Salop St C2
School St C2
Sherwood St A2
Smestow St A3
Snowhill C2
Springfield Rd A3
Stafford St B2
Staveley Rd A1
Steelhouse La C3
Stephenson St C1
Stewart St C2
Sun St B3
Sutherland Pl C3
Tempest St C2
Temple St C2
Tettenhall Rd B1
The Maltings B2
The Royal (Metro) C3
Thomas St C1
Thornley St B2
Tower St C2
Town Hall B2
University B2
Upper Zoar St C1
Vicarage Rd C3
Victoria St C2
Walpole St A1
Walsall St C3
Ward St C2
Warwick St C3
Water St A3
Waterloo Rd B2
Wednesfield Rd B3
West Park
  (not A&E) 🏥 B1
West Park Swimming
  Pool B1
Wolverhampton
  St. Georges (Metro) . C2
Wharf St C3
Whitmore Hill B2
Wolverhampton ⇌ . . B3
Wolverhampton
  Wanderers Football
  Gnd. (Molineux) . . . B2
Worcester St C2
Wulfrun Centre C2
Yarwell Cl A3
York St C3
Zoar St C1

Worcester

Albany Terr A1
Alice Otley School . . . A2
Angel Pl B2
Angel St B2
Ashcroft Rd A2
Athelstan Rd C3
Back Lane North A1
Back Lane South A1
Barbourne Rd A2
Bath Rd C2
Battenhall Rd C3
Bridge St B2
Britannia Sq A1
Broad St B2
Bromwich La C1
Bromwich Rd C1
Bromyard Rd C1
Bus Station B2
Carden St B3
Castle St A2
Cathedral † C2
Cathedral Plaza B2
Charles St B3
Chequers La B1
Chestnut St A2
Chestnut Walk A2
Citizens' Advice
  Bureau B2
City Walls Rd B2
Cole Hill C3
College of
  Technology B2
College St C2
Commandery 🏛 C3
County Cricket
  Ground C1

Cripplegate Park B1
Croft Rd B1
Cromwell St B3
Crowngate Centre . . . B2
Deansway B2
Diglis Pde C2
Diglis Parade C2
Edgar Tower ♦ C2
Farrier St B2
Fire Station B2
Foregate St B2
Foregate Street ⇌ . . . B2
Fort Royal Hill C3
Fort Royal Park C3
Foundry St B2
Friar St C2
George St B3
Grand Stand Rd B1
Greenhill C3
Greyfriars 🏛 B2
Guildhall 🏛 B2
Henwick Rd B1
High St B2
Hill St B3
Huntingdon Hall 🎭 . . B2
Hylton Rd B1
Information Ctr ℹ B2
King's School C2
King's School
  Playing Field C2
Kleve Walk C2
Lansdowne Cr A3
Lansdowne Rd A3
Lansdowne Walk A3
Laslett St B3
Leisure Centre A3
Library, Museum &
  Art Gallery 🏛 A2

Little Chestnut St A2
Little London A2
London Rd C3
Lowell St A3
Lowesmoor B2
Lowesmoor Terr A3
Lowesmoor Wharf . . . A3
Magistrates Court B2
Midland Rd B3
Mill St C2
Moors Severn Terr . . . A1
New Rd C1
New St B2
Northfield St A2
Odeon 🎬 B2
Old Palace 🏛 B2
Padmore St B3
Park St C3
Pheasant St B3
Pitchcroft
  Racecourse A1
Police Station 🚓 A2
Portland St C2
Post Office 📮 . A1/A2/B2
Quay St B2
Queen St B2
Rainbow Hill A3
Recreation Ground . . . A2
Reindeer Court B2
Rogers Hill A3
Royal Porcelain
  Works 🏛 C2
Sabrina Rd A1
St Dunstan's Cr C3
St John's C1
St Martin's Gate B3
St Oswald's Rd A2
St Paul's St B3

St Wulstans Cr C3
Sansome Walk A2
Severn St C2
Shaw St B2
Shire Hall A2
Shrub Hill ⇌ B3
Shrub Hill Retail Park . B3
Shrub Hill Rd B3
Slingpool Walk C1
South Quay B2
Southfield St A2
Sports Ground A2/C3
Stanley Rd B3
Swimming Pool A2
Swan, The 🎭 A1
Tallow Hill B3
Tennis Walk A2
The Avenue C1
The Butts B2
The Cross B2
The Shambles B2
The Tything A2
Tolladine Rd B3
Tybridge St B1
Vincent Rd B3
Vue 🎬 C2
Washington St A3
Woolhope Rd C3
Worcester Bridge B2
Worcester Library &
  History Centre B3
Worcester Royal
  Grammar School . . . A2
Wylds La C3

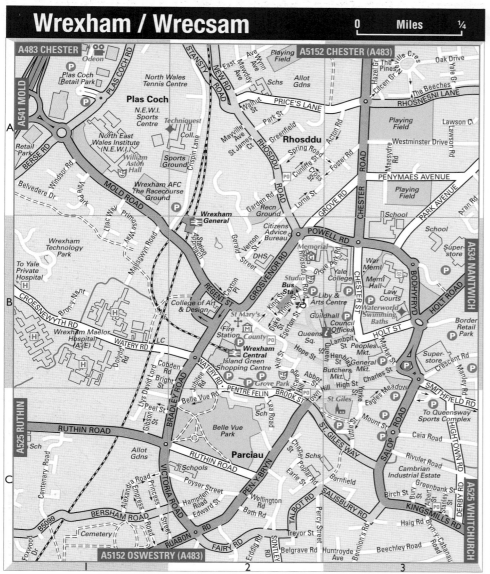

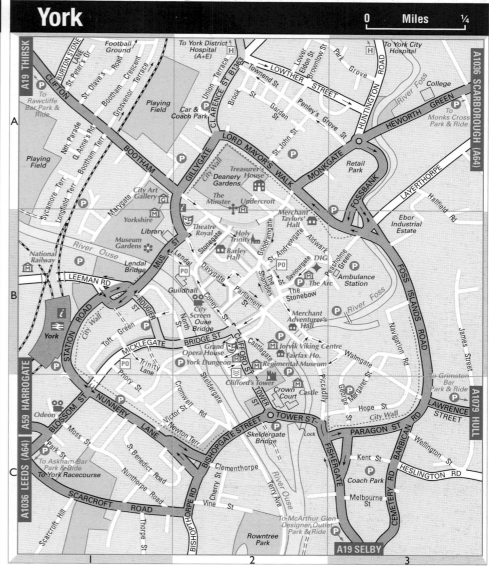

Wrexham / Wrecsam

York

Heathrow Airport (London)

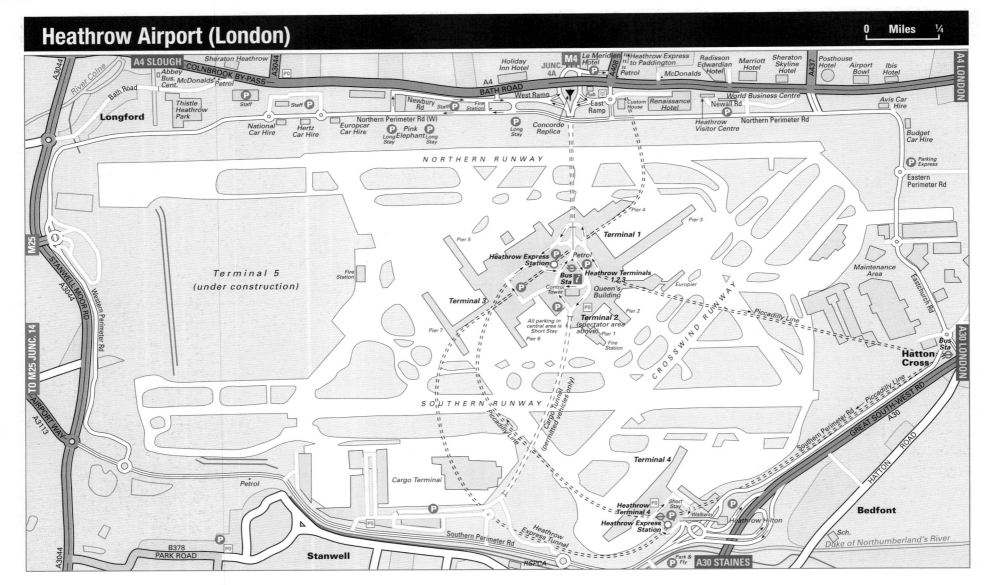

Gatwick Airport (London)

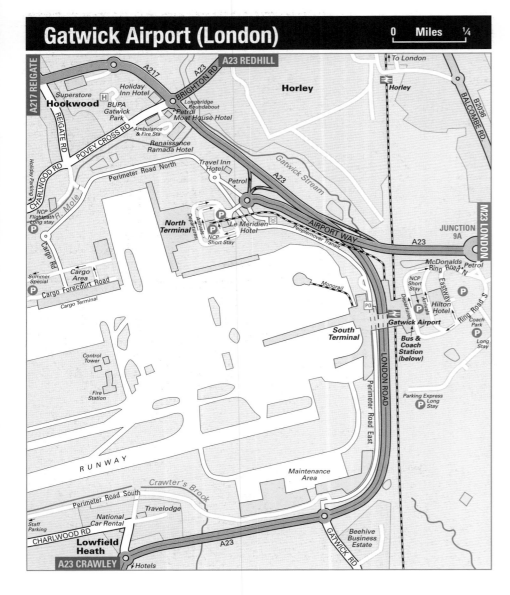

Manchester Airport

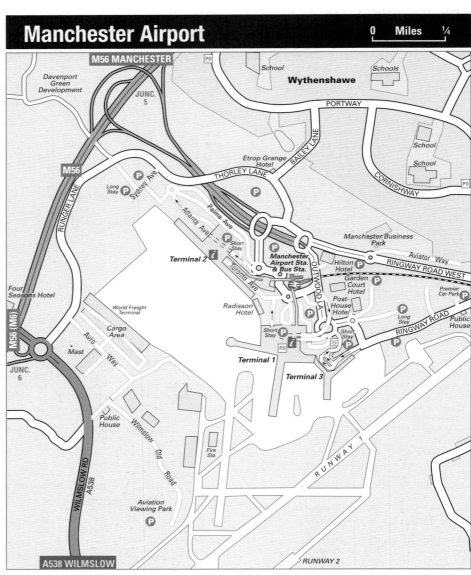

Dover road map page 55 • **Felixstowe** road map page 108 • **Portsmouth** road map page 33 • **Southampton** road map page 32

383

Port of Dover

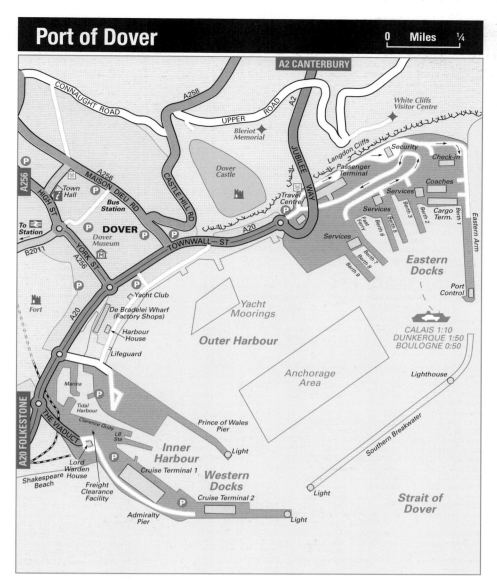

Port of Felixstowe

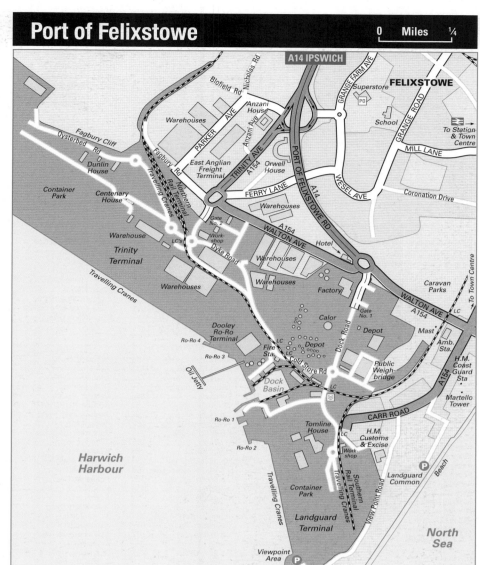

Portsmouth-Continental Ferry Port

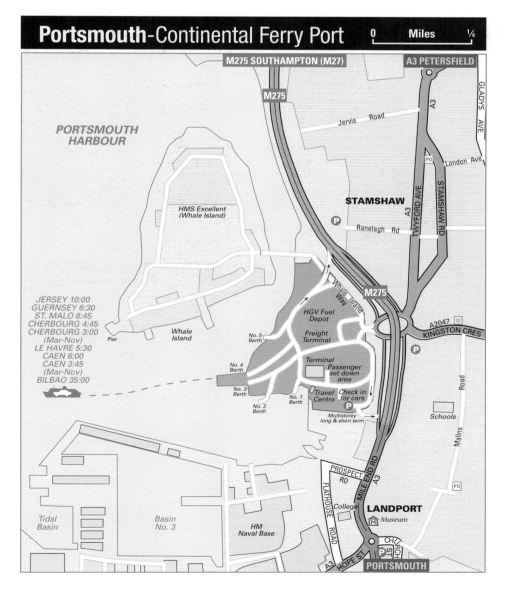

Port of Southampton

Index to road maps of Britain

Abbreviations used in the index

Aberdeen	Aberdeen City	Clack	Clackmannanshire
Aberds	Aberdeenshire	Conwy	Conwy
Ald	Alderney	Corn	Cornwall
Anglesey	Isle of Anglesey	Cumb	Cumbria
Angus	Angus	Darl	Darlington
Argyll	Argyll and Bute	Denb	Denbighshire
Bath	Bath and North East Somerset	Derby	City of Derby
Beds	Bedfordshire	Derbys	Derbyshire
Bl Gwent	Blaenau Gwent	Devon	Devon
Blkburn	Blackburn with Darwen	Dorset	Dorset
Blkpool	Blackpool	Dumfries	Dumfries and Galloway
Bmouth	Bournemouth	Dundee	Dundee City
Borders	Scottish Borders	Durham	Durham
Brack	Bracknell	E Ayrs	East Ayrshire
Bridgend	Bridgend	E Dunb	East Dunbartonshire
Brighton	City of Brighton and Hove	E Loth	East Lothian
Bristol	City and County of Bristol	E Renf	East Renfrewshire
Bucks	Buckinghamshire	E Sus	East Sussex
Caerph	Caerphilly	E Yorks	East Riding of Yorkshire
Cambs	Cambridgeshire	Edin	City of Edinburgh
Cardiff	Cardiff	Essex	Essex
Carms	Carmarthenshire	Falk	Falkirk
Ceredig	Ceredigion	Fife	Fife
Ches	Cheshire	Flint	Flintshire
		Glasgow	City of Glasgow
		Glos	Gloucestershire
		Gtr Man	Greater Manchester

Guern	Guernsey	N Som	North Somerset
Gwyn	Gwynedd	N Yorks	North Yorkshire
Halton	Halton	NE Lincs	North East Lincolnshire
Hants	Hampshire	Neath	Neath Port Talbot
Hereford	Herefordshire	Newport	City and County of Newport
Herts	Hertfordshire	Norf	Norfolk
Highld	Highland	Northants	Northamptonshire
Hrtlpl	Hartlepool	Northumb	Northumberland
Hull	Hull	Nottingham	City of Nottingham
I o M	Isle of Man	Notts	Nottinghamshire
I o W	Isle of Wight	Orkney	Orkney
Invclyd	Inverclyde	Oxon	Oxfordshire
Jersey	Jersey	P'boro	Peterborough
Kent	Kent	Pembs	Pembrokeshire
Lancs	Lancashire	Perth	Perth and Kinross
Leicester	City of Leicester	Plym	Plymouth
Leics	Leicestershire	Poole	Poole
Lincs	Lincolnshire	Powys	Powys
London	Greater London	Ptsmth	Portsmouth
Luton	Luton	Reading	Reading
M Keynes	Milton Keynes	Redcar	Redcar and Cleveland
M Tydf	Merthyr Tydfil	Renfs	Renfrewshire
M'bro	Middlesbrough	Rhondda	Rhondda Cynon Taff
Medway	Medway	Rutland	Rutland
Mers	Merseyside	S Ayrs	South Ayrshire
Midloth	Midlothian	S Glos	South Gloucestershire
Mon	Monmouthshire	S Lnrk	South Lanarkshire
Moray	Moray	S Yorks	South Yorkshire
N Ayrs	North Ayrshire	Scilly	Scilly
N Lincs	North Lincolnshire	Shetland	Shetland
N Lnrk	North Lanarkshire		

Shrops	Shropshire	V Glam	The Vale of Glamorgan
Slough	Slough	W Berks	West Berkshire
Som	Somerset	W Dunb	West Dunbartonshire
Soton	Southampton	W Isles	Western Isles
Staffs	Staffordshire	W Loth	West Lothian
Sthend	Southend-on-Sea	W Mid	West Midlands
Stirl	Stirling	W Sus	West Sussex
Stockton	Stockton-on-Tees	W Yorks	West Yorkshire
Stoke	Stoke-on-Trent	Warks	Warwickshire
Suff	Suffolk	Warr	Warrington
Sur	Surrey	Wilts	Wiltshire
Swansea	Swansea	Windsor	Windsor and Maidenhead
T & W	Tyne and Wear	Wokingham	Wokingham
Telford	Telford and Wrekin	Worcs	Worcestershire
Thamesdown	Thamesdown	Wrex	Wrexham
Thurrock	Thurrock	York	City of York
Torbay	Torbay		
Torf	Torfaen		

How to use the index

Example

Muddlebridge Devon **40 G4**
- grid square
- page number
- county or unitary authority

Places of special interest are highlighted in *magenta*

Allison Lane End ER Yorks 209 B9
Allithwaite Cumb 211 D7
Allmore Green Staffs 151 F7
Alloa Clack 279 C7
Allonby Cumb 229 C7
Allostock Ches 184 G2
Alloway S Ayrs 257 F8
Allowenshay Som'set 28 E5
Allscott Telford 150 G2
Allt Carms 75 E9
Allt na h-Airbhe H'land 307 K6
Alltami Flints 166 B3
Alltbeithe H'land 290 C2
Alltchaorunn H'land 284 B5
Alltmawr Powys 95 B11
Alltnacaillich H'land 308 E4
Allt-na-giubhsaich Aberds 292 E4
Allt-nan-sùgh H'land 295 C11
Alltrech Arg/Bute 289 F8
Alltsigh H'land 290 B6
Alltwalis Carms 93 E8
Alltwen Neath P Talb 76 E2
Alltyblaca Ceredig'n 93 B10
Allt-yr-yn Newp 59 B9
Allweston Dorset 29 E11
Allwood Green Suffolk 125 C10
Alma Park Estate Lincs 155 B8
Almagill Dumf/Gal 238 B3
Almeley Heref'd 114 G6
Almeley Wooton Heref'd 114 G6
Almer Dorset 18 B4
Almholme S Yorks 198 F5
Almhouse Green Essex 106 E5
Almington Staffs 150 C4
Alminstone Cross Devon 24 C5
Almodington W Sussex 22 D4
Almondbank Perth/Kinr 286 E4
Almondbury W Yorks 197 D7
Almondsbury S Glos 60 C6
Almondvale W Loth 269 B10
Alne N Yorks 215 F9
Alne End Warwick 118 F2
Alness H'land 300 C6
Alnessferry H'land 300 C6
Alney Island Glos 80 B4
Alnham Northum 263 G11
Alnmouth Northum 264 G6
Alnwick Northum 264 G5
Alperton London 67 C7
Alphamstone Essex 107 D7
Alpheton Suffolk 125 G7
Alphington Devon 14 D4
Alpington Norfolk 142 C5
Alport Derby 170 C2
Alpraham Ches 167 D9
Alresford Essex 107 G11
Alrewas Staffs 152 F3
Alsager Ches 168 E4
Alsagers Bank Staffs 168 F4
Alsop en le Dale Derby 169 D11
Alston Cumb 231 B10
Alston Devon 28 G4
Alston Sutton Som'set 44 C2
Alstone Glos 99 G8
Alstone Glos 99 E9
Alstone Som'set 43 D10
Alstonefield Staffs 169 D10
Alswear Devon 26 C2
Alt Hill Gtr Man 196 G2
Altandhu H'land 307 H4
Altanduin H'land 311 G2
Altarnun Cornw'l 11 E10
Altass H'land 309 J4
Altdargue Aberds 293 C7
Alterwall H'land 310 C6
Altham Lancs 203 G11
Althorne Essex 88 F6
Althorp House, Great Brington Northants 120 D3
Althorpe N Lincs 199 F10
Alticry Dumf/Gal 236 D4
Altnabreac Station H'land 310 E4
Altnacealgach Hotel H'land 307 H7
Altnacraig Arg/Bute 289 G10
Altnafeadh H'land 284 B6
Altnaharra H'land 308 F5
Altofts W Yorks 197 C11
Alton Derby 170 C5
Alton Hants 49 F8
Alton Staffs 169 G9
Alton Barnes Wilts 62 G6
Alton Pancras Dorset 29 G11
Alton Priors Wilts 62 G6
Alton Towers Staffs 169 G9
Altonhill E Ayrs 257 B10
Altonside Moray 302 D2
Altour H'land 290 E4
Altrincham Gtr Man 184 D3
Altrua H'land 290 E4
Altskeith Stirl 285 G8
Altyre Ho. Moray 301 D10
Alum Rock W Midlands 134 F2
Alva Clack 279 B7
Alvanley Ches 183 G7
Alvaston Derby C 153 C7
Alvechurch Worcs 117 C10
Alvecote Warwick 134 C4
Alvediston Wilts 31 C7
Alveley Shrops 132 G5
Alverdiscott Devon 25 B8
Alverstoke Hants 21 B8
Alverstone I/Wight 21 D7
Alverthorpe W Yorks 197 C10
Alverton Notts 172 G3
Alves Moray 301 C11
Alvescot Oxon 82 E3
Alveston S Glos 60 B6
Alveston Warwick 118 F4
Alveston Down S Glos 60 B6
Alvie H'land 291 C10
Alvingham Lincs 190 C5
Alvington Devon 24 C6
Alvington Glos 79 E10
Alwalton Peterbro 138 D2
Alway Newp 59 B10
Alwinton Northum 251 B10
Alwoodley W Yorks 205 E11
Alwoodley Gates W Yorks 206 E2
Alwoodley Park W Yorks 205 E11
Alwyn Lawn Bucks 84 C3
Alyth Perth/Kinr 286 C6
Am Baile W Isles 297 K3
Am Buth Arg/Bute 289 G10
Amatnatua H'land 309 K4
Ambaston Derby 153 C8
Amber Hill Lincs 174 F2
Ambergate Derby 170 E5
Amberley Glos 80 E5
Amberley W Sussex 35 E8
Amble Northum 253 C7
Amblecote Worcs 133 F7
Ambler Thorn W Yorks 196 B5
Ambleside Cumb 221 E7
Ambleston Pembs 91 F10
Ambrosden Oxon 83 B10
Amcotts N Lincs 199 E11
Amen Corner Brackn'l 65 F10
American Adventure, Ilkeston Derby 170 G6
American Air Museum, Duxford Cambs 105 B9
Amersham Bucks 85 F7
Amersham Common Bucks 85 F7
Amersham Old Town Bucks 85 F7
Amersham on the Hill Bucks 85 F7
Amerton Staffs 151 D9
Amerton Working Farm, Stowe-by-Chartley Staffs 151 D9
Amesbury Wilts 47 E7
Ameysford Dorset 31 G9
Amington Staffs 134 C4
Amisfield Dumf/Gal 248 G2
Amlwch Angl 178 C6
Amlwch Port Angl 179 C7
Ammanford = Rhydaman Carms 75 C10
Amod Arg/Bute 255 D8
Amotherby N Yorks 216 E5
Ampfield Hants 32 C6
Ampleforth N Yorks 215 D11
Ampney Crucis Glos 81 E9
Ampney St. Mary Glos 81 E9
Ampney St. Peter Glos 81 E9
Amport Hants 47 E9
Ampthill Beds 103 D10
Ampton Suffolk 125 C7
Amroth Pembs 73 D11
Amulree Perth/Kinr 286 D2
Amwell Herts 85 C11
An Caol H'land 298 D6
An Cnoc W Isles 304 E6
An Gleann Ur W Isles 304 E6
An Leth Meadhanach W Isles 297 K3
An t-Ob = Leverburgh W Isles 296 C6
Anagach H'land 301 G10
Anaheilt H'land 289 C10
Anancaun H'land 299 C10
Ancarraig H'land 300 G4
Ancaster Lincs 173 G7
Anchor Shrops 130 G3
Anchor Corner Norfolk 141 D10
Anchor Street Norfolk 160 E6
Anchorsholme Blackp'l 202 E2
Ancoats Gtr Man 184 B5
Ancroft Northum 273 F10
Ancrum Scot Borders 262 E4
Ancton W Sussex 35 G7
Ancumtoun Orkney 312 C8
Anderby Lincs 191 F8
Anderby Creek Lincs 191 F8
Andersea Som'set 43 G10
Andersfield Som'set 43 G8
Anderson Dorset 18 B3
Anderton Ches 183 F10
Anderton Cornw'l 7 E8
Anderton's Mill Lancs 194 E4
Andover Hants 47 D11
Andover Down Hants 47 D11
Andoversford Glos 81 B8
Andreas I/Man 192 C5
Anerley London 67 F10
Anfield Mersey 182 C5
Angarrack Cornw'l 2 B3
Angarrick Cornw'l 3 B7
Angelbank Shrops 115 B11
Angersleigh Som'set 27 D11
Angerton Cumb 238 F6
Angle Pembs 72 E5
Anglesey Sea Zoo Angl 163 B7
Angmering W Sussex 35 G9
Angram N Yorks 206 D6
Angram N Yorks 223 F7
Anick Northum 241 D11
Anie Stirl 285 F9
Ankerbold Derby 170 B5
Ankerville H'land 301 B8
Anlaby ER Yorks 200 B4
Anlaby Park Kingston/Hull 200 B5
Anmer Norfolk 158 D4
Anmore Hants 33 E11
Anna Valley Hants 47 E10
Annan Dumf/Gal 238 D5
Annaside Cumb 210 B1
Annat Arg/Bute 284 E4
Annat H'land 290 D5
Annat H'land 299 D8
Annbank S Ayrs 257 E10
Anne Hathaway's Cottage, Stratford-upon-Avon Warwick 118 G3
Annesley Notts 171 E8
Annesley Woodhouse Notts 171 E7
Annfield Plain Durham 242 G5
Anniesland Glasg C 267 B10
Annifirth Shetl'd 315 J3
Annis Hill Suffolk 143 F7
Annishader H'land 298 D4
Annitsford Tyne/Wear 243 C7
Ann's Hill Hants 33 G9
Annscroft Shrops 131 B9
Ansdell Lancs 193 B10
Ansdore Kent 54 D6
Ansells End Herts 85 B11
Ansford Som'set 44 G6
Ansley Warwick 134 E5
Ansley Common Warwick 134 E6
Anslow Staffs 152 D4
Anslow Gate Staffs 152 E3
Ansteadbrook Surrey 50 G2
Anstey Hants 49 E8
Anstey Herts 105 E8
Anstey Leics C 135 B11
Anstruther Easter Fife 287 G9
Anstruther Wester Fife 287 G9
Ansty Warwick 135 G7
Ansty Wilts 31 B7
Ansty W Sussex 36 C3
Ansty Coombe Wilts 30 B6
Ansty Cross Dorset 30 G3
Anthill Common Hants 33 E10
Anthony's Surrey 66 G4
Anthorn Cumb 238 F5
Antingham Norfolk 160 C5
Anton's Gowt Lincs 174 F3
Antonshill Falk 279 E7
Antony Cornw'l 7 E7
Antrobus Ches 183 F10
Antron Cornw'l 2 D4
Anvil Green Kent 54 D6
Anwick Lincs 173 E11
Anwoth Dumf/Gal 237 D7
Aonachan H'land 290 E4
Aoradh Arg/Bute 274 G3
Apes Dale Worcs 117 C9
Apethorpe Northants 137 D10
Apeton Staffs 151 F7
Apley Lincs 189 F10
Apperknowle Derby 186 F5
Apperley Glos 99 F7
Apperley Bridge W Yorks 205 F9
Apperley Dene Northum 242 F3
Appersett N Yorks 223 G7
Appin Arg/Bute 289 E11
Appin House Arg/Bute 289 E11
Appleby N Lincs 200 E3
Appleby Magna Leics 134 B6
Appleby Parva Leics 134 B6
Appleby-in-Westmorland Cumb 231 G9
Applecross H'land 299 E7
Applecross Ho. H'land 299 E7
Appledore Devon 27 E9
Appledore Devon 40 G3
Appledore Kent 39 B7
Appledore Heath Kent 54 G2
Appleford Oxon 83 G8
Applegarthtown Dumf/Gal 248 G4
Applehaigh W Yorks 197 E10
Applehouse Hill Windsor 65 C10
Applemore Hants 32 F5
Appleshaw Hants 47 D10
Applethwaite Cumb 229 F11
Appleton Halton 183 D8
Appleton Oxon 82 E6
Appleton Park Warrington 183 E10
Appleton Roebuck N Yorks 207 E7
Appleton Thorn Warrington 183 E10
Appleton Wiske N Yorks 225 E7
Appleton-le-Moors N Yorks 216 B4
Appleton-le-Street N Yorks 216 E4
Appletree Northants 101 B9
Appletreehall Scot Borders 262 F2
Appletreewick N Yorks 213 G11
Appley I/Wight 21 C8
Appley Som'set 27 C9
Appley Bridge Lancs 194 F4
Apse Hill I/Wight 21 E7
Apsey Green Suffolk 126 E5
Apsley Herts 85 E9
Apsley End Beds 104 E2
Apuldram W Sussex 34 G4
Aquhythie Aberds 293 B9
Arabella H'land 301 B8
Arbeadie Aberds 293 D8
Arbeia Roman Fort and Museum Tyne/Wear 243 D9
Arberth = Narberth Pembs 73 C10
Arbirlot Angus 287 C10
Arboll H'land 311 L2
Arborfield Wokingham 65 F9
Arborfield Cross Wokingham 65 F9
Arborfield Garrison Wokingham 65 G9
Arbourthorne S Yorks 186 D5
Arbroath Angus 287 C10
Arbury Cambs 123 E9
Arbuthnott Aberds 293 F9
Archavandra Muir H'land 309 K7
Archdeacon Newton D'lington 224 B5
Archiestown Moray 302 E2
Archnalea H'land 289 C10
Ardachu H'land 309 J6
Ardailly Arg/Bute 255 B7
Ardalanish Arg/Bute 288 H5
Ardallie Aberds 303 F10
Ardalum Ho Arg/Bute 288 F6
Ardamaleish Arg/Bute 275 G11
Ardanaiseig Arg/Bute 284 E4
Ardaneaskan H'land 295 B10
Ardanstur Arg/Bute 275 B9
Ardargie House Hotel Perth/Kinr 286 F4
Ardarroch H'land 295 B10
Ardban H'land 295 B9
Ardbeg Arg/Bute 254 C5
Ardbeg Arg/Bute 266 B1
Ardbeg Arg/Bute 276 E3
Ardbeg Distillery, Port Ellen Arg/Bute 254 C5
Ardcharnich H'land 307 L6
Ardchiavaig Arg/Bute 288 H5
Ardchonnell Arg/Bute 275 B10
Ardchronie H'land 309 L6
Ardchuilk H'land 300 F2
Ardchullarie More Stirl 285 F9
Ardchyle Stirl 285 E9
Ardclach H'land 301 E9
Ard-dhubh H'land 299 E7
Arddleen Powys 148 F5
Ardechvie H'land 290 D3
Ardeley Herts 104 F6
Ardelve H'land 295 C10
Arden Arg/Bute 277 E7
Arden Glasg C 267 D10
Ardencaple Ho Arg/Bute 275 B8
Ardendrain H'land 300 F5
Ardens Grafton Warwick 118 G2
Ardentallen Arg/Bute 289 G10
Ardentinny Arg/Bute 276 D3
Ardentraive Arg/Bute 275 F11
Ardeonaig Stirl 285 D10
Ardersier H'land 301 D7
Ardery H'land 289 C9
Ardessie H'land 307 L5
Ardfern Arg/Bute 275 C9
Ardfernal Arg/Bute 274 F6
Ardgartan Arg/Bute 284 G6
Ardgay H'land 309 K5
Ardglassie Aberds 303 C10
Ardgour H'land 290 G2
Ardgye Moray 301 C11
Ardheslaig H'land 299 D7
Ardiecow Moray 302 C5
Ardinamir Arg/Bute 275 B8
Ardindrean H'land 307 L6
Ardingly W Sussex 36 B4
Ardington Oxon 64 B2
Ardintoul H'land 295 C10
Ardlair Aberds 302 G5
Ardlair H'land 299 B9
Ardlamey Arg/Bute 255 C7
Ardlamont Ho. Arg/Bute 275 G10
Ardlawhill Aberds 303 C8
Ardleigh Essex 107 F10
Ardleigh Green London 68 B4
Ardleigh Heath Essex 107 E10
Ardler Perth/Kinr 286 C6
Ardley Oxon 101 F10
Ardlui Arg/Bute 285 F7
Ardlussa Arg/Bute 275 E7
Ardmair H'land 307 K6
Ardmay Arg/Bute 284 G6
Ardmenish Arg/Bute 274 F6
Ardminish Arg/Bute 255 C7
Ardmolich H'land 289 B9
Ardmore Arg/Bute 289 G9
Ardmore H'land 306 D7
Ardmore H'land 309 L7
Ardnacross Arg/Bute 289 E7
Ardnadam Arg/Bute 276 E3
Ardnagowan Arg/Bute 284 G4
Ardnagrask H'land 300 E5
Ardnarff H'land 295 B10
Ardnastang H'land 289 C10
Ardnave Arg/Bute 274 F3
Ardno Arg/Bute 284 G5
Ardo Aberds 303 F8
Ardo Ho. Aberds 303 G9
Ardoch Arg/Bute 277 F7
Ardoch Perth/Kinr 286 D4
Ardoch Stirl 285 F9
Ardochy House H'land 290 C4
Ardoyne Aberds 302 G6
Ardpatrick Arg/Bute 275 G8
Ardpatrick Ho. Arg/Bute 255 B8
Ardpeaton Arg/Bute 276 D4
Ardradnaig Perth/Kinr 285 C11
Ardrishaig Arg/Bute 275 E9
Ardross Fife 287 G9
Ardross H'land 300 B6
Ardross Castle H'land 300 B6
Ardrossan N Ayrs 266 G4
Ardshave H'land 309 K7
Ardsheal H'land 289 D11
Ardshealach H'land 289 C8
Ardskenish Arg/Bute 274 D4
Ardsley S Yorks 197 F11
Ardslignish H'land 289 C7
Ardtalla Arg/Bute 254 B5
Ardtalnaig Perth/Kinr 285 D11
Ardtaraig Arg/Bute 275 E11
Ardtoe H'land 289 B8
Ardtreck H'land 294 B5
Ardtrostan Perth/Kinr 285 E10
Ardtur Arg/Bute 289 E11
Arduaine Arg/Bute 275 B8
Ardullie H'land 300 C5
Ardvannie H'land 309 L6
Ardvar H'land 306 F6
Ardvasar H'land 295 E8
Ardveich Stirl 285 E10
Ardverikie H'land 291 E7
Ardvorlich Perth/Kinr 285 E10
Ardwell Dumf/Gal 236 E3
Ardwell Moray 302 F3
Ardwell Mains Dumf/Gal 236 E3
Ardwick Gtr Man 184 B5
Areley Kings Worcs 116 C6
Arford Hants 49 F10
Argoed Caerph 77 F11
Argoed Powys 113 E9
Argyll & Sutherland Highlanders Museum (See Stirling Castle) Stirl 278 C5
Arichamish Arg/Bute 275 C10
Arichastlich Arg/Bute 284 D6
Aridhglas Arg/Bute 288 G5
Arieniskill H'land 295 G9
Arileod Arg/Bute 288 D3
Arinacrinachd H'land 299 D7
Arinagour Arg/Bute 288 D4
Arineckaig H'land 299 E9
Arion Orkney 312 G3
Arisaig H'land 295 G8
Ariundle H'land 289 C10
Arivegaig H'land 289 C8
Arivoichallum Arg/Bute 254 C4
Arkendale N Yorks 215 G7
Arkesden Essex 105 E9
Arkholme Lancs 211 E11
Arkle Town N Yorks 223 E10
Arkleby Cumb 229 D8
Arkleside N Yorks 213 C10
Arkleton Dumf/Gal 249 E9
Arkley London 86 F2
Arksey S Yorks 198 F5
Arkwright Town Derby 186 G6
Arle Glos 99 G8
Arlecdon Cumb 219 B10
Arlescote Warwick 101 B7
Arlesey Beds 104 D3
Arleston Telford 150 G3
Arley Ches 183 E11
Arley Green Ches 183 E11
Arlingham Glos 80 C2
Arlington Devon 40 E6
Arlington E Sussex 23 D8
Arlington Glos 81 D10
Arlington Becott Devon 40 E6
Arlington Court Devon 40 E6
Armadale H'land 308 C7
Armadale W Loth 269 B8
Armadale Castle H'land 295 E8
Armathwaite Cumb 230 B6
Arminghall Norfolk 142 C4
Armitage Staffs 151 F11
Armitage Bridge W Yorks 196 E6
Armley W Yorks 205 G11
Armscote Warwick 100 C4
Armston Northants 137 F11
Armthorpe S Yorks 198 G6
Arnabost Arg/Bute 288 D4
Arnaby Cumb 210 C3
Arncliffe N Yorks 213 E8
Arncroach Fife 287 G9
Arndilly Ho. Moray 302 E2
Arne Dorset 18 D5
Arnesby Leics 136 E2
Arnfield Derby 185 B8
Arngask Perth/Kinr 286 F5
Arnisdale H'land 295 D10
Arnish H'land 298 E5
Arniston Engine Midloth 270 C6
Arnol W Isles 304 D5
Arnold ER Yorks 209 E8
Arnold Notts 171 F9
Arnolfini Gallery Bristol 60 E5
Arno's Vale Bristol 60 E6
Arnprior Stirl 278 B2
Arnside Cumb 211 D9
Aros Mains Arg/Bute 289 E7
Arowry Wrex 149 B9
Arpafeelie H'land 300 D6
Arpinge Kent 55 F7
Arpinge Kent 55 F8
Arrad Foot Cumb 210 C6
Arram ER Yorks 208 E6
Arrathorne N Yorks 224 G4
Arreton I/Wight 20 D6
Arrington Cambs 122 G6
Arrivain Arg/Bute 284 D6
Arrochar Arg/Bute 284 G6
Arrow Warwick 117 F11
Arrowe Hill Mersey 182 D3
Arrowfield Top Worcs 117 C10
Arrunden W Yorks 196 F6
Arscaig H'land 309 H5
Arscott Shrops 131 B8
Arthill Ches 184 D2
Arthington W Yorks 205 E11
Arthingworth Northants 136 G5
Arthog Gwyn 146 G2
Arthrath Aberds 303 F9
Arthursdale W Yorks 206 F3
Arthurstone Perth/Kinr 286 C6
Arthurville H'land 309 L7
Artrochie Aberds 303 F10
Arundel W Sussex 35 F8
Arundel Castle W Sussex 35 F8
Arwick Orkney 312 F4
Aryhoulan H'land 290 G2
Asby Cumb 229 G7
Ascog Arg/Bute 266 C2
Ascoil H'land 311 H2
Ascot Windsor 66 F2
Ascot Racecourse Windsor 66 F2
Ascott Warwick 100 E6
Ascott d'Oyley Oxon 82 B4
Ascott Earl Oxon 82 B3
Ascott under Wychwood Oxon 82 B4
Asenby N Yorks 215 D7
Asfordby Leics 154 F4
Asfordby Hill Leics 154 F4
Asgarby Lincs 174 B4
Asgarby Lincs 173 F10
Ash Dorset 30 E5
Ash Devon 8 F6
Ash Kent 55 B9
Ash Kent 68 G5
Ash Som'set 28 C3
Ash Som'set 29 C7
Ash Surrey 49 C11
Ash Bank Staffs 168 F6
Ash Corner Suffolk 126 F6
Ash Green Surrey 50 C3
Ash Green Warwick 134 G6
Ash Hill Devon 14 G4
Ash Magna Shrops 149 B11
Ash Mill Devon 26 C3
Ash Parva Shrops 149 B11
Ash Priors Som'set 27 B11
Ash Street Suffolk 107 B10
Ash Thomas Devon 27 E8
Ash Vale Bl Gwent 77 C10
Ash Vale Surrey 49 C11
Ash Wharf Surrey 49 C11
Ashaig H'land 295 C8
Ashampstead W Berks 64 D5
Ashampstead Green W Berks 64 D5
Ashbank Ches 167 D11
Ashbank Ches 183 G10
Ashbocking Suffolk 126 G3
Ashbourne Derby 169 F11
Ashbrittle Som'set 27 C8
Ashbrook Herts 104 F4
Ashbrook Shrops 131 E9
Ashbrooke Tyne/Wear 243 F9
Ashburton Devon 8 B5
Ashbury Devon 12 B6
Ashbury Oxon 63 B9
Ashby N Lincs 200 F2
Ashby by Partney Lincs 174 B6
Ashby cum Fenby NE Lincs 201 G9
Ashby de la Launde Lincs 173 D9
Ashby de la Zouch Leics 153 F7
Ashby Folville Leics 154 G4
Ashby Hill NE Lincs 201 G8
Ashby Magna Leics 135 E11
Ashby Parva Leics 135 G10
Ashby Puerorum Lincs 190 G4
Ashby St. Ledgers Northants 119 D11
Ashby St. Mary Norfolk 142 B6
Ashchurch Glos 99 E8
Ashcombe Devon 14 F4
Ashcott Som'set 44 F2
Ashcott Corner Som'set 44 F3
Ashday W Yorks 196 C6
Ashdon Essex 105 C11
Ashe Hants 48 C4
Asheldham Essex 89 E7
Ashen Essex 106 C4
Ashendon Bucks 84 C2
Ashey I/Wight 21 D7
Ashfield Arg/Bute 275 E8
Ashfield Carms 94 F3
Ashfield Heref'd 97 G11
Ashfield Suffolk 126 E4
Ashfield Stirl 285 G11
Ashfield Green Suffolk 126 C5
Ashfield Green Suffolk 124 F5
Ashfold Crossways W Sussex 36 B2
Ashford Devon 8 F3
Ashford Devon 40 F4
Ashford Kent 54 E4
Ashford Surrey 66 E5
Ashford Bowdler Shrops 115 C10
Ashford Carbonell Shrops 115 C10
Ashford Common Surrey 66 F5
Ashford Hill Hants 64 G5
Ashford in the water Derby 169 B11
Ashgate Derby 186 G5
Ashgill S Lanarks 268 E5
Ashgrove Bath/NE Som'set 45 B8
Ashill Devon 27 E9
Ashill Norfolk 141 C7
Ashill Som'set 28 D4
Ashingdon Essex 88 G5
Ashington Northum 253 F7
Ashington Som'set 29 C9
Ashington W Sussex 35 D10
Ashington End Lincs 175 B8
Ashintully Castle Perth/Kinr 292 G3
Ashkirk Scot Borders 261 E11
Ashlett Hants 33 G7
Ashleworth Glos 98 F6
Ashleworth Quay Glos 98 F6
Ashley Cambs 124 E3
Ashley Ches 184 E3
Ashley Dorset 31 G10
Ashley Glos 80 G6
Ashley Hants 47 G11
Ashley Hants 19 C11
Ashley Kent 55 D10
Ashley Northants 136 E5
Ashley Staffs 150 B5
Ashley Wilts 61 F10
Ashley Dale Staffs 150 B5
Ashley Down Bristol 60 D5
Ashley Green Bucks 85 D7
Ashley Heath Dorset 31 G10
Ashley Heath Gtr Man 184 D3
Ashley Heath Staffs 150 B4
Ashley Park Surrey 66 F6
Ashmanhaugh Norfolk 160 E6
Ashmansworth Hants 48 B2
Ashmansworthy Devon 24 D4
Ashmead Green Glos 80 F3
Ashmill Devon 12 B3
Ashmore Dorset 30 D6
Ashmore Green W Berks 64 F4
Ashmore Lake W Midlands 133 D9
Ashmore Park W Midlands 133 C9
Ashnashellach Lodge H'land 299 E10
Ashorne Warwick 118 F6
Ashover Derby 170 C5
Ashow Warwick 118 C6
Ashperton Heref'd 98 C2
Ashprington Devon 8 D6
Ashreigney Devon 25 E10
Ashstead Surrey 51 B7
Ashton Ches 167 B8
Ashton Cornw'l 2 D4
Ashton Hants 33 D8
Ashton Invercl 276 F4
Ashton Northants 137 F11
Ashton Northants 102 B5
Ashton Peterbro 138 B2
Ashton Som'set 44 D2
Ashton Common Wilts 45 B10
Ashton Hill Wilts 46 B3
Ashton Keynes Wilts 81 G9
Ashton under Hill Worcs 99 D9
Ashton upon Mersey Gtr Man 184 C3
Ashton Vale Bristol 60 E5
Ashton-in-Makerfield Gtr Man 183 B9
Ashton's Green Mersey 183 B8
Ashton-under-Lyne Gtr Man 184 B6
Ashurst Hants 32 E4
Ashurst Kent 52 F4
Ashurst Mersey 194 F3
Ashurst W Sussex 35 D11
Ashurst Bridge Hants 32 E4
Ashurstwood W Sussex 52 F2
Ashwater Devon 12 B3
Ashway Gap Gtr Man 196 G4
Ashwell Herts 104 D5
Ashwell Rutl'd 155 G7
Ashwell Som'set 28 D5
Ashwell End Herts 104 C5
Ashwellthorpe Norfolk 142 D2
Ashwick Som'set 44 D6
Ashwicken Norfolk 158 F4
Ashwood Staffs 133 F7
Ashybank Scot Borders 262 F2
Askern S Yorks 198 E5
Askerswell Dorset 16 C6
Askett Bucks 84 D4
Askham Cumb 230 G6
Askham Notts 188 G2
Askham Bryan C/York 207 D7
Askham in Furness Cumb 210 D4
Askham Richard C/York 206 D6
Asknish Arg/Bute 275 D10
Askrigg N Yorks 223 G8
Askwith N Yorks 205 D9
Aslackby Lincs 155 C11
Aslacton Norfolk 142 E3
Aslockton Notts 172 G2
Asloun Aberds 293 B7
Asney Som'set 44 F3
Aspall Suffolk 126 D3
Aspatria Cumb 229 C8
Aspenden Herts 105 F7
Asperton Lincs 156 B5
Aspey Green Suffolk 126 E5
Aspley Nott'ham 171 G8
Aspley Guise Beds 103 D8
Aspley Heath Beds 103 E8
Aspley Heath Warwick 118 C2
Aspull Gtr Man 194 F6
Aspull Common Gtr Man 183 B10
Assater Shetl'd 314 F4
Asselby ER Yorks 199 B8
Asserby Lincs 191 F7
Assington Suffolk 107 D8
Assington Green Suffolk 124 F5
Assynt Ho. H'land 300 C5
Astbury Ches 168 C4
Astcote Northants 120 G3
Asterby Lincs 190 F3
Asterley Shrops 131 B7
Asterton Shrops 131 E7
Asthall Oxon 82 C3
Asthall Leigh Oxon 82 C4
Astle H'land 309 K7
Astley Gtr Man 195 G8
Astley Shrops 149 F10
Astley Warwick 134 F6
Astley Worcs 116 D5
Astley W Yorks 197 B11
Astley Abbotts Shrops 132 D4
Astley Bridge Gtr Man 195 E8
Astley Cross Worcs 116 D6
Astley Green Gtr Man 184 B2
Astmoor Halton 183 E8
Aston Ches 167 F10
Aston Ches 183 F9
Aston Derby 152 C3
Aston Derby 185 E11
Aston Flints 166 B4
Aston Heref'd 115 E9
Aston Heref'd 115 C9
Aston Herts 104 G5
Aston Oxon 82 E4
Aston Shrops 132 E6
Aston Shrops 149 D10
Aston Staffs 168 G3
Aston S Yorks 187 E7
Aston Telford 132 B2
Aston W Midlands 133 F11
Aston Abbotts Bucks 102 G6
Aston Botterell Shrops 132 G2
Aston Cantlow Warwick 118 F2
Aston Clinton Bucks 84 C5
Aston Crews Heref'd 98 G3
Aston Cross Glos 99 E8
Aston End Herts 104 G5
Aston Eyre Shrops 132 E3
Aston Fields Worcs 117 D9
Aston Flamville Leics 135 E9
Aston Ingham Heref'd 98 G3
Aston Juxta Mondrum Ches 167 D10
Aston le Walls Northants 119 G9
Aston Magna Glos 100 D3
Aston Munslow Shrops 131 F10
Aston on Carrant Glos 99 E8
Aston on Clun Shrops 131 G7
Aston Pigott Shrops 130 B6
Aston Rogers Shrops 130 B6
Aston Rowant Oxon 84 F2
Aston Sandford Bucks 84 D3
Aston Somerville Worcs 99 D10
Aston Square Shrops 148 D6
Aston Subedge Glos 100 C2
Aston Tirrold Oxon 64 B5
Aston Upthorpe Oxon 64 B5
Aston-By-Stone Staffs 151 C8
Aston-on-Trent Derby 153 D8
Astrop Northants 101 D10
Astrope Herts 84 C5
Astwick Beds 104 D4
Astwith Derby 170 C6
Astwood M/Keynes 103 B9
Astwood Worcs 117 F7
Astwood Bank Worcs 117 E10
Aswarby Lincs 155 B11
Aswardby Lincs 190 G5
Atch Lench Worcs 117 G10
Atcham Shrops 131 B10
Athelhampton Dorset 17 C11
Athelington Suffolk 126 C4
Athelstaneford E Loth 281 F10
Atherfield Green I/Wight 20 F5
Atherington Devon 25 C9
Athersley North S Yorks 197 F10
Athersley South S Yorks 197 F11
Atherstone Som'set 28 D5
Atherstone Warwick 134 D6
Atherstone on Stour Warwick 118 G4
Atherton Gtr Man 195 G7
Athnamulloch H'land 299 G11
Athron Hall Perth/Kinr 286 G4
Atlow Derby 170 F2
Atrim Dorset 16 B5
Attadale H'land 295 B11
Attadale Ho. H'land 295 B11
Attenborough Notts 153 C10
Atterby Lincs 189 C7
Attercliffe S Yorks 186 D5
Atterton Leics 134 D6
Attleborough Norfolk 141 D10
Attleborough Warwick 135 E7
Attlebridge Norfolk 160 F2
Attleton Green Suffolk 124 G4
Atwick ER Yorks 209 C9
Atworth Wilts 61 F11
Auberrow Heref'd 97 B9
Aubourn Lincs 172 C6
Auch Arg/Bute 285 D7
Auchagallon N Ayrs 255 D9
Auchallater Aberds 292 E3
Auchareoch N Ayrs 255 E10
Aucharnie Aberds 302 E6
Auchattie Aberds 293 D8
Auchavan Angus 292 G3
Auchbreck Moray 302 G2
Auchenback E Renf 267 D10
Auchenbainzie Dumf/Gal 247 D8
Auchenblae Aberds 293 F9
Auchenbowie Stirl 278 D5
Auchenbrack Dumf/Gal 247 D7
Auchenbreck Arg/Bute 255 C8
Auchenbreck Arg/Bute 275 E11
Auchencairn Dumf/Gal 237 D9
Auchencairn Dumf/Gal 247 G11
Auchencairn N Ayrs 256 D2
Auchencairn Ho Dumf/Gal 237 D10
Auchencar N Ayrs 255 D9
Auchencarroch W Dunb 277 E8
Auchencrosh S Ayrs 236 B3
Auchendinny Midloth 270 C5
Auchengray S Lanarks 269 E9
Auchenhalrig Moray 302 C3
Auchenharvie N Ayrs 266 G5
Auchenheath S Lanarks 268 G6
Auchenlaich Stirl 285 G10
Auchenleck Dumf/Gal 237 D9
Auchenlochan Arg/Bute 275 F10
Auchenmalg Dumf/Gal 236 D4
Auchensoul S Ayrs 245 E7
Auchentibber S Lanarks 268 E3
Auchentiber N Ayrs 267 F7
Auchertyre H'land 295 C10
Auchessan Stirl 285 E8
Auchgourish H'land 291 B11
Auchinairn Glasg C 268 B2
Auchindrain Arg/Bute 284 G4
Auchindrean H'land 307 L6
Auchininna Aberds 302 E6
Auchinleck Dumf/Gal 236 B6
Auchinleck E Ayrs 258 E3
Auchinloch N Lanarks 278 G3
Auchinner Perth/Kinr 285 F10
Auchinraith S Lanarks 268 D3
Auchinreoch E Dunb 278 F3
Auchinroath Moray 302 D2
Auchinstarry N Lanarks 278 F4
Auchintoul Aberds 293 B7
Auchintoul H'land 309 K5
Auchiries Aberds 303 F10
Auchlee Aberds 293 D10
Auchleeks Ho. Perth/Kinr 291 G9
Auchleven Aberds 302 G6
Auchlinn Aberds 303 D7
Auchlossan Aberds 293 C7
Auchlunachan H'land 307 L6
Auchlunies Aberds 293 D10

Auchlyne Stirl 285 E9
Auchmacoy Aberds 303 F9
Auchmair Moray 302 G3
Auchmantle Dumf/Gal 236 C3
Auchmenzie Aberds 302 G5
Auchmillan E Ayrs 258 D2
Auchmithie Angus 287 C10
Auchmore H'land 300 D4
Auchmuirbridge Fife 286 G6
Auchmull Angus 293 F7
Auchmuty Fife 280 A5
Auchnacraig Arg/Bute 289 G9
Auchnacree Angus 292 G6
Auchnafree Perth/Kinr 286 D2
Auchnagallin H'land 301 F10
Auchnagarron Arg/Bute 275 E11
Auchnagatt Aberds 303 E9
Auchnaha Arg/Bute 275 E10
Auchnahillin H'land 301 F7
Auchnarrow Moray 302 G2
Auchnashelloch Perth/Kinr 285 F11
Auchnotteroch Dumf/Gal 236 C1
Aucholzie Aberds 292 D5
Auchrannie Angus 286 B6
Auchroisk H'land 301 G10
Auchronie Angus 292 E6
Auchterarder Perth/Kinr 286 F3
Auchteraw H'land 290 C5
Auchterderran Fife 280 B4
Auchterhouse Angus 287 D7
Auchtermuchty Fife 286 F6
Auchterneed H'land 300 D4
Auchtertool Fife 280 C4
Auchtertyre Moray 301 D11
Auchtertyre Stirl 285 E7
Auchtubh Stirl 285 E9
Auckengill H'land 310 C7
Auckland Park Durham 233 F10
Auckley S Yorks 199 G7
Audenshaw Gtr Man 184 B6
Audlem Ches 167 G11
Audley Staffs 168 E3
Audley End Essex 105 D10
Audley End Essex 106 D6
Audley End Suffolk 125 G7
Audley End House Essex 105 D10
Audmore Staffs 150 E6
Audnam W Midlands 133 F7
Auds Aberds 302 C6
Aughertree Cumb 229 D11
Aughton ER Yorks 207 F10
Aughton Lancs 211 F11
Aughton Lancs 193 F11
Aughton S Yorks 187 D7
Aughton Wilts 47 B8
Aughton Park Lancs 194 F2
Auldearn H'land 301 D9
Aulden Heref'd 115 G9
Auldgirth Dumf/Gal 247 F10
Auldhame E Loth 281 E11
Auldhouse S Lanarks 268 E2
Auldtown of Carnoustie Aberds 302 E6
Ault a'chruinn H'land 295 C11
Ault Hucknall Derby 171 B7
Aultanrynie H'land 308 F3
Aultbea H'land 307 L3
Aultdearg H'land 300 C2
Aultgrishan H'land 307 L2
Aultguish Inn H'land 300 B3
Aultibea H'land 311 G4
Aultiphurst H'land 310 C2
Aultivullin H'land 310 C2
Aultmore H'land 301 G10
Aultmore Moray 302 D4
Aultnagoire H'land 300 G5
Aultnamain Inn H'land 309 L6
Aultnaslat H'land 290 C3
Aulton Aberds 302 G6
Aulton of Atherb Aberds 303 E9
Aultvaich H'land 300 E5
Aunby Lincs 155 G10
Aundorach H'land 291 B11
Aunk Devon 27 G8
Aunsby Lincs 155 B10
Auquhorthies Aberds 303 G8
Aust S Glos 60 B5
Austerfield Notts 187 C11
Austerlands Gtr Man 196 F3
Austhorpe W Yorks 206 G3
Austrey Warwick 134 B5
Austwick N Yorks 212 F5
Authorpe Lincs 190 E6
Authorpe Row Lincs 191 G8
Avebury Wilts 62 F6
Avebury Trusloe Wilts 62 F5
Aveley Thurr'k 68 C5
Avening Glos 80 F5
Avening Green S Glos 80 G2
Averham Notts 172 E3
Averham Park Notts 172 D2
Avernish H'land 295 C10
Avery Hill London 68 E2
Aveton Gifford Devon 8 F3
Avielochan H'land 291 B11
Aviemore H'land 291 B10
Avington Hants 48 G4
Avington W Berks 63 F11
Avoch H'land 301 D7
Avon Wilts 62 D3
Avon Dassett Warwick 119 G8
Avonbridge Falk 279 G8
Avoncliffe Wilts 45 B10
Avonmouth Bristol 60 D4
Avonwick Devon 8 D4
Awbridge Hants 32 C4
Awhirk Dumf/Gal 236 D2
Awkley S Glos 60 B5
Awliscombe Devon 27 G10
Awre Glos 80 D2
Awsworth Notts 171 G7
Axbridge Som'set 44 C2
Axford Hants 48 E6
Axford Wilts 63 E8
Axminster Devon 15 B11
Axmouth Devon 15 C11
Axton Flints 181 E10
Axtown Devon 7 B10
Axwell Park Tyne/Wear 242 E5
Axworthy Devon 12 D5
Aycliff Kent 55 E10
Aycliffe Village Durham 233 G11
Aydon Northum 242 D2
Aykley Heads Durham 233 C11
Aylburton Glos 79 E10
Ayle Northum 231 B10
Aylesbeare Devon 14 C6
Aylesbury Bucks 84 C4
Aylesby NE Lincs 201 F8
Aylesford Kent 53 B8
Aylesham Kent 55 C8
Aylestone Leics C 135 C11
Aylestone Hill Heref'd 97 C10
Aylestone Park Leics C 135 C11
Aylmerton Norfolk 160 B3
Aylsham Norfolk 160 D3
Aylton Heref'd 98 D3
Aymestrey Heref'd 115 D8
Aynho Northants 101 E10
Ayot Green Herts 86 C2
Ayot St. Lawrence Herts 85 B11
Ayot St. Peter Herts 86 B2
Ayr S Ayrs 257 E8
Ayr Racecourse S Ayrs 257 E9
Ayre of Atler Shetl'd 315 G6
Ayres Shetl'd 315 H5
Ayres of Selivoe Shetl'd 315 J4
Ayreville Torbay 8 C6
Aysgarth N Yorks 213 B10
Ayshford Devon 27 D8
Ayside Cumb 211 C7
Ayston Rutl'd 137 C7
Aythorpe Roding Essex 87 B9
Ayton Scot Borders 273 C8
Ayton Tyne/Wear 243 F7
Aywick Shetl'd 314 E7
Azerley N Yorks 214 E5

B

Babbacombe Torbay 9 B8
Babbinswood Shrops 148 C6
Babb's Green Herts 86 B5
Babcary Som'set 29 B9
Babel Carms 94 D6
Babel Green Suffolk 106 B4
Babell Flints 181 G11
Babingley Norfolk 158 D3
Babraham Cambs 123 G10
Babworth Notts 187 E11
Babylon Flints 166 C4
Bac W Isles 304 D6
Bacchus Glos 80 C4
Bachau Angl 178 E6
Bacheldre Powys 130 E4
Back Muir Fife 279 D11
Back o' th' Brook Staffs 169 E9
Back of Keppoch H'land 295 G8
Back Rogerton E Ayrs 258 E3
Back Street Suffolk 124 F4
Backaland Orkney 312 E6
Backaskaill Orkney 312 C5
Backbarrow Cumb 211 C7
Backbower Gtr Man 185 C7
Backe Carms 74 B3
Backfolds Aberds 303 D10
Backford Ches 182 G6
Backford Cross Ches 182 G5
Backhill Aberds 303 F10
Backhill Aberds 303 F7
Backhill of Clackriach Aberds 303 E9
Backhill of Fortree Aberds 303 E9
Backhill of Trustach Aberds 293 D8
Backies H'land 311 J2
Backlass H'land 310 D6
Backlass H'land 310 E4
Backney Heref'd 97 F11
Back's Green Suffolk 143 G7
Backwell N Som'set 60 F3
Backwell Green N Som'set 60 F4
Backwell Hill N Som'set 60 F3
Backworth Tyne/Wear 243 C8
Bacon End Essex 87 B10
Baconend Green Essex 87 B10
Bacon's End W Midlands 134 F3
Baconsthorpe Norfolk 160 B2
Bacton Heref'd 97 E7
Bacton Norfolk 160 C6
Bacton Suffolk 125 D11
Bacton Green Norfolk 160 C6
Bacton Green Suffolk 125 D10
Bacup Lancs 195 C11
Badachonacher H'land 300 B6
Badachro H'land 299 B7
Badanloch Lodge H'land 308 F7
Badarach H'land 309 K5
Badavanich H'land 299 D11
Badbea H'land 307 K5
Badbury Swindon 63 C7
Badbury Wick Swindon 63 C7
Badby Northants 119 F11
Badcall H'land 306 D7
Badcaul H'land 307 K5
Baddeley Green Stoke 168 E6
Baddesley Clinton Warwick 118 C4
Baddesley Clinton Warwick 118 C4
Baddesley Ensor Warwick 134 D5
Baddidarach H'land 307 G5
Baddoch Aberds 292 E3
Baddock H'land 301 D7
Badeach Moray 302 F2
Badenscallie H'land 307 J5
Badenscoth Aberds 303 F7
Badentoy Park Aberds 293 D11
Badenyon Aberds 292 B5
Badgall Cornw'l 11 D10
Badgeney Cambs 139 D8
Badger Shrops 132 D5
Badger Street Som'set 28 D3
Badgergate Stirl 285 H11
Badger's Mount Kent 68 G3
Badgeworth Glos 80 B6
Badgworth Som'set 43 C11
Badharlick Cornw'l 11 D11
Badicaul H'land 295 C9
Badingham Suffolk 126 D6
Badintagairt H'land 309 H4
Badlesmere Kent 54 C4
Badlipster H'land 310 E6
Badluarach H'land 307 K4
Badminton S Glos 61 C10
Badnaban H'land 307 G5
Badnabay H'land 306 E7
Badnagie H'land 310 F5
Badninish H'land 309 K7
Badrallach H'land 307 K5
Badsey Worcs 99 C11
Badshot Lea Surrey 49 D11
Badsworth W Yorks 198 D3
Badwell Ash Suffolk 125 D9
Badwell Green Suffolk 125 D10
Bae Cinmel = Kinmel Bay Conwy 181 E7
Bae Colwyn = Colwyn Bay Conwy 180 F5
Bae Penrhyn = Penrhyn Bay Conwy 180 E4
Baffins Hants 33 G11
Bag Enderby Lincs 190 G5
Bagber Dorset 30 E3
Bagby N Yorks 215 C9
Bagendon Glos 81 D8
Bàgha Chàise W Isles 296 D5
Bagh a Chaisteil = Castlebay W Isles 297 M2
Bagh Mor W Isles 296 F4
Bagh Shiarabhagh W Isles 297 L3
Bagham Kent 54 C5
Baghasdal W Isles 297 K3
Bagillt Flints 182 F2
Baginton Warwick 118 C6
Baglan Rh Cyn Taff 76 G2
Bagley Shrops 149 D8
Bagley Som'set 44 D3
Bagley W Yorks 205 F10
Bagley Green Som'set 27 D10
Bagmore Hants 49 E7
Bagnall Staffs 168 E6
Bagnor W Berks 64 F2
Bagpath Glos 80 G4
Bagpath Glos 80 E5
Bagshaw Derby 185 E9
Bagshot Surrey 66 G2
Bagshot Wilts 63 F10
Bagslate Moor Gtr Man 195 E11
Bagstone S Glos 61 B7
Bagthorpe Norfolk 158 C5
Bagthorpe Notts 171 E7
Baguley Gtr Man 184 D4
Bagworth Leics 135 B8
Bagwyllydiart Heref'd 97 F8
Bail Àrd Bhuirgh W Isles 304 C6
Bail Uachdraich W Isles 296 E4
Bailbrook Bath/NE Som'set 61 F9
Baildon W Yorks 205 F9
Baildon Green W Yorks 205 F8
Baile W Isles 296 C5
Baile a Mhanaich W Isles 296 F3
Baile Ailein W Isles 304 F4
Baile an Truiseil W Isles 304 C5
Baile Boidheach Arg/Bute 275 F8
Baile Gharbhaidh W Isles 297 G3
Baile Glas W Isles 296 F4
Baile Mhartainn W Isles 296 D3
Baile Mhic Phail W Isles 296 D4
Baile Mor Arg/Bute 288 G4
Baile Mor W Isles 296 E3
Baile na Creige W Isles 297 L2
Baile nan Cailleach W Isles 296 F3
Baile Raghaill W Isles 296 D3
Bailebeag H'land 291 B7
Bailey Cumb 240 B2
Bailey Green Hants 33 B11
Bailey Hill Essex 106 D4
Bailiesward Aberds 302 F4
Bailiff Bridge W Yorks 196 C6
Baillieston Glasg C 268 C3
Bail'lochdrach W Isles 296 F4
Bailrigg Lancs 202 B5
Bail'Ur Tholastaidh W Isles 304 D7
Bainbridge N Yorks 223 G8
Bainsford Falk 279 E7
Bainshole Aberds 302 F6
Bainton ER Yorks 208 C5
Bainton Oxon 101 F11
Bainton Peterbro 137 B11
Baintown Fife 287 G7
Baker Street Thurr'k 68 C6
Baker's End Herts 86 B5
Baker's Hill Glos 79 C9
Baker's Wood Bucks 66 B4
Bakestone Moor Derby 187 F8
Bakewell Derby 170 B2
Bala = Y Bala Gwyn 147 B8
Balachroick H'land 291 C10
Balachuirn H'land 298 E5
Balavil H'land 291 C9
Balavoulin Perth/Kinr 291 G10
Balbeg H'land 300 F4
Balbeg H'land 300 G4
Balbeggie Perth/Kinr 286 E5
Balbegno Castle Aberds 293 F8
Balbithan Aberds 293 B9
Balbithan Ho. Aberds 293 B10
Balblair H'land 300 E5
Balblair H'land 301 C7
Balblair H'land 309 K5
Balby S Yorks 198 G5
Balcherry H'land 311 L2
Balchladich H'land 306 F5
Balchraggan H'land 300 E5
Balchraggan H'land 300 F5
Balchraggan H'land 300 G5
Balchrick H'land 306 D6
Balchrystie Fife 287 G8
Balcladaich H'land 300 G2
Balcombe W Sussex 51 G10
Balcombe Lane W Sussex 51 G10
Balcomie Fife 287 F10
Balcraggie Lodge H'land 310 F5
Balcurvie Fife 287 G7
Balderfield Notts 172 F4
Baldersby N Yorks 215 D7
Baldersby St. James N Yorks 215 D7
Balderstone Gtr Man 196 E2
Balderstone Lancs 203 G8
Balderton Ches 166 C5
Balderton Notts 172 E4
Baldhu Cornw'l 4 G5
Baldingstone Gtr Man 195 E10
Baldinnie Fife 287 F8
Baldock Herts 104 E5
Baldon Row Oxon 83 E9
Baldoon H'land 300 B6
Baldovie Dundee C 287 D8
Baldrine I/Man 192 D5
Baldslow E Sussex 38 E4
Baldwin I/Man 192 D4
Baldwinholme Cumb 239 G8
Baldwin's Gate Staffs 150 B5
Baldwins Hill Surrey 51 F11
Bale Norfolk 159 B10
Balearn Aberds 303 D10
Balemartine Arg/Bute 288 E1
Balephuil Arg/Bute 288 E1
Balerno C/Edinb 270 B3
Balerominhor Arg/Bute 274 D4
Balevullin Arg/Bute 288 E1
Balfield Angus 293 G7
Balfour Orkney 312 G5
Balfour Mains Orkney 312 G5
Balfron Stirl 277 D10
Balfron Station Stirl 277 D10
Balgaveny Aberds 302 E6
Balgavies Angus 287 B9
Balgonar Fife 279 C10
Balgove Aberds 303 F8
Balgowan H'land 291 D8
Balgowan Perth/Kinr 286 E3
Balgown H'land 298 C3
Balgrennie Aberds 292 C6
Balgrochan E Dunb 278 F2
Balgy H'land 299 D8
Balhaldie Stirl 286 G2
Balhalgardy Aberds 303 G7
Balham London 67 E9
Balhary Perth/Kinr 286 C6
Baliasta Shetl'd 314 C8
Baligill H'land 310 C2
Baligortan Arg/Bute 288 E5
Baligrundle Arg/Bute 289 E10
Balindore Arg/Bute 289 F11
Balingham Hill Heref'd 97 E11
Balinoe Arg/Bute 288 E1
Balintore Angus 286 B6
Balintore H'land 301 B8
Balintraid H'land 301 B7
Balintuim Aberds 292 E3
Balk N Yorks 215 C9
Balk Field Notts 188 E2
Balkeerie Angus 287 C7
Balkemback Angus 287 D7
Balkholme ER Yorks 199 B9
Balkissock S Ayrs 244 G4
Ball Shrops 148 D6
Ball Green Stoke 168 E5
Ball Haye Green Staffs 169 D7
Ball Hill Hants 64 G2
Ball o' Ditton Halton 183 D8
Ballabeg I/Man 192 E3
Ballacannel I/Man 192 D5
Ballachraggan Moray 301 E11
Ballachrochin H'land 301 F8
Ballachulish H'land 284 B4
Ballajora I/Man 192 C5
Ballaleigh I/Man 192 D4
Ballamodha I/Man 192 E3
Ballantrae S Ayrs 244 G3
Ballaquine I/Man 192 D5
Ballards Gore Essex 88 G6
Ballard's Green Warwick 134 E5
Ballasalla I/Man 192 C4
Ballasalla I/Man 192 E3
Ballater Aberds 292 D5
Ballathie Perth/Kinr 286 D5
Ballaugh I/Man 192 C4
Ballaveare I/Man 192 E4
Ballcorach Moray 301 G11
Ballechin Perth/Kinr 286 B3
Balleich Stirl 285 H9
Balleigh H'land 309 L7
Ballencrieff E Loth 281 F9
Ballencrieff Toll W Loth 279 G9
Ballentoul Perth/Kinr 291 G10
Ballhill Devon 24 C3
Ballidon Derby 170 E2
Balliekine N Ayrs 255 D9
Balliemeanoch Arg/Bute 276 A2
Balliemore Arg/Bute 275 E11
Balliemore Arg/Bute 289 G10
Ballikinrain Stirl 277 D11
Ballimeanoch Arg/Bute 284 F4
Ballimore Arg/Bute 275 E10
Ballimore Stirl 285 F9
Ballinaby Arg/Bute 274 G3
Ballinbreich Fife 286 E6
Ballindean Perth/Kinr 286 E6
Ballingdon Suffolk 107 C7
Ballinger Common Bucks 84 E6
Ballingham Heref'd 97 E11
Ballingry Fife 280 B3
Ballinlick Perth/Kinr 286 C3
Ballinluig Perth/Kinr 286 B3
Ballintean H'land 291 C10
Ballintuim Perth/Kinr 286 B5
Balliveolan Arg/Bute 289 E10
Balloch Angus 287 B7
Balloch H'land 301 E7
Balloch N Lanarks 278 G4
Balloch W Dunb 277 E7
Ballochan Aberds 293 D7
Ballochearn Stirl 277 D11
Ballochford Moray 302 F3
Ballochmorrie S Ayrs 244 G6
Ballogie Aberds 293 D7
Balls Cross W Sussex 35 B7
Balls Green E Sussex 52 F3
Balls Green Essex 107 G11
Ball's Green Glos 80 F5
Balls Hill W Midlands 133 E9
Ballygown Arg/Bute 288 E6
Ballygrant Arg/Bute 274 G4
Ballygroggan Arg/Bute 255 F7
Ballyhaugh Arg/Bute 288 D3
Balmacara H'land 295 C10
Balmacara Square H'land 295 C10
Balmaclellan Dumf/Gal 237 B8
Balmacneil Perth/Kinr 286 B3
Balmacqueen H'land 298 B4
Balmae Dumf/Gal 237 E8
Balmaha Stirl 277 C8
Balmalcolm Fife 287 G7
Balmalloch N Lanarks 278 F4
Balmeanach Arg/Bute 288 F6
Balmeanach Arg/Bute 289 E8
Balmeanach H'land 295 B7
Balmeanach H'land 298 E3
Balmeanach H'land 298 E5
Balmedie Aberds 293 B11
Balmer Heath Shrops 149 C8
Balmerino Fife 287 E7
Balmerlawn Hants 32 G4
Balmesh Dumf/Gal 236 D3
Balmichael N Ayrs 255 D10
Balminnoch Dumf/Gal 236 C4
Balmirmer Angus 287 D9
Balmoral Castle and Gardens Aberds 292 D4
Balmore E Dunb 278 G2
Balmore H'land 298 E2
Balmore H'land 300 F3
Balmore H'land 301 E8
Balmore Perth/Kinr 286 B3
Balmule Fife 280 D4
Balmullo Fife 287 E8
Balmungie H'land 301 D7
Balmurrie Dumf/Gal 236 C4
Balnaboth Angus 292 G5
Balnabreich Moray 302 D3
Balnabruaich H'land 301 C7
Balnabruich H'land 311 G5
Balnacarn H'land 290 B4
Balnacoil H'land 311 H2
Balnacra H'land 299 E9
Balnacruie H'land 301 G9
Balnafoich H'land 300 F6
Balnagall H'land 311 L2
Balnagowan Aberds 293 C7
Balnagrantach H'land 300 F4
Balnaguard Perth/Kinr 286 B3
Balnahanaid Perth/Kinr 285 C10
Balnahard Arg/Bute 274 D5
Balnahard Arg/Bute 288 F6
Balnain H'land 300 F4
Balnakeil H'land 308 C3
Balnakelly Aberds 293 B7
Balnaknock H'land 298 C4
Balnamoon Aberds 303 D9
Balnamoon Angus 293 G7
Balnapaling H'land 301 C7
Balochroy Arg/Bute 255 B8
Balole Arg/Bute 274 G4
Balone Fife 287 F8
Balornock Glasg C 268 B2
Balquharn Perth/Kinr 286 D4
Balquhidder Stirl 285 E9
Balquhidder Station Stirl 285 E9
Balquhindachy Aberds 303 E8
Balrownie Angus 293 G7
Balsall W Midlands 118 B4
Balsall Common W Midlands 118 B4
Balsall Heath W Midlands 133 G11
Balsall Street W Midlands 118 B4
Balscote Oxon 101 C7
Balsham Cambs 123 G11
Balsporran Cottages H'land 291 F8
Balstonia Thurr'k 69 C7
Baltasound Shetl'd 314 C8
Balterley Staffs 168 E3
Balterley Heath Staffs 168 E2
Baltersan Dumf/Gal 236 C6
Balthangie Aberds 303 D8
Balthayock Perth/Kinr 286 E5
Baltonsborough Som'set 44 G4
Balure Arg/Bute 289 E11
Balvaird H'land 300 D5
Balvenie Moray 302 E3
Balvicar Arg/Bute 275 B8
Balvraid H'land 295 D10
Balvraid H'land 301 F8
Balwest Cornw'l 2 C3
Bamber Bridge Lancs 194 B5
Bamber's Green Essex 105 G11
Bamburgh Northum 264 B5
Bamburgh Castle Northum 264 B5
Bamff Perth/Kinr 286 B6
Bamford Derby 186 E2
Bamford Gtr Man 195 E11
Bamfurlong Glos 99 G8
Bamfurlong Gtr Man 194 G5
Bampton Cumb 221 B10
Bampton Devon 27 C7
Bampton Oxon 82 E4
Bampton Grange Cumb 221 B10
Banavie H'land 290 F3
Banbury Oxon 101 C9
Banburylane Northants 120 F3
Bancffosfelen Carms 75 C7
Banchor H'land 301 E9
Banchory Aberds 293 D8
Banchory-Devenick Aberds 293 C11
Bancroft M/Keynes 102 C6
Bancycapel Carms 74 B6
Bancyfelin Carms 74 B4
Bandeath Industrial Estate Stirl 278 C6
Bandirran Perth/Kinr 286 D6
Bandon Hill London 67 G10
Bandrake Head Cumb 210 B6
Bandry Arg/Bute 277 C7
Banff Aberds 302 C6
Bangor Gwyn 179 G9
Bangor on Dee Racecourse Wrex 166 G5
Bangor Teifi Ceredig'n 93 C7
Bangor-is-y-coed Wrex 166 F4
Bangors Cornw'l 11 B10
Bangor's Green Lancs 193 F11
Bangrove Suffolk 125 C8
Banham Norfolk 141 F11
Banham Zoo, Diss Norfolk 141 F11
Bank Hants 32 F3
Bank End Cumb 210 B4
Bank Fold Blackb'n 195 C8
Bank Hey Blackb'n 203 G9
Bank Lane Gtr Man 195 D10
Bank Newton N Yorks 204 C4
Bank Street Worcs 116 E2
Bank Top Derby 186 E2
Bank Top Gtr Man 195 E8
Bank Top Lancs 194 F4
Bank Top Tyne/Wear 242 D5
Bank Top W Yorks 196 C6
Bank Top W Yorks 205 F9
Bankend Dumf/Gal 238 D2
Bankfoot Perth/Kinr 286 D4
Bankglen E Ayrs 258 G3
Bankhead Aberds 293 C8
Bankhead Aberd C 293 B10
Bankhead Dumf/Gal 236 C2
Bankhead Falk 278 E6
Bankhead S Lanarks 269 G7
Bankland Som'set 43 G10
Banklands Norfolk 157 E11
Banknock Falk 278 E5
Banknock Falk 278 F5
Banks Cumb 240 E3
Banks Lancs 193 C11
Banks Orkney 312 E5
Bankshill Dumf/Gal 248 G5
Bankside Falk 279 E7
Banners Gate W Midlands 133 D11
Banningham Norfolk 160 D4
Banniskirk Ho. H'land 310 D5
Banniskirk Mains H'land 310 D5
Bannister Green Essex 106 G3
Bannockburn Stirl 278 C6
Banstead Surrey 51 B9
Bantam Grove W Yorks 197 B9
Bantaskin Falk 279 F7
Bantham Devon 8 G3
Banton N Lanarks 278 F5
Banwell N Som'set 44 B2
Banwen Pyrddin Neath P Talb 76 D5
Banyard's Green Suffolk 126 C6
Bapchild Kent 70 G2
Baptist End W Midlands 133 F8
Bapton Wilts 46 F3
Bar End Hants 33 B7
Bar Hill Cambs 123 E7
Bar Moor Tyne/Wear 242 E4
Barabhas W Isles 304 D5
Barabhas Iarach W Isles 304 D5
Barabhas Uarach W Isles 304 C5
Barachandroman Arg/Bute 289 G8
Baramore H'land 289 B8
Barassie S Ayrs 257 C8
Baravullin Arg/Bute 289 F10
Barbaraville H'land 301 B7
Barbauchlaw W Loth 269 B8
Barber Booth Derby 185 E10
Barber Green Cumb 211 C7
Barbican Plym'th 7 E9
Barbieston S Ayrs 257 F10
Barbon Cumb 212 C2
Barbreck Ho Arg/Bute 275 C9
Barbridge Ches 167 D10
Barbrook Devon 41 D8
Barby Northants 119 C10
Barby Nortoft Northants 119 C11
Barcaldine Arg/Bute 289 E11
Barcheston Warwick 100 D5
Barclose Cumb 239 E10
Barcombe E Sussex 36 E6
Barcombe Cross E Sussex 36 D6
Barcroft W Yorks 204 F6
Barden N Yorks 205 B7
Barden N Yorks 224 G2
Barden Park Kent 52 D5
Bardennoch Dumf/Gal 246 E3
Bardfield End Green Essex 106 E2
Bardfield Saling Essex 106 F3
Bardister Shetl'd 314 F5
Bardnabeinne H'land 309 K7
Bardney Lincs 173 B10
Bardon Leics 153 G8
Bardon Mill Northum 241 E7
Bardowie E Dunb 277 G11
Bardown E Sussex 37 B11
Bardrainney Invercl 276 G6
Bardrishaig Arg/Bute 275 B8
Bardsea Cumb 210 E6
Bardsey W Yorks 206 E3
Bardsley Gtr Man 196 G2
Bardwell Suffolk 125 C8
Bare Lancs 211 G9
Barelees Northum 263 B9
Barepot Cumb 228 F6
Bareppa Cornw'l 3 D7
Barfad Arg/Bute 275 G9
Barfad Dumf/Gal 236 C5
Barford Hants 49 F10
Barford Norfolk 142 B2
Barford Warwick 118 E5
Barford St. John Oxon 101 E8
Barford St. Martin Wilts 46 G5
Barford St. Michael Oxon 101 E8
Barfrestone Kent 55 C9
Bargaly Dumf/Gal 236 C6
Bargarran Renf 277 G9
Bargeddie N Lanarks 268 C4
Bargod = Bargoed Caerph 77 F10
Bargoed = Bargod Caerph 77 F10
Bargrennan Dumf/Gal 236 B5
Barham Cambs 122 B2
Barham Kent 55 C8
Barham Suffolk 126 G2
Barharrow Dumf/Gal 237 D8
Barhill Dumf/Gal 237 C10
Barholm Dumf/Gal 237 D7
Barholm Lincs 155 G11
Barhough Northum 240 G5
Barkby Leics 136 B2
Barkby Thorpe Leics 136 B2
Barkers Green Shrops 149 D10
Barkestone-le-Vale Leics 154 C5
Barkham Wokingham 65 G9
Barkham Common Wokingham 65 G9
Barking London 68 C2
Barking Suffolk 125 G11
Barking Tye Suffolk 125 G11
Barkingside London 68 B2
Barkisland W Yorks 196 D5
Barkla Shop Cornw'l 4 E4
Barklye E Sussex 37 C10
Barkston Lincs 172 G6
Barkston N Yorks 206 F5
Barkway Herts 105 D7
Barlanark Glasg C 268 C3
Barlaston Staffs 151 B7
Barlavington W Sussex 35 D7
Barlborough Derby 187 F7
Barlby N Yorks 207 G8
Barlestone Leics 135 B8
Barley Herts 105 D8
Barley Lancs 204 E2
Barley Green Suffolk 126 C4
Barley Mow Tyne/Wear 243 G7
Barleycroft End Herts 105 F8
Barleythorpe Rutl'd 137 B6
Barling Essex 70 B2
Barlings Lincs 189 G9
Barlow Derby 186 G4
Barlow N Yorks 198 B6
Barlow Tyne/Wear 242 E5
Barlow Moor Gtr Man 184 C4
Barmby Moor ER Yorks 207 D11
Barmby on the Marsh ER Yorks 199 B7
Barmer Norfolk 158 C6
Barming Heath Kent 53 B8
Barmolloch Arg/Bute 275 D9
Barmouth = Abermaw Gwyn 146 F2
Barmpton D'lington 224 B6
Barmston ER Yorks 209 B9
Barmston Tyne/Wear 243 F8
Barmulloch Glasg C 268 B2
Barn Hill Worcs 117 B11
Barnaby Green Suffolk 127 B9
Barnack Peterbro 137 C11
Barnacle Warwick 135 G7
Barnaline Arg/Bute 275 B10
Barnard Castle Durham 223 B11
Barnard Gate Oxon 82 C6
Barnardiston Suffolk 106 B4
Barnard's Green Worcs 98 B5
Barnbarroch Dumf/Gal 237 D10
Barnburgh S Yorks 198 G3
Barnby Suffolk 143 F9
Barnby Dun S Yorks 198 F6
Barnby in the Willows Notts 172 E5
Barnby Moor Notts 187 E11
Barne Barton Plym'th 7 D8
Barnehurst London 68 D4
Barnes London 67 D8
Barnes Street Kent 52 D6
Barnet London 86 F2
Barnet Gate London 86 F2
Barnetby-le-Wold N Lincs 200 F5
Barnettbrook Worcs 117 B7
Barney Norfolk 159 C9
Barnfield Lancs 195 B9
Barnfields Staffs 169 D7
Barnham Suffolk 125 B7
Barnham W Sussex 35 G7
Barnham Broom Norfolk 141 B11
Barnhead Angus 287 B10
Barnhill Dundee C 287 D8
Barnhill Moray 301 D11
Barnhill S Lanarks 268 D3
Barnhills Dumf/Gal 236 B1
Barningham Durham 223 C11
Barningham Suffolk 125 B9
Barningham Green Norfolk 160 C2
Barnmoor Green Warwick 118 D3
Barnoldby le Beck NE Lincs 201 G8
Barnoldswick Lancs 204 D3
Barnoldswick N Yorks 212 E3
Barns Green W Sussex 35 B10
Barnsbury London 67 C10
Barnsden E Sussex 37 B7
Barnsley Glos 81 D9
Barnsley Shrops 132 E5
Barnsley S Yorks 197 F11
Barnsole Kent 55 B9
Barnstaple Devon 40 G5
Barnston Essex 87 B10
Barnston Mersey 182 E3
Barnstone Notts 154 B4
Barnt Green Worcs 117 C10
Barnton C/Edinb 280 F3
Barnton Ches 183 F10
Barnwell Cambs 123 F9
Barnwell Northants 137 G10
Barnwood Glos 80 B5
Barnyards Fife 281 A9
Barochreal Arg/Bute 289 G10
Barons Cross Heref'd 115 F9
Barr H'land 289 D8
Barr S Ayrs 245 E7
Barr Som'set 27 C11
Barr Common W Midlands 133 D11
Barra Airport W Isles 297 L2
Barra Castle Aberds 303 G7
Barrachan Dumf/Gal 236 E5
Barrachnie Glasg C 268 C3
Barrack Aberds 303 E8
Barrack Hill Newp 59 B10
Barraer Dumf/Gal 236 C5
Barraglom W Isles 304 E3
Barrahormid Arg/Bute 275 E8
Barran Arg/Bute 289 G10
Barranrioch Arg/Bute 289 G10
Barrapol Arg/Bute 288 E1
Barras Aberds 293 E10
Barras Cumb 222 C6
Barrasford Northum 241 C10
Barravullin Arg/Bute 275 C9
Barregarrow I/Man 192 D4
Barrhead E Renf 267 D10
Barrhill S Ayrs 244 G6
Barrington Cambs 105 B7
Barrington Som'set 28 D5
Barripper Cornw'l 2 B4
Barrmill N Ayrs 267 E7
Barrock H'land 310 B6
Barrock Ho. H'land 310 C6
Barrow Glos 99 G7
Barrow Lancs 203 F10
Barrow Rutl'd 155 F7
Barrow Shrops 132 C3
Barrow Suffolk 124 E5
Barrow Som'set 44 E5
Barrow S Yorks 186 B5
Barrow Bridge Gtr Man 195 E7
Barrow Common N Som'set 60 F4
Barrow Green Kent 70 G3
Barrow Gurney N Som'set 60 F4
Barrow Haven N Lincs 200 C5
Barrow Hill Derby 186 F6
Barrow Hill Dorset 18 B5
Barrow Hill Hants 32 D4
Barrow Hill Suffolk 107 B7
Barrow Island Cumb 210 F3
Barrow Nook Lancs 194 G2
Barrow Street Wilts 45 G10
Barrow upon Humber N Lincs 200 C5
Barrow upon Soar Leics 153 F11
Barrow upon Trent Derby 152 D6
Barrow Vale Bath/NE Som'set 60 G6
Barroway Drove Norfolk 139 C11
Barrowby Lincs 155 B7
Barrowcliff N Yorks 217 B10
Barrowden Rutl'd 137 C8
Barrowford Lancs 204 F3
Barrowhill Kent 54 F6
Barrow-in-Furness Cumb 210 E4
Barrows Green Ches 167 D11
Barrows Green Cumb 211 B10
Barrow's Green Halton 183 D8
Barrows Green Notts 170 E6
Barry Angus 287 D9
Barry V/Glam 58 F6
Barry Docks V/Glam 58 F6
Barry Island V/Glam 58 F6

Birdingbury Warwick 119 D8
Birdland Park, Bourton-on-the-Water Glos 100 G3
Birdlip Glos 80 C6
Birds Edge W Yorks 197 F8
Birds Green Essex 87 D9
Birdsall N Yorks 216 F6
Birdsend Glos 98 G5
Birdsgreen Shrops 132 G5
Birdsmoor Gate Dorset 28 G5
Birdston E Dunb 278 F3
Birdwell S Yorks 197 G10
Birdwood Glos 80 B2
Birdworld and Underwaterworld, Farnham Hants 49 E10
Birgham Scot Borders 263 B7
Birichen H'land 309 K7
Birkacre Lancs 194 E5
Birkby Cumb 229 D7
Birkby N Yorks 224 E6
Birkby W Yorks 196 D6
Birkdale Mersey 193 E10
Birkenbog Aberds 302 C5
Birkenhead Mersey 182 D4
Birkenhills Aberds 303 E7
Birkenshaw S Lanarks 268 C3
Birkenshaw S Lanarks 268 F5
Birkenshaw W Yorks 197 B8
Birkett Mire Cumb 230 G2
Birkhall Aberds 292 D5
Birkhill Angus 287 D7
Birkhill Dumf/Gal 260 F6
Birkholme Lincs 155 E9
Birkin N Yorks 198 B4
Birks W Yorks 197 B9
Birkshaw Northum 241 D7
Birley Heref'd 115 G9
Birley Carr S Yorks 186 C4
Birley Edge S Yorks 186 C4
Birleyhay Derby 186 E5
Birling Kent 69 G7
Birling Northum 253 B7
Birling Gap E Sussex 23 F9
Birlingham Worcs 99 C8
Birmingham W Midlands 133 F10
Birmingham Botanical Gardens W Midlands 133 F10
Birmingham International Airport W Midlands 134 G3
Birmingham Museum and Art Gallery W Midlands 133 F11
Birmingham Museum of Science and Technology W Midlands 133 F11
Birnam Perth/Kinr 286 C4
Birniehill S Lanarks 268 E2
Birse Aberds 293 D7
Birsemore Aberds 293 D7
Birstall Leics 135 B11
Birstall W Yorks 197 B8
Birstall Smithies W Yorks 197 B8
Birstwith N Yorks 205 B10
Birthorpe Lincs 156 C2
Birtle Gtr Man 195 E10
Birtley Heref'd 115 D7
Birtley Northum 241 B9
Birtley Tyne/Wear 243 F7
Birts Street Worcs 98 D5
Birtsmorton Worcs 98 D6
Bisbrooke Rutl'd 137 D7
Biscathorpe Lincs 190 E2
Biscombe Som'set 27 E11
Biscot Luton 103 G11
Biscovey Cornw'l 5 E11
Bish Mill Devon 26 B2
Bisham Windsor 65 C10
Bishampton Worcs 117 G9
Bishop Auckland Durham 233 F9
Bishop Burton ER Yorks 208 E5
Bishop Kinkell H'land 300 D5
Bishop Middleham Durham 234 E2
Bishop Monkton N Yorks 214 F6
Bishop Norton Lincs 189 C7
Bishop Sutton Bath/NE Som'set 44 B5
Bishop Thornton N Yorks 214 G5
Bishop Wilton ER Yorks 207 B11
Bishopbridge Lincs 189 C8
Bishopbriggs E Dunb 278 G2
Bishopdown Wilts 47 G7
Bishopmill Moray 302 C2
Bishops Cannings Wilts 62 G4
Bishop's Castle Shrops 130 F6
Bishop's Caundle Dorset 29 E11
Bishop's Cleeve Glos 99 F8
Bishops Frome Heref'd 98 B3
Bishops Gate Surrey 66 E3
Bishop's Green Essex 87 B10
Bishop's Green Hants 64 G3
Bishop's Hull Som'set 28 C2
Bishop's Itchington Warwick 119 F7
Bishops Lydeard Som'set 27 B11
Bishop's Norton Glos 98 G6
Bishop's Nympton Devon 26 C3
Bishop's Offley Staffs 150 D5
Bishop's Stortford Herts 105 G9
Bishops Sutton Hants 48 G6
Bishop's Tachbrook Warwick 118 E6
Bishop's Tawton Devon 25 B9
Bishop's Waltham Hants 33 D8
Bishop's Wood Staffs 132 B6
Bishopsbourne Kent 55 C7
Bishopsgarth Stockton 234 G4
Bishopsteignton Devon 14 G4
Bishopstoke Hants 33 D7
Bishopston Bristol 60 D5
Bishopston Swan 56 D5
Bishopstone Bucks 84 C4
Bishopstone E Sussex 37 G7
Bishopstone Heref'd 97 C8
Bishopstone Kent 71 F8
Bishopstone Swindon 63 C8
Bishopstone Wilts 31 B9
Bishopstrow Wilts 45 E11
Bishopswood Som'set 28 E3
Bishopsworth Bristol 60 F5
Bishopthorpe C/York 207 D7
Bishopton D'lington 234 G3
Bishopton Dumf/Gal 236 E6
Bishopton N Yorks 214 E5
Bishopton Renf 277 G8
Bishopton Warwick 118 F3
Bishopwearmouth Tyne/Wear 243 F9
Bishpool Newp 59 B10
Bishton Newp 59 B11
Bishton Staffs 151 E10
Bisley Glos 80 D6
Bisley Surrey 50 B3
Bisley Camp Surrey 50 B2
Bispham Blackp'l 202 E2
Bispham Green Lancs 194 E3
Bissoe Cornw'l 4 G5
Bisterne Hants 31 G10
Bisterne Close Hants 32 G2
Bitchet Green Kent 52 C5
Bitchfield Lincs 155 D9
Bittadon Devon 40 E4
Bittaford Devon 8 D3
Bitterley Shrops 115 B11
Bitterne S'thampton 32 E6
Bitterne Park S'thampton 32 E6
Bitterscote Staffs 134 C4
Bitteswell Leics 135 G10
Bittles Green Dorset 30 B5
Bitton S Glos 61 F7
Bix Oxon 65 B8
Bixter Shetl'd 315 H5
Blaby Leics 135 D11
Black Bank Cambs 139 F10
Black Bank Warwick 135 F7
Black Barn Lincs 157 D8
Black Bourton Oxon 82 E3
Black Bridge Pembs 72 D6
Black Callerton Tyne/Wear 242 D5
Black Carr Norfolk 141 D11
Black Clauchrie S Ayrs 245 G7
Black Corner W Sussex 51 E9
Black Corries Lodge H'land 284 B6
Black Crofts Arg/Bute 289 F11
Black Cross Cornw'l 5 C8
Black Dog Devon 26 F4
Black Heddon Northum 242 B3
Black Hill W Yorks 205 E7
Black Lane Gtr Man 195 F9
Black Lane Ends Lancs 204 E4
Black Moor W Yorks 205 F11
Black Mount Arg/Bute 284 C6
Black Notley Essex 106 G5
Black Pill Swan 75 G10
Black Pole Lancs 202 G5
Black Rock Brighton/Hove 36 G4
Black Rock Monmouths 60 B4
Black Street Suffolk 143 F10
Black Tar Pembs 73 D7
Black Torrington Devon 25 F7
Black Vein Caerph 78 G2
Blackacre Dumf/Gal 248 E2
Blackadder West Scot Borders 272 E6
Blackawton Devon 8 E6
Blackbeck Cumb 219 D10
Blackborough Devon 27 G9
Blackborough Norfolk 158 G3
Blackborough End Norfolk 158 G3
Blackboys E Sussex 37 C8
Blackbraes Aberds 293 B10
Blackbraes Falk 279 F8
Blackbrook Derby 170 F4
Blackbrook Derby 185 E9
Blackbrook Mersey 183 B8
Blackbrook Surrey 51 D7
Blackbrook Staffs 150 B5
Blackburn Aberds 293 B10
Blackburn Aberds 293 D10
Blackburn Aberds 302 F5
Blackburn Blackb'n 195 B7
Blackburn S Yorks 186 C5
Blackburn W Loth 269 B9
Blackchambers Aberds 293 B9
Blackcraig Dumf/Gal 246 G6
Blackcraigs Angus 293 E7
Blackden Heath Ches 184 G3
Blackditch Oxon 82 D6
Blackdog Aberds 293 B11
Blackdown Dorset 28 G5
Blackdyke Cumb 238 G4
Blackenhall Ches 168 F2
Blackenhall W Midlands 133 D8
Blacker S Yorks 197 F10
Blacker Hill S Yorks 197 G11
Blackfell Tyne/Wear 243 F7
Blackfen London 68 E3
Blackfield Hants 32 G6
Blackford Cumb 239 E9
Blackford Perth/Kinr 286 G2
Blackford Som'set 44 D2
Blackford Som'set 29 B11
Blackford Bridge Gtr Man 195 F9
Blackfordby Leics 152 F6
Blackgang I/Wight 20 F5
Blackgang Chine Fantasy Park I/Wight 20 F5
Blackgate Angus 287 B8
Blackhall Aberds 293 D8
Blackhall C/Edinb 280 G4
Blackhall Herts 105 E8
Blackhall Renf 267 C9
Blackhall Colliery Durham 234 D4
Blackhall Mill Tyne/Wear 242 F4
Blackhall Rocks Durham 234 D5
Blackham E Sussex 52 F3
Blackhaugh Scot Borders 261 B10
Blackheath Essex 107 G10
Blackheath London 67 D11
Blackheath Suffolk 127 B8
Blackheath W Midlands 133 F9
Blackhill Aberds 303 D10
Blackhill Aberds 303 E10
Blackhill Aberds 303 F10
Blackhill Durham 242 G3
Blackhill H'land 298 D3
Blackhillock Moray 302 E4
Blackhills H'land 301 D9
Blackhills Moray 302 D2
Blackhills Swan 75 G9
Blackhorse Devon 14 C5
Blackhorse S Glos 61 D7
Blackjack Lincs 156 B5
Blackland Som'set 41 F10
Blackland Wilts 62 F4
Blacklaw Aberds 302 D6
Blackleach Lancs 202 G5
Blackley Gtr Man 195 G11
Blackley W Yorks 196 D6
Blacklunans Perth/Kinr 292 G3
Blackmanston Dorset 18 E4
Blackmarstone Heref'd 97 D10
Blackmill Bridg 58 B2
Blackmoor Gtr Man 195 G7
Blackmoor Hants 49 G9
Blackmoor N Som'set 60 G3
Blackmoor Som'set 27 D11
Blackmoorfoot W Yorks 196 E6
Blackmore Essex 87 E10
Blackmore Shrops 130 B6
Blackmore End Essex 106 E4
Blackmore End Herts 85 B11
Blackmore End Worcs 98 C6
Blackness Aberds 293 D8
Blackness E Sussex 37 B8
Blackness Falk 279 E10
Blacknest Hants 49 E9
Blacknest Windsor 66 F3
Blackney Dorset 16 B4
Blacknoll Dorset 18 D2
Blacko Lancs 204 E3
Blackpark Dumf/Gal 236 C5
Blackpole Worcs 117 F7
Blackpool Blackp'l 202 F2
Blackpool Devon 9 F7
Blackpool Devon 14 G2
Blackpool Pembs 73 C9
Blackpool Airport Lancs 202 G2
Blackpool Corner Devon 16 B2
Blackpool Pleasure Beach Blackp'l 202 G2
Blackpool Sea Life Centre Blackp'l 202 F2
Blackpool Tower Blackp'l 202 F2
Blackpool Zoo Park Blackp'l 202 F2
Blackridge W Loth 269 B7
Blackrock Arg/Bute 274 G4
Blackrock Monmouths 78 C2
Blackrod Gtr Man 194 E6
Blackshaw Dumf/Gal 238 D3
Blackshaw Head W Yorks 196 C2
Blacksmith's Corner Suffolk 108 C2
Blacksmith's Green Suffolk 126 D2
Blacksnape Blackb'n 195 C8
Blackstone W Sussex 36 D2
Blackthorn Oxon 83 B10
Blackthorpe Suffolk 125 E8
Blacktoft ER Yorks 199 C10
Blacktop Aberd C 293 C10
Blacktown Newp 59 C9
Blackwall London 67 C11
Blackwall Tunnel London 67 C11
Blackwater Cornw'l 4 F4
Blackwater Dorset 19 B8
Blackwater Hants 49 B10
Blackwater I/Wight 20 D6
Blackwater Norfolk 159 E11
Blackwater Som'set 28 D3
Blackwater Lodge Moray 302 G3
Blackwaterfoot N Ayrs 255 E9
Blackwell Cumb 239 G10
Blackwell D'lington 224 C5
Blackwell Derby 170 D6
Blackwell Derby 185 G10
Blackwell Som'set 27 B8
Blackwell Warwick 100 C4
Blackwell Worcs 117 C9
Blackwell W Sussex 51 F11
Blackwell's End Green Glos 98 F5
Blackwood = Coed Duon Caerph 77 F11
Blackwood S Lanarks 268 G5
Blackwood Warrington 183 C10
Blackwood Hill Staffs 168 D6
Blacky Moor Northants 120 D5
Blacon Ches 166 B5
Bladbean Kent 55 D7
Blades N Yorks 223 F9
Bladnoch Dumf/Gal 236 D6
Bladon Oxon 82 C6
Blaen Clydach Rh Cyn Taff 77 G7
Blaenannerch Ceredig'n 92 B4
Blaenau Bl Gwent 78 E2
Blaenau Dolwyddelan Conwy 164 E2
Blaenau Ffestiniog Gwyn 164 F2
Blaenau Uchaf Wrex 166 G3
Blaenavon Torf 78 D3
Blaencaerau Bridg 76 F5
Blaencarno Caerph 77 D9
Blaencelyn Ceredig'n 111 G7
Blaencwm Rh Cyn Taff 76 F6
Blaendulais = Seven Sisters Neath P Talb 76 D4
Blaendyryn Powys 95 D8
Blaenffos Pembs 92 D3
Blaengarw Bridg 76 G6
Blaengavenny Monmouths 78 B4
Blaen-geuffordd Ceredig'n 128 G2
Blaengwawr Rh Cyn Taff 77 E8
Blaengwrach Neath P Talb 76 D5
Blaengwynfi Neath P Talb 76 F5
Blaenllechau Rh Cyn Taff 77 F8
Blaenpennal Ceredig'n 112 E2
Blaenplwyf Ceredig'n 111 B11
Blaenporth Ceredig'n 92 B5
Blaenrhondda Rh Cyn Taff 76 F6
Blaenwaun Carms 92 F4
Blaen-y-Coed Carms 92 F6
Blaen-y-cwm Bl Gwent 77 C10
Blaenycwm Ceredig'n 112 B6
Blaen-y-cwm Torf 78 E2
Blagdon N Som'set 44 B4
Blagdon Torbay 9 C7
Blagdon Hill Som'set 28 D2
Blagill Cumb 231 B10
Blaguegate Lancs 194 F3
Blaich H'land 290 F2
Blain H'land 289 C8
Blaina Bl Gwent 78 D2
Blainacraig Ho Aberds 293 D7
Blair Atholl Perth/Kinr 291 G10
Blair Castle, Blair Atholl Perth/Kinr 291 G10
Blair Drummond Stirl 278 B4
Blair Drummond Safari Park, Dunblane Stirl 278 B4
Blairanbolch Arg/Bute 266 B2
Blairbeg N Ayrs 256 C2
Blairburn Fife 279 D9
Blairdaff Aberds 293 B8
Blairdryne Aberds 293 D9
Blairgorm H'land 301 G10
Blairgowrie Perth/Kinr 286 C5
Blairhall Fife 279 D10
Blairhill N Lanarks 268 B4
Blairingone Perth/Kinr 279 B9
Blairland N Ayrs 266 F6
Blairlinn N Lanarks 278 G5
Blairlogie Stirl 278 B6
Blairlomond Arg/Bute 276 B3
Blairmore Arg/Bute 276 E3
Blairmore H'land 306 D6
Blairnamarrow Moray 292 B4
Blair's Ferry Arg/Bute 275 G10
Blairskaith E Dunb 277 F11
Blaisdon Glos 80 C2
Blaise Hamlet Bristol 60 D4
Blaize Bailey Glos 79 C11
Blake End Essex 106 G4
Blakebrook Worcs 116 B6
Blakedown Worcs 117 B7
Blakelands M/Keynes 103 C7
Blakelaw Scot Borders 263 C7
Blakelaw Tyne/Wear 242 D6
Blakeley Staffs 133 E7
Blakeley Lane Staffs 169 F7
Blakelow Ches 167 E11
Blakemere Heref'd 97 C7
Blakenall Heath W Midlands 133 C10
Blakeney Glos 79 D11
Blakeney Norfolk 177 E8
Blakeney Hill Glos 79 D11
Blakeney Point NNR Norfolk 177 D8
Blakeshall Worcs 132 G6
Blakesley Northants 120 G2
Blanchland Northum 241 G11
Bland Hill N Yorks 205 C10
Blandford Camp Dorset 30 F6
Blandford Forum Dorset 30 F5
Blandford St. Mary Dorset 30 F5
Blandy H'land 308 D6
Blanefield Stirl 277 F11
Blanerne Scot Borders 272 D6
Blankney Lincs 173 C9
Blantyre S Lanarks 268 D3
Blar a'Chaorainn H'land 290 G3
Blaran Arg/Bute 275 B9
Blarghour Arg/Bute 275 B10
Blarmachfoldach H'land 290 G2
Blarnalearoch H'land 307 K6
Blasford Hill Essex 88 C2
Blashford Hants 31 F10
Blaston Leics 136 D6
Blatherwycke Northants 137 D9
Blawith Cumb 210 C4
Blaxhall Suffolk 127 F7
Blaxton S Yorks 199 G7
Blaydon Tyne/Wear 242 E5
Blaydon Burn Tyne/Wear 242 E5
Blazefield N Yorks 214 F3
Bleach Green Cumb 219 B9
Bleach Green Suffolk 126 B4
Bleadney Som'set 44 D3
Bleadon N Som'set 43 B10
Bleak Hey Nook Gtr Man 196 F4
Bleak Hill Hants 31 E10
Bleak Street Som'set 45 G9
Blean Kent 70 G6
Bleasby Lincs 189 E10
Bleasby Notts 172 F2
Bleasby Moor Lincs 189 E10
Bleasdale Lancs 203 D7
Bleatarn Cumb 222 C4
Blebocraigs Fife 287 F8
Bleddfa Powys 114 D4
Bledington Glos 100 G4
Bledlow Bucks 84 E3
Bledlow Ridge Bucks 84 F3
Bleet Wilts 45 B10
Blegbie E Loth 271 C9
Blencarn Cumb 231 E8
Blencogo Cumb 229 B9
Blendworth Hants 34 E2
Blenheim Palace, Woodstock Oxon 82 B6
Blenheim Park Norfolk 158 C6
Blennerhasset Cumb 229 C9
Blervie Castle Moray 301 D10
Bletchingdon Oxon 83 B8
Bletchingley Surrey 51 C10
Bletchley M/Keynes 103 E7
Bletchley Shrops 150 C2
Bletherston Pembs 91 G11
Bletsoe Beds 121 F10
Blewbury Oxon 64 B4
Blickling Norfolk 160 D3
Blickling Hall, Aylsham Norfolk 160 D3
Blidworth Notts 171 D9
Blidworth Bottoms Notts 171 E9
Blindcrake Cumb 229 E9
Blindley Heath Surrey 51 D11
Blindmore Som'set 28 E3
Blingery H'land 310 E7
Blisland Cornw'l 11 G7
Bliss Gate Worcs 116 C4
Blissford Hants 31 E11
Blisworth Northants 120 G4
Blithbury Staffs 151 E11
Blitterlees Cumb 238 G4
Blo' Norton Norfolk 125 B10
Blockley Glos 100 E3
Blofield Norfolk 142 B6
Blofield Corner Norfolk 160 G6
Blofield Heath Norfolk 160 G6
Bloodman's Corner Suffolk 143 D10
Bloomfield Scot Borders 262 E3
Bloomfield Dumf/Gal 238 B1
Bloomfield W Midlands 133 E9
Bloomsbury London 67 C10
Blore Staffs 169 F10
Blossomfield W Midlands 118 B2
Blount's Green Staffs 151 C11
Blowick Mersey 193 D11
Bloxham Oxon 101 D8
Bloxholm Lincs 173 E9
Bloxwich W Midlands 133 C9
Bloxworth Dorset 18 C3
Blubberhouses N Yorks 205 B9
Blue Anchor Cornw'l 5 D8
Blue Anchor Som'set 42 E4
Blue Anchor Swan 75 F8
Blue Bank N Yorks 227 D7
Blue Bell Hill Kent 69 G8
Blue Bridge M/Keynes 102 C6
Blue Planet Aquarium Ches 182 G6
Blue Reef Aquarium, Newquay Cornw'l 4 C6
Blue Reef Aquarium, Portsmouth Portsm'th 33 H10
Blue Reef Aquarium, Tynemouth Tyne/Wear 243 C9
Blue Row Essex 89 C8
Blue Town Kent 70 D2
Blue Vein Wilts 61 F10
Bluetown Kent 54 B2
Blughasary H'land 307 J6
Blundell's Hill Mersey 183 C7
Blundellsands Mersey 182 B4
Blundeston Suffolk 143 D10
Blunham Beds 122 G3
Blunsdon St. Andrew Swindon 62 B6
Bluntington Worcs 117 C7
Bluntisham Cambs 123 C7
Blunt's Cornw'l 6 C6
Blunt's Green Warwick 118 D2
Blurton Stoke 168 G5
Blyborough Lincs 188 C6
Blychau Conwy 165 C7
Blyford Suffolk 127 B8
Blymhill Staffs 150 G6
Blymhill Common Staffs 150 G5
Blymhill Lawn Staffs 150 G6
Blyth Notts 187 D10
Blyth Northum 253 G8
Blyth Bridge Scot Borders 270 F2
Blyth End Warwick 134 E4
Blythburgh Suffolk 127 B8
Blythe Bridge Staffs 169 G7
Blythe Marsh Staffs 169 G7
Blythswood Renf 267 B10
Blyton Lincs 188 C5
Boarhills Fife 287 F9
Boarhunt Hants 33 F10
Boar's Head Gtr Man 194 F5
Boars Hill Oxon 83 E7
Boarshead E Sussex 52 G4
Boarstall Bucks 83 C10
Boasley Cross Devon 12 C5
Boat of Garten H'land 291 B11
Boath H'land 300 B5
Bobbing Kent 69 F11
Bobbington Staffs 132 E6
Bobbingworth Essex 87 D8
Bobby Hill Suffolk 125 C10
Boblainy H'land 300 F4
Bocaddon Cornw'l 6 D3
Bochastle Stirl 285 G10
Bocking Essex 106 G5
Bocking Churchstreet Essex 106 F5
Bockings Elm Essex 89 B11
Bockleton Worcs 115 E11
Bockmer End Bucks 65 B10
Bodantionail H'land 299 B7
Boddam Aberds 303 E11
Boddam Shetl'd 315 M5
Bodden Som'set 44 E6
Boddington Glos 99 G7
Bodedern Angl 178 E4
Bodelwyddan Denbs 181 F8
Bodenham Heref'd 115 G10
Bodenham Arboretum and Earth Centre Worcs 132 G6
Bodenham Bank Heref'd 98 E3
Bodenham Moor Heref'd 115 G10
Bodernham Wilts 31 B11
Bodewryd Angl 178 C5
Bodfari Denbs 181 G9
Bodffordd Angl 178 F6
Bodham Norfolk 177 E10
Bodiam E Sussex 38 B3
Bodiam Castle E Sussex 38 B3
Bodicote Oxon 101 D9
Bodiechell Aberds 303 E7
Bodieve Cornw'l 10 G5
Bodilly Cornw'l 2 C5
Bodiniel Cornw'l 5 B11
Bodinnick Cornw'l 6 E2
Bodle Street Green E Sussex 37 E11
Bodley Devon 41 D7
Bodlith Powys 148 D4
Bodlondeb Conwy 180 G4
Bodmin Cornw'l 5 B11
Bodnant Conwy 180 G4
Bodnant Garden, Colwyn Bay Conwy 180 G3
Bodney Norfolk 140 D6
Bodrane Cornw'l 6 C4
Bodsham Kent 54 D6
Boduan Gwyn 144 B6
Boduel Cornw'l 6 C4
Bodwen Cornw'l 5 C10
Bodymoor Heath Warwick 134 D3
Bofarnel Cornw'l 6 C2
Bogallan H'land 300 D6
Bogbrae Aberds 303 F10
Bogend Notts 171 F7
Bogend S Ayrs 257 C9
Bogentory Aberds 293 C9
Boghall Midloth 270 B4
Boghall W Loth 269 B9
Boghead Aberds 293 D8
Boghead E Dunb 278 G2
Boghead S Lanarks 268 G5
Bogmarsh Heref'd 97 D10
Bogmoor Moray 302 C3
Bogniebrae Aberds 302 E5
Bogniebrae Aberds 302 E6
Bognor Regis W Sussex 22 D6
Bograxie Aberds 293 B9
Bogs Aberds 302 G5
Bogside N Lanarks 268 E6
Bogthorn W Yorks 204 F6
Bogton Aberds 302 D6
Bogtown Aberds 302 C5
Bogtown Devon 12 B5
Bogue Dumf/Gal 246 G4
Bohemia E Sussex 38 F4
Bohemia Wilts 32 D2
Bohenie H'land 290 E4
Bohetherick Cornw'l 7 B8
Boholt Gtr Man 195 E9
Bohortha Cornw'l 3 C9
Bohuntine H'land 290 E4
Bohuntinville H'land 290 E4
Boirseam W Isles 296 C6
Bojewyan Cornw'l 1 C3
Bokiddick Cornw'l 5 C10
Bolam Durham 233 G9
Bolam Northum 252 G3
Bolberry Devon 8 H3
Bold Heath Mersey 183 D8
Boldmere W Midlands 134 E2
Boldon Colliery Tyne/Wear 243 E8
Boldre Hants 20 B2
Boldron Durham 223 C10
Bole Notts 188 D3
Bolehall Staffs 134 C4
Bolehill Derby 170 D3
Bolehill S Yorks 186 E5
Bolenowe Cornw'l 2 B5
Boleside Scot Borders 261 C11
Bolham Devon 27 E7
Bolham Notts 188 E2
Bolham Water Devon 27 E11
Bolingey Cornw'l 4 E5
Bollihope Durham 232 E6
Bollington Ches 184 F6
Bollington Cross Ches 184 F6
Bollow Glos 80 C2
Bolney W Sussex 36 C3
Bolnhurst Beds 121 F11
Bolshan Angus 287 B10
Bolsover Derby 187 G7
Bolster Moor W Yorks 196 D5
Bolsterstone S Yorks 186 B3
Bolstone Heref'd 97 E10
Boltby N Yorks 215 B9
Bolter End Bucks 84 G3
Boltgate N Lincs 199 D10
Bolton Cumb 231 G9
Bolton E Loth 281 G10
Bolton ER Yorks 207 C11
Bolton Gtr Man 195 F8
Bolton Northum 264 G4
Bolton W Yorks 205 F9
Bolton Abbey N Yorks 205 C7
Bolton Abbey, Skipton N Yorks 205 C7
Bolton Bridge N Yorks 205 C7
Bolton by Bowland Lancs 203 D11
Bolton Castle, Leyburn N Yorks 223 G10
Bolton Green Lancs 194 D5
Bolton Low Houses Cumb 229 C10
Bolton New Houses Cumb 229 C10
Bolton Percy N Yorks 206 E6
Bolton Town End Lancs 211 F9
Bolton upon Dearne S Yorks 198 G2
Bolton Wood Lane Cumb 229 C11
Bolton Woods W Yorks 205 F9
Boltonfellend Cumb 239 D11
Boltongate Cumb 229 C10
Bolton-le-Sands Lancs 211 F9
Bolton-on-Swale N Yorks 224 F5
Boltshope Park Durham 232 B4
Bolventor Cornw'l 11 F9
Bomarsund Northum 253 G7
Bombie Dumf/Gal 237 D9
Bomby Cumb 221 B10
Bomere Heath Shrops 149 F9
Bonar Bridge H'land 309 K6
Bonawe Arg/Bute 284 D4
Bonbusk Notts 187 G8
Bonby N Lincs 200 D4
Bonc Wrex 148 B3
Boncath Pembs 92 D4
Bonchester Bridge Scot Borders 262 G3
Bonchurch I/Wight 21 F7
Bond End Staffs 152 F2
Bondend Glos 80 B5
Bondleigh Devon 25 G10
Bonds Lancs 202 D5
Bonehayne Devon 15 C10
Bonehill Devon 13 F10
Bonehill Staffs 134 C3
Bo'ness Falk 279 E9
Boney Hay Staffs 151 G11
Bonhill W Dunb 277 F7
Boningale Shrops 132 C6
Bonjedward Scot Borders 262 E5
Bonkle N Lanarks 268 D6
Bonnavoulin H'land 289 D7
Bonning Gate Cumb 221 F9
Bonnington C/Edinb 270 B2
Bonnington Kent 54 F5
Bonnybank Fife 287 G7
Bonnybridge Falk 278 E6
Bonnykelly Aberds 303 D8
Bonnyrigg Midloth 270 B6
Bonnyton Aberds 302 F6
Bonnyton Angus 287 B10
Bonnyton Angus 287 D7
Bonnyton E Ayrs 257 B10
Bonsall Derby 170 D3
Bonskeid House Perth/Kinr 291 G10
Bonson Som'set 43 E8
Bont Monmouths 78 B5
Bont Dolgadfan Powys 129 C7
Bont Newydd Gwyn 164 G2
Bontddu Gwyn 146 F3
Bont-goch = Elerch Ceredig'n 128 F3
Bonthorpe Lincs 191 G7
Bont-newydd Conwy 181 G8
Bontnewydd Ceredig'n 112 D2
Bontnewydd Gwyn 163 D7
Bontuchel Denbs 165 D9
Bonvilston V/Glam 58 E5
Bonwm Denbs 165 G10
Bon-y-maen Swan 75 F11
Boode Devon 40 F4
Booker Bucks 84 G4
Boomer Som'set 43 G9
Boon Scot Borders 271 F11
Boon Hill Staffs 168 E4
Boorley Green Hants 33 E8
Boosbeck Redcar/Clevel'd 226 B3
Boose's Green Essex 106 E6
Boot Cumb 220 E3
Boot Street Suffolk 108 B4
Booth W Yorks 196 B4
Booth Bank Ches 184 D2
Booth Green Ches 184 E6
Booth Wood W Yorks 196 D4
Boothby Graffoe Lincs 173 D7
Boothby Pagnell Lincs 155 C9
Boothen Stoke 168 G5
Boothferry ER Yorks 199 B8
Boothroyd W Yorks 197 C8
Booth's Hill Warrington 183 D11
Boothsdale Ches 167 B8
Boothstown Gtr Man 195 G8
Boothtown W Yorks 196 B5
Boothville Northants 120 E5
Bootle Cumb 210 B2
Bootle Mersey 182 C4
Booton Norfolk 160 E2
Boots Green Ches 184 G3
Booze N Yorks 223 E10
Boquhan Stirl 277 D10
Boquhapple Stirl 278 A3
Boraston Shrops 116 D2
Borden Kent 69 G11
Borden W Sussex 34 C4
Border Cumb 238 G5
Bordesley Green W Midlands 134 F2
Bordley N Yorks 213 G8
Bordon Hants 49 F10
Bordon Camp Hants 49 F9
Boreham Essex 88 D3
Boreham Wilts 45 E11
Boreham Street E Sussex 37 E11
Borehamwood Herts 85 F11
Boreland Dumf/Gal 236 C5
Boreland Dumf/Gal 248 E5
Boreland Fife 280 C6
Boreland Stirl 285 D9
Boreland of Southwick Dumf/Gal 237 C11
Borestone Stirl 278 C5
Borgh W Isles 296 C5
Borgh W Isles 297 L2
Borghasdal W Isles 296 C6
Borghastan W Isles 304 D4
Borgie H'land 308 D6
Borgue Dumf/Gal 237 E8
Borgue H'land 311 G5
Borley Essex 106 C6
Borley Green Essex 106 C6
Borley Green Herts 105 E8
Borley Green Suffolk 125 E9
Bornais W Isles 297 J3
Bornesketaig H'land 298 B3
Borness Dumf/Gal 237 E8
Borough Green Kent 52 B6
Boroughbridge N Yorks 215 F7
Borras Wrex 166 E4
Borreraig H'land 296 F7
Borrobol Lodge H'land 311 G2
Borrodale H'land 297 G7
Borrohill Aberds 303 D9
Borrowash Derby 153 C8
Borrowby N Yorks 215 B8
Borrowby N Yorks 226 B5
Borrowcop Hill Staffs 134 B2
Borrowfield Aberds 293 D10
Borrowston H'land 310 E7
Borrowstoun Mains Falk 279 E10
Borstal Medway 69 F8
Borth = Y Borth Ceredig'n 128 E2
Borthwick Midloth 271 D7
Borthwickbrae Scot Borders 261 G10
Borthwickshiels Scot Borders 261 F10
Borthwnog Gwyn 146 F3
Borth-y-Gest Gwyn 145 B11
Borve H'land 298 E4
Borve Lodge W Isles 305 J2
Borwick Lancs 211 E10
Borwick Rails Cumb 210 D3
Bosavern Cornw'l 1 C3
Bosbury Heref'd 98 C3
Boscarne Cornw'l 5 B10
Boscastle Cornw'l 11 C7
Boscombe Bournem'th 19 C8
Boscombe Wilts 47 F8
Boscomoor Staffs 151 G8
Boscoppa Cornw'l 5 E10
Boscreege Cornw'l 2 C3
Bosham W Sussex 34 G4
Bosherston Pembs 73 G7
Boskenna Cornw'l 1 E4
Bosleake Cornw'l 4 G3
Bosley Ches 168 B6
Bossall N Yorks 216 G4
Bossiney Cornw'l 11 D7
Bossingham Kent 55 D7
Bossington Hants 47 G10
Bossington Kent 55 B8
Bossington Som'set 41 D11
Bostadh W Isles 304 D3
Bostock Green Ches 167 B11
Boston Lincs 174 G4
Boston Long Hedges Lincs 174 F4
Boston Spa W Yorks 206 D4
Boswarthen Cornw'l 1 C4
Boswinger Cornw'l 5 G9
Botallack Cornw'l 1 C3
Botany Bay Bristol 60 D5
Botany Bay London 86 F3
Botany Bay Monmouths 79 E8
Botcherby Cumb 239 F10
Botcheston Leics 135 B9
Botely Oxon 83 D7
Botesdale Suffolk 125 B10
Bothal Northum 252 F6
Bothampstead W Berks 64 D4
Bothamsall Notts 187 G11
Bothel Cumb 229 D9
Bothenhampton Dorset 16 C5
Bothwell S Lanarks 268 D4
Bothy H'land 290 F4
Botley Bucks 85 E7
Botley Hants 33 E8
Botloe's Green Glos 98 F4
Botolph Bridge Peterbro 138 D3
Botolph Claydon Bucks 102 G4
Botolphs W Sussex 35 F11
Botolph's Bridge Kent 54 G6
Bottacks H'land 300 C4
Botternell Cornw'l 11 G11
Bottesford Leics 154 B6
Bottesford N Lincs 200 F2
Bottisham Cambs 123 E10
Bottlesford Wilts 46 B6
Bottom Boat W Yorks 197 C11
Bottom House Staffs 169 E8
Bottom of Hutton Lancs 194 B3
Bottom o'th'Moor Gtr Man 195 E7
Bottomcraig Fife 287 E7
Bottomley W Yorks 196 C2
Bottoms Cornw'l 1 E3
Botton N Yorks 226 E3
Botusfleming Cornw'l 7 C8
Botwnnog Gwyn 144 C5
Bough Beech Kent 52 D3
Boughrood Powys 96 D2
Boughrood Brest Powys 96 D2
Boughspring Glos 79 F9
Boughton Norfolk 140 C4
Boughton Northants 120 D5

Crewgarth Cumb 231 E7
Crewgreen Powys 148 F6
Crewkerne Som'set 28 F6
Crew's Hole Bristol 60 E6
Crewton Derby C 153 C7
Crianlarich Stirl 285 E7
Cribyn Ceredig'n 111 G11
Criccieth Gwyn 145 B10
Crich Derby 170 E5
Crich Carr Derby 170 E4
Crich Common Derby 170 E5
Crich Tramway Village Derby 170 D4
Crichie Aberds 303 E9
Crichmere Surrey 49 G11
Crichton Midloth 271 C7
Crick Monmouths 79 G7
Crick Northants 119 C11
Crickadarn Powys 95 C11
Cricket Malherbie Som'set 28 E5
Cricket St. Thomas Som'set 28 F5
Crickham Som'set 44 C2
Crickheath Shrops 148 E5
Crickhowell Powys 78 B2
Cricklade Wilts 81 G9
Cricklewood London 67 B8
Cricladarn Powys 95 C11
Criddlestyle Hants 31 E11
Cridling Stubbs N Yorks 198 C4
Crieff Perth/Kinr 286 E2
Crieff Visitors' Centre Perth/Kinr 286 E2
Criggan Cornw'l 5 C10
Criggion Powys 148 F5
Crigglestone W Yorks 197 D10
Crimble Gtr Man 195 E11
Crimchard Som'set 28 F4
Crimond Aberds 303 D10
Crimonmogate Aberds 303 D10
Crimp Cornw'l 24 D3
Crimplesham Norfolk 140 C3
Crimscote Warwick 100 B4
Crinan Arg/Bute 275 D8
Crinan Ferry Arg/Bute 275 D8
Crindau Newp 59 B10
Crindledyke N Lanarks 268 D6
Cringleford Norfolk 142 B3
Cringles W Yorks 204 D6
Crinow Pembs 73 C10
Cripple Corner Essex 107 E7
Cripplesease Cornw'l 2 B2
Cripplestyle Dorset 31 E9
Cripp's Corner E Sussex 38 C3
Crispie Arg/Bute 275 F10
Critchell's Green Hants 32 B3
Crizeley Heref'd 97 E8
Croanford Cornw'l 10 G6
Croasdale Cumb 219 B11
Crobeag W Isles 304 F5
Crock Street Som'set 28 E4
Crockenhill Kent 68 F4
Crockenwell Devon 13 C11
Crocker End Oxon 65 B8
Crockerhill Hants 33 F9
Crockerhill W Sussex 34 F6
Crocker's Ash Heref'd 79 B8
Crockerton Wilts 45 E11
Crockerton Green Wilts 45 E11
Crocketford or Ninemile Bar Dumf/Gal 237 B10
Crockett Cornw'l 12 G3
Crockey Hill C/York 207 D8
Crockham Hill Kent 52 C2
Crockhurst Street Kent 52 E6
Crockleford Heath Essex 107 F10
Crockleford Hill Essex 107 F10
Crockness Orkney 313 J4
Croes Hywel Monmouths 78 C4
Croesau Bach Shrops 148 D4
Croeserw Neath P Talb 76 F5
Croes-goch Pembs 90 E6
Croes-lan Ceredig'n 93 C7
Croesor Gwyn 163 G10
Croespenmaen Caerph 77 F11
Croes-wian Flints 181 G10
Croesyceiliog Carms 74 B6
Croesyceiliog Torf 78 F4
Croes-y-mwyalch Torf 78 G4
Croes-y-pant Monmouths 78 E4
Croesywaun Gwyn 163 D8
Croford Som'set 27 B10
Croft Leics 135 D10
Croft Lincs 175 C8
Croft Pembs 92 C3
Croft Warrington 183 C10
Croft End Lincs 175 C7
Croft Motor Racing Circuit N Yorks 224 D5
Croft of Tillymaud Aberds 303 F11
Croft Outerly Fife 280 A4
Croft West Cornw'l 4 F5
Croftamie Stirl 277 D9
Croftfoot Glasg C 268 C2
Crofthandy Cornw'l 4 G4
Croftlands Cumb 210 D5
Croftmalloch W Loth 269 C8
Croftmoraig Perth/Kinr 285 C11
Crofton Cumb 239 G8
Crofton London 68 F2
Crofton Wilts 63 G9
Crofton W Yorks 197 D11
Croft-on-Tees N Yorks 224 D5
Crofts Dumf/Gal 237 B9
Crofts Bank Gtr Man 184 B3
Crofts of Benachielt H'land 310 F5
Crofts of Haddo Aberds 303 F8
Crofts of Inverthernie Aberds 303 E7
Crofts of Meikle Ardo Aberds 303 E8
Crofty Swan 75 F8
Crogen Iddon Wrex 148 B5
Croggan Arg/Bute 289 G9
Croglin Cumb 231 B7
Croich H'land 309 K4
Croick H'land 310 D2
Croig Arg/Bute 288 D5
Crois Dughaill W Isles 297 J3
Cromarty H'land 301 C7
Cromasaig H'land 299 C10
Crombie Fife 279 D10
Crombie Castle Aberds 302 D5
Cromblet Aberds 303 F7
Cromdale H'land 301 G10
Cromer Herts 104 F5
Cromer Norfolk 160 A4
Cromford Derby 170 D3
Cromhall S Glos 79 G11
Cromhall Common S Glos 61 B7
Cromor W Isles 304 F6
Crompton Fold Gtr Man 196 F3
Cromra H'land 291 D7
Cromwell Notts 172 C3
Cromwell Bottom W Yorks 196 C6
Crondall Hants 49 D9
Cronk-y-Voddy I/Man 192 D4
Cronton Halton 183 D8
Crook Cumb 221 F9
Crook Durham 233 D9
Crook of Devon Perth/Kinr 286 G4
Crookdale Cumb 229 C9
Crooke Gtr Man 194 F4
Crooked End Glos 79 B10
Crooked Soley Wilts 63 E10
Crooked Withies Dorset 31 F9
Crookedholm E Ayrs 257 B11
Crookes S Yorks 186 D4
Crookfur E Renf 267 D10
Crookhall Durham 242 G4
Crookham Northum 263 B10
Crookham W Berks 64 G4
Crookham Eastfield Northum 263 B10
Crookham Village Hants 49 C9
Crookhaugh Scot Borders 260 D4
Crookhill Tyne/Wear 242 E5
Crooklands Cumb 211 C10
Crook's Marsh Bristol 60 C4
Crooksmoor S Yorks 186 D4
Crookston Glasg C 267 C10
Croome Park, Pershore Worcs 99 C7
Cropredy Oxon 101 B9
Cropston Leics 153 G11
Cropthorne Worcs 99 C9
Cropton N Yorks 216 B5
Cropwell Bishop Notts 154 B3
Cropwell Butler Notts 154 B3
Cros W Isles 304 B7
Crosben H'land 289 D9
Crosbost W Isles 304 F5
Crosby Cumb 229 D7
Crosby I/Man 192 E4
Crosby Mersey 182 B4
Crosby N Lincs 199 E11
Crosby Garrett Cumb 222 D4
Crosby Ravensworth Cumb 222 B2
Crosby Villa Cumb 229 D7
Croscombe Som'set 44 E5
Crosemere Shrops 149 D8
Crosland Edge W Yorks 196 E6
Crosland Hill W Yorks 196 E6
Crosland Moor W Yorks 196 D6
Cross Devon 40 F3
Cross Devon 40 G6
Cross Som'set 28 E5
Cross Som'set 44 C2
Cross Ash Monmouths 78 B6
Cross at Hand Kent 53 D9
Cross Bank Worcs 116 C4
Cross Coombe Cornw'l 4 E4
Cross End Beds 121 F11
Cross End Essex 107 E7
Cross End M/Keynes 103 D8
Cross Gates W Yorks 206 G3
Cross Green Suffolk 125 F7
Cross Green Suffolk 124 G6
Cross Green Suffolk 125 G9
Cross Green Staffs 133 B8
Cross Green Warwick 119 F7
Cross Green W Yorks 206 G2
Cross Hands Carms 75 C9
Cross Hands Pembs 73 C9
Cross Heath Staffs 168 F4
Cross Hill Derby 170 F6
Cross Hill ER Yorks 198 D6
Cross Hill Glos 79 F9
Cross Hills N Yorks 204 E6
Cross Houses Shrops 132 E3
Cross Houses Shrops 131 B10
Cross in Hand E Sussex 37 C9
Cross Inn Ceredig'n 111 E10
Cross Inn Ceredig'n 111 F7
Cross Inn Rh Cyn Taff 58 C5
Cross Keys Kent 52 C4
Cross Keys Wilts 61 E11
Cross Lane Powys 130 C3
Cross Lane Head Shrops 132 D4
Cross Lanes Bucks 84 E3
Cross Lanes Cornw'l 2 E5
Cross Lanes Dorset 30 G3
Cross Lanes Durham 223 C11
Cross Lanes N Yorks 215 G10
Cross Lanes Wrex 166 F5
Cross Oak Powys 96 G2
Cross of Jackston Aberds 303 F7
Cross Roads Devon 12 D5
Cross Roads W Yorks 204 F6
Cross Stone Aberds 303 G9
Cross Street Suffolk 126 B3
Cross Town Ches 184 F3
Crossaig Arg/Bute 255 B9
Crossal H'land 294 B6
Crossapol Arg/Bute 288 E1
Crossbarrow Cumb 228 F6
Crossbrae Aberds 302 D6
Crossburn Falk 279 G7
Crossbush W Sussex 35 F8
Crosscanonby Cumb 229 D7
Crosscynon Powys 114 C3
Crossdale Street Norfolk 160 B4
Crossens Mersey 193 C11
Crossflatts W Yorks 205 E8
Crossford Fife 279 D11
Crossford S Lanarks 268 F6
Crossgate Lincs 156 D4
Crossgate Orkney 312 G5
Crossgate Staffs 151 B8
Crossgatehall E Loth 271 B7
Crossgates Cumb 229 G7
Crossgates Fife 280 D2
Crossgates Powys 113 E11
Crossgill Cumb 231 C10
Crossgill Lancs 211 G11
Crossgreen Shrops 149 F9
Crosshands Carms 92 G3
Crosshill Glasg C 268 C3
Crosshill E Ayrs 257 E11
Crosshill Fife 280 B3
Crosshill S Ayrs 245 B8
Crosshill S Lanarks 268 E2
Crosshouse E Ayrs 257 B9
Crosskeys Caerph 78 G2
Crosskirk H'land 310 B4
Crosslands Cumb 210 B6
Crosslands Park Cumb 210 E4
Crosslanes Shrops 148 F6
Crosslee Scot Borders 261 F8
Crosslee Renf 267 B8
Crosslees E Renf 267 E11
Crossley W Yorks 197 C8
Crossley Hall W Yorks 205 G8
Crossmichael Dumf/Gal 237 C9
Crossmill E Renf 267 D10
Crossmoor Lancs 202 F4
Crossmount Perth/Kinr 285 B11
Crossmyloof Glasg C 267 C11
Crossport W Sussex 36 C3
Crossroads Aberds 293 D9
Crossroads E Ayrs 257 E11
Crossroads Fife 281 B7
Crosston Angus 287 B9
Crosstown Cornw'l 24 E2
Crosstown V/Glam 58 E4
Crossway Heref'd 98 E2
Crossway Monmouths 78 B6
Crossway Powys 113 F10
Crossway Green Monmouths 79 G8
Crossway Green Worcs 116 D6
Crossways Dorset 17 D11
Crossways Glos 79 C9
Crossways S Glos 79 G11
Crosswell Pembs 92 D2
Crosswood Ceredig'n 112 C3
Crosthwaite Cumb 221 G8
Croston Lancs 194 D3
Crostwick Norfolk 160 F5
Crostwight Norfolk 160 D6
Crothair W Isles 304 E3
Crouch Kent 52 B6
Crouch Kent 54 B4
Crouch End London 67 B9
Crouch Green Herts 104 G4
Crouch Hill Dorset 30 E2
Croucheston Wilts 31 B9
Croughly Moray 301 G11
Croughton Northants 101 E10
Crovie Aberds 303 C8
Crow Hants 31 G11
Crow Edge S Yorks 197 G7
Crow Green Essex 87 F9
Crow Hill Heref'd 98 F2
Crow Nest W Yorks 205 F8
Crow Wood Halton 183 D8
Crowan Cornw'l 2 C4
Crowborough E Sussex 52 G4
Crowborough Warren E Sussex 52 G4
Crowcombe Som'set 42 F6
Crowdecote Derby 169 B10
Crowden Derby 185 B9
Crowden Devon 12 B5
Crowdhill Hants 33 D7
Crowdhole Devon 26 D4
Crowdleham Kent 52 B5
Crowdon N Yorks 227 F9
Crowell Oxon 84 F2
Crowfield Northants 102 C2
Crowfield Suffolk 126 F2
Crowgate Street Norfolk 160 E6
Crowhill Gtr Man 184 B6
Crowhurst E Sussex 38 E3
Crowhurst Surrey 51 D11
Crowhurst Lane End Surrey 51 D11
Crowland Lincs 156 G4
Crowlas Cornw'l 2 C2
Crowle N Lincs 199 E9
Crowle Worcs 117 F8
Crowle Green Worcs 117 F8
Crowmarsh Gifford Oxon 64 B6
Crown Corner Suffolk 126 C5
Crownfield Bucks 84 F4
Crownhill M/Keynes 102 D6
Crownhill Plym'th 7 D9
Crownland Suffolk 125 C10
Crownpits Surrey 50 E3
Crownthorpe Norfolk 141 C11
Crowntown Cornw'l 2 C4
Crow's Green Essex 106 F3
Crow's Nest Cornw'l 6 B5
Crows-an-wra Cornw'l 1 D3
Crowshill Norfolk 141 B8
Crowsnest Shrops 131 C7
Crowther's Pool Powys 96 B4
Crowthorne Wokingham 65 G10
Crowton Ches 183 G9
Croxall Staffs 152 G3
Croxby Lincs 189 B11
Croxdale Durham 233 D11
Croxden Staffs 151 B11
Croxley Green Herts 85 F9
Croxteth Mersey 182 B6
Croxton Cambs 122 F4
Croxton Norfolk 141 F7
Croxton Norfolk 159 C9
Croxton N Lincs 200 E5
Croxton Staffs 150 C5
Croxton Green Ches 167 E9
Croxton Kerrial Leics 154 D6
Croxtonbank Staffs 150 C5
Croy H'land 301 E7
Croy N Lanarks 278 F4
Croyde Devon 40 F2
Croyde Bay Devon 40 F2
Croydon Cambs 104 B6
Croydon London 67 G10
Crozen Heref'd 97 B11
Crubenbeg H'land 291 D8
Crubenmore Lodge H'land 291 D8
Cruckmeole Shrops 131 B8
Cruckton Shrops 149 G8
Cruden Bay Aberds 303 F10
Crudgington Telford 150 F2
Crudie Aberds 303 D7
Crudwell Wilts 81 G7
Crugmeer Cornw'l 10 F4
Crugybar Carms 94 D3
Crûg Powys 114 C3
Crulabhig W Isles 304 E3
Crumbles E Sussex 23 E10
Crumlin Caerph 78 F2
Crumplehorn Cornw'l 6 E4
Crumpsall Gtr Man 195 G10
Crumpton Hill Worcs 98 B5
Crundale Kent 54 D5
Crundale Pembs 73 B7
Crungoed Powys 114 C3
Crunwere Pembs 73 C11
Cruse Heref'd 79 B9
Cruwys Morchard Devon 26 E5
Crux Easton Hants 48 B2
Cruxton Dorset 17 B7
Crwbin Carms 75 C7
Crya Orkney 313 H4
Cryers Hill Bucks 84 F5
Crymych Pembs 92 E3
Crynant = Creunant Neath P Talb 76 E3
Crynfryn Ceredig'n 111 E11
Crystal Palace National Sports Centre London 67 E10
Cuaich H'land 291 E8
Cuaig H'land 299 D7
Cuan Arg/Bute 275 B8
Cubbington Warwick 118 D6
Cubeck N Yorks 213 B9
Cubert Cornw'l 4 D5
Cubitt Town London 67 D11
Cubley S Yorks 197 G8
Cublington Bucks 102 G6
Cublington Heref'd 97 D8
Cuck Hill Som'set 44 B2
Cuckfield W Sussex 36 B4
Cucklington Som'set 30 B3
Cuckney Notts 187 G9
Cuckold's Green Suffolk 143 G9
Cuckold's Green Wilts 46 B3
Cuckoo Bridge Lincs 156 E4
Cuckoo Green Suffolk 143 D10
Cuckoo's Corner Hants 49 E8
Cuckoo's Corner Wilts 46 B4
Cuckron Shetl'd 315 H6
Cuddesdon Oxon 83 E9
Cuddington Bucks 84 C2
Cuddington Ches 183 G9
Cuddington Heath Ches 167 F7
Cuddra Cornw'l 5 E11
Cuddy Hill Lancs 202 F5
Cudham London 52 B2
Cudliptown Devon 12 F6
Cudworth Som'set 28 E5
Cudworth Surrey 51 E8
Cudworth S Yorks 197 F11
Cuerdley Cross Warrington 183 D8
Cufaude Hants 48 B6
Cuffern Pembs 91 G7
Cuffley Herts 86 E4
Cùl Doirlinn H'land 289 B8
Cuiashader W Isles 304 C7
Cuidhir W Isles 297 L2
Cuidhtinis W Isles 296 C6
Cuiken Midloth 270 C4
Cuilcheanna Ho. H'land 290 G2
Cuin Arg/Bute 288 D6
Cul na h-Aird W Isles 305 H3
Culbo H'land 300 C6
Culbokie H'land 300 D6
Culburnie H'land 300 E4
Culcabock H'land 300 E6
Culcairn H'land 300 C6
Culcharry H'land 301 D8
Culcheth Warrington 183 B11
Culcronchie Dumf/Gal 237 C7
Culdrain Aberds 302 F5
Culduie H'land 299 E7
Culeave H'land 309 K5
Culford Suffolk 124 C6
Culfordheath Suffolk 125 B7
Culfosie Aberds 293 C9
Culgaith Cumb 231 F8
Culham Oxon 83 F8
Culkein H'land 306 F5
Culkein Drumbeg H'land 306 F6
Culkerton Glos 80 F6
Cullachie H'land 301 G9
Cullen Moray 302 C5
Cullercoats Tyne/Wear 243 C9
Cullicudden H'land 300 C6
Cullingworth W Yorks 205 F7
Cullipool Arg/Bute 275 B8
Cullivoe Shetl'd 314 C7
Culloch Perth/Kinr 285 F11
Culloden H'land 301 E7
Culloden Battlefield, Inverness H'land 301 E7
Cullompton Devon 27 F8
Culm Davy Devon 27 E10
Culmaily H'land 311 K2
Culmazie Dumf/Gal 236 D5
Culmer Surrey 50 F3
Culmers Kent 70 G5
Culmington Shrops 131 G9
Culmstock Devon 27 E9
Culnacraig H'land 307 J5
Culnaightrie Dumf/Gal 237 D9
Culnaknock H'land 298 C5
Culnaneam H'land 294 C6
Culpho Suffolk 108 B4
Culra Lodge H'land 291 F7
Culrain H'land 309 K5
Culross Fife 279 D9
Culroy S Ayrs 257 G8
Culscadden Dumf/Gal 236 E6
Culsh Aberds 292 D5
Culsh Aberds 303 E8
Culshabbin Dumf/Gal 236 D4
Culswick Shetl'd 315 J4
Cultercullen Aberds 303 G9
Cults Aberds 302 F5
Cults Aberd C 293 C10
Cults Dumf/Gal 236 E6
Cults Fife 287 G7
Culverhouse Cross Card 58 E6
Culverlane Devon 8 C4
Culverstone Green Kent 68 G6
Culverthorpe Lincs 173 G8
Culworth Northants 101 B10
Culzean Castle, Maybole S Ayrs 256 G6
Culzie Lodge H'land 300 B5
Cumberlow Green Herts 104 E6
Cumbernauld N Lanarks 278 G5
Cumbernauld Village N Lanarks 278 F5
Cumber's Bank Wrex 149 B8
Cumberworth Lincs 191 G8
Cumdivock Cumb 230 B2
Cumeragh Village Lancs 203 F7
Cuminestown Aberds 303 D8
Cumlewick Shetl'd 315 L6
Cumlodden Arg/Bute 275 D11
Cumloden Dumf/Gal 236 C6
Cummersdale Cumb 239 G9
Cummerton Aberds 303 C8
Cummertrees Dumf/Gal 238 D4
Cummingston Moray 301 C11
Cumnock E Ayrs 258 F3
Cumnor Oxon 83 E7
Cumrew Cumb 240 G2
Cumrue Dumf/Gal 248 F3
Cumwhinton Cumb 239 G10
Cumwhitton Cumb 240 G2
Cundall N Yorks 215 E8
Cundy Cross S Yorks 197 F11
Cunning Park S Ayrs 257 F8
Cunninghamhead N Ayrs 267 G7
Cunnister Shetl'd 314 D7
Cupar Fife 287 F7
Cupar Muir Fife 287 F7
Cupernham Hants 32 C5
Cupid Green Herts 85 D9
Curbar Derby 186 G3
Curbidge Oxon 82 D4
Curborough Staffs 152 G2
Curbridge Hants 33 E8
Curdleigh Devon 28 D2
Curdridge Hants 33 E8
Curdworth Warwick 134 E3
Curgurrel Cornw'l 3 B9
Curin H'land 300 D3
Curland Som'set 28 D3
Curlew Green Suffolk 127 D7
Curling Tye Green Essex 88 D4
Curlott Hill Som'set 28 F6
Currarie S Ayrs 244 E5
Currian Vale Cornw'l 5 D9
Curridge W Berks 64 E3
Currie C/Edinb 270 B3
Currock Cumb 239 G10
Curry Mallet Som'set 28 C4
Curry Rivel Som'set 28 B5
Cursiter Orkney 312 G4
Curteis Corner Kent 53 F10
Curtisden Green Kent 53 E8
Curtisknowle Devon 8 E4
Curtismill Green Essex 87 F8
Cury Cornw'l 2 E5
Cusbay Orkney 312 E6
Cusgarne Cornw'l 4 G5
Cushnie Aberds 303 C7
Cushuish Som'set 43 G7
Cusop Heref'd 96 C4
Custards Hants 32 F4
Custom House London 68 C2
Cusworth S Yorks 198 G4
Cutcloy Dumf/Gal 236 F6
Cutcombe Som'set 42 F2
Cutgate Gtr Man 195 E11
Cuthill E Loth 281 G7
Cutiau Gwyn 146 F2
Cutlers Green Essex 105 E11
Cutler's Green Som'set 44 C5
Cutmadoc Cornw'l 5 C11
Cutmere Cornw'l 6 C6
Cutnall Green Worcs 117 D7
Cutsdean Glos 99 E11
Cutsyke W Yorks 198 C2
Cutthorpe Green Derby 186 G4
Cuttivett Cornw'l 7 C7
Cutts Shetl'd 315 K6
Cutts End Oxon 83 E7
Cutty Sark, Greenwich London 67 D11
Cuttybridge Pembs 72 B6
Cuttyhill Aberds 303 D10
Cuxham Oxon 83 F11
Cuxton Medway 69 F8
Cuxwold Lincs 201 G7
Cwm Bl Gwent 77 D11
Cwm Denbs 181 F9
Cwm Swan 75 F11
Cwm Capel Carms 75 E7
Cwm Collo Shrops 114 B4
Cwm Dulais Swan 75 E10
Cwm Gelli Caerph 77 F11
Cwm Penmachno Conwy 164 F3
Cwm Plysgog Pembs 92 C3
Cwmafan Rh Cyn Taff 76 G3
Cwmaman Rh Cyn Taff 77 F8
Cwmann Carms 93 C11
Cwmavon Torf 78 D3
Cwmbach Carms 75 E7
Cwmbach Carms 92 F5
Cwmbach Powys 113 G10
Cwmbach Powys 96 D3
Cwmbach Rh Cyn Taff 77 E8
Cwmbelan Powys 129 G8
Cwm-brain Shrops 114 B4
Cwmbran Torf 78 F3
Cwmbrwyno Ceredig'n 128 G4
Cwmcarn Caerph 78 G2
Cwmcarvan Monmouths 79 D7
Cwm-celyn Bl Gwent 78 D2
Cwm-Cewydd Gwyn 147 G7
Cwm-cou Ceredig'n 92 C5
Cwmcrawnon Powys 77 B10
Cwmcych Pembs 92 D5
Cwm-cynnar Swan 75 G8
Cwmdare Rh Cyn Taff 77 D7
Cwm-dows Caerph 78 F2
Cwmdu Carms 94 E2
Cwmdu Powys 96 G3
Cwmdu Swan 75 G10
Cwmduad Carms 93 E7
Cwmdwr Carms 94 E4
Cwmerfyn Ceredig'n 128 G3
Cwmfelin Boeth Carms 73 B11
Cwmfelin Mynach Carms 92 G4
Cwmfelinfach Caerph 77 G11
Cwmffrwd Carms 74 B6
Cwm-Ffrwd-oer Torf 78 E3
Cwm-Fields Torf 78 E3
Cwmgiedd Powys 76 C3
Cwmgors Neath P Talb 76 C2
Cwmgwili Carms 75 C9
Cwmgwrach Neath P Talb 76 E5
Cwmheyope Powys 114 C4
Cwmhiraeth Carms 92 D6
Cwm-hwnt Rh Cyn Taff 76 D6
Cwmifor Carms 94 F3
Cwmisfael Carms 75 B7
Cwm-Llinau Powys 128 B6
Cwmllyfri Carms 74 C4
Cwmllynfell Neath P Talb 76 C2
Cwmmawr Carms 75 C8
Cwmmiles Carms 92 G3
Cwmnantyrodyn Caerph 77 F11
Cwmorgan Carms 92 E5
Cwmparc Rh Cyn Taff 76 F6
Cwmpennar Rh Cyn Taff 77 E8
Cwmpenraig Carms 92 D6
Cwmrhos Powys 96 G3
Cwmrhydyceirw Swan 75 F11
Cwmsychbant Ceredig'n 93 B9
Cwmsyfiog Caerph 77 E11
Cwmsymlog Ceredig'n 128 G4
Cwmtillery Bl Gwent 78 D2
Cwmtwrch-isaf Neath P Talb 76 C3
Cwmtwrch-uchaf Powys 76 C3
Cwmwysg Powys 95 F7
Cwm-y-gaist Powys 114 C2
Cwm-y-glo Carms 75 C9
Cwm-y-glo Gwyn 163 C9
Cwmynyscoy Torf 78 F3
Cwmyoy Monmouths 96 G6
Cwm-yr-Eglwys Pembs 91 D10
Cwmystwyth Ceredig'n 112 C5
Cwrt Gwyn 128 C3
Cwrt-newydd Ceredig'n 93 B9
Cwrt-y-Cadno Carms 94 C3
Cwrt-y-carne Swan 75 E9
Cwrt-y-gollen Monmouths 78 B2
Cydweli = Kidwelly Carms 74 D6
Cyffordd Llandudno = Llandudno Junction Conwy 180 F4
Cyffylliog Denbs 165 D9
Cyfronydd Powys 130 B2
Cymau Flints 166 D3
Cymbyr Carms 94 E2
Cymdda Bridg 58 C2
Cymer Neath P Talb 76 F5
Cymfelin Bridg 57 D11
Cymfelin Merth Tyd 77 E9
Cymmer Rh Cyn Taff 77 G8
Cyncoed Card 59 C7
Cynghordy Carms 94 D6
Cynheidre Carms 75 D7
Cynonville Neath P Talb 76 F4
Cyntwell Card 58 D6
Cynwyd Denbs 165 G9
Cynwyl Elfed Carms 93 F7
Cywarch Gwyn 147 F7

D

Daccombe Devon 9 B8
Dacre Cumb 230 F5
Dacre N Yorks 214 G3
Dacre Banks N Yorks 214 G3
Daddry Shield Durham 232 D3
Dadford Bucks 102 D3
Dadlington Leics 135 D8
Dafen Carms 75 E8
Daffy Green Norfolk 141 B9
Dagdale Staffs 151 C11
Dagenham London 68 C3
Daggons Dorset 31 E10
Daglingworth Glos 81 D7
Dagnall Bucks 85 B7
Dagtail End Worcs 117 E10
Dagworth Suffolk 125 E10
Dail Beag W Isles 304 D4
Dail bho Dheas W Isles 304 B6
Dail bho Thuath W Isles 304 B6
Dail Mor W Isles 304 D4
Daill Arg/Bute 274 G4
Dailly S Ayrs 245 C7
Dainton Devon 9 B7
Dairsie or Osnaburgh Fife 287 F8
Daisy Bank W Midlands 133 D10
Daisy Green Essex 107 F8
Daisy Green Suffolk 125 D10
Daisy Green Suffolk 125 D11
Daisy Hill Gtr Man 195 G7
Daisy Hill W Yorks 205 G8
Daisy Hill W Yorks 197 B9
Daisy Nook Gtr Man 196 G2
Dalabrog W Isles 297 J3
Dalavich Arg/Bute 275 B10
Dalbeattie Dumf/Gal 237 C10
Dalbeg H'land 291 B8
Dalblair E Ayrs 258 F4
Dalbog Angus 293 F7
Dalbrack Stirl 285 G11
Dalbury Derby 152 C5
Dalby I/Man 192 E3
Dalby Lincs 190 G6
Dalby N Yorks 216 E2
Dalchalloch Perth/Kinr 291 G9
Dalchalm H'land 311 J3
Dalchenna Arg/Bute 284 G4
Dalchirach Moray 301 F11
Dalchonzie Perth/Kinr 285 E11
Dalchork H'land 309 H5
Dalchreichart H'land 290 B4
Dalchruin Perth/Kinr 285 F11
Dalderby Lincs 174 B3
Dale Cumb 230 C6
Dale Gtr Man 196 F3
Dale Pembs 72 D4
Dale Shetl'd 314 G6
Dale Abbey Derby 153 B8
Dale Bottom Cumb 229 G11
Dale End Derby 170 C2
Dale End Derby 185 E11
Dale End N Yorks 204 D5
Dale Hill E Sussex 53 G8
Dale Moor Derby 153 B8
Dale of Walls Shetl'd 315 H3
Dalehouse N Yorks 226 B5
Dalelia H'land 289 C9
Dalemain Cumb 230 F5
Dales Brow Gtr Man 195 G9
Daless H'land 301 F8
Dalestie Moray 292 B3
Dalfaber H'land 291 B11
Dalganachan H'land 310 E4
Dalgarven N Ayrs 266 F5
Dalgety Bay Fife 280 E2
Dalginross Perth/Kinr 285 E11
Dalguise Perth/Kinr 286 C3
Dalhalvaig H'land 310 D2
Dalham Suffolk 124 E4
Dalhastnie Angus 293 F7
Dalhenzean Perth/Kinr 292 G3
Dalkeith Midloth 270 B6
Dallam Warrington 183 C9
Dallam Tower Cumb 211 C9
Dallas Moray 301 D11
Dallas Lodge Moray 301 D11
Dallcharn H'land 308 D6
Dalleagles E Ayrs 258 G3
Dallinghoo Suffolk 126 F5
Dallington E Sussex 37 D11
Dallington Northants 120 E4
Dallow N Yorks 214 E3
Dalmadilly Aberds 293 B9
Dalmahoy C/Edinb 270 B2
Dalmally Arg/Bute 284 E5
Dalmarnock Glasg C 268 C2
Dalmarnock Perth/Kinr 286 C3
Dalmary Stirl 277 B10
Dalmellington E Ayrs 245 B11
Dalmeny C/Edinb 280 F2
Dalmigavie H'land 291 B9
Dalmigavie Lodge H'land 301 G7
Dalmilling S Ayrs 257 E9
Dalmore H'land 300 C6
Dalmuir W Dunb 277 G9
Dalnabreck H'land 289 C8
Dalnacardoch Lodge Perth/Kinr 291 F9
Dalnacroich H'land 300 D3
Dalnaglar Castle Perth/Kinr 292 G3
Dalnahaitnach H'land 301 G8
Dalnamein Lodge Perth/Kinr 291 G9
Dalnarrow Arg/Bute 289 F9
Dalnaspidal Lodge Perth/Kinr 291 F8
Dalnavaid Perth/Kinr 292 G2
Dalnavie H'land 300 B6
Dalnaw Dumf/Gal 236 B5
Dalnawillan Lodge H'land 310 E4
Dalness H'land 284 B5
Dalnessie H'land 309 H6
Dalphaid H'land 309 H3
Dalqueich Perth/Kinr 286 G4
Dalrannoch Arg/Bute 289 E11
Dalreavoch H'land 309 J7
Dalriach H'land 301 F10
Dalrigh Stirl 285 E7
Dalry C/Edinb 280 G4
Dalry N Ayrs 266 F5
Dalrymple E Ayrs 257 G9
Dalscote Northants 120 G3
Dalserf S Lanarks 268 E5
Dalshannon N Lanarks 278 G4
Dalston Cumb 239 G9
Dalston London 67 C10
Dalswinton Dumf/Gal 247 F10
Dalton Cumb 211 D10
Dalton Dumf/Gal 238 C4
Dalton Lancs 194 F3
Dalton Northum 241 F10
Dalton Northum 242 C4
Dalton N Yorks 215 D8
Dalton N Yorks 224 D2
Dalton S Lanarks 268 D3
Dalton S Yorks 187 C7
Dalton W Yorks 197 D7
Dalton Gates N Yorks 224 D5
Dalton Magna S Yorks 187 C7
Dalton Parva S Yorks 187 C7
Dalton Piercy Hartlep'l 234 E5
Dalton-in-Furness Cumb 210 E4
Dalton-le-Dale Durham 234 B4
Dalton-on-Tees N Yorks 224 D5
Dalveallan H'land 300 F6
Dalveich Stirl 285 E10
Dalvina Lo. H'land 308 E6
Dalwhinnie H'land 291 E8
Dalwood Devon 28 G2
Dalwyne S Ayrs 245 D8
Dam Green Norfolk 141 F11
Dam Head W Yorks 196 B6
Dam Mill Staffs 133 C7
Dam of Quoiggs Perth/Kinr 286 G2
Dam Side Lancs 202 D4
Damask Green Herts 104 F5
Damerham Hants 31 D10
Damery Glos 80 G2
Damgate Norfolk 143 B8
Damgate Norfolk 161 F9
Damhead Moray 301 D10
Damhead Holdings Midloth 270 B5
Damnaglaur Dumf/Gal 236 F3
Damsbrook Derby 187 G7
Damside Scot Borders 270 F3
Dan Caerlan Rh Cyn Taff 58 C4
Danaway Kent 69 G11
Danbury Essex 88 D2
Danby N Yorks 226 D4
Danby Botton N Yorks 226 E3
Danby Wiske N Yorks 224 F6
Dancers Hill Herts 86 F2
Dancing Green Heref'd 98 G2
Dandaleith Moray 302 E2
Danderhall Midloth 270 B6
Dane Bank Gtr Man 184 B6
Dane Chantry Kent 54 D6
Dane End Herts 104 G6
Dane End Herts 104 D6
Dane Hills Leics C 135 C11
Dane in Shaw Ches 168 C5
Dane Street Kent 54 C5
Danebank Ches 185 E7
Danebridge Ches 169 B7
Danehill E Sussex 36 B6
Danemoor Green Norfolk 141 B11
Danesbury Herts 86 B2
Daneshill Hants 49 C7
Danesmoor Derby 170 C6
Daneway Glos 80 E6
Dangerous Corner Gtr Man 195 G7
Dangerous Corner Lancs 194 E4
Daniel's Water Kent 54 E3
Danna na Cloiche Arg/Bute 275 F7
Danskine E Loth 271 B11
Danthorpe ER Yorks 209 G10
Danygraig Torf 78 G2
Danzey Green Warwick 118 D2
Darby End Worcs 133 F9
Darby Green Hants 65 G10
Darbys Green Worcs 116 F4
Darby's Hill W Midlands 133 F9
Darcy Lever Gtr Man 195 F8
Dardy Powys 78 B2
Darenth Kent 68 E5
Darenthdale Kent 68 G4
Daresbury Halton 183 E9
Darfield S Yorks 198 G2
Dargate Kent 70 G5
Dargate Common Kent 70 G5
Darite Cornw'l 6 B5
Dark Hill Glos 79 D9
Darkland Moray 302 C2
Darland Medway 69 F9
Darlaston Staffs 151 B7
Darlaston W Midlands 133 D9
Darlaston Green W Midlands 133 D9
Darley N Yorks 205 B10
Darley Abbey Derby C 153 B7
Darley Bridge Derby 170 C3
Darley Dale Derby 170 C3
Darley Green Warwick 118 C3
Darley Head N Yorks 205 B9
Darley Hillside Derby 170 C3
Darley Moor Motor Racing Circuit Derby 169 G11
Darleyford Cornw'l 11 G11
Darleyhall Herts 104 G2
Darlingscott Warwick 100 C4
Darlington D'lington 224 C5
Darliston Shrops 149 C11
Darlton Notts 188 G3
Darmsden Suffolk 125 G11
Darn Hill Gtr Man 195 E10
Darnall S Yorks 186 D5
Darnaway Castle Moray 301 D9
Darnick Scot Borders 262 C2

Dudley Wood W Midlands 133 F8
Dudley Zoological Gardens W Midlands 133 E8
Dudlow's Green Warrington 183 E10
Dudsbury Dorset 19 B7
Dudswell Herts 85 D7
Dudwells Pembs 91 G8
Duffield Derby 170 G4
Duffryn Neath P Talb 76 F4
Duffryn Newp 59 B9
Duffryn Shrops 130 G4
Dufftown Moray 302 F3
Duffus Moray 301 C11
Dufton Cumb 231 F9
Duggleby N Yorks 217 F7
Duich Arg/Bute 254 B4
Duilletter Arg/Bute 284 D5
Duinish Perth/Kinr 291 G8
Duirinish H'land 295 B9
Duisdalebeg H'land 295 D8
Duisdalemore H'land 295 D9
Duisky H'land 290 F2
Duke End Warwick 134 F4
Duke Street Suffolk 107 C11
Dukesfield Northum 241 F10
Dukestown Bl Gwent 77 C10
Dukinfield Gtr Man 184 B6
Dulas Angl 179 D7
Dulcote Som'set 44 E5
Dulford Devon 27 G9
Dull Perth/Kinr 286 C2
Dullatur N Lanarks 278 F4
Dullingham Cambs 124 F2
Dullingham Ley Cambs 124 F2
Dulnain Bridge H'land 301 G9
Duloch Fife 280 D2
Duloe Beds 122 E3
Duloe Cornw'l 6 D4
Dulsie H'land 301 E9
Dulverton Som'set 26 B6
Dulwich Village London 67 E10
Dumbarton W Dunb 277 F7
Dumbleton Glos 99 D10
Dumbreck Glasg C 267 C11
Dumcrieff Dumf/Gal 248 C4
Dumfries Dumf/Gal 237 B11
Dumgoyne Stirl 277 E10
Dummer Hants 48 D5
Dumpford W Sussex 34 C4
Dumpling Green Norfolk 159 G10
Dumplington Gtr Man 184 B3
Dumpton Kent 71 F11
Dun Angus 287 B10
Dun Charlabhaigh W Isles 304 D3
Dunach Arg/Bute 289 G10
Dunadd Arg/Bute 275 D9
Dunain Ho. H'land 300 E6
Dunalastair Perth/Kinr 285 B11
Dunan H'land 295 C7
Dunans Arg/Bute 275 D11
Dunans Arg/Bute 275 D9
Dunball Som'set 43 E10
Dunbar E Loth 282 F3
Dunbeath H'land 311 G5
Dunbeg Arg/Bute 289 F10
Dunblane Stirl 285 G11
Dunbog Fife 286 F6
Dunbridge Hants 32 B4
Dunburgh Norfolk 143 E8
Duncan Down Kent 70 F6
Duncansclett Shetl'd 315 K5
Duncanston Aberds 302 G5
Duncanston H'land 300 D5
Dunchurch Warwick 119 C9
Duncote Northants 120 G3
Duncow Dumf/Gal 247 G11
Duncraggan Stirl 285 G9
Duncrievie Perth/Kinr 286 G5
Duncroisk Stirl 285 D9
Duncton W Sussex 35 D7
Dundas Ho. Orkney 313 K5
Dundee Dundee C 287 D8
Dundee Airport Dundee C 287 E7
Dundeugh Dumf/Gal 246 F4
Dundon Som'set 44 G3
Dundon Hayes Som'set 44 G3
Dundonald Fife 280 C4
Dundonald S Ayrs 257 C9
Dundonald Camp N Ayrs 257 C8
Dundonnell H'land 307 L5
Dundonnell Hotel H'land 307 L5
Dundonnell House H'land 307 L6
Dundraw Cumb 229 B10
Dundreggan H'land 290 B5
Dundreggan Lodge H'land 290 B5
Dundrennan Dumf/Gal 237 E9
Dundridge Hants 33 D9
Dundry N Som'set 60 F5
Dundurn Perth/Kinr 285 E11
Dundyvan N Lanarks 268 C4
Dunecht Aberds 293 C9
Dunfermline Fife 279 D11
Dunfield Glos 81 F10
Dungate Kent 54 B2
Dunge Wilts 45 C11
Dungeness Kent 39 D9
Dungworth S Yorks 186 D3
Dunham Massey Gtr Man 184 D2
Dunham on Trent Notts 188 G4
Dunham Town Gtr Man 184 D2
Dunham Woodhouses Gtr Man 184 D2
Dunham-on-the-Hill Ches 183 G7
Dunhampton Worcs 117 D7
Dunholme Lincs 189 F8
Dunino Fife 287 F9
Dunipace Falk 278 E6
Dunira Perth/Kinr 285 E11
Dunkeld Perth/Kinr 286 C4
Dunkerton Bath/NE Som'set 45 B8
Dunkeswell Devon 27 F10
Dunkeswick W Yorks 206 D2
Dunkirk Cambs 139 F10
Dunkirk Ches 182 G5
Dunkirk Kent 54 B5
Dunkirk Norfolk 160 D4
Dunkirk S Glos 61 B9
Dunkirk Wilts 62 G3
Dunk's Green Kent 52 C6
Dunlappie Angus 293 G7
Dunley Hants 48 C3
Dunley Worcs 116 D5
Dunlichity Lodge H'land 300 F6
Dunlop E Ayrs 267 F8
Dunmaglass Lodge H'land 300 G5
Dunmere Cornw'l 5 B10
Dunmore Arg/Bute 275 G8
Dunmore Falk 279 D7
Dunmore H'land 300 E5
Dunn Street Kent 54 D3
Dunn Street Kent 69 G9
Dunnet H'land 310 B6
Dunnichen Angus 287 C9
Dunnikier Fife 280 C5
Dunninald Angus 287 B11
Dunning Perth/Kinr 286 F4
Dunnington C/York 207 C9
Dunnington ER Yorks 209 C9
Dunnington Warwick 117 G11
Dunningwell Cumb 210 C3
Dunnockshaw Lancs 195 B10
Dunollie Arg/Bute 289 F10
Dunoon Arg/Bute 276 F3
Dunragit Dumf/Gal 236 D3
Dunrobin Castle Museum & Gardens H'land 311 J2
Dunrobin Mains H'land 311 J2
Dunrostan Arg/Bute 275 E8
Duns Scot Borders 272 E5
Duns Tew Oxon 101 F9
Dunsby Lincs 156 D2
Dunscar Gtr Man 195 E8
Dunscore Dumf/Gal 247 G9
Dunscroft S Yorks 199 F7
Dunsdale Redcar/Clevel'd 226 B2
Dunsden Green Oxon 65 D8
Dunsfold Surrey 50 F4
Dunsfold Green Surrey 50 F4
Dunsford Devon 14 D2
Dunshalt Fife 286 F6
Dunshill Notts 171 C7
Dunshill Worcs 98 E6
Dunshillock Aberds 303 E9
Dunsinnan Perth/Kinr 286 D5
Dunskey Ho. Dumf/Gal 236 D2
Dunsley N Yorks 227 C7
Dunsley Staffs 133 G7
Dunsmore Bucks 84 D5
Dunsop Bridge Lancs 203 C9
Dunstable Beds 103 G10
Dunstall Staffs 152 E3
Dunstall Green Suffolk 124 E4
Dunstall Hill W Midlands 133 D8
Dunstall Hill W Midlands 133 C8
Dunstan Northum 264 F6
Dunstan Staffs 151 F8
Dunster Som'set 42 E3
Dunster Beach Som'set 42 E4
Dunster Castle, Minehead Som'set 42 E3
Dunston Derby 186 G5
Dunston Lincs 173 C9
Dunston Norfolk 142 C4
Dunston Tyne/Wear 242 E6
Dunston Hill Tyne/Wear 242 E6
Dunstone Devon 7 E11
Dunstone Devon 13 F10
Dunsville S Yorks 198 F6
Dunswell ER Yorks 209 F7
Dunsyre S Lanarks 269 F11
Dunterton Devon 12 F3
Dunthrop Oxon 101 F7
Duntisborne Abbots Glos 81 D7
Duntisbourne Leer Glos 81 D7
Duntisbourne Rouse Glos 81 D7
Duntish Dorset 29 F11
Duntocher W Dunb 277 G9
Dunton Beds 104 C4
Dunton Bucks 102 G6
Dunton Norfolk 159 C7
Dunton Bassett Leics 135 E10
Dunton Green Kent 52 B4
Dunton Patch Norfolk 159 C7
Dunton Wayletts Essex 87 G11
Duntrune Castle Arg/Bute 275 D8
Duntulm H'land 298 B4
Dunure S Ayrs 257 F7
Dunvant = Dynfant Swan 75 G9
Dunvegan H'land 298 E2
Dunvegan Castle H'land 298 E2
Dunwear Som'set 43 F10
Dunwich Suffolk 127 C9
Duporth Cornw'l 5 E10
Dupplin Castle Perth/Kinr 286 F4
Durdar Cumb 239 G10
Durgan Cornw'l 3 D7
Durgates E Sussex 52 G6
Durham Durham 233 C11
Durham Cathedral Durham 233 C11
Durham Tees Valley Airport Stockton 225 C7
Durisdeer Dumf/Gal 247 C9
Durisdeermill Dumf/Gal 247 C9
Durkar W Yorks 197 D10
Durleigh Som'set 43 F9
Durley Hants 33 D8
Durley Wilts 63 G8
Durley Hill Bath/NE Som'set 60 F6
Durlock Kent 71 G10
Durlock Kent 55 B9
Durlow Common Heref'd 98 D2
Durn Gtr Man 196 D2
Durnamuck H'land 307 K5
Durness H'land 308 C4
Durno Aberds 303 G7
Durns Town Hants 19 B11
Durns Town Hants 19 B11
Duror H'land 289 D11
Durran Arg/Bute 275 C10
Durran H'land 310 C5
Durrant Green Kent 53 F11
Durrants Hants 34 F2
Durrington Wilts 47 E7
Durrington W Sussex 35 G10
Durrisdale Orkney 312 F4
Dursley Glos 80 F3
Dursley Cross Glos 79 B11
Durston Som'set 28 B3
Durweston Dorset 30 F5
Dury Shetl'd 315 G6
Duston Northants 120 E4
Duthil H'land 301 G9
Dutlas Powys 114 B4
Duton Hill Essex 106 F2
Dutson Cornw'l 12 D2
Dutton Warrington 183 F9
Dutwoods Derby 152 E4
Duxford Cambs 105 B9
Duxford Oxon 82 F5
Duxford Airfield (Imperial War Museum), Sawston Cambs 105 B9
Duxmoor Shrops 115 B8
Dwygyfylchi Conwy 180 F2
Dwyran Angl 162 B6
Dyce Aberd C 293 B10
Dye House Northum 241 F10
Dyer's Common S Glos 60 C5
Dyfatty Carms 75 E7
Dyffryn Bridg 76 G5
Dyffryn Carms 92 G6
Dyffryn Pembs 91 D8
Dyffryn Powys 148 G2
Dyffryn Powys 96 G5
Dyffryn V/Glam 58 E5
Dyffryn Ardudwy Gwyn 145 E11
Dyffryn Castell Ceredig'n 128 G5
Dyffryn Cellwen Neath P Talb 76 D5
Dyke Devon 24 C4
Dyke Lincs 156 E2
Dyke Moray 301 D9
Dykehead Angus 292 G5
Dykehead N Lanarks 269 D7
Dykehead Stirl 277 B11
Dykelands Aberds 293 G9
Dykends Angus 286 B6
Dykesfield Cumb 239 F8
Dykeside Aberds 303 E7
Dykesmains N Ayrs 266 G4
Dylife Powys 129 E7
Dymchurch Kent 39 B10
Dymock Glos 98 E3
Dynfant = Dunvant Swan 75 G9
Dyrham S Glos 61 D8
Dyrham Park S Glos 61 D8
Dysart Fife 280 C6
Dyserth Denbs 181 F9

E

Eabost H'land 294 B5
Eabost West H'land 298 E3
Each End Kent 55 B10
Eachway Worcs 117 B9
Eachwick Northum 242 C4
Eadar Dha Fhadhail W Isles 304 E2
Eagland Hill Lancs 202 D4
Eagle Lincs 172 B5
Eagle Barnsdale Lincs 172 B5
Eagle Hall Lincs 172 B5
Eagle Moor Lincs 172 B5
Eaglescliffe Stockton 225 B8
Eaglesfield Cumb 229 F7
Eaglesfield Dumf/Gal 238 C6
Eaglesham E Renf 267 E11
Eaglestone M/Keynes 103 D7
Eaglethorpe Northants 137 E11
Eagley Gtr Man 195 E8
Eairy I/Man 192 E3
Eakley M/Keynes 120 G6
Eakring Notts 171 C11
Ealand N Lincs 199 E9
Ealing London 67 C7
Ealing Common London 67 C7
Eals Northum 240 F5
Eamont Bridge Cumb 230 F6
Earby Lancs 204 D4
Earcroft Blackb'n 195 C7
Eardington Shrops 132 E4
Eardisland Heref'd 115 F8
Eardisley Heref'd 96 B6
Eardiston Shrops 149 E7
Eardiston Worcs 116 D3
Earith Cambs 123 B7
Earl Shilton Leics 135 D9
Earl Soham Suffolk 126 E4
Earl Sterndale Derby 169 B9
Earl Stonham Suffolk 126 F2
Earle Northum 263 D11
Earlesfield Lincs 155 B7
Earlestown Mersey 183 B9
Earley Wokingham 65 E9
Earlham Norfolk 142 B3
Earlish H'land 298 C3
Earls Barton Northants 121 E7
Earls Colne Essex 107 F7
Earl's Common Worcs 117 F9
Earl's Court London 67 D9
Earl's Croome Worcs 99 C7
Earl's Down E Sussex 37 D11
Earl's Green Suffolk 125 D10
Earlsdon W Midlands 118 B6
Earlsferry Fife 281 B9
Earlsfield London 67 E9
Earlsford Aberds 303 F8
Earlsheaton W Yorks 197 C9
Earlsmill Moray 301 D9
Earlston Scot Borders 262 B3
Earlston E Ayrs 257 B10
Earlswood Monmouths 79 F7
Earlswood Surrey 51 D9
Earlswood Warwick 118 C2
Earnley W Sussex 22 D4
Earnock S Lanarks 268 E3
Earnshaw Bridge Lancs 194 C4
Earsairidh W Isles 297 M3
Earsdon Northum 252 E6
Earsdon Tyne/Wear 243 C8
Earsham Norfolk 142 F6
Earsham Street Suffolk 126 B4
Earswick C/York 207 B8
Eartham W Sussex 34 F6
Earthcott Green S Glos 60 B6
Easby N Yorks 224 E3
Easby N Yorks 225 D11
Easdale Arg/Bute 275 B8
Easebourne W Sussex 34 C5
Easenhall Warwick 119 B9
Eashing Surrey 50 E2
Easington Bucks 83 C11
Easington Durham 234 C4
Easington ER Yorks 201 D11
Easington Northum 264 C4
Easington Oxon 83 F11
Easington Oxon 101 D9
Easington Redcar/Clevel'd 226 B4
Easington Colliery Durham 234 C4
Easington Lane Tyne/Wear 234 B3
Easingwold N Yorks 215 F10
Easole Street Kent 55 C9
Eassie Angus 287 C7
East Aberthaw V/Glam 58 F4
East Acton London 67 C8
East Adderbury Oxon 101 D9
East Allington Devon 8 F5
East Amat H'land 309 K4
East Anstey Devon 26 B5
East Anton Hants 47 D11
East Appleton N Yorks 224 F4
East Ardsley W Yorks 197 B9
East Ashling W Sussex 34 F4
East Ashton Hants 48 D2
East Auchronie Aberds 293 C10
East Ayton N Yorks 217 B9
East Bank Bl Gwent 78 D2
East Barkwith Lincs 189 E11
East Barming Kent 53 C8
East Barnby N Yorks 226 C6
East Barnet London 86 F3
East Barns E Loth 282 F4
East Barsham Norfolk 159 C8
East Barton Suffolk 125 D8
East Beach W Sussex 22 E5
East Beckham Norfolk 177 E11
East Bedfont London 66 E5
East Bergholt Suffolk 107 D11
East Bierley W Yorks 197 B7
East Bilney Norfolk 159 F9
East Blackdene Durham 232 D3
East Blackdene Durham 232 D3
East Blatchington E Sussex 37 G7
East Bloxworth Dorset 18 C3
East Boldon Tyne/Wear 243 E9
East Boldre Hants 32 G5
East Bonhard Perth/Kinr 286 E5
East Bower Som'set 43 F10
East Brent Som'set 43 C10
East Bridgeford Notts 171 G11
East Briscoe Durham 223 B9
East Buckland Devon 41 G7
East Budleigh Devon 15 E7
East Burnham Bucks 66 C3
East Burrafirth Shetl'd 315 H5
East Burton Dorset 18 D2
East Butsfield Durham 233 B8
East Butterleigh Devon 27 F7
East Butterwick N Lincs 199 F10
East Cairnbeg Aberds 293 F9
East Calder W Loth 269 B11
East Carleton Norfolk 142 C3
East Carlton Northants 136 F6
East Carlton W Yorks 205 E10
East Chaldon Dorset 17 E11
East Challow Oxon 63 B11
East Charleton Devon 8 G5
East Chelborough Dorset 29 F9
East Chiltington E Sussex 36 E5
East Chinnock Som'set 29 E7
East Chisenbury Wilts 46 C6
East Cholderton Hants 47 D9
East Clandon Surrey 50 C5
East Claydon Bucks 102 F4
East Clevedon N Som'set 60 E2
East Clyne H'land 311 J3
East Clyth H'land 310 F7
East Coker Som'set 29 E8
East Combe Som'set 43 G7
East Common N Yorks 207 G8
East Compton Dorset 30 D5
East Compton Som'set 44 E6
East Cornworthy Devon 8 D6
East Cottingwith ER Yorks 207 E10
East Coulston Wilts 46 C3
East Cowes I/Wight 20 B6
East Cowick ER Yorks 199 C7
East Cowton N Yorks 224 E6
East Cramlington Northum 243 B7
East Cranmore Som'set 45 E7
East Creech Dorset 18 E4
East Croachy H'land 300 G6
East Croftmore H'land 291 B11
East Curthwaite Cumb 230 B2
East Dean E Sussex 23 F9
East Dean Glos 98 G3
East Dean Hants 32 B3
East Dean W Sussex 34 E6
East Dene S Yorks 186 C6
East Denton Tyne/Wear 242 D6
East Didsbury Gtr Man 184 D5
East Down Devon 40 E6
East Drayton Notts 188 F3
East Dulwich London 67 E10
East Dundry N Som'set 60 F5
East Ella Kingston/Hull 200 B5
East End Beds 103 C9
East End Beds 122 F2
East End Bucks 84 B4
East End Cambs 124 C3
East End Dorset 18 B5
East End Essex 89 D8
East End ER Yorks 201 B9
East End ER Yorks 209 G9
East End ER Yorks 209 B9
East End Glos 81 E11
East End Hants 33 C11
East End Hants 64 G2
East End Hants 20 B3
East End Herts 105 G9
East End Kent 53 F10
East End Kent 70 E3
East End M/Keynes 103 C8
East End N Som'set 60 E3
East End Oxon 82 C5
East End Oxon 101 E7
East End Oxon 82 B6
East End Oxon 101 D9
East End Suffolk 107 D11
East End Suffolk 126 F3
East End S Glos 61 E9
East End Som'set 45 D7
East End Som'set 44 C5
East End Green Herts 86 C3
East Everleigh Wilts 47 C6
East Ewell Surrey 67 G8
East Farleigh Kent 53 C8
East Farndon Northants 136 F4
East Ferry Lincs 188 B4
East Finchley London 67 B9
East Flexford Surrey 50 D2
East Fortune E Loth 281 F10
East Garforth W Yorks 206 G4
East Garston W Berks 63 D11
East Garston Woodlands W Berks 63 E11
East Gateshead Tyne/Wear 243 E7
East Gillibrands Lancs 194 F3
East Ginge Oxon 64 B2
East Gores Essex 107 G7
East Goscote Leics 154 G2
East Grafton Wilts 63 G9
East Grange Moray 301 C10
East Green Hants 49 E10
East Green Suffolk 127 D8
East Green Suffolk 124 G3
East Grimstead Wilts 32 B2
East Grinstead W Sussex 51 F11
East Guldeford E Sussex 38 B6
East Haddon Northants 120 D3
East Hagbourne Oxon 64 B4
East Halton N Lincs 200 D6
East Ham London 68 C2
East Hampnett W Sussex 34 F6
East Hanney Oxon 82 G6
East Hanningfield Essex 88 E3
East Hardwick W Yorks 198 D3
East Harling Norfolk 141 F9
East Harlsey N Yorks 225 F8
East Harnham Wilts 31 B10
East Harptree Bath/NE Som'set 44 B5
East Hartford Northum 243 B7
East Harting W Sussex 34 D3
East Hatch Wilts 30 B6
East Hatley Cambs 122 G5
East Hauxwell N Yorks 224 G3
East Haven Angus 287 D9
East Heckington Lincs 173 G11
East Hedleyhope Durham 233 C9
East Helmsdale H'land 311 H4
East Hendred Oxon 64 B3
East Herringthorpe S Yorks 187 C7
East Herrington Tyne/Wear 243 G9
East Heslerton N Yorks 217 D8
East Hewish N Som'set 59 G11
East Hill Hants 34 B3
East Hill Kent 68 G5
East Hoathly E Sussex 37 D8
East Hogaland Shetl'd 315 K5
East Holme Dorset 18 D3
East Holywell Northum 243 C8
East Horrington Som'set 44 D5
East Horsley Surrey 50 C5
East Horton Northum 264 C2
East Howdon Tyne/Wear 243 D8
East Howe Bournem'th 19 B7
East Huntspill Som'set 43 E10
East Hyde Beds 85 B10
East Ilsley W Berks 64 C3
East Keal Lincs 174 C5
East Kennett Wilts 62 F6
East Keswick W Yorks 206 E2
East Ketton D'lington 234 G2
East Kilbride S Lanarks 268 E2
East Kingston W Sussex 35 G9
East Kirkby Lincs 174 C4
East Knapton N Yorks 217 D7
East Knighton Dorset 18 D2
East Knowstone Devon 26 C4
East Knoyle Wilts 45 G11
East Kyloe Northum 264 B3
East Kyo Durham 242 G5
East Lambrook Som'set 28 D6
East Lamington H'land 301 B7
East Langdon Kent 55 D10
East Langton Leics 136 E4
East Langwell H'land 309 J7
East Lavant W Sussex 34 F5
East Lavington W Sussex 34 D6
East Law Durham 242 G3
East Layton N Yorks 224 D3
East Leake Notts 153 D11
East Learmouth Northum 263 B9
East Leigh Devon 8 E3
East Leigh Devon 25 F11
East Lenham Kent 54 C2
East Lexham Norfolk 159 F7
East Lilburn Northum 264 E2
East Linton E Loth 281 F11
East Liss Hants 34 B3
East Lockinge Oxon 64 B2
East Loftus Redcar/Clevel'd 226 B4
East Looe Cornw'l 6 E5
East Lound N Lincs 188 B3
East Lulworth Dorset 18 E3
East Lutton N Yorks 217 F8
East Lydford Som'set 44 G5
East Lynch Som'set 42 D2
East Lyng Som'set 28 B4
East Mains Aberds 293 D8
East Mains S Lanarks 268 E2
East Malling Kent 53 B8
East Malling Heath Kent 53 B7
East March Angus 287 D8
East Marden W Sussex 34 E4
East Markham Notts 188 G2
East Marsh NE Lincs 201 F9
East Martin Hants 31 D9
East Marton N Yorks 204 C4
East Meon Hants 33 C11
East Mere Devon 27 D7
East Mersea Essex 89 C9
East Mey H'land 310 B7
East Molesey Surrey 66 F6
East Moor W Yorks 197 C10
East Morden Dorset 18 C4
East Morton W Yorks 205 E8
East Ness N Yorks 216 D3
East Newton ER Yorks 209 F11
East Newton N Yorks 216 D2
East Norton Leics 136 C5
East Nynehead Som'set 27 C11
East Oakley Hants 48 C5
East Ogwell Devon 14 G2
East Orchard Dorset 30 D4
East Ord Northum 273 E9
East Parley Dorset 19 B8
East Peckham Kent 53 D7
East Pennard Som'set 44 F5
East Perry Cambs 122 D3
East Portlemouth Devon 9 G9
East Prawle Devon 9 G10
East Preston W Sussex 35 G9
East Pulham Dorset 30 F2
East Putford Devon 24 D5
East Quantoxhead Som'set 42 E6
East Rainton Tyne/Wear 234 B2
East Ravendale NE Lincs 190 B2
East Raynham Norfolk 159 D7
East Rhidorroch Lodge H'land 307 K7
East Rigton W Yorks 206 E2
East Rolstone N Som'set 59 G11
East Rounton N Yorks 225 E8
East Row N Yorks 227 C7
East Rudham Norfolk 158 D6
East Runton Norfolk 177 E11
East Ruston Norfolk 160 D6
East Saltoun E Loth 271 B9
East Scrafton N Yorks 213 C11
East Sheen London 67 D7
East Shefford W Berks 63 D11
East Sleekburn Northum 253 G7
East Somerton Norfolk 161 F9
East Stanley Durham 242 G6
East Stockwith Lincs 188 C3
East Stoke Dorset 18 D3
East Stoke Notts 172 F3
East Stoke Som'set 29 D7
East Stour Dorset 30 C3
East Stourmouth Kent 71 G9
East Stowford Devon 25 B10
East Stratton Hants 48 F4
East Street Kent 55 B10
East Street Som'set 44 F4
East Studdal Kent 55 D10
East Suisnish H'land 295 B7
East Taphouse Cornw'l 6 C3
East Third Scot Borders 262 B4
East Thirston Northum 252 D5
East Tilbury Thurr'k 69 D7
East Tisted Hants 49 G8
East Torrington Lincs 189 E10
East Town Som'set 42 G6
East Town Som'set 44 E6
East Tuddenham Norfolk 159 G11
East Tytherley Hants 32 B3
East Tytherton Wilts 62 D3
East Village Devon 26 F4
East Village V/Glam 58 E3
East Wall Shrops 131 E10
East Walton Norfolk 158 F4
East Water Som'set 44 C4
East Week Devon 13 C9
East Wellow Hants 32 C4
East Wemyss Fife 280 B6
East Whitburn W Loth 269 B9
East Wickham London 68 D3
East Williamston Pembs 73 E9
East Winch Norfolk 158 F3
East Winterslow Wilts 47 G8
East Wittering W Sussex 22 D4
East Witton N Yorks 214 B2
East Woodburn Northum 251 F10
East Woodhay Hants 64 G2
East Woodlands Som'set 45 E9
East Worldham Hants 49 F8
East Worlington Devon 26 E3
East Worthing W Sussex 35 G11
Eastacombe Devon 25 B8
Eastbourne D'lington 224 C6
Eastbourne E Sussex 23 F10
Eastbridge Suffolk 127 D8
Eastbrook Som'set 28 C2
Eastbrook V/Glam 59 E7
Eastburn ER Yorks 208 B5
Eastburn W Yorks 204 E6
Eastbury Herts 85 G9
Eastbury W Berks 63 D10
Eastby N Yorks 204 C6
Eastchurch Kent 70 E3
Eastcombe Glos 80 E5
Eastcote London 66 B6
Eastcote Northants 120 G3
Eastcote W Midlands 118 B3
Eastcote Village London 66 B6
Eastcott Cornw'l 24 D3
Eastcott Devon 12 E5
Eastcott Wilts 46 B4
Eastcotts Beds 103 B11
Eastcourt Wilts 63 G8
Eastcourt Wilts 81 G7
Eastend Essex 86 C6
Eastend Green Essex 89 B9
Easter Aberchalder H'land 291 B7
Easter Ardross H'land 300 B6
Easter Balgedie Perth/Kinr 286 G5
Easter Balmoral Aberds 292 D4
Easter Boleskine H'land 300 G5
Easter Brackland Stirl 285 G10
Easter Brae H'land 300 C6
Easter Bush Midloth 270 C5
Easter Carbeth Stirl 277 F10
Easter Cardno Aberds 303 C9
Easter Compton S Glos 60 C5
Easter Cringate Stirl 278 D4
Easter Culfosie Aberds 293 C9
Easter Davoch Aberds 292 C6
Easter Earshaig Dumf/Gal 248 C2
Easter Ellister Arg/Bute 254 B3
Easter Fearn H'land 309 L6
Easter Galcantray H'land 301 E8
Easter Howgate Midloth 270 C4
Easter Kinkell H'land 300 D5
Easter Knox Angus 287 D9
Easter Lednathie Angus 292 G5
Easter Milton H'land 301 D9
Easter Moniack H'land 300 E5
Easter Ord Aberds 293 C10
Easter Quarff Shetl'd 315 K6
Easter Rhynd Perth/Kinr 286 F5
Easter Row Stirl 278 B5
Easter Silverford Aberds 303 C7
Easter Skeld Shetl'd 315 J5
Easter Tulloch H'land 291 B11
Easter Whyntie Aberds 302 C6
Eastergate W Sussex 35 F7
Easterhouse Glasg C 268 B3
Easterside Middlesbro 225 B10
Easterton Wilts 46 B4
Easterton of Lenabo Aberds 303 E10
Easterton Sands Wilts 46 B4
Eastertown Som'set 43 C10
Eastertown of Auchleuchries Aberds 303 F10
Eastfield Bristol 60 D5
Eastfield N Lanarks 269 C7
Eastfield N Lanarks 278 F4
Eastfield Northum 243 B7
Eastfield N Yorks 217 C10
Eastfield Peterbro 138 D4
Eastfield S Lanarks 268 C2
Eastfield S Yorks 197 G9
Eastfield S Yorks 187 C9
Eastgate Durham 232 D5
Eastgate Norfolk 160 E2
Easthall Herts 104 G4
Eastham Mersey 182 E5
Eastham Worcs 116 D3
Eastham Ferry Mersey 182 E5
Easthampstead Brackn'l 65 F11
Easthampton Heref'd 115 E8
Easthaugh Norfolk 159 F11
Eastheath Wokingham 65 F10
Easthope Shrops 131 D11
Easthorpe Essex 107 G9
Easthorpe ER Yorks 208 D3
Easthorpe Leics 154 B6
Easthorpe Notts 172 E2
Easthouse Shetl'd 315 J5
Easthouses Midloth 270 B6
Easting Orkney 312 C8
Eastington Devon 26 F2
Eastington Glos 80 D3
Eastington Glos 81 C10
Eastleach Martin Glos 82 D2
Eastleach Turville Glos 81 D11
Eastleaze Swindon 62 C6
Eastleigh Devon 25 B7
Eastleigh Hants 33 D7
Eastling Kent 54 B3
Eastly End Surrey 66 F4
Eastmoor Derby 186 G4
Eastmoor Norfolk 140 C4
Eastney Portsm'th 21 B9
Eastnor Heref'd 98 D4
Eastoft N Lincs 199 D10
Eastoke Hants 22 D2
Easton Cambs 122 C2
Easton Cumb 239 F7
Easton Cumb 239 C10
Easton Dorset 17 G9
Easton Devon 13 D10
Easton Hants 48 G4
Easton I/Wight 20 D2
Easton Lincs 155 D8
Easton Norfolk 160 G2
Easton Suffolk 126 F5
Easton Som'set 44 D4
Easton W Berks 64 E2
Easton Wilts 61 E11
Easton Grey Wilts 61 B11
Easton Maudit Northants 121 F7
Easton on the Hill Northants 137 B10
Easton Royal Wilts 63 G8
Easton Town Som'set 44 G6
Easton Town Wilts 61 B11
Easton-in-Gordano N Som'set 60 D4
Eastrea Cambs 138 D5
Eastriggs Dumf/Gal 238 D6
Eastrington ER Yorks 199 B9
Eastrip Wilts 61 E10
Eastrop Wilts 82 G2
Eastry Kent 55 C10
East-the-Water Devon 25 B7
Eastville Bristol 60 D6
Eastville Lincs 174 D6
Eastwell Leics 154 D5
Eastwick Herts 86 C6
Eastwick Shetl'd 314 F5
Eastwood Notts 171 F7
Eastwood Southend 69 B11
Eastwood S Yorks 186 C6
Eastwood End Cambs 139 E8
Eastwood Park S Glos 79 G11
Eathorpe Warwick 119 D7
Eaton Ches 167 C9
Eaton Ches 168 B5
Eaton Heref'd 115 F10
Eaton Leics 154 D5
Eaton Norfolk 142 B4
Eaton Norfolk 158 B3
Eaton Notts 188 F2
Eaton Oxon 82 E6
Eaton Shrops 131 F7
Eaton Bishop Heref'd 97 D8
Eaton Bray Beds 103 G9
Eaton Constantine Shrops 131 B11
Eaton Green Beds 103 G9
Eaton Hastings Oxon 82 F3
Eaton Socon Cambs 122 F3
Eaton upon Tern Shrops 150 E3
Eau Brink Norfolk 157 F11
Eau Well Lincs 156 E2
Eau Withington Heref'd 97 C10
Eaves Green W Midlands 134 G5
Eaves Hall Lancs 203 E10
Eavestone N Yorks 214 F4
Ebberston N Yorks 217 C7
Ebbesbourne Wake Wilts 31 C7
Ebblake Dorset 31 F10
Ebbw Vale = Glyn Ebwy Bl Gwent 77 D11
Ebchester Durham 242 F4
Ebdon N Som'set 59 G11
Ebford Devon 14 D5
Ebley Glos 80 E4
Ebnal Ches 167 F7
Ebreywood Shrops 149 F10
Ebrington Glos 100 C3
Ecchinswell Hants 48 B3
Ecclefechan Dumf/Gal 238 C5
Eccles Scot Borders 272 G5
Eccles Gtr Man 184 B3
Eccles Kent 69 G8
Eccles Green Heref'd 97 B7
Eccles on Sea Norfolk 161 D8
Eccles Road Norfolk 141 E10
Ecclesall S Yorks 186 E4
Ecclesfield S Yorks 186 C5
Ecclesgreig Aberds 293 G9
Eccleshall Staffs 150 D6
Eccleshill W Yorks 205 F9
Ecclesmachan W Loth 279 G11
Eccleston Ches 166 C6
Eccleston Lancs 194 D4
Eccleston Mersey 183 B7
Eccleston Park Mersey 183 C7
Eccliffe Dorset 30 B4
Eccup W Yorks 205 E11
Echt Aberds 293 C9
Eckford Scot Borders 262 D6
Eckington Derby 186 F6
Eckington Worcs 99 C8
Ecton Northants 120 E6
Ecton Brook Northants 120 E6
Edale Derby 185 D10
Edbrook Som'set 43 E8
Edbrooke Som'set 42 G2
Edburton W Sussex 36 E2
Edderside Cumb 229 B8
Edderthorpe S Yorks 198 F2
Edderton H'land 309 L7
Eddington Kent 71 F7
Eddington W Berks 63 F10
Eddlestone Scot Borders 270 F4
Eddlewood S Lanarks 268 E4
Eden Camp, Malton N Yorks 216 E5

Eden Mount Cumb 211 D8
Eden Vale Durham 234 D4
Eden Vale Wilts 45 C11
Edenbridge Kent 52 D2
Edenfield Lancs 195 D10
Edenhall Cumb 231 E7
Edenham Lincs 155 E11
Edensor Derby 186 G2
Edenthorpe S Yorks 198 F6
Edentown Cumb 239 F9
Ederline Arg/Bute 275 C9
Edern Gwyn 144 B5
Edford Som'set 45 D7
Edgarley Som'set 44 F4
Edgbaston W Midlands 133 G11
Edgcote Northants 101 B10
Edgcott Bucks 102 G3
Edgcott Som'set 41 F10
Edgcumbe Cornw'l 2 C6
Edge Glos 80 D4
Edge Shrops 131 B7
Edge End Glos 79 C9
Edge End Lancs 203 G10
Edge Fold Blackb'n 195 D8
Edge Fold Gtr Man 195 F7
Edge Green Norfolk 141 G10
Edge Green Warrington 183 B10
Edge Hill Mersey 182 D5
Edge Hill Warwick 134 D4
Edgebolton Shrops 149 E11
Edgefield Norfolk 159 C11
Edgefield S Yorks 186 B3
Edgefield Street Norfolk 159 C11
Edgehill Derby 170 G5
Edgeley Gtr Man 184 D5
Edgerston Scot Borders 262 G5
Edgerton W Yorks 196 D6
Edgeside Lancs 195 C10
Edgeworth Glos 80 D6
Edginswell Devon 9 B7
Edgiock Worcs 117 E10
Edgmond Telford 150 F4
Edgmond Marsh Telford 150 E4
Edgton Shrops 131 G7
Edgware London 85 G11
Edgworth Blackb'n 195 D8
Edinample Stirl 285 E9
Edinbane H'land 298 D3
Edinburgh C/Edinb 280 G4
Edinburgh Airport C/Edinb 280 G2
Edinburgh Castle C/Edinb 280 G5
Edinburgh Crystal Visitor Centre, Penicuik Midloth 270 C4
Edinburgh Hill Kent 55 E10
Edinburgh Zoo C/Edinb 280 G4
Edinchip Stirl 285 E9
Edingale Staffs 152 G4
Edingight Ho. Moray 302 D5
Edinglassie Ho. Aberds 292 B5
Edingley Notts 171 D11
Edingthorpe Norfolk 160 C6
Edingthorpe Green Norfolk 160 C6
Edington Som'set 43 F11
Edington Wilts 46 C2
Edingworth Som'set 43 C11
Edintore Moray 302 E4
Edistone Devon 24 C2
Edith Weston Rutl'd 137 B8
Edithmead Som'set 43 D10
Edlaston Derby 169 G11
Edlesborough Bucks 85 B7
Edlingham Northum 252 B4
Edlington Lincs 190 G2
Edmondsham Dorset 31 E9
Edmondsley Durham 233 B10
Edmondstown Rh Cyn Taff 77 G8
Edmondthorpe Leics 155 F7
Edmonstone C/Edinb 280 G6
Edmonstone Orkney 312 F6
Edmonstown Rh Cyn Taff 77 G8
Edmonton Cornw'l 10 G5
Edmonton London 86 G4
Edmund Hill Som'set 44 F4
Edmundbyers Durham 232 B6
Ednam Scot Borders 262 B6
Ednaston Derby 170 G2
Edney Common Essex 87 E11
Edradynate Perth/Kinr 286 B2
Edrom Scot Borders 272 D6
Edstaston Shrops 149 C10
Edstone Warwick 118 E3
Edvin Loach Heref'd 116 F3
Edwalton Notts 153 B11
Edwardstone Suffolk 107 C8
Edwardsville Merth Tyd 77 F9
Edwinstowe Notts 171 B10
Edworth Beds 104 C4
Edwyn Ralph Heref'd 116 F2
Edzell Angus 293 G7
Efail Isaf Rh Cyn Taff 58 C5
Efail-fach Rh Cyn Taff 76 F3
Efailnewydd Gwyn 145 B7
Efail-rhyd Powys 148 D3
Efailwen Carms 92 F2
Efenechtyd Denbs 165 D10
Effingham Surrey 50 C6
Effirth Shetl'd 315 H5
Efflinch Staffs 152 F3
Efford Plym'th 7 D10
Egbury Hants 48 C2
Egde Green Ches 167 E7
Egdean W Sussex 35 C7
Egdon Worcs 117 G8
Egerton Gtr Man 195 E8
Egerton Kent 54 D2
Egerton Forstal Kent 53 D11
Egerton Green Ches 167 E8
Eggborough N Yorks 198 C5
Eggbuckland Plym'th 7 D9
Eggington Beds 103 G9
Eggington Derby 152 D5
Egglesburn Durham 232 G5
Egglescliffe Stockton 225 C8
Eggleston Durham 232 G6
Egham Surrey 66 E4
Egham Wick Surrey 66 E3
Egleton Rutl'd 137 B7
Eglingham Northum 264 F4
Egloshayle Cornw'l 10 G6
Egloskerry Cornw'l 11 D11
Eglwys Cross Wrex 167 G7
Eglwys Fach Ceredig'n 128 D3
Eglwysbach Conwy 180 G4
Eglwys-Brewis V/Glam 58 F4
Eglwyswen Pembs 92 D3
Eglwyswrw Pembs 92 D2
Egmanton Notts 172 B2
Egremont Cumb 219 C10
Egremont Mersey 182 C4
Egton N Yorks 226 D6
Egton Bridge N Yorks 226 D6
Egypt Hants 48 F3
Eiden H'land 309 J7
Eight Ash Green Essex 107 F8
Eighton Banks Tyne/Wear 243 F7
Eign Hill Heref'd 97 D10
Eignaig H'land 289 E9
Eil H'land 291 B10
Eilanreach H'land 295 D10
Eildon Scot Borders 262 C3
Eilean Anabaich W Isles 305 H4
Eilean Darach H'land 307 L6
Eilean Shona Ho H'land 289 B8
Eileanach Lodge H'land 300 C5
Einacleite W Isles 304 F3
Eisgean W Isles 305 G5
Eisingrug Gwyn 146 C2
Elan Village Powys 113 D8
Eland Green Northum 242 C5
Elberton S Glos 60 B6
Elborough N Som'set 43 B11
Elburton Plym'th 7 E10
Elcho Perth/Kinr 286 E5
Elcombe Glos 80 F3
Elcombe Swindon 62 C6
Elcot W Berks 63 F11
Eldene Swindon 63 C7
Elder Street Essex 105 E11
Eldernell Cambs 138 D6
Eldersfield Worcs 98 E6
Elderslie Renf 267 C8
Eldon Durham 233 F10
Eldon Lane Durham 233 F10
Eldroth N Yorks 212 F5
Eldwick W Yorks 205 E8
Elemore Vale Tyne/Wear 234 B3
Elerch = Bont-goch Ceredig'n 128 F3
Elerch Ceredig'n 128 F3
Elfhowe Cumb 221 F9
Elford Northum 264 C5
Elford Staffs 152 G3
Elford Closes Cambs 123 C10
Elgin Moray 302 C2
Elgol H'land 295 D7
Elham Kent 55 E7
Eliburn W Loth 269 B10
Elie Fife 287 G8
Elim Angl 178 E5
Eling Hants 32 E5
Eling W Berks 64 D4
Elishader H'land 298 C5
Elishaw Northum 251 D9
Elizafield Dumf/Gal 238 C2
Elkesley Notts 187 F11
Elkington Northants 120 B2
Elkins Green Essex 87 E10
Elkstone Glos 81 C7
Ellacombe Torbay 9 C8
Ellan H'land 301 G8
Ellanbrook Gtr Man 195 G8
Elland W Yorks 196 C6
Elland Lower Edge W Yorks 196 C6
Elland Upper Edge W Yorks 196 C6
Ellary Arg/Bute 275 F8
Ellastone Staffs 169 G10
Ellbridge Cornw'l 7 C8
Ellel Lancs 202 B5
Ellenborough Cumb 228 D6
Ellenbrook Herts 86 D2
Ellenbrook I/Man 192 E4
Ellenglaze Cornw'l 4 D5
Ellenhall Staffs 150 D6
Ellen's Green Surrey 50 F5
Ellerbeck N Yorks 225 F8
Ellerburn N Yorks 216 C6
Ellerby N Yorks 226 C5
Ellerdine Telford 150 E2
Ellerdine Heath Telford 150 E2
Ellergreen Cumb 221 F10
Ellerhayes Devon 27 G7
Elleric Arg/Bute 284 C4
Ellerker ER Yorks 200 B2
Ellers N Yorks 204 E6
Ellerton ER Yorks 207 F10
Ellerton N Yorks 224 F5
Ellesborough Bucks 84 D4
Ellesmere Shrops 149 C7
Ellesmere Park Gtr Man 184 B3
Ellesmere Port Ches 182 F6
Ellicombe Som'set 42 E3
Ellinge Kent 55 E8
Ellingham Hants 31 F10
Ellingham Norfolk 143 E7
Ellingham Northum 264 D5
Ellingstring N Yorks 214 C3
Ellington Cambs 122 C3
Ellington Northum 253 E7
Ellington Thorpe Cambs 122 C3
Elliot Angus 287 D10
Elliots Green Som'set 45 D9
Ellisfield Hants 48 D6
Ellistown Leics 153 G8
Ellon Aberds 303 F9
Ellonby Cumb 230 D4
Ellough Suffolk 143 F8
Ellough Moor Suffolk 143 F8
Elloughton ER Yorks 200 B2
Ellwood Glos 79 D9
Elm Cambs 139 B9
Elm Corner Surrey 50 B5
Elm Park London 68 B4
Elmbridge Glos 80 B5
Elmbridge Worcs 117 D8
Elmdon Essex 105 D9
Elmdon W Midlands 134 G3
Elmdon Heath W Midlands 134 G3
Elmer W Sussex 35 G7
Elmers End London 67 F11
Elmer's Green Lancs 194 F4
Elmesthorpe Leics 135 D9
Elmfield I/Wight 21 C8
Elmhurst Bucks 84 B4
Elmhurst Staffs 152 G2
Elmley Castle Worcs 99 C9
Elmley Lovett Worcs 117 D7
Elmore Glos 80 B3
Elmore Back Glos 80 B3
Elms Farm Beds 121 G11
Elmscott Devon 24 C2
Elmsett Suffolk 107 B11
Elmslack Lancs 211 D9
Elmstead Essex 107 F11
Elmstead Kent 54 D6
Elmstead London 68 E2
Elmstead Heath Essex 107 G11
Elmstead Market Essex 107 G11
Elmstone Kent 71 G9
Elmstone Hardwicke Glos 99 F8
Elmswell ER Yorks 208 B5
Elmswell Suffolk 125 E9
Elmton Derby 187 G8
Elmton Park Derby 187 G7
Elness Orkney 312 E7
Elphin H'land 307 H7
Elphinstone E Loth 281 G7
Elrick Aberds 293 C10
Elrig Dumf/Gal 236 E5
Elrigbeag Arg/Bute 284 F5
Elrington Northum 241 E9
Elsdon Heref'd 114 G6
Elsdon Northum 251 E10
Elsecar S Yorks 197 G11
Elsenham Essex 105 F10
Elsfield Oxon 83 D8
Elsham N Lincs 200 E4
Elsing Norfolk 159 F11
Elslack N Yorks 204 D4
Elson Portsm'th 33 G10
Elson Shrops 149 B7
Elsrickle S Lanarks 269 G11
Elstead Surrey 50 E2
Elsted W Sussex 34 D4
Elsted Marsh W Sussex 34 C4
Elsthorpe Lincs 155 E11
Elstob Durham 234 G2
Elston Lancs 203 G8
Elston Notts 172 F3
Elston Wilts 46 E5
Elstone Devon 25 D11
Elstow Beds 103 B11
Elstree Herts 85 F11
Elstronwick ER Yorks 209 G10
Elswick Lancs 202 F4
Elswick Tyne/Wear 242 E6
Elsworth Cambs 122 E6
Elterwater Cumb 220 E6
Eltham London 68 E2
Eltisley Cambs 122 F5
Elton Cambs 137 E11
Elton Ches 183 F7
Elton Derby 170 C2
Elton Glos 79 C11
Elton Gtr Man 195 E9
Elton Heref'd 115 C9
Elton Notts 154 B5
Elton Stockton 225 B8
Elton Green Ches 183 G7
Elton's Marsh Heref'd 97 C9
Eltringham Northum 242 E3
Elvanfoot S Lanarks 259 F10
Elvaston Derby 153 C8
Elveden Suffolk 140 G6
Elverland Kent 54 B3
Elvingston E Loth 281 G9
Elvington C/York 207 D9
Elvington Kent 55 C9
Elwell Dorset 17 D9
Elwick Hartlep'l 234 E5
Elwick Northum 264 B4
Elworth Ches 168 C2
Elworthy Som'set 42 G5
Ely Cambs 139 G10
Ely Card 58 D6
Ely Cathedral and Museum Cambs 139 G10
Emberton M/Keynes 103 B7
Embleton Cumb 229 E9
Embleton Durham 234 F4
Embleton Northum 264 E6
Embo H'land 311 K2
Embo Street H'land 311 K2
Emborough Som'set 44 C6
Embsay N Yorks 204 C6
Emerson Park London 68 B4
Emery Down Hants 32 F3
Emley W Yorks 197 E8
Emmbrook Wokingham 65 F10
Emmer Green Wokingham 65 D8
Emmets Nest Brackn'l 65 E10
Emmett Carr Derby 187 F7
Emmington Oxon 84 E2
Emneth Norfolk 139 B9
Emneth Hungate Norfolk 139 B10
Emorsgate Norfolk 157 E10
Empingham Rutl'd 137 B9
Empshott Hants 49 G9
Empshott Green Hants 49 G8
Emstrey Shrops 149 G10
Emsworth Hants 34 F2
Enborne W Berks 64 F2
Enborne Row W Berks 64 G2
Enchmarsh Shrops 131 D10
Enderby Leics 135 D10
Endmoor Cumb 211 C10
Endon Staffs 168 E6
Endon Bank Staffs 168 E6
Energlyn Caerph 59 B7
Enfield London 86 F4
Enfield Worcs 117 D10
Enfield Highway London 86 F5
Enfield Island Village Essex 86 F5
Enfield Lock London 86 F5
Enfield Town London 86 F4
Enfield Wash London 86 F5
Enford Wilts 46 C6
Engamoor Shetl'd 315 H4
Engedi Angl 178 F5
Engine Common S Glos 61 C7
Englefield W Berks 64 E6
Englefield Green Surrey 66 E3
Englemere Brackn'l 66 F2
Engleseabrook Ches 168 E3
English Bicknor Glos 79 B9
English Frankton Shrops 149 D9
Englishcombe Bath/NE Som'set 61 G8
Engollen Cornw'l 5 B7
Enham-Alamein Hants 47 D11
Enisfirth Shetl'd 314 F5
Enmore Som'set 43 F8
Enmore Green Dorset 30 C5
Ennerdale Bridge Cumb 219 B11
Enniscaven Cornw'l 5 D9
Enoch Dumf/Gal 247 C9
Enochdhu Perth/Kinr 292 G2
Ensay Arg/Bute 288 E5
Ensbury Bournem'th 19 B7
Ensbury Park Dorset 19 C7
Ensdon Shrops 149 F8
Enslow Oxon 83 B7
Enson Staffs 151 D8
Enstone Oxon 101 G7
Enterkinfoot Dumf/Gal 247 C9
Enterpen N Yorks 225 D9
Enton Green Surrey 50 E3
Enville Staffs 132 F6
Eòropaidh W Isles 304 B7
Eolaigearraidh W Isles 297 L3
Eorabus Arg/Bute 288 G5
Epney Glos 80 C3
Eppelby N Yorks 224 C3
Epperstone Notts 171 F11
Epping Essex 87 E7
Epping Green Essex 86 D6
Epping Green Herts 86 D3
Epping Upland Essex 86 E6
Eppleworth ER Yorks 208 G6
Epsom Surrey 67 G8
Epsom Racecourse Surrey 67 H8
Epwell Oxon 101 C7
Epworth N Lincs 199 G9
Epworth Turbary N Lincs 199 G9
Erbistock Wrex 166 G5
Erbusaig H'land 295 C9
Erchless Castle H'land 300 E4
Erddig Wrex 166 F4
Erdington W Midlands 134 E2
Eredine Arg/Bute 275 C10
Eriboll H'land 308 D4
Ericstane Dumf/Gal 260 G3
Eridge Green E Sussex 52 F5
Erines Arg/Bute 275 F9
Eriswell Suffolk 124 B4
Erith London 68 D4
Erlestoke Wilts 46 C3
Ermine Lincs 189 G7
Ermington Devon 8 E2
Ernesettle Plym'th 7 D8
Erpingham Norfolk 160 C3
Erriottwood Kent 54 B2
Errogie H'land 300 G5
Errol Perth/Kinr 286 E6
Errol Station Perth/Kinr 286 E6
Erskine Renf 277 G9
Erskine Bridge Renf 277 G9
Ervie Dumf/Gal 236 C2
Erwarton Suffolk 108 D4
Erwood Powys 95 C11
Eryholme N Yorks 224 D6
Eryrys Denbs 166 D2
Escalls Cornw'l 1 D3
Escomb Durham 233 E9
Escott Som'set 42 F5
Escrick N Yorks 207 E8
Esgair Carms 93 F7
Esgairgeiliog Powys 128 B5
Esgyryn Conwy 180 F4
Esh Durham 233 C9
Esh Winning Durham 233 C9
Esher Surrey 66 G6
Esholt W Yorks 205 E9
Eshott Northum 252 D6
Eshton N Yorks 204 B4
Esk Valley N Yorks 226 E6
Eskadale H'land 300 F4
Eskbank Midloth 270 B6
Eskdale Green Cumb 220 E2
Eskdalemuir Dumf/Gal 249 D7
Eskeleth N Yorks 223 E9
Eskett Cumb 219 B11
Eskham Lincs 190 B5
Eskholme S Yorks 198 D6
Esknish Arg/Bute 274 G4
Esperley Lane Ends Durham 233 G8
Esprick Lancs 202 F4
Essendine Rutl'd 155 G10
Essendon Herts 86 D3
Essich H'land 300 F6
Essington Staffs 133 C9
Esslemont Aberds 303 G9
Eston Redcar/Clevel'd 225 B11
Estover Plym'th 7 D10
Eswick Shetl'd 315 H6
Etal Northum 263 B10
Etchilhampton Wilts 62 G4
Etchingham E Sussex 38 B2
Etchinghill Kent 55 F7
Etchinghill Staffs 151 F10
Etchingwood E Sussex 37 C8
Etherley Dene Durham 233 F9
Etherley Grange Durham 233 F9
Ethie Castle Angus 287 C10
Ethie Mains Angus 287 C10
Etling Green Norfolk 159 G10
Etloe Glos 79 D11
Eton Windsor 66 D3
Eton Wick Windsor 66 D2
Etrop Green Gtr Man 184 D4
Etruria Stoke 168 F5
Etterby Cumb 239 F9
Etteridge H'land 291 D8
Ettersgill Durham 232 F3
Ettiley Heath Ches 168 C2
Ettingshall W Midlands 133 D8
Ettingshall Park W Midlands 133 D8
Ettington Warwick 100 B5
Etton ER Yorks 208 E5
Etton Peterbro 138 B2
Ettrick Scot Borders 261 G7
Ettrickbridge Scot Borders 261 E9
Ettrickdale Arg/Bute 275 G11
Ettrickhill Scot Borders 261 G7
Etwall Derby 152 C5
Eudon George Shrops 132 F3
Eureka!, Halifax W Yorks 196 C5
Euston Suffolk 125 B7
Euximoor Drove Cambs 139 D9
Euxton Lancs 194 D5
Evancoyd Powys 114 E5
Evanstown Bridg 58 B3
Evanton H'land 300 C6
Eve Hill W Midlands 133 E8
Evedon Lincs 173 F9
Evelix H'land 309 K7
Even Swindon Swindon 62 B6
Evendine Heref'd 98 C5
Evenjobb Powys 114 E5
Evenley Northants 101 E11
Evenlode Glos 100 F4
Evenwood Durham 233 F9
Evenwood Gate Durham 233 G9
Ever Green Suffolk 124 G3
Everbay Orkney 312 F7
Evercreech Som'set 44 F6
Everdon Northants 119 F11
Everingham ER Yorks 208 E2
Everland Shetl'd 314 D8
Everleigh Wilts 47 C8
Eversholt Beds 103 E9
Evershot Dorset 29 G9
Eversley Hants 65 G9
Eversley Cross Hants 65 G9
Everthorpe ER Yorks 208 G4
Everton Beds 122 G4
Everton Hants 19 C11
Everton Mersey 182 C5
Everton Notts 187 C11
Evertown Dumf/Gal 239 B9
Eves Corner Essex 88 D2
Eves Corner Essex 88 F6
Evesbatch Heref'd 98 B3
Evesham Worcs 99 C10
Evington Leics C 136 C2
Ewanrigg Cumb 228 D6
Ewden Village S Yorks 186 B3
Ewell Surrey 67 G8
Ewell Minnis Kent 55 E9
Ewelme Oxon 83 G10
Ewen Glos 81 F8
Ewenny V/Glam 58 D2
Ewerby Lincs 173 F10
Ewerby thorpe Lincs 173 F10
Ewes Dumf/Gal 249 E9
Ewhurst Surrey 50 E5
Ewhurst Green E Sussex 38 C3
Ewhurst Green Surrey 50 F5
Ewloe Flints 166 B4
Ewloe Green Flints 166 C3
Ewood Blackb'n 195 B7
Ewood Bridge Lancs 195 C9
Eworthy Devon 12 B4
Ewshot Hants 49 D10
Ewyas Harold Heref'd 97 F7
Exbourne Devon 25 G10
Exbury Hants 32 G6
Exbury Gardens, Fawley Hants 32 G6
Exebridge Som'set 26 C6
Exelby N Yorks 214 B5
Exeter Devon 14 C4
Exeter Cathedral Devon 14 C4
Exeter International Airport Devon 14 C6
Exford Som'set 41 F11
Exfords Green Shrops 131 B9
Exhall Warwick 118 F2
Exhall Warwick 134 F6
Exlade Street Oxon 65 C7
Exley W Yorks 196 C5
Exley Head W Yorks 204 E6
Exminster Devon 14 D4
Exmouth Devon 14 E6
Exnaboe Shetl'd 315 M5
Exning Suffolk 124 D2
Explosion, Gosport Hants 33 G10
Exted Kent 55 E7
Exton Devon 14 D5
Exton Hants 33 C10
Exton Rutl'd 155 G8
Exton Som'set 42 G2
Exwick Devon 14 C4
Eyam Derby 186 F2
Eydon Northants 119 G10
Eye Heref'd 115 E9
Eye Peterbro 138 C4
Eye Suffolk 126 C2
Eye Green Peterbro 138 C4
Eye Kettleby Leics 154 F4
Eyemouth Scot Borders 273 C8
Eyeworth Beds 104 B5
Eyhorne Street Kent 53 C10
Eyke Suffolk 126 G6
Eynesbury Cambs 122 F3
Eynort H'land 294 C5
Eynsford Kent 68 F4
Eynsham Oxon 82 D6
Eype Dorset 16 C5
Eyre H'land 295 B7
Eyre H'land 298 D4
Eyres Monsell Leics 135 D11
Eythorne Kent 55 D9
Eyton Heref'd 115 E9
Eyton Shrops 131 F7
Eyton Shrops 149 G7
Eyton Wrex 166 G5
Eyton on Severn Shrops 131 B11
Eyton upon the Weald Moors Telford 150 G3

F

Faberstown Hants 47 C9
Faccombe Hants 47 B11
Faceby N Yorks 225 E9
Fachwen Gwyn 163 C9
Facit Lancs 195 D11
Faddiley Ches 167 E9
Faddonch H'land 295 C11
Fadmoor N Yorks 216 B3
Faerdre Swan 75 E11
Fagley W Yorks 205 F9
Fagwyr Swan 75 E11
Faichem H'land 290 C4
Faifley W Dunb 277 G10
Fail S Ayrs 257 D10
Failand N Som'set 60 E4
Failford S Ayrs 257 D11
Failsworth Gtr Man 196 G2
Fain H'land 299 B11
Faindouran Lodge Moray 292 C2
Fair Cross W Berks 65 G7
Fair Green Norfolk 158 F3
Fair Hill Cumb 230 E6
Fair Moor Northum 252 F5
Fair Oak Hants 64 G5
Fair Oak Hants 33 D7
Fair Oak Lancs 203 D9
Fair Oak Green Hants 65 G7
Fairbourne Gwyn 146 G2
Fairbourne Heath Kent 53 C11
Fairburn N Yorks 198 B3
Fairburn House H'land 300 D4
Fairfield Clack 279 C7
Fairfield Derby 185 G9
Fairfield Gtr Man 195 E10
Fairfield Gtr Man 184 B6
Fairfield Kent 39 B7
Fairfield Mersey 182 C5
Fairfield Stockton 225 B8
Fairfield Worcs 99 C10
Fairfield Worcs 116 B6
Fairfield Worcs 117 B9
Fairfield Park Bath/NE Som'set 61 F9
Fairford Glos 81 E11
Fairhaven Lancs 193 B10
Fairhaven N Ayrs 255 C10
Fairhill S Lanarks 268 E4
Fairlands Surrey 50 C3
Fairlie N Ayrs 266 D4
Fairlight E Sussex 38 E5
Fairlight Cove E Sussex 38 E5
Fairlop London 87 G7
Fairmile Devon 15 B7
Fairmile Surrey 66 G6
Fairmile Common Surrey 66 G6
Fairmilehead C/Edinb 270 B4
Fairoak Caerph 77 F11
Fairoak Staffs 150 C5
Fairseat Kent 68 G6
Fairstead Essex 88 B3
Fairstead Norfolk 158 F2
Fairwarp E Sussex 37 B7
Fairwater Card 58 D6
Fairwater Torf 78 G3
Fairy Cottage I/Man 192 D5
Fairy Cross Cornw'l 6 C2
Fairy Cross Devon 24 C6
Fakenham Norfolk 159 C8
Fakenham Magna Suffolk 125 B8
Fakenham Racecourse Norfolk 159 D8
Fala Midloth 271 C8
Fala Dam Midloth 271 C8
Falahill Scot Borders 271 D7
Falcon Heref'd 98 E2
Falcon Lodge W Midlands 134 D2
Falconwood London 68 D2
Faldingworth Lincs 189 E9
Falfield Fife 287 G8
Falfield S Glos 79 G11
Falkenham Suffolk 108 D5
Falkirk Falk 279 F7
Falkland Fife 286 G6
Falkland Palace Fife 286 G6
Fallin Stirl 278 C6
Fallings Heath W Midlands 133 D9
Fallowfield Gtr Man 184 C5
Fallowfield Northum 241 D10
Fallside N Lanarks 268 C4
Falmer E Sussex 36 F5
Falmouth Cornw'l 3 C8
Falnash Scot Borders 249 B9
Falsgrave N Yorks 217 B10
Falside W Loth 269 B9
Falstone Northum 250 F6
Fanagmore H'land 306 E6
Fancott Beds 103 F10
Fangdale Beck N Yorks 225 G11
Fangfoss ER Yorks 207 C11
Fanich H'land 311 J2
Fankerton Falk 278 E5
Fanmore Arg/Bute 288 E6
Fanner's Green Essex 87 C11
Fannich Lodge H'land 300 C2
Fans Scot Borders 272 G2
Fanshawe Ches 184 F5
Fant Kent 53 C8
Faoilean H'land 295 C7
Far Bletchley M/Keynes 102 E6
Far Cotton Northants 120 F4
Far End Cumb 220 F6
Far End Derby 186 G3
Far Forest Worcs 116 B4
Far Green Glos 80 E3
Far Hoarcross Staffs 152 E2
Far Moor Gtr Man 194 G4
Far Oakridge Glos 80 E6
Far Royds W Yorks 205 G11
Far Sawrey Cumb 221 F7
Farcet Cambs 138 E4
Farden Shrops 115 B11
Fareham Hants 33 F9
Farewell Staffs 151 G11
Farforth Lincs 190 F4
Faringdon Oxon 82 F3
Farington Lancs 194 C5
Farlam Cumb 240 F3
Farlands Booth Derby 185 D9
Farlary H'land 309 J7
Farleigh N Som'set 60 F3
Farleigh Surrey 67 G11
Farleigh Green Kent 53 C8
Farleigh Hungerford Som'set 45 B10
Farleigh Wallop Hants 48 D6
Farleigh Wick Wilts 61 G10
Farlesthorpe Lincs 191 G7
Farleton Cumb 211 C10
Farleton Lancs 211 F11
Farley N Som'set 60 E2
Farley Shrops 131 B7
Farley Staffs 169 G9
Farley Wilts 32 B2
Farley Common Kent 52 C2
Farley Green Suffolk 124 G4
Farley Green Surrey 50 D5
Farley Hill Luton 103 G11
Farley Hill Wokingham 65 G9
Farlington N Yorks 216 F2
Farlington Portsm'th 33 F11
Farlow Shrops 132 G2
Farm Town Leics 153 F7
Farmborough Bath/NE Som'set 61 G7
Farmbridge End Essex 87 C10
Farmcote Glos 99 F11
Farmington Glos 81 B10
Farmoor Oxon 83 D7
Farms Common Cornw'l 2 C5
Farmtown Moray 302 D5
Farnborough Hants 49 C11
Farnborough London 68 G2
Farnborough Warwick 101 B8
Farnborough W Berks 64 C2
Farnborough Green Herts 49 B11
Farnborough Park Hants 49 B11
Farncombe Surrey 50 D3
Farndish Beds 121 E8
Farndon Ches 166 E6
Farndon Notts 172 E3
Farnell Angus 287 B10
Farneyside Northum 241 G7
Farnham Dorset 31 D7
Farnham Essex 105 G9
Farnham N Yorks 214 G6
Farnham Suffolk 127 E7
Farnham Surrey 49 D10
Farnham Common Bucks 66 B3
Farnham Green Essex 105 G9
Farnham Royal Bucks 66 C3
Farnhill N Yorks 204 D6
Farningham Kent 68 F4
Farnley N Yorks 205 D10
Farnley W Yorks 205 G11
Farnley Tyas W Yorks 197 E7
Farnsfield Notts 171 D11
Farnworth Gtr Man 195 F8
Farnworth Halton 183 D8
Farr H'land 291 C10
Farr H'land 300 F6
Farr H'land 308 C7
Farr House H'land 300 F6
Farraline H'land 300 G5
Farringdon Devon 14 C6
Farringdon Tyne/Wear 243 G9
Farringdon Cross Devon 14 C6
Farrington Gurney Bath/NE Som'set 44 B6
Farsley W Yorks 205 F10
Farsley Beck Bottom W Yorks 205 F10
Farther Howegreen Essex 88 E4
Farthing Common Kent 54 E6
Farthing Corner Medway 69 G10
Farthing Green Kent 53 D10
Farthinghoe Northants 101 D10
Farthingloe Kent 55 E9
Farthingstone Northants 120 G2
Fartown W Yorks 196 D6
Farway Devon 15 B9
Fasach H'land 297 G7
Fasag H'land 299 D8
Fascadale H'land 289 B7
Faslane Port Arg/Bute 276 D4
Fasnacloich Arg/Bute 284 C4
Fasnakyle Ho H'land 300 G3
Fassfern H'land 290 F2
Fatfield Tyne/Wear 243 G8
Fattahead Aberds 302 D6
Faucheldean W Loth 279 G11
Faugh Cumb 240 F2
Fauld Staffs 152 D3
Fauldhouse W Loth 269 C8
Fauldiehill Angus 287 D9
Faulkbourn Essex 88 B3
Faulkland Som'set 45 B9
Fauls Shrops 149 C11
Faulston Wilts 31 B9
Faverdale D'lington 224 B5
Faversham Kent 70 G4
Favillar Moray 302 F2
Fawdington N Yorks 215 E8
Fawdon Northum 264 F2
Fawdon Tyne/Wear 242 D6
Fawfieldhead Staffs 169 C9
Fawkham Kent 68 F5
Fawler Oxon 63 B10
Fawler Oxon 82 B5
Fawley Bucks 65 B9
Fawley Hants 33 G7
Fawley W Berks 63 C11
Fawley Bottom Bucks 65 B8
Fawley Chapel Heref'd 97 F11
Fawton Cornw'l 6 B3
Faxfleet ER Yorks 199 C11
Faxton Northants 120 B5
Faygate W Sussex 51 G8
Fazakerley Mersey 182 B5
Fazeley Staffs 134 C4
Feagour H'land 291 D7
Fearby N Yorks 214 C3
Fearn H'land 301 B8
Fearn Lodge H'land 309 L6
Fearn Station H'land 301 B8
Fearnan Perth/Kinr 285 C11
Fearnbeg H'land 299 D7
Fearnhead Warrington 183 C10
Fearnmore H'land 299 C7
Featherstone Staffs 133 C8
Featherstone W Yorks 198 C2
Feckenham Worcs 117 E10
Fedw Monmouths 79 F8
Feering Essex 107 G7
Feetham N Yorks 223 F9
Fegg Hayes Stoke 168 E5
Fèith Mhor H'land 301 G8
Feizor N Yorks 212 F5
Felbridge Surrey 51 F11
Felbrigg Norfolk 160 B4
Felcourt Surrey 51 E11
Felday Surrey 50 E6
Felden Herts 85 E8
Felderland Kent 55 B10
Felhampton Shrops 131 F8
Felin-Crai Powys 95 G7
Felindre Bridg 58 C3
Felindre Carms 93 G11
Felindre Carms 92 D6
Felindre Carms 94 E3
Felindre Carms 94 F4
Felindre Ceredig'n 111 F11
Felindre Powys 130 C3
Felindre Powys 130 G3
Felindre Powys 96 G3
Felindre Swan 75 E10
Felindre Farchog Pembs 92 D2
Felinfach Ceredig'n 111 F10
Felinfach Powys 95 E11
Felinfoel Carms 75 E8
Felingwmisaf Carms 93 G10
Felingwmuchaf Carms 93 G10
Felin-Wnda Ceredig'n 92 B6
Felinwynt Ceredig'n 110 G4
Felixkirk N Yorks 215 C9
Felixstowe Suffolk 108 D5
Felixstowe Ferry Suffolk 108 D6
Felkington Northum 273 G8
Felkirk W Yorks 197 E11
Fell Beck N Yorks 214 F4
Fell Lane W Yorks 204 E6
Fell Side Cumb 230 D2
Felldyke Cumb 219 B11
Fellgate Tyne/Wear 243 E8
Felling Tyne/Wear 243 E7
Felling Shore Tyne/Wear 243 E7
Fellside Tyne/Wear 242 E5
Felmersham Beds 121 F9
Felmingham Norfolk 160 D4
Felpham W Sussex 35 H7
Felsham Suffolk 125 F8
Felsted Essex 106 G3
Feltham London 66 E6
Feltham Som'set 28 D2
Felthamhill London 66 E6
Felthorpe Norfolk 160 F3
Felton Heref'd 97 B11
Felton N Som'set 60 F4
Felton Northum 252 C5
Felton Butler Shrops 149 F7
Feltwell Norfolk 140 E4
Fen Ditton Cambs 123 E9
Fen Drayton Cambs 122 D6
Fen End Lincs 156 E4
Fen End W Midlands 118 B4
Fen Side Cambs 123 C11
Fen Side Lincs 174 D4
Fen Street Norfolk 141 G11
Fen Street Suffolk 125 B9
Fen Street Suffolk 125 B11
Fenay Bridge W Yorks 197 D7
Fence Lancs 204 F2
Fence S Yorks 186 D6
Fence Houses Tyne/Wear 243 G8
Fencott Oxon 83 B9

Funtington W Sussex 34 F3
Funtley Hants 33 F9
Funtullich Perth/Kinr 285 E11
Funzie Shetl'd 314 D8
Furley Devon 28 G3
Furnace Arg/Bute 284 G4
Furnace Carms 75 E8
Furnace Ceredig'n 128 D3
Furnace H'land 299 B9
Furnace End Warwick 134 E4
Furnace Green W Sussex 51 F9
Furneaux Pelham Herts 105 F8
Furner's Green E Sussex 36 B6
Furness Vale Derby 185 E8
Furnham Som'set 28 F4
Further Ford End Essex 105 E8
Further Quarter Kent 53 F11
Furze Green Norfolk 142 G4
Furze Platt Windsor 65 C11
Furzebrook Dorset 18 E4
Furzehill Dorset 31 G8
Furzeley Corner Hants 33 E11
Furzley Hants 32 D3
Furzton M/Keynes 102 D6
Futho Northants 102 C5
Fyfett Som'set 28 E2
Fyfield Essex 87 D9
Fyfield Hants 47 D9
Fyfield Oxon 82 F6
Fyfield Wilts 63 G7
Fyfield Wick Oxon 82 F6
Fyling Park N Yorks 227 E8
Fylingthorpe N Yorks 227 E8
Fyning W Sussex 34 C4
Fyvie Aberds 303 F7

G

Gabalfa Card 59 D7
Gabhsann bho Dheas W Isles 304 C6
Gabhsann bho Thuath W Isles 304 C6
Gable Head Hants 22 D2
Gablon H'land 309 K7
Gabroc Hill E Ayrs 267 E9
Gadbrook Surrey 51 D8
Gaddesby Leics 154 G3
Gadebridge Herts 85 D8
Gadfa Angl 179 D7
Gadlas Shrops 149 B7
Gadlys Rh Cyn Taff 77 E7
Gadshill Kent 69 E8
Gaer Newp 59 B9
Gaer Powys 96 G3
Gaer-fawr Monmouths 78 F6
Gaerllwyd Monmouths 79 F6
Gaerwen Angl 179 G7
Gagingwell Oxon 101 F8
Gaick Lodge H'land 291 E9
Gailey Staffs 151 G8
Gain Hill Kent 53 D8
Gainford Durham 224 B3
Gainsborough Lincs 188 C4
Gainsborough Suffolk 108 C3
Gainsford End Essex 106 D4
Gairloch H'land 299 B8
Gairlochy H'land 290 E3
Gairney Bank Perth/Kinr 280 B2
Gairnshiel Lodge Aberds 292 C4
Gaisgill Cumb 222 D2
Gaitsgill Cumb 230 B3
Galashiels Scot Borders 261 B11
Gale Gtr Man 196 D2
Gale Green Gtr Man 184 D5
Galgate Lancs 202 B5
Galhampton Som'set 29 B10
Gallaberry Dumf/Gal 247 G11
Gallachoille Arg/Bute 275 E8
Gallanach Arg/Bute 288 C4
Gallanach Arg/Bute 289 G10
Gallanach H'land 294 G6
Gallantry Bank Ches 167 E8
Gallatown Fife 280 C5
Galley Common Warwick 134 E6
Galley Hill Cambs 122 D6
Galley Hill Lincs 173 F9
Galleyend Essex 88 E2
Galleywood Essex 88 E2
Galligill Cumb 231 C11
Gallin Perth/Kinr 285 C9
Gallovie H'land 291 E7
Gallowfauld Angus 287 C8
Gallowhill Glasg C 268 D2
Gallowhill Renf 267 B9
Gallowhills Aberds 303 D10
Gallows Green Essex 106 F2
Gallows Green Essex 107 F8
Gallows Green Staffs 169 G9
Gallows Inn Derby 171 G7
Gallowsgreen Torf 78 D3
Gallowstree Common Oxon 65 C7
Gallt Melyd = Meliden Denbs 181 E9
Galltair H'land 295 C10
Galltegfa Denbs 165 D10
Gallt-y-foel Gwyn 163 C9
Gallypot Street E Sussex 52 F3
Galmington Som'set 28 C2
Galmisdale H'land 294 G6
Galmpton Devon 8 G3
Galmpton Torbay 9 D7
Galmpton Warborough Torbay 9 D7
Galon Uchaf Merth Tyd 77 D9
Galphay N Yorks 214 E4
Galston E Ayrs 258 B2
Galton Dorset 17 D11
Galtrigill H'land 296 F7
Gamble Hill W Yorks 205 G11
Gamble's Green Essex 88 C3
Gamblesby Cumb 231 D8
Gamelsby Cumb 239 G7
Gamesley Derby 185 C8
Gamlingay Cambs 122 G4
Gamlingay Cinques Cambs 122 G4
Gamlingay Great Heath Cambs 122 G4
Gammersgill N Yorks 213 C11
Gamston Notts 154 B2
Gamston Notts 188 F2
Ganavan Arg/Bute 289 F10
Ganborough Glos 100 F3
Gandale N Yorks 224 G3
Gang Cornw'l 6 B6
Ganllwyd Gwyn 146 E4
Gannochy Angus 293 F7
Gannochy Perth/Kinr 286 E5
Gannow Hill Shrops 149 C7
Gansclet H'land 310 E7
Ganstead ER Yorks 209 G9
Ganthorpe N Yorks 216 E3
Ganton N Yorks 217 D9
Gants Hill London 68 B2
Ganwick Corner Herts 86 F3
Gaodhail Arg/Bute 289 F8
Gappah Devon 14 F3
Garafad H'land 298 C4
Garamor H'land 295 F8
Garaway Hill Heref'd 97 F8
Garazim Conwy 179 F11
Garbat H'land 300 C4
Garbhallt Arg/Bute 275 D11
Garboldisham Norfolk 141 G10
Garbole H'land 301 G7
Garden City Bl Gwent 77 D11
Garden City Flints 166 B4
Garden Village S Yorks 186 B3
Garden Village Swan 75 F9
Garden Village Wrex 166 E4
Garden Village W Yorks 206 G4
Gardener's Green Wokingham 65 F10
Gardenstown Aberds 303 C7
Garderhouse Shetl'd 315 J5
Gardham ER Yorks 208 E5
Gardie Shetl'd 314 D7
Gardin Shetl'd 314 G6
Gare Hill Som'set 45 E9
Garelochhead Arg/Bute 276 C4
Garford Oxon 82 F6
Garforth W Yorks 206 G4
Gargrave N Yorks 204 C4
Gargunnock Stirl 278 C4
Garker Cornw'l 5 E10
Garlandhayes Devon 27 D11
Garlands Cumb 239 G10
Garlic Street Norfolk 142 G4
Garlieston Dumf/Gal 236 E6
Garlinge Kent 71 F10
Garlinge Green Kent 54 C6
Garlogie Aberds 293 C9
Garmond Aberds 303 D8
Garmondsway Durham 234 E2
Garmony Arg/Bute 289 E8
Garmouth Moray 302 C3
Garmston Shrops 132 B2
Garnant Carms 75 C11
Garndiffaith Torf 78 E3
Garndolbenmaen Gwyn 163 G7
Garnett Bridge Cumb 221 F10
Garnfadryn Gwyn 144 C5
Garnkirk N Lanarks 268 B3
Garnlydan Bl Gwent 77 C11
Garnsgate Lincs 157 E8
Garnswilt Swan 75 D10
Garn-yr-erw Torf 78 C3
Garra Ellabus Arg/Bute 274 F3
Garrabost W Isles 304 E7
Garrachoran Arg/Bute 276 E2
Garrachra Arg/Bute 275 E11
Garralburn Moray 302 D4
Garraron Arg/Bute 275 C9
Garras Cornw'l 2 E6
Garreg Gwyn 163 G10
Garrett's Green W Midlands 134 F2
Garrick Perth/Kinr 286 F2
Garrigill Cumb 231 C10
Garrison Stirl 285 G7
Garriston N Yorks 224 G3
Garroch Dumf/Gal 246 G3
Garrogie Lodge H'land 291 B7
Garros H'land 298 C4
Garrow Perth/Kinr 286 C2
Garrowhill Glasg C 268 C3
Garrygualach H'land 290 C3
Garryhorn Dumf/Gal 246 E2
Garsdale Cumb 212 B4
Garsdale Head Cumb 222 G5
Garsdon Wilts 62 B3
Garshall Green Staffs 151 C9
Garsington Oxon 83 E9
Garstang Lancs 202 D5
Garston Herts 85 E10
Garston Mersey 182 E6
Garswood Mersey 183 B9
Gartbreck Arg/Bute 254 B3
Gartcosh N Lanarks 268 B3
Garth Brigd 76 G5
Garth Ceredig'n 128 G2
Garth Gwyn 179 G9
Garth Monmouths 78 G4
Garth Perth/Kinr 285 B11
Garth Powys 128 C5
Garth Powys 95 B9
Garth Powys 114 C5
Garth Shetl'd 315 H4
Garth Shetl'd 315 H6
Garth Wrex 166 G3
Garth Owen Powys 130 E2
Garth Place Caerph 59 B7
Garth Row Cumb 221 F10
Garth Trevor Wrex 166 G3
Garthamlock Glasg C 268 B3
Garthbeg H'land 291 B7
Garthbrengy Powys 95 E10
Garthdee Aberd C 293 C11
Gartheli Ceredig'n 111 F11
Garthmyl Powys 130 D3
Garthmyn Conwy 164 D4
Garthocharn W Dunb 277 D8
Garthorpe Leics 154 E6
Garthorpe N Lincs 199 D10
Gartlea N Lanarks 268 C5
Gartly Aberds 302 F5
Gartmore Stirl 277 B10
Gartmore Ho. Stirl 285 H9
Gartnagrenach Arg/Bute 255 B8
Gartness N Lanarks 268 C5
Gartness Stirl 277 D10
Garton ER Yorks 209 F11
Garton-on-the-Wolds ER Yorks 208 B5
Gartsherrie N Lanarks 268 B4
Gartur Stirl 285 H9
Gartymore H'land 311 H4
Garvald Scot Borders 270 F2
Garvald E Loth 281 G11
Garvamore H'land 291 D7
Garvard Arg/Bute 274 D4
Garvault Hotel H'land 308 F7
Garve H'land 300 C3
Garvestone Norfolk 141 B10
Garvock Aberds 293 F9
Garvock Hill Fife 280 D2
Garway Heref'd 97 G9
Garway Common Heref'd 97 G9
Garwick Lincs 173 G11
Gas Terminal Aberds 303 D10
Gascote W Midlands 133 C10
Gaskan H'land 289 B9
Gasper Wilts 45 G9
Gasstown Dumf/Gal 238 B1
Gastard Wilts 61 F11
Gasthorpe Norfolk 141 G9
Gaston Green Essex 87 B7
Gatcombe I/Wight 20 E5
Gate Burton Lincs 188 E4
Gate Helmsley N Yorks 207 B9
Gateacre Mersey 182 D6
Gatebeck Cumb 211 B10
Gateford Common Notts 187 E9
Gateforth N Yorks 198 B5
Gatehead E Ayrs 257 B9
Gatehouse of Fleet Dumf/Gal 237 D8
Gatelawbridge Dumf/Gal 247 D10
Gateley Norfolk 159 E9
Gatenby N Yorks 214 B6
Gateshead Tyne/Wear 243 E7
Gateshead International Stadium Tyne/Wear 243 E7
Gatesheath Ches 167 C7
Gateside Aberds 293 B8
Gateside Angus 287 C8
Gateside E Renf 267 D9
Gateside Fife 286 G5
Gateside N Ayrs 267 E7
Gateside Shetl'd 314 F4
Gathurst Gtr Man 194 F4
Gatley Gtr Man 184 D4
Gatley End Cambs 104 C5
Gattonside Scot Borders 262 B2
Gatwick Glos 80 C2
Gatwick Airport W Sussex 51 E9
Gaufron Powys 113 D9
Gaulby Leics 136 C3
Gauldry Fife 287 E7
Gauntons Bank Ches 167 F9
Gaunt's Common Dorset 31 F8
Gaunt's Earthcott S Glos 60 C6
Gaunt's End Essex 105 F10
Gautby Lincs 189 G11
Gavinton Scot Borders 272 E5
Gawber S Yorks 197 F10
Gawcott Bucks 102 E3
Gawsworth Ches 168 B5
Gawthorpe W Yorks 197 D7
Gawthorpe W Yorks 197 C9
Gawthrop Cumb 212 B3
Gawthwaite Cumb 210 C5
Gay Bowers Essex 88 E3
Gay Street W Sussex 35 C9
Gaydon Warwick 119 G7
Gayfield Orkney 312 C5
Gayhurst M/Keynes 102 B6
Gayle N Yorks 213 B7
Gayles N Yorks 224 D2
Gayton Mersey 182 E3
Gayton Norfolk 158 F4
Gayton Northants 120 G4
Gayton Staffs 151 D9
Gayton Engine Lincs 191 D7
Gayton le Marsh Lincs 190 E6
Gayton le Wold Lincs 190 D2
Gayton Thorpe Norfolk 158 F4
Gayton Top Lincs 190 E6
Gaywood Norfolk 158 E2
Gaza Shetl'd 314 F5
Gazeley Suffolk 124 E4
Geàrraidh Sheilidh W Isles 297 J3
Geanies House H'land 301 B8
Gear Sands Cornw'l 4 D5
Gearraidh Bhailteas W Isles 297 J3
Gearraidh Bhaird W Isles 304 F5
Gearraidh Dubh W Isles 296 F4
Gearraidh na h-Aibhne W Isles 304 E4
Gearraidh na Monadh W Isles 297 K3
Geary H'land 298 C2
Geddes House H'land 301 D8
Gedding Suffolk 125 F8
Geddington Northants 137 F7
Gedintailor H'land 295 B7
Gedling Notts 171 G10
Gedney Lincs 157 E8
Gedney Broadgate Lincs 157 E8
Gedney Drove End Lincs 157 D9
Gedney Dyke Lincs 157 D8
Gedney Hill Lincs 156 G6
Gee Cross Gtr Man 185 C7
Geenmoor Hill Oxon 64 C6
Geeston Rutl'd 137 C9
Gefnan Gwyn 163 B10
Geilston Inverc'l 276 F6
Geirinis W Isles 297 G3
Geise H'land 310 C5
Geisiadar W Isles 304 E3
Geldeston Norfolk 143 E7
Gell Conwy 164 B5
Gelli Pembs 73 B9
Gelli Rh Cyn Taff 77 G7
Gellideg Merth Tyd 77 D8
Gellifor Denbs 165 C10
Gelligaer Caerph 77 F10
Gelligroes Caerph 77 F11
Gelli-haf Caerph 77 F11
Gellilydan Gwyn 146 B3
Gellinudd Neath P Talb 76 E2
Gellyburn Perth/Kinr 286 D4
Gellywen Carms 92 G5
Gelston Dumf/Gal 237 D9
Gelston Lincs 172 F6
Gembling ER Yorks 209 B8
Gendros Swan 75 F10
Genesis Green Suffolk 124 F5
Geneva Ceredig'n 111 F9
Gentleshaw Staffs 151 G11
Geocrab W Isles 305 J3
George Green Bucks 66 C4
George Nympton Devon 26 C2
Georgefield Dumf/Gal 249 E7
Georgeham Devon 40 F3
Georgetown Bl Gwent 77 D10
Georgetown Dumf/Gal 238 B1
Gergask H'land 291 D8
Gerlan Gwyn 163 B10
Germansweek Devon 12 C4
Germiston Glasg C 268 B2
Germoe Cornw'l 2 D3
Gerrans Cornw'l 3 B9
Gerrard's Cross Bucks 66 B3
Gerrick Redcar/Clevel'd 226 B4
Gestingthorpe Essex 106 D6
Gesto Ho H'land 294 B5
Geuffordd Powys 148 G4
Gib Heath W Midlands 133 F11
Gibb Hill Ches 183 F10
Gibbet Hill Som'set 45 D9
Gibbshill Dumf/Gal 237 B9
Gibraltar Beds 103 B10
Gibraltar Bucks 84 C3
Gibraltar Kent 55 F8
Gibraltar Oxon 83 B7
Gibraltar Suffolk 126 G3
Gibshill Inverc'l 276 G6
Giddeahall Wilts 61 E11
Giddy Green Dorset 18 D2
Gidea Park London 87 G8
Gidleigh Devon 13 D9
Giffnock E Renf 267 D11
Gifford E Loth 271 B10
Giffordland N Ayrs 266 F5
Giffordtown Fife 286 F6
Gigg Gtr Man 195 F10
Giggleswick N Yorks 212 G6
Giggshill Surrey 67 F7
Gignog Pembs 91 G7
Gilbent Gtr Man 184 E5
Gilberdyke ER Yorks 199 B10
Gilbert Street Hants 49 G7
Gilbert's Coombe Cornw'l 4 G3
Gilbert's End Worcs 98 C6
Gilbert's Green Warwick 118 C2
Gilbertstone W Midlands 134 G2
Gilchriston E Loth 271 B9
Gilcrux Cumb 229 D8
Gildersome W Yorks 197 B8
Gildersome Street W Yorks 197 B8
Gildingwells S Yorks 187 D9
Gilesgate Durham 233 C11
Gilesgate Moor Durham 233 C11
Gileston V/Glam 58 F4
Gilfach Caerph 77 F11
Gilfach Goch Rh Cyn Taff 58 B3
Gilfachrheda Ceredig'n 111 F8
Gilgarran Cumb 228 G6
Gill N Yorks 204 E5
Gillamoor N Yorks 216 B3
Gillan Cornw'l 3 D7
Gillar's Green Mersey 183 C7
Gillbank Cumb 221 F7
Gillen H'land 298 D2
Gillesbie Dumf/Gal 248 E5
Gillham Kent 53 E11
Gilling East N Yorks 216 D2
Gilling West N Yorks 224 D3
Gillingham Dorset 30 B4
Gillingham Medway 69 F9
Gillingham Norfolk 143 E8
Gillmoss Mersey 182 B6
Gillock H'land 310 D6
Gillow Heath Staffs 168 D5
Gills H'land 310 B7
Gill's Green Kent 53 G9
Gilmanscleuch Scot Borders 261 E8
Gilmerton C/Edinb 270 B5
Gilmerton Perth/Kinr 286 E2
Gilmonby Durham 223 C9
Gilmorton Leics 135 F11
Gilmourton S Lanarks 258 B3
Gilnow Gtr Man 195 F8
Gilridge Kent 52 E3
Gilroyd S Yorks 197 G10
Gilslake S Glos 60 C5
Gilsland Cumb 240 D4
Gilson Warwick 134 E3
Gilstead W Yorks 205 F8
Gilston Scot Borders 271 D8
Gilston Herts 87 C7
Giltbrook Notts 171 F7
Gilver's Lane Worcs 98 C6
Gilwern Monmouths 78 C2
Gimingham Norfolk 160 B5
Gin Pit Gtr Man 195 G7
Ginclough Ches 185 F7
Ginger's Green E Sussex 37 E10
Giosla W Isles 304 F3
Gipping Suffolk 125 E11
Gipsey Bridge Lincs 174 F3
Gipsy Row Suffolk 107 D11
Gipsyville Kingston/Hull 200 B5
Gipton W Yorks 206 F2
Girdle Toll N Ayrs 266 G6
Girlington W Yorks 205 G8
Girlsta Shetl'd 315 H6
Girsby N Yorks 225 D7
Girtford Beds 122 G2
Girthon Dumf/Gal 237 D8
Girton Cambs 123 E8
Girton Notts 172 B4
Girvan S Ayrs 244 D5
Gisburn Lancs 204 D2
Gisburn Cotes Lancs 204 D2
Gisleham Suffolk 143 F10
Gislingham Suffolk 125 C11
Gissing Norfolk 142 F2
Gissing Common Norfolk 142 F3
Gittisham Devon 15 B8
Givons Grove Surrey 51 C7
Glachavoil Arg/Bute 275 F11
Glack of Midthird Moray 302 E3
Glackmore H'land 300 D6
Gladestry Powys 114 F4
Gladsmuir E Loth 281 G9
Glaichbea H'land 300 F5
Glais Swan 76 E2
Glaisdale N Yorks 226 D5
Glaisdale Side N Yorks 226 E5
Glame H'land 298 E5
Glamis Angus 287 C7
Glamis Castle Angus 287 C7
Glan Duar Carms 93 C10
Glan Dwyfach Gwyn 163 G7
Glan yr afon Gwyn 145 B10
Glanaber Angl 179 F7
Glanaber Terrace Conwy 164 F3
Glan-Adda Gwyn 179 G9
Glanafon Pembs 73 B7
Glanaman Carms 75 C11
Glandford Norfolk 177 E8
Glandwr Bl Gwent 78 E2
Glandwr Pembs 92 F3
Glandy Cross Carms 92 F2
Glaneirw Ceredig'n 92 B5
Glangrwyney Monmouths 78 B2
Glanllynfi Bridg 76 G5
Glanmule Powys 130 E3
Glanpwllafon Pembs 92 C3
Glanrafon Ceredig'n 128 G2
Glan-rhyd Gwyn 163 D7
Glanrhyd Pembs 92 C2
Glan-rhyd Powys 76 D3
Glanton Northum 264 G3
Glanvilles Wootton Dorset 29 F11
Glanwern Ceredig'n 128 F2
Glan-wr-afon Denbs 165 G8
Glanwydden Conwy 180 E4
Glan-y-don Flints 181 F11
Glan-y-Fferi = Ferryside Carms 74 D5
Glan-y-llyn Rh Cyn Taff 58 C6
Glan-y-nant Caerph 77 F10
Glan-y-nant Powys 129 G8
Glan-yr-afon Gwyn 164 G3
Glan-yr-afon Angl 178 F5
Glan-yr-afon Angl 179 E10
Glanyrafon Powys 148 D4
Glan-y-wern Gwyn 146 C2
Glapthorn Northants 137 E10
Glapwell Derby 171 B7
Glas-allt Shiel Aberds 292 E4
Glasbury Powys 96 D3
Glaschoil H'land 301 F10
Glascoed Denbs 181 G7
Glascoed Monmouths 78 E4
Glascoed Powys 130 B2
Glascoed Powys 148 G2
Glascoed Wrex 166 E3
Glascorrie Aberds 292 D5
Glascorrie Perth/Kinr 286 E2
Glascote Staffs 134 C4
Glascote Heath Staffs 134 C4
Glascwm Powys 114 G3
Glasdrum Arg/Bute 284 C4
Glasfryn Conwy 164 E6
Glasgoforest Aberds 293 B10
Glasgow Glasg C 267 B11
Glasgow Airport Renf 267 B9
Glasgow Art Gallery & Museum Glasg C 267 B11
Glasgow Botanic Gardens Glasg C 267 B11
Glasgow Bridge E Dunb 278 G2
Glasgow Cathedral Glasg C 268 B2
Glasgow Prestwick International Airport S Ayrs 257 D9
Glashvin H'land 298 C4
Glasinfryn Gwyn 163 B9
Glasllwch Newp 59 B9
Glasnacardoch H'land 295 F8
Glasnakille H'land 295 D7
Glasphein H'land 297 G7
Glaspwll Powys 128 D4
Glass Houghton W Yorks 198 C2
Glassburn H'land 300 F3
Glassenbury Kent 53 F9
Glasserton Dumf/Gal 236 F6
Glassford S Lanarks 268 F4
Glassgreen Moray 302 C2
Glasshouse Glos 98 G4
Glasshouse Hill Glos 98 G4
Glasshouses N Yorks 214 G3
Glasslie Fife 286 G6
Glasson Cumb 239 D7
Glasson Lancs 202 B4
Glassonby Cumb 231 D7
Glasterlaw Angus 287 B9
Glaston Rutl'd 137 C7
Glastonbury Som'set 44 F4
Glastonbury Abbey Som'set 44 F4
Glatton Cambs 138 F3
Glazebrook Warrington 183 C11
Glazebury Warrington 183 B11
Glazeley Shrops 132 F4
Gleadless S Yorks 186 E5
Gleadless Valley S Yorks 186 E5
Gleadsmoss Ches 168 B4
Gleann Tholàstaidh W Isles 304 D7
Gleaston Cumb 210 E5
Glebe Shetl'd 315 J6
Glebe Tyne/Wear 243 F8
Glebe Cliff Cornw'l 10 D7
Glebe Farm W Midlands 134 F2
Glecknabae Arg/Bute 275 G11
Gledhow W Yorks 206 F2
Gleiniant Powys 129 E9
Glemsford Suffolk 106 B6
Glen Dumf/Gal 237 B10
Glen Dumf/Gal 237 D7
Glen Auldyn I/Man 192 C5
Glen Bernisdale H'land 298 E4
Glen Ho Scot Borders 261 C7
Glen Mona I/Man 192 D5
Glen Mor H'land 295 B10
Glen Nevis House H'land 290 F3
Glen of Newmill Moray 302 D4
Glen Parva Leics C 135 D11
Glen Sluain Arg/Bute 275 D11
Glen Tanar House Aberds 292 D6
Glen Vic Askil H'land 298 E3
Glen Village Falk 279 F7
Glen Vine I/Man 192 E4
Glenallachie Moray 302 E2
Glenalmond College Perth/Kinr 286 E3
Glenalmond Ho. Perth/Kinr 286 E3
Glenamachrie Arg/Bute 289 G11
Glenample Stirl 285 E9
Glenancross H'land 295 F8
Glenaros Ho Arg/Bute 289 E7
Glenbarr Arg/Bute 255 D7
Glenbeg H'land 289 C7
Glenbeg H'land 301 G10
Glenbervie Aberds 293 E9
Glenboig N Lanarks 268 B4
Glenborrodale H'land 289 C8
Glenbranter Arg/Bute 276 B2
Glenbreck Scot Borders 260 E3
Glenbrein Lodge H'land 290 B6
Glenbrittle House H'land 294 C6
Glenbuchat Castle Aberds 292 B5
Glenbuchat Lodge Aberds 292 B5
Glenbuck E Ayrs 259 D7
Glenburn Renf 267 C9
Glenbyre Arg/Bute 289 G7
Glencalvie Lodge H'land 309 L4
Glencanisp Lodge H'land 307 G6
Glencaple Dumf/Gal 237 C11
Glencarron Lodge H'land 299 D10
Glencarse Perth/Kinr 286 E5
Glencassley Castle H'land 309 J4
Glencat Aberds 293 D7
Glenceitlein H'land 284 C5
Glencoe H'land 284 B4
Glencraig Fife 280 C3
Glencripesdale H'land 289 D8
Glencrosh Dumf/Gal 247 F7
Glendavan Ho. Aberds 292 C6
Glendevon Perth/Kinr 286 G3
Glendoe Lodge H'land 290 C6
Glendoebeg H'land 290 C6
Glendoick Perth/Kinr 286 E6
Glendoll Lodge Angus 292 F4
Glendon Hall Northants 136 G6
Glendoune S Ayrs 244 D5
Glenduckie Fife 286 F6
Glendye Lodge Aberds 293 E8
Gleneagles Hotel Perth/Kinr 286 F3
Gleneagles House Perth/Kinr 286 G3
Glenearn Perth/Kinr 286 F5
Glenegedale Arg/Bute 254 B4
Glenelg H'land 295 D10
Glenernie Moray 301 E10
Glenfarg Perth/Kinr 286 F5
Glenfarquhar Lodge Aberds 293 E9
Glenferness House H'land 301 E9
Glenfeshie Lodge H'land 291 D10
Glenfiddich Distillery, Dufftown Moray 302 E3
Glenfiddich Lodge Moray 302 F3
Glenfield Leics 135 B10
Glenfinnan H'land 295 G10
Glenfinnan Lodge H'land 295 G11
Glenfintaig Ho. H'land 290 E4
Glenfoot Perth/Kinr 286 F5
Glenfyne Lodge Arg/Bute 284 F6
Glengap Dumf/Gal 237 D8
Glengarnock N Ayrs 266 E6
Glengolly H'land 310 C5
Glengorm Castle Arg/Bute 288 D6
Glengoulandie Perth/Kinr 285 B11
Glengrasco H'land 298 E4
Glenhead Farm Angus 292 G4
Glenholt Plym'th 7 C10
Glenhoul Dumf/Gal 246 F4
Glenhurich H'land 289 C10
Glenkerry Scot Borders 261 G7
Glenkiln Dumf/Gal 237 B10
Glenkindie Aberds 292 B6
Glenlair Dumf/Gal 237 B9
Glenlatterach Moray 301 D11
Glenlee Dumf/Gal 246 G4
Glenleraig H'land 306 F6
Glenlichorn Perth/Kinr 285 F11
Glenlicht Ho. H'land 290 B2
Glenlivet Moray 301 G11
Glenlochar Dumf/Gal 237 C9
Glenlochsie Perth/Kinr 292 F2
Glenlocksie Lodge Perth/Kinr 292 F2
Glenloig N Ayrs 255 D10
Glenlomond Perth/Kinr 286 G5
Glenluce Dumf/Gal 236 D4
Glenlussa Ho Arg/Bute 255 E8
Glenmallan Arg/Bute 276 B4
Glenmark Angus 292 E6
Glenmarkie Lodge Angus 292 G4
Glenmarksie H'land 300 D3
Glenmassan Arg/Bute 276 D2
Glenmavis N Lanarks 268 B5
Glenmavis W Loth 269 B9
Glenmaye I/Man 192 E3
Glenmeanie H'land 300 D2
Glenmidge Dumf/Gal 247 F9
Glenmoidart Ho H'land 289 B9
Glenmore Arg/Bute 275 B9
Glenmore Arg/Bute 275 G11
Glenmore H'land 298 E4
Glenmore Lodge H'land 291 C11
Glenmoy Angus 292 G6
Glennoe Arg/Bute 284 D4
Glenogil Angus 292 G6
Glenprosen Lodge Angus 292 G4
Glenprosen Village Angus 292 G5
Glenquaich Lodge Perth/Kinr 286 D2
Glenquiech Angus 292 G6
Glenquithlie Aberds 303 C8
Glenrazie Dumf/Gal 236 C5
Glenreasdell Mains Arg/Bute 255 B9
Glenree N Ayrs 255 E10
Glenridding Cumb 221 B7
Glenrosa N Ayrs 255 D10
Glenrossal H'land 309 J4
Glenrothes Fife 286 G6
Glensanda H'land 289 E10
Glensaugh Aberds 293 F8
Glensburgh Falk 279 E8
Glenshero Lodge H'land 291 D7
Glenshoe Lodge Perth/Kinr 292 G3
Glenstockadale Dumf/Gal 236 C2
Glenstriven Arg/Bute 275 F11
Glentaggart S Lanarks 259 D8
Glentarkie Perth/Kinr 286 F5
Glentham Lincs 189 C8
Glentirranmuir Stirl 278 C3
Glenton Aberds 302 G6
Glentress Scot Borders 261 B7
Glentromie Lodge H'land 291 D9
Glentrool Village Dumf/Gal 236 B5
Glentruan I/Man 192 B5
Glentruim House H'land 291 D8
Glenturret Distillery, Crieff Perth/Kinr 286 E2
Glentworth Lincs 188 D6
Glenuaig Lodge H'land 299 E11
Glenuig H'land 289 B8
Glenure Arg/Bute 284 C4
Glenurquhart H'land 301 C7
Glenview Arg/Bute 284 E5
Glespin S Lanarks 259 D8
Gletness Shetl'd 315 H6
Glewstone Heref'd 97 G11
Glinton Peterboro 138 B3
Glodwick Gtr Man 196 G2
Glogue Pembs 92 E4
Glooston Leics 136 D5
Glossop Derby 185 C8
Gloucester Glos 80 B4
Gloucester Cathedral Glos 80 B4
Gloucestershire Airport Glos 99 G7
Gloup Shetl'd 314 C7
Glover's Hawes Kent 52 E3
Gloweth Cornw'l 4 G5
Glusburn N Yorks 204 D6
Glutt Lodge H'land 310 F3
Glutton Bridge Derby 169 B9
Gluvian Cornw'l 5 C8
Glympton Oxon 101 G8
Glyn Ceiriog Wrex 148 B4
Glyn Ebwy = Ebbw Vale Bl Gwent 77 D11
Glynarthen Ceredig'n 92 B6
Glynbrochan Powys 129 G8
Glyncoch Rh Cyn Taff 77 G9
Glyncorrwg Neath P Talb 76 F5
Glynde E Sussex 37 E7
Glyndebourne E Sussex 37 E7
Glyndyfrdwy Denbs 165 G10
Glynedd = Glyn-neath Neath P Talb 76 D5
Glynmorlas Shrops 148 B6
Glyn-neath = Glynedd Neath P Talb 76 D5
Glynogwr Bridg 58 B3
Glyntaff Rh Cyn Taff 58 B5
Glyntawe Powys 76 B4
Gnosall Staffs 150 E6
Gnosall Heath Staffs 150 E6
Goadby Leics 136 D5
Goadby Marwood Leics 154 D5
Goadsbarrow Cumb 210 F5
Goat Lees Kent 54 D4
Goatacre Wilts 62 D4
Goatham Green E Sussex 38 D4
Goathill Dorset 29 D11
Goathland N Yorks 226 E6
Goathurst Som'set 43 G9
Goathurst Common Kent 52 C3
Gobernuisgach Lodge H'land 308 E4
Gobernuisgeach H'land 310 F3
Gobhaig W Isles 305 H2
Gobowen Shrops 148 C6
Godalming Surrey 50 E3
Goddard's Corner Suffolk 126 D5
Goddard's Green Kent 53 F9
Goddard's Green Kent 53 G10
Goddard's Green W Berks 65 F7
Goddard's Green W Sussex 36 C3
Godden Green Kent 52 B5
Goddington London 68 F3
Godford Cross Devon 27 G10
Godington Oxon 102 F2
Godley Gtr Man 185 B7
Godmanchester Cambs 122 C4
Godmanstone Dorset 17 B9
Godmersham Kent 54 C5
Godney Som'set 44 E3
Godolphin Cross Cornw'l 2 C4
Godre'r-graig Neath P Talb 76 D2
Godshill Hants 31 E11
Godshill I/Wight 20 E6
Godstone Surrey 51 C10
Godstone Staffs 151 C10
Godstone Farm Surrey 51 C11
Godsworthy Devon 12 F6
Godwell Devon 8 D2
Godwinscroft Hants 19 B9
Goetre Monmouths 78 D4
Goff's Oak Herts 86 E4
Gogar C/Edinb 280 G3
Gogarth Conwy 180 E3
Goginan Ceredig'n 128 G3
Goirtean a'Chladaich H'land 290 F2
Golan Gwyn 163 G8
Golant Cornw'l 6 D2
Golberdon Cornw'l 12 G2
Golborne Gtr Man 183 B10
Golcar W Yorks 196 D5
Gold Hill Cambs 139 E10
Gold Hill Dorset 30 E4
Goldcliff Newp 59 C11
Golden Cross E Sussex 37 E8
Golden Green Kent 52 D6
Golden Grove Carms 75 B9
Golden Hill Bristol 60 D5
Golden Hill Hants 19 B11
Golden Hill Pembs 73 E7
Golden Hill Pembs 91 G9
Golden Pot Hants 49 E8
Golden Square Devon 28 G2
Golden Valley Derby 170 E6
Golden Valley Glos 99 G8
Golden Valley Heref'd 98 B3
Golden Valley S Glos 61 E7
Goldenhill Stoke 168 E4
Golders Green London 67 B8
Goldfinch Bottom W Berks 64 G4
Goldhanger Essex 88 D6
Goldington Beds 121 G11
Golds Green W Midlands 133 E9
Goldsborough N Yorks 206 B3
Goldsborough N Yorks 226 C6
Goldsithney Cornw'l 2 C2
Goldstone Shrops 150 D4
Goldsworth Park Surrey 50 B3
Goldthorn Park W Midlands 133 D8
Goldthorpe S Yorks 198 G3
Goldwick Glos 80 F2
Goldworthy Devon 24 C5
Golfa Powys 148 D3
Golford Kent 53 F10
Golftyn Flints 166 B3
Golgotha Kent 55 D9
Gollanfield H'land 301 D8
Gollawater Cornw'l 4 E5
Gollinglith Foot N Yorks 214 C2
Golly Wrex 166 D4
Golsoncott Som'set 42 F4
Golspie H'land 311 J2
Golval H'land 310 C2
Golynus Torf 78 E3
Gomeldon Wilts 47 F7
Gomersal W Yorks 197 B8
Gometra Ho Arg/Bute 288 E5
Gomshall Surrey 50 D5
Gonalston Notts 171 F11
Gonamena Cornw'l 11 G11
Gonerby Hill Foot Lincs 155 B8

Gonfirth Shetl'd 315 G5
Good Easter Essex 87 C10
Gooderstone Norfolk 140 C5
Goodleigh Devon 40 G5
Goodmanham ER Yorks 208 E3
Goodmayes London 68 B3
Goodnestone Kent 55 C9
Goodnestone Kent 70 G4
Goodrich Heref'd 79 B9
Goodrington Torbay 9 D7
Goodshaw Lancs 195 B10
Goodshaw Chapel Lancs 195 B10
Goodshaw Fold Lancs 195 B10
Goodstone Devon 13 G11
Goodwick = Wdig Pembs 91 D8
Goodwood Racecourse W Sussex 34 E5
Goodworth Clatford Hants 47 E11
Goodyers End Warwick 134 F6
Goodyhills Cumb 229 B8
Goole ER Yorks 199 C8
Goole Fields ER Yorks 199 C9
Goonabarn Cornw'l 5 E9
Goonbell Cornw'l 4 F4
Goonhavern Cornw'l 4 E5
Goonown Cornw'l 4 E4
Goonpiper Cornw'l 3 B8
Goonvrea Cornw'l 4 F4
Goose Eye W Yorks 204 E6
Goose Green Essex 108 F2
Goose Green Gtr Man 194 G5
Goose Green Hants 32 F4
Goose Green Herts 86 D5
Goose Green Kent 53 F10
Goose Green Kent 52 C6
Goose Green Norfolk 142 F2
Goose Green S Glos 61 E7
Goose Green S Glos 61 C8
Goose Green W Sussex 35 D10
Goose Pool Heref'd 97 D9
Gooseberry Green Essex 87 F11
Gooseham Cornw'l 24 D2
Goosehill W Yorks 197 C11
Goosemoor Devon 15 D7
Goosemoor Green Staffs 151 G11
Goosenford Som'set 28 B2
Goosewell Plym'th 7 E10
Goosey Oxon 82 G5
Goosnargh Lancs 203 G7
Goostrey Ches 184 G3
Gorbals Glasg C 267 C11
Gorcott Hill Worcs 117 D11
Gord Shetl'd 315 L6
Gorddinog Conwy 179 G11
Gordon Scot Borders 272 G2
Gordonbush H'land 311 J2
Gordonsburgh Moray 302 C4
Gordonstoun Moray 301 C11
Gordonstown Aberds 302 D5
Gordonstown Aberds 303 F7
Gore Kent 55 B10
Gore End Hants 64 G2
Gore Houses Mersey 193 G11
Gore Pit Essex 88 B5
Gore Street Kent 71 F9
Gorebridge Midloth 270 C6
Gorefield Cambs 157 G8
Gores Wilts 46 B6
Gorgie C/Edinb 280 G4
Goring Oxon 64 C6
Goring Heath Oxon 65 D7
Goring-by-Sea W Sussex 35 G10
Gorleston-on-Sea Norfolk 143 C10
Gornalwood W Midlands 133 E8
Gorrachie Aberds 303 D7
Gorran Churchtown Cornw'l 5 G9
Gorran Haven Cornw'l 5 G10
Gorran High Lanes Cornw'l 5 G9
Gorrenberry Scot Borders 249 D11
Gors Ceredig'n 112 B2
Gorse Covert Warrington 183 C11
Gorse Hill Gtr Man 184 B4
Gorse Hill Swindon 63 B7
Gorsedd Flints 181 F11
Gorseinon Swan 75 F9
Gorseness Orkney 312 G5
Gorsey Bank Shrops 150 G5
Gorseybank Derby 170 E3
Gorsgoch Ceredig'n 111 G9
Gorslas Carms 75 C9
Gorsley Glos 98 F3
Gorsley Common Heref'd 98 F3
Gorstage Ches 183 G10
Gorstan H'land 300 C3
Gorstanvorran H'land 289 B10
Gorstella Ches 166 C5
Gorsty Hill Staffs 152 D2
Gortan Arg/Bute 274 G3
Gortantaoid Arg/Bute 274 F4
Gortenacullish H'land 295 G8
Gorteneorn H'land 289 C8
Gortenfern H'land 289 C8
Gortinanane Arg/Bute 255 C8
Gortleigh Devon 25 F7
Gorton Gtr Man 184 B5
Gortonallister N Ayrs 256 D2
Gosbeck Suffolk 126 F3
Gosberton Lincs 156 C4
Gosberton Cheal Lincs 156 D4
Gosberton Clough Lincs 156 D3
Goseley Dale Derby 152 E6
Gosfield Essex 106 F5
Gosford Devon 15 B7
Gosford Heref'd 115 D10
Gosford Oxon 83 C8
Gosford Green W Midlands 118 B6
Gosforth Cumb 219 E11
Gosforth Tyne/Wear 242 D6
Gosforth Valley Derby 186 F4
Gosland Green Ches 167 D9
Gosland Green Suffolk 124 G5
Gosling Green Suffolk 107 C9
Gosmore Herts 104 F3
Gospel End Staffs 133 E7
Gospel Oak London 67 B9
Gosport Hants 32 C5
Gosport Hants 21 B8
Gossabrough Shetl'd 314 E7
Gossard's Green Beds 103 C9
Gossington Glos 80 E2
Gossops Green W Sussex 51 F8
Goswick Northum 273 F11
Gotham Dorset 31 E9
Gotham E Sussex 38 F2
Gotham Notts 153 C10
Gothelney Green Som'set 43 F9
Gotherington Glos 99 F9
Gothers Cornw'l 5 D9
Gott Arg/Bute 288 E2
Gott Shetl'd 315 J6
Gotton Som'set 28 B2
Goudhurst Kent 53 F8
Goukstone Moray 302 D4
Goulceby Lincs 190 F3
Goulton N Yorks 225 E9
Gourdas Aberds 303 E7
Gourdon Aberds 293 F10
Gourock Inverci 276 F4
Govan Glasg C 267 B11
Govanhill Glasg C 267 C11
Gover Valley Cornw'l 5 E9
Goverton Notts 172 E2
Goveton Devon 8 F5
Govilon Monmouths 78 C3
Gowanhill Aberds 303 C10
Gowanwell Aberds 303 E8
Gowdall ER Yorks 198 C6
Gowerton = Tre-Gwyr Swan 75 F9
Gowkhall Fife 279 D11
Gowkthrapple N Lanarks 268 E5
Gowthorpe ER Yorks 207 C11
Goxhill ER Yorks 209 E9
Goxhill N Lincs 200 C6
Goxhill Haven N Lincs 200 B6
Goytre Neath P Talb 57 D9
Gozzard's Ford Oxon 83 F7
Grabhair W Isles 305 G5
Graby Lincs 155 D11
Gracca Cornw'l 5 D10
Grade Cornw'l 2 G6
Gradeley Green Ches 167 E9
Graffham W Sussex 34 D6
Grafham Cambs 122 D3
Grafham Surrey 50 E4
Grafton Bucks 84 C5
Grafton Heref'd 97 D9
Grafton N Yorks 215 G8
Grafton Oxon 82 E3
Grafton Shrops 149 F8
Grafton Worcs 99 D9
Grafton Flyford Worcs 117 F9
Grafton Regis Northants 102 B5
Grafton Underwood Northants 137 G8
Grafty Green Kent 53 D11
Grahamston Falk 279 E7
Graianrhyd Denbs 166 D2
Graig Carms 74 E6
Graig Conwy 180 G4
Graig Denbs 181 G9
Graig Rh Cyn Taff 58 B5
Graig Shrops 114 B5
Graig Felen Swan 75 E11
Graig Penllyn V/Glam 58 D3
Graig Trewyddfa Swan 75 F11
Graig-Fawr Swan 75 E10
Graig-fechan Denbs 165 E10
Grain Medway 69 D11
Grains Bar Gtr Man 196 F3
Grainsby Lincs 190 B3
Grainthorpe Lincs 190 B5
Graizelound N Lincs 188 B3
Grampound Cornw'l 5 F8
Grampound Road Cornw'l 5 E8
Gramsdal W Isles 296 F4
Granborough Bucks 102 F5
Granby Notts 154 B5
Grandborough Warwick 119 D9
Grandpont Oxon 83 D8
Grandtully Perth/Kinr 286 B3
Grange Cumb 220 B5
Grange Dorset 31 G8
Grange E Ayrs 257 B10
Grange Fife 287 G8
Grange Halton 183 E8
Grange Lancs 202 F3
Grange Lancs 203 G7
Grange Mersey 182 D2
Grange Medway 69 F9
Grange NE Lincs 201 F9
Grange N Yorks 223 G8
Grange N Yorks 225 F11
Grange Perth/Kinr 286 E6
Grange Warrington 183 C10
Grange Crossroads Moray 302 D4
Grange Estate Dorset 31 G10
Grange Hall Moray 301 C10
Grange Hill Durham 233 F10
Grange Hill Essex 86 G6
Grange Moor W Yorks 197 D8
Grange of Cree Dumf/Gal 236 D6
Grange of Lindores Fife 286 F6
Grange Park London 86 F4
Grange Park Mersey 183 C7
Grange Park Swindon 62 C6
Grange Villa Durham 242 G6
Grangemill Derby 170 D2
Grangemouth Falk 279 E8
Grangemuir Fife 287 G9
Grange-over-Sands Cumb 211 D8
Grangepans Falk 279 E10
Grangetown Card 59 E7
Grangetown Redcar/Clevel'd 235 G7
Grangetown Tyne/Wear 243 G10
Granish H'land 291 B11
Gransmoor ER Yorks 209 B8
Gransmore Green Essex 106 G3
Granston = Treopert Pembs 91 E7
Grant Thorold NE Lincs 201 F9
Grantchester Cambs 123 F8
Grantham Lincs 155 B8
Granthouse Scot Borders 272 B6
Grantley N Yorks 214 F4
Grantlodge Aberds 293 B9
Granton C/Edinb 280 F4
Grantown Aberds 302 D5
Grantown-on-Spey H'land 301 G10
Graplin Dumf/Gal 237 E8
Grappenhall Warrington 183 D10
Grasby Lincs 200 G5
Grasmere Cumb 220 D6
Grass Green Essex 106 D4
Grasscroft Gtr Man 196 G3
Grassendale Mersey 182 D5
Grassgarth Cumb 221 F8
Grassgarth Cumb 230 C2
Grasshill Derby 170 B6
Grassington N Yorks 213 G10
Grassmoor Derby 170 B6
Grassthorpe Notts 172 B3
Grasswell Tyne/Wear 243 G8
Grateley Hants 47 E9
Gratton Devon 24 E5
Gratwich Staffs 151 C10
Gravel Castle Kent 55 D8
Gravel Hill Bucks 85 G8
Gravel Hole Gtr Man 196 F2
Graveley Cambs 122 E4
Graveley Herts 104 F4
Gravelly Hill W Midlands 134 E2
Gravelsbank Shrops 130 C6
Graven Shetl'd 314 F6
Graveney Kent 70 G5
Graveney Hill Kent 70 G5
Gravesend Herts 105 F8
Gravesend Kent 68 E6
Grayingham Lincs 188 B6
Grayrigg Cumb 221 F11
Grays Thurr'k 68 D6
Grayshott Hants 49 F11
Grayson Green Cumb 228 F5
Grayswood Surrey 50 G2
Graythorp Hartlep'l 234 F6
Graze Hill Beds 121 G11
Grazeley Wokingham 65 F7
Greagdhubh Lodge H'land 291 D8
Greamchary H'land 310 F2
Greasbrough S Yorks 186 B6
Greasby Mersey 182 D3
Greasley Notts 171 F7
Great Abington Cambs 105 B10
Great Addington Northants 121 B9
Great Alne Warwick 118 F2
Great Altcar Lancs 193 F10
Great Amwell Herts 86 C5
Great Asby Cumb 222 C3
Great Ashfield Suffolk 125 D9
Great Ayton N Yorks 225 C11
Great Baddow Essex 88 E2
Great Bardfield Essex 106 E3
Great Barford Beds 122 G2
Great Barr W Midlands 133 D10
Great Barrington Glos 82 C2
Great Barrow Ches 167 B7
Great Barton Suffolk 125 D7
Great Barugh N Yorks 216 D4
Great Bavington Northum 251 G11
Great Bealings Suffolk 108 B4
Great Bedwyn Wilts 63 G9
Great Bentley Essex 108 G2
Great Billing Northants 120 E6
Great Bircham Norfolk 158 C5
Great Blakenham Suffolk 126 G2
Great Blencow Cumb 230 E5
Great Bolas Telford 150 E3
Great Bookham Surrey 50 C6
Great Bourton Oxon 101 B9
Great Bowden Leics 136 F4
Great Bradley Suffolk 124 G3
Great Braxted Essex 88 C5
Great Bricett Suffolk 125 G10
Great Brickhill Bucks 103 E8
Great Bridge W Midlands 133 E9
Great Bridgeford Staffs 151 D7
Great Brington Northants 120 D3
Great Bromley Essex 107 F11
Great Broughton Cumb 229 E7
Great Broughton N Yorks 225 D11
Great Buckland Kent 69 G7
Great Budworth Ches 183 F11
Great Burdon D'lington 224 B6
Great Burgh Surrey 51 B8
Great Burstead Essex 87 G11
Great Busby N Yorks 225 D10
Great Cambourne Cambs 122 F6
Great Canfield Essex 87 B9
Great Carlton Lincs 190 D6
Great Casterton Rutl'd 137 B10
Great Chart Kent 54 E3
Great Chatfield Wilts 61 G11
Great Chatwell Staffs 150 G5
Great Chell Staffs 168 E5
Great Chesterford Essex 105 C10
Great Cheverell Wilts 46 C3
Great Chilton Durham 233 E11
Great Chishill Cambs 105 D8
Great Clacton Essex 89 B11
Great Cliff W Yorks 197 D10
Great Clifton Cumb 228 F6
Great Coates NE Lincs 201 E8
Great Comberton Worcs 99 C9
Great Common Suffolk 143 F7
Great Corby Cumb 239 F11
Great Cornard Suffolk 107 C7
Great Cowden ER Yorks 209 E10
Great Coxwell Oxon 82 G3
Great Crakehall N Yorks 214 B5
Great Cransley Northants 120 B6
Great Cressingham Norfolk 141 C7
Great Crosby Mersey 182 B4
Great Crosthwaite Cumb 229 G11
Great Cubley Derby 152 B3
Great Dalby Leics 154 G4
Great Doddington Northants 121 E7
Great Doward Heref'd 79 B9
Great Dunham Norfolk 159 G7
Great Dunmow Essex 106 G2
Great Durnford Wilts 46 F6
Great Easton Essex 106 F2
Great Easton Leics 137 E6
Great Eccleston Lancs 202 E4
Great Edstone N Yorks 216 C4
Great Ellingham Norfolk 141 D10
Great Elm Som'set 45 D8
Great Eppleton Tyne/Wear 234 B3
Great Eversden Cambs 123 G7
Great Fen Cambs 123 B11
Great Fencote N Yorks 224 G5
Great Finborough Suffolk 125 F10
Great Fransham Norfolk 159 G7
Great Gaddesden Herts 85 C8
Great Gidding Cambs 138 G2
Great Givendale ER Yorks 208 C2
Great Glemham Suffolk 126 E6
Great Glen Leics 136 D3
Great Gonerby Lincs 155 B7
Great Gransden Cambs 122 F5
Great Green Cambs 104 C5
Great Green Norfolk 142 F5
Great Green Suffolk 125 B11
Great Green Suffolk 126 B2
Great Green Suffolk 125 F8
Great Green Suffolk 125 D8
Great Habton N Yorks 216 D5
Great Hale Lincs 173 G10
Great Hallingbury Essex 87 B8
Great Hampden Bucks 84 E5
Great Harrowden Northants 121 C7
Great Harwood Lancs 203 G10
Great Haseley Oxon 83 E10
Great Hatfield ER Yorks 209 E9
Great Haywood Staffs 151 E9
Great Heath W Midlands 134 G6
Great Heck N Yorks 198 C5
Great Henny Essex 107 D7
Great Hinton Wilts 46 B2
Great Hivings Bucks 85 E7
Great Hockham Norfolk 141 E9
Great Holland Essex 89 B12
Great Hollands Brackn'l 65 F11
Great Holm M/Keynes 102 D6
Great Horkesley Essex 107 E9
Great Hormead Herts 105 E8
Great Horton W Yorks 205 G8
Great Horwood Bucks 102 E5
Great Houghton Northants 120 F5
Great Houghton S Yorks 198 F2
Great Howarth Gtr Man 196 D2
Great Hucklow Derby 185 F11
Great Job's Cross Kent 38 B4
Great Kelk ER Yorks 209 B8
Great Kimble Bucks 84 D4
Great Kingshill Bucks 84 F5
Great Langdale Cumb 220 D6
Great Langton N Yorks 224 F5
Great Lea Common Wokingham 65 F8
Great Leighs Essex 88 B2
Great Leighs Racecourse Essex 88 B2
Great Lever Gtr Man 195 F8
Great Limber Lincs 200 F6
Great Linford M/Keynes 103 C7
Great Livermere Suffolk 125 C7
Great Longstone Derby 186 G2
Great Lumley Durham 233 B11
Great Malvern Worcs 98 B5
Great Maplestead Essex 106 E6
Great Marton Blackp'l 202 F2
Great Marton Moss Lancs 202 G3
Great Massingham Norfolk 158 E5
Great Melton Norfolk 142 B2
Great Milton Oxon 83 E10
Great Missenden Bucks 84 E5
Great Mitton Lancs 203 E10
Great Mongeham Kent 55 C10
Great Moor Gtr Man 184 D6
Great Moulton Norfolk 142 E3
Great Munden Herts 105 G7
Great Musgrave Cumb 222 C5
Great Ness Shrops 149 F7
Great Norman Street Kent 52 C3
Great Notley Essex 106 G4
Great Oak Monmouths 78 D5
Great Oakley Essex 108 F3
Great Oakley Northants 137 F7
Great Offley Herts 104 F2
Great Orme Tramway, Llandudno Conwy 180 E3
Great Ormside Cumb 222 B3
Great Orton Cumb 239 G8
Great Ouseburn N Yorks 215 G8
Great Oxendon Northants 136 G4
Great Oxney Green Essex 87 D11
Great Parndon Essex 86 D6
Great Pattenden Kent 53 D8
Great Paxton Cambs 122 E4
Great Plumpton Lancs 202 G3
Great Plumstead Norfolk 160 G6
Great Ponton Lincs 155 C8
Great Preston W Yorks 198 B2
Great Purston Northants 101 D10
Great Raveley Cambs 138 G5
Great Rissington Glos 81 B11
Great Rollright Oxon 100 E6
Great Ryburgh Norfolk 159 D9
Great Ryle Northum 264 G2
Great Ryton Shrops 131 C9
Great Saling Essex 106 F4
Great Salkeld Cumb 230 D6
Great Sampford Essex 106 D2
Great Sankey Warrington 183 D9
Great Saredon Staffs 133 B9
Great Saxham Suffolk 124 E5
Great Shefford W Berks 63 D11
Great Shelford Cambs 123 G9
Great Smeaton N Yorks 225 E7
Great Snoring Norfolk 159 C8
Great Somerford Wilts 62 C3
Great Stainton D'lington 234 G2
Great Stambridge Essex 88 G6
Great Staughton Cambs 122 E2
Great Steeping Lincs 174 C6
Great Stoke S Glos 60 C6
Great Stonar Kent 55 B10
Great Strickland Cumb 231 G7
Great Stukeley Cambs 122 C4
Great Sturton Lincs 190 F2
Great Sutton Ches 182 F5
Great Sutton Shrops 131 G10
Great Swinburne Northum 241 B10
Great Tew Oxon 101 F7
Great Tey Essex 107 F7
Great Thorness I/Wight 20 C5
Great Thurlow Suffolk 124 G3
Great Torrington Devon 25 D7
Great Tosson Northum 252 C2
Great Totham Essex 88 C5
Great Tows Lincs 190 C2
Great Tree Cornw'l 6 D5
Great Urswick Cumb 210 E5
Great Wakering Essex 70 B2
Great Waldingfield Suffolk 107 C8
Great Walsingham Norfolk 159 B8
Great Waltham Essex 87 C11
Great Warley Essex 87 G9
Great Washbourne Glos 99 E9
Great Watersend Kent 55 E9
Great Weeke Devon 13 D10
Great Welnetham Suffolk 125 F7
Great Wenham Suffolk 107 D11
Great Whittington Northum 242 C2
Great Wigborough Essex 89 C7
Great Wilbraham Cambs 123 F10
Great Wilne Derby 153 C9
Great Wishford Wilts 46 F5
Great Witchingham Norfolk 160 F2
Great Witcombe Glos 80 C6
Great Witley Worcs 116 D5
Great Wolford Warwick 100 E5
Great Wratting Suffolk 106 B3
Great Wymondley Herts 104 F4
Great Wyrley Staffs 133 B9
Great Wytheford Shrops 149 F11
Great Yarmouth Norfolk 143 B10
Great Yarmouth Sea Life Centre Norfolk 143 B10
Great Yeldham Essex 106 D5
Greatfield Wilts 62 B5
Greatford Lincs 155 G11
Greatgap Bucks 84 B6
Greatgate Staffs 169 G9
Greatham Hants 49 G9
Greatham Hartlep'l 234 F5
Greatham W Sussex 35 D8
Greatness Kent 52 B4
Greatstone-on-Sea Kent 39 C9
Greatworth Northants 101 C11
Greave Gtr Man 184 C6
Greave Lancs 195 C11
Grebby Lincs 174 B6
Greeba I/Man 192 D4
Green Denbs 165 B9
Green Bottom Cornw'l 4 F5
Green Bottom Glos 79 B11
Green Cross Surrey 49 F11
Green End Beds 103 B10
Green End Beds 121 E11
Green End Beds 122 G2
Green End Beds 122 E2
Green End Bucks 103 E8
Green End Cambs 122 C4
Green End Cambs 123 D9
Green End Cambs 123 F7
Green End Herts 104 E5
Green End Herts 104 E6
Green End Lancs 204 D4
Green End N Yorks 226 E6
Green End Warwick 134 F5
Green Gate Devon 27 D8
Green Hailey Bucks 84 E4
Green Hammerton N Yorks 206 B5
Green Haworth Lancs 195 B9
Green Head Cumb 230 B3
Green Heath Staffs 151 G9
Green Hill Lincs 155 B8
Green Hill Wilts 62 B5
Green Hill Worcs 99 B10
Green Lane Devon 13 F11
Green Lane Heref'd 98 B2
Green Lane Powys 130 D3
Green Lane Worcs 117 E11
Green Moor S Yorks 186 B3
Green Ore Som'set 44 C5
Green Quarter Cumb 221 E9
Green Street E Sussex 38 E3
Green Street Essex 87 F10
Green Street Glos 80 E3
Green Street Glos 80 B5
Green Street Herts 105 G9
Green Street Worcs 99 B7
Green Street W Sussex 35 C10
Green Street Green Kent 68 E5
Green Street Green London 68 G3
Green Tye Herts 86 B6
Greenacres Gtr Man 196 F2
Greenan Arg/Bute 275 G11
Greenbank Shetl'd 314 C7
Greenburn W Loth 269 C8
Greencroft Durham 242 G5
Greencroft Norfolk 177 E8
Greendown Som'set 44 C5
Greendykes Northum 264 D3
Greenend Oxon 100 G6
Greenfaulds N Lanarks 278 G5
Greenfield Beds 103 E11
Greenfield Flints 181 F11
Greenfield Gtr Man 196 G3
Greenfield H'land 289 D11
Greenfield H'land 290 C4
Greenfield Oxon 84 G2
Greenfoot N Lanarks 268 B4
Greenford London 66 C6
Greengairs N Lanarks 278 G5
Greengate Gtr Man 196 D2
Greengate Norfolk 159 F10
Greengates W Yorks 205 F9
Greenhalgh Lancs 202 F4
Greenham Dorset 28 F6
Greenham Som'set 27 C9
Greenham W Berks 64 F3
Greenhaugh Northum 251 F7
Greenhead Dumf/Gal 247 D9
Greenhead N Lanarks 268 D6
Greenhead Northum 240 D5
Greenheyes Gtr Man 195 G8
Greenhill Dumf/Gal 248 G4
Greenhill Durham 234 B3
Greenhill Falk 278 F6
Greenhill Heref'd 98 B4
Greenhill Kent 71 F7
Greenhill Leics 153 F8
Greenhill London 67 B7
Greenhill S Glos 60 B6
Greenhill S Yorks 186 E4
Greenhill Worcs 116 B6
Greenhillocks Derby 170 F6
Greenhills N Ayrs 267 E7
Greenhithe Kent 68 D5
Greenholm E Ayrs 258 B2
Greenholme Cumb 221 D11
Greenhouse Scot Borders 262 E3
Greenhow Hill N Yorks 214 G2
Greenigoe Orkney 313 H5
Greenland H'land 310 C6
Greenland S Yorks 186 D5
Greenland Mains H'land 310 C6
Greenlands Worcs 117 D11
Greenlaw Aberds 302 D6
Greenlaw Scot Borders 272 F4
Greenlea Dumf/Gal 238 B2
Greenleys M/Keynes 102 C6
Greenloaning Perth/Kinr 286 G2
Greenmeadow Swindon 62 B6
Greenmeadow Torf 78 F3
Greenmeadow Community Farm, Pontnewydd Torf 78 F3
Greenmount Gtr Man 195 E9
Greenmow Shetl'd 315 L6
Greenoak ER Yorks 199 B10
Greenock Inverci 276 F5
Greenock West Inverci 276 F5
Greenodd Cumb 210 C6
Greenrigg W Loth 269 C8
Greenrow Cumb 238 G4
Greens Norton Northants 102 B3
Greensforge Staffs 133 F7
Greenshills S Lanarks 268 F2
Greenside Cumb 222 E4
Greenside Derby 186 F5
Greenside Tyne/Wear 242 E4
Greenside W Yorks 197 D7
Greenstead Essex 107 F10
Greenstead Green Essex 106 F6
Greensted Essex 87 E8
Greensted Green Essex 87 E8
Greensted Log Church, Chipping Ongar Essex 87 E8
Greenstreet Green Suffolk 125 G10
Greenway Glos 98 E4
Greenway Som'set 28 C4
Greenway V/Glam 58 E5
Greenway Worcs 116 C4
Greenways Som'set 27 B11
Greenwell Cumb 240 F2
Greenwich London 67 D11
Greenwich Wilts 46 G2
Greenwith Common Cornw'l 4 G5
Greeny Orkney 312 F3
Greep H'land 298 E2
Greet Glos 99 E10
Greete Shrops 115 C11
Greetham Lincs 190 G4
Greetham Rutl'd 155 G8
Greetland W Yorks 196 C5
Greetland Wall Nook W Yorks 196 C5
Greetwell N Lincs 200 G2
Grèin W Isles 297 L2
Gregson Lane Lancs 194 B5
Gregynog Powys 129 D11
Greinetobht W Isles 296 D4
Greinton Som'set 44 F2
Gremista Shetl'd 315 J6
Grenaby I/Man 192 E3
Grendon Northants 121 E7
Grendon Warwick 134 C5
Grendon Bishop Heref'd 115 F11
Grendon Common Warwick 134 D5
Grendon Underwood Bucks 102 G3
Grenend N Lanarks 268 C4
Grenofen Devon 12 G5
Grenoside S Yorks 186 C4
Greosabhagh W Isles 305 J3
Gresford Wrex 166 E5
Gresham Norfolk 160 B3
Greshornish H'land 298 D3
Gressenhall Norfolk 159 F9
Gressingham Lancs 211 F11
Greta Bridge Durham 223 C11
Gretna Dumf/Gal 239 D8
Gretna Green Dumf/Gal 239 D8
Gretton Glos 99 E10
Gretton Northants 137 E7
Gretton Shrops 131 D10
Gretton Field Glos 99 E10
Grewelthorpe N Yorks 214 D4
Grey Green N Lincs 199 F9
Greyfriars Surrey 50 D4
Greygarth N Yorks 214 E3
Greylake Som'set 43 G11
Greylake Fosse Som'set 44 F2
Greynor Carms 75 D9
Greyrigg Dumf/Gal 248 F3
Greys Green Oxon 65 C8
Greysouthern Cumb 229 F7
Greystoke Cumb 230 E4
Greystoke Gill Cumb 230 F4
Greystone Aberds 292 D6
Greystone Aberds 302 F6
Greystone Angus 287 C9
Greystone Dumf/Gal 237 B11
Greystones S Yorks 186 D4
Greytree Heref'd 97 F11
Greywell Hants 49 C8
Griais W Isles 304 D6
Grianan W Isles 304 E6
Grianllyn Conwy 180 F4
Gribb Dorset 28 G5
Gribbleford Bridge Devon 25 G8
Gribthorpe ER Yorks 207 F11
Griff Warwick 135 F7
Griff Hollow Warwick 135 F7
Griffithstown Torf 78 F3
Griffydam Leics 153 F8
Griggs Green Hants 49 G10
Grimbister Orkney 312 G4
Grimblethorpe Lincs 190 D2
Grimeford Village Lancs 194 E6
Grimesthorpe S Yorks 186 C5
Grimethorpe S Yorks 198 F2
Griminis W Isles 296 D3
Griminis W Isles 296 F3
Grimister Shetl'd 314 D6
Grimley Worcs 116 E6
Grimness Orkney 313 J5
Grimoldby Lincs 190 D5
Grimpo Shrops 149 D7
Grimsargh Lancs 203 G7
Grimsbury Oxon 101 C9
Grimsby NE Lincs 201 E9
Grimscote Northants 120 G2
Grimscott Cornw'l 24 F3
Grimshaw Blackb'n 195 C8
Grimshaw Green Lancs 194 E3
Grimsthorpe Lincs 155 E10
Grimston ER Yorks 209 F11
Grimston Leics 154 E3
Grimston Norfolk 158 E4
Grimstone Dorset 17 C8
Grimstone End Suffolk 125 D8
Grindale ER Yorks 218 E2
Grindigar Orkney 313 H6
Grindiscol Shetl'd 315 K6
Grindle Shrops 132 C5
Grindleford Derby 186 F2
Grindleton Lancs 203 D11
Grindley Staffs 151 D10
Grindley Brook Shrops 167 G8
Grindlow Derby 185 F11
Grindon Northum 273 G8
Grindon Stockton 234 F3
Grindon Staffs 169 E9
Grindon Tyne/Wear 243 F9
Grindsbrook Booth Derby 185 D10
Gringley on the Hill Notts 188 C2
Grinnacombe Moor Devon 12 C4
Grinshill Shrops 149 E10
Grinton N Yorks 223 F10
Griomasaigh W Isles 297 G4
Griomsidar W Isles 304 F5
Grisdale Cumb 222 G5
Grishipoll Arg/Bute 288 D3
Grisling Common E Sussex 36 C6
Gristhorpe N Yorks 217 C11
Griston Norfolk 141 D8
Gritley Orkney 313 H6
Grittenham Wilts 62 C4
Grittlesend Heref'd 98 B4
Grittleton Wilts 61 C11
Grizebeck Cumb 210 B4
Grizedale Cumb 220 G6
Groam H'land 300 E5
Grobister Orkney 312 F7
Grobsness Shetl'd 315 G5
Groby Leics 135 B10
Groes Conwy 165 C8
Groes Neath P Talb 57 D9
Groes Efa Denbs 165 B10
Groesfaen Rh Cyn Taff 58 C5
Groesffordd Conwy 180 F3
Groesffordd Gwyn 144 B5
Groeslon Gwyn 163 C8
Groeslon Gwyn 163 D7
Groes-lwyd Powys 148 G4
Groespluan Powys 130 B4
Groes-wen Caerph 58 B6
Grogoth Wallas Cornw'l 5 G8
Grogport Arg/Bute 255 C9
Gronant Flints 181 E9
Groombridge E Sussex 52 F4
Groomford Suffolk 127 F7
Grosmont Monmouths 97 G8
Grosmont N Yorks 226 D6
Grosvenor Museum, Chester Ches 166 B6
Grotaig H'land 300 G4
Groton Suffolk 107 C9
Grotton Gtr Man 196 G3
Groudle Glen Railway I/Man 192 E5
Grougfoot Falk 279 F10
Grove Dorset 17 G9
Grove Kent 71 G8
Grove Notts 188 F2
Grove Oxon 82 G5
Grove Pembs 73 E7
Grove End Bucks 84 D2
Grove End Warwick 134 D3
Grove Green Kent 53 B9
Grove Park London 68 E2
Grove Town W Yorks 198 C3
Grove Vale W Midlands 133 E10
Grovehill ER Yorks 208 F6
Grovehill Herts 85 D9
Grovehurst Kent 53 E8
Groves Kent 55 B9
Grovesend S Glos 61 B7
Grovesend Swan 75 E9
Grub Street Kent 68 F5
Grudie H'land 300 C3
Gruids H'land 309 J5
Gruinard House H'land 307 K4
Gruinards H'land 309 K5
Grula H'land 294 C5
Gruline Arg/Bute 289 E7
Gruline Ho Arg/Bute 289 F7
Grumbeg H'land 308 F6
Grumbla Cornw'l 1 D4
Grunasound Shetl'd 315 K5
Grundisburgh Suffolk 126 G4
Gruting Shetl'd 315 J4
Grutness Shetl'd 315 N6
Gualachulain H'land 284 C5
Gualin Ho. H'land 308 D3
Guard House W Yorks 204 E6
Guardbridge Fife 287 F8
Guarlford Worcs 98 B6
Guay Perth/Kinr 286 C4
Gubbions Green Essex 88 B2
Gubblacote Herts 84 B6
Guesachan H'land 289 B10
Guestling Green E Sussex 38 E4
Guestling Thorn E Sussex 38 D5
Guestwick Norfolk 159 D11
Guestwick Green Norfolk 159 D11
Guide Blackb'n 195 B8
Guide Bridge Gtr Man 184 B6
Guide Post Northum 253 F7
Guilden Morden Cambs 104 C5
Guilden Sutton Ches 167 B7
Guildford Surrey 50 D4
Guildford Park Surrey 50 D3
Guildiehaugh W Loth 269 B9
Guildtown Perth/Kinr 286 D5
Guilford Pembs 73 D7
Guilsborough Northants 120 C3
Guilsfield = Cegidfa Powys 148 G4
Guilthwaite S Yorks 186 D6
Guilton Kent 55 B9
Guineaford Devon 40 F5
Guisachan H'land 300 G3
Guisborough Redcar/Clevel'd 226 B2
Guiseley W Yorks 205 E9
Guist Norfolk 159 D9
Guith Orkney 312 E6
Guiting Power Glos 99 G11
Gulberwick Shetl'd 315 K6
Gullane E Loth 281 E9
Guller's End Worcs 99 D7
Gulling Green Suffolk 124 F6
Gully W Yorks 196 F6
Gulpher Suffolk 108 D6
Gulval Cornw'l 1 C5

Gulworthy Devon 12 G5
Gumfreston Pembs 73 E10
Gumley Leics 136 E3
Gummow's Shop Cornw'l 5 D7
Gun Green Kent 53 G9
Gun Hill E Sussex 37 E9
Gun Hill Warwick 134 F5
Gunby Lincs 175 B7
Gunby Lincs 155 E8
Gundleton Hants 48 G6
Gunn Devon 41 G6
Gunnerby NE Lincs 190 B2
Gunnersbury London 67 D7
Gunnerside N Yorks 223 F8
Gunnerton Northum 241 B10
Gunness N Lincs 199 E10
Gunnislake Cornw'l 12 G4
Gunnista Shetl'd 315 J7
Guns Village W Midlands 133 E9
Gunthorpe Norfolk 159 C10
Gunthorpe N Lincs 188 B4
Gunthorpe Notts 171 G11
Gunthorpe Peterbro 138 C3
Gunthorpe Rutl'd 137 B7
Gunton Suffolk 143 D10
Gunville I/Wight 20 D5
Gunwalloe Cornw'l 2 E5
Gunwalloe Fishing Cove Cornw'l 2 E5
Gupworthy Som'set 42 G3
Gurnard I/Wight 20 B5
Gurnett Ches 184 G6
Gurney Slade Som'set 44 D6
Gurney Street Som'set 43 F9
Gurnos Merth Tyd 77 D8
Gurnos Powys 76 D3
Gushmere Kent 54 B5
Gussage All Saints Dorset 31 E8
Gussage St. Andrew Dorset 31 E7
Gussage St. Michael Dorset 31 E7
Guston Kent 55 E10
Gutcher Shetl'd 314 D7
Guthram Gowt Lincs 156 E3
Guthrie Angus 287 B9
Guyhirn Cambs 139 C8
Guyhirn Gull Cambs 139 C7
Guy's Marsh Dorset 30 C4
Guyzance Northum 252 C6
Gwaelod-y-garth Rh Cyn Taff 58 C6
Gwaenysgor Flints 181 E9
Gwaithla Powys 114 F4
Gwalchmai Angl 178 F5
Gwar-cwm Ceredig'n 128 E3
Gwarn-Leisian Neath P Talb 76 C2
Gwarthlow Shrops 130 D4
Gwastad Pembs 91 G10
Gwastadgoed Gwyn 128 A1
Gwastadnant Gwyn 163 D10
Gwaun Leisian Carms 76 C2
Gwaun Meisgyn Rh Cyn Taff 58 C5
Gwaun-Cae-Gurwen Neath P Talb 76 C2
Gwbert Ceredig'n 92 B3
Gweek Cornw'l 2 D6
Gwehelog Monmouths 78 E5
Gweithdy Angl 179 F8
Gwenddwr Powys 95 C11
Gwennap Cornw'l 4 G4
Gwent Bl Gwent 78 E2
Gwenter Cornw'l 2 F6
Gwernaffel Powys 114 C5
Gwernaffield Flints 166 C2
Gwernau Caerph 77 G11
Gwerneirin Powys 129 F10
Gwerneirin Powys 130 G3
Gwernesney Monmouths 78 E6
Gwern-Estyn Flints 166 D4
Gwernogle Carms 93 E10
Gwernymynydd Flints 166 C2
Gwern-y-Steeple V/Glam 58 D5
Gwersyllt Wrex 166 E4
Gwespyr Flints 181 E10
Gwindra Cornw'l 5 E9
Gwinear Cornw'l 2 B3
Gwithian Cornw'l 2 A3
Gwredog Angl 178 D6
Gwrhay Caerph 77 F11
Gwrhyd Mawr Pembs 90 F5
Gwyddelwern Denbs 165 F9
Gwyddgrug Carms 93 D9
Gwydir Gwyn 162 F5
Gwynfryn Wrex 166 E3
Gwystre Powys 113 D11
Gwytherin Conwy 164 C5
Gyfelia Wrex 166 F4
Gyffin Conwy 180 F3
Gylen Park Arg/Bute 289 G10
Gyre Orkney 313 H4
Gyrn Goch Gwyn 162 F6

H

Habberley Shrops 131 C8
Habberley Worcs 116 B6
Habergham Lancs 204 G2
Habertoft Lincs 175 B8
Habin W Sussex 34 C4
Habrough NE Lincs 200 E6
Haccombe Devon 14 G3
Hacconby Lincs 156 D2
Haceby Lincs 155 B10
Hacheston Suffolk 126 F6
Hackbridge London 67 F9
Hackenthorpe S Yorks 186 E6
Hackford Norfolk 141 C11
Hackforth N Yorks 224 G4
Hackland Orkney 312 F4
Hackleton Northants 120 F6
Hacklinge Kent 55 C10
Hackman's Gate Worcs 117 B7
Hackness N Yorks 227 G9
Hackness Orkney 313 J4
Hackness Som'set 43 D10
Hackney London 67 C10
Hackney Wick London 67 C11
Hackthorn Lincs 189 E7
Hackthorpe Cumb 230 G6
Hackwood Northum 241 E10
Haclait W Isles 297 G4
Hacton London 68 C5
Hadden Scot Borders 263 B7
Haddenham Bucks 84 D2
Haddenham Cambs 123 B9
Haddington E Loth 281 G10
Haddington Lincs 172 C6
Haddiscoe Norfolk 143 D8
Haddoch Aberds 302 E5
Haddon Cambs 138 E2
Haddon Hall Derby 170 B2
Hademore Staffs 134 B3
Haden Cross W Midlands 133 F9
Hadfield Derby 185 B8
Hadham Cross Herts 86 B6
Hadham Ford Herts 105 G8
Hadleigh Essex 69 B10
Hadleigh Suffolk 107 C10
Hadleigh Heath Suffolk 107 C9
Hadley London 86 F2
Hadley Telford 150 G3
Hadley Worcs 117 E7
Hadley Castle Telford 150 G3
Hadley End Staffs 152 E2
Hadley Wood London 86 F3
Hadlow Kent 52 D6
Hadlow Down E Sussex 37 C8
Hadlow Stair Kent 52 D6
Hadnall Shrops 149 E10
Hadspen Som'set 45 G7
Hadstock Essex 105 C11
Hadston Northum 253 D7
Hady Derby 186 G5
Hadzor Worcs 117 E8
Haffenden Quarter Kent 53 E11
Hafod Swan 75 G11
Hafod Dinbych Conwy 164 E5
Hafodrisclawdd Caerph 77 E11
Hafodyrynys Torf 78 F2
Hag Fold Gtr Man 195 G7
Hagg Hill Derby 170 B6
Haggate Gtr Man 196 F2
Haggate Lancs 204 F3
Haggbeck Cumb 239 C11
Haggersta Shetl'd 315 J5
Haggerston London 67 C10
Haggerston Northum 273 G10
Hagget End Cumb 219 C10
Haggington Hill Devon 40 D5
Haggrister Shetl'd 314 F5
Haggs Falk 278 F5
Hagley Heref'd 97 C11
Hagley Worcs 133 G8
Hagmore Green Suffolk 107 D8
Hagnaby Lincs 174 C4
Hagnaby Lincs 191 F7
Hague Bar Derby 185 D7
Hagworthingham Lincs 174 B4
Haigh Gtr Man 194 F6
Haigh S Yorks 197 E9
Haigh Moor W Yorks 197 C9
Haighton Green Lancs 203 G7
Hail Weston Cambs 122 E3
Haile Cumb 219 D10
Hailey Herts 86 C5
Hailey Oxon 64 B6
Hailey Oxon 82 C5
Hailsham E Sussex 23 D9
Haimer H'land 310 C5
Hainault London 87 G7
Haine Kent 71 F11
Haines Hill Som'set 28 C2
Hainford Norfolk 160 F4
Hainton Lincs 189 E11
Hainworth W Yorks 205 F7
Haisthorpe E Yorks 218 G2
Hakin Pembs 72 D5
Halabezack Cornw'l 2 C6
Halam Notts 171 E11
Halamanning Cornw'l 2 C3
Halbeath Fife 280 D2
Halberton Devon 27 E8
Halcon Som'set 28 B2
Halcro H'land 310 C6
Haldens Herts 86 C2
Hale Cumb 211 D10
Hale Gtr Man 184 D3
Hale Hants 31 D11
Hale Halton 183 E7
Hale Kent 71 F9
Hale Medway 69 F9
Hale Som'set 30 B3
Hale Surrey 49 D10
Hale Bank Halton 183 E7
Hale End London 86 G5
Hale Green E Sussex 37 E9
Hale Mills Cornw'l 4 G5
Hale Nook Lancs 202 E3
Hale Street Kent 53 D7
Halebarns Gtr Man 184 D3
Halehird Cumb 221 E8
Hales Norfolk 143 D7
Hales Staffs 150 C4
Hales Green Derby 169 G11
Hales Park Worcs 116 B5
Hales Place Kent 54 B6
Hales Street Norfolk 142 F3
Halesfield Telford 132 C4
Halesgate Lincs 156 D6
Halesowen W Midlands 133 G9
Halesworth Suffolk 127 B7
Halewood Halton 183 D7
Halford Devon 14 G2
Halford Shrops 131 G8
Halford Warwick 100 B5
Halfpenny Furze Carms 74 C3
Halfpenny Green Staffs 132 E6
Halfway Carms 75 E8
Halfway Carms 94 E2
Halfway Carms 94 E6
Halfway S Yorks 186 E6
Halfway W Berks 64 F2
Halfway Bridge W Sussex 34 C6
Halfway House Shrops 148 G6
Halfway Houses Kent 70 E2
Halfway Houses Lincs 172 C5
Halfway Street Kent 55 D9
Halgabron Cornw'l 11 D7
Halifax W Yorks 196 C5
Halket E Ayrs 267 E8
Halkirk H'land 310 D5
Halkyn Flints 182 G2
Hall E Renf 267 D8
Hall Suffolk 125 G11
Hall Bower W Yorks 196 E6
Hall Common Norfolk 161 F7
Hall Cross Lancs 202 G4
Hall Dunnerdale Cumb 220 F4
Hall End Beds 103 D11
Hall End Beds 103 B9
Hall End Lincs 174 E6
Hall End S Glos 61 B8
Hall End Warwick 134 C5
Hall Green Ches 168 D4
Hall Green Essex 106 D5
Hall Green Lancs 194 C3
Hall Green Lancs 194 F4
Hall Green Norfolk 159 F8
Hall Green S Yorks 197 E10
Hall Green W Midlands 134 G2
Hall Green W Midlands 135 G7
Hall Green Wrex 167 G8
Hall Grove Herts 86 C3
Hall of Clestrain Orkney 313 H3
Hall of Tankerness Orkney 313 H6
Hall Stanton Cumb 220 E2
Hall Waberthwaite Cumb 219 F11
Hallam Fields Derby 171 G7
Halland E Sussex 37 D8
Hallaton Leics 136 D5
Hallatrow Bath/NE Som'set 44 B6
Hallbankgate Cumb 240 F3
Hallbeck Cumb 212 B2
Hallen S Glos 60 C4
Hallew Cornw'l 5 D10
Hallfield Gate Derby 170 D5
Hallgarth Durham 234 C2
Hallglen Falk 279 F7
Hallin H'land 298 D2
Halling Medway 69 G8
Hallingbury Street Essex 87 B8
Hallington Lincs 190 D4
Hallington Northum 241 B11
Halliwell Gtr Man 195 E8
Halloughton Notts 171 E11
Hallow Worcs 116 F6
Hallow Heath Worcs 116 F6
Hallowes Derby 186 F5
Hallowsgate Ches 167 B8
Hallrule Scot Borders 262 G3
Halls E Loth 282 G3
Halls Green Essex 86 D6
Hall's Green Herts 104 F5
Hall's Green Kent 52 D4
Hallsands Devon 9 G11
Hallside S Lanarks 268 C3
Hallspill Devon 25 C7
Hallthwaites Cumb 210 B3
Hallwood Green Heref'd 98 E3
Hallwood Park Halton 183 E8
Hallworthy Cornw'l 11 D9
Hallyburton House Perth/Kinr 286 D6
Hallyne Scot Borders 270 G3
Halmer End Staffs 168 F3
Halmond's Frome Heref'd 98 B3
Halmore S Glos 79 E11
Halmyre Mains Scot Borders 270 F3
Halnaker W Sussex 34 F6
Halpenny Cumb 211 B10
Halsall Lancs 193 E11
Halse Northants 101 C11
Halse Som'set 27 B10
Halsetown Cornw'l 2 B2
Halsfordwood Devon 14 C3
Halsham E Yorks 201 B9
Halsinger Devon 40 F4
Halstead Essex 106 E6
Halstead Kent 68 G3
Halstead Leics 136 B5
Halstock Dorset 29 F8
Halsway Som'set 42 F6
Haltcliff Bridge Cumb 230 D3
Halterworth Hants 32 C5
Haltham Lincs 174 C2
Haltoft End Lincs 174 F5
Halton Bucks 84 C5
Halton Halton 183 E8
Halton Lancs 211 G10
Halton Northum 241 D11
Halton Wrex 148 B6
Halton W Yorks 206 G2
Halton Brook Halton 183 E8
Halton East N Yorks 204 C6
Halton Fenside Lincs 174 C6
Halton Gill N Yorks 213 D7
Halton Green Lancs 211 F10
Halton Holegate Lincs 174 B6
Halton Moor W Yorks 206 G2
Halton Park Lancs 211 F10
Halton Shields Northum 242 D2
Halton View Halton 183 D8
Halton West N Yorks 204 C2
Halton-Lea-Gate Northum 240 F5
Haltwhistle Northum 240 E6
Halvergate Norfolk 143 B8
Halwell Devon 8 E5
Halwill Devon 12 B4
Halwill Junction Devon 12 B4
Ham Devon 28 G2
Ham Glos 79 F11
Ham Glos 99 G9
Ham H'land 310 B6
Ham Kent 55 C10
Ham London 67 E7
Ham Plym'th 7 D9
Ham Shetl'd 315 K1
Ham Som'set 28 E3
Ham Som'set 27 C11
Ham Som'set 28 B3
Ham Som'set 45 D7
Ham Som'set 43 C10
Ham Wilts 63 G10
Ham Common Dorset 30 B4
Ham Green Bristol 60 D4
Ham Green Hants 48 G2
Ham Green Kent 38 B5
Ham Green Kent 69 F10
Ham Green Worcs 117 E10
Ham Hill Medway 69 G8
Ham Street Som'set 44 G5
Hamar Shetl'd 314 F5
Hamarhill Orkney 312 E6
Hamars Shetl'd 315 G6
Hambleden Bucks 65 B9
Hambledon Hants 33 D10
Hambledon Surrey 50 F3
Hamble-le-Rice Hants 33 F7
Hambleton Lancs 202 E3
Hambleton N Yorks 207 G7
Hambleton Moss Side Lancs 202 E3
Hambridge Som'set 28 C5
Hambrook S Glos 60 D6
Hambrook W Sussex 34 F3
Hameringham Lincs 174 B4
Hamerton Cambs 122 B2
Hametoun Shetl'd 315 K1
Hamilton Leics C 136 B2
Hamilton S Lanarks 268 D4
Hamilton Park Racecourse S Lanarks 268 D4
Hamister Shetl'd 315 G7
Hamlet Dorset 29 F9
Hamlet of Shell Ness Kent 70 F5
Hammer W Sussex 49 G11
Hammer Bottom Hants 49 G11
Hammerpot W Sussex 35 F9
Hammersmith Derby 170 E5
Hammersmith London 67 D8
Hammerwich Staffs 133 B11
Hammerwood E Sussex 52 F2
Hammill Kent 55 B9
Hammond Street Herts 86 E4
Hammond's Green Hants 32 E4
Hammoon Dorset 30 E4
Hamnavoe Shetl'd 314 E4
Hamnavoe Shetl'd 314 E6
Hamnavoe Shetl'd 314 F6
Hamnavoe Shetl'd 315 K5
Hamnish Clifford Heref'd 115 F10
Hamp Som'set 43 F10
Hampden National Stadium Glasg C 267 C11
Hampden Park E Sussex 23 E10
Hamperden End Essex 105 E11
Hampnett Glos 81 B10
Hampole S Yorks 198 E4
Hampreston Dorset 19 B7
Hampsfield Cumb 211 C8
Hampson Green Lancs 202 C5
Hampstead London 67 B9
Hampstead Garden Suburb London 67 B9
Hampstead Norreys W Berks 64 D4
Hampsthwaite N Yorks 205 B11
Hampt Cornw'l 12 G3
Hampton Devon 15 B11
Hampton Kent 71 F7
Hampton London 66 E6
Hampton Shrops 132 F4
Hampton Swindon 81 G11
Hampton Worcs 99 C10
Hampton Bishop Heref'd 97 D11
Hampton Court Palace, Teddington London 67 F7
Hampton Fields Glos 80 F5
Hampton Gay Oxon 83 B7
Hampton Green Ches 167 F8
Hampton Heath Ches 167 F8
Hampton Hill London 66 E6
Hampton in Arden W Midlands 134 G4
Hampton Loade Shrops 132 F5
Hampton Lovett Worcs 117 D7
Hampton Lucy Warwick 118 F5
Hampton Magna Warwick 118 D5
Hampton on the Hill Warwick 118 E5
Hampton Park S'thampton 32 D6
Hampton Park Wilts 47 G7
Hampton Poyle Oxon 83 B8
Hampton Wick London 67 F7
Hamptons Kent 52 C6
Hamptworth Wilts 32 D2
Hamrow Norfolk 159 E8
Hams Som'set 28 D6
Hamsey E Sussex 36 E6
Hamsey Green Surrey 51 B11
Hamshill Glos 80 E3
Hamstall Ridware Staffs 152 F2
Hamstead W Midlands 133 E10
Hamstead Marshall W Berks 64 F2
Hamsterley Durham 233 E8
Hamsterley Durham 242 F4
Hamsterley Mill Durham 242 F4
Hamstreet Kent 54 G4
Hamwood N Som'set 43 B11
Hamworthy Poole 18 C5
Hanbury Staffs 152 D3
Hanbury Worcs 117 E9
Hanbury Woodend Staffs 152 D3
Hanby Lincs 155 C10
Hanchet End Suffolk 106 B3
Hanchurch Staffs 168 G4
Hand and Pen Devon 14 B6
Hand Green Ches 167 C8
Handale Redcar/Clevel'd 226 B4
Handbridge Ches 166 B6
Handcross W Sussex 36 B3
Handforth Ches 184 E5
Handley Ches 167 D7
Handley Derby 170 C5
Handley Green Essex 87 E11
Handsacre Staffs 151 F11
Handside Herts 86 C2
Handsworth S Yorks 186 D6
Handsworth W Midlands 133 E10
Handy Cross Bucks 84 G4
Handy Cross Devon 24 B6
Hanford Dorset 30 E4
Hanford Stoke 168 G5
Hangersley Hants 31 F11
Hanging Bank Kent 52 C3
Hanging Heaton W Yorks 197 C9
Hanging Houghton Northants 120 C5
Hanging Langford Wilts 46 F4
Hangleton Brighton/Hove 36 F3
Hangleton W Sussex 35 G9
Hanham S Glos 60 E6
Hanham Green S Glos 60 E6
Hankelow Ches 167 F11
Hankerton Wilts 81 G7
Hankham E Sussex 23 D10
Hanley Stoke 168 F5
Hanley Castle Worcs 98 C6
Hanley Child Worcs 116 D3
Hanley Swan Worcs 98 C6
Hanley William Worcs 116 D3
Hanlith N Yorks 213 G8
Hanmer Wrex 149 B9
Hannaford Devon 25 B10
Hannafore Cornw'l 6 E5
Hannah Lincs 191 F8
Hanningfields Green Suffolk 125 G7
Hannington Hants 48 B4
Hannington Northants 120 C6
Hannington Swindon 81 G11
Hannington Wick Swindon 81 F11
Hanscombe End Beds 104 D2
Hansel Village S Ayrs 257 C9
Hanslope M/Keynes 102 B6
Hanthorpe Lincs 155 E11
Hanwell London 67 C7
Hanwell Oxon 101 C8
Hanwood Shrops 131 B8
Hanwood Bank Shrops 149 G9
Hanworth London 66 E6
Hanworth Norfolk 160 B3
Happendon S Lanarks 259 C9
Happisburgh Norfolk 161 C7
Happisburgh Common Norfolk 161 D7
Hapsford Ches 183 G7
Hapton Lancs 203 G11
Hapton Norfolk 142 D3
Harberton Devon 8 D5
Harbertonford Devon 8 D5
Harbledown Kent 54 B6
Harborne W Midlands 133 G10
Harborough Magna Warwick 119 B9
Harborough Parva Warwick 119 B9
Harbottle Northum 251 C10
Harbour Park, Littlehampton W Sussex 35 G8
Harbourland Kent 53 B9
Harbourneford Devon 8 C4
Harbours Hill Worcs 117 D9
Harbridge Hants 31 E10
Harbridge Green Hants 31 E10
Harburn W Loth 269 C10
Harbury Warwick 119 F7
Harby Leics 154 C4
Harby Notts 188 G5
Harcombe Devon 14 E3
Harcombe Devon 15 C9
Harcombe Bottom Devon 16 B2
Harcourt Cornw'l 3 B8
Hardbreck Orkney 313 H5
Harden W Midlands 133 C10
Harden W Yorks 205 F7
Harden Park Ches 184 G4
Hardendale Cumb 221 C11
Hardengreen Midloth 270 B6
Hardenhuish Wilts 62 E2
Hardgate Aberds 293 C9
Hardgate Dumf/Gal 237 C10
Hardgate N Yorks 214 G5
Hardgate W Dunb 277 G10
Hardham W Sussex 35 D8
Hardhorn Lancs 202 F3
Hardingham Norfolk 141 C10
Hardings Booth Staffs 169 C9
Hardings Wood Ches 168 E4
Hardingstone Northants 120 F5
Hardington Som'set 45 C8
Hardington Mandeville Som'set 29 E8
Hardington Marsh Som'set 29 F8
Hardington Moor Som'set 29 E8
Hardley Hants 32 G6
Hardley Street Norfolk 143 C7
Hardmead M/Keynes 103 B8
Hardraw N Yorks 223 G7
Hardstoft Derby 170 C6
Hardstoft Common Derby 170 C6
Hardway Portsm'th 33 G10
Hardway Som'set 45 G8
Hardwick Bucks 84 B4
Hardwick Cambs 123 F7
Hardwick Cambs 122 D3
Hardwick Lincs 188 F5
Hardwick Norfolk 142 E4
Hardwick Norfolk 158 F2
Hardwick Northants 121 D7
Hardwick Oxon 82 E5
Hardwick Oxon 101 C8
Hardwick Oxon 101 F11
Hardwick Stockton 234 G4
Hardwick S Yorks 187 D7
Hardwick W Midlands 133 D11
Hardwick Green Worcs 98 E6
Hardwick Hall Derby 171 C7
Hardwick Village Notts 187 G10
Hardwicke Glos 80 C3
Hardwicke Glos 99 F8
Hardwicke Heref'd 96 C5
Hardy's Green Essex 107 G9
Hare Green Essex 107 G11
Hare Hatch Wokingham 65 D10
Hare Street Essex 86 D6
Hare Street Herts 105 F7
Hareby Lincs 174 B4
Harecroft W Yorks 205 F7
Harefield London 85 G9
Harefield S'thampton 33 E7
Haregate Staffs 169 D7
Harehill Derby 152 B3
Harehills W Yorks 206 G2
Harelaw Durham 242 G5
Hareleeshill S Lanarks 268 E5
Hareplain Kent 53 F10
Hare's Down Devon 14 C3
Harescough Cumb 231 C8
Harescombe Glos 80 C4
Haresfield Glos 80 C4
Haresfinch Mersey 183 B8
Hareshaw N Lanarks 268 C6
Harestanes E Dunb 278 G3
Harestock Hants 48 G3
Harewood Windsor 66 F3
Harewood W Yorks 206 E2
Harewood End Heref'd 97 F10
Harewood House, Wetherby W Yorks 206 E2
Harford Carms 94 C2
Harford Devon 8 D2
Hargate Norfolk 142 E2
Hargatewall Derby 185 F10
Hargrave Ches 167 C7
Hargrave Northants 121 C10
Hargrave Suffolk 124 F5
Harker Cumb 239 E9
Harker Marsh Cumb 229 E7
Harkland Shetl'd 314 E6
Harknett's Gate Essex 86 D6
Harkstead Suffolk 108 E3
Harlaston Staffs 152 G4
Harlaw Ho. Aberds 303 G7
Harlaxton Lincs 155 C7
Harle Syke Lancs 204 F3
Harlech Gwyn 145 C11
Harlech Castle Gwyn 145 C11
Harlequin Notts 154 B3
Harlescott Shrops 149 F10
Harlesden London 67 C8
Harlesthorpe Derby 187 F7
Harleston Devon 8 F5
Harleston Norfolk 142 G4
Harleston Suffolk 125 E10
Harleston Common Norfolk 142 G4
Harlestone Northants 120 E4
Harley Shrops 131 C11
Harley S Yorks 186 B5
Harley Shute E Sussex 38 F3
Harleywood Glos 80 F4
Harling Road Norfolk 141 F9
Harlington Beds 103 E10
Harlington London 66 D5
Harlington S Yorks 198 G3
Harlington Woodend Beds 103 E10
Harlosh H'land 298 E2
Harlow Essex 87 C7
Harlow Carr RHS Garden, Harrogate N Yorks 205 C11
Harlow Green Tyne/Wear 243 F7
Harlow Hill Northum 242 D3
Harlow Hill N Yorks 205 C11
Harlthorpe ER Yorks 207 F10
Harlton Cambs 123 G7
Harlyn Cornw'l 10 F3
Harman's Corner Kent 69 G11
Harman's Cross Dorset 18 E5
Harmans Water Brackn'l 65 F11
Harmby N Yorks 214 B2
Harmer Green Herts 86 B3
Harmer Hill Shrops 149 E9
Harmondsworth London 66 D5
Harmston Lincs 173 C7
Harnage Shrops 131 C11
Harnham Northum 252 G3
Harnham Wilts 31 B10
Harnhill Glos 81 E9
Harold Hill London 87 G8
Harold Park London 87 G9
Harold Wood London 87 G9
Haroldston West Pembs 72 B5
Haroldswick Shetl'd 314 B8
Harome N Yorks 216 C2
Harpenden Herts 85 C10
Harper Green Gtr Man 195 F8
Harperley Durham 242 G5
Harper's Hill Devon 8 C5
Harpford Devon 15 C7
Harpham ER Yorks 217 G11
Harpley Norfolk 158 D5
Harpley Worcs 116 E3
Harpole Northants 120 E3
Harpsdale H'land 310 D5
Harpsden Oxon 65 C9
Harpsden Bottom Oxon 65 C8
Harpswell Lincs 188 D6
Harpur Hill Derby 185 G9
Harpurhey Gtr Man 195 G11
Harraby Cumb 239 G10
Harracott Devon 25 B9
Harrapool H'land 295 C8
Harras Cumb 219 B9
Harraton Tyne/Wear 243 G7
Harrier Shetl'd 315 J1
Harrietfield Perth/Kinr 286 E3
Harrietsham Kent 53 C11
Harringay London 67 B10
Harrington Cumb 228 F5
Harrington Lincs 190 G5
Harrington Northants 120 B5
Harringworth Northants 137 D8
Harris H'land 294 F5
Harris Green Norfolk 142 F4
Harris Museum, Preston Lancs 194 B4
Harriseahead Staffs 168 D5
Harriston Cumb 229 C9
Harrogate N Yorks 206 B2
Harrold Beds 121 F8
Harrop Dale Gtr Man 196 F4
Harrow H'land 310 B6
Harrow London 66 B6
Harrow Green Suffolk 125 G7
Harrow Hill Glos 79 B10
Harrow on the Hill London 67 B7
Harrow Weald London 85 G10
Harrowbarrow Cornw'l 7 B7
Harrowbeer Devon 7 B10
Harrowden Beds 103 B11
Harrowgate Hill D'lington 224 B5
Harrowgate Village D'lington 224 B5
Harry Stoke S Glos 60 D6
Harsley Castle N Yorks 225 F8
Harston Cambs 123 G8
Harston Leics 154 C6
Harswell ER Yorks 208 E2
Hart Hartlep'l 234 E5
Hart Common Gtr Man 194 G6
Hart Hill Luton 104 G2
Hart Station Hartlep'l 234 D5
Hartbarrow Cumb 221 G8
Hartbarrow Cumb 221 G8
Hartburn Northum 252 F3
Hartburn Stockton 225 B8
Hartcliffe Bristol 60 F5
Hartest Suffolk 124 G6
Hartest Hill Suffolk 124 G6
Hartfield E Sussex 52 F3
Hartfield H'land 299 E7
Hartford Cambs 122 C4
Hartford Ches 183 G10
Hartford Som'set 27 B7
Hartford End Essex 87 B11
Hartfordbeach Ches 183 G10
Hartfordbridge Hants 49 B9
Hartforth N Yorks 224 D3
Hartgrove Dorset 30 D4
Harthill Ches 167 D8
Harthill Derby 185 D8
Harthill N Lanarks 269 C8
Harthill S Yorks 187 E7
Hartington Derby 169 C10
Hartland Devon 24 C3
Hartland Quay Devon 24 C2
Hartlands Hill Glos 80 B3
Hartle Worcs 117 B8
Hartlebury Worcs 116 C6
Hartlepool Hartlep'l 234 E6
Hartlepool's Maritime Experience Hartlep'l 234 E6
Hartley Cumb 222 D5
Hartley Kent 53 G9
Hartley Kent 68 F6
Hartley Northum 243 B8
Hartley Plym'th 7 D9
Hartley W Yorks 196 B2
Hartley Green Kent 68 F5
Hartley Green Staffs 151 D9
Hartley Mauditt Hants 49 F8
Hartley Wespall Hants 49 B8
Hartley Wintney Hants 49 B9
Hartlington N Yorks 213 G10
Hartlip Kent 69 G10
Hartlip Hill Kent 69 G10
Hartmount H'land 301 B7
Hartoft End N Yorks 226 G4
Harton N Yorks 216 G4
Harton Shrops 131 F9
Harton Tyne/Wear 243 E9
Hartpury Glos 98 G6
Hart's Green Suffolk 125 F7
Hartshead W Yorks 197 C7
Hartshead Green Gtr Man 196 G3
Hartshill Warwick 134 E6
Hartsholme Lincs 172 B6
Hartshorne Derby 152 E6
Hartsop Cumb 221 C8
Hartswell Som'set 27 B9
Hartwell Northants 120 G5
Hartwith N Yorks 214 G4
Hartwood Lancs 194 D5
Hartwood N Lanarks 269 D7
Harvel Kent 68 G6
Harvieston Stirl 277 D11
Harvington Worcs 99 B11
Harvington Worcs 117 C7
Harwell Notts 187 B10
Harwell Oxon 64 B3
Harwich Essex 108 E5
Harwood Durham 232 E2
Harwood Gtr Man 195 E8
Harwood Northum 251 E11
Harwood Dale N Yorks 227 F9
Harwood Lee Gtr Man 195 E8
Harworth Notts 187 B10
Hasbury W Midlands 133 G9
Hascombe Surrey 50 E3
Haselbech Northants 120 B4
Haselbury Plucknett Som'set 29 E7
Haseley Warwick 118 D4
Haseley Green Warwick 118 D4
Haseley Knob Warwick 118 C4
Haselor Warwick 118 F2
Hasendean Scot Borders 262 E2
Hasfield Glos 98 F6
Hasguard Pembs 72 D5
Hasguard Cross Pembs 72 C4
Haskayne Lancs 193 F11
Hasketon Suffolk 126 G5
Hasland Derby 170 B5
Hasland Green Derby 170 B5
Haslemere Surrey 49 G11
Hasleston Suffolk 125 E10
Haslingden Lancs 195 C9
Haslingden Grane Lancs 195 C9
Haslingfield Cambs 123 G8
Haslington Ches 168 D2
Hasluck's Green W Midlands 118 B2
Hassal Ches 168 D3
Hassal Green Ches 168 D3
Hassell Street Kent 54 D5
Hassingham Norfolk 143 B7
Hassocks W Sussex 36 D4
Hassop Derby 186 G2
Haster H'land 310 D7
Hasthorpe Lincs 175 B7
Hastigrow H'land 310 C6
Hasting Hill Tyne/Wear 243 G9
Hastingleigh Kent 54 E5
Hastings E Sussex 38 F4
Hastings Som'set 28 D4
Hastings Castle E Sussex 38 F4
Hastings Sea Life Centre E Sussex 38 F4
Hastingwood Essex 87 D7
Hastoe Herts 84 D6
Haswell Durham 234 C3
Haswell Moor Durham 234 C3
Haswell Plough Durham 234 C3
Hatch Beds 104 B3
Hatch Hants 49 C7
Hatch Beauchamp Som'set 28 C4
Hatch Bottom Hants 33 D7
Hatch End Beds 121 E11
Hatch End London 85 G10
Hatch Green Som'set 28 D4
Hatch Warren Hants 48 D6
Hatchet Gate Hants 32 G5
Hatchet Green Hants 31 D11
Hatching Green Herts 85 C10
Hatchmere Ches 183 G9
Hatcliffe NE Lincs 201 G8
Hatfield Heref'd 115 F11
Hatfield Herts 86 D2
Hatfield S Yorks 199 E7
Hatfield Worcs 117 G7
Hatfield Broad Oak Essex 87 B8
Hatfield Garden Village Herts 86 D2
Hatfield Heath Essex 87 C8
Hatfield House Herts 86 D2
Hatfield Hyde Herts 86 C2
Hatfield Peverel Essex 88 C3
Hatfield Woodhouse S Yorks 199 F7
Hatford Oxon 82 G4
Hatherden Hants 47 C10
Hatherleigh Devon 25 G8
Hatherley Glos 99 G8
Hathern Leics 153 E10
Hatherop Glos 81 D11
Hathersage Derby 186 E2
Hathersage Booths S Yorks 186 E2
Hathershaw Gtr Man 196 G2
Hatherton Ches 167 F11
Hatherton Staffs 151 G9
Hatley St. George Cambs 122 G5
Hatston Orkney 312 G5
Hatt Cornw'l 7 C7
Hatt Hill Hants 32 B4
Hatterseat Aberds 303 G9
Hattersley Gtr Man 185 C7
Hattingley Hants 48 F6
Hatton Aberds 303 F10
Hatton Angus 287 D9
Hatton Derby 152 C4
Hatton Lincs 189 F11
Hatton London 66 D6
Hatton Moray 301 D11
Hatton Shrops 131 E9
Hatton Warwick 118 D4
Hatton Warrington 183 E9
Hatton Castle Aberds 303 E7
Hatton Country World Warwick 118 D4
Hatton Heath Ches 167 C7
Hatton of Fintray Aberds 293 B10
Hattonburn Aberds 293 C9
Hattoncrook Aberds 303 G8
Hattonrig N Lanarks 268 C4
Haugh E Ayrs 257 D11
Haugh Gtr Man 196 E2
Haugh Lincs 190 F6
Haugh Head Northum 264 D2
Haugh of Glass Moray 302 F4
Haugh of Kilnmaichlie Moray 301 F11
Haugh of Urr Dumf/Gal 237 C10

Haugham Lincs 190 E4
Haughhead E Dunb 278 F2
Haughland Orkney 312 G6
Haughley Suffolk 125 E10
Haughley Green Suffolk 125 E10
Haughley New Street Suffolk 125 E10
Haughs of Clinterty Aberd C 293 B10
Haughton Notts 187 G11
Haughton Powys 148 F6
Haughton Shrops 149 D7
Haughton Shrops 149 F11
Haughton Shrops 132 B4
Haughton Staffs 151 E7
Haughton Green Gtr Man 184 C6
Haughton Le Skerne D'lington 224 B6
Haughton Moss Ches 167 D9
Haulkerton Aberds 293 F9
Haultwick Herts 104 G6
Haunn Arg/Bute 288 E5
Haunn W Isles 297 K3
Haunton Staffs 152 G5
Hauxton Cambs 123 F8
Havannah Ches 168 C5
Havant Hants 34 F2
Haven Heref'd 115 G8
Haven Bank Lincs 174 E2
Havenside ER Yorks 201 B7
Havenstreet I/Wight 21 C7
Haverbrack Cumb 211 C9
Havercroft N Yorks 197 E11
Haverfordwest = Hwlffordd Pembs 72 B6
Haverhill Suffolk 106 B3
Haverholme Priory Lincs 173 F10
Haverigg Cumb 210 D3
Havering-atte-Bower London 87 G8
Haversham M/Keynes 102 C6
Haverthwaite Cumb 210 C6
Haverton Hill Stockton 234 G5
Haviker Street Kent 53 D8
Havyatt Som'set 44 F4
Havyatt Green N Som'set 60 G3
Hawarden = Penarlâg Flints 166 B4
Hawbridge Worcs 99 B8
Hawbush Green Essex 106 G5
Hawcoat Cumb 210 E4
Hawen Ceredig'n 92 B6
Hawes N Yorks 213 B7
Hawe's Green Norfolk 142 D4
Hawes Side Blackp'l 202 G2
Hawford Worcs 116 E6
Hawick Scot Borders 262 G2
Hawk Green Gtr Man 185 D7
Hawkchurch Devon 28 G4
Hawkcombe Som'set 41 D11
Hawkedon Suffolk 124 G6
Hawkenbury Kent 53 E10
Hawkenbury Kent 52 F6
Hawkeridge Wilts 45 C11
Hawkerland Devon 15 D7
Hawkes End W Midlands 134 G5
Hawkesbury S Glos 61 B9
Hawkesbury Warwick 135 G7
Hawkesbury Common S Glos 61 B9
Hawkesbury Upton S Glos 61 B9
Hawkhill N Ayrs 266 G5
Hawkhill Northum 264 G6
Hawkhurst Kent 53 G9
Hawkinge Kent 55 E8
Hawkley Gtr Man 194 G5
Hawkley Hants 34 B2
Hawkridge Som'set 41 G11
Hawks Green Staffs 151 G9
Hawks Hill Bucks 66 B2
Hawksdale Cumb 230 B3
Hawkshaw Gtr Man 195 E9
Hawkshead Cumb 220 F6
Hawkshead Hill Cumb 220 F6
Hawkshill Down Kent 55 D11
Hawksland S Lanarks 269 G6
Hawkspur Green Essex 106 E3
Hawkswick N Yorks 213 E9
Hawkswick Cote N Yorks 213 E8
Hawksworth Notts 172 G3
Hawksworth W Yorks 205 E9
Hawksworth W Yorks 205 F11
Hawkwell Essex 88 G5
Hawkwell Northum 242 C3
Hawley Hants 49 B11
Hawley Kent 68 E4
Hawley's Corner London 52 B2
Hawling Glos 99 G11
Hawn Orkney 312 F5
Hawnby N Yorks 215 B10
Haworth W Yorks 204 F6
Haws Bank Cumb 220 F6
Hawser Bottoms N Yorks 227 D8
Hawstead Suffolk 125 F7
Hawstead Green Suffolk 125 F7
Hawthorn Durham 234 B4
Hawthorn Hants 49 G7
Hawthorn Rh Cyn Taff 58 B5
Hawthorn Wilts 61 F10
Hawthorn Corner Kent 71 F8
Hawthorn Hill Brackn'l 65 E11
Hawthorn Hill Lincs 174 D2
Hawthorpe Lincs 155 D10
Hawton Notts 172 E3
Haxby C/York 207 B8
Haxby Gates C/York 207 B8
Haxey N Lincs 188 B3
Haxey Turbary N Lincs 199 G9
Haxted Surrey 52 D2
Haxton Wilts 47 D6
Hay Green Essex 87 E10
Hay Green Herts 104 D6
Hay Green Norfolk 157 F10
Hay Mills W Midlands 134 G2
Hay on Wye = Y Gelli Gandryll Powys 96 C4
Hay Street Herts 105 F7
Haybridge Shrops 116 C2
Haybridge Som'set 44 D4
Haybridge Telford 150 G3
Hayden Glos 99 G8
Haydock Mersey 183 B9
Haydock Park Racecourse Mersey 183 B9
Haydon Bath/NE Som'set 45 C7
Haydon Dorset 29 D11
Haydon Devon 26 D6
Haydon Som'set 28 C3
Haydon Swindon 62 B6
Haydon Bridge Northum 241 E8
Haydon Wick Swindon 62 B6
Haye Cornw'l 12 G2
Hayes London 68 F2
Hayes London 66 C5
Hayes End London 66 C5
Hayes End Som'set 28 D6
Hayes Green Warwick 134 F6
Hayes Knoll Wilts 81 G10
Hayes Town London 66 C6
Hayfield Derby 185 D8
Hayfield Fife 280 C5
Haygate Telford 150 G2
Hayhill E Ayrs 257 F11
Hayhillock Angus 287 C9
Haylands I/Wight 21 C7
Hayle Cornw'l 2 B3
Hayley Green W Midlands 133 G9
Haymoor Bottom Poole 18 C6
Haymoor End Som'set 28 B4
Hayne Devon 26 F5
Hayne Devon 27 D7
Hayne Som'set 28 D2
Haynes Beds 103 C11
Haynes Church End Beds 103 C11
Haynes West End Beds 103 C11
Hayscastle Pembs 91 F7
Hayscastle Cross Pembs 91 F8
Haysden Kent 52 D5
Haysford Pembs 91 G8
Hayshead Angus 287 C10
Hayston E Dunb 278 G2
Haythorn Dorset 31 F8
Hayton Aberd C 293 C11
Hayton Cumb 229 C8
Hayton Cumb 240 F2
Hayton ER Yorks 208 D2
Hayton Notts 188 E2
Hayton's Bent Shrops 131 G10
Haytor Vale Devon 13 F11
Haytown Devon 24 E5
Haywards Heath W Sussex 36 C4
Haywood S Lanarks 269 E9
Haywood S Yorks 186 B3
Haywood S Yorks 198 E5
Hazard's Green E Sussex 37 E11
Hazel Grove Gtr Man 184 D6
Hazel Head Cumb 220 G3
Hazel Street Kent 53 F7
Hazel Stub Suffolk 106 B3
Hazelbank S Lanarks 268 F6
Hazelbeach Pembs 73 E6
Hazelbury Bryan Dorset 30 F2
Hazeleigh Essex 88 E4
Hazeley Hants 49 B8
Hazeley Heath Hants 49 B9
Hazelford Ferry Notts 172 F2
Hazelgrove Notts 171 F8
Hazelhead S Yorks 197 G7
Hazelhurst Gtr Man 195 G9
Hazelhurst Gtr Man 195 D9
Hazelhurst Gtr Man 196 G3
Hazelmere Bucks 84 G5
Hazelslack Cumb 211 D9
Hazelslade Staffs 151 G10
Hazelton Walls Fife 287 E7
Hazelwood Derby 170 F4
Hazelwood Devon 8 E4
Hazelwood London 68 G2
Hazler Shrops 131 E9
Hazlerigg Tyne/Wear 242 C6
Hazleton Glos 81 B9
Hazlewood N Yorks 205 C7
Heacham Norfolk 158 B3
Head of Muir Falk 278 E6
Headbourne Worthy Hants 48 G3
Headcorn Kent 53 E10
Headham Durham 224 B3
Headingley W Yorks 205 F11
Headington Oxon 83 D8
Headington Hill Oxon 83 D8
Headless Cross Worcs 117 D10
Headley Hants 49 F10
Headley Hants 64 G4
Headley Surrey 51 C8
Headley Down Hants 49 F10
Headley Heath Worcs 117 B11
Headley Park Bristol 60 F5
Headon Devon 24 G5
Headon Notts 188 F2
Heads S Lanarks 268 F4
Heads Nook Cumb 239 F11
Headstone London 66 B6
Headwell Fife 279 D11
Heady Hill Gtr Man 195 E10
Heage Derby 170 E5
Healaugh N Yorks 206 D5
Healaugh N Yorks 223 F10
Heald Green Gtr Man 184 D5
Healds Green Gtr Man 195 F11
Heale Devon 40 D6
Heale Som'set 28 B5
Heale Som'set 45 E7
Healey Lancs 195 D11
Healey Northum 242 F3
Healey N Yorks 214 C3
Healey W Yorks 197 D9
Healey W Yorks 197 C8
Healeyfield Durham 233 B7
Healing NE Lincs 201 E8
Heamoor Cornw'l 1 C5
Heaning Cumb 221 F8
Heanish Arg/Bute 288 E2
Heanor Derby 170 F6
Heanor Gate Derby 170 F6
Heap Bridge Gtr Man 195 E10
Heapham Lincs 188 D5
Hearn Hants 49 F10
Hearnden Green Kent 53 D10
Hearthstane Scot Borders 260 D4
Hearts Delight Kent 69 G11
Heasley Mill Devon 41 G8
Heast H'land 295 D8
Heath Card 59 D7
Heath Derby 170 B6
Heath W Yorks 197 C11
Heath and Reach Beds 103 F8
Heath Charnock Lancs 194 E5
Heath Common Devon 28 G3
Heath Common W Sussex 35 E10
Heath Cross Devon 13 B10
Heath End Bucks 84 F5
Heath End Bucks 85 D7
Heath End Hants 64 G2
Heath End Hants 64 G5
Heath End Leics 153 E7
Heath End S Glos 61 B7
Heath End Surrey 49 D10
Heath End Warwick 118 E4
Heath End W Midlands 133 C10
Heath End W Sussex 35 D7
Heath Green Hants 48 F6
Heath Green Worcs 117 C11
Heath Hayes Staffs 151 G10
Heath Hill Shrops 150 G5
Heath House Som'set 44 D2
Heath Park London 68 B4
Heath Town W Midlands 133 D8
Heathbrook Shrops 150 D2
Heathcot Aberds 293 C10
Heathcote Derby 169 C10
Heathcote Warwick 118 E6
Heathencote Northants 102 B4
Heather Leics 153 G7
Heather Row Hants 49 C8
Heatherfield H'land 298 E4
Heatherside Surrey 50 B2
Heatherwood Park H'land 311 K2
Heatherybanks Aberds 303 E7
Heathfield Devon 14 F2
Heathfield E Sussex 37 C9
Heathfield N Yorks 214 F2
Heathfield S Ayrs 257 E9
Heathfield Som'set 27 B11
Heathhall Dumf/Gal 237 B11
Heathlands Wokingham 65 F10
Heathrow Airport London 66 D5
Heathstock Devon 28 G2
Heathton Shrops 132 E6
Heathtop Derby 152 C4
Heathwaite Cumb 221 F8
Heathy Brow E Sussex 36 G6
Heatley Ches 184 D2
Heatley Staffs 151 D11
Heaton Gtr Man 195 F8
Heaton Lancs 211 G8
Heaton Staffs 169 C7
Heaton Tyne/Wear 243 D7
Heaton W Yorks 205 F8
Heaton Chapel Gtr Man 184 C5
Heaton Mersey Gtr Man 184 C5
Heaton Moor Gtr Man 184 C5
Heaton Norris Gtr Man 184 C5
Heaton Punchardon Devon 40 F4
Heaton's Bridge Lancs 194 E2
Heaverham Kent 52 B5
Heaviley Gtr Man 184 D6
Heavitree Devon 14 C4
Hebburn Tyne/Wear 243 E8
Hebburn Colliery Tyne/Wear 243 D8
Hebburn Hall Ponds Tyne/Wear 243 E8
Hebburn New Town Tyne/Wear 243 E8
Hebden N Yorks 213 G10
Hebden Bridge W Yorks 196 B3
Hebden Green Ches 167 B10
Hebing End Herts 104 G6
Hebron Carms 92 F3
Hebron Angl 179 E7
Hebron Northum 252 F5
Heck Dumf/Gal 248 G3
Heckdyke Notts 188 B3
Heckfield Hants 65 G8
Heckfield Green Suffolk 126 B3
Heckfordbridge Essex 107 G8
Heckingham Norfolk 143 D7
Heckington Lincs 173 G10
Heckmondwike W Yorks 197 C8
Heddington Wilts 62 F4
Heddington Wick Wilts 62 F3
Heddle Orkney 312 G4
Heddon Devon 25 B11
Heddon Oak Som'set 42 F6
Heddon-on-the-Wall Northum 242 D4
Hedenham Norfolk 142 E6
Hedge End Hants 33 E7
Hedgefield Tyne/Wear 242 E4
Hedgerley Bucks 66 B3
Hedgerley Green Bucks 66 B3
Hedging Som'set 28 B4
Hedley on the Hill Northum 242 F3
Hednesford Staffs 151 G9
Hedon ER Yorks 201 B7
Hedsor Bucks 66 B2
Hedworth Tyne/Wear 243 E8
Heelands M/Keynes 102 D6
Heeley S Yorks 186 E5
Heeley City Farm, Sheffield S Yorks 186 D5
Heggle Lane Cumb 230 D3
Heglibister Shetl'd 315 H5
Heighington D'lington 233 G10
Heighington Lincs 173 B8
Height End Lancs 195 C9
Heightington Worcs 116 C5
Heights of Brae H'land 300 C5
Heights of Kinlochewe H'land 299 C10
Heilam H'land 308 C4
Heiton Scot Borders 262 C6
Helbeck Cumb 222 B5
Hele Devon 13 G10
Hele Devon 12 C2
Hele Devon 27 G7
Hele Devon 40 D4
Hele Som'set 27 C10
Hele Torbay 9 B8
Hele Lane Devon 26 E3
Helebridge Cornw'l 24 G2
Helensburgh Arg/Bute 276 E6
Helentongate S Ayrs 257 C9
Helford Cornw'l 3 D7
Helford Passage Cornw'l 3 D7
Helham Green Herts 86 B6
Helhoughton Norfolk 159 D7
Helions Bumpstead Essex 106 C3
Hell Corner W Berks 63 G11
Hellaby S Yorks 187 C9
Helland Cornw'l 11 G7
Helland Som'set 28 C4
Hellandbridge Cornw'l 11 G7
Hellescott Cornw'l 11 D11
Hellesdon Norfolk 160 G4
Hellesveor Cornw'l 2 A2
Hellgill Cumb 222 F5
Hellidon Northants 119 F10
Hellifield N Yorks 204 B3
Hellifield Green N Yorks 204 B3
Hellingly E Sussex 37 E9
Hellington Norfolk 142 C6
Hellington Corner Norfolk 142 C6
Hellister Shetl'd 315 J5
Helm Northum 252 D5
Helmdon Northants 101 C11
Helme W Yorks 196 E5
Helmingham Suffolk 126 F3
Helmington Row Durham 233 D9
Helmsdale H'land 311 H4
Helmshore Lancs 195 C9
Helmsley N Yorks 216 C2
Helperby N Yorks 215 F8
Helperthorpe N Yorks 217 D9
Helpringham Lincs 173 G10
Helpston Peterbro 138 B2
Helsby Ches 183 F7
Helsey Lincs 191 G8
Helston Cornw'l 2 D5
Helston Water Cornw'l 4 G5
Helstone Cornw'l 11 E7
Helton Cumb 230 G6
Helwith N Yorks 223 E11
Helwith Bridge N Yorks 212 F6
Hem Powys 130 C4
Hem Heath Stoke 168 G5
Hemble Hill Redcar/Clevel'd 225 B11
Hemblington Norfolk 160 G6
Hemblington Corner Norfolk 160 G6
Hemel Hempstead Herts 85 D9
Hemerdon Devon 7 D11
Hemingbrough N Yorks 207 G9
Hemingby Lincs 190 F2
Hemingfield S Yorks 197 G11
Hemingford Abbots Cambs 122 C5
Hemingford Grey Cambs 122 C5
Hemingstone Suffolk 126 G2
Hemington Leics 153 D9
Hemington Northants 137 F11
Hemington Som'set 45 C8
Hemley Suffolk 108 C5
Hemlington Middlesbro 225 C10
Hemp Green Suffolk 127 D7
Hempholme ER Yorks 209 C7
Hempnall Norfolk 142 E4
Hempnall Green Norfolk 142 E4
Hempriggs House H'land 310 E7
Hemp's Green Essex 107 F8
Hempstead Essex 106 D2
Hempstead Medway 69 G9
Hempstead Norfolk 160 B2
Hempstead Norfolk 161 D8
Hempsted Glos 80 B4
Hempton Norfolk 159 D8
Hempton Oxon 101 E8
Hempton Wainhill Bucks 84 E3
Hemsby Norfolk 161 F9
Hemsted Kent 54 E6
Hemswell Lincs 188 C6
Hemswell Cliff Lincs 189 D7
Hemsworth Dorset 31 F7
Hemsworth S Yorks 186 E5
Hemsworth W Yorks 198 E2
Hemyock Devon 27 E10
Hen Bentref Llandegfan Angl 179 F9
Henbrook Worcs 117 D8
Henbury Bristol 60 D5
Henbury Ches 184 F5
Henbury Kent 55 E7
Hendomen Powys 130 D4
Hendon London 67 B8
Hendon Tyne/Wear 243 F10
Hendra Cornw'l 10 E6
Hendra Cornw'l 2 B6
Hendra Cornw'l 5 D9
Hendra Croft Cornw'l 4 D5
Hendrabridge Cornw'l 6 B5
Hendre Bridg 58 C2
Hendre Flints 165 B11
Hendre Heref'd 97 G10
Hendre-ddu Conwy 164 B5
Hendreforgan Rh Cyn Taff 58 B3
Hendre-hen Powys 148 G4
Hendy Carms 75 E9
Hendy-Gwyn = Whitland Carms 73 B11
Heneglwys Angl 178 F6
Henfield S Glos 61 D7
Henfield W Sussex 36 D2
Henford Devon 12 C3
Henfords Marsh Wilts 45 E11
Henghurst Kent 54 F3
Hengoed Caerph 77 F11
Hengoed Shrops 148 C5
Hengrave Suffolk 124 D6
Hengrove Bristol 60 F6
Hengrove Park Bristol 60 F5
Henham Essex 105 F10
Heniarth Powys 130 B2
Henlade Som'set 28 C3
Henley Dorset 29 G11
Henley Glos 80 B6
Henley Shrops 131 F9
Henley Suffolk 126 G3
Henley Som'set 28 F6
Henley Som'set 44 G2
Henley Wilts 61 F10
Henley W Sussex 34 B5
Henley Green W Midlands 135 G7
Henley in Arden Warwick 118 D2
Henley Park Surrey 50 C2
Henley Street Kent 69 F7
Henley-on-Thames Oxon 65 C9
Henley's Down E Sussex 38 E2
Henllan Ceredig'n 93 C7
Henllan Denbs 165 B8
Henllan Amgoed Carms 73 B11
Henllys Torf 78 G3
Henllys Vale Torf 78 G3
Henlow Beds 104 D3
Hennock Devon 14 E2
Henny Street Essex 107 D7
Henryd Conwy 180 G3
Henry's Moat Pembs 91 F10
Hensall N Yorks 198 C5
Henshaw Northum 241 E7
Henshaw W Yorks 205 E9
Hensingham Cumb 219 B9
Hensington Oxon 83 B7
Henstead Suffolk 143 F9
Hensting Hants 33 C7
Henstridge Som'set 30 D2
Henstridge Ash Som'set 30 C2
Henstridge Bowden Som'set 29 C11
Henstridge Marsh Som'set 30 C2
Henton Oxon 84 E3
Henton Som'set 44 D3
Henwood Cornw'l 11 G11
Henwood Oxon 83 E7
Henwood Green Kent 52 E6
Henzleaze Bristol 60 D5
Heogan Shetl'd 315 J6
Heol Senni Powys 95 G8
Heolgerrig Merth Tyd 77 D8
Heol-laethog Bridg 58 C2
Heol-las Bridg 58 C2
Heol-y-Cyw Bridg 58 C2
Hepburn Northum 264 E3
Hepple Northum 251 C11
Hepscott Northum 252 G6
Hepthorne Lane Derby 170 C6
Heptonstall W Yorks 196 B3
Hepworth Suffolk 125 C9
Hepworth W Yorks 197 F7
Herbrandston Pembs 72 D5
Hereford Heref'd 97 D10
Hereford Cathedral Heref'd 97 D10
Hereford Racecourse Heref'd 97 C10
Heribusta H'land 298 B4
Heriot Scot Borders 271 E7
Heritage Motor Centre, Gaydon Warwick 119 G7
Hermiston C/Edinb 280 G3
Hermit Hill S Yorks 197 G10
Hermitage Scot Borders 250 D2
Hermitage Dorset 29 F10
Hermitage W Berks 64 E4
Hermitage W Sussex 34 F3
Hermitage Green Warrington 183 C10
Hermon Carms 93 E7
Hermon Carms 94 F3
Hermon Angl 162 B5
Hermon Pembs 92 E4
Herne Kent 71 F7
Herne Bay Kent 71 F7
Herne Common Kent 71 G7
Herne Hill London 67 E10
Herne Pound Kent 53 C7
Hernhill Kent 70 G5
Hernston V/Glam 58 D2
Herodsfoot Cornw'l 6 C4
Heronden Kent 55 C9
Herongate Essex 87 G10
Heron's Ghyll E Sussex 37 B7
Heronsford S Ayrs 244 G4
Heronsgate Herts 85 G8
Herra Shetl'd 314 D8
Herriard Hants 49 D7
Herringfleet Suffolk 143 D9
Herring's Green Beds 103 C11
Herringswell Suffolk 124 D4
Herringthorpe S Yorks 187 C7
Hersden Kent 71 G8
Hersham Cornw'l 24 F3
Hersham Surrey 66 G6
Herstmonceux E Sussex 37 E10
Herston Dorset 18 F6
Herston Orkney 313 J5
Hertford Herts 86 C4
Hertford Heath Herts 86 C4
Hertingfordbury Herts 86 C4
Hesket Newmarket Cumb 230 D2
Hesketh Bank Lancs 194 C2
Hesketh Lane Lancs 203 E8
Heskin Green Lancs 194 D4
Hesleden Durham 234 D4
Heslington C/York 207 C8
Hessay C/York 206 C6
Hessenford Cornw'l 6 D6
Hessett Suffolk 125 E8
Hessilhead N Ayrs 267 E7
Hessle ER Yorks 200 B4
Hessle W Yorks 198 D2
Hest Bank Lancs 211 F9
Hester's Way Glos 99 G8
Hestinsetter Shetl'd 315 J4
Hestley Green Suffolk 126 D3
Heston London 66 D6
Hestwall Orkney 312 G3
Heswall Mersey 182 E3
Hethe Oxon 101 F11
Hethel Norfolk 142 C3
Hethelpit Cross Glos 98 F5
Hethersett Norfolk 142 C2
Hethersgill Cumb 239 D11
Hetherside Cumb 239 D10
Hetherson Green Ches 167 F8
Hethpool Northum 263 D9
Hett Durham 233 D11
Hetton N Yorks 204 B5
Hetton Downs Tyne/Wear 234 B3
Hetton le Hill Tyne/Wear 234 C3
Hetton-le-Hole Tyne/Wear 234 B3
Heugh Northum 242 C3
Heugh-head Aberds 292 B5
Heveningham Suffolk 126 C6
Hever Kent 52 E3
Hever Castle and Gardens Kent 52 D3
Heversham Cumb 211 C9
Hevingham Norfolk 160 E3
Hewas Cornw'l 5 E8
Hewas Water Cornw'l 5 F9
Hewelsfield Glos 79 E9
Hewelsfield Common Glos 79 E8
Hewer Hill Cumb 230 D3
Hewish Som'set 28 F6
Hewood Dorset 28 G5
Heworth C/York 207 C8
Heworth Tyne/Wear 243 E7
Hexham Northum 241 E10
Hexham Abbey Northum 241 E10
Hexham Racecourse Northum 241 E10
Hextable Kent 68 E4
Hexthorpe S Yorks 198 G5
Hexton Herts 104 E2
Hexworthy Devon 13 G9
Hey Gtr Man 196 G3
Hey Lancs 204 E3
Hey Green W Yorks 196 E4
Hey Houses Lancs 193 B10
Heybridge Essex 87 F10
Heybridge Essex 88 D5
Heybridge Basin Essex 88 D5
Heybrook Bay Devon 7 F9
Heydon Cambs 105 D8
Heydon Norfolk 160 D2
Heydour Lincs 155 B10
Heyhead Gtr Man 184 D4
Heyheads Gtr Man 196 G3
Heyhouses Lancs 203 F11
Heylipol Arg/Bute 288 E1
Heylor Shetl'd 314 E4
Heyop Powys 114 C4
Heyrod Gtr Man 185 B7
Heysham Lancs 211 G8
Heyshaw N Yorks 214 G3
Heyshott W Sussex 34 D5
Heyshott Green W Sussex 34 D5
Heyside Gtr Man 196 F2
Heytesbury Wilts 46 E2
Heythrop Oxon 101 F7
Heywood Gtr Man 195 E11
Heywood Wilts 45 C11
Hibaldstow N Lincs 200 G3
Hibb's Green Suffolk 125 G7
Hickford Hill Essex 106 C5
Hickleton S Yorks 198 F3
Hickling Norfolk 161 E8
Hickling Notts 154 D3
Hickling Green Norfolk 161 E8
Hickling Heath Norfolk 161 E8
Hickmans Green Kent 54 B5
Hicks Forstal Kent 71 G7
Hick's Mill Cornw'l 4 G5
Hickstead W Sussex 36 C3
Hidcote Bartrim Glos 100 C3
Hidcote Boyce Glos 100 C3
Hidcote Manor Garden, Moreton-in-Marsh Glos 100 C3
Higford Shrops 132 C5
Higginshaw Gtr Man 196 F2
High Ackworth W Yorks 198 D2
High Angerton Northum 252 F3
High Bankhill Cumb 231 C7
High Banton N Lanarks 278 E5
High Barnes Tyne/Wear 243 F9
High Barnet London 86 F2
High Beach Essex 86 F6
High Beechburn Durham 233 E9
High Bentham N Yorks 212 F3
High Bickington Devon 25 C9
High Biggins Cumb 212 D2
High Blantyre S Lanarks 268 D3
High Bonnybridge Falk 278 F6
High Borrans Cumb 221 E8
High Bradfield S Yorks 186 B3
High Bradley N Yorks 204 D6
High Bray Devon 41 G7
High Brooms Kent 52 E5
High Bullen Devon 25 C8
High Buston Northum 252 B6
High Callerton Northum 242 C5
High Casterton Cumb 212 D2
High Catton ER Yorks 207 C10
High Church Northum 252 F5
High Clarence Stockton 234 G5
High Close N Yorks 224 B3
High Cogges Oxon 82 D5
High Common Norfolk 141 B9
High Common Norfolk 142 G3
High Common Suffolk 143 F7
High Condurrow Cornw'l 2 B5
High Coniscliffe D'lington 224 B4
High Crompton Gtr Man 196 F2
High Crosby Cumb 239 F11
High Cross Cornw'l 2 D6
High Cross Hants 34 B2
High Cross Herts 85 F10
High Cross Herts 86 B5
High Cross Lancs 202 F2
High Cross Leics 135 F9
High Cross Newp 59 B9
High Cross Warwick 118 D3
High Cross W Sussex 36 D3
High Cross Bank Derby 152 F5
High Crosshill S Lanarks 268 C2
High Dubmire Tyne/Wear 234 B2
High Dyke Cumb 230 E5
High Dyke Durham 232 F5
High Easter Essex 87 C10
High Eldrig Dumf/Gal 236 C4
High Ellington N Yorks 214 C3
High Entercommon N Yorks 224 D6
High Ercall Telford 149 F11
High Etherley Durham 233 F9
High Ferry Lincs 174 F4
High Flatts W Yorks 197 F8
High Fremington N Yorks 223 F10
High Friarside Durham 242 F5
High Gallowhill E Dunb 278 G3
High Garrett Essex 106 F5
High Grange Durham 233 E9
High Green Cumb 221 E8
High Green Norfolk 141 B8
High Green Norfolk 142 B2
High Green Shrops 132 G4
High Green Suffolk 125 E7
High Green S Yorks 186 B4
High Green Worcs 99 B7
High Green W Yorks 197 E7
High Halden Kent 53 F11
High Halstow Medway 69 E9
High Ham Som'set 44 G2
High Harrington Cumb 228 F6
High Harrogate N Yorks 206 B2
High Haswell Durham 234 C3
High Hatton Shrops 150 E2
High Hauxley Northum 253 C7
High Hawsker N Yorks 227 D8
High Heath Shrops 150 D3
High Heath W Midlands 133 C10
High Hesket Cumb 230 C5
High Hesleden Durham 234 D5
High Hoyland S Yorks 197 E9
High Hunsley ER Yorks 208 F5
High Hurstwood E Sussex 37 B7
High Hutton N Yorks 216 F5
High Ireby Cumb 229 D10
High Kelling Norfolk 177 E10
High Kilburn N Yorks 215 D10
High Knipe Cumb 221 B10
High Lands Durham 233 F8
High Lane Derby 170 G6
High Lane Gtr Man 185 D7
High Lane Heref'd 116 E3
High Lanes Cornw'l 2 B3
High Laver Essex 87 D8
High Leas Lincs 190 E5
High Legh Ches 184 E2
High Leven Stockton 225 C9
High Littleton Bath/NE Som'set 44 B6
High Longthwaite Cumb 229 B11
High Lorton Cumb 229 F9
High Marishes N Yorks 216 D6
High Marnham Notts 188 G4
High Melton S Yorks 198 G4
High Melwood N Lincs 199 G9
High Mickley Northum 242 E3
High Mindork Dumf/Gal 236 D5
High Moor C/York 206 C6
High Moor Lancs 194 E4
High Moorland Visitor Centre, Princetown Devon 13 G7
High Moorsley Tyne/Wear 234 C2
High Nash Glos 79 C9
High Newport Tyne/Wear 243 G9
High Newton Cumb 211 C9
High Newton-by-the-Sea Northum 264 D6
High Nibthwaite Cumb 210 C4
High Offley Staffs 150 D5
High Ongar Essex 87 E9
High Onn Staffs 150 F6
High Orchard Glos 80 B4
High Park Mersey 193 D11
High Risby N Lincs 200 E2
High Rocks Kent 52 F4
High Roding Essex 87 B10
High Rougham Suffolk 125 E8
High Row Cumb 230 G3
High Row Cumb 230 D3
High Salvington W Sussex 35 F10
High Scales Cumb 229 B9
High Sellafield Cumb 219 E10
High Shaw N Yorks 223 G7
High Shields Tyne/Wear 243 D9
High Shincliffe Durham 234 D2
High Side Cumb 229 E10
High Southwick Tyne/Wear 243 F9
High Spen Tyne/Wear 242 F4
High Stakesby N Yorks 227 C7
High Stittenham N Yorks 216 F3
High Street Cornw'l 5 E9
High Street Kent 53 G8
High Street Suffolk 127 C8
High Street Suffolk 143 G7
High Street Suffolk 127 F8
High Street Suffolk 107 B7
High Street Green Suffolk 125 F10
High Throston Hartlep'l 234 E5
High Tirfergus Arg/Bute 255 F7
High Town Staffs 151 G9
High Toynton Lincs 174 B3
High Urpeth Durham 242 G6
High Valleyfield Fife 279 D10
High Westwood Durham 242 F4
High Whinnow Cumb 239 G8
High Woolaston Glos 79 F9
High Worsall N Yorks 225 D7
High Wray Cumb 221 E7
High Wych Herts 87 C7
High Wycombe Bucks 84 G5
High Yarridge Northum 241 E10
Higham Derby 170 D5
Higham Fife 286 F6
Higham Kent 69 E8
Higham Lancs 204 F2
Higham Suffolk 107 D10
Higham Suffolk 124 D4
Higham S Yorks 197 F10
Higham Common S Yorks 197 F10
Higham Cross M/Keynes 102 B5
Higham Ferrers Northants 121 D9
Higham Gobion Beds 104 E2
Higham Hill London 86 G5
Higham on the Hill Leics 135 D7
Higham Park Northants 121 E9
Higham Wood Kent 52 D6
Highams Park London 86 G5
Highbridge Cumb 230 C3
Highbridge Hants 33 C7
Highbridge H'land 290 E3
Highbridge Som'set 43 D10
Highbrook W Sussex 51 G11
Highburton W Yorks 197 E7
Highbury London 67 B10
Highbury Som'set 45 D7
Highbury Vale Nott'ham 171 G8
Highclere Hants 64 G2
Highcliffe Dorset 19 C10
Highcliffe Northum 273 E10
Higher Alham Som'set 45 E7
Higher Ansty Dorset 30 G3
Higher Ashton Devon 14 E3
Higher Audley Blackb'n 195 B7
Higher Bal Cornw'l 4 E4
Higher Ballam Lancs 202 G3
Higher Bartle Lancs 202 G6
Higher Bebington Mersey 182 D4
Higher Berry End Beds 103 E9
Higher Blackley Gtr Man 195 G10
Higher Boarshaw Gtr Man 195 F11
Higher Bockhampton Dorset 17 C10
Higher Boscaswell Cornw'l 1 C3
Higher Broughton Gtr Man 195 G10
Higher Burrow Som'set 28 C6
Higher Burwardsley Ches 167 D8
Higher Change Lancs 195 C11
Higher Cheriton Devon 27 G10
Higher Chisworth Derby 185 C7
Higher Crackington Cornw'l 11 B9
Higher Croft Blackb'n 195 B7
Higher Denham Bucks 66 B4
Higher Dinting Derby 185 C8
Higher Disley Ches 185 E7
Higher Downs Cornw'l 2 C3
Higher End Gtr Man 194 G4
Higher Folds Gtr Man 195 G7
Higher Gabwell Devon 9 B8
Higher Green Gtr Man 195 G8
Higher Halstock Leigh Dorset 29 F8
Higher Heysham Lancs 211 G8
Higher Holnest Dorset 29 F10
Higher Holton Som'set 29 B11

404 Hig – Hos

Higher Hurdsfield Ches 184 G6
Higher Kingcombe Dorset 29 G8
Higher Kinnerton Flints 166 C4
Higher Marsh Som'set 30 C2
Higher Marston Ches 183 F11
Higher Melcombe Dorset 30 G2
Higher Metcombe Devon 15 C7
Higher Muddiford Devon 40 F5
Higher Northcott Devon 12 C2
Higher Nyland Dorset 30 C2
Higher Penwortham Lancs 194 B4
Higher Porthpean Cornw'l 5 E10
Higher Poynton Ches 184 E6
Higher Priestacott Devon 12 B3
Higher Rocombe Barton Devon 9 B8
Higher Row Dorset 31 G8
Higher Runcom Halton 183 E8
Higher Sandford Dorset 29 C10
Higher Shotton Flints 166 B4
Higher Shurlach Ches 183 G11
Higher Slade Devon 40 D4
Higher Stanbear Cornw'l 11 G11
Higher Street Som'set 42 E6
Higher Tale Devon 27 G9
Higher Town Cornw'l 5 C10
Higher Town I/Scilly 1 F4
Higher Town Som'set 42 D3
Higher Tremarcoombe Cornw'l 6 B5
Higher Vexford Som'set 42 F6
Higher Walton Lancs 194 B5
Higher Walton Warrington 183 D9
Higher Wambrook Som'set 28 F3
Higher Warcombe Devon 40 D3
Higher Waterston Dorset 17 B10
Higher Whatcombe Dorset 30 G4
Higher Wheelton Lancs 194 C6
Higher Whitley Ches 183 E10
Higher Wincham Ches 183 F11
Higher Woodhill Gtr Man 195 E9
Higher Wraxall Dorset 29 G9
Higher Wych Ches 167 G7
Higherfence Ches 184 G6
Higherford Lancs 204 E3
Highertown Cornw'l 11 E8
Highertown Cornw'l 4 G6
Highfield ER Yorks 207 F10
Highfield Gtr Man 195 F8
Highfield Gtr Man 194 G5
Highfield Herts 85 D9
Highfield N Ayrs 266 E6
Highfield Oxon 101 G11
Highfield S'thampton 32 E6
Highfield Stockton 225 C8
Highfield S Yorks 186 D5
Highfield Tyne/Wear 242 F5
Highfields Cambs 123 F7
Highfields Derby 170 B6
Highfields Northum 273 E9
Highfields Staffs 151 E8
Highfields S Yorks 198 F4
Highgate E Sussex 52 G2
Highgate Kent 53 G9
Highgate London 67 B9
Highgate N Ayrs 267 E7
Highgate N Yorks 198 D5
Highgate Powys 130 D2
Highgate S Yorks 198 G3
Highhampton Devon 25 G7
Highland Folk Museum, Aultlarie H'land 291 D9
Highland Folk Museum, Kingussie H'land 291 C9
Highlane Ches 168 B5
Highlane Derby 186 E6
Highlaws Cumb 229 B8
Highleadon Glos 98 G5
Highleigh W Sussex 22 D4
Highley Shrops 132 G4
Highmoor Cumb 229 B11
Highmoor Oxon 65 B7
Highmoor Cross Oxon 65 C8
Highmoor Hill Monmouths 60 B3
Highnam Glos 98 G5
Highnam Green Glos 80 B3
Highridge Bristol 60 F5
Highstead Kent 71 F8
Highsted Kent 70 G2
Highstreet Kent 70 G5
Highstreet Green Essex 106 E5
Highstreet Green Surrey 50 F3
Hightae Dumf/Gal 238 B3
Highters Heath W Midlands 117 B11
Hightown Ches 168 C5
Hightown Hants 31 G11
Hightown Mersey 193 G10
Hightown S'thampton 33 E7
Hightown Wrex 166 F4
Hightown W Yorks 197 C7
Hightown Green Suffolk 125 F9
Hightown Heights W Yorks 197 C7
Highway Cornw'l 4 G4
Highway Cornw'l 6 E2
Highway Heref'd 97 B9
Highway Wilts 62 E4
Highweek Devon 14 G2
Highwood Dorset 18 D3
Highwood Hants 31 F11
Highwood Staffs 151 C11
Highwood Worcs 116 D3
Highwood Hill London 86 G2
Highworth Swindon 81 G11
Hilborough Norfolk 140 C6
Hilcote Derby 171 D7
Hilcott Wilts 46 B6
Hilden Park Kent 52 D5
Hildenborough Kent 52 D5
Hildersham Cambs 105 B10
Hildersley Heref'd 98 G2
Hilderstone Staffs 151 C8
Hilderthorpe ER Yorks 218 F3
Hilgay Norfolk 140 D2
Hill Devon 25 B11
Hill S Glos 79 F10
Hill Warwick 119 D9
Hill Worcs 99 B9
Hill Bottom Oxon 64 D6
Hill Brow W Sussex 34 B3
Hill Chorlton Staffs 150 B5
Hill Common Norfolk 161 E8
Hill Cottages N Yorks 226 F4
Hill Crest Worcs 116 B6
Hill Croome Worcs 99 C7
Hill Dale Lancs 194 E3
Hill Deverill Wilts 45 E11
Hill End Durham 232 D6
Hill End Fife 279 B10
Hill End Glos 99 D8
Hill End London 85 G9
Hill End N Yorks 205 C7
Hill End Shrops 131 E10
Hill End Worcs 117 E8
Hill Gate Heref'd 97 F9
Hill Green Essex 105 E9
Hill Green Kent 69 G10
Hill Head Hants 33 G8
Hill Head Kent 52 E3
Hill Houses Derby 170 B5
Hill Houses Shrops 116 B2
Hill Mountain Pembs 73 D7
Hill of Beath Fife 280 C2
Hill of Fearn H'land 301 B8
Hill of Keillor Angus 286 C6
Hill of Mountblairy Aberds 302 D6
Hill of Overbrae Aberds 303 C8
Hill Park Kent 52 B2
Hill Ridware Staffs 151 F11
Hill Side Hants 34 B3
Hill Side Hants 49 C9
Hill Side S Yorks 197 G8
Hill Side W Yorks 197 D7
Hill Somersal Derby 152 C2
Hill Street Dorset 30 E2
Hill Street Kent 54 D6
Hill Top Derby 186 F5
Hill Top Durham 232 G5
Hill Top Durham 242 G5
Hill Top Durham 233 C10
Hill Top Gtr Man 195 G8
Hill Top Hants 32 G6
Hill Top Notts 171 F7
Hill Top S Yorks 197 F9
Hill Top S Yorks 186 D3
Hill Top W Midlands 133 E9
Hill Top W Yorks 196 E5
Hill Top W Yorks 197 D10
Hill Top W Yorks 205 G7
Hill Top W Yorks 205 G11
Hill Top, Sawrey Cumb 221 F7
Hill View Dorset 18 B5
Hill Wootton Warwick 118 D6
Hillam N Yorks 198 B4
Hillborough Kent 71 F8
Hillbourne Dorset 18 C6
Hillbrae Aberds 302 E6
Hillbrae Aberds 303 G7
Hillbutts Dorset 31 G7
Hillcliffe Warrington 183 D10
Hillcommon Som'set 27 B10
Hillcross Derby C 152 C6
Hilldyke Lincs 174 F4
Hillend Fife 280 E3
Hillend N Lanarks 268 B6
Hillend N Som'set 43 B11
Hillend Green Glos 98 F4
Hillersland Glos 79 C9
Hillerton Devon 13 B10
Hillesden Bucks 102 F3
Hillesley Glos 61 B9
Hillfarrance Som'set 27 C11
Hillfield Dorset 29 F10
Hillfield Devon 8 E6
Hillfields Bristol 60 D6
Hillfields W Berks 65 F7
Hillfoot Aberds 303 D9
Hillfoot W Yorks 205 G10
Hillfoot End Beds 104 D2
Hillgreen W Berks 64 D3
Hillgrove W Sussex 34 B6
Hillhampton Heref'd 97 B11
Hillhead Aberds 302 F5
Hillhead Aberds 303 G8
Hillhead Cornw'l 5 C11
Hillhead Devon 9 E8
Hillhead E Ayrs 257 B10
Hillhead S Ayrs 257 F10
Hillhead of Auchentumb Aberds 303 D9
Hillhead of Blairy Aberds 302 D6
Hillhead of Cocklaw Aberds 303 E10
Hillhouse Scot Borders 271 D10
Hilliard's Cross Staffs 152 G2
Hilliclay H'land 310 C5
Hillier Gardens and Arboretum Hants 32 C5
Hillingdon London 66 C5
Hillingdon Heath London 66 C5
Hillington Glasg C 267 C10
Hillington Norfolk 158 D4
Hillington Industrial Estate Glasg C 267 B10
Hillis Corner I/Wight 20 C5
Hillmorton Warwick 119 C10
Hillock Vale Lancs 195 B9
Hillockhead Aberds 292 B6
Hillockhead Aberds 292 C5
Hillpool Worcs 117 B7
Hill's End Beds 103 E9
Hills Town Derby 171 B7
Hillsborough S Yorks 186 C4
Hillside Aberds 293 D11
Hillside Angus 293 G9
Hillside Devon 8 C4
Hillside Orkney 312 F4
Hillside Orkney 313 J5
Hillside Shetl'd 315 G6
Hillside Wilts 81 G9
Hillside Worcs 116 E5
Hillstreet Hants 32 D4
Hillswick Shetl'd 314 F4
Hillview Tyne/Wear 243 F9
Hillway I/Wight 21 D8
Hillwell Shetl'd 315 M5
Hilmarton Wilts 62 D4
Hilperton Wilts 45 B10
Hilperton Marsh Wilts 61 G11
Hilsea Portsm'th 33 G11
Hilston ER Yorks 209 G11
Hiltingbury Hants 32 C6
Hilton Aberds 303 F9
Hilton Cambs 122 D5
Hilton Cumb 231 G10
Hilton Derby 152 C4
Hilton Dorset 30 G3
Hilton Durham 233 G9
Hilton H'land 309 L7
Hilton H'land 311 L3
Hilton Shrops 132 D5
Hilton Stockton 225 C9
Hilton Staffs 133 B11
Hilton House Gtr Man 194 F6
Hilton Lodge H'land 300 G2
Hilton of Cadboll H'land 301 B8
Hilton Park Gtr Man 195 G10
Himbleton Worcs 117 F8
Himley Staffs 133 D7
Hincaster Cumb 211 C10
Hinchley Wood Surrey 67 G7
Hinchwick Glos 100 E2
Hinckley Leics 135 E8
Hinderclay Suffolk 125 B10
Hinderton Ches 182 F4
Hinderwell N Yorks 226 B5
Hindford Shrops 148 C6
Hindhead Surrey 49 F11
Hindle Fold Lancs 203 G10
Hindley Gtr Man 194 G6
Hindley Northum 242 F3
Hindley Green Gtr Man 194 G6
Hindolveston Norfolk 159 D10
Hindon Wilts 46 G2
Hindringham Norfolk 159 B9
Hindsford Gtr Man 195 G7
Hingham Norfolk 141 C10
Hinlip Worcs 117 F7
Hinstock Shrops 150 D3
Hintlesham Suffolk 107 C11
Hinton Glos 79 E11
Hinton Hants 19 B10
Hinton Heref'd 96 D6
Hinton Northants 119 G10
Hinton Shrops 131 B8
Hinton S Glos 61 D8
Hinton Som'set 29 C9
Hinton Ampner Hants 33 B9
Hinton Blewett Bath/NE Som'set 44 B5
Hinton Charterhouse Bath/NE Som'set 45 B9
Hinton Green Worcs 99 C10
Hinton Martell Dorset 31 F8
Hinton on the Green Worcs 99 D10
Hinton Parva Dorset 31 G7
Hinton Parva Swindon 63 C8
Hinton St. George Som'set 28 E6
Hinton St. Mary Dorset 30 D3
Hinton Waldrist Oxon 82 F5
Hinton-in-the-Hedges Northants 101 D11
Hints Staffs 134 C3
Hinwick Beds 121 E8
Hinxhill Kent 54 E5
Hinxton Cambs 105 B9
Hinxworth Herts 104 C4
Hipperholme W Yorks 196 B6
Hipsburn Northum 264 G6
Hipswell N Yorks 224 F3
Hirael Gwyn 179 G9
Hiraeth Carms 92 G3
Hirn Aberds 293 C9
Hirnant Powys 147 E10
Hirst N Lanarks 269 C7
Hirst Northum 253 F7
Hirst Courtney N Yorks 198 C6
Hirwaen Denbs 165 C10
Hirwaun Rh Cyn Taff 77 D7
Hiscott Devon 25 B8
Histon Cambs 123 E8
Hitcham Suffolk 125 G9
Hitcham Causeway Suffolk 125 G9
Hitchill Dumf/Gal 238 D4
Hitchin Herts 104 F3
Hither Green London 67 E11
Hittisleigh Devon 13 C10
Hive ER Yorks 208 G2
Hixon Staffs 151 D10
HMS Victory Portsm'th 33 G10
HMY Britannia C/Edinb 280 F5
Hoaden Kent 55 B9
Hoar Cross Staffs 152 E2
Hoarwithy Heref'd 97 F10
Hoath Kent 71 G8
Hoath Corner Kent 52 E3
Hobarris Shrops 114 B6
Hobbister Orkney 313 H4
Hobbles Green Suffolk 124 G4
Hobbs Cross Essex 87 F7
Hobbs Cross Essex 87 C7
Hobbs Point Pembs 73 E7
Hobkirk Scot Borders 262 G3
Hobroyd Derby 185 C8
Hobson Durham 242 F5
Hoby Leics 154 F3
Hoccombe Som'set 27 B10
Hockenden London 68 F3
Hockerill Herts 105 G9
Hockering Norfolk 159 G11
Hockering Heath Norfolk 159 G11
Hockerton Notts 172 D2
Hockholler Som'set 27 C11
Hockleton Shrops 130 C5
Hockley Ches 184 E6
Hockley Derby 170 B5
Hockley Essex 88 G4
Hockley Kent 54 B3
Hockley Staffs 134 C4
Hockley W Midlands 118 B5
Hockley Heath W Midlands 118 C3
Hockliffe Beds 103 F9
Hockwold cum Wilton Norfolk 140 F4
Hockworthy Devon 27 D8
Hoddesdon Herts 86 D5
Hoddlesden Blackb'n 195 C8
Hoddom Mains Dumf/Gal 238 C5
Hodgehill Ches 168 B4
Hodgehill W Midlands 134 F2
Hodgeston Pembs 73 F8
Hodley Powys 130 E3
Hodnet Shrops 150 D2
Hodnetheath Shrops 150 D2
Hodsall Street Kent 68 G6
Hodsock Notts 187 E10
Hodson Swindon 63 C7
Hodthorpe Derby 187 F9
Hoe Hants 33 D9
Hoe Norfolk 159 F9
Hoe Benham W Berks 64 E2
Hoe Gate Hants 33 E10
Hoel-ddu Swan 75 F11
Hoff Cumb 222 B3
Hog Hatch Surrey 49 D10
Hog Hill E Sussex 38 D5
Hogbarn Kent 53 B11
Hogben's Hill Kent 54 B4
Hogganfield Glasg C 268 B2
Hoggard's Green Suffolk 125 F7
Hoggeston Bucks 102 F6
Hoggrill's End Warwick 134 E4
Hogha Gearraidh W Isles 296 D3
Hoghton Lancs 194 B6
Hoghton Bottoms Lancs 194 B6
Hogland Shetl'd 314 F5
Hogley Green W Yorks 196 F6
Hognaston Derby 170 E2
Hogspit Bottom Herts 85 E8
Hogsthorpe Lincs 191 G8
Holbeach Lincs 157 E7
Holbeach Bank Lincs 157 D7
Holbeach Clough Lincs 156 D6
Holbeach Drove Lincs 156 G6
Holbeach Hurn Lincs 157 D7
Holbeach St. Johns Lincs 156 F6
Holbeach St. Marks Lincs 157 C7
Holbeach St. Matthew Lincs 157 C8
Holbeache Worcs 116 B5
Holbeck Notts 187 G8
Holbeck W Yorks 205 G11
Holbeck Woodhouse Notts 187 G8
Holberrow Green Worcs 117 F10
Holbeton Devon 8 E2
Holborn London 67 C10
Holborough Kent 69 G7
Holbrook Derby 170 F5
Holbrook Suffolk 108 D3
Holbrook S Yorks 186 E6
Holbrook Common S Glos 61 E7
Holbrooks W Midlands 134 G6
Holburn Northum 264 B2
Holbury Hants 32 G6
Holbury Purlieu Hants 32 G6
Holcombe Devon 14 G5
Holcombe Devon 16 C2
Holcombe Gtr Man 195 D9
Holcombe Som'set 45 D7
Holcombe Brook Gtr Man 195 D9
Holcombe Burnell Barton Devon 14 C3
Holcombe Rogus Devon 27 D9
Holcot Northants 120 D5
Holden Lancs 203 D11
Holden Fold Gtr Man 196 F2
Holdenby Northants 120 D3
Holdenhurst Bournem'th 19 B8
Holder's Green Essex 106 F2
Holders Hill London 86 G2
Holdgate Shrops 131 F11
Holdingham Lincs 173 F9
Holditch Dorset 28 G4
Holdsworth W Yorks 196 B5
Hole Devon 27 E11
Hole Bottom W Yorks 196 C2
Hole in the Wall Heref'd 98 F2
Hole Street W Sussex 35 E10
Holefield Scot Borders 263 C8
Holehills N Lanarks 268 B5
Holehouse Derby 185 C7
Holehouse E Renf 267 D9
Holemill Aberd C 293 C10
Holemoor Devon 24 F6
Holestane Dumf/Gal 247 D9
Holford Som'set 43 E7
Holgate C/York 207 C7
Holincote Som'set 42 D2
Holker Cumb 211 D7
Holkham Norfolk 176 E5
Hollacombe Devon 24 G5
Holland Orkney 312 C5
Holland Orkney 312 F7
Holland Surrey 52 C2
Holland Fen Lincs 174 F2
Holland Lees Lancs 194 F4
Holland Moor Lancs 194 G4
Holland Park W Midlands 133 B10
Holland-on-Sea Essex 89 B12
Hollandstoun Orkney 312 C9
Hollee Dumf/Gal 239 D7
Hollesley Suffolk 109 C6
Hollicombe Torbay 9 C7
Hollin Green Ches 167 E9
Hollin Hall Lancs 204 F4
Hollinfare Warrington 183 C11
Hollingbourne Kent 53 B10
Hollingbury Brighton/Hove 36 F4
Hollingdon Bucks 103 F7
Hollingrove E Sussex 37 C11
Hollington Derby 152 B4
Hollington E Sussex 38 E3
Hollington Hants 64 G2
Hollington Staffs 151 B11
Hollington Grove Derby 152 B4
Hollingwood Derby 186 G6
Hollingworth Gtr Man 185 B8
Hollins Cumb 222 G3
Hollins Derby 186 G4
Hollins Gtr Man 195 F8
Hollins Gtr Man 195 F11
Hollins Gtr Man 195 F10
Hollins Staffs 168 E4
Hollins End S Yorks 186 E5
Hollins Green Warrington 183 C11
Hollins Lane Lancs 202 C5
Hollinsclough Staffs 169 B9
Hollinswood Telford 132 B4
Hollinthorpe W Yorks 206 G3
Hollinwood Gtr Man 196 G2
Hollinwood Shrops 149 B10
Hollis Head Devon 27 G7
Hollocombe Devon 25 E10
Hollocombe Town Devon 25 E10
Hollow Oak Dorset 18 C2
Hollow Street Kent 71 G8
Holloway Derby 170 D4
Holloway Wilts 45 G11
Holloway Windsor 65 C10
Holloway End W Midlands 133 G7
Holloway Hill Surrey 50 E3
Hollowell Northants 120 C3
Hollows Dumf/Gal 239 B9
Hollowsgate Ches 167 B8
Holly Bank W Midlands 133 C11
Holly Brook Som'set 44 D4
Holly Cross Wokingham 65 C10
Holly End Norfolk 139 B9
Holly Green Bucks 84 E3
Holly Green Worcs 99 C7
Holly Hill Norfolk 142 E6
Holly Hill N Yorks 224 E3
Hollybed Common Worcs 98 D5
Hollyberry End W Midlands 134 G5
Hollybush Caerph 77 E11
Hollybush E Ayrs 257 G9
Hollybush Stoke 168 G5
Hollybush Worcs 98 D5
Hollybush Corner Bucks 66 B3
Hollybush Corner Suffolk 125 F8
Hollybush Hill Essex 89 B10
Hollybushes Kent 54 B2
Hollym ER Yorks 201 B10
Hollywater Hants 49 G10
Hollywood Worcs 117 B11
Holman Clavel Som'set 28 D2
Holmbridge W Yorks 196 F6
Holmbury St. Mary Surrey 50 E6
Holmbush Cornw'l 5 E10
Holmcroft Staffs 151 D8
Holme Beds 104 C3
Holme Cambs 138 F3
Holme Cumb 211 D10
Holme Lancs 195 C9
Holme N Lincs 200 F2
Holme Notts 172 D4
Holme N Yorks 215 C7
Holme S Yorks 198 E5
Holme W Yorks 196 F6
Holme W Yorks 205 G9
Holme Bank Ches 167 B7
Holme Chapel Lancs 195 B11
Holme Green N Yorks 207 E7
Holme Green Wokingham 65 F10
Holme Hale Norfolk 141 B7
Holme Hill NE Lincs 201 F9
Holme Lacy Heref'd 97 D11
Holme Marsh Heref'd 114 G6
Holme Mills Cumb 211 D10
Holme next the Sea Norfolk 176 E2
Holme on the Wolds ER Yorks 208 D5
Holme Pierrepont Notts 154 B2
Holme St. Cuthbert Cumb 229 B8
Holme Slack Lancs 203 G7
Holme Wood W Yorks 205 G9
Holmebridge Dorset 18 D3
Holme-on-Spalding-Moor ER Yorks 208 F2
Holmer Heref'd 97 C9
Holmer Green Bucks 84 F6
Holmes Chapel Ches 168 B3
Holme's Hill E Sussex 37 E8
Holmescales Cumb 211 B11
Holmesdale Derby 186 F5
Holmesfield Derby 186 F4
Holmeswood Lancs 194 D2
Holmethorpe Surrey 51 C9
Holmewood Derby 170 B6
Holmfield W Yorks 196 B5
Holmfirth W Yorks 196 F6
Holmhead Angus 293 F7
Holmhead Dumf/Gal 246 F6
Holmhead E Ayrs 258 E3
Holmhurst St. Mary E Sussex 38 E4
Holmisdale H'land 297 G7
Holmley Common Derby 186 F5
Holmpton ER Yorks 201 C11
Holmrook Cumb 219 F11
Holmsgarth Shetl'd 315 J6
Holmside Durham 233 B10
Holmston S Ayrs 257 E9
Holmwood Corner Surrey 51 E7
Holmwrangle Cumb 230 B6
Holne Devon 8 B4
Holnest Dorset 29 E11
Holsworthy Devon 24 G4
Holsworthy Beacon Devon 24 F5
Holt Dorset 31 G8
Holt Hants 49 C8
Holt Mersey 183 C7
Holt Norfolk 159 B11
Holt Wilts 61 G11
Holt Worcs 116 E6
Holt Wrex 166 E6
Holt End Hants 49 F7
Holt End Worcs 117 D11
Holt Fleet Worcs 116 E6
Holt Green Lancs 193 G11
Holt Head W Yorks 196 E5
Holt Heath Dorset 31 G9
Holt Heath Worcs 116 E6
Holt Park W Yorks 205 E11
Holt Pound Hants 49 E10
Holt Street Kent 55 C9
Holt Wood Dorset 31 F8
Holtby C/York 207 C9
Holtby Grange N Yorks 224 G5
Holton Oxon 83 D10
Holton Suffolk 127 B8
Holton Som'set 29 B11
Holton cum Beckering Lincs 189 D10
Holton Heath Dorset 18 C5
Holton Hill E Sussex 37 B11
Holton le Clay NE Lincs 201 G9
Holton le Moor Lincs 189 B9
Holton St. Mary Suffolk 107 D11
Holts Gtr Man 196 G3
Holtsmere End Herts 85 C9
Holtwood W Berks 64 G2
Holtye E Sussex 52 F3
Holway Flints 181 F11
Holway Som'set 28 C2
Holwellbury Beds 104 D3
Holwell Dorset 30 E2
Holwell Herts 104 E3
Holwell Leics 154 E4
Holwell Oxon 82 D2
Holwell Som'set 45 D8
Holwick Durham 232 F4
Holwood Cornw'l 7 C7
Holy City Devon 28 G3
Holy Cross Tyne/Wear 243 D8
Holy Cross Worcs 117 B8
Holy Island Northum 273 B11
Holybourne Hants 49 E8
Holyfield Essex 86 E5
Holyhead = Caergybi Angl 178 E3
Holymoorside Derby 170 B4
Holyport Windsor 65 D11
Holystone Northum 251 C11
Holytown N Lanarks 268 C5
Holywell Beds 85 B8
Holywell Cambs 122 C6
Holywell Cornw'l 4 D5
Holywell Dorset 29 G9
Holywell Glos 80 G3
Holywell Northum 243 C8
Holywell = Treffynon Flints 181 F11
Holywell Warwick 118 D3
Holywell Bay Fun Park, Newquay Cornw'l 4 D5
Holywell Green W Yorks 196 D5
Holywell Lake Som'set 27 C10
Holywell Row Suffolk 124 B4
Holywood Dumf/Gal 247 G10
Hom Green Heref'd 97 G11
Home End Cambs 123 F10
Homer Shrops 132 C2
Homer Green Mersey 193 G10
Homersfield Suffolk 142 F5
Homerton London 67 C11
Homestead Hants 47 G10
Homington Wilts 31 B10
Honey Hill Kent 70 G6
Honey Street Wilts 62 G6
Honey Tye Suffolk 107 D9
Honeybourne Worcs 100 C2
Honeychurch Devon 25 G10
Honeydon Beds 122 G2
Honicknowle Plym'th 7 D9
Honiley Warwick 118 C4
Honing Norfolk 160 D6
Honingham Norfolk 160 G2
Honington Lincs 172 G6
Honington Suffolk 125 C8
Honington Warwick 100 C5
Honiton Devon 27 G10
Honkley Wrex 166 D4
Honley W Yorks 196 E6
Honor Oak London 67 E11
Hoo Suffolk 126 F5
Hoo End Herts 104 G3
Hoo Green Ches 184 E2
Hoo St. Werburgh Medway 69 E9
Hoober S Yorks 186 B6
Hoobrook Worcs 116 C6
Hood Green S Yorks 197 G10
Hood Hill S Yorks 186 B5
Hood Manor Warrington 183 D9
Hooe E Sussex 23 D11
Hooe Plym'th 7 E10
Hooe Common E Sussex 37 E11
Hoohill Blackp'l 202 F2
Hook Cambs 139 E8
Hook Devon 28 F4
Hook ER Yorks 199 B9
Hook Hants 49 C8
Hook Hants 33 F8
Hook London 67 G7
Hook Pembs 73 C7
Hook Wilts 62 C5
Hook Common Worcs 98 C6
Hook End Essex 87 F9
Hook End Oxon 65 C7
Hook Green Kent 53 F7
Hook Green Kent 68 E4
Hook Green Kent 68 F6
Hook Green Kent 68 E6
Hook Heath Surrey 50 B3
Hook Norton Oxon 101 E7
Hook Street Glos 79 F11
Hook Street Wilts 62 C5
Hook-a-gate Shrops 131 B9
Hooke Dorset 16 B6
Hooke Dorset 29 F8
Hooker Gate Tyne/Wear 242 F4
Hookgate Staffs 150 B4
Hookhills Torbay 9 D7
Hook's Cross Herts 104 G5
Hookway Devon 14 B3
Hookwood Surrey 51 E9
Hoole Ches 166 B6
Hooley London 51 B9
Hooley Bridge Gtr Man 195 E10
Hooley Brow Gtr Man 195 E11
Hooley Hill Gtr Man 184 B6
Hoop Monmouths 79 D8
Hooton Ches 182 F5
Hooton Levitt S Yorks 187 C8
Hooton Pagnell S Yorks 198 F3
Hooton Roberts S Yorks 187 B7
Hop Pole Lincs 156 G3
Hope Derby 185 E11
Hope H'land 308 D4
Hope Powys 130 B5
Hope Shrops 130 C6
Hope Staffs 169 D10
Hope = Yr Hôb Flints 166 D4
Hope Bagot Shrops 115 C11
Hope Bowdler Shrops 131 E9
Hope End Green Essex 105 G11
Hope Green Ches 184 E6
Hope Mansell Heref'd 79 B10
Hope under Dinmore Heref'd 115 G10
Hopebeck Cumb 229 G9
Hopeman Moray 301 C11
Hope's Green Essex 69 B9
Hope's Rough Heref'd 98 B2
Hopesay Shrops 131 G7
Hopetown W Yorks 198 C2
Hopkinstown Rh Cyn Taff 77 G9
Hoplands Hants 32 B5
Hopleys Staffs 134 C4
Hopley's Green Heref'd 114 G6
Hopperton N Yorks 206 B4
Hopsford Warwick 135 G8
Hopstone Shrops 132 E5
Hopton Derby 170 E3
Hopton Shrops 149 E7
Hopton Suffolk 125 B9
Hopton Staffs 151 D8
Hopton Cangeford Shrops 131 G10
Hopton Castle Shrops 115 B7
Hopton on Sea Norfolk 143 C10
Hopton Wafers Shrops 116 B2
Hoptonheath Shrops 115 B7
Hopwas Staffs 134 C3
Hopwood Gtr Man 195 F11
Hopwood Worcs 117 B10
Hopworthy Devon 24 G4
Horam E Sussex 37 D9
Horbling Lincs 156 B2
Horbury W Yorks 197 D9
Horbury Bridge W Yorks 197 D9
Horbury Junction W Yorks 197 D10
Horcott Glos 81 E10
Horden Durham 234 C4
Horderley Shrops 131 F8
Hordle Hants 19 B11
Hordley Shrops 149 C7
Horeb Carms 75 D7
Horeb Carms 93 F10
Horeb Ceredig'n 93 C7
Horeb Flints 166 D3
Horfield Bristol 60 D5
Horgabost W Isles 305 J2
Horham Suffolk 126 C4
Horingford I/Wight 20 D6
Horkesley Heath Essex 107 F9
Horkstow N Lincs 200 D3
Horley Oxon 101 C8
Horley Surrey 51 E9
Horn Som'set 28 F4
Horn Hill Bucks 85 G8
Horn Street Kent 55 F7
Horn Street Kent 69 G7
Hornblotton Som'set 44 G5
Hornblotton Green Som'set 44 G5
Hornby Lancs 211 F11
Hornby N Yorks 224 G4
Hornby N Yorks 225 D7
Horncastle Lincs 174 B3
Hornchurch London 68 B4
Horncliffe Northum 273 F8
Horndean Scot Borders 273 F7
Horndean Hants 33 E11
Horndon Devon 12 E6
Horndon on the Hill Thurr'k 69 C7
Horne Surrey 51 E10
Horne Row Essex 88 E3
Horner Devon 8 E5
Horner Som'set 41 D11
Horner's Green Suffolk 107 C9
Hornestreet Essex 107 E10
Horngrove Worcs 116 C6
Hornick Cornw'l 5 E9
Horniehaugh Angus 292 G6
Horning Norfolk 161 F6
Horninghold Leics 136 D6
Horninglow Staffs 152 E4
Horningsea Cambs 123 E9
Horningsham Wilts 45 D10
Horningtoft Norfolk 159 E8
Horningtops Cornw'l 6 C5
Horns Corner Kent 38 B2
Horns Cross Devon 24 C5
Horns Cross Kent 38 C4
Horns Cross Kent 68 E5
Horns Green London 52 B2
Hornsbury Som'set 28 E4
Hornsby Cumb 240 G2
Hornsea ER Yorks 209 D10
Hornsea Burton ER Yorks 209 D10
Hornsey London 67 B10
Hornton Oxon 101 C7
Horpit Swindon 63 C8
Horrabridge Devon 12 G7
Horringer Suffolk 124 D6
Horrocks Fold Gtr Man 195 E7
Horrocksford Lancs 203 E10
Horsebridge Devon 12 G4
Horsebridge Hants 47 G10
Horsebrook Devon 8 D4
Horsebrook Staffs 151 G7
Horsecastle N Som'set 60 F2
Horsedowns Cornw'l 2 C4
Horsehay Telford 132 B3
Horseheath Cambs 106 B2
Horseholm Dumf/Gal 237 B12
Horsehouse N Yorks 213 C10
Horselees Kent 54 B5
Horseley Heath W Midlands 133 E9
Horsell Surrey 50 B3
Horseman Side Essex 87 F8
Horseman's Green Wrex 166 G6
Horsemoor W Berks 64 E3
Horsendon Bucks 84 E3
Horseshoe Green Kent 52 E3
Horseway Cambs 139 F8
Horsey Norfolk 161 E9
Horsey Som'set 43 F10
Horsey Corner Norfolk 161 E9
Horsey Down Wilts 81 G9
Horsford Norfolk 160 F3
Horsforth W Yorks 205 F10
Horsforth Woodside W Yorks 205 F11
Horsham W Sussex 51 G7
Horsham St. Faith Norfolk 160 G4
Horsington Lincs 173 B11
Horsington Som'set 30 C2
Horsington Marsh Som'set 30 C2
Horsley Derby 170 G5
Horsley Glos 80 F4
Horsley Northum 242 D3
Horsley Northum 251 D8
Horsley Cross Essex 108 F2
Horsley Hill Tyne/Wear 243 D9
Horsley Woodhouse Derby 170 G5
Horsleycross Street Essex 108 F2
Horsleygate Derby 186 F4
Horsleyhill Scot Borders 262 F2
Horsleyhope Durham 233 B7
Horsleys Green Bucks 84 F3
Horsmonden Kent 53 E8
Horspath Oxon 83 E9
Horstead Norfolk 160 F5
Horsted Keynes W Sussex 36 B5
Horton Bucks 84 B6
Horton Dorset 31 F8
Horton Kent 54 B6
Horton Lancs 204 C3
Horton Northants 120 G6
Horton Shrops 149 C9
Horton S Glos 61 C9
Horton Som'set 28 E4
Horton Staffs 168 D6
Horton Swan 56 D3
Horton Telford 150 G3
Horton Wilts 62 G5
Horton Windsor 66 D4
Horton Cross Som'set 28 D4
Horton Green Ches 167 F7
Horton Heath Dorset 31 F9
Horton Heath Hants 33 D7
Horton in Ribblesdale N Yorks 212 E6
Horton Kirby Kent 68 F5
Horton-cum-Studley Oxon 83 C9
Hortonlane Shrops 149 G8
Hortonwood Telford 150 G3
Horwich Gtr Man 194 E6
Horwich End Derby 185 E8
Horwood Devon 25 B8
Hoscar Lancs 194 E3
Hose Leics 154 D4

Kirkoswald S Ayrs 244 B6
Kirkpatrick Dumf/Gal 247 E10
Kirkpatrick Durham Dumf/Gal 237 B9
Kirkpatrick-Fleming Dumf/Gal 239 C7
Kirksanton Cumb 210 C2
Kirkshaw N Lanarks 268 C4
Kirkstall W Yorks 205 F11
Kirkstile Aberds 302 F5
Kirkstyle H'land 310 B7
Kirkthorpe W Yorks 197 C11
Kirkton Aberds 302 E6
Kirkton Aberds 302 G6
Kirkton Angus 286 C6
Kirkton Angus 287 C8
Kirkton Angus 287 D8
Kirkton Arg/Bute 275 C8
Kirkton Scot Borders 262 G2
Kirkton Dumf/Gal 247 G11
Kirkton Fife 287 E7
Kirkton Fife 287 F8
Kirkton H'land 295 C10
Kirkton H'land 299 E9
Kirkton H'land 301 D7
Kirkton H'land 309 K7
Kirkton N Ayrs 266 D3
Kirkton Perth/Kinr 286 F3
Kirkton Stirl 285 G9
Kirkton S Lanarks 259 E10
Kirkton W Loth 269 B10
Kirkton Manor Scot Borders 260 B6
Kirkton of Airlie Angus 287 B7
Kirkton of Auchterhouse Angus 287 D7
Kirkton of Auchterless Aberds 303 E7
Kirkton of Barevan H'land 301 E8
Kirkton of Bourtie Aberds 303 G8
Kirkton of Collace Perth/Kinr 286 D5
Kirkton of Craig Angus 287 B11
Kirkton of Culsalmond Aberds 302 F6
Kirkton of Durris Aberds 293 D9
Kirkton of Glenbuchat Aberds 292 B5
Kirkton of Glenisla Angus 292 G4
Kirkton of Kingoldrum Angus 287 B7
Kirkton of Largo Fife 287 G8
Kirkton of Lethendy Perth/Kinr 286 C5
Kirkton of Logie Buchan Aberds 303 G9
Kirkton of Maryculter Aberds 293 D10
Kirkton of Menmuir Angus 293 G7
Kirkton of Monikie Angus 287 D9
Kirkton of Oyne Aberds 302 G6
Kirkton of Rayne Aberds 302 G6
Kirkton of Skene Aberds 293 C10
Kirkton of Tough Aberds 293 B8
Kirktonhill Scot Borders 271 E9
Kirktonhill W Dunb 277 G7
Kirktoun E Ayrs 267 G8
Kirktown Aberds 303 D10
Kirktown of Alvah Aberds 302 C6
Kirktown of Deskford Moray 302 C5
Kirktown of Fetteresso Aberds 293 E10
Kirktown of Mortlach Moray 302 F3
Kirktown of Slains Aberds 303 G10
Kirkud Scot Borders 270 G2
Kirkwall Orkney 312 G5
Kirkwall Airport Orkney 313 H5
Kirkwhelpington Northum 251 G11
Kirkwood Dumf/Gal 238 B4
Kirkwood N Lanarks 268 C4
Kirmington N Lincs 200 E6
Kirmond le Mire Lincs 189 C11
Kirn Arg/Bute 276 F3
Kirriemuir Angus 287 B7
Kirstead Green Norfolk 142 D5
Kirtlebridge Dumf/Gal 238 C6
Kirtleton Dumf/Gal 249 G7
Kirtling Cambs 124 F3
Kirtling Green Cambs 124 F3
Kirtlington Oxon 83 B7
Kirtomy H'land 308 C7
Kirton Lincs 156 B6
Kirton Notts 171 B11
Kirton Suffolk 108 D5
Kirton End Lincs 156 B5
Kirton Holme Lincs 174 G3
Kirton in Lindsey N Lincs 188 B6
Kiskin Cumb 210 B1
Kislingbury Northants 120 F4
Kitchenroyd W Yorks 197 F8
Kites Hardwick Warwick 119 D9
Kit's Coty Kent 69 G8
Kitt Green Gtr Man 194 F5
Kittisford Som'set 27 C9
Kittisford Barton Som'set 27 C9
Kittle Swan 56 D5
Kitt's End Herts 86 F2
Kitt's Green W Midlands 134 F3
Kitt's Moss Gtr Man 184 E5
Kittwhistle Dorset 28 G5
Kittybrewster Aberd C 293 C11
Kitwood Hants 49 G7
Kivernoll Heref'd 97 E9
Kiveton Park S Yorks 187 E7
Knackers Hole Dorset 30 E3
Knaith Lincs 188 E4
Knaith Park Lincs 188 D4
Knap Corner Dorset 30 C4
Knaphill Surrey 50 B3
Knapp Hants 32 C6
Knapp Perth/Kinr 286 D6
Knapp Som'set 28 B3
Knapthorpe Notts 172 D2
Knapton C/York 207 C7
Knapton Norfolk 160 C6
Knapton Green Heref'd 115 G8
Knapwell Cambs 122 E6
Knaresborough N Yorks 206 B3
Knarsdale Northum 240 G5
Knatts Valley Kent 68 G5
Knauchland Moray 302 D5
Knaven Aberds 303 E8
Knave's Ash Kent 71 G8
Knaves Green Suffolk 126 D2
Knavesmire C/York 207 D7
Knayton N Yorks 215 B8
Knebworth Herts 104 G5
Knebworth House, Stevenage Herts 104 G4
Knedlington ER Yorks 199 B8
Kneesall Notts 172 C2
Kneesworth Cambs 104 B6
Kneeton Notts 172 F2
Knelston Swan 56 D3
Knenhall Staffs 151 B8
Knettishall Suffolk 141 G9
Knightacott Devon 41 F6
Knightcote Warwick 119 G7
Knightcott N Som'set 43 B11
Knightley Staffs 150 D6
Knightley Dale Staffs 150 E6
Knighton Dorset 29 E10
Knighton Devon 7 F10
Knighton Leics C 136 C2
Knighton Oxon 63 B9
Knighton Poole 19 B7
Knighton Som'set 43 E7
Knighton Staffs 150 D4
Knighton Staffs 168 G2
Knighton = Tref-y-Clawdd Powys 114 C5
Knighton Wilts 63 E9
Knighton Worcs 117 F10
Knighton Fields Leics C 135 C11
Knighton on Teme Worcs 116 C2
Knight's End Cambs 139 E8
Knights Enham Hants 47 D11
Knight's Green Glos 98 E4
Knightshayes Court Devon 27 D7
Knightsridge W Loth 269 B10
Knightswood Glasg C 267 B10
Knill Heref'd 114 E5
Knipoch Arg/Bute 289 G10
Knipton Leics 154 C6
Knitsley Durham 233 B8
Kniveton Derby 170 E2
Knocharthur H'land 309 J7
Knock Arg/Bute 289 F7
Knock Cumb 231 F9
Knock Moray 302 D5
Knockally H'land 311 G5
Knockan H'land 307 H7
Knockandhu Moray 302 G2
Knockando Moray 301 E11
Knockando Ho. Moray 302 E2
Knockandoo H'land 301 G7
Knockbain H'land 300 D6
Knockbreck H'land 298 C2
Knockbrex Dumf/Gal 237 E7
Knockcarrach H'land 290 B6
Knockdee H'land 310 C5
Knockdolian S Ayrs 244 F4
Knockdow Arg/Bute 276 G2
Knockdown Wilts 61 B10
Knockenbaird Aberds 302 G6
Knockenkelly N Ayrs 256 E2
Knockentiber E Ayrs 257 B9
Knockespock Ho. Aberds 302 G5
Knockfarrel H'land 300 D5
Knockglass Dumf/Gal 236 D2
Knockhall Kent 68 E5
Knockhall Castle Aberds 303 G9
Knockhill Motor Racing Circuit Fife 279 C11
Knockholt London 52 B3
Knockholt Pound London 52 B3
Knockie Lodge H'land 290 B6
Knockin Shrops 148 E6
Knockinlaw E Ayrs 257 B10
Knockinnon H'land 310 F5
Knocklearn Dumf/Gal 237 B9
Knocklearoch Arg/Bute 274 G4
Knockmill Kent 68 G5
Knocknaha Arg/Bute 255 F7
Knocknain Dumf/Gal 236 C1
Knockothie Aberds 303 F9
Knockrome Arg/Bute 274 F6
Knocksharry I/Man 192 D3
Knockstapplemore Arg/Bute 255 F7
Knockvologan Arg/Bute 288 H5
Knodishall Suffolk 127 E8
Knokan Arg/Bute 288 G6
Knole Som'set 29 B7
Knole House & Gardens Kent 52 C4
Knoll Green Som'set 43 F8
Knollbury Monmouths 60 B2
Knolls Green Ches 184 F4
Knolton Wrex 149 B7
Knolton Bryn Wrex 149 B7
Knook Wilts 46 E2
Knossington Rutl'd 136 B6
Knotbury Staffs 169 B8
Knotlow Derby 169 B10
Knott End-on-Sea Lancs 202 D3
Knott Lanes Gtr Man 196 G2
Knott Side N Yorks 214 F3
Knotting Beds 121 E10
Knotting Green Beds 121 E10
Knottingley W Yorks 198 C4
Knotts Cumb 230 G4
Knotty Ash Mersey 182 C6
Knotty Green Bucks 84 G6
Knowbury Shrops 115 C11
Knowe Dumf/Gal 236 B5
Knowe Shetl'd 315 G5
Knowefield Cumb 239 F10
Knowehead Aberds 302 D5
Knowehead Aberds 293 C7
Knowehead Dumf/Gal 246 E4
Knowes of Elrick Aberds 302 D6
Knowesgate Northum 251 F11
Knoweton N Lanarks 268 D5
Knowhead Aberds 303 D9
Knowl Green Essex 106 C5
Knowl Hill Flints 166 C3
Knowl Hill Windsor 65 D10
Knowl Wood W Yorks 196 C2
Knowle Bristol 60 E6
Knowle Devon 27 F8
Knowle Devon 15 E7
Knowle Devon 26 G3
Knowle Devon 40 F3
Knowle Shrops 115 C11
Knowle Som'set 42 E3
Knowle Som'set 43 F10
Knowle Wilts 63 G7
Knowle W Midlands 118 B3
Knowle Cross Devon 14 B6
Knowle Green Lancs 203 F8
Knowle Green Surrey 66 E4
Knowle Hill Surrey 66 F3
Knowle Park W Yorks 205 E7
Knowle St. Giles Som'set 28 E4
Knowle Top S Yorks 186 D4
Knowle Village Hants 33 F9
Knowles Hill Devon 14 G3
Knowlton Kent 55 C9
Knowsley Mersey 182 B6
Knowsley Industrial Estate Mersey 182 B6
Knowsley Safari Park Mersey 183 C7
Knowsthorpe W Yorks 206 G2
Knowstone Devon 26 C4
Knox N Yorks 205 B11
Knox Bridge Kent 53 E9
Knucklas Powys 114 C5
Knuston Northants 121 D8
Knutsford Ches 184 F3
Knutton Staffs 168 F4
Knuzden Brook Lancs 195 B8
Knypersley Staffs 168 D5
Kraiknish H'land 294 C5
Krumlin W Yorks 196 E4
Kuggar Cornw'l 2 F6
Kyle of Lochalsh H'land 295 C9
Kyleakin H'land 295 C9
Kylepark S Lanarks 268 C3
Kylerhea H'land 295 C9
Kylesknoydart H'land 295 F10
Kylesku H'land 306 F7
Kylesmorar H'land 295 F10
Kylestrome H'land 306 F7
Kyllachy House H'land 301 G7
Kymin Monmouths 79 C8
Kynaston Heref'd 97 F10
Kynaston Heref'd 98 D2
Kynaston Shrops 149 E7
Kynnersley Telford 150 F3
Kyre Green Worcs 116 E2
Kyrewood Worcs 116 D2
Kyrle Som'set 27 C9

L

Labost W Isles 304 D4
Lacasaidh W Isles 304 F5
Lacasdal W Isles 304 E6
Laceby NE Lincs 201 F8
Lacey Green Bucks 84 E4
Lacey Green Ches 184 E4
Lach Dennis Ches 184 G2
Lache Ches 166 C5
Lackenby Redcar/Clevel'd 225 B11
Lackford Suffolk 124 C5
Lacock Wilts 62 F2
Ladbroke Warwick 119 F8
Laddingford Kent 53 D7
Lade Bank Lincs 174 E5
Ladock Cornw'l 5 E7
Ladwood Kent 55 E8
Lady Orkney 312 D7
Lady Balk W Yorks 198 C3
Lady Green Mersey 193 G10
Lady Hall Cumb 210 B3
Lady House Gtr Man 196 E2
Ladybank Fife 287 F7
Ladybrook Notts 171 C8
Ladyburn Inverci 276 F6
Ladycross Cornw'l 12 D2
Ladykirk Scot Borders 273 F7
Ladyridge Heref'd 97 E11
Lady's Green Suffolk 124 F5
Ladysford Aberds 303 C9
Ladywell London 67 E11
Ladywell W Loth 269 B10
Ladywood W Midlands 133 F11
Ladywood Worcs 117 E7
Laga H'land 289 C8
Lagafater Lodge Dumf/Gal 236 B3
Lagalochan Arg/Bute 275 B9
Lagavulin Arg/Bute 254 C5
Lagg Arg/Bute 274 F6
Lagg N Ayrs 255 E10
Laggan Arg/Bute 254 B3
Laggan H'land 289 B9
Laggan H'land 290 D4
Laggan H'land 291 D8
Laggan Lodge Arg/Bute 289 G8
Laggania H'land 291 C10
Lagganmullan Dumf/Gal 237 D7
Lagganulva Arg/Bute 288 E6
Lagness W Sussex 34 G5
Laide H'land 307 K3
Laig H'land 294 G6
Laigh Fenwick E Ayrs 267 G9
Laigh-Glengall S Ayrs 257 F8
Laighmuir E Ayrs 267 F9
Laighstonehall S Lanarks 268 E4
Laindon Essex 69 B7
Lair H'land 299 E10
Lair Perth/Kinr 292 G3
Laira Plym'th 7 D10
Lairg H'land 309 J5
Lairg Lodge H'land 309 J5
Lairg Muir H'land 309 J5
Lairgmore H'land 300 F5
Laisterdyke W Yorks 205 G9
Laithes Cumb 230 E5
Laithkirk Durham 232 G5
Laity Moor Cornw'l 3 B7
Lake Devon 40 G5
Lake I/Wight 21 E7
Lake Poole 18 C5
Lake Wilts 46 F6
Lake End Windsor 66 D2
Lakenham Norfolk 142 B4
Lakenheath Suffolk 140 G4
Lakesend Norfolk 139 D10
Lakeside Cumb 211 B7
Lakeside Worcs 117 D11
Lakeside and Haverthwaite Railway Cumb 210 B6
Laleham Surrey 66 F5
Laleston Bridg 57 F11
Lamarsh Essex 107 D7
Lamas Norfolk 160 E4
Lamb Corner Essex 107 E10
Lamb Roe Lancs 203 F10
Lambden Scot Borders 272 G4
Lamberhead Green Gtr Man 194 G4
Lamberhurst Kent 53 F7
Lamberhurst Quarter Kent 53 F7
Lamberton Scot Borders 273 D9
Lambert's End W Midlands 133 E9
Lambeth London 67 D10
Lambfair Green Suffolk 124 G4
Lambfoot Cumb 229 E9
Lambhill Glasg C 267 B11
Lambley Notts 171 G10
Lambley Northum 240 F5
Lambourn W Berks 63 D10
Lambourn Woodlands W Berks 63 D10
Lambourne Cornw'l 4 E5
Lambourne End Essex 87 G7
Lambridge Bath/NE Som'set 61 F9
Lamb's Green Dorset 18 B5
Lambs Green W Sussex 51 F8
Lambston Pembs 72 B6
Lambton Tyne/Wear 243 G7
Lamellion Cornw'l 6 C4
Lamerton Devon 12 F5
Lamesley Tyne/Wear 243 F7
Laminess Orkney 312 E7
Lamington H'land 301 B7
Lamington S Lanarks 259 C11
Lamlash N Ayrs 256 C2
Lamledra Cornw'l 5 G10
Lamloch Dumf/Gal 246 D2
Lamonby Cumb 230 D4
Lamorick Cornw'l 5 C10
Lamorna Cornw'l 1 E4
Lamorran Cornw'l 5 G7
Lampardbrook Suffolk 126 E5
Lampen Cornw'l 6 B3
Lampeter = Llanbedr Pont Steffan Ceredig'n 93 B11
Lampeter Velfrey Pembs 73 C11
Lamphey Pembs 73 E8
Lamplugh Cumb 229 G7
Lamport Northants 120 C5
Lampton London 66 D6
Lamyatt Som'set 45 F7
Lana Devon 12 B2
Lana Devon 24 F4
Lanark S Lanarks 269 G7
Lancaster Lancs 211 G9
Lancaster Leisure Park Lancs 202 A5
Lanchester Durham 233 B9
Lancing W Sussex 35 F11
Land Gate Gtr Man 194 G5
Land Side Gtr Man 183 B11
Landbeach Cambs 123 D9
Landcross Devon 25 C7
Landerberry Aberds 293 C9
Landford Wilts 32 D3
Landford Common Wilts 32 D3
Landfordwood Wilts 32 C3
Landican Mersey 182 D3
Landimore Swan 75 G7
Landkey Devon 40 G5
Landkey Newland Devon 40 G5
Landore Swan 75 F11
Landport E Sussex 36 E6
Landport Portsm'th 33 G10
Landrake Cornw'l 7 C7
Land's End Cornw'l 1 D2
Land's End Airport Cornw'l 1 D3
Landscove Devon 8 B5
Landshipping Pembs 73 C8
Landulph Cornw'l 7 C8
Landwade Cambs 124 D2
Landywood Staffs 133 B9
Lane Cornw'l 4 C6
Lane Bottom Lancs 204 F3
Lane End Bucks 84 G4
Lane End Cumb 220 G2
Lane End Derby 170 C6
Lane End Dorset 18 C3
Lane End Flints 166 C3
Lane End Gtr Man 184 C5
Lane End Gtr Man 195 F11
Lane End Hants 33 B9
Lane End Heref'd 79 B10
Lane End I/Wight 21 D9
Lane End Kent 68 E5
Lane End Lancs 204 D3
Lane End N Yorks 225 F8
Lane End Surrey 49 E10
Lane End Wilts 45 D10
Lane End W Yorks 204 F6
Lane Ends Ches 185 E7
Lane Ends Derby 152 C4
Lane Ends Derby 170 E5
Lane Ends Gtr Man 185 C7
Lane Ends Lancs 203 G8
Lane Ends Lancs 203 G11
Lane Ends Lancs 203 C10
Lane Ends Lancs 194 D6
Lane Ends N Yorks 204 E5
Lane Ends W Yorks 205 F10
Lane Green Staffs 133 C7
Lane Head Derby 185 F11
Lane Head Durham 233 F7
Lane Head Durham 224 C2
Lane Head Gtr Man 183 B10
Lane Head W Midlands 133 C9
Lane Head W Yorks 197 E7
Lane Head W Yorks 197 F7
Lane Heads Lancs 202 F4
Lane Side Lancs 195 C9
Lane Side Lancs 195 C9
Laneast Cornw'l 11 E10
Lane-end Cornw'l 5 B10
Laneham Notts 188 F4
Lanehead Durham 232 C2
Lanehead Northum 251 F7
Lanercost Cumb 240 E3
Lanescot Cornw'l 5 D11
Lanesend Pembs 73 D9
Lanesfield W Midlands 133 D8
Laneshaw Bridge Lancs 204 E4
Laney Green Staffs 133 B9
Langaford Devon 12 B4
Langal H'land 289 C9
Langaller Som'set 28 B3
Langar Notts 154 C4
Langbank Renf 277 G7
Langbar N Yorks 205 C7
Langbaurgh N Yorks 225 C11
Langbridge I/Wight 21 D7
Langburnshiels Scot Borders 250 C2
Langcliffe N Yorks 212 G6
Langdale H'land 308 E6
Langdon Cornw'l 12 D2
Langdon Beck Durham 232 E3
Langdon Hills Essex 69 B7
Langdown Hants 32 F6
Langdyke Fife 287 G7
Langeitho Ceredig'n 112 F2
Langenhoe Essex 89 B8
Langford Beds 104 C3
Langford Devon 27 G8
Langford Essex 88 D4
Langford Notts 172 D4
Langford Oxon 82 E2
Langford Som'set 28 B2
Langford Budville Som'set 27 C10
Langford Green N Som'set 44 B3
Langham Dorset 30 B3
Langham Essex 107 E10
Langham Norfolk 177 E8
Langham Rutl'd 154 G6
Langham Suffolk 125 D9
Langhaugh Scot Borders 260 C6
Langho Lancs 203 G10
Langholm Dumf/Gal 249 G9
Langlees Falk 279 E7
Langley Ches 184 G6
Langley Derby 170 F6
Langley Essex 105 D8
Langley Glos 99 F10
Langley Gtr Man 195 F11
Langley Hants 32 G6
Langley Herts 104 G4
Langley Kent 53 C9
Langley Northum 241 E8
Langley Slough 66 D4
Langley Som'set 27 B9
Langley Warwick 118 E3
Langley W Midlands 133 F9
Langley Burrell Wilts 62 D2
Langley Common Derby 152 B5
Langley Common Wokingham 65 G9
Langley Corner Bucks 66 B4
Langley Green Derby 152 B5
Langley Green Essex 107 G7
Langley Green Norfolk 143 C7
Langley Green W Sussex 51 F9
Langley Heath Kent 53 C10
Langley Marsh Som'set 27 B9
Langley Mill Derby 170 F6
Langley Moor Durham 233 C10
Langley Park Durham 233 C11
Langley Street Norfolk 143 C7
Langley Vale Surrey 51 B8
Langleyfield Telford 132 B3
Langloan N Lanarks 268 C4
Langmere Norfolk 142 G3
Langney E Sussex 23 E10
Langold Notts 187 D9
Langore Cornw'l 11 D11
Langport Som'set 28 B6
Langrick Lincs 174 F3
Langridge Bath/NE Som'set 61 F8
Langridgeford Devon 25 C9
Langrigg Cumb 222 C5
Langrigg Cumb 229 B9
Langrish Hants 34 C2
Langsett S Yorks 197 G8
Langshaw Scot Borders 262 B2
Langside Glasg C 267 C11
Langside Perth/Kinr 285 F11
Langskaill Orkney 312 D5
Langstone Hants 34 F2
Langstone Newp 59 B11
Langthorne N Yorks 224 G5
Langthorpe N Yorks 215 F7
Langthwaite N Yorks 223 E10
Langtoft ER Yorks 217 F10
Langtoft Lincs 156 G2
Langton Durham 224 B3
Langton Lincs 174 B2
Langton Lincs 190 G5
Langton N Yorks 216 F5
Langton by Wragby Lincs 189 F10
Langton Green Kent 52 F4
Langton Green Suffolk 126 C2
Langton Herring Dorset 17 E8
Langton Long Blandford Dorset 30 F5
Langton Matravers Dorset 18 F5
Langtree Devon 24 D7
Langtree Week Devon 25 D7
Langwathby Cumb 231 E7
Langwell Ho. H'land 311 G5
Langwell Lodge H'land 307 J6
Langwith Derby 171 B8
Langwith Junction Derby 171 B8
Langworth Lincs 189 F9
Lanham Green Essex 106 G5
Lanhydrock House, Bodmin Cornw'l 5 C11
Lanivet Cornw'l 5 C10
Lanjeth Cornw'l 5 E9
Lank Cornw'l 11 F7
Lanlivery Cornw'l 5 D11
Lanmack Blackb'n 195 B7
Lanner Cornw'l 2 B6
Lanoy Cornw'l 11 F11
Lanreath Cornw'l 6 D3
Lanrick Stirl 285 G10
Lansallos Cornw'l 6 E3
Lansbury Park Caerph 59 B7
Lansdown Bath/NE Som'set 61 F8
Lansdown Glos 99 G8
Lansdown Glos 100 G3
Lanstephan Cornw'l 12 D2
Lanteglos Cornw'l 11 E7
Lanton Scot Borders 262 E4
Lanton Northum 263 C10
Lanvean Cornw'l 5 B7
Lapal W Midlands 133 G9
Lapford Devon 26 F2
Laphroaig Arg/Bute 254 C4
Lapley Staffs 151 G7
Lapworth Warwick 118 C3
Larachbeg H'land 289 E8
Larbert Falk 279 E7
Larbreck Lancs 202 E4
Larches Lancs 202 G6
Larden Green Ches 167 E9
Larg H'land 292 B2
Largie Aberds 302 F6
Largiebaan Arg/Bute 255 F7
Largiemore Arg/Bute 275 E10
Largoward Fife 287 G8
Largs N Ayrs 266 D4
Largue Aberds 302 E6
Largybeg N Ayrs 256 E3
Largymeanoch N Ayrs 255 E11
Largymore N Ayrs 256 E2
Larkbeare Devon 15 B7
Larkfield Inverci 276 F4
Larkfield Kent 53 B8
Larkhall Bath/NE Som'set 61 F9
Larkhall S Lanarks 268 E5
Larkhill Wilts 46 E6
Larkhill Worcs 116 B6
Larklands Derby 171 G7
Larling Norfolk 141 F9
Larport Heref'd 97 D11
Larrick Cornw'l 12 F2
Larriston Scot Borders 250 E2
Lartington Durham 223 B10
Lary Aberds 292 C5
Lasborough Glos 80 G4
Lasham Hants 49 E7
Lashenden Kent 53 E11
Laskill N Yorks 225 G11
Lassington Glos 98 G5
Lasswade Midloth 270 B6
Lastingham N Yorks 226 G4
Latcham Som'set 44 D2
Latchford Herts 105 G7
Latchford Oxon 83 E11
Latchford Warrington 183 D10
Latchingdon Essex 88 E5
Latchley Cornw'l 12 G4
Latchmore Bank Essex 87 B7
Latchmore Green Hants 48 B6
Lately Common Warrington 183 B11
Lathallan Mill Fife 287 G8
Lathbury Durham 223 B10
Lathbury M/Keynes 103 B7
Latheron H'land 310 F5
Latheronwheel H'land 310 F5
Latheronwheel Ho. H'land 310 F5
Lathones Fife 287 G8
Latimer Bucks 85 F7
Latteridge S Glos 61 C7
Lattersey Hill Cambs 138 D5
Lattiford Som'set 29 B11
Latton Wilts 81 F9
Latton Bush Essex 87 D7
Lauchintilly Aberds 293 B9
Laudale Ho H'land 289 D9
Lauder Scot Borders 271 F10
Laugharne = Talacharn Carms 74 C4
Laugherton Lincs 188 F4
Laughton E Sussex 37 E7
Laughton Leics 136 F3
Laughton Lincs 155 C11
Laughton Lincs 188 B4
Laughton Common E Sussex 37 E7
Laughton Common S Yorks 187 D9
Laughton en le Morthen S Yorks 187 D9
Launcells Cornw'l 24 F2
Launceston Cornw'l 12 E2
Launcherley Som'set 44 E5
Laund Lancs 195 C10
Laund Lancs 204 E3
Launton Oxon 102 G2
Laurel Street Som'set 44 F4
Laurencekirk Aberds 293 F9
Laurieston Dumf/Gal 237 C8
Laurieston Falk 279 F8
Lavendon M/Keynes 121 G8
Lavenham Suffolk 107 B8
Laverackloch Moray 301 C11
Laverhay Dumf/Gal 248 D4
Laversdale Cumb 239 E11
Laverstock Wilts 47 G7
Laverstoke Hants 48 D3
Laverton Glos 99 D11
Laverton N Yorks 214 E4
Laverton Som'set 45 C9
Lavister Wrex 166 D5
Law S Lanarks 268 E6
Law Hill S Lanarks 268 E6
Lawers Perth/Kinr 285 D10
Lawers Perth/Kinr 285 E11
Lawford Essex 107 E11
Lawford Som'set 42 F6
Lawhill Perth/Kinr 286 F3
Lawhitton Cornw'l 12 E3
Lawkland N Yorks 212 F5
Lawkland Green N Yorks 212 F5
Lawley Telford 132 B3
Lawn Swindon 63 C7
Lawnhead Staffs 150 D6
Lawnswood W Yorks 205 F11
Lawrence Weston Bristol 60 D4
Lawrenny Pembs 73 D8
Lawshall Suffolk 125 G7
Lawshall Green Suffolk 125 G7
Lawson Street Kent 70 G3
Lawton Heath End Ches 168 D3
Lawtongate Ches 168 D4
Laxey I/Man 192 D5
Laxey Wheel and Mines I/Man 192 D5
Laxfield Suffolk 126 C5
Laxfirth Shetl'd 315 H6
Laxfirth Shetl'd 315 J6
Laxford Bridge H'land 306 E7
Laxo Shetl'd 315 G6
Laxobigging Shetl'd 314 F6
Laxton ER Yorks 199 B9
Laxton Northants 137 D9
Laxton Notts 172 B2
Laycock W Yorks 204 E6
Layer Breton Essex 88 B6
Layer Breton Heath Essex 88 B6
Layer de la Haye Essex 89 B7
Layer Marney Essex 88 B6
Layerthorpe C/York 207 C8
Layham Suffolk 107 C10
Laymore Dorset 28 G5
Layter's Green Bucks 85 G7
Laytham ER Yorks 207 F10
Layton Blackp'l 202 F2
Lazenby Redcar/Clevel'd 225 B11
Lazonby Cumb 231 D7
Lea Derby 170 D4
Lea Devon 15 B10
Lea Heref'd 98 G3
Lea Lancs 202 G5
Lea Lincs 188 D4
Lea Shrops 131 F7
Lea Shrops 131 B8
Lea Warwick 134 E4
Lea Wilts 62 B3
Lea Bridge London 67 B11
Lea Brook S Yorks 186 B6
Lea End Worcs 117 B10
Lea Green Mersey 183 C8
Lea Hall Derby 170 D4
Lea Hall W Midlands 134 F2
Lea Heath Staffs 151 D10
Lea Marston Warwick 134 E3
Lea Town Lancs 202 G5
Lea Yeat Cumb 212 B5
Leabrooks Derby 170 E6
Leac a Li W Isles 305 J3
Leacainn W Isles 305 H3
Leachkin H'land 300 E6
Leacnasaide H'land 299 B7
Leadburn Midloth 270 D4
Leaden Roding Essex 87 C9
Leadenham Lincs 172 E6
Leaderfoot Scot Borders 262 C3
Leadgate Cumb 231 C10
Leadgate Durham 242 G4
Leadgate Northum 242 F4
Leadhills S Lanarks 259 F9
Leadingcross Green Kent 53 C11
Leadmill Flints 166 C2
Leadmill S Yorks 186 E2
Leafield Oxon 82 B4
Leafield Wilts 61 F11
Leagrave Luton 103 G10
Leake N Yorks 225 G8
Leake Commonside Lincs 174 E5
Leake Fold Hill Lincs 174 E6
Leake Gride Lincs 174 E5
Leake Hurn's End Lincs 174 F6
Lealholm N Yorks 226 D5
Lealholm Side N Yorks 226 D5
Lealt Arg/Bute 275 D7
Lealt H'land 298 C5
Leam Derby 186 F2
Leam Lane Tyne/Wear 243 E7
Leamington Hastings Warwick 119 D8
Leamonsley Staffs 134 B2
Leamoor Common Shrops 131 F8
Leamore W Midlands 133 C9
Leamside Durham 234 C2
Leanach Arg/Bute 275 D11
Leanachan H'land 290 F4
Leanaig H'land 300 D5
Leargybreck Arg/Bute 274 F6
Lease Rigg N Yorks 226 E6
Leasgill Cumb 211 C9
Leasingham Lincs 173 F9
Leasingthorne Durham 233 F11
Leasowe Mersey 182 C3
Leatherhead Surrey 51 B7
Leatherhead Common Surrey 51 B7
Leathern Bottle Glos 80 E2
Leathley N Yorks 205 D10
Leaths Dumf/Gal 237 C9
Leaton Shrops 149 F9
Leaton Telford 150 G2
Leaveland Kent 54 C4
Leavenheath Suffolk 107 D9
Leavening N Yorks 216 G5
Leaves Green London 68 G2
Leavesden Green Herts 85 E9
Leazes Durham 242 F5
Leazes Northum 241 E10
Lebberston N Yorks 217 C11
Lechlade-on-Thames Glos 82 F2
Leck Lancs 212 D2
Leckford Hants 47 F11
Leckfurin H'land 308 D7
Leckgruinart Arg/Bute 274 G3
Leckhampstead Bucks 102 D4
Leckhampstead W Berks 64 D2
Leckhampstead Street W Berks 64 D2
Leckhampstead Thicket W Berks 64 D2
Leckhampton Glos 80 B6
Leckie H'land 299 C10
Leckmelm H'land 307 K6
Leckuary Arg/Bute 275 D9
Leckwith V/Glam 59 E7
Leconfield ER Yorks 208 E6
Ledaig Arg/Bute 289 F11
Ledburn Bucks 103 G8
Ledbury Heref'd 98 D4
Ledcharrie Stirl 285 E9
Ledgemoor Heref'd 115 G8
Ledgowan H'land 299 D11
Ledicot Heref'd 115 E8
Ledmore Angus 293 G7
Ledmore H'land 307 H7
Lednagullin H'land 308 C7
Ledsham Ches 182 G5
Ledsham W Yorks 198 B3
Ledston W Yorks 198 B2
Ledstone Devon 8 F4
Ledwell Oxon 101 F8
Lee Arg/Bute 288 G6
Lee Devon 40 D3
Lee Devon 40 D5
Lee Devon 26 B4
Lee Hants 32 D5
Lee Lancs 203 B7
Lee London 67 E11
Lee Northum 241 F10
Lee Shrops 149 C8
Lee Brockhurst Shrops 149 D10
Lee Chapel Essex 69 B7
Lee Clump Bucks 84 E6
Lee Green Medway 69 E8
Lee Ground Hants 33 F8
Lee Head Derby 185 C8
Lee Mill Devon 7 D11
Lee Moor Devon 7 C11
Leeans Shetl'd 315 J5
Leebotten Shetl'd 315 L6
Leebotwood Shrops 131 D9
Leece Cumb 210 F4
Leech Pool Pembs 73 B7
Leechpool Monmouths 60 B4
Leedon Beds 103 F8
Leeds Kent 53 C10
Leeds W Yorks 206 F2
Leeds Bradford International Airport W Yorks 205 E10
Leeds Castle Kent 53 C10
Leeds City Art Gallery W Yorks 206 G2
Leedstown Cornw'l 2 C4
Leeford Devon 41 D9
Leegomery Telford 150 G3
Leeholme Durham 233 E10
Leek Staffs 169 D7
Leek Wootton Warwick 118 D5
Leekbrook Staffs 169 E7
Leeming N Yorks 214 B5
Leeming W Yorks 204 G6
Leeming Bar N Yorks 224 G5
Lee-on-the-Solent Hants 33 G9
Lee-over-Sands Essex 89 C10
Lees Derby 152 B5
Lees Gtr Man 196 G3

Lixwm Flints 181 G11
Lizard Cornw'l 2 G6
Llaingarreglwyd Ceredig'n 111 F8
Llaingoch Angl 178 E2
Llaithddu Powys 129 G11
Llampha V/Glam 58 D2
Llan Powys 129 C7
Llan Rh Cyn Taff 58 B4
Llan Ffestiniog Gwyn 164 G2
Llanaber Gwyn 146 F2
Llanaelhaearn Gwyn 162 G5
Llanaeron Ceredig'n 111 E9
Llanafan Ceredig'n 112 C3
Llanafan-fawr Powys 113 F9
Llanallgo Angl 179 D8
Llanandras = Presteigne Powys 114 E6
Llananno Powys 113 C11
Llanarmon Gwyn 145 B8
Llanarmon Dyffryn Ceiriog Wrex 148 C3
Llanarmon Mynydd-Mawr Powys 148 D2
Llanarmon-yn-Ial Denbs 165 D11
Llanarth Ceredig'n 111 F8
Llanarth Monmouths 78 C5
Llanarthne Carms 93 G10
Llanasa Flints 181 E10
Llanbabo Angl 178 D5
Llanbad Bridg 58 C3
Llanbadarn Fawr Ceredig'n 128 G2
Llanbadarn Fynydd Powys 113 B11
Llanbadarn-y-garreg Powys 96 B2
Llanbadoc Monmouths 78 E5
Llanbadrig Angl 178 C5
Llanbeder Newp 78 G5
Llanbedr Gwyn 145 D11
Llanbedr Powys 96 B2
Llanbedr Powys 96 G4
Llanbedr Pont Steffan = Lampeter Ceredig'n 93 B11
Llanbedr-Dyfryn-Clwyd Denbs 165 D10
Llanbedrgoch Angl 179 E8
Llanbedrog Gwyn 144 C6
Llanbedr-y-cennin Conwy 164 B3
Llanberis Gwyn 163 C9
Llanbethery V/Glam 58 F4
Llanbister Powys 114 C3
Llanblethian V/Glam 58 E3
Llanboidy Carms 92 G4
Llanbradach Caerph 77 G10
Llanbrynmair Powys 129 C7
Llancadle V/Glam 58 F4
Llancaiach Merth Tyd 77 F10
Llancarfan V/Glam 58 E5
Llancayo Monmouths 78 E5
Llancloudy Heref'd 97 G9
Llancoch Powys 114 C4
Llancynfelyn Ceredig'n 128 E2
Llan-dafal Bl Gwent 77 E11
Llandaff Card 59 D7
Llandaff North Card 59 D7
Llandanwg Gwyn 145 D11
Llandarcy Rh Cyn Taff 76 F2
Llandawke Carms 74 C3
Llanddaniel Fab Angl 179 G7
Llanddarog Carms 75 B8
Llanddeiniol Ceredig'n 111 C11
Llanddeiniolen Gwyn 163 B8
Llandderfel Gwyn 147 B9
Llanddeusant Carms 94 G5
Llanddeusant Angl 178 D4
Llanddew Powys 95 E11
Llanddewi Swan 56 D3
Llanddewi Brefi Ceredig'n 112 F3
Llanddewi Rhydderch Monmouths 78 C4
Llanddewi Velfrey Pembs 73 B10
Llanddewi Ystradenni Powys 114 D2
Llanddewi'r-Cwm Powys 95 B10
Llanddoged Conwy 164 C4
Llanddona Angl 179 F9
Llanddowror Carms 74 C3
Llanddulas Conwy 180 F6
Llanddwywe Gwyn 145 E11
Llanddygfael Hir Angl 178 C5
Llandecwyn Gwyn 146 B2
Llandefaelog Powys 95 E10
Llandefaelogtre'r-graig Powys 96 F2
Llandefalle Powys 96 D2
Llandegfan Angl 179 G9
Llandegla Denbs 165 E11
Llandegley Powys 114 E2
Llandegveth Monmouths 78 F4
Llandegwning Gwyn 144 D5
Llandeillo'r-Fan Powys 95 E7
Llandeilo Carms 94 G2
Llandeilo Graban Powys 95 C11
Llandeloy Pembs 91 F7
Llandenny Monmouths 78 E6
Llandevaud Newp 78 G6
Llandevenny Monmouths 60 B2
Llandilo Carms 92 F2
Llandinabo Heref'd 97 F10
Llandinam Powys 129 F10
Llandissilio Pembs 92 G2
Llandogo Cleddon Monmouths 79 E8
Llandough V/Glam 58 E3
Llandough V/Glam 59 E7
Llandovery = Llanymddyfri Carms 94 E5
Llandow V/Glam 58 E2
Llandre Carms 94 C3
Llandre Ceredig'n 128 F2
Llandrillo Denbs 147 B10
Llandrillo-yn-Rhôs Conwy 180 E4
Llandrindod = Llandrindod Wells Powys 113 E11
Llandrindod Wells = Llandrindod Powys 113 E11
Llandrinio Powys 148 F5
Llandudno Conwy 180 E3
Llandudno Junction = Cyffordd Llandudno Conwy 180 F4
Llandudoch = St. Dogmaels Pembs 92 B3
Llandwrog Gwyn 163 D7
Llandybie = Llandybïe Carms 75 B10
Llandybïe = Llandybie Carms 75 B10
Llandyfaelog Carms 74 C6
Llandyfan Carms 75 B10
Llandyfriog Ceredig'n 92 C6
Llandyfrydog Angl 178 D6
Llandygai Gwyn 179 G9
Llandygwydd Ceredig'n 92 C4
Llandynan Denbs 165 G11
Llandyrnog Denbs 165 B10
Llandyry Carms 74 E6
Llandysilio Powys 148 F5
Llandyssil Powys 130 D3
Llandysul Ceredig'n 93 C8
Llanedeyrn Card 59 C8
Llanedi Carms 75 D9
Llaneglwys Powys 95 D11
Llanegryn Gwyn 110 B2
Llanegwad Carms 93 G10
Llaneilian Angl 179 C7
Llanelian-yn-Rhos Conwy 180 F5
Llanelidan Denbs 165 E10
Llanelieu Powys 96 E3
Llanellen Monmouths 78 C4
Llanelli Carms 75 E8
Llanelltyd Gwyn 146 F4
Llanelly Monmouths 78 C2
Llanelly Hill Monmouths 78 C2
Llanelwedd Powys 113 G11
Llanelwy = St. Asaph Denbs 181 G8
Llanenddwyn Gwyn 145 E11
Llanengan Gwyn 144 D5
Llanerch Emrys Powys 148 E4
Llanerchymedd Angl 178 E6
Llanerch-y-môr Flints 181 F11
Llanerfyl Powys 129 B10
Llaneuddog Angl 179 D7
Llan-eurgain = Northop Flints 166 B2
Llanfach Caerph 78 F2
Llanfachraeth Angl 178 E4
Llanfachreth Gwyn 146 E5
Llanfaelog Angl 178 G4
Llanfaelrhys Gwyn 144 D4
Llanfaenor Monmouths 78 B6
Llanfaes Angl 179 F10
Llanfaes Powys 95 F10
Llanfaethlu Angl 178 D4
Llanfaglan Gwyn 163 C7
Llanfair Gwyn 145 D11
Llanfair Caereinion Powys 130 B2
Llanfair Clydogau Ceredig'n 112 G2
Llanfair Dyfryn Clwyd Denbs 165 D10
Llanfair Kilgeddin Monmouths 78 D4
Llanfair Talhaiarn Conwy 180 G6
Llanfair Waterdine Shrops 114 B4
Llanfairfechan Conwy 179 F11
Llanfair-Nant-Gwyn Pembs 92 D3
Llanfairpwllgwyngyll Angl 179 G8
Llanfair-ym-Muallt = Builth Wells Powys 113 G10
Llanfairyneubwll Angl 178 F4
Llanfairynghornwy Angl 178 C4
Llanfallteg Carms 73 B11
Llanfaredd Powys 113 G11
Llanfarian Ceredig'n 111 B11
Llanfechain Powys 148 E3
Llanfechan Powys 113 G9
Llanfechell Angl 178 C5
Llanfendigaid Gwyn 110 C2
Llanferres Denbs 165 C11
Llanfflewyn Angl 178 D5
Llanfihangel Crucorney Monmouths 96 G6
Llanfihangel Glyn Myfyr Conwy 165 F7
Llanfihangel Nant Bran Powys 95 E8
Llanfihangel Rhydithon Powys 114 D3
Llanfihangel Tal-y-llyn Powys 96 F2
Llanfihangel yn Nhowyn Angl 178 F4
Llanfihangel-ar-arth Carms 93 D9
Llanfihangel-helygen Powys 113 E10
Llanfihangel-nant-Melan Powys 114 F3
Llanfihangel-y-Creuddyn Ceredig'n 112 B3
Llanfihangel-yng-Ngwnfa Powys 147 F11
Llanfihangel-y-pennant Gwyn 128 B3
Llanfihangel-y-pennant Gwyn 163 G8
Llanfilo Powys 96 E2
Llanfoist Monmouths 78 C3
Llanfor Gwyn 147 B8
Llanfrechfa Torf 78 G4
Llanfrothen Gwyn 163 G10
Llanfrynach Powys 95 F11
Llanfwrog Denbs 165 D10
Llanfwrog Angl 178 E4
Llanfyllin Powys 148 F2
Llanfynydd Carms 93 F11
Llanfynydd Flints 166 D3
Llanfyrnach Pembs 92 E4
Llangadfan Powys 147 G10
Llangadog Carms 74 D6
Llangadog Carms 94 F4
Llangadwaladr Angl 162 B5
Llangadwaladr Powys 148 C3
Llangaffo Angl 162 B6
Llangain Carms 74 B5
Llangammarch Wells Powys 95 B8
Llangan V/Glam 58 D3
Llangarron Heref'd 97 G10
Llangasty-Talyllyn Powys 96 F2
Llangathen Carms 93 G11
Llangattock Powys 78 B2
Llangattock Lingoed Monmouths 97 F7
Llangedwyn Powys 148 E3
Llangefni Angl 179 F7
Llangeinor Bridg 58 B2
Llangeler Carms 93 D7
Llangelynnin Gwyn 110 B2
Llangendeirne Carms 75 C7
Llangennech Carms 75 E9
Llangennith Carms 74 G6
Llangenny Powys 78 B2
Llangernyw Conwy 164 B5
Llangeview Monmouths 78 E6
Llangian Gwyn 144 D5
Llangiwg Neath P Talb 76 D2
Llangloffan Pembs 91 E8
Llanglydwen Carms 92 F3
Llangoed Angl 179 F10
Llangoedmor Ceredig'n 92 B4
Llangollen Denbs 166 G2
Llangolman Pembs 92 F2
Llangors Powys 96 F2
Llangorwen Ceredig'n 128 G2
Llangovan Monmouths 79 D7
Llangower Gwyn 147 C8
Llangrannog Ceredig'n 110 G6
Llangristiolus Angl 178 G6
Llangrove Heref'd 79 B8
Llangua Monmouths 97 F7
Llangunllo Powys 114 C4
Llangunnor Carms 93 G8
Llangurig Powys 129 G8
Llangwm Conwy 165 G7
Llangwm Monmouths 78 F6
Llangwm Pembs 73 D7
Llangwnnadl Gwyn 144 C4
Llangwyfan Denbs 165 B10
Llangwyllog Angl 178 F6
Llangwyryfon Ceredig'n 112 C2
Llangybi Ceredig'n 112 G2
Llangybi Gwyn 162 G6
Llangybi Monmouths 78 F5
Llangyfelach Swan 75 F10
Llangynhafal Denbs 165 C10
Llangynidr Powys 77 B11
Llangynin Carms 74 B3
Llangynllo Ceredig'n 93 C7
Llangynog Carms 74 B4
Llangynog Powys 147 D11
Llangynwyd Bridg 57 D11
Llanhamfach Powys 95 F11
Llanharan Rh Cyn Taff 58 C4
Llanharry Rh Cyn Taff 58 C4
Llanhennock Monmouths 78 G5
Llanhilleth Bl Gwent 78 E2
Llanidloes Powys 129 G9
Llaniestyn Gwyn 144 C5
Llanifihangel-uwch-Gwili Carms 93 G9
Llanifyny Powys 129 G7
Llanigon Powys 96 C4
Llanilar Ceredig'n 112 B2
Llanilid Rh Cyn Taff 58 C3
Llanion Pembs 73 E7
Llanishen Card 59 C7
Llanishen Monmouths 79 E7
Llanllawddog Carms 93 F9
Llanllechid Gwyn 163 B10
Llanllowell = Llanllywell Monmouths 78 F5
Llanllugan Powys 129 C11
Llanllwch Carms 74 B5
Llanllwchaiarn Powys 130 E2
Llanllwni Carms 93 D9
Llanllyfni Gwyn 163 E7
Llanllywell = Llanllowell Monmouths 78 F5
Llanmadoc Carms 74 G6
Llanmaes V/Glam 58 F3
Llanmartin Newp 59 B11
Llanmihangel V/Glam 58 E3
Llan-mill Pembs 73 C10
Llanmiloe Carms 74 D3
Llanmorlais Swan 75 G8
Llannant Swan 75 E9
Llannefydd Conwy 181 G7
Llannon Carms 75 D8
Llan-non = Llanon Ceredig'n 111 D10
Llannor Gwyn 145 B7
Llanon = Llan-non Ceredig'n 111 D10
Llanover Monmouths 78 D4
Llanpumpsaint Carms 93 F8
Llanreath Pembs 73 E7
Llanreithan Pembs 91 F7
Llanrhaeadr Denbs 165 C9
Llanrhaeadr-ym-Mochnant Powys 148 D2
Llanrhian Pembs 90 E6
Llanrhidian Swan 75 G7
Llanrhos Conwy 180 E3
Llanrhyddlad Angl 178 D4
Llanrhystud Ceredig'n 111 D10
Llanrosser Heref'd 96 D5
Llanrothal Heref'd 79 B7
Llanrug Gwyn 163 C8
Llanrumney Card 59 C8
Llanrwst Conwy 164 C4
Llansadurnen Carms 74 C3
Llansadwrn Carms 94 E3
Llansadwrn Angl 179 F9
Llansaint Carms 74 D5
Llansanffraid Glan Conwy Conwy 180 F4
Llansannan Conwy 164 B6
Llansannor V/Glam 58 D3
Llansantffraed Ceredig'n 111 D10
Llansantffraed Powys 96 G2
Llansantffraed-Cwmdeuddwr Powys 113 D9
Llansantffraed-in-Elwel Powys 113 G11
Llansantffraid-ym-Mechain Powys 148 E4
Llansawel = Briton Ferry Rh Cyn Taff 76 G2
Llansawel Carms 94 D2
Llansilin Powys 148 D4
Llansoy Monmouths 78 E6
Llanspyddid Powys 95 F10
Llanstadwell Pembs 73 D7
Llansteffan Carms 74 C5
Llanstephan Powys 96 C2
Llantarnam Torf 78 G4
Llanteg Pembs 73 C11
Llanteglos Pembs 73 D11
Llanthony Monmouths 96 F5
Llantilio Crossenny Monmouths 78 C5
Llantilio Pertholey Monmouths 78 B4
Llantood Pembs 92 C3
Llantrisant Angl 178 E5
Llantrisant Monmouths 78 F5
Llantrisant Rh Cyn Taff 58 C4
Llantrithyd V/Glam 58 E4
Llantwit Fardre Rh Cyn Taff 58 C5
Llantwit Major V/Glam 58 F3
Llanuwchllyn Gwyn 147 C7
Llanvaches Newp 78 G6
Llanvair Discoed Monmouths 78 G6
Llanvapley Monmouths 78 C5
Llanvetherine Monmouths 78 B5
Llanveynoe Heref'd 96 E6
Llanvihangel Gobion Monmouths 78 D4
Llanvihangel Pontymoel Torf 78 E4
Llanvihangel-Ystern-Llewern Monmouths 78 C6
Llanwarne Heref'd 97 F10
Llanwddyn Powys 147 F10
Llanwenarth Monmouths 78 C3
Llanwenog Ceredig'n 93 B9
Llanwern Newp 59 B11
Llanwinio Carms 92 F5
Llanwnda Gwyn 163 D7
Llanwnda Pembs 91 D8
Llanwnnen Ceredig'n 93 B10
Llanwnog Powys 129 E10
Llanwonno Rh Cyn Taff 77 F8
Llanwrda Carms 94 E4
Llanwrin Powys 128 C5
Llanwrthwl Powys 113 E9
Llanwrtud = Llanwrtyd Wells Powys 95 B7
Llanwrtyd Powys 95 B7
Llanwrtyd Wells = Llanwrtud Powys 95 B7
Llanwryglyn Powys 129 E8
Llanwyddelan Powys 129 C11
Llanyblodwel Shrops 148 E4
Llanybri Carms 74 C4
Llanybydder Carms 93 C10
Llanycefn Pembs 91 G11
Llanychaer Pembs 91 D9
Llanycil Gwyn 147 C8
Llanycrwys Carms 94 B2
Llanymawddwy Gwyn 147 F8
Llanymddyfri = Llandovery Carms 94 E5
Llanymynech Shrops 148 E5
Llanynghenedl Angl 178 E4
Llanynys Denbs 165 C10
Llan-y-pwll Wrex 166 E5
Llanyrafon Torf 78 F4
Llanyre Powys 113 E10
Llanystumdwy Gwyn 145 B9
Llanywern Powys 96 F2
Llawhaden Pembs 73 B9
Llawndy Flints 181 E10
Llawnt Shrops 148 C5
Llay Wrex 166 D4
Llechcynfarwy Angl 178 E5
Llecheiddior Gwyn 163 G7
Llechfaen Powys 95 F11
Llechfraith Gwyn 146 F3
Llechryd Caerph 77 D10
Llechryd Ceredig'n 92 C4
Llechwedd Conwy 180 F3
Llechwedd Slate Caverns, Blaenau Ffestiniog Gwyn 164 F2
Lledrod Ceredig'n 112 C2
Llenmerewig Powys 130 E3
Llethrid Swan 75 G8
Lletty Brongu Bridg 57 D11
Llidiadnenog Carms 93 D10
Llidiardau Gwyn 147 B7
Llidiart-y-Parc Denbs 165 G10
Llidiartywaen Powys 129 G10
Llingattock-Vibon-Avel Monmouths 79 B7
Llithfaen Gwyn 162 G5
Lloc Flints 181 F10
Llong Flints 166 C3
Llowes Powys 96 C3
Lloyney Powys 114 B4
Llugwy Gwyn 128 C4
Llundain-fach Ceredig'n 111 F11
Llwydcoed Rh Cyn Taff 77 E7
Llwyn Gwyn 146 B3
Llwyncelyn Ceredig'n 111 F8
Llwyndafydd Ceredig'n 111 F7
Llwynderw Powys 130 C4
Llwyndrain Carms 92 E5
Llwyn-du Monmouths 78 B3
Llwyn-du Swan 76 E2
Llwyndyrys Gwyn 162 G5
Llwyneinion Wrex 166 F3
Llwyngwril Gwyn 110 B2
Llwynhendy Carms 75 E8
Llwynmawr Wrex 148 B4
Llwyn-on-village Merth Tyd 77 C8
Llwyn-y-brain Carms 73 B11
Llwyn-y-Groes Ceredig'n 111 F11
Llwynymaen Shrops 148 D5
Llwynypia Rh Cyn Taff 77 G7
Llynclys Shrops 148 E5
Llynfaes Angl 178 F6
Llyn-y-Pandy Flints 166 B2
Llysdinam Powys 113 F10
Llysfaen Conwy 180 F5
Llysnewydd Carms 93 D7
Llyswen Powys 96 D2
Llysworney V/Glam 58 E3
Llys-y-Fran Pembs 91 G10
Llywel Powys 95 E7
Llywernog Ceredig'n 128 G4
Loan Falk 279 F9
Loandhu H'land 301 B8
Loanhead Aberds 302 D6
Loanhead Midloth 270 B5
Loanhead Perth/Kinr 286 D5
Loanreoch H'land 300 B6
Loans S Ayrs 257 C8
Loans of Tullich H'land 301 B8
Loansdean Northum 252 G5
Lobb Devon 40 F3
Lobhillcross Devon 12 D5
Lobley Hill Tyne/Wear 242 E6
Lobthorpe Lincs 155 E9
Loch a Charnain W Isles 297 G4
Loch a'Ghainmhich W Isles 304 F4
Loch Baghasdail = Lochboisdale W Isles 297 K3
Loch Choire Lodge H'land 308 F6
Loch Eil H'land 290 F2
Loch Euphoirt W Isles 296 E4
Loch Head Dumf/Gal 236 E5
Loch Loyal Lodge H'land 308 E6
Loch nam Madadh = Lochmaddy W Isles 296 E5
Loch Ness Monster Exhibition, Drumnadrochit H'land 300 F5
Loch Sgioport W Isles 297 H4
Lochailort H'land 295 G9
Lochaline H'land 289 E8
Lochanhully H'land 301 G9
Lochans Dumf/Gal 236 D2
Locharbriggs Dumf/Gal 247 G11
Lochassynt Lodge H'land 307 G6
Lochavich Ho Arg/Bute 275 B10
Lochawe Arg/Bute 284 E5
Lochboisdale = Loch Baghasdail W Isles 297 K3
Lochbuie Arg/Bute 289 G8
Lochbuie Ho Arg/Bute 289 G8
Lochcallater Lodge Aberds 292 E3
Lochcarron H'land 295 B10
Lochdhu H'land 310 E4
Lochdochart House Stirl 285 E8
Lochdon Arg/Bute 289 F9
Lochdrum H'land 300 B2
Lochead Arg/Bute 275 E11
Lochead Arg/Bute 275 F8
Lochearnhead Stirl 285 E9
Lochee Dundee C 287 D7
Lochend H'land 300 F5
Lochend H'land 310 C6
Lochend Ho. Stirl 285 H9
Lochetive Ho. H'land 284 C5
Lochfoot Dumf/Gal 237 B10
Lochgair Arg/Bute 275 D10
Lochgarthside H'land 291 B7
Lochgelly Fife 280 C3
Lochgilphead Arg/Bute 275 E9
Lochgoilhead Arg/Bute 284 G6
Lochhill Moray 302 C2
Lochhussie H'land 300 D4
Lochinch Castle Dumf/Gal 236 C3
Lochindorb Lodge H'land 301 F9
Lochinver H'land 307 G5
Lochlane Perth/Kinr 286 E2
Lochletter H'land 300 G4
Lochluichart H'land 300 C3
Lochmaben Dumf/Gal 248 G3
Lochmaddy = Loch nam Madadh W Isles 296 E5
Lochmore Cottage H'land 310 E4
Lochmore Lodge H'land 306 F7
Lochnell Ho Arg/Bute 289 F10
Lochore Fife 280 B3
Lochorodale Arg/Bute 255 F7
Lochportain W Isles 296 D5
Lochranza N Ayrs 255 B10
Lochs Crofts Moray 302 C3
Lochside Aberds 293 G9
Lochside Dumf/Gal 247 H11
Lochside H'land 301 D8
Lochside H'land 308 D4
Lochside H'land 310 F2
Lochslin H'land 311 L2
Lochstack Lodge H'land 306 E7
Lochton Aberds 293 D9
Lochton Scot Borders 263 B7
Lochty Angus 293 G7
Lochty Fife 287 G9
Lochty Perth/Kinr 286 E4
Lochuisge H'land 289 D9
Lochurr Dumf/Gal 247 F7
Lochwinnoch Renf 267 D7
Lochwood Glasg C 268 B3
Lochwood Dumf/Gal 248 D3
Lochyside H'land 290 F3
Lockengate Cornw'l 5 C10
Lockerbie Dumf/Gal 248 G4
Lockeridge Wilts 62 F6
Lockerley Hants 32 B3
Lockhills Cumb 230 B6
Locking N Som'set 43 B11
Locking Stumps Warrington 183 C10
Lockington ER Yorks 208 D5
Lockington Leics 153 D9
Lockleaze Bristol 60 D6
Lockleywood Shrops 150 D3
Locks Heath Hants 33 F8
Locksbottom London 68 G2
Locksbrook Bath/NE Som'set 61 F8
Locksgreen I/Wight 20 C4
Lockton N Yorks 216 B6
Lockwood W Yorks 196 D6
Lockwood W Yorks 196 D6
Locomotion Museum, Shildon Durham 233 F10
Loddington Leics 136 C5
Loddington Northants 120 B6
Loddiswell Devon 8 F4
Loddon Norfolk 143 D7
Lode Cambs 123 E10
Lode Heath W Midlands 134 G3
Loders Dorset 16 C5
Lodge Green W Midlands 134 G5
Lodge Hill Cornw'l 6 C4
Lodge Hill W Midlands 133 G10
Lodge Lees Kent 55 D8
Lodsworth W Sussex 34 C6
Lodway N Som'set 60 D4
Lofthouse N Yorks 214 E2
Lofthouse W Yorks 197 B10
Lofthouse Gate W Yorks 197 C10
Loftus Redcar/Clevel'd 226 B4
Logan E Ayrs 258 E3
Logan Mains Dumf/Gal 236 E2
Loganlea W Loth 269 C9
Logaston Heref'd 114 G6
Loggerheads Staffs 150 B4
Logie Angus 293 G8
Logie Fife 287 E8
Logie Moray 301 D10
Logie Coldstone Aberds 292 C6
Logie Hill H'land 301 B7
Logie Newton Aberds 302 F6
Logie Pert Angus 293 G8
Logiealmond Lodge Perth/Kinr 286 D3
Logierait Perth/Kinr 286 B3
Login Carms 92 G3
Loidse Mhorsgail W Isles 304 F3
Lolworth Cambs 123 E7
Lonbain H'land 298 D6
Londesborough ER Yorks 208 D3
London Apprentice Cornw'l 5 E10
London Beach Kent 53 F11
London City Airport London 68 C2
London Colney Herts 85 E11
London Fields W Midlands 133 E8
London Gatwick Airport W Sussex 51 E9
London Heathrow Airport London 66 D5
London Luton Airport Luton 104 G2
London Minstead Hants 32 E3
London Stansted Airport Essex 105 G10
London Zoo London 67 C9
Londonderry N Yorks 214 B6
Londonderry W Midlands 133 F10
Londonthorpe Lincs 155 B9
Londubh H'land 307 L3
Lonemore H'land 299 B7
Lonemore H'land 309 L7
Long Ashton N Som'set 60 E4
Long Bank Worcs 116 C5
Long Bennington Lincs 172 G4
Long Bredy Dorset 17 C7
Long Buckby Northants 120 D2
Long Buckby Wharf Northants 120 D2
Long Clawson Leics 154 D4
Long Common Hants 33 E8
Long Compton Staffs 151 E7
Long Compton Warwick 100 E5
Long Crendon Bucks 83 D11
Long Crichel Dorset 31 E7
Long Cross N Som'set 60 F4
Long Cross Wilts 45 G9
Long Dean Wilts 61 D11
Long Ditton Surrey 67 F7
Long Drax N Yorks 199 B7
Long Duckmanton Derby 186 G6
Long Eaton Derby 153 C9
Long Gardens Essex 106 D6
Long Green Ches 183 G7
Long Green Worcs 98 E6
Long Hanborough Oxon 82 C6
Long Honeyborough Pembs 73 D7
Long Itchington Warwick 119 D8
Long John's Hill Norfolk 142 B4
Long Lane Telford 150 F2
Long Lawford Warwick 119 B9
Long Load Som'set 29 C7
Long Marston Herts 84 B5
Long Marston N Yorks 206 C6
Long Marston Warwick 100 B3
Long Marton Cumb 231 G9
Long Meadow Cambs 123 E10
Long Meadowend Shrops 131 G8
Long Melford Suffolk 107 B7
Long Moor Wokingham 65 G9
Long Newnton Glos 80 G6
Long Newton E Loth 271 C10
Long Park Hants 48 G2
Long Preston N Yorks 204 B2
Long Riston ER Yorks 209 E8
Long Sandall S Yorks 198 F6
Long Sight Gtr Man 196 F2
Long Stratton Norfolk 142 E3
Long Street M/Keynes 102 B5
Long Sutton Hants 49 D8
Long Sutton Lincs 157 E8
Long Sutton Som'set 29 B7
Long Thurlow Suffolk 125 D10
Long Whatton Leics 153 E9
Long Wittenham Oxon 83 G8
Longbar N Ayrs 266 E6
Longbenton Tyne/Wear 243 D7
Longborough Glos 100 F3
Longbridge Plym'th 7 D10
Longbridge Staffs 151 F8
Longbridge Warwick 118 E5
Longbridge W Midlands 117 B10
Longbridge Deverill Wilts 45 E11
Longburgh Cumb 239 F8
Longburton Dorset 29 E10
Longcause Devon 8 C5
Longcliffe Derby 170 D2
Longcombe Devon 8 D6
Longcot Oxon 82 G3
Longcroft Cumb 238 F6
Longcroft Falk 278 F5
Longcross Surrey 66 F3
Longdale Cumb 222 D2
Longdales Cumb 230 C6
Longden Shrops 131 B8
Longden Common Shrops 131 C8
Longdenwood Shrops 131 B9
Longdon Staffs 151 G11
Longdon Worcs 98 D6
Longdon Green Staffs 151 G11
Longdon Heath Worcs 98 D6
Longdon-on-Tern Telford 150 F2
Longdown Devon 14 C3
Longdowns Cornw'l 2 C6
Longdrum Angus 292 G4
Longfield Kent 68 F6
Longfield Shetl'd 315 M5
Longfield Wilts 45 B10
Longfield Hill Kent 68 F6
Longfleet Poole 18 C6
Longford Derby 152 B4
Longford Glos 98 G6
Longford Kent 52 B4
Longford London 66 D5
Longford Shrops 150 C2
Longford Telford 150 F4
Longford W Midlands 135 G7
Longford Warrington 183 C10
Longforgan Perth/Kinr 287 E7
Longformacus Scot Borders 272 D3
Longframlington Northum 252 C4
Longham Dorset 19 B7
Longham Norfolk 159 F8
Longhaven Aberds 303 F11
Longhedge Wilts 45 E10
Longhill Aberds 303 D9
Longhill S Ayrs 257 F8
Longhirst Northum 252 F6
Longhope Glos 79 B11
Longhope Orkney 313 J4
Longhorsley Northum 252 E5
Longhoughton Northum 264 F6
Longlands Cumb 229 D11
Longlands Lincs 191 E7
Longlands London 68 E3
Longlane Derby 152 B5
Longlane W Berks 64 E4
Longleat House Wilts 45 E10
Longlevens Glos 99 G7
Longley W Yorks 196 F6
Longley W Yorks 196 C4
Longley Estate S Yorks 186 C5
Longley Green Worcs 116 G4
Longleys Perth/Kinr 286 C6
Longmanhill Aberds 303 C7
Longmoor Camp Hants 49 G9
Longmorn Moray 302 D2
Longmoss Ches 184 G5
Longnewton Scot Borders 262 D3
Longnewton Stockton 225 B7
Longney Glos 80 C3
Longniddry E Loth 281 F8
Longnor Shrops 131 C9
Longnor Staffs 169 C9
Longparish Hants 48 E2
Longpark Cumb 239 E10
Longpark E Ayrs 257 B10
Longport Stoke 168 F5
Longridge Glos 80 D5
Longridge Lancs 203 F8
Longridge W Loth 269 C8
Longridge End Glos 98 G6
Longrigg N Lanarks 278 G6
Longriggend N Lanarks 278 G6
Longrock Cornw'l 1 C5
Longsdon Staffs 169 E7
Longshaw Gtr Man 194 G4
Longside Aberds 303 E10
Longsight Gtr Man 184 C5
Longslow Shrops 150 B3
Longsowerby Cumb 239 G9
Longstanton Cambs 123 D7
Longstock Hants 47 F11
Longstone C/Edinb 280 G4
Longstone Cornw'l 11 G7
Longstone Cornw'l 2 B2
Longstone Pembs 73 D10
Longstowe Cambs 122 G6
Longstreet Wilts 46 C6
Longthorpe Peterbro 138 D3
Longton Lancs 194 B3
Longton Stoke 168 G6
Longton Hill End Worcs 98 D6
Longtown Cumb 239 D9
Longtown Heref'd 96 F6
Longtownmail Orkney 313 H5
Longview Mersey 182 C6
Longville in the Dale Shrops 131 E10
Longwell Green S Glos 61 E7
Longwick Bucks 84 D3
Longwitton Northum 252 F3
Longwood W Yorks 196 D6
Longwood Edge W Yorks 196 D6
Longworth Oxon 82 F5
Longyester E Loth 271 B10
Lon-las Rh Cyn Taff 76 F2
Lonmay Aberds 303 D10
Lonmore H'land 298 E2
Looe Cornw'l 6 E5
Looe Mills Cornw'l 6 C4
Loose Kent 53 C9
Loosebeare Devon 26 F2
Loosegate Lincs 156 D6
Loosley Row Bucks 84 E4
Lopcombe Corner Wilts 47 F9
Lopen Som'set 28 E6
Loppington Shrops 149 D9
Lopwell Devon 7 B9
Lordington W Sussex 34 F3
Lord's Cricket Ground London 67 C9
Lord's Hill S'thampton 32 D5
Lords Wood Medway 69 G9
Lordsbridge Norfolk 157 G11
Lornty Perth/Kinr 286 C5
Loscoe Derby 170 F6
Loscombe Dorset 16 B6
Losgaintir W Isles 305 J2
Lossiemouth Moray 302 B2
Lossit Arg/Bute 254 B2
Lossit Lodge Arg/Bute 274 G5
Lostock Gralam Ches 183 F11
Lostock Green Ches 183 G11
Lostock Hall Lancs 194 B4
Lostock Junction Gtr Man 195 F7
Lostwithiel Cornw'l 6 D2
Loth Orkney 312 E7
Lothbeg H'land 311 H3
Lothersdale N Yorks 204 D5
Lothianbridge Midloth 270 B6
Lothmore H'land 311 H3
Lottisham Som'set 44 G5
Loudwater Bucks 84 G6
Loudwater Herts 85 F9
Loughborough Leics 153 F10
Loughor Swan 75 F9
Loughton Essex 86 F6
Loughton Lincs 155 C11
Loughton M/Keynes 102 D6
Loughton Shrops 132 G2
Louis Tussaud's Waxworks Blackp'l 202 F2
Lound Lincs 155 F11
Lound Notts 187 D11
Lound Suffolk 143 D10
Lount Leics 153 F7
Lour Angus 287 C8
Louth Lincs 190 D4
Lovat H'land 300 E5
Love Clough Lancs 195 B10
Love Green Bucks 66 C4
Lovedean Hants 33 E11
Lover Wilts 32 C2
Loversall S Yorks 187 B9
Loves Green Essex 87 E10
Loveston Pembs 73 D9
Lovington Som'set 44 G5
Low Ackworth W Yorks 198 D3
Low Angerton Northum 252 G3
Low Bentham N Yorks 212 F3
Low Biggins Cumb 212 D2
Low Blantyre S Lanarks 268 D3
Low Bolton N Yorks 223 F10
Low Borrowbridge Cumb 222 E2
Low Bradfield S Yorks 186 B3
Low Bradley N Yorks 204 D6
Low Braithwaite Cumb 230 C4
Low Brunton Northum 241 D10
Low Burnham N Lincs 199 G9
Low Catton ER Yorks 207 C10
Low Clanyard Dumf/Gal 236 F3
Low Common Norfolk 141 G11
Low Common Norfolk 142 E2
Low Common Norfolk 160 C4
Low Compton Gtr Man 196 F2
Low Coniscliffe N Yorks 224 C5
Low Cotehill Cumb 239 G11

Manningford Bruce Wilts 46 B6
Manningham W Yorks 205 G9
Manning's Common Devon 28 E2
Mannings Heath W Sussex 36 B2
Mannington Dorset 31 F9
Manningtree Essex 108 E2
Mannofield Aberd C 293 C11
Manor Bourne Devon 7 F9
Manor Estate S Yorks 186 D5
Manor Park Bucks 84 C4
Manor Park Ches 167 B11
Manor Park Halton 183 E8
Manor Park London 68 B2
Manor Park Notts 153 C11
Manor Park Slough 66 C3
Manor Park S Yorks 186 D5
Manor Parsley Cornw'l 4 F4
Manor Powis Stirl 278 B6
Manorbier = Maenorbŷr Pembs 73 F9
Manorbier Newton Pembs 73 F8
Manordeifi Pembs 92 C4
Manordeilo Carms 94 F3
Manselfield Swan 56 D5
Mansell Gamage Heref'd 97 C7
Mansell Lacy Heref'd 97 B8
Manselton Swan 75 F11
Mansergh Cumb 212 C2
Mansewood Glasg C 267 C11
Mansfield E Ayrs 258 G4
Mansfield Notts 171 C8
Mansfield Woodhouse Notts 171 C8
Manson Green Norfolk 141 C10
Mansriggs Cumb 210 C5
Manston Dorset 30 D4
Manston Kent 71 F11
Manston W Yorks 206 F3
Manswood Dorset 31 F7
Manthorpe Lincs 155 F11
Mantles Green Bucks 85 F7
Manton Notts 187 G10
Manton Rutl'd 137 C7
Manton Wilts 63 F7
Manuden Essex 105 G9
Manwood Green Essex 87 C8
Manx Electric Railway I/Man 192 C5
Maperton Som'set 29 B11
Maple Cross Herts 85 G8
Maple End Essex 105 D11
Maplebeck Notts 172 C2
Mapledurham Oxon 65 D7
Mapledurwell Hants 49 C7
Maplehurst W Sussex 35 C11
Maplescombe Kent 68 G4
Mapleton Derby 169 F11
Mapleton Kent 52 D3
Mapperley Nott'ham 171 G9
Mapperley Derby 170 G6
Mapperley Park Nott'ham 171 G9
Mapperton Dorset 16 B6
Mapperton Dorset 18 B4
Mappleborough Green Warwick 117 D11
Mappleton ER Yorks 209 E10
Mapplewell S Yorks 197 F10
Mappowder Dorset 30 F2
Mar Lodge Aberds 292 D2
Maraig W Isles 305 H3
Marazanvose Cornw'l 4 E6
Marazion Cornw'l 2 C3
Marbhig W Isles 305 G6
Marbury Ches 167 F9
March Cambs 139 D8
March S Lanarks 259 G11
Marcham Oxon 83 F7
Marchamley Shrops 149 D11
Marchamley Wood Shrops 149 C11
Marchington Staffs 152 C2
Marchington Woodlands Staffs 152 D2
Marchwiel Wrex 166 F5
Marchwood Hants 32 E5
Marcle Hill Heref'd 98 E2
Marcross V/Glam 58 F2
Marden Heref'd 97 B10
Marden Kent 53 E8
Marden Tyne/Wear 243 C9
Marden Wilts 46 B5
Marden Ash Essex 87 E9
Marden Beech Kent 53 E8
Marden Thorn Kent 53 E9
Marden's Hill E Sussex 52 G4
Mardleybury Herts 86 B3
Mardon Northum 263 B10
Mardu Shrops 130 G5
Mardy Monmouths 78 B4
Marefield Bucks 65 B10
Marefield Leics 136 B4
Mareham Gate Lincs 174 D3
Mareham le Fen Lincs 174 C3
Mareham on the Hill Lincs 174 B3
Marehay Derby 170 F5
Marehill W Sussex 35 D9
Maresfield E Sussex 37 C7
Marfleet Kingston/Hull 200 B6
Marford Wrex 166 D5
Margam Neath P Talb 57 D9
Margaret Marsh Dorset 30 D4
Margaret Roding Essex 87 C9
Margaretta Norfolk 157 F11
Margaretting Essex 87 E11
Margaretting Tye Essex 87 E11
Margate Kent 71 E11
Margery Surrey 51 C9
Margnaheglish N Ayrs 256 C2
Margreig Dumf/Gal 237 B10
Margrove Park Redcar/Clevel'd 226 B3
Marham Norfolk 140 B4
Marhamchurch Cornw'l 24 G2
Marholm Peterbro 138 C2
Marian Denbs 181 F9
Marian Cwm Denbs 181 F9
Marian Ffrith Denbs 181 F9
Marianglas Angl 179 E8
Mariansleigh Devon 26 C2
Marian-y-de Gwyn 145 C7
Marian-y-mor Gwyn 145 C7
Marine Town Kent 70 E2
Marionburgh Aberds 293 C9
Marishader H'land 298 C4
Marjoriebanks Dumf/Gal 248 G3
Mark Dumf/Gal 236 D3
Mark Dumf/Gal 237 C7
Mark S Ayrs 236 B2
Mark Som'set 43 D11
Mark Causeway Som'set 43 D11
Mark Cross E Sussex 37 E7
Mark Cross E Sussex 52 G5
Mark Hall North Essex 87 C7
Mark Hall South Essex 87 C7
Markbeech Kent 52 E3
Markby Lincs 191 F7
Markeaton Derby C 152 B6
Market Bosworth Leics 135 C8
Market Deeping Lincs 156 G2
Market Drayton Shrops 150 C3
Market End Warwick 134 F6
Market Harborough Leics 136 F4
Market Lavington Wilts 46 C4
Market Overton Rutl'd 155 F7
Market Rasen Lincs 189 D10
Market Rasen Racecourse Lincs 189 D10
Market Stainton Lincs 190 F2
Market Warsop Notts 171 B9
Market Weighton ER Yorks 208 E3
Market Weston Suffolk 125 B9
Markethill Perth/Kinr 286 D6
Markfield Leics 153 G9
Markham Caerph 77 E11
Markham Moor Notts 188 G2
Markinch Fife 286 G6
Markington N Yorks 214 G5
Markland Hill Gtr Man 195 F7
Marks Gate London 87 G7
Marks Tey Essex 107 G8
Marksbury Bath/NE Som'set 61 G7
Markyate Herts 85 B9
Marl Bank Worcs 98 C5
Marland Gtr Man 195 E11
Marlas Heref'd 97 F8
Marlborough Wilts 63 F7
Marlbrook Heref'd 115 G10
Marlbrook Worcs 117 C9
Marlcliff Warwick 117 G11
Marldon Devon 9 C7
Marle Green E Sussex 37 D9
Marle Hill Glos 99 G8
Marlesford Suffolk 126 F6
Marley Kent 55 C7
Marley Kent 55 C10
Marley Green Ches 167 F9
Marley Hill Tyne/Wear 242 F6
Marlingford Norfolk 142 B2
Marloes Pembs 72 D3
Marlow Bucks 65 B11
Marlow Heref'd 115 B8
Marlow Bottom Bucks 65 B10
Marlpit Hill Kent 52 D2
Marlpits E Sussex 38 E2
Marlpits E Sussex 37 B7
Marlpool Derby 170 F6
Marnhull Dorset 30 D3
Marnoch Aberds 302 D5
Marnock N Lanarks 268 B4
Marple Gtr Man 185 D7
Marple Bridge Gtr Man 185 D7
Marpleridge Gtr Man 185 D7
Marr S Yorks 198 F4
Marrel H'land 311 H4
Marrick N Yorks 223 F11
Marridge Hill Wilts 63 E9
Marrister Shetl'd 315 G7
Marros Carms 74 D2
Marsden Tyne/Wear 243 E9
Marsden W Yorks 196 E4
Marsden Hall Lancs 204 F3
Marsden Height Lancs 204 F3
Marsett N Yorks 213 B8
Marsh Bucks 84 D4
Marsh Devon 28 E3
Marsh W Yorks 196 D6
Marsh W Yorks 204 F6
Marsh W Yorks 197 B7
Marsh Baldon Oxon 83 F9
Marsh Benham W Berks 64 F2
Marsh End Worcs 98 D6
Marsh Gibbon Bucks 102 G2
Marsh Green Ches 183 F8
Marsh Green Devon 14 C6
Marsh Green Gtr Man 194 F5
Marsh Green Kent 52 E2
Marsh Green Staffs 168 D5
Marsh Green Telford 150 G2
Marsh Lane Derby 186 F6
Marsh Lane Glos 79 D9
Marsh Leys Beds 103 B10
Marsh Street Som'set 42 E3
Marshall's Cross Mersey 183 C8
Marshall's Elm Som'set 44 G3
Marshall's Heath Herts 85 C11
Marshalswick Herts 85 D11
Marsham Norfolk 160 E3
Marshaw Lancs 203 C7
Marshborough Kent 55 B10
Marshbrook Shrops 131 F8
Marshchapel Lincs 190 B5
Marshfield Newp 59 C9
Marshfield S Glos 61 E9
Marshgate Cornw'l 11 C9
Marshland St. James Norfolk 139 B10
Marshside Kent 71 F8
Marshside Mersey 193 D11
Marshwood Dorset 16 B3
Marske N Yorks 224 E2
Marske-by-the-Sea Redcar/Clevel'd 235 G8
Marsland Green Gtr Man 183 B11
Marston Ches 183 F11
Marston Heref'd 115 F7
Marston Lincs 172 G5
Marston Oxon 83 D8
Marston Staffs 150 G6
Marston Staffs 151 D8
Marston Warwick 134 E4
Marston Wilts 46 B3
Marston Bigot Som'set 45 E9
Marston Doles Warwick 119 F9
Marston Green W Midlands 134 F3
Marston Hill Glos 81 F10
Marston Jabbett Warwick 135 F7
Marston Junction Warwick 135 F7
Marston Magna Som'set 29 C9
Marston Meysey Wilts 81 F10
Marston Montgomery Derby 152 B2
Marston Moretaine Beds 103 C9
Marston on Dove Derby 152 D4
Marston St. Lawrence Northants 101 C10
Marston Trussell Northants 136 F3
Marstow Heref'd 79 B9
Marsworth Bucks 84 C6
Marten Wilts 63 G9
Marthall Ches 184 F4
Martham Norfolk 161 F9
Marthwaite Cumb 222 G2
Martin Hants 31 D9
Martin Kent 55 D10
Martin Lincs 174 B2
Martin Lincs 173 C10
Martin Drove End Hants 31 C9
Martin Hussingtree Worcs 117 F7
Martin Mill Kent 55 D10
Martindale Cumb 221 B8
Martinhoe Devon 41 D7
Martinscroft Warrington 183 D10
Martinslade Wilts 62 G3
Martinstown Dorset 17 D8
Martlesham Suffolk 108 B5
Martlesham Heath Suffolk 108 B5
Martletwy Pembs 73 C8
Martley Worcs 116 F5
Martock Som'set 29 D7
Marton Ches 168 B5
Marton Cumb 210 D4
Marton ER Yorks 209 F9
Marton Lincs 188 E4
Marton Middlesbro 225 B10
Marton N Yorks 215 G8
Marton N Yorks 216 C4
Marton Shrops 130 C5
Marton Shrops 149 E8
Marton Warwick 119 D8
Marton Grove Middlesbro 225 B9
Marton Moss Side Blackp'l 202 G2
Marton-in-the-Forest N Yorks 216 F2
Marton-le Moor N Yorks 215 E7
Martyr Worthy Hants 48 G4
Martyr's Green Surrey 50 B5
Marus Bridge Gtr Man 194 G5
Marwell Zoo, Bishop's Waltham Hants 33 C8
Marwick Orkney 312 F3
Marwood Devon 40 F4
Mary Arden's House, Wilmcote Warwick 118 F3
Mary Rose Portsm'th 33 G10
Mary Tavy Devon 12 F6
Marybank H'land 300 D4
Marybank H'land 301 B7
Maryburgh H'land 300 D5
Maryfield Aberds 293 D7
Maryfield Cornw'l 7 D8
Maryhill Glasg C 267 B11
Marykirk Aberds 293 G8
Maryland Monmouths 79 D8
Marylebone Gtr Man 194 F5
Marylebone London 67 C9
Marypark Moray 301 F11
Maryport Cumb 228 D6
Maryport Dumf/Gal 236 F3
Marystow Devon 12 E4
Maryton Angus 287 B10
Maryton Angus 287 B7
Marywell Aberds 293 D11
Marywell Aberds 293 D7
Marywell Angus 287 C10
Masbrough S Yorks 186 C6
Masham N Yorks 214 C4
Mashbury Essex 87 C11
Mason Tyne/Wear 242 C6
Masongill N Yorks 212 D2
Masonhill S Ayrs 257 E9
Mastin Moor Derby 187 F7
Mastrick Aberd C 293 C10
Matchborough Worcs 117 D11
Matching Essex 87 C8
Matching Green Essex 87 C8
Matching Tye Essex 87 C8
Matfen Northum 242 C2
Matfield Kent 53 E7
Mathern Monmouths 79 G8
Mathon Heref'd 98 B4
Mathrafal Powys 148 G2
Mathry Pembs 91 E7
Matlaske Norfolk 160 C3
Matlock Derby 170 C4
Matlock Bank Derby 170 C3
Matlock Bath Derby 170 D3
Matlock Bridge Derby 170 D3
Matlock Dale Derby 170 D3
Matlock Moor Derby 170 C4
Matravers Dorset 16 C6
Matshead Lancs 202 E6
Matson Glos 80 B4
Matterdale End Cumb 230 G3
Mattersey Notts 187 D11
Mattersey Thorpe Notts 187 C11
Matthewsgreen Wokingham 65 F10
Mattingley Hants 49 B8
Mattishall Norfolk 159 G10
Mattishall Burgh Norfolk 159 G11
Mauchline E Ayrs 258 D2
Maud Aberds 303 E9
Maudlin Cornw'l 5 C11
Maudlin W Sussex 34 F5
Maugersbury Glos 100 F4
Maughold I/Man 192 C5
Mauld H'land 300 F4
Maulden Beds 103 D11
Maulds Meaburn Cumb 222 B2
Maunby N Yorks 215 B7
Maund Bryan Heref'd 115 G10
Maundown Som'set 27 B8
Mautby Norfolk 161 G9
Mavesyn Ridware Staffs 151 F11
Mavis Enderby Lincs 174 B5
Maviston H'land 301 D9
Maw Green Ches 168 D2
Mawbray Cumb 229 B7
Mawdesley Lancs 194 E3
Mawdlam Bridg 57 E10
Mawgan Cornw'l 2 E6
Mawgan Porth Cornw'l 4 B6
Mawla Cornw'l 4 F4
Mawnan Cornw'l 3 D7
Mawnan Smith Cornw'l 3 D7
Mawsley Northants 120 B6
Mawthorpe Lincs 191 G7
Maxey Peterbro 138 B2
Maxstoke Warwick 134 F4
Maxted Street Kent 54 E6
Maxton Scot Borders 262 C4
Maxton Kent 55 E10
Maxwellheugh Scot Borders 262 C6
Maxwelltown Dumf/Gal 237 B11
Maxworthy Cornw'l 11 C11
May Bank Staffs 168 F5
May Hill Monmouths 79 C8
Mayals Swan 75 G10
Maybole S Ayrs 245 B8
Maybury Surrey 50 B4
Maybush S'thampton 32 E5
Mayes Green Surrey 50 F6
Mayeston Pembs 73 E8
Mayfair London 67 C9
Mayfield E Sussex 37 B9
Mayfield Midloth 271 C7
Mayfield N Ayrs 266 G5
Mayfield Northum 243 B7
Mayfield Staffs 169 F11
Mayfield W Loth 269 B8
Mayford Surrey 50 B3
Mayhill Swan 75 G10
Mayland Essex 88 E6
Maylandsea Essex 88 E6
Maynard's Green E Sussex 37 D9
Mayne Ho. Moray 302 C2
Mayon Cornw'l 1 D3
Maypole Kent 71 G7
Maypole Kent 68 E4
Maypole London 68 G3
Maypole Monmouths 79 B7
Maypole W Midlands 117 B11
Maypole Green Essex 107 G9
Maypole Green Norfolk 143 D8
Maypole Green Suffolk 126 D5
Maypole Green Suffolk 125 F8
May's Green N Som'set 59 G11
Mays Green Oxon 65 D8
Mayshill S Glos 61 C7
Maythorn S Yorks 197 F7
Maywick Shetl'd 315 L5
Mead Devon 13 G11
Mead Devon 24 D2
Mead End Hants 19 B11
Mead End Hants 33 E11
Mead End Wilts 31 C8
Mead Vale Surrey 51 D9
Meadgate Bath/NE Som'set 45 B7
Meadle Bucks 84 D4
Meadow Derby 185 G10
Meadow Green Heref'd 116 F4
Meadow Head S Yorks 186 E4
Meadowbank Ches 167 B10
Meadowfield Durham 233 D10
Meadowfoot N Ayrs 266 F4
Meadowmill E Loth 281 G8
Meadows Nott'ham 153 B11
Meadowtown Shrops 130 C6
Meads E Sussex 23 F10
Meadside Oxon 83 G9
Meadwell Devon 12 E4
Meal Bank Cumb 221 F10
Mealabost W Isles 304 E6
Mealabost Bhuirgh W Isles 304 C6
Mealasta W Isles 304 F1
Mealrigg Cumb 229 B8
Mealsgate Cumb 229 C10
Mean Ham Glos 80 B4
Meanwood W Yorks 205 F11
Mearbeck N Yorks 212 G6
Meare Som'set 44 E3
Meare Green Som'set 28 C3
Meare Green Som'set 28 B4
Mearns E Renf 267 D10
Mears Ashby Northants 120 D6
Measborough Dike S Yorks 197 F11
Measham Leics 152 G6
Meath Green Surrey 51 E9
Meathop Cumb 211 C9
Meaux ER Yorks 209 F7
Meavy Devon 7 B10
Medbourne Leics 136 E5
Medburn Northum 242 C4
Meddon Devon 24 D3
Meden Vale Notts 171 B9
Medlam Lincs 174 D4
Medlar Lancs 202 F4
Medlock Vale Gtr Man 184 B6
Medlyn Cornw'l 2 C6
Medmenham Bucks 65 C10
Medomsley Durham 242 G4
Medstead Hants 49 F7
Meer Common Heref'd 115 G7
Meer End W Midlands 118 C4
Meerbrook Staffs 169 C7
Meers Bank Lincs 191 D7
Meers Bridge Lincs 191 D7
Meersbrook S Yorks 186 E4
Meesden Herts 105 E8
Meeth Devon 25 F8
Meethe Devon 25 C11
Meeting Green Suffolk 124 F4
Meeting House Hill Norfolk 160 D6
Meggernie Castle Perth/Kinr 285 C9
Meggethead Scot Borders 260 E5
Meidrim Carms 92 G5
Meifod Powys 148 G3
Meigle Perth/Kinr 286 C6
Meikle Earnock S Lanarks 268 E4
Meikle Ferry H'land 309 L7
Meikle Forter Angus 292 G3
Meikle Gluich H'land 309 L6
Meikle Obney Perth/Kinr 286 D4
Meikle Pinkerton E Loth 282 F4
Meikle Strath Aberds 293 F8
Meikle Tarty Aberds 303 G9
Meikle Wartle Aberds 303 F7
Meikleour Perth/Kinr 286 D5
Meinciau Carms 75 C7
Meir Stoke 168 G6
Meir Heath Staffs 151 B8
Melbourn Cambs 105 C7
Melbourne Derby 153 D7
Melbourne ER Yorks 207 E10
Melbourne S Lanarks 269 G11
Melbury Abbas Dorset 30 C5
Melbury Bubb Dorset 29 F9
Melbury Osmond Dorset 29 F9
Melbury Sampford Dorset 29 F9
Melby Shetl'd 315 H3
Melchbourne Beds 121 D10
Melcombe Som'set 43 G9
Melcombe Bingham Dorset 30 G3
Melcombe Regis Dorset 17 E9
Meldon Devon 13 C7
Meldon Northum 252 G4
Meldreth Cambs 105 B7
Meldrum Ho. Aberds 303 G8
Meledor Cornw'l 5 E8
Melfort Arg/Bute 275 B9
Melgarve H'land 290 D6
Meliden = Gallt Melyd Denbs 181 E9
Melin Meredydd Denbs 165 D10
Melinbyrhedyn Powys 128 D6
Melincourt Neath P Talb 76 E4
Melincryddan Rh Cyn Taff 76 F2
Melin-y-coed Conwy 164 C4
Melin-y-ddôl Powys 129 B11
Melin-y-Grogue Shrops 114 B4
Melin-y-wig Denbs 165 F8
Melkinthorpe Cumb 231 F7
Melkridge Northum 240 E6
Melksham Wilts 62 G2
Melksham Forest Wilts 62 G2
Mell Green W Berks 64 D3
Mellangaun H'land 307 L3
Melldalloch Arg/Bute 275 F10
Mellguards Cumb 230 B4
Melling Lancs 211 E11
Melling Mersey 193 G11
Melling Mount Mersey 194 G2
Mellis Suffolk 126 C2
Mellon Charles H'land 307 K3
Mellon Udrigle H'land 307 K3
Mellor Gtr Man 185 D7
Mellor Lancs 203 G9
Mellor Brook Lancs 203 G8
Mells Som'set 45 D8
Mells Green Som'set 45 D8
Melmerby Cumb 231 D8
Melmerby N Yorks 214 D6
Melmerby N Yorks 213 B11
Melon Green Suffolk 124 F6
Melplash Dorset 16 B5
Melrose Scot Borders 262 C2
Melsetter Orkney 313 K3
Melsonby N Yorks 224 D3
Meltham W Yorks 196 E5
Meltham Mills W Yorks 196 E6
Melton ER Yorks 200 B3
Melton Suffolk 126 G5
Melton Constable Norfolk 159 C10
Melton Mowbray Leics 154 F5
Melton Ross N Lincs 200 E5
Meltonby ER Yorks 207 C11
Melvaig H'land 307 L2
Melverley Shrops 148 F6
Melverley Green Shrops 148 F6
Melvich H'land 310 C2
Membland Devon 7 F11
Membury Devon 28 G3
Memsie Aberds 303 C9
Memus Angus 287 B8
Menabilly Cornw'l 6 E2
Menagissey Cornw'l 4 F4
Menai Bridge = Porthaethwy Angl 179 G9
Mendham Suffolk 142 G5
Mendlesham Suffolk 126 D2
Mendlesham Green Suffolk 125 E11
Menethorpe N Yorks 216 F5
Mengham Hants 22 D2
Menheniot Cornw'l 6 C5
Menherion Cornw'l 2 B6
Menithwood Worcs 116 D4
Menna Cornw'l 5 E8
Mennock Dumf/Gal 247 B8
Menston W Yorks 205 E9
Menstrie Clack 279 B7
Mentmore Bucks 84 B6
Meoble H'land 295 G9
Meole Brace Shrops 149 G9
Meols Mersey 182 C2
Meonstoke Hants 33 D10
Meopham Kent 68 F6
Meopham Green Kent 68 F6
Meopham Station Kent 68 F6
Mepal Cambs 139 G8
Meppershall Beds 104 D2
Merbach Heref'd 96 B6
Merchiston C/Edinb 280 G4
Mere Ches 184 E2
Mere Wilts 45 G10
Mere Brow Lancs 194 D2
Mere Green W Midlands 134 D2
Mere Green Worcs 117 E8
Mere Heath Ches 183 G11
Mereclough Lancs 204 G3
Merefield Northants 120 F4
Meresborough Medway 69 G10
Mereside Blackp'l 202 G2
Mereworth Kent 53 C7
Mergie Aberds 293 E9
Meriden W Midlands 134 G4
Merkadale H'land 294 B5
Merkland Dumf/Gal 237 B9
Merkland N Ayrs 256 B2
Merkland S Ayrs 244 E6
Merkland Lodge H'land 309 G4
Merley Poole 18 B6
Merlin Haven Glos 80 G2
Merlin's Bridge Pembs 72 C6
Merlins Cross Pembs 73 E7
Merridge Som'set 43 G8
Merrifield Devon 8 F6
Merrifield Devon 24 G3
Merrington Shrops 149 E9
Merrion Pembs 72 F6
Merriott Som'set 28 E6
Merriottsford Som'set 28 E6
Merritown Dorset 19 B8
Merrivale Devon 12 F6
Merrivale Heref'd 98 G2
Merrow Surrey 50 C4
Merry Field Corner Som'set 45 D7
Merry Hill Dorset 31 G8
Merry Hill Herts 85 G10
Merry Hill Staffs 133 D7
Merrybent Durham 224 C4
Merryhill Green Wokingham 65 E9
Merrylee E Renf 267 D11
Merrymeet Cornw'l 6 B5
Merseyside Maritime Museum Mersey 182 D4
Mersham Kent 54 F5
Merstham Surrey 51 C9
Merston W Sussex 34 G5
Merstone I/Wight 20 D6
Merther Cornw'l 5 G7
Merther Lane Cornw'l 5 G7
Merthyr Carms 93 G7
Merthyr Cynog Powys 95 D9
Merthyr Dyfan V/Glam 58 F6
Merthyr Mawr Bridg 57 F11
Merthyr Tudful = Merthyr Tydfil Merth Tyd 77 D9
Merthyr Tydfil = Merthyr Tudful Merth Tyd 77 D9
Merton Devon 25 E8
Merton London 67 F8
Merton Norfolk 141 D8
Merton Oxon 83 B9
Merton Park London 67 F8
Meshaw Devon 26 D3
Messing Essex 88 B5
Messingham N Lincs 199 G11
Mesty Croft W Midlands 133 D9
Metcombe Devon 15 C7
Metfield Suffolk 142 G5
Metfield Common Suffolk 126 B5
Metherell Cornw'l 7 B8
Metheringham Lincs 173 C9
Methersgate Suffolk 108 B5
Methil Fife 281 B7
Methilhill Fife 281 A7
Methley W Yorks 197 B11
Methley Junction W Yorks 197 B11
Methlick Aberds 303 F8
Methven Perth/Kinr 286 E4
Methwold Norfolk 140 E4
Methwold Hythe Norfolk 140 D4
Metroland, Gateshead Tyne/Wear 242 E6
Mettingham Suffolk 143 F7
Metton Norfolk 160 B4
Mevagissey Cornw'l 5 G10
Mewith Head N Yorks 212 F4
Mexborough S Yorks 198 G3
Mey H'land 310 B6
Meyllteyrn Gwyn 144 C4
Meysey Hampton Glos 81 F10
Miabhag W Isles 305 H2
Miabhag W Isles 305 J3
Miabhig W Isles 304 E2
Mial H'land 299 B7
Michaelchurch Heref'd 97 F10
Michaelchurch Escley Heref'd 96 E6
Michaelchurch-on-Arrow Powys 114 G4
Michaelston-le-pit V/Glam 58 E6
Michaelston-super-Ely Card 58 D6
Michaelston-y-Fedw Newp 59 C8
Michaelstow Cornw'l 11 F7
Michel Troy Monmouths 79 C7
Michelcombe Devon 8 B3
Micheldever Hants 48 F4
Micheldever Station Hants 48 E4
Michelmersh Hants 32 B5
Mickfield Suffolk 126 E2
Mickle Trafford Ches 166 B6
Micklebring S Yorks 187 B8
Mickleby N Yorks 226 C6
Micklefield Bucks 84 G5
Micklefield Green Herts 85 F9
Mickleham Surrey 51 C7
Micklehurst Gtr Man 196 G3
Mickleover Derby C 152 C6
Micklethwaite Cumb 239 G7
Micklethwaite W Yorks 205 E8
Mickleton Durham 232 G5
Mickleton Glos 100 C3
Mickletown W Yorks 197 B11
Mickley Derby 186 F4
Mickley N Yorks 214 D5
Mickley Green Suffolk 124 F6
Mickley Square Northum 242 E3
Mid Ardlaw Aberds 303 C9
Mid Auchinlek Inverclyd 276 G6
Mid Beltie Aberds 293 C8
Mid Calder W Loth 269 B11
Mid Cloch Forbie Aberds 303 D7
Mid Clyth H'land 310 F6
Mid Garrary Dumf/Gal 237 B7
Mid Lavant W Sussex 34 F5
Mid Letter Arg/Bute 284 G4
Mid Main H'land 300 F4
Mid Shandon Stirl 277 C9
Mid Urchany H'land 301 E8
Mid Walls Shetl'd 315 H4
Mid Yell Shetl'd 314 D7
Midanbury S'thampton 33 E7
Midbea Orkney 312 D5
Middle Assendon Oxon 65 B8
Middle Aston Oxon 101 F9
Middle Balnald Perth/Kinr 286 B4
Middle Barton Oxon 101 F8
Middle Bickenhill W Midlands 134 G4
Middle Bockhampton Dorset 19 B9
Middle Bridge N Som'set 60 D3
Middle Burnham Som'set 43 C10
Middle Cairncake Aberds 303 E8
Middle Chinnock Som'set 29 E7
Middle Claydon Bucks 102 F4
Middle Drums Angus 287 B9
Middle Duntisbourne Glos 81 D7
Middle Green Suffolk 124 E4
Middle Green Slough 66 C3
Middle Green Som'set 27 D10
Middle Handley Derby 186 F6
Middle Harling Norfolk 141 F9
Middle Herrington Tyne/Wear 243 G9
Middle Hill Pembs 73 C7
Middle Kames Arg/Bute 275 E10
Middle Lambrook Som'set 28 D6
Middle Littleton Worcs 99 B11
Middle Maes-coed Heref'd 96 E6
Middle Marwood Devon 40 F4
Middle Mayfield Staffs 169 G10
Middle Mill Pembs 90 F6
Middle Quarter Kent 53 F11
Middle Rainton Tyne/Wear 234 C2
Middle Rasen Lincs 189 D9
Middle Rigg Perth/Kinr 286 G4
Middle Rocombe Devon 9 B8
Middle Stoford Som'set 27 C11
Middle Stoke Medway 69 D10
Middle Stoke W Midlands 119 B7
Middle Stoughton Som'set 44 D2
Middle Street Glos 80 E3
Middle Street Norfolk 160 B5
Middle Taphouse Cornw'l 6 C3
Middle Town I/Scilly 1 F4
Middle Town Warwick 117 E11
Middle Tysoe Warwick 100 C6
Middle Wallop Hants 47 F9
Middle Weald M/Keynes 102 D5
Middle Wick Glos 80 F2
Middle Winterslow Wilts 47 G8
Middle Woodford Wilts 46 F6
Middlebie Dumf/Gal 238 B6
Middlecave N Yorks 216 E5
Middlecliffe S Yorks 198 F2
Middlecott Devon 13 D10
Middlecroft Derby 186 G6
Middlefield Falk 279 E7
Middlefield Leics 135 E8
Middleforth Green Lancs 194 B4
Middleham N Yorks 214 B2
Middlehill Cornw'l 6 B5
Middlehill Wilts 61 F10
Middlehope Shrops 131 F9
Middlemarsh Dorset 29 F11
Middlemore Devon 12 G5
Middlemuir Aberds 303 D9
Middlemuir Aberds 303 E8
Middlemuir Aberds 303 G9
Middleport Stoke 168 F5
Middlesbrough Middlesbro 225 B10
Middlesceugh Cumb 230 C3
Middleshaw Cumb 211 B11
Middleshaw Dumf/Gal 238 B4
Middlesmoor N Yorks 213 E11
Middlestone Durham 233 E11
Middlestone Moor Durham 233 E10
Middlestown W Yorks 197 D9
Middlethorpe C/York 207 D7
Middleton Aberds 293 B10
Middleton Arg/Bute 288 E1
Middleton Cumb 212 B2
Middleton Derby 170 D3
Middleton Derby 169 C11
Middleton Essex 107 D7
Middleton Gtr Man 195 F11
Middleton Hants 48 E2
Middleton Heref'd 115 D10
Middleton Hartlep'l 234 E6
Middleton I/Wight 20 D2
Middleton Lancs 202 B4
Middleton Midloth 271 D7
Middleton Norfolk 158 F3
Middleton Northants 136 E6
Middleton Northum 252 F3
Middleton Northum 264 B4
Middleton N Yorks 204 E5
Middleton N Yorks 205 D8
Middleton N Yorks 216 C5
Middleton Perth/Kinr 286 C5
Middleton Perth/Kinr 286 F2
Middleton Perth/Kinr 286 G5
Middleton Shrops 115 B10
Middleton Shrops 148 D6
Middleton Suffolk 127 D8
Middleton Swan 56 D2
Middleton Warwick 134 D3
Middleton W Yorks 197 B10
Middleton Cheney Northants 101 C10
Middleton Green Staffs 151 B9
Middleton Hall Northum 263 D11
Middleton Junction Gtr Man 195 G11
Middleton Moor Suffolk 127 D8
Middleton of Rora Aberds 303 E10
Middleton on the Hill Heref'd 115 E10
Middleton One Row D'lington 225 C7
Middleton Place Cumb 219 G11
Middleton Quernhow N Yorks 214 D6
Middleton Railway, Hunslet W Yorks 206 G2
Middleton St. George D'lington 225 C7
Middleton Scriven Shrops 132 F3
Middleton Stoney Oxon 101 G10
Middleton Tyas N Yorks 224 D4
Middleton-in-Teesdale Durham 232 F5
Middleton-on-Leven N Yorks 225 D9
Middleton-on-Sea W Sussex 35 H7
Middleton-on-the-Wolds ER Yorks 208 D4
Middletown Cumb 219 D9
Middletown N Som'set 60 E2
Middletown Powys 148 G6
Middlewich Ches 168 B2
Middlewood Ches 184 E6
Middlewood Cornw'l 11 F11
Middlewood Heref'd 96 C5
Middlewood S Yorks 186 C4
Middlewood Green Suffolk 125 E11
Middleyard Glos 80 E4
Middlezoy Som'set 43 G11
Middridge Durham 233 F11
Midfield H'land 308 C5
Midford Bath/NE Som'set 61 G9
Midge Hall Lancs 194 C4
Midgehole W Yorks 196 B3
Midgeholme Cumb 240 F4
Midgham W Berks 64 F5
Midgham Green W Berks 64 F5
Midgley W Yorks 197 E9
Midgley W Yorks 196 B4
Mid-Hants Railway (Watercress Line), New Alresford Hants 48 G5
Midhopestones S Yorks 186 B2
Midhurst W Sussex 34 C5
Midland Orkney 313 H
Midlem Scot Borders 262
Midmar Aberds 293
Midmuir Arg/Bute 289
Midney Som'set
Midpark Arg/Bute 2
Midplaugh Aberds
Midsomer Norton Bath/NE Som'set
Midton Invercl

Muddlebridge Devon 40 G4
Muddles Green E Sussex 37 E8
Mudeford Dorset 19 C9
Mudford Som'set 29 D9
Mudford Sock Som'set 29 D9
Mudgley Som'set 44 D2
Mugdock Stirl 277 F11
Mugeary H'land 294 B6
Mugginton Derby 170 G3
Muggintonlane End Derby 170 G3
Muggleswick Durham 232 B6
Muie H'land 309 J6
Muir Aberds 292 E2
Muir of Alford Aberds 293 B7
Muir of Fairburn H'land 300 D4
Muir of Fowlis Aberds 293 B7
Muir of Kinellar Aberds 293 B10
Muir of Miltonduff Moray 301 D11
Muir of Ord H'land 300 D5
Muir of Pert Angus 287 D8
Muirden Aberds 303 D7
Muirdrum Angus 287 D9
Muirend Glasg C 267 C11
Muirhead Angus 287 D7
Muirhead Glasg C 268 C3
Muirhead Fife 286 G6
Muirhead Fife 287 F8
Muirhead N Lanarks 268 B3
Muirhead S Ayrs 257 C8
Muirhouse C/Edinb 280 F4
Muirhouse N Lanarks 268 E5
Muirhouses Falk 279 E10
Muirkirk E Ayrs 258 D5
Muirmill Stirl 278 E4
Muirshearlich H'land 290 E3
Muirskie Aberds 293 D10
Muirtack Aberds 303 F9
Muirton Aberds 303 D7
Muirton H'land 301 C7
Muirton Perth/Kinr 286 E5
Muirton Perth/Kinr 286 F3
Muirton Mains H'land 300 D4
Muirton of Ardblair Perth/Kinr 286 C5
Muirton of Ballochy Angus 293 G8
Muiryfold Aberds 303 D7
Muker N Yorks 223 F8
Mulbarton Norfolk 142 C3
Mulben Moray 302 D3
Mulgrave Castle N Yorks 226 C6
Mulindry Arg/Bute 254 B4
Mulla Shetl'd 315 G6
Mullardoch House H'land 300 F2
Mullion Cornw'l 2 F5
Mullion Cove Cornw'l 2 F5
Mumby Lincs 191 G8
Mumps Gtr Man 196 F2
Muncaster Owl Trust World HQ Cumb 219 F6
Mundale Moray 301 D10
Munday Bois Kent 54 D2
Munderfield Row Heref'd 116 G3
Munderfield Stocks Heref'd 116 G3
Mundesley Norfolk 160 B6
Mundford Norfolk 140 E6
Mundham Norfolk 142 D6
Mundon Essex 88 E5
Mundurno Aberd C 293 B11
Munerigie H'land 290 C4
Muness Shetl'd 314 C8
Mungasdale H'land 307 K4
Mungrisdale Cumb 230 E3
Munlochy H'land 300 D6
Munsary Cottage H'land 310 E6
Munsley Heref'd 98 C3
Munslow Shrops 131 F10
Munstead Heath Surrey 50 E3
Munstone Heref'd 97 C10
Murch V/Glam 59 E7
Murchington Devon 13 D9
Murcot Worcs 99 C11
Murcott Oxon 83 B9
Murcott Wilts 81 G7
Murdishaw Wood Halton 183 E9
Murieston W Loth 269 C11
Murkle H'land 310 C5
Murlaggan H'land 290 D2
Murlaggan H'land 290 E5
Murra Orkney 313 H3
Murrayfield C/Edinb 280 G4
Murrayfield Stadium C/Edinb 280 G4
Murrays Motorcycle Museum I/Man 192 D4
Murrayshall Perth/Kinr 286 E5
Murraythwaite Dumf/Gal 238 C4
Murrell Green Hants 49 B8
Murrion Shetl'd 314 F4
Murrow Cambs 139 B7
Mursley Bucks 102 F6
Murston Kent 70 G2
Murthill Angus 287 B8
Murthly Perth/Kinr 286 D4
Murton Cumb 231 G10
Murton C/York 207 C9
Murton Durham 234 B3
Murton Swan 56 D5
Murton Tyne/Wear 243 C8
Musbury Devon 15 C11
Muscliff Bournem'th 19 B7
Muscoates N Yorks 216 C3
Muscott Northants 120 E2
Musdale Arg/Bute 289 G11
Museum of the Broads, Sutton Norfolk 161 E7
Musselburgh E Loth 280 G6
Musselburgh Racecourse E Loth 280 G6
Mustard Hyrn Norfolk 161 F8
Muston Leics 154 B6
Muston N Yorks 217 D11
Mustow Green Worcs 117 C7
Muswell Hill London 67 B9
Mutehill Dumf/Gal 237 E8
Mutford Suffolk 143 F9
Muthill Perth/Kinr 286 F2
Mutley Plym'th 7 D9
Mutterton Devon 27 F8
Mutton Hall E Sussex 37 C9
Muxton Telford 150 G4
Mwnt Ceredig'n 110 G3
Mybster H'land 310 D5
Mychett Surrey 49 B11
Myddfai Carms 94 E5
Myddle Shrops 149 E9
Myddlewood Shrops 149 E9
Mydroilyn Ceredig'n 111 F9
Myerscough Lancs 202 F5
Myerscough Lancs 203 G8
Mylor Bridge Cornw'l 3 B8
Mylor Churchtown Cornw'l 3 B8
Mynachlog-ddu Pembs 92 E2
Mynydd Alltir-fach Newp 78 G6
Mynydd Bach Ceredig'n 112 B4
Mynydd Cilan Gwyn 144 E5
Mynydd Isa Flints 166 C3
Mynydd Llandegai Gwyn 163 B10
Mynydd Marian Conwy 180 F5
Mynydd-bach Monmouths 79 G7
Mynydd-Bach Swan 75 F11
Mynydd-bach-y-glo Swan 75 F10
Mynyddislwyn Caerph 77 F11
Mynydd-llan Flints 181 G11
Mynydd-y-briw Powys 148 D3
Mynyddygarreg Carms 74 D6
Mynytho Gwyn 144 C6
Myrebird Aberds 293 D9
Myrelandhorn H'land 310 D6
Myreside Perth/Kinr 286 E6
Mytholm W Yorks 196 B3
Mytholmes W Yorks 204 F6
Mytholmroyd W Yorks 196 B4
Mythop Lancs 202 G3
Mytice Aberds 302 F4
Myton Warwick 118 E6
Myton-on Swale N Yorks 215 F8
Mytton Shrops 149 F8

N

Na Gearrannan W Isles 304 D3
Naast H'land 307 L3
Nab Wood W Yorks 205 F8
Nab's Head Lancs 194 B6
Naburn C/York 207 D7
Naccolt Kent 54 E5
Nackington Kent 55 C7
Nacton Suffolk 108 C4
Nacton Heath Suffolk 108 C4
Nadderwater Devon 14 C3
Nafferton ER Yorks 209 B7
Nags Head Glos 80 F5
Nailbridge Glos 79 B10
Nailsbourne Som'set 28 B2
Nailsea N Som'set 60 E3
Nailstone Leics 135 B8
Nailsworth Glos 80 F5
Nairn H'land 301 D8
Nalderswood Surrey 51 D8
Nancegollan Cornw'l 2 C4
Nancledra Cornw'l 1 B5
Nangreaves Lancs 195 D10
Nanhoron Gwyn 144 C5
Nannerch Flints 165 B11
Nannerth Powys 113 C8
Nanpantan Leics 153 F10
Nanpean Cornw'l 5 D9
Nanstallon Cornw'l 5 B10
Nant Denbs 165 D11
Nant Alyn Flints 165 B11
Nant Ddu Rh Cyn Taff 77 C7
Nant Mawr Flints 166 C3
Nant Peris = Old Llanberis Gwyn 163 D9
Nanternis Ceredig'n 111 F7
Nantffyllon Bridg 76 G5
Nantgaredig Carms 93 G9
Nantgarw Rh Cyn Taff 58 B6
Nant-glas Powys 113 D9
Nantglyn Denbs 165 C8
Nantgwyn Powys 113 B9
Nantlle Gwyn 163 E8
Nantmawr Shrops 148 E5
Nantmel Powys 113 D10
Nantmor Gwyn 163 F10
Nantwich Ches 167 E11
Nant-y-Bai Carms 94 C5
Nant-y-Bwch Bl Gwent 77 C10
Nant-y-Cafn Neath P Talb 76 D4
Nant-y-Caws Shrops 148 D5
Nant-y-derry Monmouths 78 E4
Nant-y-felin Conwy 179 G11
Nant-y-ffin Carms 93 E11
Nantyglesaid Caerph 59 B8
Nantyglo Bl Gwent 77 C11
Nant-y-gollen Shrops 148 D4
Nant-y-Moel Bridg 76 G6
Nant-y-pandy Conwy 179 G11
Napchester Kent 55 D10
Naphill Bucks 84 F5
Napleton Worcs 99 B7
Nappa N Yorks 204 C3
Napton on the Hill Warwick 119 E9
Narberth = Arberth Pembs 73 C10
Narberth Bridge Pembs 73 C10
Narborough Leics 135 D10
Narborough Norfolk 158 G4
Narkurs Cornw'l 6 D6
Narracott Devon 24 D5
Narrowgate Corner Norfolk 161 F8
Nasareth Gwyn 163 E7
Naseby Northants 120 B3
Nash Bucks 102 E5
Nash Kent 55 B9
Nash London 68 G2
Nash Newp 59 C10
Nash Shrops 116 C2
Nash Som'set 29 E8
Nash End Worcs 132 G5
Nash Lee Bucks 84 D4
Nash Street Kent 68 F6
Nashend Glos 80 E6
Nashes Green Hants 49 D7
Nassington Northants 137 D11
Nastend Glos 80 D3
Nasty Herts 105 G7
Natcott Devon 24 C3
Nateby Cumb 222 D5
Nateby Lancs 202 E5
Nately Scures Hants 49 C8
National Agricultural Centre, Stoneleigh Warwick 118 C6
National Botanic Garden of Wales Carms 75 B8
National Cycle Collection, Llandrindod Wells Powys 113 E11
National Exhibition Centre, Birmingham W Midlands 134 G3
National Fishing Heritage Centre, Grimsby NE Lincs 201 F9
National Forest Discovery Centre Leics 152 F6
National Gallery London 67 C9
National Hockey Stadium M/Keynes 102 D6
National Ice Centre Nott'ham 153 B11
National Maritime Museum London 67 D11
National Maritime Museum, Falmouth Cornw'l 3 C8
National Motor Museum, Beaulieu Hants 32 G5
National Museum of Photography, Bradford W Yorks 205 G9
National Museum of Wales Card 59 D7
National Portrait Gallery (See National Gallery) London 67 C9
National Railway Museum C/York 207 C7
National Seal Sanctuary, Gweek Cornw'l 2 D6
National Space Science Centre Leics 135 B11
National Squash Centre Gtr Man 184 B5
National Waterfront Museum Swan 57 C7
Natland Cumb 211 B10
Natural History Museum London 67 D9
Natureland Seal Sanctuary, Skegness Lincs 175 C9
Naughton Suffolk 107 B10
Naunton Glos 100 G2
Naunton Worcs 99 D7
Naunton Beauchamp Worcs 117 G9
Navarino Cornw'l 11 D11
Navenby Lincs 173 D7
Navestock Essex 87 F9
Navestock Heath Essex 87 F9
Navidale H'land 311 H4
Navity H'land 301 C7
Nawton N Yorks 216 C3
Nayland Suffolk 107 E9
Nazeing Essex 86 D6
Nazeing Gate Essex 86 E6
Nazeing Long Green Essex 86 E6
Nazeing Mead Essex 86 D5
Neacroft Hants 19 B9
Nealhouse Cumb 239 G8
Neal's Green Warwick 134 G6
Neames Forstal Kent 54 B4
Neap Shetl'd 315 H7
Near Sawrey Cumb 221 F7
Nearton End Bucks 102 F6
Neasden London 67 B8
Neasham D'lington 224 C6
Neat Enstone Oxon 101 G7
Neath = Castell-nedd Rh Cyn Taff 76 F3
Neath Abbey Rh Cyn Taff 76 F2
Neath Hill M/Keynes 103 C7
Neatham Hants 49 E8
Neatishead Norfolk 160 E6
Neaton Norfolk 141 C8
Nebo Conwy 164 D4
Nebo Ceredig'n 111 D10
Nebo Gwyn 163 E7
Nebo Angl 179 C7
Nechells W Midlands 133 F11
Necton Norfolk 141 B7
Nedd H'land 306 F6
Nedderton Northum 252 G6
Nedging Suffolk 107 B9
Nedging Tye Suffolk 107 B10
Needham Norfolk 142 G4
Needham Green Essex 87 B9
Needham Market Suffolk 125 F11
Needham Street Suffolk 124 D4
Needingworth Cambs 122 C6
Needwood Staffs 152 E3
Neen Savage Shrops 116 B3
Neen Sollars Shrops 116 C3
Neenton Shrops 132 F2
Neep's Bridge Norfolk 139 B11
Neeston Pembs 72 D5
Nefyn Gwyn 162 G4
Neilston E Renf 267 D9
Neithrop Oxon 101 C8
Nelly Andrews Green Powys 130 B5
Nelson Caerph 77 F10
Nelson Lancs 204 F3
Nelson Village Northum 242 B6
Nemphlar S Lanarks 269 G7
Nempnett Thrubwell Bath/NE Som'set 60 G4
Nene Terrace Lincs 138 B4
Nenthall Cumb 231 B11
Nenthead Cumb 231 C11
Nenthorn Scot Borders 262 B5
Neopardy Devon 13 B11
Nep Town W Sussex 36 D2
Nepcote W Sussex 35 F10
Nepgill Cumb 229 F7
Nerabus Arg/Bute 254 B3
Nercwys Flints 166 C2
Nerston S Lanarks 268 D2
Nesbit Northum 263 C11
Nesbitt Hill Head Northum 242 E3
Nesfield N Yorks 205 D7
Ness Ches 182 F4
Ness Orkney 312 E5
Ness Gardens, Connah's Quay Ches 182 F4
Nesscliffe Shrops 149 F7
Nessholt Ches 182 F4
Nesstoun Orkney 312 C8
Neston Ches 182 F3
Neston Wilts 61 F11
Nether Fife 280 B5
Nether Alderley Ches 184 F4
Nether Blainslie Scot Borders 271 G10
Nether Booth Derby 185 D10
Nether Broughton Leics 154 D3
Nether Burrow Lancs 212 D2
Nether Burrows Derby 152 B5
Nether Cerne Dorset 17 B9
Nether Compton Dorset 29 D9
Nether Crimond Aberds 303 G8
Nether Dalgliesh Scot Borders 249 B7
Nether Dallachy Moray 302 C3
Nether Edge S Yorks 186 E4
Nether End Derby 186 G3
Nether End Leics 154 G4
Nether End W Yorks 197 F9
Nether Exe Devon 26 G6
Nether Glasslaw Aberds 303 D8
Nether Hall Leics C 136 B2
Nether Handwick Angus 287 C7
Nether Haugh S Yorks 186 B6
Nether Headon Notts 188 F2
Nether Heage Derby 170 E5
Nether Hesleden N Yorks 213 E7
Nether Heyford Northants 120 F3
Nether Howecleuch S Lanarks 260 G2
Nether Kellet Lancs 211 F10
Nether Kinmundy Aberds 303 E10
Nether Kirkton E Renf 267 D9
Nether Langwith Notts 187 G8
Nether Leask Aberds 303 F10
Nether Lenshie Aberds 302 E6
Nether Liberton C/Edinb 280 G5
Nether Moor Derby 170 B5
Nether Padley Derby 186 F2
Nether Park Aberds 303 D10
Nether Poppleton C/York 207 C7
Nether Row Cumb 230 D2
Nether Savock Aberds 303 E10
Nether Silton N Yorks 225 G9
Nether Skyborry Shrops 114 C5
Nether Stowey Som'set 43 F7
Nether Street Essex 87 C9
Nether Street Herts 86 B6
Nether Street Suffolk 125 E8
Nether Urquhart Fife 286 G5
Nether Wallop Hants 47 F10
Nether Wasdale Cumb 220 E2
Nether Welton Cumb 230 B3
Nether Westcote Glos 100 G4
Nether Whitacre Warwick 134 E4
Nether Worton Oxon 101 E8
Nether Yeadon W Yorks 205 E10
Netheravon Wilts 46 D6
Netherbrae Aberds 303 D7
Netherbrough Orkney 312 G4
Netherburn S Lanarks 268 F6
Netherbury Dorset 16 B5
Netherby Cumb 239 C9
Netherby N Yorks 206 D2
Netherclay Som'set 28 C3
Nethercote Glos 100 G3
Nethercote Warwick 119 E10
Nethercott Devon 40 F3
Nethercott Oxon 101 G9
Netherdale Shetl'd 315 H3
Netherend Glos 79 E9
Netherfield E Sussex 38 D2
Netherfield M/Keynes 103 D7
Netherfield Notts 171 G10
Nethergate Norfolk 159 D11
Netherhall N Ayrs 266 C4
Netherhampton Wilts 31 B10
Netherhay Dorset 28 F6
Netherland Green Staffs 152 C2
Netherlaw Dumf/Gal 237 E9
Netherlee E Renf 267 D11
Netherley Aberds 293 D10
Netherley Mersey 182 D6
Nethermill Dumf/Gal 248 F2
Nethermills Moray 302 D5
Nethermuir Aberds 303 E9
Netheroyd Hill W Yorks 196 D6
Netherplace E Renf 267 D10
Netherseal Derby 152 G5
Netherthird E Ayrs 258 F3
Netherthong W Yorks 196 F6
Netherthorpe Derby 186 G6
Netherthorpe S Yorks 187 E8
Netherton Aberds 303 E8
Netherton Angus 287 B9
Netherton Ches 183 F8
Netherton Cumb 228 D6
Netherton Cornw'l 11 G11
Netherton Devon 14 G3
Netherton Hants 47 B11
Netherton Heref'd 97 F10
Netherton Mersey 193 G11
Netherton N Lanarks 268 E5
Netherton Northum 251 B11
Netherton Oxon 82 F6
Netherton Perth/Kinr 286 B5
Netherton Shrops 132 G4
Netherton Stirl 277 F11
Netherton W Midlands 133 F8
Netherton Worcs 99 C9
Netherton W Yorks 196 E6
Netherton W Yorks 197 D9
Netherton of Lonmay Aberds 303 C10
Nethertown Cumb 219 D9
Nethertown H'land 310 B7
Nethertown Lancs 203 F10
Nethertown Staffs 152 F2
Netherwitton Northum 252 E4
Netherwood E Ayrs 258 D5
Nethy Bridge H'land 301 G10
Netley Hants 33 F7
Netley Marsh Hants 32 E4
Netteswell Essex 87 C7
Nettlebed Oxon 65 B7
Nettlebridge Som'set 45 D6
Nettlecombe Dorset 16 B6
Nettlecombe I/Wight 20 F6
Nettleden Herts 85 C8
Nettleham Lincs 189 F8
Nettlehirst N Ayrs 267 E7
Nettlestead Kent 53 C7
Nettlestead Suffolk 107 B11
Nettlestead Green Kent 53 C7
Nettlestone I/Wight 21 C8
Nettlesworth Durham 233 B11
Nettleton Glos 80 C6
Nettleton Lincs 189 B10
Nettleton Wilts 61 D10
Nettleton Green Wilts 61 D10
Nettleton Shrub Wilts 61 D10
Nettleton Top Lincs 189 B10
Netton Wilts 46 F6
Neuadd Carms 94 G4
Nevendon Essex 88 G2
Nevern Pembs 91 C11
Nevill Holt Leics 136 E6
Nevilles Cross Durham 233 C11
Nevis Range Ski Centre, Torlundy H'land 290 F3
New Abbey Dumf/Gal 237 C11
New Aberdour Aberds 303 C8
New Addington London 67 G11
New Alresford Hants 48 G5
New Alyth Perth/Kinr 286 C6
New Arley Warwick 134 F5
New Arram ER Yorks 208 E6
New Ash Green Kent 68 F6
New Balderton Notts 172 E4
New Barn Kent 68 F6
New Barnet London 86 F3
New Barnetby N Lincs 200 E5
New Barton Northants 121 E7
New Basford Nott'ham 171 G9
New Beckenham London 67 E11
New Belses Scot Borders 262 D3
New Bewick Northum 264 E3
New Bilton Warwick 119 B9
New Bolingbroke Lincs 174 D4
New Bolsover Derby 187 G7
New Boston Mersey 183 B9
New Boultham Lincs 189 G7
New Bradwell M/Keynes 102 C6
New Brancepath Durham 233 C10
New Bridge ER Yorks 199 D7
New Bridge N Yorks 216 B6
New Brighton Flints 166 B3
New Brighton Hants 34 F2
New Brighton Mersey 182 C4
New Brighton N Yorks 204 C4
New Brighton Wrex 166 E3
New Brighton W Yorks 205 F8
New Brighton W Yorks 197 B9
New Brimington Derby 186 G6
New Brinsley Notts 171 E7
New Brotton Redcar/Clevel'd 235 G9
New Broughton Wrex 166 E4
New Buckenham Norfolk 141 E11
New Buildings Bath/NE Som'set 45 B7
New Bury Gtr Man 195 F8
New Byth Aberds 303 D8
New Catton Norfolk 160 G4
New Cheriton Hants 33 B9
New Chesterton Cambs 123 F8
New Costessey Norfolk 160 G3
New Coundon Durham 233 E10
New Cowper Cumb 229 B8
New Crofton W Yorks 197 D11
New Cross London 67 D11
New Cross Som'set 28 D6
New Cubbington Warwick 118 D6
New Cummock E Ayrs 258 G4
New Cut E Sussex 38 D4
New Deer Aberds 303 E8
New Delaval Northum 243 B7
New Delph Gtr Man 196 F3
New Denham Bucks 66 C4
New Duston Northants 120 E4
New Earswick C/York 207 B8
New Eastwood Notts 171 F7
New Edlington S Yorks 187 B8
New Elgin Moray 302 C2
New Ellerby ER Yorks 209 F9
New Eltham London 68 E2
New End Worcs 117 F10
New England Essex 106 C4
New England Lincs 175 D8
New England Peterbro 138 C3
New England Surrey 66 G2
New Farm Loch E Ayrs 257 B10
New Farnley W Yorks 205 G10
New Ferry Mersey 182 D4
New Fletton Peterbro 138 D3
New Fryston W Yorks 198 B3
New Galloway Dumf/Gal 237 B8
New Gilston Fife 287 G8
New Greens Herts 85 D10
New Grimsby I/Scilly 1 F3
New Hall Warrington 183 D9
New Hall Hey Lancs 195 C10
New Hartley Northum 243 B8
New Haw Surrey 66 G5
New Headington Oxon 83 D8
New Hedges Pembs 73 E10
New Herrington Tyne/Wear 243 G8
New Hinksey Oxon 83 E8
New Holkham Norfolk 176 F5
New Holland N Lincs 200 C5
New Horwich Derby 185 E8
New Houghton Derby 171 B8
New Houghton Derby 171 B7
New Houghton Norfolk 158 D5
New House Durham 233 C9
New House Green Wilts 62 D2
New Houses Gtr Man 194 G5
New Humberstone Leics C 136 B2
New Hunwick Durham 233 E9
New Hutton Cumb 221 G11
New Hythe Kent 53 B8
New Inn Carms 93 D9
New Inn Carms 94 F2
New Inn Devon 24 F6
New Inn Pembs 91 E11
New Inn Torf 78 F4
New Invention W Midlands 133 C9
New Kelso H'land 299 E9
New Kingston Notts 153 D10
New Kyo Durham 242 G5
New Lambton Tyne/Wear 243 G8
New Lanark S Lanarks 269 G7
New Lanark World Heritage Village, Lanark S Lanarks 269 G7
New Lane Lancs 194 E2
New Lane End Warrington 183 C10
New Langholm Dumf/Gal 249 G9
New Leake Lincs 174 D6
New Leeze S Glos 60 B5
New Leeds Aberds 303 D9
New Lodge S Yorks 197 F10
New Longton Lancs 194 B4
New Luce Dumf/Gal 236 C3
New Malden London 67 F8
New Marske Redcar/Clevel'd 235 G8
New Marston Oxon 83 D8
New Marton Shrops 148 C6
New Micklefield W Yorks 206 G4
New Mill Aberds 293 E9
New Mill Cumb 219 E11
New Mill Cornw'l 1 C5
New Mill Cornw'l 4 F6
New Mill Herts 84 C6
New Mill Wilts 63 G7
New Mill W Yorks 197 F7
New Mill End Beds 85 B10
New Mills Ches 184 E3
New Mills Cornw'l 5 E8
New Mills Derby 185 D7
New Mills Powys 129 C11
New Mills Powys 148 F2
New Milton Hants 19 B10
New Mistley Essex 108 E2
New Moat Pembs 91 F11
New Moston Gtr Man 195 G11
New Ollerton Notts 171 B11
New Oscott W Midlands 133 E11
New Park N Yorks 206 B2
New Parks Leics C 135 B11
New Pitsligo Aberds 303 D8
New Polzeath Cornw'l 10 F4
New Quay = Ceinewydd Ceredig'n 111 E7
New Quay Devon 8 G4
New Rackheath Norfolk 160 G5
New Radnor Powys 114 E4
New Rent Cumb 230 D5
New Ridley Northum 242 F3
New Road Side N Yorks 204 E5
New Road Side W Yorks 196 B6
New Romney Kent 39 C9
New Rossington S Yorks 187 B10
New Row Ceredig'n 112 C4
New Sawley Derby 153 C9
New Scarbro W Yorks 205 G10
New Sharlston W Yorks 197 C11
New Silksworth Tyne/Wear 243 G9
New Skelton Redcar/Clevel'd 226 B3
New Smithy Derby 185 E9
New Southgate London 86 G3
New Springs Gtr Man 194 F6
New Sprowston Norfolk 160 G4
New Stanton Derby 153 B9
New Stevenston N Lanarks 268 D5
New Street Heref'd 114 F6
New Street Staffs 169 E9
New Sulehay Northants 137 D11
New Swanage Dorset 18 E6
New Swannington Leics 153 F8
New Thirsk N Yorks 215 C8
New Thundersley Essex 69 B9
New Totley S Yorks 186 F4
New Town Bath/NE Som'set 60 G5
New Town C/Edinb 280 G5
New Town Dorset 30 D4
New Town Dorset 31 F7
New Town Dorset 31 D7
New Town Dorset 31 D7
New Town Dorset 30 C3
New Town E Loth 281 G8
New Town E Sussex 37 C7
New Town Glos 99 E10
New Town Kent 53 B7
New Town Lancs 203 F8
New Town Luton 103 G11
New Town Medway 69 G8
New Town Shetl'd 314 E6
New Town Som'set 29 D9
New Town Som'set 44 D3
New Town Swindon 63 C7
New Town Tyne/Wear 234 B2
New Town Tyne/Wear 243 E8
New Town W Berks 64 D6
New Town Wokingham 65 E8
New Town Wilts 29 D11
New Town Wilts 63 E9
New Town Wilts 61 C11
New Town W Midlands 133 E9
New Town W Sussex 51 G7
New Town W Yorks 198 C3
New Tredegar = Tredegar Newydd Caerph 77 E10
New Trows S Lanarks 259 B8
New Ulva Arg/Bute 275 E8
New Village ER Yorks 209 G7
New Village S Yorks 198 F5
New Waltham NE Lincs 201 F9
New Whittington Derby 186 F5
New Wimpole Cambs 122 G6
New Winton E Loth 281 G8
New Woodhouse Shrops 167 G9
New World Cambs 139 E7
New Yatt Oxon 82 C5
New York Lincs 174 D2
New York N Yorks 214 G3
New York Tyne/Wear 243 C8
New Zealand Derby C 152 B6
New Zealand Wilts 62 D4
Newall W Yorks 205 D9
Newall Green Gtr Man 184 D4
Newark Orkney 312 D8
Newark Peterbro 138 C4
Newark Castle Notts 172 E3
Newark-on-Trent Notts 172 E3
Newarthill N Lanarks 268 D5
Newball Lincs 189 F9
Newbarn Kent 55 E7
Newbarns Cumb 210 E4
Newbattle Midloth 270 B6
Newbiggin Cumb 210 F5
Newbiggin Cumb 219 G11
Newbiggin Cumb 230 F5
Newbiggin Cumb 231 F8
Newbiggin Cumb 231 B7
Newbiggin Durham 232 F4
Newbiggin Durham 233 B8
Newbiggin Northum 232 B5
Newbiggin N Yorks 218 C2
Newbiggin N Yorks 223 G9
Newbiggin N Yorks 213 B10
Newbiggin Hall Estate Tyne/Wear 242 D6
Newbiggin-by-the-Sea Northum 253 F8
Newbigging Aberds 303 G7
Newbigging Angus 286 C6
Newbigging Angus 287 D8
Newbigging Angus 287 D8
Newbigging S Lanarks 269 F10
Newbiggings Orkney 312 D7
Newbiggin-on-Lune Cumb 222 D4
Newbold Derby 186 G5
Newbold Gtr Man 196 E2
Newbold Leics 153 F8
Newbold Leics 136 B5
Newbold on Avon Warwick 119 B9
Newbold on Stour Warwick 100 B4
Newbold Pacey Warwick 118 F5
Newbold Verdon Leics 135 C8
Newborough = Niwbwrch Angl 162 B6
Newborough Peterbro 138 B4
Newborough Staffs 152 D2
Newbottle Northants 101 D10
Newbottle Tyne/Wear 243 G8
Newbourne Suffolk 108 C5
Newbridge C/Edinb 280 G2
Newbridge Caerph 78 F2
Newbridge Ceredig'n 111 F10
Newbridge Cornw'l 1 C4
Newbridge Cornw'l 4 G5
Newbridge Cornw'l 6 B6
Newbridge Dumf/Gal 237 B11
Newbridge E Sussex 52 G3
Newbridge Hants 32 D3
Newbridge I/Wight 20 D4
Newbridge Lancs 204 F3
Newbridge Oxon 82 E6
Newbridge Pembs 91 E8
Newbridge W Midlands 133 D7
Newbridge Wrex 166 G3
Newbridge Green Worcs 98 D6
Newbridge on Wye Powys 113 F10
Newbridge-on-Usk Monmouths 78 G5
Newbrough Northum 241 D9
Newbuildings Devon 26 G3
Newburgh Aberds 303 D9
Newburgh Aberds 303 G9
Newburgh Scot Borders 261 E8
Newburgh Fife 286 F6
Newburgh Lancs 194 E3
Newburn Tyne/Wear 242 D5
Newbury Kent 54 B2
Newbury Som'set 45 C7
Newbury W Berks 64 F3
Newbury Wilts 45 E10
Newbury Park London 68 B2
Newbury Racecourse W Berks 64 F3
Newby Cumb 231 G7
Newby Lancs 204 D2
Newby N Yorks 205 D11
Newby N Yorks 212 E4
Newby N Yorks 227 G10
Newby N Yorks 225 C10
Newby Bridge Cumb 211 B7
Newby Cote N Yorks 212 E4
Newby East Cumb 239 F11
Newby Hall & Gardens, Ripon N Yorks 214 F6
Newby Head Cumb 231 G7
Newby West Cumb 239 G9
Newby Whiske N Yorks 215 B7
Newcastle Bridg 57 F11
Newcastle Monmouths 78 B6
Newcastle Shrops 130 G4
Newcastle Emlyn = Castell Newydd Emlyn Carms 92 C6
Newcastle International Airport Tyne/Wear 242 C5
Newcastle Racecourse Tyne/Wear 243 C7
Newcastle upon Tyne Tyne/Wear 242 D6
Newcastleton = Copshaw Holm Scot Borders 249 F11
Newcastle-under-Lyme Stoke 168 F4
Newchapel Pembs 92 D4
Newchapel Powys 129 G9
Newchapel Surrey 51 E11
Newchapel Staffs 168 E5
Newchurch Bl Gwent 77 C11
Newchurch Carms 93 G7
Newchurch Heref'd 115 G7
Newchurch I/Wight 21 D7
Newchurch Kent 54 G5
Newchurch Lancs 195 C10
Newchurch Monmouths 79 F7
Newchurch Powys 114 G4
Newchurch Staffs 152 E2
Newchurch in Pendle Lancs 204 F2
Newcott Devon 28 F2
Newcraighall E Loth 280 G6
Newdigate Surrey 51 E7
Newell Green Brackn'l 65 E11
Newenden Kent 38 B4
Newent Glos 98 F4
Newerne Glos 79 E10
Newfield Durham 233 E10
Newfield Durham 242 G6
Newfield H'land 301 B7
Newfield Stoke 168 E5
Newfield Green S Yorks 186 E5
Newfound Hants 48 C5
Newgale Pembs 91 G7
Newgarth Orkney 312 G3
Newgate Derby 186 G4
Newgate Lancs 194 F4
Newgate Norfolk 177 E9
Newgate Street Herts 86 D3
Newhailes E Loth 280 G6
Newhall Ches 167 F10
Newhall Derby 152 E5
Newhall House H'land 300 C6
Newhall Point H'land 301 C7
Newham Cornw'l 4 G6
Newham Lincs 174 E3
Newham Northum 264 D5
Newhaven C/Edinb 280 F5
Newhaven Derby 169 D11
Newhaven E Sussex 36 G6
Newhey Gtr Man 196 E2
Newhill Fife 286 F6
Newhill Perth/Kinr 286 G5
Newhill S Yorks 186 B6
Newhills Aberd C 293 C10
Newholm N Yorks 227 C7
Newhouse N Lanarks 268 C5
Newhouse Shetl'd 315 G6
Newick E Sussex 36 C6
Newingreen Kent 54 F6
Newington C/Edinb 280 G5
Newington Kent 71 F11
Newington Kent 55 F7

Norton-in-the-Moors Stoke 168 E5
Norton-le-Clay N Yorks 215 E8
Norton-on-Derwent N Yorks 216 E6
Norwell Notts 172 C3
Norwell Woodhouse Notts 172 C2
Norwich Norfolk 142 B4
Norwich Castle Museum Norfolk 142 B4
Norwich Cathedral Norfolk 142 B4
Norwich International Airport Norfolk 160 G4
Norwick Shetl'd 314 B8
Norwood Derby 187 E7
Norwood End Essex 87 D9
Norwood Green London 66 D6
Norwood Green W Yorks 196 B6
Norwood Hill Surrey 51 E8
Norwood Park Som'set 44 F4
Norwoodside Cambs 139 D8
Noseley Leics 136 D4
Noss H'land 310 D7
Noss Shetl'd 315 M5
Noss Mayo Devon 7 F11
Nosterfield N Yorks 214 C5
Nosterfield End Cambs 106 C2
Nostie H'land 295 C10
Notgrove Glos 100 G2
Nothe Fort, Weymouth Dorset 17 F9
Nottage Brigd 57 F10
Notter Cornw'l 7 C7
Notting Hill London 67 C8
Nottingham Nott'ham 171 G9
Nottingham Castle Museum Nott'ham 153 B11
Nottingham East Midlands Airport Leics 153 D8
Nottingham Racecourse Nott'ham 153 B11
Nottington Dorset 17 E9
Notton Wilts 62 F2
Notton W Yorks 197 E10
Nounsley Essex 88 C3
Noutard's Green Worcs 116 D6
Nova Scotia Ches 167 B10
Novar House H'land 300 C6
Novers Park Bristol 60 F5
Noverton Glos 99 G9
Nowton Suffolk 125 E7
Nox Shrops 149 G8
Noyadd Trefawr Ceredig'n 92 B5
Nuffield Oxon 65 B7
Nun Hills Lancs 195 C11
Nun Monkton N Yorks 206 B6
Nunburnholme ER Yorks 208 D2
Nuncargate Notts 171 E8
Nunclose Cumb 230 B5
Nuneaton Warwick 135 E7
Nuneham Courtenay Oxon 83 F8
Nuney Green Oxon 65 D7
Nunhead London 67 E11
Nunney Som'set 45 D8
Nunney Catch Som'set 45 D8
Nunnington N Yorks 216 D3
Nunnington Park Som'set 27 B9
Nunsthorpe NE Lincs 201 F9
Nunthorpe C/York 207 D7
Nunthorpe Middlesbro 225 C10
Nunton Wilts 31 B11
Nunwick N Yorks 214 E6
Nup End Bucks 84 B5
Nup End Herts 86 B2
Nupdown S Glos 79 F10
Nupend Glos 80 D3
Nupend Glos 80 F4
Nuptown Brackn'l 65 E11
Nursling Hants 32 D5
Nursted Hants 34 C3
Nursteed Wilts 62 G4
Nurston V/Glam 58 F5
Nut Grove Mersey 183 C7
Nutbourne W Sussex 34 F3
Nutbourne W Sussex 35 D9
Nutbourne Common W Sussex 35 D9
Nutburn Hants 32 D5
Nutfield Surrey 51 C10
Nuthall Notts 171 F8
Nuthampstead Herts 105 E8
Nuthurst Warwick 118 C2
Nuthurst W Sussex 35 B11
Nutley E Sussex 36 B6
Nutley Hants 48 E6
Nuttall Gtr Man 195 D9
Nutwell S Yorks 198 G6
Nybster H'land 310 C7
Nyetimber W Sussex 22 D5
Nyewood W Sussex 34 C4
Nyland Som'set 44 C3
Nymans Garden, Crawley W Sussex 36 B3
Nymet Rowland Devon 26 F2
Nymet Tracy Devon 26 G2
Nympsfield Glos 80 E4
Nynehead Som'set 27 C10
Nythe Som'set 44 G2
Nythe Swindon 63 B7
Nyton W Sussex 34 F6

O

Oad Street Kent 69 G11
Oadby Leics 136 C2
Oak Bank Gtr Man 195 F10
Oak Hill Suffolk 109 B7
Oak Hill Stoke 168 G5
Oak Tree Durham 225 C7
Oakamoor Staffs 169 G9
Oakbank W Loth 269 B11
Oakdale Caerph 77 F11
Oakdale Poole 18 C6
Oake Som'set 27 B11
Oake Green Som'set 27 B11
Oaken Staffs 133 C7
Oakenclough Lancs 202 D6
Oakengates Telford 150 G4
Oakenholt Flints 182 G3
Oakenshaw Durham 233 D9
Oakenshaw Lancs 203 G11
Oakenshaw Worcs 117 D10
Oakenshaw W Yorks 197 B7
Oakerthorpe Derby 170 E5
Oakes W Yorks 196 D6
Oakfield I/Wight 21 C7
Oakfield Torf 78 G3
Oakford Ceredig'n 111 F9
Oakford Devon 26 C6
Oakfordbridge Devon 26 C6
Oakgrove Ches 168 B6
Oakhall Green Worcs 116 E6
Oakham Rutl'd 137 B7
Oakham W Midlands 133 F9
Oakhanger Hants 49 F9
Oakhill Som'set 44 D6
Oakhill W Sussex 51 G7
Oakhurst Kent 52 C5
Oakington Cambs 123 E8
Oaklands Flints 182 G2
Oaklands Herts 86 B2
Oaklands Powys 113 G10
Oakle Street Glos 80 B3
Oakleigh Park London 86 G3
Oakley Beds 121 G10
Oakley Bucks 83 C10
Oakley Fife 279 D10
Oakley Glos 99 G9
Oakley Hants 48 C5
Oakley Oxon 84 E2
Oakley Poole 18 B6
Oakley Suffolk 126 B3
Oakley Staffs 133 B7
Oakley Green Windsor 66 D2
Oakley Park Powys 129 F9
Oakmere Ches 167 B9
Oakridge Glos 80 E6
Oakridge Hants 48 C6
Oaks Shrops 131 C8
Oaks Green Derby 152 C3
Oaks in Charnwood Leics 153 F9
Oaksey Wilts 81 G7
Oakshaw Ford Cumb 240 B2
Oakshott Hants 34 B2
Oakthorpe Leics 152 G6
Oakwell W Yorks 197 B8
Oakwood Derby C 153 B7
Oakwood London 86 F3
Oakwood Northum 241 D10
Oakwood Warrington 183 B10
Oakwood W Yorks 206 F2
Oakwood Adventure Park, Narberth Pembs 73 C9
Oakwoodhill Surrey 50 F6
Oakworth W Yorks 204 F6
Oape H'land 309 J4
Oare Kent 70 G4
Oare Som'set 41 D10
Oare W Berks 64 E4
Oare Wilts 63 G7
Oareford Som'set 41 D10
Oasby Lincs 155 B10
Oat Hill Ches 167 F7
Oatfield Glos 80 D3
Oath Som'set 28 B5
Oathill Dorset 28 F6
Oathlaw Angus 287 B8
Oatlands Glasg C 267 C11
Oatlands N Yorks 206 C2
Oatlands Park Surrey 66 F5
Oban Arg/Bute 289 G10
Oban H'land 295 G10
Oban W Isles 305 H3
Oborne Dorset 29 D11
Obridge Som'set 28 B2
Obthorpe Lincs 155 F11
Occold Suffolk 126 C3
Ocean Beach Amusement Park, Rhyl Denbs 181 E7
Ochiltree E Ayrs 258 E2
Ochrwyth Caerph 59 B8
Ochr-y-foel Denbs 181 F9
Ochtermuthill Perth/Kinr 286 F2
Ochtertyre Perth/Kinr 286 E2
Ochtow H'land 309 J4
Ockbrook Derby 153 B8
Ocker Hill W Midlands 133 E9
Ockeridge Worcs 116 E5
Ockford Ridge Surrey 50 E3
Ockham Surrey 50 B5
Ockle H'land 289 B7
Ockley Kent 53 G9
Ockley Surrey 50 F6
Ocle Pychard Heref'd 97 B11
Octon ER Yorks 217 F10
Odcombe Som'set 29 D8
Odd Down Bath/NE Som'set 61 G8
Oddendale Cumb 221 C11
Odder Lincs 188 F6
Oddingley Worcs 117 F8
Oddington Oxon 83 C9
Odell Beds 121 F9
Odgen Gtr Man 196 E3
Odham Devon 25 G7
Odie Orkney 312 F7
Odiham Hants 49 C8
Odsal W Yorks 197 B7
Odsey Cambs 104 D5
Odstock Wilts 31 B10
Odstone Leics 135 B7
Offchurch Warwick 119 D7
Offenham Worcs 99 B11
Offenham Cross Worcs 99 B11
Offerton Gtr Man 184 D6
Offerton Tyne/Wear 243 F8
Offerton Green Gtr Man 184 D6
Offham E Sussex 36 E5
Offham Kent 53 B7
Offham W Sussex 35 F8
Offley Chase Herts 104 G2
Offley Hoo Herts 104 F3
Offleyhay Staffs 150 D5
Offleymarsh Staffs 150 D5
Offleyrock Staffs 150 D5
Offmore Farm Worcs 116 B6
Offord Cluny Cambs 122 D4
Offord D'Arcy Cambs 122 D4
Offton Suffolk 107 B11
Offwell Devon 15 B9
Ogbourne Maizey Wilts 63 E7
Ogbourne St. Andrew Wilts 63 E7
Ogbourne St. George Wilts 63 E7
Ogden W Yorks 205 G7
Ogdens Hants 31 E11
Ogden's Purlieu Hants 31 E11
Ogil Angus 292 G6
Ogle Northum 242 B4
Ogmore V/Glam 57 F11
Ogmore Vale Bridg 58 B2
Ogmore-by-Sea = Aberogwr V/Glam 57 G11
Okeford Fitzpaine Dorset 30 E4
Okehampton Devon 13 C7
Okehampton Camp Devon 13 C7
Oker Derby 170 C3
Okle Green Glos 98 F5
Okraquoy Shetl'd 315 K6
Olchfa Swan 75 G10
Old Northants 120 C5
Old Aberdeen Aberd C 293 C11
Old Alresford Hants 48 G5
Old Arley Warwick 134 E5
Old Basford Notts 171 G9
Old Basing Hants 49 C7
Old Belses Scot Borders 262 D3
Old Bewick Northum 264 E3
Old Blacksmith's Shop Centre, Gretna Green Dumf/Gal 239 D8
Old Blair Perth/Kinr 291 G10
Old Bolingbroke Lincs 174 B5
Old Boston Mersey 183 B9
Old Bramhope W Yorks 205 E10
Old Brampton Derby 186 G4
Old Bridge of Tilt Perth/Kinr 291 G10
Old Bridge of Urr Dumf/Gal 237 C9
Old Buckenham Norfolk 141 E11
Old Burdon Tyne/Wear 243 G9
Old Burghclere Hants 48 B3
Old Byland N Yorks 215 B10
Old Cambus Scot Borders 272 B6
Old Carlisle Cumb 229 B11
Old Cassop Durham 234 D2
Old Castleton Scot Borders 250 E2
Old Catton Norfolk 160 G4
Old Chalford Oxon 100 F6
Old Church Stoke Powys 130 D5
Old Clee NE Lincs 201 F9
Old Cleeve Som'set 42 E4
Old Clipstone Notts 171 C9
Old Colwyn Conwy 180 F5
Old Corry H'land 295 C8
Old Coulsdon London 51 B10
Old Craig Aberds 303 G9
Old Craig Angus 292 G4
Old Craighall E Loth 280 G6
Old Crombie Aberds 302 D5
Old Cullen Moray 302 C5
Old Dailly S Ayrs 244 D6
Old Dalby Leics 154 E3
Old Dam Derby 185 F10
Old Deer Aberds 303 E9
Old Denaby S Yorks 187 B7
Old Dilton Wilts 45 D11
Old Ditch Som'set 44 D4
Old Dolphin W Yorks 205 G8
Old Down S Glos 60 B6
Old Down Som'set 44 C6
Old Duffus Moray 301 C11
Old Edlington S Yorks 187 B8
Old Eldon Durham 233 F10
Old Ellerby ER Yorks 209 F9
Old Fallings W Midlands 133 C8
Old Farm Park M/Keynes 103 D8
Old Felixstowe Suffolk 108 D6
Old Field Shrops 115 B9
Old Field Carr Lancs 202 F3
Old Fletton Peterbro 138 D3
Old Fold Tyne/Wear 243 E7
Old Ford London 67 C11
Old Forge Heref'd 79 B9
Old Furnace Heref'd 97 G9
Old Furnace Torf 78 E3
Old Gate Lincs 157 E8
Old Glossop Derby 185 C8
Old Goginan Ceredig'n 128 G3
Old Goole ER Yorks 199 C8
Old Gore Heref'd 98 F2
Old Graitney Dumf/Gal 239 D8
Old Grimsbury Oxon 101 C9
Old Grimsby I/Scilly 1 F3
Old Hall Powys 129 G8
Old Hall Green Herts 105 G7
Old Hall Street Norfolk 160 C6
Old Hatfield Herts 86 D2
Old Heath Essex 107 G10
Old Heathfield E Sussex 37 C9
Old Hill W Midlands 133 F9
Old House, Rochford Essex 88 G5
Old Hunstanton Norfolk 175 G11
Old Hurst Cambs 122 B6
Old Hutton Cumb 211 B11
Old Hyton Cumb 210 B2
Old Kea Cornw'l 4 G6
Old Kilpatrick W Dunb 277 G9
Old Kinnernie Aberds 293 C9
Old Knebworth Herts 104 G4
Old Langho Lancs 203 F10
Old Laxey I/Man 192 D5
Old Leake Lincs 174 E6
Old Lindley W Yorks 196 D5
Old Linslade Beds 103 F8
Old Llanberis = Nant Peris Gwyn 163 D9
Old Malden London 67 F8
Old Malton N Yorks 216 E5
Old Micklefield W Yorks 206 G4
Old Milton Hants 19 C10
Old Milverton Warwick 118 D5
Old Monkland N Lanarks 268 C4
Old Netley Hants 33 F7
Old Newton Suffolk 125 E11
Old Oak Common London 67 C8
Old Passage S Glos 60 B5
Old Pentland Midloth 270 B5
Old Philipstoun W Loth 279 F11
Old Quarrington Durham 234 D2
Old Radnor Powys 114 F5
Old Rattray Aberds 303 D10
Old Rayne Aberds 302 G6
Old Romney Kent 39 B8
Old Sarum, Salisbury Wilts 46 G6
Old Shirley S'hampton 32 E5
Old Sodbury S Glos 61 C9
Old Somerby Lincs 155 C9
Old Stillington Stockton 234 G3
Old Stratford Northants 102 C5
Old Struan Perth/Kinr 291 G10
Old Swan Mersey 182 C5
Old Swarland Northum 252 C5
Old Swinford W Midlands 133 G9
Old Tame Gtr Man 196 F3
Old Tebay Cumb 222 D2
Old Thirsk N Yorks 215 C8
Old Toll S Ayrs 257 E9
Old Town C/Edinb 280 G5
Old Town Cumb 211 C11
Old Town Cumb 230 C5
Old Town E Sussex 23 F9
Old Town ER Yorks 218 F3
Old Town I/Scilly 1 G4
Old Town Northants 101 D11
Old Town Som'set 28 F4
Old Town S Yorks 197 F10
Old Town W Yorks 196 B3
Old Trafford Gtr Man 184 B4
Old Tree Kent 71 G8
Old Tupton Derby 170 B5
Old Warden Beds 104 C2
Old Weston Cambs 122 B2
Old Whittington Derby 186 G5
Old Wick H'land 310 D7
Old Windsor Windsor 66 E3
Old Wingate Durham 234 D3
Old Wives Lees Kent 54 C5
Old Woking Surrey 50 B4
Old Wolverton M/Keynes 102 C6
Old Woodbury Beds 122 G4
Old Woodhall Lincs 174 B2
Old Woodhouse Shrops 167 G9
Old Woods Shrops 149 E9
Old Woodstock Oxon 82 B6
Oldany H'land 306 F6
Oldberrow Warwick 118 D2
Oldborough Devon 26 F3
Oldbury Kent 52 B5
Oldbury Shrops 132 E4
Oldbury Warwick 134 E6
Oldbury W Midlands 133 F9
Oldbury Naite S Glos 79 G10
Oldbury on Severn S Glos 79 G10
Oldbury on the Hill Glos 61 B10
Oldcastle Bridg 58 D2
Oldcastle Monmouths 96 G6
Oldcastle Heath Ches 167 F7
Oldcotes Notts 187 E8
Oldcroft Glos 79 D10
Oldeamere Cambs 138 D6
Oldend Glos 80 D3
Oldfallow Staffs 151 G9
Oldfield Mersey 182 E3
Oldfield Shrops 132 F3
Oldfield Worcs 116 E6
Oldfield W Yorks 196 E6
Oldfield W Yorks 204 F6
Oldfield Brow Gtr Man 184 D2
Oldford Som'set 45 C9
Oldfurnace Staffs 169 G8
Oldhall Renf 267 B10
Oldhall Green Suffolk 125 F7
Oldhall Ho H'land 310 D6
Oldham Gtr Man 196 G2
Oldham Edge Gtr Man 196 F2
Oldhamstocks E Loth 282 G4
Oldland S Glos 61 E7
Oldland Common S Glos 61 E7
Oldmeldrum Aberds 303 G8
Oldmill Cornw'l 12 G3
Oldmixon N Som'set 43 B10
Oldpark Telford 132 B3
Oldridge Devon 14 B2
Oldshore Beg H'land 306 D6
Oldshoremore H'land 306 D7
Oldstead N Yorks 215 C10
Oldtown Aberds 293 C7
Oldtown Aberds 302 G5
Oldtown H'land 309 L5
Oldtown of Ord Aberds 302 D6
Oldwall Cumb 239 E11
Oldwalls Swan 75 G7
Oldway Swan 56 D5
Oldway Torbay 9 C7
Oldways End Devon 26 C5
Oldwhat Aberds 303 D8
Oldwich Lane W Midlands 118 C4
Olgrinmore H'land 310 D4
Oliver's Battery Hants 33 B7
Ollaberry Shetl'd 314 E5
Ollag W Isles 297 G3
Ollerbrook Booth Derby 185 E10
Ollerton Ches 184 F3
Ollerton Notts 171 B11
Ollerton Shrops 150 D3
Olmarch Ceredig'n 112 F2
Olmstead Green Cambs 106 C2
Olney M/Keynes 121 G7
Olrig Ho. H'land 310 C5
Olton W Midlands 134 G2
Olveston S Glos 60 B6
Ombersley Worcs 116 E6
Ompton Notts 171 B11
Omunsgarth Shetl'd 315 J5
Onchan I/Man 192 E4
Onecote Staffs 169 D8
Onehouse Suffolk 125 F10
Onen Monmouths 78 C6
Ongar Street Heref'd 115 D7
Ongley Kent 53 F10
Onibury Shrops 115 B9
Onich H'land 290 G2
Onllwyn Neath P Talb 76 C4
Onneley Staffs 168 G3
Onslow Village Surrey 50 D3
Onston Ches 183 G9
Onthank E Ayrs 267 G8
Onziebust Orkney 312 F5
Openshaw Gtr Man 184 C5
Openwoodgate Derby 170 F5
Opinan H'land 299 B7
Opinan H'land 307 K3
Orange Lane Scot Borders 272 G5
Orange Row Norfolk 157 E10
Orasaigh W Isles 305 G5
Orbiston N Lanarks 268 D4
Orbliston Moray 302 D3
Orbost H'land 298 E2
Orby Lincs 175 B7
Orchard Hill Devon 24 B6
Orchard Leigh Bucks 85 E7
Orchard Portman Som'set 28 C2
Orcheston Wilts 46 D5
Orcop Heref'd 97 F9
Orcop Hill Heref'd 97 F9
Ord H'land 295 D8
Ordale Shetl'd 314 C8
Ordhead Aberds 293 B8
Ordie Aberds 292 C6
Ordiequish Moray 302 D3
Ordiqhill Aberds 302 D5
Ordley Northum 241 F10
Ordsall Gtr Man 184 B4
Ordsall Notts 188 F2
Ore E Sussex 38 E4
Oreston Plym'th 7 E10
Oreton Shrops 132 G3
Orford Lincs 190 C2
Orford Suffolk 109 B8
Orford Warrington 183 C10
Organford Dorset 18 C4
Orgreave Staffs 152 F3
Oridge Street Glos 98 F5
Orleton Heref'd 115 D9
Orleton Worcs 116 D3
Orlingbury Northants 121 C7
Ormacleit W Isles 297 H3
Ormathwaite Cumb 229 F11
Ormesby Redcar/Clevel'd 225 B10
Ormesby St. Margaret Norfolk 161 G9
Ormesby St. Michael Norfolk 161 G9
Ormiclate Castle W Isles 297 H3
Ormidale Lodge Arg/Bute 275 F11
Ormiscaig H'land 307 K3
Ormiston E Loth 271 B8
Ormsaigbeg H'land 288 C6
Ormsaigmore H'land 288 C6
Ormsary Arg/Bute 275 F8
Ormsgill Cumb 210 E3
Ormskirk Lancs 194 F2
Ornsby Hill Durham 233 B9
Orpington London 68 F3
Orrell Gtr Man 194 G4
Orrell Mersey 182 B4
Orrell Post Gtr Man 194 F4
Orrisdale I/Man 192 C4
Orrock Fife 280 D4
Orroland Dumf/Gal 237 E9
Orsett Thurr'k 68 C6
Orsett Heath Thurr'k 68 E6
Orslow Staffs 150 F6
Orston Notts 172 G2
Orthwaite Cumb 229 E11
Ortner Lancs 202 C6
Orton Cumb 222 D2
Orton Northants 120 B6
Orton Staffs 133 D7
Orton Brimbles Peterbro 138 D2
Orton Goldhay Peterbro 138 D3
Orton Longueville Peterbro 138 D3
Orton Malborne Peterbro 138 D3
Orton on the Hill Leics 134 C6
Orton Rigg Cumb 239 G8
Orton Waterville Peterbro 138 D3
Orton Wistow Peterbro 138 D2
Orwell Cambs 123 G7
Osbaldeston Lancs 203 G8
Osbaldeston Green Lancs 203 G8
Osbaldwick C/York 207 C8
Osbaston Leics 135 C8
Osbaston Telford 150 F2
Osbaston Hollow Leics 135 B8
Osborne House I/Wight 20 C6
Osbournby Lincs 155 B11
Oscroft Ches 167 B8
Ose H'land 298 E3
Osgathorpe Leics 153 F8
Osgodby Lincs 189 C9
Osgodby N Yorks 207 G8
Osgodby N Yorks 217 C11
Osidge London 86 G3
Oskaig H'land 295 B7
Oskamull Arg/Bute 288 E6
Osleston Derby 152 B4
Osmaston Derby 169 G11
Osmaston Derby C 153 C7
Osmington Dorset 17 E10
Osmington Mills Dorset 17 E10
Osmondthorpe W Yorks 206 G2
Osmotherley N Yorks 225 F9
Osney Oxon 83 D7
Ospisdale H'land 309 L7
Ospringe Kent 70 G3
Ossett W Yorks 197 C9
Ossett Spa W Yorks 197 D9
Ossett Street Side W Yorks 197 C9
Ossington Notts 172 C3
Ostend Essex 88 F6
Ostend Norfolk 161 C7
Osterley London 66 D6
Oswaldkirk N Yorks 216 D2
Oswaldtwistle Lancs 195 B8
Oswestry Shrops 148 D5
Otby Lincs 189 C10
Otford Kent 52 B4
Otham Kent 53 C9
Otham Hole Kent 53 C9
Othery Som'set 43 G11
Otley Suffolk 126 F4
Otley W Yorks 205 E9
Otter Ferry Arg/Bute 275 E10
Otter Ho Arg/Bute 275 F10
Otterbourne Hants 33 C7
Otterburn Northum 251 E9
Otterburn N Yorks 204 B3
Otterburn Camp Northum 251 D9
Otterham Cornw'l 11 C9
Otterham Quay Kent 69 F10
Otterhampton Som'set 43 E8
Ottershaw Surrey 66 G4
Otterspool Mersey 182 D5
Otterswick Shetl'd 314 E7
Otterton Devon 15 D7
Otterwood Hants 32 G6
Ottery St. Mary Devon 15 B8
Ottinge Kent 55 E7
Ottringham ER Yorks 201 C9
Oughterby Cumb 239 F7
Oughtershaw N Yorks 213 C7
Oughterside Cumb 229 C8
Oughtibridge S Yorks 186 C4
Oughtrington Warrington 183 D11
Oulston N Yorks 215 E10
Oulton Cumb 238 G6
Oulton Norfolk 160 D2
Oulton Suffolk 143 E10
Oulton Staffs 151 B8
Oulton W Yorks 197 B11
Oulton Broad Suffolk 143 E10
Oulton Heath Staffs 151 B8
Oulton Park Motor Racing Circuit Ches 167 C9
Oulton Street Norfolk 160 D3
Oultoncross Staffs 151 C8
Oundle Northants 137 F10
Ousby Cumb 231 E8
Ousdale H'land 311 G4
Ousden Suffolk 124 F4
Ousefleet ER Yorks 199 C10
Ouston Durham 243 G7
Ouston Northum 241 G7
Ouston Northum 242 C3
Out Elmstead Kent 55 C8
Out Gate Cumb 221 F7
Out Newton ER Yorks 201 C11
Out Rawcliffe Lancs 202 E4
Outchester Northum 264 C4
Outer Hope Devon 8 G3
Outertown Orkney 312 G3
Outhgill Cumb 222 E5
Outhill Warwick 118 D2
Outhills Aberds 303 D10
Outlane W Yorks 196 D5
Outwell Norfolk 139 C10
Outwick Hants 31 D10
Outwood Gtr Man 195 F9
Outwood Surrey 51 D10
Outwood W Yorks 197 C10
Outwoods Leics 153 F8
Outwoods Staffs 150 F5
Outwoods Warwick 134 G4
Ouzlewell Green W Yorks 197 B10
Ovenden W Yorks 196 B5
Ovenden Wood W Yorks 196 B5
Ovenscloss Scot Borders 261 C11
Over Cambs 123 C7
Over Ches 167 B10
Over Glos 80 B4
Over S Glos 60 C5
Over Burrow Lancs 212 D2
Over Burrows Derby 152 B5
Over Compton Dorset 29 D9
Over End Cambs 137 D11
Over End Derby 186 G3
Over Green W Midlands 134 E3
Over Haddon Derby 170 B2
Over Hall Suffolk 108 D4
Over Hulton Gtr Man 195 F7
Over Kellet Lancs 211 F10
Over Kiddington Oxon 101 G8
Over Knutsford Ches 184 F3
Over Leck Lancs 212 D3
Over Monnow Monmouths 79 C8
Over Norton Oxon 100 F6
Over Silton N Yorks 225 G9
Over Stowey Som'set 43 F7
Over Stratton Som'set 28 D6
Over Tabley Ches 184 E2
Over Town Lancs 195 B11
Over Wallop Hants 47 F9
Over Whitacre Warwick 134 E5
Over Worton Oxon 101 F8
Overbister Orkney 312 D7
Overbury Worcs 99 D9
Overcombe Dorset 17 E9
Overend W Midlands 133 G8
Overgreen Derby 186 G4
Overleigh Som'set 44 F3
Overpool Ches 182 F5
Overscaig Hotel H'land 309 G4
Overseal Derby 152 F5
Overslade Warwick 119 C9
Oversland Kent 54 B5
Oversley Green Warwick 117 F11
Overstone Northants 120 D6
Overstrand Norfolk 160 A4
Overthorpe Northants 101 C9
Overthorpe W Yorks 197 D8
Overthwaite Cumb 211 C10
Overton Aberds 293 B9
Overton Aberd C 293 B10
Overton Ches 183 F8
Overton Dumf/Gal 237 C11
Overton Glos 80 C2
Overton Hants 48 D4
Overton Lancs 202 B4
Overton N Yorks 207 B7
Overton = Owrtyn Wrex 166 G5
Overton Shrops 115 C10
Overton Staffs 151 B11
Overton Swan 56 D3
Overton W Yorks 197 D9
Overtown Lancs 212 D2
Overtown N Lanarks 268 E6
Overtown Swindon 63 D7
Overy Oxon 83 G9
Oving Bucks 102 G5
Oving W Sussex 34 F6
Ovingdean Brighton/Hove 36 G5
Ovingham Northum 242 E3
Ovington Durham 224 C2
Ovington Essex 106 C5
Ovington Hants 48 G5
Ovington Norfolk 141 C8
Ovington Northum 242 E3
Ower Hants 32 D4
Owermoigne Dorset 17 D11
Owl End Cambs 122 B4
Owlcotes Derby 170 B6
Owler Bar Derby 186 F3
Owlerton S Yorks 186 D4
Owlet W Yorks 205 F9
Owletts End Worcs 99 C10
Owl's Green Suffolk 126 D5
Owlsmoor Brackn'l 65 G11
Owlswick Bucks 84 D3
Owlthorpe S Yorks 186 E6
Owmby Lincs 200 G5
Owmby-by-Spital Lincs 189 D8
Ownham W Berks 64 E2
Owrtyn = Overton Wrex 166 G5
Owslebury Hants 33 C8
Owston Leics 136 B5
Owston S Yorks 198 E4
Owston Ferry N Lincs 199 G10
Owstwick ER Yorks 209 G11
Owthorne ER Yorks 201 B10
Owthorpe Notts 154 C3
Owton Manor Hartlep'l 234 F5
Oxborough Norfolk 140 C4
Oxburgh Hall Norfolk 140 C4
Oxclose S Yorks 186 E6
Oxclose Tyne/Wear 243 F7
Oxcombe Lincs 190 F4
Oxcroft Derby 187 G7
Oxen End Essex 106 F3
Oxen Park Cumb 210 B6
Oxenhall Glos 98 F4
Oxenholme Cumb 221 G10
Oxenhope W Yorks 204 F6
Oxenpill Som'set 44 E2
Oxenton Glos 99 E9
Oxenwood Wilts 47 B10
Oxford Oxon 83 D8
Oxford University Botanic Garden Oxon 83 D8
Oxgang E Dunb 278 G3
Oxgangs C/Edinb 270 B4
Oxhey Herts 85 F10
Oxhill Durham 242 G5
Oxhill Warwick 100 B6
Oxlease Herts 86 D2
Oxley W Midlands 133 C8
Oxley Green Essex 88 C6
Oxley's Green E Sussex 37 C11
Oxlode Cambs 139 F9
Oxnam Scot Borders 262 F5
Oxnead Norfolk 160 E4
Oxshott Surrey 66 G6
Oxspring S Yorks 197 G9
Oxted Surrey 51 C11
Oxton Scot Borders 271 E9
Oxton Mersey 182 D3
Oxton Notts 171 E11
Oxton N Yorks 206 E6
Oxwich Swan 56 D3
Oxwich Green Swan 56 D3
Oxwick Norfolk 159 D8
Oykel Bridge H'land 309 J3
Oyne Aberds 302 G6
Oystermouth Swan 56 D6
Ozleworth Glos 80 G3

P

Pabail Iarach W Isles 304 E7
Pabail Uarach W Isles 304 E7
Packers Hill Dorset 30 E2
Packington Leics 153 G7
Packmoor Stoke 168 E5
Packmores Warwick 118 D5
Packwood W Midlands 118 C3
Padanaram Angus 287 B8
Padbury Bucks 102 E4
Paddington London 67 C9
Paddington Warrington 183 D10
Paddlesworth Kent 55 E7
Paddlesworth Kent 69 G7
Paddock Kent 54 C3
Paddock W Yorks 196 D6
Paddock Wood Kent 53 E7
Paddockhaugh Moray 302 D2
Paddockhole Dumf/Gal 248 G6
Paddolgreen Shrops 149 C10
Padfield Derby 185 B8
Padgate Warrington 183 C10
Padham's Green Essex 87 F10
Padiham Lancs 203 G11
Padog Conwy 164 E4
Padside N Yorks 205 B9
Padside Green N Yorks 205 B9
Padstow Cornw'l 10 F4
Padworth W Berks 64 F6
Paganhill Glos 80 D4
Page Bank Durham 233 D10
Page Moss Mersey 182 C6
Page's Green Suffolk 126 D2
Pagham W Sussex 22 D5
Paglesham Churchend Essex 88 G6
Paglesham Eastend Essex 88 G6
Paibeil W Isles 296 E3
Paible W Isles 305 J2
Paignton Devon 9 C7
Paignton Zoo Devon 9 D7
Pailton Warwick 135 G9
Painleyhill Staffs 151 C10
Pains Hill Surrey 52 C2
Painscastle Powys 96 B3
Painshawfield Northum 242 E3
Painsthorpe ER Yorks 208 B2
Painswick Glos 80 D5
Painter's Forstal Kent 54 B3
Painter's Green Herts 86 B3
Painthorpe W Yorks 197 D10
Pairc Shiaboist W Isles 304 D4
Paisley Renf 267 C9
Pakefield Suffolk 143 E10
Pakenham Suffolk 125 D8
Palace House, Beaulieu Hants 32 G5
Palace of Holyroodhouse C/Edinb 280 G5
Palacefields Halton 183 E9
Pale Gwyn 147 B9
Pale Green Essex 106 C3
Palehouse Common E Sussex 37 D7
Palestine Hants 47 E9
Paley Street Windsor 65 D11
Palfrey W Midlands 133 D10
Palgowan Dumf/Gal 245 G9
Palgrave Suffolk 126 B2
Palla Flat Cumb 219 C9
Pallion Tyne/Wear 243 F9
Palmarsh Kent 54 G6
Palmers Devon 26 G6
Palmers Cross Staffs 133 C7
Palmer's Flat Glos 79 D9
Palmer's Green Kent 53 E7
Palmer's Green London 86 G4
Palmerstown V/Glam 58 F6
Palmersville Tyne/Wear 243 C7
Palnackie Dumf/Gal 237 D10
Palnure Dumf/Gal 236 C6
Palterton Derby 171 B7
Pamber End Hants 48 B6
Pamber Green Hants 48 B6
Pamber Heath Hants 64 G6
Pamington Glos 99 E8
Pamphill Dorset 31 G7
Pampisford Cambs 105 B8
Pan Orkney 313 J4
Panborough Som'set 44 D3
Panbride Angus 287 D9
Pancakehill Glos 81 C9
Pancrasweek Devon 24 F3
Pancross V/Glam 58 F4
Pandy Gwyn 128 C2
Pandy Gwyn 147 D7
Pandy Monmouths 96 G6
Pandy Powys 129 C8
Pandy Wrex 148 B3
Pandy Tudur Conwy 164 C5
Pandy'r Capel Denbs 165 E9
Panfield Essex 106 F4
Pangbourne W Berks 64 D6
Pangelly Cornw'l 11 E7
Panhall Fife 280 C6
Pannal N Yorks 206 C2
Pannal Ash N Yorks 205 C11
Panshanger Herts 86 C3
Pant Caerph 78 F2
Pant Denbs 166 E2
Pant Flints 181 G10
Pant Gwyn 144 C4
Pant Merth Tyd 77 D9
Pant Shrops 148 E5
Pant Wrex 166 F3
Pant Mawr Powys 129 G7
Panta Monmouths 79 F7
Pantasaph Flints 181 F11
Panteg Ceredig'n 111 E9
Panteg Torf 78 F4
Pantersbridge Cornw'l 6 B3

418 Qua – Roc

Quarndon Common Derby 170 G4
Quarr Dorset 30 B3
Quarr Hill I/Wight 21 C7
Quarrelton Renf 267 C8
Quarrelwood Dumf/Gal 247 G11
Quarrendon Bucks 84 B4
Quarrier's Village Invercl 267 B7
Quarrington Lincs 173 G9
Quarrington Hill Durham 234 D2
Quarry Bank W Midlands 133 F8
Quarry Bank Mill, Wilmslow Ches 184 E4
Quarry Hill Staffs 134 C4
Quarrybank Ches 167 B9
Quarryford E Loth 271 B11
Quarryhead Aberds 303 C9
Quarryhill H'land 309 L7
Quarrywood Moray 301 C11
Quarter S Lanarks 268 E4
Quatford Shrops 132 E4
Quatquoy Orkney 312 G4
Quatt Shrops 132 F5
Quebb Heref'd 114 G6
Quebec Durham 233 C9
Quedgeley Glos 80 C4
Queen Adelaide Cambs 139 G11
Queen Camel Som'set 29 C9
Queen Charlton Bath/NE Som'set 60 F6
Queen Dart Devon 26 D4
Queen Oak Dorset 45 G9
Queen Street Kent 53 D7
Queen Street Wilts 62 B4
Queenborough Kent 70 E2
Queenhill Worcs 99 D7
Queen's Bower I/Wight 21 E7
Queen's Head Shrops 148 D6
Queen's Park Blackb'n 195 B7
Queen's Park Beds 103 B10
Queens Park Ches 166 B6
Queens Park Essex 87 F11
Queen's Park Northants 120 E5
Queen's View Centre, Loch Tummel Perth/Kinr 286 B2
Queensbury London 67 B7
Queensbury W Yorks 205 G7
Queensferry C/Edinb 280 F2
Queensferry Flints 166 B4
Queenstown Blackp'l 202 F2
Queensville Staffs 151 E8
Queensway Fife 280 A5
Queenzieburn N Lanarks 278 F3
Quemerford Wilts 62 E4
Quenchwell Cornw'l 4 G5
Quendale Shetl'd 315 M5
Quendon Essex 105 E10
Queniborough Leics 154 G2
Quenington Glos 81 E10
Quernmore Lancs 202 B6
Queslett W Midlands 133 E11
Quethiock Cornw'l 6 C6
Quham Shetl'd 314 G6
Quholm Orkney 312 G3
Quick Gtr Man 196 G3
Quick Edge Gtr Man 196 G3
Quick's Green W Berks 64 D5
Quidenham Norfolk 141 F10
Quidhampton Hants 48 C4
Quidhampton Wilts 46 G6
Quilquox Aberds 303 F9
Quina Brook Shrops 149 C10
Quindry Orkney 313 J5
Quinton Northants 120 G5
Quinton W Midlands 133 G9
Quinton Green Northants 120 G5
Quintrell Downs Cornw'l 5 D7
Quixhill Staffs 169 G10
Quoditch Devon 12 B4
Quoig Perth/Kinr 286 E2
Quorndon Leics 153 F11
Quothquan S Lanarks 259 B11
Quoyloo Orkney 312 F3
Quoynee H'land 310 D6
Quoyness Orkney 313 H3
Quoys Shetl'd 314 B8
Quoys Shetl'd 315 G6

R

Raasay Ho. H'land 295 B7
Rabbit's Cross Kent 53 D9
Rableyheath Herts 86 B2
Raby Cumb 238 G5
Raby Mersey 182 F4
Racecourse Suffolk 108 C3
Rachan Mill Scot Borders 260 C4
Rachub Gwyn 163 B10
Rack End Oxon 82 E6
Rackenford Devon 26 D5
Rackham W Sussex 35 E9
Rackheath Norfolk 160 G5
Rackley Som'set 43 C11
Racks Dumf/Gal 238 C2
Rackwick Orkney 312 D5
Rackwick Orkney 313 J3
Radbourne Derby 152 B5
Radcliffe Gtr Man 195 F9
Radcliffe Northum 253 C7
Radcliffe on Trent Notts 154 B2
Radclive Bucks 102 E3
Radcot Oxon 82 F3
Raddery H'land 301 D7
Raddington Som'set 27 B8
Radernie Fife 287 G8
Radfall Kent 70 G6
Radford Blackb'n 195 C7
Radford Bath/NE Som'set 45 B7
Radford Notts 171 G9
Radford Oxon 101 G8
Radford W Midlands 134 G6
Radford Worcs 117 F10
Radford Semele Warwick 118 E6
Radipole Dorset 17 E9
Radlet Som'set 43 F8
Radlett Herts 85 E11
Radley Oxon 83 F8
Radley Green Essex 87 D10
Radmanthwaite Notts 171 C8
Radmoor Shrops 150 E2
Radmore Green Ches 167 E9
Radmore Wood Staffs 151 D11
Radnage Bucks 84 F3
Radnor Park W Dunb 277 G9
Radstock Bath/NE Som'set 45 B7
Radstone Northants 101 C11
Radway Warwick 101 B7
Radwell Beds 121 F10
Radwell Herts 104 D4
Radwinter Essex 106 D2
Radwinter End Essex 106 D2
Radyr Card 58 C6
Raera Arg/Bute 289 G10
RAF Museum, Cosford Shrops 132 C5
RAF Museum, Hendon London 67 A8
Rafford Moray 301 D10
Raftra Cornw'l 1 E3
Raga Shetl'd 314 D6
Ragdale Leics 154 F3
Ragged Appleshaw Hants 47 D10
Raginnis Cornw'l 1 D5
Raglan Monmouths 78 D6
Ragley Hall Warwick 117 F11
Ragmere Norfolk 141 E11
Ragnall Notts 188 G4
Rahoy H'land 289 D8
Raigbeg H'land 301 G8
Rain Shore Gtr Man 195 D11
Rainbow Hill Worcs 117 F7
Rainford Mersey 194 G3
Rainford Junction Mersey 194 G3
Rainham London 68 C4
Rainham Medway 69 F10
Rainhill Mersey 183 C7
Rainhill Stoops Mersey 183 C8
Rainow Ches 185 F7
Rainowlow Ches 184 F7
Rainsough Gtr Man 195 G10
Rainton Dumf/Gal 237 D8
Rainton N Yorks 215 D7
Rainton Bridge Tyne/Wear 234 C2
Rainworth Notts 171 E9
Raisbeck Cumb 222 D2
Raise Cumb 231 B10
Rait Perth/Kinr 286 E6
Raithby Lincs 174 B5
Raithby Lincs 190 E4
Raithwaite N Yorks 227 C7
Rake W Sussex 34 B4
Rake End Staffs 151 F11
Rake Head Lancs 195 C10
Rakes Dale Staffs 169 G9
Rakeway Staffs 169 G8
Rakewood Gtr Man 196 E2
Ralia Lodge H'land 291 D9
Rallt Swan 75 G8
Ram Carms 93 B11
Ram Alley Wilts 63 G8
Ram Hill S Glos 61 D7
Ram Lane Kent 54 D3
Ramasaig H'land 297 G7
Rame Cornw'l 2 C6
Rame Cornw'l 7 F8
Rameldry Mill Bank Fife 287 G7
Ramley Hants 19 B11
Ramnageo Shetl'd 314 C8
Rampisham Dorset 29 G9
Rampside Cumb 210 F4
Rampton Cambs 123 D8
Rampton Notts 188 F3
Ramsbottom Gtr Man 195 D10
Ramsburn Moray 302 D5
Ramsbury Wilts 63 E9
Ramscraigs H'land 311 G5
Ramsdean Hants 34 C2
Ramsdell Hants 48 B5
Ramsden London 68 F3
Ramsden Oxon 82 B5
Ramsden Bellhouse Essex 88 G2
Ramsden Heath Essex 88 F2
Ramsey Cambs 138 F5
Ramsey Essex 108 E4
Ramsey I/Man 192 C5
Ramsey Forty Foot Cambs 138 F6
Ramsey Heights Cambs 138 F5
Ramsey Island Essex 88 D6
Ramsey Mereside Cambs 138 F5
Ramsey St. Mary's Cambs 138 F5
Ramseycleuch Scot Borders 261 G7
Ramsgate Kent 71 G11
Ramsgill N Yorks 214 E2
Ramshaw Durham 232 B5
Ramsholt Suffolk 108 C6
Ramshorn Staffs 169 F9
Ramsley Devon 13 C8
Ramslye Kent 52 F5
Ranais W Isles 304 F6
Ranby Lincs 190 F2
Ranby Notts 187 E11
Rand Lincs 189 F10
Randlay Telford 132 B4
Randwick Glos 80 D4
Ranfurly Renf 267 C7
Rangag H'land 310 E5
Rangemore Staffs 152 E3
Rangeworthy S Glos 61 B7
Rankinston E Ayrs 257 G11
Rank's Green Essex 88 B2
Ranmoor S Yorks 186 D4
Ranmore Common Surrey 50 C6
Rannerdale Cumb 220 B3
Rannoch Lodge Perth/Kinr 285 B9
Rannoch Station Perth/Kinr 285 B8
Ranochan H'land 295 G10
Ranscombe Som'set 42 E2
Ranskill Notts 187 E11
Ranton Staffs 151 E7
Ranton Green Staffs 150 E6
Ranworth Norfolk 161 G7
Raploch Stirl 278 C5
Rapness Orkney 312 D6
Rapps Som'set 28 D4
Rascal Moor ER Yorks 208 F2
Rascarrel Dumf/Gal 237 E9
Rashfield Arg/Bute 276 E2
Rashielee Renf 277 G9
Rashiereive Aberds 303 G9
Rashwood Worcs 117 D8
Raskelf N Yorks 215 E9
Rassal H'land 299 E8
Rassau Bl Gwent 77 C11
Rastrick W Yorks 196 C6
Ratagan H'land 295 D11
Ratby Leics 135 B10
Ratcliffe Culey Leics 134 D6
Ratcliffe on Soar Notts 153 D9
Ratcliffe on the Wreake Leics 154 G2
Ratford Wilts 62 E3
Ratfyn Wilts 46 E7
Rathen Aberds 303 C10
Rathillet Fife 287 E7
Rathmell N Yorks 204 B2
Ratho C/Edinb 280 G2
Ratho Byres C/Edinb 280 G2
Ratho Station C/Edinb 280 G2
Rathven Moray 302 C4
Ratlake Hants 32 C6
Ratley Warwick 101 B7
Ratling Kent 55 C8
Ratlinghope Shrops 131 D8
Ratsloe Devon 14 B5
Rattar H'land 310 B6
Ratten Row Cumb 230 C2
Ratten Row Cumb 230 B3
Ratten Row Lancs 202 E4
Ratten Row Norfolk 157 G10
Rattery Devon 8 C4
Rattlesden Suffolk 125 F9
Ratton Village E Sussex 23 E9
Rattray Perth/Kinr 286 C5
Raughton Cumb 230 B3
Raughton Head Cumb 230 B3
Raunds Northants 121 C9
Ravelston C/Edinb 280 G4
Ravenfield S Yorks 187 B7
Ravenglass Cumb 219 F11
Ravenglass and Eskdale Railway & Museum Cumb 219 F11
Ravenhead Mersey 183 C9
Raveningham Norfolk 143 D7
Raven's Green Essex 108 G2
Ravenscar N Yorks 227 E9
Ravenscliffe W Yorks 205 F9
Ravenscraig Invercl 276 G4
Ravensdale I/Man 192 C4
Ravensden Beds 121 G11
Ravenseat N Yorks 223 E7
Ravenshead Notts 171 E9
Ravenshills Green Worcs 116 G4
Ravensmoor Ches 167 E10
Ravensthorpe Northants 120 C3
Ravensthorpe Peterbro 138 C3
Ravensthorpe W Yorks 197 C8
Ravenstone Leics 153 G8
Ravenstone M/Keynes 120 G6
Ravenstonedale Cumb 222 E4
Ravenstown Cumb 211 D7
Ravenstruther S Lanarks 269 F8
Ravenswick N Yorks 216 B3
Ravensworth N Yorks 224 D2
Raw N Yorks 227 D8
Rawcliffe C/York 207 C7
Rawcliffe ER Yorks 199 C7
Rawcliffe Br ER Yorks 199 C7
Rawdon W Yorks 205 F10
Rawgreen Northum 241 F10
Rawmarsh S Yorks 186 B6
Rawnsley Staffs 151 G10
Rawreth Essex 88 G3
Rawridge Devon 28 F2
Rawson Green Derby 170 F5
Rawtenstall Lancs 195 C10
Rawthorpe W Yorks 197 D7
Raxton Aberds 303 F8
Raydon Suffolk 107 D10
Raylees Northum 251 E10
Rayleigh Essex 88 G4
Rayne Essex 106 G4
Rayners Lane London 66 B6
Raynes Park London 67 F8
Rea Glos 80 B4
Rea Hill Torbay 9 D8
Reach Cambs 123 D11
Read Lancs 203 G11
Reader's Corner Essex 88 E2
Reading Reading 65 E8
Reading Green Suffolk 126 C4
Reading Street Kent 71 F11
Reading Street Kent 54 G2
Readings Glos 79 B10
Readymoney Cornw'l 6 E2
Reagill Cumb 222 B2
Rearquhar H'land 309 K7
Rearsby Leics 154 G3
Reasby Lincs 189 F9
Reaster H'land 310 C6
Reaulay H'land 299 D7
Reawick Shetl'd 315 J5
Reawla Cornw'l 2 B4
Reay H'land 310 C3
Rechullin H'land 299 D8
Reculver Kent 71 F8
Red Ball Devon 27 D9
Red Bull Ches 168 D4
Red Bull Staffs 150 B4
Red Dial Cumb 229 B11
Red Hill Bournem'th 19 B7
Red Hill Hants 34 E2
Red Hill Heref'd 97 D10
Red Hill W Berks 64 G2
Red Hill W Midlands 117 B10
Red Hill W Yorks 198 B2
Red House Glass Cone, Wordsley W Midlands 133 F7
Red Lake Telford 150 G3
Red Lodge Suffolk 124 C3
Red Lumb Gtr Man 195 D10
Red Pits Norfolk 159 D11
Red Post Bath/NE Som'set 45 B8
Red Rail Heref'd 97 F10
Red Rock Gtr Man 194 F5
Red Roses Carms 74 C2
Red Row Northum 253 D7
Red Scar Lancs 203 G7
Red Street Staffs 168 E4
Red Wharf Bay Angl 179 E8
Redberth Pembs 73 E9
Redbourn Herts 85 C10
Redbournbury Herts 85 C10
Redbourne N Lincs 200 G3
Redbridge Dorset 17 D11
Redbridge London 68 B2
Redbridge S'thampton 32 E5
Redbrook Glos 79 C8
Redbrook S Yorks 197 F10
Redbrook Wrex 167 G8
Redburn H'land 300 C5
Redburn H'land 301 E9
Redburn Northum 241 E7
Redcar Redcar/Clevel'd 235 F8
Redcar Racecourse Redcar/Clevel'd 235 G8
Redcastle Angus 287 B10
Redcastle H'land 300 E5
Redcliff Bay N Som'set 60 D2
Redcroft Dumf/Gal 237 B9
Redden Scot Borders 263 B7
Reddicap Heath W Midlands 134 D2
Redding Falk 279 F8
Reddingmuirhead Falk 279 F8
Reddish Gtr Man 184 C5
Redditch Worcs 117 D11
Rede Suffolk 124 F6
Redenhall Norfolk 142 G5
Redenham Hants 47 D10
Redesdale Camp Northum 251 D8
Redesmouth Northum 251 G9
Redford Aberds 293 F9
Redford Angus 287 C9
Redfordgreen Scot Borders 261 F9
Redgate Cornw'l 6 B4
Redgorton Perth/Kinr 286 E4
Redgrave Suffolk 125 B10
Redheugh Angus 292 G6
Redhill Aberds 293 C9
Redhill Aberds 302 F6
Redhill Herts 104 E6
Redhill N Som'set 60 G4
Redhill Notts 171 G9
Redhill Surrey 51 C9
Redhills Cumb 230 F6
Redhills Devon 14 C4
Redhouse Arg/Bute 275 G9
Redhouses Arg/Bute 274 G4
Redisham Suffolk 143 G8
Redland Bristol 60 E5
Redland Orkney 312 F4
Redland End Bucks 84 E4
Redlingfield Suffolk 126 C3
Redlynch Som'set 45 G8
Redlynch Wilts 32 C2
Redmain Cumb 229 E8
Redmarley Worcs 116 D5
Redmarley D'Abitot Glos 98 E5
Redmarshall Stockton 234 G3
Redmile Leics 154 B5
Redmire N Yorks 223 G10
Redmoor Cornw'l 5 C11
Redmoss Aberds 303 F8
Rednal Shrops 149 D7
Rednal W Midlands 117 B10
Redpath Scot Borders 262 B3
Redpoint H'land 299 C7
Redruth Cornw'l 4 G4
Redstocks Wilts 62 G2
Redtye Cornw'l 5 C10
Redvales Gtr Man 195 F9
Redwick Newp 60 C2
Redwick S Glos 60 B4
Redworth D'lington 233 G10
Reed Herts 105 D7
Reed End Herts 104 D6
Reed Point Lincs 156 B5
Reedham Lincs 174 D2
Reedham Norfolk 143 C8
Reedley Lancs 204 F3
Reedness ER Yorks 199 C9
Reeds Beck Lincs 174 B2
Reeds Holme Lancs 195 C10
Reedy Devon 14 D2
Reen Sands Cornw'l 4 E5
Reepham Lincs 189 G8
Reepham Norfolk 159 E11
Reeth N Yorks 223 F10
Reeves Green W Midlands 118 B5
Refail Powys 130 C3
Regaby I/Man 192 C5
Regoul H'land 301 D8
Reiff H'land 307 H4
Reigate Surrey 51 D8
Reighton N Yorks 218 D2
Reinigeadal W Isles 305 H4
Reisque Aberds 293 B10
Reiss H'land 310 D7
Rejerrah Cornw'l 4 D5
Releath Cornw'l 2 C5
Relubbus Cornw'l 2 C3
Relugas Moray 301 E9
Remenham Wokingham 65 C9
Remenham Hill Wokingham 65 C9
Remony Perth/Kinr 285 C11
Rempstone Notts 153 E11
Remusaig H'land 309 J7
Rendcomb Glos 81 D8
Rendham Suffolk 126 E6
Rendlesham Suffolk 126 G6
Renfrew Renf 267 B10
Renhold Beds 121 G11
Renishaw Derby 186 F6
Renmure Angus 287 B10
Rennington Northum 264 F6
Renton W Dunb 277 F7
Renville Kent 55 C7
Renwick Cumb 231 C7
Repps Norfolk 161 F8
Repton Derby 152 D6
Reraig H'land 295 C10
Reraig Cot H'land 295 B10
Rerwick Shetl'd 315 M5
Rescassa Cornw'l 5 G9
Rescobie Angus 287 B9
Rescorla Cornw'l 5 D10
Resipole H'land 289 C9
Reskadinnick Cornw'l 4 G2
Resolfen = Resolven Neath P Talb 76 E4
Resolis H'land 300 C6
Resolven = Resolfen Neath P Talb 76 E4
Restalrig C/Edinb 280 G5
Reston Scot Borders 273 C7
Reston Cumb 221 F9
Restrop Wilts 62 B5
Resugga Green Cornw'l 5 D10
Reswallie Angus 287 B9
Retford Notts 188 E2
Retire Cornw'l 5 C10
Rettendon Essex 88 F3
Revesby Lincs 174 C4
Revesby Bridge Lincs 174 C4
Revidge Blackb'n 195 B7
Rew Street I/Wight 20 C5
Rewe Devon 14 B4
Rexon Devon 12 D4
Reybridge Wilts 62 F2
Reydon Suffolk 127 B9
Reydon Smear Suffolk 127 B9
Reymerston Norfolk 141 B10
Reynalton Pembs 73 D9
Reynoldston Swan 56 D3
Rezare Cornw'l 12 F3
Rhadyr Monmouths 78 E5
Rhaeadr Gwy = Rhayader Powys 113 D9
Rhandirmwyn Carms 94 C5
Rhayader = Rhaeadr Gwy Powys 113 D9
Rhegreanoch H'land 307 H5
Rhemore H'land 289 D7
Rhencullen I/Man 192 C4
Rhenetra H'land 298 D4
Rhes-y-cae Flints 181 G11
Rhewl Denbs 165 C10
Rhewl Denbs 165 F11
Rhewl Shrops 148 C6
Rhewl-Mostyn Flints 181 E11
Rhian H'land 309 H5
Rhicarn H'land 307 G5
Rhiconich H'land 306 D7
Rhicullen H'land 300 B6
Rhidorroch Ho. H'land 307 K6
Rhifail H'land 308 E7
Rhigolter H'land 308 D3
Rhigos Rh Cyn Taff 76 D6
Rhilochan H'land 309 J7
Rhiroy H'land 307 L6
Rhiston Shrops 130 E5
Rhitongue H'land 308 D6
Rhivichie H'land 306 D7
Rhiw Gwyn 144 D4
Rhiwabon = Ruabon Wrex 166 G4
Rhiwbina Card 59 C7
Rhiwbryfdir Gwyn 163 F11
Rhiwceiliog Bridg 58 C3
Rhiwderin Newp 59 B9
Rhiwen Gwyn 163 C9
Rhiwinder Rh Cyn Taff 58 B4
Rhiwlas Gwyn 147 B8
Rhiwlas Gwyn 163 B9
Rhiwlas Powys 148 C3
Rhiwnachor Powys 147 F11
Rhiwsaeson Rh Cyn Taff 58 C5
Rhode Som'set 43 G9
Rhode Common Kent 54 B5
Rhodes Gtr Man 195 F10
Rhodes Minnis Kent 54 E6
Rhodesia Notts 187 E9
Rhodiad-y-Brenin Pembs 90 F5
Rhodmad Ceredig'n 111 C11
Rhôs Common Powys 148 F5
Rhôs Lligwy Angl 179 D7
Rhôs on Sea Conwy 180 E4
Rhôs-y-llan Gwyn 144 B4
Rhonadale Arg/Bute 255 D8
Rhondda Rh Cyn Taff 77 F7
Rhonehouse or Kelton Hill Dumf/Gal 237 D9
Rhoose V/Glam 58 F5
Rhos Carms 93 D7
Rhos Neath P Talb 76 E2
Rhos Powys 148 F5
Rhos Powys 96 E3
Rhos Shrops 148 B5
Rhos Hamminiog Ceredig'n 111 E10
Rhosaman Carms 76 C2
Rhosbeirio Angl 178 C5
Rhoscefnhir Angl 179 F8
Rhoscolyn Angl 178 F3
Rhoscrowther Pembs 72 E6
Rhos-ddu Wrex 166 E4
Rhos-ddû Gwyn 144 B5
Rhosdylluan Gwyn 147 D7
Rhosesmor Flints 166 B2
Rhosfach Pembs 92 F2
Rhos-fawr Gwyn 145 B7
Rhosgadfan Gwyn 163 D8
Rhosgoch Angl 178 D6
Rhos-goch Powys 96 B3
Rhosgyll Gwyn 163 G7
Rhos-hill Pembs 92 C3
Rhoshirwaun Gwyn 144 D3
Rhoslan Bl Gwent 77 C10
Rhoslan Gwyn 163 G7
Rhoslefain Gwyn 110 B2
Rhosllanerchrugog Wrex 166 F4
Rhosmaen Carms 94 G2
Rhosmeirch Angl 179 F7
Rhosneigr Angl 178 G4
Rhosnesni Wrex 166 E4
Rhosrobin Wrex 166 E4
Rhossili Swan 56 D2
Rhosson Pembs 90 F4
Rhostrehwfa Angl 178 G6
Rhostryfan Gwyn 163 D7
Rhostyllen Wrex 166 F4
Rhosweil Shrops 148 B5
Rhosybol Angl 178 D6
Rhos-y-brithdir Powys 148 E2
Rhos-y-brwyner Flints 166 C3
Rhos-y-garth Ceredig'n 112 C2
Rhos-y-gwaliau Gwyn 147 C8
Rhos-y-madoc Wrex 166 G4
Rhosymedre Wrex 166 G3
Rhos-y-meirch Powys 114 D5
RHS Garden, Wisley Surrey 66 H5
Rhu Arg/Bute 275 G9
Rhu Arg/Bute 276 E5
Rhuallt Denbs 181 G9
Rhubodach Arg/Bute 275 F11
Rhuddall Heath Ches 167 C9
Rhuddlan Ceredig'n 93 C9
Rhuddlan Denbs 181 F8
Rhue H'land 307 K5
Rhulen Powys 96 B2
Rhunahaorine Arg/Bute 255 C8
Rhyd Ceredig'n 92 C5
Rhyd Gwyn 163 G10
Rhyd y golau Flints 166 B2
Rhydaman = Ammanford Carms 75 C10
Rhydargaeau Carms 93 F8
Rhydcymerau Carms 93 D11
Rhydd Worcs 98 B6
Rhydd Green Worcs 98 C6
Rhyd-Ddu Gwyn 163 E9
Rhydding Rh Cyn Taff 76 F3
Rhydgaled Conwy 165 C7
Rhydleos Powys 148 C4
Rhydlewis Ceredig'n 92 B6
Rhydlios Gwyn 144 C3
Rhyd-Lydan Conwy 164 E5
Rhydlydan Powys 129 E11
Rhyd-meirionydd Ceredig'n 128 F2
Rhydowen Carms 92 F3
Rhydowen Ceredig'n 93 B8
Rhyd-Rosser Ceredig'n 111 D11
Rhydspence Heref'd 96 B4
Rhydtalog Flints 166 E2
Rhyd-uchaf Gwyn 147 B7
Rhydwyn Angl 178 D4
Rhyd-y-clafdy Gwyn 144 C6
Rhydycroesau Shrops 148 C4
Rhyd-y-cwm Shrops 130 G3
Rhydyfelin Ceredig'n 111 B11
Rhydyfelin Rh Cyn Taff 58 B5
Rhyd-y-foel Conwy 180 F6
Rhyd-y-fro Neath P Talb 76 D2
Rhydygele Pembs 91 G7
Rhyd-y-groes Gwyn 163 B9
Rhyd-y-groes Powys 130 C4
Rhyd-y-gwin Swan 75 E11
Rhyd-y-gwystl Gwyn 145 B8
Rhydymain Gwyn 146 E6
Rhyd-y-meirch Monmouths 78 D4
Rhydymwyn Flints 166 B2
Rhyd-y-pandy Swan 75 E11
Rhyd-yr-onen Gwyn 128 C2
Rhyd-y-Sarn Gwyn 164 G2
Rhydywrach Carms 73 B11
Rhyd-y-meudwy Denbs 165 E10
Rhyl = Y Rhyl Denbs 181 E8
Rhymney = Rhymni Caerph 77 D10
Rhymni = Rhymney Caerph 77 D10
Rhynd Fife 287 E8
Rhynd Perth/Kinr 286 E5
Rhynie Aberds 302 G4
Rhynie H'land 301 B8
Ribbesford Worcs 116 C5
Ribblehead N Yorks 212 D5
Ribbleton Lancs 203 G7
Ribby Lancs 202 G4
Ribchester Lancs 203 F8
Ribigill H'land 308 D5
Riby Lincs 201 F7
Riby Cross Roads Lincs 201 F7
Riccall N Yorks 207 F8
Riccarton E Ayrs 257 B10
Richard's Castle Heref'd 115 D9
Richborough Port Kent 71 G10
Richings Park Bucks 66 D4
Richmond London 67 E7
Richmond N Yorks 224 E3
Richmond S Yorks 186 D6
Richmond Hill S Yorks 198 G5
Richmond's Green Essex 106 F2
Rich's Holford Som'set 42 G6
Rickard's Down Devon 24 B6
Rickarton Aberds 293 E10
Rickerby Cumb 239 F10
Rickerscote Staffs 151 E8
Rickford N Som'set 44 B3
Rickinghall Suffolk 125 B10
Rickleton Durham 243 G7
Rickling Essex 105 E9
Rickling Green Essex 105 F10
Rickmansworth Herts 85 G8
Riddings Derby 170 E6
Riddlecombe Devon 25 E10
Riddlesden W Yorks 205 E7
Riddrie Glasg C 268 B2
Ridgacre W Midlands 133 G10
Ridge Dorset 18 D4
Ridge Devon 28 F3
Ridge Hants 32 D4
Ridge Herts 86 E2
Ridge Lancs 204 E3
Ridge Lancs 211 G9
Ridge Wilts 46 G3
Ridge Common Hants 34 B2
Ridge Green Surrey 51 D10
Ridge Hill Gtr Man 185 B7
Ridge Lane Warwick 134 E5
Ridge Row Kent 55 E8
Ridgehill N Som'set 60 G4
Ridgeway Derby 170 E5
Ridgeway Derby 186 E5
Ridgeway Newp 59 B9
Ridgeway Pembs 73 D10
Ridgeway Stoke 168 E5
Ridgeway Som'set 45 E9
Ridgeway Cross Heref'd 98 B4
Ridgeway Moor Derby 186 E6
Ridgewell Essex 106 C4
Ridgewood E Sussex 37 D7
Ridgmont Beds 103 D9
Ridgway Surrey 50 B4
Riding Gate Som'set 30 B2
Riding Mill Northum 242 E2
Ridley Kent 68 G6
Ridley Northum 241 E7
Ridley Green Ches 167 E9
Ridlington Norfolk 160 C6
Ridlington Rutl'd 136 C6
Ridlington Street Norfolk 161 C6
Ridsdale Northum 251 G10
Riechip Perth/Kinr 286 C4
Riemore Perth/Kinr 286 C4
Rienachait H'land 306 F5
Rievaulx N Yorks 215 B11
Rievaulx Abbey N Yorks 215 C11
Riff Orkney 312 G5
Riffin Aberds 303 E7
Rifle Green Torf 78 D3
Rift House Hartlep'l 234 E5
Rifton Devon 26 D5
Rigg Dumf/Gal 239 D7
Riggend N Lanarks 278 G5
Rigsby Lincs 190 F6
Rigside S Lanarks 259 C9
Rigton Hill W Yorks 206 E3
Riley Green Lancs 194 B6
Rileyhill Staffs 152 F2
Rilla Mill Cornw'l 11 G11
Rillaton Cornw'l 11 G11
Rillington N Yorks 217 E7
Rimbleton Fife 280 A5
Rimington Lancs 204 D2
Rimpton Som'set 29 C10
Rimswell ER Yorks 201 B10
Ring o'Bells Lancs 194 E3
Ringasta Shetl'd 315 M5
Ringford Dumf/Gal 237 D8
Ringinglow S Yorks 186 E3
Ringland Norfolk 160 G2
Ringland Newp 59 B11
Ringles Cross E Sussex 37 C7
Ringlestone Kent 53 B11
Ringley Gtr Man 195 G9
Ringmer E Sussex 37 E7
Ringmore Devon 8 F3
Ringmore Devon 14 G4
Ringorm Moray 302 E2
Ring's End Cambs 139 C7
Ringsfield Suffolk 143 F8
Ringsfield Corner Suffolk 143 F8
Ringshall Herts 85 C7
Ringshall Suffolk 125 G10
Ringshall Stocks Suffolk 125 G11
Ringstead Norfolk 176 E2
Ringstead Northants 121 B9
Ringtail Green Essex 87 B11
Ringwood Hants 31 F11
Ringwould Kent 55 D11
Rinmore Aberds 292 B6
Rinnigill Orkney 313 J4
Rinsey Cornw'l 2 D3
Rinsey Croft Cornw'l 2 D4
Riof W Isles 304 E3
Ripe E Sussex 37 E8
Ripley Derby 170 E6
Ripley Hants 19 B9
Ripley N Yorks 214 G5
Ripley Surrey 50 B4
Ripley Green Surrey 50 B5
Riplingham ER Yorks 208 G4
Ripon N Yorks 214 E6
Ripon Cathedral N Yorks 214 E6
Ripon Racecourse N Yorks 214 F6
Rippingale Lincs 156 D2
Ripple Kent 55 C10
Ripple Worcs 99 D7
Ripponden W Yorks 196 D4
Rireavach H'land 307 K5
Risabus Arg/Bute 254 C4
Risbury Heref'd 115 F10
Risby ER Yorks 208 G6
Risby Lincs 189 C11
Risby Suffolk 124 D6
Risca Caerph 78 G2
Rise ER Yorks 209 E9
Rise Carr D'lington 224 B5
Rise End Derby 170 D3
Rise Park Notts 171 G9
Riseden E Sussex 52 G6
Riseden Kent 53 F8
Risegate Lincs 156 D4
Riseholme Lincs 189 F7
Risehow Cumb 228 E6
Riseley Beds 121 E10
Riseley Wokingham 65 G8
Rishangles Suffolk 126 D3
Rishton Lancs 203 G10
Rishworth W Yorks 196 D4
Rising Bridge Lancs 195 B9
Rising Sun Cornw'l 12 G3
Risinghurst Oxon 83 D9
Risley Derby 153 B9
Risley Warrington 183 C11
Rispith N Yorks 214 F4
Rispond H'land 308 C4
Rivar Wilts 63 G10
Rivenhall Essex 88 B4
Rivenhall End Essex 88 B4
River Kent 55 E9
River W Sussex 34 C6
River Bank Cambs 123 D10
River Hall Herts 85 B9
Riverhead Kent 52 B4
River's Corner Dorset 30 E3
Riverside Card 59 D7
Riverside Plym'th 7 D8
Riverside Stirl 278 C6
Riverview Park Kent 69 E7
Rivington Lancs 194 E6
Rixton Warrington 183 C11
Roa Island Cumb 210 F4
Roach Bridge Lancs 194 B5
Roaches Gtr Man 196 G3
Roachill Devon 26 C4
Road Green Devon 15 C10
Road Green Norfolk 142 E5
Road Weedon Northants 120 F2
Roade Northants 120 G5
Roadhead Cumb 240 C2
Roadmeetings S Lanarks 269 E7
Roadside H'land 310 C5
Roadside of Catterline Aberds 293 F10
Roadside of Kinneff Aberds 293 F10
Roadwater Som'set 42 F4
Roag H'land 298 E2
Roast Green Essex 105 E9
Roath Card 59 D8
Rob Roy and Trossachs Visitor Centre, Callander Stirl 285 G10
Rob Roy's House Arg/Bute 284 F5
Robert Burns Centre, Dumfries Dumf/Gal 237 B11
Roberton Scot Borders 261 G10
Roberton S Lanarks 259 D10
Robertsbridge E Sussex 38 C2
Robertstown Moray 302 E2
Robertstown Rh Cyn Taff 77 E8
Roberttown W Yorks 197 C7
Robeston Back Pembs 73 B9
Robeston Wathen Pembs 73 B9
Robeston West Pembs 72 D5
Robin Hood Derby 186 G3
Robin Hood Lancs 194 E4
Robin Hood W Yorks 197 B10
Robin Hood Doncaster Sheffield Airport S Yorks 187 B11
Robin Hood's Bay N Yorks 227 D9
Robinhood End Essex 106 D4
Robinson's End Warwick 134 E6
Roborough Devon 7 C10
Roborough Devon 25 D9
Robroyston Glasg C 268 B2
Roby Mersey 182 C6
Roby Mill Lancs 194 F4
Rocester Staffs 152 B2
Roch Pembs 91 G7
Rochdale Gtr Man 195 E11
Roche Cornw'l 5 C9
Rochester Medway 69 F8
Rochester Northum 251 D8
Rochester Castle Medway 69 F8
Rochester Cathedral Medway 69 F8
Rochford Essex 88 G5
Rochford Worcs 116 D2
Rock Caerph 77 F11
Rock Cornw'l 10 F4
Rock Devon 28 G3
Rock Northum 264 E6
Rock Worcs 116 C4
Rock W Sussex 35 E10
Rock Ferry Mersey 182 D4
Rock Hall Dumf/Gal 238 B3
Rockbeare Devon 14 B6
Rockbourne Hants 31 D10
Rockcliffe Cumb 239 E8
Rockcliffe Dumf/Gal 237 D10
Rockcliffe Cross Cumb 239 E8
Rockfield H'land 311 L3
Rockfield Monmouths 79 C7
Rockford Hants 31 F11
Rockgreen Shrops 115 B10
Rockhampton S Glos 79 G11
Rockhead Cornw'l 11 E7
Rockhill Shrops 114 B5
Rockingham Northants 137 E7
Rockingham Motor Speedway Northants 137 E8
Rockland All Saints Norfolk 141 D9

Rockland St. Mary Norfolk 142 C6
Rockland St. Peter Norfolk 141 D9
Rockley Notts 188 G2
Rockley Wilts 63 E7
Rockliffe Lancs 195 C11
Rockness Glos 80 F4
Rockrobin E Sussex 52 G6
Rocks Park E Sussex 37 C7
Rocksley M/Keynes 102 D6
Rockstowes Glos 80 F3
Rockwell Cornw'l 12 D2
Rockwell End Bucks 65 B9
Rockwell Green Som'set 27 B10
Rodborough Glos 80 E4
Rodbourne Swindon 62 B6
Rodbourne Wilts 62 C2
Rodbourne Cheney Swindon 62 B6
Rodbridge Corner Suffolk 107 C7
Roddam Northum 264 E2
Rodden Dorset 17 E8
Roddymoor Durham 233 D9
Rode Som'set 45 C10
Rode Heath Ches 168 D4
Rode Hill Som'set 45 C10
Rodeheath Ches 168 B5
Roden Telford 149 F11
Rodford S Glos 61 C8
Rodhuish Som'set 42 F4
Rodington Telford 149 G11
Rodington Heath Telford 149 G11
Rodley Glos 80 C2
Rodley W Yorks 205 F10
Rodmarton Glos 80 F6
Rodmell E Sussex 36 F6
Rodmersham Kent 70 G2
Rodmersham Green Kent 70 G2
Rodney Stoke Som'set 44 C3
Rodsley Derby 170 G2
Rodway Som'set 43 E9
Rodwell Dorset 17 F9
Roe Cross Gtr Man 185 B7
Roe End Herts 85 B8
Roe Green Gtr Man 195 G9
Roe Green Herts 86 D2
Roe Green Herts 104 E6
Roe Lee Blackb'n 203 G9
Roebuck Low Gtr Man 196 F3
Roecliffe N Yorks 215 F7
Roedean Brighton/Hove 36 G4
Roehampton London 67 E8
Roesound Shetl'd 314 G5
Roestock Herts 86 D2
Roffey W Sussex 51 G7
Rogart H'land 309 J7
Rogart Station H'land 309 J7
Rogate W Sussex 34 C4
Roger Ground Cumb 221 F7
Rogerstone Newp 59 B9
Rogerton S Lanarks 268 D2
Roghadal W Isles 296 C6
Rogiet Monmouths 60 B3
Rogues Alley Cambs 139 B7
Roke Oxon 83 G10
Rokemarsh Oxon 83 G10
Roker Tyne/Wear 243 F10
Rollesby Norfolk 161 F8
Rolleston Leics 136 C4
Rolleston Notts 172 E2
Rolleston on Dove Staffs 152 D4
Rollestone Wilts 46 E5
Rolls Park Essex 86 G6
Rolston ER Yorks 209 D10
Rolstone N Som'set 59 G11
Rolvenden Kent 53 G10
Rolvenden Layne Kent 53 G10
Romaldkirk Durham 232 G5
Roman Bank Shrops 131 E10
Roman Baths & Pump Room, Bath Bath/NE Som'set 61 F9
Roman Hill Suffolk 143 E10
Romanby N Yorks 225 G7
Romannobridge Scot Borders 270 F3
Romansleigh Devon 26 C2
Rome Angus 293 G7
Romesdal H'land 298 D4
Romford Dorset 31 F9
Romford Kent 52 E6
Romford London 68 B4
Romiley Gtr Man 184 C6
Romney, Hythe and Dymchurch Light Railway Kent 54 G6
Romney Street Kent 68 G4
Rompa Shetl'd 315 L6
Romsey Hants 32 C4
Romsey Town Cambs 123 F9
Romsley Shrops 132 G5
Romsley Worcs 117 B9
Ronachan Ho Arg/Bute 255 B8
Ronague I/Man 192 E3
Ronkswood Worcs 117 F7
Rood Ashton Wilts 45 B11
Rood End W Midlands 133 F10
Rook Devon 8 C2
Rook End Essex 105 E11
Rookhope Durham 232 C4
Rooking Cumb 221 B8
Rookley I/Wight 20 E6
Rookley Green I/Wight 20 E6
Rooks Bridge Som'set 43 C11
Rook's Nest Som'set 42 G5
Rook's Street Wilts 45 G10
Rooksmoor Glos 80 E4
Rookwith N Yorks 214 B4
Rookwood W Sussex 22 D3
Roos ER Yorks 209 G11
Roose Cumb 210 F4
Roosebeck Cumb 210 F5
Roosecote Cumb 210 F4
Roost End Essex 106 C4
Rootham's Green Beds 122 G2
Rooting Street Kent 54 D3
Rootpark S Lanarks 269 E9
Ropley Hants 48 G6
Ropley Dean Hants 48 G6
Ropley Stoke Hants 49 G7
Ropsley Lincs 155 C9
Rora Aberds 303 D10
Rorandle Aberds 293 B8
Rorrington Shrops 130 C6
Rosarie Moray 302 E3
Roscroggan Cornw'l 4 G2
Rose Cornw'l 4 E5
Rose Ash Devon 26 C3
Rose Green Essex 107 F8
Rose Green Suffolk 107 C9
Rose Green Suffolk 107 D8
Rose Green W Sussex 22 D6
Rose Grove Lancs 204 G2
Rose Hill Derby C 153 B7
Rose Hill E Sussex 37 D7
Rose Hill Gtr Man 195 F8
Rose Hill Lancs 204 G2
Rose Hill Oxon 83 E8
Rose Hill Suffolk 108 C3
Rose Hill Surrey 51 D7
Rose Hill Stockton 225 C8
Roseacre Kent 53 B9
Roseacre Lancs 202 F4
Rose-an-Grouse Cornw'l 2 B2
Rosebank E Dunb 278 G3
Rosebank S Lanarks 268 F6
Rosebrae Moray 301 C11
Rosebush Pembs 91 F11
Rosecare Cornw'l 11 B9
Rosedale Abbey N Yorks 226 F4
Roseden Northum 264 E2
Rosedinnick Cornw'l 5 B8
Rosedown Devon 24 C3
Rosefield H'land 301 D8
Rosehall H'land 309 J4
Rosehall N Lanarks 268 C4
Rosehaugh Mains H'land 300 D6
Rosehearty Aberds 303 C9
Rosehill Blackb'n 195 C8
Rosehill Cornw'l 4 E5
Rosehill London 67 F9
Rosehill Shrops 149 F9
Rosehill Tyne/Wear 243 D8
Roseisle Moray 301 C11
Roseland Cornw'l 6 C5
Roselands E Sussex 23 E10
Rosemarket Pembs 73 D7
Rosemarkie H'land 301 D7
Rosemary Lane Devon 27 E11
Rosemount Perth/Kinr 286 C5
Rosenannon Cornw'l 5 B9
Rosenithon Cornw'l 3 E8
Roser's Cross E Sussex 37 C9
Rosevean Cornw'l 5 D10
Rosevidney Cornw'l 2 C2
Roseville W Midlands 133 E8
Rosevine Cornw'l 3 B9
Rosewarne Cornw'l 4 G2
Rosewarne Cornw'l 2 B4
Rosewell Midloth 270 C5
Roseworth Stockton 234 G4
Roseworthy Cornw'l 4 F5
Roseworthy Cornw'l 2 B4
Rosgill Cumb 221 B10
Roshven H'land 289 B9
Roskhill H'land 298 E2
Roskill House H'land 300 D6
Roskorwell Cornw'l 3 E7
Rosley Cumb 230 B2
Roslin Midloth 270 C5
Rosliston Derby 152 F4
Rosneath Arg/Bute 276 E5
Ross Dumf/Gal 237 E8
Ross Northum 264 B4
Ross Perth/Kinr 285 E11
Ross Green Worcs 116 E5
Ross on Wye Heref'd 98 G2
Rossett Wrex 166 D4
Rossett Green N Yorks 206 C2
Rossie Ochill Perth/Kinr 286 F4
Rossie Priory Perth/Kinr 286 D6
Rossington S Yorks 187 B11
Rosskeen H'land 300 C6
Rossland Renf 277 G8
Rossmore Poole 19 C7
Roster H'land 310 F6
Rostherne Ches 184 E2
Rostholme S Yorks 198 F5
Rosthwaite Cumb 210 B4
Rosthwaite Cumb 220 C5
Roston Derby 169 G10
Rosudgeon Cornw'l 2 D3
Rosyth Fife 280 E2
Rotcombe Bath/NE Som'set 45 B7
Rothbury Northum 252 C3
Rotherby Leics 154 F3
Rotherfield E Sussex 37 B9
Rotherfield Greys Oxon 65 C8
Rotherfield Peppard Oxon 65 C8
Rotherham S Yorks 186 C6
Rotherhithe London 67 D11
Rothersthorpe Northants 120 F4
Rotherwas Heref'd 97 D10
Rotherwick Hants 49 B8
Rothes Moray 302 E2
Rothesay Arg/Bute 275 G11
Rothiebrisbane Aberds 303 F7
Rothiemay Crossroads Moray 302 E5
Rothiemurchus Estate Visitor Centre H'land 291 C11
Rothiemurchus Lodge H'land 291 C11
Rothienorman Aberds 303 F7
Rothiesholm Orkney 312 F7
Rothley Leics 153 G11
Rothley Northum 252 F2
Rothmaise Aberds 302 F6
Rothwell Lincs 189 B11
Rothwell Northants 136 G6
Rothwell W Yorks 197 B10
Rothwell Haigh W Yorks 197 B10
Rotsea ER Yorks 209 C7
Rottal Angus 292 G5
Rotten End Suffolk 127 D7
Rotten Green Hants 49 B9
Rotten Row Norfolk 159 G11
Rottingdean Brighton/Hove 36 G5
Rottington Cumb 219 C9
Rotton Row W Berks 64 E5
Rotton Row W Midlands 118 B3
Rotunda, Folkestone Kent 55 F8
Roud I/Wight 20 E6
Rough Close Staffs 151 B8
Rough Common Kent 54 B6
Rough Haugh H'land 308 E7
Rough Hay Staffs 152 E4
Rougham Norfolk 158 E6
Rougham Suffolk 125 E8
Rougham Green Suffolk 125 E8
Roughbirchworth S Yorks 197 G9
Roughburn H'land 290 E5
Roughlee Lancs 204 E2
Roughley W Midlands 134 D2
Roughrigg N Lanarks 278 F6
Roughsike Cumb 240 B2
Roughton Lincs 174 C2
Roughton Norfolk 160 B4
Roughton Shrops 132 E5
Roughway Kent 52 C6
Round Bush Herts 85 F11
Round Maple Suffolk 107 C9
Round Oak Shrops 131 G7
Round Oak W Berks 64 F6
Round Oak W Midlands 133 F8
Round Spinney Northants 120 D5
Round Street Kent 69 F7
Roundbush Essex 88 E5
Roundbush Glos 98 F5
Roundbush Green Essex 87 C9
Roundham Som'set 28 F6
Roundhay W Yorks 206 F2
Roundstonefoot Dumf/Gal 248 B4
Roundstreet Common W Sussex 35 B9
Roundswell Devon 40 G4
Roundthorn Gtr Man 184 D4
Roundthwaite Cumb 222 E2
Roundway Wilts 62 G4
Roundyhill Angus 287 B7
Rous Lench Worcs 117 G10
Rousdon Devon 15 C11
Rousham Oxon 101 G9
Routenburn N Ayrs 266 C3
Routh ER Yorks 209 D7
Rout's Green Bucks 84 F3
Row Cumb 219 E11
Row Cumb 211 B9
Row Cumb 231 E8
Row Cornw'l 11 F7
Row Ash Hants 33 E8
Row Brow Cumb 229 D7
Row Green Essex 106 G4
Row Heath Essex 89 B10
Row Town Surrey 66 G4
Rowanburn Dumf/Gal 239 B10
Rowanfield Glos 99 G8
Rowardennan Stirl 277 B7
Rowarth Derby 185 D8
Rowbarns Surrey 50 C6
Rowbarton Som'set 28 B2
Rowberrow Som'set 44 B3
Rowde Wilts 62 G3
Rowden N Yorks 205 B11
Rowden Down Wilts 62 E2
Rowell Cumb 211 C10
Rowen Conwy 180 G3
Rowfoot Northum 240 E5
Rowford Som'set 28 B2
Rowhedge Essex 107 G10
Rowhill Surrey 66 G4
Rowhook W Sussex 50 G6
Rowington Warwick 118 D4
Rowington Green Warwick 118 C4
Rowland Derby 186 G2
Rowlands Castle W Sussex 34 E2
Rowlands Gill Tyne/Wear 242 F5
Rowledge Surrey 49 E10
Rowlestone Heref'd 97 F7
Rowley Durham 233 B7
Rowley ER Yorks 208 G5
Rowley Shrops 130 B6
Rowley Hill W Yorks 197 E7
Rowley Park Staffs 151 E8
Rowley Regis W Midlands 133 F9
Rowley's Green Warwick 134 G6
Rowly Surrey 50 E4
Rowmore Arg/Bute 276 D4
Rowner Hants 33 G9
Rowney Green Worcs 117 C10
Rownhams Hants 32 D5
Row-of-Trees Ches 184 F4
Rowrah Cumb 219 B11
Rowsham Bucks 84 B5
Rowsley Derby 170 B3
Rowstock Oxon 64 B3
Rowston Lincs 173 D9
Rowthorn Derby 171 C7
Rowton Ches 166 C6
Rowton Shrops 149 G7
Rowton Telford 150 F2
Roxburgh Scot Borders 262 C5
Roxby N Lincs 200 D2
Roxby N Yorks 226 B5
Roxeth London 66 B6
Roxton Beds 122 G3
Roxwell Essex 87 D10
Royal Botanic Gardens C/Edinb 280 F4
Royal British Legion Village Kent 53 B8
Royal Leamington Spa Warwick 118 E6
Royal Museum of Scotland C/Edinb 280 G5
Royal Oak Durham 233 G10
Royal Oak Lancs 194 G2
Royal Oak N Yorks 218 D2
Royal Pavilion, Brighton Brighton/Hove 36 G4
Royal Tunbridge Wells = Tunbridge Wells Kent 52 F5
Royal Welch Fusiliers Regimental Museum (See Caernarfon Castle) Gwyn 163 C7
Royal Worcester Porcelain, Worcester Worcs 117 G7
Royal's Green Ches 167 G10
Roybridge H'land 290 E4
Roydhouse W Yorks 197 E8
Roydon Essex 86 C6
Roydon Norfolk 141 G11
Roydon Norfolk 158 E4
Roydon Hamlet Essex 86 D6
Royston Herts 105 C7
Royston S Yorks 197 E11
Royston Water Som'set 28 E2
Royton Gtr Man 196 F2
Ruabon = Rhiwabon Wrex 166 G4
Ruaig Arg/Bute 288 E2
Ruan High Lanes Cornw'l 3 B10
Ruan Lanihorne Cornw'l 5 G7
Ruan Major Cornw'l 2 F6
Ruan Minor Cornw'l 2 F6
Ruarach H'land 295 C11
Ruardean Glos 79 B10
Ruardean Hill Glos 79 B10
Ruardean Woodside Glos 79 B10
Rubery Worcs 117 B9
Rubha Ghaisinis W Isles 297 G4
Rubha Stoer H'land 306 F5
Ruchazie Glasg C 268 B3
Ruchill Glasg C 267 B11
Ruckcroft Cumb 230 C6
Ruckhall Heref'd 97 D8
Ruckinge Kent 54 G4
Ruckland Lincs 190 F4
Rucklers Green Herts 85 E9
Rudbaxton Pembs 91 G9
Rudby N Yorks 225 D9
Ruddle Glos 79 C11
Ruddington Notts 153 C11
Ruddlemoor Cornw'l 5 D10
Rudford Glos 98 G5
Rudge Shrops 132 D6
Rudge Som'set 45 C10
Rudgeway S Glos 60 B6
Rudgwick W Sussex 50 G5
Rudhall Heref'd 98 F2
Rudheath Ches 183 G11
Rudhja Garbh Arg/Bute 289 E11
Rudley Green Essex 88 E4
Rudloe Wilts 61 E10
Rudry Caerph 59 B7
Rudston ER Yorks 217 F11
Rudyard Staffs 168 D6
Ruffets Monmouths 60 B4
Rufford Lancs 194 D3
Rufforth C/York 206 C6
Ruffs Notts 171 F8
Ruffside Durham 241 G11
Rugby Warwick 119 C10
Rugeley Staffs 151 F11
Ruggin Som'set 27 D11
Ruglen S Ayrs 245 C7
Ruilick H'land 300 E5
Ruishton Som'set 28 C3
Ruisigearraidh W Isles 296 C5
Ruislip London 66 B5
Ruislip Common London 66 B5
Ruislip Gardens London 66 B5
Ruislip Manor London 66 B6
Ruiton W Midlands 133 E8
Rumach H'land 295 G8
Rumbling Bridge Perth/Kinr 279 B10
Rumburgh Suffolk 142 G6
Rumer Hill Staffs 133 B9
Rumford Cornw'l 10 G3
Rumford Falk 279 F8
Rumney Card 59 D8
Rumsam Devon 40 G5
Rumwell Som'set 27 C11
Runcorn Halton 183 E8
Runcton W Sussex 34 G5
Runcton Bottom Norfolk 140 B2
Runcton Holme Norfolk 140 B2
Rundlestone Devon 13 F7
Runfold Surrey 49 D11
Runhall Norfolk 141 B11
Runham Norfolk 143 B10
Runham Norfolk 161 G9
Running Waters Durham 234 C2
Runnington Som'set 27 C10
Runsell Green Essex 88 E3
Runshaw Moor Lancs 194 D4
Runswick Bay N Yorks 226 B6
Runwell Essex 88 G3
Ruscombe Glos 80 D4
Ruscombe Wokingham 65 D10
Ruscote Oxon 101 C8
Rush Green Essex 89 B11
Rush Green Herts 104 G4
Rush Green Herts 104 F6
Rush Green London 68 B4
Rush Green Norfolk 141 B11
Rush Hill Bath/NE Som'set 61 G8
Rushall Heref'd 98 E2
Rushall Norfolk 142 G3
Rushall Wilts 46 B6
Rushall W Midlands 133 C10
Rushbrooke Suffolk 125 E7
Rushbury Shrops 131 E10
Rushden Herts 104 E6
Rushden Northants 121 D9
Rushenden Kent 70 E2
Rusher's Cross E Sussex 37 B10
Rushey Mead Leics C 136 B2
Rushford Devon 12 F4
Rushford Norfolk 141 G8
Rushgreen Warrington 183 D11
Rush-head Aberds 303 E8
Rushington Hants 32 E5
Rushlake Green E Sussex 37 D10
Rushley Green Essex 106 D5
Rushmere Beds 103 F8
Rushmere Suffolk 143 F9
Rushmere St. Andrew Suffolk 108 B3
Rushmere Street Suffolk 108 B4
Rushmoor Surrey 49 E11
Rushock Worcs 117 C7
Rusholme Gtr Man 184 B5
Rushton Northants 136 G6
Rushton Shrops 132 B2
Rushton Spencer Staffs 168 B6
Rushwick Worcs 116 G6
Rushy Green E Sussex 37 E7
Rushyford Durham 233 F11
Ruskie Stirl 285 G10
Ruskington Lincs 173 E9
Rusland Cumb 210 B6
Rusper W Sussex 51 F8
Ruspidge Glos 79 C11
Russ Hill Surrey 51 E8
Russel H'land 299 E8
Russell's Green E Sussex 38 E2
Russell's Hall W Midlands 133 F8
Russell's Water Oxon 65 B8
Russel's Green Suffolk 126 C5
Rusthall Kent 52 F5
Rustington W Sussex 35 G9
Ruston N Yorks 217 C9
Ruston Parva ER Yorks 217 G11
Ruswarp N Yorks 227 D7
Rutherglen Glasg C 268 C2
Ruthernbridge Cornw'l 5 B10
Ruthin Denbs 165 D10
Ruthin V/Glam 58 D3
Ruthin Craft Centre Denbs 165 D10
Ruthrieston Aberd C 293 C11
Ruthven Aberds 302 E5
Ruthven Angus 286 C6
Ruthven H'land 291 D9
Ruthven H'land 301 F8
Ruthven House Angus 287 C7
Ruthvoes Cornw'l 5 C8
Ruthwaite Cumb 229 D10
Ruthwell Dumf/Gal 238 D4
Ruxley London 68 E3
Ruxton Green Heref'd 79 B8
Ruyton-XI-Towns Shrops 149 E7
Ryal Northum 242 C2
Ryall Worcs 99 C7
Ryarsh Kent 69 G7
Rychraggan H'land 300 F4
Rydal Cumb 221 D7
Ryde I/Wight 21 C7
Rye E Sussex 38 B6
Rye Foreign E Sussex 38 B6
Rye Harbour E Sussex 38 D6
Rye Hill Essex 87 D7
Rye Park Herts 86 D5
Rye Street Worcs 98 D5
Ryebank Shrops 149 C10
Ryecroft W Yorks 205 F7
Ryeford Glos 80 E4
Ryeford Heref'd 98 G2
Ryehill ER Yorks 201 B8
Ryeish Green Wokingham 65 F8
Ryeworth Glos 99 G9
Ryhall Rutl'd 155 G10
Ryhill W Yorks 197 E11
Ryhope Tyne/Wear 243 G10
Ryhope Colliery Tyne/Wear 243 G10
Rylah Derby 171 B7
Rylands Notts 153 B10
Rylstone N Yorks 204 B5
Ryme Intrinseca Dorset 29 E9
Ryther N Yorks 207 F7
Ryton Glos 98 E4
Ryton N Yorks 216 D5
Ryton Shrops 132 C5
Ryton Tyne/Wear 242 E5
Ryton Warwick 135 F7
Ryton on Dunsmore Warwick 119 C7
Ryton Woodside Tyne/Wear 242 E4

S

Saasaig H'land 295 E8
Sabden Lancs 203 F11
Sabine's Green Essex 87 F8
Sackers Green Suffolk 107 D8
Sacombe Herts 86 B4
Sacombe Green Herts 86 B4
Sacriston Durham 233 B10
Sadberge D'lington 224 B6
Saddell Arg/Bute 255 D8
Saddell Ho Arg/Bute 255 D8
Saddington Leics 136 E3
Saddle Bow Norfolk 158 F2
Saddlescombe W Sussex 36 E3
Sadgill Cumb 221 D9
Saffron Walden Essex 105 D10
Sageston Pembs 73 E9
Saham Grove Norfolk 141 B8
Saham Hills Norfolk 141 C8
Saham Toney Norfolk 141 C8
Saighdinis W Isles 296 E4
Saighton Ches 166 C6
St. Abbs Scot Borders 273 B8
St. Abb's Haven Scot Borders 273 B8
St. Agnes Cornw'l 4 E4
St. Albans Herts 85 D10
St Alban's Abbey Herts 85 D10
St. Allen Cornw'l 4 E6
St. Andrews Fife 287 F9
St. Andrew's Major V/Glam 58 E6
St. Andrew's Well Dorset 16 C5
St. Anne's Lancs 193 B10
St. Anne's Park Bristol 60 E6
St. Ann's Nott'ham 171 G9
St. Ann's Dumf/Gal 248 E3
St. Ann's Chapel Cornw'l 12 G4
St. Ann's Chapel Devon 8 F3
St. Anthony Cornw'l 3 C9
St. Anthony-in-Meneage Cornw'l 3 D7
St. Anthony's Tyne/Wear 243 E7
St. Anthony's Hill E Sussex 23 E10
St. Arvans Monmouths 79 F8
St. Asaph = Llanelwy Denbs 181 G8
St. Athan V/Glam 58 F4
St. Austell Cornw'l 5 E10
St. Bartholomew's Hill Wilts 30 B5
St. Bees Cumb 219 C9
St. Blazey Cornw'l 5 E11
St. Blazey Gte Cornw'l 5 E11
St. Boswells Scot Borders 262 C3
St. Breock Cornw'l 10 G5
St. Breward Cornw'l 11 F7
St. Briavels Glos 79 E9
St. Briavels Common Glos 79 E8
St. Brides Pembs 72 C3
St. Bride's Major = Saint-y-Brid V/Glam 57 G11
St. Bride's Netherwent Monmouths 60 B2
St. Bride's Wentllooge Newp 59 C9
St. Bride's-super-Ely V/Glam 58 D5
St. Budeaux Plym'th 7 D8
St. Buryan Cornw'l 1 D4
St. Catherine Bath/NE Som'set 61 E9
St. Catherine's Arg/Bute 284 G5
St. Chloe Glos 80 E4
St. Clears = Sanclêr Carms 74 B3
St. Cleer Cornw'l 6 B4
St. Clement Cornw'l 5 G6
St Clement's Caves, Hastings E Sussex 38 F4
St. Clether Cornw'l 11 E10
St. Colmac Arg/Bute 275 G11
St. Columb Major Cornw'l 5 C8
St. Columb Minor Cornw'l 4 C6
St. Columb Road Cornw'l 5 D8
St. Combs Aberds 303 C10
St. Cross Hants 33 B7
St. Cross South Elmham Suffolk 142 G6
St. Cyrus Aberds 293 G9
St. David's Perth/Kinr 286 E3
St. David's = Tyddewi Pembs 90 F5
St. Day Cornw'l 4 G4
St. Decumans Som'set 42 E5
St. Dennis Cornw'l 5 D9
St. Denys S'thampton 32 E6
St. Dials Torf 78 G3
St. Dogmaels = Llandudoch Pembs 92 B3
St. Dominick Cornw'l 7 B8
St. Donats V/Glam 58 F2
St. Edith's Marsh Wilts 62 G3
St. Endellion Cornw'l 10 F5
St. Enoder Cornw'l 5 D7
St. Erme Cornw'l 4 F6
St. Erney Cornw'l 7 D7
St. Erth Cornw'l 2 B3
St. Erth Praze Cornw'l 2 B3
St. Ervan Cornw'l 10 G3
St. Eval Cornw'l 5 B7
St. Ewe Cornw'l 5 F9
St. Fagans Card 58 D6
St Fagans Museum of Welsh Life Card 58 D6
St. Fergus Aberds 303 D10
St. Fillans Perth/Kinr 285 E10
St. Florence Pembs 73 E9
St. Gennys Cornw'l 11 B8
St. George Bristol 60 E6
St. George Conwy 181 F7
St. George's N Som'set 59 G11
St. George's Telford 150 G4
St. George's V/Glam 58 D5
St. George's Hill Surrey 66 G5
St. Germans Cornw'l 7 D7
St. Giles Lincs 189 G7
St Giles Cathedral C/Edinb 280 G5
St. Giles in the Wood Devon 25 D8
St. Giles on the Heath Devon 12 C3
St. Giles's Hill Hants 33 B7
St. Gluvias Cornw'l 3 C7
St. Harmon Powys 113 C9
St. Helen Auckland Durham 233 F9
St. Helena Warwick 134 C5
St. Helens Cumb 228 E6
St. Helen's E Sussex 38 E4
St. Helen's I/Wight 21 D8
St. Helens Mersey 183 C9
St. Helen's S Yorks 197 F11
St. Helen's Wood E Sussex 38 E4
St. Helier London 67 F9
St. Hilary Cornw'l 2 C3
St. Hilary V/Glam 58 E4
St. Hill Devon 27 G9
St. Ibbs Herts 104 F3
St. Illtyd Bl Gwent 78 E2
St. Ippollitts Herts 104 F4
St. Ishmael Carms 74 D5
St. Ishmael's Pembs 72 D4
St. Issey Cornw'l 10 G4
St. Ive Cornw'l 6 B6
St. Ive Cross Cornw'l 6 B6
St. Ives Cambs 122 C6
St. Ives Cornw'l 2 A2
St. Ives Dorset 31 G10
St. James Dorset 30 C5
St. James Norfolk 160 E5
St. James South Elmham Suffolk 142 G6
St. James's End Northants 120 E4
St. James's Park Notts 154 B3
St. Jidgey Cornw'l 5 B8
St. John Cornw'l 7 E8
St. John's E Sussex 52 G4
St. John's I/Man 192 D3
St. John's Kent 52 B4
St. John's London 67 D11
St. John's Suffolk 108 C3
St. John's Surrey 50 B3
St. John's W Yorks 206 F4
St. John's Chapel Durham 232 D3
St. John's Fen End Norfolk 157 G10
St. John's Highway Norfolk 157 G10
St. John's Town of Dalry Dumf/Gal 246 G4
St. John's Wells Aberds 303 F7
St. John's Wood London 67 C9
St. Judes I/Man 192 C4
St. Julians Herts 85 D10
St. Julian's Newp 59 B10
St. Just Cornw'l 1 C3
St. Just in Roseland Cornw'l 3 B9
St Just In Roseland Cornw'l 3 B9
St. Katherine's Aberds 303 F7
St. Keverne Cornw'l 3 E7
St. Kew Cornw'l 10 F6
St. Kew Highway Cornw'l 10 F6
St. Keyne Cornw'l 6 C4
St. Lawrence Essex 89 E7
St. Lawrence I/Wight 20 F6
St. Lawrence Kent 71 F11
St. Leonards Bucks 84 D6
St. Leonards Dorset 31 G10
St. Leonards E Sussex 38 F4
St. Leonards S Lanarks 268 E2
St. Leonard's Street Kent 53 B7
St. Levan Cornw'l 1 E3
St. Loy Cornw'l 1 E4
St. Lukes Derby C 152 B6
St. Lythans Card 58 E6
St. Mabyn Cornw'l 10 G6
St. Madoes Perth/Kinr 286 E5
St. Margaret South Elmham Suffolk 142 G6
St. Margaret's Heref'd 97 E7
St. Margarets Herts 86 C5
St. Margaret's Wilts 63 F7
St. Margaret's at Cliffe Kent 55 E11
St. Margaret's Hope Orkney 313 J5
St. Mark's Glos 99 G8
St. Mark's I/Man 192 E3
St. Martin Cornw'l 6 D5
St. Martin Cornw'l 2 E6
St. Martins Perth/Kinr 286 D5
St. Martin's Shrops 148 B6
St. Martin's Wilts 63 F7
St. Martin's Moor Shrops 148 B6
St. Martin's Plain Kent 55 F7
St. Mary Bourne Hants 48 C2
St. Mary Church V/Glam 58 E4
St. Mary Cray London 68 F3
St. Mary Hill V/Glam 58 D3
St. Mary Hoo Medway 69 D10
St. Mary in the Marsh Kent 39 B9
St. Marychurch Torbay 9 B8
St. Mary's Orkney 313 H5
St. Mary's Bay Kent 39 B9
St Mary's Church Warwick 118 D5
St. Mary's Grove N Som'set 60 F3
St. Maughans Monmouths 79 B7
St. Maughans Green Monmouths 79 B7
St. Mawes Cornw'l 3 C8
St. Mawgan Cornw'l 5 B7
St. Mellion Cornw'l 7 B7
St. Mellons Card 59 C8
St. Merryn Cornw'l 10 G3
St. Mewan Cornw'l 5 E9
St. Michael Caerhays Cornw'l 5 G9
St. Michael Church Som'set 43 G10
St. Michael Penkevil Cornw'l 5 G7
St. Michael South Elmham Suffolk 142 G6
St. Michaels Kent 53 F11
St. Michael's Torbay 9 C7
St. Michael's Worcs 115 D11
St. Michael's Hamlet Mersey 182 D5
St. Michael's Mead Herts 87 B7
St Michael's Mount, Penzance Cornw'l 2 D2
St. Michael's-on-Wyre Lancs 202 E5
St. Minver Cornw'l 10 F5
St. Monans Fife 287 G9
St. Neot Cornw'l 6 B3
St. Neots Cambs 122 F2
St. Nicholas Pembs 91 D8
St. Nicholas V/Glam 58 E5
St. Nicholas at Wade Kent 71 F9
St. Nicholas South Elmham Suffolk 142 G6
St. Nicolas Park Warwick 135 E7
St. Ninians Stirl 278 C6
St. Olaves Norfolk 143 D9
St. Osyth Essex 89 B10
St. Osyth Heath Essex 89 B10
St. Owen's Cross Heref'd 97 G10
St Paul's Cathedral London 67 C10
St. Paul's Cray London 68 F3
St. Paul's Walden Herts 104 G4
St. Peter South Elmham Suffolk 142 G6
St. Peter The Great Worcs 117 G7
St. Peters Glos 99 G8
St. Peters Kent 71 F11
St. Peter's Tyne/Wear 243 E7
St. Petrox Pembs 73 F7
St. Pinnock Cornw'l 6 C4
St. Quivox S Ayrs 257 E9
St. Ruan Cornw'l 2 F6
St. Stephen Cornw'l 5 E8
St. Stephens Cornw'l 12 D2
St. Stephens Cornw'l 7 D8
St. Stephen's Herts 85 D10
St. Teath Cornw'l 11 E7
St. Thomas Devon 14 C4
St. Tudy Cornw'l 11 F7
St. Twynnells Pembs 73 F7
St. Veep Cornw'l 6 D2
St. Vigeans Angus 287 C10
St. Vincent's Hamlet Essex 87 G9
St. Wenn Cornw'l 5 C9
St. Weonards Heref'd 97 G9
St. Winnow Cornw'l 6 D2
Saintbridge Glos 80 B5
Saintbury Glos 100 D2
Saint-y-Brid = St. Bride's Major V/Glam 57 G11
Saith Ffynnon Flints 181 F11
Salcombe Devon 9 G9
Salcombe Regis Devon 15 D8
Salcott Essex 89 C7
Sale Gtr Man 184 C3
Sale Ees Gtr Man 184 C3
Sale Green Worcs 117 F8
Saleby Lincs 191 F7
Salehurst E Sussex 38 C2
Salem Carms 94 F2
Salem Ceredig'n 128 G3
Salem Cornw'l 4 G4
Salen Arg/Bute 289 E7
Salen H'land 289 C8
Salendine Nook W Yorks 196 D6
Salesbury Lancs 203 G9
Saleway Worcs 117 F8
Salford Beds 103 D8
Salford Gtr Man 184 B4
Salford Oxon 100 F5
Salford Priors Warwick 117 G11
Salford Quays Gtr Man 184 B4
Salfords Surrey 51 D9
Salhouse Norfolk 160 G6
Saligo Arg/Bute 274 G3
Saline Fife 279 C10
Salisbury Wilts 47 G7
Salisbury Cathedral Wilts 31 B10
Salisbury Racecourse Wilts 31 B10
Salisbury Street Dorset 30 D3
Salkeld Dykes Cumb 230 D6
Sallachan H'land 289 C11
Sallachy H'land 295 B11
Sallachy H'land 309 J5
Salle Norfolk 160 E2
Salmonby Lincs 190 G4
Salmond's Muir Angus 287 D9
Salperton Glos 99 G11
Salph End Beds 121 G11
Salsburgh N Lanarks 268 C6
Salt Staffs 151 D9
Salt Cotes Cumb 238 G5
Salt Hill Slough 66 C3
Salta Cumb 229 B7
Saltaire W Yorks 205 F8
Saltaire 1853 Gallery W Yorks 205 F8
Saltash Cornw'l 7 D8
Saltburn H'land 301 C7
Saltburn-by-the-Sea Redcar/Clevel'd 235 G9
Saltby Leics 155 D7
Saltcoats Cumb 219 F11
Saltcoats E Loth 281 E9
Saltcoats N Ayrs 266 G4
Saltcotes Lancs 193 B11
Saltdean Brighton/Hove 36 G5

Salter Street W Midlands 118 C2
Salterbeck Cumb 228 F5
Salterforth Lancs 204 D3
Saltergate N Yorks 227 G7
Saltergate Hill N Yorks 205 B11
Salters Heath Hants 48 B6
Salters Heath Kent 52 C4
Salters Lode Norfolk 139 C11
Salterswall Ches 167 B10
Salterton Wilts 46 F6
Saltfleet Lincs 191 C7
Saltfleetby All Saints Lincs 191 C7
Saltfleetby St. Clements Lincs 191 C7
Saltfleetby St. Peter Lincs 190 D6
Saltford Bath/NE Som'set 61 F7
Salthouse Cumb 210 F4
Salthouse Norfolk 177 E9
Saltley W Midlands 133 F11
Saltmarsh Newp 59 C11
Saltmarshe ER Yorks 199 C9
Saltmead Card 59 D7
Saltness Orkney 313 J3
Saltness Shetl'd 315 J4
Saltney Flints 166 C5
Salton N Yorks 216 C4
Saltrens Devon 25 C7
Saltwell Tyne/Wear 243 E7
Saltwick Northum 242 B5
Saltwood Kent 55 F7
Salum Arg/Bute 288 E2
Salvington W Sussex 35 F10
Salwarpe Worcs 117 E7
Salwayash Dorset 16 B5
Salwick Lancs 202 G5
Sambourne Warwick 117 E11
Sambourne Wilts 45 E11
Sambrook Telford 150 E4
Samhla W Isles 296 E3
Samlesbury Lancs 203 G7
Samlesbury Bottoms Lancs 194 B6
Sammy Miller Motorcycle Museum Hants 19 B10
Sampford Arundel Som'set 27 D10
Sampford Brett Som'set 42 E5
Sampford Chapple Devon 25 G10
Sampford Courtenay Devon 25 G10
Sampford Moor Som'set 27 D10
Sampford Peverell Devon 27 E8
Sampford Spiney Devon 12 G7
Samuel's Corner Essex 70 B3
Samuelston E Loth 281 G9
Sanachan H'land 299 E8
Sanaigmore Arg/Bute 274 F3
Sanclêr = St. Clears Carms 74 B3
Sancreed Cornw'l 1 D4
Sancton ER Yorks 208 F4
Sand H'land 307 K4
Sand Shetl'd 315 J5
Sand Som'set 44 D2
Sand Acre Cottages Lincs 156 C3
Sand Beds W Midlands 133 D9
Sand Hill ER Yorks 199 D10
Sand Hole ER Yorks 208 F2
Sand Hutton N Yorks 207 B9
Sand Side Cumb 210 C4
Sandaig H'land 295 E9
Sandal Magna W Yorks 197 D10
Sandale Cumb 229 C11
Sandavore H'land 294 G6
Sanday Airport Orkney 312 D7
Sandbach Ches 168 C3
Sandbach Heath Ches 168 C3
Sandbank Arg/Bute 276 E3
Sandbanks Poole 18 D6
Sandbraes Lincs 200 G6
Sandend Aberds 302 C5
Sanderstead London 67 G10
Sandfields Rh Cyn Taff 76 G2
Sandfields Staffs 134 B2
Sandford Cumb 222 B4
Sandford Dorset 18 D4
Sandford Devon 26 G4
Sandford Hants 31 G11
Sandford I/Wight 20 E6
Sandford N Som'set 44 B2
Sandford Shrops 148 E6
Sandford Shrops 149 C11
Sandford S Lanarks 268 G4
Sandford Hill Stoke 168 G6
Sandford on Thames Oxon 83 E8
Sandford Orcas Dorset 29 C10
Sandford St. Martin Oxon 101 F8
Sandfordhill Aberds 303 E11
Sandgate Kent 55 F8
Sandgreen Dumf/Gal 237 D7
Sandhaven Aberds 303 C9
Sandhead Dumf/Gal 236 E2
Sandhill Bucks 102 F4
Sandhill Cambs 139 F11
Sandhill S Yorks 186 B6
Sandhill S Yorks 198 F2
Sandhills Dorset 29 G9
Sandhills Dorset 29 E11
Sandhills Oxon 83 D9
Sandhills Surrey 50 F2
Sandhills W Yorks 206 F3
Sandhoe Northum 241 D11
Sandhole Arg/Bute 275 D11
Sandholme ER Yorks 208 G2
Sandholme Lincs 156 B6
Sandholme Landing ER Yorks 208 G2
Sandhurst Brackn'l 65 G10
Sandhurst Glos 98 G6
Sandhurst Kent 38 B3
Sandhurst Cross Kent 38 B3
Sandhutton N Yorks 215 C7
Sandiacre Derby 153 B9
Sandilands Lincs 191 E8
Sandilands S Lanarks 259 B9
Sandiway Ches 183 G10
Sandleford Close W Berks 64 F3
Sandleheath Hants 31 E10
Sandling Kent 53 B9
Sandlow Green Ches 168 B3
Sandness Shetl'd 315 H3
Sandon Essex 88 E2
Sandon Herts 104 E6
Sandon Staffs 151 D8
Sandown I/Wight 21 E7
Sandown Park Kent 52 E6
Sandown Park Surrey 66 F6
Sandown Park Racecourse Surrey 66 F6
Sandplace Cornw'l 6 D5
Sandridge Herts 85 C11
Sandringham Norfolk 158 D3
Sands Bucks 84 G4
Sandsend N Yorks 227 C7
Sandside Cumb 211 C9
Sandside Orkney 313 H3
Sandside Ho. H'land 310 C3
Sandsound Shetl'd 315 J5
Sandtoft N Lincs 199 F8
Sandvoe Shetl'd 314 D5
Sandway Dorset 45 G9
Sandway Kent 53 C11
Sandwell W Midlands 133 F10
Sandwich Kent 55 B10
Sandwich Bay Est Kent 55 B11
Sandwick Cumb 221 B8
Sandwick Orkney 313 K5
Sandwick Shetl'd 315 L6
Sandwith Cumb 219 C9
Sandwith Newton Cumb 219 C9
Sandy Beds 104 B3
Sandy Carms 75 E7
Sandy Bank Lincs 174 D3
Sandy Bank Shrops 149 B10
Sandy Carrs Durham 234 C3
Sandy Cross E Sussex 37 C9
Sandy Cross Surrey 49 D11
Sandy Gate Devon 14 C5
Sandy Haven Pembs 72 D5
Sandy Lane Wilts 62 F3
Sandy Lane Wrex 166 G6
Sandy Lane W Yorks 205 F8
Sandy Way I/Wight 20 E5
Sandybank Orkney 312 G6
Sandycroft Flints 166 B4
Sandyford Dumf/Gal 248 E6
Sandyford Stoke 168 E5
Sandygate Devon 14 G3
Sandygate I/Man 192 C4
Sandygate S Yorks 186 D4
Sandyhills Dumf/Gal 237 D10
Sandylake Cornw'l 6 C2
Sandylands Lancs 211 G8
Sandylane Swan 56 D5
Sandypark Devon 13 D10
Sandysike Cumb 239 D9
Sandystones Scot Borders 262 D3
Sandyway Heref'd 97 F9
Sanford Batch N Som'set 44 B2
Sangobeg H'land 308 C4
Sangomore H'land 308 C4
Sanham Green W Berks 63 F10
Sankey Bridges Warrington 183 D9
Sankyn's Green Worcs 116 D5
Sanna H'land 288 C6
Sanndabhaig W Isles 297 G4
Sanndabhaig W Isles 304 E6
Sannox N Ayrs 255 C11
Sanquhar Dumf/Gal 247 B7
Santa Barbara W Midlands 118 B3
Santa Pod Raceway Beds 121 E9
Santon Cumb 220 E2
Santon N Lincs 200 E2
Santon Bridge Cumb 220 E2
Santon Downham Norfolk 140 F6
Sapcote Leics 135 E9
Sapey Common Worcs 116 E4
Sapiston Suffolk 125 B8
Sapley Cambs 122 C4
Sapperton Glos 80 E6
Sapperton Lincs 155 C10
Saracen's Head Lincs 156 D6
Sarclet H'land 310 E7
Sardis Carms 75 E9
Sardis Pembs 73 D7
Sardis Mountain Pembs 73 D10
Sarisbury Hants 33 F8
Sarn Brigd 58 C2
Sarn Flints 181 F10
Sarn Powys 130 E4
Sarn Bach Gwyn 144 D6
Sarn Meyllteyrn Gwyn 144 C4
Sarnau Ceredig'n 110 G6
Sarnau Gwyn 147 B9
Sarnau Powys 148 F4
Sarnau Powys 95 E10
Sarnesfield Heref'd 115 G7
Saron Carms 93 D7
Saron Carms 75 C9
Saron Gwyn 163 B8
Saron Gwyn 163 D7
Sarratt Herts 85 F8
Sarratt Bottom Herts 85 F8
Sarre Kent 71 F9
Sarsden Oxon 100 G5
Sarsgrum H'land 308 C3
Satley Durham 233 C8
Satmar Kent 55 F9
Satran H'land 294 B6
Satron N Yorks 223 F8
Satterleigh Devon 25 C11
Satterthwaite Cumb 220 G6
Satwell Oxon 65 C8
Sauchen Aberds 293 B8
Saucher Perth/Kinr 286 D5
Sauchie Clack 279 C8
Sauchieburn Aberds 293 G8
Saughall Ches 182 G5
Saughall Massie Mersey 182 D3
Saughton C/Edinb 280 G4
Saughtree Scot Borders 250 D3
Saul Glos 80 D2
Saundby Notts 188 D3
Saundersfoot Pembs 73 E10
Saunderton Bucks 84 E3
Saunderton Lee Bucks 84 F3
Saunton Devon 40 F3
Sausthorpe Lincs 174 B5
Saval H'land 309 J5
Savary H'land 289 E8
Saveock Cornw'l 4 F5
Saverley Green Staffs 151 B9
Savile Park W Yorks 196 C5
Savile Town W Yorks 197 C8
Sawbridge Warwick 119 D10
Sawbridgeworth Herts 87 B7
Sawdon N Yorks 217 C8
Sawley Derby 153 C9
Sawley Lancs 203 D11
Sawley N Yorks 214 F4
Sawston Cambs 105 B9
Sawtry Cambs 138 G3
Saxby Leics 154 F6
Saxby Lincs 189 D8
Saxby All Saints N Lincs 200 D3
Saxelbye Leics 154 E4
Saxham Street Suffolk 125 E11
Saxilby Lincs 188 F5
Saxlingham Norfolk 159 B10
Saxlingham Green Norfolk 142 D4
Saxlingham Nethergate Norfolk 142 D4
Saxlingham Thorpe Norfolk 142 D4
Saxmundham Suffolk 127 E7
Saxon Street Cambs 124 F3
Saxondale Notts 154 B3
Saxtead Suffolk 126 D5
Saxtead Green Suffolk 126 E5
Saxtead Little Green Suffolk 126 D5
Saxthorpe Norfolk 160 C2
Saxton N Yorks 206 F5
Sayers Common W Sussex 36 D3
Scackleton N Yorks 216 E2
Scadabhagh W Isles 305 J3
Scaftworth Notts 187 C11
Scagglethorpe N Yorks 216 E6
Scaitcliffe Lancs 195 B9
Scaladal W Isles 305 G3
Scalan Moray 292 B4
Scalasaig Arg/Bute 274 D4
Scalby ER Yorks 199 B10
Scalby N Yorks 227 G10
Scalby Mills N Yorks 227 G10
Scald End Beds 121 F10
Scaldwell Northants 120 C5
Scale Hall Lancs 211 G9
Scaleby Cumb 239 E11
Scaleby Hill Cumb 239 E10
Scales Cumb 210 E5
Scales Cumb 230 F2
Scales Lancs 202 G5
Scalford Leics 154 E5
Scaling Redcar/Clevel'd 226 C4
Scaling Dam Redcar/Clevel'd 226 C4
Scaliscro W Isles 304 F3
Scallasaig H'land 295 D10
Scallastle Arg/Bute 289 F8
Scalloway Shetl'd 315 K6
Scalpay W Isles 305 J4
Scalpay Ho. H'land 295 C8
Scalpsie Arg/Bute 255 B11
Scamadale H'land 295 F9
Scamblesby Lincs 190 F3
Scammadale Arg/Bute 289 G10
Scamodale H'land 289 B10
Scampston N Yorks 217 D7
Scampton Lincs 189 F7
Scaniport H'land 300 F6
Scapa Orkney 313 H5
Scapegoat Hill W Yorks 196 D5
Scar Orkney 312 D7
Scarborough N Yorks 217 B10
Scarborough Sea Life Centre N Yorks 227 G10
Scarcewater Cornw'l 5 E8
Scarcliffe Derby 171 B7
Scarcroft W Yorks 206 E3
Scardroy H'land 300 D2
Scarff Shetl'd 314 E4
Scarfskerry H'land 310 B6
Scargill Durham 223 C11
Scarinish Arg/Bute 288 E2
Scarisbrick Lancs 193 E11
Scarletts Wokingham 65 D10
Scarness Cumb 229 E10
Scarning Norfolk 159 G9
Scarrington Notts 172 G3
Scarth Hill Lancs 194 F2
Scarthin Nick Derby 170 D3
Scarthingwell N Yorks 206 F5
Scartho NE Lincs 201 F9
Scarvister Shetl'd 315 J5
Scarwell Orkney 312 F3
Scatness Shetl'd 315 M5
Scatraig H'land 301 F7
Scatwell Ho H'land 300 D3
Scawby N Lincs 200 F3
Scawby Brook N Lincs 200 F3
Scawsby S Yorks 198 G4
Scawthorpe S Yorks 198 F5
Scawton N Yorks 215 C11
Scayne's Hill W Sussex 36 C5
Scethrog Powys 96 F2
Scholar Green Ches 168 D4
Scholemoor W Yorks 205 G8
Scholes Gtr Man 194 F5
Scholes S Yorks 186 B5
Scholes W Yorks 197 F7
Scholes W Yorks 204 F6
Scholes W Yorks 197 B7
Scholes W Yorks 206 F3
Scholey Hill W Yorks 197 B11
School Aycliffe Durham 233 G11
School Green Ches 167 C10
School Green Essex 106 E4
School Green I/Wight 20 D2
School House Dorset 28 G5
School Lane Lancs 194 B5
Schoolgreen Wokingham 65 F8
Schoolhill Aberds 293 D11
Sciberscross H'land 309 H7
Science & Industry Museum, Manchester Gtr Man 184 B4
Science Centre Glasg C 267 B11
Science Museum London 67 D9
Scilly Bank Cumb 219 B9
Scissett W Yorks 197 E9
Scleddau Pembs 91 E8
Sco Ruston Norfolk 160 E5
Scofton Notts 187 D11
Scole Norfolk 126 B3
Scole Common Norfolk 142 G2
Scolpaig W Isles 296 D3
Scone Perth/Kinr 286 E5
Scone Palace, Perth Perth/Kinr 286 E5
Sconser H'land 295 B7
Scoonie Fife 287 G7
Scoor Arg/Bute 288 H6
Scopwick Lincs 173 D9
Scoraig H'land 307 K5
Scorborough ER Yorks 208 D6
Scorrier Cornw'l 4 G4
Scorriton Devon 8 B4
Scorton Lancs 202 D6
Scorton N Yorks 224 E5
Scot Hay Staffs 168 F4
Scot Lane End Gtr Man 196 F6
Scotbheinn W Isles 296 F4
Scotby Cumb 239 G10
Scotch Corner N Yorks 224 D4
Scotforth Lancs 202 B5
Scothern Lincs 189 F8
Scotland Leics 136 D3
Scotland Lincs 155 C10
Scotland End Oxon 100 E6
Scotland Gate Northum 253 G7
Scotlandwell Perth/Kinr 286 G5
Scotney Castle Garden Kent 53 F7
Scot's Gap Northum 252 F2
Scotsburn H'land 301 B7
Scotscalder Station H'land 310 D4
Scotscraig Fife 287 E8
Scotsdike Cumb 239 C9
Scotston Aberds 293 F9
Scotston Perth/Kinr 286 C3
Scotstoun Glasg C 267 B10
Scotstown H'land 289 C10
Scotswood Tyne/Wear 242 E6
Scott Willoughby Lincs 155 B11
Scottas H'land 295 E9
Scotter Lincs 199 G11
Scotterthorpe Lincs 199 G11
Scottish Sea Life Sanctuary, Barcaldine Arg/Bute 284 C3
Scottlethorpe Lincs 155 E11
Scotton Lincs 188 B5
Scotton N Yorks 206 B2
Scotton N Yorks 224 F3
Scottow Norfolk 160 E5
Scoughall E Loth 282 E2
Scoulag Arg/Bute 266 D2
Scoulton Norfolk 141 C9
Scounslow Green Staffs 151 D11
Scourie H'land 306 E6
Scourie More H'land 306 E6
Scousburgh Shetl'd 315 M5
Scout Dike S Yorks 197 F8
Scout Green Cumb 221 D11
Scouthead Gtr Man 196 F3
Scowles Glos 79 C9
Scrabster H'land 310 B4
Scrafield Lincs 174 B4
Scragged Oak Kent 69 G10
Scrainwood Northum 251 B11
Scrane End Lincs 174 G5
Scrapsgate Kent 70 E2
Scraptoft Leics 136 B2
Scratby Norfolk 161 F10
Scrayingham N Yorks 216 G4
Scredington Lincs 173 G9
Scremby Lincs 174 B6
Scremerston Northum 273 F10
Screveton Notts 172 G2
Scrivelsby Lincs 174 B3
Scriven N Yorks 206 B3
Scriventon Kent 52 E5
Scronkey Lancs 202 D4
Scrooby Notts 187 C11
Scropton Derby 152 C3
Scrub Hill Lincs 174 D2
Scruton N Yorks 224 G6
Scrwgan Powys 148 E3
Scuddaborg H'land 298 C3
Scuggate Cumb 239 C10
Sculcoates Kingston/Hull 209 G7
Sculthorpe Norfolk 159 C7
Scunthorpe N Lincs 199 E11
Scupholme Lincs 190 C6
Scurlage Swan 56 D3
Sea Som'set 28 E4
Sea Mills Bristol 60 D5
Sea Palling Norfolk 161 D8
Seaborough Dorset 28 F6
Seabridge Staffs 168 G4
Seabrook Kent 55 G7
Seaburn Tyne/Wear 243 F10
Seacombe Mersey 182 C4
Seacox Heath Kent 53 G8
Seacroft Lincs 175 C9
Seacroft W Yorks 206 F3
Seadyke Lincs 156 B6
Seafar N Lanarks 278 G5
Seafield H'land 311 L3
Seafield Midloth 270 C5
Seafield S Ayrs 257 E8
Seafield W Loth 269 B10
Seaford E Sussex 23 F7
Seaforth Mersey 182 B5
Seagrave Leics 154 F2
Seagry Heath Wilts 62 C3
Seaham Durham 234 B4
Seahouses Northum 264 C6
Seal Kent 52 B5
Sealand Flints 166 B5
Seale Surrey 49 D11
Seamer N Yorks 217 C10
Seamer N Yorks 225 C10
Seamill N Ayrs 266 F3
Searby Lincs 200 F5
Seasalter Kent 70 F5
Seascale Cumb 219 E10
Seaside Carms 75 F8
Seathorne Lincs 175 B9
Seathwaite Cumb 220 F4
Seathwaite Cumb 220 C4
Seatle Cumb 211 C7
Seatoller Cumb 220 C4
Seaton Cumb 228 E6
Seaton Cornw'l 6 E6
Seaton Devon 15 C10
Seaton ER Yorks 209 D9
Seaton Kent 55 B8
Seaton Northum 243 B8
Seaton Rutl'd 137 D8
Seaton Burn Tyne/Wear 242 C6
Seaton Carew Hartlep'l 234 E6
Seaton Delaval Northum 243 B8
Seaton Junction Devon 15 B10
Seaton Ross ER Yorks 207 E11
Seaton Sluice Northum 243 B8
Seaton Terrace Northum 243 B8
Seatown Aberds 302 C5
Seatown Aberds 303 D11
Seatown Dorset 16 C4
Seave Green N Yorks 225 E11
Seaview I/Wight 21 C8
Seaville Cumb 238 G5
Seavington St. Mary Som'set 28 E5
Seavington St. Michael Som'set 28 D6
Seawick Essex 89 C10
Sebastopol Torf 78 F3
Sebay Orkney 313 H6
Sebergham Cumb 230 C3
Sebiston Velzian Orkney 312 F3
Seckington Warwick 134 B5
Second Coast H'land 307 K3
Sector Devon 16 B2
Sedbergh Cumb 222 G3
Sedbury Glos 79 G8
Sedbusk N Yorks 223 G7
Seddington Beds 104 B3
Sedgeberrow Worcs 99 D10
Sedgebrook Lincs 155 B7
Sedgecroft Devon 28 G4
Sedgefield Durham 234 F3
Sedgefield Racecourse Durham 234 F2
Sedgeford Norfolk 158 B4
Sedgehill Wilts 30 B5
Sedgemere W Midlands 118 B4
Sedgley W Midlands 133 E8
Sedgley Park Gtr Man 195 G10
Sedgwick Cumb 211 B10
Sedlescombe E Sussex 38 D3
Seed Kent 54 B2
Seedley Gtr Man 184 B4
Seend Wilts 62 G2
Seend Cleeve Wilts 62 G2
Seend Row Wilts 62 G2
Seer Green Bucks 85 G7
Seething Norfolk 142 D6
Sefton Mersey 193 G11
Seggat Aberds 303 E7
Seghill Northum 243 C7
Seighford Staffs 151 E7
Seilebost W Isles 305 J2
Seion Gwyn 163 B8
Seisdon Staffs 132 E6
Seisiadar W Isles 304 E7
Selattyn Shrops 148 C5
Selborne Hants 49 G8
Selby N Yorks 207 G8
Selham W Sussex 34 C6
Selhurst London 67 F10
Selkirk Scot Borders 261 D11
Selkirk Glass Scot Borders 261 D11
Sellack Heref'd 97 F11
Sellack Marsh Heref'd 97 F11
Sellafirth Shetl'd 314 D7
Sellibister Orkney 312 D8
Sellick's Green Som'set 28 D2
Sellindge Kent 54 F6
Selling Kent 54 B4
Sells Green Wilts 62 G2
Selly Hill N Yorks 227 D7
Selly Oak W Midlands 133 G10
Selly Park W Midlands 133 G11
Selmeston E Sussex 23 D8
Selsdon London 67 G11
Selsey Glos 80 E4
Selsey W Sussex 22 E5
Selsfeild Common W Sussex 51 G10
Selside Cumb 221 F10
Selside N Yorks 212 D5
Selsmore Hants 22 D2
Selson Kent 55 B10
Selstead Kent 55 E8
Selston Notts 171 E7
Selston Common Notts 171 E7
Selston Green Notts 171 E7
Selwick Orkney 313 H3
Selworthy Som'set 42 D2
Semblister Shetl'd 315 H5
Semer Suffolk 107 B9
Semere Green Norfolk 142 G3
Semington Wilts 61 G11
Semley Wilts 30 B5
Send Surrey 50 B4
Send Marsh Surrey 50 B4
Senghenydd Caerph 77 G10
Sennen Cornw'l 1 D3
Sennen Cove Cornw'l 1 D3
Sennicotts W Sussex 34 F4
Sennybridge = Pont Senni Powys 95 F8
Serlby Notts 187 D11
Serrington Wilts 46 F5
Sessay N Yorks 215 D9
Setchey Norfolk 158 G2
Setley Hants 32 G4
Seton E Loth 281 G8
Seton Mains E Loth 281 F8
Setter Shetl'd 314 E6
Setter Shetl'd 315 H5
Setter Shetl'd 315 J7
Setter Shetl'd 315 L6
Settiscarth Orkney 312 G4
Settle N Yorks 212 G6
Settrington N Yorks 216 E6
Seven Ash Som'set 43 G7
Seven Kings London 68 B3
Seven Sisters = Blaendulais Neath P Talb 76 D4
Seven Springs Glos 81 B7
Seven Star Green Essex 107 F8
Sevenhampton Glos 99 G10
Sevenhampton Swindon 82 G2
Sevenoaks Kent 52 B4
Sevenoaks Weald Kent 52 C4
Severn Beach S Glos 60 C4
Severn Bridges Visitor Centre S Glos 60 B4
Severn Stoke Worcs 99 C7
Severn Valley Railway Worcs 116 B5
Sevick End Beds 121 G11
Sevington Kent 54 E4
Sevington Wilts 61 D11
Sewards End Essex 105 D11
Sewardstone Essex 86 F5
Sewardstonebury Essex 86 F5
Sewell Beds 103 G10
Sewerby ER Yorks 218 F3
Sewerby Hall and Gardens, Bridlington ER Yorks 218 F4
Seworgan Cornw'l 2 C6
Sewstern Leics 155 E7
Sexhow N Yorks 225 D9
Sgarasta Mhor W Isles 305 J2
Sgiogarstaigh W Isles 304 B7
Shabbington Bucks 83 D11
Shackerley Shrops 132 B6
Shackerstone Leics 135 B7
Shacklecross Derby 153 C8
Shackleford Surrey 50 D2
Shacklewell London 67 B10
Shade W Yorks 196 C2
Shadforth Durham 234 C2
Shadingfield Suffolk 143 G8
Shadoxhurst Kent 54 F3
Shadsworth Blackb'n 195 B8
Shadwell Glos 80 F3
Shadwell London 67 C11
Shadwell Norfolk 141 G8
Shadwell W Yorks 206 F2
Shaftenhoe End Herts 105 D8
Shaftesbury Dorset 30 C5
Shaftholme S Yorks 198 F5
Shafton S Yorks 197 E11
Shafton Two Gates S Yorks 197 E11
Shaggs Dorset 18 E3
Shakerley Gtr Man 195 G7
Shakesfield Glos 98 E3
Shakespeare's Birthplace, Stratford-upon-Avon Warwick 118 G3
Shalbourne Wilts 63 G10
Shalcombe I/Wight 20 D3
Shalden Hants 49 E7
Shalden Green Hants 49 E7
Shaldon Devon 14 G4
Shalfleet I/Wight 20 D4
Shalford Essex 106 F4
Shalford Som'set 45 G8
Shalford Surrey 50 D4
Shalford Green Essex 106 F4
Shalloch Moray 302 D3
Shallowford Devon 13 F9
Shallowford Staffs 151 D7
Shalmsford Street Kent 54 C5
Shalstone Bucks 102 D2
Shamley Green Surrey 50 E4
Shandon Arg/Bute 276 D5
Shandwick H'land 301 B8
Shangton Leics 136 D4
Shankhouse Northum 243 B7
Shanklin I/Wight 21 E7
Shanklin Chine I/Wight 21 E7
Shannochie N Ayrs 255 E10
Shanquhar Aberds 302 F5
Shanwell Fife 287 E8
Shanzie Perth/Kinr 286 B6
Shap Cumb 221 B11
Shapridge Glos 79 B11
Shapwick Dorset 30 G6
Shapwick Som'set 44 F2
Sharcott Wilts 46 B7
Shard End W Midlands 134 F3
Shardlow Derby 153 C8
Shareshill Staffs 133 B8
Sharlston W Yorks 197 D11
Sharlston Common W Yorks 197 E11
Sharman's Cross W Midlands 118 B2
Sharnal Street Medway 69 E9
Sharnbrook Beds 121 F9
Sharneyford Lancs 195 C11
Sharnford Leics 135 E9
Sharnhill Green Dorset 30 F2
Sharoe Green Lancs 202 G6
Sharow N Yorks 214 E6
Sharp Street Norfolk 161 E7
Sharpenhoe Beds 103 E11
Sharperton Northum 251 C11
Sharples Gtr Man 195 E8
Sharpness Glos 79 E11
Sharp's Corner E Sussex 37 D9
Sharpsbridge E Sussex 36 C6
Sharpstone Bath/NE Som'set 45 B9
Sharpthorne W Sussex 51 G11
Sharptor Cornw'l 11 G11
Sharpway Gate Worcs 117 D9
Sharrington Norfolk 159 B10
Sharrow S Yorks 186 D4
Shatton Gtr Man 184 D4
Shatterford Worcs 132 G5
Shatterling Kent 55 B9
Shatton Derby 185 E11
Shaugh Prior Devon 7 C10
Shave Cross Dorset 16 B4
Shavington Ches 168 E2
Shaw Gtr Man 196 F2
Shaw Swindon 62 B6
Shaw W Berks 64 F3
Shaw Wilts 61 F11
Shaw W Yorks 204 F6
Shaw Common Glos 98 F3
Shaw Green Herts 104 E5
Shaw Green Lancs 194 D4
Shaw Green N Yorks 205 C11
Shaw Heath Ches 184 F3
Shaw Heath Gtr Man 184 D5
Shaw Lands S Yorks 197 F10
Shaw Mills N Yorks 214 G5
Shaw Side Gtr Man 196 F2
Shawbirtch Telford 150 G2
Shawbury Shrops 149 E11
Shawclough Gtr Man 195 E11
Shawell Leics 135 G10
Shawfield Gtr Man 195 E11
Shawfield Head N Yorks 205 C11
Shawford Hants 33 C7
Shawforth Lancs 195 C11
Shawhead Dumf/Gal 237 B10
Shawhead N Lanarks 268 C4
Shawhill Dumf/Gal 238 D6
Shawlands Glasg C 267 C11
Shawsburn S Lanarks 268 E5
Shawton S Lanarks 268 F3
Shawtonhill S Lanarks 268 F3
Sheandow Moray 302 F2
Shear Cross Wilts 45 E11
Shearington Dumf/Gal 238 D2
Shearsby Leics 136 E2
Shearston Som'set 43 G9
Shebbear Devon 24 F6
Shebdon Staffs 150 D5
Shebster H'land 310 C4
Sheddens E Renf 267 D11
Shedfield Hants 33 E9
Sheen Staffs 169 C10
Sheep Hill Durham 242 F5
Sheepbridge Derby 186 G5
Sheepcote Close N Yorks 225 F7
Sheeplane Beds 103 E8
Sheepridge W Yorks 196 D6
Sheepscar W Yorks 206 G2
Sheepscombe Glos 80 C5
Sheepstor Devon 7 B10
Sheeptick End Beds 103 D9
Sheepwash Devon 25 F7
Sheepwash Northum 253 F7
Sheepway N Som'set 60 D3
Sheepy Magna Leics 134 C6
Sheepy Parva Leics 134 C6
Sheering Essex 87 C8
Sheerness Kent 70 D2
Sheerwater Kent 71 G9
Sheerwater Surrey 66 G4
Sheet Hants 34 C3
Sheet Shrops 115 C10
Sheets Heath Surrey 50 B3
Sheffield Cornw'l 1 D5
Sheffield S Yorks 186 D5
Sheffield Bottom W Berks 65 F7
Sheffield Common Essex 87 G9
Sheffield Green E Sussex 36 B6
Sheffield Park S Yorks 186 D5
Sheffield Park, Uckfield E Sussex 36 C6
Shefford Beds 104 D2
Shefford Woodlands W Berks 63 E11
Sheigra H'land 306 C6
Sheinton Shrops 132 C2
Shelderton Shrops 115 B8
Sheldon Derby 169 B11
Sheldon Devon 27 F10
Sheldon W Midlands 134 G3
Sheldwich Kent 54 B4
Sheldwich Lees Kent 54 B4
Shelf Bridg 58 C2
Shelf W Yorks 196 B6
Shelfanger Norfolk 142 G2
Shelfield Warwick 118 E2
Shelfield W Midlands 133 C10
Shelfield Green Warwick 118 E2
Shelfleys Northants 120 F4
Shelford Notts 171 G11
Shelford Warwick 135 F8
Shell Green Halton 183 D8
Shelley Essex 87 D9
Shelley Suffolk 107 D10
Shelley W Yorks 197 E8
Shellingford Oxon 82 G4
Shellow Bowells Essex 87 D10
Shellthorn Som'set 43 G8
Shelly Green W Midlands 118 B2
Shelsley Beauchamp Worcs 116 E4
Shelsley Walsh Worcs 116 E4
Shelthorpe Leics 153 F10
Shelton Beds 121 D10
Shelton Norfolk 142 E4
Shelton Notts 172 G3
Shelton Shrops 149 G9
Shelton Common Norfolk 142 E4
Shelton Green Norfolk 142 E4
Shelton Lock Derby C 153 C7
Shelton under Harley Staffs 150 B6
Shelve Shrops 130 D6
Shelvingford Kent 71 F8
Shelwick Heref'd 97 C10
Shelwick Green Heref'd 97 C10
Shenfield Essex 87 G9
Shenington Oxon 101 C7
Shenley Herts 85 E11
Shenley Brook End M/Keynes 102 E6
Shenley Church End M/Keynes 102 D6
Shenley Fields W Midlands 133 G10
Shenley Lodge M/Keynes 102 D6
Shenleybury Herts 85 E11
Shenmore Heref'd 97 D7
Shennanton Dumf/Gal 236 C5
Shennanton Ho. Dumf/Gal 236 C5
Shenstone Staffs 134 C2
Shenstone Worcs 117 C7
Shenstone Woodend Staffs 134 C2
Shenton Leics 135 C7
Shenval H'land 300 G4
Shenval Moray 302 G2
Shenvault Moray 301 E10
Shepard Hill N Yorks 225 E9
Shepard Hill W Yorks 197 C9
Shepeau Stow Lincs 156 G6
Shephall Herts 104 G5
Shepherds Cornw'l 4 E6
Shepherd's Bush London 67 C8
Shepherd's Gate Norfolk 157 F11
Shepherd's Green Oxon 65 C8
Shepherd's Patch Glos 80 E2
Shepherd's Port Norfolk 158 C3
Shepherdswell or Sibertswold Kent 55 D9
Shepley W Yorks 197 F7
Shepperdine S Glos 79 F10
Shepperton Surrey 66 F5
Shepperton Green Surrey 66 F5
Shepreth Cambs 105 B7
Shepshed Leics 153 F9
Shepton Beauchamp Som'set 28 D6
Shepton Mallet Som'set 44 E6
Shepton Montague Som'set 45 G7
Shepway Kent 53 C9
Sheraton Durham 234 D4
Sherborne Dorset 29 D10
Sherborne Glos 81 C11
Sherborne Causeway Dorset 30 C4
Sherborne St. John Hants 48 B6
Sherborne Street Suffolk 107 C9
Sherbourne Warwick 118 E5
Sherburn Durham 234 C2
Sherburn N Yorks 217 D9
Sherburn Hill Durham 234 C2
Sherburn in Elmet N Yorks 206 G5
Shere Surrey 50 D5
Shereford Norfolk 159 D7
Sherfield English Hants 32 C3
Sherfield Hill Hants 49 B7
Sherfield on Loddon Hants 49 B7
Sherfin Lancs 195 B9
Sherford Devon 8 G5
Sherford Som'set 28 C2
Sheriff Hill Tyne/Wear 243 E7
Sheriff Hutton N Yorks 216 F3
Sheriffhales Shrops 150 G5
Sheringham Norfolk 177 E11
Sherington M/Keynes 103 B7
Sheringwood Norfolk 177 E11
Shernal Green Worcs 117 E8
Shernborne Norfolk 158 C4
Sherrard's Green Worcs 98 B6
Sherrardspark Herts 86 C2
Sherrington Wilts 46 F3
Sherston Wilts 61 B11
Sherston Parva Wilts 61 B11
Sherwood Nott'ham 171 G9
Sherwood Lancs 202 G6
Sherwood Park Kent 52 E6
Shettleston Glasg C 268 C2
Shevington Gtr Man 194 F4
Shevington Moor Gtr Man 194 E4
Shevington Vale Gtr Man 194 F4

Sheviock Cornw'l 7 D7
Shewalton N Ayrs 257 B8
Shibden Head W Yorks 196 B5
Shide I/Wight 20 D5
Shiel Aberds 292 B4
Shiel Bridge H'land 295 D11
Shield Row Durham 242 G6
Shieldaig H'land 299 B8
Shieldaig H'land 299 D8
Shieldhall Glasg C 267 B10
Shieldhall Falk 279 F7
Shieldhill Dumf/Gal 248 F2
Shieldhill S Lanarks 269 G10
Shieldmuir N Lanarks 268 D5
Shielfoot H'land 289 C8
Shielhill Angus 287 B8
Shifford Oxon 82 E5
Shifnal Shrops 132 B5
Shilbottle Northum 252 B5
Shilbottle Grange Northum 252 B6
Shildon Durham 233 F10
Shillford E Renf 267 D8
Shillingford Devon 27 C7
Shillingford Oxon 83 G9
Shillingford Abbot Devon 14 D4
Shillingford St. George Devon 14 D4
Shillingstone Dorset 30 E4
Shillington Beds 104 D2
Shillmoor Northum 251 B9
Shilton Oxon 82 D3
Shilton Warwick 135 G8
Shilvinghampton Dorset 17 E8
Shilvington Northum 252 G5
Shimpling Norfolk 142 G3
Shimpling Suffolk 125 G7
Shimpling Street Suffolk 125 G7
Shincliffe Durham 233 C11
Shiney Row Tyne/Wear 243 G8
Shinfield Wokingham 65 F8
Shingay Cambs 104 B6
Shingham Norfolk 140 B5
Shingle Street Suffolk 109 C7
Shinner's Bridge Devon 8 C5
Shinness H'land 309 H5
Shipbourne Kent 52 C5
Shipbrookhill Ches 183 G11
Shipdham Norfolk 141 B9
Shipham Som'set 44 B2
Shiphay Torbay 9 B7
Shiplake Oxon 65 D9
Shiplake Bottom Oxon 65 C8
Shiplake Row Oxon 65 D9
Shiplate N Som'set 43 B11
Shipley Northum 264 F4
Shipley Shrops 132 D6
Shipley W Sussex 35 C10
Shipley W Yorks 205 F8
Shipley Bridge Surrey 51 E10
Shipley Common Derby 171 G7
Shipmeadow Suffolk 143 F7
Shipmeadow Common Suffolk 143 F7
Shippon Oxon 83 F7
Shipston on Stour Warwick 100 C5
Shipton Bucks 102 F5
Shipton Glos 81 B8
Shipton N Yorks 207 B7
Shipton Shrops 131 E11
Shipton Bellinger Hants 47 D8
Shipton Gorge Dorset 16 C5
Shipton Green W Sussex 22 D3
Shipton Moyne Glos 61 B11
Shipton Oliffe Glos 81 B8
Shipton on Cherwell Oxon 83 B7
Shipton Solers Glos 81 B8
Shipton under Wychwood Oxon 82 B3
Shiptonthorpe ER Yorks 208 E3
Shirburn Oxon 84 F2
Shirdley Hill Lancs 193 E11
Shire Cumb 231 D8
Shire Horse Centre, Stratford-upon-Avon Warwick 118 G4
Shire Oak W Midlands 133 C11
Shirebrook Derby 171 B8
Shirecliffe S Yorks 186 C4
Shiregreen S Yorks 186 C5
Shirehampton Bristol 60 D4
Shiremoor Tyne/Wear 243 C8
Shirenewton Monmouths 79 G7
Shireoaks Notts 187 E9
Shirkoak Kent 54 F2
Shirl Heath Heref'd 115 F8
Shirland Derby 170 D5
Shirlett Shrops 132 D3
Shirley Derby 170 G2
Shirley Hants 19 B9
Shirley S'thampton 32 E6
Shirley W Midlands 118 B2
Shirley Heath W Midlands 118 B2
Shirley Warren S'thampton 32 E6
Shirrell Heath Hants 33 E9
Shirwell Devon 40 F5
Shirwell Cross Devon 40 F5
Shiskine N Ayrs 255 E10
Shittlehope Durham 232 D6
Shobdon Heref'd 115 E7
Shobley Hants 31 F11
Shobnall Staffs 152 E4
Shobrooke Devon 26 G5
Shoby Leics 154 E3
Shocklach Ches 166 F6
Shocklach Green Ches 166 F6
Shoeburyness Southend 70 C2
Sholden Kent 55 C11
Sholing S'thampton 33 E7
Sholing Common S'thampton 33 E7
Sholver Gtr Man 196 F2
Shoot Hill Shrops 149 G8
Shootash Hants 32 C4
Shooter's Hill London 68 D2
Shootersway Herts 85 D7
Shop Cornw'l 10 G3
Shop Cornw'l 24 E2
Shop Devon 24 E5
Shop Corner Suffolk 108 D4
Shopford Cumb 240 C3
Shopnoller Som'set 43 G7
Shore Gtr Man 196 D2
Shore W Yorks 196 B2
Shore Mill H'land 301 C7
Shoreditch London 67 C10
Shoreditch Som'set 28 C2
Shoregill Cumb 222 E5
Shoreham Kent 68 G4
Shoreham Airport W Sussex 36 F2
Shoreham Beach W Sussex 36 G2
Shoreham-by-Sea W Sussex 36 G2
Shoresdean Northum 273 F9
Shoreside Shetl'd 315 J4
Shoreswood Northum 273 F8
Shoreton H'land 300 C6
Shorley Hants 33 B9
Shorncote Glos 81 F8
Shorne Kent 69 E7
Shorne Ridgeway Kent 69 E7
Short Cross W Midlands 133 G9
Short Heath Leics 152 G6
Short Heath W Midlands 133 E11
Short Street Wilts 45 D10
Shorta Cross Cornw'l 6 D5
Shortacombe Devon 12 D6
Shortbridge E Sussex 36 C6
Shortfield Common Surrey 49 E10
Shortgate E Sussex 37 D7
Shorthampton Oxon 100 G6
Shortheath Hants 49 F9
Shortheath Surrey 49 E10
Shortlands London 67 F11
Shortlanesend Cornw'l 4 F6
Shortlees E Ayrs 257 B10
Shorton Torbay 9 C7
Shortroods Renf 267 B9
Short's Corner Lincs 174 E4
Shortstanding Glos 79 C9
Shortstown Beds 103 B11
Shortwood Glos 80 F4
Shortwood S Glos 61 D7
Shorwell I/Wight 20 E5
Shoscombe Bath/NE Som'set 45 B8
Shoscombe Vale Bath/NE Som'set 45 B8
Shotesham Norfolk 142 D5
Shotford Heath Suffolk 142 G4
Shotgate Essex 88 G3
Shotley Northants 137 D8
Shotley Suffolk 108 D4
Shotley Bridge Northum 242 G3
Shotley Gate Suffolk 108 D4
Shotleyfield Northum 242 G3
Shottenden Kent 54 C4
Shottermill Surrey 49 G11
Shottery Warwick 118 F3
Shotteswell Warwick 101 B8
Shottisham Suffolk 108 C6
Shottle Derby 170 F4
Shottlegate Derby 170 F4
Shotton Durham 234 D4
Shotton Durham 234 F3
Shotton Flints 166 B4
Shotton Northum 242 B6
Shotton Northum 263 C8
Shotton Colliery Durham 234 C3
Shotts N Lanarks 269 C7
Shotwick Ches 182 G4
Shouldham Norfolk 140 B3
Shouldham Thorpe Norfolk 140 B3
Shoulton Worcs 116 F6
Shover's Green E Sussex 52 G6
Shraleybrook Staffs 168 F3
Shrawardine Shrops 149 F8
Shrawley Worcs 116 D6
Shreding Green Bucks 66 C4
Shrewley Warwick 118 D4
Shrewsbury Shrops 149 G10
Shrewton Wilts 46 E5
Shripney W Sussex 34 G6
Shrivenham Oxon 63 B8
Shropham Norfolk 141 E9
Shroton Dorset 30 E4
Shrub End Essex 107 G9
Shrubs Hill Surrey 66 F3
Shuart Kent 71 F9
Shucknall Heref'd 97 C11
Shudy Camps Cambs 106 C2
Shulishadermor H'land 298 E4
Shulista H'land 298 B4
Shuna Ho Arg/Bute 275 C8
Shurdington Glos 80 B6
Shurlock Row Windsor 65 E10
Shurnock Worcs 117 E10
Shurrery H'land 310 D4
Shurrery Lodge H'land 310 D4
Shurton Som'set 43 E8
Shustoke Warwick 134 E4
Shute Devon 15 B11
Shute Devon 26 G5
Shute End Wilts 31 B11
Shutford Oxon 101 C7
Shutheath Staffs 151 E7
Shuthonger Glos 99 D7
Shutlanger Northants 102 B4
Shutta Cornw'l 6 E5
Shuttington Warwick 134 B5
Shuttlesfield Kent 55 E7
Shuttlewood Derby 187 G7
Shuttleworth Lancs 195 D10
Shwt Bridg 57 D11
Siabost bho Dheas W Isles 304 D4
Siabost bho Thuath W Isles 304 D4
Siadar W Isles 304 C5
Siadar Iarach W Isles 304 C5
Siadar Uarach W Isles 304 C5
Sibbaldbie Dumf/Gal 248 F4
Sibbertoft Northants 136 G3
Sibdon Carwood Shrops 131 G8
Sibford Ferris Oxon 101 D7
Sibford Gower Oxon 101 D7
Sible Hedingham Essex 106 E5
Sibley's Green Essex 106 F2
Sibsey Lincs 174 E5
Sibsey Fen Side Lincs 174 E4
Sibson Cambs 137 D11
Sibson Leics 135 C7
Sibster H'land 310 D7
Sibthorpe Notts 172 F3
Sibthorpe Notts 188 G2
Sibton Suffolk 127 D7
Sibton Green Suffolk 127 C7
Sicklesmere Suffolk 125 E7
Sicklinghall N Yorks 206 D3
Sid Devon 15 D8
Sidbrook Som'set 28 B3
Sidbury Devon 15 C8
Sidbury Shrops 132 F3
Sidcot N Som'set 44 B2
Sidcup London 68 E3
Siddal W Yorks 196 C6
Siddick Cumb 228 E6
Siddington Ches 184 G4
Siddington Glos 81 F8
Side of the Moor Gtr Man 195 E8
Sidemoor Worcs 117 C8
Sidestrand Norfolk 160 B5
Sideway Stoke 168 G5
Sidford Devon 15 C8
Sidlesham W Sussex 22 D5
Sidley E Sussex 38 F2
Sidlow Surrey 51 D9
Sidmouth Devon 15 D8
Siefton Shrops 131 G9
Sigford Devon 13 G11
Sigglesthorne ER Yorks 209 D9
Sighthill C/Edinb 280 G3
Sigingstone V/Glam 58 E3
Signet Oxon 82 C2
Silchester Hants 64 G6
Sildinis W Isles 305 G4
Sileby Leics 154 F2
Silecroft Cumb 210 C2
Silfield Norfolk 142 D2
Silford Devon 24 B6
Silian Ceredig'n 111 G11
Silk Willoughby Lincs 173 G9
Silkstead Hants 32 C6
Silkstone S Yorks 197 F9
Silkstone Common S Yorks 197 G9
Sill Field Cumb 211 B11
Sillaton Cornw'l 7 C7
Sillerhole Fife 281 A7
Silloth Cumb 238 G4
Sillyearn Moray 302 D5
Siloh Carms 94 D4
Silpho N Yorks 227 G9
Silsden W Yorks 204 D6
Silsoe Beds 103 D11
Silver End Essex 88 B4
Silver Green Norfolk 142 E5
Silver Hill E Sussex 38 B2
Silver Street Glos 80 E3
Silver Street Kent 69 G11
Silver Street Som'set 27 C11
Silver Street Som'set 44 G4
Silver Street Worcs 117 B11
Silverburn Midloth 270 C4
Silverdale Lancs 211 D9
Silverdale Staffs 168 F4
Silverdale Green Lancs 211 E9
Silvergate Norfolk 160 D3
Silverhill E Sussex 38 E4
Silverhill Park E Sussex 38 E4
Silverknowes C/Edinb 280 F4
Silverlace Green Suffolk 126 E6
Silverley's Green Suffolk 126 B5
Silverstone Northants 102 C3
Silverstone Motor Racing Circuit Northants 102 C3
Silverton Devon 27 G7
Silverton W Dunb 277 F8
Silvertonhill S Lanarks 268 E4
Silvertown London 68 C2
Silverwell Cornw'l 4 F4
Silvington Shrops 116 B2
Silwick Shetl'd 315 J4
Simister Gtr Man 195 F10
Simmondley Derby 185 C8
Simm's Cross Halton 183 D8
Simm's Lane End Mersey 194 G4
Simonburn Northum 241 C9
Simonsbath Som'set 41 F9
Simonside Tyne/Wear 243 E8
Simonstone Lancs 203 G11
Simonstone N Yorks 223 G7
Simprim Scot Borders 273 F7
Simpson M/Keynes 103 D7
Simpson Pembs 72 B5
Simpson Cross Pembs 72 B5
Simpson Green W Yorks 205 F9
Sinclair's Hill Scot Borders 272 E6
Sinclairston E Ayrs 257 F11
Sinclairtown Fife 280 C5
Sinderby N Yorks 214 C6
Sinderhope Northum 241 G8
Sinderland Green Gtr Man 184 C2
Sindlesham Wokingham 65 F9
Sinfin Derby C 152 C6
Singdean Scot Borders 250 C3
Singleborough Bucks 102 E5
Singledge Kent 55 D9
Singleton Lancs 202 G2
Singleton W Sussex 34 E5
Singlewell Kent 69 E7
Singret Wrex 166 D4
Sinkhurst Green Kent 53 E10
Sinnahard Aberds 292 B6
Sinnington N Yorks 216 B4
Sinton Worcs 116 E6
Sinton Green Worcs 116 E6
Sion Hill Bath/NE Som'set 61 F8
Sion Hill N Yorks 215 C7
Sipson London 66 D5
Sirhowy Bl Gwent 77 D10
Sisland Norfolk 142 D6
Sissinghurst Kent 53 F9
Sissinghurst Castle Garden Kent 53 F10
Siston S Glos 61 D7
Sithney Cornw'l 2 D4
Sithney Green Cornw'l 2 D4
Sitterton Dorset 18 C2
Sittingbourne Kent 70 G2
Sitwell Grange Derby 170 C6
Six Ashes Staffs 132 F5
Six Bells Bl Gwent 78 E2
Six Mile Bottom Cambs 123 F10
Sixhills Lincs 189 D10
Sixmile Kent 54 E6
Sixpenny Handley Dorset 31 D7
Sizewell Suffolk 127 E9
Skail H'land 308 E7
Skaill Orkney 312 E5
Skaill Orkney 312 G3
Skaill Orkney 313 H6
Skara Brae Orkney 312 G3
Skares E Ayrs 258 F2
Skateraw E Loth 282 F4
Skaw Shetl'd 314 B8
Skaw Shetl'd 314 G7
Skeabost H'land 298 E4
Skeabrae Orkney 312 F3
Skeeby N Yorks 224 E4
Skeete Kent 54 E6
Skeffington Leics 136 C4
Skeffling ER Yorks 201 D11
Skegby Notts 171 C8
Skegness Lincs 175 C9
Skelberry Shetl'd 315 G6
Skelberry Shetl'd 315 M5
Skelbo H'land 309 K7
Skelbo Street H'land 309 K7
Skelbrooke S Yorks 198 E4
Skeldyke Lincs 156 B6
Skelfhill Scot Borders 249 C11
Skellingthorpe Lincs 188 G6
Skellister Shetl'd 315 H6
Skellorn Green Ches 184 E6
Skellow S Yorks 198 E4
Skelmanthorpe W Yorks 197 E8
Skelmersdale Lancs 194 F3
Skelmonae Aberds 303 F8
Skelmorlie N Ayrs 266 B3
Skelmuir Aberds 303 E9
Skelpick H'land 308 D7
Skelton Cumb 230 D4
Skelton C/York 207 B7
Skelton ER Yorks 199 B9
Skelton N Yorks 215 F7
Skelton N Yorks 223 E11
Skelton Redcar/Clevel'd 226 B3
Skelton Green Redcar/Clevel'd 226 B3
Skelton Wood End Cumb 230 D4
Skelwick Orkney 312 D5
Skelwith Bridge Cumb 220 E6
Skendleby Lincs 174 B6
Skendleby Psalter Lincs 190 G6
Skene Ho. Aberds 293 C9
Skenfrith Monmouths 97 G9
Skerne ER Yorks 208 B6
Skeroblingarry Arg/Bute 255 E8
Skerray H'land 308 C6
Skerricha H'land 306 D7
Skerton Lancs 211 G9
Sketchley Leics 135 E8
Sketchley Hill Leics 135 E8
Sketty Swan 75 G10
Skewen Rh Cyn Taff 76 F2
Skewsby N Yorks 216 E2
Skeyton Norfolk 160 D4
Skeyton Corner Norfolk 160 D5
Skiag Bridge H'land 307 G7
Skibo Castle H'land 309 L7
Skidbrooke Lincs 190 C6
Skidbrooke North End Lincs 190 B6
Skidby ER Yorks 208 G6
Skilgate Som'set 27 B7
Skillington Lincs 155 E7
Skinburness Cumb 238 F4
Skinflats Falk 279 E8
Skinidin H'land 298 E2
Skinnand Lincs 172 D6
Skinner's Bottom Cornw'l 4 F4
Skinners Green W Berks 64 F3
Skinnet H'land 308 C5
Skinningrove Redcar/Clevel'd 226 B4
Skipness Arg/Bute 255 B9
Skippool Lancs 202 E2
Skiprigg Cumb 230 B3
Skipsea ER Yorks 209 C9
Skipsea Brough ER Yorks 209 C9
Skipton N Yorks 204 C5
Skipton-on-Swale N Yorks 215 D7
Skipwith N Yorks 207 F9
Skirbeck Lincs 174 G4
Skirbeck Quarter Lincs 174 G4
Skireholme N Yorks 213 G11
Skirethorns N Yorks 213 G9
Skirlaugh ER Yorks 209 F8
Skirling Scot Borders 260 B3
Skirmett Bucks 65 B9
Skirpenbeck ER Yorks 207 B10
Skirwith N Yorks 212 E4
Skirwith Cumb 231 E8
Skirza H'land 310 C7
Skitby Cumb 239 D10
Skitham Lancs 202 E4
Skittle Green Bucks 84 E3
Skrinkle Pembs 73 F9
Skulamus H'land 295 C8
Skullomie H'land 308 C6
Skyborry Green Shrops 114 C5
Skye Green Essex 107 G7
Skye of Curr H'land 301 G9
Skyfog Pembs 90 F6
Slack W Yorks 196 B3
Slack Head Cumb 211 D9
Slackcote Gtr Man 196 F3
Slackhall Derby 185 E9
Slackhead Moray 302 C4
Slackholme End Lincs 191 G8
Slacks of Cairnbanno Aberds 303 E8
Slad Glos 80 D5
Slade Kent 54 C2
Slade Pembs 72 B6
Slade Swan 56 D3
Slade End Oxon 83 G9
Slade Green London 68 D4
Slade Heath Staffs 133 B8
Slade Hooton S Yorks 187 E9
Slades Green Worcs 99 E7
Sladesbridge Cornw'l 10 G6
Slaggyford Northum 240 G5
Slaid Hill W Yorks 206 E2
Slaidburn Lancs 203 C10
Slaithwaite W Yorks 196 E5
Slaley Derby 170 D3
Slaley Northum 241 F11
Slamannan Falk 279 G7
Slapeworth Redcar/Clevel'd 226 B2
Slapton Bucks 103 G8
Slapton Devon 8 F6
Slapton Northants 102 B2
Slate Haugh Moray 302 C4
Slatepit Dale Derby 170 B4
Slattocks Gtr Man 195 F11
Slaugham W Sussex 36 B3
Slaughterford Wilts 61 E10
Slawston Leics 136 E5
Slay Pits S Yorks 199 F7
Slea View Lincs 173 F9
Sleaford Hants 49 F10
Sleaford Lincs 173 F9
Sleagill Cumb 221 B11
Sleap Shrops 149 D9
Sleapford Telford 150 F2
Sleapshyde Herts 86 D2
Sleastary H'land 309 K6
Sledge Green Worcs 98 E6
Sledmere ER Yorks 217 G8
Sleeches Cross E Sussex 52 G5
Sleet Moor Derby 170 E6
Sleight Dorset 18 B5
Sleights N Yorks 227 D7
Slepe Dorset 18 C4
Slerra Devon 24 C4
Sliabhna h-Airde W Isles 296 F3
Slickly H'land 310 C6
Sliddery N Ayrs 255 E10
Sligachan Hotel H'land 294 C6
Sligneach Arg/Bute 288 G4
Slimbridge Glos 80 E2
Slimbridge Wildfowl & Wetlands Centre, Frampton on Severn Glos 80 E2
Slindon Staffs 150 C6
Slindon W Sussex 35 F7
Slindon Common W Sussex 35 F7
Slinfold W Sussex 50 G6
Sling Glos 79 D9
Sling Gwyn 163 B10
Slingsby N Yorks 216 D4
Slioch Aberds 302 F5
Slip End Beds 85 B9
Slip End Herts 104 D5
Slipperhill Cornw'l 11 F11
Slipton Northants 121 B9
Slitting Mill Staffs 151 F10
Sloadlane Derby 186 E5
Slochd H'land 301 G8
Slockavullin Arg/Bute 275 D9
Slogan Moray 302 E3
Sloley Norfolk 160 E5
Sloncombe Devon 13 D10
Sloothby Lincs 191 G7
Slough Windsor 66 C3
Slough Green Som'set 28 C3
Slough Green W Sussex 36 B3
Sluggan H'land 301 G8
Sluggans H'land 298 E4
Slumbay H'land 295 B10
Slyfield Surrey 50 C3
Slyne Lancs 211 F9
Smailholm Scot Borders 262 B4
Small Dole W Sussex 36 E2
Small End Lincs 174 D6
Small Heath W Midlands 133 F11
Small Hythe Kent 53 G11
Small Way Som'set 44 G6
Smallbridge Gtr Man 196 E2
Smallbrook Devon 14 B3
Smallbrook Glos 79 E9
Smallburgh Norfolk 160 E6
Smallburn Aberds 303 E10
Smallburn E Ayrs 258 D5
Smalldale Derby 185 F9
Smalldale Derby 185 E11
Smalley Derby 170 G6
Smalley Common Derby 170 G6
Smalley Green Derby 170 G6
Smallfield Surrey 51 E10
Smallford Herts 85 D11
Smallholm Dumf/Gal 238 B3
Smallridge Devon 28 G3
Smallshaw Gtr Man 196 G2
Smallwood Worcs 117 D10
Smallwood Green Suffolk 125 F8
Smallwood Hey Lancs 202 D3
Smallworth Norfolk 141 G10
Smannell Hants 47 D11
Smardale Cumb 222 D4
Smarden Kent 53 E11
Smarden Bell Kent 53 E11
Smart's Hill Kent 52 E4
Smaull Arg/Bute 274 G3
Smeatharpe Devon 27 E11
Smeaton Fife 280 C5
Smeeth Kent 54 F5
Smeeton Westerby Leics 136 E3
Smelthouses N Yorks 214 G3
Smercleit W Isles 297 K3
Smerral H'land 310 F5
Smestow Staffs 133 E7
Smethcott Shrops 131 D8
Smethwick W Midlands 133 F10
Smirisary H'land 289 B8
Smisby Derby 153 F7
Smith End Green Worcs 116 G5
Smith Green Lancs 202 B5
Smithaleigh Devon 7 D11
Smithbrook W Sussex 34 C6
Smithfield Cumb 239 D10
Smithies S Yorks 197 F11
Smithincott Devon 27 E9
Smithley S Yorks 197 G11
Smith's End Herts 105 D7
Smith's Green Essex 105 G11
Smith's Green Essex 106 C3
Smithston Aberds 302 G5
Smithstown H'land 299 B7
Smithton H'land 301 E7
Smithwood Green Suffolk 125 G8
Smithy Bridge Gtr Man 196 D2
Smithy Gate Flints 181 F11
Smithy Green Ches 184 G2
Smithy Green Cumb 210 C6
Smithy Green Gtr Man 184 D5
Smithy Hill Derby 185 E11
Smithy Lane Ends Lancs 194 E2
Smockington Leics 135 F8
Smoky Row Bucks 84 D4
Smoogro Orkney 313 H4
Smythe's Green Essex 88 B6
Snaefell Mountain Railway I/Man 192 D5
Snaigow House Perth/Kinr 286 C4
Snailbeach Shrops 131 C7
Snailswell Herts 104 E3
Snailwell Cambs 124 D2
Snainton N Yorks 217 C8
Snaisgill Durham 232 F5
Snaith ER Yorks 198 C6
Snape N Yorks 214 C5
Snape Suffolk 127 F7
Snape Green Lancs 193 E11
Snape Hill Derby 186 F5
Snape Hill S Yorks 198 G2
Snape Watering Suffolk 127 F7
Snapper Devon 40 G6
Snaresbrook London 67 B11
Snarestone Leics 134 B6
Snarford Lincs 189 E9
Snargate Kent 39 B7
Snarraness Shetl'd 315 H4
Snatchwood Torf 78 E3
Snave Kent 39 B8
Sneachill Worcs 117 G8
Snead Common Heref'd 116 D4
Sneath Common Norfolk 142 F3
Sneaton N Yorks 227 D8
Sneatonthorpe N Yorks 227 D8
Sneedham's Green Glos 80 C4
Sneinton Nott'ham 153 B11
Snelland Lincs 189 E9
Snelston Derby 169 G11
Snetterton Norfolk 141 E9
Snetterton Motor Racing Circuit Norfolk 141 F10
Snettisham Norfolk 158 C3
Sneyd Green Stoke 168 F5
Sneyd Park Bristol 60 D5
Snibston Discovery Park, Coalville Leics 153 G8
Snig's End Glos 98 F5
Snipeshill Kent 70 G2
Sniseabhal W Isles 297 H3
Snitter Northum 252 C2
Snitterby Lincs 189 C7
Snitterfield Warwick 118 F4
Snittlegarth Cumb 229 D10
Snodhill Heref'd 96 C6
Snodland Kent 69 G7
Snods Edge Northum 242 G3
Snow End Herts 105 E8
Snow Hill W Yorks 197 C10
Snow Lea W Yorks 196 D5
Snow Street Norfolk 142 G2
Snowden Hill S Yorks 197 G9
Snowdon Mountain Railway, Llanberis Gwyn 163 D9
Snowdown Kent 55 C8
Snowhill Telford 150 G4
Snowshill Glos 99 E11
Snowshill Manor Glos 99 E11
Snydale W Yorks 198 C2
Soake Hants 33 E11
Soar Card 58 C5
Soar Carms 94 F2
Soar Gwyn 146 B2
Soar Angl 178 G5
Soar Powys 95 E9
Soar-y-Mynydd Ceredig'n 112 G5
Soberton Hants 33 D10
Soberton Heath Hants 33 E10
Sockbridge Cumb 230 F5
Sockburn N Yorks 224 D6
Sodom Shetl'd 315 G7
Sodom Wilts 62 C4
Soham Cambs 123 C11
Soham Cotes Cambs 123 B11
Soho London 67 C9
Soho Som'set 45 D7
Solas W Isles 296 D4
Soldon Cross Devon 24 E4
Soldridge Hants 49 G7
Sole Street Kent 54 D5
Sole Street Kent 69 F7
Solent Breezes Hants 33 G8
Solfach = Solva Pembs 90 G5
Solihull W Midlands 118 B2
Solihull Lodge W Midlands 117 B11
Sollers Dilwyn Heref'd 115 F8
Sollers Hope Heref'd 98 E2
Sollom Lancs 194 D3
Solva = Solfach Pembs 90 G5
Somerby Leics 154 G5
Somerby Lincs 200 F5
Somercotes Derby 170 E6
Somerford Dorset 19 C9
Somerford Keynes Glos 81 F8
Somerley W Sussex 22 D4
Somerleyton Suffolk 143 D9
Somersal Herbert Derby 152 B2
Somersby Lincs 190 G4
Somersham Cambs 123 B7
Somersham Suffolk 107 B11
Somerton Newp 59 B10
Somerton Oxon 101 F9
Somerton Suffolk 124 G6
Somerton Som'set 29 B7
Somerwood Shrops 149 G11
Sompting W Sussex 35 G11
Sompting Abbots W Sussex 35 F11
Sonning Wokingham 65 D9
Sonning Common Oxon 65 C8
Sonning Eye Oxon 65 D9
Sookholme Notts 171 B8
Sopley Hants 19 B9
Sopwell Herts 85 D11
Sopworth Wilts 61 B10
Sorbie Dumf/Gal 236 E6
Sordale H'land 310 C5
Sorisdale Arg/Bute 288 C4
Sorley Devon 8 F4
Sorn E Ayrs 258 D3
Sornhill E Ayrs 258 B2
Sortat H'land 310 C6
Sotby Lincs 190 F2
Sothell S Yorks 186 E6
Sots Hole Lincs 173 C10
Sotterley Suffolk 143 G9
Soudley Shrops 150 D4
Soughton = Sychdyn Flints 166 B2
Soulbury Bucks 103 F7
Soulby Cumb 230 F5
Soulby Cumb 222 C4
Souldern Oxon 101 E10
Souldrop Beds 121 E9
Sound Shetl'd 315 H5
Sound Shetl'd 315 J6
Sound Heath Ches 167 F10
Soundwell S Glos 61 D7
Sourhope Scot Borders 263 E8
Sourin Orkney 312 E5
Sourton Devon 12 C6
Soutergate Cumb 210 C4
South Acre Norfolk 158 G6
South Acton London 67 D8
South Alkham Kent 55 E9
South Allington Devon 9 G10
South Alloa Falk 279 C7
South Ambersham W Sussex 34 C6
South Anston S Yorks 187 E9
South Ascot Windsor 66 F2
South Ashford Kent 54 E4
South Auchmachar Aberds 303 E9
South Baddesley Hants 20 B3
South Ballachulish H'land 284 B4
South Balloch S Ayrs 245 D8
South Bank C/York 207 C7
South Bank Redcar/Clevel'd 234 G6
South Barham Kent 55 D7
South Barrow Som'set 29 B10
South Beddington London 67 G10
South Benfleet Essex 69 B9
South Bents Tyne/Wear 243 E10
South Bersted W Sussex 34 G6
South Bockhampton Dorset 19 B9
South Bowood Dorset 16 B4
South Bramwith S Yorks 198 E6
South Brent Devon 8 C3
South Brewham Som'set 45 F8
South Broomage Falk 279 E7
South Broomhill Northum 252 D6
South Burlingham Norfolk 143 B7
South Cadbury Som'set 29 B10
South Cairn Dumf/Gal 236 C1
South Carlton Lincs 189 F7
South Carlton Notts 187 E9
South Cave ER Yorks 208 G4
South Cerney Glos 81 F8
South Chailey E Sussex 36 D5
South Chard Som'set 28 F4
South Charlton Northum 264 E5
South Cheriton Som'set 29 C11
South Church Durham 233 F10
South Cleatlam Durham 224 B2
South Cliffe ER Yorks 208 F3
South Clifton Notts 188 G4
South Clunes H'land 300 E5
South Cockerington Lincs 190 D5
South Common Devon 28 G4
South Cornelly Bridg 57 E10
South Corriegills N Ayrs 256 C2
South Cove Suffolk 143 G9
South Creagan Arg/Bute 289 E11
South Creake Norfolk 159 B7
South Crosland W Yorks 196 E6
South Croxton Leics 154 G3
South Croydon London 67 G10
South Cuil H'land 298 C3
South Dalton ER Yorks 208 D5
South Darenth Kent 68 F5
South Devon Railway Devon 8 C5
South Duffield N Yorks 207 G9
South Dunn H'land 310 D5
South Elkington Lincs 190 D3
South Ella ER Yorks 200 B4
South Elmsall W Yorks 198 E3
South End Beds 103 B10
South End Bucks 103 G7
South End ER Yorks 201 D11
South End ER Yorks 209 E9
South End Hants 31 E10
South End Leics 153 G11
South End Norfolk 141 E9
South End N Lincs 200 C6
South End W Berks 64 E5
South Erradale H'land 299 B7
South Fambridge Essex 88 F5
South Fawley W Berks 63 C11
South Ferriby N Lincs 200 C3
South Field ER Yorks 200 B4
South Flobbets Aberds 303 F7
South Garth Shetl'd 314 D7
South Garvan H'land 289 B11
South Glendale W Isles 297 K3
South Gluss Shetl'd 314 F5
South Godstone Surrey 51 D11
South Gorley Hants 31 E11
South Gosforth Tyne/Wear 242 D6
South Green Essex 87 G11
South Green Essex 89 B8
South Green Kent 69 G10
South Green Norfolk 157 F10
South Green Norfolk 142 G4
South Green Norfolk 159 G11
South Green Norfolk 159 G9
South Green Suffolk 126 C3
South Ham Hants 48 C6
South Hanningfield Essex 88 F2
South Harefield London 66 B5
South Harrow London 66 B6
South Harting W Sussex 34 D3
South Hatfield Herts 86 D2
South Hayling Hants 22 D2
South Hazelrigg Northum 264 C3
South Heath Bucks 84 E6
South Heighton E Sussex 37 G7
South Hetton Durham 234 B3
South Hiendley W Yorks 197 E11
South Hill Cornw'l 12 G2
South Hill Som'set 29 B7
South Hinksey Oxon 83 E8
South Hole Devon 24 D2
South Holme N Yorks 216 D4
South Holmwood Surrey 51 D7
South Hornchurch London 68 C4
South Huish Devon 8 G3
South Hykeham Lincs 172 C6
South Hylton Tyne/Wear 243 F9
South Kelsey Lincs 189 B8
South Kensington London 67 D9
South Kessock H'land 300 E6
South Killingholme N Lincs 200 D6
South Kilvington N Yorks 215 C8
South Kilworth Leics 136 G2
South Kirkby W Yorks 198 E3
South Kirkton Aberds 293 C9
South Kiscadale N Ayrs 256 D2
South Knighton Devon 14 G2
South Knighton Leics C 136 C2
South Kyme Lincs 173 F11
South Lambeth London 67 D10
South Lancing W Sussex 35 G11
South Lane S Yorks 197 F9
South Leigh Oxon 82 D5
South Leverton Notts 188 E3
South Littleton Worcs 99 B11
South Loftus Redcar/Clevel'd 226 B4
South Lopham Norfolk 141 G10
South Luffenham Rutl'd 137 C8
South Malling E Sussex 36 E6
South Marston Swindon 63 B7
South Merstham Surrey 51 C9
South Middleton Northum 263 E11
South Milford N Yorks 206 G5

Tafarnaubach Bl Gwent 77 C10
Tafarn-y-Bwlch Pembs 91 E11
Tafarn-y-Gelyn Denbs 165 C11
Taff Merthyr Garden Village Merth Tyd 77 F10
Taff's Well Card 58 C6
Tafolwern Powys 129 C7
Tàbost W Isles 304 B7
Tai Conwy 164 C3
Taibach Neath P Talb 57 D9
Tai-bach Powys 148 D3
Taicynhaeaf Gwyn 146 F3
Taigh a Ghearraidh W Isles 296 D3
Taigh Bhalaigh W Isles 296 D3
Taillwyd Rh Cyn Taff 76 F2
Tai-morfa Gwyn 144 D5
Tain H'land 309 L7
Tain H'land 310 C6
Tai'n Lon Gwyn 162 E6
Tairbeart = Tarbert W Isles 305 H3
Tai'r-Bull Powys 95 F9
Tairgwaith Neath P Talb 76 C2
Tai'r-heol Caerph 77 G10
Tai'r-waun Caerph 77 G10
Tai'r-ysgol Swan 75 F11
Takeley Essex 105 G11
Takeley Street Essex 105 G10
Talacharn = Laugharne Carms 74 C4
Talachddu Powys 95 E11
Talacre Flints 181 E10
Talardd Gwyn 147 D7
Talaton Devon 15 B7
Talbenny Pembs 72 C4
Talbot Green Rh Cyn Taff 58 C4
Talbot Village Bournem'th 19 C7
Talbot's End S Glos 80 G2
Talerddig Powys 129 C8
Talewater Devon 15 B7
Talgarreg Ceredig'n 111 G8
Talgarth Powys 96 E3
Taliesin = Tre Taliesin Ceredig'n 128 E3
Talisker H'land 294 B5
Talke Staffs 168 E4
Talke Pits Stoke 168 E4
Talkin Cumb 240 F2
Talladale H'land 299 B9
Tallarn Green Wrex 166 G6
Tallentire Cumb 229 D8
Talley Carms 94 E2
Tallington Lincs 137 B11
Tallistown Bl Gwent 77 D11
Talmine H'land 308 C5
Talog Carms 92 F6
Talsarn Carms 94 F5
Tal-sarn Ceredig'n 111 F10
Talsarnau Gwyn 146 B2
Talskiddy Cornw'l 5 B8
Talwrn Angl 179 F7
Talwrn Wrex 166 F3
Talwrn Wrex 166 E3
Tal-y-Bont Conwy 164 B3
Tal-y-bont Ceredig'n 128 F3
Tal-y-bont Gwyn 145 E11
Tal-y-bont Gwyn 179 G10
Talybont-on-Usk Powys 96 G2
Tal-y-cafn Conwy 180 G3
Tal-y-coed Monmouths 78 B6
Talyllyn Powys 96 F2
Tal-y-llyn Gwyn 128 B4
Talysarn Gwyn 163 E7
Tal-y-Waenydd Gwyn 163 F11
Talywain Torf 78 E3
Tamanabhagh W Isles 304 F2
Tame Bridge N Yorks 225 D10
Tame Water Gtr Man 196 F3
Tamer Lane End Gtr Man 194 G6
Tamerton Foliot Plym'th 7 C9
Tamfourhill Falk 279 F7
Tamworth Staffs 134 C4
Tamworth Green Lincs 174 G5
Tan Hills Durham 233 B11
Tan Office Suffolk 126 E2
Tan Office Green Suffolk 124 F5
Tandem W Yorks 197 E7
Tandlehill Renf 267 C8
Tandridge Surrey 51 C10
Tanerdy Carms 93 G8
Tanfield Durham 242 F5
Tanfield Lea Durham 242 G5
Tang N Yorks 205 B10
Tang Hall C/York 207 C8
Tangasdal W Isles 297 M2
Tangier Som'set 28 C2
Tangiers Pembs 73 B7
Tangley Hants 47 C10
Tanglwst Carms 92 E6
Tangmere W Sussex 34 F6
Tangwick Shetl'd 314 F4
Tangy Arg/Bute 255 E7
Tanhouse Lancs 194 F3
Tanis Wilts 62 G3
Tank Museum, Bovington Dorset 18 D2
Tankersley S Yorks 186 B4
Tankerton Kent 70 F6
Tan-lan Conwy 164 C3
Tan-lan Flints 181 E10
Tan-lan Gwyn 163 G10
Tannach H'land 310 E7
Tannachie Aberds 293 E9
Tannadice Angus 287 B8
Tanner's Green Worcs 117 C11
Tannington Suffolk 126 D4
Tannington Green Suffolk 126 D4
Tannochside N Lanarks 268 C4
Tanshall Fife 280 A5
Tansley Derby 170 D4
Tansley Hill W Midlands 133 F9
Tansley Knoll Derby 170 C4
Tansor Northants 137 E11
Tanterton Lancs 202 G6
Tantobie Durham 242 G5
Tanton N Yorks 225 C10
Tanvats Lincs 173 C10
Tanworth in Arden Warwick 118 C2
Tan-y-Bwlch Gwyn 163 B10
Tan-y-bwlch Gwyn 163 G11
Tan-y-coed Gwyn 163 C8
Tan-y-fron Conwy 165 C7
Tan-y-fron Wrex 166 E3
Tanygrisiau Gwyn 163 F11
Tan-y-groes Ceredig'n 92 B5
Tan-y-Lôn Gwyn 179 G10
Tan-yr-allt Denbs 181 E9
Tan-yr-allt Gwyn 163 E7
Taobh a Chaolais W Isles 297 K3
Taobh a Thuath Loch Aineort W Isles 297 J3
Taobh a Tuath Loch Baghasdail W Isles 297 J3
Taobh a'Ghlinne W Isles 305 G5
Taobh Siar W Isles 305 H3
Taobh Tuath W Isles 296 C5
Taplow Bucks 66 C2
Tapton Derby 186 G5
Tapton Hill S Yorks 186 D4
Tarbat Ho. H'land 301 B7
Tarbert Arg/Bute 255 B7
Tarbert Arg/Bute 275 E7
Tarbert Arg/Bute 275 G9
Tarbert = Tairbeart W Isles 305 H3
Tarbet Arg/Bute 285 G7
Tarbet H'land 295 F9
Tarbet H'land 306 E6
Tarbock Green Mersey 183 D7
Tarbolton S Ayrs 257 D10
Tarbrax S Lanarks 269 D10
Tardebigge Worcs 117 D9
Tardy Gate Lancs 194 B4
Tarfside Angus 292 F6
Tarland Aberds 292 C6
Tarleton Lancs 194 C2
Tarlogie H'land 309 L7
Tarlscough Lancs 194 E2
Tarlton Glos 81 F7
Tarn W Yorks 205 F9
Tarnbrook Lancs 203 B7
Tarnock Som'set 43 C11
Tarns Cumb 229 B8
Tarnside Cumb 221 G8
Tarporley Ches 167 C9
Tarpots Essex 69 B9
Tarr Som'set 42 G6
Tarraby Cumb 239 F10
Tarrant Crawford Dorset 30 G6
Tarrant Gunville Dorset 30 E6
Tarrant Hinton Dorset 30 E6
Tarrant Keyneston Dorset 30 G6
Tarrant Launceston Dorset 30 F6
Tarrant Monkton Dorset 30 F6
Tarrant Rawston Dorset 30 F6
Tarrant Rushton Dorset 30 F6
Tarrel H'land 311 L2
Tarring Neville E Sussex 36 G6
Tarrington Heref'd 98 C2
Tarryblake Ho. Moray 302 E5
Tarsappie Perth/Kinr 286 E5
Tarskavaig H'land 295 E7
Tarves Aberds 303 F8
Tarvie H'land 300 D4
Tarvie Perth/Kinr 292 G2
Tarvin Ches 167 B7
Tarvin Sands Ches 167 B7
Tasburgh Norfolk 142 D3
Tasley Shrops 132 E3
Taston Oxon 101 G7
Tat Bank W Midlands 133 F9
Tate Gallery London 67 D9
Tate Gallery, Albert Dock Mersey 182 D4
Tate Modern London 67 C10
Tate St Ives Cornw'l 2 A2
Tatenhill Staffs 152 E4
Tathall End M/Keynes 102 B6
Tatham Lancs 212 F2
Tathwell Lincs 190 E4
Tatling End Bucks 66 B4
Tatlingbury Kent 52 D6
Tatmore Place Herts 104 F3
Tatsfield Surrey 52 B2
Tattenhall Ches 167 D7
Tattenhoe M/Keynes 102 E6
Tatterford Norfolk 159 D7
Tattersett Norfolk 158 D6
Tattershall Lincs 174 D2
Tattershall Bridge Lincs 173 D11
Tattershall Thorpe Lincs 174 D2
Tattingstone Suffolk 108 D2
Tattingstone White Horse Suffolk 108 D2
Tatton Dale Ches 184 E2
Tatton Park Ches 184 E2
Tatworth Som'set 28 F4
Taunton Gtr Man 196 G2
Taunton Som'set 28 B2
Taunton Racecourse Som'set 28 C2
Taverham Norfolk 160 G3
Taverners Green Essex 87 B9
Tavernspite Pembs 73 C11
Tavistock Devon 12 G5
Taw Green Devon 13 B9
Tawd Bridge Lancs 194 F3
Tawstock Devon 25 B8
Taxal Derby 185 F8
Tay Bridge Dundee C 287 E8
Tayinloan Arg/Bute 255 C7
Taymouth Castle Perth/Kinr 285 C11
Taynish Arg/Bute 275 E8
Taynton Glos 98 G4
Taynton Oxon 82 C2
Taynuilt Arg/Bute 284 D4
Tayport Fife 287 E8
Tayvallich Arg/Bute 275 E8
Tea Green Herts 104 G2
Tealby Lincs 189 C11
Tealby Thorpe Lincs 189 C10
Tealing Angus 287 D8
Team Valley Tyne/Wear 242 E6
Teams Tyne/Wear 242 E6
Teanford Staffs 169 G8
Teangue H'land 295 E8
Teanna Mhachair W Isles 296 E3
Tebay Cumb 222 E2
Tebworth Beds 103 F9
Tedburn St. Mary Devon 14 C2
Teddington Glos 99 E9
Teddington London 67 E7
Tedstone Delamere Heref'd 116 F3
Tedstone Wafre Heref'd 116 F3
Teesport Redcar/Clevel'd 234 G6
Teesville Redcar/Clevel'd 225 B10
Teeton Northants 120 C3
Teffont Evias Wilts 46 G3
Teffont Magna Wilts 46 G3
Tegiskey Cornw'l 5 F10
Tegryn Pembs 92 E4
Teigh Rutl'd 155 F7
Teign Village Devon 14 E2
Teigncombe Devon 13 D9
Teigngrace Devon 14 G3
Teignmouth Devon 14 G4
Telford Shrops 150 G4
Telham E Sussex 38 E3
Tellisford Som'set 45 B9
Telscombe E Sussex 36 G6
Telscombe Cliffs E Sussex 36 G5
Templand Dumf/Gal 248 F3
Temple Glasg C 267 B10
Temple Cornw'l 11 G8
Temple Midloth 270 D6
Temple Wilts 45 E10
Temple Windsor 65 C10
Temple Balsall W Midlands 118 B4
Temple Bar Carms 75 B9
Temple Bar Ceredig'n 111 F11
Temple Bar Pembs 91 D11
Temple Bar W Sussex 34 F6
Temple Bruer Lincs 173 E8
Temple Cloud Bath/NE Som'set 44 B6
Temple Cowley Oxon 83 E8
Temple End Suffolk 124 G3
Temple Ewell Kent 55 E9
Temple Fields Essex 87 C7
Temple Grafton Warwick 118 G2
Temple Guiting Glos 99 F11
Temple Herdewyke Warwick 119 G7
Temple Hill Kent 68 D4
Temple Hirst N Yorks 198 C6
Temple Normanton Derby 170 B6
Temple Sowerby Cumb 231 F8
Templeborough S Yorks 186 C6
Templecombe Som'set 30 C2
Templehall Fife 280 C5
Templeton Devon 26 E5
Templeton Pembs 73 C10
Templeton Bridge Devon 26 E5
Templetown Durham 233 B8
Tempsford Beds 122 G3
Ten Acres W Midlands 133 G11
Ten Mile Bank Norfolk 139 D11
Tenandry Perth/Kinr 291 G11
Tenbury Wells Worcs 115 D11
Tenby = Dinbych-y-Pysgod Pembs 73 E10
Tendring Essex 108 G2
Tendring Green Essex 108 F2
Tendring Heath Essex 108 F2
Tenston Orkney 312 G3
Tenterden Kent 53 G11
Terfyn Conwy 180 F6
Terhill Som'set 43 G7
Terling Essex 88 B3
Terlingham Kent 55 F8
Ternhill Shrops 150 C2
Terpersie Castle Aberds 302 G5
Terras Cornw'l 5 E8
Terregles Banks Dumf/Gal 237 B11
Terrick Bucks 84 D4
Terrick Shrops 167 G8
Terrier's End Bucks 84 D6
Terrington N Yorks 216 E3
Terrington St. Clement Norfolk 157 E10
Terrington St. John Norfolk 157 G10
Terryhorn Aberds 302 F4
Terry's Green Warwick 118 C2
Terwick Common W Sussex 34 C4
Teston Kent 53 C7
Testwood Hants 32 E5
Tetbury Glos 80 G5
Tetbury Upton Glos 80 F5
Tetchill Shrops 149 C7
Tetchwick Bucks 83 B11
Tetcott Devon 12 B2
Tetford Lincs 190 G4
Tetney Lincs 201 G10
Tetney Lock Lincs 201 G10
Tetsworth Oxon 83 E11
Tettenhall W Midlands 133 C7
Tettenhall Wood W Midlands 133 D7
Tetworth Cambs 122 G4
Tetworth Windsor 66 F2
Teuchan Aberds 303 F10
Teversal Notts 171 C7
Teversham Cambs 123 F9
Teviothead Scot Borders 249 B10
Tevorrick Cornw'l 10 G4
Tewel Aberds 293 E10
Tewin Herts 86 C3
Tewitfield Lancs 211 E10
Tewkesbury Glos 99 E7
Tewkesbury Abbey Glos 99 E7
Teynham Kent 70 G2
Teynham Street Kent 70 G3
Thackley W Yorks 205 F9
Thackley End W Yorks 205 F9
Thackthwaite Cumb 229 G8
Thackthwaite Cumb 230 F4
Thainston Aberds 293 F8
Thakeham W Sussex 35 D10
Thame Oxon 84 D2
Thames Ditton Surrey 66 F6
Thames Haven Thurr'k 69 C8
Thamesmead London 68 C3
Thankerton S Lanarks 259 B11
Thannington Kent 54 B6
Tharbies Herts 87 B7
Tharston Norfolk 142 E3
Thatcham W Berks 64 F4
Thatto Heath Mersey 183 C8
Thaxted Essex 106 E2
The Aird H'land 298 D4
The All England Jumping Course, Hickstead W Sussex 36 D3
The Bage Heref'd 96 C5
The Balloch Perth/Kinr 286 F2
The Bank Ches 168 D4
The Bank Shrops 132 D2
The Banks Gtr Man 185 D7
The Banks Wilts 62 D4
The Barony Orkney 312 F3
The Barton Wilts 62 D5
The Batch S Glos 61 E7
The Batch Som'set 44 C4
The Bell Gtr Man 194 F4
The Bent Derby 152 C4
The Bluebell Railway, Sheffield Park E Sussex 36 C6
The Blyth Staffs 151 D11
The Bourne Surrey 49 D10
The Bourne Worcs 117 F9
The Bows Stirl 285 G11
The Braes H'land 295 B7
The Bratch Staffs 133 E7
The Breaches Worcs 117 D11
The Breck Orkney 313 H4
The Brushes Derby 186 F5
The Bryn Monmouths 78 D4
The Burf Worcs 116 D6
The Burrell Collection Glasg C 267 C11
The Bury Herts 104 F4
The Butts Som'set 45 D9
The Camp Glos 80 D6
The Camp Herts 85 D11
The Cape Warwick 118 D5
The Chequer Wrex 167 G7
The Children's Village E Loth 271 C9
The Chuckery W Midlands 133 D10
The City Beds 122 F2
The City Bucks 84 F3
The City Suffolk 143 F7
The Cleaver Heref'd 97 F10
The Common Bucks 102 E5
The Common Oxon 100 F5
The Common Surrey 51 G7
The Common Wilts 47 G8
The Common Wilts 62 B4
The Corner Kent 53 E8
The Corner Shrops 131 F8
The Craigs H'land 309 K4
The Cronk I/Man 192 C4
The Dams Cambs 139 E9
The Dell Suffolk 143 D9
The Delves W Midlands 133 E10
The Den N Ayrs 266 E6
The Dene Durham 242 G4
The Dicker E Sussex 23 D9
The Dinosaur Museum, Dorchester Dorset 17 C9
The Down Kent 53 F7
The Dunks Wrex 166 E4
The Eaves Glos 79 D10
The Fall W Yorks 197 B10
The Fence Glos 79 D8
The Flat Glos 80 B3
The Folly Som'set 44 C5
The Folly W Berks 64 F3
The Ford Bucks 84 E3
The Forstal E Sussex 52 F4
The Forstal Kent 54 F5
The Four Alls Shrops 150 C3
The Fox Wilts 62 B6
The Foxholes Shrops 116 B2
The Frenches Hants 32 C4
The Friars, Aylesford Kent 53 B8
The Garths Shetl'd 314 B8
The Gibb Wilts 61 D10
The Graig Monmouths 79 D8
The Green Beds 85 B8
The Green Cambs 122 D5
The Green Cumb 210 C3
The Green Essex 88 B3
The Green Flints 166 B2
The Green Glos 99 F9
The Green Hants 32 B4
The Green M/Keynes 103 C7
The Green Norfolk 141 C11
The Green Norfolk 159 B11
The Green Northants 102 C5
The Green Notts 188 G4
The Green Oxon 84 E3
The Green S Glos 61 E7
The Green S Yorks 197 G8
The Green Warwick 118 F4
The Green Wilts 45 G11
The Grove Dumf/Gal 237 B11
The Grove Durham 242 G3
The Grove Worcs 99 C7
The Hall Suffolk 126 F4
The Hall Shetl'd 314 D8
The Hallands N Lincs 200 C5
The Ham Wilts 45 C11
The Haven W Sussex 50 G5
The Hawkhills N Yorks 215 F10
The Headland Hartlep'l 234 E6
The Heath Norfolk 159 D8
The Heath Norfolk 160 E3
The Heath Norfolk 160 E4
The Heath Suffolk 108 D2
The Heath Staffs 151 C11
The Heavens Notts 153 D11
The Hem Shrops 132 B4
The Herberts V/Glam 58 E4
The High Essex 86 C6
The Highlands E Sussex 38 F2
The Hill Cumb 210 C3
The Hill Worcs 98 D6
The Holt Hants 64 G5
The Holt W Berks 63 E10
The Holt Wokingham 65 D10
The Hoo Glos 100 D3
The Hook Worcs 98 C6
The Howe Cumb 211 B9
The Howe I/Man 192 F2
The Hundred Heref'd 115 E10
The Hyde London 67 B8
The Hythe Essex 107 G10
The Kendals Dorset 30 B4
The Knapp S Glos 79 G11
The Knowle W Midlands 133 F9
The Lake Dumf/Gal 237 E8
The Lakes Worcs 116 B5
The Lawe Tyne/Wear 243 D9
The Leacon Kent 54 G3
The Lee Bucks 84 E6
The Lees Kent 54 C4
The Leigh Glos 99 F7
The Leys Staffs 134 C4
The Lhen I/Man 192 B4
The Lindens Lincs 201 F7
The Lindens W Midlands 133 D11
The Ling Norfolk 142 D6
The Lings Norfolk 141 B10
The Lings S Yorks 199 F7
The Linleys Wilts 61 F11
The Living RainForest W Berks 64 D4
The Lodge Wrex 166 E3
The Long Man of Wilmington E Sussex 37 G8
The Lost Gardens of Heligan, Mevagissey Cornw'l 5 F9
The Lowry, Salford Gtr Man 184 B4
The Lunt W Midlands 133 D9
The Marsh Heref'd 115 F9
The Marsh Powys 130 D6
The Marsh Shrops 150 D3
The Marsh Suffolk 125 B11
The Marsh Wilts 62 C5
The Middles Durham 242 G6
The Moor Cambs 105 B7
The Moor E Sussex 38 D4
The Moor Kent 38 B3
The Moors Heref'd 97 E10
The Moors Centre, Danby N Yorks 226 D4
The Mount Dorset 16 B5
The Mount Hants 64 G2
The Mount London 52 B3
The Mount Reading 65 E8
The Mount Worcs 116 C6
The Mumbles = Y Mwmbwls Swan 56 D6
The Murray S Lanarks 268 E2
The Mythe Glos 99 E7
The Nant Wrex 166 E3
The North Monmouths 79 D8
The National Archives, Kew London 67 D7
The Needles Old Battery I/Wight 20 E1
The Neuk Aberds 293 D9
The Node Herts 104 G4
The Oval Bath/NE Som'set 61 G8
The Oval Cricket Ground London 67 D10
The Oxford Story, Oxford Oxon 83 D8
The Park Glos 99 G8
The Park Glos 99 F8
The Park N Som'set 60 E2
The Parks S Yorks 198 F6
The Pentre Monmouths 78 B3
The Pill Monmouths 60 B3
The Pitts Wilts 31 B9
The Platt Kent 52 G5
The Point Devon 14 E5
The Pole of Itlaw Aberds 302 D6
The Pound Glos 98 E4
The Pound Powys 114 C3
The Purlieu Glos 79 D11
The Quarry Glos 80 F2
The Quarter Kent 53 E11
The Ramplings Worcs 99 E7
The Reddings Glos 99 G8
The Rhos Pembs 73 C8
The Rhydd Heref'd 97 E9
The Ridge Wilts 61 F11
The Rise Windsor 66 F2
The Rock Shrops 132 B3
The Rocks Kent 53 B8
The Rocks S Glos 61 C8
The Rookery Herts 85 F10
The Rookery Staffs 168 D5
The Roundabout S Glos 60 B6
The Row Lancs 211 D9
The Row Oxon 82 C6
The Rowe Staffs 150 B6
The Ryde Herts 86 D2
The Sale Staffs 152 G3
The Sands Surrey 49 D11
The Scarr Glos 98 F4
The Shoe Wilts 61 E10
The Shruggs Staffs 151 C8
The Slack Durham 233 F8
The Slade W Berks 64 F4
The Spa Wilts 62 G2
The Square Torf 78 F3
The Stocks Kent 38 B6
The Stocks Wilts 62 G2
The Straits W Midlands 133 E8
The Strand Wilts 46 B2
The Swillett Herts 85 G8
The Tales of Robin Hood Nott'ham 153 B11
The Thorn Heref'd 97 G11
The Three Crossways Suffolk 126 F2
The Thrift Herts 104 D6
The Throat Wokingham 65 F10
The Tutankhamun Exhibition, Dorchester Dorset 17 C9
The Tynings Glos 80 B6
The Vale W Sussex 35 F10
The Valley Ches 167 D11
The Valley Kent 54 C3
The Valley Pembs 73 D10
The Verne Dorset 17 G9
The Village Newp 78 G4
The Village Surrey 66 E3
The Village W Midlands 133 F7
The Vyne Hants 48 B6
The Walshes Worcs 116 C6
The Warren Flints 181 E10
The Warren Reading 65 D7
The Wern Wrex 166 E3
The Willows NE Lincs 201 F8
The Woodlands Suffolk 107 C11
The Woods W Midlands 133 D10
The World of Beatrix Potter, Bowness-on-Windermere Cumb 221 F8
The Wrangle Bath/NE Som'set 44 B4
The Wrythe London 67 F9
The Wyke Shrops 132 B4
Theakston N Yorks 214 B6
Thealby N Lincs 199 D11
Theale Som'set 44 D3
Theale W Berks 64 E6
Theale Green W Berks 64 E6
Thearne ER Yorks 209 F7
Theberton Suffolk 127 D8
Theddingworth Leics 136 F3
Theddlethorpe All Saints Lincs 191 D7
Theddlethorpe St. Helen Lincs 191 D7
Thelnetham Suffolk 125 B10
Thelveton Norfolk 142 G3
Thelwall Warrington 183 D10
Themelthorpe Norfolk 159 E11
Thenford Northants 101 C10
Theobald's Green Wilts 62 F4
Therfield Herts 104 D6
Thetford Lincs 156 G2
Thetford Norfolk 141 G7
Thethwaite Cumb 230 C3
Theydon Bois Essex 86 F6
Thick Hollins W Yorks 196 E6
Thicket Mead Bath/NE Som'set 45 B7
Thickwood Wilts 61 E10
Thimble End W Midlands 134 E2
Thimbleby Lincs 174 B2
Thimbleby N Yorks 225 F9
Thingwall Mersey 182 E3
Third Dumf/Gal 248 F3
Thirdpart N Ayrs 266 F3
Thirkleby N Yorks 215 D9
Thirlby N Yorks 215 C9
Thirlestane Scot Borders 271 F11
Thirn N Yorks 214 B4
Thirsk N Yorks 215 C8
Thirsk Racecourse N Yorks 215 C8
Thirtleby ER Yorks 209 G9
Thisleton Lancs 202 F4
Thistleton Rutl'd 155 F8
Thistley Green Essex 88 B2
Thistley Green Suffolk 124 B3
Thixendale N Yorks 216 G6
Thockrington Northum 241 B11
Tholomas Drove Cambs 139 B8
Tholthorpe N Yorks 215 F9
Thomas Chapel Pembs 73 D10
Thomas Close Cumb 230 C4
Thomas Town Warwick 117 E11
Thomastown Aberds 302 F5
Thomastown Rh Cyn Taff 58 B4
Thompson Norfolk 141 D8
Thomshill Moray 302 D2
Thong Kent 69 E7
Thongsbridge W Yorks 197 F7
Thoralby N Yorks 213 B10
Thoresby Notts 187 G11
Thoresthorpe Lincs 191 F7
Thoresway Lincs 189 B11
Thorganby Lincs 190 B2
Thorganby N Yorks 207 E9
Thorgill N Yorks 226 F4
Thorington Suffolk 127 C8
Thorington Street Suffolk 107 D10
Thorlby N Yorks 204 C5
Thorley Herts 87 B7
Thorley I/Wight 20 D3
Thorley Houses Herts 105 G9
Thorley Street Herts 87 B7
Thorley Street I/Wight 20 D3
Thormanby N Yorks 215 E9
Thorn Beds 103 G10
Thorn Powys 114 E5
Thorn Green Northum 232 B2
Thornaby-on-Tees Stockton 225 B9
Thornage Norfolk 159 B11
Thornaugh Peterbro 137 C11
Thornborough Bucks 102 E4
Thornborough N Yorks 214 D5
Thornbury Devon 24 F6
Thornbury Heref'd 116 F2
Thornbury S Glos 79 G10
Thornbury W Yorks 205 G9
Thornbury Park S Glos 79 G10
Thornby Cumb 239 G7
Thornby Northants 120 B3
Thornby Wood Stockton 225 C8
Thorncliff Staffs 169 D8
Thorncliff W Yorks 197 E8
Thorncombe Street Surrey 50 E4
Thorncote Green Beds 104 B3
Thorncross I/Wight 20 E4
Thorndon Suffolk 126 D2
Thorndon Cross Devon 12 C6
Thorne S Yorks 199 E7
Thorne Abbotts Norfolk 126 B3
Thorne Coffin Som'set 29 D8
Thorne St. Margaret Som'set 27 C9
Thornecombe Dorset 28 G5
Thornend Wilts 62 D3
Thorner W Yorks 206 E3
Thornes Staffs 133 C11
Thornes W Yorks 197 D10
Thorney Bucks 66 D4
Thorney Notts 188 G5
Thorney Peterbro 138 C5
Thorney Som'set 28 C6
Thorney Close Tyne/Wear 243 G9
Thorney Crofts ER Yorks 201 C8
Thorney Green Suffolk 125 E11
Thorney Hill Hants 19 B10
Thorney Toll Cambs 138 C6
Thorneywood Notts 171 G9
Thornfalcon Som'set 28 C3
Thornford Dorset 29 E10
Thorngill N Yorks 213 B11
Thorngrafton Northum 241 D7
Thorngrove Som'set 43 G11
Thorngumbald ER Yorks 201 B8
Thornham Norfolk 176 E2
Thornham Fold Gtr Man 195 F11
Thornham Magna Suffolk 126 C2
Thornham Parva Suffolk 126 C2
Thornhill Caerph 59 C7
Thornhill Cumb 219 D10
Thornhill Derby 185 E11
Thornhill Dumf/Gal 247 D9
Thornhill Stirl 278 B3
Thornhill S'thampton 33 E7
Thornhill Wilts 62 D5
Thornhill W Yorks 197 D9
Thornhill Edge W Yorks 197 D9
Thornhill Head Devon 24 D6
Thornhill Lees W Yorks 197 D8
Thornhill Park S'thampton 33 E7
Thornhills W Yorks 197 C7
Thornholme ER Yorks 218 G2
Thornicombe Dorset 30 G5
Thornington Northum 263 C9
Thornley Durham 233 D8
Thornley Durham 234 D3
Thornley Gate Northum 241 F8
Thornliebank E Renf 267 D11
Thornly Park Renf 267 C9
Thornroan Aberds 303 F8
Thorns N Yorks 223 E7
Thorns Suffolk 124 F4
Thorns Beach Hants 20 B4
Thorns Green Ches 184 E3
Thornsett Derby 185 D8
Thornship Cumb 221 C11
Thornthwaite Cumb 229 F10
Thornthwaite N Yorks 205 B9
Thornton Angus 287 C7
Thornton Bucks 102 D5
Thornton E Loth 282 G4
Thornton ER Yorks 207 D11
Thornton Fife 280 B5
Thornton Lancs 202 E2
Thornton Leics 135 B9
Thornton Lincs 174 B2
Thornton Middlesbro 225 C9
Thornton Mersey 193 G10
Thornton Northum 273 F9
Thornton Pembs 72 D6
Thornton W Yorks 205 G8
Thornton Curtis N Lincs 200 D5
Thornton Heath London 67 F10
Thornton Hough Mersey 182 E4
Thornton in Craven N Yorks 204 D4
Thornton in Lonsdale N Yorks 212 E3
Thornton Rust N Yorks 213 B9
Thornton Steward N Yorks 214 B3
Thornton Watlass N Yorks 214 B4
Thorntonhall S Lanarks 267 D11
Thornton-le-Beans N Yorks 225 G7
Thornton-le-Clay N Yorks 216 F3
Thornton-le-Dale N Yorks 216 C6
Thornton-le-Moor Lincs 189 B8
Thornton-le-Moor N Yorks 215 B7
Thornton-le-Moors Ches 182 G6
Thornton-le-Street N Yorks 215 B8
Thorntonloch E Loth 282 G5
Thornwood Common Essex 87 E7
Thoroton Notts 172 G3
Thorp Gtr Man 196 F2
Thorp Arch W Yorks 206 D4
Thorpe Cumb 230 F5
Thorpe Derby 169 E11
Thorpe ER Yorks 208 D5
Thorpe Lincs 191 E7
Thorpe Norfolk 143 D8
Thorpe Notts 172 F3
Thorpe N Yorks 213 G10
Thorpe Surrey 66 F4
Thorpe Acre Leics 153 E10
Thorpe Arnold Leics 154 E5
Thorpe Audlin W Yorks 198 D3
Thorpe Bassett N Yorks 217 E7
Thorpe Bay Southend 70 B2
Thorpe by Water Rutl'd 137 D7
Thorpe Common Suffolk 108 D5
Thorpe Constantine Staffs 134 B5
Thorpe Culvert Lincs 175 C7
Thorpe Edge W Yorks 205 F9
Thorpe End Norfolk 160 G5
Thorpe Fendykes Lincs 175 C7
Thorpe Green Essex 108 G3
Thorpe Green Suffolk 125 G8
Thorpe Green Surrey 66 F4
Thorpe Hamlet Norfolk 142 B4
Thorpe Hesley S Yorks 186 B5
Thorpe in Balne S Yorks 198 E5
Thorpe Langton Leics 136 E4
Thorpe Larches Durham 234 F3
Thorpe le Fallows Lincs 188 E6
Thorpe le Street ER Yorks 208 E2
Thorpe le Vale Lincs 190 C2
Thorpe Lea Surrey 66 E4
Thorpe Malsor Northants 120 B6
Thorpe Mandeville Northants 101 B10
Thorpe Market Norfolk 160 B4
Thorpe Marriot Norfolk 160 G3
Thorpe Morieux Suffolk 125 G8
Thorpe on the Hill Lincs 172 B6
Thorpe on the Hill W Yorks 197 B10
Thorpe Park, Chertsey Surrey 66 F4
Thorpe Row Norfolk 141 B9
Thorpe St. Andrew Norfolk 142 B5
Thorpe St. Peter Lincs 175 C7
Thorpe Salvin S Yorks 187 E9
Thorpe Satchville Leics 154 G4
Thorpe Street Suffolk 125 B10
Thorpe Thewles Stockton 234 G4
Thorpe Tilney Lincs 173 D10
Thorpe Tilney Dales Lincs 173 D11
Thorpe Underwood Northants 136 G5
Thorpe Underwood N Yorks 206 B5
Thorpe Waterville Northants 137 G10
Thorpe Willoughby N Yorks 207 G7
Thorpe-le-Soken Essex 108 G3
Thorpeness Suffolk 127 F9
Thorpland Norfolk 140 B2
Thorrington Essex 89 B9
Thorverton Devon 26 G6
Thrandeston Suffolk 126 B2
Thrapston Northants 121 B9
Thrashbush N Lanarks 268 B5
Threapland Cumb 229 D9
Threapland N Yorks 213 G9
Threapwood Staffs 169 G8
Threapwood Wrex 166 F6
Threave Gardens Dumf/Gal 237 C9
Three Ashes Hants 64 G6
Three Ashes Heref'd 97 G10
Three Ashes Som'set 45 D7
Three Bridges Arg/Bute 284 F4
Three Bridges Lincs 190 D6
Three Bridges W Sussex 51 F9
Three Burrows Cornw'l 4 F4
Three Chimneys Kent 53 F10
Three Cocks Powys 96 D3
Three Counties Showground, Malvern Worcs 98 C5
Three Crosses Swan 75 G9
Three Cups Corner E Sussex 37 C10
Three Gates Shrops 130 F5
Three Hammers Cornw'l 11 D10
Three Holes Norfolk 139 C10
Three Horse Shoes Devon 14 B4
Three Leg Cross E Sussex 53 G7
Three Legged Cross Dorset 31 F9
Three May Poles W Midlands 118 B2
Three Mile Cross Wokingham 65 F8
Three Oaks E Sussex 38 E4
Threehammer Common Norfolk 160 F6
Threekingham Lincs 155 B11

Threemilestones Cornw'l 4 G5
Threemiletown W Loth 279 F11
Threewaters Cornw'l 5 B10
Threlkeld Cumb 230 F2
Threshers Bush Essex 87 D8
Threshfield N Yorks 213 G9
Thrigby Norfolk 161 G9
Thrimby Cumb 231 G7
Thringarth Durham 232 G4
Thringstone Leics 153 F8
Thrintoft N Yorks 224 G6
Thriplow Cambs 105 B8
Throapham S Yorks 187 E9
Throckenholt Lincs 139 B7
Throcking Herts 104 E6
Throckley Tyne/Wear 242 D5
Throckmorton Worcs 99 B9
Throop Dorset 18 C2
Throphill Northum 252 F4
Thropton Northum 252 C2
Throsk Stirl 279 C7
Throughgate Dumf/Gal 247 G9
Throwleigh Devon 13 C9
Throwley Kent 54 B3
Throwley Forstal Kent 54 C3
Thrumpton Notts 153 C10
Thrumpton Notts 188 E2
Thrumster H'land 310 E7
Thrunton Northum 264 G3
Thrupe Som'set 44 D6
Thrupp Glos 80 E5
Thrupp Oxon 82 F3
Thrupp Oxon 83 B7
Thruscross N Yorks 205 B9
Thrushelton Devon 12 D4
Thrussington Leics 154 F3
Thruxted Kent 54 C6
Thruxton Hants 47 D9
Thruxton Heref'd 97 E8
Thruxton Motor Racing Circuit Hants 47 D9
Thrybergh S Yorks 187 B7
Thulston Derby 153 C8
Thunder Bridge W Yorks 197 E7
Thundergay N Ayrs 255 C9
Thundersley Essex 69 B9
Thundridge Herts 86 B5
Thurcaston Leics 153 G11
Thurcroft S Yorks 187 E7
Thurdon Cornw'l 24 E3
Thurgarton Notts 171 G11
Thurgarton Norfolk 160 C3
Thurgoland S Yorks 197 G9
Thurlaston Leics 135 D10
Thurlaston Warwick 119 C9
Thurlbear Som'set 28 C3
Thurlby Lincs 191 F7
Thurlby Lincs 155 F11
Thurlby Lincs 172 C6
Thurleigh Beds 121 F11
Thurlestone Devon 8 G3
Thurloxton Som'set 43 G9
Thurlstone S Yorks 197 G8
Thurlton Norfolk 143 D8
Thurlwood Ches 168 D5
Thurmaston Leics 136 B2
Thurnby Leics 136 C2
Thurne Norfolk 161 F8
Thurnham Kent 53 B10
Thurning Norfolk 159 D11
Thurning Northants 137 F11
Thurnscoe S Yorks 198 F3
Thurnscoe East S Yorks 198 F3
Thursby Cumb 239 G8
Thursden Lancs 204 F4
Thursford Norfolk 159 C9
Thursford Collection, Fakenham Norfolk 159 C9
Thursford Green Norfolk 159 C9
Thursley Hants 50 F2
Thurso H'land 310 C5
Thurso East H'land 310 C5
Thurstaston Mersey 182 E2
Thurston Pembs 73 D7
Thurston Suffolk 125 D8
Thurston Clough Gtr Man 196 F3
Thurston End Suffolk 124 G5
Thurston Planche Suffolk 125 E8
Thurstonfield Cumb 239 F8
Thurstonland W Yorks 197 E7
Thurton Norfolk 142 C6
Thurvaston Derby 152 B4
Thuxton Norfolk 141 B10
Thwaite Durham 223 C10
Thwaite N Yorks 223 F7
Thwaite Suffolk 126 D2
Thwaite Head Cumb 220 G6
Thwaite St. Mary Norfolk 142 D6
Thwaites W Yorks 205 E7
Thwaites Brow W Yorks 205 E7
Thwing ER Yorks 217 E11
Tibbermore Perth/Kinr 286 E4
Tibberton Glos 98 G5
Tibberton Telford 150 E3
Tibberton Worcs 117 F8
Tibenham Norfolk 142 F2
Tibshelf Derby 170 C6
Tibthorpe ER Yorks 208 B5
Ticehurst E Sussex 53 G7
Tichborne Hants 48 G5
Tickencote Rutl'd 137 B9
Tickenham N Som'set 60 E3
Tickenhurst Kent 55 C9
Tickford End M/Keynes 103 C7
Tickhill S Yorks 187 B9
Ticklerton Shrops 131 E9
Tickmorend Glos 80 F4
Ticknall Derby 153 E7
Tickton ER Yorks 209 D7
Tidbury Green W Midlands 118 B2
Tidcombe Wilts 47 B9
Tiddington Oxon 83 E11
Tiddington Warwick 118 F4
Tiddleywink Wilts 61 D11
Tidebrook E Sussex 37 B10
Tideford Cornw'l 6 D6
Tideford Cross Cornw'l 6 C6
Tidenham Glos 79 F9
Tideswell Derby 185 F11
Tidmarsh W Berks 64 E6
Tidmington Warwick 100 D5
Tidnor Heref'd 97 D11
Tidpit Hants 31 D9
Tidworth Wilts 47 D8
Tiers Cross Pembs 72 C6
Tiffield Northants 120 G3
Tifty Aberds 303 E7
Tigerton Angus 293 G7
Tigh-na-Blair Perth/Kinr 285 F11
Tighnabruaich Arg/Bute 275 F10
Tighnacachla Arg/Bute 274 G3
Tighnafiline H'land 307 L3
Tighness Arg/Bute 284 G6
Tigley Devon 8 C5
Tilbrook Cambs 121 D11
Tilbrook M/Keynes 103 E8
Tilbrook Grange Cambs 121 C11
Tilbury Thurr'k 68 D6
Tilbury Green Essex 106 C4
Tile Cross W Midlands 134 F3
Tile Hill W Midlands 118 B5
Tilegate Green Essex 87 D8
Tilehouse Green W Midlands 118 B3
Tilehurst Reading 65 E7
Tilekiln Essex 106 E4
Tilekiln Green Essex 105 G10
Tilford Surrey 49 E11
Tilgate W Sussex 51 G9
Tilgate Forest Row W Sussex 51 G9
Tilkey Essex 106 G6
Tilland Cornw'l 6 C6
Tillathrowie Aberds 302 F4
Tillicoultry Clack 279 B8
Tillers Green Glos 98 E3
Tilley Shrops 149 D10
Tilley Green Shrops 149 D10
Tillingham Essex 89 E7
Tillington Heref'd 97 B9
Tillington Staffs 151 E8
Tillington W Sussex 35 C7
Tillington Common Heref'd 97 B9
Tilly Lo. Aberds 293 C7
Tillyarblet Angus 293 G7
Tillybirloch Aberds 293 C8
Tillycorthie Aberds 303 G9
Tillydrine Aberds 293 D8
Tillyfour Aberds 293 B7
Tillyfourie Aberds 293 B8
Tillygarmond Aberds 293 D8
Tillygreig Aberds 303 G8
Tillykerrie Aberds 303 G8
Tillynaught Aberds 302 C5
Tilmanstone Kent 55 C10
Tiln Notts 188 E2
Tilney All Saints Norfolk 157 F11
Tilney Cum Islington Norfolk 157 G11
Tilney Fen End Norfolk 157 G10
Tilney High End Norfolk 157 F11
Tilney St. Lawrence Norfolk 157 G10
Tilsdown Glos 80 F3
Tilshead Wilts 46 D4
Tilsmore E Sussex 37 C9
Tilstock Shrops 149 B10
Tilston Ches 167 E7
Tilstone Bank Ches 167 D9
Tilstone Fearnall Ches 167 C9
Tilsworth Beds 103 G9
Tilton on the Hill Leics 136 B4
Tiltups End Glos 80 F4
Tilty Essex 105 F11
Timbercombe Som'set 43 G8
Timberden Bottom Kent 68 G4
Timberland Lincs 173 D10
Timbersbrook Ches 168 C5
Timberscombe Som'set 42 E3
Timble N Yorks 205 C9
Timperley Gtr Man 184 D3
Timsbury Bath/NE Som'set 45 B7
Timsbury Hants 32 C4
Timsgearraidh W Isles 304 E2
Timworth Suffolk 125 D7
Timworth Green Suffolk 125 D7
Tincleton Dorset 17 C11
Tindale Cumb 240 F4
Tindale Crescent Durham 233 F9
Tingewick Bucks 102 E3
Tingley W Yorks 197 B9
Tingon Shetl'd 314 E4
Tingrith Beds 103 E10
Tingwall Orkney 312 F4
Tinhay Devon 12 D3
Tinkers End Bucks 102 F5
Tinkers Hill Hants 47 D11
Tinshill W Yorks 205 F11
Tinsley S Yorks 186 C6
Tinsley Green W Sussex 51 F9
Tintagel Cornw'l 11 D7
Tintagel Castle Cornw'l 11 D7
Tintern Abbey Monmouths 79 E8
Tintern Parva Monmouths 79 E8
Tintinhull Som'set 29 D7
Tintwistle Derby 185 B8
Tinwald Dumf/Gal 248 G2
Tinwell Rutl'd 137 B10
Tipperty Aberds 302 C6
Tipperty Aberds 303 G9
Tip's Cross Essex 87 E9
Tips End Norfolk 139 E10
Tiptoe Hants 19 B11
Tipton W Midlands 133 E8
Tipton Cross Devon 15 C7
Tipton Green W Midlands 133 E9
Tipton St. John Devon 15 C7
Tiptree Essex 88 B5
Tiptree Heath Essex 88 C5
Tirabad Powys 95 C7
Tiraghoil Arg/Bute 288 G5
Tircanol Swan 75 F11
Tirdeunaw Swan 75 F10
Tiree Airport Arg/Bute 288 E1
Tirinie Perth/Kinr 291 G10
Tirley Glos 98 F6
Tiroran Arg/Bute 288 G6
Tirphil Caerph 77 E10
Tirril Cumb 230 F6
Tirryside H'land 309 H5
Tir-y-dail Carms 75 C10
Tir-y-fron Flints 166 D3
Tisbury Wilts 30 B6
Tisman's Common W Sussex 50 G5
Tissington Derby 169 E11
Titchberry Devon 24 B2
Titchfield Hants 33 F8
Titchfield Common Hants 33 F8
Titchmarsh Northants 121 B10
Titchwell Norfolk 176 E3
Titcomb W Berks 63 F11
Tithby Notts 154 B3
Tithe Barn Hillock Mersey 183 B9
Tithebarn Staffs 169 G9
Tithill Som'set 27 B11
Titley Heref'd 114 F6
Titmore Green Herts 104 F4
Titsey Surrey 52 C2
Titson Cornw'l 24 G2
Tittenhurst Windsor 66 F2
Tittensor Staffs 151 B7
Tittleshall Norfolk 159 E7
Titton Worcs 116 D6
Tiverton Ches 167 C9
Tiverton Devon 27 E7
Tivetshall Norfolk 142 F3
Tivetshall St. Margaret Norfolk 142 F3
Tividale W Midlands 133 E9
Tivington Som'set 42 D2
Tivoli Cumb 219 B9
Tixall Staffs 151 E9
Tixover Rutl'd 137 C9
Toab Orkney 313 H6
Toab Shetl'd 315 M5
Toad Row Suffolk 143 F10
Toadmoor Derby 170 E5
Tobermory Arg/Bute 289 D7
Toberonochy Arg/Bute 275 C8
Tobha Beag W Isles 296 D5
Tobha Mor W Isles 297 H3
Tobhtarol W Isles 304 E3
Tobson W Isles 304 E3
Toby's Hill Lincs 191 C7
Tocher Aberds 302 F6
Tockenham Wilts 62 D4
Tockenham Wick Wilts 62 C4
Tockholes Blackb'n 195 C7
Tockington S Glos 60 B6
Tockwith N Yorks 206 C5
Todber Dorset 30 C3
Todding Heref'd 115 B8
Toddington Beds 103 F10
Toddington Glos 99 E10
Toddington W Sussex 35 G8
Toddlehills Aberds 303 E10
Todd's Green Herts 104 F4
Todenham Glos 100 D4
Todhill Angus 287 D8
Todhills Cumb 239 E9
Todhills Durham 233 E10
Todlachie Aberds 293 B8
Todmorden W Yorks 196 C2
Todrig Scot Borders 261 F10
Todwick S Yorks 187 E7
Toft Cambs 123 F7
Toft Lincs 155 F11
Toft Shetl'd 314 F6
Toft Warwick 119 C9
Toft Hill Durham 233 F9
Toft Hill Lincs 174 C2
Toft Monks Norfolk 143 E8
Toft next Newton Lincs 189 D8
Toftrees Norfolk 159 D7
Tofts H'land 310 C7
Tofts Northum 241 D8
Toftwood Norfolk 159 G9
Tog Hill S Glos 61 E8
Togston Northum 252 B6
Tokavaig H'land 295 D8
Tokers Green Oxon 65 D8
Tolastadh a Chaolais W Isles 304 E3
Tolastadh bho Thuath W Isles 304 D7
Tolborough Cornw'l 11 F9
Toldish Cornw'l 5 D8
Tolgus Mount Cornw'l 4 G3
Tolhurst E Sussex 53 G7
Toll Bar Mersey 183 C7
Toll Bar S Yorks 198 F5
Toll End W Midlands 133 E9
Toll of Birness Aberds 303 F10
Tolladine Worcs 117 F7
Tolland Som'set 42 G6
Tollard Farnham Dorset 31 D7
Tollard Royal Wilts 30 D6
Tollbar End W Midlands 119 B7
Toller Fratrum Dorset 17 B7
Toller Porcorum Dorset 17 B7
Toller Whelme Dorset 29 G8
Tollerford Dorset 17 B7
Tollerton Notts 154 C2
Tollerton N Yorks 215 G10
Tollesbury Essex 89 C7
Tollesby Middlesbro 225 B10
Tolleshunt D'Arcy Essex 88 C6
Tolleshunt Knights Essex 88 B6
Tolleshunt Major Essex 88 C6
Tollie H'land 300 D5
Tollingham ER Yorks 208 F2
Tolm W Isles 304 E6
Tolpuddle Dorset 17 C11
Tolvah H'land 291 D10
Tolworth London 67 F7
Tom an Fhuadain W Isles 305 G5
Tomaknock Perth/Kinr 286 E2
Tomatin H'land 301 G8
Tombreck H'land 300 F6
Tombui Perth/Kinr 286 B2
Tomchrasky H'land 290 B4
Tomdoun H'land 290 C3
Tomich H'land 300 B6
Tomich H'land 300 G3
Tomich House H'land 300 E5
Tomintoul Aberds 292 D3
Tomintoul Moray 292 B3
Tomlow Warwick 119 E9
Tomnaven Moray 302 F4
Tomnavoulin Moray 302 G2
Tomsleibhe Arg/Bute 289 F8
Ton Monmouths 78 F5
Tonbridge Kent 52 D5
Tonderghie Dumf/Gal 236 F6
Tondu Bridg 57 E11
Tone Som'set 27 C10
Tone Green Som'set 27 C11
Tonedale Som'set 27 C10
Tonfanau Gwyn 110 C2
Tong Kent 53 D10
Tong Shrops 132 B5
Tong W Yorks 205 G10
Tong End Lancs 195 D11
Tong Green Kent 54 C3
Tong Norton Shrops 132 B5
Tong Park W Yorks 205 F9
Tong Street W Yorks 205 G9
Tongdean Brighton/Hove 36 F3
Tonge Leics 153 E8
Tonge Fold Gtr Man 195 F8
Tonge Moor Gtr Man 195 E8
Tongham Surrey 49 D11
Tongland Dumf/Gal 237 D8
Tongue H'land 308 D5
Tongue End Lincs 156 F3
Tongwell M/Keynes 103 C7
Tongwynlais Card 58 C6
Tonmawr Rh Cyn Taff 76 F4
Tonna = Tonnau Rh Cyn Taff 76 F3
Tonnau = Tonna Rh Cyn Taff 76 F3
Ton-Pentre Rh Cyn Taff 77 F7
Ton-teg Rh Cyn Taff 58 B5
Tontine Lancs 194 G4
Ton-ty'r-bel Caerph 78 F2
Tonwell Herts 86 B4
Tonypandy Rh Cyn Taff 77 G7
Ton-y-pistyll Caerph 77 F11
Tonyrefail Rh Cyn Taff 58 B4
Toot Baldon Oxon 83 E9
Toot Hill Essex 87 E8
Toothill Hants 32 D5
Toothill Swindon 62 C6
Toothill W Yorks 196 C6
Tooting Graveney London 67 E9
Top End Beds 121 E10
Top Green Notts 172 F3
Top Lock Gtr Man 194 F6
Top of Hebers Gtr Man 195 F11
Top o'th'Lane Lancs 194 C5
Top Valley Nott'ham 171 G9
Topcliffe N Yorks 215 D8
Topcliffe W Yorks 197 B9
Topcroft Norfolk 142 E5
Topcroft Street Norfolk 142 E5
Topham S Yorks 198 D6
Toppesfield Essex 106 D4
Toppings Gtr Man 195 E8
Toprow Norfolk 142 D3
Topsham Devon 14 D5
Top-y-rhos Flints 166 D3
Torbay Torbay 9 C8
Torbeg N Ayrs 255 E10
Torboll Farm H'land 309 K7
Torbothie N Lanarks 269 D7
Torbreck H'land 309 J7
Torbrex Stirl 278 C5
Torbryan Devon 8 B6
Torbush N Lanarks 268 D6
Torcross Devon 8 G6
Torcroy H'land 291 D9
Tore H'land 300 D6
Torfrey Cornw'l 6 E2
Torgyle H'land 290 B5
Torinturk Arg/Bute 275 G9
Torkington Gtr Man 184 D6
Torksey Lincs 188 F4
Torlum W Isles 296 F3
Torlundy H'land 290 F3
Tormarton S Glos 61 D9
Tormisdale Arg/Bute 254 B2
Tormitchell S Ayrs 244 E6
Tormore H'land 295 E8
Tormore N Ayrs 255 D9
Tornagrain H'land 301 E7
Tornahaish Aberds 292 C4
Tornapress H'land 299 E8
Tornaveen Aberds 293 C8
Torness H'land 300 G5
Toronto Durham 233 E9
Torpenhow Cumb 229 D10
Torphichen W Loth 279 G9
Torphin Midloth 270 B4
Torphins Aberds 293 C8
Torpoint Cornw'l 7 D8
Torquay Torbay 9 C8
Torquhan Scot Borders 271 F8
Torr Devon 7 E11
Torr Devon 8 C2
Torra Arg/Bute 254 B4
Torran Arg/Bute 275 C9
Torran H'land 298 E5
Torran H'land 301 B7
Torrance E Dunb 278 G2
Torrans Arg/Bute 288 G6
Torranyard N Ayrs 267 G7
Torre Som'set 42 E4
Torre Torbay 9 B8
Torridon H'land 299 D9
Torridon Ho. H'land 299 D8
Torries Aberds 293 B8
Torrin H'land 295 C7
Torrisdale H'land 308 C6
Torrisdale Castle Arg/Bute 255 D8
Torrisdale-Square Arg/Bute 255 D8
Torrish H'land 311 H3
Torrisholme Lancs 211 G9
Torroble H'land 309 J5
Torroy H'land 309 K5
Torry Aberds 302 F4
Torry Aberd C 293 C11
Torryburn Fife 279 D10
Torterston Aberds 303 E10
Torthorwald Dumf/Gal 238 B2
Tortington W Sussex 35 F7
Torton Worcs 116 C6
Tortworth S Glos 80 G2
Torvaig H'land 298 E4
Torver Cumb 220 G5
Torwood Falk 278 D6
Torworth Notts 187 E11
Tosberry Devon 24 C3
Toscaig H'land 295 B9
Toseland Cambs 122 E4
Tosside N Yorks 203 B11
Tostock Suffolk 125 E9
Totaig H'land 295 C10
Totaig H'land 298 D2
Totardor H'land 294 B5
Tote H'land 298 E4
Totegan H'land 310 C2
Totford Hants 48 F5
Totgarrick Cornw'l 5 E8
Totham Hill Essex 88 C5
Totham Plains Essex 88 C5
Tothill Lincs 190 E6
Totland I/Wight 20 D2
Totley Bents S Yorks 186 E4
Totley Brook S Yorks 186 E4
Totley Rise S Yorks 186 E4
Totnell Dorset 29 F10
Totnes Devon 8 C6
Toton Notts 153 C10
Totronald Arg/Bute 288 D3
Totscore H'land 298 C3
Tottenham London 86 G4
Tottenhill Norfolk 158 G2
Tottenhill Row Norfolk 158 G2
Totteridge Bucks 84 G5
Totteridge Park London 86 G2
Totternhoe Beds 103 G9
Totties W Yorks 197 F7
Tottington Gtr Man 195 E9
Tottlebank Cumb 210 C6
Totton Hants 32 E5
Touchen-end Windsor 65 D11
Touches Som'set 28 F4
Toulton Som'set 43 G7
Toulvaddie H'land 311 L2
Tournaig H'land 307 L3
Toux Aberds 303 D9
Tovil Kent 53 C8
Tow House Northum 241 E7
Tow Law Durham 233 D8
Towan Cornw'l 10 G3
Towan Cross Cornw'l 4 F4
Toward Arg/Bute 266 B2
Towcester Northants 102 B3
Towcester Racecourse Northants 102 B4
Towednack Cornw'l 1 B5
Tower End Norfolk 158 F3
Tower Hamlets Kent 55 E10
Tower Hill Ches 184 F6
Tower Hill Essex 108 E5
Tower Hill Herts 85 E8
Tower Hill Mersey 194 G2
Tower Hill W Midlands 133 D11
Tower Hill W Sussex 35 B11
Tower Knowe Visitor Centre, Kielder Water Northum 250 F5
Tower of London London 67 C10
Towerhead N Som'set 44 B2
Towersey Oxon 84 D2
Towie Aberds 292 B6
Towie Aberds 302 G5
Towie Aberds 303 C8
Towiemore Moray 302 E3
Town Bent Lancs 195 B8
Town End Bucks 84 F3
Town End Cambs 139 D8
Town End Cumb 211 B7
Town End Cumb 221 F7
Town End Cumb 220 D6
Town End Cumb 211 C8
Town End Cumb 221 E8
Town End Cumb 212 C2
Town End Cumb 230 F6
Town End Cumb 231 F8
Town End Derby 185 F11
Town End Lincs 173 G7
Town End Mersey 183 D7
Town End W Yorks 196 D5
Town End Farm Tyne/Wear 243 F8
Town Fields Ches 167 B10
Town Green Gtr Man 183 B9
Town Green Lancs 194 F2
Town Green Norfolk 160 C4
Town Green Norfolk 161 G7
Town-head Arg/Bute 275 G11
Town Head Cumb 222 C3
Town Head Cumb 220 D6
Town Head Cumb 221 E8
Town Head Cumb 231 F7
Town Head Cumb 222 C2
Town Head Cumb 231 F8
Town Head Derby 185 F11
Town Head N Yorks 212 F5
Town Head N Yorks 204 B2
Town Hill N Yorks 213 G10
Town Kelloe Durham 234 D3
Town Lane Gtr Man 195 G7
Town Littleworth E Sussex 36 D6
Town of Lowton Gtr Man 183 B10
Town Park Telford 132 B4
Town Row E Sussex 52 G5
Town Street Glos 98 F6
Town Yetholm Scot Borders 263 D8
Townend Derby 185 E9
Townend W Dunb 277 F7
Townend W Dunb 277 F8
Townfield Durham 232 B5
Towngate Cumb 230 B6
Towngate Lincs 156 G2
Townhead Arg/Bute 266 C1
Townhead Cumb 229 D7
Townhead Cumb 230 D6
Townhead Cumb 231 E8
Townhead Dumf/Gal 237 E8
Townhead Lancs 203 C10
Townhead N Lanarks 268 B4
Townhead S Ayrs 244 C6
Townhead S Yorks 197 G7
Townhead S Yorks 186 E4
Townhead of Greenlaw Dumf/Gal 237 C9
Townhill Fife 280 D2
Townhill Swan 75 G10
Townhill Park Hants 33 E7
Townlake Devon 12 F4
Townland Green Kent 54 G2
Town's End Bucks 84 D2
Town's End Bucks 102 G2
Town's End Dorset 18 B3
Town's End Dorset 18 E5
Town's End Dorset 29 F9
Towns End Hants 48 B5
Town's End Som'set 42 E6
Town's End Som'set 45 D7
Towns End Som'set 30 D2
Townsend Bath/NE Som'set 44 B5
Townsend Herts 85 D10
Townsend Oxon 63 B11
Townsend S Glos 60 C5
Townsend Stoke 168 F6
Townsend Som'set 44 C4
Townsend Som'set 28 E5
Townsend Som'set 43 G11
Townsend Wilts 46 B3
Townsend Fold Lancs 195 C10
Townshend Cornw'l 2 C3
Townwell S Glos 79 G11
Towthorpe C/York 207 B8
Towthorpe ER Yorks 217 G8
Towton N Yorks 206 F5
Towyn Conwy 181 F7
Toxteth Mersey 182 D5
Toynton All Saints Lincs 174 C5
Toynton Fen Side Lincs 174 C5
Toynton Ings Lincs 174 C6
Toynton St. Peter Lincs 174 C6
Toy's Hill Kent 52 C3
Trabboch E Ayrs 257 E10
Traboe Cornw'l 2 E6
Tracebridge Som'set 27 C9
Tradespark H'land 301 D8
Tradespark Orkney 313 H5
Trafford Park Gtr Man 184 B3
Trago Mills, Newton Abbot Devon 14 G2
Traigh Ho H'land 295 F8
Trallong Powys 95 F9
Trallwn Swan 75 F11
Tram Inn Heref'd 97 E9
Tranch Torf 78 E3
Tranent E Loth 281 G8
Tranmere Mersey 182 D4
Trantlebeg H'land 310 D2
Trantlemore H'land 310 D2
Tranwell Northum 252 G5
Trapp Carms 75 B11
Traprain E Loth 281 F11
Trap's Green Warwick 118 D2
Trapshill W Berks 63 G11
Traquair Scot Borders 261 C8
Trash Green W Berks 65 F7
Travellers Rest Carms 74 B5
Travelmond Cornw'l 6 C4
Trawden Lancs 204 F4
Trawscoed Powys 95 E11
Trawsfynydd Gwyn 146 B4
Trawsmawr Carms 93 G8
Trawsnant Ceredig'n 111 D11
Tre Taliesin = Taliesin Ceredig'n 128 E3
Treaddow Heref'd 97 G10
Trealaw Rh Cyn Taff 77 G8
Treales Lancs 202 G4
Treamble Cornw'l 4 D5
Trearddur Angl 178 F3
Treaslane H'land 298 D3
Treator Cornw'l 10 F4
Tre-Aubrey V/Glam 58 E4
Trebah Garden, Mawnan Smith Cornw'l 3 D7
Trebahwartha Cornw'l 3 D7
Trebanog Rh Cyn Taff 76 D6
Trebanog Rh Cyn Taff 77 G8
Trebanos Neath P Talb 76 E2
Trebarber Cornw'l 5 C7
Trebartha Cornw'l 11 F11
Trebarvah Cornw'l 2 D2
Trebarvah Cornw'l 2 C6
Trebarwith Cornw'l 11 D7
Trebeath Cornw'l 11 D11
Tre-Beferad V/Glam 58 F3
Trebehor Cornw'l 1 E3
Trebetherick Cornw'l 10 F4
Treble's Holford Som'set 42 G6
Tre-boeth Swan 75 F11
Treborough Som'set 42 F4
Trebudannon Cornw'l 5 C7
Trebullett Cornw'l 12 F2
Treburley Cornw'l 12 F2
Treburrick Cornw'l 10 G3
Trebyan Cornw'l 5 C11
Trecastle Powys 95 F7
Trecenydd Caerph 58 B6
Trecrogo Cornw'l 12 E2
Trecwn Pembs 91 E9
Trecynon Rh Cyn Taff 77 E7
Tredarrup Cornw'l 11 C9
Tredaule Cornw'l 11 E10
Tredavoe Cornw'l 1 D5
Tredegar Bl Gwent 77 D10
Tredegar Newydd = New Tredegar Caerph 77 E10
Trederwen Powys 148 F5
Tredington Glos 99 F8
Tredington Warwick 100 C5
Tredinnick Cornw'l 1 C4
Tredinnick Cornw'l 6 B3
Tredinnick Cornw'l 6 D4
Tredogan V/Glam 58 F5
Tredomen Powys 96 E2
Tredrizzick Cornw'l 10 F5
Tredunnock Monmouths 78 G5
Tredustan Powys 96 E2
Tredworth Glos 80 B4
Treen Cornw'l 1 E3
Treen Cornw'l 1 B4
Treesmill Cornw'l 5 D11
Tre-Essey Heref'd 97 G10
Treeton S Yorks 186 D6
Trefaes Gwyn 144 C5
Trefaldwyn = Montgomery Powys 130 D4
Trefasser Pembs 91 D7
Trefdraeth Angl 178 G6
Trefdraeth = Newport Pembs 91 D11
Trefeca Powys 96 E2
Trefechan Ceredig'n 128 G1
Trefechan Merth Tyd 77 D8
Trefeglwys Powys 129 E9
Trefeitha Powys 96 E2
Trefelyn Pembs 91 E7
Trefenter Ceredig'n 112 D2
Treffanney Powys 148 F4
Treffany Hill Cornw'l 6 D4
Treffgarne Pembs 91 G9
Treffynnon Pembs 90 F6
Treffynnon = Holywell Flints 181 F11
Trefgarn Owen Pembs 91 F7
Trefil Bl Gwent 77 C10
Trefilan Ceredig'n 111 F10
Trefin = Trevine Pembs 90 E6
Treflach Shrops 148 D5
Trefnant Denbs 181 G8
Trefonen Shrops 148 D5
Trefor Gwyn 162 F5
Trefor Angl 178 E5
Trefor Angl 179 F8
Treforest Rh Cyn Taff 58 B5
Tre-Forgan Neath P Talb 76 D3
Treforys = Morriston Swan 75 F11
Trefriw Conwy 164 C3
Tref-y-Clawdd = Knighton Powys 114 C5
Tref-y-nant Wrex 166 G3
Tregada Cornw'l 12 E2
Tregadillet Cornw'l 11 E11
Tre-gagle Monmouths 79 D8
Tregaian Angl 179 F7
Tregajorran Cornw'l 4 G3
Tregare Monmouths 78 C6
Tregarland Cornw'l 6 D5
Tregarne Cornw'l 3 E7
Tregaron Ceredig'n 112 E3
Tregarth Gwyn 163 B10
Tregaswith Cornw'l 5 C7
Tregatta Cornw'l 11 D7
Tregavarras Cornw'l 5 G9
Tregear Cornw'l 5 E7
Tregeare Cornw'l 11 D10
Tregeiriog Wrex 148 C3
Tregele Angl 178 C5
Tregellist Cornw'l 10 F6
Tregenna Cornw'l 11 G7
Tregeseal Cornw'l 1 C3
Tre-Gibbon Rh Cyn Taff 77 D7
Tregonce Cornw'l 10 G4
Tregonetha Cornw'l 5 C9
Tregonhawke Cornw'l 7 E8
Tregonna Cornw'l 10 G4
Tregony Cornw'l 5 G8
Tregoodwell Cornw'l 11 E8
Tregorrick Cornw'l 5 E10
Tregoss Cornw'l 5 C9
Tregowris Cornw'l 3 E7
Tregoyd Powys 96 D3
Tregoyd Mill Powys 96 D3
Tregrehan Mills Cornw'l 5 E10
Tregroes Ceredig'n 93 C8
Tregullon Cornw'l 5 C11
Tregunna Cornw'l 10 G5
Tregunnon Cornw'l 11 E10
Tregurrian Cornw'l 5 B7
Tre-Gwyr = Gowerton Swan 75 F9
Tregynon Powys 129 D11
Tre-gynwer Carms 74 B6
Trehafod Rh Cyn Taff 77 G8
Trehan Cornw'l 7 D8
Treharris Merth Tyd 77 F9
Trehemborne Cornw'l 10 G3
Treherbert Rh Cyn Taff 77 F6
Treheveras Cornw'l 4 F6
Trehill V/Glam 58 E5
Trehilyn Pembs 91 D8
Trehunist Cornw'l 6 C6
Tre-Ifor Rh Cyn Taff 77 D7
Trekeivesteps Cornw'l 6 B4
Trekelland Cornw'l 11 F11
Trekelland Cornw'l 12 E2
Trekenner Cornw'l 12 F2
Treknow Cornw'l 11 D7
Trelan Cornw'l 2 F6
Tre-lan Flints 165 B11
Trelash Cornw'l 11 C9
Trelassick Cornw'l 5 E7
Trelawnyd Flints 181 F9
Trelech Carms 92 E5
Trelech-a'r-Bettws Carms 92 F6
Treleddyd fawr Pembs 90 F5
Treleigh Cornw'l 4 G4
Treletert = Letterston Pembs 91 F8
Trelewis Merth Tyd 77 F10
Treligga Cornw'l 10 E7
Trelights Cornw'l 10 F5
Trelill Cornw'l 10 F6
Trelinnoe Cornw'l 12 E2
Trelion Cornw'l 5 E8
Trelissick Cornw'l 3 B8
Trelissick Garden, Feock Cornw'l 3 B8
Trellech Monmouths 79 D8
Trelleck Cross Monmouths 79 E8
Trelleck Grange Monmouths 79 E7
Trelogan Flints 181 E10
Trelonk Cornw'l 5 G7
Trelowia Cornw'l 6 D5
Trelowth Cornw'l 5 E9
Trelowthas Cornw'l 5 F7
Treluggan Cornw'l 3 B9
Trelydan Powys 148 G4
Tremadog Gwyn 163 G9
Tremail Cornw'l 11 D9
Tremain Ceredig'n 92 B4
Tremaine Cornw'l 11 D10
Tremar Cornw'l 6 B5
Trematon Cornw'l 7 D7
Trembraze Cornw'l 6 B5
Tremeirchion Denbs 181 G9
Tremollett Cornw'l 11 F11
Tremore Cornw'l 5 C10
Tremorfa Card 59 D8
Tre-Mostyn Flints 181 F10
Trenale Cornw'l 11 D7
Trenance Cornw'l 10 G4
Trenance Cornw'l 5 C6
Trenant Cornw'l 6 B4
Trenarren Cornw'l 5 F10
Trenarrett Cornw'l 11 E10
Trenault Cornw'l 11 E11
Trench Telford 150 G3
Trench Green Oxon 65 D7
Trench Wood Kent 52 D5
Trencreek Cornw'l 4 C6
Trendeal Cornw'l 5 E7
Trendrean Cornw'l 4 D6
Treneague Cornw'l 10 G5
Trenear Cornw'l 2 C5
Treneglos Cornw'l 11 D10
Trenewan Cornw'l 6 E3
Trengune Cornw'l 11 C9
Trenhorne Cornw'l 11 F11
Treninnick Cornw'l 4 C6
Trenode Cornw'l 6 D5
Trenoweth Cornw'l 3 C7
Trent Dorset 29 D9
Trent Vale Stoke 168 G5
Trentham Staffs 168 G5
Trentham Gardens, Newcastle-under-Lyme Staffs 168 G5
Trentishoe Devon 40 D6
Trentlock Derby 153 C9
Trenwheal Cornw'l 2 C4
Treoes V/Glam 58 D2
Treopert = Granston Pembs 91 E7
Treorchy = Treorci Rh Cyn Taff 77 F7
Treorci = Treorchy Rh Cyn Taff 77 F7
Treowen Caerph 78 F2
Treowen Powys 130 E2
Trequite Cornw'l 10 F6
Trerank Moor Cornw'l 5 D9
Tre'r-ddol Ceredig'n 128 E3
Trerhyngyll V/Glam 58 D4
Trerose Cornw'l 3 D7
Trerulefoot Cornw'l 6 D6
Tresaith Ceredig'n 110 G5
Tresawle Cornw'l 5 F7
Tresawsen Cornw'l 4 F5
Trescott Staffs 132 D6
Trescowe Cornw'l 2 C3
Tresean Cornw'l 4 D5
Tresevern Croft Cornw'l 2 B6
Tresham S Glos 80 G3
Tresillian Cornw'l 5 F7
Treskillard Cornw'l 2 B5
Treskinnick Cross Cornw'l 11 B10
Tresmeer Cornw'l 11 D10
Tresowes Green Cornw'l 2 D3
Tresoweshill Cornw'l 2 D3
Tresparrett Cornw'l 11 C8
Tresparrett Posts Cornw'l 11 C8
Trespeane Cornw'l 11 E10
Tressady H'land 309 J7
Tressait Perth/Kinr 291 G10
Tressinney Cornw'l 11 E8
Tresta Shetl'd 314 D8
Tresta Shetl'd 315 H5
Treswell Notts 188 F3
Treswithian Cornw'l 4 G2
Treswithian Downs Cornw'l 4 G2
Trethevy Cornw'l 11 D7
Trethewey Cornw'l 1 E3
Trethomas Caerph 59 B7
Trethosa Cornw'l 5 E8
Trethowel Cornw'l 5 E10

Trethurgy Cornw'l 5 D10
Tretio Pembs 90 F5
Tretire Heref'd 97 G10
Tretower Powys 96 G3
Treuddyn Flints 166 D3
Trevadlock Cornw'l 11 F11
Trevalga Cornw'l 11 C7
Trevalyn Wrex 166 D5
Trevance Cornw'l 10 G4
Trevanger Cornw'l 10 F5
Trevanson Cornw'l 10 G5
Trevarrack Cornw'l 1 C5
Trevarren Cornw'l 5 C8
Trevarrian Cornw'l 5 B7
Trevarrick Cornw'l 5 G9
Trevarth Cornw'l 4 G4
Trevaughan Carms 73 B11
Trevaughan Carms 93 G8
Treveal Cornw'l 4 D5
Treveddw Monmouths 96 G6
Treveighan Cornw'l 11 F7
Trevellas Cornw'l 4 E4
Trevemper Cornw'l 4 D6
Treverbyn Cornw'l 5 D10
Treverbyn Cornw'l 6 B4
Treverva Cornw'l 3 C7
Trevescan Cornw'l 1 E3
Trevethan Cornw'l 4 G4
Trevethin Torf 78 E3
Trevia Cornw'l 11 E7
Trevigro Cornw'l 12 G2
Trevilla Cornw'l 3 B8
Trevillian Cornw'l 11 C9
Trevilson Cornw'l 4 D6
Trevine = Trefin Pembs 90 E6
Treviscoe Cornw'l 5 D8
Treviscoe Barton Cornw'l 5 D8
Trevithal Cornw'l 1 D5
Trevivian Cornw'l 11 D9
Trevoll Cornw'l 4 D6
Trevone Cornw'l 10 F3
Trevor Wrex 166 G3
Trevor Gardens E Sussex 37 F7
Trevor Uchaf Denbs 166 G2
Trevowah Cornw'l 4 D5
Trew Cornw'l 2 D4
Trewalder Cornw'l 11 E7
Trewarlett Cornw'l 12 E2
Trewarmett Cornw'l 11 D7
Trewassa Cornw'l 11 D8
Treween Cornw'l 11 E10
Trewellard Cornw'l 1 C3
Trewen Cornw'l 11 E11
Trewennack Cornw'l 2 D5
Tre-wern Powys 148 D2
Trewern Powys 114 F4
Trewern Powys 148 G5
Trewetha Cornw'l 10 E6
Trewethern Cornw'l 10 F6
Trewidland Cornw'l 6 D5
Trewint Cornw'l 11 B9
Trewint Cornw'l 11 E10
Trewint Cornw'l 6 C5
Trewithian Cornw'l 3 B9
Trewoodloe Cornw'l 12 G2
Trewoofe Cornw'l 1 D4
Trewoon Cornw'l 5 E9
Treworga Cornw'l 5 G7
Treworlas Cornw'l 3 B9
Treworthal Cornw'l 3 B9
Tre-wyn Monmouths 96 G6
Treyarnon Cornw'l 10 G3
Treyford W Sussex 34 D4
Triangle Staffs 133 B10
Triangle W Yorks 196 C4
Trickett's Cross Dorset 31 G9
Tricombe Devon 15 B10
Trill Devon 15 B11
Trimdon Durham 234 E3
Trimdon Colliery Durham 234 D3
Trimdon Grange Durham 234 D3
Trimingham Norfolk 160 B5
Trimley Lower Street Suffolk 108 D5
Trimley St. Martin Suffolk 108 D5
Trimley St. Mary Suffolk 108 D5
Trimpley Worcs 116 B5
Trims Green Herts 87 B7
Trimsaran Carms 74 E7
Trimstone Devon 40 E3
Trinafour Perth/Kinr 291 G9
Trinant Caerph 78 F2
Tring Herts 84 C6
Tring Wharf Herts 84 C6
Tringford Herts 84 C6
Trinity Angus 293 G8
Trinity C/Edinb 280 F4
Trinity Devon 27 F7
Trinity Fields Staffs 151 D8
Trisant Ceredig'n 112 B4
Triscombe Som'set 43 F7
Trislaig H'land 290 F2
Trispen Cornw'l 4 E6
Tritlington Northum 252 E6
Troan Cornw'l 5 D7
Trochry Perth/Kinr 286 C3
Trodigal Arg/Bute 255 E7
Troedrhiwdalar Powys 113 G9
Troedrhiwfuwch Caerph 77 E10
Troedrhiwgwair Bl Gwent 77 D11
Troedyraur Ceredig'n 92 B6
Troed-y-rhiw Ceredig'n 111 G10
Troedyrhiw Merth Tyd 77 E9
Trofarth Conwy 180 G5
Trolway Heref'd 97 G9
Tromode I/Man 192 E4
Trondavoe Shetl'd 314 F5
Troon Cornw'l 2 B5
Troon S Ayrs 257 C8
Trosaraidh W Isles 297 K3
Trossachs Hotel Stirl 285 G9
Troston Suffolk 125 C8
Trostre Carms 75 F8
Trostrey Common Monmouths 78 E5
Troswell Cornw'l 11 C11
Trotten Marsh W Sussex 34 B4
Trottiscliffe Kent 68 G6
Trotton W Sussex 34 C4
Trough Gate Lancs 195 C11
Troutbeck Cumb 221 E8
Troutbeck Cumb 230 F3
Troutbeck Bridge Cumb 221 E7
Trow Devon 15 D9
Trow Green Glos 79 D9
Troway Derby 186 F5
Trowbridge Card 59 C8
Trowbridge Wilts 45 B10
Trowell Notts 153 B9
Trowle Common Wilts 45 B10
Trowley Bottom Herts 85 C9
Trowse Newton Norfolk 142 B4
Troy W Yorks 205 F10
Troy Town Kent 52 D2
Troydale W Yorks 205 G10
Trub Gtr Man 195 F11
Trubshaw Staffs 168 D5
Trudoxhill Som'set 45 E9
True Streek Devon 8 C6
Trueman's Heath Worcs 117 B11
Trull Som'set 28 C2
Trumaisgearraidh W Isles 296 D4
Trumfleet S Yorks 198 E6
Trumpan H'land 298 C2
Trumpet Heref'd 98 D3
Trumpington Cambs 123 F8
Trumps Green Surrey 66 F4
Trunch Norfolk 160 C5
Trunnah Lancs 202 E2
Truro Cornw'l 4 G6
Truro Cathedral Cornw'l 4 G6
Truscott Cornw'l 12 D2
Trusham Devon 14 E3
Trusley Derby 152 B5
Trusthorpe Lincs 191 E8
Truthwall Cornw'l 2 C2
Tryfil Angl 178 E6
Trysull Staffs 133 E7
Trythogga Cornw'l 1 C5
Tubney Oxon 82 F6
Tuckenhay Devon 8 D6
Tuckermarsh Devon 7 B8
Tuckhill Staffs 132 F5
Tuckingmill Cornw'l 11 C10
Tuckingmill Cornw'l 4 G3
Tuckingmill Wilts 30 B6
Tuckton Bournem'th 19 C8
Tuddenham Suffolk 124 C4
Tuddenham St. Martin Suffolk 108 B3
Tudeley Kent 52 D6
Tudeley Hale Kent 52 D6
Tudhoe Durham 233 D11
Tudhoe Grange Durham 233 E11
Tudor Hill W Midlands 134 D2
Tudorville Heref'd 97 G11
Tudweiliog Gwyn 144 B4
Tuebrook Mersey 182 C5
Tuffley Glos 80 B4
Tufnell Park London 67 B9
Tufton Hants 48 D3
Tufton Pembs 91 F10
Tugby Leics 136 C5
Tugford Shrops 131 F11
Tughall Northum 264 D6
Tulchan Lodge Angus 292 F3
Tullibardine Perth/Kinr 286 F3
Tullibody Clack 279 B7
Tullich Arg/Bute 284 F4
Tullich H'land 299 E9
Tullich H'land 300 G6
Tullich Muir H'land 301 B7
Tullie House Museum, Carlisle Cumb 239 F9
Tulliemet Perth/Kinr 286 B3
Tulloch Aberds 293 F9
Tulloch Aberds 303 F8
Tulloch H'land 290 E5
Tulloch Perth/Kinr 286 E4
Tulloch Castle H'land 300 C5
Tulloch-gribban H'land 301 G9
Tullochgorm Arg/Bute 275 D10
Tullochroisk Perth/Kinr 285 B11
Tullochvenus Aberds 293 C7
Tulloes Angus 287 C9
Tullybannocher Perth/Kinr 285 E11
Tullybelton Perth/Kinr 286 D4
Tullyfergus Perth/Kinr 286 C6
Tullymurdoch Perth/Kinr 286 B5
Tullynessle Aberds 293 B7
Tulse Hill London 67 E10
Tumble = Y Tymbl Carms 75 C8
Tumblers Green Essex 106 F6
Tumby Lincs 174 C2
Tumby Woodside Lincs 174 D3
Tummel Bridge Perth/Kinr 285 B11
Tumpy Green Glos 80 E2
Tunbridge Wells Kent 52 F5
Tunbridge Wells = Royal Tunbridge Wells Kent 52 F5
Tunga W Isles 304 E6
Tungate Norfolk 160 D5
Tunley Bath/NE Som'set 45 B7
Tunnel End W Yorks 196 E4
Tunnel Hill Worcs 98 C6
Tunshill Gtr Man 196 E2
Tunstall E Yorks 209 G12
Tunstall Kent 70 G2
Tunstall Lancs 212 E2
Tunstall Norfolk 143 B8
Tunstall N Yorks 224 F4
Tunstall N Yorks 225 C10
Tunstall Suffolk 127 F7
Tunstall Stoke 168 E5
Tunstall Tyne/Wear 243 G9
Tunstall Hills Tyne/Wear 243 G9
Tunstead Gtr Man 196 G4
Tunstead Norfolk 160 E5
Tunstead Milton Derby 185 E8
Tunworth Hants 49 D7
Tupsley Heref'd 97 C10
Tupton Derby 170 B5
Tur Langton Leics 136 E4
Turf Hill Gtr Man 196 E2
Turfdown Cornw'l 5 B11
Turfholm S Lanarks 259 B8
Turfmoor Devon 28 G3
Turgis Green Hants 49 B8
Turin Angus 287 B9
Turkdean Glos 81 B10
Turkey Island Hants 33 E9
Turkey Island W Sussex 34 D3
Turleigh Wilts 61 G10
Turleygreen Shrops 132 F5
Turlin Moor Poole 18 C5
Turmer Hants 31 F10
Turn Lancs 195 D10
Turnalt Arg/Bute 275 C9
Turnant Heref'd 96 F6
Turnastone Heref'd 97 D7
Turnberry S Ayrs 244 B6
Turnchapel Plym'th 7 E9
Turnditch Derby 170 F3
Turner Green Lancs 203 G8
Turnerheath Ches 184 F6
Turner's Green E Sussex 37 D10
Turner's Green Warwick 118 D3
Turner's Green W Berks 64 F4
Turners Hill W Sussex 51 F10
Turners Puddle Dorset 18 C2
Turner's Tump Glos 79 B10
Turnford Herts 86 E5
Turnhouse C/Edinb 280 G3
Turnhurst Stoke 168 E5
Turnworth Dorset 30 F4
Turrerich Perth/Kinr 286 D2
Turriff Aberds 303 D7
Tursdale Durham 234 D2
Turton Bottoms Blackb'n 195 D8
Turves Green W Midlands 117 B10
Turvey Beds 121 G8
Turville Bucks 84 G3
Turweston Bucks 102 D2
Tushielaw Scot Borders 261 F8
Tutbury Staffs 152 D4
Tutnall Worcs 117 C9
Tutnalls Glos 79 E10
Tutshill Glos 79 F8
Tutt Hill Kent 54 D3
Tuttington Norfolk 160 D4
Tutts Clump W Berks 64 E5
Tutwell Cornw'l 12 F3
Tuxford Notts 188 G2
Twatt Orkney 312 F3
Twatt Shetl'd 315 H5
Twechar E Dunb 278 F4
Tweedmouth Northum 273 E9
Tweedsmuir Scot Borders 260 E3
Tweenaways Torbay 9 D7
Twelve Oaks E Sussex 37 C11
Twelveheads Cornw'l 4 G5
Twemlow Green Ches 168 B3
Twenty Lincs 156 E3
Twerton Bath/NE Som'set 61 G8
Twickenham London 66 E6
Twickenham Stadium London 67 E7
Twig Side Bucks 84 G3
Twigworth Glos 98 G6
Twineham W Sussex 36 D3
Twineham Green W Sussex 36 C3
Twinhoe Bath/NE Som'set 45 B8
Twinstead Essex 107 D7
Twinstead Green Essex 107 D7
Twiss Green Warrington 183 B11
Twiston Lancs 204 E2
Twitchen Devon 41 G9
Twitchen Shrops 115 B7
Twitham Kent 55 B9
Twitton Kent 52 B4
Two Bridges Devon 13 G9
Two Burrows Cornw'l 4 F4
Two Dales Derby 170 C3
Two Gates Staffs 134 C4
Two Mile Ash M/Keynes 102 D6
Two Mile Oak Cross Devon 8 B6
Two Mills Ches 182 G5
Two Waters Herts 85 D9
Twycross Leics 134 C6
Twycross Zoo, Ashby-de-la-Zouch Leics 134 B6
Twydall Medway 69 F9
Twyford Bucks 102 F3
Twyford Dorset 30 D5
Twyford Hants 33 C7
Twyford Leics 154 G4
Twyford Lincs 155 E8
Twyford Norfolk 159 E10
Twyford Oxon 101 D9
Twyford Staffs 152 D6
Twyford Wokingham 65 D9
Twyford Common Heref'd 97 D10
Twyn Allws Monmouths 78 C3
Twyn Shon-Ifan Caerph 77 G11
Twynersh Surrey 66 F4
Twyn-gwyn Torf 78 E3
Twynholm Dumf/Gal 237 D8
Twyning Glos 99 D7
Twyning Green Glos 99 D8
Twynllanan Carms 94 G5
Twynmynydd Carms 75 C11
Twynrodyn Merth Tyd 77 D9
Twyn-yr-odyn V/Glam 58 E6
Twyn-y-Sheriff Monmouths 78 D6
Twywell Northants 121 B9
Tyberton Heref'd 97 D7
Tyburn W Midlands 134 E2
Tyby Norfolk 159 D11
Ty-coch Torf 78 G3
Tycroes Carms 75 C10
Tycrwyn Powys 148 F2
Tydd Gote Lincs 157 F9
Tydd St. Giles Cambs 157 F8
Tydd St. Mary Lincs 157 F8
Tyddewi = St. David's Pembs 90 F5
Tyddyn Powys 129 F9
Tyddyn Dai Angl 178 C6
Tyddyn Llewely Gwyn 145 C7
Tyddyn Sieffre Gwyn 146 G2
Tye Hants 34 G2
Tye Common Essex 87 G11
Tye Green Essex 87 D7
Tye Green Essex 105 G10
Tye Green Essex 105 D11
Tye Green Essex 87 C10
Tye Green Essex 106 G5
Tyes Cross E Sussex 51 G11
Ty-hen Carms 92 G6
Tŷ-gwyn Powys 148 E5
Tyldesley Gtr Man 195 G7
Tyler Hill Kent 70 G6
Tylers Causeway Herts 86 D3
Tyler's Green Bucks 84 G6
Tyler's Green Essex 87 D8
Tyler's Green Surrey 51 C10
Tyllwyd Ceredig'n 92 B5
Tylorstown Rh Cyn Taff 77 F8
Tylwch Powys 129 G9
Ty-Mawr Carms 93 C10
Ty-mawr Denbs 181 F7
Ty-mawr Angl 179 D7
Ty'n Coed Angl 179 E8
Ty-nant Conwy 165 G7
Ty-nant Denbs 165 F9
Tynant Rh Cyn Taff 58 B5
Tyndrum Stirl 285 D7
Tyne Dock Tyne/Wear 243 D9
Tyne Tunnel Tyne/Wear 243 D8
Tyneham Dorset 18 E3
Tynehead Midloth 271 D7
Tynemouth Tyne/Wear 243 D9
Tynewydd Rh Cyn Taff 76 F6
Tyning Bath/NE Som'set 45 B7
Tyninghame E Loth 282 F2
Tyn-lôn Gwyn 163 D7
Tynron Dumf/Gal 247 E8
Tyntesfield N Som'set 60 E4
Tyntetown Rh Cyn Taff 77 F9
Ty'n-y-bryn Rh Cyn Taff 58 B4
Ty'n-y-ffridd Powys 148 C2
Ty'n-y-garn Bridg 57 E11
Tynygongl Angl 179 E8
Tynygraig Ceredig'n 112 D3
Ty'n-y-graig Powys 95 B10
Ty'n-y-groes Conwy 180 G3
Ty'n-y-maes Gwyn 163 C10
Ty'n-y-maes Powys 148 D2
Tyn-y-Pistyll Conwy 165 F7
Ty'n-yr-eithin Ceredig'n 112 E3
Tyn-y-Rhos Shrops 148 B5
Tynywain Powys 114 D3
Tyrie Aberds 303 C9
Tyringham M/Keynes 103 B7
Tyrrell's Wood Surrey 51 B7
Tyseley W Midlands 134 G2
Ty-Sign Caerph 78 G2
Tythe Luton 103 G10
Tythecott Devon 24 D6
Tythegston Bridg 57 F11
Tytherington Ches 184 F6
Tytherington S Glos 61 B7
Tytherington Som'set 45 D9
Tytherington Wilts 46 E2
Tytherleigh Devon 28 G4
Tyttenhanger Herts 85 D11
Tywardreath Cornw'l 5 E11
Tywardreath Highway Cornw'l 5 D11
Tywyn Conwy 180 F3
Tywyn Gwyn 110 C2

U

Uachdar W Isles 296 F3
Uags H'land 295 B9
Ubberley Stoke 168 F6
Ubbeston Green Suffolk 126 C6
Ubley Bath/NE Som'set 44 B4
Uckerby N Yorks 224 E4
Uckfield E Sussex 37 C7
Uckinghall Worcs 99 D7
Uckington Glos 99 F8
Uddingston S Lanarks 268 C3
Uddington S Lanarks 259 C9
Udimore E Sussex 38 D5
Udley N Som'set 60 G3
Udny Green Aberds 303 G8
Udny Station Aberds 303 G9
Udston S Lanarks 268 D3
Udstonhead S Lanarks 268 F4
Uffcott Wilts 62 D6
Uffculme Devon 27 E9
Uffington Lincs 137 B11
Uffington Oxon 63 B10
Uffington Shrops 149 G10
Ufford Peterbro 137 C11
Ufford Suffolk 126 G5
Ufton Warwick 119 E7
Ufton Green W Berks 64 F6
Ufton Nervet W Berks 64 F6
Ugadale Arg/Bute 255 E8
Ugborough Devon 8 D3
Ugford Wilts 46 G5
Uggeshall Suffolk 143 G8
Ugglebarnby N Yorks 227 D7
Ughill S Yorks 186 B3
Ugley Essex 105 F10
Ugley Green Essex 105 F10
Ugthorpe N Yorks 226 C5
Uidh W Isles 297 M2
Uig Arg/Bute 288 D3
Uig Arg/Bute 276 E2
Uig H'land 296 F7
Uig H'land 298 C3
Uigen W Isles 304 E2
Uigshader H'land 298 E4
Uisken Arg/Bute 288 H5
Ulaw Aberds 303 G9
Ulbster H'land 310 E7
Ulcat Row Cumb 230 G4
Ulceby Lincs 190 G6
Ulceby N Lincs 200 E6
Ulceby Skitter N Lincs 200 D6
Ulcombe Kent 53 D10
Uldale Cumb 229 D10
Uley Glos 80 F3
Ulgham Northum 252 E6
Ullapool H'land 307 K6
Ullcombe Devon 28 F2
Ullenhall Warwick 118 D2
Ullenwood Glos 80 B6
Ulleskelf N Yorks 206 F6
Ullesthorpe Leics 135 G10
Ulley S Yorks 187 D7
Ullingswick Heref'd 97 B11
Ullinish H'land 294 B5
Ullock Cumb 229 G7
Ullock Cumb 229 G10
Ulnes Walton Lancs 194 D4
Ulpha Cumb 220 G3
Ulrome ER Yorks 209 B9
Ulsta Shetl'd 314 E6
Ulting Essex 88 D4
Ulva House Arg/Bute 288 F6
Ulverley Green W Midlands 134 G2
Ulverston Cumb 210 D5
Ulwell Dorset 18 E6
Umberleigh Devon 25 C10
Unapool H'land 306 F7
Unasary W Isles 297 J3
Uncleby ER Yorks 208 B2
Under Tofts S Yorks 186 D4
Underbarrow Cumb 221 G9
Undercliffe W Yorks 205 G9
Underdale Shrops 149 G10
Underdown Devon 13 C10
Underhill London 86 F3
Underhoull Shetl'd 314 C7
Underling Green Kent 53 D9
Underriver Kent 52 C5
Underwood Newp 59 B11
Underwood Notts 171 E7
Underwood Plym'th 7 D10
Undley Suffolk 140 G3
Undy Monmouths 60 B2
Ungisiadar W Isles 304 F3
Unifirth Shetl'd 315 H4
Union Cottage Aberds 293 D10
Union Mills I/Man 192 E4
Union Street E Sussex 53 G8
University Museum, Oxford Oxon 83 D8
Unst Airport Shetl'd 314 C8
Unstone Derby 186 F5
Unstone Green Derby 186 F5
Unsworth Gtr Man 195 F10
Unthank Cumb 230 D4
Unthank Cumb 230 B3
Unthank Cumb 231 C8
Unthank Derby 186 F4
Unthank End Cumb 230 D5
Up Cerne Dorset 29 G11
Up End M/Keynes 103 B8
Up Exe Devon 26 G6
Up Exe Devon 26 G6
Up Green Hants 65 G9
Up Hatherley Glos 99 G8
Up Holland Lancs 194 G4
Up Marden W Sussex 34 E3
Up Mudford Som'set 29 D9
Up Nately Hants 49 C7
Up Somborne Hants 47 G11
Up Sydling Dorset 29 G10
Upavon Wilts 46 C7
Upchurch Kent 69 F10
Upcott Devon 25 F9
Upcott Heref'd 114 G6
Upcott Som'set 26 B6
Upcott Som'set 27 C11
Upend Cambs 124 F3
Upgate Norfolk 160 F2
Upgate Street Norfolk 141 E11
Upgate Street Norfolk 142 E5
Uphall Dorset 29 G9
Uphall W Loth 279 G11
Uphall Station W Loth 279 G11
Upham Devon 26 F5
Upham Hants 33 C8
Uphampton Heref'd 115 E8
Uphampton Worcs 116 E6
Uphempston Devon 8 C6
Uphill N Som'set 43 B10
Uplands Glos 80 D5
Uplands Swan 75 G10
Uplawmoor E Renf 267 D8
Upleadon Glos 98 F5
Upleatham Redcar/Clevel'd 226 B2
Uplees Kent 70 G3
Uploders Dorset 16 B6
Uplowman Devon 27 D8
Uplyms Devon 16 C2
Upminister London 68 B5
Upottery Devon 28 F2
Uppark, Petersfield Hants 34 D3
Uppat H'land 311 J2
Upper Affcot Shrops 131 F8
Upper Ardchronie H'land 309 L6
Upper Ardgrain Aberds 303 F9
Upper Ardroscadale Arg/Bute 275 G11
Upper Arley Worcs 132 G5
Upper Armley W Yorks 205 G11
Upper Arncott Oxon 83 B10
Upper Astley Shrops 149 F10
Upper Astrop Northants 101 D10
Upper Badcall H'land 306 E6
Upper Bangor Gwyn 179 G9
Upper Basildon W Berks 64 D5
Upper Batley W Yorks 197 B8
Upper Battlefield Shrops 149 F10
Upper Beeding W Sussex 35 E11
Upper Benefield Northants 137 F9
Upper Bentley Worcs 117 D9
Upper Bighouse H'land 310 D2
Upper Birchwood Derby 170 E6
Upper Boat Rh Cyn Taff 58 B6
Upper Boddam Aberds 302 F6
Upper Boddington Northants 119 G9
Upper Bogrow H'land 309 L7
Upper Bogside Moray 302 D2
Upper Borth Ceredig'n 128 F2
Upper Boyndlie Aberds 303 C9
Upper Brailes Warwick 100 D6
Upper Breakish H'land 295 C8
Upper Breinton Heref'd 97 C9
Upper Broadheath Worcs 116 F6
Upper Broughton Notts 154 D3
Upper Broxwood Heref'd 115 G7
Upper Brynamman Carms 76 C2
Upper Buckenhill Heref'd 97 E11
Upper Bucklebury W Berks 64 F4
Upper Burgate Hants 31 D10
Upper Burnhaugh Aberds 293 D10
Upper Caldecote Beds 104 B3
Upper Canada N Som'set 43 B11
Upper Canterton Hants 32 E3
Upper Catesby Northants 119 F10
Upper Catshill Worcs 117 C9
Upper Chapel Powys 95 C10
Upper Cheddon Som'set 28 B2
Upper Chicksgrove Wilts 31 B7
Upper Church Village Rh Cyn Taff 58 B5
Upper Chute Wilts 47 B9
Upper Clapton London 67 B10
Upper Clatford Hants 47 E11
Upper Coberley Glos 81 B7
Upper Cokeham W Sussex 35 F11
Upper Colwall Heref'd 98 C5
Upper Common Hants 48 D6
Upper Cotburn Aberds 303 D7
Upper Cotton Staffs 169 F9
Upper Coullie Aberds 293 B9
Upper Cound Shrops 131 C10
Upper Cudworth S Yorks 197 G11
Upper Culphin Aberds 302 D6
Upper Cumberworth W Yorks 197 F8
Upper Cwmbran Torf 78 F3
Upper Dallachy Moray 302 C3
Upper Deal Kent 55 C10
Upper Dean Beds 121 D10
Upper Denby W Yorks 197 F8
Upper Denton Cumb 240 D4
Upper Derraid H'land 301 F10
Upper Diabaig H'land 299 C8
Upper Dicker E Sussex 37 E9
Upper Dounreay H'land 310 C4
Upper Dovercourt Essex 108 E4
Upper Druimfin Arg/Bute 289 D7
Upper Dunsforth N Yorks 215 G8
Upper Eashing Surrey 50 E3
Upper Eastwood W Yorks 196 B3
Upper Eathie H'land 301 C7
Upper Edmonton London 86 G4
Upper Egleton Heref'd 98 B2
Upper Elkstone Staffs 169 D9
Upper Ellastone Staffs 169 G10
Upper Elmers End London 67 F11
Upper End Derby 185 F9
Upper End Glos 81 C10
Upper End Leics 154 G4
Upper Enham Hants 47 D11
Upper Farringdon Hants 49 F8
Upper Feorlig H'land 298 E2
Upper Fivehead Som'set 28 C4
Upper Framilode Glos 80 C2
Upper Froyle Hants 49 E9
Upper Gills H'land 310 B7
Upper Glenfintaig H'land 290 E4
Upper Godney Som'set 44 E3
Upper Goldstone Kent 71 G9
Upper Gornal W Midlands 133 E8
Upper Gravenhurst Beds 104 D2
Upper Green Essex 105 E8
Upper Green Monmouths 78 B5
Upper Green Suffolk 124 E4
Upper Green W Berks 63 G11
Upper Green W Yorks 197 B9
Upper Grove Common Heref'd 97 F11
Upper Guist Norfolk 159 D10
Upper Hackney Derby 170 C3
Upper Hale Surrey 49 D10
Upper Halistra H'land 298 D2
Upper Halliford Surrey 66 F5
Upper Halling Medway 69 G7
Upper Ham Worcs 99 D7
Upper Ham Worcs 99 B7
Upper Hambleton Rutl'd 137 B8
Upper Harbledown Kent 54 B6
Upper Hartfield E Sussex 52 G3
Upper Hartshay Derby 170 E5
Upper Haugh S Yorks 186 C6
Upper Hawkhillock Aberds 303 F10
Upper Haysden Kent 52 E5
Upper Hayton Shrops 131 G10
Upper Heaton W Yorks 197 D7
Upper Hellesdon Norfolk 160 G4
Upper Helmsley N Yorks 207 B9
Upper Hengoed Shrops 148 C5
Upper Hergest Heref'd 114 G5
Upper Heyford Northants 120 F3
Upper Heyford Oxon 101 F9
Upper Hiendley W Yorks 197 E11
Upper Hill Heref'd 115 G9
Upper Hill S Glos 79 F11
Upper Holloway London 67 B9
Upper Holton Suffolk 127 B8
Upper Hopton W Yorks 197 D7
Upper Horsebridge E Sussex 37 E9
Upper Howsell Worcs 98 B5
Upper Hoyland S Yorks 197 G11
Upper Hulme Staffs 169 C8
Upper Ifield Kent 69 E7
Upper Ifold Surrey 50 G4
Upper Inglesham Swindon 82 F2
Upper Inverbrough H'land 301 F8
Upper Kergord Shetl'd 315 H6
Upper Kilcott Glos 61 B9
Upper Killay Swan 75 G9
Upper Killeyan Arg/Bute 254 C3
Upper Kinsham Heref'd 115 D7
Upper Kirton N Ayrs 266 D3
Upper Knockando Moray 301 E11
Upper Lambourn W Berks 63 C10
Upper Landywood Staffs 133 B9
Upper Langford N Som'set 44 B3
Upper Leigh Staffs 151 B10
Upper Lenie H'land 300 G5
Upper Ley Glos 80 B2
Upper Littleton N Som'set 60 G5
Upper Llanover Monmouths 78 D4
Upper Lochton Aberds 293 D8
Upper Longdon Staffs 151 G11
Upper Longwood Shrops 132 B2
Upper Lybster H'land 310 F6
Upper Lydbrook Glos 79 B10
Upper Maes-coed Heref'd 96 E6
Upper Marsh W Yorks 204 F6
Upper Midhope S Yorks 186 B2
Upper Midway Derby 152 E5
Upper Milovaig H'land 297 G7
Upper Milton Oxon 82 B3
Upper Milton Som'set 44 D4
Upper Minety Wilts 81 G8
Upper Moor Worcs 99 B9
Upper Moor Side W Yorks 205 G10
Upper Morton S Glos 79 G11
Upper Nash Pembs 73 E8
Upper Newbold Derby 186 G5
Upper Nobut Staffs 151 B10
Upper North Dean Bucks 84 F5
Upper Norwood London 67 E10
Upper Norwood W Sussex 34 D6
Upper Obney Perth/Kinr 286 D4
Upper Oddington Glos 100 F4
Upper Ollach H'land 295 B7
Upper Outwoods Staffs 152 D4
Upper Padley Derby 186 F2
Upper Pennington Hants 20 B2
Upper Pollicott Bucks 84 C2
Upper Poppleton C/York 207 C7
Upper Port H'land 301 G10
Upper Quinton Warwick 100 B3
Upper Race Torf 78 F3
Upper Ratley Hants 32 C4
Upper Ridinghill Aberds 303 D10
Upper Rochford Worcs 116 D2
Upper Sandaig H'land 295 D9
Upper Sanday Orkney 313 H6
Upper Sapey Heref'd 116 E3
Upper Saxondale Notts 154 B3
Upper Seagry Wilts 62 C2
Upper Shelton Beds 103 C9
Upper Sheringham Norfolk 177 E10
Upper Shirley London 67 F11
Upper Shirley S'thampton 32 E6
Upper Shuckburgh Warwick 119 E9
Upper Siddington Glos 81 F8
Upper Skelmorlie N Ayrs 266 B3
Upper Slackstead Hants 32 B5
Upper Slaughter Glos 100 G3
Upper Soudley Glos 79 C11
Upper Spond Heref'd 114 G6
Upper Stanton Drew Bath/NE Som'set 60 G6
Upper Stoke Norfolk 142 C4
Upper Stoke W Midlands 119 B7
Upper Stondon Beds 104 D3
Upper Stonnall Staffs 133 C11
Upper Stowe Northants 120 F2
Upper Stratton Swindon 63 B7
Upper Street Hants 31 D10
Upper Street Norfolk 126 B3
Upper Street Norfolk 160 E7
Upper Street Norfolk 160 F6
Upper Street Norfolk 161 F7
Upper Street Suffolk 108 D2
Upper Street Suffolk 124 G5
Upper Street Suffolk 126 F2
Upper Strensham Worcs 99 D8
Upper Studley Wilts 45 B10
Upper Sundon Beds 103 F10
Upper Swell Glos 100 F3
Upper Sydenham London 67 E10
Upper Tean Staffs 151 B10
Upper Threapwood Ches 166 F6
Upper Thurnham Lancs 202 C5
Upper Tillyrie Perth/Kinr 286 G5
Upper Tooting London 67 E9
Upper Tote H'land 298 D5
Upper Town Derby 170 E2
Upper Town Durham 233 D7
Upper Town Heref'd 97 B11
Upper Town N Som'set 60 F4
Upper Town Suffolk 125 D8
Upper Town Wilts 62 D3
Upper Town W Yorks 204 G6
Upper Treverward Shrops 114 B5
Upper Tysoe Warwick 100 C6
Upper Upham Wilts 63 D8
Upper Upnor Medway 69 E9
Upper Vobster Som'set 45 D8
Upper Walthamstow London 67 B11
Upper Wardington Oxon 101 B9
Upper Waterhay Wilts 81 G9
Upper Weald M/Keynes 102 D5
Upper Weedon Northants 120 F2
Upper Welland Worcs 98 C5
Upper Wellingham E Sussex 36 E6
Upper Welson Heref'd 114 G5
Upper Weston Bath/NE Som'set 61 F8
Upper Weybread Suffolk 126 B4
Upper Whiston S Yorks 187 D7
Upper Wick Glos 80 F2
Upper Wick Worcs 116 G6
Upper Wield Hants 48 F6
Upper Wilcove Cornw'l 7 D8
Upper Winchendon Bucks 84 C2
Upper Witton W Midlands 133 E11
Upper Wolvercote Oxon 83 C7
Upper Woodend Aberds 293 B8
Upper Woodford Wilts 46 F6
Upper Woolhampton W Berks 64 F5
Upper Wootton Hants 48 C5
Upper Wraxhall S Glos 61 E10
Upper Wyche Worcs 98 C5
Upperby Cumb 239 G10
Uppermill Gtr Man 196 F3
Uppersound Shetl'd 315 J6
Upperthong W Yorks 196 F6
Upperthorpe Derby 187 E7
Upperthorpe N Lincs 199 G9
Upperton E Sussex 23 E10
Upperton W Sussex 35 C7
Uppertown Derby 170 B4
Uppertown H'land 300 F4
Uppertown H'land 310 B7
Uppertown Northum 241 C9
Uppertown Orkney 313 J5
Uppincott Devon 26 G5
Uppingham Rutl'd 137 D7
Uppington Dorset 31 F8
Uppington Shrops 131 B11
Upsall N Yorks 215 B9
Upsettlington Scot Borders 273 F7
Upsher Green Suffolk 107 C8
Upshire Essex 86 E6
Upstreet Kent 71 G8
Upthorpe Glos 80 E3
Upthorpe Suffolk 125 C9
Upton Cambs 122 B3
Upton Ches 166 B6
Upton Cumb 230 D2
Upton Cornw'l 11 G11
Upton Cornw'l 24 G2
Upton Dorset 17 E10
Upton Dorset 18 C5
Upton Devon 8 G4
Upton Devon 27 G9
Upton ER Yorks 209 C8
Upton Hants 47 B11
Upton Hants 32 D5
Upton Halton 183 D7
Upton Kent 71 F11
Upton Leics 135 D7
Upton Lincs 188 E5
Upton London 68 C2
Upton Mersey 182 D3
Upton Norfolk 161 G7
Upton Northants 120 E4
Upton Notts 172 E2
Upton Notts 188 F2

Wellsborough Leics 135 C7
Wells-next-the-Sea Norfolk 176 E6
Wellstye Green Essex 87 B10
Wellswood Torbay 9 C8
Wellsworth Hants 34 E2
Wellwood Fife 279 D11
Welney Norfolk 139 E10
Welsford Devon 24 C3
Welsh Bicknor Heref'd 79 B9
Welsh End Shrops 149 B10
Welsh Frankton Shrops 149 C7
Welsh Highland Railway, Caernarfon Gwyn 163 C7
Welsh Highland Railway, Porthmadog Gwyn 163 H9
Welsh Hook Pembs 91 F8
Welsh National Velodrome Newp 59 B10
Welsh Newton Heref'd 79 B7
Welsh Newton Common Heref'd 79 B8
Welsh St. Donats V/Glam 58 D4
Welshampton Shrops 149 B8
Welshpool = Y Trallwng Powys 130 B4
Welstor Devon 13 G10
Welton Bath/NE Som'set 45 C7
Welton Cumb 230 C3
Welton ER Yorks 200 B3
Welton Lincs 189 F8
Welton Northants 119 D11
Welton Hill Lincs 189 E8
Welton le Marsh Lincs 175 B7
Welton le Wold Lincs 190 D3
Welwick ER Yorks 201 B10
Welwyn Herts 86 B2
Welwyn Garden City Herts 86 C3
Wem Shrops 149 D10
Wembdon Som'set 43 F9
Wembley London 67 B7
Wembley Park London 67 B7
Wembley Stadium London 67 B7
Wembury Devon 7 F10
Wembworthy Devon 25 F11
Wemyss Bay Inverci 266 B3
Wenallt Ceredig'n 112 C3
Wendens Ambo Essex 105 D10
Wendlebury Oxon 83 B9
Wendling Norfolk 159 G8
Wendover Bucks 84 D5
Wendover Dean Bucks 84 E5
Wendron Cornw'l 2 C5
Wendy Cambs 104 B6
Wenfordbridge Cornw'l 11 F7
Wenhaston Suffolk 127 B8
Wennington Cambs 122 B4
Wennington Lancs 212 E2
Wennington London 68 C4
Wensley Derby 170 C3
Wensley N Yorks 213 B11
Wentbridge W Yorks 198 D3
Wentnor Shrops 131 E7
Wentworth Cambs 123 B9
Wentworth S Yorks 186 C5
Wenvoe V/Glam 58 E6
Weobley Heref'd 115 G8
Weobley Marsh Heref'd 115 G8
Weoley Castle W Midlands 133 G10
Wepham W Sussex 35 F8
Wepre Flints 166 B3
Wereham Norfolk 140 C3
Wereton Staffs 168 E3
Wergs W Midlands 133 C7
Wern Gwyn 145 B10
Wern Powys 148 G5
Wern Powys 148 E5
Wern Shrops 148 C5
Wern Gifford Monmouths 96 G6
Wern Tarw Bridg 58 C3
Werneth Gtr Man 196 G2
Werneth Low Gtr Man 185 C7
Wernffrwd Swan 75 G8
Wern-gerhynt Powys 129 D7
Wernheolydd Monmouths 78 C4
Wern-olau Swan 75 F9
Wern-y-cwrt Monmouths 78 D5
Wern-y-gaer Flints 166 B2
Werrington Cornw'l 12 D2
Werrington Peterbro 138 C3
Werrington Staffs 168 F6
Wervin Ches 182 G6
Wescoe Cumb 230 F2
Wesham Lancs 202 G4
Wessington Derby 170 D5
West Aberthaw V/Glam 58 F4
West Acre Norfolk 158 F5
West Acton London 67 C7
West Adderbury Oxon 101 D9
West Allerdean Northum 273 F9
West Allotment Tyne/Wear 243 C8
West Alvington Devon 8 G4
West Amesbury Wilts 47 E6
West Anstey Devon 26 B4
West Appleton N Yorks 224 G4
West Ardhu Arg/Bute 288 D6
West Ardsley W Yorks 197 B9
West Ardwell Dumf/Gal 236 E2
West Arthurlie E Renf 267 D9
West Ashby Lincs 190 G3
West Ashford Devon 40 F4
West Ashling W Sussex 34 F4
West Ashton Wilts 45 B11
West Auckland Durham 233 F9
West Ayton N Yorks 217 C9
West Bagborough Som'set 43 G7
West Bank Bl Gwent 78 D2
West Bank Halton 183 E8
West Barkwith Lincs 189 E11
West Barnby N Yorks 226 C6
West Barnes London 67 F8
West Barns E Loth 282 F3
West Bay Dorset 16 C5
West Beckham Norfolk 160 B2
West Bedfont Surrey 66 E5
West Benhar N Lanarks 269 C7
West Bergholt Essex 107 F9
West Bexington Dorset 16 D6
West Bilney Norfolk 158 F4
West Blackdene Durham 232 D3
West Blatchington Brighton/Hove 36 F3
West Boldon Tyne/Wear 243 E9
West Bourton Dorset 30 B3
West Bowling W Yorks 205 G9
West Bradford Lancs 203 E10
West Bradley Som'set 44 F5
West Brasham Norfolk 159 C8
West Bretton W Yorks 197 E9
West Bridgford Notts 153 B11
West Brigg's Norfolk 158 G3
West Bromwich W Midlands 133 E10
West Buckland Devon 41 G7
West Buckland Som'set 27 C11
West Burnside Aberds 293 F8
West Burrafirth Shetl'd 315 H4
West Burton N Yorks 213 B10
West Burton W Sussex 35 E8
West Butsfield Durham 233 C8
West Butterwick N Lincs 199 F10
West Byfleet Surrey 66 G4
West Caister Norfolk 161 G10
West Calder W Loth 269 C10
West Camel Som'set 29 C9
West Carr Kingston/Hull 209 G7
West Carr N Lincs 199 F8
West Chadsmoor Staffs 151 G9
West Chaldon Dorset 17 E11
West Challow Oxon 63 B11
West Charleton Devon 8 G5
West Chelborough Dorset 29 F8
West Chevington Northum 252 D6
West Chiltington W Sussex 35 D9
West Chiltington Common W Sussex 35 D9
West Chinnock Som'set 29 E7
West Chirton Tyne/Wear 243 D8
West Chisenbury Wilts 46 C6
West Clandon Surrey 50 C4
West Cliff N Yorks 227 C7
West Cliffe Kent 55 E11
West Clyne H'land 311 J2
West Clyth H'land 310 F6
West Coker Som'set 29 E8
West Cornforth Durham 234 E2
West Common Hants 32 G6
West Compton Dorset 17 C7
West Compton Som'set 44 E5
West Cowick ER Yorks 198 C6
West Creech Dorset 18 E3
West Cross Kent 53 G10
West Cross Swan 56 D6
West Cullery Aberds 293 C9
West Curry Cornw'l 11 C11
West Curthwaite Cumb 230 B2
West Darlochan Arg/Bute 255 E7
West Dean Wilts 32 B3
West Dean W Sussex 34 E5
West Deeping Lincs 138 B2
West Dennant Pembs 72 C6
West Denton Tyne/Wear 242 D5
West Derby Mersey 182 C6
West Dereham Norfolk 140 C2
West Didsbury Gtr Man 184 C4
West Down Devon 40 E4
West Drayton London 66 D5
West Drayton Notts 188 G2
West Dulwich London 67 E10
West Ealing London 67 C7
West Ella ER Yorks 200 B4
West End Beds 121 G9
West End Beds 122 E2
West End Brackn'l 65 E11
West End Bucks 102 F3
West End Caerph 78 F2
West End Cumb 239 F8
West End Dorset 30 G6
West End ER Yorks 201 B9
West End ER Yorks 208 G4
West End ER Yorks 209 G9
West End ER Yorks 217 G11
West End ER Yorks 209 B9
West End Glos 80 F5
West End Hants 48 E6
West End Hants 33 E7
West End Hants 33 F9
West End Herts 86 D3
West End Kent 54 B2
West End Kent 71 F7
West End Lancs 195 B8
West End Lancs 211 G8
West End Leics 153 F8
West End Lincs 174 F5
West End Lincs 190 B5
West End Norfolk 141 B8
West End Norfolk 161 G9
West End Northants 102 C3
West End N Som'set 60 F3
West End N Yorks 206 E6
West End N Yorks 205 B8
West End Oxon 82 E6
West End Oxon 64 B5
West End Suffolk 143 G9
West End S Glos 61 B8
West End Som'set 28 E5
West End Som'set 29 B7
West End Som'set 45 F7
West End Som'set 44 C5
West End S Lanarks 269 F9
West End Surrey 66 G2
West End Surrey 66 G6
West End S Yorks 199 F7
West End Wilts 30 C6
West End Wilts 31 C7
West End Wilts 62 D3
West End Windsor 65 D10
West End Worcs 99 D11
West End W Sussex 36 D2
West End W Yorks 197 B7
West End W Yorks 205 F10
West End Green Hants 65 G7
West Ewell Surrey 67 G8
West Farleigh Kent 53 C8
West Farndon Northants 119 G10
West Felton Shrops 148 D6
West Fenton E Loth 281 E9
West Ferry Dundee C 287 D8
West Firle E Sussex 37 F7
West Fleetham Northum 264 D5
West Garforth W Yorks 206 G3
West Gillibrands Lancs 194 F3
West Ginge Oxon 64 B2
West Grafton Wilts 63 G8
West Green Hants 49 B8
West Green London 67 B10
West Green W Sussex 51 F9
West Greenskares Aberds 303 C7
West Grimstead Wilts 32 B2
West Grinstead W Sussex 35 C11
West Haddlesey N Yorks 198 B5
West Haddon Northants 120 C2
West Hagbourne Oxon 64 B4
West Hagley Worcs 117 B8
West Hale N Lincs 199 F8
West Hall Cumb 240 D3
West Hallam Derby 170 G6
West Halton N Lincs 200 C2
West Ham London 68 C2
West Hampstead London 67 C9
West Handley Derby 186 F5
West Hanney Oxon 82 G6
West Hanningfield Essex 88 F2
West Hardwick W Yorks 198 D2
West Harnham Wilts 31 B10
West Harptree Bath/NE Som'set 44 B5
West Harrow London 66 B6
West Harting W Sussex 34 C3
West Harton Tyne/Wear 243 E9
West Hatch Som'set 28 C3
West Hatch Wilts 30 B6
West Hay N Som'set 60 G3
West Head Norfolk 139 B11
West Heath Ches 168 C4
West Heath Hants 48 B5
West Heath Hants 49 B11
West Heath London 68 D3
West Heath W Midlands 117 B10
West Helmsdale H'land 311 H4
West Hendon London 67 B8
West Hendred Oxon 64 B2
West Herrington Tyne/Wear 243 G8
West Heslerton N Yorks 217 D8
West Hewish N Som'set 59 G11
West Hill Devon 15 C7
West Hill ER Yorks 218 F3
West Hill London 67 E8
West Hill N Som'set 60 E3
West Hill N Som'set 60 D3
West Hill Staffs 151 G9
West Hill Wilts 61 F11
West Hill W Sussex 51 G10
West Hoathly W Sussex 51 G11
West Holme Dorset 18 D3
West Holywell Tyne/Wear 243 C8
West Horndon Essex 68 B6
West Horrington Som'set 44 D5
West Horsley Surrey 50 C5
West Horton Northum 264 C2
West Hougham Kent 55 E9
West Houlland Shetl'd 315 H4
West Houses Lincs 174 E4
West Howe Bournem'th 19 B7
West Howetown Som'set 42 F2
West Huntspill Som'set 43 E10
West Hurn Dorset 19 B8
West Hyde Herts 85 G8
West Hynish Arg/Bute 288 F1
West Hythe Kent 54 G6
West Ilsley W Berks 64 C3
West Itchenor W Sussex 34 G3
West Jesmond Tyne/Wear 243 D7
West Keal Lincs 174 C5
West Kennett Wilts 62 F6
West Kilbride N Ayrs 266 F4
West Kingsdown Kent 68 G5
West Kington Wilts 61 D10
West Kington Wick Wilts 61 D10
West Kinharrachie Aberds 303 F9
West Kirby Mersey 182 D2
West Knapton N Yorks 217 D7
West Knighton Dorset 17 D10
West Knoyle Wilts 45 G11
West Kyo Durham 242 G5
West Lambrook Som'set 28 D6
West Langdon Kent 55 D10
West Langwell H'land 309 J6
West Lavington Wilts 46 C4
West Lavington W Sussex 34 C5
West Layton N Yorks 224 D2
West Lea Durham 234 B4
West Leake Notts 153 D10
West Learmouth Northum 263 B8
West Leigh Devon 25 F11
West Leigh Hants 34 F2
West Lexham Norfolk 158 F6
West Lilling N Yorks 216 F2
West Linton Scot Borders 270 E3
West Liss Hants 34 B3
West Littleton S Glos 61 D9
West Lockinge Oxon 64 B2
West Looe Cornw'l 6 E5
West Luccombe Som'set 42 D2
West Lulworth Dorset 18 E3
West Lutton N Yorks 217 F8
West Lydford Som'set 44 G5
West Lydiatt Heref'd 97 C11
West Lyn Devon 41 D8
West Lyng Som'set 28 B4
West Lynn Norfolk 158 E2
West Mains S Lanarks 268 E2
West Malling Kent 53 B7
West Malvern Worcs 98 B5
West Marden W Sussex 34 E3
West Marina E Sussex 38 F3
West Markham Notts 188 G2
West Marsh NE Lincs 201 F9
West Marton N Yorks 204 C3
West Mathers Aberds 293 G9
West Melbury Dorset 30 C5
West Melton S Yorks 198 G2
West Meon Hants 33 C10
West Meon Woodlands Hants 33 B10
West Merkland H'land 308 F3
West Mersea Essex 89 C8
West Midland Safari Park, Kidderminster Worcs 116 B6
West Mill Herts 104 E3
West Milton Dorset 16 B6
West Minster Kent 70 E2
West Molesey Surrey 66 F6
West Monkseaton Tyne/Wear 243 C8
West Monkton Som'set 28 B3
West Moor Tyne/Wear 243 C7
West Moors Dorset 31 G9
West Morden Dorset 18 B4
West Morriston Scot Borders 271 G11
West Morton W Yorks 205 E7
West Mudford Som'set 29 C9
West Muir Angus 293 G7
West Myreriggs Perth/Kinr 286 C6
West Ness N Yorks 216 D3
West Newton ER Yorks 209 F9
West Newton Norfolk 158 D3
West Newton Som'set 28 B3
West Norwood London 67 E10
West Ogwell Devon 14 G2
West Orchard Dorset 30 D4
West Overton Wilts 62 F6
West Panson Devon 12 C2
West Park Hartlep'l 234 E5
West Park Mersey 183 B7
West Park Tyne/Wear 243 D9
West Park W Yorks 205 F11
West Parley Dorset 19 B7
West Peckham Kent 52 C6
West Pelton Durham 242 G6
West Pennard Som'set 44 F4
West Pentire Cornw'l 4 C5
West Perry Cambs 122 D2
West Poringland Norfolk 142 C5
West Porlock Som'set 41 D11
West Pulham Dorset 30 F2
West Putford Devon 24 D5
West Quantoxhead Som'set 42 E6
West Rainton Durham 234 B2
West Rasen Lincs 189 D9
West Ravendale NE Lincs 190 B2
West Raynham Norfolk 159 D7
West Retford Notts 187 E11
West Rounton N Yorks 225 E8
West Row Suffolk 124 B3
West Royd W Yorks 205 F9
West Rudham Norfolk 158 D6
West Ruislip London 66 B5
West Runton Norfolk 177 E11
West Saltoun E Loth 271 B9
West Sandford Devon 26 G4
West Sandwick Shetl'd 314 E6
West Scholes W Yorks 205 G7
West Scrafton N Yorks 213 C11
West Shepton Som'set 44 E6
West Side Orkney 312 E6
West Sleekburn Northum 253 F7
West Somerset Railway, Minehead Som'set 42 E4
West Somerton Norfolk 161 F9
West Stafford Dorset 17 D10
West Stockwith Notts 188 B3
West Stoke Som'set 29 D7
West Stoke W Sussex 34 F4
West Stonesdale N Yorks 223 E7
West Stoughton Som'set 44 D2
West Stour Dorset 30 C3
West Stourmouth Kent 71 G9
West Stow Suffolk 124 C6
West Stowell Wilts 62 G6
West Strathan H'land 308 C5
West Stratton Hants 48 E4
West Street Kent 55 B10
West Street Kent 54 C2
West Street Medway 69 D8
West Street Suffolk 125 C9
West Street Suffolk 125 C10
West Tanfield N Yorks 214 D5
West Taphouse Cornw'l 6 C3
West Tarbert Arg/Bute 275 G9
West Tarring W Sussex 35 G10
West Third Scot Borders 262 B4
West Thirston Northum 252 D5
West Thorney W Sussex 34 G3
West Thurrock Thurr'k 68 D5
West Tilbury Thurr'k 69 D7
West Tisted Hants 33 B10
West Tofts Norfolk 140 E6
West Tofts Perth/Kinr 286 D5
West Tolgus Cornw'l 4 G3
West Torrington Lincs 189 E10
West Town Bath/NE Som'set 60 G4
West Town Bucks 66 C2
West Town Devon 14 B3
West Town Devon 24 C4
West Town Hants 22 D2
West Town Heref'd 115 E8
West Town N Som'set 60 F3
West Town Som'set 44 F4
West Town W Sussex 36 D3
West Tytherley Hants 32 B3
West Tytherton Wilts 62 E3
West Vale W Yorks 196 C5
West View Hartlep'l 234 D5
West Village V/Glam 58 E3
West Walton Norfolk 157 G9
West Wellow Hants 32 D3
West Wembury Devon 7 F10
West Wemyss Fife 280 C6
West Wick N Som'set 59 G11
West Wickham Cambs 106 B2
West Wickham London 67 F11
West Williamston Pembs 73 D8
West Willoughby Lincs 173 G7
West Winch Norfolk 158 F2
West Winterslow Wilts 47 G8
West Wittering W Sussex 22 D3
West Witton N Yorks 213 C10
West Woodburn Northum 251 F9
West Woodhay W Berks 63 G11
West Woodlands Som'set 45 E9
West Worldham Hants 49 F8
West Worlington Devon 26 E3
West Worthing W Sussex 35 G10
West Wratting Cambs 124 G2
West Wycombe Bucks 84 G4
West Wylam Northum 242 E4
West Yatton Wilts 61 D11
West Yell Shetl'd 314 E6
West Yeo Som'set 43 G10
Westbere Kent 71 G7
Westborough Lincs 172 G5
Westbourne Bournem'th 19 C7
Westbourne Suffolk 108 B2
Westbourne W Sussex 34 F3
Westbrook Heref'd 96 C5
Westbrook Kent 71 E11
Westbrook Surrey 50 E3
Westbrook W Berks 64 E2
Westbrook Wilts 62 F3
Westbrook Warrington 183 C9
Westbrook Green Norfolk 142 G2
Westburn S Lanarks 268 C3
Westbury Bucks 102 D2
Westbury Shrops 131 B7
Westbury Wilts 45 C11
Westbury Leigh Wilts 45 C11
Westbury on Trym Bristol 60 D5
Westbury Park Bristol 60 D5
Westbury-on-Severn Glos 80 C2
Westbury-sub-Mendip Som'set 44 D4
Westby Lancs 202 G3
Westby Lincs 155 D9
Westcliff I/Wight 20 F6
Westcliff-on-Sea Southend 69 B11
Westcombe Som'set 29 B7
Westcombe Som'set 45 F7
Westcot Oxon 63 B10
Westcote Glos 100 G4
Westcott Bucks 84 B2
Westcott Devon 13 D11
Westcott Devon 27 G8
Westcott Surrey 50 D6
Westcott Barton Oxon 101 F8
Westcourt Wilts 63 G8
Westcraigs W Loth 269 B8
Westcroft M/Keynes 102 E6
Westdean E Sussex 23 F8
Westdene Brighton/Hove 36 F3
Westdowns Cornw'l 10 E7
Westend Glos 80 D3
Westend Oxon 100 G6
Westend S Glos 79 G10
Westend Town Northum 241 D7
Westend Town S Glos 61 E9
West-end-Town V/Glam 58 F3
Westenhanger Kent 54 F6
Wester Aberchalder H'land 300 G5
Wester Arboll H'land 311 L2
Wester Auchinloch N Lanarks 278 G3
Wester Auchnagallin H'land 301 F10
Wester Balgedie Perth/Kinr 286 G5
Wester Brae H'land 300 C6
Wester Craiglands H'land 301 D7
Wester Culbeuchly Aberds 302 C6
Wester Dalvoult H'land 291 B11
Wester Dechmont W Loth 279 G10
Wester Denoon Angus 287 C7
Wester Ellister Arg/Bute 254 B2
Wester Essendy Perth/Kinr 286 C5
Wester Feddal Perth/Kinr 286 G2
Wester Fintray Aberds 293 B10
Wester Galgantray H'land 301 E8
Wester Gospetry Fife 286 G5
Wester Gruinards H'land 309 K5
Wester Hailes C/Edinb 270 B4
Wester Lealty H'land 300 B6
Wester Lix Stirl 285 E9
Wester Milton H'land 301 D9
Wester Mosshead Aberds 302 F5
Wester Newburn Fife 287 G8
Wester Ord Aberds 293 C10
Wester Quarff Shetl'd 315 K6
Wester Skeld Shetl'd 315 J4
Wester Strath H'land 300 D6
Wester Watten H'land 310 D6
Westerdale H'land 310 D5
Westerdale N Yorks 226 D3
Westerfield Suffolk 108 B3
Westerfield Shetl'd 315 H5
Westerfolds Moray 301 C11
Westergate W Sussex 34 F6
Westerham Kent 52 C2
Westerhope Tyne/Wear 242 D5
Westerleigh S Glos 61 D8
Westerleigh Common S Glos 61 C8
Westerleigh Hill S Glos 61 D8
Western Bank Cumb 229 B10
Western Downs Staffs 151 E8
Western Heights Kent 55 E10
Western Hill Durham 233 C11
Western Point Halton 183 E7
Westerton Aberds 293 B9
Westerton Aberds 302 E5
Westerton Angus 287 B10
Westerton Durham 233 E10
Westerton Moray 302 D3
Westerton Stirl 278 B5
Westerton W Sussex 34 F5
Westertown Aberds 303 F7
Westerwick Shetl'd 315 J4
Westfield Bath/NE Som'set 45 C7
Westfield Cumb 228 F5
Westfield E Sussex 38 D4
Westfield Hants 22 D2
Westfield Heref'd 98 B4
Westfield H'land 310 C4
Westfield Norfolk 141 B9
Westfield N Lanarks 278 G4
Westfield N Lincs 200 D6
Westfield Redcar/Clevel'd 235 G7
Westfield Surrey 50 B4
Westfield S Yorks 186 E6
Westfield W Loth 279 G8
Westfield W Yorks 205 E9
Westfield W Yorks 197 C8
Westfield Sole Kent 69 G9
Westfields Dorset 30 F2
Westfields Heref'd 97 C10
Westfields of Rattray Perth/Kinr 286 C5
Westford Som'set 27 C10
Westgate Durham 232 D4
Westgate Norfolk 177 E7
Westgate N Lincs 199 F9
Westgate Hill W Yorks 197 B8
Westgate on Sea Kent 71 E10
Westgate Street Norfolk 160 E3
Westhall Aberds 302 G6
Westhall Suffolk 143 G8
Westhall Hill Oxon 82 C2
Westham Dorset 17 F9
Westham E Sussex 23 E10
Westham Som'set 44 D2
Westhampnett W Sussex 34 F5
Westhay Som'set 44 E2
Westhead Lancs 194 F2
Westhide Heref'd 97 C11
Westhill Aberds 293 C10
Westhill H'land 301 E7
Westholme Som'set 44 E5
Westhope Heref'd 115 G9
Westhope Shrops 131 F9
Westhorp Northants 119 G10
Westhorpe Derby 187 F7
Westhorpe Lincs 156 C4
Westhorpe Suffolk 125 D10
Westhoughton Gtr Man 195 F7
Westhouse N Yorks 212 E3
Westhouses Derby 170 D6
Westhumble Surrey 51 C7
Westing Shetl'd 314 C7
Westlake Devon 8 E2
Westland Arg/Bute 275 G11
Westland Green Herts 105 G8
Westlands Cambs 139 F10
Westlands Staffs 168 G4
Westlands Worcs 117 E7
Westlea Swindon 62 C6
Westleigh Devon 27 D9
Westleigh Devon 25 B7
Westleigh Gtr Man 195 G7
Westleigh Gtr Man 194 G6
Westleton Suffolk 127 D8
Westley Shrops 131 B7
Westley Suffolk 124 E6
Westley Heights Essex 69 B7
Westley Waterless Cambs 124 G2
Westlington Bucks 84 C3
Westlinton Cumb 239 E9
Westmancote Worcs 99 D8
Westmarsh Kent 71 G9
Westmeston E Sussex 36 E4
Westmill Herts 105 F7
Westminster London 67 D9
Westminster Cathedral London 67 D9
Westmoor End Cumb 229 D8
Westmuir Angus 287 B7
Westness Orkney 312 F4
Westnewton Cumb 229 C8
Westnewton Northum 263 C10
Westoe Tyne/Wear 243 D9
Weston Bath/NE Som'set 61 F8
Weston Ches 168 E2
Weston Ches 184 G5
Weston Dorset 17 G9
Weston Devon 15 D9
Weston Devon 27 G10
Weston Hants 34 C2
Weston Heref'd 115 F7
Weston Halton 183 E8
Weston Herts 104 E5
Weston Lincs 156 D5
Weston Northants 101 B11
Weston Notts 172 B3
Weston N Yorks 205 D9
Weston Shrops 114 C6
Weston Shrops 131 E11
Weston Shrops 149 D11
Weston S Lanarks 269 F10
Weston S'thampton 32 E6
Weston Staffs 151 D9
Weston W Berks 63 E11
Weston Bampfylde Som'set 29 B10
Weston Beggard Heref'd 97 C11
Weston by Welland Northants 136 E5
Weston Colley Hants 48 F4
Weston Colville Cambs 124 G2
Weston Corbett Hants 49 D7
Weston Coyney Stoke 168 G6
Weston Ditch Suffolk 124 B3
Weston Favell Northants 120 E5
Weston Green Cambs 124 G2
Weston Green Norfolk 160 G2
Weston Green Surrey 67 F7
Weston Heath Shrops 149 D11
Weston Heath Shrops 150 G5
Weston Hills Lincs 156 E5
Weston in Arden Warwick 135 F7
Weston Jones Staffs 150 E5
Weston Longville Norfolk 160 F2
Weston Lullingfields Shrops 149 E8
Weston Mill Plym'th 7 D9
Weston on the Green Oxon 83 B8
Weston on Trent Derby 153 D8
Weston Park Bath/NE Som'set 61 F8
Weston Park Staffs 150 G6
Weston Patrick Hants 49 D7
Weston Point Halton 183 E7
Weston Rhyn Shrops 148 B5
Weston Subedge Glos 100 C2
Weston Town Som'set 45 E8
Weston Turville Bucks 84 C5
Weston under Lizard Staffs 150 G6
Weston under Penyard Heref'd 98 G2
Weston under Wetherley Warwick 119 D7
Weston Underwood Derby 170 G3
Weston Underwood M/Keynes 121 G7
Westonbirt Glos 61 B11
Westonbirt Arboretum, Tetbury Glos 61 B11
Westoning Beds 103 E10
Weston-in-Gordano N Som'set 60 E2
Weston-on-Avon Warwick 118 G3
Weston-super-Mare N Som'set 59 G10
Westonzoyland Som'set 43 F11
Westover Hants 47 E11
Westow N Yorks 216 F5
Westowe Som'set 42 G6
Westown Devon 27 E10
Westown Perth/Kinr 286 E6
Westport Arg/Bute 255 E7
Westport Som'set 28 C5
Westquarter Falk 279 F8
Westra V/Glam 58 E6
Westray Airport Orkney 312 C5
Westridge Green W Berks 64 D5
Westrigg W Loth 269 B8
Westrip Glos 80 D4
Westrop Swindon 82 G2
Westrop Wilts 61 E11
Westruther Scot Borders 272 F2
Westry Cambs 139 D8
Westvale Mersey 182 B6
Westville Notts 171 F8
Westward Cumb 229 B11
Westward Ho! Devon 24 B6
Westwell Kent 54 D3
Westwell Oxon 82 D2
Westwell Leacon Kent 54 D3
Westwells Wilts 61 F11
Westwick Cambs 123 D8
Westwick Durham 223 B11
Westwick Norfolk 160 D5
Westwood Devon 26 G4
Westwood Devon 14 B6
Westwood Kent 71 F10
Westwood Kent 68 E5
Westwood Notts 171 E7
Westwood Peterbro 138 D3
Westwood S Lanarks 268 E2
Westwood Wilts 45 B10
Westwood Wilts 46 G6
Westwood Heath W Midlands 118 B5
Westwood Park Gtr Man 184 B3
Westwoodside N Lincs 188 B2
Westy Warrington 183 D10
Wetham Green Kent 69 F10
Wetheral Cumb 239 F11
Wetheral Plain Cumb 239 F11
Wetherby W Yorks 206 D4
Wetherby Racecourse W Yorks 206 D4
Wetherden Suffolk 125 E10
Wetheringsett Suffolk 126 D2
Wethersfield Essex 106 E4
Wethersta Shetl'd 314 G5
Wetherup Street Suffolk 126 E2
Wetley Rocks Staffs 169 F7
Wetmore Staffs 152 E5
Wetreins Green Ches 166 E6
Wettenhall Ches 167 C10
Wetton Staffs 169 D10
Wetwang ER Yorks 208 B4
Wetwood Staffs 150 C5
Wexcombe Wilts 47 B9
Wexham Street Bucks 66 C3
Weybourne Norfolk 177 E10
Weybourne Surrey 49 D11
Weybread Suffolk 142 G4
Weybridge Surrey 66 G5
Weycroft Devon 28 G4
Weydale H'land 310 C5
Weyhill Hants 47 D10
Weymouth Dorset 17 F9
Weymouth Sea Life Park Dorset 17 E9
Weythel Powys 114 F4
Whaddon Bucks 102 E6
Whaddon Cambs 104 B6
Whaddon Glos 80 C4
Whaddon Glos 99 G9
Whaddon Wilts 31 B11
Whaddon Wilts 61 G11
Whaddon Gap Cambs 104 B6
Whale Cumb 230 G6
Whalecombe Pembs 73 D8
Whaley Derby 187 G8
Whaley Bridge Derby 185 E8
Whaley Thorns Derby 187 G8
Whaligoe H'land 310 E7
Whalley Lancs 203 F10
Whalley Banks Lancs 203 F10
Whalley Range Gtr Man 184 C4
Whalleys Mersey 194 F3
Whalsay Airport Shetl'd 314 G7
Whalton Northum 252 G4
Whaplode Lincs 156 E6
Whaplode Drove Lincs 156 G6
Whaplode St. Catherine Lincs 156 E6
Wharf Warwick 119 G8
Wharfe N Yorks 212 F5
Wharles Lancs 202 F4
Wharley End Beds 103 C8
Wharmley Northum 241 D9
Wharncliffe Side S Yorks 186 C3
Wharram le Street N Yorks 217 F7
Wharton Ches 167 B11
Wharton Lincs 188 C4
Wharton Green Ches 167 B11
Whashton N Yorks 224 D3
Whashton Green N Yorks 224 D2
Whasset Cumb 211 C10
Whatcote Warwick 100 C6
Whateley Warwick 134 D4
Whatfield Suffolk 107 B10
Whatley Som'set 28 F5
Whatley Som'set 45 D8
Whatlington E Sussex 38 D3
Whatsole Street Kent 54 E6
Whatstandwell Derby 170 E4
Whatton Notts 154 B4
Whauphill Dumf/Gal 236 E6
Whaw N Yorks 223 E9
Wheal Baddon Cornw'l 4 G5
Wheal Busy Cornw'l 4 G4
Wheal Frances Cornw'l 4 E5
Wheal Rose Cornw'l 4 G4
Wheal Vor Cornw'l 2 C4
Wheatacre Norfolk 143 E9
Wheatcroft Derby 170 D5
Wheatenhurst Glos 80 D3
Wheatfield Oxon 83 F11
Wheathampstead Herts 85 C11
Wheathill Shrops 132 G2
Wheathill Som'set 44 G5
Wheatley Devon 14 C4
Wheatley Hants 49 E9
Wheatley Oxon 83 D9
Wheatley S Yorks 198 G5
Wheatley W Yorks 196 B5
Wheatley Hill Durham 234 D3
Wheatley Hill W Yorks 197 F9
Wheatley Hills S Yorks 198 G5
Wheatley Lane Lancs 204 F2
Wheatley Park S Yorks 198 F5
Wheaton Aston Staffs 150 G6
Wheatridge Glos 80 B4
Wheddon Cross Som'set 42 F2
Wheedlemont Aberds 302 G4
Wheelbarrow Town Kent 54 D6
Wheelerend Common Bucks 84 G4
Wheelerstreet Surrey 50 E2
Wheelock Ches 168 D3
Wheelock Heath Ches 168 D3
Wheelton Lancs 194 C6
Wheen Angus 292 F5
Wheldale W Yorks 198 B3

Wheldrake C/York 207 D9
Whelford Glos 81 F11
Whelley Gtr Man 194 F5
Whelp Street Suffolk 107 B8
Whelpley Hill Bucks 85 E7
Whelpo Cumb 230 D2
Whelprigg Cumb 212 C2
Whelston Flints 182 F2
Whenby N Yorks 216 F2
Whepstead Suffolk 124 F6
Wherry Town Cornw'l 1 D5
Wherstead Suffolk 108 C3
Wherwell Hants 47 E11
Wheston Derby 185 F10
Whetley Cross Dorset 29 G7
Whetsted Kent 53 D7
Whetstone Leics 135 D11
Whetstone London 86 G3
Whicham Cumb 210 C2
Whichford Warwick 100 E6
Whickham Tyne/Wear 242 E6
Whickham Fell Tyne/Wear 242 F6
Whiddon Devon 40 G5
Whiddon Down Devon 13 C9
Whifflet N Lanarks 268 C4
Whigstreet Angus 287 C8
Whilton Northants 120 E2
Whiltonlocks Northants 120 E2
Whimble Devon 24 G5
Whimple Devon 14 B6
Whimpwell Green Norfolk 161 D7
Whin Lane End Lancs 202 E3
Whinburgh Norfolk 141 B10
Whinfield D'lington 224 B6
Whinhall N Lanarks 268 B5
Whinmoor W Yorks 206 F3
Whinney Hill S Yorks 187 C7
Whinnieliggate Dumf/Gal 237 D9
Whinny Heights Blackb'n 195 B7
Whinny Hill D'lington 225 B7
Whinny Hill Notts 171 B9
Whinnyfold Aberds 303 F10
Whins of Milton Stirl 278 C5
Whins Wood W Yorks 205 F7
Whipcott Devon 27 D9
Whippingham I/Wight 30 C6
Whipps Cross London 67 B11
Whipsiderry Cornw'l 4 C6
Whipsnade Beds 85 B8
Whipsnade Wild Animal Park, Dunstable Beds 85 B8
Whipton Devon 14 C4
Whirley Grove Ches 184 F5
Whirlow S Yorks 186 E4
Whirlow Brook S Yorks 186 E4
Whisby Lincs 172 B6
Whissendine Rutl'd 154 G6
Whissenthorpe Leics 154 G5
Whissonsett Norfolk 159 E8
Whisterfield Ches 184 G4
Whistlefield Arg/Bute 276 C4
Whistley Green Wokingham 65 E10
Whiston Mersey 183 C7
Whiston Northants 121 E7
Whiston Staffs 151 G7
Whiston Staffs 169 F8
Whiston S Yorks 187 D7
Whiston Cross Mersey 183 C7
Whitacre Heath Warwick 134 E4
Whitbeck Cumb 210 C2
Whitbourne Heref'd 116 F4
Whitbourne Ford Heref'd 116 F4
Whitbread Hop Farm, Beltring Kent 53 D7
Whitburn Tyne/Wear 243 E10
Whitburn W Loth 269 C8
Whitburn Colliery Tyne/Wear 243 E10
Whitby Ches 182 F5
Whitby N Yorks 227 C8
Whitby Abbey N Yorks 227 C8
Whitbyheath Ches 182 G5
Whitchurch Bucks 102 G6
Whitchurch Bristol 60 F6
Whitchurch Card 59 D7
Whitchurch Devon 12 G5
Whitchurch Hants 48 D3
Whitchurch Heref'd 79 B8
Whitchurch Oxon 64 D6
Whitchurch Pembs 90 F5
Whitchurch Shrops 167 G8
Whitchurch Warwick 100 B4
Whitchurch Cannonicorum Dorset 16 B3
Whitchurch Hill Oxon 64 D6
Whitcombe Dorset 17 D10
Whitcott Keysett Shrops 130 G5
White Ball Devon 27 D9
White Colne Essex 107 F7
White Cross Bath/NE Som'set 44 B6
White Cross Cornw'l 2 E5
White Cross Cornw'l 5 D7
White Cross Heref'd 97 C9
White Cross Wilts 45 G9
White End Glos 98 F6
White Gate Gtr Man 195 G11
White Hill Wilts 45 G10
White Hills Northants 120 E4
White Horse Common Norfolk 160 D6
White House Suffolk 108 B2
White Houses Notts 188 F2
White Kirkley Durham 232 D6
White Lackington Dorset 17 B10
White Ladies Aston Worcs 117 G8
White Lee W Yorks 197 B8
White Lund Lancs 211 G8
White Mill Carms 93 G9
White Moor Derby 170 F5
White Moss Cumb 239 E11
White Ness Shetl'd 315 J5
White Notley Essex 88 B3
White Ox Mead Bath/NE Som'set 45 B8
White Pit Lincs 190 F5
White Post Notts 171 D10
White Post Farm Centre, Farnsfield Notts 171 D10
White Rocks Heref'd 97 G8
White Roding Essex 87 C9
White Stake Lancs 194 B4
White Stone Heref'd 97 C11
White Waltham Windsor 65 D11
Whiteacen Moray 302 E2
Whiteacre Kent 54 D6
Whiteash Green Essex 106 E5
Whitebirk Blackb'n 195 B8
Whitebog H'land 301 C7
Whitebridge H'land 290 B6
Whitebrook Monmouths 79 D8
Whiteburn Scot Borders 271 F11
Whitecairn Dumf/Gal 236 D4
Whitecairns Aberds 293 B11
Whitecastle S Lanarks 269 G10
Whitechapel Lancs 203 E7
Whitechapel London 67 C10
Whitechurch Som'set 30 C2
Whitecleat Orkney 313 H6
Whitecliff Glos 79 C9
Whiteclosegate Cumb 239 F10
Whitecote W Yorks 205 F10
Whitecraigs E Renf 267 D11
Whitecroft Glos 79 D10
Whitecrook Renf 267 B10
Whitecross Cornw'l 10 G5
Whitecross Cornw'l 2 C2
Whitecross Dorset 16 B5
Whitecross Falk 279 F9
Whitecross Staffs 151 E7
Whitecross Green Oxon 83 C9
Whiteface H'land 309 L7
Whitefarland N Ayrs 255 C9
Whitefaulds S Ayrs 245 B7
Whitefield Aberds 303 G7
Whitefield Dorset 18 C4
Whitefield Gtr Man 195 F10
Whitefield Perth/Kinr 286 D5
Whitefield Som'set 27 B9
Whitefield Lane End Mersey 183 D7
Whitefield Lane End Mersey 183 D7
Whiteford Aberds 303 G7
Whitegate Ches 167 B10
Whitehall Devon 27 E10
Whitehall Devon 40 F4
Whitehall Hants 49 C8
Whitehall Herts 104 E6
Whitehall Lancs 195 C7
Whitehall W Sussex 35 C10
Whitehall Village Orkney 312 F7
Whitehaven Cumb 219 B9
Whitehaven Shrops 148 E5
Whiteheath Gate W Midlands 133 F9
Whitehill E Sussex 37 B8
Whitehill Hants 49 G9
Whitehill Kent 54 B4
Whitehill Midloth 271 B7
Whitehill Moray 302 D5
Whitehill S Lanarks 268 D4
Whitehills Aberds 302 C6
Whitehills S Lanarks 268 E2
Whitehills Tyne/Wear 243 E7
Whitehough Derby 185 E8
Whitehouse Aberds 293 B8
Whitehouse Arg/Bute 275 G9
Whitehouse Common W Midlands 134 D2
Whitehouse Green W Berks 65 F7
Whiteinch Glasg C 267 B10
Whitekirk E Loth 281 E11
Whiteknights Reading 65 E8
Whiteknowes Aberds 293 C7
Whitelackington Som'set 28 D5
Whitelaw S Lanarks 268 G2
Whiteleaf Bucks 84 E4
Whiteleas Tyne/Wear 243 E9
Whiteleaved Oak Heref'd 98 D5
White-le-Head Durham 242 G5
Whiteless S Ayrs 257 C9
Whiteley Bank I/Wight 21 E7
Whiteley Green Ches 184 F6
Whiteley Village Surrey 66 G5
Whitelye Monmouths 79 E8
Whitemans Green W Sussex 36 B4
Whitemire Moray 301 D9
Whitemoor Nott'ham 171 G8
Whitemoor Cornw'l 5 D9
Whitenap Hants 32 C5
Whiteoak Green Oxon 82 C4
Whiteparish Wilts 32 C3
Whiterashes Aberds 303 G8
Whiterow H'land 310 E7
Whites Som'set 43 G10
Whiteshill Glos 80 D4
Whiteshill S Glos 60 D6
Whiteside W Loth 269 B9
Whitesmith E Sussex 37 E8
Whitestaunton Som'set 28 E3
Whitestone Devon 14 C3
Whitestone Aberds 293 D8
Whitestone Devon 40 D3
Whitestone Warwick 135 F7
Whitestone Cross Devon 14 C4
Whitestones Aberds 303 D8
Whitestreet Green Suffolk 107 D9
Whitewall Common Monmouths 60 B2
Whitewall Corner N Yorks 216 E5
Whiteway Bath/NE Som'set 61 G8
Whiteway Glos 80 F4
Whiteway Glos 80 C6
Whitewayhead Shrops 115 C11
Whitewell Aberds 303 C9
Whitewell H'land 291 C11
Whitewell Lancs 203 D9
Whitewell Bottom Lancs 195 C10
Whiteworks Devon 13 G8
Whitfield Heref'd 97 G11
Whitfield Kent 55 D10
Whitfield Northants 102 D2
Whitfield Northum 241 F7
Whitfield S Glos 79 G11
Whitfield Stoke 168 E4
Whitford Devon 15 B11
Whitford Flints 181 F10
Whitgift ER Yorks 199 C10
Whitgreave Staffs 151 D7
Whithebeir Orkney 312 E6
Whithorn Dumf/Gal 236 E6
Whiting Bay N Ayrs 256 D2
Whitkirk W Yorks 206 G3
Whitland = Hendy-Gwyn Carms 73 B11
Whitle Derby 185 D7
Whitlea Northum 243 B7
Whitleigh Plym'th 7 C9
Whitletts S Ayrs 257 E9
Whitley Gtr Man 194 F5
Whitley N Yorks 198 C5
Whitley Reading 65 E8
Whitley Wilts 61 F11
Whitley W Midlands 119 B7
Whitley Bay Tyne/Wear 243 C9
Whitley Chapel Northum 241 F10
Whitley Heath Staffs 150 D6
Whitley Lower W Yorks 197 D8
Whitley Reed Ches 183 E10
Whitley Row Kent 52 C4
Whitley Thorpe N Yorks 198 C5
Whitley Wood Reading 65 F8
Whitlock's End W Midlands 118 B2
Whitminster Glos 80 D3
Whitmoor Devon 27 E9
Whitmore Dorset 31 F9
Whitmore Staffs 168 G4
Whitmore Heath Staffs 168 G3
Whitmore Park W Midlands 134 G6
Whitnage Devon 27 D8
Whitnash Warwick 118 E6
Whitnell Som'set 43 F8
Whitney Bottom Som'set 28 E4
Whitney-on-Wye Heref'd 96 B5
Whitrigg Cumb 229 D10
Whitrigg Cumb 238 F6
Whitsbury Hants 31 D10
Whitsome Scot Borders 273 E7
Whitsomehill Scot Borders 273 F7
Whitson Newp 59 C11
Whitstable Kent 70 F6
Whitstone Cornw'l 11 B11
Whittaker Gtr Man 196 D2
Whittingham Northum 264 G3
Whittingslow Shrops 131 F8
Whittington Glos 99 G10
Whittington Lancs 212 D2
Whittington Norfolk 140 D4
Whittington Shrops 148 C6
Whittington Staffs 133 G7
Whittington Staffs 134 B3
Whittington Warwick 134 D5
Whittington Moor Derby 186 G5
Whittle Hill Gtr Man 195 F10
Whittlebury Northants 102 C3
Whittleford Warwick 134 E6
Whittle-le-Woods Lancs 194 C5
Whittlesey Cambs 138 D5
Whittlesford Cambs 105 B9
Whittlestone Head Blackb'n 195 D8
Whitton Scot Borders 263 E7
Whitton London 66 E6
Whitton N Lincs 200 C2
Whitton Northum 252 C3
Whitton Powys 114 D5
Whitton Shrops 115 C11
Whitton Suffolk 108 B2
Whitton Stockton 234 G3
Whittonditch Wilts 63 E9
Whittonstall Northum 242 F3
Whitway Hants 48 B3
Whitwell Derby 187 G9
Whitwell Herts 104 G3
Whitwell I/Wight 20 F6
Whitwell N Yorks 224 F5
Whitwell Rutl'd 137 B8
Whitwell Common Norfolk 159 E11
Whitwell Street Norfolk 160 E2
Whitwell-on-the-Hill N Yorks 216 F4
Whitwick Leics 153 F8
Whitwood W Yorks 198 C2
Whitworth Lancs 195 D11
Whixall Shrops 149 C10
Whixley N Yorks 206 B4
Whoberley W Midlands 118 B6
Wholeflats Falk 279 E8
Whome Orkney 313 J4
Whorlton Durham 224 C2
Whorlton N Yorks 225 E9
Whydown E Sussex 38 F2
Whyke W Sussex 34 G5
Whyle Heref'd 115 E11
Whyteleafe Surrey 51 B11
Wibsey W Yorks 205 G8
Wibtoft Warwick 135 F9
Wichenford Worcs 116 E5
Wichling Kent 54 B2
Wick Bournem'th 19 C9
Wick Devon 27 G11
Wick H'land 310 D7
Wick Shetl'd 315 K6
Wick S Glos 61 E8
Wick Som'set 43 E8
Wick Som'set 28 B6
Wick Som'set 44 F4
Wick Som'set 43 C10
Wick V/Glam 58 E2
Wick Wilts 31 C11
Wick Worcs 99 B9
Wick W Sussex 35 G8
Wick Airport H'land 313 N4
Wick End Beds 121 G9
Wick Hill Brackn'l 65 E11
Wick Hill Kent 53 E10
Wick Hill Wokingham 65 G10
Wick Hill Wilts 62 E3
Wick St. Lawrence N Som'set 59 F11
Wick Street Glos 80 D5
Wicken Cambs 123 C11
Wicken Northants 102 D4
Wicken Bonhunt Essex 105 E10
Wicken Green Village Norfolk 158 C6
Wickenby Lincs 189 E9
Wicker Street Green Suffolk 107 C9
Wickersley S Yorks 187 C7
Wickford Essex 88 G2
Wickham Hants 33 E9
Wickham W Berks 63 E11
Wickham Bishops Essex 88 C4
Wickham Green Suffolk 125 D11
Wickham Green W Berks 63 E11
Wickham Heath W Berks 64 F2
Wickham Market Suffolk 126 F5
Wickham St. Paul Essex 106 D6
Wickham Skeith Suffolk 125 D11
Wickham Street Suffolk 125 D11
Wickham Street Suffolk 124 G5
Wickhambreaux Kent 55 B8
Wickhambrook Suffolk 124 G4
Wickhamford Worcs 99 C11
Wickhampton Norfolk 143 B8
Wicklane Bath/NE Som'set 45 B7
Wicklewood Norfolk 141 C11
Wickmere Norfolk 160 C3
Wickridge Street Glos 98 F6
Wicksgreen Glos 80 C3
Wicksteed Park, Kettering Northants 121 B7
Wickstreet E Sussex 23 D8
Wickwar S Glos 61 B8
Widcombe Bath/NE Som'set 61 G9
Widcombe Som'set 28 D2
Widdenham Wilts 61 E10
Widdington Essex 105 E10
Widdop W Yorks 204 G4
Widdrington Northum 253 D7
Widdrington Station Northum 252 E6
Wide Open Tyne/Wear 242 C6
Widecombe in the Moor Devon 13 F10
Widegate's Cornw'l 6 D5
Widemarsh Heref'd 97 C10
Widemouth Bay Cornw'l 24 G2
Widewall Orkney 313 J5
Widewell Plym'th 7 C9
Widford Essex 87 E11
Widford Herts 86 B6
Widford Oxon 82 C3
Widham Wilts 62 B5
Widley Hants 33 F11
Widmer End Bucks 84 F5
Widmerpool Notts 154 D2
Widnes Halton 183 E8
Widworthy Devon 15 B10
Wig Powys 130 F2
Wigan Gtr Man 194 F5
Wigan Pier Gtr Man 194 G5
Wigbeth Dorset 31 F8
Wigborough Som'set 28 D6
Wig-Fach Bridg 57 F10
Wiggaton Devon 15 C8
Wiggenhall St. Germans Norfolk 157 G11
Wiggenhall St. Mary Magdalen Norfolk 157 G11
Wiggenhall St. Mary the Virgin Norfolk 157 G11
Wiggenhall St. Peter Norfolk 158 G2
Wiggens Green Essex 106 C3
Wigginton C/York 207 B7
Wigginton Herts 84 C6
Wigginton Oxon 101 E7
Wigginton Staffs 134 B4
Wigginton Bottom Herts 84 D6
Wigglesworth N Yorks 204 B2
Wiggonby Cumb 239 G7
Wiggonholt W Sussex 35 D9
Wighill N Yorks 206 D5
Wighton Norfolk 176 E6
Wightwick W Midlands 133 D7
Wigley Hants 32 D4
Wigmore Heref'd 115 D8
Wigmore Medway 69 G10
Wigsley Notts 188 G5
Wigsthorpe Northants 137 G10
Wigston Leics 136 D2
Wigston Fields Leics C 135 C11
Wigston Harcourt Leics 136 D2
Wigston Magna Leics 136 D2
Wigston Parva Leics 135 F9
Wigthorpe Notts 187 E9
Wigtoft Lincs 156 B5
Wigton Cumb 229 B11
Wigtown Dumf/Gal 236 D6
Wîg Powys 147 G11
Wike W Yorks 206 E2
Wike Well End S Yorks 199 E7
Wilbarston Northants 136 F6
Wilberfoss ER Yorks 207 C10
Wilberlee W Yorks 196 E5
Wilburton Cambs 123 C9
Wilby Norfolk 141 F10
Wilby Northants 121 D7
Wilby Suffolk 126 C4
Wilcot Wilts 62 G6
Wilcot Green Wilts 62 G6
Wilcott Shrops 149 F7
Wilcrick Newp 60 B2
Wild Mill Bridg 58 C2
Wildboarclough Ches 169 B7
Wilde Street Suffolk 124 B4
Wilden Beds 121 F11
Wilden Worcs 116 C6
Wildern Hants 33 E7
Wildernesse Kent 52 B4
Wilderspool Warrington 183 D10
Wildfowl and Wetland Centre, Martin Mere Lancs 194 E2
Wildhern Hants 47 C11
Wildhill Herts 86 D3
Wildlife & Dinosaur Park, Combe Martin Devon 40 E6
Wildmanbridge S Lanarks 268 E6
Wildmoor Hants 49 B7
Wildmoor Oxon 83 F7
Wildmoor Worcs 117 B9
Wildridings Brackn'l 65 F11
Wildsworth Lincs 188 B4
Wildwood Staffs 151 E8
Wilford Notts 153 B11
Wilkesley Ches 167 G10
Wilkhaven H'land 311 L3
Wilkieston W Loth 270 B2
Wilkin Throop Som'set 29 C11
Wilksby Lincs 174 C3
Willacy Lane End Lancs 202 F5
Willand Devon 27 E8
Willand Som'set 27 E11
Willand Moor Devon 27 E8
Willards Hill E Sussex 38 C2
Willaston Ches 167 E11
Willaston Ches 182 F4
Willaston Shrops 149 B11
Willen M/Keynes 103 C7
Willenhall W Midlands 133 D9
Willenhall W Midlands 119 B7
Willerby ER Yorks 208 G6
Willerby N Yorks 217 D10
Willersey Glos 100 D2
Willersley Heref'd 96 B6
Willesborough Kent 54 E4
Willesborough Lees Kent 54 E4
Willesden London 67 B8
Willesden Green London 67 C8
Willesleigh Devon 40 G5
Willesley Glos 61 B11
Willestrew Devon 12 F4
Willett Som'set 42 G6
Willey Shrops 132 D3
Willey Warwick 135 G9
Willey Green Surrey 50 C3
William Herts 104 E4
William's Green Suffolk 107 C9
Williamscot Oxon 101 B9
Williamstown Rh Cyn Taff 77 G8
Williamthorpe Derby 170 B6
Williamwood E Renf 267 D11
Willingale Essex 87 D9
Willingcott Devon 40 E3
Willingdon E Sussex 23 E9
Willingham Cambs 123 B8
Willingham by Stow Lincs 188 D5
Willingham Green Cambs 124 G2
Willington Beds 104 B2
Willington Derby 152 D5
Willington Durham 233 D9
Willington Kent 53 C9
Willington Tyne/Wear 243 D8
Willington Warwick 100 D5
Willington Corner Ches 167 B8
Willington Quay Tyne/Wear 243 D8
Willisham Suffolk 125 G11
Willisham Tye Suffolk 125 G11
Willitoft ER Yorks 207 F10
Williton Som'set 42 E5
Willoughbridge Staffs 168 G2
Willoughby Lincs 191 G7
Willoughby Warwick 119 D10
Willoughby Hills Lincs 174 F5
Willoughby on the Wolds Notts 154 D2
Willoughby Waterleys Leics 135 E11
Willoughton Lincs 188 C6
Willoughton Cliff Lincs 188 C6
Willow Green Ches 183 F10
Willow Holme Cumb 239 F9
Willowbank Bucks 66 B5
Willows Gtr Man 195 F8
Willows Green Essex 88 B2
Willsbridge S Glos 61 E7
Willslock Staffs 151 C11
Willtown Som'set 28 C5
Wilmcote Warwick 118 F3
Wilmington Bath/NE Som'set 61 G7
Wilmington Devon 15 B10
Wilmington E Sussex 23 E9
Wilmington Kent 68 E4
Wilminstone Devon 12 F5
Wilmslow Ches 184 E4
Wilmslow Park Ches 184 E5
Wilnecote Staffs 134 C4
Wilney Green Norfolk 141 G11
Wilpshire Lancs 203 G9
Wilsden W Yorks 205 F7
Wilsford Lincs 173 G8
Wilsford Wilts 46 F6
Wilsford Wilts 46 B5
Wilshaw W Yorks 196 F6
Wilsill N Yorks 214 G3
Wilsley Green Kent 53 F9
Wilsley Pound Kent 53 F9
Wilsom Hants 49 F8
Wilson Heref'd 97 G11
Wilson Leics 153 E8
Wilsontown S Lanarks 269 D8
Wilstead Beds 103 C11
Wilsthorpe Derby 153 C9
Wilsthorpe Lincs 155 G11
Wilstone Herts 84 C6
Wilstone Green Herts 84 C6
Wilthorpe S Yorks 197 F10
Wilton Scot Borders 261 G11
Wilton Cumb 219 C10
Wilton Heref'd 97 G11
Wilton N Yorks 217 C7
Wilton Redcar/Clevel'd 225 B11
Wilton Som'set 28 C2
Wilton Wilts 63 G9
Wilton Wilts 46 G5
Wilton House, Salisbury Wilts 46 G5
Wiltown Devon 27 D11
Wimbish Essex 105 D11
Wimbish Green Essex 106 D2
Wimblebury Staffs 151 G10
Wimbledon London 67 E8
Wimbledon All England Tennis Club London 67 E8
Wimblington Cambs 139 E8
Wimborne Minster Dorset 18 B6
Wimborne Minster Dorset 18 B6
Wimborne St. Giles Dorset 31 E8
Wimbotsham Norfolk 140 B2
Wimpole Hall and Home Farm, Royston Cambs 122 G6
Wimpson S'thampton 32 E5
Wimpstone Warwick 100 B4
Wincanton Som'set 30 B2
Wincanton Racecourse Som'set 45 G8
Winceby Lincs 174 B4
Winch Fawr Merth Tyd 77 D8
Wincham Ches 183 F11
Winchburgh W Loth 279 F11
Winchcombe Glos 99 F10
Winchelsea E Sussex 38 D6
Winchelsea Beach E Sussex 38 D6
Winchester Hants 33 B7
Winchester Cathedral Hants 33 B7
Winchestown Bl Gwent 77 C11
Winchet Hill Kent 53 E8
Winchfield Hants 49 C9
Winchmore Hill Bucks 84 F6
Winchmore Hill London 86 G4
Wincle Ches 169 B7
Wincobank S Yorks 186 C5
Wincombe Wilts 30 C5
Wind Mill Durham 233 F8
Windcross Glos 98 E3
Winder Cumb 219 B10
Windermere Cumb 221 F8
Winderton Warwick 100 C6
Windfallwood Common W Sussex 34 B6
Windhill H'land 300 E5
Windhill S Yorks 198 G3
Windhill W Yorks 205 F9
Windhouse Shetl'd 314 D6
Windle Hill Ches 182 F4
Windlehurst Gtr Man 185 D7
Windlesham Surrey 66 G2
Windley Derby 170 F4
Windmill Cornw'l 10 G3
Windmill Derby 185 F11
Windmill Hill Bristol 60 E5
Windmill Hill E Sussex 37 E11
Windmill Hill Halton 183 E9
Windmill Hill Kent 69 F10
Windmill Hill Som'set 28 D4
Windmill Hill S Yorks 198 F2
Windmill Hill Worcs 99 B8
Windmill Hill W Yorks 197 E11
Windrush Glos 81 C11
Windsor N Lincs 199 E9
Windsor Windsor 66 D2
Windsor Castle Windsor 66 D3
Windsor Green Suffolk 125 G7
Windsor Racecourse Windsor 66 D2
Windsoredge Glos 80 E4
Windy Arbor Mersey 183 D7
Windy Arbour Warwick 118 C5
Windy Hill Wrex 166 E4
Windy Nook Tyne/Wear 243 E7
Windygates Fife 287 G7
Windyharbour Ches 184 G4
Windyknowe W Loth 269 B9
Windywalls Scot Borders 263 C7
Wineham W Sussex 36 C2
Winestead ER Yorks 201 C9
Winewall Lancs 204 E4
Winfarthing Norfolk 142 F2
Winford I/Wight 21 E7
Winford N Som'set 60 F4
Winforton Heref'd 96 B5
Winfrith Newburgh Dorset 18 E2
Wing Bucks 103 G7
Wing Rutl'd 137 C7
Wingate Durham 234 D3
Wingates Gtr Man 195 F7
Wingates Northum 252 D4
Wingerworth Derby 170 B5
Wingfield Beds 103 F10
Wingfield Suffolk 126 B4
Wingfield S Yorks 186 C6
Wingfield Wilts 45 B10
Wingfield Green Suffolk 126 B4
Wingfield Park Derby 170 E5
Wingham Kent 55 B8
Wingham Green Kent 55 B8
Wingham Well Kent 55 B8
Wingmore Kent 55 D7
Wingrave Bucks 84 B5
Winkburn Notts 172 D2
Winkfield Brackn'l 66 E2
Winkfield Row Brackn'l 65 E11
Winkfield Street Brackn'l 66 E2
Winkhill Lincs 173 F10
Winkhill Staffs 169 E9
Winkhurst Green Kent 52 D3
Winklebury Hants 48 C6
Winkleigh Devon 25 F10
Winksley N Yorks 214 E4
Winkton Dorset 19 B9
Winkton Common Dorset 19 C9
Winlaton Tyne/Wear 242 E5
Winlaton Mill Tyne/Wear 242 E5
Winless H'land 310 D7
Winmarleigh Lancs 202 D5
Winnal Heref'd 97 E9
Winnal Common Heref'd 97 E9
Winnall Worcs 116 D6
Winnersh Wokingham 65 E9
Winnington Ches 183 G10
Winnington Shrops 148 G6
Winnothdale Staffs 169 G8
Winscales Cumb 228 F6
Winscombe N Som'set 44 B2
Winsdon Hill Luton 103 G11
Winsford Ches 167 B11
Winsford Som'set 42 G2
Winsham Devon 40 F3
Winsham Som'set 28 F5
Winshill Staffs 152 E5
Winsh-wen Swan 75 F11
Winsick Derby 170 B6
Winskill Cumb 231 E7
Winslade Hants 48 D6
Winsley N Yorks 214 G4
Winsley Wilts 61 G10
Winslow Bucks 102 F5
Winson Glos 81 D9
Winson Green W Midlands 133 F10
Winsor Hants 32 E4
Winstanley Gtr Man 194 G5
Winster Cumb 221 G8
Winster Derby 170 C2
Winston Durham 224 B2
Winston Suffolk 126 E3
Winston Green Suffolk 126 E3
Winstone Glos 81 D7
Winswell Devon 25 E7
Winter Gardens Essex 69 C9
Winter Well Som'set 28 C3
Winterborne Clenston Dorset 30 G4
Winterborne Herringston Dorset 17 D9
Winterborne Houghton Dorset 30 G4
Winterborne Kingston Dorset 18 B3
Winterborne Monkton Dorset 17 D9
Winterborne Stickland Dorset 30 G4
Winterborne Whitechurch Dorset 30 G4
Winterborne Zelston Dorset 18 B3
Winterbourne S Glos 60 B6
Winterbourne W Berks 64 E2
Winterbourne Abbas Dorset 17 C8
Winterbourne Bassett Wilts 62 D5
Winterbourne Dauntsey Wilts 47 G7
Winterbourne Down S Glos 61 D7
Winterbourne Earls Wilts 47 G7
Winterbourne Gunner Wilts 47 F7
Winterbourne Monkton Wilts 62 E5
Winterbourne Steepleton Dorset 17 D8
Winterbourne Stoke Wilts 46 E5
Winterbrook Oxon 64 B5
Winterburn N Yorks 204 B4
Winterhay Green Som'set 28 D5
Winteringham N Lincs 200 C2
Winterley Ches 168 D2
Wintersett W Yorks 197 E11
Wintershill Hants 33 D8
Winterton N Lincs 200 D2
Winterton-on-Sea Norfolk 161 F9
Winthorpe Lincs 175 B9
Winthorpe Notts 172 D4
Winton Bournem'th 19 C7
Winton Cumb 222 C5
Winton E Sussex 23 E8
Winton Gtr Man 184 B3
Winton N Yorks 225 F8
Wintringham N Yorks 217 E7
Winwick Cambs 138 G2
Winwick Northants 120 C2
Winwick Warrington 183 C10
Winwick Quay Warrington 183 C9
Winyates Worcs 117 D11
Winyates Green Worcs 117 D11
Wirksworth Derby 170 E3
Wirksworth Moor Derby 170 E4
Wirswall Ches 167 G8
Wisbech Cambs 139 B9
Wisbech St. Mary Cambs 139 B8
Wisborough Green W Sussex 35 B8
Wiseton Notts 188 D2
Wishanger Glos 80 D6
Wishaw N Lanarks 268 E5
Wishaw Warwick 134 E2
Wisley Surrey 50 B5
Wispington Lincs 190 G2
Wissenden Kent 54 E2
Wissett Suffolk 127 B7
Wistanstow Shrops 131 F8
Wistanswick Shrops 150 D3
Wistaston Ches 167 E11
Wistaston Green Ches 167 E11
Wiston Pembs 73 B8
Wiston S Lanarks 259 C11
Wiston W Sussex 35 E10
Wistow Cambs 138 G5
Wistow Leics 136 D2
Wistow N Yorks 207 F7
Wistow Lordship N Yorks 207 F8
Wiswell Lancs 203 F10
Witcham Cambs 123 B9
Witchampton Dorset 31 F7
Witchford Cambs 123 B9
Witcombe Som'set 29 C7
Withacott Devon 24 D6
Witham Essex 88 C4
Witham Friary Som'set 45 E8
Witham on the Hill Lincs 155 F11
Witham St. Hughes Lincs 172 C5
Withcall Lincs 190 E3
Withdean Brighton/Hove 36 F4
Withecombe Devon 13 D9
Witherenden Hill E Sussex 37 B10
Withergate Norfolk 160 D5
Witheridge Devon 26 E4
Witheridge Hill Oxon 65 C7
Witherley Leics 134 D6
Withermarsh Green Suffolk 107 D10
Withern Lincs 190 E6
Withernsea ER Yorks 201 B10
Withernwick ER Yorks 209 E9
Withersdale Street Suffolk 142 G5
Withersdane Kent 54 D5
Withersfield Suffolk 106 B3
Witherslack Cumb 211 C9
Witherwack Tyne/Wear 243 F9
Withiel Cornw'l 5 B9
Withiel Florey Som'set 42 G3
Withielgoose Mills Cornw'l 5 B10
Withington Ches 168 B4
Withington Glos 81 B8
Withington Gtr Man 184 C5
Withington Heref'd 97 C11
Withington Shrops 149 G11
Withington Staffs 151 B10
Withington Green Ches 184 G4
Withington Marsh Heref'd 97 C11
Withleigh Devon 26 E6
Withnell Lancs 194 C6
Withnell Fold Lancs 194 C6
Withybrook Som'set 45 D7
Withybrook Warwick 135 G8
Withybush Pembs 73 B7
Withycombe Som'set 42 E4
Withycombe Raleigh Devon 14 E6
Withyditch Bath/NE Som'set 45 B8
Withyham E Sussex 52 F3
Withymoor Village W Midlands 133 F8
Withypool Som'set 41 F10
Withywood Bristol 60 F5
Witley Surrey 50 F2
Witnell's End Worcs 132 G5
Witnesham Suffolk 126 G3
Witney Oxon 82 C5
Witney Green Essex 87 D9
Wittensford Hants 32 E3
Wittering Peterbro 137 C11
Wittersham Kent 38 B5
Witton Angus 293 F7
Witton Norfolk 142 B6
Witton Worcs 117 E7
Witton Bridge Norfolk 160 C6
Witton Gilbert Durham 233 B10
Witton le Wear Durham 233 E8
Witton Park Durham 233 E9
Wiveliscombe Som'set 27 B9
Wivelrod Hants 49 F7
Wivelsfield E Sussex 36 C4
Wivelsfield Green E Sussex 36 D5
Wivenhoe Essex 107 G10
Wivenhoe Cross Essex 107 G10
Wiveton Norfolk 177 E8
Wix Essex 108 F3
Wixford Warwick 117 G11

County and unitary authority boundaries

Greater London

Hertfordshire

Essex

Surrey

Kent

1 City and County of the City of London
2 Hackney
3 Tower Hamlets
4 Southwark
5 Lambeth
6 Wandsworth
7 Hammersmith and Fulham
8 Royal Borough of Kensington and Chelsea
9 City of Westminster
10 Camden
11 Islington
12 Haringey
13 Waltham Forest
14 Newham
15 Greenwich
16 Lewisham
17 Merton
18 Richmond upon Thames
19 Hounslow
20 Ealing
21 Brent
22 Barnet
23 Enfield
24 Redbridge
25 Barking and Dagenham
26 Havering
27 Bexley
28 Bromley
29 Croydon
30 Sutton
31 Kingston upon Thames
32 Hillingdon
33 Harrow

1 Central Scotland

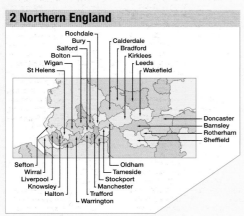

East Dunbartonshire
West Dunbartonshire
Inverclyde
Falkirk
Clackmannanshire
East Lothian
Renfrewshire
East Renfrewshire
Glasgow City
North Lanarkshire
Midlothian
City of Edinburgh
West Lothian

2 Northern England

Rochdale
Bury
Salford
Bolton
Wigan
St Helens
Calderdale
Bradford
Kirklees
Leeds
Wakefield
Doncaster
Barnsley
Rotherham
Sheffield
Sefton
Wirral
Liverpool
Knowsley
Halton
Oldham
Tameside
Stockport
Manchester
Trafford
Warrington

3 West Midlands

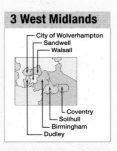

City of Wolverhampton
Sandwell
Walsall
Coventry
Solihull
Birmingham
Dudley

4 South Wales and Bristol area

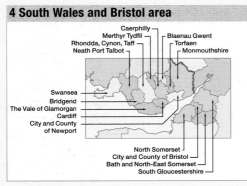

Caerphilly
Merthyr Tydfil
Rhondda, Cynon, Taff
Neath Port Talbot
Blaenau Gwent
Torfaen
Monmouthshire
Swansea
Bridgend
The Vale of Glamorgan
Cardiff
City and County of Newport
North Somerset
City and County of Bristol
Bath and North-East Somerset
South Gloucestershire

5 Thames Valley

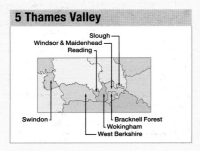

Slough
Windsor & Maidenhead
Reading
Swindon
Bracknell Forest
Wokingham
West Berkshire

Ordnance Survey National Grid

The blue lines which divide the Navigator map pages into squares for indexing match the Ordnance Survey National Grid and correspond to the small squares on the boundary map below. Each side of a grid square measures 10km on the ground.

The National Grid 100-km square letters and kilometre values are indicated for the grid intersection at the outer corners of each page. For example, the intersection SP1020 at the lower right corner of page 99 is 10km East and 20km North of the south-west corner of National Grid square SP.

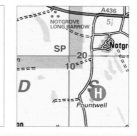

Using GPS with Navigator mapping

Since Navigator Britain is based on Ordnance Survey mapping, and rectified to the National Grid, it can be used with in-car or handheld GPS for locating identifiable waypoints such as road junctions, bridges, railways and farms, or assessing your position in relation to any of the features shown on the map.

On your receiver, choose British Grid as the location format and for map datum select Ordnance Survey (this may be described as Ord Srvy GB or similar, or more specifically as OSGB36). Your receiver will automatically convert the latitude/longitude co-ordinates transmitted by GPS into compatible National Grid data.

Positional accuracy of any particular feature is limited to 50–100m, due to the limitations of the original survey and the scale of Navigator mapping.

For further information see www.gps.gov.uk

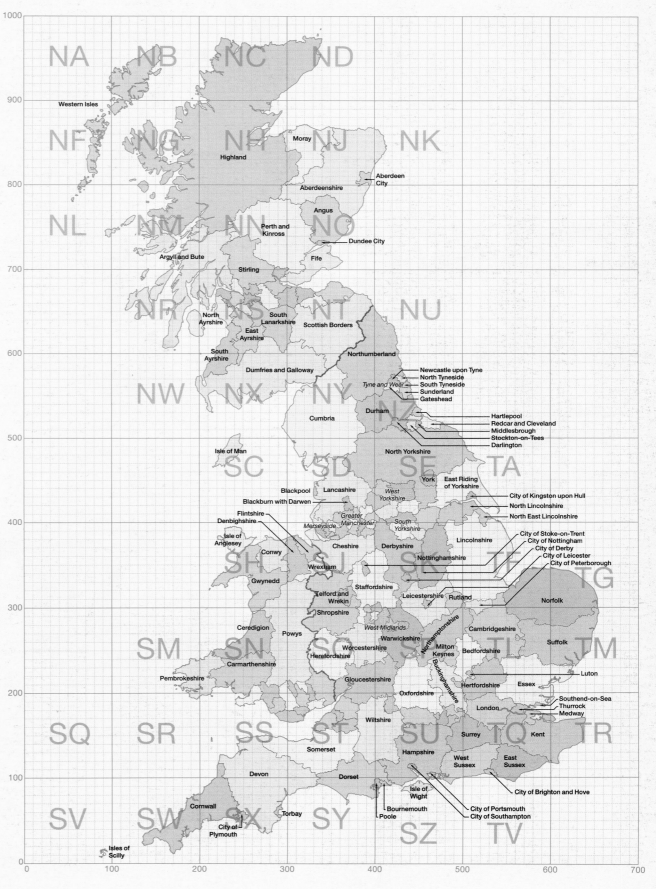

PHILIP'S MAPS
the Gold Standard for serious driving

◆ **Philip's street atlases cover every county in England, Wales, Northern Ireland and much of Scotland**

- ◆ Every named street is shown, including alleys, lanes and walkways

- ◆ Thousands of additional features marked: stations, public buildings, car parks, places of interest

- ◆ Route-planning maps to get you close to your destination

- ◆ Postcodes on the maps and in the index

- ◆ Widely used by the emergency services, transport companies and local authorities

BEST BUY • BEST BUY
Auto EXPRESS
BEST BUY • BEST BUY

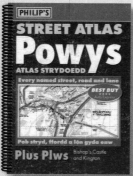

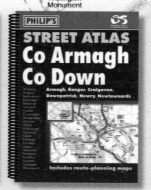

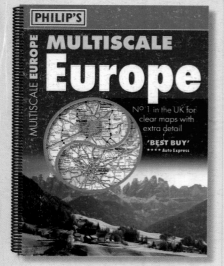

For European mapping, choose
Philip's Multiscale Europe

This best-selling atlas contains clear, detailed road maps of the whole of Europe, large-scale approach maps and street-level city centre plans of major cities.

How to order Philip's maps and atlases are available from bookshops, motorway services and petrol stations. You can order direct from the publisher by phoning **01903 828503** or online at **www.philips-maps.co.uk** For bulk orders only, e-mail philips@philips-maps.co.uk

Street atlases currently available

England
Bedfordshire
Berkshire
Birmingham and West Midlands
Bristol and Bath
Buckinghamshire
Cambridgeshire
Cheshire
Cornwall
Cumbria
Derbyshire
Devon
Dorset
County Durham and Teesside
Essex
North Essex
South Essex
Gloucestershire
Hampshire
North Hampshire
South Hampshire
Herefordshire Monmouthshire
Hertfordshire
Isle of Wight
Kent
East Kent
West Kent
Lancashire
Leicestershire and Rutland
Lincolnshire
London
Greater Manchester
Merseyside
Norfolk
Northamptonshire
Northumberland
Nottinghamshire
Oxfordshire
Shropshire
Somerset
Staffordshire
Suffolk
Surrey
East Sussex
West Sussex
Tyne and Wear
Warwickshire
Birmingham and West Midlands
Wiltshire and Swindon
Worcestershire
East Yorkshire
Northern Lincolnshire
North Yorkshire
South Yorkshire
West Yorkshire

Wales
Anglesey, Conwy and Gwynedd
Cardiff, Swansea and The Valleys
Carmarthenshire, Pembrokeshire and Swansea
Ceredigion and South Gwynedd
Denbighshire, Flintshire, Wrexham
Herefordshire Monmouthshire
Powys

Scotland
Aberdeenshire
Ayrshire
Dumfries and Galloway
Edinburgh and East Central Scotland
Fife and Tayside
Glasgow and West Central Scotland
Inverness and Moray
Lanarkshire
Scottish Borders

Northern Ireland
County Antrim and County Londonderry
County Armagh and County Down
Belfast
County Tyrone and County Fermanagh

Bridge heights

This chart converts between metric and Imperial bridge heights. Each small division in blue represents 1cm, each small division in red represents 1 inch.

The range of heights shown starts at the height at which a driver's cab must have a plate indicating vehicle height (3 metres) and ends at the maximum height at which a bridge will have a low bridge warning sign (16ft 6in).

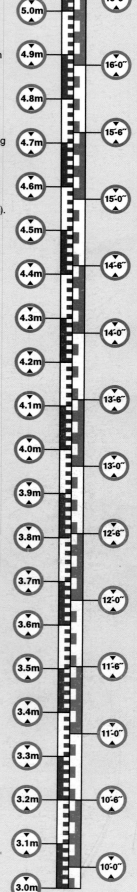

Conversion factors

To convert from Imperial to metric units, **multiply** by the figure shown. To convert from metric to Imperial units, **divide** by the figure shown.

Imperial	✕	Metric
inches	2.54	centimetres
feet	0.3048	metres
yards	0.9144	metres
miles	1.6093	kilometres
cubic feet	0.0283	cubic metres
cubic yards	0.7646	cubic metres
pints (UK)	0.568	litres
gallons (UK)	4.55	litres
pounds	0.4536	kilograms